# ENCYCLOPEDIA OF
# SPECIAL EDUCATION

# ENCYCLOPEDIA OF SPECIAL EDUCATION

## A REFERENCE FOR THE EDUCATION OF THE HANDICAPPED AND OTHER EXCEPTIONAL CHILDREN AND ADULTS

### VOLUME 1

EDITORS

**CECIL R. REYNOLDS, Ph.D.**
Texas A&M University

**LESTER MANN, Ph.D.**
Hunter College,
City University of New York

A WILEY-INTERSCIENCE PUBLICATION
**JOHN WILEY & SONS**
NEW YORK · CHICHESTER · BRISBANE · TORONTO · SINGAPORE

**Library of Congress Cataloging-in-Publication Data**

Encyclopedia of special education.

   "A Wiley–Interscience publication."
    1. Handicapped children—Education—United States—
Dictionaries.  2. Exceptional children—Education—
United States—Dictionaries.  3. Handicapped—Education—
United States—Dictionaries.  I. Reynolds, Cecil R.,
1952–     II. Mann, Lester.
LC4007.E53   1987   371.9′03′21     86-33975
ISBN  0471-63004-7 (Vol. 1)
ISBN  0471-82858-0 (Set)

Printed in the United States of America

10  9  8  7  6  5  4  3  2  1

*Some may consider it inappropriate to dedicate the writings of others, yet we feel that we would be remiss if we did not dedicate such a large work to those so clearly deserving: to the teachers and mentors of exceptional children throughout the world we dedicate this labor—may it serve you in some way as you foster the growth of your charges. We extend a special dedication to two great pioneers, mentors, and teachers of our age, the late Captain Dick Scobee, a special friend of the College of Education at Texas A & M University, and Professor E. Paul Torrance, a special friend of exceptional students everywhere.*

# CONTRIBUTORS

Susanne Blough Abbott, Ed.D.
Bedford Central School District
Mt. Kisco, New York

Marty Abramson, Ph.D.
University of Wisconsin, Stout
Menomonie, Wisconsin

Patricia Ann Abramson, M.A.
Hudson Public Schools
Hudson, Wisconsin

Patricia A. Alexander, Ph.D.
Texas A&M University
College Station, Texas

Thomas E. Allen, Ph.D.
Gallaudet College
Washington, D.C.

Geri R. Alvis, M.S.
University of Tennessee
Memphis State University
Memphis, Tennessee

C. H. Ammons, Ph.D.
Psychological Reports/Perceptual and
    Motor Skills
Missoula, Montana

Carol Anderson, Ph.D.
Texas A&M University
College Station, Texas

Peggy L. Anderson, Ph.D.
University of New Orleans, Lakefront
New Orleans, Louisiana

J. Appelboom-Fondu, Ph.D.
Université Libre de Bruxelles
Brussels, Belgium

James M. Applefield, Ph.D.
University of North Carolina
Wilmington, North Carolina

Pauline F. Applefield, Ph.D.
University of North Carolina
Wilmington, North Carolina

John Arena, M.A.
Academic Therapy Publications
Novato, California

Bernice Arricale, M.A.
Hunter College, City University
    of New York
New York, New York

H. Roberta Arrigo, M.A.
Hunter College, City University
    of New York
New York, New York

Michael J. Ash, Ph.D.
Texas A&M University
College Station, Texas

Adel E. Ashawal, Ph.D.
Ain Shams University
Cairo, Egypt

William G. Austin, Ph.D.
Cape Fear Psychological Services
Wilmington, North Carolina

Anna H. Avant, Ed.S.
University of Alabama
University, Alabama

Rebecca Bailey, B.S.
Texas A&M University
College Station, Texas

Timothy A. Ballard, Ph.D.
University of North Carolina
Wilmington, North Carolina

Russell A. Barkley, Ph.D.
University of Massachusetts Medical
    Center
Worchester, Massachusetts

Charles P. Barnard, Ed.D.
University of Wisconsin, Stout
Menomonie, Wisconsin

David W. Barnett, Ph.D.
University of Cincinnati
Cincinnati, Ohio

Ellis I. Barowsky, Ph.D.
Hunter College, City University
    of New York
New York, New York

Lyle E. Barton, Ed.D.
Kent State University
Kent, Ohio

Vicki Bartosik, B.S.
Stanford University
Stanford, Connecticut

Paul Bates, Ph.D.
Southern Illinois University
Carbondale, Illinois

Anne M. Bauer, Ed.D.
University of Cincinnati
Cincinnati, Ohio

Elizabeth R. Bauerschmidt, M.S.
University of North Carolina
Wilmington, North Carolina

Michael Bauerschmidt, M.D.
Brunswick Hospital
Wilmington, North Carolina

Monique Bauters, Ph.D.
Centre d'Etude et de Reclassement
Brussels, Belgium

John R. Beattie, Ph.D.
University of North Carolina
Charlotte, North Carolina

George R. Beauchamp, M.D.
Cleveland Clinic Foundation
Cleveland, Ohio

Ana Yeraldina Beneke
University of Oklahoma
Norman, Oklahoma

Randy Elliot Bennett, Ed.D.
Educational Testing Service
Princeton, New Jersey

Richard A. Berg, Ph.D.
West Virginia University Medical
    Center, Charleston Division
Charleston, West Virginia

John R. Bergan, Ph.D.
University of Arizona
Tucson, Arizona

Dianne E. Berkell, Ph.D.
C. W. Post Campus, Long Island
    University
Greenvale, New York

Gary Berkowitz, Ph.D.
Temple University
Philadelphia, Pennsylvania

Shari A. Bevins, M.Ed.
Texas A&M University
College Station, Texas

Erin D. Bigler, Ph.D.
Austin Neurological Clinic
University of Texas
Austin, Texas

L. Worth Bolton, M.S.W.
Cape Fear Substance Abuse Center
Wilmington, North Carolina

Gwyneth M. Boodoo, Ph.D.
Texas A&M University
College Station, Texas

Nancy Bordier, Ph.D.
Hunter College, City University
    of New York
New York, New York

Jeannie Bormans, Ph.D.
Center for Developmental Problems
Brussels, Belgium

Morton Botel, Ph.D.
University of Pennsylvania
Philadelphia, Pennsylvania

Michael Bourdot, Ph.D.
Centre d'Etude et de Reclassement
Brussels, Belgium

Bruce A. Bracken, Ph.D.
University of Wisconsin
Milwaukee, Wisconsin

**Mary Brady, M.S.**
Pennsylvania Special Education
  Assistive Device Center
Elizabethtown, Pennsylvania

**Janet S. Brand, M.A.**
Hunter College, City University
  of New York
New York, New York

**Don Braswell, M.S.A.**
Research Foundation, City University
  of New York
New York, New York

**T. Berry Brazelton, M.D.**
Children's Hospital
Boston, Massachusetts

**Warner H. Britton, M.Ed.**
Auburn University
Auburn, Alabama

**Michael G. Brown, Ph.D.**
Central Wisconsin Center for the
  Developmentally Disabled
Madison, Wisconsin

**Robert T. Brown, Ph.D.**
University of North Carolina
Wilmington, North Carolina

**Ronald T. Brown, Ph.D.**
Emory University School of Medicine
Atlanta, Georgia

**Tina L. Brown, B.S.**
University of Tennessee
Memphis State University
Memphis, Tennessee

**Robert G. Brubaker, Ph.D.**
Eastern Kentucky University
Richmond, Kentucky

**Catherine O. Bruce, M.S.**
Hunter College, City University
  of New York
New York, New York

**Andrew R. Brulle, Ed.D.**
Eastern Illinois University
Charleston, Illinois

**Laura Kinzie Brutting, Ph.D.**
University of Wisconsin
Madison, Wisconsin

**Donna M. Bryant, Ph.D.**
University of North Carolina
Chapel Hill, North Carolina

**Milton Budoff, Ph.D.**
Research Institute for Educational
  Problems
Cambridge, Massachusetts

**Carolyn Bullard, Ph.D.**
Lewis & Clark College
Portland, Oregon

**Thomas Burke, Ph.D.**
Hunter College, City University
  of New York
New York, New York

**Alois Bürli, Ph.D.**
Swiss Institute for Special Education
Lucerne, Switzerland

**Thomas A. Burton, Ed.D.**
University of Georgia
Athens, Georgia

**James Button, Ed.D.**
United States Department of Education
Washington, D.C.

**Anne Campbell, Ph.D.**
Purdue University
West Lafayette, Indiana

**Frances A. Campbell, Ph.D.**
University of North Carolina
Chapel Hill, North Carolina

**Steven A. Carlson, Ph.D.**
Beaverton Schools
Beaverton, Oregon

**Douglas Carnine, Ph.D.**
University of Oregon
Eugene, Oregon

**Janet Carpenter, M.A.**
University of Oklahoma
Norman, Oklahoma

**Tracy Calpin Castle, M.A.**
Eastern Kentucky University
Richmond, Kentucky

**John F. Cawley, Ph.D.**
University of New Orleans
New Orleans, Louisiana

**Constance Y. Celaya, M.S.**
Texas A&M University
College Station, Texas

**James C. Chalfant, Ph.D.**
University of Arizona
Tucson, Arizona

**Chris Cherrington, Ph.D.**
Lycoming College
Williamsport, Pennsylvania

**LeRoy Clinton, Ed.D.**
Boston University
Boston, Massachusetts

**Shirley Cohen, Ph.D.**
Hunter College, City University
  of New York
New York, New York

**Ginga L. Colcough, R.N., F.N.P.**
University of North Carolina
Wilmington, North Carolina

**Christine L. Cole, Ph.D.**
University of Wisconsin
Madison, Wisconsin

**Rhonda Collins, M.S.**
Florida State University
Tallahassee, Florida

**Jane Close Conoley, Ph.D.**
University of Nebraska
Lincoln, Nebraska

**Vivian I. Correa, Ph.D.**
University of Florida
Gainesville, Florida

**Lawrence S. Cote, Ed.D.**
Pennsylvania State University
University Park, Pennsylvania

**Katherine D. Couturier, Ph.D.**
Pennsylvania State University
King of Prussia, Pennsylvania

**J. Michael Coxe, M.Ed.**
University of South Carolina
Columbia, South Carolina

**Anne B. Crabbe, Ed.D.**
St. Andrews College
Laurinburg, North Carolina

**Jack A. Cummings, Ph.D.**
Indiana University
Bloomington, Indiana

**Jacqueline Cunningham, M.S.**
University of Texas
Austin, Texas

**Susan Curtiss, Ph.D.**
University of California
Los Angeles, California

**Rik Carl D'Amato, Ed.D.**
Ball State University
Muncie, Indiana

**Elizabeth Dane, B.S.W.**
Hunter College, City University
  of New York
New York, New York

**Craig Darch, Ph.D.**
Auburn University
Auburn, Alabama

**Jacqueline E. Davis, Ph.D.**
Boston University
Boston, Massachusetts

**Raymond S. Dean, Ph.D.**
Ball State University
Indiana University School of Medicine
Muncie, Indiana

**Lizanne DeStefano, Ph.D.**
University of Illinois, Urbana-
  Champaign
Champaign, Illinois

**S. De Vriendt, Ph.D.**
Vrije Universiteit Brussel
Brussels, Belgium

**Caroline D'Ippolito, M.S.**
Eastern Pennsylvania Special Education
  Resources Center
King of Prussia, Pennsylvania

**Mary D'Ippolito, M.Ed.**
Montgomery County Intermediate Unit
Norristown, Pennsylvania

**Marilyn P. Dornbush, Ph.D.**
Atlanta, Georgia

**Mary K. Dykes, Ph.D.**
University of Florida
Gainesville, Florida

**Peg Eagney, Ph.D.**
School for the Deaf
New York, New York

**Ronald C. Eaves, Ph.D.**
Auburn University
Auburn, Alabama

**John M. Eells, Ph.D.**
Souderton Area School District
Souderton, Pennsylvania

**Stephen N. Elliott, Ph.D.**
Louisiana State University
Baton Rouge, Louisiana

**Carol Sue Englert, Ph.D.**
Michigan State University
East Lansing, Michigan

**Christine A. Espin, B.S.**
University of Minnesota
Minneapolis, Minnesota

**Rand B. Evans, Ph.D.**
Texas A&M University
College Station, Texas

**MaryAnn C. Farthing, Ph.D.**
University of North Carolina
Chapel Hill, North Carolina

**Mary Grace Feely, M.S.**
School for the Deaf
New York, New York

**John F. Feldhusen, Ph.D.**
Purdue University
West Lafayette, Indiana

**Britt-Inger Fex, Ph.D.**
University of Lund
Sweden

**Donna Filips, M.S.**
Steger, Illinois

**Sally L. Flagler, M.Ed.**
University of Oklahoma
Norman, Oklahoma

**Dennis M. Flanagan, Ph.D.**
Montgomery County Intermediate Unit
Norristown, Pennsylvania

**David Fletcher-Janzen, M.Ed.**
San Marcos Treatment Center
San Marcos, Texas

**Elaine Fletcher-Janzen, M.Ed.**
Texas A&M University
College Station, Texas

**Thomas A. Frank. Ph.D.**
Pennsylvania State University
University Park, Pennsylvania

**Mary M. Frasier, Ph.D.**
University of Georgia
Athens, Georgia

**Joseph L. French, Ph.D.**
Pennsylvania State University
University Park, Pennsylvania

**Alice G. Friedman, Ph.D.**
University of Oklahoma Health Services
  Center
Norman, Oklahoma

**Douglas L. Friedman, M.S.**
Fordham University
Bronx, New York

**Douglas Fuchs, Ph.D.**
Peabody College, Vanderbilt University
Nashville, Tennessee

**Lynn S. Fuchs, Ph.D.**
Peabody College, Vanderbilt University
Nashville, Tennessee

**Gerald B. Fuller, Ph.D.**
Central Michigan University
Mt. Pleasant, Illinois

**Rosemary Gaffney, Ph.D.**
Hunter College, City University
  of New York
New York, New York

**Diego Gallegos, M.S.**
Texas A&M University

College Station, Texas
San Antonio Independent School District
San Antonio, Texas

**Katherine Garnett, Ed.D.**
Hunter College, City University
  of New York
New York, New York

**Melissa M. George, Ph.D.**
Montgomery County Intermediate Unit
Norristown, Pennsylvania

**Harvey R. Gilbert, Ph.D.**
Pennsylvania State University
University Park, Pennsylvania

**Elizabeth Girshick, Ph.D.**
Montgomery County Intermediate Unit
Norristown, Pennsylvania

**Joni J. Gleason, Ed.D.**
University of West Florida
Pensacola, Florida

**Sharon L. Glennen, M.S.**
Pennsylvania State University
University Park, Pennsylvania

**Rick Gonzales, B.S.**
Texas A&M University
College Station, Texas

**Libby Goodman, Ph.D.**
Pennsylvania State University
King of Prussia, Pennsylvania

**Carole Reiter Gothelf, Ed.D.**
Hunter College, City University
  of New York
New York, New York

**Steve Graham, Ph.D.**
University of Maryland
College Park, Maryland

**Jeffrey W. Gray, M.A.**
Ball State University
Muncie, Indiana

**P. Allen Gray, Jr., Ph.D.**
University North Carolina
Wilmington, North Carolina

**Laurence C. Grimm, Ph.D.**
University of Illinois
Chicago, Illinois

**Lindsay S. Gross, M.A.**
University of Wisconsin
Milwaukee, Wisconsin

**Norma Guerra, M.A.**
Texas A&M University
College Station, Texas

**John Guidubaldi, D.Ed.**
Kent State University
Kent, Ohio

**Steven Gumerman, M.Ed.**
Temple University
Philadelphia, Pennsylvania

**Terry B. Gutkin, Ph.D.**
University of Nebraska
Lincoln, Nebraska

**Patricia A. Haensly, Ph.D.**
Texas A&M University
College Station, Texas

**George James Hagerty, Ed.D.**
Stonehill College
North Easton, Massachusetts

**Robert Hall, Ph.D.**
Texas A&M University
College Station, Texas

**Richard E. Halmstad, M.S.**
University of Wisconsin, Stout
Menomonie, Wisconsin

**Glennelle Halpin, Ph.D.**
Auburn University
Auburn, Alabama

**Donald D. Hammill, Ed.D.**
PRO-ED, Inc.
Austin, Texas

**Harold Hanson, M.S.**
Southern Illinois University
Carbondale, Illinois

**Janice Harper, Ph.D.**
North Carolina Central University
Durham, North Carolina

**Gale A. Harr, Ed.S.**
Maple Heights City Schools
Maple Heights, Ohio

**Karen L. Harrell, Ed.D.**
University of Georgia
Athens, Georgia

**Frances T. Harrington, Ph.D.**
Radford University
Blacksberg, Virginia

**Karen R. Harris, Ph.D.**
University of Maryland
College Park, Maryland

**Patti L. Harrison, Ph.D.**
University of Alabama
University, Alabama

**Lawrence C. Hartlage, Ph.D.**
Evans, Georgia

**Dan Hatt,**
University of Oklahoma
Norman, Oklahoma

**Jeff Heinzen, M.S.**
Indianhead Enterprise
Menomonie, Wisconsin

**Rhonda Hennis, B.A.**
University of North Carolina
Wilmington, North Carolina

**Arthur Hernandez, M.A.**
Texas A&M University
College Station, Texas

**E. Valerie Hewitt, M.Ed.**
Texas A&M University
College Station, Texas

**Julia A. Hickman, Ph.D.**
University of Texas
Austin, Texas

**Craig S. Higgins, Ph.D.**
Stonehill College
North Easton, Massachusetts

**Alan Hilton, Ed.D.**
Seattle University
Seattle, Washington

**Harold E. Hoff, Jr., M.A.**
Eastern Pennsylvania Special Education
  Resources Center
King of Prussia, Pennsylvania

**E. Wayne Holden, Ph.D.**
University of Oklahoma Health Sciences
  Center
Norman, Oklahoma

**Ivan Z. Holowinsky, Ph.D.**
Rutgers University
New Brunswick, New Jersey

**Thomas F. Hopkins, Ph.D.**
Center for Behavioral Psychotherapy
White Plains, New York

**Charles A. Hughes, Ph.D.**
Pennsylvania State University
University Park, Pennsylvania

**Jan N. Hughes, Ph.D.**
Texas A&M University
College Station, Texas

**Nancy L. Hutchinson, Ph.D.**
Simon Fraser University
Buraby, British Columbia

**Paul Irvine, Ph.D.**
Katonah, New York

**Lee Anderson Jackson, Jr., Ph.D.**
University of North Carolina
Wilmington, North Carolina

**Diane Jarvis, M.A.**
State University of New York
Buffalo, New York

**Phillip Jenkins, B.S.**
University of Kentucky
Lexington, Kentucky

**Elizabeth Jones, B.S.**
Texas A&M University
College Station, Texas

**Gideon Jones, Ed.D.**
Florida State University
Tallahassee, Florida

**Philip R. Jones, Ed.D.**
Virginia Polytechnic Institute and State
  University
Blacksburg, Virginia

**Shirley A. Jones, J.D.**
Virginia Polytechnic Institute and State
  University
Blacksburg, Virginia

**James W. Kalat, Ph.D.**
North Carolina State University
Raleigh, North Carolina

**Randy W. Kamphaus, Ph.D.**
Eastern Kentucky University
Richmond, Kentucky

**Stan A. Karcz, Ph.D.**
University of Wisconsin, Stout
Menomonie, Wisconsin

**Maribeth Montgomery Kasik, Ph.D.**
Governors State University
University Park, Illinois

**Alan S. Kaufman, Ph.D.**
University of Alabama
University, Alabama

**Nancy J. Kaufman, Ph.D.**
University of Wisconsin
Stevens Point, Wisconsin

**Kenneth A. Kavale, Ph.D.**
University of Iowa
Iowa City, Iowa

**Forrest E. Keesbury, Ph.D.**
Lycoming College
Williamsport, Pennsylvania

**Barbara Keogh, Ph.D.**
University of California
Los Angeles, California

**Margie K. Kitano, Ph.D.**
New Mexico State University
Las Cruces, New Mexico

**F. J. Koopmans-Van Beinum, Ph.D.**
Amsterdam, The Netherlands

**Mark A. Koorland, Ph.D.**
Florida State University
Tallahassee, Florida

**L. Koulischer, Ph.D.**
Institut de Morphologie Pathologique
Belgium

**Howard M. Knoff, Ph.D.**
University of South Florida
Tampa, Florida

**Thomas R. Kratochwill, Ph.D.**
University of Wisconsin
Madison, Wisconsin

**James P. Krouse, Ed.D.**
Clarion University of Pennsylvania
Clarion, Pennsylvania

**Louis J. Kruger, Psy.D.**
Tufts University
Medford, Pennsylvania

**Timothy D. Lackaye, M.A.**
Hunter College, City University
  of New York
New York, New York

**C. Sue Lamb, Ph.D.**
University of North Carolina
Wilmington, North Carolina

**Nadine M. Lambert, Ph.D.**
University of California
Berkeley, California

**Louis J. LaNunziata, Ph.D.**
University of North Carolina
Wilmington, North Carolina

**Jeff Laurent, M.S.**
University of Texas
Austin, Texas

**Samuel LeBaron, Ph.D.**
University of Texas Health Science
  Center
San Antonio, Texas

**Yvan Lebrun, Ph.D.**
School of Medicine, V.U.B.
Brussels, Belgium

**Ronald S. Lenkowsky, Ed.D.**
Hunter College, City University
  of New York
New York, New York

**Mary Louise Lennon, M.A.**
Educational Testing Service
Princeton, New Jersey

**Allison Lewis**
University of North Carolina
Wilmington, North Carolina

**Janet A. Lindow, M.S.**
University of Wisconsin
Madison, Wisconsin

**Daniel D. Lipka, M.Ed.**
Lincoln Way Special Education Regional
  Resources Center
Louisville, Ohio

**Cornelia Lively, M.S.**
University of Illinois, Urbana-
  Champaign
Champaign, Illinois

**Charles J. Long, Ph.D.**
University of Tennessee
Memphis State University
Memphis, Tennessee

**Linda R. Longley, B.A.**
University of North Carolina
Wilmington, North Carolina

**Emilia C. Lopez, M.S.**
Fordham University
New York, New York

**Marsha H. Lupi, Ed.D.**
Hunter College, City University
  of New York
New York, New York

**Ann E. Lupkowski, Ph.D.**
Texas A&M University
College Station, Texas

**Philip E. Lyon, Ph.D.**
College of St. Rose
Albany, New York

**Charles A. MacArthur, Ph.D.**
University of Maryland
College Park, Maryland

**John MacDonald, Ph.D.**
Eastern Kentucky University
Richmond, Kentucky

**Ghislain Magerotte, Ph.D.**
Mons State University
Mons, Belgium

**Susan Mahanna-Boden, M.S.**
Eastern Kentucky University
Richmond, Kentucky

**Charles A. Maher, Psy.D.**
Rutgers University
Piscataway, New Jersey

**David C. Mann, D.D.M.**
St. Francis Hospital
Pittsburgh, Pennsylvania

**Douglas L. Mann, M.D.**
V. A. Medical Center, Medical
  University of South Carolina
Charleston, South Carolina

**Lester Mann, Ph.D.**
Hunter College, City University
  of New York
New York, New York

Donald S. Marozas, Ed.D.
State University of New York
Geneseo, New York

Ellen B. Marriott, B.A.
University of North Carolina
Wilmington, North Carolina

Margo A. Mastropieri, Ph.D.
Purdue University
Lafayette, Indiana

Deborah C. May, Ed.D.
State University of New York
Albany, New York

James K. McAfee, Ph.D.
Pennsylvania State University
King of Prussia, Pennsylvania

Eileen F. McCarthy, Ph.D.
University of Wisconsin
Madison, Wisconsin

Elizabeth McClellan, Ph.D.
Council for Exceptional Children
Reston, Virginia

George McCloskey, Ph.D.
American Guidance Service
Circle Pines, Minnesota

Linda McCormick, Ph.D.
University of Hawaii, Manoa
Honolulu, Hawaii

Paul A. McDermott, Ph.D.
University of Pennsylvania
Philadelphia, Pennsylvania

Phillip J. McLaughlin, Ed.D.
University of Georgia
Athens, Georgia

James A. McLoughlin, Ph.D.
University of Louisville
Louisville, Kentucky

Paolo Meazzini, Ph.D.
University of Rome
Rome, Italy

Frederic J. Medway, Ph.D.
University of South Carolina
Columbia, South Carolina

James F. Merritt, Ph.D.
University of North Carolina
Wilmington, North Carolina

Danielle Michaux, Ph.D.
Vrije Universiteit Brussel
Brussels, Belgium

James H. Miller, Ph.D.
University of New Orleans
New Orleans, Louisiana

Ted L. Miller, Ph.D.
University of Tennessee
Chattanooga, Tennessee

Norris Minick, Ph.D.
Center for Psychosocial Studies
The Spencer Foundation
Chicago, Illinois

Lisa Monda, M.S.
Florida State University
Tallahassee, Florida

Richard J. Morris, Ph.D.
University of Arizona
Tucson, Arizona

Lonny W. Morrow, Ed.D.
Northeast Missouri State University
Kirksville, Missouri

Sue Ann Morrow, Ph.D.
EDGE, Inc.
Bradshaw, Michigan

Mary Murray, B.S.
Journal of Special Education
Ben Salem, Pennsylvania

Michael Nall, M.D.
Louisville, Kentucky

Robert T. Nash, Ph.D.
University of Wisconsin
Oshkosh, Wisconsin

Bonnie K. Nastasi, Ph.D.
Kent State University
Kent, Ohio

Joyce Ness, M.Ed.
Montgomery County Intermediate Unit
Norristown, Pennsylvania

Ulrika Nettelbladt, Ph.D.
University of Lund
Sweden

Robert C. Nichols, Ph.D.
State University of New York
Buffalo, New York

Etta Lee Nurick, Ph.D.
Montgomery County Intermediate Unit
Norristown, Pennsylvania

Thomas Oakland, Ph.D.
University of Texas
Austin, Texas

John O'Neill, Ph.D.
Hunter College, City University
of New York
New York, New York

Andrew Oseroff, Ed.D.
Florida State University
Tallahassee, Florida

Lawrence J. O'Shea, Ph.D.
University of Florida
Gainesville, Florida

Ellis B. Page, Ed.D.
Duke University
Durham, North Carolina

Kathleen D. Paget, Ph.D.
University of South Carolina
Columbia, South Carolina

Douglas J. Palmer, Ph.D.
Texas A&M University
College Station, Texas

Hagop S. Pambookian, Ph.D.
Elizabeth City, North Carolina

Ernest L. Pancsofar, Ph.D.
University of Connecticut
Storrs, Connecticut

Sara Pankaskie, M.S.
Florida State University
Tallahassee, Florida

Linda H. Parrish, Ph.D.
Texas A&M University
College Station, Texas

Daniel R. Paulson, Ed.D.
University of Wisconsin, Stout
Menomonie, Wisconsin

Mary Leon Peery, M.S.
Texas A&M University
College Station, Texas

Olivier Périer, Ph.D.
Université Libre de Bruxelles
Centre Comprendre et Parler
Brussels, Belgium

Joseph D. Perry, Ph.D.
Kent State University
Kent, Ohio

Richard G. Peters, Ed.D.
Ball State University
Muncie, Indiana

Faith L. Phillips, Ph.D.
University of Oklahoma Health Science
    Center
Norman, Oklahoma

Jeffrey L. Phillips, Ph.D.
University of North Carolina
Wilmington, North Carolina

John J. Pikulski, Ph.D.
University of Delaware
Newark, Delaware

Sally E. Pisarchick, Ph.D.
Cuyahoga Special Education Service
    Center
Maple Heights, Ohio

Brenda M. Pope, R.N., A.D.N.
New Hanover Memorial Hospital
Wilmington, North Carolina

John E. Porcella, Ph.D.
Rhinebeck Country School
Rhinebeck, New York

James A. Poteet, Ph.D.
Ball State University
Muncie, Indiana

David P. Prasse, Ph.D.
University of Wisconsin
Milwaukee, Wisconsin

Marianne Price, Ed.D.
Montgomery County Intermediate Unit
Norristown, Pennsylvania

Elisabeth A. Prinz, B.S.
Pennsylvania State University
University Park, Pennsylvania

Philip M. Prinz, Ph.D.
Pennsylvania State University
University Park, Pennsylvania

Antonio E. Puente, Ph.D.
University of North Carolina
Wilmington, North Carolina

Nuri Puig
University of Oklahoma
Norman, Oklahoma

Craig T. Ramey, Ph.D.
University of North Carolina
Chapel Hill, North Carolina

Sylvia Z. Ramirez, M.S.
University of Wisconsin
Madison, Wisconsin

**Arlene I. Rattan, M.S.**
Ball State University
Muncie, Indiana

**Gurmal Rattan, Ed.D.**
Indiana University of Pennsylvania
Indiana, Pennsylvania

**Robert R. Reilley, Ed.D.**
Texas A&M University
College Station, Texas

**Fredricka K. Reisman, Ph.D.**
Drexel University
Philadelphia, Pennsylvania

**Daniel J. Reschly, Ph.D.**
Iowa State University
Ames, Iowa

**Cecil R. Reynolds, Ph.D.**
Texas A&M University
College Station, Texas

**William S. Rholes, Ph.D.**
Texas A&M University
College Station, Texas

**James R. Ricciuti, Ph.D.**
United States Office of Management
    and Budget
Washington, D.C.

**Teresa K. Rice, B.S.**
Texas A&M University
College Station, Texas

**Paul C. Richardson, M.A.**
Elwyn Institutes
Elwyn, Pennsylvania

**Sylvia O. Richardson, M.D.**
University of South Florida
Tampa, Florida

**Bert O. Richmond, Ph.D.**
University of Georgia
Athens, Georgia

**Catherine Hall Rikhye, Ph.D.**
Hunter College, City University
    of New York
New York, New York

**Gary J. Robertson, Ph.D.**
American Guidance Service
Circle Pines, Minnesota

**Kathleen Rodden-Nord, Ph.D.**
University of Oregon
Eugene, Oregon

**Jean A. Rondal, Ph.D.**
Laboratory for Language, Psychology,
    and Logopedics
University of Liege
Liege, Belgium

**Sheldon Rosenberg, Ph.D.**
University of Illinois
Chicago, Illinois

**Bruce P. Rosenthal, O.D.**
State University of New York
New York, New York

**Kathy L. Ruhl, Ph.D.**
Pennsylvania State University
University Park, Pennsylvania

**Joseph M. Russo, Ed.M.**
Hunter College, City University
    of New York
New York, New York

**Robert B. Rutherford, Jr., Ph.D.**
Arizona State University
Tempe, Arizona

**Anne Sabatino, E.Ad.**
Hudson, Wisconsin

**David A. Sabatino, Ph.D.**
West Virginia College of Graduate
    Studies
Institute, West Virginia

**Lisa J. Sampson, B.A.**
Eastern Kentucky University
Richmond, Kentucky

**Polly E. Sanderson, M.S.**
Research Triangle Institute
Research Triangle Park, North Carolina

**Scott W. Sautter, Ph.D.**
Peabody College, Vanderbilt University
Nashville, Tennessee

**Robert F. Sawicki, Ph.D.**
Lake Erie Institute of Rehabilitation
Lake Erie, Pennsylvania

**Patrick J. Schloss, Ph.D.**
Pennsylvania State University
University Park, Pennsylvania

**Ronald V. Schmelzer, Ph.D.**
Eastern Kentucky University
Richmond, Kentucky

**Carol S. Schmitt, M.S.**
Eastern Kentucky University
Richmond, Kentucky

**Sue A. Schmitt, Ed.D.**
University of Wisconsin, Stout
Menomonie, Wisconsin

**Lyle F. Schoenfeldt, Ph.D.**
Texas A&M University
College Station, Texas

**Eric Schopler, Ph.D.**
University of North Carolina
Chapel Hill, North Carolina

**Louis Schwartz, Ed.D.**
Florida State University
Tallahassee, Florida

**June Scobee, Ph.D.**
University of Houston, Clear Lake
Houston, Texas

**Thomas E. Scruggs, Ph.D.**
Purdue University
Lafayette, Indiana

**Denise M. Sedlak, M.S.**
United Way of Dunn County
Menomonie, Wisconsin

**Robert A. Sedlak, Ph.D.**
University of Wisconsin, Stout
Menomonie, Wisconsin

**John D. See, Ph.D.**
University of Wisconsin, Stout
Menomonie, Wisconsin

**Sandra B. Sexton, M.D.**
Emory University School of Medicine
Atlanta, Georgia

**Susan Shandelmier, M.A.**
Eastern Pennsylvania Special Education
    Regional Resources Center
King of Prussia, Pennsylvania

**Deborah A. Shanley, Ed.D.**
Medgar Evers College, City University
    of New York
New York, New York

**William J. Shaw, Psy.D.**
University of Oklahoma
Norman, Oklahoma

**Susan M. Sheridan, M.S.**
University of Wisconsin
Madison, Wisconsin

**Dakum Shown, Ph.D.**
University of Jos
Nigeria

**Lawrence J. Siegel, Ph.D.**
University of Texas Medical Branch
Galveston, Texas

**Rosanne K. Silberman, Ed.D.**
Hunter College, City University
    of New York
New York, New York

**Lissen Simonsen, B.A.**
University of North Carolina
Wilmington, North Carolina

**Paul T. Sindelar, Ph.D.**
Florida State University
Tallahassee, Florida

**Jerry L. Sloan, Ph.D.**
Wilmington Psychiatric Associates
Wilmington, North Carolina

**Craig D. Smith, Ph.D.**
Georgia College
Milledgeville, Georgia

**Maureen A. Smith, Ph.D.**
Pennsylvania State University
University Park, Pennsylvania

**Judy Smith-Davis, Ph.D.**
Counterpoint Communications Company
Reno, Nevada

**Jane Sparks, B.A.**
University of North Carolina
Wilmington, North Carolina

**Barbara S. Speer, M.Ed.**
Shaker Heights City School District
Shaker Heights, Ohio

**Harrison C. Stanton, M.Ed.**
Texas A&M University
College Station, Texas

**J. Todd Stephens, Ph.D.**
University of Wisconsin
Madison, Wisconsin

**Cecelia Steppe-Jones, Ph.D.**
North Carolina Central University
Durham, North Carolina

**Linda J. Stevens, B.A.**
University of Minnesota
Minneapolis, Minnesota

**Rachael J. Stevenson, M.A.**
Bedford, Ohio

**Mary E. Stinson, M.A.**
University of Alabama
University, Alabama

**Roberta C. Stokes, B.S.**
Texas A&M University
College Station, Texas

**Doretha McKnight Stone, M.S.N.**
University of North Carolina
Wilmington, North Carolina

**Michael L. Stowe, M.S.**
Texas A&M University
College Station, Texas

**Edythe A. Strand, Ph.D.**
University of Wisconsin
Madison, Wisconsin

**Dorothy A. Strom, M.S.**
Ball State University
Indiana School of Medicine
Muncie, Indiana

**Kathryn A. Sullivan, M.A., Ed.S.**
Texas A&M University
College Station, Texas

**Emily G. Sutter, Ph.D.**
University of Houston, Clear Lake
Houston, Texas

**Mark E. Swerdlik, Ph.D.**
Illinois State University
Normal, Illinois

**Henri B. Szliwowski, M.D.**
Hôpital Erasme, Université Libre de
   Bruxelles
Brussels, Belgium

**Pearl E. Tait, Ph.D.**
Florida State University
Tallahassee, Florida

**Paula Tallal, Ph.D.**
University of California
San Diego, California

**Mary K. Tallent, Ph.D.**
Texas Tech University
Lubbock, Texas

**C. Mildred Tashman, Ph.D.**
College of Saint Rose
Albany, New York

**James W. Tawney, Ph.D.**
Pennsylvania State University
University Park, Pennsylvania

**Cathy F. Telzrow, Ph.D.**
Cuyahoga Special Education Service
   Center
Maple Heights, Ohio

**Steven R. Timmermans, Ph.D.**
Mary Free Bed Hospital and
   Rehabilitation Center
Grand Rapids, Michigan

**Gerald Tindal, Ph.D.**
University of Oregon
Eugene, Oregon

**Francine Tomkins, Ph.D.**
University of Cincinnati
Cincinnati, Ohio

**Carol Tomlinson-Keasey, Ph.D.**
University of California
Riverside, California

**Raymond Toraille, Ph.D.**
Public Education
Paris, France

**Jose Luis Torres, M.Ed.**
Texas A&M University
College Station, Texas

**Timothy L. Turco, M.S.**
Louisiana State University
Baton Rouge, Louisiana

**Lori E. Unruh, M.S.**
Eastern Kentucky University
Richmond, Kentucky

**Cynthia Vail, M.S.**
Florida State University
Tallahassee, Florida

**Greg Valcante, Ph.D.**
University of Florida
Tallahassee, Florida

**Hubert B. Vance, Ph.D.**
East Tennessee State University
Johnson City, Tennessee

**Aryan Van Der Leij, Ph.D.**
Free University
Amsterdam, The Netherlands

**K. Sandra Vanta, M.S.**
Cleveland Public Schools
Cleveland, Ohio

**Emily Wahlen, M.S.**
Hunter College, City University
   of New York
New York, New York

**Deborah Klein Walker, Ed.D.**
Harvard University
Cambridge, Massachusetts

**Marjorie E. Ward, Ph.D.**
The Ohio State University
Columbus, Ohio

**Sue Allen Warren, Ph.D.**
Boston University
Boston, Massachusetts

**Danny Wedding, Ph.D.**
Marshall University
Huntington, Virginia

**Frederick F. Weiner, Ph.D.**
Pennsylvania State University
University Park, Pennsylvania

**Marjorie Weintraub, M.S.Ed.**
Montgomery County Intermediate Unit
Norristown, Pennsylvania

**Bahr Weiss, B.S.**
University of North Carolina
Chapel Hill, North Carolina

**Shirley Parker Wells, B.A.**
University of North Carolina
Wilmington, North Carolina

**Louise H. Werth, Ph.D.**
Florida State University
Tallahassee, Florida

**Catherine Wetzburger, Ph.D.**
Université Libre de Bruxelles
Brussels, Belgium

**Larry J. Wheeler, Ed.D.**
Southwest Texas State University
San Marcos, Texas

**Thomas M. Whitten, Ph.D.**
Florida State University
Tallahassee, Florida

**Greta N. Wilkening, Ph.D.**
Children's Hospital
Denver, Colorado

**Mary Clare Williams, R.N.**
Ramey, Pennsylvania

**Diane J. Willis, Ph.D.**
University of Oklahoma Health Sciences
   Center
Oklahoma City, Oklahoma

**Victor L. Willson, Ph.D.**
Texas A&M University
College Station, Texas

**John D. Wilson, M.A.**
Elwyn Institutes
Elwyn, Pennsylvania

**Margo E. Wilson, Ph.D.**
Lexington, Kentucky

**Joseph C. Witt, Ph.D.**
Louisiana State University
Baton Rouge, Louisiana

**Bencie Woll, Ph.D.**
University of Bristol
England

**Bernice Y. L. Wong, Ph.D.**
Simon Fraser University
Buraby, British Columbia

**Mary M. Wood, Ph.D.**
University of Georgia
Athens, Georgia

**Diane E. Woods, M.Ed.**
World Rehabilitation Fund
New York, New York

**Frances F. Worchel, Ph.D.**
Texas A&M University
College Station, Texas

**Eleanor Boyd Wright, Ph.D.**
University of North Carolina
Wilmington, North Carolina

**Logan Wright, Ph.D.**
University of Oklahoma
Norman, Oklahoma

**Karen F. Wyche, Ph.D.**
Hunter College, City University
   of New York
New York, New York

**Martha Ellen Wynne, Ph.D.**
Loyola University of Chicago
Chicago, Illinois

**Roland K. Yoshida, Ph.D.**
Fordham University
New York, New York

**Thomas Zane, Ph.D.**
Johns Hopkins University
Baltimore, Maryland

**Lonnie K. Zeltzer, M.D.**
University of Texas Health Science
   Center
San Antonio, Texas

**Paul M. Zeltzer, M.D.**
University of Texas Health Science
   Center
San Antonio, Texas

**Kenneth A. Zych, Ph.D.**
Walter Reed Army Medical Center
Washington, D.C.

# FOREWORD

The creation of the *Encyclopedia of Special Education* represents a coming of age for a field of endeavor that not so many years ago was a focus of limited public interest and concern, both for society at large and for education in particular.

Those of use who served in special education during its earlier years, when public concern and commitment to its needs were minimal or even lacking, cannot help but be both pleased and astonished at the vast enterprise that it has now become.

The growth of special education has developed very gradually over the past 150 years. From approximately 1850 to 1900, the care, management, and education of handicapped children was conducted primarily in residential institutions for the deaf, the blind, the mentally deficient, and the delinquent, and in religious-sponsored facilities. From 1900 to approximately 1950, public schools in large cities began to educate a small percentage of handicapped and gifted children. After 1950 some states began to subsidize local public schools to encourage the establishment of special education to decrease the demands made on overcrowded and dilapidated state residential schools. During this period the federal government gave no financial assistance to the states, believing that education was a state responsibility, and that federal aid would lead to federal control of education.

In the 1950s the precedent of the denial of federal aid was discarded. Parents began to organize and to demand services for their handicapped children. Their demands extended beyond state legislators and finally reached the White House. President Eisenhower listened and consequently requested Congress to help. Congress responded by appropriating several million dollars to be used for research and the preparation of professional personnel.

The major expansion and social revolution came in the 1960s during the administration of John F. Kennedy. Following the beginnings made by President Eisenhower, President Kennedy dispatched task forces to several countries around the world to survey their programs for handicapped children. The task force to the Soviet Union, of which I was fortunate enough to be a member, visited laboratories and schools in that country for 3 weeks, and returned to report their findings to the President. On hearing the reports of Soviet advances, President Kennedy asked, "Do you mean to tell me that the greatest and richest country in the world is not doing as good a job as the Soviet Union?" The following January, he presented to Congress a comprehensive bill for research and training entitled Mental Retardation Facilities and Community Mental Health Centers Construction Act of 1963. This was followed by a number of congressional acts to encompass many kinds of services. In 1975 Congress enacted PL 94-142, The Education for All Handicapped Children Act. Interestingly, this act follows the time-honored Declaration of Independence. It has been paraphrased as follows:

> We hold these truths to be self-evident, that all children, handicapped and nonhandicapped, are created equal; that they are endowed by their creator with certain inalienable rights, among these are the right to equal education to the maximum of each child's capability. To secure these rights, Public Law 94-142 was established. We, the people of these United States, solemnly declare that all exceptional children shall be educated at public expense, and that their education will be in the least restrictive environment. (Kirk & Gallagher, *Educating Exceptional Children,* 3rd ed., 1979, xi)

It is particularly gratifying to observe that special education has become a major public commitment for exceptional students, not just in the United States but throughout much of the rest of the world as well. This is true not only in Canada and western Europe, whose achievements in many areas of special education service often preceded and inspired those of the United States, but also in Japan, Indonesia, and less advanced and less affluent parts of the globe. There, too, concerned professionals and parents seek to provide for the education of handicapped children and youths, often in spite of extremely limited resources.

The growth of special education, and the extraordinary commitment of financial and human resources to service and research over the past two decades, has meant an explosion of information. This scattered information in a wide variety of journals and books is extremely difficult for professionals to amass and acquire. A variety of efforts have been made to bring this information under control. The contributions of abstracting services, databases, reviews, and handbooks have helped greatly to manage special education's knowledge base. At the same time, such efforts have not been entirely successful in bringing the information under coherent control, or in making it readily accessible to professionals in related fields or to interested lay persons.

The *Encyclopedia of Special Education* is designed to present a comprehensive vision of what special education is about in a readily understandable, usable, summative form. It makes it possible for any intelligent seeker of information about special education to grasp both the broad scope and specific details of those areas of endeavor identified with special education. Comprehensive yet succinct, the encyclopedia literally provides an A to Z examination of what special education is all about. Furthermore, it does so by serving its readers with explanations that are succinct and devoid of unnecessary detail.

The *Encyclopedia of Special Education* provides a scope and view of special education not readily obtained from other sources. It provides a thorough and summative view of special education and succinct access to needed current information. Its issuance comes at a most propitious time because special education has now taken directions that are likely to persist well into the next century.

The *Encyclopedia of Special Education* will be an essential reference tool, not only for professionals working in special education but for lawyers, physicians, psychologists, social workers, school board members, and others who assist in or formulate policies for the education of the handicapped and gifted. It is the type of reference that the everyday citizen will find both useful and informative, since it is the informed citizen who, ultimately, is the guardian of special education.

The *Encyclopedia of Special Education* will likely find a welcome niche in public as well as college and professional libraries. Reynolds and Mann and their consulting editors should be congratulated for taking the time and effort to compile this gargantuan encyclopedia.

SAMUEL A. KIRK

*University of Arizona, Tucson*
*April 1987*

# PREFACE

Exceptional children, i.e., handicapped or gifted individuals between the ages of birth and 23, constitute (depending on various types of estimation) nearly 10% of children and adolescents who receive educational services throughout the world. The field of endeavor concerned with this education is generally designated as special education.

Special education is a broad domain encompassing many different concerns and types of children. There long has been a need for a publication that provides ready access to authoritative and comprehensive, yet current and succinct, information about this category of education and its many related aspects. The *Encyclopedia of Special Education* is just such a publication. It is intended as a primary reference for many disciplines and professions concerned with the education of exceptional children and with their special characteristics, needs, and problems. The *Encyclopedia* will continue to serve for many years as a desktop reference containing essential information for educators, psychologists, physicians, social workers, occupational and physical therapists, lawyers, and ministers.

The *Encyclopedia of Special Education* is, however, more than just a professional reference book. It also is intended for use by intelligent lay people, including parents, school board members, advocates of handicapped persons' rights, legislators, and concerned citizens seeking to be more knowledgeable about the education of exceptional children. Indeed, as Raymond J. Corsini, editor of the *Encyclopedia of Psychology* (1984) (Wiley-Interscience) wrote in his preface to that valuable reference work, it can be argued that "professionals [themselves] are lay people when not reading in their own specialized field." It was on this basis that he sought to make his encyclopedia "understandable to the average intelligent layperson (Corsini, p. xxi). It is on this basis, too, that we have prepared the *Encyclopedia of Special Education* as a source of authentic and authoritative information expressed with clarity and conciseness. Though technical language is used, the level of presentation was carefully reviewed to achieve this goal of utility and readability.

The preparation of the *Encyclopedia of Special Education* presented many challenges. Among the foremost was the fact that over the past two decades or so, the needs and rights of exceptional children have moved from a position of relative obscurity and neglect to a position in the center of public consciousness and obligation to a degree unanticipated and even inconceivable in earlier generations.

Originally, special education was a small, poorly understood, and underfunded field that attempted to meet the needs of but a few children, first under the rubric of "the education of exceptional children" and then, in recent years, under that of "special education." Over the course of several decades, special education has become a massive multidimensional movement involving many different groups and interests and making important claims on public attention and funding. Thus, the *Encyclopedia of Special Education* has a broad scope. Though it is primarily concerned with the education and training of gifted and handicapped children, it also extends into psychology, medicine, and politics, to mention but a few of the non-educational fields. The inclusion of these fields is critical to an appreciation of special education. Indeed, the *Encyclopedia of Special Education* attempts to touch on all areas and fields deemed relevant to an understanding of what late twentieth century and early twenty-first century special education is about.

The volumes each follow a traditional encyclopedic structure and are organized alphabetically. Each topic is covered succinctly, giving the most crucial information and directing the reader to more extensive treatments of the issues. There are more than two thousand included in the work. Although presented alphabetically, the various entries can be grouped conceptually into seven major catagories.

1. *Biographies*—brief descriptions of key figures in the field, both living and deceased, and their key contributions to special education.
2. *Educational and psychological tests*—brief descriptions and commentary on tests with applications to special education are provided, but more extensive discussions are given of tests with widespread use or with a particularly complex structure. Tests are given under their proper titles and not by acronyms or popular titles. Acronyms are indexed and cross-referenced in most cases for ease of locating information.
3. *Interventions and service delivery*—techniques of intervention and the delivery of special education services to individuals are discussed and reviewed.

4. *Handicapping conditions*—conditions that require special education services are described.

5. *Related services*—services necessary to support the effectiveness of special education but not usually deemed to be special education services per se are described and their relevance to special education noted.

6. *Legal*—major court cases, legislation, and legal concepts related to the field of special education are noted and their implications for special education are reviewed.

7. *Miscellaneous entries*—this category includes special education topics that are not classified under the previous categories but that are substantive and relevant to the field (e.g., measurement terms, prevention projects, major works, journals, professional associations, and terms such as epidemiology, school psychology, vocational counselor, naturalistic observation, and effectiveness of special education).

These categories were derived primarily for the use of editors, consulting editors, and the publisher's staff. However, they are valuable to the users of the *Encyclopedia* as well as they help to locate items of interest. To address such a diverse array of topics and to maintain a balanced view on what can be a controversial field, two groups of advisers were formed: the Board of Consulting Editors, who had important writing and supervisory responsibilities shared with the editors, and the the Editorial Advisory Board, professionals who advised the editors, did limited writing, and provided specialty reviewing for a variety of topics. These individuals were chosen to represent a host of theoretical positions, areas of expertise, disciplines (special education, psychology, medicine, speech pathology, physical therapy, educational psychology, and school psychology, to name a few), demographic and ethnic characteristics, and national origins. Practitioners, academicians, administrators, and others are represented here as well. Experts from many disciplines of science, education, politics, and philosophy contributed to the *Encyclopedia*. Each author is credited with a byline at the end of each entry. Those entries listed as authored by Staff were prepared by Elaine Fletcher-Janzen, E. Valerie Hewitt, Angela Bailey, and Cecil Reynolds, with the assistance of various sources. Many of these entries are biographies in which the staff was assisted by the biographees. All living biographees were asked to review their entries for factual accuracy; most were extremely helpful and cooperative in this regard.

A great challenge in the creation of the *Encyclopedia of Special Education* was the recognition that special education is a worldwide concern rather than a concern narrowly defined and interpreted in terms of events proceeding within the boundaries of the United States. Fortunately, the *Encyclopedia* was able to draw on the expertise of authorities familiar with the international aspects of special education to assist in providing access to information worldwide about developments relevant to special education.

Still another challenge to the *Encyclopedia of Special Education* was to respond to the historical antecedents and roots of special education as well as to current issues. A significant effort, and a successful one was to ensure that the *Encyclopedia* would provide its users with succinct, pertinent information relative to the foundations of special education in addition to information bearing on its immediate concerns.

Indeed, the *Encyclopedia of Special Education* has gone to great lengths to give all of the aspects of special education their due. It is hoped that the *Encyclopedia* will serve as an efficient and effective aide for practitioners, scientists, parents, and intelligent laypersons alike, and for many years to come. We have been helped in this task by the expert opinions and advice of authorities across a broad range of disciplines. Recommendations for topics to be included in the *Encyclopedia* and opinions about those topics were sought from many experts, going far beyond even the insightful comments of our consulting editors and Editorial Advisory Board. Indexes of all major works in the field were examined, computer searches were conducted, and practitioners in special education were asked their opinion. Reference librarians throughout the United States were consulted. As preparation of the *Encyclopedia* proceeded, further topics were solicited and prepared as late as 2 weeks prior to the publisher's final deadline for submission. Inevitably, something will be missing and we, the editors, accept full responsibility for any such sins of omission.

As a consequence of the broad diversity of sources for the topics suggested, the *Encyclopedia* is an ecumenical work, a manifestation of many divergent streams of thought brought together in a flow of convergent achievement. There are more than 380 contributors all concerned, though often in quite different ways, with the education, training, and management of exceptional individuals. Users of the *Encyclopedia of Special Education* will find that it serves a variety of purposes. The *Encyclopedia* serves the profession and the public:

1. *As a source of basic summative information.* Users of the *Encyclopedia of Special Education* will find it valuable first and foremost as an immediate source of concise summative information about special education, rehabilitation, and childhood exceptionality; it covers topics in these areas literally from A to Z. The *Encyclopedia*'s information is presented in ways that make it very accessible. Readers seeking information will find it available in quick and easy to comprehend form, whether the information they seek concerns definitions or concepts, theories or historical personages, critical assessment techniques,

issues of intervention techniques employed in special education, laws and regulations, or key projects and key persons. Great effort was made to ensure that the *Encyclopedia*'s entries are as contemporary as possible. In many instances, the *Encyclopedia*'s users will find the information offered on most topics to be sufficient for their purposes. When more extensive information is required, the *Encyclopedia* will guide its users to other sources of information both through cross-references within the *Encyclopedia* itself and to other texts as well.

2. *As a basic spot reference.* A most important use of the *Encyclopedia of Special Education* is to serve as a source for spot references. Using its entries or its extensive index, the user can look up and check out particular topics for names, definitions, and the like. The user can identify other topics related to a particular area and learn quickly how to access them. The *Encyclopedia* is more useful, in many ways, than abstracts or abstract services for tracking down information.

3. *As a textbook.* The *Encyclopedia* is not intended to serve as a primary text for a basic or core course in childhood exceptionality or special education. However, it will serve as a useful supplementary text for almost any course at either undergraduate or graduate levels, serving to amplify the topics in such courses or to extend the knowledge networks of concepts, practices, and research. The *Encyclopedia* also can serve as a primary text for advanced courses or seminars; as such, the student will be left with a set of books that will serve him or her long into a professional career. The *Encyclopedia* also should be helpful to students and scholars who need a concise yet precise guide to information in education, psychology, etc., for review purposes, either for comprehensives or licensure or certification. Graduate students approaching comprehensive exams should find the work useful, especially on their reference shelves as they move ahead toward the practice of special education.

4. *As a continuing information-support system.* Well beyond the immediate needs of knowledge and information, the *Encyclopedia of Special Education* will serve as a source of continuing education for its owners. Regular, even review of its contents will ensure its readers of a deeper understanding relative to special education and related fields. In professional and public libraries, it will serve as a network control system permitting the management of other resources concerning the education of exceptional children.

A project as massive as the *Encyclopedia* requires the joint work of an inordinate number of individuals. To our authors we must offer our first round of thanks. They worked in a timely manner, jovially revising their first efforts in many cases and under tight editorial guidelines. Our Editorial Advisory Board gave excellent advice in reviewing, writing, and generally advising at various stages of the project. All are listed in the front matter. The Board of Consulting Editors gave a yeoman's effort in all cases. Each consulting editor had significant supervisory and writing responsibilities; without their help we would still be struggling.

Many others deserve our thanks. Joan Kappus gave hours and hours to the development of the master list of entries. E. Valerie Hewitt began working with us only during the last 6 months of manuscript preparation, but was a godsend nevertheless. Mike Ash, Head of the Department of Educational Psychology at Texas A&M University, was instrumental in obtaining the university support necessary for such a large project. Mike's support, moral and professional, and as a friend, was necessary and welcomed—and very typical of this extraordinary department head. The Research Assistance Laboratory of the College of Education at Texas A&M University, under the direction of Victor Willson, graciously gave us cherished space for housing the *Encyclopedia* office and operations. Hugh J. Scott, dean of the Division of Programs in Education at Hunter College, provided an encouragement of scholarship in special education that was inspirational and deserving of our appreciation.

Angela Bailey was our administrative editor and was responsible for coordinating all aspects of the day-to-day operations of the office. She corresponded with hundreds of authors, cajoled the tardy, smoothed ruffled feathers, and served as chief operations officer, making everyone adhere to schedule, the editors included. She handled all with humor, aplomb, and efficiency. We could not have done it without her and consider ourselves fortunate to have had the insight to have hired her.

Elaine Fletcher-Janzen, senior editorial associate, read and edited every piece of manuscript for content and for style. She coordinated writing assignments and consistently performed well beyond the expected. Elaine prepared background material for more entries than any individual author and prepared her own entries, while also coordinating the review process. Elaine is truly the proverbial gem. She is the kind of graduate assistant and doctoral student that we came to academia hoping to mentor; we hope she has learned as much from us as we have learned from her while she progressed through her doctoral studies—and all while starting her family—another successful venture we are sure.

The overall guidance of the work can be ascribed to Dr. Martin Grayson, editor of the Encyclopedia Division of John Wiley & Sons. Martin believed in us and the project from the beginning. A journal and an encyclopedia editor as well as a scholar in his own field, Martin gave essential guidance, urging us on through inspiration as well as an occasional shove when our labors flagged. The staff of production editors at Wiley was most helpful as well, consistent with our experience with a half dozen other Wiley projects. In particular, Cary Weinberger and her predecessor April Kelliher deserve recognition for their coordination from the publisher's office. Margery Carazzone, Production Manager and Rosalind Greenberg, Production Editor, performed superbly.

To our families, our friends, and our secretaries, we needed your patience and understanding as we struggled to meet deadlines and asked more than we should have from you. You so graciously accommodated us. Thank you. And, Julia, thanks for the crucial times of sanity you bring

to a very crazy life. CRR would like to express a special note of appreciation to his mentors, Alan S. Kaufman and E. Paul Torrance, who continue to inspire. To the users of the *Encyclopedia*, we await your comments on this work and hope that you will find it helpful to you in helping children grow and develop to the utmost of their potential.

CECIL R. REYNOLDS
LESTER MANN

*College Station, Texas*
*New York, New York*
*April 1987*

# ENCYCLOPEDIA OF
# SPECIAL EDUCATION

# A

## AAAS

See AMERICAN ASSOCIATION FOR THE ADVANCEMENT OF SCIENCE.

## AAMD ADAPTIVE BEHAVIOR SCALES

Two adaptive behavior scales were developed by the American Association on Mental Deficiency (AAMD) to measure adaptive and maladaptive behavior of the retarded, disturbed, and developmentally disabled. One scale was developed for use in institutions and the other for use in public schools.

The AAMD Adaptive Behavior Scale (institution version) was developed in 1969 by Nihira, Foster, Shellhaas, and Leland. The scale is designed to provide a description of the way an individual maintains personal independence in daily living or of how he or she meets the social expectations of the environment. Part 1 consists of 66 items grouped into 10 domains that measure adaptive behavior: independent functioning, physical development, economic activity, language development, numbers and time, domestic activity, vocational activity, self-direction, responsibility, and socialization. Part 2 consists of 42 items grouped into 14 domains that measure maladaptive behavior: violent and destructive behavior, antisocial behavior, rebellious behavior, untrustworthy behavior, withdrawal, stereotyped behavior and odd mannerisms, inappropriate interpersonal manners, unacceptable vocal habits, unacceptable or eccentric habits, self-abusive behavior, hyperactive tendencies, sexually aberrant behavior, psychological disturbances, and use of medication.

The AAMD Adaptive Behavior Scale was revised in 1974 (Lambert, Windmiller, Cole, & Figueroa, 1975) for use in the public schools. The latest edition was prepared by Lambert and Windmiller (1981) and the instructional planning manual was developed by Lambert, Windmiller, Tharinger, & Cole (1981). This scale is intended to provide information about students' personal independence and social skills and to reveal areas of functioning where special program planning is needed.

The school edition contains essentially the same items found in the institutional version from which it was derived. Three domains, domestic activity, self-abusive behavior, and sexually aberrant behavior, perceived by the authors to be not pertinent to public schools, were omitted.

## REFERENCES

Lambert, N., & Windmiller, M. (1981). *Diagnostic and technical manual, revised AAMD Adaptive Behavior Scale-School Edition.* Monterey, CA: CTB/McGraw-Hill.

Lambert, N., Windmiller, M., Cole, L., & Figueroa, R. (1975). *Manual for AAMD Adaptive Behavior Scale—Public School Version (1974 revision).* Washington, DC: American Association on Mental Deficiency.

Lambert, N., Windmiller, M., Tharinger, D., & Cole, L. (1981). *Administration and instructional planning manual, AAMD Adaptive Behavior Scale-School Edition.* Monterey, CA: CTB/McGraw-Hill.

Nihira, K., Foster, R., Shellhaas, M., & Leland, H. (1969). *Adaptive Behavior Scale.* Washington, DC: American Association on Mental Deficiency.

Nihira, K., Foster, R., Shellhaas, M., & Leland, H. (1974). *Adaptive Behavior Scale manual.* Washington, DC: American Association on Mental Deficiency.

CECELIA STEPPE-JONES
*North Carolina Central University*

AAMD CLASSIFICATION SYSTEMS
ADAPTIVE BEHAVIOR

## AAMD CLASSIFICATION SYSTEMS

The American Association on Mental Deficiency (AAMD) was founded in 1876 to support and promote the general welfare of people who are mentally retarded through professional programs, dissemination of research and program advances, and development of standards for services and facilities. The organization is comprised of approximately 10,000 professionals from many different disciplines who are concerned with the prevention and treatment of mental retardation. The association publishes two research journals, *Mental Retardation* and *American Journal of Mental Deficiency.* A national conference, along

1

with many regional and state conferences, is held each year to give professionals the opportunity to share significant information regarding the education and welfare of children and adults with mental retardation.

The first diagnostic and classification system was published in 1921. It was reviewed and revised in 1933, 1941, 1957, 1959, 1973, 1977, and 1983. In each case, the manual was revised based on new developments in philosophy and knowledge of the field. To make the revisions and clarify important issues, input is culled from presentations at national and regional meetings of the AAMD, national and local hearings, and discussions with representatives of many professional, social, and political action groups. All revisions are made by the AAMD's Terminology and Classification Committee after a careful examination of the present classification system and the new data. Major revisions over the years have centered around the presentation of a dual classification system, medical and behavioral; clarification of the definitions of adaptive and measured intelligence; the addition of an extensive glossary; an illustration of levels of adaptive behavior; and procedures for diagnosing mental retardation in the behavioral system. With this last example, it is important that clinicians understand, in diagnosing mental retardation, the concept of standard error of measurement and its use in making a clinical determination of retardation and level of functioning.

The 1983 AAMD classification system developed by the AAMD's Terminology and Classification Committee has been written to reflect current thinking in the field. This latest edition has three distinct purposes. First, the 1983 edition was an attempt to provide an acceptable system to be used worldwide. It was developed in coordination with the International Classification of Diseases-9 (ICD-9) of the World Health Organization, the American Psychiatric Association's *Diagnostic and Statistical Manual-III* (DSM-III), and the American Association on Mental Deficiency's Classification in Mental Retardation.

The second purpose was to improve opportunities to gather and disseminate information regarding diagnosis, treatment, and research activities. The third purpose of this classification system was to provide opportunities for the identification of causes of mental retardation with implications for prevention.

The definition of mental retardation accepted by most authorities is the one used by the American Association on Mental Deficiency. The definition was presented first by Heber in 1961 and later revised by Grossman in 1973 to read: "Mental retardation refers to significantly subaverage general intellectual functioning resulting in or associated with concurrent impairments in adaptive behavior and manifested during the developmental period." Based on the definition, to be classified mentally retarded, the person must be below average in both measured intelligence and adaptive behavior.

The AAMD classification of the retarded has been use-

ful to professionals as well because it is based on the severity of retardation. The terms used by the AAMD are mild, moderate, severe, and profound.

The AAMD causal classification scheme centers around nine general groupings for mental retardation. These groups include infections and intoxication, trauma or physical agent, metabolism or nutrition, gross brain disease, unknown prenatal influence, chromosomal anomalies, other conditions originating in the perinatal period following psychiatric disorder, and environmental influences.

**REFERENCES**

Grossman, H. (Ed.). (1983). *Classification in mental retardation.* Washington, DC: American Association on Mental Deficiency.

CECELIA STEPPE-JONES
*North Carolina Central University*

**AAMD ADAPTIVE BEHAVIOR SCALES MENTAL RETARDATION**

## ABAB DESIGN

The ABAB design is one of the oldest and most widely used single-case designs developed in behavioral psychology. It was initially used in laboratory studies with animals (Sidman, 1960); however, as the applied behavior analysis movement got under way (Baer, Wolf, & Risley, 1968), it became a prototype for applied behavioral investigations conducted in the natural environment. Although the number of single-case designs has increased markedly since the early days of applied behavior analysis (e.g., Kazdin, 1980; Kratochwill, 1978), the ABAB design still occupies a prominent place in applied behavioral research. Moreover, because of the high degree of experimental control that it provides, it has been widely used with individuals manifesting various types of handicaps (Bergan, 1977). For example, the ABAB design has been particularly useful in studying environmental variables affecting language acquisition in retarded children (Bergan, 1977).

The ABAB design is intended to reveal a functional relationship between an experimental treatment and a behavior targeted for change. For example, it might be used to establish a functional relationship between the use of the plural form of a noun and a treatment such as praise following the occurrence of a plural noun. The demonstration of a functional relationship between praise and plural nouns would require an association between the frequency of plural-noun production and the occurrence of verbal praise. Given that a functional relationship were established, verbal praise could be assumed to function as a positive reinforcer increasing the probability of occurrence of plural nouns by the subject or subjects participating in the experiment.

The ABAB technique has often been referred to as a single-case design (e.g., Kratochwill, 1978). However, it may be applied with more than one subject. Thus, the term single case is a bit misleading. Glass, Wilson, and Gottman (1975) among others called attention to the fact that the ABAB design is a time-series design in that it reflects an effort to determine changes in behavior occurring across a series of points in time. Recognition of the ABAB design as a time-series design opened the way for linking the design to the statistical procedures associated with time-series analysis (see, for example, Glass, Wilson, & Gottman, 1975). Application of time-series analysis procedures affords a statistical test for hypotheses that may be investigated with the ABAB design. However, despite this advantage, time-series techniques have not been widely used in applied investigations involving the ABAB design. There are a variety of reasons for this. Among them is the fact that the graphing techniques suggested by behavioral psychologists (e.g., Parsonson & Baer, 1978) as an alternative to statistical analysis are easier to implement and to interpret than time-series statistics. Nonetheless, time-series procedures constitute a potentially powerful tool for applied behavioral research and their use can be expected to increase in the future.

As the letters in its name suggest, the ABAB design includes four phases. The initial A phase is a baseline period that records behavior across a series of points in time in the absence of intervention. The length of the baseline period varies depending on the variability of the behavior being recorded. If the behavior is highly variable, a longer baseline is required than if the behavior is highly stable. More data are required to get a sense of the fluctuations that may be expected without intervention for a highly variable behavior than for a highly stable behavior. The second phase, denoted by the letter B, is a treatment phase. During this phase the treatment is introduced. The treatment may be implemented in accordance with a variety of different schedules. For example, treatment may be implemented with every occurrence of the target behavior. For instance, praise might be given following every occurrence of a plural noun. On the other hand, treatment might be implemented in accordance with one of the many available partial reinforcement schedules. Thus, praise might be given after every third occurrence of a plural noun. The third phase, also denoted by the letter A, constitutes a return to baseline. The return to baseline may be brought about by various means. One is to withdraw the treatment. For instance, praise might not be given following plural-noun utterances during the return-to-baseline phase. Another procedure is to introduce another treatment intended to bring the target behavior back to baseline level. For example, reinforcement of a behavior that is incompatible with the target behavior

may be introduced during the return-to-baseline phase. The final phase in the ABAB design, denoted by the second occurrence of the letter B, is a second implementation of the treatment. The second implementation is intended to demonstrate treatment control over the target behavior by minimizing the possibility that environmental influences occurring coincidentally with the treatment could be responsible for the observed behavior change.

The major advantage of the ABAB design lies in the fact that it minimizes the likelihood of coincidental environmental influences on the target behavior. There are two potential disadvantages to the approach (Kazdin, 1973). One is that some behaviors are not easily reversed. For example, a skill that has been well-learned may not be easy to unlearn. The second disadvantage is that there are cases in which it may not be practical to carry out a return-to-baseline even if it is possible to do so. For instance, a teacher may not want to return a child's performance of an academic skill to baseline even for a short period of time. Despite these shortcomings, the ABAB design has been shown to be useful in establishing a functional relationship between a treatment and behavior in countless applications. It is truly a mainstay in applied behavioral research and will continue to be used widely.

## REFERENCES

Baer, D. M., Wolf, M. M., & Risley, T. R. (1968). Some current dimensions of applied behavior analysis. *Journal of Applied Behavior Analysis, 8,* 387–398.

Bergan, J. R. (1977). *Behavioral consultation.* Columbus, OH: Merrill.

Glass, G. V., Wilson, V. L., & Gottman, J. M. (1975). *Design and analysis of time-series experiments.* Boulder: Colorado Associated University Press.

Kazdin, A. E. (1973). Methodological and assessment considerations in evaluating reinforcement programs in applied settings. *Journal of Applied Behavior Analysis, 6,* 517–531.

Kazdin, A. E. (1980). *Research design in clinical psychology.* New York: Harper & Row.

Kratochwill, T. R. (1978). *Single-subject research: Strategies for evaluating change.* New York: Academic.

Parsonson, B. S., & Baer, D. M. (1978). The analysis and presentation of graphic data. In T. R. Kratochwill (Ed.), *Single-subject research: Strategies for evaluating change.* New York: Academic.

Sidman, M. (1960). *Tactics of scientific research.* New York: Basic.

JOHN R. BERGAN
University of Arizona

**RESEARCH IN SPECIAL EDUCATION**

# ABECEDARIAN PROJECT

For the past quarter century, American education has been especially concerned with the academic performance of children from disadvantaged families. This special concern stems from the well-established fact that this group of children typically performs well below average on standardized tests of academic achievement. They also are overrepresented in special education classes. The root causes of this poor performance are not well understood but their consequences are costly, in terms both of economics and psychological dysfunction. Such consequences have frequently been called developmental retardation.

To ameliorate these costly consequences, a wide variety of special education programs have been investigated under the rubric of compensatory education. Most of these programs have concentrated on the so-called preschool and/or early elementary school years. The primary hypothesis has been that educational experiences that augment and/or supplement the educational experiences of the home will better prepare disadvantaged children for academic accomplishment in the public schools. The Abecedarian project has been such an experiment. Abecedarian means one learning the rudiments of something (the alphabet).

The specific aims of the Abecedarian project have been:

To determine whether developmental retardation and school failure can be prevented in children from socially and economically high-risk families by means of educational day care.

To determine whether a follow-through program for early elementary school is necessary to maintain preschool intellectual gains in high-risk children.

To determine whether school-age intervention alone can significantly improve academic and/or intellectual performance in children who did not have preschool intervention.

To identify a sample of families at high risk for having a developmentally retarded child, a high-risk screening index (Ramey & Smith, 1977) was developed. This index included social, environmental, and psychological factors judged on the basis of the developmental literature to be associated with poor intellectual and scholastic progress. Each factor was assigned a weight based on professional consensus as to its likely importance in determining intellectual and scholastic outcomes. Thirteen factors were included; among them were paternal and maternal education; family income; father's absence; retardation among other family members; family disorganization; maladaptive or antisocial behavior within the family; and unstable job history.

Based on the high-risk index, families were judged to be at elevated risk and eligible for inclusion in the study. Characteristics of the 109 families (111 children) eventually enrolled in the study are given in the following Table. As may be seen in the Table, the families in the sample were predominantly black (98%), were headed by

Entry Level Demographic Data for Experimental and Control Families

| Experimental Variable | Group | | |
|---|---|---|---|
| | Control (N = 55) | Experimental (N = 54) | Total (N = 109) |
| 1. Mean high-risk index | 20.08 (5.72) | 21.41 (5.88) | 20.75 (5.81) |
| 2. Mean maternal age (years) | 19.62 (3.87) | 20.28 (5.77) | 19.94 (4.89) |
| 3. Mean maternal education (years) | 10.46 (1.75) | 10.00 (1.89) | 10.23 (1.83) |
| 4. Mean maternal IQ (WAIS full scale) | 85.49 (12.43) | 84.18 (10.78) | 84.84 (11.61) |
| 5. Percent female-headed family | 78% | 65% | 72% |
| 6. Percent black families | 96% | 100% | 98% |

a single female (72%) who was young (20 years) and who had less than a high school education (10.23 years).

It is a special feature of the Abecedarian project that participants were assigned to the preschool experimental educational treatment or control condition at random. Fifty-seven children were randomly assigned to the preschool experimental group, 54 were preschool controls. Ninety-six children remained in the study to be randomly assigned to a school-age treatment group.

At public school entry, Abecedarian children within the two preschool groups were rank-ordered according to 48-month Stanford-Binet IQ's; each consecutive pair was randomly assigned to the school-age experimental or control groups. All families accepted their school-age assignment, but three children assigned to the preschool control-school-age experimental condition (CE) moved away and did not participate in the school-age phase.

Figure 1 gives the overall design of the Abecedarian study, including the preschool and school-age treatment programs and the number of children randomly assigned to each condition. The Abecedarian study can be conceptualized as a 2 × 2 factorial design. The factors are preschool educational treatment versus no preschool treatment and school-age educational treatment versus no school-age treatment. Thus, there were two preschool groups, the experimental (E) and control (C) groups, and

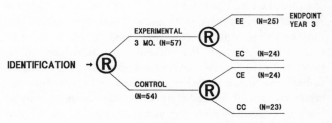

Figure 1. Research design of Carolina Abecedarian Project.

four school-age conditions: preschool experimental school-age experimental (EE); preschool experimental school-age control (EC); preschool control school-age experimental (CE); and preschool control school-age control (CC). These groups varied in the intensity (defined as number of years) of intervention: 8 years for the EE group; 5 years for the EC group; 3 years for the CE group; none for the CC group.

The preschool program may be characterized as a comprehensive, whole child program. The aim was to create a rich, stimulating, yet orderly environment in which the children could grow and learn. The curriculum was designed to enhance cognitive and linguistic development and to provide the children with many opportunities for successful mastery experiences. The curriculum materials included those for infants and preschoolers developed by Sparling and Lewis (1979). In addition, there was an enriched language environment that was responsive to the children's needs and interests (Ramey, et al., 1982).

In many ways the program was not unlike other high-quality infant daycare and preschool programs. Child/caregiver ratios ranged from 1:3 for infants to 1:6 for four year olds. Teachers typically had early childhood education experience and participated in an extensive in-service education program. The children's experiences became increasingly more structured over the preschool years, eventually coming to include prephonics programs and science and math experiences in addition to an emphasis on language and linguistic development. The presumption was that when the child left the preschool, he or she would be able to enter kindergarten without experiencing an abrupt transition.

Children attended the preschool program beginning between 6 weeks and 3 months of age. Children attended the daycare program 5 days per week, 50 weeks per year. The center was open from 7:30 A.M. to 5:15 P.M. Free transportation to and from the center was provided for families who needed it. Almost all of the children were transported by center staff. This portion of the program has been described in more detail by Ramey, MacPhee, and Yeates (1982).

The school-age intervention program began in kindergarten. It consisted of providing a home/school resource teacher to each child and family in the two Abecedarian school-age experimental groups (EE and CE) shown in Figure 1. These teachers filled many roles: they were curriculum developers who prepared an individualized set of home activities to supplement the school's basic curriculum in reading and math; they taught parents how to use these activities with their children; they tutored children directly; they met regularly with classroom teachers to ensure that home activities matched the skills being taught in the classroom; they served as consultants for the classroom teacher when problems arose; and they advocated for the child and family within the school and community. Thus, they facilitated communication between teacher and parent, providing an important support for disadvantaged parents who frequently lacked the skills and confidence needed to advocate for their children within the school system, an institution seen by many as both monolithic and difficult to comprehend. Each home/school resource teacher had a caseload of approximately 12 families per year. The home/school resource teachers were experienced educators familiar with the local school system.

The supplemental curriculum delivered as home activities concentrated on two basic subjects: reading and math. These subjects were emphasized because it seemed likely that high-risk children might need extra reinforcement of these basic concepts to master and to remember them. The program sought to provide such reinforcement, presuming that scholastic performance would best be enhanced by direct teaching and practice of needed basic skills. The curriculum packets contained teaching activities that parents and children could share and enjoy. In addition, work sheets to give extra drill and practice were often included.

Home/school teachers made approximately 17 school visits per year for each child. During these visits they met with the classroom teacher to identify the skills currently being taught and to learn which areas needed extra work or review. A variety of specialists within the system were contacted, including special education resource personnel, reading teachers, and school counselors. Efforts were made to coordinate the child's program and to make sure the best available resources were being used.

The home component of the program was equally intense. Home visits were made about 15 times each school year. A typical visit lasted approximately 30 to 45 minutes, with the mother being the most likely participant. Teachers reviewed the classroom situation and showed the parent the materials in the activity packet, explaining the purpose and directions for each activity. The child was present and participated in about one-quarter of the home visits; this was often helpful because it allowed the teacher to demonstrate how an activity was to be carried out. Parents reported spending an average of 15 minutes a day working with their children on home activities. Parent response to the activities was very positive; very few reported that they failed to use the activities although direct verification was not possible.

Many forces other than intellectual ability and encouragement to learn can have an impact on a child's scholastic performance: emotional upset within the home, parental unemployment, the death of a family member, or instability of living arrangements, to name a few. Home/school resource teachers sometimes helped families deal with personal crises. Extra home visits occurred if and when the home/school teacher attempted to help the family solve such real-life problems. Home/school teachers also helped to provide the children with a variety of summer experiences, including summer activity packets, sum-

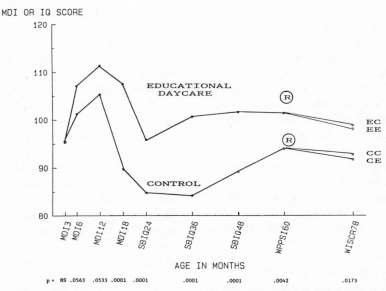

Figure 2. Mean mental development (MDI's) and IQ scores for randomly assigned high-risk children from 3 to 78 months of age in the Abecedarian Project.

mer camp, trips to the public library, and, for some children, a six-week tutorial in reading.

The results to be included here cover the intellectual and academic outcomes for Abecedarian children through the first 2 years in public school. Many other results are available, but these have been chosen because they represent the primary outcome hypotheses under investigation.

Figure 2 gives the IQ results for Abecedarian children from infancy through age 6½ years (78 months). In Figure 2, the mean IQs are graphed by preschool group up to the age of 60 months and by the four school-age groups thereafter. The scores are Bayley Mental Developmental Indices at 3, 6, 9, 12, and 18 months, Binet IQs at 24, 36, and 48 months, and full-scale IQ's on the Wechsler Preschool and Primary Scale of Intelligence at 60 months and the Wechsler Intelligence Scale for Children-Revised at 78 months.

The preschool intervention had a positive effect on intellectual development of the high-risk children in the ex-

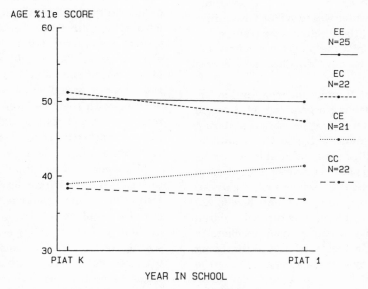

Figure 3. Mean age-referenced percentile scores on the Peabody Individual Achievement Test by year in school for the groups in the Abecedarian Project.

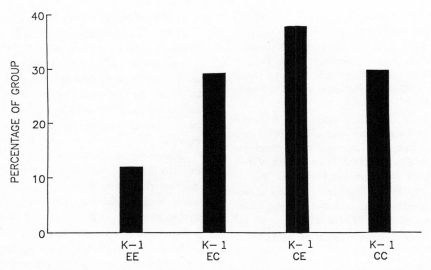

Figure 4. Percentage of high-risk children retained in grades as a function of experimental educational conditions.

perimental group, as may be seen in Figure 2. Throughout the preschool period, at every testing occasion after 12 months, significant mean differences on standardized test scores were found between the two Abecedarian preschool groups (Ramey & Campbell, 1984). The primary form of this effect was to reduce the drop in mental test scores evidenced by the control group. It is now apparent that this preschool effect persists up through 78 months (Ramey & Campbell, in press). There is no evidence, however, that the school-age intervention significantly impacted children's intellectual performance during the first year and half of public school. No significant effect of the school-age program was found at 78 months. Thus regardless of school-age intervention status, the two groups who had preschool intervention maintained their relative superiority in tested intelligence over children who were preschool controls.

Figure 3 from Ramey and Campbell (in press) contains the kindergarten and first grade Peabody Individual Achievement Test results in terms of age-referenced percentile scores. Examination of this figure reveals that the preschool groups are near national average whereas the preschool control groups are below national average. Thus during the first 2 years in public school, positive preschool treatment effects on academic achievement were observed.

Figure 4 presents the percentage of children retained in either kindergarten or first grade for each of the four experimental conditions. One-eighth, or 12%, of the children in the EE group were retained in grade during the first 2 years of public school, compared with approximately one-third in the other three groups. Although it is very early in these children's public school careers, it is remarkable that the academic failure rate is so high in the groups that did not receive early and continuing supplemental education. The one-third grade retention rate

is clearly costly and apparently reducible through intensive early education. Such a high retention rate also buttresses the initial judgment that these children were indeed at elevated risk for school failure.

Together, the data on IQs, academic achievement, and retention in grade suggest that preschool intervention exerts a positive influence on intelligence and school success in the first 2 years of public school. Preschool intervention supplemented by continued help in the early grades via a home/school resource teacher program shows promise for being the most effective intervention. This intensity of effort apparently enabled the high-risk children in this sample to maintain a level of achievement near the national average. In addition, the likelihood of being retained in grade was less by a factor of approximately three for children who had early and continued educational intervention.

We are currently in the process of analyzing data for the final year of the school-age intervention. When those analyses are completed and we have systematically examined the family, school, and child factors associated with academic performance, we hope to have a better understanding of the forces that are associated with the academic performance of children from disadvantaged families and the ability of educational intervention to ameliorate those forces.

## REFERENCES

Ramey, C. T., & Campbell, F. A. (1984). Preventive education for high-risk children: Cognitive consequences of the Carolina Abecedarian project [Special issue]. *American Journal of Mental Deficiency, 88*(5), 515–523.

Ramey, C. T., & Campbell, F. A. (in press). The Carolina Abecedarian project: An educational experiment concerning human malleability. In J. J. Gallagher (Ed.). *The malleability of children*. Baltimore, MD: Brookes.

Ramey, C. T., MacPhee, D., & Yeates, K. O. (1982). Preventing developmental retardation: A general systems model. In L. A. Bond & J. M. Joffe (Eds.), *Facilitating infant and early childhood development* (pp. 343–401). Hanover, NH: University Press of New England.

Ramey, C. T., McGinness, G. D., Cross, L., Collier, A. M., & Barrie-Blackley, S. (1982). The Abecedarian approach to social competence: Cognitive and linguistic intervention for disadvantaged preschoolers. In K. Borman (Ed.), *The social life of children in a changing society*. Hillsdale, NJ: Erlbaum.

Ramey, C. T. & Smith, B. (1977). Assessing the intellectual consequences of early intervention with high-risk infants. *American Journal of Mental Deficiency, 81*, 318–324.

Sparling, J., & Lewis, I. (1979, February). Six learning games to play with your baby. *Parents*, pp. 35–38.

CRAIG T. RAMEY
FRANCES A. CAMPBELL
DONNA M. BRYANT
*University of North Carolina,
Chapel Hill*

**MENTAL RETARDATION**

# ABILITY TRAINING

Many educators believe that most academic and social learning is based on factors such as student aptitudes or abilities, instructional environment, and teaching methodology. While these three variables do not form a complete structure capable of containing all those factors contributing to learning, they certainly account for many of the variables educators would agree are important to success in school.

Learner aptitudes or abilities are those personological variables that frequently are called intelligence(s), traits, gifts, and characteristics. Frequently, educators will talk about a child's potential to learn, using the term ability as if it were a predetermined factor waiting to be drawn on at some point. The logic, then, is that if learning is a result of the presence and development of certain mental abilities, school failure (both academic and social) may be the result of disabilities, with disability implying an academic or social handicap.

If regular (elementary and secondary) educators teach to the abilities of students to learn, then special educators may direct more of their instruction to the disabilities that inhibit learning, hence the term and concept of ability training. How valid is this construct of ability training? A short response to that question is impossible. Any field involving relatively newly defined services to persons, especially children, in particular handicapped children, will generate professional controversy. Any field struggling

with the pressures associated with economic, political, social, legislative, litigative, and basic human rights and values will face diversity. Any field that requires its many disciplines to unite in purpose will experience communicative stress. But, few professionals will purposely question their field's major methodology to the degree special and remedial educators have, for the period of time they have done so, and in the face of such a degree of controversy.

Some special educators believe avidly in ability training of all types; some reject it totally; but almost all, no matter what they believe, practice ability training. The truth in that observation is vividly displayed when we recognize that the value of ability training to handicapped persons has been questioned repeatedly for over the last 100 years. What then is in ability training that has caused the field of special education to tenaciously and steadfastly maintain its cause? Ability training is routed in the historic search for the structure and function of the mind. Educators, in particular special educators, have sought to diagnose specific abilities and provide remediation to those abilities, or disabilities as the case may be.

Mental ability (aptitude), concerns those components that are assumed to constitute the mind, and therefore explain learning. Mental-ability structures, in more scientific parlance, may be referred to as information-processing behaviors. Mental processes or information processes are those theoretical or conceptual acts (processes) by which information is transmitted from the peripheral (to the central nervous system) sensory organs (i.e., eyes, ears, fingers [tactile], muscles, [kinesthetic]) perceived, labeled, stored, provided mediated meaning, conceptually associated, and expressed as language or motoric responses. It is not unusual for practitioners to reference most psychological functions synonymously with mental abilities. Hence, the very definition of learning disabilities refers to "basic psychological processes."

The history of man, at least those aspects related to the structures of the mind, how it works, and therefore how these processes can be measured, begins with the early Greek philosophers. Pythagoras placed the "mind" in the brain in the sixth century BC. Most of the processes described then were hypotheoretical, related to this assumed function. Therefore, the names given these processes sometimes sound as if they had been isolated neurologically or psychoneurologically. The truth is that the majority of the commonly referenced mental processes, that is, perception and language, are not simple, easily explained constructs. They are complex concepts that may contain hundreds of component subparts. The major issues relating to ability training have been the long-standing arguments regarding the mind, its disabilities, and the habilitation or rehabilitation needed. A case in point is that while simple tests are designed to ascertain visual perceptual-motor development, visual perception is not a simple discriminate function. In a general sense, perception requires the discrimination of distinctive features, wherein a specific symbolic meaning can be assigned each distinct stimuli. Logically then, once perceptual information has been discriminated, it may be stored for some short-term reference, or it may be assigned a permanent symbolism, then converted to a language concept. Logically then, too, there may be both visual and auditory perception. These two processes may need to be coordinated when auditory and visual information is presented in an integrated manner. Perception, however, is not logically complex in contrast to the explanations of the structure and function of language.

A mental ability may also be referred to as a faculty. Mann (1979) credits Aristotle for establishing the basis for modern faculty psychology. The Romans further refined and added descriptors such as intellect, attention, and language. St. Thomas Aquinas, during the Middle Ages, although poorly credited, began to amplify and extend faculty psychology by dividing it into two parts: the *intellectus*, which carries out abstractions and functions of the possible intellect; and the *ratio*, which is directed toward understanding, judgment, and reasoning. The intellect is active and creative, the ratio, passive and receptive, i.e., sensory stimuli must be perceptually assigned symbolic meaning/value before they have intellectual meaning.

Faculty psychology, the theoretical basis for mental process, was soundly criticized by many of the seventeenth-, eighteenth-, and nineteenth-century scholars. Hobbes (1558–1679) displaced it with his theories of automotion in the brain set off by sensory stimulation. Locke (1632–1704) was a sensationalist, and an arch antifacilist. Hume (1715–1776), also a sensationalist in the British tradition, condemned faculties, basing mental response solely in sensory stimulation. By the mid-nineteenth century, the psychologist and educator Herbart attempted to destroy for all time the residual of faculty psychology.

One of the predominate figures in mental measurement, Spearman, writing in 1927, notes that faculty psychology seems to persist, no matter what the criticism.

> One curious feature about these formal faculties has yet to be mentioned. The doctrine loses every battle—so to speak—but always wins the war. It will bend to the slightest breath of criticism; but not the most violent storm can break it. The attacks made long ago by the Herbartians appeared to be irresistible; no serious defense was even attempted. Yet the sole permanent effect of these attacks was only to banish the word "faculty," leaving the doctrine represented by this word to escape scot free. (pp. 38–39)

However, other early forces in the field such as Thorndike continued to be critical. As a quote from Mann (1979) notes,

> The science of education should at once rid itself of its con-

ception of the mind as a sort of machine, different parts of which sense, perceive, discriminate, imagine, remember, conceive, associate, reason about, desire, choose, form habits, attend to. . . . There is no power of sense discrimination to be delicate or coarse. . . . There are only the connections between separate sense stimuli and our separate senses and human judgments thereof. . . . There is no memory to hold in a uniformly tight and loose grip the experiences of the past. There are only the particular connections between particular mental events and others. (Klein, 1970, p. 662)

Though an out-and-out antifaculist, Thorndike, interestingly enough, could not shake the ingrained habit of his times of speaking about "faculties." Thus, he described his bonds as faculties in the 1903 edition of *Education Psychology* (p. 30) "the mind is a host of highly particularized and independent faculties" (Spearman, 1927, p. 36).

Yet, it is faculty psychology that provided the definition for twentieth-century mental measurement. On the basis of his inquiries, Galton described what, in essence, is a superfaculty, which he called "general ability," assigning to this faculty the name intelligence (a term popularized by Spencer). Galton distinguished this superfaculty from special aptitudes. He was more interested in the first, since he believed that general ability inevitably set a limit to accomplishment of any kind. He complained that most writers emphasized specific aptitudes or skill, that they

> lay too much stress upon apparent specialties, thinking that because a man is devoted to some particular pursuit, he could not have succeeded in anything else; they might as well say that, because a youth has fallen in love with a brunette, he could not possibly have fallen in love with a blonde. He may or may not have had any more natural liking for the former type of beauty than for the latter; but it is as probable as not that the affair was mainly or wholly due to a general amorousness. It is just the same with intellectual pursuits. (Burt, 1955, p. 85)

Galton most certainly did not deny the existence of special capacities or their potential importance. He cited instances in which memory, musical ability, and artistic and literary talent ran within several members of the same family. Home environment or family tradition could not explain all such cases, for example, "prodigies of memory." However, his studies in the main had convinced him "in how small a degree intellectual eminence can be considered as due to purely special powers" (Burt, 1955, p. 85).

As to the measurement of both general and special abilities, Galton suggested that individual differences in both are distributed in accordance with the normal curve, much as other human characteristics such as size or height are distributed. He printed a tabular classification of frequencies which he held "may apply to special just as truly as to general ability" (Burt, 1955, p. 85). Thus we see the beginnings of psychometric assessment of both general ability and specific abilities.

About 1880, the German psychiatrist Kraeplin, one of Wundt's students, began to use different tests to describe higher cognitive functions (Guilford, 1967). His testing interests were directed to such processes as general memory, specific memory, attention, and task-directed behaviors. However, it was James McKeen Cattell who first formulated the term "mental tests." Cattell's extension of Galton's simple tests began the modern practice of psychometrics as we know it today. Others such as DeSanctis attacked the realms of higher cognitive functioning. DeSanctis published a series of six tests including (1) memory for colors, (2) recognition of forms, (3) sustained attention, (4) reasoning involving relations, (5) following instructions, and (6) thinking.

At the turn of the twentieth century, the French Minister of Public Instruction was still wrestling with an age-old problem: how to consistently identify the handicapped. Having agreed on the terminology to be used (idiot for the lowest level; imbecile for the intermediate level; and moron for the mildly mentally retarded), a psychologist, Alfred Binet, and physician, Theodore Simon, were commissioned to develop a consistent means of classifying children. Binet and Simon (1905, 1908) produced, through a standardized procedure of observation, a psychological classification of quantifiable differences in children's intellectual characteristics (traits). By 1905 Binet and Simon had developed 29 such tests designed to measure specific traits; by 1908 they had developed a classification of tests beginning at age three and continuing through age 13. Thus, the work preceding 1905 established human intelligence as a comprehensive integration of several traits including memory, attention, comprehension, muscular coordination, spatial relations, judgment, initiative, and ability to adapt. Further, the criteria for measurement of these traits were standardized at various chronological age levels. From this procedure the measurement of human performance took a great leap forward.

Binet carried his interest in higher processes into his work of developing mental tests for use in Paris schools. He and his associates criticized tests of the Galton type as being too simple, too sensory-motor, and too dependent on associationistic dogma. They expressed their own preference for the complex cognitive functions, proposing that 10 categories be explored by mental tests: (1) memory, (2) imagery, (3) imagination, (4) attention, (5) comprehension, (6) suggestibility, (7) aesthetic appreciation, (8) moral sentiment, (9) muscular force, force of will, and motor skill, and (10) judgment of visual space.

Modern psychoeducational assessment and remedial practices, indeed the very content of most perceptual, motor, language, vocational, and academic remedial curricula, are based on Binet's work. Two of the major issues are the specificity with which mental ability processes can reliably be ascertained and the desirability of remediating the specific perceptual or language processes in terms of their transferability and ultimate academic and social learning transfer.

But, it is clear that abilities had been identified by tests and that ability training was to become a crucial issue facing the twentieth century. The main philosophic question is, do mental abilities really exist in nature? The second question is, do they respond to specific training once they are described, measured, observed, and, in short, isolated as specific mental abilities? These two questions constitute the major issues facing special educators today. Since mental abilities are developmentally linked to chronological growth, culture, and experience, they may be encouraged by structured educational experiences. Conversely, when developmentally arrested, culturally neglected, or denied sequenced experiential practice, they may become deficient. Mental ability deficiencies may then be the principal characteristics associated with handicapping conditions such as learning and behavioral disorders. The entire nervous system develops only when each aspect or component necessary to successfully decode information (perceive its symbolic features) provides that symbol a language construct and a mechanism by which encoding of the mediated concept through motoric or verbal language permits communication. Therefore, specific reference is made in the definition of mental retardation and learning disabilities, two of the largest categories of handicapping conditions, to dysfunction of perceptual, perceptual-motor, or language abilities.

Philosophically, then, it appears that a leap in logic is *not* required to assume that if a disability exists, relative to causing a handicap, it should be corrected. That is exactly what ability training implies. It would appear that it was incorrectly named to begin with. It should be called disability training.

The history of ability training parallels that of the field of special education. The pioneers in ability training were the pioneers of the field. Itard, Howe, Sequin, Montessori, Binet, Wepman, Kirk, Strauss, Fernald, Frostig, and Cruickshank were all advocates of special education as it grew, and responsible for advancing ability training simultaneously. Tests used to describe a disability were followed by commercially prepared curricula to train the ability and remove the disability. The logic is obvious. The problem is in the scientific validation, or lack of it.

The early 1960s brought with it a concern for neurologically impaired children. The mid-1960s added the term learning disabled as a category of handicapping conditions. Both of these conditions required an increased emphasis on psychoneurological and psychoeducational assessment. Those that developed psychoeducational and psychoneurological tests to diagnose these conditions fueled the fire for ability training by describing conditions which, by their description, must exist.

Curricula designed to modify and treat patterns of disability were soon commercially available. Whole classes of children were exposed to Montessori, Frostig, and Fernald techniques, and administered Frostig, Kephart, and Delaccato assessment procedures. Tests such as the Illinois Test of Psycholinguistic Abilities became common place, much as the Woodcock-Johnson test batteries of today. The prevailing belief was that specific mental processes must be diagnosed in order for modification of a specific disability to result in quantum jumps in academic remedial achievement and potential normalization. Thus, the so-called diagnostic-prescriptive process is one form of ability training.

What then is the difficulty with visual and auditory perceptual training, perceptual motor training, language training, and the other forms of sensory, motor, perceptual, and language ability training? The problem is that data arrived at through quasi-scientific means are controversial concerning the results of ability training. There are data to support ability training, if the objective to be achieved is a change in an ability, and that ability alone. There are relatively few data to support that transfer of training occurs between training of a perceptual or cognitive ability and an academic achievement skill, for instance reading.

It is not clear which age groups profit most; there are some data to suggest that perceptual motor training is most effective between 3 and 7 years of age, and language training, 18 months to 14 or 15 years of age. There is no clear pattern as to the intelligence level needed for a student to profit from ability training, since specific abilities constitute statements of global intelligence. Cultural and ethnic factors have been found: urban black children may need auditory perceptual training; Native Americans outperform age norms of Anglos on visual perceptual tests.

The overall interaction among these abilities being training and other abilities remains unknown, except it does seem that auditory perceptual training is related to language growth much more than visual perceptual training. Language training seemingly has the greatest transference to academic remediation. But even the search for generalities would produce only controversy. The fact is, ability training makes sense logically but has not been sufficiently researched devoid of other educational practices with school-age children to permit definitive statements. And yet, the practice does not only continue, it continues to thrive.

**REFERENCES**

Binet, A., & Simon, T. (1905). Methodes nouvelles pour le diagnostic du niveau intellectuel des anomaux. *L'anne psychologque, 11*, 191–244.

Binet, A., & Simon, T. (1908). Le developpement de l'intelligence chez les infants. *L'anne psychologque, 14*, 1–94.

Burt, C. (1955). The evidence for the concept of intelligence. *British Journal of Educational Psychology, 25*, 158–177.

Klein, D. B. (1970). *A history of scientific psychology.* New York: Basic Books.

Mann, L. (1970). *On the trail of process.* New York: Grune & Stratton.

Spearman, C. (1927). *The abilities of man: Their nature and measurement.* London: Macmillan.

DAVID A. SABATINO
*West Virginia College
of Graduate Studies*

DIAGNOSTIC-PRESCRIPTIVE TEACHING
FERNALD METHOD
ILLINOIS TEST OF PSYCHOLINGUISTIC
    ABILITIES
INTELLIGENCE

## ABNORMALITIES, NEUROPHYSIOLOGICAL

The human nervous system consists of the brain, the spinal cord, and an intricate network of nerve fibers projecting from the brain and spinal cord. Structurally, the brain is differentiated into the two cerebral hemispheres, the brain stem and the cerebellum. The brain, together with the spinal cord, traditionally has been conceptualized as the central nervous system (CNS). The entire network of nerve fibers is then referred to as the peripheral nervous system (PNS). The brief discussion regarding normal neurological structure and function that follows is meant as an aid in the appreciation of neurophysiological disorders. The intent here is to offer an overview; for a more detailed account of the nervous system, the reader is referred to one of a number of neurophysiological texts (e.g., Bickerstaff, 1978; Lindsley & Holmes, 1984).

Peripheral nerves are referred to by the direction the impulses flow and the site of their termination. Specifically, the direction of the impulses carried in relation to the CNS, the originating structure, or final destination of the impulse, and the nature of the impulse itself, are used to classify peripheral nerves. For instance, the PNS contains sensory nerves that carry impulses from the sense organs (eyes, ears, nose, etc.) to the CNS. By way of contrast, the motor nerves travel from the CNS to the periphery, exciting both skeletal (voluntary) and smooth muscle (involuntary) muscle into movement. Included in PNS, the cranial nerves arise from or travel to the brain stem (connecting structure between spinal cord and cerebrum). Similarly, the spinal nerves travel to or from the spinal cord. The group of peripheral nerves that carry impulses to smooth muscle (causing involuntary movements of the intestines, heartbeat, constriction of the pupils, etc.) and those that incite the secretion of glands cause automatic changes in the body. These peripheral nerves are sometimes referred to collectively as the autonomic nervous system.

Functionally, the fundamental building block of the

nervous system is the neuronal circuit. The simplest neuronal circuit contains only two interconnected nerve cells, involving an input and an output cell (e.g., simple knee jerk reflex). Local circuits exist at all levels of the nervous system and, in fact, such circuits in the spinal cord connect the cerebral cortex, brain stem, and cerebellum. These connections can function as modules in more complex circuits. Indeed, these integrated networks are capable of sustaining complex behavior (Gaddes, 1985).

As an example, sensory impulses traveling from the various sense organs to the brain are integrated, recorded, recognized, stored or remembered, as interpreted by the cerebral cortex. Moreover, skeletal movement may be affected by motor nerves traveling by way of the spinal cord. Generally, the entire system works to regulate and coordinate bodily responses to both internal and external changes in the environment (Taber, 1970). A malfunctioning neurological system results in an impaired capacity for responding adaptively to a changing environment.

Neurophysiological abnormality may occur by means of many agents and during various stages of the life process; some stages offer more vulnerability than others. Antenatal agents (occurring before birth) described by Nelson (1969) include genetic factors, chromosomal aberrations, placental disease, maternal complications, number of previous pregnancies, age of both mother and father, intrauterine infection, toxic agents (including certain drugs and alcohol), and radiation. Various organ systems begin and end their prenatal development at different times, therefore their sensitivity to agents varies with maturity of the fetus. The most vulnerable period for the brain is from 15 to 25 days of gestation but, clearly, damage can occur at any time during the development of the nervous system (Hetherington & Parke, 1979).

Perinatal (occurring just before or after birth) vulnerability to neurological insult is accentuated by premature birth. Inadequate oxygen during this stage, hemorrhage, trauma, and infection are the principal offenders (Nelson, 1969). Postnatal (occurring after birth) damage to the neurological system may include damage incurred after birth, during childhood, or throughout the various stages of adulthood. Infections, principally meningitis and encephalitis, injuries, and degenerative neurological disease have also been implicated (Nelson, 1969).

Weller, Swash, McLellan and Scholtz (1983) estimated that 40% of developmental malformations of the CNS arise from genetic abnormality. The most common genetic abnormality is Down's syndrome. This disorder is associated with a group of chromosomal aberrations involving the 21st chromosome pair. In the great majority of cases, a failure to join occurs during the meiosis process, resulting in a trisomy (additional chromosome) of the 21st chromosome pair. Translocation and mosaician represent less frequently occurring aberrations of the 21st chromosome pair, also associated with Down's syndrome (Kopp & Parmelee, 1979).

The incidence of Down's syndrome is between one and two per thousand live births for all races and ethnic groups (Norman, 1963). Although there is some variability in incidence, most researchers cite an increase in relation to maternal age (Benda, 1960; Lawrence, 1981; Weller et al., 1983). A gradual increase begins with maternal age of 35 and escalates drastically after 45. Metabolic or environmental factors in the mothers' ovaries have been suggested as causes for the syndrome (Benda, 1960; Lawrence, 1981; Nelson, 1969; Norman, 1963; Weller, Swash, McLellan, & Scholtz, 1983). Structural inspection of the Down's syndrome brain suggests impairment of both growth and differentiation (Benda, 1960). The brain is generally low in weight and the normal convolutional pattern of the brain is simplified. The density of the nerve cells in the cerebral cortex is reduced (Weller et al., 1983).

Rate of mental development is not only slower than normal but also deteriorates progressively with age in Down's syndrome (Cornwell & Birch, 1969; Dicks-Mireaux, 1972). Many explanations, including neurophysiologic changes, have been offered as explanation for this progressive deterioration. Weller et al. (1983) noted that the microscopic study of brain tissue of Down's syndrome victims during autopsy reveals patterns of neurofibrillary tangles, senile plaques, and granulovacular degeneration such as are found in Alzheimer's disease (deteriorative disease of the elderly involving degeneration of the smaller blood vessels of the brain). Kopp and Parmelee (1979) suggest that the severe limitations in higher level integrative abilities evident in Down's syndrome may cause deficits in information processing (e.g., use of language) that could have progressive detrimental effects on the child's intellectual development over time. The child's capacity for responding adaptively to changing stimulus conditions, a necessity for proper intellectual development, may be impaired directly by the nature of the syndrome. However, the nature of the environment in which these children find themselves, whether it is enriched or impoverished, also can affect development.

In contrast to Down's syndrome, which is genetically related, spina bifida seems to be more influenced by environmental factors. Although genetic factors are suggested by the higher incidence in infants born to parents with a family history of such lesions, it seems that racial, geographical, and even seasonal factors also may be implicated (Kopp & Parmelee, 1979; Weller et al., 1983). Clearly, the interaction of genetic and environmental factors has recently been given prominence. Genetic predisposition combined with certain environmental factors may be the causal condition for spina bifida occurrence (Carter, 1974).

Spina bifida represents a malformation of the nervous system that appears to be more localized and variable in effect than that of Down's syndrome. This defect occurs as a result of faulty prenatal development, in which the lower end of embryotic CNS fails to close. The contents of the spinal column (nerve fibers, meninges, and fluid) may protrude from the lower back in a sac (meningomyelocele). Individual defects vary depending on the extent of damage to the nerve fibers and the existence of other associated conditions (Kleinberg, 1982). The spinal cord is frequently abnormal above and below the level of the spina bifida (Weller et al., 1983). Hydrocephalus, abnormal accumulation of cerebral spinal fluid, frequently is associated with spina bifida. Untreated hydrocephalus creates severe enlargement of the head, increased pressure, and subsequent damage to the brain (Kleinberg, 1982).

Intellectual levels of victims with spina bifida are variable, ranging from an IQ of 137 to severe subnormality (Hunt, 1981). More specifically, Spain (1974) associates mental retardation with protrusion of a portion of the brain (cranial meningocele and cephalocele), whereas infants with other forms are considered to have potentially normal intellect. Many individuals with spina bifida are incontinent of urine and feces, and have weakness of their legs with sensory loss below the level of the lesion (Kleinberg, 1982). Owing to the presence of the typical locomotor problems in spina bifida, it is unclear whether some deficits are due to neurological impairment or environmental influence. Spain's (1974) longitudinal spina bifida studies have revealed significant deficits in spatial and manipulative development. The fact that the disorder limits the individual's experience may, in fact, cause or influence the specific deficits in spatial and manipulative development. Among the educational problems noted are difficulties with arithmetic and perseveration in language, as well as emotionality and poor motivation (Kopp & Parmelee, 1979).

Primary disorders of the CNS, like Down's syndrome and spina bifida, represent a relatively small proportion of the neurological problems in infants (Horwitz, 1973). More frequently, the genetic programs for potentially normal neurological development are subverted by adverse prenatal or birthing conditions such as lack of oxygen (hypoxia). Cerebral hemorrhage often occurs during prolonged hypoxia. The accumulation of stagnate blood that follows circulatory collapse may cause bleeding and ultimate damage to brain tissue (Weller et al., 1983). Premature infants are especially vulnerable to hypoxia. Since the respiratory system is not fully perfected until the last four to six weeks of gestation, these infants are often born without an optimally functioning respiratory system. Postmortem studies on premature children show that the bleeding usually occurs within one of the cavities of the brain or the space below the arachnoid membrane that contains cerebrospinal fluid (subarachnoid space [Horwitz, 1973]). Later complications of such subarachnoid hemorrhage involve epilepsy, dementia, and hydrocephalus (Weller et al., 1983). Full-term infants are more likely to suffer from hemorrhage in the mid-brain stem (pons) and the posterior portion of the cerebral cortex (hip-

pocampus). Cause for these differences are not, as yet, fully understood.

The location and size of brain lesions at or soon after birth are the primary determinants of the extent of nervous system impairment. The results may range from a gross alteration of brain organization to more minimal effects such as motor overactivity, shortened attention span, or slight muscle impairment (Pincus & Tucker, 1974; Teberg et al., 1982). Large injuries in infants tend to produce more widespread deficits in intellectual abilities than similar injuries in adults. Dulling of many areas of intellectual functioning, as opposed to having an effect in specific functioning (e.g., language development, visual-spatial relationship comprehension), is also a hallmark effect of the diffuse damage that follows hypoxia (Rapin, 1982).

Neurological deficiencies from early injury are difficult to predict. The nervous system of the newborn infant is extremely immature, functioning largely at brain stem and spinal cord level. The neurologic reflexes such as Moro, grasping, and stepping represent primitive neuronal function that is largely uninhibited by higher cerebral control. Changes in these reflexes are usually not helpful in localizing the lesion, and may occur with either cortical or subcortical dysfunction (Horwitz, 1973). Damage to the cerebral cortex, for instance, may not be evident until the age when behavior dependent on the damaged part makes its developmental appearance. Thus, pathology of fine motor coordination, speech, and cognition is unlikely to be diagnosed in infancy (Rapin, 1982). However, changes in reflexes and disorganized activity of the subcortical structures expressed as a movement disorder or spasticity continue to be used as indicators of neurological damage. In Teberg et al.'s study of low birth weight infants (1982), spastic quadiplegia did, in fact, emerge as the indicative diagnosis of neurological handicap. Churchill, Masland, Naylor, and Ashworth (1974) support this finding.

The electroencephalogram (EEG), a measure of brain activity, has been recognized as a predictor of neurologic outcome for neonates with seizures. Irritative effects on the tissue surrounding brain damage may precipitate a variety of seizure activities (Rapin, 1982). Rose and Lombrosco (1970) found that newborns with seizures and a normal EEG had a 0.86 chance of normal development at age four, regardless of any other data.

Turkewitz (1974) contended that the standard methods used for the early identification of neurologic handicaps are insensitive to many forms of neurological involvement. Infants who have had difficulties shortly before or during the birth process frequently appear to recover in a few days. However, abnormalities in motor, language, and intellectual functioning become apparent later in infancy and childhood. Studies using indicators of higher levels of neurological organization (e.g., left/right preference) are being investigated in an effort to identify infants who have experienced neurological damage that is normally not expressed until later in life. However, normative patterns of left/right preference for infants must be established first, before atypical patterns can be interpreted.

The possibilities for neurophysiological dysfunction are limitless; the pathologies presented should not be considered as inclusive by any means. However, it is hoped that an appreciation of the complexity of cerebral neural structure and the corresponding intricacies of impairment resulting from neurophysiological dysfunction will encourage the reader to treat each impaired patient as a unique individual, for heterogeneity of outcome is common (Gaddes, 1985; Kopp & Parmelee, 1979).

## REFERENCES

Benda, C. E. (1960). *The child with mongolism (congenital acromicria)*. New York: Grune & Stratton.

Bickerstaff, E. R. (1978). *Neurology* (3rd ed.). Bungay, England: Chaucer.

Carter, C. O. (1974). Clues to the aetiology of neural tube malformations: Studies in hydrocephalus and spina bifida. *Developmental Medicine and Child Neurology, 16* (Suppl. 32), 3–15.

Churchill, J. A., Masland, R. L., Naylor, A. A., & Ashworth, M. R. (1974). The etiology of cerebral palsy in pre-term infants. *Developmental Medicine and Child Neurology, 16,* 143–149.

Cornwell, A. C., & Birch, H. G. (1969). Psychological and social development in home-reared children with Down's syndrome (mongolism). *American Journal of Mental Deficiencies, 74,* 341–350.

Dicks-Mireaux, M. J. (1972). Mental development of infants with Down's syndrome. *American Journal of Mental Deficiencies, 77,* 26–32.

Gaddes, W. H. (1985). *Learning disabilities and brain function: A neuropsychological approach* (2nd ed.). New York: Springer-Verlag.

Hetherington, E. M., & Parke, R. D. (1979). *Child psychology: A contemporary viewpoint* (2nd ed.). New York: McGraw-Hill.

Horwitz, S. J. (1973). Neurologic problems. In M. H. Klaus & A. A. Fanaroff (Eds.), *Care of the high risk neonate* (pp. 287–300). Philadelphia: Saunders.

Hunt, G. (1981). Spina bifida: Implications for 100 children at school. *Developmental Medicine and Child Neurology, 23,* 160–172.

Kleinberg, S. B. (1982). *Educating the chronically ill child*. Rockville, MD: Aspen Systems.

Kopp, C. B., & Parmelee, A. H. (1979). Prenatal and perinatal influences on infant behavior. In J. D. Osofsky (Ed.), *Handbook of infant development* (pp. 29–75). New York: Wiley.

Lawrence, K. M. (1981). Abnormalities of the central nervous system. In A. P. Norman (Ed.), *Congenital abnormalities in infancy* (pp. 21–81). Oxford, England: Blackwell.

Lindsley, D. F., & Holmes, J. E. (1984). *Basic human neurophysiology*. Amsterdam: Elsevier Science.

Nelson, W. E. (Ed.) (1969). *Textbook of pediatrics* (9th ed.). Philadelphia: Saunders.

Norman, A. P. (1963). *Congenital abnormalities in infancy*. Philadelphia: Davis.

Pincus, J. H., & Tucker, G. J. (1974). *Behavioral neurology*. New York: Oxford University Press.

Rapin, I. (1982). *Children with brain dysfunction: Neurology, cognition, language and behavior*. New York: Raven.

Rose, A., & Lombrosco, C. (1970). Neonatal seizure states: A study of clinical, pathological and electroencephalographic features in 137 full term babies with long-term follow-up. *Pediatrics, 45,* 404–425.

Spain, B. (1974). Verbal performance ability in pre-school children with spina bifida. *Developmental Medicine and Child Neurology, 16,* 773–780.

Taber, C. W. (1970). *Taber's cyclopedic medical dictionary* (11th ed.). Philadelphia: Davis.

Teberg, A. J., Wu, P. Y. K., Hodgman, J. E., Mich, C., Garfinkle, J., Azen, S., & Wingert, W. A. (1982). Infants with birth weight under 1500 grams: Physical, neurological and developmental outcome. *Critical Care Medicine, 10,* 10–14.

Turkewitz, G. (1974). The detection of brain dysfunction in the newborn infant. In D. P. Purpura & G. P. Reaser (Eds.), *Methodological approaches to the study of brain maturation and its abnormalities* (pp. 125–130). Baltimore: University.

Weller, R. O., Swash, M., McLellan, D. S., & Scholtz, C. L. (1983). *Clinical neuropathology*. New York: Overwallop, Great Britain: BAS.

DOROTHY A. STROM
RAYMOND S. DEAN
*Ball State University*
*Indiana University School*
*of Medicine*

**ADAPTED PHYSICAL EDUCATION**
**HEALTH MAINTENANCE PROCEDURES**
**PHYSICAL ANOMALIES**

## ABPP

See AMERICAN BOARD OF PROFESSIONAL PSYCHOLOGY.

## ABROMS, KIPPY I. (1942–        )

Kippy I. Abroms received her BA in psychology from the University of New Hampshire in 1962, MEd in reading from Tulane University in 1973, and PhD in special education from the University of South Mississippi in 1977. Abroms also completed post doctoral training at the University of California, Riverside in 1977 where she worked with Jane Mercer on the System of Multiple Pluralistic Assessment (SOMPA). Abroms is presently an associate professor at Tulane University where she has been teach-

**Kippy I. Abroms**

ing since 1975. She has directed several projects for the Office of Special Education and Rehabilitation Services and the Bureau of Education for the Handicapped.

Abroms conducted research with J. W. Bennett (1981) that dispelled the well-entrenched notion of exclusive maternal etiology in Down's syndrome. Abroms and Bennett found that in a significant number of cases the extra #21 chromosome, the immediate cause of Down's syndrome, comes from the sperm. Thus there can be a maternal or paternal contribution to the etiology of Trisomy 21.

Abroms is presently conducting a longitudinal study on the social development of preschool gifted children, and, as a member of the cranio-facial team at the Tulane University Medical Center, is involved in research on the relationship between cognitive functioning, self concept, and cranio-facial intervention.

**REFERENCES**

Abroms, K. I., & Bennett, J. W. (1981). Parental contributions to Trisomy 21: Review of recent cytological and statistical findings. In P. Mittler (Ed.), *Frontiers of knowledge in mental retardation, Vol. 2. Biomedical aspects.* (pp. 149–157). Baltimore: University Park.

ELAINE FLETCHER-JANZEN
*Texas A&M University*

## ABSENCE OF SPEECH

See SPEECH, ABSENCE OF.

## ABSENCE SEIZURES

Absence seizures (also known as petit mal seizures) are a form of epilepsy characterized by brief losses of consciousness unaccompanied by large convulsive movements. Absence seizures are generalized; involving abnormal activity throughout the brain. They are characterized by lack of any aura (sensation that a seizure is to occur), brevity (absence seizures typically last 5–10 seconds [Menkes, 1985]), and abrupt termination. After an absence seizure has occurred, there is no postictal period, the individual does not complain of fatigue or the need to sleep, and he or she can resume the activity being engaged in prior to the seizure. Children with absence seizures often are unaware of their lapses of consciousness.

Although absence seizures are nonconvulsive during the seizure, some movement will be seen in about 70% of diagnosed children. When the seizure begins, an observer may notice a vacant look in the child's eyes. Minor motor movements such as lip smacking, eye blinking, or twitching of the eyelids or face sometimes occur. There may be a slight loss of body tone, with the child perhaps dropping something he or she is holding. Absence seizures often can be precipitated by sustained hyperventilation, and less frequently by photic stimulation.

Absence seizures are more common in girls, and onset is generally between 5 and 15 years of age. There frequently is a family history of a seizure disorder. Most often the neurologic exam and CAT scan is normal. The EEG shows a characteristic three-cycle per second spike and wave pattern during seizures. Generally IQs are reported to be within normal limits, though some studies suggest a mild depression when compared with siblings (Dreifuss, 1983). The most frequent school problem is difficulty in paying attention. There is some evidence that this is related to abnormal brain function (Mirsky, 1969). With frequent seizures, schoolwork often is disrupted.

The medications used in absence seizures include ethosuximide (Zarontin), valproate (Depakene), clonazepam (Clonopin), paramethadione (Paradione), and methsuximide (Celontin). There are other types of seizures that include staring, but these are not simple absence seizures.

**REFERENCES**

Dreifuss, F. E. (1983). *Pediatric epileptology*. Boston: Wright.

Menkes, J. H. (1985). *Textbook of child neurology*. Philadelphia: Lee & Febiger.

Mirsky, A. F. (1969). Studies of paroxysmal EEG phenomena and background EEG in relation to impaired attention. In C. R. Evans & T. P. Mullholland (Eds.), *Attention in neurophysiology* (pp. 310–322). London: Butterworth.

GRETA N. WILKENING
*Children's Hospital, Denver,
Colorado*

## ELECTROENCEPHALOGRAPH
## GRAND MAL SEIZURES

## ABSENTEEISM/ATTENDANCE OF HANDICAPPED CHILDREN

Compulsory school attendance laws have been enacted in all states. The scope of those laws was narrowed in most states by the introduction of exemption clauses. These clauses excuse children considered unfit or uneducable because of physical or mental handicaps from school attendance. Legal challenges by handicapped children for extension and protection of the right established under state law of equal access to educational opportunity ensued during the early 1970s. Those cases were followed by federal and state laws that mandate free appropriate public education to handicapped children and ensure their right to attend school regardless of the severity or type of their disability.

Under Part B of the Education of the Handicapped Act (EHA) and Section 504 of the Rehabilitation Act of 1973, a handicapped child must be educated in the least restrictive environment his or her needs allow. Children with serious, often chronic, health impairments who require special education and related services may receive instruction in hospitals or in the home. Schools use various approaches, including home visitations, school-to-home telephone communication, and interactive television to connect a homebound or hospitalized student with the classroom. Federal law recognizes that there are instances when, because of the nature or severity of a child's handicap, the child must be educated in a setting other than the regular classroom. However, the least restrictive environment provisions prohibit placement of a child on homebound instruction or other exclusion from the regular educational environment solely because the child is handicapped. Homebound instruction may not be appropriate for the instructional needs of that child.

There have been few studies of program and school attendance as a factor in the achievement of handicapped students. There is some evidence that handicapped students attending regular schools are no more likely to be absent from school than nonhandicapped students (Sullivan & McDaniel, 1983). High rates of school attendance do not necessarily ensure high rates of program attendance or achievement. Sullivan and McDaniel (1983) concluded that handicapped children served in resource rooms may be receiving up to one-quarter less schooling time than is prescribed in their individualized education programs because of competing school activities and absences of either the resource room teacher or the student during a scheduled period. In various studies involving handicapped or nonhandicapped learners (Ivarie, Hogue, & Brulle, 1984; Rosenshine, 1979), investigators in the area of academic learning time as it relates to academic achievement have found a positive correlation between the learning of basic skills and the number of minutes students spend on academically relevant tasks. Research-

ers are continuing their study of increased active learning time as a powerful intervention technique for handicapped and nonhandicapped students.

Under the EHA and Section 504, mandatory procedural safeguards exist that allow parents to challenge school disciplinary actions that would interrupt a handicapped child's education. Expulsions, suspensions, and transfers to settings outside a regular classroom or school are considered placement changes since such measures remove students from their current school program or curtail attendance (Simon, 1984). A series of court decisions on this sensitive area have provided important guidelines for determining when and for what length of time handicapped students may be expelled or suspended under federal law (Simon, 1984).

### REFERENCES

Ivarie, J., Hogue, D., & Brulle, A. (1984). Investigation of mainstream teacher time spent with students labeled learning disabled. *Exceptional Children, 51*, 142–149.

Rosenshine, B. V. (1979). Content, time, and direct instruction. In P. L. Peterson & H. J. Walberg (Eds.), *Research on teaching* (pp. 28–56). Berkeley, CA: McCutchan.

Simon, S. G. (1984). Discipline in the public schools: A dual standard for handicapped and nonhandicapped students? *Journal of Law & Education, 13*, 209–237.

Sullivan, P. D., & McDaniel, E. A. (1983). Pupil attendance in resource rooms as one measure of the time on task variable. *Journal of Learning Disabilities, 16*, 398–399.

SHIRLEY A. JONES
*Virginia Polytechnic Institute
and State University*

**HOMEBOUND INSTRUCTION
SUMMER SCHOOL FOR HANDICAPPED**

## ABSTRACTION, CAPACITY FOR

Abstract reasoning refers to the ability to identify common features of two or more concepts, and has been considered an essential component of intelligence (e.g., Thorndike, 1927). Abstract reasoning ability can be assessed through at least three types of tasks: those which require a person to identify a general concept common to several exemplars, e.g., sorting objects according to categories; to state common features among different concepts, e.g, the Similarities subtest of the Wechsler Intelligence Scale for Children-Revised; or to state examples or features of a given concept (Burger, Blackman, Clark, & Reis, 1982).

While general abstraction ability varies across persons, ability to reason abstractly in specific tasks appears to vary with subject area expertise. For example, in studying the superior memory of chess masters for the configuration of briefly presented game arrangements, Chi, Glaser, and Rees (1981) suggest that experts form abstract, organized representations of the field of play, while novices retain only the surface features of the problem. Adelson (1984) found that novice computer programming students actually had better recall for the details of a briefly presented program than did expert programmers, but that the experts had better recall for what the programs were designed to do. Ability to make abstractions about information seems to improve with experience; as one gains more experience with an area of knowledge, one becomes familiar with the organization of it, and is able to integrate new information with greater success.

Burger, Blackman, Clark, and Reis (1982) found that educable mentally retarded (EMR) adolescents could be trained to improve their abstract reasoning abilities. This training consisted of telling oneself to label the pictures or objects presented, tell about the picture or object, tell in what way the pictures are the same, and checking that one had identified similarities. Further research is needed to describe the extent to which such learning can transfer to other concept learning tasks.

### REFERENCES

Adelson, B. (1984). When novices surpass experts: The difficulty of a task may increase with expertise. *Journal of Experimental Psychology: Learning, Memory, and Cognition, 10,* 483–495.

Burger, A. L., Blackman, L. S., Clark, H. T., & Reis, E. (1982). Effects of hypothesis testing and variable format training on generalization of a verbal abstraction strategy by EMR learners. *American Journal on Mental Deficiency, 86,* 405–413.

Chi, M. T. H., Glaser, R. & Rees, E. (1981). Expertise in problem solving. In R. Sternberg (Ed.), *Advances in the psychology of human intelligence* (Vol. 1, pp. 7–75). Hillsdale, NJ: Erlbaum.

Thorndike, E. L. (1927). *The measurement of intelligence.* New York: Bureau of Publications, Teachers College, Columbia University.

JOHN MACDONALD
*Eastern Kentucky University*

INTELLIGENCE TESTING
EDUCABLE MENTALLY RETARDED

## ABSTRACT THINKING, IMPAIRMENT IN

Those who work with children having learning problems are interested in trying to understand their thinking processes. Three groups of children have been of particular interest—deaf, mentally retarded, and learning disabled. Children with these disorders have all exhibited difficulty acquiring academic skills. One hypothesis for their difficulty is that they may not be processing information normally. Some assert these children have deficiencies in abstract reasoning.

A theory of abstract reasoning hinges on the notion that human thinking is a process of conceptualization. Concept formation is the organization of data into categories. To know a concept is to know the characteristics of an entity that either include it or exclude it from a category. To know the concept of "dog" is to know that animals with four legs, hair, and the ability to bark belong together in a category. Some argue that forming a concept is a process of abstracting. To learn the concept of dog requires noticing common characteristics of different dogs, as well as noticing that cats have some characteristics that eliminate them from that category. However, not all concepts are created equally. Some are based on immediate, sensory experience. For example, a child may form a category of "doggy" by directly experiencing dogs and pictures of dogs. This is considered to be a concrete concept. On the other hand, there are concepts that are built from other concepts, for example, the notion of "mammal." A concept even further removed from direct experience is "democracy." The more removed the concept from direct experience, the more abstract it is. The term *abstract,* then, is used in two different ways. On the one hand, it is used to mean the process by which the salient characteristics of entities are identified in order to form concepts. On the other hand, it is used in contrast with the term *concrete* to indicate the role of direct experience.

Another factor related to abstract reasoning is the role of symbolization. Luria (1961) stated that the development of more abstract concepts was dependent on symbolization—more specifically the use of language. In fact, he felt that higher level concept formation was probably dependent on the mediation of language. For example, Luria would contend that a concept such as democracy more than likely requires language for acquisition.

Those dealing with children having difficulties with learning have tried to understand the role of conceptualization and symbolization in the development of abstract reasoning. Johnson and Myklebust (1967) were particularly interested in the conceptualization problems of learning-disabled children. They asserted that some have difficulties in the process of concept formation itself. They argued that any deficit in the processes of perception, imagery, symbolization, or abstracting could interfere with conceptualization. Others have difficulty not so much in the process of conceptualization as in dealing with the more abstract concepts. As Johnson and Myklebust point out, an individual with disturbances in the processes of abstracting or conceptualizing may be identified as a concrete thinker.

Myers and Hammill (1982) note that children who cannot form abstract concepts are generally labeled as being mentally retarded rather than learning disabled. Nonetheless, learning-disabled children are often described as having "concrete behavior characterized by a dependence upon immediate experience as opposed to abstract behavior that transcends any given immediate experience and results in the formation of conceptual categories" (p. 39). Many would argue that the difficulty exhibited by learning-disabled children is caused by a developmental lag and is not a permanent problem. In the case of mentally retarded children, however, the conceptualization problem may be permanent. Further, a body of research has been dedicated to trying to determine whether the conceptual behavior of mentally retarded children represents simply a delay or difference (Zigler & Balla, 1982). To understand this problem researchers may, for example, look at how mentally retarded children use the role of language as a mediation device for concept formation (Field, 1977).

It is not uncommon for those working with hearing-impaired children to describe their cognitive behavior as being concrete (Johnson & Myklebust, 1967). There are several difficulties with this notion, however. Hearing-impaired children, because of their limited input, may simply not have had a sufficient experiential base to adequately form concepts that would be expected of hearing children. Another problem in understanding the hearing-impaired child's conceptualization is that these children live in a visual linguistic world. What may appear to be concrete behavior on the part of the child may simply be an artifact of one of the underlying rules of natural sign language systems. The rule is that the structure of an utterance cannot violate the visual world. For example, the word order of the structure "I finished my work, then watched television" is directly translatable into American Sign Language. "I watched television after I finished my work" is not, because it violates the visual sequence of events. Difficulties that hearing-impaired children have with the latter structure, when encountering it in English, are sometimes interpreted as evidence that the child is a concrete thinker. In truth, it may be simply that the child is having difficulty in dealing with a structure that violates the child's linguistic rules.

It is important to note that the relationship between sensory information, concept formation, and symbolization is not well understood. Research has given us only the most sketchy idea of what the relationship among the three might be. One field of philosophy, epistemology, has been dedicated to trying to understand these relationships. Introspection and logical reasoning remain the most powerful tools available to both psychology and philosophy for describing concept development and abstract reasoning.

In summary, the notion of abstract reasoning is used in two different ways. It can mean the process by which one identifies the salient characteristics in entities for purposes of categorization. Abstract reasoning can also be the process by which individuals deal with concepts that are based on other concepts, rather than concepts that are based on direct experience. Children with learning problems can have difficulties with either type of abstract reasoning. When difficulties are exhibited, the question arises as to whether the difference is simply developmental delay or a difference in cognitive processing. Some people working with learning-disabled children contend that they eventually outgrow problems in these areas. Mentally retarded children may not necessarily do so. Children who are hearing impaired have also been described as "concrete" learners. However, their difficulties may be a result of too little experience and their use of visually based linguistic rules.

### REFERENCES

Field, D. (1977). The importance of verbal content in the training of Piagetian conservation skills. *Child Development*, 1583–1592.

Johnson, D. J., & Myklebust, H. R. (1967). *Learning disabilities: Educational principles and practices*. New York: Grune & Stratton.

Luria, A. R. (1961). *The role of speech in the regulation of normal and abnormal behavior*. New York: Liveright (Pergamon Press).

Myers, P. I., & Hammill, D. D. (1982). *Learning disabilities: Basic concepts, assessment practices, and instructional strategies*. Austin, TX: PRO-ED.

Zigler, E., & Balla, D. (1982). *Mental retardation: The developmental-difference controversy*. Hillsdale, NJ: Lawrence Erlbaum.

CAROLYN BULLARD
*Lewis & Clark College*

CONCRETE OPERATIONS
LEARNING DISIBILITIES

# ABUSED CHILDREN

Today abused children are typically regarded as suffering from a primary illness (Quirk, 1980). A primary illness refers to the notion that living with a certain circumstance for a prolonged period of time creates a situation in the victim requiring primary treatment. The primary illness of child abuse has identifiable symptoms and etiology along with an official diagnosis and prescribed treatments.

An orderly treatment for abused children and adults who were abused as children involves the ability of the clinician to identify and properly diagnose the dilemma and its ramifications and to facilitate the natural healing process from trauma. Thus the first step in treatment is proper identification of child abuse as the problem to be treated.

Children who have been abused relive their abuse over and over in clear or symbolic ways. They dream abusive dreams, remember abusive situations, and in adulthood go so far as to recreate abusive relationships. They manifest little positive affect in interpersonal relationships, and they lack intimacy and express difficulty in trusting others (Herman, 1981). They are depressed and have difficulty in developing meaningful relationships or experiences in their lives. Adults who were abused children are often defensive, suspicious, nervous, and overly alert. They seem to be preoccupied with their bodily functions and are frequently labeled hypochondriacs. Insomnia is another frequently reported symptom, even in the absence of distressing nightmares. Abused children are also guilt-ridden, and experience much shame and self-hatred. Concentrating and following a task through to its completion is another problem area for this population (Mrazek & Kempe, 1981; Williams & Money, 1980).

Acting out the abuse in self-destructive ways such as drug abuse is frequently observed in this population, which is disproportionately represented in chemical dependency treatment facilities. As teenagers, abused children often become runaways and act out their rage in criminal behavior. Abused children are also disproportionately represented in facilities for delinquents. A disproportionately large group in this population may attempt suicide, hallucinate, manifest seizures, and ultimately be placed in psychiatric hospitals. While these obvious problematic behaviors will occur at high rates, another observed phenomena of this population is the frequency with which they become quiet, good children who then marry an abusive partner. Other compulsive behaviors are frequently manifested by these children and subsequently they will be found as adults in Al-anon, Alcoholics Anonymous, Narcotics Anonymous, Overeaters Anonymous, Gamblers Anonymous, and other self-help treatment programs.

Abused children as adults have difficulty with parenting. Appropriate discipline is difficult for them because it is too restimulating. Consequently, they will abdicate their parenting until the children eventually become abusive toward them (Justice & Justice, 1976). This promotes another likely place for adult abused children to reflect inadequacies—as parents of children in trouble. On the other hand, adult abused children may become abusive parents themselves. The inordinate numbers of child abusers that were themselves abused has been widely documented.

Because young and abused children live and grow with a wounded and fragmented personality, they often need intensive treatment efforts. The client who clings or annoys the clinician, reporting that something is missing from treatment, will often be a person who was abused. This person will often complain about the deficiencies of treatment and report that he or she has not been responded to reasonably. This type of reporting should be expected in view of the fact that abused children are wounded people who will have difficulty objectifying their relations: after all, their primary objects, mom or dad, abused them.

Treatment programs and clinicians should routinely be sensitive in recognizing and treating child abuse. When working with clients the following questions should be a routine part of the interview. What was your childhood like? How did your parents treat you? How were you disciplined? What were the punishments employed by your parents? Were you ever raped or seduced? Those who report having difficulty recalling all or crucial parts of their childhood should definitely be regarded as potentially having been abused. This self-induced amnesia is a primitive form of defense against the pain and discomfort resulting from recall of an abusive situation. Naturally, this needs to be dealt with in a sensitive manner by the clinician, and the client should not be prematurely pushed into acknowledging information or feelings they are not prepared to confront.

Abused children often feel at fault for their experience of child abuse. They live with much guilt, shame, self-blame, and self-loathing. Often their abusers told them it was their fault. Child molesters use guilt as a tool with their victims in order to keep the secret, while parents who physically beat their children do so in the name of discipline. Yet, abused children mentally make their parents correct and good. Generally, therapists should enjoy relationships with people, but it is even more important for therapists of abused children to like their clients. While one might think that all therapists would like their clients, fragile clients often find themselves disliked by their therapists. Since they do not grow as the therapist expects, they experience rejection in the context of the therapeutic relationship.

Adults who were abused in childhood have unusual difficulty in establishing trust with the therapist, identifying and discussing feelings, and cooperating with the therapeutic process. Because their tormentors were often people they trusted (e.g., parents), abused children may recoil at the need to trust the therapist. Therefore, an unusually long working-through process is frequently required. This is often difficult for the novice therapist, educator, or other professional lacking information about child abuse and its symptoms.

Most children learn to cope by making decisions separate from the influence of their parents. Abused children have more to cope with, and fewer skills to do so. Reparenting applies here also. Regardless of age, abused children need to learn to live and cope in the real world, and come to recognize that not all people are as threatening as their abusive parents. Therefore, learning coping skills is essential to any successful treatment program. The following are examples of important coping skills to be addressed: learning to trust one's own instincts; learning to identify one's own needs; and learning to proceed to satisfy those needs. Another essential component to treatment is the development of an ability to identify and avoid close contact with abusive people.

Because abuse occurs in the context of an interpersonal relationship, the environment of a therapeutic group has proven itself a particularly helpful treatment modality. In view of the characteristics of this population, the following are important considerations for the leader of a group of abused children. The group should be initially supportive, gentle, homogeneous, and closed to new members after the group has begun. These elements are necessary to address the difficulty in trusting manifested by this population. The group needs to project an image of safety and members must be monitored from inappropriately expressing the rage some may possess. Confrontation must be kept well managed to further reduce regression that may be promoted by some of the more fragmented members. The group leader must monitor the development of any situation that may resemble the childhood abuse of any member in the group. A primary goal of the group is to develop understanding of the personal dynamics of abuse and coping skills that may prevent the development of similar abusive situations in the future.

### REFERENCES

Herman, J. L. (1981). *Father-daughter incest.* Cambridge, MA: Harvard University Press.

Justice, B., & Justice, R. (1976). *The abusing family.* New York: Human Sciences.

Mrazek, P. B., & Kempe C. H. (Eds.). (1981). *Sexually abused children and their families.* New York: Pergamon.

Quirk, J. P. (Ed.). (1980). *Reading in child abuse.* Guilford, CT: Special Learning.

Williams, J. W., & Money, J. (Eds.). (1980). *Traumatic abuse and neglect of children at home.* Baltimore, MD: John Hopkins University Press.

CHARLES P. BARNARD
*University of Wisconsin, Stout*

ACTING OUT
CHILD ABUSE
CHILD CARETAKER
ETIOLOGY

## ACADEMICALLY TALENTED CHILDREN

Academically talented children usually possess superior intellectual ability or a specific subject matter aptitude. This point of view is supported by the general acceptance of Witty's (1940) definition of giftedness as performance by a child that is consistently remarkable in a potentially valuable line of human activity. Included in the scope of Witty's definition are those who are academically talented, and, therefore, have the ability to do well in one or more academic subjects in school. This label distinguishes these children from those who may be talented in other areas designated by the U.S. Office of Education such as creative or productive thinking, leadership, visual and performing arts, and psychomotor activities (Renzulli, 1978).

Identification of academic ability can include the use of IQ tests, achievement test scores, evidence of academic achievement, and products successfully completed in an academic area. In addition, students who are academically talented are sometimes 2 to 8 years ahead of chronological age peers in academic subjects (Clark, 1983).

It must be noted that academic talent in one subject matter area does not always mean talent in another academic area. For example, children with a high mathematical aptitude may not perform equally well in other subject matter classes. Once identified, academically talented children require acceleration and/or enrichment in each area of strength.

### REFERENCES

Clark, B. (1983). *Growing up gifted.* Columbus, OH: Merrill.

Renzulli, J. S. (1978). What makes giftedness? Reexamining a definition. *Phi Delta Kappan, 60,* 180–184.

Witty, P. (1940). Some considerations in the education of gifted children. *Educational Administration and Supervision, 26,* 512–521.

MARY K. TALLENT
*Texas Tech University*

ACCELERATION OF GIFTED CHILDREN
GIFTED AND TALENTED CHILDREN
GIFTED CHILDREN

## ACADEMIC ASSESSMENT

The global function of achievement testing is to assess a student's attainment of academic content areas. Reading, written language, and mathematical functioning are the major domains under the rubric of academic achievement. Anastasi (1982) notes that traditionally academic assessment has been differentiated from aptitude/ability testing by the degree to which a measure is designed to assess uniform versus diverse antecedent experiences. To be categorized as a measure of academic achievement, a measure is designed to test a fairly uniform previous experience (e.g., first grade instruction in reading). In contrast, an aptitude test would be designed to assess the impact of multiple or diverse antecedent experiences. Contemporary measurement specialists recognize that both achievement and aptitude tests assess acquired knowledge, but differ on the degree of specificity and abstraction.

Salvia and Ysseldyke (1981) have described four functions that achievement tests fulfill within the schools. They are used for screening students who may need more in-depth assessment to determine whether special services are appropriate; determining whether a child is eligible for placement in a special education class based on local criteria; assessing a child's strengths and weaknesses to facilitate decisions regarding his or her placement in an instructional sequence; and determining the impact of educational intervention on a class or group of students.

Achievement testing may be conceptualized along several lines: norm-referenced versus criterion referenced; individual versus group administered; and informal teacher-constructed versus standardized instruction. Each of these dimensions will be discussed to highlight the multifaceted construct of academic achievement assessment.

Norm-referenced testing began to play a prominent role in American education after World War I. Army Alpha and Beta tests were used for the classification of recruits during the war. The Otis Group Intelligence Scale was published in 1918 by the World Book Company. This scale employed such advances as multiple choice questions, answer sheets, test booklets, and improved normative sampling procedures (Cunningham, 1986). These advances were adapted for the first norm-referenced, standardized measure of academic achievement, the Stanford Achievement Test, published in 1923.

The most salient characteristic of norm-referenced achievement tests is that an examinee's performance on the test is interpreted by comparing his or her relative standing to a given reference group. The reference group or standardization sample is usually composed of representative peers of the same chronological age, or peers in the same grade placement. Performance on a norm-referenced test is typically expressed in scores based on the normal curve such as stanines, T-scores, and/or standard scores (which usually have a mean of 100 and a standard deviation of 15, or sometimes 16). Performance on a norm-referenced test may also be expressed in percentiles, which tell a student's standing relative to a hypothetical group of 100 children. For instance, a score at the 86th percentile indicates that the examinee scored better than 86 out of 100 of his or her hypothetical same-aged peers.

The major norm-referenced group achievement tests include the California Achievement Test (CTB/McGraw-Hill, 1985); the Comprehensive Test of Basic Skills (CTB/McGraw-Hill, 1981); the Iowa Test of Basic Skills (Hieronymus, Lindquist, & Hoover, 1983); the Metropolitan Achievement Test (Barlow, Farr, Hogan, & Prescott, 1978); and the Stanford Achievement Test (Gardner, Rudman, Karlsen, & Merwin, 1982).

These group-administered tests have multiple levels, each designated for a specified grade range. For instance, the Stanford Achievement Test series has six levels: Primary Level 1 for grades 1.5–2.9; Primary Level 2 for 2.5–3.9; Primary Level 3 for 3.5–4.9; Intermediate Level 1 for 4.5–5.9; Intermediate Level 2 for 5.5–7.9; and Intermediate Level 3 for 7.0–9.9. Generally, these tests have gone through several revisions. The Stanford Achievement Test, for example, is in its seventh revision and has been in use in the public schools for over 60 years.

A primary difference between norm-referenced and criterion-referenced tests lies in the way they are interpreted. As noted, the norm-referenced achievement test is designed to give information on a given student's performance relative to a representative group of same-aged peers. In contrast, the criterion-referenced achievement test is designed to give information on a given student's performance in terms of whether he or she has learned a given concept or skill. Thus, the criterion-referenced measure is designed to tell what the student can and cannot do. For instance, the student can add single digit numerals with sums less than 10, but has not learned to regroup or perform simple subtraction problems. Since discrimination among students is not the purpose of a criterion-referenced test, the difficulty level of items and the power of items to separate students are not as important as they are in norm-referenced measures. The major issue in criterion-referenced measurement is whether items reflect a specified instructional domain. Most of the major group-administered achievement tests have been adapted to yield criterion-referenced information. The problem with adapting norm-referenced tests is that there are a multiplicity of instructional objectives (Cunningham, 1986). Since each objective requires several test items to achieve an adequate level of reliability, the length of the test becomes unmanageable.

Up to this point group-administered measures have been used to illustrate the norm- versus criterion-referenced dimensions of academic assessment. Academic achievement testing may also be examined from the viewpoint of the administration format, either individual or group. While group achievement tests are usually given to a whole class by the regular education teacher, individual achievement measures are administered by specially trained personnel (special education teachers, educational diagnosticians, and school psychologists) to a child on a one-to-one basis. Typically, the child has been referred for testing because of academic or behavioral problems manifested in the regular classroom. A general distinction between group and individual measures relates to their use in the decision-making process. Group measures are designed to make decisions about groups, while individual tests are more appropriate for decisions concerning an individual. Therefore, caution must be exercised when attempting to interpret the results of a single child's performance on a group-administered measure. There are many variables that may influence a child's performance on a group-administered measure and result in an inaccurate portrayal of that child's academic skills. Misunderstanding instructions, fatigue, random guessing, class distractions, looking on a neighbor's response sheet, etc., may invalidate a child's scores. When a child is being considered for placement in a special education program, a poor performance on a group-administered measure should be followed up with an individual assessment.

Individual measures of academic achievement commonly used within the context of the special education eligibility process include the Peabody Individual Achievement Test-Revised (Dunn & Markwardt, 1970; Wide Range Achievement Test-Revised (Jastak & Wilkinson, 1984); Part II of the Woodcock-Johnson Psycho-Educational Battery (Woodcock & Johnson, 1977); and the Basic Achievement Skills Individual Screener (Psychological Corporation, 1983), a test that has recently gained acceptance in the schools. All of these instruments are norm-referenced and designed to provide information at a screening level, not a comprehensive diagnostic level. Only limited information that has value for placing a child at a given point in an instructional sequence may be gleaned from these measures. More in-depth information may be obtained through the use of individually administered specialized measures, e.g., KeyMath Diagnostic Arithmetic Test (Connolly, Nachtman, & Pritchett, 1971), the Woodcock Reading Mastery Test (Woodcock, 1973), and informal assessment. For instance, if a child's performance on a screening measure indicates potential difficulties in reading, then the Woodcock Reading Mastery Test, in conjunction with an informal reading inventory measure, would be appropriate for gaining a fuller understanding of the child's difficulties with word attack skills, word comprehension, or reading comprehension.

Finally, the academic achievement test may be approached by examining the degree to which the directions to students are standardized. The standardized test is one where the instructions and test questions are presented in the same manner to all examinees. On the other hand, in the teacher-constructed test, there is unlimited latitude in the construction and administration of test items. Both standardized and informal teacher-made tests have advantages and disadvantages. However, they should share certain attributes, i.e., clear directions to students, careful development of items based on a table of specifications, and the type or format of test items.

Whether the directions to an achievement test are standardized or constructed by the teacher, building a table of specifications represents the first step in test construction. A table of specifications contains a listing of instructional objects as well as the relative emphasis to be assigned to each objective. For standardized measures of achievement, the table of specification is based on an examination of major textbook series used across the country. For instance, when reading subtests are constructed, the most widely used basal reading series are reviewed by the test developer. Note is taken at what point in the curricula various concepts are introduced. Invariably, decisions and compromises have to be made regarding content, because all basal reading series are not identical. As such, the consumer of both individual and group standardized achievement tests must examine the available measures, not just in terms of quality of standardization and reliability, but also with respect to the match between the concepts assessed by the test and those taught within the framework of the local curriculum. See Table 1 for selected

Table 1. Selected objectives from the California Achievement Tests, Forms E and F

*Visual Recognition*
1. Single letters
2. Upper, lowercase letters
3. Letter combinations

*Sound Recognition*
4. Initial consonant sounds
5. Final consonant sounds
6. Rhyming

*Word Analysis*
7. Single consonants/oral
8. Consonant clusters, digraphs/oral
9. Consonant clusters
10. Variant consonant sounds
11. Long vowels/oral
12. Long vowels
13. Short vowels/oral
14. Short vowels
15. Diphthongs, variant vowel sounds
16. Sight words
17. Compound words
18. Root words/affixes

*Reading Comprehension*
Literal comprehension
32. Passage details
33. Stated main idea
Inferential Comprehension
34. Passage analysis/oral
35. Character analysis
36. Central thought
37. Interpreting events
Critical Comprehension
38. Forms of writing
39. Writing techniques

*Spelling*
40. Vowel sounds
41. Consonant sounds
42. Structural units

objectives covered by Forms E and F of the California Achievement Test.

A major difference between standardized and informal, teacher-developed tests is that the former usually represents many more hours of item development, refinement, empirical tryouts, and final selection of test items. In developing standardized achievement tests, considerable weight is placed on both content validity (the representativeness of the items to the domain being tested, and the appropriateness of the format and wording of items relative to the age level of the prospective examinees), and the empirical tryout of the items in terms of reliability. The advantage of the standardized test lies in its documented reliability (presented in an accompanying technical manual), and its ability to compare a student's performance with that of a reference group or specified criterion. Whereas standardized tests measure content that is common to reading and mathematics programs from around the country, the teacher-constructed tests can be specifically targeted to the content of the local curriculum, or to a specific teacher's class.

In addition to defining informal assessment as the administration of a teacher-constructed measure, the term may also be applied to diagnostic processes. These include error analysis, behavioral observation, and the learner's relations to various instructional strategies (Sedlak, Sedlak, & Steppe-Jones, 1982). This last process is flexible and dynamic. A psychoeducational examiner presents tasks to the student in a branching manner similar to the operation of a branching computer-assisted instructional program. Information about the student's mastery of various skills is gleaned from analysis of his or her errors. Error analysis has been applied to reading, writing, mathematics, second language learning, and spelling (Bejar,

1984). The analysis is usually conducted within a "content" framework, such as an educational taxonomy.

Mathematical functioning is a key area where error analysis has been profitably employed (Brown & Van-Lehn, 1982). Ashlock (1976) offers useful exercises in a semiprogrammed text to help detect common error patterns in computation. See Table 2 for exemplars of common errors that give insight into the students' problems. Lankford (1974) demonstrated the value of having a student think aloud while solving arithmetic problems. Thus, when an error is made, the computation strategy used by the student becomes apparent. Roberts (1968) has noted four common error categories for arithmetic computation: selecting the wrong operation; erring in recalling a specific arithmetic fact; attempting the correct operation but using an inappropriate algorithm; and random responding that has no apparent relationship to the problem.

In summary, academic achievement assessment is used to make decisions about students. These decisions may be made from a normative perspective or in terms of students' mastery of a specified skill. Depending on the administration, format decisions can be made for an individual student or for groups of students. Norm-referenced achievement tests provide information about a student's relative standing compared with that of a reference group, while criterion-referenced tests and informal assessments may be used to make informed decisions about a student's future instructional needs.

Table 2. Samples of common arithmetic error patterns that give insight into the student's incorrect problem-solving strategy

*Addition*

$$\begin{array}{r} 56 \\ +\ 7 \\ \hline 513 \end{array}$$

(Failure to regroup)

$$\begin{array}{r} 24 \\ +\ 5 \\ \hline 11 \end{array}$$

(Addition of all numerals without regard for place value)

*Subtraction*

$$\begin{array}{r} 53 \\ -\ 5 \\ \hline 52 \end{array}$$

(Failure to group)

$$\begin{array}{r} 522 \\ -101 \\ \hline 401 \end{array}$$

(Misunderstanding of zero as a subtrahend)

*Multiplication*

$$\begin{array}{r} 34 \\ \times\ 3 \\ \hline 122 \end{array}$$

(Addition of the regrouped number prior to multiplication)

$$\begin{array}{r} 93 \\ \times\ 8 \\ \hline 101 \end{array}$$

(Use of inappropriate algorithm)

*Division*

$$\begin{array}{r} 21 \\ 2\overline{)24} \\ 20 \\ \hline 4 \end{array}$$

(A right to left recording pattern is employed)

$$\begin{array}{r} 5 \\ 3\overline{)18} \end{array}$$

(Basic fact mistake)

## REFERENCES

Anastasi, A. (1982). *Psychological testing* (5th ed.). New York: Macmillan.

Ashlock, R. B. (1976). *Error patterns in computation: A semi-programmed approach* (2nd ed.). Columbus, OH: Merrill.

Barlow, I. H., Farr, R., Hogan, T. P., & Prescott, G. A. (1978). *Metropolitan Achievement Tests* (5th ed.). New York: Psychological Corp.

Bejar, I. I. (1984). Educational diagnostic assessment. *Journal of Educational Measurement, 21,* 175–189.

Brown, J. S., & VanLehn, K. (1982). Toward a generative theory of "bugs." In T. P. Carpenter, J. M. Moser, & T. A. Romberg (Eds.), *Addition and subtraction: A cognitive perspective.* Hillsdale, NJ: Erlbaum.

Connolly, A. J., Nachtman, W., & Pritchett, E. M. (1971). *KeyMath Diagnostic Arithmetic Test.* Circle Pines, MN: American Guidance Service.

CTB/McGraw-Hill. (1981). *The Comprehensive Tests of Basic Skills.* New York: Author.

CTB/McGraw-Hill. (1985). *California Achievement Tests.* New York: Author.

Cunningham, G. K. (1986). *Educational and psychological measurement.* New York: Macmillan.

Dunn, L. M., & Markwardt, F.C. (1970). *Peabody Individual Achievement Test.* Circle Pines, MN: American Guidance Service.

Gardner, E. G., Rudman, H. C., Karlsen, B., & Merwin, J. C.

(1982). *Stanford Achievement Test* (1982 ed.). New York: Psychological Corp.

Hieronymus, A. N., Lindquist, E. F., & Hoover, H. D. (1983). *Iowa Tests of Basic Skills*. Chicago: Riverside.

Jastak, S., & Wilkinson, G. S. (1984). *The Wide Range Achievement Test-Revised* (1984 revised ed.). Wilmington, DE: Jastak Associates.

Lankford, F. G. (1974). What can a teacher learn about a pupil's thinking through oral interviews? *Arithmetic Teacher, 21,* 26–32.

Psychological Corporation (1983). *Basic Achievement Skills Individual Screener*. New York: Author.

Roberts, G. H. (1968). The failure strategies of third grade arithmetic pupils. *Arithmetic Teacher, 15,* 442–446.

Salvia, J., & Ysseldyke, J. E. (1981). *Assessment in special and remedial education* (2nd ed.). Boston: Houghton Mifflin.

Sedlak, R. A., Sedlak, D. M., & Steppe-Jones, C. (1982). Informal assessment. In D. A. Sabatino & L. Mann (Eds.), *A handbook of diagnostic and prescriptive teaching*. Rockville, MD: Aspen Systems.

Woodcock, R. W. (1973). *Woodcock Reading Mastery Tests*. Circle Pines, MN: American Guidance Service.

Woodcock, R. W., & Johnson, M. B. (1977). *Woodcock-Johnson Psycho-Educational Battery*. Hingham, MA: Teaching Resources.

JACK A. CUMMINGS
*Indiana University*

ACHIEVEMENT TESTS
CRITERION-REFERENCED TESTING
NORM REFERENCED TESTING

# ACADEMIC SKILLS

While to some individuals the definition of academic skills conjours up the three Rs, to others the delineation of the academic skills most important to the process of special education is a task that poses an awesome definitional problem. To the preschool special educator, for example, certain fine motor skills may be defined as important academic skills. On the other hand, for the special educator working at the secondary level, the ability to accept positive and negative feedback (social skills), driving skills, or home economics may be considered important academic skills that warrant inclusion in the secondary special education curriculum.

A recent comprehensive sourcebook on research on teaching presents detailed analyses of seven academic skill areas: written composition, reading, mathematics, natural sciences, arts and aesthetics, moral and values education, and social studies (Wittrock, 1986). At least a few of these areas would be considered by most individuals to be core or basic academic skills. The fact that these

academic skill areas have entire chapters devoted to them also indicates that there is enough research, theory, or perhaps controversy regarding them as to allow them to be studied and discussed extensively.

Beyond the issue of defining academic skills are the related issues of the rise and fall of skills across generations (which is constantly addressed by the popular media), and equally important, the procedures by which these skills are taught and acquired by students in special education. Cartwright, Cartwright, and Ward (1981) list several approaches used by special education teachers to impart academic skills; these include the diagnostic teaching model, remedial and compensatory education models, direct instruction, task analysis, perceptual-motor training, inquiry, modeling, media-based instruction, education games, and computer-assisted and computer-managed instruction. Two additional instructional approaches that were popularized in the 1970s include mastery learning and cooperative learning (Stallings & Stipek, 1986).

With regard to learner characteristics that affect the acquisition of academic skills, Wittrock (1986) suggests the following broad categories for consideration: students' perceptions and expectations, attention, motivation, learning and memory, comprehension and knowledge acquisition, learning strategies, and metacognitive processes. In summary, special educators must first define the academic skills that their students must acquire and then consider instructional, student, and other variables in planning for the optimal acquisition of academic skills.

**REFERENCES**

Cartwright, P. G., Cartwright, C. A., & Ward, M. E. (1981). *Educating special learners*. Belmont, CA: Wadsworth.

Stallings, J. A., & Stipek, D. (1986). Research on early childhood and elementary school teaching programs. In M. C. Wittrock (Ed.), *Handbook of research on teaching*. New York: Macmillan.

Wittrock, M. C. (1986). Students' thought processes. In M. C. Wittrock (Ed.), *Handbook of research on teaching*. New York: Macmillan.

RANDY W. KAMPHAUS
*Eastern Kentucky University*

METACOGNITION

# ACADEMIC THERAPY

*Academic Therapy* was the first journal designed for specialists (special education teachers, educational diagnosticians, psychologists, resource room specialists, practitioners in speech, language, communication, vision, and hearing) who are in direct contact with children manifesting learning, language, and communication difficulties. Since 1965, it has established a reputation for easy-to-read and practical articles that focus on "what works" in the special clinical, therapeutic, or classroom setting. Contributors are teachers, professors, and specialists. Articles are short and are selected on the basis of their usefulness and ability to be put into immediate use by the journal reader. Each issue includes listings of new materials, current news on the national level, and ideas for home management. *Academic Therapy* is published five times during the year: September, November, January, March, and May.

JOHN ARENA
*Academic Therapy Publications,
Novato, California*

## ACADEMIC THERAPY PUBLICATIONS (ATP)

Since 1965, Academic Therapy Publications (ATP) has served specialists, diagnosticians, private clinics and schools, teachers in mainstream and self-contained classes, and others who work in special settings. It has a wide variety of publications designed to address classroom aids, auditory learning, language, math, vocational/career, secondary/adult, professional texts, parent brochures, and reading programs. Academic Therapy Publication has a Computer Software Division for students and professionals and a Test Division which offers diagnostic instruments for assessing academic achievement. Every two years, ATP publishes the *Directory of Facilities and Services for the Learning Disabled* (Kratoville, 1985), a widely used referral source on the subject of learning disabilities.

### REFERENCES

Kratoville, B. L., (Ed.). (1985). *Directory of facilities and Services for the learning disabled* (11th ed.). Novato, CA: Academic Therapy Publications.

JOHN ARENA
*Academic Therapy Publications,
Novato, California*

## ACALCULIA

Acalculia is defined by Hallahan, Kauffman, and Lloyd (1985) as "complete inability to use mathematic symbols and perform mathematical computations" (p. 267). Hallahan et al. distinguish acalculia from dyscalculia by stating that the term dyscalculia is "reserved for less severe problems in these areas" (p. 267).

One of the earliest uses of the term acalculia comes from the work of Henschen (Cohn, 1961). According to Cohn's description, Henschen used the term acalculia to include disturbances in number recognition as well as problems with specific arithmetic operations. This was re-

ported by Henschen to be a manifestation of lesions in different regions of the brain, but primarily involved with the caudal portion of the left cerebral hemisphere (Cohn, 1961).

Strauss and Werner (1938) described acalculia as "deficiency in number operations" (p. 719) and provided evidence of the association between acalculia and finger agnosia (inability to recognize fingers on one's own hands), which was said to be caused by a lesion within an area around the angular gyrus. Strauss and Werner (1938) provided some evidence of a correlation between finger agnosia and acalculia.

According to Strauss and Lehtinen (1948), disturbance in visual perception was a major contributing factor to acalculia. They developed several principles for instruction based on organized perceptual experiences. Terms such as acalculia and dyscalculia have declined in popularity with the increasing attention given to more educationally relevant orientations. Generally, deficits in mathematical functioning have been remediated with the use of task-specific instructional strategies. Mercer (1979, chapter 8) provides an overview of some of these strategies.

### REFERENCES

Cohn, R. (1961). Dyscalculia. *Archives of Neurology, 4,* 301–307.

Hallahan, D. P., Kauffman, J. M., & Lloyd, J. W. (1985). *Introduction to learning disabilities* (2nd ed.). Englewood Cliffs, NJ: Prentice Hall.

Mercer, C. (1979). *Children and adolescents with learning disabilities.* Columbus, OH: Merrill.

Strauss, A. A., & Lehtinen, L. E. (1948). *Psychopathology and education of the brain-injured child.* New York: Grune & Stratton.

Strauss, A. A., & Werner, H. (1938). Deficiency in the finger schema in relation to arithmetic disability (finger agnosia and acalculia). *American Journal of Orthopsychiatry, 8,* 719–724.

THOMAS E. SCRUGGS
MARGO A. MASTROPIERI
*Purdue University*

**ARITHMETIC REMEDIATION
DYSCALCULIA**

## ACCELERATION OF GIFTED CHILDREN

Acceleration is any process whereby a child makes educational progress faster than usual, whether measured by advancement in school grade or by actual achievement (Ward, 1980). Presently, there are numerous avenues for acceleration in schools for those students who exhibit general intellectual ability and/or outstanding aptitude in one or more subject areas.

For students who exhibit general intellectual ability, three of the existing options are telescoping, grade skipping, and early admission to formal schooling. Telescoping involves the completion of three years of schooling in two years or four years of schooling in three years (Fox, 1979). Those who skip grades are promoted two grade levels in one year. These children are usually given credit for the skipped year and are able to complete formal schooling in fewer years than usual. Early entrance to formal schooling occurs when children are allowed to enter kindergarten or first grade at an age lower than is usually allowed by the school or school system. These children may merit early entrance because of advanced scores on IQ or abilities tests.

For pupils with outstanding aptitude in one or more subject areas, six options exist: concurrent enrollment, correspondence courses, special schools or classes, independent study, tutorials, and credit by exam. Other options may be created within each individual class, school, or school system.

Concurrent enrollment for secondary school students occurs when high schools and universities cooperate to allow students to be concurrently enrolled both in a high school and in a college. These pupils receive college credit for courses taken on the college campus; in some cases they receive college credit for courses taught by a university faculty member on the high school campus. Correspondence courses provide another option for acceleration when secondary school students enroll through the continuing education division of participating universities. They receive lessons by mail, and, on completion of all requirements, receive a grade after taking a final examination graded by the same university professor who planned the lessons.

Another acceleration practice takes place in special schools or classes where students are allowed to complete more than one year of credit in a subject area class by working in a compacted curriculum and successfully passing examinations. One of the most well known of these special school and class arrangements is Julian Stanley's Study of Mathematically Precocious Youth, conducted at Johns Hopkins University (Stanley, 1977). Students who have qualified for participation in this program by scoring at least 550 on the Scholastic Aptitude Test in mathematics have the opportunity to study higher level mathematics in college classes during the summer and/or complete college correspondence courses during the school year. Since the inception of the program at Johns Hopkins, it has expanded to include students with high verbal aptitude, and subjects other than mathematics are offered. Two other programs have replicated Stanley's work: the Midwest Talent Search at Illinois' Northwestern University and the Talent Identification Program at North Carolina's Duke University.

Talented students may also do independent study or be provided with a special tutor to complete course requirements in an advanced curriculum area. Finally, other credit-by-examination options are available to students who wish to advance beyond their peers through acceleration. These include advanced placement in secondary schools in states that provide their own examinations to receive credit for high school classes, advanced placement in college courses through the Advanced Placement Program, and the College Level Examination Program that allows students to receive credit in 15 fields by taking exams at university testing centers.

In the early 1900s the most frequent accommodation for gifted and talented children was to allow rapid acceleration through the standard curriculum (Whitmore, 1980). The popular belief that acceleration is socially detrimental to the child later curbed much of this acceleration. There are conflicting views on this subject. Kulik and Kulik (1984) concluded that the research they reviewed offered no real answers to this debate, with some studies showing small positive effects and some showing small negative effects in affective areas. However, following the work pioneered by Julian Stanley and his colleagues, acceleration has become more acceptable again.

Although there are no clear answers concerning the effects of acceleration on social and emotional growth, there are answers to questions about whether acceleration is beneficial academically. In a meta-analysis of 26 controlled studies, evidence showed that examination performance of accelerates surpassed by nearly one grade level the performance of nonaccelerates of equivalent age and intelligence. Furthermore, the examination scores of accelerates were equivalent to those of same-grade, but older, talented nonaccelerates (Kulik & Kulik, 1984).

## REFERENCES

Fox, L. H. (1979). Programs for the gifted and talented. In A. H. Passow (Ed.), *The gifted and talented: Their education and development*. Chicago: National Society for the Study of Education.

Kulik, J. A., & Kulik, C. C. (1984). Effects of accelerated instruction on students. *Review of Educational Research, 54,* 409–425.

Stanley, J. C. (1977). Rationale of the study of mathematically precocious youth (SMPY) during its first five years of promoting educational acceleration. In J. C. Stanley, W. C. George, & C. H. Solano (Eds.), *The gifted and creative: A fifty-year perspective*. Baltimore, MD: Johns Hopkins University Press.

Ward, V. S. (1980). *Differential education for the gifted*. Ventura, CA: Ventura County Superintendent of Schools Office.

Whitmore, J. R. (1980). *Giftedness, conflict, and underachievement*. Boston: Allyn & Bacon.

MARY K. TALLENT
*Texas Tech University*

ACADEMICALLY TALENTED CHILDREN
GIFTED AND TALENTED CHILDREN

## ACCESSIBILITY OF BUILDINGS

The accessible building is a structure that is readily usable by individuals possessing a wide range of physical disabilities or other limitations (such as sensory handicaps). Although estimates vary widely as to the number of citizens whose temporary or permanent impairments inhibit their mobility, the U.S. Department of Housing and Urban Development (1978) projects that at least 30 million people possess conditions that demand barrier-free facilities. A building or other site designed to accommodate ambulant or sensorily disabled persons is equally convenient and accessible to the nonhandicapped population. The design criteria used to meet the needs of handicapped populations are essentially no different from those of the general, nondisabled citizenry; they are only more pronounced.

The generally accepted minimum standards for ensuring the accessibility of buildings are incorporated in the American National Standards Institute (ANSI) specifications. Originally adopted in 1961 and subsequently revised and expanded during 1970s, the ANSI standards serve as a foundation for state laws and federal guidelines concerning building accessibility. A federal entity, the National Commission on Architectural Barriers (CAB), was created by an act of Congress to promote and evaluate voluntary and, in the case of federally owned or subsidized buildings, mandatory compliance with the ANSI standards.

The CAB's primary function has been to oversee the implementation of the Architectural Barriers Act of 1968 and related federal legislation designed to foster the accessibility of buildings and other environments.

The economic and human benefits of a site design that is barrier free are substantial. Data from the U.S. Office of Housing and Urban Development (1978) suggest that the initial costs of remodeling existing structures or designing and constructing new, fully accessible facilities are minimal when compared with the benefits derived by the disabled, their families, friends and colleagues, educational and other service agencies, and employers. The initial, one-time investment in a barrier-free design provides long-term benefits in terms of personal comfort, mobility, maximization of educational, social and employment options, and (particularly important for business) an expansion in the pool of active consumers.

Guided by the ANSI standards, architects and facility planners must ensure that the entrances to and the interiors of buildings allow for the uninhibited mobility, orientation, comfort, and performance of all facility users. As reviewed by Cotler and DeGraff (1976), the structural dimensions, interior design, entranceways and the layout of furniture in all buildings should be integrated to accommodate the physical limitations in mobility, reach and posture experienced by most wheelchair users and individuals aided by crutches, walkers and canes. It is of equal importance to the sensorily handicapped population (e.g., individuals who are blind or deaf) that building environments offer a simple, regular, well-lighted and marked design that enhances orientation and ready access to sources of visual, aural and tactile information.

### REFERENCES

Cotler, S. R., & DeGraff, A. H. (1976). *Architectural accessibility for the disabled on college campuses*. Albany, NY: State University Construction Fund.

U.S. Department of Housing and Urban Development (1978). *Access to the environment*. Washington, DC: U.S. Government Printing Office.

GEORGE JAMES HAGERTY
*Stonehill College*

ARCHITECTURAL BARRIERS
ARCHITECTURE AND THE HANDICAPPED

## ACCESSIBILITY OF PROGRAMS

Section 504 of the Rehabilitation Act of 1973, as amended, provides that

> no otherwise qualified handicapped individual . . . shall, solely by reason of his handicap, be excluded from participation in, be denied the benefits of, or be subjected to discrimination under any program or activity receiving federal financial assistance or under any program or activity conducted by any executive agency or the United States Postal Service.

The substantive provisions apply to two distinct sets of entities: recipients of federal financial assistance (federally assisted programs) and the operations of government agencies (federally conducted programs).

The concept of program accessibility is a key requirement of the implementing regulations for both federally assisted and federally conducted programs (U.S. Government, 1978; U.S. Government, 1985). In both cases, the requirement is not that every existing building or classroom be physically accessible, but rather that "the program or activity, when viewed in its entirety, is readily accessible to and usable by handicapped persons" (28 CFR 41.57(a)). All new buildings and facilities must be designed and constructed to be readily accessible to and usable by handicapped persons.

Since the late 1970s, federal court decisions and regulatory policy have interpreted and qualified the precise requirements of program accessibility. Of particular importance is the U.S. Supreme Court decision in *Southeastern Community College* v. *Davis* (1979), which held that the school was not required to modify a nurse training program as sought by a hearing-impaired individual because such modification would constitute "a fundamental alteration in the nature of the program." In discussing program modification, the Court also referenced attaining desirable goals "without imposing undue financial and administrative burdens" (pp. 410, 412).

In a prototype regulation distributed to all agencies as nonbinding guidance, and in its own regulation on federally conducted programs promulgated in 1984 (U.S. Government, 1985), the Department of Justice employs criteria from the *Davis* decision. The program accessibility requirement for existing programs explicitly does not "require the agency to taken any action that it can demonstrate would result in a fundamental alteration in the nature of the program or in undue financial and administrative burdens" (28 CFR 39.150(a)(2)).

Some commentators on the Department of Justice's proposed regulation objected to the inclusion of the *Davis* criteria. They argued that the language must be identical to the Department of Justice's government-wide coordinating regulation on federally assisted programs, which does not include such criteria (U.S. Government, 1985, p. 357). The Department of Justice's position is that "judicial interpretation of Section 504 [including circuit court decisions following *Davis*] compels it to incorporate the new language" and that the regulations for federally assisted programs must now be interpreted consistent with the federally conducted rule and *Davis* (U.S. Government, 1985, p. 357).

A good discussion of these issues is in the editorial note to 28 CFR 39 (U.S. Government, 1985). Litigation is pending.

**REFERENCES**

*Southeastern Community College v. Davis* (1979). United States Supreme Court, 442 U.S. 397.
U.S. Government. (1978). Code of Federal Regulations Title 28, Part 41. *Implementation of Executive Order 12250, Non-Discrimination on the Basis of Handicap in Federally Assisted Programs.*
U.S. Government (1985). Code of Federal Regulations Title 28, Part 39. *Enforcement of Non-Discrimination on the Basis of Handicap in Programs or Activities Conducted by the Department of Justice.*

JAMES R. RICCIUTI
*United States Office of
Management and Budget*

ACCESSIBILITY OF BUILDINGS
SPECIAL EDUCATION, LEGAL REGULATION OF

# ACCOMMODATION

Accommodation is one of two complementary processes proposed by Jean Piaget to account for an individual's adaptation to the environment; its counterpart is assimilation. Accommodation involves changing or transforming cognitive or sensorimotor schemes according to the demands of the environment; assimilation involves incorporating external elements into existing conceptual schemes.

The difference between accommodation and assimilation can be illustrated by an example of an infant's response to a rattle (Ginsburg & Opper, 1969). When a rattle suspended from an infant's crib begins to shake after the infant's arm movement causes it to move, the infant looks at and listens to the toy rattling, assimilating the event into his or her schemes of looking and listening. To repeat the movement of the rattle, the infant must make the necessary hand and arm movements, accommodating his or her actions according to the demands of the situation.

Assimilation and accommodation were viewed by Piaget as inseparable aspects of a single process of adaptation, separable only for purposes of discussion (Brainerd, 1978). Assimilation and accommodation occur simultaneously; a balance between the two is necessary for adaptation. A scheme must accommodate itself to the specific characteristics of the object or event it is attempting to assimilate; accommodation guides the eventual change in structures (Gelman & Baillargeon, 1983).

**REFERENCES**

Brainerd, C. J. (1978). *Piaget's theory of intelligence.* Englewood Cliffs, NJ: Prentice-Hall.
Gelman, R., & Baillargeon, R. (1983). A review of some Piagetian concepts. In P. H. Mussen (Ed.), *Handbook of child psychology: Vol. III. Cognitive development* (pp. 167–230). New York: Wiley.
Ginsburg, H., & Opper, S. (1969). *Piaget's theory of intellectual development: An introduction.* Englewood Cliffs, NJ: Prentice-Hall.

LINDA J. STEVENS
*University of Minnesota*

ASSIMILATION
COGNITIVE DEVELOPMENT
PIAGET, JEAN

# ACETYLCHOLINE

Acetylcholine (ACh) is a neurotransmitter, a chemical that is released from one neuron to pass a message to another neuron. Acetylcholine is naturally synthesized in living cells in cholinergic nerve terminals that are located primarily in the autonomic nervous system. It also is evident at parasympathetic postganglionic synapses, and at neuromuscular junctures (Cooper, Bloom, & Roth, 1982).

The autonomic nervous system is involved in what appears to be functionally reflexive responses directed toward energy conservation or preparation for possible trauma. Thus, with cholinergic stimulation, pupils contract, heart rate slows, and muscular contraction is facilitated (Katzung, 1982). Experimental work by Deutsch (1984) suggests the possibility of an indirect, environmental role for ACh in the development of memories. Results of animal studies indicate that drugs that block cholinergic action tend to increase low rates of response and decrease high rates of response among behaviors that were maintained through food reinforcers (Seiden & Dykstra, 1977). Such findings are consistent with the likelihood that ACh plays a role in creating a chemical environmental context for learning by mediating autonomic responsiveness. A role in pain perception also has been postulated (Cooper et al., 1982). Myasthenia gravis, a disease characterized by fluctuating muscle weakness, especially in muscles innervated by the motor nuclei of the brain stem (Adams & Victor, 1981), is a model of ACh dysfunction. Observed involvement of cholinergic systems in tardive dyskinesia, Huntington's chorea, and Alzheimer's dementia has led to experimental administration of drugs that facilitate ACh; however, no consistent results have been observed in such studies (Cooper et al., 1982).

**REFERENCES**

Adams, R. D., & Victor, M. (1981). *Principles of neurology.* New York: McGraw-Hill.

Cooper, J. R., Bloom, F. E., & Roth, R. H. (1982). *The biochemical basis of neuropharmocology.* New York: Oxford University Press.

Deutsch, J. A. (1984). Amnesia and a theory for dating memories. In G. Lynch, J. L. McGaugh, & N. M. Weinberger (Eds.), *Neurobiology of learning and memory* (pp. 105–110). New York: Guilford Press.

Katzung, B. G. (1982). *Basic and clinical pharmacology.* Los Altos, CA: Lange Medical Publications.

Seiden, L. S., & Dykstra, L. A. (1977). *Psychopharmocology: A biochemical and behavioral approach.* New York: Van Nostrand Reinhold.

ROBERT F. SAWICKI
*Lake Erie Institute of
Rehabilitation, Lake Erie,
Pennsylvania*

# ACHIEVEMENT NEED

Achievement need is also known as achievement motivation, the need for achievement and n:Ach. The concept was first defined by Murray (1938) as the need, "to overcome obstacles, to exercise power, to strive to do something difficult as well and as quickly as possible" (pp. 80–81). Murray, however, chose not to attempt to conduct applied research in achievement motivation and the concept did not receive much attention until McClelland (1951) developed a cognitive theory of motivation in which the need for achievement is one element. McClelland's theory states that a person's tendency to approach a task (effort) is a function of the strength of the achievement need, the strength of the need to avoid failure, the person's subjective belief about the probability of success or failure, and the value of the incentives associated with either success or failure. According to McClelland (1951) and Atkinson (1964), achievement need is intrinsic. It is not associated with extrinsic rewards that accrue as a result of achievement. Achievement need is generally measured through the Thematic Apperception Test (TAT), although Hermans (1970) developed a paper and pencil test for this purpose called n:Ach.

Many researchers have attempted to determine how achievement need develops. Crandall (1963) discovered that children with high achievement needs had mothers who rewarded achievement and achievement activities at an early age. These mothers also did not attend to their children's pleas for help when the children faced a difficult problem. Crandall further concluded that middle- and upper-class parents were more likely to engage in behaviors that develop achievement motivation than were parents of lower economic status.

A number of studies have been conducted to determine the effects of achievement on task performance and personality. Weiner (1970) found that high-need achievement persons persist in the face of failure while low-need achievement persons become more inhibited in their responses. He further found that low-need achievement persons will engage in achievement activity when success and reinforcement rates approach 100%, but high-need achievement persons work best when reinforcement is attained approximately 50% of the time. Weiner & Kukla (1970) related achievement need research to Rotter's (1966) research in locus of control. Using elementary school children, they concluded that high-need achievement children viewed their successes as resulting from their effort. Both high- and low-achievement need children attributed failure to themselves, but high-need achievement children attributed failure to lack of effort while low-achievement children attributed it to lack of ability.

**REFERENCES**

Atkinson, J. W. (1964). *An introduction to motivation.* Princeton, NJ: Van Nostrand.

Crandall, V. J. (1963). Achievement. In H. W. Stevenson (Ed.), *Child psychology* (pp. 416–459). Chicago: University of Chicago Press.

Hermans, H. J. M. A. (1970). A questionnaire measure of achievement motivation. *Journal of Applied Psychology, 54,* 353–363.

McClelland, D. C. (1951). *Personality.* New York: Dryden.

Murray, H. A. (1938). *Exploration in personality.* New York: Oxford University Press.

Rotter, J. B. (1966). Generalized expectancies for internal versus external control of reinforcement. *Psychology Monographs, 80.*

Weiner, B. (1970). New conceptions in the study of achievement motivation. In B. A. Maher (Ed.), *Progress in experimental personality research; Volume 5.* New York: Academic.

Weiner, B., & Kukla, A. (1970). An attributional analysis of achievement motivation. *Journal of Personality and Social Psychology, 15,* 1–20.

JAMES K. MCAFEE
*Pennsylvania State University*

## LEARNED HELPLESSNESS MOTIVATION

## ACHIEVEMENT TESTS

Achievement tests are the most frequent forms of standardized assessment in education and the 1980s is a popular decade for the publication of achievement tests. New editions for nearly all major tests have been published or are in process. Standardized tests are typically classified into group-administered measures or individually administered measures. The mid 1980s have witnessed new editions of group-administered tests by all of the major publishers: CTB/McGraw Hill; The Psychological Corporation; Riverside Publishing Company; and Science Research Associates (SRA). Riverside and SRA each publish one major series (e.g., Riverside's Iowa Test of Basic Skills). The Psychological Corporation and CTB/McGraw Hill have two major series (e.g., CTB's California Achievement Tests and the Comprehensive Test of Basic Skills).

The first major achievement series, the Stanford Achievement Test, was published in 1923 by World Books Company. This instrument is in its seventh edition. The Stanford Achievement Test series includes the seventh edition, the second edition of the Stanford Early School Achievement Test, and the second edition of Stanford Test of Academic Skills. The new Stanford series, like its predecessor, is an overall measure of achievement in the basic skills of reading, mathematics, and language arts, as well as science and social science. The SESAT/STANFORD/TASK series spans all grades from kindergarten through 13, and provides continuous assessment by means of a common scaled score system. Ten articulated levels are provided, with two equivalent forms at each level of Stanford and TASK.

Two levels of SESAT are designed for use from the beginning of kindergarten through grade 1. The Stanford Achievement Test comprises six battery levels that measure basic skills in the major school subjects at grades 1.5 to 9.9. Two levels of TASK, for grades 8 to 13, are designed to provide information about students' basic school-related skills. Stanford measures listening skills, a concept it pioneered in the 1973 edition, with measures of listening vocabulary, listening comprehension and total listening in grades K–9.

Stanford makes it easy to use test results effectively in the classroom by providing reading prescriptions in words, not numbers, for each student. This information was formerly available only from diagnostic tests.

Stanford yields a reading skills group placement for every pupil based on all reading subtests, and gives teachers a quick reference for grouping pupils needing similar skills instruction. A variety of reading passages provide insight into pupils' reading skills and content preferences. Separate performance ratings are provided for textual, functional, and recreational reading. Textual passages are typical of the kinds of material found in grade-appropriate textbooks. Functional reading selections include such items as coupons and directions for assembling things. Recreational reading passages represent the kinds of material one reads for enjoyment, such as fiction or poetry.

The Stanford Writing Assessment Program Guide, offered as an option for Primary 3 through TASK 2, provides teachers with insight into students' writing samples. The writing exercises included in this guide cover four forms of writing: describing, explaining, narrating, and reasoning.

Words on Stanford's spelling test were selected from textbook spelling lists, not from reading vocabulary lists. Distractors portray most typical spelling errors, enabling teachers to analyze pupils' errors in terms of phonics and structure. Stanford measures science and social science in grades 3 to 12. The environment test has also been expanded to cover K to 3.

The series provides a normed score for "using information" without requiring administration of a separate test. The score is based on questions measuring reference study, and inquiry skills objectives included in mathematics, science, social science, and language subtests.

Group-administered tests provide elaborate scoring and reporting systems. These reports are generated to meet diverse needs such as evaluating funded programs and audiences (e.g., teachers, principals, parents). Individually administered tests are more typically given to pupils who have been referred for evaluation. The 1980s have also witnessed an expansion in these offerings. There are many small publishers and a multitude of individual tests on the market. Examples of widely used instruments are the Wide Range Achievement Tests of Jostals Associates and DLM's Woodcock Johnson Psycho-Educational Battery: Tests of Achievement.

The major publisher in this area is American Guidance Services, with such offerings as the Peabody Individual

Achievement Test and the Woodcock Reading and the Key Math tests. A recent publication is the Kaufman Test of Educational Achievement with a brief form and a comprehensive form. The brief form meets screening and placement needs. This form provides a 30-minute measure of global achievement in reading, mathematics, and spelling, and yields norm-referenced subtest scores and a battery composite.

The Comprehensive form is ideal for determining the most likely areas in which a student needs remediation. Student errors are categorized on the error analysis form and provide a basis for formulating hypotheses of possible strengths and weaknesses, documented by standardization data as well as other evidence gathered by the examiner. An extensive section of the manual is devoted to interpreting these results.

The comprehensive form also provides norm-referenced scores. In addition to the reading composite, math composite, and battery composite scores, separate scores for reading decoding, reading comprehension, math computation, math applications, and spelling are given. Administration time averages 30 to 60 minutes for grades 1 to 3 and 60 to 75 minutes for grades 4 to 12.

### REFERENCES

Gardner, E. F., Rudman, H. C., & Karlsen, B. (1982). *Stanford Achievement Test* (7th ed.). San Antonio: Psychological Corporation.

Kaufman, A. S., & Kaufman, N. L. (1985). *Kaufman Test of Educational Achievement*. Circle Pines, Minnesota: American Guidance Service.

THOMAS F. HOPKINS
*Center for Behavioral
Psychotherapy, White Plains,
New York*

**ASSESSMENT
CRITERION-REFERENCED TESTS
NORM-REFERENCED TESTS**

## ACHONDROPLASIA

Achondroplasia, also called chondrodystrophy, refers to a defect in the formation of cartilage in the epiphyses of long bones, such that a type of dwarfism results. This most common form of dwarfism is usually inherited as an autosomal dominant trait, or it may result from spontaneous mutation (Avioli, 1979; Magalini, 1971). Clinical features of achondroplasia include absolute diminution of extremities; normal trunk and head size; a prominent, bulging forehead; and a flattened, saddle nose. Hands and feet typically are short, and fingers tend to be nearly equal in length (trident hands). Adult height generally does not exceed 1.4 meters.

The intelligence of affected persons is reported to be normal (Avioli, 1979; Lubs, 1977), although there is evidence of occasional neurologic complications during early adulthood (Magalini, 1971). The fertility of achondroplastic dwarfs is reported to be 30% of normal. Of offspring of two affected persons, two-thirds will exhibit the syndrome (Lubs, 1977). In educational settings, afflicted children may require adaptive equipment to accommodate their short stature. While there is no evidence to suggest that achondroplasia places individuals at increased risk for learning problems, a multifactored evaluation is appropriate for children who experience difficulty in school.

### REFERENCES

Avioli, L. V. (1979). Diseases of bone. In P. B. Beeson, W. McDermott, & J. B. Wyngaarden (Eds.), *Cecil textbook of medicine* (pp. 2225–2265). Philadelphia: Saunders.

Lubs, M. (1977). Genetic disorders. In M. J. Krajicek & A. I. Tearney (Eds.), *Detection of developmental problems in children* (pp. 55–77). Baltimore, MD: University Park Press.

Magalini, S. (1971). *Dictionary of medical syndromes*. Philadelphia: Lippincott.

CATHY F. TELZROW
*Cuyahoga Special Education
Service Center, Maple
Heights, Ohio*

**CONGENITAL DISORDERS
MINOR PHYSICAL ANOMALIES**

## ACQUIRED APHASIA

Acquired aphasia refers to a communication disorder resulting from a neurologic injury or disease that is not caused by a primary sensory deficit (e.g., deafness) or pervasive cognitive impairment (e.g., mental retardation). It is contrasted with congenital or developmental aphasia and described as the unique failure of the growth of language in an otherwise normally developing child (Nicolosi, Harryman, & Kresheck, 1978). Gaddes (1985) identifies acquired or traumatic aphasia as that resulting from neurologic impairment occurring between age two and puberty.

Acquired aphasia is a rare phenomenon in preschool and primary-aged children (Gaddes, 1985). The reason for this observation probably concerns the progression of language lateralization during the developmental period. Thus, children who incurred unilateral lesions at a young age (e.g., below age six) demonstrated fewer lateralized findings (e.g., aphasia subsequent to left hemisphere lesions) on neuropsychological evaluation than children who suffered trauma at a later age (Satz, 1985). Nevertheless, some residual language deficits are evident in youngsters with early left-hemisphere damage (Aram, Ekelman, Rose, & Whitaker, 1985), a finding consistent with the invariant hypothesis of cerebral specialization (Seron, 1981). Gaddes (1985) describes such children with early left lateralized lesions as "aphasoid," and suggests they comprise a subgroup of the learning-disabled population.

The clinical features of acquired aphasia include non-fluent spontaneous speech, accompanied by such disturbances as dysarthria (disorders of articulation), hesitations, and limited vocabulary (Hecaen, 1979). Complete absence of spoken language (mutism) may occur, particularly as an early symptom of acquired aphasia. Paraphasias, errors in the use or construction of single words (e.g., substituting the word "ford" for "fork"), are not commonly observed in acquired aphasia in children, although these are characteristic of fluent aphasia in adults (Hecaen, 1979). Some chidren with acquired aphasia demonstrate significant language comprehension disorders, while others do not. Hecaen (1979) reported more than one-third of his sample of children with acquired aphasia exhibited auditory comprehension disorders. Concomitant disturbances of reading and writing are commonplace, and the latter, in particular, tend to be pervasive and resistant to intervention (Gaddes, 1985: Hecaen, 1979).

The prognosis for children with acquired aphasia is mixed. Gaddes (1985) reports aphasic symptoms may resolve a year or two following the onset of traumatic aphasia, although disorders of reading and written language may persist. Hecaen (1979) suggests recovery from the most common motor (Broca's) aphasia may be complete and rapid, although the prognoses for other types of aphasia are less positive. Myklebust (1971) describes remediation approaches for children with aphasia. He suggests intervention must be intensive, necessitating a comprehensive special education program rather than intermittent sessions of speech therapy. Myklebust (1971) also cautions that childhood aphasics have an altered process of learning, and hence require a significantly modified approach to instruction. In planning educational programs for children with acquired aphasia, special educators should be cognizant of the pervasive nature of this neurologic disorder and the need for an integrated program tha can undergo modification as recovery occurs.

## REFERENCES

Aram, D. M., Ekelman, B. L., Rose, D. F., & Whitaker, H. A. (1985). Verbal and cognitive sequelae following unilateral lesions acquired in early childhood. *Journal of Clinical and Experimental Neuropsychology, 7*(1), 55–78.

Gaddes, W. H. (1985). *Learning disabilities and brain function: A neuropsychological approach* (2nd ed.). New York: Springer-Verlag.

Hecaen, H. (1979). Aphasias. In M. S. Gazzaniga (Ed.), *Handbook of Behavioral Neurobiology. Vol. 2 Neuropsychology* (pp. 239–292). New York: Plenum.

Myklebust, H. R. (1971). Childhood aphasia: Identification diagnosis, remediation. In L. E. Travis (Ed.), *Handbook of speech pathology and audiology* (pp. 1203–1217). New York: Appleton-Century-Crofts.

Nicolosi, L., Harryman, E., & Kresheck, J. (1978). *Terminology of communication disorders*. Baltimore, MD: Williams & Wilkins.

Satz, P. (1985, August). *Recovery from early brain damage: Some facts and reflections*. Invited address at the meeting of the American Psychological Association, Los Angeles.

Seron, X. (1981). Children's acquired aphasia: Is the initial equipotentiality theory still tenable? In Y. Lebrun & O. Zangwill (Eds.), *Lateralization of language in the child* (pp. 39–50). Lisse, Netherlands: Swets & Zeitlinger.

CATHY F. TELZROW
*Cuyahoga Special Education
Service Center, Maple
Heights, Ohio*

DEVELOPMENTAL APHASIA
LANGUAGE DELAYS
LANGUAGE DISORDERS

# ACTING OUT

Acting out has been defined by Harriman (1975) as the "direct expression of conflicted tensions in annoying or antisocial behavior in fantasies" (p. 30). A child who exhibits acting-out behavior is one who cannot easily accept structural limits and is difficult to manage in the classroom. Acting-out behaviors are similar to conduct disorders, but not necessarily as severe. One reason for the similarity is that acting-out behavior is one of the characteristics clustered under the broader grouping of conduct disorders. Acting-out behaviors usually are of high frequency and of significant duration, and do not include minor daily misbehavior.

Usually, when a behavior is identified as an acting-out behavior, it is operationally defined, observed, and recorded by the classroom teacher in specific and observable terms. Some of the behaviors that can be identified as acting-out behaviors include fighting, lying, temper tantrums, pouting, stealing, hyperactivity, threatening, and bullying (Quay, 1979).

## REFERENCES

Harriman, P. L. (1975). *Handbook of psychological terms*. Totowa, NJ: Littlefield, Adams.

Quay, H. C. (1979). Classification. In H. C. Quay & J. S. Werry (Eds.), *Psychopathological disorders of childhood* (2nd ed.). New York: Wiley.

MARIBETH MONTGOMERY KASIK
*Governors State University*

APPLIED BEHAVIOR ANALYSIS
CONDUCT DISORDER

# ACTUARIAL ASSESSMENT

Actuarial assessment bases diagnostic decisions on statistical relationships among current behaviors and future behaviors. As used in clinical assessment, the purpose is to classify clients into treatment-useful categories with as little error as possible. Any data that are quantifiable, available, and statistically related to diagnostic categories can be used. A widely used test designed for actuarial use with adults is the Minnesota Multiphasic Personality Inventory (MMPI [Hathaway & McKinley, 1967]). Current uses of actuarial assessment with children and adolescents primarily involves general diagnosis of learning and behavior problems (Hale & McDermott, 1984; Lachar & Gdowski, 1979; McDermott & Hale, 1982), but more narrow-band assessment applications have also been reported, for example, identification of potential dropouts (Lloyd, 1978), and potentially abusive parents (Stringer & LaGreca, 1985).

These approaches have attempted to "bootstrap" diagnostic systems from empirical relationships among child behaviors (Achenbach & Edelbrock, 1978) instead of basing diagnoses on traditional, nonempirical classification systems. Data having the highest utility are based on observable, verifiable behavior collected over a period of time, on multiple methods of assessment (McDermott, 1983), and on data that are deliberately sought after or routinely collected, rather than on data such as case notes or anecdotal records (Gdowski, Lachar, & Butkis, 1980).

Assessment packages developed for diagnoses of behavior problems include the Personality Inventory for Children (PIC [Lachar & Gdowski, 1979; Wirt, Lachar, Klinedinst, & Seat, 1984]) and the McDermott Multidimensional Actuarial Classification System (M-MAC [McDermott & Watkins, 1985]). The PIC was developed as a downward extension of the MMPI for 6 to 16 year olds, using parent reports rather client self-reports. Data regarding four "broad-band" symptom clusters are provided (I: Undisciplined/Poor Self-Control; II: Social Competence; III: Internalization/Somatic Symptoms; and IV: Cognitive Development), as well as 12 clinical (narrow-band) scales, validity scales (as with the MMPI), and a number of experimental scales. The full scale contains 600 items, but three short forms are available. The M-MAC incorporates computer-assisted diagnostic decision making. Decisions are based on cutoff scores set by the user, the standard error of the measures used, and statistical relationships among domains assessed. Diagnoses include normal, slow learner, conduct disorder, learning disability, anxiety-withdrawal, mental retardation, and communication disorder.

Child actuarial assessment packages are very new, and evaluative data is still scarce. There will undoubtedly be a great deal of literature over the next five years regarding their validity.

## REFERENCES

Achenbach, T. M., & Edelbrock, C. S. (1978). The classification of child psychopathology: A review and analysis of empirical efforts. *Psychological Bulletin, 85*, 1275–1301.

Gdowski, C. L., Lachar, D., & Butkis, M. (1980). A methodological consideration in the construction of actuarial interpretation systems. *Journal of Personality Assessment, 44*, 427–432.

Hale, R. L., & McDermott, P. A. (1984). Pattern-analysis of an actuarial strategy for computerized diagnosis of childhood exceptionality. *Journal of Learning Disabilities, 17*, 30–37.

Hathaway, S. R., & McKinley, J. C. (1967). *Minnesota Multiphasic Personality Inventory*. New York: Psychological Corporation.

Lachar, D., & Gdowski, C. L. (1979). *Actuarial assessment of child and adolescent personality: An interpretive guide for the Personality Inventory for Children profile*. Los Angeles: Western Psychological Services.

Lloyd, D. N. (1978). Prediction of school failure from third-grade data. *Educational and Psychological Measurement, 38*, 1193–1200.

McDermott, P. A. (1983). A syndromic typology for analyzing school children's disturbed social behavior. *School Psychology Review, 12*, 250–259.

McDermott, P. A., & Hale, R. L. (1982). Validity of a systems actuarial computer process for multidimensional classification of child psychopathology. *Journal of Clinical Psychology, 38*, 477–486.

McDermott, P. A., & Watkins, M. W. (1985). *McDermott Multidimensional Assessment of Children*. New York: Psychological Corporation.

Stringer, S. A., & LaGreca, A. M. (1985). Correlates of child abuse potential. *Journal of Abnormal Child Psychology, 13*, 217–226.

Wirt, R. D., Lachar, D., Klinedinst, J. K., & Seat, P. D. (1984). *Multidimensional description of child personality: A manual for the Personality Inventory for Children*. Los Angeles: Western Psychological Assessment.

ROBERT G. BRUBAKER
*Eastern Kentucky University*

ASSESSMENT
CLINICAL PSYCHOLOGY
DIAGNOSIS IN SPECIAL EDUCATION

# ADAPTED PHYSICAL EDUCATION

Adapted physical education is a

diversified program of developmental activities, games, sports, and rhythms suited to the interests, capacities, and limitations of students with disabilities who may not safely and successfully engage in unrestricted participation in vigorous activities of the general physical education program. (Hurley, 1981, p. 43)

The focus of adapted physical education is on the development of motor and physical fitness and fundamental motor patterns and skills in a sportslike environment (Sherrill, 1985).

Adapted physical education implies the modification of physical activities, rules, and regulations to meet existing limiting factors of specific handicapped populations. By definition, adapted physical education includes activities planned for persons with learning problems owed to mental, motor, or emotional impairment, disability, or dysfunction; planned for the purpose of rehabilitation, habilitation, or remediation; modified so the handicapped can participate; and designed for modifying movement capabilities.

Adapted physical education primarily occurs within a school setting, but it may also occur in clinics, hospitals, residential facilities, daycare centers, or other centers where the primary intent is to influence learning or movement potential through motor activity (AAHPER, 1952).

In the school setting, adapted physical education differs from regular physical education in the following manner. It has a federally mandated base through PL 94-142. It serves students who are primarily identified as having a handicapping condition but may serve students such as the obese, who are not identified as handicapped but are in need of physical activity modification within a restricted environment. Adapted physical education classes are usually separate and educationally distinct from regular physical education owing to the need to modify the curriculum to suit the individual interests and capabilities of the student.

The basic elements in curriculum planning are individuality, flexibility, and educational accountability. Because of the intra- and intervariability of individual differences within and across handicaps, activities must be designed and programmed to fit each child's motor capabilities. For instance, children within a particular handicapped group may be able to throw a ball, but each within the group, because of motor limitations, may throw the ball differently while still achieving the objective of distance and accuracy. Second, adapted physical education activities are designed to be flexible enough to achieve educational goals. For instance, for basketball, a smaller ball is provided and baskets are lowered so that students may be able to score more baskets in a game, thereby increasing their enjoyment in the sport (Auxter & Pyer, 1985).

Adapted physical education for students classified as handicapped implies accountability via the individualized educational plan (IEP). Objectives stated on an IEP ensure that the student is receiving instruction in activities where there is the greatest physical, motor, and social need. The student is evaluated periodically to assess progress toward the short- and long-term goals stated in the IEP.

## REFERENCES

AAHPER. (1952, April). *Guiding principles for a physical education journal of health, physical education, recreation.* Author.

Auxter, D., & Pyer, J. (1985). *Adapted physical education.* St. Louis: (1981, June). Mosby.

Hurley, D. (1981). *Guidelines for adapted physical education.* New York: *Journal of Health, Physical Education, Recreation, and Dance.* pp. 43–45.

Sherrill, C. (1985). *Adapted physical education and recreation* (3rd ed.). Dubuque, IA: Brown.

THOMAS R. BURKE
*Hunter College, City University of New York*

# ADAPTIVE BEHAVIOR

Adaptive behavior, or the daily activities required for personal and social sufficiency, is an integral part of the evaluation and planning for handicapped and nonhandicapped individuals. It is not a new concept and has its roots in historical views concerning the treatment of the mentally retarded. The increased emphasis now placed on the use of the adaptive behavior concept in special education and programs for the handicapped is resulting in attempts to better understand the characteristics of adaptive behavior and in the publication of many new instruments for measuring adaptive behavior (Meyers, Nihira, & Zetlin, 1979).

Present concepts of adaptive behavior are traced to early attempts to describe the mentally retarded (Harrison, 1985). As early as the Renaissance and Reformation, language and law defined mental retardation in terms of adaptive behavior, or a person's ability to take care of himself or herself and get along with others. Legal reforms for the mentally retarded during the 1800s resulted in continued attention to adaptive behavior. However, in the early 1900s, the development of the Binet intelligence scales and its counterparts led to a prevalent practice of defining mental retardation solely in terms of IQ; this practice continued for many years.

Edgar Doll, the major pioneer in adaptive behavior assessment, disagreed with the use of IQs only, and, in the 1930s, indicated that a person's social competence, or adaptive behavior, should be the first and most important criterion for mental retardation. It was not until 1959 that the American Association on Mental Deficiency published its official manual and formally included deficits in adaptive behavior, in addition to low intelligence, as an integral part of the definition of mental retardation (Heber, 1961). Subsequent editions of the manual have further emphasized the importance of adaptive behavior.

Several issues in the 1960s and 1970s precipitated an upsurge of interest in adaptive behavior and adaptive behavior assessment (Witt & Martens, 1984). A concern arose about "6-hour retarded children" or minority group and low socioeconomic status children who were labeled as retarded in the public schools but exhibited adequate adaptive behavior at home and in the community (Mercer, 1973). This concern eventually led to litigation such as the Guadalupe and Larry P. cases and court decisions that indicated that results of intelligence tests cannot be the primary basis for classifying children as mentally retarded and that adaptive behavior must be assessed. The 1960s and 1970s saw a trend toward the normalization of handicapped individuals and the awareness that effective programs for teaching adaptive skills allow handicapped individuals to participate as fully as possible in normal environments. A third issue was the need for a nonbiased and multifaceted assessment of all handicapped children to facilitate the fairness of decisions based on the results of tests and to investigate functioning in all areas related to a particular handicap.

The passage of the Education of All Handicapped Children Act of 1975 (Public Law 94-142) represented the culmination of the issues of the 1960s and 1970s. Public Law 94-142 has stringent guides for the assessment of handicapped children and stipulates that deficits in adaptive behavior must be substantiated before a child is classified as mentally retarded. Further, it recognizes the importance of adaptive behavior assessment for children other than the mentally retarded. Since the passage of the law, most states have developed guidelines for adaptive behavior assessment (Patrick & Reschley, 1982) and many have strict criteria for the types of adaptive behavior instruments and scores to be used.

Sparrow, Balla, and Cicchetti (1984) discuss several characteristics that are inherent in present concepts of adaptive behavior. Adaptive behavior is an age-related construct; as normally developing children grow older, adaptive behavior increases and becomes more complex. Adaptive behavior is determined by the standards of other people, those who live, work, play, teach, and interact with an individual. Finally, adaptive behavior is defined as what an individual does day by day, not by an individual's ability or what he or she can do. If a person has the ability to perform a daily task, but does not do it, adaptive behavior is considered to be inadequate.

An important issue in the description of adaptive behavior is the distinction between adaptive behavior and intelligence (Meyers, Nihira, & Zetlin, 1979). Adaptive behavior and intelligence have several important differences. First, adaptive behavior focuses on everyday behavior and intelligence on thought processes. Adaptive behavior is based on concrete environmental demands while intelligence focuses on academic demands. Adaptive behavior assessment involves common, typical, and everyday behaviors, whereas intelligence scales attempt to measure a person's potential, or his or her best possible performance.

Since the passage of Public Law 94-142, a large number of adaptive behavior scales have been published or developed for local use. Most adaptive behavior scales are administered to a respondent such as a parent or teacher who is familiar with the daily activities of the person. Some are administered directly to the person whose adaptive behavior is being assessed. The Vineland Adaptive Behavior Scales (Sparrow, et al., 1984) measure adaptive behavior in the areas of communication, daily living skills, socialization, motor skills, and maladaptive behavior. The Adaptive Behavior Inventory for Children (Mercer & Lewis, 1977) assesses a child's adaptation to family, community, and peer social systems. The AAMD Adaptive Behavior Scale (Lambert & Windmiller, 1981) evaluates personal sufficiency, social sufficiency, responsibility, and personal and social adjustment. The Scales of Independent Behavior (Bruininks, Woodcock, Weatherman, & Hill, 1984) include measures of motor skills, social interaction and communication, personal and community independence, and problem behaviors. The Children's Adaptive Behavior Scale (Richmond & Kicklighter, 1980) contains scales for language, independent functioning, family roles, economic vocational activity, and socialization.

## REFERENCES

Bruininks, R. J., Woodcock, R. W., Weatherman, R. F., & Hill, B. K. (1984). *Scales of independent behavior*. Allen, TX: DLM Teaching Resources.

Harrison, P. L. (1985). *Vineland Adaptive Behavior Scales, Classroom Edition Manual*. Circle Pines, MN: American Guidance Service.

Heber, R. F. (1961). A manual on terminology and classification in mental retardation (Monograph Suppl.). *American Journal of Mental Deficiency*.

Lambert, N., & Windmiller, M. (1981). *AAMD Adaptive Behavior Scale—School Edition*. Monterey, CA: Publishers Test Service.

Mercer, J. R. (1973). *Labeling the mentally retarded*. Berkeley, CA: University of California Press.

Mercer, J. R., & Lewis, J. E. (1977). *Adaptive Behavior Inventory for Children*. New York: Psychological Corporation.

Meyers, C. E., Nihira, K., & Zetlin, A. (1979). The measurement of adaptive behavior. In N. R. Ellis (Eds.), *Handbook of mental deficiency: Psychological theory and research* (2nd ed.) (pp. 215–253). Hillside, NJ: Erlbaum.

Patrick, J. L., & Reschley, D. J. (1982). Relationship of state educational criteria and demographic variables to school system prevalence of mental retardation. *American Journal of Mental Deficiency, 86*, 351–360.

Richmond, B. O., & Kicklighter, R. H. (1980). *Children's Adaptive Behavior Scale*. Atlanta: Humanics Limited.

Sparrow, S. S., Balla, D. A., & Cicchetti, D. V. (1984). *Vineland Adaptive Behavior Scales*. Circle Pines, MN: American Guidance Service.

Witt, J. C., & Martens, B. K. (1984). Adaptive behavior: Test and assessment issues. *School Psychology Review, 13*, 478–484.

PATTI L. HARRISON
*University of Alabama*

ADAPTIVE BEHAVIOR INVENTORY FOR CHILDREN
MENTAL RETARDATION

ADAPTIVE BEHAVIOR
BEHAVIORAL OBSERVATION
SYSTEM OF MULTICULTURAL PLURALISTIC
     ASSESSMENT
VINELAND SOCIAL MATURITY SCALE

## ADAPTIVE BEHAVIOR INVENTORY FOR CHILDREN (ABIC)

The Adaptive Behavior Inventory for Children (ABIC), a component of the System of Multicultural Pluralistic Assessment (Mercer & Lewis, 1977), is a 242-item rating scale for children ages 5 to 11 years. It provides an indication of a child's adaptation to social systems involving the family, peer group, and community. The ABIC items are administered to a child's parents or guardians; the questions are read to a parent and he or she indicates whether the child's role in the activity described by the item is latent, emergent, or mastered. The administration requires about 1 hour. The ABIC contains six scales: Family, Community, Peer Relations, Nonacademic School Roles, Earner Consumer, and Self-Maintenance. A measure of veracity (or a lie scale) is also included.

Scaled scores (with a mean of 50 and a standard deviation of 15) are available for each of the six scales; the ABIC Average Scaled Score, a measure of overall adaptive behavior, is the mean of the six scaled scores. The ABIC was standardized with a sample of 2085 California schoolchildren (696 black, 700 Spanish surname, and 689 white). The SOMPA *Technical Manual* reports average split-half reliability coefficients ranging from 0.82 to 0.89 for the six scales and a reliability coefficient of 0.97 for the ABIC Average Scaled Score. No validity data are reported in the manual, but the ABIC has been used in numerous studies that investigated, for example, the relationship between the ABIC and intelligence and achievement (e.g., Harrison, 1981; Oakland, 1983) and the representativeness of the ABIC norms (Oakland, 1979).

### REFERENCES

Harrison, P. L. (1981). Mercer's adaptive behavior inventory, the McCarthy scales, and dental development as predictors of first grade achievement. *Journal of Educational Psychology, 73*, 78–82.

Mercer, J. R., & Lewis, J. E. (1977). *System of Multicultural Pluralistic Assessment*. New York: Psychological Corporation.

Oakland, T. (1979). Research on the adaptive behavior inventory for children and the estimated learning potential. *School Psychology Digest, 8*, 63–78.

Oakland, T. (1983). Joint use of adaptive behavior and IQ to predict achievement. *Journal of Consulting and Clinical Psychology, 51*, 298–301.

PATTI L. HARRISON
*University of Alabama*

## ADAPTIVE BEHAVIOR SCALE

See VINELAND ADAPTIVE BEHAVIOR SCALES.

## ADAPTIVE DEVICES

Adaptive, assistive, augmentative, prosthetic, and orthotic devices are all aids to help those with a variety of disabilities to overcome problems of everyday living. Examples range from leg braces to highly sophisticated microcomputers adapted for the disabled. Included are hearing aids, Braille books, glasses, wheelchairs, specialized eating utensils, braces, positioning devices, page turners, tape recorders, typewriters, and the artificial larynx.

Two sources of information for this wide range of adaptive devices are *The Directory of Living Aids for the Disabled Person*, published by the Veterans Administration (U.S. Government Printing Office, 1982), which provides an extensive list of aids for daily living, and *The Information System for Adaptive, Assistive and Rehabilitative Equipment (ISAARE)* (Melichar, 1977, 1978), an information storage and retrieval system that lists devices by categories such as "travel" and "communication."

The type of adaptive devices currently experiencing the greatest technological advances as well as the greatest emphasis in rehabilitation is augmentative communication systems. Three general modes of nonvocal or augmentative communication have been developed for those for whom intelligible speech is not an option. They are manual communication, communication boards, and electronic systems. Manual communication includes gestures, signs, and finger spelling; it is used extensively with nonhearing-impaired as well as hearing-impaired populations, but it does not include an adaptive device. Communication boards are boards, or booklets, that come in a wide range of sizes, shapes, and materials, and make use of a variety of symbol systems. These symbols include objects, drawings and photographs, rebus symbols, Blissymbols, letters, and words. Sources of information on the design and use of communication boards include the *Language Board Instruction Kit* (Oaklander, 1980); Carlson, 1981; Musselwhite & St. Louis, 1982; Silverman, 1980; and *Non Oral Communication* (Plavan Schools, 1980).

The tremendous growth of computer technology is providing the impetus for the development of communication systems for the physically disabled that can be individually tailored to their abilities. Input devices for those who do not have sufficient motor control for direct selection (pointing or using a keyboard) include paddle switches, joy sticks, moisture switches, optical switches, eyebrow or tongue-controlled switches, sip and puff switches, and voice-controlled switches, among others. These augmentative systems are also tailored to the user's output needs and may include a combination of hard copy printout, synthesized speech output, display screens, and so on. The selection of an appropriate system to include the most effective and efficient symbol system, input technique, and output capabilities is a complex process requiring the services of a team of experts. The American Speech-Language-Hearing Association (ASHA) Ad Hoc Committee on Communication Processes and Non-Speaking Persons (1980) identifies possible team members as well as essential components of the assessment process. Depending on the individual's needs, most of the following people should be involved in the assessment and training process: speech-language pathologist, occupational therapist, physical therapist, parents, teacher, system user, psychologist, rehabilitation engineer, and social worker.

Ongoing research on the design and use of augmentative communication systems makes any list or discussion of specific systems quickly obsolete. The sources in the References list will provide further background reading. The most current information can be obtained through the following: *Communication Outlook*, a monthly publication from the Artificial Language Laboratory, Computer Science Department, Michigan State University, East Lansing, MI 48824; National Rehabilitation Information Center (NARIC), The Catholic University of America, 4407 8th Street NE, Washington, DC 20064; *The Resource Guide, Rehabilitation Engineering and Product Information* (Publication No. E-80-2205, September 1980), U.S. Dept. of Education, Office of Special Education and Rehabilitation Services, Office for Handicapped Individuals, Washington, DC 20202; *Augmentative & Alternative Communication*, the official journal of the International Society for Augmentative and Alternative Communication, Baltimore: Williams & Wilkins; and the Trace Research and Development Center University of Wisconsin, Madison, WI.

## REFERENCES

American Speech-Language-Hearing Association (1980). Nonspeech communication: a position paper. *ASHA*, 22, 267–272.

Carlson, F. (1981). *Alternate methods of communication*. Danville, IL: Interstate.

*Directory of living aids for the disabled person* (1982). U.S. Government Printing Office.

Fraser, B. A., & Hensinger, R. N. (1983). *Managing physical handicaps: A practical guide for parents, care providers, and educators*. Baltimore, MD: Brookes.

Haring, N. G. (Ed.) (1982). *Exceptional children and youth*. Columbus, OH: Merrill.

Melichar, J. F. (1977). *ISAARE*, San Mateo, CA: Adaptive Systems.

Melichar, J. F. (1978). *Challenges in mental retardation: Progressive ideology and sources*. New York: Human Services Press.

Musselwhite, C. R., & St. Louis, K. W. (1982). *Communication programming for the severely handicapped: Vocal and nonvocal strategies*. San Diego: College Hill Press.

*Non Oral Communication: A Training Guide for the Child Without Speech* (1980). Plavan School, 9675 Warner Ave., Fountain Valley, CA 92708.

Oakander, S. (1980). *Language Board Instruction Kit*. Non-Oral Communication Center, 9675 Warner Ave., Fountain Valley, CA 92708.

Silverman, F. H. (1980). *Communication for the speechless*. Englewood Cliffs, NJ: Prentice-Hall.

MARGO E. WILSON
*Lexington, Kentucky*

**AUGMENTATIVE COMMUNICATION SYSTEMS**
**BLISSYMBOLS**
**COMMUNICATION BOARDS**

# ADAPTIVE PE

See ADAPTED PHYSICAL EDUCATION.

# ADDITIVE-FREE DIETS

During the past decade, one very important and particularly controversial theory of the management of learning and behavioral disorders in children has been the theory of the additive-free diet proposed by Feingold (1975). Specifically, Feingold has maintained that children with hyperactivity and other behavioral disorders have a natural toxic reaction to artificial food colors, flavorings, preservatives, and other substances that are added to food to enhance their shelf-life. The additive-free diet regimen proposed by Feingold purports to eliminate artificial flavors and salicylates (compounds naturally occurring in certain fruits and vegetables) from a child's diet as a treatment for hyperactivity and learning disabilities. It is also noteworthy that Feingold has advocated his additive-free diet for a number of other conditions, including mental retardation, early infantile autism, and delinquency (Barkley, 1981).

Despite the widespread appeal of the additive-free diet

among the lay community and the Feingold Association, this treatment has been widely assailed in scholarly literature. On the basis of empirically unsubstantiated claims concerning the efficacy of this diet, Feingold has insisted that nearly 50% of hyperactive children in his clinical private practice sample displayed a complete remission of symptoms as a result of the additive-free dietary regimen. Such improved symptoms, according to the Feingold group, include markedly enhanced cognitive and academic functioning. Further, Feingold has insisted that the younger the child, the more expedient and complete the improvement that occurs. Nonetheless, several investigators (Harley & Matthews, 1980) have attributed this dramatic success to a placebo effect, or even the changed aspects of family dynamics that often result from the additive-free diet. Also contributing to widespread acceptance of the Feingold diet is our culture's current obsession with diet consciousness and health food fads.

The publicity and heated debate resulting from Feingold's claims have resulted in a proliferation of empirical studies among investigators in the scientific community that have assessed the efficacy of additive-free diets in hyperactive children (Conners, 1980; Conners, Goyette, Southwick, Lees, & Andrulonis, 1976). In a cogent summary of a series of studies conducted by these researchers, Conners (1980) has concluded that only a small number of children (less than 5%) respond specifically to the additive-free diet. More important, many investigators now recognize that those foods that Feingold has recommended be eliminated from children's diets are often high in important nutrients necessary for normal growth and development. Thus, placing children on the additive-free diet may even compromise their nutritional needs. Nonetheless, despite the "gross overstatements by Dr. Feingold" (Conners, 1980, p. 109) and the proliferation of weak studies in this area, one must be cognizant of the fact that for a small subgroup of hyperactive children (Ross & Ross, 1982) diet management may be a useful form of intervention. It remains unclear whether it is the additive-free diet itself that is responsible for the observed improvements or the behavioral regimen associated with this special diet. As a result, Conners (1980) has recommended that limited empirical investigations still be continued in this controversial area. Practitioners and researchers concerned with this topic will want to examine Conners' (1980) important work in this field.

## REFERENCES

Barkley, R. A. (1981). *Hyperactive children: A handbook for diagnosis and treatment.* New York: Guilford.

Conners, C. K. (1980). *Food additives and hyperactive children.* New York: Plenum.

Conners, C. K., Goyette, C. H., Southwick, D. A., Lees, J. M., & Andrulonis, P. (1976). Food additives and hyperkinesis. *Pediatrics, 58,* 154–166.

Feingold, B. F. (1975). *Why your child is hyperactive.* New York: Random House.

Harley, J. P., & Matthews, C. G. (1980). Food additives and hyperactivity in children. In R. M. Knights & D. J. Bakker (Eds.), *Treatment of hyperactive and learning disordered children.* Baltimore, MD: University Park Press.

Ross, D. M., & Ross, S. A. (1982). Hyperactivity: Current issues, research and theory (2nd ed.). New York: Wiley-Interscience.

RONALD T. BROWN
*Emory University School
of Medicine*

**HYPERACTIVITY
FEINGOLD DIET**

# ADJUSTMENT OF THE HANDICAPPED

By virtue of their "differentness," handicapped individuals and their families must make certain special adjustments to lead fulfilling and satisfying lives. The most obvious and important of these adjustments is the appraisal and acceptance of the handicapping condition itself. Such acceptance is prerequisite to seeking and obtaining appropriate care and services.

Another necessary adjustment requires recognizing and dealing with influences of a handicapping condition on all aspects of the individual's development. For example, a physical handicap affects social development and interactions in ways that have only recently been addressed scientifically and professionally, but have long been sources of confusion and frustration to the handicapped.

It has become fashionable among educators and developmental psychologists to refer to the "whole child" in nurturing and/or describing the development of "normal," i.e., nonhandicapped, children. Some (e.g., Shontz, 1980) have advocated this integrated approach in understanding the development of handicapped children and adolescents. However, two factors make it especially difficult to grasp specific implications of particular handicapping conditions for domains not directly affected by the conditions. One difficulty is that the interrelationships among the various developmental domains are subtle and complex; another is that the exceptional child's development is affected by special social and internal forces. Therefore, our ability to recommend theoretically based prescriptions for professional and parenting practices that will promote maximal development in indirectly affected domains is limited by the lack of empirical evidence comparing particular approaches to raising, treating, and educating the "whole" handicapped child.

The development of the child with a handicap occurs along the same lines as that of the nonhandicapped child.

However, an individual handicapped child's development will exhibit qualitative variations from the norm. The specific deviations from typical development depend both on the nature and severity of the handicapping condition and on the level of adjustment achieved by the child and his or her family and teachers. Of particular significance in the adjustment of the handicapped child are personality and social development. Also of concern are possible physical and/or medical adjustments that may be required, and special educational adjustments.

Normal personal-social development includes the emergence of the individual's self-concept and self-esteem. These beliefs about one's characteristics, relative worth, and competence are acquired by internalizing an image of one's self as it is reflected by important adults and peers. Bartel and Guskin (1980) emphasize that the feedback one receives from the social environment is a crucial factor in the development of a positive self-concept and high self-esteem, for it creates an expectation and interpretive schema for self-evaluation of one's abilities and efforts. The self-concept of a handicapped child is at risk because society's negative evaluations of individuals who are different from the norm are systematically, if unconsciously, transmitted to him or her (Gliedman & Roth, 1980). Because the development of high self-esteem is based on what an individual *can* do, a handicapping condition may endanger a child's self-esteem by focusing attention on what the child cannot do.

The social side of personal-social development includes the acquisition of skills for interacting socially. Two forces interact to interfere with normal social experiences and therefore place the handicapped child at a disadvantage for acquiring appropriate social skills. On the one hand is a cultural tendency, described by Bartel and Guskin (1980), to stigmatize a handicapped individual; this often results in deliberate as well as unconscious social rejection of the child. Therefore, he or she may experience decreased opportunities to participate in the sorts of activities through which social skills are acquired and refined. On the other hand, some researchers (Field, 1980; Novak, Olley, & Kearney, 1980) have demonstrated that handicapped children are less likely to initiate social interaction with peers, preferring instead object-oriented activities. Such reserve is self-defeating, for the child denies himself or herself opportunities that are available. In sum, the rejection of others and the child's own reluctance to join in the usual social activities interfere with normal personal-social development by reducing opportunities for social participation.

A handicapping condition may limit a child's or adolescent's physical activities. The handicap may impose restrictions owing to physical limitations or medical complications that limit freedom to get about in the environment. Physical and/or medical limitations may reduce opportunities for interaction and exploration in both the physical and social realms and thus curtail experiences that stimulate and promote cognitive growth and personal-social development. Handicapped children must be encouraged not to retreat from any activities that are accessible, although inconvenient, because of physical restrictions. Professionals and others can help them to participate in an adapted way, if necessary, in order not to deprive them of beneficial experiences.

Handicapped children may have to adjust medical interventions or therapies such as drugs, braces, physical therapy, surgical procedures, hearing appliances, etc. The child's adjustment to the medical aspect of his or her program is absolutely essential because the child must cooperate in order to achieve the maximum benefits of the prescribed treatment(s).

A handicapped child is very likely to have to make an adjustment involving his or her educational programs. The adjustment may range from simply modifying his or her study habits or methods to full-time participation in a special self-contained program. Professionals who work with the child should strive to minimize whatever educational disadvantage(s) may be imposed by the handicap. The goals of the child's educational program should emphasize activities to compensate for and/or overcome his or her handicap.

The effectiveness of the child's program will be amplified by the active involvement of parents in consistently following through on behavioral and educational interventions in the home environment. Concrete benefits are derived from the parents' participation. Parents are able to provide additional reinforcement and practice for skills learned during the school day, helping their child consolidate gains more rapidly. In addition, their involvement is a signal to the child of their commitment to his or her development and the high value they place on educational achievement. These attitudes are highly motivating and will help see the child through difficult periods.

Parents who do not accept and adjust to the child's handicap escalate their child's difficulties. Maladaptive behavior patterns that emerge in the relationship between parents and their handicapped child can arise from either of two opposite, but equally harmful, reactions. Parents may either overestimate or underestimate their child's abilities and potential. Overestimates may be due to parents' denial of their child's problems. Such parents are prone to establish unreasonably high standards for their child's behavior or development. Because the child wants to please the parents but is not capable of fulfilling their expectations, he or she continually faces feelings of frustration, inadequacy, and other negative emotions such as guilt, disappointment, and uncertainty as to his or her place in the affections of the parents. On the other hand, some parents seem to overcompensate for their handicapped child. Some typical behaviors of these parents include setting goals that are too easily attained, praising or rewarding the child for work that is below his or her level of functioning, and intervening unnecessarily when the child is working on difficult tasks. Such behaviors convey the message, albeit indirectly, that the parents do not recognize or appreciate the child's actual abilities. These signals undermine the development of high self-esteem and a positive self-concept.

Adjusting to the child's handicap is difficult, but Kogan (1980) has shown that parents can learn and use techniques for interacting with their child in ways that promote an adaptive relationship. General guidelines for parents in nurturing optimum development include realistically accepting the child, including abilities and disabilities. Parents should be sympathetic, but must encourage independence in order to enhance the child's self-esteem and promote his or her success in the "real" world.

Parents also have a crucial role in setting the stage for good sibling relationships. They must not show favoritism toward any of their children. Although they may enjoy different activities with their individual children, they should not give their attention preferentially to any single child. In particular, parents must avoid making comparisons among their children, and instead emphasize each child's individual strengths. All children will benefit when parents provide experiences and delegate responsibilities in accordance with each child's developmental level and needs.

Over and above the special methods and materials teachers use in working with the handicapped child, perhaps the most important element of the handicapped child's educational experience is a positive social climate. Teachers can provide a model for accepting individual differences in general and specifically valuing each child's, including the handicapped child's, abilities and contributions. The child's classmates will imitate the teacher and assimilate the underlying nondiscriminatory attitudes. Being accepted by one's teachers and classmates nourishes the handicapped child's self-concept and self-esteem, thereby promoting not only social development, but also cognitive growth and educational achievement. Thus, the handicapped child will be more willing to take the necessary risks associated with attempting challenging tasks, and through accepting such challenges will be stretched to reach his or her full potential.

**REFERENCES**

Bartel, N. R., & Guskin, S. L. (1980). A handicap as a social phenomenon. In W. M. Cruickshank (Ed.), *Psychology of exceptional children and youth* (pp. 45–73). Englewood Cliffs, NJ: Prentice-Hall.

Field, T. (1980). Self, teacher, toy, and peer-directed behaviors of handicapped preschool children. In T. Field, S. Goldberg, D. Stern, & A. M. Sostek (Eds.), *High risk infants and children: Adult and peer interactions* (pp. 313–326). New York: Academic.

Gliedman, J., & Roth, W. (1980). *The unexpected minority: Handicapped children in America.* New York: Harcourt Brace Jovanovich.

Kogan, K. L. (1980). Interaction systems between preschool handicapped or developmentally delayed children and their parents. In T. Field, S. Goldberg, D. Stern, & A. M. Sostek (Eds.), *High risk infants and children: Adult and peer interactions* (pp. 227–247). New York: Academic.

Novak, M. A., Olley, G., & Kearney, D. S. (1980). Social skills of children with special needs in integrated separate preschools. In T. Field, S. Goldberg, D. Stern, & A. M. Sostek (Eds.), *High risk infants and children: Adult and peer interactions* (pp. 327–346). New York: Academic.

Shontz, F. C. (1980). Theories about adjustment to having a disability. In W. M. Cruickshank (Ed.), *Psychology of exceptional children and youth* (pp. 3–44). Englewood Cliffs, NJ: Prentice-Hall.

PAULINE F. APPLEFIELD
*University of North Carolina,
Wilmington*

**FAMILY RESPONSE TO A HANDICAPPED CHILD
HANDICAPISM
TEACHER EXPECTANCIES**

# ADLER, ALFRED (1870–1937)

Alfred Adler, an Austrian psychiatrist, severed an early connection with Freudian psychoanalysis to develop his more socially oriented Individual Psychology, which was a powerful influence in the development of the field of social psychology. Adler's work in education and child guidance is less well known, but it contributed greatly to the development of school services in Austria and it had worldwide significance for the education and treatment of children.

At the Pedagogical Institute of the City of Vienna, he helped to train thousands of teachers and established the first child guidance clinics in the Vienna school system. In 1935, with the coming of a fascist regime in Austria, Adler left Vienna for the United States, where he established a private practice and served as professor of medical psychology at the Long Island College of Medicine.

**REFERENCES**

Ansbacher, H. L. & R. R. (1956). *The individual psychology of Alfred Adler.* New York: Basic Books.

Watson, R. I. (1963). *The great psychologists.* New York: Lippincott.

PAUL IRVINE
*Katonah, New York*

# ADMINISTRATION OF SPECIAL EDUCATION

Prior to the advent of public school programs for the handicapped in the late nineteenth and early twentieth centuries, administration of special education programs was usually executed by persons who were not administrators. Because many of the early programs were provided by religious organizations (Hewett & Forness, 1977), the earliest administrators were probably monks, nuns, or other religious figures (e.g., Pedro Ponce deLeon, a Spanish monk who worked with the deaf in the sixteenth century). During the late eighteenth and early nineteenth centuries, philosophical changes and a new attention to science changed attitudes toward the handicapped and their treatment. These changes, evidenced in the French and American revolutions, created a reverence for the individual and a belief that the lives of handicapped persons could be significantly improved through the application of science. Thus a new wave of administrators arose. These administrators were not interested primarily in running a program, but in teaching, scientific inquiry, and having an impact on contemporary thought through their writings. Thus a time was born in which most programs were managed by scientists, physicians, and philosophers such as Edouard Sequin, Valentin Hauy, and Samuel Gridley Howe. During the nineteenth century a great number of public and private residential schools/institutions were developed. For the most part, these institutions (which remained the dominant force in special education until the middle of the twentieth century) were administered by physicians. This was especially true for institutions for the mentally retarded, the emotionally disturbed, and the physically handicapped.

Public school services for exceptional children began in the latter part of the nineteenth century (Gearheart & Wright, 1979). By the middle of the twentieth century, public school classes became the primary mode of education for exceptional children. With this change, the administration of special education programs fell to educators and school psychologists. Although special education programs were held in public school buildings, they were usually separate, and writers of the time advocated separate administration and supervision systems (Ayer & Barr, 1928).

The rise of special education administration as a discipline occurred simultaneously with the rise of segregated public school programs. Special education administrators during the first quarter of the twentieth century were not trained generally as administrators; it was not until 1938 that any professional identity was established. In that year, the National Association of State Directors of Special Education was founded (Burrello & Sage, 1979). In 1951 the Council of Administrators of Special Education (CASE) convened as a special interest group within the Council for Exceptional Children (Burello & Sage, 1979).

During the 1950s, 1960s, and 1970s, special education administration grew as a result of the increase in public special-education programs brought about by the increased federal role in programs for the handicapped. In the 1950s, the U.S. Office of Education conducted several large-scale studies of special education and special-education administration (Mackie & Engel, 1956; Mackie & Snyder, 1957). These studies helped to establish the roles of administrators of programs for exceptional children and the need for professional training. Many more studies were conducted during the 1960s and 1970s (e.g., Kohl & Marro, 1971; Sage, 1968; Wisland & Vaughan, 1964). It was, however, the passage of PL 94-142, The Education of All Handicapped Children Act of 1975, that brought special education administration to its current state. This legislation, and others that followed, together with numerous lawsuits, created a demand for administrators who were specifically trained to manage special-education programs.

Although special education administration has developed a uniqueness and identity, there is considerable variety within the discipline. This variety is expressed across governmental levels and organizational arrangements. There are three governmental levels in special education administration: federal, state, and local. Within each level the tasks of the administrator may vary considerably depending on the specific role of the administrator, the organization of the agency for which the administrator works, and the ways in which the agency delivers services.

Presently, the federal role in special education administration is executed primarily by the Office of Special Education and Rehabilitation of the U.S. Department of Education. The administrative roles of this office include monitoring state compliance with PL 94-142; generating research; providing public information; formulating regulations; promoting personnel development; and drafting legislation. As a result of PL 94-142, the federal role in administration of special education has grown substantially. Nearly every administrative decision in special education must be made with consideration for the regulations propagated by PL 94-142. Because of this, the majority of the administrators at the federal level are involved in activities related to providing services to the states in order that they may carry out the provisions of PL 94-142, or in evaluating/monitoring the state's efforts.

Administration of special education programs at the state level occurs in three places: at the state education agency (SEA); at state-operated schools; and at state-operated regional centers. At the SEA, the roles of administration are to develop legislation; to develop state plans; to obtain and administer financial resources; to develop personnel preparation systems and standards; to develop plans for improving instruction; to enforce and monitor regulations; and to develop public relations (Gearhart & Wright, 1979; Podemski, Price, Smith, & Marsh, 1984). The SEAs also directly administer programs such as state schools for the deaf or blind (e.g., Pennsylvania). These programs are usually for low-incidence populations. In Georgia, the SEA administers both state schools and regional centers that provide direct service to low-incidence populations, especially in rural areas. Regional centers also serve as resource centers for local education agencies (LEAs).

Some state-operated programs in special education are not administered by the SEA. These programs, usually serving the mentally retarded or the emotionally disturbed, may be managed by state agencies such as a department of mental retardation, mental health, and juvenile services. Such programs are generally subject to the same regulations (primarily PL 94-142) as programs operated by the SEA. In many instances, however, the programs are not managed by educators. The practice of employing physicians, psychologists, or social workers to manage state residential programs is a vestige of a tradition in state institutions and is justifiable for programs that are not chiefly educational.

At the local level, there are a number of different administrative arrangements and even more varied service delivery arrangements (Burello & Sage, 1979). The simplest administrative arrangement is the LEA. The LEA, also known as the local school district, provides direct services to exceptional children through various delivery systems. Administration at the local level may be centralized or decentralized. In a centralized system, persons (i.e., teachers) who provide services to exceptional children are managed by a district-wide special education director (coordinator). The special education director in a centralized system exercises a great amount of control over special education personnel and programs. In a decentralized system, the special education administrator serves in a coordinating/supporting/advising role. This administrator may have some authority over personnel but it is generally a building administrator (principal) who oversees daily operations.

More complex local administrative arrangements include intermediate educational units (IEU) and cooperative programs. Intermediate units exist in approximately 35 states (Podemski et al., 1984). In some states (e.g., Georgia) these units may be state-operated regional programs. In other states (e.g., New York, Texas, Wisconsin, Pennsylvania) the intermediate units are administered as a separate level of education agency. Intermediate units may be known by several names (e.g., Board of Cooperative Educational Services in New York, Regional Education Service Centers in Texas). According to Podemski et al. (1984), intermediate units were developed to pool resources and to share costs. In some states (e.g., Pennsylvania) intermediate units provide more than special education services and were developed for political as well as educational reasons during a time of district consolidation. Intermediate units have been criticized as arrangements that violate the principle of least restrictive environment because their services often require removing a child from his or her home school. Among the problems facing administrators of intermediate units are competition with LEAs for funds and students, potential

conflict in lines of authority, communication gaps with the LEA, and salary variations that influence competition with LEAs for teachers.

Many rural school systems and suburban systems enter into cooperative agreements in order to provide more cost-effective programs, especially for low-incidence populations (Howe, 1981). Cooperative programs engender the same problems as do IEUs. Additionally, they must often contend with long distances for busing students.

The competencies of LEA and IEU special education administrators are similar. The differences are probably in terms of the amount of time devoted to different tasks rather than the tasks themselves. This may be true also for administrators of state-operated direct service programs (e.g., state schools). The competency areas for such administrators include organization theory and behavior; budget development; curriculum development; supervision; personnel administration; community relations; community resources; change processes; physical plant management; research; professional standards; and policy development.

Public Law 94-142 requires all LEAs to have available the complete range of service-delivery options. This includes self-contained classes, resource rooms, part-time classes, residential programs, and other options (Deno, 1970). Before PL 94-142 it was possible for LEAs to offer only one service-delivery option (most often self-contained classes). This change and the variability of placement options has brought new problems to the forefront of special education administration. These problems include teamwork with regular educators; appropriate placement; coordination with general education administrators; and increased parental involvement (Ysseldyke, Algozzine, & Allen, 1982; Mingo & Burrello, 1985).

Specialized graduate training for administrators of programs for exceptional children began in 1965. The impetus for such training was provided by a journal article by Milazzo and Blessing (1964). Subsequent to the publishing of that article, the U.S. Office of Education awarded grants to universities for the purpose of developing training programs (Burrello & Sage, 1979). Although these training programs have existed for 20 years, it is apparent that most persons in special education leadership positions have not come through such programs but rather have progressed through the ranks as teachers or as general education administrators (Burrello & Sage, 1979). Furthermore, as of 1971, only slightly more than 50% of the graduates of doctoral programs in special education administration actually became special education administrators (Vance & Howe, 1974). Although most states do have certification requirements for special education leadership positions, requirements can be met with a general administrative certificate or a collection of courses and experience. Because market demands are limited, most training programs have not reached a high degree of articulation, sophistication, or visibility. A number of writers have articulated the desired content of special education administration training programs. Among the more notable training programs is the Special Education Supervisory Training Project (SEST, 1974), which was based on a human/conceptual/technical model (Burrello & Sage, 1979).

## REFERENCES

Ayer, F. C., & Barr, A. S. (1928). *The organization of supervision.* New York: Appleton.

Burrello, L. C., & Sage, D. D. (1979). *Leadership and change in special education.* Englewood Cliffs, NJ: Prentice-Hall.

Deno, E. (1970). Special education for the mildly retarded: Is much of it justifiable? *Exceptional Children, 37(3),* 229–237.

Gearheart, B. R., & Wright, W. S. (1979). *Organization and administration of educational programs for exceptional children* (2nd ed.). Springfield, IL: Thomas.

Hewett, F. M., & Forness, S. R. (1977). *Education of exceptional learners.* Boston: Allyn & Bacon.

Howe, C. (1981). *Administration of special education.* Denver: Love.

Kohl, J. W., & Marro, T. D. (1971). *A normative study of the administrative position in special education.* Grant No. OEG-0-70-2467 (607), U.S. Office of Education, Pennsylvania State University.

Mackie, R. P., & Engel, A. M. (1956). *Directors and supervisors of special education in local school systems.* U.S. Office of Education Bulletin 1955, No. 13. Washington, DC: U.S. Government Printing Office.

Mackie, R. P., & Snyder, W. E. (1957). *Special education personnel in state departments of education.* U.S. Office of Education Bulletin 1956, No. 6. Washington, DC: U.S. Government Printing Office.

Milazzo, T. C., & Blessing, K. R. (1964). The training of directors and supervisors of special education programs. *Exceptional Children, 31,* 129–141.

Mingo, J., & Burrello, L. C. (1985). *Determining the relationship between special education administrator, supervisor, and building principal role and responsibilities in the administration of educational programs for the handicapped.* Bloomington, IN: Council of Administrators of Special Education, Inc., Indiana University.

Podemski, R. S., Price, B. J., Smith, T. E. C., & Marsh, G. E. (1984). *Comprehensive administration of special education.* Rockville, MD: Aspen.

Sage, D. D. (1968). Functional emphasis in special education administration. *Exceptional Children, 35,* 69–70.

SEST Project (1974). *Professional supervisor competencies.* Austin, TX: University of Texas.

Vance, V. L., & Howe, C. E. (1974). Status of special education administration students who received USOE/BEH training grants. *Exceptional Children, 41(2),* 120–121.

Wisland, M. V., & Vaughan, T. D. (1964). Administrative problems in special education. *Exceptional Children, 31,* 87–89.

Ysseldyke, J., Algozzine, B., & Allen, D. (1982). Participation of regular education teachers in special education team decision making. *Exceptional Children, 48(4),* 365–366.

JAMES K. MCAFEE
*Pennsylvania State University*

**POLITICS AND SPECIAL EDUCATION**
**SPECIAL EDUCATION PROGRAMS**
**SUPERVISION IN SPECIAL EDUCATION**

## ADOLESCENCE AND SPECIAL PROBLEMS OF THE HANDICAPPED

Adolescence is the period extending from puberty (about 12 years of age) to age 18 through 20. Crises during adolescence, according to McDowell (1981), generally involve two common elements, physiological and psychological development. Physiological development involves definition of concepts such as identity, relationships, and independence; psychological development involves definition of concepts such as identity, relationships, and independence. The physiological changes include development of sex characteristics. Changes in the body build and structure are very prominent during this period. Much of the stress and anxiety during this period revolve around a general lack of understanding about what adolescents can expect to happen; an impatience with nature in the developmental process; and possible ridicule if an adolescent does not meet certain standards.

Havinghurst (1972) outlined several tasks associated with adolescent development. They include the following:

Achieving new and more mature relations with age-mates of both sexes.

Achieving a masculine or feminine social role.

Accepting one's physique and using the body effectively.

Achieving emotional independence of parents and other adults.

Preparing for marriage and family life.

Preparing for a career.

Acquiring a set of values and an ethical system.

Desiring and achieving socially responsible behavior (pp. 45–75).

These developmental tasks are considered crucial stages in development that require a great deal of adjustment and decision making. However, there are critical problems that many adolescents may be confronted with during this stage. According to McDowell (1981), one major problem adolescents have to deal with is the lack of support systems to meet their needs. Many programs for adolescents were originally designed for children or adults. Three major agencies that adolescents may be involved with are the public schools, mental health facilities, and the legal system. Only recently have the public schools begun to develop appropriate educational alternatives for handicapped adolescents. Many mental health agencies are still in the process of revising child and adult programs to meet the needs of adolescents. The legal system is confronted with deciding whether an adolescent is a child or an adult.

Other problem areas frequently encountered by adolescents include alcohol and drug abuse, crime, suicide, teenage pregnancy, and marriage. Alcohol and drug abuse has been a major problem for many years. Drug abuse surfaced during the late 1960s. The use of drugs by adolescents can lead to emotional and physical problems. Some youngsters may ocasionally experiment with drugs; others may become drug abusers to escape from personal problems. Adolescent crime usually involves minor offenses. Only a small number of youngsters are brought to court for serious crimes such as assault, rape, or murder. Adolescent suicide is usually the result of extreme depression and is often related to a relationship problem. Teenage pregnancy can be a traumatic experience for a young girl. Information about sex and birth control are easily available, therefore many adults think adolescents have adequate knowledge. However, many adolescents are not educated about sex and birth control and tend not to admit their lack of knowledge.

Adolescence is often a difficult period for the nonhandicapped child, therefore it is reasonable to assume that it may be even more difficult for the handicapped child. The handicapped adolescent experiences all of the developmental stages and general needs characterized by this period of growth, plus problems relating to exceptionality (Smith & Payne, 1980). According to Cartwright, Cartwright, and Payne (1984), handicapped adolescents may be classified into two groups, the mildly vocationally handicapped and the seriously vocationally handicapped. Those individuals with a strong chance of becoming independent and self-supporting are classified as mildly vocationally handicapped. Those students will be able to get and maintain a job with the proper counseling, career and vocational training, and compensatory skills. Many others may be able to attend technical and trade schools. The seriously vocationally handicapped have severe disabilities that offer little hope for independent living. This group includes the severely and profoundly retarded, multihandicapped, and severely physically handicapped.

Prior to the 1970s, the educational programs for handicapped adolescents were very limited. During the 1950s and 1960s, educational programs for severely handicapped adolescents were minimal. During this time, handicapped youths who attended special classes in public schools were often socially promoted. Many dropped out of school at age 16. The impact of parent groups and the passage of PL 94-142 has created many more special programs for handicapped adolescents of every level of severity and handi-

capping condition (Cartwright et al., 1984). Traditional secondary programs for handicapped adolescents are being rejected by many special educators. These programs are often inappropriate for handicapped students. The lack of relevant subject matter, materials, instructional practices, and testing methods are often major problem areas that offer little or no assistance in meeting the needs of the handicapped (Laurie, Buchwach, Silverman, & Zigmond, 1978).

Mandell & Gold (1984) emphasized that the handicapped adolescent's needs, skills, and future goals are essential components that must be considered when selecting the most appropriate service delivery model. The mildly handicapped student may be served in the mainstream with supplementary assistance. Some students may benefit from a combination of regular secondary and vocational education with supplementary assistance. The more severely handicapped student may benefit from self-contained and special classes or special vocational training centers.

Career and vocational education is an essential component of the secondary education program for the handicapped adolescent. McDowell (1979) stated that for handicapped adolescents, the following behaviors are essential for survival on the job and in today's society.

1. Be able to establish eye contact if required by the situation.
2. Demonstrate respect for others and their property.
3. Be attentive to authority figures in appropriate ways.
4. Exhibit good manners.
5. Use appropriate manners.
6. Discriminate between behaviors as to time and place (i.e., recognize that certain behaviors are appropriate at different times and places).
7. Achieve a reasonable balance between dependence and independence.
8. Learn to accept directions and take orders.
9. Learn to accept and follow the work schedule established by an employer.
10. See a task through to its completion (p. 2.).

A great deal of emphasis should be placed on helping the handicapped adolescent learn behaviors and skills essential to independence. However, many handicapped people are underemployed and unable to find jobs within their range of abilities (Razeghi & Davis, 1979). Another essential component of a secondary program for handicapped adolescents is social skills. Many handicapped children have problems developing appropriate social skills. Difficulties in these areas lead to problems with integration into the mainstream and peer relationships.

## REFERENCES

Cartwright, G. P. (1984). *Educating special learners* (2nd ed.). Belmont, CA: Wadsworth.

Havinghurst, R. J. (1972). *Developmental tasks and education* (3rd ed.). New York: Mckay.

Laurie, T. E., Buchwach, L., Silverman, R., & Zigmond, N. (1978). Teaching secondary learning disabled students in the mainstream. *Learning Disabilities Quarterly, 1,* 62–72.

Mandell, C. J., & Gold, V. (1984). *Teaching handicapped students.* St. Paul, MN: West.

McDowell, R. L. (1979). *The emotionally disturbed adolescent.* PRISE Reporter, No. 3, May 1979. King of Prussia, PA: Pennsylvania Resources and Information Center for Special Education.

McDowell, R. L. (1981). Adolescence. In G. Brown, R. L. McDowell, & J. Smith (Eds.), *Educating adolescents with behavior disorders.* Columbus, OH: Merrill.

Razeghi, J. A., & Davis, S. (1979). Federal mandates for the handicapped: Vocational education opportunity and employment. *Exceptional Children, 45,* 353–359.

Smith, J. E., & Payne, J. S. (1980). *Teaching exceptional adolescents.* Columbus, OH: Merrill.

JANICE HARPER
*North Carolina Central
University*

**AFFECTIVE EDUCATION
FAMILY RESPONSE TO A HANDICAPPED CHILD
SOCIAL SKILLS
VOCATIONAL TRAINING OF HANDICAPPED**

## ADOPTEES

The practice of adoption is centuries old, but our understanding of the impact of this form of child care continues to be without definitive answers. At the theoretical level, adoption has often been associated with increased risk for psychological maladjustment. Psychoanalytic theory, for example, suggests that the experience of adoption sets the stage for disturbances in personality and identity development. This is especially true because of doubt surrounding the true circumstances of the child's origins, and because the child has two sets of parents instead of one with whom to identify. Bowlby's work (1969) suggests that adopted children are at risk for emotional problems, but only in cases where there is disruption in the development and continuity of primary attachment relationships. Consequently, infants adopted soon after birth and cared for continually by affectionate and competent parents would not be viewed as being at risk in terms of possible maladjustment. However, individuals raised by multiple caregivers, or separated from caregivers after a secure attachment has developed, would be perceived as being at risk.

In contrast to the theoretical literature, the results of empirical research have produced an inconsistent picture of the effects of adoption on an individual's psychological development. After reviewing the social work literature on the success of adoption placements, both Mech (1973) and Kadushin (1974) concluded that the majority of placements were satisfactory. However, an examination of the records of mental-health clinics reveals that adopted children are referred to these clinics at disproportionate rates. Mech (1973) reported that while adopted children reared by nonrelatives constitute approximately 1% of the population, they account for over 4% of the children seen in clinics. Researchers have also reported that there are differences in types of problems presented by adopted children versus those who are nonadopted. Adopted children typically manifest more aggressive and acting-out problems, as well as learning-related difficulties. In fact, a recent study has even reported an elevated number of pediatric health conditions among adopted children (Dalby, Fox, & Haslam, 1982).

While there are those studies available that validate these findings, there are also those such as Aumend and Barrett's (1984) that provide a contrary set of findings. In their study of adult adoptees they reported the following: the majority of those in their study scored above the 60th percentile on the Tennessee Self Concept Scale; had positive scores on the Attitude Toward Parents Scales; were happy growing up, with only 12% reporting that they were unhappy; and did not report revelation of their adoptive status as being disruptive or traumatic. These findings were consistent with those of Norvell and Guy (1977), who determined there were no significant differences between self-concepts of an adopted and nonadopted population, aged 18 to 25. They concluded that problems of a negative identity seemed to stem more from problems within the home, rather than an association with adoption.

Because of a lack of definitive empirical information, the issue of open records, or allowing adopted children to learn about their biological parents at a particular point in time, continues to be controversial. As has been the case in the past, this issue will probably be resolved in the courts. Another issue unique to adoption is when children should be informed of their adoptive status. Currently, most specialists on adoption advocate telling children before they are 5 years of age. The specialists believe this promotes the development of a trusting relationship within the context of a warm and supportive family and eliminates the possibility that the child will hear of his or her unique family status from nonfamily members under less than desirable conditions. While many advocate telling the child during the preschool years, recent studies such as that by Brodzinsky, Schechter, Braff, & Singer (1984) suggest that a child's cognitive development during the preschool years may mitigate against his or her understanding of the nature of adoption. Their concern is that parents may relate this information to children and then feel the "job is done," failing to understand that advanced stages of cognitive development call for further explanations and sequential exploration of concerns the child might harbor.

While the data are not as definitive as might be liked, it certainly seems that adoption is a legitimate way of building families and caring for young children. It is superior to alternatives such as serial placements in a number of homes, or large-scale institutional care. Assuming the family is capable of providing a stable environment that is free of debilitating or otherwise pathological features, and relates the information on adoption in a facilitative fashion, there seems to be little reason to expect greater childhood problems than experienced in biologically created families.

## REFERENCES

Aumend, S. A., & Barrett, M. C. (1984). Self-concept and attitudes toward adoption: A comparison of searching and nonsearching adult adoptees. *Child Welfare, 63*, 251–259.

Bowlby, J. (1969). *Attachment and loss: Volume 1 attachment.* New York: Basic Books.

Brodzinsky, D. M., Schechter, D. E., Braff, A. M., & Singer, L. M. (1984). Psychological and academic adjustment in adopted children. *Journal of Consulting and Clinical Psychology, 52*, 582–589.

Dalby, J. T., Fox, S. L., & Haslam, R. H. (1982). Adoption and foster care rates in pediatric disorders. *Developmental and Behavioral Pediatrics, 3*, 61–64.

Kadushin, A. (1974). *Child welfare services.* New York: Macmillan.

Mech, E. V. (1973). Adoption: A policy perspective. In B. Caldwell & H. Ricuitti (Eds.), *Review of child development research* (Vol. 3). Chicago: University of Chicago Press.

Norvell, M., & Guy, R. F. (1977). A comparison of self concept in adopted and nonadopted adolescents. *Adolescence, 12*, 443–448.

CHARLES P. BARNARD
*University of Wisconsin, Stout*

## CHILD CARE AGENCIES
## CHILD CARETAKER
## CHILD GUIDANCE CLINIC

## ADULT BASIC EDUCATION (ABE)

Adult basic education (ABE), a part of the adult education movement, is designed and intended for those individuals who may lack the basic education needed to function appropriately in society. For many adults, particularly those with handicapping conditions, adult education serves as a substitute for the education that was missed in earlier years or never completed. For others, adult education implies further or continuing education.

Adult education encompasses all organized learning, including vocational education (Stubblefield, 1981). During the formative years of what became the adult education movement (mid-to-late 1920s), adult education revolved around a belief that individual growth and improvement was paramount; that is, individuals would respond to education that would assist in helping them to understand their life experiences and improve themselves through the acquisition of knowledge, enjoyment, power, etc.

Later, the adult education movement emphasized a variety of other themes, including psychological and physical maturity, service to society, and civic life. Those who have tried to identify a central focus within adult education have most often portrayed the adult learner as an individual who seeks out education and has a desire to accommodate to a changing society and value system. Thus one major issue has centered around whether the goal of adult education should be to satisfy individual needs or societal needs.

The content of adult education varies from the simple to the complex. In fact, any content that is reflective of the adult's interest and desire to know is legitimate (Schroeder, 1970). At times, content is selected to achieve cognitive objectives (i.e., facts, knowledge of principles) while, at other times, content is selected to achieve affective objectives (i.e., interests, values, or psychomotor objectives or skills). Similarly, adult education can involve hobby learning (e.g., learning to play golf or bridge), literacy learning (e.g., learning at the academic level of elementary and secondary schools), occupational learning (e.g., learning manual and clerical skills), and higher learning (e.g., learning beyond the secondary and vocational level) (Bowen, 1980). It is literacy learning that constitutes adult basic education.

There are many adult education service providers, although most can be assigned to one of four categories: (1) agencies that serve the needs of adults; (2) agencies that serve the needs of adolescents, but have some responsibility for serving the needs of adults; (3) agencies that serve the educational and noneducational needs of the community; and (4) agencies that serve the special interest needs of particular groups. In the first category are agencies such as proprietary schools (i.e., business schools, technical schools) and independent education centers. The second category consists of public schools, community colleges, and institutions of higher education. The third category includes libraries and museums, while the fourth category includes unions, churches, business and industry, and so on. In essence, adult education is found in a variety of organizations that provide education for adults.

There are numerous categories of individuals who provide potential populations of adult learners. These include:

Those desiring to overcome educational limitations
College and high school dropouts
Career changers or career updaters
Institutionalized populations
Elderly persons
Those who simply enjoy learning
The handicapped.

Adult basic education coupled with programs for speakers of other languages long have been features of adult education. The rationale behind ABE programs is based on the demonstrated correlation between years of schooling and income. That is, there is a presumed relationship between the length of time spent in school and the amount of income earned. Consequently, ABE programs are directed toward assisting individuals to enter or upgrade their skills for the labor market. A further rationale for ABE programs is that every adult has a basic right to acquire skills in written and verbal communication and computation. Therefore, ABE programs are directed toward undereducated adults. Although this can include those adult individuals having known handicapping conditions, the majority of clients are poor, from a minority background, and possibly defeatist.

All possible knowledge could be included in an ABE program. However, few programs have the resources to provide such an extensive range of services for all types of adult learners. Limiting services, however, tends to limit the types of individuals who can participate; thus, handicapped adults may not be recruited for ABE programs that require students who have needs that are linked to a program's goals or capacities. While some ABE programs for adult handicapped persons are available, they have not been a major focus of ABE programs.

**REFERENCES**

Bowen, H. R. (1980). *Adult learning, higher education, and the economics of unused capacity.* New York: College Entrance Examination Board.

Schroeder, W. L. (1970). Adult education defined and described. In R. M. Smith, G. F. Aker, & J. R. Kidd (Eds.), *Handbook of adult education.* New York: Macmillan.

Stubblefield, H. W. (1981). The focus should be on life fulfillment. In B. W. Kreitlow and Associates (Eds.), *Examining controversies in adult education.* San Francisco: Jossey-Bass.

Shworles, T. R., & Wang, P. H. (1980). Education for handicapped adults. In E. J. Boon, R. W. Shearon, & E. E. White (Eds.), *Serving personal and community needs through adult education.* San Francisco, Jossey-Bass.

MARTY ABRAMSON
*University of Wisconsin, Stout*

COMMUNITY-BASED SERVICES
REHABILITATION
VOCATIONAL VILLAGE

## ADULT PROGRAMS FOR THE DISABLED

There are numerous programs of several types that serve adults with disabilities. Many such programs are financed by federal, state, and local governments; many others are funded by private business, private nonprofit organizations, and charities. The following is a summary of major programs organized by function and financing source. It will not capture the complexity and breadth of these programs, especially at the state and local level.

The Social Security Act authorizes several major programs providing cash payments and health insurance to adults on the basis of disability. The disability insurance (DI) program replaces in part income lost when a person with a work history can no longer work because of a physical or mental impairment. Many individuals, of course, have separate commercial disability insurance policies provided by an employer or purchased on their own. After receiving Social Security DI benefits for 24 months, regardless of age, an individual becomes eligible for government-provided health insurance under the Medicare program, which normally covers persons 65 and over. The Social Security Act also contains the Supplemental Security Income (SSI) program, which provides cash income support payments to needy individuals who are aged, blind, or disabled. Income is provided regardless of work history to those who meet means and asset requirements. In most states, with SSI eligibility comes eligibility for the Medicaid program (federal-state matching required), which provides health insurance for low-income individuals. Included in Medicaid is support for intermediate care facilities for the mentally retarded (ICFs/MR), which provide residential care and service programs. Many disabled individuals benefit from programs for which they may be eligible without regard to their disability, for example, Social Security Old Age and Survivors insurance payments and Medicare (persons 65 and older).

Finally, there are four other major federal programs of this type for special groups of disabled individuals. Veterans with service-connected disabilities are eligible for special cash payments under the Veterans Compensation program. Veterans of wartime service with nonservice-connected disabilities are eligible for a special pension program. Coal miners disabled by black lung or other lung disease are eligible for one of two separate special payment programs (one administered by the Social Security Administration, the other by the Labor Department), depending on circumstances.

Special programs of postsecondary education for the deaf and hearing impaired, supported with significant federal funding, are provided at Gallaudet College, the National Technical Institute for the Deaf, and four special regional postsecondary institutions. In addition, educational programs that are recipients of federal financial assistance at public and private colleges and universities must be accessible to and usable by individuals with disabilities of all types. Some schools are making adaptations and providing support services that go beyond legal requirements.

Rehabilitation and job training services are available from a number of sources. Under Title I of the Rehabilitation Act, the federal government and the states provide vocational rehabilitation services such as physical restoration, job training, and placement to persons with mental and physical disabilities, regardless of prior work history. Physical rehabilitation is covered by most accident and health insurance policies; vocational rehabilitation is sometimes covered. Rehabilitation is available and in fact required under some state workers' compensation laws. Rehabilitation services financed by various forms of insurance are provided by private, for-profit companies and facilities, private nonprofit agencies, and state agencies. Provision of rehabilitation services by private, profit-making (proprietary) firms is a growing phenomenon (Taylor, et al., 1985).

Private nonprofit entities play a significant role in providing job training, rehabilitation, and other skill development to adults with disabilities. Included in this group are organizations such as the Association for Retarded Citizens, Easter Seals, Goodwill Industries, and United Cerebral Palsy. Some activities of these organizations are financed by the government; others are funded by contracts with businesses for work performed.

Major employers, faced with rising costs of disability, will find it in their interest to pay greater attention to management, rehabilitation, and disability prevention (Schwartz, 1984). Many are increasing efforts in these areas, including rehabilitation, job, and work-site modification efforts to facilitate entry or return to jobs by individuals with disabilities. Contracts with the federal government of more than $2500 must operate with an affirmative action program to employ and advance individuals with disabilities.

Self-help, referral, and training services are available to people with very severe disabilities to improve their capacity for independent living. These services are available through a network of community-based nonprofit centers and from state rehabilitation agencies. In addition, supported employment is an important new program for individuals with disabilities so severe they were previously thought incapable of working. These individuals (especially those with mental impairments) are likely to need continual support, but they are able to work on regular jobs in integrated settings if given a highly structured training program and some support on the job site (Mank 1986).

Special housing and transportation programs are available for individuals with disabilities, financed by both the federal government and states and localities. The same is true for special recreation programs for the disabled, in which local governments, service organizations, charities, and private businesses play a large role. Therapeutic recreation is also part of some rehabilitation programs. In addition, many local recreation facilities and organizations, including those involved with the arts, are adapting programs so that the disabled can participate or attend with the general public.

## REFERENCES

General Services Administration. (1985). *Catalog of federal domestic assistance.* Washington, DC: U.S. Government Printing Office.

Mank, D. (1986). Four supported employment alternatives. In W. Kiernan & J. Stark (Eds.), *Pathways to employment for developmentally disabled adults.* Baltimore, MD: Brooks.

National Council on the Handicapped. (1986). *Toward independence: An assessment of federal laws and programs affecting persons with disabilities.* Washington, DC: U.S. Government Printing Office.

Schwartz, G. (1984, May). Disability costs: The impending crisis. *Business and Health*, pp. 25–28.

Taylor, L. J., Golter, M., Golter, G., & Backer, T. (Eds.). (1985). *Handbook of private sector rehabilitation.* New York: Springer.

JAMES R. RICCIUTI
*United States Office of
Management and Budget*

**ACCESSIBILITY OF PROGRAMS**
· **HABILITATION OF THE HANDICAPPED**
**REHABILITATION**

# ADVANCED PLACEMENT PROGRAM

The Advanced Placement Program was established in 1955 as a program of college-level courses and examinations for secondary school students. It is administered by the College Board, a nonprofit membership organization composed of public and private secondary schools, colleges, and universities. This program gives high school students the opportunity to receive advanced placement and/or credit on entering college.

The essential premise of the Advanced Placement Program is that college-level courses can be successfully taught to high school students by high school teachers on high school campuses (College Entrance Examination Board, 1985). Descriptions and examinations on 26 introductory college courses in 14 fields are disseminated. These fields include art, biology, chemistry, computer science, English, French, German, government and politics, history, Latin, mathematics, music, physics, and Spanish. Course descriptions are prepared, with the help of the Educational Testing Service, by working committees of school and college teachers appointed by the College Board. Exams are administered by the Educational Testing Service.

Most participating high schools, offering one or more advanced placement courses (called AP courses) are larger schools with enough students to qualify for a class. Smaller schools usually provide independent study for those students wishing to take advanced placement exams. The AP course teachers are provided with course descriptions and teachers' guides that state curricular goals and suggest strategies to achieve them. Teachers are not required to follow a detailed plan of assignments and classroom activities; however, seven Advanced Placement Regional Offices and Advanced Placement Program conferences are available to assist teachers.

Advanced Placement courses offer demanding academic opportunities for abler students. Students who complete these courses are not required to take advanced placement examinations, but those who choose to take them and who receive a passing score, have the opportunity to receive advanced placement and/or credit on entering college.

REFERENCES

College Entrance Examination Board (1985). *School administrator's guide to the advanced placement program* (Edition G). New York: Author.

*The College Board Review* (quarterly publication)
The College Board
888 Seventh Avenue
New York, NY 10106

Advanced Placement Program
Harlan P. Hanson, Director
45 Columbus Avenue
New York, NY 10023-6917

MARY K. TALLENT
*Texas Tech University*

## ACCELERATION OF GIFTED CHILDREN
## GIFTED AND TALENTED CHILDREN

# ADVANCE ORGANIZERS

Advance organizers are concepts or orienting information presented prior to a new lesson. They make the new material more meaningful and have been found to improve reading comprehension with reading disabled (Risko & Alvarez, 1982) and deaf (Biser, 1984) children, and with average learners who are being introduced to an unfamiliar topic (Mayer, 1979). Teachers have found advance organizers helpful in making a disorganized text more sensible, and in facilitating transfer of learning (Mayer, 1979).

Ausabel (1960) wrote that advance organizers aid comprehension and retention by anchoring newly learned material to existing knowledge structures. In contrast to simple outlines, advance organizers are presented at a higher level of abstraction and generality than the task itself.

Ausabel has discussed two general categories of organizers, each relevant to specific learning conditions. The first, termed expository or correlative organizers, are used when students have no context within which to frame new material. Expository organizers may be preliminary discussions or readings presenting the new material in global terms. Once the general concepts have been explored, the learner can organize the factual content within a meaningful structure.

The second category of advance organizers, referred to as comparative organizers, also bridges new knowledge with existing structures. In contrast to expository organizers, comparative organizers capitalize on schema that have been developed with related factual material. Rather than building a new conceptual framework, comparative organizers highlight similarities and differences between mastered concepts and those to be learned.

A third type of advance organizer, the graphic organizer, has gained popularity in recent years in programs for disabled readers (Vick & Lynn, 1983) and for deaf students (Biser, 1984). Graphic organizers, presented as visual displays, are used to preview vocabulary words and to represent the flow of ideas from one level of abstraction to another. Biser suggests that deaf and language deficient children, who may lack access to subtle differences in linguistic meanings, can use advance graphic organizers to enrich their comprehension.

Children with limited intellectual capacity clearly have more difficulty in using advance organizers effectively. Lacking the conceptual sophistication needed to relate facts to general concepts, slow learners may fail to grasp the intent of the organizer (Risko & Alvarez, 1982). Miller and Schloss (1982) have highlighted the importance of addressing language deficits in preparing organizers for limited children, and in building on previously presented content.

REFERENCES

Ausabel, D. P. (1960). Use of advance organizers in the learning and retention of meaningful verbal material. *Journal of Educational Psychology, 51,* 267–272.

Biser, E. (1984, June). *Application of Ausabel's theory of meaningful verbal learning to curriculum, teaching, and learning of deaf students.* Paper presented at the International Symposium on Cognition, Education, and Deafness, Washington, D.C. (ERIC Document Reproduction Service No. ED 247 712).

Mayer, R. E. (1979). *Twenty years of research on advance organizers: Technical report series in learning and cognition* (Report

No. 79-1). Washington, DC National Science Foundation (ERIC Document Reproduction Service No. ED 206 691).

Miller, S. R., & Schloss, P. J. (1982). *Career-vocational education for handicapped youths*. Rockville, MD: Aspen.

Risko, V. J., & Alvarez, M. C. (1982, Dec.). *Thematic organizers: Application to remedial reading*. Paper presented at the American Reading Forum, Lido Beach, FL (ERIC Document Reproduction Service No. ED 227 438).

Vick, M. L., & Lynn, J. A. (1983, May). *Developing comprehension skills via advance organizers*. Paper presented at the 2nd annual meeting of the International Reading Association, Anaheim, CA (ERIC Document Reproduction Service No. ED 243 069).

GARY BERKOWITZ
*Temple University*

## ADVENTITIOUS DISABILITIES

Disabilities may present themselves at birth or be acquired through disease or accident. Those acquired later in life are known as adventitious disabilities. Among these is brain damage produced by extremely high and consistent temperatures or a lack of needed oxygen to the brain. Adventitious disabilities may also be a consequence of trauma to the brain or injury to other parts of the body (Hallahan & Kauffman, 1986).

A major cause of adventitious disabilities is child abuse, which effects one out of every 100 children in the United States under 18 years of age (Kneedler, Hallahan, & Kauffman, 1984). Child abuse is emotionally or physically damaging and can cause perdurable learning problems. Such abuse occurs most often in lower socioeconomic strata.

An area of childhood exceptionality often associated with an adventitious disability is hearing impairment or deafness. Hearing losses may be present at birth or adventitiously acquired later on in life through disease or accident (Kirk & Gallagher, 1983). If a child is unable to hear from birth, he or she will not be able to learn speech and language spontaneously. In contrast, a child suffering from adventitious disabilities will require assistance in adjusting to his or her hearing loss and in maintaining the ability to speak clearly.

### REFERENCES

Hallahan, D. P., & Kauffman, J. M. (1986). *Exceptional children*. Englewood Cliffs, NJ: Prentice-Hall.

Kirk, S. A., & Gallagher, J. (1983). *Educating exceptional children*. Boston: Houghton-Mifflin.

Kneedler, R. D., Hallahan, D. P., & Kauffman, J. M. (1984). *Special education today*. Englewood Cliffs, NJ: Prentice-Hall.

JOSEPH M. RUSSO
*Hunter College, City University
of New York*

**BRAIN DAMAGE**
**CHILD ABUSE**

## ADVOCACY FOR HANDICAPPED CHILDREN

Advocacy for handicapped people has become a multifaceted reality in today's world of concern about the legal rights of those with disabilities. The term actually has a variety of meanings, depending on who is providing the advocacy. In its essence, advocacy refers to attempts by an individual handicapped person, by another person, or by a group to guarantee that all rights due a handicapped person are realized. Roos (1983) traces the origins of the advocacy movement to the 1930s, when parents of mentally retarded children began to react against neglectful or inappropriate actions by professionals who claimed to be helping these children and their families. Frustrated with the professionals' response, parents turned to each other for help.

In 1933, the Cuyahoga County (Ohio) Council for the Retarded Child was founded by parents as the forerunner of today's Association for Retarded Citizens (*ARC*). Other local, grass-roots organizations sprang up in different communities, and later, in 1950, joined together to form what was then known as the National Association of Parents and Friends of Mentally Retarded Children. At that time, similar organizational activity sprung up with parents of children with cerebral palsy.

Recently groups have been formed to advocate the interests of learning disabled, deaf, blind, and autistic children, and those with a variety of medical and physical anomalies. The early parent movements had at least three effects in the 1950s, at the same time as they formed a base on which later governmental and judicial action would be built. First, local ARCs extended emotional support to families with retarded members, providing information about available resources and bringing the issue of mental retardation into public view. This helped remove some of the stigma of having a handicapped child. Second, they encouraged state legislatures to adopt mandatory legislation for public school programs for retarded children, to enforce existing legislation, and to increase state appropriations for publicly funded programs. Third, parents developed preschool, school-age, and adult programs that became models for professionals, and public education and voluntary agencies (Lippman & Goldberg, 1973).

The role of ARC as a direct service provider has declined recently. Greater emphasis is now placed on information and public education services, advocacy, legislation, and funding (Roos, 1983). Advocacy efforts by ARC and other such groups today focus on citizen advocacy and self-advocacy. Professionals and volunteers have joined with parents to change the makeup of many groups formerly consisting exclusively of parents of handicapped children. Various advocacy groups and professional associations have formed coalitions to increase their political and public influence, with many organizations maintaining full- or part-time offices in Washington, DC, as well as in state capitals. These groups may be closely linked with legal advocacy agencies and may be represented on state and national advisory panels, accrediting boards, and monitoring bodies, often by state or federal regulation or court order. Advocacy groups have been instrumental in initiating litigation, often through the use of class-action suits, to guarantee that the existing rights of handicapped persons are safeguarded, to obtain new rights or services, or to enhance currently available programs. In some cases, international societies have been formed by national advocacy groups representing several nations (Roos, 1983).

Herr (1983) describes several different kinds of advocacy that have evolved from earlier movements. Though definitions and actual practice may vary, the following types of advocacy approaches for the handicapped can be identified:

1. *Self-advocacy*: "part consciousness-raising, assertiveness-training . . . and springboard to direct consumer involvement. . . ." (Herr, 1983).
2. *Family advocacy*: the oldest and most well understood.
3. *Friend advocacy*: personal, voluntary assistance by altruistic citizens; also referred to as *citizen advocacy*.
4. *Disability rights advocacy*: trained advocacy specialists dealing with individual needs and human service systems.
5. *Human rights advocacy*: usually citizen review committees composed of volunteers and professionals.
6. *Internal advocacy*: individuals within, rather than external to, human service agencies who attempt to guarantee clients' rights (sometimes referred to as ombudsmen).
7. *Legal advocacy*; primarily nonprofit, public-interest law projects, including some private or government lawyers (Herr, 1983).

Although individual special educators, acting alone or through professional organizations, may also view themselves as advocates for the handicapped children they serve, there may be inherent conflicts in attempting to play the two roles simultaneously (Bateman, 1982). Special educators must keep current on ethical practices and legal developments in their field, and on law and education in general.

## REFERENCES

Bateman, B. (1982). Legal and ethical dilemmas of special educators. *Exceptional Education Quarterly, 2(4)*, 57–67.

Herr, S. S. (1983). *Rights and advocacy for retarded people.* Lexington, MA: Lexington Books.

Lippman, L., & Goldberg, I. I. (1973). *Right to education: Anatomy of the Pennsylvania case and its implications for exceptional children.* New York: Teachers College Press.

Roos, P. R. (1983). Advocate groups. In J. L. Matson & J. A. Mulick (Eds.), *Handbook of mental retardation.* New York: Pergamon.

JOHN D. WILSON
*Elwyn Institutes,
Elwyn, Pennsylvania*

## ADVOCACY GROUPS, CITIZEN

A citizen advocacy group may be defined in general as any organization that has as its purpose to increase the quality of life for a specified handicapped population. Two examples of citizen advocacy groups containing both parents and professionals, and formally organized, are the Association for Children With Learning Disorders (ACLD) and the American Association on Mental Deficiency. These two groups have national headquarters but are organized state by state, having local chapters at county, city, or regional levels. They are not, however, classified as grass-roots advocacy groups.

An example of an informal organization is Youth Advocacy in the Washington, DC, area, a group of citizens (nonparents), with paid professional leadership, that provides services for adjudicated youths. They may represent an alternative to incarceration, providing community-based rehabilitation and supporting school, work, and living arrangements for youths in the area. Another example of a grass-roots nationally organized group is the Association for Autistic children. The chief characteristic of the organization is that the majority of local support groups are informally organized, and indeed are parents, while the leadership has national consolidation. There are formal and informal advocacy groups at national, regional, and local levels serving handicapped students representing all disability groups. The purposes for each group may vary considerably, depending on the perceived needs of the group.

The work of advocacy groups includes seeking federal or state legislation, developing policy or ordinances at the community level, supporting parental work, and intervening directly for students. One example of a community-based advocacy group is the Lion's Club, which supports the visually handicapped. Other social clubs support the hearing impaired (Rotary), the mentally retarded (Civitian), or orthopedically impaired (Shriners) by paying for services, prostheses, or therapy. Another example is the Junior Chamber of Commerce, a group that raises partial or full support for group homes, sheltered employment centers, or residential or day schools for the emotionally disturbed.

Providing funds for services or a community-support base are two of the major purposes of advocacy organizations. The definition of a community-support base varies with the particular advocacy group and community. Certainly, providing emotional support for parents is a major consideration. Obtaining legislation also is a primary function, given the fact that all legislation for the handicapped was provided and obtained by parents, not professionals. Advocacy groups may purchase direct services or even provide direct services, but that has not been their major role in the past. It is becoming more of a major role though, and represents a trend toward advocacy in the United States.

DAVID A. SABATINO
*West Virginia College
of Graduate Studies*

# ADVOCACY ORGANIZATIONS

Advocacy organizations are organizations that devote themselves to advocacy for individuals or groups who have needs for which their own resources may not be sufficient. The establishment of these organizations has proceeded on "the assumption that classes of persons exist with similar needs and similar inability to speak effectively for themselves" (Sage & Burello, 1986).

Many, if not most, of the services currently available to handicapped children and adolescents either began or succeeded because of the efforts of advocacy groups. Much of special education history represents the efforts of advocacy groups, including church, parent, and charitable groups. The Association for Retarded Citizens, in its national, state, and local forms, is an example of an advocacy organization that has altered educational practices in major ways.

Increasing growth in all sorts of advocacy groups has taken place since the 1960s, with an acceleration in the last decade. Not all groups, of course, deal with the handicapped. There are environmental advocacy groups, groups concerned with product safety, with the elimination of drunk driving, etc. However, advocacy groups for the handicapped have been among the most vociferous and successful.

Many of these advocacy groups began and sustained themselves through grants from the federal government. This was particularly true during the 1960s and 1970s, when they were financially encouraged as part of the social legislation of the times. Some were started or supported through funds provided by foundations or their own fund-raising activities.

The nature of advocacy is such that agencies are likely to be activist, to aggressively seek to achieve long-range changes in the social system to benefit their clients, and to immediately help those clients. Thus they often seek to influence legislation. Some advocacy agencies have special service missions, but modern agencies are more likely to intercede with a particular service or political system so as to obtain services and other needed benefits for their clients rather than provide those benefits themselves. They also make efforts to educate both their clients and the systems with which they interact so as to facilitate their working relationships. Professional advocacy groups usually assume major informational roles. They provide forums for speakers and disseminate information and literature, including manuals that assist their audiences to assist themselves in achieving their goals.

Advocacy organizations often have been successful in obtaining services for their clients, either through their own intercessions or by educating and supporting the services' "consumers" or their representatives so as to make them more effective. Such organizations as Closer Look Information Center for the Handicapped and the National Center for Law and the Handicapped have been instrumental in making public schools more responsive to the needs of handicapped students. They also have played major roles in disseminating information to the individuals whose advocacies they are assuming, to the general public, and to the legislative bodies whose laws and regulations may affect their constituencies.

**REFERENCE**

Sage, D. D., & Burello, L. C. (1986). *Policy and management in special education.* Englewood Cliffs, NJ: Prentice-Hall.

LESTER MANN
*Hunter College, City University
of New York*

# ADVOCATES (parents and others)

See ADVOCACY FOR HANDICAPPED CHILDREN.

# AFFECTIVE DISORDERS

Affect is the externally observable, immediately expressed component of human emotion (e.g., facial expression, tone of voice). Mood is considered to be a sustained emotion that pervades an individual's perception of the world. Affective disorders, as defined by the American Psychiatric Association (*Diagnostic and Statistical Manual*, 3rd ed.), are the class of mental disorders where "the essential feature . . . is a disturbance of mood" (p. 205).

Emotions and their expression are an integral part of human experience. It is only under certain conditions that the expression of emotion is considered maladaptive; in some instances, in fact, a lack of affect might be viewed as abnormal. It is only when an emotional reaction is disproportionate to the event, when the duration of the reaction is atypical, or when it interferes with a person's psychological, social, or occupational functioning that an emotional response may be labeled symptomatic of an affective disorder.

Affective disorders are comprised of two basic elements, depression and mania, which can be conceptualized as opposite ends of a continuum paralleling the normal happiness/sadness continuum. Both depression and mania have their counterparts in everyday life: The parallels for depression are grief and dejection; the experience corresponding to mania is less clear-cut, but probably could be described as the feverish activity with which people sometimes respond to stress.

Formally, both mania and depression can be characterized by symptoms at the emotional, cognitive, and somatic/motivational levels. The major emotional components of depression are sadness and melancholy, often accompanied by feelings of guilt and worthlessness. These emotions permeate the individual's total experience of life. Cognitively, depressed persons are characterized by a negatively distorted view of themselves, the world, and the future. Their outlook is generally one of unrealistic hopelessness. In terms of their physical functioning, depressed persons frequently suffer appetite and sleep disturbances, fatigue, apathy, and a general loss of energy.

In certain aspects, the symptoms of mania could be viewed as opposite to those of depression. For instance, people suffering a manic episode often are in a highly elevated mood, seeming to experience life with an intense euphoria. However, it generally takes little frustration to shift this elated enthusiasm to irritability or tears, which suggests that mania may be closer to depression than initially seems apparent. In fact, it has been suggested by a number of theorists that mania is a defense against depression, that it is an attempt to ward off depressive feelings through feverish activity.

Cognitively, manic individuals characteristically show wildly inflated self-esteem, believing themselves to be capable of great accomplishments or possessed of exceptional talent. Manic individuals act on their high opinion of themselves. They behave recklessly, involving themselves in unwise business deals or sexual liaisons, wasting large sums of money on shopping sprees or gambling. When experiencing a manic episode, individuals often have a decreased need for sleep, sometimes going for days without rest.

Within the affective disorders, there are two major syndromes: major depression (or unipolar depression as it has traditionally been called) and bipolar disorder (or manic-depressive disorder). In unipolar depression, an individual experiences one or more episodes of depression without ever experiencing an episode of mania. Approximately half of the people who suffer major depression will undergo only one episode of depression: Their first episode will be their last. In general, even without intervention, most people will recover from an occurrence of unipolar depression within 3 to 6 months.

In bipolar disorder, an individual experiences both manic and depressive episodes. In rare cases, an individual vacillates between manic and depressive episodes without an intervening period of normal functioning. More often, there are periods of normality interspersed between the manic and/or depressive episodes. There is no separate diagnostic category for persons who experience only manic episodes; this occurs only rarely. In such instances, an assumption is made that the person will ultimately experience a depressive episode, and a diagnosis of bipolar disorder will be made.

Of the two disorders, bipolar disorder is the more serious and debilitating. People with bipolar disorder, in comparison with those with unipolar disorder, experience more episodes, and their interepisode functioning is worse. Further, such people are more likely to have serious alcohol abuse problems and attempt and commit suicide at a higher rate than persons with unipolar disorder.

Depression has been referred to as the common cold of mental illness. Around 10% of the males and perhaps 22% of the females living in the United States will at some point in their lives experience an episode of major depression. This one-to-two ratio has been found in many different cultures, in Europe and Africa as well as North America. (There are, however, a few notable exceptions such as the Amish in Pennsylvania.) It has been hypothesized that more women experience depression than men because it is more socially acceptable for women to respond to negative life experiences with passive, depressive symptoms. Men may be less likely to experience or express depressive symptoms because they may receive more social rejection (or less social reinforcement) than women for acting depressed. Instead, men may respond to stressful events more actively, with substance abuse (e.g., alcoholism) or antisocial behavior.

Bipolar disorder is much less common than unipolar disorder; slightly less than 1% percent of the U.S. population will experience bipolar disorder at some point in their lives. Unlike unipolar disorder, bipolar disorder occurs with approximately the same frequency in men as in women. Both unipolar and bipolar disorder tend to run in families, though bipolar disorder probably has a significantly larger genetic component than unipolar disorder.

At present, the nature of the genetic mechanisms underlying the affective disorders is not clear. It is known, however, that in both mania and depression there are abnormalities in the level of neurotransmitters in the brain.

Beyond the possibility noted that mania is a defense against depression, there has been relatively little psychological theorizing about the causes of mania and bipolar disorder. This is not the case with unipolar depression, for which a number of etiological theories have been developed. From a Freudian perspective, depression is viewed as the punishment an overly punitive superego inflicts on the ego for the ego's failure to properly treat a lost love. The superego's harshness is seen also as a means of preventing the ego's feelings of anger and aggression from being expressed (Freud, 1917).

From a more behavioral perspective, Lewinsohn (1974) has hypothesized that depression is the result of a low rate of response-contingent reinforcement, caused by either a lack of social skills or a deficient environment, which results in the person experiencing behavioral extinction. Rather than being a function of the rate of reinforcement, Seligman et al. (Abramson, Seligman, & Teasdale, 1978) believe that it is the individual's lack of control over his or her environment and the attributions that this person makes about this lack of control that results in depression. Seligman believes that a lack of control that is attributed to causes that are internal (the self), global (some general quality), and stable (not likely to change) will result in depression.

Most theorists believe that the cognitions that depressed persons experience are a consequence of depression. Beck (1967), however, believes that negative cognitions and thought patterns are the cause of unipolar depression rather than a consequence of depression. He has proposed that individuals prone to depression have negative schema that are activated by stress. Once activated, the individual tends to interpret his or her experience in the worst possible light, using errors of logic (e.g., drawing sweeping conclusions based on one or two events) to do so. This negative interpretation occurs even when more plausible explanations for experiences are available; the person chooses his or her explanation on the basis of its negativity rather than its validity.

From the viewpoint of the individual working with children, what may be most important regarding affective disorders is an awareness of and ability to recognize signs of childhood affective disorders. It should be noted first that it is rare for children, particularly prior to puberty, to experience manic episodes. When a young child exhibits overactive behavior that appears manic, it is probably more appropriately considered a symptom of hyperactivity. (It is also possible for overactive behavior to result from an endocrine dysfunction.) Depressivelike syndromes, on the other hand, have been reported in children 3 years of age and younger. The symptoms of these syndromes vary in part as a function of age; the older a depressed child, the

more closely his or her symptoms will parallel those of adults. Consequently, this discussion will focus on the symptoms of younger school-aged children (i.e., approximately ages 6 to 14).

A major distinction between depressed children and adults is that children, in contrast to adults, seldom seek help or complain about feelings of depression. Instead, they may become apathetic regarding school or socially withdrawn, sometimes preferring to remain in their rooms at home rather than playing with friends. They may make vague physical complaints about head or stomach pains, seem overly self-conscious, and cry inexplicably. Older children may see themselves as bad kids—incompetent in school and unworthy of the love of adults or the friendship of other children. Some, but not all, depressed children may simply look sad, particularly in their facial expressions, for extended periods of time with little apparent fluctuation in mood. Overall, a child will usually exhibit only some of the symptoms noted, and the symptom pattern may vary across a period of weeks.

Such symptoms are expressed in what is essentially a passive manner. Though there is far from universal agreement on the issue, certain professionals believe that in some instances children may express depression through aggressive misbehavior. While it is usually difficult to distinguish between genuine misbehavior and misbehavior that is an expression of so-called masked depression, children who are acting out as a symptom of depression often are more responsive to firm (but not overly authoritarian) limit-setting than children who are misbehaving for other reasons.

A technique that is sometimes useful in determining if a child is feeling depressed is to ask the child where he or she stands on a scale of 1 to 10, with 10 being children who are very happy, and 1 being children who are very sad. (This technique presupposes a certain level of cognitive development in the child.) On an informal level, there are several things a teacher can do for a depressed child. With children who appear apathetic and low in self-esteem, it may be useful to set lower standards for praising their accomplishments in school, or to praise them for their efforts in addition to their finished products. It is important, however, to strike a balance between setting criteria that allow an increase in praise and avoiding reinforcement of the child's symptoms. The latter may lead to the child using the symptoms as an excuse to perform at a level significantly below his or her ability level. Children may also respond to messages from the teacher that suggest that the child is an important, valued person. Overall, it is important to make sure that such interactions with the child are honest and nonpatronizing; if it is not possible to do something in this manner, it is probably better not to do it.

If a teacher feels that a child needs more assistance than the teacher has the training or experience to render, there is a wide range of professional treatments for depression, many with proven efficacy (though the majority of treatment research has focused on adults rather than children). These treatments range from medication to psychotherapy and behavior therapy. Tricyclic antidepressants are often prescribed in the treatment of unipolar depression. Less frequently prescribed because of the danger of side effects are monoamine oxidase-inhibitors. Both of these classes of drugs are known to work at the neurotransmitter level. Lithium carbonate is usually prescribed for bipolar disorder in adults; it has an effect on both the depressive and manic symptoms, and is probably the treatment of choice for bipolar disorder. The exact mechanism for lithium's action is unknown. In a few instances, lithium may be used to successfully treat adult unipolar depression.

The variety of psychological and behavioral therapies used in the treatment of depression is vast. Techniques such as social skills training, modification of negative cognitions through cognitive restructuring and reality testing, and the teaching of self-control strategies (to name just a few) have been used. Treatment may occur individually or in groups, and many of the therapies have been empirically tested, often with results supporting their value as treatments for depression.

## REFERENCES

Abramson, L. Y., Seligman, M. E. P., & Teasdale, J. D. (1978). Learned helplessness in humans: Critique and reformulation. *Journal of Abnormal Psychology, 87,* 49–74.

American Psychiatric Association. (1980). *Diagnostic and statistical manual of mental disorders* (3rd ed.). Washington, DC: Author.

Beck, A. T. (1967). *Depression: Clinical, experimental, and theoretical aspects.* New York: Harper & Row.

Freud, S. (1976). Mourning and melancholia. In J. Strachey (Ed. and Trans.), *The complete psychological works.* New York: Norton. (Original work published 1917).

Lewinsohn, P. M. (1974). A behavioral approach to depression. In R. J. Friedman & M. Katz (Eds.), *The psychology of depression: Contemporary theory and research.* Washington, DC: Winston-Wiley.

BAHR WEISS
*University of North Carolina,
Chapel Hill*

**CHILDHOOD NEUROSIS**
**CHILDHOOD PSYCHOSIS**
**DEPRESSION**
**EMOTIONAL DISORDERS**

# AFFECTIVE EDUCATION

Affective education promotes emotional development by educating students about attitudes, thoughts, values, feelings, beliefs, and interpersonal relationships (Morse, Ardizzone, Macdonald, & Pasick, 1980). Through it, students are provided experiences in which cognitive, motor, social, and emotional elements are interrelated and balanced (Morse et al., 1980), leading to the enhancement of self-concept (what one is) and self-esteem (how one feels about what one is) and the development of social skills essential to meeting basic needs in a satisfying and socially responsible way (Wood, 1982). Affective education helps youngsters to establish value systems, morals, independence, a sense of responsibility, and self-direction (Morse et al., 1980; Wood, 1982). Although the need for affective education is not limited to students in special education programs, it is especially relevant for them because social skills are essential for success in mainstream placements.

Although most educators agree on the importance of affective education and understand its general purpose, there is less agreement among them on the specific objectives or how best to realize them. In part, this ambiguity derives from the persistent difficulty of defining such terms as self-concept, self-esteem, affect, and attitude. The general lack of systematic programming should not, however, be an indication that affective goals are unimportant (Francescani, 1982). Morse et al. (1980) have argued that affective education represents "a new effort and serious obligation" and is "an essential component of special education as it is formulated under the mandate of Public Law 94-142" (p. 2). Essentially, all children deserve the right to more "systematic assistance with their affective growth" (Morse et al., 1980, p. 6).

Nonetheless, affective goals are often subordinated to academic objectives, as the following example (Reinert, 1982) illustrates. Ann, age 10, was known by her teacher to display many different types of inappropriate behavior in the classroom. She talked out loud, pushed and shoved other children, would not share, and cried for no apparent reason. During evaluation, it was discovered that Ann was reading and spelling on a kindergarten level and her arithmetic skills were two years below grade level. In addition, Ann's parents were divorced and she was often absent from school because she had to babysit for her younger sister while her mother worked. She seldom came to school appropriately groomed or attired. Ann was either unwilling or unable to speak to adults or peers in a normal, conversational tone of voice; she had a poor self-concept and relatively few friends. Upon staffing, her Individual Education Plan (IEP) prescribed 60 minutes in a resource room for remedial help in arithmetic and reading skills, but no emphasis on affective problems. Although affective needs should be a part of an IEP, they are seldom systematically delineated.

Systematic instruction in the affective domain is especially important for emotionally handicapped students like Ann. Emotionally handicapped students include those who have not learned essential skills for social and emotional growth, or how to control their behavior in times of stress, how to communicate their feelings and needs in a socially acceptable manner, how to bring interpersonal problems to a satisfying solution, or how to encounter others without conflict (Francescani, 1982). It is difficult to imagine how a student with deficits as pervasive as these can survive in an environment for which he or she is so poorly equipped. Yet it is in the highly socialized classroom world in which affective education must occur, and most proponents recognize the need to integrate affective learning into everyday classroom life.

Integrated affective learning lies at one end of the intrinsic/extrinsic dimension of affective education. Morse et al. (1980) defined this dimension as the extent "to which (affective education) grows naturally out of what is going on in the educational life space versus how much is added as a special function" (p. 16). Ideally, affective lessons should derive naturally from school activities, using materials already in the curriculum in harmony with the philosophy of the program (Morse et al., 1980; Schlindler, 1982). Teachers should capitalize on naturally occurring opportunities spending time motivating the uninvolved student, resolving peer conflicts, encouraging a reluctant student to join in group activity, or trying to enliven a depressed student. A teacher should not rely on an added-on or extrinsic curriculum to accomplish affective goals.

Affective educators stress the need for developing empathetic relationships between teachers and students in order to convey fundamental human relationships where the "sense of relationship dominates authoritarianism" (Morse et al. 1980, p. 15). Teachers and students share responsibilities, goals, and rules for living together (Morse et al., 1980; Reinert, 1982; Sarason, 1971).

However, to expect all teachers to act at all times with the spontaneity, sensitivity, and astuteness that the ideal intrinsic approach requires is unrealistic. This expectation belies the human limitations of teachers and assumes a degree of training rare if not unknown in teacher preparation programs. Approximations to this intrinsic ideal may be found in curricular approaches to affective education and in strategies such as role playing and sociodrama (Wood, 1982) that allow for the exploration of new solutions to familiar problems.

Among the most popular and widely used curricula is *DUSO* (Developing Understanding of Self and Others). It is designed to be used by teachers or counselors as an add-on to the academic curriculum. Throughout the school year, eight themes (e.g., Developing Self-Concept, Understanding Peers) are explored through listening, modeling, discussion, and role-playing activities. Everyday problems of classroom life are described through pictures, stories, and puppetry, and solutions are discussed, modeled, and role played. The elements of the lessons are carefully prescribed and the materials are attractive and engaging to a primary-aged audience. Although the curriculum is extrinsic, it does provide a structure through which problems

may be simulated and the values of alternative solutions weighed.

Only one of many such curricula, DUSO is singled out here for illustration only. For more complete treatments of the available curricula, see Morse et al. (1980) or Reinert (1980). Suffice it to say that they are diverse in objectives, activities, and the sophistication of their intended audiences. It is difficult to compare extrinsic programs because the materials themselves provide content and continuity in their individual components (Reinert, 1982). Most seek to enhance self-concept, encourage positive socialization, recognize and understand basic feelings, and model appropriate responses to given situations through practice and role playing. Few have substantial data bases.

Affective education has grown out of the school mental health movement, but has not yet evolved into a well-formulated program intrinsic to the ongoing school process (Morse, 1980). Instead it tends to be relegated to the periphery of the basic curriculum. If affective education is to realize its potential, deliberate efforts must replace the haphazard, casual, and indirect approaches currently in operation (Morse et al., 1980).

## REFERENCES

Francescani, C. (1982). M A R C: An affective curriculum for emotionally disturbed adolescents. *Teaching Exceptional Children, 14*, 217–222.

Morse, W. C., Ardizzone, J., Macdonald, C., & Pasick, P. (1980). *Affective education for special children and youth.* Reston, VA: Council for Exceptional Children.

Reinert, H. R. (1980). *Children in conflict* (2nd ed.). St. Louis: Mosby.

Reinert, H. R. (1982). The development of affective skills. In T. L. Miller & E. E. Davis (Eds.), *The mildly handicapped student* (pp. 421–451). New York: Grune & Stratton.

Sarason, S. B. (1971). *The culture of schools and the problem of change.* Boston: Allyn & Bacon.

Schlindler, P. J. (1982). Affective growth in the preschool years. *Teaching Exceptional Children, 14*, 226–232.

Wood, F. H. (1982). Affective education and social skills training. *Teaching Exceptional Children, 14*, 212–216.

LOUISE H. WERTH
PAUL T. SINDELAR
*Florida State University*

**DEVELOPING UNDERSTANDING OF SELF AND OTHERS**
**SELF-CONCEPT**
**SOCIAL SKILLS**

# AFRICA, SPECIAL EDUCATION IN

Special education is relatively new in most African countries. The need for a major commitment to special education by African countries to provide handicapped learners with a variety of programs and services has been recognized for some time now (Anderson, 1983; Joy, 1979; Shown, 1980; UNESCO, 1979, 1986), though progress toward realization has been slow and halting. The UNESCO definition of special education is one that generally adheres to western European and American expectations. Thus the Nigerian National Policy on Education (1981) has defined special education as "education of children and adults who have learning difficulties as a result of not coping with the normal school organization and methods" (Nigerian Year Book, 1984). In Nigeria's Plateau State (Nigeria), special education is defined as including "the course and content of education, including specially defined classroom, material, and equipment designed to meet the unique needs of a handicapped child" (Shown, 1986).

Despite such broad perspectives, special education in Africa is more likely to be concerned with children who are physically and sensorially handicapped rather than suffering from mild cognitive deficits. Children with more severe cognitive deficits are likely to be cared for in other contexts than those of formal special education. Expressing this fact, Shown observes: "To acquire education in the modern sense one must possess and make full use of all his senses. This is beside being fully mobile" (Shown, in press). Sambo (1981) has pointed out "when one loses two or more of these senses, then the acqusition of education in the normal sense becomes a problem entirely different from those problems normally encountered in the acquistion of education. For such a person, there is a need for a viable alternative for educating him."

Anderson (1973) observed that the majority of African teachers were not familiar with the special techniques and methods required to assist handicapped students to become educationally competent. Furthermore, as Shown (1986) has pointed out, a lack of clear educational objectives has hampered the delivery of educational services to handicapped learners.

Because most African nations have faced major fiscal difficulties for many years, improvements in special education have been difficult to achieve. Nations like Nigeria have, however, made serious efforts at both federal and local levels to teach the elements of special education in teacher training institutions (Nigeria Federal Ministry, 1977). Nigeria has established training programs at the universities of Jos and Ibadan. These universities provide training and research on scientific education of the handicapped at undergraduate and graduate levels.

In most places in Africa, there are not likely to be clearly defined admission policies for the handicapped or age limits for education of the handicapped as it now exists in Africa. It is not uncommon, therefore, to find a handicapped adult in a special education class with much younger students. Furthermore, the personnel providing special education services are likely to come from the middle or lower ranks of school staffs rather than the higher. The burden of education for handicapped students is thus frequently carried by less well-trained aides and members of the local community, rather than by highly skilled teachers.

Special education teachers working in regular school settings have been reported to be facing emotional and psychological problems (Joy, 1972). They may face neglect and even hostility on the part of other teachers who resent having handicapped students and special education teachers in regular schools. Also, nonspecialist teachers are often resentful of the fact that special education teachers receive extra pay.

Many of the special education services provided in Africa on a noninstitutional basis must be on an itinerant basis because of the scarcity of educational facilities able to serve handicapped students. A dearth of itinerant teachers has limited the extent and effectiveness of such education. Recent efforts have been made in certain African countries to mainstream handicapped students. Thus the Federal Ministry of Information, Lagos, Nigeria (1977) mandates that handicapped school children, where possible, should be mainstreamed along with their nonhandicapped peers. Some African educators have expressed disagreement with this policy (Shown, 1980). There is concern about the dangers that the physical hazards of African terrain may pose for mainstreamed handicapped students who are not carefully supervised, e.g., most parts of Nigeria have dangerous structures and hazards such as rocks, forests, and rivers. Also, the application of mainstreaming policies in Africa places an inordinate burden on most handicapped students unless they are able to use the same materials as their nonhandicapped peers or can be assisted to achieve comparable levels of attainment; this is difficult to achieve in light of the current dearth of trained professionals and the lack of proper facilities and materials. As UNESCO has pointed out (1979), mere physical placement in a mainstreamed school environment is not an answer to providing services to handicapped African children. Provisions at African colleges for handicapped students are essentially nonexistent. There are no ramps, suitable steps elevators, or toilet facilities with special accommodations.

Despite efforts to improve the education of the handicapped, the outlook of Africans respecting the needs of handicapped students and adults is not such as to raise hopes for serious concern regarding their transition into productive roles in society. As Shown has observed regarding the largest nation in Africa, "Nigerians are immensely practical people caluing something or someone only if it is seen to be economically useful. With this in mind, the outlook for the handicapped would seem to be bleak" (Shown, in press).

## REFERENCES

Anderson, E. (1983). *The disabled school child. A study in integration*. Open University Set Book, Jos, Nigeria.

Federal Government of Nigeria. (1984). *Nigerian year book*: Lagos, Nigeria: Author.

Joy, D. C. (1979, August 9). Experiment with blind children. *New Nigerian*.

Nigeria Federal Ministry of Information. (1977). *The republic of nigeria national policy on education*, Lagos, Nigeria: Author.

Sambo, E. W. (1981, April). *What is special education*? Paper presented at the workshop on the integration of elements of special education into teachers education curriculum in plateau state, University of Jos, Jos, Nigeria.

Shown, D. G. (1980). *A study of effectiveness of mainstreaming of visually handicapped children in Plateau State of Nigeria with a view toward determining quality education for these children.* Jos, Nigeria: University of Jos.

Shown, D. G. (1986, April) *Integrating handicapped children in Plateau State*. Paper presented at the workshop on the integration of elements of special education into teachers education curriculum in plateau state, University of Jos, Jos, Nigeria.

UNESCO. (1979, October 15–20). Expert meetings of special education, UNESCO headquarters, Paris. *Final Report*.

UNESCO. (1981, July 20–31). *Sub-regional seminar on planning for special education*. Nairobi, Kenya.

UNESCO (1986, April). *Expert meeting on special education*. Plateau State, Nigeria: University of Jos.

DAKUM SHOWN
*University of Jos, Nigeria*

**NIGERIA, SPECIAL EDUCATION IN**


# AGE-APPROPRIATE CURRICULUM

An age-appropriate curriculum is a special-education curriculum that consists of activities that are matched to both the students' chronological ages and their developmental or skill levels. This match has been difficult to achieve, especially for older trainable and severely handicapped students who continue to function on preschool levels. The older students with severe handicaps often need continued training in fine motor, cognitive, and language skills, but also need to acquire skills that can be used immediately and will transfer to later community and vocational placements (Drew, Logan, & Hardman, 1984).

Public law 94–142 has mandated an appropriate education for all handicapped students, but wide differences remain when defining this term. The justification for using an age-appropriate education lies in the principle of normalization, which Nirje (1979) has defined as follows: "Making available to all mentally retarded people patterns of life and conditions of everyday living which are as close as possible to the regular circumstances of society" (p. 73). Although it may appear unrealistic to teach age-appropriate behaviors to students with severe developmental delays, Larsen and Jackson (1981) argue that this is the mission of special education: "No, we will not be completely successful (but) . . . our goals for students will stress skills relevant to the general culture, rather than skills that have a proven value only in special-education classrooms" (p. 1).

Our current knowledge of developmental milestones, task analysis procedures, and behavior modification principles can be used in adopting this approach if we also examine the "age-appropriateness" of the materials, skills, activities, environments, and reinforcers used during instruction. For example, in learning visual discrimination of shapes, elementary-age students may use form boards and shape sorters, while older students use community signs and mosaic art activities. For other skills, calculators may be used instead of number lines; colored clothing can be sorted rather than colored cubes; and the assembly of vocational products may replace peg boards and beads (Bates, Renzaglia, & Wehman, 1981).

Because there are many skills that older severely handicapped youths will never acquire (e.g., reading a newspaper and buying groceries), the curriculum focuses on those abilities that can be learned (e.g., reading survival signs or following directions). To identify these skills for each group of students, Brown et al. (1979) employ an ecological inventory approach listing the environments and subenvironments where the students currently (or will eventually) function. An inventory of the activities in each environment and a listing of skills needed to participate in those activities provide the framework for selecting curriculum goals. In this approach, for example, the basic skill of matching pictures leads to finding grooming items in a drugstore, and identifying different foods leads to ordering in a fast-food restaurant.

Classroom design and decor also should reflect the chronological age of the students. For older youths, pictures of teen activities and movie celebrities are more age-appropriate decorations than cartoon characters. Since PL 94–142, many special-education classrooms have moved into secondary buildings, opening up opportunities to use age-appropriate training sites such as home economics rooms.

Severely handicapped students have extremely slow learning rates and much difficulty in generalizing learned skills to new situations. Therefore, their education must include the teaching of critical skill clusters and opportunities to practice functional skills in natural settings such as sheltered workshops, supermarkets, and public transportation. For a more detailed description of curricular approaches to teaching functional skill clusters see Guess and Noonan (1982).

**REFERENCES**

Bates, P., Renzaglia, A., & Wehman, P. (1981). Characteristics of an appropriate education for severely and profoundly handicapped students. *Education & Training of the Mentally Retarded, 16,* 142–149.

Brown, L., Branston, M. B., Homre-Nietupski, S., Pumpian, I., Certo, N., & Grunewald, L. (1979). A strategy for developing chronological age appropriate and functional curriculum content for severely handicapped adolescents and young adults. *Journal of Special Education, 13,* 81–90.

Drew, C. J., Logan, D. R., Hardman, M. L. (1984). *Mental Retardation: A Life Cycle Approach* (3rd ed.). St. Louis: Times Mirror/Mosby.

Guess, D., & Noonan, M. J. (1982). Curricula and instructional procedures for severely handicapped students. *Focus on Exceptional Children, 14,* 9–10.

Larsen, L. A., & Jackson, L. B. (1981). Chronological age in the design of educational programs for severely and profoundly impaired students. *PRISE Reporter, 13,* 1–2.

Nirje, B. (1979). Changing patterns in residential services for the mentally retarded. In E. L. Meyen (Ed.), *Basic Readings in the Study of Exceptional Children and Youth.* Denver: Love.

KATHERINE D. COUTURIER
*Pennsylvania State University*

ADAPTIVE BEHAVIOR
FUNCTIONAL INSTRUCTION
FUNCTIONAL SKILLS TRAINING
MENTAL RETARDATION

## AGE AT ONSET

Age at onset refers to the point in an individual's life when a specific condition began. Age at onset can be compared with a child's chronological age to establish the duration of a condition. It is a significant variable in making diagnostic judgments and prognostic statements. Within a school setting, age at onset is typically a consideration in: (1) understanding behavioral disorders; (2) understanding the prognosis for adequate intellectual and learning performance in children with neurologic and chronic medical conditions; and (3) assessing and programming for children with learning disabilities.

In the assessment of behavioral difficulties, it is important to have an adequate history of the disorder, including an estimate of when the child began experiencing difficulties. Knowledge of age at onset allows one to assess the relationship between behavioral changes and other significant occurrences in the child's life (e.g., Did difficulties start when a sibling was born? When the child entered school?). Different psychopathologic conditions have different histories, ages at onset, and significance. For example, infrequent nightmares are not pathognomonic, in fact, they are normal in a three-year-old child (Lowrey, 1978). Infantile autism, by definition, has an age of onset prior to 30 months of age (*Diagnostic and Statistical Manual of Mental Disorders*, 1980).

Age of onset is an important variable in understanding outcome in brain damage. Though animal research suggested that brain damage sustained early in life would have less deleterious effects than that sustained later in life, recent evidence suggests that this conclusion is an over simplification and fails to address issues such as length of recovery, type of task used for assessment, and the pathologic process involved (St. James-Roberts, 1981). Early diffuse lesions often result in pervasive developmental difficulties (Witelson, 1977). Early focal deficits result in less pervasive and more subtle deficits such as those seen in learning disabilities (Dennis, Lovett, & Wiegel-Crump, 1981). Brain damage incurred during adolescence has more similarities to the consequences seen in adults than those seen in children. Classic language and visual spatial disorders are seen with lateralized left and right hemisphere lesions, respectively. Some research suggests that when a very young child has a medical disorder that results in diffuse central nervous system damage, the cognitive consequences may be more pronounced than if age of onset were later in life (Wilkening & Golden 1982).

Age at onset is an important consideration in the assessment of learning disabilities. Some research suggests that the type of difficulty discovered when a child is assessed depends on when in the course of development the child is evaluated (Satz, Taylor, Friel, & Fletcher, 1978).

### REFERENCES

American Psychiatric Association (1980). *Diagnostic and statistical manual of mental disorders* (3rd ed.). Washington, DC: Author.

Dennis, M., Lovett, M. & Wiegel-Crump, C. A. (1981). Written language acquisition after left or right hemidecortication in infancy. *Brain and Language, 12,* 54–91.

Lowrey, G. H. (1978). *Growth and development of children.* New York: Year Book Medical.

St. James-Roberts, I. (1981). A reinterpretation of hemispherectomy data without functional plasticity of the brain. *Brain and Language, 13,* 31–53.

Satz, P., Taylor, H. G., Friel, J., & Fletcher, J. M. (1978). Some developmental and predictive precursors of reading disabilities: A six year follow-up. In A. L. Benton & D. Pearl (Eds.), *Dyslexia: An appraisal of current knowledge* (pp. 315–347). New York: Oxford University Press.

Wilkening, G. N., & Golden, C. J. (1982). Pediatric neuropsychology: Status, theory and research. In P. Karoly, J. J. Steffan, & D. J. O'Grady (Eds.), *Child health psychology: Concepts and issues* (pp. 119–153). New York: Pergamon.

Witelson, S. F. (1977). Early hemisphere specialization and interhemisphere plasticity: An empirical and theoretical review. In S. J. Segalowitz & F. A. Graber (Eds.), *Language development and neurological theory* (pp. 213–287). New York: Academic.

GRETA N. WILKENING
*Children's Hospital, Denver, Colorado*

ASSESSMENT
MEDICAL HISTORY
MENTAL STATUS EXAM

# AGGRESSION

Aggression may be defined as an action that causes or has the potential to cause discomfort (physical or psychological) to someone else, or destruction to property. A second dimension of aggression is the intention behind the action. Injury or destruction resulting from the accidental behavior of others is not viewed as aggression, whereas actions intended to cause harm are viewed as aggression even though they may not culminate in injury or destruction.

The broader outlines of the concept of aggression are easily recognized, but precise definition and measurement are more difficult to achieve. For example, how does one reliably judge the intentionality of an act? How does one distinguish among assertiveness (an adaptive and often desirable attribute) competitiveness (sometimes necessary for success), and aggressiveness? Hollandsworth (1977) differentiates aggression from assertiveness by emphasizing the former's threatening, punitive, and coercive qualities.

Also noteworthy is the fact that aggression is often correlated with other disordered behavior patterns. It is frequently associated with hyperactivity and is also related to excessive distractability and impulsivity. For example, Messer and Brodzinsky (1979) found positive correlations between impulsive cognitive tempo and both aggression and lack of concern for the consequences of aggression. Children's aggression against others may be expressed as tantrums, verbal abuse, teasing, opposition (doing the opposite of what one is requested to do), and physical assault. Several categories of high-frequency behaviors that are often exhibited as aggression have been compiled after extensive observation (Patterson, Cobb, & Ray, 1972; Patterson, Reid, Jones, & Conger, 1975). These include yelling, harmful physical acts (against others), destructive behavior (of property), and the use of negative commands and threats to force compliance.

Each of these examples represents an area of behavior that is exhibited by all youngsters, but the extreme differences in frequency of the behavior tip the scale toward the aggressive rather than the nonaggressive child. Thus aggressive behavior is a common and normal part of the behavioral repertoire of children, and males in almost all cultures exhibit more aggressive behavior than females. The aggressive child label is assigned only if the frequency and/or intensity of the behavior becomes excessive (relative to age, sex, form, and culture). Aggressive children also continue to exhibit aversive behaviors at a much later age than do normal children.

Explanations of aggressive behavior can be classified into five theoretical perspectives: (1) ethological/biological, (2) psychodynamic, (3) drive theory, (4) social learning theory, and (5) social-cognitive perspective. Aggression as an instinct is a popular notion; its basic premise is that aggression stems from an innate fighting instinct (Lorenz, 1966). Aggressive energy is thought to build up over time and must eventually be released directly or indirectly. The evidence for causative evolutionary or genetic factors is weak, whereas support for experiential factors is compelling. Although certain species can be selectively bred to achieve more aggressive strains, for humans it is far more likely that environmental histories determine specific aggressive acts and targets (Simmel, Hahn, & Walters, 1983).

Biological approaches hold that aggression can be influenced by genetic factors (Olweus, 1980), biochemical factors (hormonal processes), or electrical activity in the central nervous system (Moyer, 1976). The extent of this influence varies, but most agree that the expression of biological tendencies is very much a function of the qualifying effects of the environment. Rather than providing a sufficient cause of aggression, it is more accurate to view biological factors as one of a multiple set of determinants (Parke & Slaby, 1983).

Freud believed that aggression is a basic instinctual force that creates a need for aggressive behavior. Thus aggression is viewed as a motivating force that causes behavior and may be expressed in either positive or negative ways. The demands of the environment and the controlling mechanisms of the ego and superego determine whether the expression of aggression is manifested in socially acceptable or unacceptable ways. A common example of a behavior having aggressive overtones (but one that is socially acceptable) is participation in contact sports. Occasionally excesses of aggression that are viewed as beyond the bounds of a game bring sanctions against the overly zealous competitor. In recent years the psychodynamic view of aggression has suffered diminishing influence, largely because of its untestable hypotheses.

The frustration-aggression hypothesis has been an historically important contender in explaining aggression. Frustration is hypothesized to be the cause of aggression (Dollard, Doob, Miller, Mowrer, & Sears, 1939; Berkowitz, 1962). Frustration, which is the result of the blocking or thwarting of some goal-directed activity, induces an aggressive drive that can only be reduced through the expression of aggressive behavior. Although it is certainly true that frustration can produce aggression, this explanation is far too simplistic to explain the myriad instances of aggression. Additional research has shown that aggression is not the inevitable consequence of frustration and that the frustration-aggression hypothesis has limited utility in accounting for either the onset or maintenance of aggressive behavior (Achenbach, 1982).

The most comprehensive analysis of aggression has been achieved by researchers applying social learning theory. According to this perspective, acquiring aggressive behavior is a function of learning from models, the child's reinforcement history, and current contingencies of reinforcement that maintain aggression (Bandura, 1973). Social learning theory, though heavily rooted in fundamental operant learning principles, also uses cognitive processes such as thoughts, perceptions, and attitudes. The integration of behavioral and cognitive concepts is clearly seen in Bandura's (1977) description of observational learning that includes attentional, retention, reproduction, and motivational phases. The last phase emphasizes the significance of reinforcing both the model's behavior and the observer's imitation of the model's response.

Based on research guided by social learning theory, Bandura (1973) and Goldstein (1983) have summarized major generalizations regarding the acquisition, instigation, and maintenance of aggression. It is well established that children can learn aggressive responses from live or filmed models, and from adults, peers, or cartoon characters; they are also more likely to imitate aggressive models who have high social status and who either receive no punishment or are reinforced for their behavior. Further, when specific or generalized imitation of aggression goes unpunished or is rewarded, a child will be more likely to engage in that behavior. Aversive stimulation in the form of taunts or threats, or the removal of salient reinforcers, may also evoke aggressive behavior.

Once aggression has become a regular aspect of one's behavioral repertoire, it will be perpetuated to the extent that it continues to be reinforced. Aggression can also be maintained through mental processes that serve to justify one's behavior. Paradoxically, some uses of corporal punishment can increase the probability of future aggressive behavior (Axelrod & Apsche, 1983).

The more recent social-cognitive perspective, though not fully formulated, holds much promise for the study and understanding of aggression. This model (Dodge, 1980; Dodge & Frame, 1982) focuses on social judgments and interpretations of social cues. It calls attention to the attributions and inferences that are made about the motives of others. Cognitive mediators of aggression may affect how a child first determines which social cues are relevant and then evaluates those cues to interpret a peer's intentions. Other internally mediated events involve considering alternative responses to the situation, determining when to apply one's personal response rules, and deciding on the optimal reponse given the costs and benefits of various solutions. Therefore, this view of aggression seeks to reveal the cognitive and attributional underpinnings of personal decisions regarding the expression of aggressive behavior.

Approaches to the control of aggression vary according to one's theoretical persuasion. Psychodynamic interpretations of aggression recommend that the child be helped to express aggression in constructive ways. The concept of catharsis is critical to this view. Catharsis is the dissi-

pation of built-up aggression that results from fantasy activities that permit one to vicariously express aggressive impulses (watching violent television programs or painting aggressive themes), or from the psychodynamic processes of displacement and sublimation. Building trust, communicating total acceptance of the child, and creating a permissive, noncompetitive classroom environment are also recommended as key elements for fostering insight into unconscious aggressive wishes. Empirical support for the efficacy of these approaches has not been shown, and there is some evidence that such approaches may actually increase aggressive propensities (Lefkowitz, et al., 1977).

Procedures referred to as "psychoeducational" are distinctive for their focus on cognitive and affective contributions to behavior. The premise of most of the literature and programs that apply psychoeducational methods is that cognitive awareness, feelings about aggression, and perceptions of others will influence the nature of one's behavior (Fagan, Long, & Stevens, 1975; Rezmierski, Knoblock, & Bloom, 1982). Through structured training experiences that focus on problem-solving techniques for managing aggression, the aggressive child's perception of aggression and exercise of self-control can be improved.

Extensions of the psychoeducational approach have centered on the training of explicit skills for achieving self-control over aggressive behavior (Fagan & Long, 1979; Rich, Beck, & Coleman, 1982). The self-control curriculum of Fagan and Long (1979) teaches skill clusters such as anticipating response consequences, managing frustration, inhibition, and delay, and relaxation. A variety of strategies are used to teach these skills, including many used in cognitive-behavior modification (Mahoney, 1974). Techniques for interventions with both groups and individual children have been developed. Research confirms that aggression can be decreased by altering a child's cognitive strategies and affective states (Goldstein, 1983).

Interventions based on social learning theory are used extensively and include most behavior modification techniques. All social learning strategies seek to modify the child's current social environment (Bandura, 1973; Patternson et al., 1975). The initial step in any intervention is to operationalize the offending behavior and determine its frequency. Then one or a combination of intervention strategies may be used.

Commonly used procedures include modeling or role playing nonaggressive behavior in situations likely to elicit aggressive responses. Of course, interventions frequently involve reinforcement of acceptable alternatives to aggressive behavior in conjunction with extinction procedures or some variation of punishment (presenting an aversive stimulus, response cost, time out, or overcorrection). All of these procedures are predicated on the belief that aggression and nonaggression are learned response patterns.

Behavioral interventional involve not only contingencies designed to eliminate aggressive responses, but also efforts to teach acceptable behavior. Such behavior may include building effective skills of social interaction, as well as cognitive or affective behaviors. These last areas of intervention represent a degree of significant overlap in the techniques being used by today's proponents of social learning theory and the psychoeducational perspective.

The behavioral approaches to aggression, though often effective in reducing aggression, do have some limitations. Two major limitations are a lack of adequate generalization to other environments and maintenance of behavior over time (Kazdin & Frame, 1983). Another difficulty arises when aggressive children elect to respond to the contingencies of the change strategy with counter-control measures of their own. This oppositional one-upmanship has not been adequately addressed.

## REFERENCES

Achenbach, T. M. (1982). *Developmental psychopathology* (2nd ed.). New York: Ronald.

Axelrod, S., & Apsche, J. (Eds.). 1983. *The effect of punishment on human behavior.* New York: Academic.

Bandura, A. (1973). *Aggression: A social learning analysis.* Englewood Cliffs, NJ: Prentice-Hall.

Bandura, A. (1977). *Social learning theory.* Englewood Cliffs, NJ: Prentice-Hall.

Berkowitz, L. (1962). *Aggression: A social psychological analysis.* New York: McGraw-Hill.

Dodge, K. A. (1980). Social cognition and children's aggressive behavior. *Child Development, 51*, 162–170.

Dodge, K. A., & Frame, C. L. (1982). Social cognitive biases and deficits in aggressive boys. *Child Development, 53*, 620–635.

Dollard, J., Doob, L. W., Miller, N. E., Mowrer, O. H., & Sears, R. R. (1939). *Frustration and aggression.* New Haven, CT: Yale University Press.

Fagan, S. A., & Long, N. J. (1979). A psychoeducational curriculum approach to teaching self-control. *Behavioral Disorders, 4*, 68–82.

Fagan, S. A., Long, N. J., & Stevens, D. J. (1975). *Teaching children self-control.* Columbus, OH: Merrill.

Goldstein, A. P. (Ed.). (1983). *Prevention and control of aggression.* New York: Pergamon.

Hollandsworth, J. G., Jr. (1977). Differentiating assertion and aggression: Some behavioral guidelines. *Behavior Therapy, 8*, 347–352.

Kazdin, A. E., & Frame, C. (1983). Aggressive behavior and conduct disorders. In R. J. Morris & T. R. Kratochwill (Eds.), *The practice of child therapy* (pp. 167–192). New York: Pergamon.

Lefkowitz, M. M., Eron, L. D., Walder, L. D., & Huesmann, L. R. (1977). *Growing up to be violent: A longitudinal study of the development of aggression.* New York: Pergamon.

Lorenz, K. (1966). *On aggression.* New York: Harcourt, Brace & World.

Mahoney, M. J. (1974). *Cognition and behavior modification.* Cambridge, MA: Ballinger.

Messer, S. B., & Brodzinsky, D. M. (1979). The relation of conceptual tempo to aggression and its control. *Child Development, 50*, 758–766.

Moyer, K. E. (1976). *The psychobiology of aggression.* New York: Harper & Row.

Olweus, D. (1980). Familial and temperamental determinants of aggressive behvior in adolescent boys: A causal analysis. *Developmental Psychology, 16*, 644–666.

Parke, R. D., & Slaby, R. G. (1983). The development of aggression. In P. Mussen & E. M. Heatherington (Eds.), *Handbook of child psychology. Vol. 4. Socialization, personality, and social development* (4th ed.) (pp. 547–641). New York: Wiley.

Patterson, G. R., Cobb, J. A., & Ray, R. S. (1972). Direct intervention in the classroom: A set of procedures for the aggressive child. In F. W. Clark, D. R. Evans, & L. A. Hammerlynck (Eds.), *Implementing behavioral programs in schools and clinics,* pp. 151–201. Champaign, IL: Research Press.

Patterson, G. R., Reid, J. B., Jones, R. R., & Conger, R. E. (1975). *A social learning approach to family intervention: Vol. 1. Families with aggressive children.* Eugene, OR: Castalia.

Rezmiersky, V. E., Knoblock, P., & Bloom, R. B. (1982). The psychoeducational model: Theory and historical perspective. In R. L. McDowell, G. W. Adamson, & F. W. Wood (Eds.), *Teaching emotionally disturbed cildren* (pp. 47–69). Boston: Little, Brown.

Rich, H. L., Beck, M. A., & Coleman, T. W., Jr. (1982). Behavior management: The psychoeducational model. In R. L. McDowell, G. W. Adamson, & F. W. Wood (Eds.), *Teaching emotionally disturbed children* (pp. 131–166). Boston: Little, Brown.

Simmel, E. C., Hahn, M. E., & Walters, J. K. (1983). Synthesis and new directions. In E. C. Simmel, M. E. Hahn, & J. K. Walters (Eds.), *Aggressive behavior: Genetic and neural approaches,* pp. 183–190. Hillsdale, NJ: Erlbaum.

JAMES M. APPLEFIELD
*University of North Carolina,
Wilmington*

COGNITIVE BEHAVIOR THERAPY
CONDUCT DISORDER
SOCIAL LEARNING THEORY

# AGRAPHIA

The *Cyclopedia of Education* (1915) defines agraphia as a disorder of the associations of speech in which there is a partial or complete inability to express ideas by means of written symbols in an individual who had previously acquired this mode of speech expression. Agraphia is often associated with apraxia and with so-called motor aphasia.

Orton (1937) distinguished between motor agraphia and development agraphia, or special writing disability. Orton defined motor agraphia as the loss of ability to write restricted to the motor component of writing. Orton attributed this problem to dysfunction in relevant motor control areas of the brain without accompanying dysfunction in nearby speech functioning areas. Developmental agraphia was said to manifest itself in one of two ways: the first instance characterized by an unusually slow rate of writing; the second characterized by quality of writing. Orton suggested that "shifted sinistrals," or enforced training of the right hand in left-handed children, may result in slow writing. In other cases, the lack of dominant handedness was said to result in writing problems.

Strauss and Werner (1938) suggested that finger agnosia (inability to recognize one's own fingers) may be related to agraphia. Terms such as agraphia have declined in popularity in recent years, partly as a result of a trend toward the use of more educationally relevant orientations (see Hallahan, Kauffman, & Lloyd, 1985, for a historical overview). Recently, deficits in writing performance have been defined and remediated in terms of task-specific behaviors (Mercer, 1979).

## REFERENCES

*Cyclopedia of Education* (1915). New York: Macmillan.

Hallahan, D. P., Kauffman, J. M., & Lloyd, J. W. (1985). *Introduction to learning disabilities*. Englewood Cliffs, NJ: Prentice-Hall.

Mercer, C. (1979). *Children and adolescents with learning disabilities*. Columbus, OH: Merrill.

Orton, S. T. (1937). *Reading, writing, and speech problems in children*. New York: Norton.

Strauss, A. A., & Werner, H. (1938). Deficiency in finger schema in relation to arithmetic disability (finger agnosia and acalculia). *American Journal of Orthopsychiatry, 8*, 719–724.

THOMAS E. SCRUGGS
MARGO A. MASTROPIERI
*Purdue University*

## DYSGRAPHIA
## HANDWRITING

# AIDES TO PSYCHOLINGUISTIC TEACHING

Psycholinguistics focuses on the interactions and psychological functions underlying communication. It attends to the processes by which a speaker or writer emits signals or symbols, and the interpretation of those signals by the receiver (Hammill & Larsen, 1974).

Language programs and assessment techniques have been derived from these psycholinguistic principles and have been applied to education. A basic tenet of psycholinguistics is that language is made up of discrete components that may be identified and measured; further, it is assumed that if one is deficient in a given component, the deficiency can be remediated. This leads to two more assumptions, that a child's failure to learn stems from his or her own weaknesses, and that strengthening weak areas will result in improved classroom learning (Hammill & Larsen, 1974). If these assumptions are valid, programs aimed at mitigating psycholinguistic weaknesses are both necessary and desirable. If the assumptions are invalid, however, a great deal of time and money is being wasted on the application of these programs in educational settings.

In their review of research, Hammill and Larsen (1974) showed that the efficacy of psycholinguistic training had not been adequately demonstrated. They pointed out that many exceptional children are being provided with training programs aimed at increasing their psycholinguistic competencies. On the basis of their review, the authors claimed that it is essential to determine whether the constructs are trainable by present programs. It is also necessary, they said, to identify the children for whom such training would prove worthwhile.

Arter and Jenkins (1977), in their examination of the benefits and prevalence of modality considerations in special education, concluded that research evidence failed to support the practice of basing instructional plans on modality assessment. Thirteen of the 14 studies they reviewed indicated that students were not differentially assisted by instruction congruent with their modality strengths. Further, they stated that "increased efforts in research and development of test instruments and techniques may be warranted but, as far as the practitioner is concerned, advocacy of the (modality) model cannot be justified." (p. 295)

Recent reviews using a quantitative statistic known as effect size (ES) have been conducted to summarize educational research. This statistic is computed to quantitatively determine how much improvement occurs across different investigations, based on two indices: the direction of improvement (+ or −) and the amount of improvement with an ES of 1.00 revealing a 34% improvement. Kavale and Glass (1982) refer to a meta-analysis performed by Kavale in 1981 that investigated the effectiveness of psycholinguistic training. Kavale's studies yielded 240 effect sizes with an overall ES of 0.39. Kavale and Glass conclude by asserting that there are specific situations where psycholinguistic training is effective and that it should be included within a total remedial program. The findings from this research should be qualified, however, because of the lack of consideration of research methodologies across the different investigations. Furthermore, the outcome measures were based on performance on the process tests (i.e., Illinois Test of Psycholinguistic Abilities—ITPA), not on academic tests. Further analyses of studies using achievement outcomes have found negligible effect sizes. It remains open to question whether such improvement on psycholinguistic process tasks would translate into improved performance on academic tasks in the classroom.

## REFERENCES

Arter, J. A., & Jenkins, J. R. (1977). Examining the benefits and prevalence of modality considerations in special education. *Journal of Special Education, 11*(3), 281–298.

Hammill, D. D., & Larsen, S. C. (1974). The effectiveness of psycholinguistic training. *Exceptional Children, 41*, 5–14.

Kavale, K. A., & Glass, G. V. (1982). The efficacy of special education interventions and practices: A compendium of meta-analysis findings. *Focus on Exceptional Children, 15*(4), 1–16.

KATHLEEN RODDEN-NORD
GERALD TINDAL
*University of Oregon*

**FERNALD METHOD**
**ORTON-GILLINGHAM METHOD**
**PSYCHOLINGUISTICS**

## AKINETON

Akineton is the proprietary name of *biperiden*, a skeletal muscle relaxant used in the treatment of Parkinson's disease (Modell, 1985). It is available in tablet and ampul form. Akineton is used in the treatment of all forms of parkinsonism, and it helps reduce movement disorders associated with this condition. It also is used in conjunction with antipsychotic drugs such as the phenothiazines to control extrapyramidal disturbances. Safe, effective use in children has not been established. Possible side effects associated with Akineton include dryness of the mouth, drowsiness, blurred vision, and urinary retention. Extreme adverse effects include mental confusion, agitation, and disturbed behavior.

## REFERENCES

Modell, W. (Ed.) (1985). *Drugs in current use and new drugs* (31st ed.). New York: Springer.

*Physician's desk reference* (37th ed.) (1983). Oradell, NJ: Medical Economics.

CATHY F. TELZROW
*Cuyahoga Special Education
Service Center, Maple
Heights, Ohio*

**CHOREA**
**PHENOTHIAZINES**

## AL-ANON

Al-Anon originally was an adjunct of Alcoholics Anonymous, but in 1954 it incorporated as a separate fellowship.

The central headquarters, known as the World Service Office (WSO), serves Al-Anon groups all over the world. The WSO is guided by a voluntary board of trustees, a policy committee, and an executive committee that makes administrative decisions. There is a paid staff with an executive director. Although there is a central headquarters, all local groups operate autonomously. The only requirement for membership is the belief that one's life has been or is being deeply affected by close contact with a problem drinker.

Al-Anon groups help those affected by someone else's drinking to:

> Learn the facts about alcoholism as a family illness
>
> Benefit from contact with members who have had the same problem
>
> Improve their own attitudes and personalities by the study and practice of the "twelve steps"
>
> Reduce tensions and improve the attitudes of the family through attendance at Al-Anon meetings

Al-Anon is primarily a self-help/support group that focuses on assisting family members in dealing with the problems that an alcoholic brings to the family. It is based on anonymity and sharing.

PHILIP E. LYON
*College of St. Rose*

## ALATEEN

Alateen is a self-help, self-support group for young Al-Anon members whose lives have been affected by someone else's drinking. Each Alateen group has an active, adult member of Al-Anon who serves as a sponsor and who is responsible for guiding the group and sharing knowledge of the twelve steps and traditions. The basis purpose of this group is to help Alateens to cope with the turmoil created in their lives by someone else's drinking. Meetings are voluntary and generally are held in community buildings. Alateen members openly discuss their problems, share experiences, learn effective ways to cope with their problems, encourage one another, and help each other to understand the principles of the Al-Anon program.

In a survey conducted by World Service Office in the summer of 1985, it was found that 46% of the Alateens held membership for between 1 and 4 years, 57% were female, most were children of alcoholics, 27% were the brother, sister, or other relative of an alcoholic, and the average age of a member was 14, with 71% between the ages of 13 and 17. Furthermore, 31% of the Alateen members had participated in treatment/counseling before or since coming to Alateen. Fully 94% of the Alateen respondents indicated that personal influences were responsible for their attendance at their first Alateen meeting, with Alcoholics Anonymous members, Al-Anon/Alateen members, or family members being the most frequently identified influence.

PHILIP E. LYON
*College of Saint Rose*

## AL-ANON
## ALCOHOL AND DRUG ABUSE PATTERNS

## ALBINISM

Albinism is a genetic disorder that affects the pigmentation, of the skin, hair, or eyes or any combination of the three. Individuals with albinism often have significant visual impairment. Problems with acuity are common, as is pendular nystagmus. Central nervous system involvement may be present. Although one would typically require intense illumination for such problems, persons with albinism are severely photosensitive, i.e., intolerant of light. Special education services will often be necessary, particularly if the visual impairments so often accompanying albinism are severe. Social and behavioral problems related to the odd physical appearance concomitant with albinism are common, as are problems with anxiety and self-esteem. Children with albinism will vary as much as normal individuals in the vast majority of human characteristics. Some will not require special education.

CECIL R. REYNOLDS
*Texas A&M University*

## ALBRIGHT'S HEREDITARY OSTEODYSTROPHY (PSEUDOHYPOPARATHYROIDISM)

Albright's hereditary osteodystrophy is believed to be an X-linked inherited disorder that results in a low level of calcium and a high level of phosphorus in the blood. Varying degrees of mental retardation, ranging from slight to severe, are associated with the condition, and hearing and vision problems are found in a number of afflicted children. At times, hyperthyroidism is associated with Albright's, therefore alterations in personality and behavior may be seen (Carter, 1978).

Children with this condition are usually short and stocky with skeletal abnormalities often observed in both upper and lower extremities and prominent foreheads. Calcium deposits may be present in the brain, skin, and organs. Calcification is often found in hands, wrists, and feet. Toes and fingers are short and stubby. There may be

impairment in the sense of sour and bitter taste and the sense of smell. Glandular disorders may be seen and sexual glands may be poorly developed (Lemeshaw, 1982).

Neurological, sensory, and motor problems often accompanying this syndrome will require related attention. Developmental and mental status evaluations will be necessary to measure the degree of disability each child has. Because seizures may be present, drug therapy may be necessary and must be known and monitored.

### REFERENCES

Carter, C. (Ed.). (1978). *Medical aspects of mental retardation* (2nd ed.). Springfield, IL: Thomas.

Lemeshaw, S. (1982). *The handbook of clinical types in mental retardation*. Boston: Allyn & Bacon.

Stonburg, J., & Wyngaarden, J. (1978). *Metabolic basis of inherited disease*. New York: McGraw-Hill.

SALLY L. FLAGLER
*University of Oklahoma*

## HYPERTHYROIDISM
## PHYSICAL ANOMALIES

## ALCOHOL AND DRUG ABUSE PATTERNS

Alcohol and drug abuse patterns in contemporary American society should be viewed from many perspectives in an effort to understand the multidimensional nature of the problem. Patterns of alcohol and drug use, abuse, and dependence, particularly among adolescents, have changed radically in the past 20 years. Rates of use, abuse, and dependence have all increased at an alarming rate, as has the variety of substances indulged in by young and old alike. Many theories have been developed as social scientists seek to understand and explain the upsurge in adolescent alcohol and drug use. For example, in 1980, 50 theorists described 43 different theories on drug abuse (Lettieri, Sayers, & Pearson, 1980). Similarly, a plethora of research articles have appeared on the phenomenon of alcohol use and abuse (Maisto & Caddy, 1981; Roebuck & Kessler, 1972).

To explore and explain fully the complex nature of alcohol and drug use among youths, one must look at the theoretical constructs of anthropology, economics, medicine, politics, psychology, and sociology. In a recent review of the many determinants of alcohol and drug use, Galizio and Maisto (1985) call for a "biopsychosocial" model. Given the alarming rate of acceleration in alcohol and drug use and the complexity of the issue, such a model would allow theorists and scientists from varying disciplines to study and collaborate in an effort to understand and intervene in this escalating social issue.

The third edition of the *Diagnostic and Statistical Manual of Mental Disorders* (American Psychiatric Association, 1980, pp. 163–179) clearly distinguishes among the terms, use, abuse, and dependence. Although each category of psychoactive drug use (e.g., alcohol, barbiturate, opioid, cocaine, amphetamine, phencyclidine, hallucinogen, cannabis, and tobacco) is separated within the manual, the more general term substance use, is employed when referencing the disorder as a whole. Substance use is defined as a pattern of consumption of a psychoactive substance; (i.e., one that has a mechanism of action in the brain) that does not meet the definitive criteria that follow for abuse or dependence. Substance abuse is a pattern of pathological use, (i.e., impairment in social or occupational functioning that is related to the use of the substance) that lasts at least 1 month. Substance dependence is defined by the presence of body tolerance to the drug, or evidence of withdrawal symptoms (e.g., runny nose, goose flesh, fevers and chills, gastrointestinal discomfort, muscle cramping) after cessation of use. Tolerance is defined as a state of use in which larger and larger amounts of the particular substance are required to produce the user's desired outcome. Withdrawal symptoms can be physiological, psychological, or both; several drugs, notably alcohol, heroin, opioids, barbiturates, sedatives, and some types of stimulants, frequently create both. This point is significant regarding the establishment and maintenance of specific patterns of alcohol and drug use. Cessation of use by a chemically dependent person may create such great discomfort that the user feels compelled to return to use for relief.

Patterns of alcohol and drug use among adolescents are strongly linked with delinquent behavior. Indeed, delinquent behavior and substance abuse are consistently correlated (Elliott & Ageton, 1976). At the least, use of alcohol, illicit drugs, or prescription drugs not prescribed for the individual using them is illegal. Further, other unconventional or nonconforming actions such as sexual experiences, attenuated academic performance, and flagrant violations of minor and major laws often precede involvement with illicit substances. Not all youths who experiment with alcohol and other drugs will manifest the problems associated with chronic or continued substance abuse, but current research supports a high correlation between continuing drug and alcohol use and delinquent behavior (Clayton, 1981). Initial, or trial, use of alcohol and drug is likely to occur in youths who have already participated in other minor deviant activities; those who choose a high level of peer group involvement; and those who have seen both parent and peer use. Huba, Wingard, and Bentler (1980) found that prior behavior is a much stronger predictor of intended drug behavior than is either expressed interest or desire. This factor is significant in understanding the causal relationship between criminal behavior and drug and alcohol use. Initial research suggested that drug use precedes other forms of juvenile delinquent behavior (Single & Kandel, 1978), but more recent studies indicate that delinquent subgroups establish group acceptance of continued alcohol and drug use beyond the level of what could be considered normal adolescent experimentation and curiosity (Clayton, 1981).

Initiation of alcohol and drug use can be seen as either a developmental issue of adolescence (Kandel, 1975) or as an abnormal adaptation to frustration (Hendin, 1980), among other possibilities. Numerous theories have been posited about the initial or trial stage of drug use. However, concensus has been reached as to the critical role of peer-group pressure and the addictive nature, physically and/or psychologically, of the substances used in maintaining drug use. Thus regardless of the reason for beginning drug use, acceptance and support by peers to continue use, tolerance, and aversive withdrawal symptoms are essential factors in understanding the use, abuse, and dependence continuum. The addictive potential of the substance used, amount used, frequency and duration of use, and route of administration are key factors influencing adolescents' ability to start and stop their alcohol and drug use.

Adolescents seem to follow a predictable pattern in their continued alcohol and drug use. The use of legal drugs usually precedes the use of illegal drugs, irrespective of what age the use of illegal drugs is begun. Similarly, the use of illicit drugs like marijuana rarely takes place without prior experimentation or use. However, no evidence indicates that anything inherent in the pharmacologic properties of any substance necessarily leads from use of one to the use of another (the stepping stone theory of addiction). That is, the use of tobacco leads to alcohol, alcohol to marijuana, marijuana to stronger drugs, and finally addiction and dependency. Factors such as parental role models, peer pressure, and availability and access seem to be more important than anything pharmacological (Kandel, 1975).

A further complication is that adolescents who use and abuse substances that can produce tolerance may suffer the biomedical consequences of lifelong chemical affinity for continued abuse and dependency (Cohen, 1981). Also, evidence of a biogenetic predisposition to drug dependency can be seen in patterns of use and abuse in the offspring of alcoholics and, to a lesser degree, other substance-addicted parents (Crabbe, McSwigan, & Belknap, 1985). Children of addicted parents may become addicted with fewer episodes of intoxication, smaller amounts of substances, and fewer of the factors noted previously for adolescents. A word of caution is offered by Schuckit (1980), who states that even when a predisposition or affinity for substances is noted in an adolescent, the final picture must involve not only genetics but also the careful consideration of environment, culture, and other social factors.

The range and variation of the adolescent experience is an important final concern in understanding adolescent patterns of alcohol and drug use. The period of chronological growth beginning at age 12 and continuing through age 21 is marked by great physical, emotional, and intellectual development. Early, middle, and late phase adolescents respond differently to issues such as opportunity for first use, continued use, decision making, the ability to make choices, stress and anxiety, and prevalent patterns of communication within a given peer network. Cohen (1983) and Kandel (1975) substantiate concerns about the impact of the age of first use moving downward. Data on age of admission to treatment centers and survey responses both suggest that a large number of adolescents will become dependent at an earlier age. Further research is needed to determine the impact of this trend on the rapidly developing, but fragile, systems of young people. Although some studies suggest a decline in the frequency of adolescent drug and alcohol use in this society (Johnston, Bachman, & O'Malley, 1982), more specific information is needed about high-risk youths from isolated populations that are not routinely surveyed in national studies (e.g., high school dropouts, younger members of the armed forces, and residents of college dorms). Miller (1981) indicates that the "survellience function of epidemiological research" will best be served by closer attention to special "pockets" of substance-abusing youths who have escaped close scrutiny in the recent past.

## REFERENCES

American Psychiatric Association. (1980). *Diagnostic and statistical manual of mental disorders* (3rd ed.). Washington, DC: Author.

Clayton, R. R. (1981). The delinquency and drug use relationship among adolescents: A critical review. In D. J. Lettieri & J. P. Lundford (Eds.), *Drug abuse and the American adolescent* (pp. 82–98). Rockville, MD: National Institute on Drug Abuse.

Cohen, S. (1981). Adolescence and drug abuse: Biomedical consequences. In D. J. Lettieri & J. P. Ludford (Eds.), *Drug abuse and the American adolescent* (pp. 104–109). Rockville, MD: National Institute on Drug Abuse.

Cohen, S. (1983). *The alcoholism problems*. New York: Haworth.

Crabbe, J. C., McSwigan, J. D., & Belknap, J. K. (1985). The role of genetics in substance abuse. In M. Galizio & S. A. Maisto (Eds.), *Determinants of substance abuse* (pp. 13–54). New York: Plenum.

Elliott, J. D. S., & Ageton, A. R. (1976). The relationship between drug use and crime among adolescents. In Research Triangle Institute, *Appendix to drug use and crime: Report of the Panel on Drug Use and Criminal Behavior* (pp. 297–322). VA: National Technical Information Service.

Galizio, M., & Maisto, S. A. (1985). Toward a biopsychosocial theory of substance abuse. In M. Galizio & S. A. Maisto (Eds.), *Determinants of substance abuse* (pp. 425–427) New York: Plenum.

Hendin, H. (1980). Psychosocial theory of drug abuse. In D. J. Lettieri, M. Sayers, & H. W. Pearson (Eds.), *Theories on drug abuse* (pp. 195–200). Rockville, MD: National Institute on Drug Abuse.

Huba, G. J., Wingard, J. A., & Bentler, P. M. (1980). Framework for an interactive theory of drug use. In D. J. Lettieri, M. Sayers, & H. W. Pearson (Eds.), *Theories on drug abuse* (pp. 95–101). Rockville, MD: National Institute on Drug Abuse.

Johnston, L. D., Bachman, J. G., & O'Malley, P. M. (1982). *Student drug use, attitudes, and beliefs: National trends 1975–82*. Detroit, MI: Institute for Social Research.

Kandel, D. (1975). Stages in adolescent involvement in drug use. *Science, 190*, 912–914.

Lettieri, D. J., Sayers, M., & Pearson, H. W., (Eds.). (1980). *Theories on drug abuse: Selected contemporary perspectives*. Rockville, MD: National Institute on Drug Abuse.

Maisto, S. A., & Caddy, G. R. (1981). Self-control and addictive behavior: Present status and prospects. *International Journal of the Addictions, 16*, 109–133.

Miller, J. D. (1981). Epidemiology of drug use among adolescents. In D. J. Lettieri & J. P. Ludford (Eds.), *Drug abuse and the american adolescent* (pp. 25–35). Rockville, MD: National Institute on Drug Abuse.

Roebuck, J., & Kessler, R. (1972). *The etiology of alcoholism*. Springfield, IL: Thomas.

Schuckit, M. A. (1980). A theory of alcohol and drug abuse; A genetic approach. In D. J. Lettieri, M. Sayers, & H. W. Pearson (Eds.), *Theories on drug abuse*, (pp. 297–302). Rockville, MD: National Institute on Drug Abuse.

Single, E., & Kandel, D. (1978). The role of buying and selling in illicit drug use. In A. Trebach (Ed.), *Drugs, crime and politics*. New York: Praeger.

L. WORTH BOLTON
*Cape Fear Substance Abuse
Center, Wilmington,
North Carolina*

CHEMICALLY DEPENDENT YOUTH
DRUG ABUSE
SUBSTANCE ABUSE

# ALEXANDER GRAHAM BELL ASSOCIATION

The Alexander Graham Bell Association was founded in 1890 to promote the teaching of speech, speech reading, and the use of residual hearing for deaf individuals. Contrary to popular notion, the Bell Association is not a political or consumer group advocating the use of the oral method as the only educational strategy for hearing-impaired children. Its members recognize that speech is the universal mode of communication; that development of speech during early childhood increases educational opportunities and promotes greater participation in society; and that use of the oral method to develop speech is enhanced by early identification, proper amplification, and appropriate educational programming. Toward this end, the purpose of the Alexander Graham Bell Association is

to aid any school or program for hearing impaired children in their efforts to develop or improve programs in speech communication by providing qualified speech consultants; by developing criteria for model programs for different approaches in a variety of settings; by holding local, regional, and national conferences; by sponsoring summer workshops in speech development with affiliated colleges and universities; by encouraging and supporting research designed to improve the state of the art of teaching the deaf to speak; by collecting, publishing, and disseminating information concerning methods of teaching speech communication proficiency, to the end that no deaf child in America shall be allowed to grow up "deaf and dumb" or "mute" without earnest and persistent efforts having been made to help him develop speech communication proficiency. (Flint, 1975, pp. 153–154)

The headquarters of the Bell Association is at 3517 Volta Place, NW, Washington, DC 20007. Approximately 5700 individuals are members of the Bell Association. There are four subsections: the Oral Deaf Adults Section (ODAS); the International Parents' Organization (IPO); the American Association of Teachers for the Education of the Hearing Impaired (AOEHI); and the International Committee on Auditory Verbal Communication (ICAVC). In addition to section affiliation and committee memberships, members of the association receive *Volta Review* (an educational journal) and *Newsounds* (a newsletter), have access to lending and archival libraries, and have the opportunity to attend conferences and biennial conventions.

**REFERENCE**

Flint, R. W. (1975). Association report: A. G. Bell Board re-examines the association's purpose and mission. *Volta Review*, 77, 152–154.

MAUREEN A. SMITH
*Pennsylvania State University*

## ALEXIA

Alexia is used often in a general sense to refer to reading disabilities of adult onset (Lezak, 1983). As such, the term serves to differentiate between adult reading disorders and developmental reading disabilities commonly denoted by the term dyslexia. Literally, however, the term *alexia* derives from the Greek and can be approximately translated as "no reading." Thus, in a more precise sense, alexia denotes a total inability to read brought about by an abnormality in the central nervous system (Thomas, 1977). The term can be correctly applied to individuals regardless of age.

In most individuals, the perception of verbal material is mediated by cortical association areas found in the temporal lobe of the left hemisphere of the brain (Milner, 1971). Specifically, the perception of written words appears to be dependent on the proper function of a cortical area found in the posterior temporal lobe, the angular

gyrus. As such, the presence of alexia is often seen as an indication of a cortical lesion or other abnormality associated with this particular brain region.

Not all researchers, however, agree that alexia should signify only a condition in which individuals demonstrate an inability to recognize words. It has been argued that individuals who cannot attach meanings to words that they can recognize (i.e., those who demonstrate a failure in word comprehension) are also alexic. Such an inability (whether or not one chooses to call it alexia) may also be related to cortical abnormalities in the left temporal lobe involving neural pathways connecting the angular gyrus to verbal comprehension centers such as Wernicke's area. Interestingly, individuals suffering from right temporal lobe lesions, although seldom demonstrating reading disorders, have been shown to experience related difficulties in nonverbal tasks calling for both spatial recognition and comprehension (Vignolo, 1969).

Given that the events that may lead to cortical damage (e.g., cardiovascular accident, toxic or other poisoning, head trauma) rarely are confined in their effects to any one specific brain location, alexia is generally observed in combination with related language dysfunctions, and rarely in pure form (Lezak, 1983). Dyslexia, defined as an impairment of reading ability of less than total magnitude, is a much more common occurrence.

**REFERENCES**

Lezak, M. D. (1983). *Neuropsychological assessment* (2nd ed.). New York: Oxford University Press.

Milner, B. (1971). Interhemispheric differences in the localization of psychological processes in man. *British Medical Bulletin*, 27, 272–277.

Thomas, C. L. (ed.). (1977). *Tabor's cyclopedic medical dictionary*. Philadelphia: Davis.

Vignolo, L. A. (1969). Auditory agnosia: A review and report of recent evidence. In A. L. Benton (Ed.), *Contributions to clinical neuropsychology* (pp. 172–208). Chicago: Aldine.

RICHARD G. PETERS
*Ball State University*

RAYMOND S. DEAN
*Ball State University*
*Indiana University School*
*of Medicine*

## ALGOZZINE, BOB (1946–    )

After receiving a BS in economics in 1968 from Wagner College in New York, Bob Algozzine earned his MS in educational psychology from the State University of New York, Albany in 1970 and his PhD in the education of exceptional children from Pennsylvania State University in 1975. He is presently a professor at the University of

Florida, where he is involved with training regular class teachers to work with exceptional students.

Algozzine's main interest is in working with students who fail to profit in regular classes. Much of his work has focused on the similarities between learning-disabled (LD) and low-achieving students. Algozzine contends that LD is a sophisticated term for low achievement and that it represents an oversophistication of a concept (Algozzine, Ysseldyke, & Shinn, 1982). He has shown that few differences exist in test profiles of LD and low-achieving students and that performance profiles of many normal students evidence significant discrepancies as well. He believes that schools need to spend less energy trying to identify exceptional students and place more effort on determining what to do with all students who fail to profit from their current educational placement (Algozzine & Ysseldyke, 1983).

Algozzine has written over 200 articles, research reports, monographs, final reports, and books. He is currently a member of the Council for Exceptional Children, the American Educational Research Association, and the Florida Council for Children with Behavior Disorders.

## REFERENCES

Algozzine, B., & Ysseldyke, J. E. (1983). Learning disabilities as a subset of school failure: The oversophistication of a concept. *Exceptional Children, 50,* 242–246.

Algozzine, B., Ysseldyke, J. E., & Shinn, M. (1982). Identifying children with learning disabilities: When is a discrepancy severe? *Journal of School Psychology, 20,* 299–305.

E. Valerie Hewitt
*Texas A&M University*

## ALLERGIC DISORDERS

An allergy is a hypersensitivity to a specific substance (an antigen) that in a similar quantity does not affect other people. The abnormal reactions are usually in the form of asthma, hay fever, eczema, hives, or chronic stuffy nose (allergic rhinitis). Technically, the use of the term should be limited to those conditions in which an immunological mechanism can be demonstrated. Allergies are common to 20 to 25% of the children in the United States and are inherited. The tendency to develop allergies is present at birth but may appear at any age.

Allergies can be classified into two types: immediate hypersensitivity (such as allergic rhinitis, asthma, and food allergies) and delayed hypersensitivity (such as reactions to poison ivy). Patients with the former have more of the antibody IgE in their systems. This antibody reacts with whatever patients are allergic to, whether it is something that they breathe, eat, or have skin contact with.

This reaction causes certain cells in the body to release chemical mediators such as histamine and serotonin. These chemicals cause the dilation of the small blood vessels, increased secretion from the mucous glands, and smooth muscle contractions that produce the allergy symptoms.

Allergic rhinitis is the commonest cause of nasal congestion in children. Epidemiological data indicate that in the United States alone allergic rhinitis occurs in 6 million children, accounting for 2 million days lost from school (Shapiro, 1986). An important complication of perennial allergic rhinitis is otitis media with effusion, an accumulation of fluid behind the eardrum in the middle ear. Patients usually have at least an intermittent loss of hearing and may complain of a sensation of fullness or popping and cracking noises.

Allergies often play a role in the etiology of asthma, especially in childhood. The chemical mediators released upon the allergic reaction cause contraction of the smooth muscles in the walls of the bronchial airways, swelling of the bronchial tubes, and an increase in the rate of secretion of mucous by submucosal glands. This produces obstruction and causes the characteristic wheezing and shortness of breath. Asthma may be mild (one or two mild attacks per year) or severe with intractable wheezing daily. The severe form may greatly restrict physical activity and make school attendance difficult for school-age children. Physical exertion may precipitate wheezing and become a problem in physical education classes.

Skin allergies are common, especially in younger children. Atopic dermatitis (eczema) may occur in 3 to 4% of infants and result in a dry, scaly, itchy rash involving the cheeks and extremities. While most children outgrow the rash, over 50% of them tend to develop respiratory allergies. Another common rash with an allergic origin is urticaria or hives. Possible causes are allergies to drugs like aspirin or penicillin and to foods.

Food allergies are perhaps the most controversial area of allergy study. Some allergists feel that allergic reactions to foods are rare, while others feel they are a common cause of illness. The frequency of food allergy seems to decrease as children grow older. The most common symptoms of food allergy include gastrointestinal symptoms such as abdominal pain, vomiting and diarrhea, and rashes such as hives. Food may play a role in other allergic conditions such as allergic rhinitis, asthma, and eczema, especially during the first 3 or 4 years of life. The most serious allergic reaction to foods and drugs is an anaphylactic one, in which the person experiences a shocklike reaction that can result in death. Any food can cause an allergic reaction, but the foods most apt to cause one in children include milk, eggs, fish, wheat, corn, peanuts, soy, pork, and chocolate.

Stinging insect allergies may cause a severe anaphylactic reaction to the sting of a bee, wasp, hornet, or yellow jacket. The reaction may occur within minutes after the sting and allergic persons need immediate medical attention.

A thorough history and physical examination are important components of a diagnosis. Seasonal patterns of symptoms, exposure to animals, and usual diet are useful information in identifying causes. Laboratory analysis of nasal secretions, sputum, and blood may establish the presence of eosinophil cells that appear in increased numbers with allergic reactions. Pulmonary function tests are also helpful. Scratch and intradermal skin tests for the suspected allergens can confirm a diagnosis. Another tool is the radioallergoabsorbant (RAST) test, which measures the level of IgE in the blood for a particular allergen (Tuft, 1973). The elimination-challenge diet is used for suspected food allergies; after avoiding a particular food for two to three weeks, the patient consumes it and is observed for reactions. Awareness of environmental conditions from change of seasons, foliage in different parts of the country, and environmental factors in homes, schools, and the work place also assists the diagnostician.

While there is no cure for allergies, symptoms may be controlled in a variety of ways. First, symptomatic treatment involves using medication. Antihistamines are the most commonly prescribed drugs for the treatment of allergic reactions. They inhibit some of the actions of histamine but frequently have negative side effects such as sedation, excitation, and insomnia. Antihistamines are often combined with decongestant drugs. Asthmatics are usually treated with bronchodilator drugs that cause relaxation of the smooth muscle surrounding the bronchial tubes. Acute asthmatic attacks and anaphylactic reactions are frequently treated with epinephrine. Both drugs may have negative side effects. For severe allergic problems, corticosteroids may be used, but on a limited basis because of adrenal suppression and limitation of physical growth in children.

The second method of treatment is environmental control, that is, removal of troublesome antigens such as pet hair, dust, and pollen. Good housekeeping practices, use of air conditioning at home and in the car, and other careful planning can prevent many allergic problems. A third and related approach is to teach self-regulation strategies to persons with asthma and other types of allergies. They include relaxation training, biofeedback procedures to modify physiological reactions, and general education about the medical condition (Creer, Marion, & Harm, in press). A fourth treatment is immunotherapy, which involves injecting the patient with small amounts of an antigen that has been processed into a dilute form. These injections stimulate the immune system to produce another type of antibody that inhibits the reaction between the allergic antibody and the antigen. While initially the shots are taken once or twice a week, the regimen is gradually phased out over a 2- to 3-year period (Patterson et al., 1978).

Allergies have been connected with specific learning disabilities through analyses of case studies (Rapaport & Flint, 1976). Allergic children are rated lower in reading, auditory perception, and visual perception (Harvard, 1975). Teacher and parent ratings as well as test scores indicated lower proficiency among allergic students in some areas (Rawls, Rawls, & Harrison, 1971). Learning-disabled students with recurrent otitis media may have more problems with allergies and verbal skills than non-disabled children (Loose, 1984). Geschwind and Behan (1982) associate left-handedness with reports of learning problems and immunological diseases such as thyroid and bowel disorders.

However, McLoughlin, et al. (1983) found no differences in parent reports concerning academic achievement, diagnosis for disabilities, and behavioral problems of allergic and nonallergic students. There was a tendency for children with asthma and chronic rhinitis to be rated lower in listening skills. Additionally, a comparison of group achievement scores of allergic and nonallergic students indicated no interaction of exceptional conditions and allergies (McLoughlin, Nall, & Petrosko, 1985). Some lower estimates of allergic children's school performance seem confused with the effects of socioeconomic factors.

Higher rates of school absenteeism are reported for asthmatic children (Creer, Marion, & Harm, in press) and those with chronic rhinitis (Shapiro, 1986). Creer and his colleagues estimate that asthmatic children may be absent 10% of the time and report studies that establish such absenteeism as a direct cause of school problems. Additionally, the seasonal occurrence of allergic reactions (especially in the fall) and the typical pattern of frequent, brief absences are disruptive to classroom performance, attending skills, and social development. Milder forms of allergies may not cause significant school absenteeism, particularly with improved medical treatment, self-management programs, and parent education (McLoughlin, Nall, & Petrosko, 1985). Furthermore, some previous estimates of higher absenteeism of allergic children may have been confused with the effects of socioeconomic status.

Hearing difficulties are frequently associated with otitis media resulting from allergies (Northern, 1980). Among allergic students, Szanton and Szanton (1966) found many cases of intermittent hearing loss that had been undetected on screening measures. Articulation and/or vocal quality problems have also been reported among allergic students (Baker & Baker, 1980). Recurrent otitis media among three year olds has been associated with lower speech and language performance (Teele, et al., 1984).

Allergy history seems present among cases of behavioral and emotional disorders (Mayron, 1978). King (1981) estimated that 70% of students with such disorders have personal or family allergy histories; cognitive-emotional symptoms were noted after allergic exposure under double-blind conditions. Psychological and personality changes are frequently reported by asthmatic children and their parents (Creer, Marion, & Creer, 1983). However, comparisons of reports and ratings of behavioral problems, placement in services for behavior disorders, and school suspensions between allergic and nonallergic students have not yielded significantly different profiles (McLoughlin et al., 1985).

Hyperactivity has been particularly connected with food allergies. Feingold (1975b) drew attention to the ingestion of artificial food additives (color and flavors) and naturally occurring salicylates in food and proposed the Feingold Kaiser-Permanente (K-P) diet based on clinical observations and anecdotal accounts (Crook, 1977; Feingold, 1975a). However, recent reviews of more controlled studies (Kavale & Forness, 1983; Mattes, 1983) dismiss these claims, as do the findings of the Consensus Development Conference sponsored by the National Institutes of Health (Office for Medical Applications of Research, 1982).

Allergy medication may have adverse effects on behavior and exacerbate existing behavioral problems (McLoughlin et al., 1983). Theophylline has been significantly correlated with inattentiveness, hyperactivity, irritability, drowsiness, and withdrawal behavior; the negative side effects increase with length of use. Furakawa and his colleagues (1984) found decreased test performances under the influence of theophylline. Terbutaline created socially inappropriate behavior in a comparison group (Creer, 1979), and corticosteroids negatively affected academic performance (Suess & Chai, 1981). Ladd, Leibold, Lindsey, and Ornby (1980) also reported euphoria, insomnia, and visual disturbances with corticosteroids. Antihistamines may cause sedation, dry mouth, and irritability (Weinberger & Hendeles, 1980). Visual hallucinations occur among some children receiving decongestants (Sankey, Nunn, & Sills, 1984).

Allergic disorders have important implications for the professional assessment and intervention of exceptionalities as well as for parental involvement. Certain types of allergies and/or the side effects of medication may be contributing factors in behaviors of concern and may require special consideration when designing special services. The self-monitoring and management skills taught in special education may be mutually beneficial in coping with this medical condition.

## REFERENCES

Baker, M., & Baker, C. (1980). Difficulties generated by allergies. *Journal of School Health, 50,* 583–585.

Creer, T. L. (1979). *Asthma therapy.* New York: Springer.

Creer, T. L., Marion, R. J., & Creer, P. P. (1983). The asthma problem behavior checklist: Parental perceptions of the behavior of asthmatic children. *Journal of Asthma, 20,* 97–104.

Creer, T. L., Marion, R. J., & Harm, D. L. (in press). Childhood asthma. In V. B. Van Hasselt, P. S. Strain, & M. Herson (Eds.), *Handbook of developmental and physical disabilities.* New York: Pergamon.

Crook, W. G. (1977, Jan.). Letter to the editor. *News and Comment,* American Academy of Pediatrics.

Feingold, B. F. (1975a). Hyperkinesis and learning disabilities linked to artificial food flavors and colors. *American Journal of Nursing, 75,* 797–803.

Feingold, B. F. (1975b). *Why your child is hyperactive.* New York: Random House.

Furakawa, C. T., Shapiro, G. G., DuHamel, T., Weimer, L., Pierson, W. E., & Bierman, C. W. (1984, March). Learning and behavior problems associated with theophylline therapy. *Lancet,* 621.

Geschwind, N., & Behan, P. (1982). Left-handedness: Association with immune disease, migraine, and developmental learning disorders. *Proceedings of the National Academy of Science, USA, 79,* 5097–5100.

Harvard, J. G. (1975). Relationship between allergic conditions and language and/or learning disabilities. *Dissertation Abstracts International, 35,* 6940.

Kavale, K. A., & Forness, S. R. (1983). Hyperactivity and diet treatment: A meta-analysis of the Feingold hypothesis. *Journal of Learning Disabilities, 16,* 324–330.

King, D. S. (1981). Can allergic exposure provoke psychological symptoms? *Biology Psychiatry, 16,* 3–19.

Ladd, F. T., Leibold, S. R., Lindsey, C. N., & Ornby, R. (1980). RX in the classroom. *Instructor, 90,* 58–59.

Loose, F. F. (1984). *Educational implications of recurrent otitis media among children at risk for learning disabilities.* Unpublished doctoral dissertation, Michigan State University.

Mattes, J. A. (1983). The Feingold diet: A current reappraisal. *Journal of Learning Disabilities, 16,* 319–323.

Mayron, L. (1978). Ecological factors in learning disabilities. *Journal of Learning Disabilities, 11,* 40–50.

McLoughlin, J. A., Nall, M., Isaacs, B., Petrosko, J., Karibo, J., & Lindsey, B. (1983). The relationship of allergies and allergy treatment to school performance and student behavior. *Annals of Allergy, 51,* 506–510.

McLoughlin, J. A., Nall, M., & Petrosko, J. (1985). Allergies and learning disabilities. *Learning Disability Quarterly, 8,* 255–260.

Northern, J. L. (1980). Diagnostic tests of ear disease. In C. Bierman & D. Pearlman (Eds.), *Allergic diseases of infancy, childhood and adolescence* (pp. 492–501). Philadelphia: Saunders.

Office for Medical Applications of Research, National Institutes of Health. (1982). Defined diets and childhood hyperactivity. *Journal of the American Medical Association, 245,* 290–292.

Patterson, R., Lieberman, P., Irons, J., Pruzansky, J., Melam, H., Metzger, W. J., & Zeiss, C. R. (1978). Immunotherapy. In E. Middleton, Jr., C. Reed, & E. Ellis (Eds.), *Allergy principles and practice* (Vol. 2) (pp. 877–897). St. Louis: Mosby.

Rapaport, H. G., & Flint, H. (1976). Is there a relationship between allergy and learning disabilities? *Journal of School Health, 46,* 139–141.

Rawls, D. J., Rawls, J. R., & Harrison, D. W. (1971). An investigation of 6 to 11 year old children with allergic disorders. *Journal of Consulting and Clinical Psychology, 36,* 260–264.

Sankey, R. J., Nunn, A. J., & Sills, J. A. (1984). Visual hallucinations in children receiving decongestants. *British Medical
Journal, 288*, 1369.

Shapiro, G. (1986). Understanding allergic rhinitis. *Pediatrics in
Review, 7*, 212–218.

Suess, W. M., & Chai, H. (1981). Neuropsychological correlates
of asthma: Brain damage or drug effects? *Journal of Consulting and Clinical Psychology, 49*, 135–136.

Szanton, V. J., & Szanton, W. C. (1966). Hearing disturbances in
allergic children. *Journal of Asthma Research, 4*, 25–28.

Teele, D. W., Klein, J. O., Rosner, B. A., & the Greater Boston
Otitis Media Study Group. (1984). *Pediatrics, 74*, 282–287.

Tuft, L. (1973). *Allergy management in clinical practice.* St. Louis:
Mosby.

Weinberger, M., & Hendeles, L. (1980). Pharmacologic management. In C. Bierman & D. Pearlman (Eds.), *Allergic diseases
of infancy, childhood and adolescence* (pp. 311–332). Philadelphia: Saunders.

JAMES A. MCLOUGHLIN
*University of Louisville*
MICHAEL NALL
*Louisville, Kentucky*

## ALLEY, GORDON R. (1934–      )

Gordon R. Alley received his BA in psychology in 1959
from Augustina, Illinois, and his MA in psychology in
1961 from the University of Iowa. He then went on to receive his doctorate in special education and school psychology, in 1967, from the University of Iowa.

Alley has been a teacher of the mentally retarded, a
school psychologist, and a director of special education. In
addition, he has taught at the University of Utah (1967–
1970) and has been an associate professor and full professor of special education and lecturer in pediatrics at the
University of Kansas since 1970.

Alley has published many articles at the Institute for
Research in Learning Disabilities at the University of
Kansas and coauthored 12 articles; he also contributed a
chapter to *Instructional Planning for Exceptional Children: Essays from Focus on Exceptional Children.* His
principal publication is *Teaching the Learning Disabled
Adolescent: Strategies and Methods.* He has presented numerous papers both regionally and nationally.

Alley's work promotes alternatives to the traditional,
tutorial, remedial, pursuant approach as an intervention
for learning-disabled adolescents. His work stresses the
developmental characteristics of adolescents with emphasis on learning strategies.

### REFERENCES

Alley, G., & Deshler, D. D. (1979). *Teaching the learning disabled
adolescent: Strategies and methods.* Denver: Love.

Alley, G., & Foster, C. (1979). *Instructional planning for exceptional children: Essays from focus on exceptional children.* Denver: Love.

ROBERTA C. STOKES
*Texas A&M University*

## ALPHABETIC METHOD

The alphabetic method of teaching children to read is historically connected with the development of an alphabet.
Once letters and sounds were fixed in a structure (an alphabet), a method to master this structure emerged. The
first recorded use of the alphabetic method was in ancient
Greek and Roman civilizations. Reading instruction began
by teaching children all the letters in their proper alphabetical order. After a complete mastery of the alphabet,
children learned to group the letters to form syllables,
words, and finally sentences. Reading instruction was considered primarily an oral process; the child recited the
spelling of each syllable or word and then pronounced it.
This progression of teaching letters, syllables, words, and
sentences was the predominant method of teaching reading from Greek and Roman times until the late 1800s
(Huey, 1908).

In using this method, sixteenth- and seventeenth-century teachers drilled children unmercifully on the names
of the letters (Matthews, 1966). Instructional materials
that presented lists of letters, syllables, and words to be
memorized before advancing to the text were developed.
The *New England Primer* was one of the most widely used
reading texts in seventeenth-century America. Each reading selection focused on a moral or religious lesson, and
was preceded by an alphabet, lists of the vowels and consonants, and lists of syllables such as ab, eb, and ib.The
lists of words for spelling began with one-syllable words
and progressed to two- and three-syllable words (Huey,
1980).

As the English language evolved, letter names no
longer directly represented speech sounds; therefore, children became more and more confused as they tried to read
modern literature by simply reciting the names of the letters. Realizing that this confusion hindered efforts to teach
reading effectively, the alphabetic method was gradually
replaced by phonetically based methods of reading instruction. By the beginning of the twentieth century, the classic
alphabetic method was seldom used.

### REFERENCES

Huey, E. B. (1908). *The psychology and pedagogy of reading.* New
York: Macmillan.

Matthews, M. M. (1966). *Teaching to read.* Chicago: University of Chicago Press.

CHRIS CHERRINGTON
*Lycoming College*

DISTAR
READING REMEDIATION
WHOLE WORD TEACHING

## ALTERNATIVE COMMUNICATION METHODS IN SPECIAL EDUCATION

The nonspeaking population is composed of persons who are temporarily or permanently unable to use speech to communicate, and whose handicaps are not primarily due to hearing impairment (ASHA, 1980). Prevalence figures have estimated that there are over one million such nonspeaking persons in the United States (ASHA 1980). Their lack of verbal speech severely affects their ability to communicate within their environment.

In the mid 1970s, alternative methods of communication began to be explored with the nonspeaking population. These methods are termed augmentative communication systems, or nonspeech communication systems. They are currently being used with children and adults who have physical, mental, emotional, and linguistic handicaps. Augmentative communication systems are categorized as being unaided or aided (ASHA, 1980). Unaided communication systems use only the physical body for communication. They include sign languages, gestures, and facial expressions. Aided systems require additional equipment for communication.

There are many advantages to using unaided systems for communication. Social interaction is enhanced because the rate of communication is typically fast. Speaker-listener eye contact is maintained when using unaided systems. The meaning of many signs and gestures are concrete, making learning and recall of vocabulary easier. In addition, during training, sign and gesture responses can be physically prompted and shaped by the instructor.

Sign languages such as American Sign Language (ASL) were originally developed for the hearing-impaired population. They are separate languages and not simply word-for-word manual translations of spoken English or other oral languages. Educational sign systems, or pedagogical sign systems, are designed to be manual equivalents of spoken English. Signed English and Signing Exact English (SEE 2) are two educational sign systems that are used frequently with the nonspeaking handicapped population (Musselwhite & St. Louis, 1982). The differences between true sign languages and educational sign systems include differences in word order and sign representations and changes in grammatical structures. To use sign systems as an augmentative communication system, the nonspeaking person should have good motor control of the hands, arms, and face, along with good visual acuity (Musselwhite & St. Louis, 1982). Persons who routinely interact with a signing communicator will also need to learn the system.

Gestures and facial expressions typically require less motor control than sign-language systems. Pantomime and natural gestures can often be used and understood without extensive training. Skelly and Schinsky (1979) developed a comprehensive gestural system known as Amer-Ind; it is based on American Indian hand talk. While gesture systems are initially less complex to learn, the information that can be conveyed is often constrained. Gestures and facial expressions are typically used as supplements to other communication systems, or as temporary communication methods.

Aided communication systems require additional devices or equipment for communication. Microcomputers, writing with pen and paper, and communication boards, are all examples of aided communication systems. An aided communication system consists of a communication aid, which is the mechanism used for communication, and a symbol system, which is the language used for communication.

The communication aid can consist of three major components: the interface, the communication device, and the output system. Complex electronic systems usually have all three components. Simple communication boards may consist of the communication device alone. The interface is used to control the system. A head stick, joystick, or computer keyboard are examples of interfaces. They are used to select symbols on the communication device. Direct selection allows the user to directly choose symbols for communication. Scanning systems present symbol choices to the user, who then activates a response when the desired symbol is reached. A scanning system resembles an advanced form of the guessing game "Twenty Questions."

The communication device can display all of the available vocabulary options, or it can display a few symbols that are combined into codes to access vocabulary. Electronic devices often indicate, by small lights or LCD display screens, which symbol has been selected. Once the entire message to be communicated is completed, an output device such as a speech synthesizer, computer modem, or printer is used to convey the message to others. For more information, refer to "Electronic Communication Aids" in this volume or Vanderheiden (1985).

Many symbol systems have been developed for use in aided communication systems. Symbol systems can be hierarchically ordered from linguistically simple concrete systems to complex written languages (see Table). Concrete linguistic systems are the easiest to learn. However, linguistically complex systems allow greater flexibility for communicative expression.

A Hierarchy of Aided Communication Symbol Systems

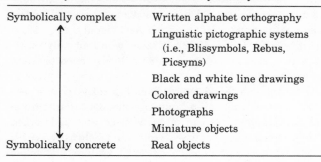

| Symbolically complex | Written alphabet orthography |
| | Linguistic pictographic systems (i.e., Blissymbols, Rebus, Picsyms) |
| | Black and white line drawings |
| | Colored drawings |
| | Photographs |
| | Miniature objects |
| Symbolically concrete | Real objects |

The advantage of aided communication systems is flexibility. The communication aid and symbol system can be adapted to meet the physical and mental skills of almost any handicapped person. The symbol system can be permanently displayed to enhance symbol recall and memory. In addition, most aided communication systems can be easily understood by others without extensive listener training.

There are also many disadvantages to using aided communication systems. The devices themselves are often physically cumbersome and difficult to transport. Communication through a mechanical device also reduces speaker–listener eye contact and affects the location and distance from the speaker or a listener. The primary disadvantage of aided communication systems is an extremely slow rate of communication. Normal verbal communication rates range from 126 to 172 words per minute (Foulds, 1980). Direct selection aided systems have rates that range from 6 to 25 words per minute; scanning systems can be as slow as two words per minute (Foulds, 1980). This slow rate of communication tends to affect the style and amount of communicative interaction that occurs when using aided communication systems. Methods of increasing communication rate will be discussed later in this entry.

Before an augmentative communication system can be developed, a complete evaluation of the user's physical, linguistic, cognitive, and academic skills must be completed. This requires a team of professionals including: speech-language pathologists, physical therapists, occupational therapists, and educational specialists. The physical evaluation should determine the user's gross motor skills, range of motion, adaptive posturing and seating, fine motor accuracy, and speed of movement. An evaluation of language skills should determine the user's current communication strategies and receptive language skills, and the communicative needs of the user (Shane, 1980). Academic and cognitive skills should be evaluated with a language specialist to determine a language symbol system that is within the user's capabilities. In addition, the academic and vocational skills and needs of the user should be identified. The evaluation results are then used to determine the communication aid, or unaided system,

and symbolic system that best fits the user's needs and skills.

When an aided communication system is being developed, the system should be designed to increase communication speed. Message cost can be used to analyze the communication speed of augmentative communication systems (Goodenough-Trepagnier & Prather, 1981). Message cost equals the number of separate motor movements necessary to encode a message. For example, the message cost of letter-by-letter encoding for *I want to go to the store* equals 25 when blank spaces between words are included. By using whole word symbols, message cost is reduced to seven. If unnecessary words are eliminated (i.e., *I want go store*), message cost is further reduced to four. Baker (1984) theorized that there is a maximum message cost limit of five to seven separate motor movements. Any system that requires more motor movements to encode messages will not result in effective communication. Recently, ideographic symbol systems such as Minspeak have been developed; they reduce message cost to three or four motor movements per message (Baker, 1984).

Once an augmentative system is developed, extensive user training is required. There are two components to the training process. The first is augmentative system training. The user needs to learn how the augmentative system functions. Communication aid operation, vocabulary training, and the production of phrases and sentences are aspects of system training. The second component is communication training. Studies have documented that many nonspeaking persons who are trained to use their augmentative communication systems are unable to communicate effectively (Calculator & Dollaghan, 1982; Harris, 1982). Normal children learn how to interact communicatively and socially with others through experience. Nonspeaking handicapped persons have limited interactive experiences and need to be taught communicative and social interaction skills. Communication training should include teaching the user how to initiate communication across many different social contexts (Yoder & Kraat, 1983). Nonspeaking persons also need to learn how to respond to others, how to maintain conversations, and how to increase intelligibility in various contexts.

The ability to communicate with others is a binding element within members of a society. The development of augmentative communication systems has opened many avenues of communication for the nonspeaking population. While most augmentative systems are not yet perfect replacements for oral speech, they do provide a means of communication and interaction with others.

## REFERENCES

American Speech-Language Hearing Association. (1980). Nonspeech communication: A position paper. *ASHA, 22,* 267–272.

Baker, B. (1984). Minspeak: An introduction to semantic compaction systems. *Speech Technology 1984,* 168–170.

Calculator, S., & Dollaghan, C. (1982). The use of communication boards in a residential setting: An evaluation. *Journal of Speech and Hearing Disorders, 47,* 281–287.

Foulds, R. (1980). *Communication rates for nonspeech expression as the result of manual tasks and linguistic constraints.* Proceedings of the International Conference on Rehabilitation Engineering, Toronto, Canada.

Goodenough-Trepagnier, C., & Prather, P. (1981). Communication systems for the nonvocal based on frequent phoneme sequences. *Journal of Speech and Hearing Research, 24,* 322–324.

Harris, D. (1982). Communicative interaction processes involving nonvocal physically handicapped persons. *Topics in Language Disorders, 14,* 389–409.

Musselwhite, C. R., & St. Louis, K. W. (1982). *Communication programming for the severely handicapped: Vocal and nonvocal strategies.* Houston: College-Hill.

Shane, H. C. (1980). Approaches to assessing the communication of people who are nonoral. In R. Schiefulbusch (Ed.), *Nonspeech language and communication: Analysis and intervention.* Baltimore, MD: University Park Press.

Skelly, M., & Schinsky, M. (1979). *Amer-Ind gestural code based on universal American Indian hand talk.* New York: Elsevier North Holland.

Vanderheiden, G. (1985). *Nonvocal communication resource book—revised.* Madison, WI: Trace Research and Development Center, University of Wisconsin.

Yoder, D., & Kraat, A. (1983). Intervention issues in nonspeech communication. In J. Miller, C. Yoder, & R. Schiefulbusch (Eds.), *Contemporary issues in language intervention.* Rockville, MD: ASHA Press.

SHARON L. GLENNEN
*Pennsylvania State University*

## AMERICAN SIGN LANGUAGE

## AUGMENTATIVE COMMUNICATION SYSTEMS

## AMBLYOPIA

Ambliopia, also called suppression blindness (Harley & Lawrence, 1977), is a visual condition that occurs when an anatomically healthy eye cannot see because of some other defect (Eden, 1978). Ambliopia is commonly called "lazy eye"; however, this is a misnomer (Eden, 1978) because it implies that ambliopia results from a muscular problem. Actually, ambliopia can have a number of causes. For example, strabismus (a condition in which the two eyes are not parallel when viewing an object) can lead to ambliopia. The brain ignores the visual signals of one of the two eyes to reduce the annoyance of double vision. Other factors such as astigmatism can also lead to ambliopia.

The degree of visual impairment associated with ambliopia can vary a great deal from losses that are just below normal to those in which only large objects can be identified. Treatment of ambliopia consists of treating the causal factors. It must be accomplished early in life, (before the age of six) because the child is likely to permanently lose the ability to process a 20/20 image from the affected eye.

### REFERENCES

Eden, J. (1978). *The eye book.* New York: Viking.

Harley, R. K., & Lawrence, G. A. (1977). *Visual impairment in the schools.* Springfield, IL: Thomas.

THOMAS E. ALLEN
*Gallaudet College*

## BLIND

## CATARACTS

## AMERICAN ACADEMY FOR CEREBRAL PALSY AND DEVELOPMENTAL MEDICINE (AACPDM)

The American Academy for Cerebral Palsy, founded in 1947, changed its name in 1976 to the American Academy for Cerebral Palsy and Developmental Medicine (AACPDM). This is a professional organization of physicians, diplomates of specialty boards, and persons holding a PhD degree in specialties concerned with diagnosis, care, treatment, and research into cerebral palsy and developmental disorders. The AACPDM's 13,000 members also include associate members from the fields of occupational and physical therapy and speech-language pathology.

The AACPDM's activities and services include the presentation of awards and grants for research, demonstration, and personnel preparation. The organization also supports or conducts continuing education activities. The AACPDM holds an annual convention and publishes the *Journal of Developmental Medicine* and *Child Neurology* (both bimonthly). The office address is P.O. Box 11083, 2315 Westwood Avenue, Richmond, VA 23230.

SHIRLEY A. JONES
*Virginia Polytechnic Institute and State University*

## AMERICAN ANNALS OF THE DEAF

The *American Annals of the Deaf* is a joint publication of the Conference of Educational Administrators Serving the Deaf and the Convention of American Instructors of the Deaf. First published in 1847, *Annals* is the oldest and most widely read English-language journal dealing with deafness and the education of deaf persons.

The current information about research and projects being conducted in the field is targeted for classroom teachers, school principals, program administrators, counselors, audiologists, speech therapists, and other specialists involved in the education and training of hearing-impaired individuals.

The special Reference Issue is used as a source of information about schools and programs for the deaf throughout the United States and Canada.

*Annals* is published in March, July, October, and December. The special Reference Issue is published in April. When a particular subject area demands attention, special bonus issues are published at no additional cost to subscribers.

ELAINE FLETCHER-JANZEN
*Texas A&M University*

DEAF

## AMERICAN ASSOCIATION FOR THE ADVANCEMENT OF SCIENCE (AAAS)

The American Association for the Advancement of Science (AAAS) was founded in 1848. With its membership of 138,285, it is the largest general scientific organization representing all fields of science. The total membership is divided into 138,000 individuals and 285 professional organizations, scientific societies, and state and city academies, many of which sponsor junior academies of science. The AAAS hopes to promote human welfare through the work of scientists and the effectiveness of science. The organization consists of 28 sections: atmospheric and hydrospheric sciences, astronomy, anthropology, agriculture, biological sciences, dentistry, chemistry, education, engineering, geology and geography, general history and philosophy of science, information, computing and communications, industrial science, mathematics, pharmaceutical sciences, medical sciences, physics, psychology, economics, political and social sciences, and statistics.

The AAAS convention meets annually in May. Its committees cover science, arms control and national security, arid lands, climate science, engineering and public policy, opportunities in science, public understanding of science, and scientific freedom and responsibility. The organization bestows the AAAS-Westinghouse Science Journalism Awards, the Newcomb-Cleveland Award, the AAAS Socio-Psychological Prize, and the AAAS Scientific Freedom and Responsibility Award.

The AAAS publications include *Science* (published weekly), *Science 83* (published monthly), Science Books and Films (five times per year), *Science Educa-News*

(quarterly), the *Handbook* (annual), *Research and Development in the Federal Budget* (annual), *Symposium Volumes*, and compendia-form general and science reference works.

MARY LEON PEERY
*Texas A&M University*

## AMERICAN ASSOCIATION FOR THE SEVERELY HANDICAPPED

See ASSOCIATION FOR PERSONS WITH SEVERE HANDICAPS.

## AMERICAN ASSOCIATION OF COLLEGES FOR TEACHER EDUCATION (AACTE)

The American Association of Colleges for Teacher Education (AACTE) is a national, voluntary organization of colleges and universities dedicated to the preparation of teachers and other educational personnel. Located at One Dupont Circle, Suite 610, Washington, DC 20036, AACTE serves as a central, professionally affiliated vehicle for the promotion of effective and innovative teacher education programs.

The AACTE and its predecessor organizations represent more than a century of service that encompasses the movement of collegiate-based teacher, counselor, and administrative training from normal schools to comprehensive universities (AACTE, 1986). The member institutions of the association reflect the diversity of personnel preparation options available in teacher education. The network of 700 nationally or regionally accredited institutional members includes small liberal arts colleges, state universities, and larger research institutions. As a group, AACTE member institutions produce more than 80% of new school personnel each academic year.

As a professional organization, AACTE (including its 44 state-level affiliates) is recognized as the primary representative of teacher education interests before Congress, state legislatures, the media, and other national and state organizations. The association's mission is directed to the development of teacher education through public advocacy at the federal, state, and local levels; professional development activities for the administration and faculty of member institutions; and data collection and analysis. It is also devoted to the publication and dissemination of reports on issues of importance to the teacher education community.

## REFERENCE

American Association of Colleges for Teacher Education. (1986). *For a profession on the move*. Washington, DC: Author.

GEORGE JAMES HAGERTY
*Stonehill College*

## AMERICAN ASSOCIATION ON MENTAL DEFICIENCY (AAMD)

The American Association on Mental Deficiency (AAMD) was founded in 1906 and was known originally as the Association of Medical Officers of American Institutions of Idiotic and Feebleminded Children. Its current name was adopted in 1933. The AAMD is a professional organization that has encouraged research in mental retardation and has been responsible for establishing many institutions for the management, training, and treatment of individuals with mental retardation (Sloan & Stevens, 1976).

It has also established guidelines for professionals interested in the diagnosis and treatment of the mentally retarded. One of its important functions has been to expand knowledge in the area of mental retardation by publishing monographs as well as two bimonthly journals, *The American Journal of Mental Deficiency* and *Mental Retardation* (Gruber & Cloyd, 1986). The AAMD maintains 14 major divisions that include administration, communication disorders, education, general, legal process, medicine, nursing, occupational and physical therapy, private residential facilities, psychology, religion, resident living, social work, and vocational rehabilitation. Membership is open to professionals in all disciplines who work with the mentally retarded. Membership fees depend on the division(s) joined. The AAMD's main office is located at 1719 Kalorama Road, NW, Washington, DC 20009.

## REFERENCES

Gruber, K., & Cloyd, I. (Eds.). (1986). *Encyclopedia of associations* (Vol. I, Part 2). Detroit, MI: Gale Research.
Sloan, W., & Stevens, H. A. (1976). *A century of concern: A history of the American Association on Mental Deficiency*. Washington, DC: American Association on Mental Deficiency.

EMILIA C. LOPEZ
*Fordham University*

## AAMD CLASSIFICATION SYSTEM

## AMERICAN BOARD OF PROFESSIONAL PSYCHOLOGY (ABPP)

Originally named the American Board of Examiners in Professional Psychology, this organization was renamed the American Board of Professional Psychology in 1968. Founded in 1947, it is comprised of a board of 10 trustees with headquarters in Washington, DC. This certification board conducts oral examinations and awards diplomas in four specialties for advanced study: clinical psychology, counseling psychology, industrial and organization psychology, and school psychology. Necessary for certification is 5 years of qualifying experience in psychological practice.

The ABPP annually presents the Distinguished Professional Achievement Award. This and other awards are presented at the annual convention in August or September. Publications of the ABPP include the *Manual for Oral Examinations* (annual), *Policies and Procedures* (annual), and the *Directory of Diplomates* (triennial).

MARY LEON PEERY
*Texas A&M University*

## AMERICAN CANCER SOCIETY (ACS)

The American Cancer Society (ACS) is a voluntary organization committed to the elimination and control of cancer. This nationwide effort is conducted through 58 largely state-incorporated divisions and is accomplished through four major activities: (1) the public education program, which emphasizes regular, preventive care for adults, attention to specific warning signals, and information regarding positive outcomes when prompt diagnosis and preventive measures are adopted; (2) a comprehensive professional education program designed to stimulate health professionals to use the best cancer detection, diagnostic, and patient management techniques available, to exchange knowledge on the latest cancer-fighting techniques, and to disseminate new ideas and developments in the community; (3) a wide range of volunteer-based service and rehabilitation programs to assist cancer patients and their families with the necessary practical and emotional support so vital to coping with the wide-ranging effects of the disease; and (4) research into all aspects of cancer, from direct clinical investigations and training to prospective cancer prevention studies.

Begun in 1913, the ACS raised $10,000 in its first year. Today, over 70 years later, the annual income of the society is over $180 million. Over $1½ billion have been invested in research since the society's first large-scale national fund campaign in 1945.

The core of the organization's effort resides in its 2 million volunteers who implement the society's public and professional education programs, service programs for patients and families, and raise funds for research programs.

## REFERENCES

American Cancer Society. *American Cancer Society—What it is, what it does, how it began, who directs it, where it is going.* New York: Author.

American Cancer Society, Massachusetts Division. (1984). *Annual Report*. Boston: Author.

American Cancer Society. (1985). *Cancer facts and figures*. New York: Author.

CRAIG S. HIGGINS
*Stonehill College*

## AMERICAN EDUCATIONAL RESEARCH ASSOCIATION (AERA)

The American Educational Research Association (AERA) was founded in 1915 as the National Association of Directors of Educational Research. The AERA is an international organization of educators, professors, research directors, specialists, and graduate students interested in educational research. The objectives of AERA include improving the status and quality of research and promoting application and findings of research to educational problems (American Education Research Association, undated).

The AERA is divided into 10 divisions: administration; counseling and human development; curriculum studies; education in the professions; history and historiography; instruction and learning; measurement and research methodology; postsecondary education; school evaluation and program development; and social context of education.

Journals published by the AERA include the *American Educational Research Journal*; *Contemporary Education Review*; *Educational Evaluation and Policy Analysis*; *Journal of Educational Statistics*; *Review of Educational Research*; *Educational Researcher*; *Review of Research in Education* (annual); *Encyclopedia of Educational Research*; and *Handbook of Research on Teaching* (both revised every 10 years).

The AERA holds an annual convention for the presentation of reports, papers, and awards. It also holds research training programs and monitors federal educational research activities.

### REFERENCE

American Educational Research Association. (Undated brochure). *American Educational Research Association: A membership for your discipline*. Washington, DC: Author.

DOUGLAS L. FRIEDMAN
*Fordham University*

## AMERICAN EDUCATIONAL RESEARCH JOURNAL (AERJ)

The *American Educational Research Journal* (AERJ) publishes original reports of empirical and theoretical studies that reflect a significant and substantial inquiry in education. Typically articles accepted are "(1) empirically test theory that has direct application to education, (2) focus on dependent variables that are relevant to classrooms and schools and (3) directly relate to improving school practice" (the editors, 1981, p. 257).

The range of topics, issues, and levels of education represented in *AERJ* tends to be broad rather than concentrated in any particular area. Articles involving research in special education occasionally appear in the journal. The *AERJ* has been published continuously since 1964 by the American Educational Research Association and appears quarterly (spring, summer, fall, and winter).

### REFERENCE

The editors. (1981). Statement from the editors. *American Educational Research Journal, 18*, 257.

DOUGLAS L. FRIEDMAN
*Fordham University*

## AMERICAN FOUNDATION FOR THE BLIND (AFB)

The American Foundation for the Blind (AFB) was established in 1921 as a nonprofit organization to serve as the national partner of local services for the blind and visually impaired. The organization traces its origin to a meeting of a group of professionals in Vinton, Iowa, in the summer of 1921 (Koestler, 1976). This meeting, comprised mainly of officers of the American Association of Workers for the Blind (AAWB), recognized the pressing need for a national organization that was not affiliated with special interest groups, professional organizations, or any local, regional, or state organization currently serving the needs of the blind.

Helen Keller was closely identified with AFB from the early 1920s until her death. Keller represented AFB in their efforts to educate legislators and the public about the services blind people need.

The AFB has national consultants in education, employment, aging, orientation and mobility, low vision, rehabilitation, special populations, radio information services, and preschool. The AFB also provides consumer resources, services, and products and carries out research in all areas of blindness. The seven regional offices of AFB provide a direct liaison with public and private institutions including schools and agencies serving the blind and visually impaired in the United States.

For more information about AFB, teachers may write AFB Headquarters at 15 West 16th Street, New York, NY 10011.

REFERENCE

Koestler, F. A. (1976). *The unseen minority*. New York: McKay.

GIDEON JONES
*Florida State University*

## AMERICAN PRINTING HOUSE FOR THE BLIND MOBILITY TRAINING

## AMERICAN GUIDANCE SERVICE

American Guidance Service (AGS), founded in 1957, is an educational publishing company located in Circle Pines, Minnesota. Using the philosophy that AGS and professionals are "partners in developing human potential," this company publishes a wide variety of instructional material and educational and psychological tests for use by teachers, counselors, psychologists, social workers, parents, and others. AGS publishes material for all ages, although much of their material is geared to children in special education or children with learning and emotional problems.

The AGS tests include those for general ability and development, educational achievement and diagnosis, speech, motor skills, and vocational interest. Examples of familiar AGS tests are the Kaufman Assessment Battery for Children, Vineland Adaptive Behavior Scales, Peabody Picture Vocabulary Test—Revised, Woodcock Reading Mastery Tests, Key-Math Diagnostic Arithmetic Tests, and Harrington–O'Shea Career Decision Making System.

Instructional materials include programs for early development, computer learning, language development, reading, writing, mathematics, personal growth, and teen guidance. Small Wonder, Peabody Language Development Kits, KeyMath Teach and Practice, Developing Understanding of Self and Others, and Bookfinder are just a few of the AGS instructional materials. Programs for parenting, marriage, and family living include Systematic Training for Effective Parenting, Training in Marriage Enrichment, and PREP for Effective Family Living.

The AGS publishes two catalogs each year: one for instructional materials and tests and another for parenting, marriage, and family living. Exhibits of AGS materials may be found at many local, state, and regional conferences, as well as at national conventions for organizations such as the Council for Exceptional Children, International Reading Association, American Association for Counseling and Development, and American Psychological Association.

PATTI L. HARRISON
*University of Alabama*

## AMERICAN INSTITUTE—THE TRAINING SCHOOL AT VINELAND

The American Institute—The Training School at Vineland, is located in Vineland, New Jersey (Main Road and Landis Avenue, Vineland, NJ 08360). The school and training facility were founded in 1887; they are under the supervision and administrative management of Elwyn Institutes. The facility serves children and adults who are mentally retarded, brain damaged, emotionally disturbed, physically handicapped, and learning disabled.

The school programs are ungraded at the elementary and secondary levels. The school features education and training programs that are designed to train young people to return to the community. The training programs serve mildly handicapped to the severely retarded students. The range of educational programs and vocational training experiences are developed with individualized educational plans and rehabilitation services. The facility is internationally recognized for the pioneering works of Binet and Doll. The Standford Binet tests were translated and norms were developed at the school. Dr. Edward Doll is recognized as the pioneer in the development of the Vineland Social Maturity Scale.

REFERENCE

Sargent, J. K. (1982). *The Directory for exceptional children* (9th ed.). Boston, MA: Porter Sargent.

PAUL C. RICHARDSON
*Elwyn Institutes,
Elwyn, Pennsylvania*

## AMERICAN JOURNAL OF MENTAL DEFICIENCY

The *American Journal of Mental Deficiency* is a professional journal that has been approved by the American Psychological Association (APA). It is published by the American Association on Mental Deficiency on a bimonthly basis. The journal's primary purpose is to publish theoretical manuscripts and research in the area of mental retardation. Its emphasis is on presenting material of an objective, scientific, and experimental nature. Books on mental retardation are also reviewed periodically. The journal address is 1719 Kalorama Road, NW, Washington, DC 20009.

EMILIA C. LOPEZ
*Fordham University*

## AMERICAN JOURNAL OF OCCUPATIONAL THERAPY

The *American Journal of Occupational Therapy* is published monthly by the American Occupational Therapy

Association, Inc., located at 1383 Piccard Drive, Rockville, MD 20850. This journal was established in 1947, and in 1978 and 1979 was published under the name *AJOT: The American Journal of Occupational Therapy*. Research relating to the field of occupational therapy is reported in the journal, which also includes book reviews and advertising. The current circulation of the journal is approximately 40,000. It is available in microform from University Microfilms (UMI).

SHIRLEY A. JONES
*Virginia Polytechnic Institute and State University*

## AMERICAN JOURNAL OF ORTHOPSYCHIATRY (AJO)

The *American Journal of Orthopsychiatry* (AJO), is the quarterly journal of the American Orthopsychiatric Association. The association was founded in 1926 and began publication of AJO in 1930. The AJO is a quarterly, refereed, scholarly journal written from a multidisciplinary perspective. The AJO is dedicated to public policy, professional practice, and information that relates to mental health and human development. Clinical, theoretical, research, review, and expository papers are published in AJO. These papers are essentially synergistic and directed at concept and theory development, reconceptualization of major issues, explanation, and interpretation.

During the first 50 years of publication, AJO has had just five editors. Lawson Lowrey was the founding editor and served the journal in this capacity for 18 years. Beginning in 1973, the association adopted a practice of appointing editors for a five-year, nonrenewable term.

The AJO concentrates on many topics of concern to special educators. During its lifetime, AJO's articles have centered around the topics of social issues and the handicapped, childhood psychosis, psychopharmacology, school phobia, depression, suicide, child abuse, mental retardation, and treatment of all of these disorders. The contributors' list and editorial board have, over the years, featured some of the finest scholars from developmental medicine, developmental psychopathology, child development, school psychology, clinical psychology, special education, neurology, psychiatry, and related mental health fields. The AJO is an influential journal that publishes top scholars' writing on special education.

CECIL R. REYNOLDS
*Texas A&M University*

## AMERICAN ORTHOPSYCHIATRIC ASSOCIATION

## AMERICAN JOURNAL OF PSYCHIATRY

The *American Journal of Psychiatry* is published monthly by the American Psychiatric Association at 1400 K Street, NW, Washington, DC 20005. This journal was first established in 1844 under the title *American Journal of Insanity*; it has been published under its current title since 1921. In addition to reports of research studies and professional articles of general interest in the field of psychiatry, the *American Journal of Psychiatry* contains book reviews and advertising. In October 1985, its circulation was approximately 44,000. This journal is available in microform from University Microfilms (UMI).

SHIRLEY A. JONES
*Virginia Polytechnic Institute and State University*

## AMERICAN OCCUPATIONAL THERAPY FOUNDATION

The American Occupational Therapy Foundation was founded in 1965 as the American Occupational Therapy Association's (AOTA) philanthropic sister organization. The foundation has devoted its energies to raising funds and resources in three program areas—scholarships, publications, and research—associated with the profession of occupational therapy and health-care delivery.

The foundation has eight active endowed scholarship funds, and other smaller funds working toward endowments. The scholarship program provides financial assistance to undergraduate and graduate students in the field of occupational therapy.

The foundation's publication program aims to increase public knowledge and understanding of the occupational therapy profession. In addition to various reports and documents, it publishes *The Occupational Therapy Journal of Research*, and has produced a major bibliography of completed research in the field. The foundation supports the Occupational Therapy Library, which supplies requested materials through interlibrary loan.

A research program is conducted through the foundation's Office of Professional Research Services. Program services include the Academy of Research, support of researchers through grant awards (in association with the AOTA), and doctoral and postdoctoral fellowship awards to support researchers.

The American Occupational Therapy Foundation is located at 1383 Piccard Drive, Rockville, MD 20850.

SHIRLEY A. JONES
*Virginia Polytechnic Institute and State University*

# AMERICAN ORTHOPSYCHIATRIC ASSOCIATION (ORTHO)

The American Orthopsychiatric Association (Ortho) was formed at the invitation of Herman Adler and Karl Menninger at the Institute for Juvenile Research in Chicago in 1924 under the name of the Association of American Orthopsychiatrists. The group operated informally, debating its name and purpose and finally founding Ortho a year later. In 1926 Ortho amended its constitution, which limited membership to physicians, to redefine membership to include psychiatrists, psychologists, social workers, and other professional persons "whose work and interests lie in the study and treatment of conduct disorders." According to Eisenberg and DeMaso (1985), the first published membership roster, published October 1, 1927, included 45 psychiatrists, 12 psychologists, 5 social workers, and several lawyers and penologists. Ortho had as its purpose the centralization of the techniques, objectives, and aspirations of psychiatrists, psychologists, and related mental health workers whose primary interests were in the area of human behavior, providing a common meeting ground for students of behavior problems and for fostering scientific research and its dissemination. The early membership included names familiar to special educators, including such notables as Edgar Doll, Lightner Witmer, and Carl Murchison.

Lightner Witmer, noted among historians of psychology as the man who coined the term clinical psychology, founded school psychology and established the first psychological clinic; he also coined the term orthogenics and established the team approach to children's problems when he invited neurologists to collaborate on case studies (Eisenberg & DeMaso, 1985). Ortho subsequently became a major force in the establishment of the child guidance movement in the early 1900s. In 1930 Ortho established the *American Journal of Orthopsychiatry*, a widely read and respected journal that in its early years vigorously debated the roles and functions of various professionals (e.g., psychiatrists, psychologists, social workers, etc.) in the treatment of childhood mental health disorders.

Presently, many special educators belong to Ortho. It is a large, robust organization of more than 10,000 members. It is involved in social, scientific, and public policy issues, including diagnosis, evaluation, and treatment, relevant to the improvement of the lives of the handicapped. The *American Journal of Orthopsychiatry* is provided as a benefit of membership; it contains many articles of interest to special educators.

## REFERENCE

Eisenberg, L., & DeMaso, D. R. (1985). Fifty years of the *American Journal of Orthopsychiatry*: An overview and introduction. In E. Flaxman & E. Herman (Eds.), *American Journal of Ortho-psychiatry: Annotated index: Vols. 1–50. 1930–1980.* Greenwich, CT: JAI.

CECIL R. REYNOLDS
*Texas A&M University*

## AMERICAN JOURNAL OF ORTHOPSYCHIATRY
WITMER, LIGHTNER

## AMERICAN PHYSICAL THERAPY ASSOCIATION

The American Physical Therapy Association (APTA) endeavors to improve physical therapy services and education through accrediting academic programs in physical therapy; assisting states in preparing certification examinations; and offering workshops and continuing education courses for therapists at the national and local level. Information is available about careers in physical therapy, accredited preparation programs, sources of student financial aid, and employment opportunities. A variety of pamphlets are available on prevention of injuries and chronic or degenerative conditions. The association publishes a newsletter and journal. Bibliographies have been prepared on topics including resources for stroke victims, quadriplegics, paraplegics, amputees, parents, and educators. Members benefit from information on questions regarding practice and disabilities. The association also serves as a referral source for individuals who require physical therapy services. Association offices are located at 1111 North Fairfax Street, Alexandria, VA 22314. Telephone: (703) 684-2782.

PHILIP R. JONES
*Virginia Polytechnic Institute and State University*

## AMERICAN PRINTING HOUSE FOR THE BLIND

The American Printing House for the Blind (APH), located in Louisville, Kentucky, was founded in 1858. It is the oldest national, private nonprofit agency for the blind in the United States and the largest publishing house for the blind in the world. In 1879 the Act to Promote the Education of the Blind was passed by Congress. This act enables the American Printing House for the Blind to receive grants from the federal government to be used for educational texts and aids for visually handicapped students. The American Printing House for the Blind annually registers all eligible blind students enrolled in public educational facilities lower than the college level. It also determines annually, on the basis of the appropriation from Congress, the current per capita quota for the purchase of books or aids for each student (American Printing House for the Blind, 1982).

The APH's activities are guided by a board of trustees consisting of seven members and by all superintendents of schools for the blind and all chief state school officers who serve as ex officio members of the board of trustees. In addition, the publications and research and development committees provide input to the APH staff by reviewing progress and projected projects (American Printing House for the Blind Annual Report, 1984).

Besides producing materials in various media and manufacturing educational aids for visually handicapped students, The American Printing House for the Blind, through its Instructional Materials Reference Center, contains a central catalog of volunteer and commercially produced school textbooks. The catalog has been transcribed into braille, large type, and cassette tapes and disk recordings. Volunteer transcribers report the books that they produce and APH in turn provides a continuous reference service to pupils, teachers, and parents in need of particular texts. The central catalog enables visually handicapped students to acquire specific materials in the least amount of time and it helps to prevent duplication of materials at numerous locations throughout the country. Other APH catalogs include lists of Braille music and magazines, talking books, and educational aids (Schrotberger, 1981). The American Printing House for the Blind, through its fund-raising efforts, also, publishes braille and recorded editions of *The Reader's Digest* and recorded copies of *Newsweek* magazine.

## REFERENCES

*American Printing House for the Blind* (1982). Louisville, KY: American Printing House for the Blind.

*American Printing House for the Blind One Hundred Sixteenth Annual Report* (1984). Louisville, KY: American Printing House for the Blind.

Nolan, C. Y. (1983). *Providing educational materials under the "Act to Promote the Education of the Blind."* Louisville, KY: American Printing House for the Blind.

Schrotberger, W. B. (1981). Sources of materials for the visually handicapped. In G. Napier, D. Kappan, D. Tuttle, W. Schrotberger, & A. Dennison (Eds.), *Handbook for teachers of the visually handicapped* (pp. 61–76). Louisville, KY: American Printing House for the Blind.

ROSANNE K. SILBERMAN
*Hunter College, City University
of New York*

## LIBRARY SERVICES FOR THE HANDICAPPED
## LIBRARY FOR THE BLIND & PHYSICALLY HANDICAPPED

## AMERICAN PSYCHIATRIC ASSOCIATION (APA)

The American Psychiatric Association (APA), founded in 1844, was originally known as the Association of Medical Superintendents of American Institutions for the Insane. Its current name came to be used in 1921. The APA was incorporated in the District of Columbia in 1927. The objectives of the association include (1) improving the treatment, rehabilitation, and care of the mentally ill, the mentally retarded, and the emotionally disturbed; (2) promoting research, professional education, and prevention of psychiatric disabilities; (3) advancing standards of services and facilities; (4) fostering cooperation of professionals concerned with medical, psychological, social, and legal aspects of mental health and illness; (5) providing information to practitioners, scientists, and the public; and (6) promoting the best interests of patients and those using or needing mental health services.

*The American Journal of Psychiatry* (the official journal of APA) has a monthly circulation of over 40,000. *Hospital and Community Psychiatry* (monthly) and *Psychiatric News* (twice monthly) are other publications. Medical student members and members in training also receive *Psychiatric Residents Newsletter*. Workshops, continuing medical education courses, seminars, and library services are available to members. The APA offices are located at 1400 K Street, NW, Washington, DC 20005.

PHILIP R. JONES
*Virginia Polytechnic Institute
and State University*

## AMERICAN PSYCHOLOGICAL ASSOCIATION

The American Psychological Association (APA) is the nation's major psychology organization. The APA works to advance psychology as a science and a profession, and to promote human welfare. When APA was established in 1892, psychology was a new profession and the organization had fewer than three dozen members. Over the years the association has grown rapidly: in 1985 the APA had more than 70,000 members, 44 divisions in specialized subfields and interest areas, and 53 affiliated state psychological associations.

The growth of the science and profession of psychology is reflected in the development of diverse programs and services administered by the association. These programs aim to disseminate psychological knowledge, promote research, improve research methods and conditions, and develop the qualifications and competence of psychologists through standards of education, ethical conduct, and professional practice.

The program and business activities of APA are coordinated at the association's central office in Washington, DC, and nearby Arlington, Virginia. These offices are headquarters for APA's programs in governance affairs, national policy studies, public affairs, communications, and financial affairs. Through these programs the central office staff provides information to members, other professionals, students, and the public through the publication of books, major journals, pamphlets, the monthly APA *Monitor* newspaper, *Psychology Today*, and a growing spectrum of bibliographic and abstracting services covering the literature of psychology.

The affairs of the association are administered by the Board of Directors, which is responsible for the work of an executive officer who administers the affairs of the central office. The Board of Directors is composed of a president, past president, and president-elect, all of whom are elected by APA members at large, and a treasurer, a secretary, and six board members who are elected by the Council of Representatives. The Council of Representatives is composed of 120 members of the association who are elected by their division and state members in proportion to the annual assignment of seats by the membership. The Council of Representatives sets policy for the association, and those policies are administered by the Board of Directors through the executive officer and the staff of the central office.

The governance affairs office of the association coordinates and directs psychology programs and activities such as accreditation of doctoral programs in professional psychology and predoctoral internship sites; supervision of educational affairs aimed at identifying and analyzing developments in higher education and training of psychologists; setting standards for scientific and professional ethics, professional affairs, scientific affairs, social and ethical responsibility of psychologists, and overseeing special issues concerning ethnic minorities and women's programs.

The national policy studies of APA help to formulate and implement federal policy and legislative activities of the association. The Office of National Policy Studies develops advocacy positions, informs Congress and federal agencies of psychology's concerns, keeps the APA membership and governance structure informed of related policy issues, and develops working coalitions with outside organizations on common legislative issues.

The Public Affairs Office works to provide overall direction on the ways organized psychology is presented to its national and international public. The office works with television, radio, and print media to demonstrate the contributions psychologists make to society and to improve public understanding of psychology's broad scope and application.

The APA publishes 27 periodicals and a variety of books, brochures, and pamphlets. Among these are *American Psychologist*, the official journal of the association, and *Psychological Abstracts*, which contains abstracts of the world's literature on psychology and related disciplines.

Each year more than 10,000 psychologists and other individuals attend the APA convention in late summer. This is the world's largest meeting of psychologists and one of the largest professional conventions in the United States. The week-long program features more than 3000 presentations through symposiums, lectures, invited addresses, specialized workshops, and other forums. Through the convention, practitioners and the public are given the opportunity to learn of the latest findings from psychological research, their applications in society, and other professional, scientific, and educational issues.

From energy conservation and industrial productivity to child development, aging, and prevention of stress and related illness, hardly a personal or national problem exists that does not demand an understanding of human behavior. Even modern technological innovations emerge from the ability of the mind to transform observations and data into action. Because of their fundamental understanding of behavior, psychologists are increasingly consulted for ways to increase human progress and well-being.

NADINE M. LAMBERT
*University of California,
Berkeley*

## AMERICAN PSYCHOLOGIST

*American Psychologist* is the official journal of the American Psychological Association. As such, it is the primary archival chronicle of the affairs of the association. It includes minutes of the annual business meeting, reports of the treasurer, executive officer, and Policy and Planning Board, lists new members and associates, and provides other reports of boards and committees that represent policies and practices affecting members of the association. In addition to reporting on the business of the association, *American Psychologist* is the primary source for more general discussions concerning psychology as a science, a profession, and a means of promoting human welfare. As the most widely circulated and most frequently cited psychological journal in the world, the editors of *American Psychologist* assume a special responsibility to inform psychologists and the public about psychology's impact and potential regarding issues and problems that involve people and human behavior.

In setting forth general editoral policy for the journal, past and present editors have agreed that *American Psychologist* should (1) contribute to enlightened participation in organized psychology and thereby to effective functioning of the association; (2) examine the relationship between psychology and society, especially as historical, cultural, and societal influences have an impact on the science and practice of psychology; (3) present the status and foster the development of the diverse applications of psychological knowledge in a form appropriate to the general membership; and (4) present the status of substantive areas of psychological knowledge in a form and style suitable to the general membership and to the interested public. Information about *American Psychologist* can be obtained from the Editor, *American Psychologist*, American

Psychological Association, 1200 Seventeenth Street N.W., Washington, DC 20036.

NADINE M. LAMBERT
*University of California,
Berkeley*

# AMERICAN SIGN LANGUAGE

During the past 20 years, there has been a rapid and widespread increase in the use of sign language as a viable means of communication by deaf and hearing individuals. American Sign Language (ASL), also known as Ameslan, has been recognized as a natural language with its own unique grammatical structure (Klima & Bellugi, 1979; Liddell, 1980; Wilbur, 1979). Approximately half a million deaf Americans and Canadians currently use ASL (Wilbur, 1979).

Systematic research on the linguistic bases of ASL and the importance of sign language to the cultural identity of the deaf community began less than two decades ago. In 1960 William Stokoe published the first linguistic analysis of American Sign Language, and in 1965 he and his associates published the first dictionary of ASL (Stokoe, Casterline, & Croneberg, 1976). The 1970s and early 1980s were an exceptionally active period in terms of deafness and sign language research. Much of the research during this period examined the linguistic aspects of ASL, while only a few studies investigated psycholinguistic, sociolinguistic, and/or developmental issues.

Sign language is composed of specific movements and shapes of the hands, arms, eyes, face, head, and body that correspond to the words and suprasegmental features of spoken languages. In delineating the major components of ASL, linguists find it useful to differentiate between manual and nonmanual aspects of signing. Sign formation, originally called "cherology" by Stokoe (1960), corresponds to the phonological system of oral languages. Each sign consists of four basic parameters: hand shape (dez); location or place of articulation (tab); movement in a particular direction (sig); and palm orientation occurring with various hand shapes.

Another way of classifying signs is on the basis of specific morphologic and/or lexical characteristics. One family of signs is that based on motion and direction differences. For example, the sign for "appear" is formed by bringing the right index finger up between the index and middle fingers of the left hand. By moving in the opposite direction, that is by drawing the right index finger down, the signer creates the sign for "disappear." Some families of signs are based on hand shape. Signs expressing emotion are produced with the open eight hand shape, where the middle fingertip touches the thumb to form the hand shape for the number eight. This hand shape occurs in the signs "excite," "depress," "feel," and "like."

Some families of signs are based on the location of the sign in space. Masculine and feminine signs are differentiated on the basis of location. For example, the sign for "man" is made at the forehead by grasping the imaginary brim of a hat with four fingers and the thumb and then bringing the flat hand, palm down, away from the head at the level of the imaginary hat. The sign of "woman" is produced at the level of the cheek by moving the inside of the thumb of the right "A" hand shape down along the right cheek toward the chin and then bringing the flat hand, palm down, away from the face.

There are similarities in some of the syntactic mechanisms used in ASL and English; others are specialized to accommodate communication in the visual–gestural mode. It has been argued that sign order is relatively flexible and that several built-in syntactic devices help to convey information efficiently. One such device is the deletion of grammatical morphemes such as articles and the copular verb "to be." Information is preserved by establishing positions of reference in space and referring to them through pointing and eye gaze. A second device is the incorporation of location, number, manner, size, and shape of signs. A third syntactic device is the use of nonmanual signals, for example, facial expressions and body posture. These are important in terms of syntactic as well as semantic and pragmatic functions in ASL, and they frequently assume a role similar to the suprasegmentals in speech (Liddell, 1980). Eye gaze is used to perform indexic reference or even to establish the reference in a conversation. Raising the eyebrow is used as a topic marker and in forming questions. Eye blinking is relevant to the proper interpretation of conditional sentences and interrogatives. A head shake over part or all of a signed utterance may negate that part or the entire sign communication. Also, certain nonmanual behaviors are associated with particular lexical items. For example, the sign for "bite" is accompanied by a biting motion of the mouth. The sign for "relieved" is accompanied by rapid exhaling and a burst of air through pursed lips. Frequently, a combination of nonmanual signals is used to convey specific linguistic constructions and semantic relations.

In addition to studies of the linguistic bases of American Sign Language, the research of the previous decade focused primarily on psycholinguistic, neurolinguistic, and sociolinguistic aspects of sign language; and studies of the acquisition of sign language in deaf children. For a review of this and related research, the reader is referred to Lane and Grosjean (1980), Prinz (1981), and Strong (in press).

## REFERENCES

Klima, E. S., & Bellugi, U. (1979). *The signs of language.* Cambridge, MA: Harvard University Press.

Lane, H., & Grosjean, F. (Eds.). (1980). *Recent perspectives on American Sign Language*. Hillsdale, NJ: Erlbaum.

Liddell, S. (1980). *American Sign Language syntax*. The Hague: Mouton.

Prinz, P. M. (1981). Recent perspectives on the development of sign language in deaf children. *Journal of the National Student Speech–Language–Hearing Association, 9*(1), 50–65.

Stokoe, W. C. (1960). Sign language structure: An outline of the visual communication systems of the American deaf. *Studies in Linguistics, Occasional Papers, 8.*

Stokoe, W. C., Casterline, D. C., & Croneberg, C. G. (1976). *A dictionary of American Sign Language on linguistic principles* (2nd ed.). Silver Spring, MD: Linstok Press.

Strong, M. A. (Ed.). (in press). *Language learning and deafness*. Cambridge, England: Cambridge University Press.

Wilbur, R. B. (1979). *American Sign Language and sign systems*. Baltimore, MD: University Park Press.

PHILIP M. PRINZ
ELISABETH A. PRINZ
*Pennsylvania State University*

## ALTERNATIVE COMMUNICATION METHODS IN SPECIAL EDUCATION
## AUGMENTATIVE COMMUNICATION SYSTEMS

# AMERICAN SPEECH–LANGUAGE–HEARING ASSOCIATION

In the early 1900s, a number of practitioners were actively engaged in the treatment of communication disorders. Unfortunately, there were also a few unscrupulous individuals who made claims about their ability to cure communication disorders for exorbitant fees. Those involved in the ethical treatment of speech disorders saw an immediate need to protect the public from this small minority of opportunistic individuals. This became the prime motivation for forming an organization of speech and hearing professionals.

The ethical practitioners of speech correction began working in public schools and publishing the scientific results of their clinical work in the 1920s. Most of these practitioners belonged to the National Association of Teachers of Speech (NATS). They published their papers in the *Quarterly Journal of Speech Education* and met as a special interest group at NATS meetings.

The increasing interest in communication disorders grew to the point where, in 1925, a small group met in Iowa City, Iowa, to propose the creation of an organization devoted entirely to the study and treatment of communication disorders. The group chose the American Academy of Speech Correctionists as its name. Its purpose was the promotion of scientifically organized work in speech communication.

In 1935 the organization, with 87 members, changed its name to the American Speech Correction Association. In 1947 the name was again changed, this time to the American Speech and Hearing Association (ASHA). The new name lasted until 1978, when the present name, American Speech–Language–Hearing Association, was adopted.

From the beginning, the members had a deep commitment to a strong code of ethics and the growth of science related to speech and hearing disorders. Today there are 35,000 members. Three quarterly journals and a monthly journal are published by ASHA. The organization has lobbied with state governments to get them to adopt license procedures for professionals in communication disorders. One of ASHA's most important actions was the development of standards for a Certificate of Clinical Competence in Speech Pathology (CCC-SP) and Audiology (CCC-A). Professionals in communication disorders must meet certain training and experience standards to qualify for these prestigious certificates. ASHA is the voice of the professions of speech-language pathology and audiology. It stimulates and polices its own members and lobbies for the profession on both state and federal levels.

### REFERENCES

American Speech–Language–Hearing Association. (1980). ASHA is 35,000 strong. *ASHA, 22,* 867.

Paden, E. P. (1970). *A history of the American Speech and Hearing Association, 1925–1958*. Washington, DC: American Speech and Hearing Association.

FREDERICK F. WEINER
*Pennsylvania State University*

# AMES, LOUISE BATES (1908–    )

Born in Portland, Maine, Louise Ames received her BA in 1930 from the University of Maine. She then went on to receive her MA in 1933 and PhD in 1937 in experimental psychology from Yale University, where she studied with Arnold Gesell. Her relationship with Gesell resulted in the founding of the Gesell Institute in 1950, along with Dr. Francis Ilg and Dr. Janet Learner. Ames was also an instructor. She was assistant professor at Yale Medical School (1936–1950) and curator of the Yale Films of Child Development (1944–1950).

Collaboration with Francis Ilg generated interests such as the individuality of ages and behavior ages; several books such as *Infant and Child in the Culture of Today* (1940) and *School Readiness* (1956) resulted. This collaboration also resulted in a syndicated newspaper column, "Child Behavior," which later became a weekly half-hour television show.

Ames had a strong interest in projective assessment

**Louise Bates Ames**

and provided normative data in *Child Rorschach Responses* (1974). This interest extended to assessment of the elderly (*Rorschach Responses in Old Age*) and a series of articles developing test batteries for assessing deterioration of functions in old age.

Ames's general interest throughout her career has been the study of development and behavior of normal children. This research developed standard references for psychologists and was translated into popular terms, in the media, for parents.

Author of some 300 articles and monographs and collaborator/co-author of 25 books, Ames has received honorary degrees and many awards for service. *Don't Rush your Preschooler* (1980), published with her daughter Joan Ames Chase, indicates the continuation of her studies in school readiness and the status of one of the most publicized women of psychology.

**REFERENCES**

Ames, L. B. (1940). *Infant and child in the culture of today.* New York: Harper & Row.

Ames, L. B. (1974). *Child Rorschach responses.* New York: Brunner/Mazel.

Ames, L. B., & Chase, J. A. (1980). *Don't rush your preschooler.* New York: Harper & Row.

Ames, L. B., & Ilg, F. (1956). *School readiness.* New York: Harper & Row.

Ames, L. B., Metraux, R. W., Rodell, J. L., & Walker, R. W. (1973). *Rorschach responses in old age.* New York: Brunner/Mazel.

ELAINE FLETCHER-JANZEN
*Texas A&M University*

## AMNESIA

Amnesia is a disorder of memory that occurs in the absence of gross disorientation, confusion, or dementia. Amnesia may be retrograde, where the individual has difficulty remembering events and information learned prior to the onset of the amnesia, or it may be anterograde, where the individual is unable to learn new information from the point of onset of the amnesia. Amnesics do not have difficulty with immediate memory. Digit span and immediate repetition are intact. Rather, individuals with amnesia are unable to remember after a delay filled with interference.

Amnesia is fascinating because observation of amnesics may help us understand how new information is learned (e.g., what brain structures are involved and what processes facilitate new learning). Amnesics are also of interest because the sense of continuity and time passing, remembering experiences, and hence, self-identity (Walton, 1977) depend on continuous access to information about the remote and recent past. The difficulties that amnesic patients encounter in awareness of their own experiences emphasizes just how important memory is.

Amnesia as an isolated neurologic symptom can be mistaken for a psychiatric disorder (DeJong, Itabashi, & Olson, 1969). There are hysterical amnesias that are a consequence of psychiatric distress alone. Fugue states are 20dissociative episodes during which an individual forgets his or her identity and past. Hysterical amnesia is discriminable from neurologic conditions causing amnesia in that the total loss of self-identity rarely occurs in neurologically based amnesias, and because the end of the fugue state is abrupt. In the neurologically based amnesias that remit, the cessation of memory loss is gradual, with the period of time for which the individual is amnesic shrinking only gradually.

Transient amnesia is a known consequence of electroconvulsive therapy (ECT shock treatment). Individuals receiving ECT have both retrograde amnesia for events occurring just prior to treatment, and anterograde amnesia for what happens subsequent to treatment. When compared with their own performance after recovery from amnesia, patients who are amnesic after receiving ECT forget more easily and at an abnormal rate (Squire, 1981). This suggests a deficit in consolidation and elaboration of memory. There is some disagreement as to whether memory loss secondary to ECT is cumulative. Transient amnesia also may occur when an individual receives general anesthesia.

Anterograde amnesia that gradually remits is a frequent occurrence after closed head injuries (Levin, Benton, & Grossman, 1982). There often is a more limited retrograde amnesia for the period just prior to the injury. Anterograde amnesia secondary to closed head injury (also called posttraumatic amnesia) is a good index of the severity of the injury and useful in the prediction of long-term recovery. After the amnesia has remitted, there is often a residual memory disorder.

Transient global amnesia is a neurologic condition that is now assumed to be a consequence of transient ischemia (Heathfield, Croft, & Swash, 1973). The presentation of an individual with transient global amnesia is characteristic. There is an abrupt onset of amnesia, both retrograde and anterograde, with perhaps only initial, mild clouding of consciousness, and no change in cognition or speech. Episodes typically last for several hours only, and the retrograde amnesia gradually shrinks, leaving individuals amnesic only for the period during which they had anterograde amnesia (Hecaen & Albert, 1978).

Amnesia is the hallmark of Korsakoff's disease. Patients with Korsakoff's have a profound anterograde amnesia. Though immediate repetition is intact, remembering what they have been told after an interference (e.g., a brief conversation) is impossible. Patients hospitalized with Korsakoff's often reintroduce themselves to their physicians when the physician who has been caring for them reenters the room after a short interval. Korsakoff's patients are notable for their tendency to confabulate (i.e., fill in the blanks in their memory with imaginary accounts). The most common etiology of Korsakoff's is thiamine deficiency as a consequence of alcoholism. Head injury, anoxia, carbon monoxide poisoning, tumors, and other pathologies involving the same brain structure are other causes of the disorder (Walton, 1977).

A great deal has been learned about amnesia and memory through the study of groups of patients with unremitting forms of amnesia: amnesia secondary to Korsakoff's syndrome, amnesia secondary to neurosurgery for control of epilepsy, traumatic brain lesions resulting in amnesia, and generalized dementing processes (especially Huntington's disease and Alzheimer's disease) in which memory deficits are disproportionately problematic (at least during specific stages of the disease). Careful investigation of these patients clearly reveals that though the average clinician thinks of memory as a unitary phenomenon, memory loss is a multidimensional symptom with different etiologies resulting in characteristic, discriminable patterns of memory loss and skill (Butters, 1984).

One pattern of amnesia reflects hemispheric differences. Individuals with amnesia secondary to isolated damage to the right hemisphere have deficient skills in nonverbal memory when the information is presented visually. Those amnesic secondary to isolated left hemisphere damage have greater difficulty with verbal memory. Verbal memory deficits are seen regardless of the sensory modality used to present the information; e.g., visual presentation of verbal information (Hecaen and Albert, 1978).

The pattern of retrograde amnesia is not the same across all amnesic populations. Butters (1984) compared remote memory functioning in Huntington's disease, Korsakoff's disease, and normal subjects by assessing their ability to recall famous people and events from past decades. Korsakoff's patients had more severe difficulties recalling past events, but there was a normal gradation in their ability to remember, with events that occurred further in the past recalled better than more recent past experiences. The Huntington's disease patients demonstrated a flat pattern. They were equally unable to remember any past event. This pattern of remote recollection occurs across the stages of Huntington's disease, though the severity increases as the disease progresses.

Amnesic patients of differing etiologies demonstrate differential responses to manipulations aimed at facilitating memory. For example, Korsakoff's amnesics are assisted in memorization by increasing rehearsal time, intertrial rest intervals, and a structured orientation procedure. They are not aided, however, by the provision of verbal mediation. Conversely, Huntington's disease patients are not assisted as are Korsakoff's patients; neither increased rehearsal time, increased intertrial intervals, nor general orientation aids their performance. They are assisted, however, by verbal mediation. Patients with Alzheimer's disease are not assisted by verbal mediation.

Another difference between amnesic syndromes is related to the ability to acquire procedural versus declarative memories (Squire, 1982). Declarative memory pertains to specific facts and data. Procedural memory refers to the rules for completing a specific type of task. Studies of amnesic patients indicate that patients with amnesia secondary to Korsakoff's disease acquire procedural information but have great difficulty in learning declarative data. Huntington's disease patients do not remember procedural rules, but do learn (or at least recognize) previously presented data of a declarative type.

The study of patient populations with known etiologies has been useful in increasing our understanding of what brain structures are involved in the elaboration and retrieval of memory. Evidence from neurosurgical intervention to control severe epilepsy has demonstrated that damage to the medial aspects of both temporal lobes, especially the hippocampus, results in profound amnesia (Hecaen & Albert, 1978; Squire, 1982). This amnesia is distinguished by rapid and abnormal forgetting. Other amnesics appear to have diencephalic damage with some disagreement as to exactly which structures are affected. The mammillary bodies and dorsal-medial nucleus of the thalamus are involved, though the relative contributions of either structure are not known. Damage to the dorsal-medial nucleus appears sufficient to cause amnesia (Squire, 1982). Amnesia secondary to diencephalic damage is notable for a normal forgetting curve, but difficulty with encoding. Identification of structures involved in memory is useful not only in terms of understanding specific syndromes, but also in considering pharmacologic manipulations to assist in treatment.

With the exception of posttraumatic amnesia, amnesia in its pure form is not reported to occur in children. Subsequent to head injuries, children do exhibit posttraumatic amnesia and have difficulty learning new information in school and remembering what they learned just prior to their injuries. Consequently, they will be confused in the school setting. Posttraumatic amnesia generally will remit. Such children should be allowed to recover after their injuries (with the most rapid recovery occurring in the first 6 months) without the expectation that by studying harder they will remember significantly better. Once the major recovery period is over (after 6 to 9 months), cognitive rehabilitation programs aimed at providing strategies to assist in memory may be useful. There are limited data available on how generalizable the effect of cognitive rehabilitation is in the adult population, and less data regarding children.

It should be clear that the short-term memory impairments described in the learning of disabled children bear little resemblance to amnesic disorders. Amnesic patients are capable of short-term memory performance. Children with severe brain injury may become amnesic, but it is most often within the context of general dementia with difficulties in a variety of areas.

**REFERENCES**

Butters, N. (1984). The clinical aspects of memory disorders: Contributions from experimental studies of amnesia and dementia. *Journal of Clinical Neuropsychology, 6*, 17–36.

DeJong, R. N., Itabashi, H. H., & Olson, J. R. (1969). Memory loss due to hippocampal lesion. *Archives of Neurology, 20*, 339–348.

Heathfield, K. W. G., Croft, P. B., & Swash, M. (1973). The syndrome of transient global amnesia. *Brain, 96*, 729–731.

Hecaen, H., & Albert, M. L. (1978). *Human neuropsychology*. New York: Wiley.

Levin, H. S., Benton, A. L., & Grossman, R. G. (1982). *Neurobehavioral consequences of closed head injury*. New York: Oxford University Press.

Milner, B., Corkin, S., & Teuber, H. L. (1968). Further analysis of the hippocampal amnesic syndrome: A 14-year followup study of H. M. *Neuropsychologia, 6*, 215–234.

Squire, L. (1981). Two forms of human amnesia: An analysis of forgetting. *Journal of Neurosciences, 1*, 635–640.

Squire, L. (1982). The neuropsychology of human memory. *Annual Review of Neurosciences, 5*, 241–273.

Walton, J. N. (1977). *Brain's diseases of the nervous system*. Oxford: Oxford University Press.

GRETA N. WILKENING
*Children's Hospital, Denver,
Colorado*

**MEMORY DISORDERS**

# AMNIOCENTESIS

Amniocentesis is the sampling of amniotic fluid surrounding a fetus. A physician anesthetizes a small area of the pregnant woman's abdomen, inserts a small needle through the abdominal wall, and, with the aid of ultrasonography, enters the amniotic sac and removes 30 ccs (approximately 1 oz) of fluid. It is performed most frequently between 15 and 18 weeks gestation to detect hereditary disease or congenital defects in the fetus. One disadvantage is that analysis of the fluid takes 2 to 4 weeks. Damage to the fetus also may occur, but the risk is small (Pritchard, MacDonald, & Gant, 1985).

Midtrimester amniocentesis plays an important role in genetic and other prenatal counseling by providing potential parents with reproductive options. It should be considered when the pregnant woman is over 35, or a family history of genetic or congenital disorders is apparent (Kaback, 1979). Cytogenetic analysis of fetal fluid leads to prevention of birth of approximately 15,000 chromosomally abnormal infants each year in the United States alone (Pritchard et al., 1985).

Amniocentesis allows identification of about 300 chromosomal, single-gene, and other congenital abnormalities (Pritchard et al., 1985). The list grows with the discovery of new markers. Chromosomally based disorders are identified through karyotyping and resultant abnormal appearance of one or more chromosomes; other disorders are identified through elevated or reduced levels of particular substances. Among the disorders that can be reliably diagnosed are (1) all chromosomally based disorders such as Down's syndrome and cri du chat; (2) about 75 inborn errors of metabolism, including galactosemia, Tay-Sachs disease, and Lesch-Nyhan syndrome (X-linked), but not phenylketonuria; (3) some central nervous system defects including meningocele (a form of spina bifida) and anencephaly; (4) some fetal infections (cytomegalovirus, herpes simplex, and rubella); (5) and some hematologic disorders (e.g., sickle-cell anemia; Pritchard et al., 1985).

The widespread availability of amniocentesis forces many women to confront the decision to terminate an advanced pregnancy. Attachment grows throughout pregnancy, and confronting the decision of choosing termination at a late stage can be emotionally painful (Brewster, 1984). Many women are unprepared for the anxiety associated with both waiting several weeks for results of their amniocentesis and choosing between life and quality of life. Optimally, women in high-risk groups should weigh this decision and discuss other reproductive options with a genetic counselor prior to conception. Some counselors suggest that health caregivers be sensitive to pregnant women's emotional reactions and not use measures such as a doppler to hear the fetus's heartbeat or ultrasonography to take pictures of the fetus, that promote maternal attachment prior to amniocentesis (Brewster, 1984).

A new diagnostic technique, chorion-villus biopsy, usable as early as 8 weeks gestation, may be preferable in some cases because of the emotional and medical problems presented with a midtrimester abortion.

**REFERENCES**

Brewster, A. (1984). After office hours: A patient's reaction to amniocentesis. *Obstetrics & Gynecology, 64,* 443–444.

Kaback, M. M. (1979). Predictors of hereditary diseases or congenital defects in antenatal diagnosis (National Institute of Child Health and Human Development, U.S. Department of HEW, NIH Publication No. 79-1973). *Antenatal Diagnosis,* 39–42.

Pritchard, J. A., MacDonald, C., & Gant, N. F. (Eds.). (1985). *Williams obstetrics* (17th ed., pp. 267–293). Englewood Cliffs, NJ: Appleton-Century-Crofts.

BRENDA POPE
*New Hanover Memorial
Hospital, Wilmington,
North Carolina*

**GENETIC COUNSELING
INBORN ERRORS OF METABOLISM**


# AMPHETAMINE PSYCHOSIS

Amphetamine psychosis results from the neurochemical and behavioral interaction of large doses of amphetamines. The toxic reaction, induced by chronic amphetamine abuse or by an acute overdose, leads to transitory symptoms that are clinically indistinguishable from those of paranoid schizophrenia. Such symptoms, occurring as early as 36 to 48 hours after a large dosage, include vivid auditory, visual, and tactile hallucinations, changes in affect, loosening of associations with reality, and paranoid thought processes (Gilman, Goodman, & Gilman, 1980). Affected individuals may also show behavioral stereotypes such as continuous rocking or polishing motions, repetitive grooming activities (rubbing or picking of the skin), and other locomotor irregularities. Biochemical correlates of amphetamine psychosis, including increased dopaminergic activity, are similar to those of schizophrenia (Kokkinidis & Anisman, 1980).

In addition to reducing amphetamine intake, treatment includes sedatives, psychotherapy, and custodial care. Acidification of the urine will speed excretion of the amphetamines. The psychotic state usually clears in about a week after beginning treatment, with hallucinations being the first symptom to disappear (American Medical Association, 1980).

**REFERENCES**

American Medical Association. (1980). *AMA drug evaluations* (4th ed.). New York: Wiley.

Gilman, A. G., Goodman, L. S., & Gilman, A. (1980). *Goodman and Gilman's pharmacological basis of therapeutics* (6th ed.). New York: Macmillan.

Kokkinidis, L., & Anisman, H. (1980). Amphetamine models of paranoid schizophrenia: An overview and elaboration of animal experimentation. *Psychological Bulletin, 88,* 551–579.

VICKI BARTOSIK
*Stanford University*

**CHILDHOOD SCHIZOPHRENIA
DRUG ABUSE
LSD
PSYCHOTROPIC DRUGS**


# AMSLAN

See AMERICAN SIGN LANGUAGE.


# ANASTASI, ANNE (1908—    )

Anne Anastasi obtained her BA from Barnard College in 1928 and her PhD from Columbia University in 1930 at the age of 21. Influenced by H. L. Hollingworth and articles about early precursors of factor analysis by C. Spearman, Anastasi changed her orientation from mathematics to psychology. She also extended her study of individual differences to include major group differences. These changes began her association with the development of differential psychology. Her major areas of study are the nature and identification of psychological traits, test construction and evaluation, and interpretation of test results with specific reference to the role of cultural factors in individual and group differences.

Anastasi's major publications include *Differential Psychology, Psychological Testing,* and *Fields of Applied Psy-*

**Anne Anastasi**

*chology*. She has also published more than 150 journal articles and monographs and is the only author who has contributed to every edition of the *Mental Measurements Yearbook* since its inception in 1938.

Professor emeritus at Fordham University and third female president of the American Psychological Association, Anastasi has received several honorary degrees and many awards such as the 1977 Educational Testing Service Award for Distinguished Service to Measurement, the American Psychological Association Distinguished Scientific Award for the Application of Psychology, the AERA Award for Distinguished Contributions to Research in Education, the E. L. Thorndike Award for Distinguished Psychological Contributions to Education (from APA Division 15), and the American Psychological Foundation Gold Medal.

## REFERENCES

Anastasi, A. (1958). *Differential psychology* (3rd. ed.). New York: Macmillan.

Anastasi, A. (1979). *Fields of applied psychology* (2nd ed.). New York: McGraw-Hill.

Anastasi, A. (1982). *Psychological testing* (5th ed.). New York: Macmillan.

ELAINE FLETCHER-JANZEN
*Texas A&M University*

## ANASTASIOW, NICHOLAS J. (1924–    )

As Thomas Hunter professor at Hunter College, City University of New York, Nicholas Anastasiow maintains his principal interest in early childhood special education and child development. He began his career as an elementary school teacher in the early 1950s and garnered various educational certifications until he received his PhD in child development and guidance from Stanford University in 1963. In 1967, he completed postdoctoral courses in neurology at Columbia University.

Anastasiow believes that "many at risk children can lead normal lives when they are provided remediation as well as support and education for their parents" (personal communication, August 2, 1985). This belief is well represented in the 200 articles, reports, and books he has published on a vast array of subjects such as language development. Some of his titles are *Language and Reading Strategies for Poverty Children* (Anastasiow, Hanes, & Hanes, 1982), *The At Risk Infant* (Harel & Anastasiow, 1984), and *Development and Disabilities* (Anastasiow, 1986).

Anastasiow is also interested in the "prevention of at risk children by educating future parents in knowledge of child development and the skills and strategies of par-

Nicholas J. Anastasiow

enting before they become parents" (personal communication, August 2, 1985). He has encouraged schools to establish child development courses for sixth and seventh graders in publications such as *The Adolescent Parent* (1982).

Asastasiow has served as a consultant to the Assistant Secretary on Human Development, the White House Conference on the Handicapped, and the President's Council for Exceptional Children—Early Childhood Division, and as an exchange delegate to the USSR.

## REFERENCES

Anastasiow, N. J. (1982). *The adolescent parent*. Baltimore, MD: Brookes.

Anastasiow, N. J. (1986). *Development and disabilities*. Baltimore, MD: Brookes.

Anastasiow, N. J., Hanes, M. L., & Hanes, M. (1982). *Language and reading strategies for in text poverty children*. Austin, TX: Pro-Ed.

Harel, S., & Anastasiow, N. J. (Eds.). (1984). *The at risk infant*. Baltimore, MD: Brookes.

ELAINE FLETCHER-JANZEN
*Texas A&M University*

## ANDERSON, META L. (1878–1942)

Meta L. Anderson, while a teacher in the New York City public schools, enrolled in a course in the education of mentally retarded children at The Training School at Vineland, New Jersey. There, Edward R. Johnstone and Henry H. Goddard, recognizing her unusual ability, recommended her to the Newark, New Jersey, Board of Education, which employed her to begin special classes for mentally retarded children. In 1910 she established two special classes and Newark joined the handful of school systems that provided special programs for handicapped students.

Anderson developed an instructional approach based on careful analysis of the abilities and limitations of each student and devised trade classes and a work experience program to provide vocational preparation. Her book, *Education of Defectives in the Public Schools* (1917), described the program and added impetus to the growing special class movement in the United States. In the closing months of World War I, Anderson was appointed head of reconstruction aid in Europe. After the war she served for a year in Serbia. She returned to the Newark schools in 1920 to become director of the city's comprehensive special education program. She received her PhD from New York University in 1922. She served as president of the American Association on Mental Deficiency in 1941.

## REFERENCES

Anderson, M. L. (1917). *Education of defectives in the public schools.* Yonkers, New York: World Book.

Whitney, E. A. (1953). Some stalwarts of the past. *American Journal of Mental Deficiency, 57,* 345–360.

PAUL IRVINE
*Katonah, New York*

## ANENCEPHALY

Anencephaly is a congenital disorder marked by the absence of the cerebral cortices. It belongs to a class of disorders that are termed neural tube defects (NTD) and results from the failure of the neural tube to close during embryogenesis. The neural tube, which is the precursor to the brain and spinal cord, usually closes by the 28th day after conception (Kloza, 1985). If this does not occur completely, various defects to the central nervous system (CNS) become manifest. If this occurs "lower" on the neural tube, spina bifida will be present. However, if the "top" of the neural tube remains open, anencephaly results. Anencephaly with spina bifida, rarely occurs (Swaiman & Wright, 1973).

As anencephaly is ostensibly marked by the absence of the cerebral cortices, the centers of higher cognitive functioning are absent. Therefore, while certain subcortical structures may remain intact (producing the reflex patterns and responses often indicative of neonates), higher cerebral activity is precluded by the absence of structures subserving those functions. Many anencephalics are stillborn, as they lack the brain structures necessary to maintain respiration and other functions vital to survival. On the occasion that the newborn is physiologically viable, it should be remembered that associative processes, reasoning, and cognitive and language development are not possible. Therefore, educational services are not a practical consideration and absolute custodial supervision and care

are indicated. Ethical considerations pertaining to care must also come into play. Anencephaly remains a medical disorder where special educational services are not practical.

The development of anencephaly and other NTDs is believed to be multifactorial. The second most common group of congenital anomalies, with environment, intrauterine environment, and genetic factors implicated in their development are NTDs. Geographically, anencephaly appears to be a more common occurrence on the East Coast of the United States. It is found more frequently in female births than male (two to one). It has been suggested that a higher prevalence of anaencephaly is found in lower socioeconomic class families (James, Nevin, Johnston, & Merrett, 1981; Nevin, Johnston, & Merrett, 1981).

While treatment of anencephaly is not feasible, prenatal screening has been effective in identifying anencephaly prior to birth. With NTDs, a substance called alpha fetoprotein (AFP) occurs in higher concentration in the amniotic fluid surrounding the fetus (Adinolfi, 1985; Kloza, 1985). The AFP enters the mother's circulation either by the amniotic fluid or the placenta; it can then be measured in the mother's blood. Higher levels of AFP in the mother's blood at certain times in fetal gestation indicate NTDs. This method of identifying anencephaly has been shown to be 99% reliable, with a reliability of similar magnitude for other NTDs such as spina bifida.

## REFERENCES

Adinolfi, M. (1985). The development of the human blood–csf–brain barrier. *Developmental Medicine and Child Neurology, 27*(4), 532–537.

James, W. H., Nevin, N. C., Johnston, W. P., & Merrett, J. D. (1981). Influence of social class on the risk of recurrence of anencephaly and spina bifida. *Developmental Medicine and Child Neurology, 23*(5), 661–662.

Kloza, E. M. (1985). Prenatal screening: neural tube defects. *Disorders of Brain Development and Cognition.* Boston: Eunice Kennedy Shriver Center and Harvard Medical School.

Nevin, N. C., Johnston, W. P., & Merrett, J. D. (1981). Influence of social class on the risk of recurrence of anencephaly and spina bifida. *Developmental Medicine and Child Neurology, 23*(2), 151–154.

Swaiman, K. F., & Wright, F. S. (1973). Neurologic diseases due to developmental and metabolic defects. In A. B. Baker & L. H. Baker (Eds.), *Clinical neurology.* New York: Harper & Row.

ELLIS I. BAROWSKY
*Hunter College, City University
of New York*

## BABY JANE DOE

## ANIMALS FOR THE HANDICAPPED

Today, animals are being used to assist the handicapped with daily living. For centuries, the blind have used dogs to assist them in ambulation. Recently, pilot programs using domesticated monkeys to assist moderately to severely disabled persons in the home to perform rote chores has been a successful innovation. Horseback riding has emerged as a leisure-time pursuit for many types of disabled persons.

The benefits of human/animal interaction are now being realized, especially for special education purposes. Lowered blood pressure has been documented in studies where the participants had regular contact with dogs. In another study, Friedman (1980) found that the survival rate of hypertensive persons increased dramatically with pet ownership. Pets have been considered effective agents in the reduction of everyday stress. They provide a sense of relaxation (Kidd, 1981). They also provide a chance to exercise, and for many a sense of security (White & Watson, 1983).

Animals provide the opportunity to communicate. This is probably the most valuable attribute of the human/animal relationship. Levinson (1969) states that an animal can have a "very positive effect on a family and that they have the potential to bridge the gap between children and adults by providing a common object of responsibility."

According to Levinson (1969), the introduction of animals into a residential setting for the handicapped indicates that the staff believes that anything of possible treatment value to the handicapped can and should be used. It reveals an awareness of the potential healing properties of pet ownership, even if those benefits have not been scientifically documented in the laboratory.

A handicapped child is not constantly reminded of his or her handicap in the interaction with a pet. A deaf child can care for a dog competently and receive all of the rewards that a hearing child would for the same efforts. The same is true for a variety of handicaps; only the type of pet might have to be changed. A child confined to a wheelchair may intefact well with a rabbit or an aquarium and achieve a sense of purpose and responsibility previously unrealized.

The teaching of the emotionally disturbed child provides a setting in which the use of animals may be especially beneficial. Typically, motivating this student to participate in class can be a difficult task for the teacher. Often, these students have never learned to care for or share with others. The animal in the class may provide both the subject matter and the motivation to learn. The child who had previously trusted no one can begin to trust the teacher for the first time when he or she sees the teacher's concern in dealing with the classroom pet. This could be the first step by the child in accepting the structure of the class (Levinson, 1969).

**REFERENCES**

Friedman, E. (1980, July/August). Animal companions and one year survival of patients after discharge from a coronary care unit. *Public Health Reports, 44*(4), 37–42.

Kidd, A. (1981). Dogs, cats and people. *Mills Quarterly, 23*(8), 23–28.

Levinson, B. (1969). Pet oriented child psychotherapy. Springfield, IL: Thomas.

White, B., & Watson, T. (1983). *Pet love, how pets take care of us.* New York: Pinnacle.

THOMAS R. BURKE
*Hunter College, City University
of New York*

EQUINE THERAPY
THERAPEUTIC RECREATION

## ANNALS OF DYSLEXIA

Originating in 1950 as the *Bulletin of the Orton Society* under the editorial leadership of June Lyday Orton, the annual periodical of the Orton Dyslexia Society was renamed *Annals of Dyslexia* in 1981. It was designed as a means to enhance communication among the members of the Orton Dyslexia Society, an organization founded in 1949 to further research and work with children with specific language disabilities.

Since its inception, the journal has been aimed at a professional multidisciplinary membership, consisting of neurologists, psychologists, pathologists, psychiatrists, educators, and social workers. As research on dyslexia has accelerated in different professional fields of inquiry, the society views the role of the periodical as increasingly important. Through concrete illustration of the practical applications of new knowledge, *Annals* serves as a bridge between the researcher and the field worker. The periodical has grown from its early circulation of 35 copies to members of the society to a circulation of 8000 to a wide interdisciplinary membership and professional libraries around the world. Although *Annals* is referred to as a periodical, it comes out once a year and is more like a book. A cumulative index is available for the first 21 volumes of the periodical, though 1975.

ELIZABETH DANE
*Hunter College, City University
of New York*

## ANNUAL DIRECTORY OF EDUCATIONAL FACILITIES FOR THE LEARNING DISABLED

The *Annual Directory of Educational Facilities for the Learning Disabled* is published by Academic Therapy. It contains a listing of nonpublic educational facilities that specialize in programs for the learning disabled. The directory lists facilities in alphabetical order by state. Following the name, location, director, and number of staff members is coded information describing the following: type of facility—educational, related professional service (diagnostic, optometric, etc.), summer camp; age ranges accepted; boys only, girls only, or coeducational; full day, part day, or residential; and fee information. A copy of the *directory* can be obtained from Academic Therapy Publications, 1539 Fourth Street, San Rafael, CA 94901.

DANIEL R. PAULSON
*University of Wisconsin, Stout*

## ANNUAL GOALS

Annual goals describe expected student performance, are an important part of an individual education plan (IEP), and are in compliance with the Education for all Handicapped Children Act, PL 94-142. Each IEP must contain a statement of annual educational goals consisting of specific objectives indicating the condition under which desired performance should occur, a description of the desired performance, and a listing of the criteria for adequate performance. Short-term instructional objectives, which should be included in the IEP, break annual goals down into smaller components, sometimes using task analysis, to provide a logical progression of objectives in a given domain, while indicating the rate at which students are expected to progress toward mastery of goals. The proportion of IEP objectives achieved by each student at the end of the term divided by the total number written at the start of the term can be used as a measure of educational progress (Brinker & Thorpe, 1984).

Public Law 94-142 mandates that pupils' rates of progress be continuously monitored so that educational programs can be reassessed and improved as students move toward goals. A common method used in instruction is the pretest, teach, posttest design. In assessing pupils, teachers in special education commonly rely on informal observation and develop curriculum-based measurement systems matched to annual goals.

Findings indicate that the use of more systematic measurement and evaluation systems than those currently in use result in better student achievement toward goals (Fuchs, Deno, & Mirkin, 1984). Another finding is that public goal setting between student and teacher is more effective than private goal setting in increasing on-task behavior in the classroom (Lyman, 1984). One suggested system is the Goal Attainment Scale (GAS), a method that can help special educators to become more accountable and effective and increase the likelihood that curricula will become student centered rather than method centered.

The method involves devising a set of goals with the involved persons, developing a set of expected outcomes for each goal, scoring the outcomes on a five-point continuum from worse than expected to better than expected, and calculating a summary score of outcomes across the goals. Mutual determination of goals and their importance by the persons involved ensures relevance and meaning to parents, students, and educators. This mutual determination also helps students to learn about alternative behaviors and helps to clarify expectations for both students and teachers. GAS is independent of theoretical predispositions and can be used by teachers to clarify specific problems, sharpen goal setting, and point out directions for action (Carr, 1979).

**REFERENCES**

Brinker, R. P., & Thorpe, M. E. (1984, Oct.). Integration of severely handicapped students and the proportion of IEP objectives achieved. *Exceptional Children, 51,* 168–175.

Carr, R. A. (1979, Oct.). Goal Attainment Scaling as a useful tool for evaluating progress in special education. *Exceptional Children, 46,* 88–95.

Fuchs, L. S., Deno, S. L., & Mirkin, P. K. (1984, Summer). The effects and frequent curriculum-based measurement and evaluation on pedagogy, student achievement and student awareness of learning. *American Education Research Journal, 21,* 449–460.

Gerardi, R. J., Grohe, B., Benedict, G. C., & Collidge, P. G. (1984, Fall). IEP—more paperwork and wasted time. *Contemporary Education, 56,* 39–42.

Jaffe, M. J., & Snelbecker, G. E. (1982, Summer). Evaluating independent education programs: A recommendation and some programmatic implications. *Urban Review, 14*(2), 73–81.

Lyman, R. D. (1984, Sept.). The effect of private and public goal setting on classroom on-task behavior of emotionally disturbed children. *Behavior Therapy, 15,* 395–402.

CATHERINE O. BRUCE
*Hunter College, City University
of New York*

## EDUCATION FOR ALL HANDICAPPED CHILDREN ACT OF 1975

## INDIVIDUAL EDUCATION PLAN

## ANOMALIES, PHYSICAL

See PHYSICAL ANOMALIES.

## ANOREXIA NERVOSA

Anorexia nervosa is an eating disorder that has underlying psychological factors. This condition was first identified by Sir William Gull in 1873; he defined it as an individual's desire to be slender and to be praised for the willpower to diet effectively, accompanied by a lack of appetite and a disturbed mental state (Abraham & Llewellyn-Jones, 1984). In recent years a greater understanding of anorexia nervosa has been achieved with effective means of diagnosis and treatment. The *Diagnostic and Statistical Manual of Mental Disorders* (1980) of the American Psychiatric Association offers specific guidelines for identifying and diagnosing anorexia nervosa.

Anorexia nervosa is characterized by severe reduction of food intake and significant weight loss, resulting in medical complications such as reduced blood pressure and blood sugar level, amenorrhea, and gastrointestinal illness. Other observable effects of anorexia nervosa include emotional lability, skin and hair problems, insomnia, dental decay, electrolyte disturbance, and vitamin deficiency. In its advanced stages, continued anorexia can create cardiac impairments and paralysis. Certain criteria are present in individuals diagnosed as having anorexia nervosa. The patient's fear of being fat leads to a drastic decrease in the amount of food eaten, self-induced vomiting, improper use of laxatives and diuretics, and overly strenuous exercise. The loss of 25% of one's ideal body weight can be determined through charts compiled with age and physical build data. The weight loss must not be due to other psychological or physical illnesses. Most anorexic women cease to menstruate. Psychological features include a distorted body image, unclear sense of self-identity, little autonomy, and a fear of loss of control (Minuchin, 1978).

Anorexia nervosa occurs in approximately one individual per two hundred. Females between the ages of 16 and 18 years are twice as likely to suffer from this disorder (Atwater, 1983). Anorexia nervosa occurs about 10 times more often in females than in males. Other frequent circumstances include all female families, older parents, high socioeconomic level, and physical or psychological illness of the parents. Anorexic patients are often good students and obedient and helpful, though over-controlled; many were previously overweight (Hall, 1978). Atwater (1983) emphasizes the significance of family stress, particularly an independence/dependence issue between the individual and one or both parents. Parents frequently communicate mixed messages regarding their perception, expectation, or approval of the individual. While ongoing problems in interpersonal relationships among family members are common, a series of stressful events can precipitate the onset of an anorexic pattern.

A psychological explanation for this disorder can classify the patient as neurotic and obsessional with introverted and dependent tendencies and extreme anxiety. To feel fullfilled and loved, as in childhood, the individual avoids physical and sexual maturity. A social learning theory of the onset of anorexia nervosa holds that the anorexic individual has learned to equate slimness with happiness, attractiveness, and popularity.

In the past, anorexia nervosa has been treated by insulin shock therapy, force feeding, tube feeding, sleep therapy, and medication to stimulate appetite. However, it has been found that the most effective way of treating this psychological illness and its accompanying physical symptoms has been through supportive therapy, counseling about eating properly, perhaps some relaxation training, and family or marital therapy. It is important for the anorexic individual to learn or relearn normal eating habits and to increase body weight to at least 90% of the average body weight for that individual's age and build. Medication may be prescribed for depression or for some medical symptoms. Treatment must focus on both the eating disturbance per se and the underlying psychological issues. A multidisciplinary approach coordinated by one primary professional is the most effective in allowing individuals with anorexia nervosa to maintain physical health and comfortable emotional ajustment.

## REFERENCES

Abraham, S., & Llewellyn-Jones, D. (1984). *Eating disorders: The facts*. Oxford, England: Oxford University Press.

American Psychiatric Association. (1980). *Diagnostic and statistical manual of mental disorders* (3rd ed.). Washington, DC: American Psychological Association.

Atwater, E. (1983). *Adolescence*. Englewood Cliffs, NJ: Prentice-Hall.

Bruch, H. (1978). *The golden cage: The enigma of anorexia nervosa*. Cambridge, MA: Harvard University Press.

Hall, A. (1978). Family structure and the relationship of 50 female anorexia nervosa patients. *Australian and New Zealand Journal of Psychiatry, 12*(4), 263–268.

Minuchin, S. (1978). *Psychosomatic families: Anorexia nervosa in context*. Cambridge, MA: Harvard University Press.

ELIZABETH GIRSHICK
*Montgomery County
Intermediate Unit,
Norristown, Pennsylvania*

**EATING DISORDERS**
**OBSESSIVE-COMPULSIVE DISORDERS**


# ANOSMIA

The term *anosmia* derives from the Greek *an* (without) and *osme* (odor); it refers to the absence or impairment of the sense of smell. Synonyms for this condition include anodmia, anosphrasia, and olfactory anesthesia (*Dorland's*, 1981). Organic forms of anosmia are categorized as afferent (related to impaired conductivity of the olfactory nerve), central (due to cerebral disease), obstructive (related to obstruction of the nasal fossae), and peripheral (due to diseases of peripheral olfactory nerves) (*Blakiston's*, 1979).

The most common cause of anosmia is a severe head cold or respiratory infection, which intranasal swelling blocks the nasal passages, preventing odors from reaching the olfactory region. This type of anosmia is temporary. Other organic causes of this condition include neoplasms (tumors), head injuries, or chronic rhinitis associated with granulomatous diseases (Levin, Benton, & Grossman, 1982; *Mosby's*, 1983; Thomson, 1979). Anosmia also is a characteristic of olfactogenital dysplasia, also known as *Kallman's syndrome* or anosmia-eunuchoidism. This condition, more prevalent in males, is associated with lack of development of secondary sexual characteristics and anosmia. The aparently *X*-linked autosomal dominant or recessive inheritable condition is associated with dysfunction of the hypothalamus and the pituitary (Magalini, 1971). Anosmia with these etiologies typically is a permanent condition.

Psychological forms of anosmia, while less common, may occur. Phobias or fears have been identified as precipitating such forms of anosmia (*Mosby's*, 1983). Specific types of anosmia include anosmia gustatoria (loss of the ability to smell foods) and preferential anosmia (loss of the ability to smell certain odors) (*Dorland's*, 1981).

## REFERENCES

*Blakiston's Gould medical dictionary* (4th ed.). (1979). New York: McGraw-Hill.

*Dorland's illustrated medical dictionary* (26th ed.). (1981). Philadelphia: Saunders.

Levin, H. A., Benton, A. L. M., & Grossman, R. G. (1982). *Neurobehavioral consequences of closed head injury.* New York: Oxford University Press.

Magalini, S. (1971). *Dictionary of medical syndromes.* Philadelphia: Lippincott.

*Mosby's medical and nursing dictionary* (1983). St. Louis: Mosby.

Thomson, W. A. R. (1979). *Black's medical dictionary* (32nd ed.). New York: Barnes & Noble.

CATHY F. TELZROW
*Cuyahoga Special Education
Service Center, Maple
Heights, Ohio*

# ANOXIA

Anoxia literally means an absence of oxygen, a condition that is incompatible with life. Recent terminology more correctly uses the term hypoxia to refer to a condition of lowered oxygen intake. Although hypoxia is compatible with life, long-term sequelae may result depending on the degree and duration of the condition.

BRENDA POPE
*New Hanover Memorial
Hospital, Wilmington,
North Carolina*

**ASPHYXIA**
**HYPOXIA**

# ANTECEDENT TEACHING

Antecedent stimuli are those events that occur before a response that affect the probability of the occurrence of that response. In his book *Science and Human Behavior*, Skinner (1953) described the response sequence as having three parts: the antecedent events, the response, and the consequences. Although much has been written concerning the management of the consequences and their effects on a student's responses, Repp (1983) emphasized that teaching is actually the effective arrangement of both antecedent *and* consequent events in a manner that allows the student to learn to the full extent of his or her capabilities.

Teachers exert tremendous control over the antecedents to which their students are exposed. Some antecedent stimuli commonly seen in classrooms include instruction, curriculum, instructional objectives, commands, modeling, and materials (Repp, 1983; Snell, 1983). As teachers manipulate these antecedents, students learn to respond differentially to the differing stimuli. When their behaviors are consistently affected by the antecedents, their responses are considered to be under stimulus control. Kazdin (1975) noted one particularly effective antecedent strategy, response priming. He stated that "response priming refers to any procedure which initiates early steps in a sequence of responses" (Kazdin, 1975, p. 135). The use of various prompts or directions, while not inclusive of the total concept of response priming, is one area that has received considerable attention.

Snell (1983) identified four different types of prompts: verbal directions; modeling, which is the demonstration of all or parts of a behavioral sequence before the subject makes an attempt; cueing, which is a procedure that helps the student to focus on the task at hand without using physical contact (e.g., pointing to the relevant materials); and physical prompting, which is the actual physical manipulation of the subject's responses. In using prompting, Snell (1983) reported that prompts may be used by themselves, in combination with other prompts (e.g., physical prompting and verbal directions), or in a hierarchical pattern. When using prompting in a hierarchical manner, one may use the least to most intrusive order (i.e., verbal directions to modeling to cueing to physical prompting) or conversely, the most to least intrusive order, also known as graduated guidance. Snell (1983) stated that both hierarchies have advantages, with the graduated guidance order being the best choice for students with lower functioning levels (e.g., those labeled severely or profoundly retarded). Snell (1983) also noted that whenever artificial prompts are used, they must be gradually faded to allow the desired behaviors to come under the control of natural stimuli.

Kazdin (1975) described another effective subset of response priming, reinforcer sampling. In this procedure, the subject is allowed to experience a small portion of the reinforcer in an effort to have the subject initiate the full sequence of responses necessary to earn the entire reinforcer. Teachers could easily incorporate this procedure into their classrooms, particularly before difficult behavioral sequences are begun (e.g., a verbal description of a movie to be seen after the upcoming math quiz has concluded).

The curriculum and materials that are used in the classroom are other powerful antecedent stimuli that can be easily controlled. In an interesting exposition on classroom materials, Vargas (1984) proposed that many current textual materials actually have a number of errors that result in faulty stimulus control. She stated that if any one of five questions could be answered affirmatively concerning particular textual material, then that material would not be appropriate for use. The questions she listed were

1. Can students use pictures or diagrams instead of text to complete an exercise?
2. Does highlighting or physical layout give away answers, making it unnecessary to read through an assignment?
3. Are students able to answer questions on a passage without reading it?
4. Do all of the problems on a page require the same process for solution, making it unnecessary to discriminate between strategies?
5. Are the questions Jabberwocky comprehension questions—that is, can they be answered using grammatical cues alone? (p. 130).

Even a casual analysis of many commercially prepared and teacher-made materials will reveal that they provide improper antecedent stimuli for the responses they were designed to elicit.

The area of antecedent teaching is both broad and important. For more information on how this strategy blends with the area of behavioral teaching, the reader is referred to Skinner (1953; 1968) and Repp (1983).

## REFERENCES

Kazdin, A. E. (1975). *Behavior modification in applied settings.* Homewood, IL: Dorsey.

Repp, A. C. (1983). *Teaching the mentally retarded.* Englewood Cliffs, NJ: Prentice-Hall.

Skinner, B. F. (1953). *Science and human behavior.* New York: Macmillan.

Skinner, B. F. (1968). *The technology of teaching.* New York: Appleton-Century-Crofts.

Snell, M. E. (1983). *Systematic instruction for the moderately and severely handicapped* (2nd ed.). Columbus, OH: Merrill.

Vargas, J. S. (1984). What are your exercises teaching? An analysis of stimulus control in instructional materials. In W. L. Heward, T. E. Heron, D. S. Hill, & J. Trap-Porter (Eds.), *Focus on behavior analysis in education.* Columbus, OH: Merrill.

ANDREW R. BRULLE
*Eastern Illinois University*

**APPLIED BEHAVIOR ANALYSIS**
**BEHAVIOR MODELING**

# ANTHROPOSOPHIC MOVEMENT

The anthroposophic movement was founded by Rudolf Steiner (1861–1925). Steiner defined anthroposophy as knowledge produced by the higher self in man, and a way of knowledge that undertakes to guide man's spirit to communion with the spirit of the cosmos (Wannamaker, 1965). Anthroposophy postulates a spiritual world beyond man's sensory experiences. Steiner proposed that, through proper training, each person could develop an enhanced consciousness that would restore values and morality to materialistic society.

Steiner became involved in the education of both adults and children. Anthroposophic education for adults took place at the Goetheanum, a school for physical science, near Basal, Switzerland. The Waldorf School, founded in Stuttgart, Germany, in 1919, was the first of several schools for children that sought to reach the inner nature of the child and provide guidance to maturity. By 1965, 80 Waldorf Schools had been attended by more than 25,000 children in the United States and Europe (Wannamaker, 1965). Eurythmy (movement of speech and music) was used to develop concentration, attention, imitation, and an awareness of position in space (Zeigler, 1979). The schools included programming for the emotionally disturbed, socially maladjusted, and other exceptional children.

During a residential tutorship, Steiner began to apply anthroposophic training to the mentally handicapped. Karl Konig, a student of Steiner's, continued the application of Steiner's techniques in an approach known as curative education (Payne & Patton, 1981). In 1939 Konig founded the first integrated community for the mentally retarded, based on the anthroposophic philosophy in Aberdeen, Scotland (Payne & Patton, 1981). This "Camphill movement" formulated anthroposophy into the following four bases of curative education:

A right to education for all children
A humanistic/developmental perspective

An accepting milieu, providing the retarded with stability and support,

Group and individual instruction, providing the retarded with a sense of integration with mankind

Camphill communities are comprised of aproximately equal numbers of retarded and normal citizens. These self-sufficient, monasticlike communes are comprised of "families" of no more than 15 persons, about half of whom are retarded. Criteria for admission include the ability to care for personal needs and adequate physical health (Zipperlen, 1975). Presently, there are 25 communities in Europe, South Africa, and the United states (Payne & Patton, 1981).

## REFERENCES

Payne, J. S., & Patton, J. R. (1981). *Mental retardation.* Columbus, OH: Merrill.

Steiner, R. (1972). *Outline of occult science.* New York: Anthroposophical Society.

Wannamaker, O. D. (1965). *The anthroposophical society: The nature of its objectives.* New York: Anthroposophical Society.

Ziegler, E. F. (1979). *A history of physical education and sport.* Englewood Cliffs, NJ: Prentice-Hall.

Zipperlan, H. R. (1975). Normalization. In J. Wortis (Ed.), *Mental retardation and developmental disabilities, Volume VII:.* New York: Brunner/Mazel.

ANNE M. BAUER
*University of Cincinnati*

## CAMPHILL COMMUNITY MOVEMENT
## HUMANISM AND SPECIAL EDUCATION

## ANTICONVULSANTS

Anticonvulsants are medications used to control seizure activity. Investigation of the possible effects of anticonvulsant medications on a person's ability to function has been complicated by certain methodological difficulties, including the use of only normal controls, the interaction of a placebo with an active agent, and the use of a limited number of performance measures. Studies tend to fall into three different groups: those that have not distinguished among different drugs, those examining the effects of specific drugs, and those that have included the measurement of serum (blood) anticonvulsant levels (Corbett & Trimble, 1983).

Phenobarbital is perhaps one of the most widely investigated anticonvulsants with regard to effects on cognitive functioning. Lennox (1940) assessed the causes of mental deterioration in 1245 individuals with epilepsy and determined that in 15% of the cases, the anticonvulsant medication was the cause. In a later publication, Lennox and Lennox (1960) reduced this number to 5%. Relatively few studies or the effects of multiple drugs on children have been carried out. Of the investigations reported, the results have been conflicting. Chaudhry and Pond (1961) examined the causes of intellectual deterioration in 28 children with epilepsy and found no evidence to suggest that anticonvulsant medications were responsible for the noted declines in functioning. Rather, these authors suggested that such declines were related to seizure frequency. In a study of 117 children with seizures in regular public school classes, Holdsworth and Whitmore (1976) reported no differences in academic achievement depending on whether or not phenobarbital had been prescribed. These findings lend support to an earlier study that assessed the psychological performance of 26 epileptic patients over a three-month period and found little effect on total environmental adjustment caused by the use of anticonvulsants (Loveland, Smith, & Forster, 1957). There were, however, no controls in the study and the majority of patients had been receiving anticonvulsant medication for several years prior to the study.

Conversely, a number of studies of multiple drug effects have reported learning impairments with specific deficits noted in visual-spatial perception and performance (Rayo & Martin, 1959; Tchicaloff & Gaillard, 1970). In a study by Hutt, Jackson, Belsham, and Higgins (1968), phenobarbital was administered to normal subjects with serum level control. Decreases in abilities were noted that were related to phenobarbital blood serum levels. These effects were seen most prominently on tasks requiring sustained attention, psychomotor performance, and spontaneous speech. The drug effects became more prominent as the tasks became longer and more difficult and as the degree of external constraint (having the examiner in the room) was decreased. It was concluded that phenobarbital has effects maximally evident on tasks requiring attention and concentration, but that it also may have pronounced effects on motor coordination.

Unfavorable behavioral changes have been estimated to occur in 20 to 75% of children receiving phenobarbital as prophylaxis for febrile convulsions in infancy (Heckmatt, Houston, & Dodds, 1976; Thorn, 1975; Wolf & Forsythe, 1978). Although no significant IQ differences were reported for groups of toddlers receiving an 8- to 12-month period of phenobarbital or placebo, there were effects on memory that were related to blood serum levels and effects on comprehension that were related to the duration of treatment (Camfield et al., 1979). There was no evidence of hyperactivity, although 15 of the 315 childrn on phenobarbital in the study did demonstrate an increase in "daytime fussiness and irritability."

Phenytoin (Dilantin) is the most widely used anticonvulsant in the world (Dodrill, 1981). It has been shown to be effective with a broad range of attacks including generalized tonic-clonic seizures, most types of partial seizures, and some other less frequently observed seizure types. Acute intoxication with phenytoin leads to a confusional state, occasionally referred to as encephalopathy, which is associated with neurological symptoms of toxicity, especially ataxia and nystagmus (Corbett & Trimble, 1983). It also has been demonstrated that prolonged use of this medication, even in low doses (Logan & Freeman, 1969; Vallarta, Bell, & Reichert, 1974), may result in a clinical picture of a progressive degenerative disorder that may occur without the classic signs of such a disorder. Rosen (1968) and Stores (1975) have both reported impaired intellectual performance on long-term treatment with phenytoin. Dodrill (1975) reports that phenytoin has behavioral effects specifically related to motor performance decrements.

Ethosuximide (Zarontin), an anticonvulsant used with children for control of absence (petit mal) seizures, has been shown to impair memory and speech as well as result in affective disturbances (Guey et al., 1967). Soulayrol and Roger (1970) reported intellectual impairment in children treated with this medication; however, other studies have not confirmed this (e.g., Brown et al., 1975).

Carbamazepine (Tegretol) has been reported to have psychotropic effects. About half of 40 studies cited by Dalby (1975), in a major review of the literature, reported a beneficial psychologic effect. Typically, improvements in mood and behavior have been noted, as manifested by greater cooperativeness, reduced irritability, and a possible decrease in aggression. There have been no reported studies of the effects of primidone (Mysoline) on behavior in children, although adults occasionally have been reported to develop a florid confusional state on doses within the normal therapeutic range (Booker, 1972). It is well recognized that the drug initially may cause drowsiness and have effects similar to phenobarbital in causing restlessness in some children.

Trimble and Corbett (1980a, 1980b) studied the relationship between anticonvulsant drug levels and the behavior and cognitive performance of 312 children with seizures. The drug most commonly prescribed was phenytoin, followed by carbamazepine, valproic acid, primidone, and phenobarbital. A decrease in IQ was noted in 15% of the 204 children studied; these children had significantly higher mean phenytoin and primidone levels than other subjects. A distinct relationship between an increase in serum drug levels and a decline in nonverbal skills was reported.

Despite these side effects associated with anticonvulsants, they are recognized as essential in the management of epilepsy. According to Dodrill (1981), when anticonvulsant blood serum levels fall within therapeutic ranges and when there are no overt signs of toxicity, the chances of deleterious effects are minimal if detectable at all. Furthermore, the deleterious effects are distinctly offset by decreased seizure frequency, which has known effects on the deterioration of mental functions. It is far preferable to have modest drug side effects than seizures.

## REFERENCES

Booker, H. E. (1972). Primidone toxicity. In D. M. Woodbury, J. K. Penry, & R. P. Schmidt (Eds.), *Antiepileptic drugs*, (pp. 169–204). New York: Raven.

Brown, T. R., Dreifuss, F. E., Dyken, P. R., Goode, D. J., Penry, J. K., Porter, R. J., White, B. J., & White, P. T. (1975). Ethosuccimide in the treatment of absence (petit mal) seizures. *Neurology, 25*, 515–525.

Camfield, C. S., Chaplin, S., Doyle, A. B., Shapiro, S. H., Cummings, C., & Camfield, P. R. (1979). Side effects of phenobarbitone in toddlers: Behavioral and cognitive effects. *Journal of Pediatrics, 95*, 361–365.

Chaudhry, M. R., & Pond, D. A. (1961). Mental deterioration in epileptic children. *Journal of Neurology, Neurosurgery, & Psychiatry, 24*, 213–219.

Corbett, J. A., & Trimble, M. R. (1983). Epilepsy and anticonvulsant medication. In M. Rutter (Eds.), *Developmental neuropsychiatry* (pp. 112–129). New York: Guilford.

Dalby, M. A. (1975). Behavioral effects of carbamazepine. In J. K. Penry & D. D. Daley (Eds.), *Advances in neurology* (Vol. 11, pp. 130–149). New York: Raven.

Dodrill, C. B. (1975). Diphenylhydantoin serum levels, toxicity, and neuropsychological performance in patients with epilepsy. *Epilepsia, 16*, 593–600.

Dodrill, C. B. (1981). Neuropsychology of epilepsy. In S. B. Filskov & T. J. Boll (Eds.), *Handbook of clinical neuropsychology* (pp. 366–395). New York: Wiley.

Guey, J., Charles, C., Coquery, C., Roger, J., & Soulayrol, R. (1967). Study of the psychological effects of ethosuccimide on 25 children suffering from petit mal epilepsy. *Epilepsia, 8*, 129–141.

Heckmatt, J., Houston, A., & Dodds, K. (1976). Failure of phenobarbitone to prevent febrile convulsions. *British Medical Journal, 1*, 559–561.

Holdsworth, L., & Whitmore, K. (1976). A study of children with epilepsy attending ordinary schools. *Developmental Medicine & Child Neurology, 16*, 746–758.

Hutt, S. J., Jackson, P. M., Belsham, A., & Higgins, G. (1968). Perceptual motor behavior in relation to blood phenobarbitone levels: A preliminary report. *Development Medicine & Child Neurology, 10*, 626–632.

Lennox, W. G. (1940). Brain injury, drugs, and environment as a cause of mental decay in epilepsy. *American Journal of Psychiatry, 99*, 174–180.

Lennox, W. G., & Lennox, M. A. (1960). *Epilepsy and related disorders*, Boston: Little, Brown.

Logan, W. J., & Freeman, J. M. (1969). Pseudodegenerative diseases due to diphenylhydantoin intoxication. *Archives of Neurology, 21*, 631–637.

Loveland, N., Smith, B., & Forster, F. (1957). Mental and emotional changes in epileptic patients on continuous anticonvulsant medication. *Neurology, 7*, 856–865.

Rayo, D., & Martin, F. (1959). Standardized psychometric tests applied to the analysis of the effects of anticonvulsant medication on the proficiency of young epileptics. *Epilepsia, 1*, 189–207.

Rosen, J. A. (1968). Dilantin dementia. *Transactions of the American Neurological Association, 93*, 273–277.

Soulayrol, R., & Roger, J. (1970). Effets psychiatriques defavorables des medications antiepileptiques. *Revue de Neuropsychiatrie Infantile* (English abstract), *18*, 599–603.

Stores, G. (1975). Behavioral effects of anticonvulsant drugs. *Developmental Medicine & Child Neurology, 17*, 547–658.

Tchicaloff, M., & Gaillard, F. (1970). Quelques effets indesirables des medicaments antiepileptiques sur les rendements intellectuels. *Revue de Neuropsychiatrie Infantile* (English abstract), *18*, 599–603.

Thorn, I. (1975). A controlled study of prophylactic longterm treatment of febrile convulsions with phenobarbital. *Acta Neurologica Scandinavica, 60*, 67–70.

Trimble, M. R., & Corbett, J. A. (1980a). Behavioral and cognitive disturbances in epileptic children. *Irish Medical Journal, 73*, 21–28.

Trimble, M. R., & Corbett, J. A. (1980b). Anticonvulsant drugs and cognitive function. In J. A. Wada & J. K. Penry (Eds.), *Advances in epileptology: The X International Symposium*, New York: Raven.

Vallarta, J. M., Bell, D. B., & Reichert, A. (1974). Progressive encephalopathy due to chronic hydantoin intoxication. *American Journal of Diseases of Children, 128*, 27–34.

Wolf, S. M., & Forsythe, A. (1978). Behavior disturbance, phenobarbital, and febrile seizures. *Pediatrics, 61*, 728–730.

RICHARD A. BERG
*West Virginia University*
*Medical Center, Charleston*
*Division*

**DILANTIN**
**DRUG THERAPY**
**EPILEPSY**
**MEDICATION**
**PHENOBARBITOL**
**TEGRETOL**

# ANTIHISTAMINES

Antihistamines are a class of pharmaceutical agents that block the effect of histamine. Histamine is a naturally occurring body substance that is released in certain allergic reactions. Typically, antihistamines are more effective in preventing rather than in reversing the action of histamine. Unfortunately, antihistamines have not been found to have any dramatic effects in children with asthma or other severe diseases of an allergic nature (Markowitz, 1983). For pediatric populations, antihistamines may be effective in the treatment of hay fever or mild recurrent hives of unknown etiology. Some research also has sug-

gested the potential efficacy of antihistamines in the prevention of motion sickness in children (Macnair, 1983).

Typically, antihistamines are found in cold preparations prescribed for children (Pruitt, 1985). Children who are treated with antihistamines are likely to have less severe runny noses, yet the other features of the common cold are not significantly affected by this class of drugs. Antihistamines have atropine like effects that diminish the amount of secretions produced by the irritated lining of the nose or bronchial passages. Although some antihistamines have been marketed as cough suppressants, a number of studies have shown that antihistamines are no better than placebos in relieving children of the symptoms of the common cold (Markowitz, 1983).

Because the use of minor and major tranquilizers carries significant disadvantages in the treatment of behavioral and anxiety disorders in children (Popper, 1985), it has been suggested that antihistamines be used short term for calming acutely anxious children and for controlling agitation in severely psychotic children (Popper, 1985). Risks of recreational abuse, management abuse, tolerance, and dependence are also lower than for anti-anxiety agents and major tranquilizers (Popper, 1985), making this class of drugs more appealing for use by the practicing physician. The enduring cognitive effects of antihistamines are not well documented in the empirical literature, although some recent research has suggested an amelioration of behavioral difficulties and improved academic performance in response to antihistamine therapy (McLoughlin, et al., 1983). Further, some investigators (Millichap, 1973; Mattes, 1979) have found antihistamines to be efficacious in the treatment and management of hyperactivity. While the effects of antihistamines on cognitive and learning outcome appear to be somewhat promising, more research must be mounted before any definitive conclusions can be made in this area. Moreover, while the use of antihistamines in the treatment of psychiatric disorders of children may provide a safer alternative than the use of other psychotropic agents, including neuroleptic agents and antianxiety drugs, it still entails some of the same risks and the physician must carefully weigh the potential benefits against any possible risks.

Although the long-term effects of antihistamines have received little systematic study, the use of these agents appear to provide primarily short-term benefits. They are typically safe and consequently are often sold without a prescription. They may have adverse effects, although these usually occur with higher doses. Sedation is the most common side effect in children, but some tolerance may develop. Combinations of antihistamines with other central nervous system depressants (e.g., alcohol) should be avoided. In high doses, or for children who are particularly sensitive to these agents, antihistamines may cause undesirable side effects. These may include excitation, nervousness, palpitations, rapid heartbeat, dryness of the mouth, urinary retention, and constipation. In rare instances, red blood cells can burst (hemolytic anemia) or bone marrow can be depleted of blood-forming cells (arganulocytosis) (Markowitz, 1983). Sustained antihistamine usage with pediatric populations may be associated with persistent daytime drowsiness, "hangover," or mild enduring effects on cognition (Popper, 1985). Although such side effects are better tolerated by younger children than by adolescents, the occurrence of these effects should result in the prompt cessation of antihistamine therapy.

## REFERENCES

Macnair, A. L. (1983). Cinnarizine in the prophylaxis of car sickness in children. *Current Medical Research Opinion, 8,* 451–455.

Markowitz, M. (1983). Immunity, allergy, and related diseases. In R. E. Behrman & V. C. Vaughn (Eds.), *Nelson textbook of pediatrics* (pp. 497–594). Philadelphia: Saunders.

Mattes, J. (1979). Trial of diphenpyraline in hyperactive children (letter). *Psychopharmacology Bulletin, 15,* 5–6.

McLoughlin, J., Nall, M., Isaacs, P., Petrosko, J., Karibo, J., & Lindsey, B. (1983). The relationship of allergies and allergy treatment to school performance and student behavior. *Annals of Allergy, 51,* 506–510.

Millichap, J. G. (1973). Drugs in management of minimal brain dysfunction. *Annals of the New York Academy of Science, 205,* 321–334.

Popper, C. W. (1985). Child and adolescent psychopharmacology. In R. Michels & J. O. Cavenar (Eds.), *Psychiatry* (Vol. 2, pp. 1–23). New York: Lippincott.

Pruitt, A. W. (1985). Rational use of cold and cough preparations. *Pediatric Annals, 14,* 289–291.

RONALD T. BROWN
*Emory University School
of Medicine*

**DRUG THERAPY
TRANQUILIZERS**

## ANTISOCIAL BEHAVIOR

A study by Peterson (1961) considered a sampling of many behaviors of children that could be considered as antisocial. More than 400 representative case folders from files of a child-guidance clinic were inspected and the referral problems of each child noted. Peterson's results indicated that the interrelationship among 58 items could be reduced to two independent clusters: conduct problems and personality problems. The two dimensions of problems most frequently reported among the public school students in these two major clusters were aggression and withdrawl. Each child could be placed somewhere in these two dimensions regardless of the number of problem behaviors

or other dimensions the child manifested. Children's behaviors differ quantitatively not qualitatively. The degree of quantitative difference between normal and abnormal is usually slight.

Definitions are particularly difficult to generate when context is general and critical, as is the case when the word "social" is used. While there is a need to convey with words what is meant by antisocial behavior, the intensity, timeliness, and impact of a behavior on others in the culture/society/group where the behavior is experienced determines the definition: therefore, a static meaning is not effective. Antisocial behaviors or misbehaving (disliked performances) are accepted daily by society. A behavior is labeled antisocial when the tolerance level of an observer is exceeded with respect to that observer's interpretation of societal rules.

For example, aggressive antisocial behavior is manifested when a student stands and yells a phrase of profanity during a school assembly. The consequences of such behavior could be removal from the audience (peer group), immediate verbal reprimand by adult authorities, a quick trip to the administrator's office, or dismissal from school. In contrast, if the same pupil were to stand during a professional ball game and yell the same phrase of profanity, not only might the audience approve of the behavior, it might even reward the verbal expressiveness.

Variables in the environment that define the tolerance level of observers when a behavior is judged antisocial are many: time, social status, money, event, location, age, reputation, intensity, duration, frequency, and group expectations. When the cumulative effect of these variables is negative, exceeding the dynamic acceptable definition of the moment, a person's behavioral performance is judged antisocial. For example, when a behavior is poorly timed, appropriate social status is not recognized, intensity is high and loud, the behavior is against school rules, reputation is known, duration is long; frequency is perceived as too often, and other students are conforming to rules of the environment, an antisocial behavior is said to exist. To identify specific factors related to perceptions of antisocial behavior, recent investigation has emphasized those behaviors that teachers and students find most disturbing. Aggressive behavior is most often primary, but withdrawl behaviors such as fear, anxiety, and tension are also defined as antisocial.

This second type of antisocial behavior is reported to be more tolerable to society. The child suffering from withdrawl may be in deeper pain, despair, or depression than an aggressive individuals, however, such a child is less aversive to adults and peers, and less likely to excite the environment into action. These children have too little behavior rather than too much. Characteristics accompanying withdrawal are feelings of inferiority and self-consciousness, social withdrawal, shyness, anxiety, weeping, hypersensitivity, infrequent social smiles, nail chewing, depression and chronic sadness, drowsiness, sluggishness, daydreaming, passivity, short attention span, preoccupation, and somber quietness. These children are also picked on by others.

The term antisocial behavior is often applied when behaviors remain inflexible, or frozen, and the person performing the behaviors continues to react to the environment in a manner judged by the group to be displeasing, inappropriate and uncomfortable. The label antisocial behavior is attached to the person displaying the behavior and the definition itself magnifies the individual's differences. Not only does the behavior classify a person, but the antisocial definition itself accentuates differences. Only if classification leads to positive action through school programs on the behalf of the child is this definition constructive.

## Characteristics

Patterns of antisocial behavior have received a variety of labels: e.g., unsocialized aggressive, conduct disorder, aggressive, unsocialized psychopathic, psychopathic delinquent, antisocially aggressive, and sadistically aggressive. Children exhibiting antisocial behaviors apparent to school officials and teachers may demonstrate one or more of the following characteristics:

1. An inability to learn that cannot be explained by conventional intellectual, sensory, or health factors. A learning-disabled child seldom escapes recognition. He or she is frequently labeled learning disabled, thus lowering self-esteem. The inability to learn is perhaps the single most significant characteristic of antisocial children, with the learning disability manifested as the inability to profit from social experiences and/or academic instruction.

2. An inability to build and maintain satisfactory interpersonal relationships with peers and teachers; to demonstrate sympathy and warmth toward others; to stand alone when necessary; to have close friends; to be aggressively constructive; to enjoy working and playing with others as well as working and playing alone. Children who are unable to build and maintain satisfactory interpersonal relationships are easily defined as different by teachers and peers.

3. "Inappropriate" behaviors or feelings that occur under normal conditions. What is appropriate is judged by the teacher and the student's peers. This judgment is sensed by children because of their ability to profit from school experiences and relate to their teachers. Children classified as antisocial often cannot learn what is appropriate because of their inability to relate to and profit from cultural experiences. This amplifies the daily failures of children who fail to conform to social/cultural rules and exacerbates their lack of socialization.

4. Lack of flexibility. When behaviors become frozen into patterns of inappropriateness of such intensity, du-

ration, and frequency that they interfere with social activities of a group, those behaviors are identified as antisocial.

5. Depression and general moods of unhappiness, characteristics of withdrawl. When children seldom smile and express unhappiness in play, art work, group discussions, and language arts, the observer should watch for antisocial expression.

6. A tendency to develop physical symptoms, pains, or fears, especially in reaction to school situations or authority figures. These symptoms may indicate potential antisocial behaviors.

7. Disobedience, disruptiveness, fighting, temper tantrums, irresponsibility, impertinence, jealousy, anger, bossiness, the use of profanity, attention-seeking behavior, boisterousness, defiance of authority, feelings of guilt and inadequacy, irritability, and quarrelsomeness. These descriptors are often associated with antisocial phenomena.

Behaviors described by these characteristics may formulate a pattern of active antisocial behavior that results in conflict with parents, peers, and social institutions. Children and adolescents who represent extreme patterns of antisocial behaviors are likely to have difficulty with law-enforcement agencies. Extreme antisocial behavior will be defined as criminal conduct and result in arrest, incarceration, recidivism, and failure to become a good citizen.

## Acquisition

The possibility of hereditary or predispositional factors cannot be ignored, neither can the contributions of organic factors be ruled out. Prematurity, (birth weight less than 5 pounds,) is regarded as an important cause of brain damage in children. Epilipsy and cerebral palsy studies report higher prevalances of antisocial behaviors among those with known brain lesions. Situations where trait patterns of deviant behavior can be studied along with the mechanisms by which the acquisition of the traits occurs is very revealing. Sociological literature has emphasized social class, deviant social organization, and social inequalities as influential. The family is also a setting where deviant behavior has been studied. It is obvious making the acquisition of principal behavioral patterns of antisocial behavior more probable. Psychiatric illness in parents reflects an increased rate of behavior problems in children. Antisocial parents tend to rear antisocial children. Childhood behavior problems are more common among lower socio-economic classes. To what extent the influence of parents' disturbances on the child's behavior is genetic and to what extent it is environmental, is speculative.

Children with antisocial behaviors are most visible when required to pay strict attention, follow directions, demonstrate control, exhibit socially acceptable behavior, and master academic skills. School, the primary social-izing agency for society, emphasizes conformity and edu-cational achievement. These expectations are basic to the order of formal training. When children are unable to meet these expectations, concerns frequently arise among teachers. Questions educators pose may include: How many children are there? How do they behave? How can they be controlled and managed in the classroom? How should they be classified to deduce effects created by la-bels? What support systems can provide these children with needed programs?

Terms used in educational settings to describe children with antisocial behaviors are emotionally disturbed, so-cially maladjusted, minimally neurologically impaired, culturally disadvantaged, behavior disordered, education-ally handicapped, and conduct disturbed. Such labels rep-resent different orientations that exist among educators confronted with the task of providing educational pro-grams for children with antisocial behaviors. All these la-bels could be used collectively for a single child experi-encing difficulty in school. For qualification for programs, labels and treatments should be closely related to how the antisocial child (in classroom, community, or at home) is perceived (by educators, social groups, or family). Edu-cational offerings frequently depend on how a child is per-ceived and the attitude of the referring school toward the child.

## Treatment

When an individual has appropriate behavioral responses in his or her repertoire and exhibits these responses under appropriate circumstances, antisocial behavior is inter-preted. Through systematic and explicit application of the principles of learning, behavior management can be ap-plied in educational settings to treat antisocial behaviors.

The individual can be helped to change deficient or mal-adaptive behavior by receiving assistance to modify his or her responses to specific sound cues. In the case of mal-adaptive behavior, for example, aggression could be mod-ified to be elicited or emitted under appropriate circum-stances only. This type of behavioral learning, unlearning, or relearning is known as behavior management. The teacher or behaviorist operates on the assumption that the behavior can be modified without understanding why the behavior is antisocial. The antecedents to the behavior need not be reconstructed to initiate corrective action. Teaching the child to react more appropriately is the only relevant issue, not finding out how the child came to be-have antisocially. The focus during behavior therapy is on teaching new behaviors and eliminating old ones. The first task of the therapist (teacher) is to decide which behavior should be modified. Once a target behavior is defined, the treatment goal can be specified. Treatments are based on principles of learning: respondent learning, operant con-ditioning, interrelationships of operation and respondent

factors, social reinforcement, desensitization, and aversive and contingency control. The treatment goal is assessed when the antisocial behavior has become adapted. If in the process of identifying target behaviors the teacher dis-covers antecedents as causes, the organization of the class-room environment, stimuli, and consequences can be ar-ranged so that the learning situation supports the child's development. An engineered, structured classroom with clear-cut expectations and rewarding consequences for ap-propriate behavior and academic accomplishment can re-sult in definite academic and behavioral gains. Primary or tangible rewards, teacher attention, "game" ap-proaches, and high-interest activities can become suc-cessful interventions for adapting antisocial behaviors. Precision teaching involves selecting a behavior, charting it on a graph, recording changes and occurrences, analyz-ing the child's performance, and changing the program according to program effects. Some schools use a resource room concept, in which the child participates part time in a special program and part time in a regular class pro-gram.

Completely self-contained classrooms for children with more severe learning and behavioral problems can be suc-cessful. The engineered classroom directs attention to the establishment of specific goals or develops a sequence of behavioral objectives, for example, attention, response, order, exploratoration, social activity, mastery, and achievement. This engineering translates behavior modi-fication strategy into realistic use in the classroom. There is constant manipulation of stimuli and intervention in the class to assure a child's continued success.

There are limitless behaviors that can disturb, inter-fere, or interrupt. There are as many interventions to at-tempt to modify disturbing behaviors. The range of chil-dren's behaviors that are judged negatively is extensive, especially in the complex social system called school. Our tendency is to cause a child to internalize his or her prob-lematic characteristics through inadvertent reinforce-ment.

Reactors classify, define, program, analyze, label, and provide some services to those identified as aggressive when threatening behaviors become a serious concern. Seldom do educators recognize the responder as a contrib-utor to the disturbances. The child judged as antisocial is the one who violates a large number of behavioral codes, yet some of the most seriously troubled go unrecognized and untreated as passive aggressors.

The intensity of observer reaction may be related to the observer's own social tolerance and his or her difficulty in controlling comparable tendencies. Certainly, the observ-er's tolerance plays a significant role in determining the services to be received by the antisocial performer.

If a tree crashes in the forest but there is no human ear to hear it, is there a noise? When an individual behaves in an antisocial fashion, does the disturbance exist without a reactor to register the event? Does the disturbance reside in the child or the reactor, or is it a product of both?

**REFERENCE**

Quay, H. C., & Werry, J. S. (1972). *Psychopathological disorders of childhood.* New York: Wiley.

ANNE SABATINO
*Hudson, Wisconsin*

**CONDUCT DISORDER
EMOTIONAL DISORDERS
SERIOUSLY EMOTIONALLY DISTURBED**

# ANTISOCIAL PERSONALITY

The antisocial personality is characterized by a recurring pattern of antisocial behaviors and a general disregard for the rights of others. This pattern of behavior has, in the past been referred to as psychopathy or sociopathy. It emerges during childhood in the form of truancy and other school-related academic and behavior problems such as delinquency, lying, fighting, sexual promiscuity, substance abuse, and running away from home. The DSM III (American Psychiatric Association, 1980) requires at least four of the following nine manifestations of the disorder be present before a diagnosis of antisocial personality disorder (APD) is made: inability to sustain consistent work behavior; lack of ability to function as a responsible parent; failure to accept social norms with respect to lawful behavior; inability to maintain enduring attachment to a sexual partner; irritability or aggressiveness; failure to honor financial obligations; failure to plan ahead, or impulsivity; disregard for the truth; and recklessness. Cleckley (1976) has identified other characteristics such as lack of remorse or shame, failure to learn from experience, poor judgment, and absence of anxiety.

The diagnosis of APD is typically reserved for individuals age 18 and over. Younger children and adolescents who manifest signs of APD are diagnosed as conduct disorder. There are four subtypes of conduct disorder depending on the presence or absence of normal social attachments and aggressive behavior. Many, but not all, children who manifest conduct disorder go on to develop an antisocial personality disorder (Loeber, 1982). Research has identified five factors that appear to play a role in the etiology of APD including heredity, brain abnormalities, autonomic nervous system underarousal, and family or environmental influences.

**REFERENCES**

American Psychiatric Association (1980). *Diagnostic and statistical manual of mental disorders (3rd ed.).* Washington, DC.

Cleckley, H. M. (1976). *The mask of sanity* (5th ed.). St. Louis: Mosby.

Loeber, R. (1982). The stability of antisocial and delinquent behavior: A review. *Child Development, 53,* 1431–1446.

ROBERT G. BRUBAKER
*Eastern Kentucky University*

**AGGRESSION
CONDUCT DISORDER**

# ANXIETY

There is probably no aspect of the human experience more universal than that of anxiety. In every culture and throughout recorded time, the human organism has been subject to real and imagined threats that may produce the arousal state that is labeled anxiety. By the midpoint of the present century, many authors, philosophers, psychologists, and others were referring to the twentieth century as the age of anxiety. Auden (1947) explained that the age of anxiety was reflected in heightened feelings of loneliness. This increase in anxiety, or perhaps an increased awareness of its existence, was often attributed to loneliness, uncertainty, and bureaucratic interference with the individual's efforts toward self-recognition and self-realization.

Both Kierkegaard (1944) and May (1977) noted the potential for human growth inherent in a satisfactory response to anxiety-producing stimuli. In support of this notion is the considerable research and theory of Torrance (1965) affirming that creative problem solving serves as an antidote for anxiety. Thus anxiety is not always defined as a destructive or debilitating force in human behavior. Many psychologists and educators today describe a curvilinear relationship between learning and anxiety. Both very high and very low levels of anxiety are negatively related to learning, resulting in the well-known inverted or U-shaped curve between anxiety and performance on complex tasks.

One of the more prevalent conceptualizations of anxiety today embodies the state-trait distinction. Here we may refer to Spielberger (1972), who states the differences between state and trait anxiety very clearly. Essentially, state anxiety is a complex system of emotional reactions that arise when an individual perceives a situation as threatening, regardless of whether a real threat exists. Thus, state anxiety is a transitory condition and may vary greatly from individual to individual and from one condition to another. Not all conditions are equally threatening to all individuals.

In contrast, anxiety may be understood to be more of a personality trait. This notion suggests that it is a more permanent construct of the individual's usual manner of functioning. Trait anxiety is a term used to define the personality of one who frequently experiences anxiety, often where the strength of the stimulus for evoking anxiety is relatively weak. It refers to the propensity of the individual to feel anxiety. This trait appears to vary among persons on a continuum from highly infrequent to an almost constant level of anxiety. Several researchers, including Gottschalk and Gleser (1969), view anxiety as a multimodal concept. It has been theorized that such emotions as anger, guilt, shame, and shyness are really components of anxiety.

In an effort to understand more clearly the nature and impact of anxiety, several researchers have developed measures of anxiety. Some of these measures record physiological manifestations of anxiety such as changes in temperature or heart rate. Taylor (1951) is credited with an early effort to measure anxiety through a self-report technique. Behavior, task performance, clinical intuition, and stress responses are also used to measure anxiety.

Among the most widely researched measures of anxiety are the *State-Trait Anxiety Inventory for Children* (Spielberger, et al., 1973), the *State-Trait Anxiety Inventory* (Spielberger, et al., 1970) and the *Revised Children's Manifest Anxiety Scale* (Reynolds & Richmond, 1978, 1985). These and other instruments continue to be used by researchers and clinicians in their efforts to specify the nature of anxiety and to record and remediate its debilitating effects on the individual.

## REFERENCES

Auden, W. H. (1947). *The age of anxiety.* New York: Random House.

Gottschalk, L. O., & Gleser, G. C. (1969). *The measurement of psychological states through the content analysis of verbal behavior.* Los Angeles: University of California Press.

Kierkegaard, S. (1944). *The concept of dread* (translated by Walter Lowrie). Princeton, NJ: Princeton University Press (originally published in Danish in 1844).

May, R. (1977). *The meaning of anxiety.* New York: Norton.

Reynolds, C. R., & Richmond, B. O. (1978). What I think and feel: A revised measure of children's manifest anxiety. *Journal of Abnormal Child Psychology, 6,* 271–280.

Reynolds, C. R., & Richmond, B. O. (1985). *Manual, revised children's manifest anxiety scale.* Los Angeles: Western Psychological Services.

Spielberger, C. D. (1972). Anxiety as an emotional state. In C. D. Spielberger (Ed.), *Anxiety: Current trends in theory and research* (p. 30). New York: Academic.

Spielberger, C. D., Edwards, C. D., Lushene, R. E., Montuori, I., & Platzek, D. (1973). *Manual, state trait anxiety inventory for children.* Palo Alto, CA: Consulting Psychologists Press.

Spielberger, C. D., Gorsuch, R. L., & Lushene, R. E. (1970). *Manual, for the state-trait Anxiety inventory,* Palo Alto, CA: Consulting Psychologists Press.

Taylor, J. A. (1951). The relationship of anxiety to the conditioned eyelid response. *Journal of Experimental Psychology, 41,* 81–92.

Torrance, E. P. (1965). *Mental health and constructive behavior.* Belmont, CA: Wadsworth.

BERT O. RICHMOND
*University of Georgia*

**FEARS AND PHOBIAS**
**TEST ANXIETY**

## ANXIETY DISORDERS

Anxiety is an emotional condition experienced by all children and adults to some degree. It results when people's responses to internal or external events produce a negative arousal state. It is a state of general emotional arousal that is experienced as unpleasant to some degree by the individual. Internal or external conditions that create fear are the most common sources of anxiety. When individuals experience anxiety to a significant degree, they often show a wide range of possible responses that are exaggerated in proportion to the objective situation. These diffuse effects may include emotional responses, including physiological changes; cognitive changes in perceptions of objects or thoughts about a situation; motor responses such as irritable behavior or hyperactivity, or the opposite including lethargy or withdrawn behavior. A certain degree of anxiety has motivating properties and can have a positive value such as enhancing performance on educational tasks. Anxiety becomes a clinical problem when it reaches a significant degree on a regular basis and interferes with normal adaptive behavior.

Anxiety can be specific to particular situations or even a specific object, or it can be generalized, undifferentiated, and "free-floating." Specific anxiety may give rise to phobias. Generalized anxiety would be part of a disorder such as an avoidant disorder, in which anxiety is part of a general response to social encounters.

The two general approaches to explaining the origins of anxiety disorders are psychoanalytic and behavioral. According to the psychoanalytic approach, anxiety, in its more significant forms, represents intrapsychic conflict between a child's ego and unconscious sexual impulses. As the developing child attempts to defend himself or herself against the unconscious impulses, the accompanying anxiety is displaced or transferred into some other form that is the behavioral manifestation of one of the anxiety disorders. The particular form of the disorder may represent a personality difference in the individual child or be the result of a traumatic incident.

The behavioral approach traces the origins of the symptom behavior to specific environmental conditions. For example, phobias are often explained as conditioned responses in which a previously neutral stimulus (e.g., a dog) is paired with a noxious stimulus to produce fear, which then may be generalized (e.g., to other animals). The concept of reinforcement is also used by learning theorists. According to this point of view, the behavior is maintained because it serves to reduce the anxiety. For example, the child who avoids a fearful object, in the case of a phobia, controls anxiety in this way. Similarly, the child who is fearful of other people learns to control anxiety by withdrawing from social contacts and acting shy. The anxiety disorders are generally classified with the psychoneurotic disorders.

## Childhood Stress

Stress refers to environmental pressures and changes that produce emotional and physiological coping responses in the child. Circumstances often produce anxiety reactions. Changes that produce stress frequently occur in normal child development. For example, the young infant experiences anxiety in the form of separation anxiety from the mother. Healthy child development depends on the child's learning effective ways to cope with stressful changes so as to keep anxiety at manageable levels.

Much research exists on the effects of change and stressors on adults, and a variety of stress scales have been developed. Less is known about the clinical effects of stress and changes in child development, although Bowlby (1980) has studied the role of separation and loss on the development of childhood depression. Clinicians, teachers, and guidance counselors should be aware of the role of change, loss, and stress in the development of anxiety disorders. The loss of a parent through death or divorce, chronic illness, and school failure all place the child at risk of developing anxiety reactions. Lanier (1984) has developed an experimental childhood stress scale that may be of assistance to school personnel in identifying children at risk.

## Separation Anxiety Disorder

The main symptom of this syndrome is excessive anxiety when the child is separated from a major attachment figure such as a parent. Common behaviors include fear that harm will come to the parent; worry that a major trauma such as an automobile accident will occur; refusal to go to school; sleep disturbance; reluctance to be left alone; physical symptoms, such as stomach aches, headaches, or dizziness; and withdrawal from normal social activities. This disorder may develop anytime from infancy through adolescence. It is usually not caused by a single event, but gradually emerges as a behavioral pattern stemming from a disturbed child-parent relationship. Cases often appear to have been set off by a particular upsetting event, but close examination reveals the longstanding pattern.

## School Phobia

Children refusing to go to school or asking to leave school once they arrive is one of the most common and sometimes most difficult to treat of childhood disorders. Children sometimes develop a negative association based on a frustrating school experience and then refuse to go to school. This could be the case where a child has a serious learning disability of an attention deficit disorder in which self-esteem is adversely affected. Generally, however, a school-refusal or school-phobic child is acting out of anxiety relating to separation.

School phobic cases can be classified into two types. The first is generally seen in younger children with more cooperative parents; it responds better to intervention. The second type occurs in late childhood (ages 10 to 12) or adolescence. The parents tend to be less cooperative; there may be conflict in the marital relationship; and response to treatment is slower and may require hospitalization.

Two cases treated by the author demonstrate the two clinical subtypes. In one, an 8-year-old girl was referred by her pediatrician because she was showing anxiety about attending school and was frequently calling her mother from school in acute distress. She worried excessively and was concerned that her mother might be in an automobile accident (her mother did a good deal of traveling as part of her job). In her rural community, a number of fatal automobile accidents had been well publicized, and the child was focusing on those traumas as she verbalized her terror. She was the youngest child in the family and the mother had a long pattern of overinvolvement and protectiveness toward her. Treatment consisted of individual psychotherapy addressing the irrational fear that the mother may die in a traffic accident, and behavioral prescriptions for the mother to be less protective of the child. The parents were supportive and responsive to identifying the problem. The child responded well to insight-oriented therapy, and the fear and phobic behavior was gradually extinguished.

A case that reflects the second type of school phobia involved a 14-year-old boy. He was referred following involvement with a school truant officer because of refusal to go to school in the grade 8. A history revealed that the child had always been reluctant to attend school. The mother had worked as a teacher's aide in the child's elementary school during his early years; this served to reduce the child's separation anxiety. Mother and child had an extremely close, enmeshed relationship. When the family moved to a different city and the mother no longer was in the school during the day, the school refusal became acute. The parents had an extremely poor marital relationship, and the mother had been diagnosed as a paranoid personality disorder. The child, as an adolescent, felt compelled to stay home from school because of his mother's worry and agitation. This case required hospitalization of the adolescent to work intensely on the overinvolvement between mother and child and to address the family problems.

## Avoidant Disorder of Childhood and Adolescence

This disorder occurs from age $2\frac{1}{2}$ through adolescence. A behavioral pattern of shrinking away from social contacts and withdrawing from others is the central characteristic. Children with this disorder are not merely shy, they actively retreat from social contacts and are very cautious in dealing with peers. Nonverbal body movements may be characterized by the avoidance of eye contact, poor posture, and childlike mannerisms.

A clinical case treated by this psychologist illustrates this disorder. A 17-year-old female was referred with the suspected problem of bulimia. She had been vomiting daily for several months because of a preoccupation with the idea that she was overweight and unattractive to others. History revealed that this seemed to be a recent pattern of behavior stemming from a longstanding pattern of social isolation. This girl and her mother described her as being rejected and isolated from others since grade 1. Her peers had seen her as "weird" and different for 12 years and had ostracized her because of her unusual behaviors. She had few friends and was performing poorly in school despite excellent academic skills and at least average intelligence. The decision to come to therapy resulted in the girl and her family finally admitting to the severity of her social isolation and unhappiness. It was followed by a suicidal gesture that resulted in hospitalization. In the hospital, the girl showed behaviors that impressed others as similar to those of schizophrenics. There was regressed, childlike behavior. As she began to adjust to the hospital setting, she showed nonverbal behaviors of avoidance of eye contact and stared at the wall when engaged in conversation with others. She would curl her legs into a fetallike position in the middle of a conversation. This case demonstrated behaviorally the psychological turmoil of the avoidant disorder. Children with this disorder are extremely sensitive to social acceptance and the judgment of others. Treatment was highly successful. A supportive hospital milieu and intensive individual psychotherapy produced fairly rapid changes in the longstanding behavioral pattern of avoiding contact with other people. The school environment was an important testing ground of the behavioral changes involving less sensitivity to the judgment of peers.

## Overanxious Disorders

Children with this syndrome show excessive worry about performance, potential injuries, and acceptance by others. The difference between this disorder and the avoidant one is that the primary problem is worry or anxiety rather than avoidant behavior. Children who show this problem syndrome tend to come from families having a high emphasis on performance, achievement, and socially accept-

able behavior. The worry tends to be generalized, not specifically associated with a particular situation. It often involves overconcern with being a highly competent individual and sensitivity to criticism. Children with this disorder also may show psychophysiological symptoms such as stomach aches or general nervousness. There are signs of obsessional thoughts about oneself, a tendency toward perfectionism, and approval-seeking behavior. Such children also are prime examples of people who are always imagining the worst; they may have fears of death or impending disaster. Children with this psychological problem share many of the same concerns as those with the avoidant disorder, but they persevere in their efforts to achieve or to please despite their excessive worry instead of withdrawing from social contacts.

## Childhood Phobias

Phobias reflect intense anxiety associated with a fear about a specific object or situation that is out of proportion to the apparent objective danger. In this sense, phobias are irrational fears. In evaluating whether or not a childhood fear is a phobia, the clinician must keep in mind the fears that normally would be apparent at different developmental ages. For example, fear of loud noises and strangers are the norm in infancy; fear of animals and fear of darkness in toddlerhood; and fear of social embarrassment in adolescence. A phobia is distinguished by the severity of the anxiety and a sense of panic that seems to overwhelm the child when faced with the object or situation. There is an obsessional quality to the phobia as the child may spend unusual amounts of time worrying about exposure to the object. Common phobias include fear of animals, heights, and insects.

Psychoanalytic theory explains the development of phobias as a process in which internal conflicts produce anxiety and are displaced onto an external object, causing an intense fear reaction. In contrast, behavior therapy proposes a conditioning theory to explain the development of phobias. Wolpe (1969) suggests that a traumatic or frightening incident occurs when a neutral stimulus or object is present at the same time. Anxiety thereafter is evoked by the presence of the previously neutral object such as a dog; a phobia is born this way. There are other variations of these two general approaches in explaining the development of phobias, many of which emphasize the development of irrational cognitive beliefs from many sources including a child's imagination.

Behavior therapy has become the most popular approach to treating phobias because of fairly high success rates. The most common behavioral therapy technique is Wolpe's (1969) systematic desensitization technique. In this approach, the clinician first constructs an anxiety hierarchy that consists of a list of objects or situations that are logically related to the phobic object and that gradually increase in the degree of anxiety that would be elicited. For example, in a social phobia, the list may begin with low levels of anxiety involving the introduction to an acquaintance and increase to a situation involving public speaking. The second step in the desensitization procedure is to train the person in techniques of relaxation. The final step in the procedure is to gradually introduce the individual to anxiety-producing objects while relaxation techniques are employed or alternated with the introduction to the objects, as it is assumed the relaxation is incompatible with anxiety.

The clinician hopes to teach the individual to control anxiety in the face of exposure to the objects, in this way desensitizing the subject to the phobic reaction. Visualization or imagery techniques are often applied. The individual is asked to visualize an anxiety-producing situation and then to practice relaxation. The person might at a later time be exposed to this actual situation. The hope is that the subject will have learned to control anxiety through practicing relaxation and also, with the help of a therapist, to be able to think through misconceptions about the irrational fear. This approach has proven effective in a wide variety of phobias, including school phobia.

## REFERENCES

American Psychiatric Association. (1980). *Diagnostic and statistical manual of mental disorders* (3rd ed.). Washington, DC: Author.

Bowlby, J. (1980). *Attachment and loss: Vol. 3. Loss: Sadness and depression.* New York: Basic Books.

Lanier, H. B. (1984). *School events as stressors: Development of a school stress rating scale.* Unpublished doctoral dissertation, Rutgers, State University of New Jersey, New Brunswick.

Wolpe, J. (1969). *The practice of behavior therapy.* New York: Pergamon.

WILLIAM G. AUSTIN
*Cape Fear Psychological
Services, Wilmington,
North Carolina*

**CHILDHOOD PSYCHOSIS**
**DEPRESSION**
**EMOTIONAL DISORDERS**
**PSYCHONEUROTIC DISORDERS**
**SCHOOL PHOBIA**

## APGAR RATING SCALE

The Apgar Rating Scale was specifically designed to assess medical distress in newborns. Ratings are made by attending nurses or physicians at 1 minute after birth, with possible further ratings at 3, 5, and 10 minutes. Five vital signs, heart rate, respiratory effort, reflex irritability, muscle tone, and color, are rated on a 3-point scale: 2 if present, 1 if not fully present, and 0 if absent. Thus the range of possible scores is 0–10, with scores greater than 7 (about 70% of all newborns) indicating excellent condition, 3–7 (24% of all newborns) indicating a moderately depressed condition, and less than 3 (6% of all newborns) indicating a severely depressed condition (Apgar, 1953; Apgar, Holaday, James & Weisbrott, 1958).

The Apgar Scale has been used extensively in research in anesthesiology, obstetrics, pediatric neurology, and developmental psychology. Apgar scores are predictive of infant mortality: 15% of neonates with severely depressed scores die within $7\frac{1}{2}$ months, compared with 0.13% of those receiving scores of 10 (Apgar, et al., 1958). There is also a moderate relationship between Apgar scores and intellectual and motor development: Edwards (1968), for example, found an Apgar correlation of 0.251 with Stanford-Binet IQ, 0.456 with a battery of fine-motor tasks, and 0.480 with gross-motor tasks at age 4. The 5-minute postnatal Apgar scores were more predictive than 1-minute scores in Edwards' study.

## REFERENCES

Apgar, V. (1953). A proposal for a new method of evaluation of the newborn infant. *Current Researches in Anesthesia and Analgesia, 32,* 260–267.

Apgar, V., Holaday, D., James, L., Weisbrott, I., & Berrien, C. (1958). Evaluation of the newborn infant—second report. *Journal of the American Medical Association, 168,* 1985–1988.

Edwards, N. (1968). The relationship between physical condition immediately after birth and mental and motor performance at age four. *Genetic Psychology Monographs, 78,* 257–289.

JOHN MACDONALD
*Eastern Kentucky University*

**NEONATAL BEHAVIORAL ASSESSMENT SCALE**
**PREMATURITY/PRETERM**

## APHASIA

Aphasia is a generic term referring to communication disorders of neurologic origin that are not explained by primary sensory deficits (e.g., deafness) or pervasive cognitive impairment (e.g., mental retardation). While disturbances of written language (e.g., reading, written expression) may be present, aphasia generally is considered a disorder of spoken communication (Myklebust, 1971). The broad term *aphasia* may be subdivided into specific types of language disturbances. Several aphasia classification systems exist, but perhaps the clearest is Geschwind's (1979) description of two basic types of aphasics. Nonfluent aphasics may communicate by single words only, or by short, incomplete phrases (Kaufman, 1981). Misarticulations may be present, and the speech that is produced may be slow, labored, and ungrammatical. In contrast, fluent aphasia is characterized by ample, well-articulated speech, although there is an absence of integrated meaning. Paraphasias (abnormalities in the use or construction of single words) are pathognomonic of fluent aphasia. Paraphasias may be literal (e.g., "spoot" for "spoon") or verbal (e.g., calling a fork a spoon) (Geschwind, 1979; Kaufman, 1981).

Geschwind (1979) identified major aphasic syndromes and their associated lesion loci. The four most common syndromes are (1) Broca's aphasia, a nonfluent aphasia resulting from lesions in the left frontal cortex (Broca's area); (2) Wernicke's aphasia, a fluent form of the disorder associated with impairment of the posterior portion of the superior temporal gyrus in the dominant hemisphere (Wernicke's area); (3) conduction aphasia, a fluent aphasia characterized by impaired ability to repeat another's words resulting from a lesion in the suprasylvian temporal region; and (4) anomic aphasia, a fluent aphasia distinguished from Broca's type by preserved repetition ability. This last type may be observed in patients recovering from other aphasias, and may arise from variable loci (Geschwind, 1979; Hecaen, 1979). Geshwind (1979) cautions that fluent aphasia is a rare phenomenon in children, and that the associated lesion loci outlined previously are less clear in pediatric populations.

Traditional aphasia classifications are not directly applicable to children. Communication disorders in children may be divided into acquired disorders (those that develop subsequent to the capacity for understanding and using language) and congenital or developmental disorders, characterized by the failure of development of age-appropriate language skills (Hecaen, 1979). Rapin and Allen (1983) described seven developmental language disorders in children based on clinical observations and longitudinal investigations. Aphasic children exhibit severe communication disorders that seriously interfere with their learning. An integrated, comprehensive special education program derived from a multifactored evaluation of neuropsychological abilities is recommended for such children.

## REFERENCES

Geschwind, N. (1979). Focal disturbances of higher nervous function. In P. B. Beeson, W. McDermott, & J. B. Wyngaarden (Eds.), *Cecil textbook of medicine* (pp. 656–659). Philadelphia: Saunders.

Hecaen, H. (1979). Aphasias. In M. S. Gazzaniga (Ed.), *Handbook of behavioral neurobiology. Vol. 2 Neuropsychology* (pp. 239–292). New York: Plenum.

Kaufman, D. M. (1981). *Clinical neurology for psychiatrists.* New York: Grune & Stratton.

Myklebust, H. R. (1971). Childhood aphasia: An evolving concept. In L. E. Travis (Ed.), *Handbook of speech pathology and audiology* (pp. 1181–1202). New York: Appleton-Century-Crofts.

Rapin, I., & Allen, D. A. (1983). Developmental language disorders: Nosologic considerations. In U. Kirk (Ed.), *Neuropsy-chology of language, reading, and spelling* (pp. 155–184). New York: Academic.

CATHY F. TELZROW
*Cuyahoga Special Education
Service Center, Maple
Heights, Ohio*

DEVELOPMENTAL APHASIA
LANGUAGE DISORDERS

## APHASIA, DEVELOPMENTAL

See DEVELOPMENTAL APHASIA.

## APNEA

Apnea is defined as a lack of respiration for a period of 20 to 30 seconds with or without an accompanied decrease in heart rate to $\leq$ 80 beats per minute with resultant cyanosis. Twenty-five percent of infants in premature nurseries, but only a small percentage of full-term infants, exhibit apnea. Apnea, therefore, appears in most cases to stem from actual immaturity of the neural mechanism responsible for regulation of respiration. When immature, this mechanism is vulnerable to metabolic disturbances in calcium and blood-sugar levels, changes in body temperature, or disturbances in brain-wave patterns that occur during seizures or normal REM (rapid eye movement) sleep. The association between apnea and sleep is significant because premature sleep up to 80% of the time and REM sleep are the predominant sleep states of these infants (Parry, Baldy, & Gardner, 1985). Apnea is less frequently caused by actual obstruction of the airway itself either from excessive mucus or improper body positioning, as premature infants have very flexible tracheas.

Apnea owed to immaturity or genetic influences appears to be a possible cause of sudden infant death syndrome (SIDS). The fact that SIDS occurs most frequently in children less than 1 year of age supports this theory. Treatment focuses on prevention and involves general measures to promote adequate respiration until the infant "outgrows" the condition. Correction of existing chemical imbalances may be all that is required. Theophylline, a stimulant drug, decreases apnea and is widely used. Most infants reinstitute breathing with gentle tactile stimulation such as stroking or jostling, but at times they require manual ventilation to prevent prolonged anoxia and to restore breathing. Occasionally apnea becomes so severe that the child has to be temporarily placed on a respirator (Volpe & Koenigsberger, 1981). Generally, the heart and respiratory rates of premature infants should be closely monitored for signs of apnea. A home monitor may be necessary for infants with persistent apnea. Full-term infants who are at high risk for *SIDS* should also be monitored for apnea (Spitzer & Fox, 1984).

Prognosis is generally good for infants who do not experience prolonged apnea and who are otherwise healthy. It becomes less favorable with increased frequency and duration of apneic episodes (Parry, et al., 1984). However, at least one study suggests that infantile apnea may be associated with deficiences in later gross motor, and perhaps some cognitive, functions and behavior (Deykin, Bauman, Kelly, Hsieh, & Shannon, 1984). Since apnea produces transient anoxia, it can, when extensive, cause many of the problems associated with that disorder.

### REFERENCES

Deykin, E., Bauman, M., Kelly, D., Hsieh, C., & Shannon, D. (1984). Apnea of infancy and subsequent neurologic, cognitive and behavioral status. *Pediatrics, 73,* 638–645.

Parry, W., Baldy, M., & Gardner, S. (1985). Respiratory diseases. In G. B. Merenstein, & S. L. Gardner (Eds.), *Handbook of neonatal intensive care.* St. Louis: Mosby.

Spitzer, A., & Fox, W. (1984). Infant apnea, an approach to management. *Clinical Pediatrics, 23,* 374–380.

Volpe, J., & Koenigsberger, R. (1981). Neurologic disorders. In G. B. Avery (Ed), *Neonatology: Pathophysiology and management of the newborn,* (2nd ed.). (pp. 920–923). Philadelphia: Lippincott.

BRENDA M. POPE
*New Hanover Memorial
Hospital, Wilmington,
North Carolina*

ANOXIA
INFANT STIMULATION

## APPLIED BEHAVIOR ANALYSIS

Applied behavior analysis is an approach for changing behavior that involves the systematic application of a set of principles derived from psychological theories of learning. Applied behavior analysis has been demonstrated to be a highly effective management system in both school (Alberto & Troutman, 1982) and home situations (Becker, 1971). Its principles have been successfully applied to a wide range of children's problems, including academic problems such as reading, handwriting, and task completion, and social and behavioral problems such as aggression, shyness, and school avoidance.

Applied behavior analysis and behavior modification are closely related terms. Both involve the application of principles of learning to the changing of behavior. Technically, behavior modification is the broader term, including behavior change strategies that are not based on learning principles (e.g., chemotherapy, the use of physical restraints, and brain surgery). Behavior modification in schools has become synonymous with reinforcement programs derived from operant conditioning principles. Operant conditioning procedures change behavior through changing the events that follow behaviors (i.e., consequences of behavior). Applied behavior analysis applies principles derived from operant conditioning, social learning theory, and respondent conditioning. The applied behavior analyst assesses and treats behavior in terms of both consequences and antecedents (i.e., events that precede behavior). These antecedent events may be environmental events or cognitive events (i.e., thoughts, attitudes, or perceptions) that are thought to influence behavior.

The principles of learning that are applied to problem behaviors include positive reinforcement, negative reinforcement, shaping, prompting, fading, extinction, punishment, modeling, discrimination learning, task analysis, and self-instructional talk. Most of these terms are dscribed in more detail in separate entries in this encyclopedia but they are summarized here. Then the steps in behavior analysis are outlined. Finally, applied behavior analysis is illustrated with a case study.

*Positive reinforcement* involves presenting a reward to a child after the child performs a specific desired behavior. If that behavior occurs more frequently after the reward, positive reinforcement has occurred. A reinforcer, or reward, is defined in terms of its effect on the behavior it follows. If something (a stimulus) follows a specific behavior and the rate of that behavior increases, that stimulus is a reinforcer. Ther are no universal reinforcers; children can react differently to such potential reinforcers as adult praise and bubble gum. Allowing a child 5 extra minutes of free time when he or she completes an arithmetic assignment with 80% accuracy is an example of positive reinforcement. It is important that the positive reinforcer be contingent on the specific desired behavior. If the behavior occurs, then the reinforcer is given. If the behavior does not occur, or does not occur at the specified frequency, then the reinforcer is not given. Sometimes teachers and parents will inadvertently follow an undesired behavior with a positive reinforcer. For example, when a child gets out of his or her seat, the teacher calls out that child's name. If the out-of-seat behavior occurs more frequently, the teacher calling out the child's name is a reinforcer. When reinforcement is used, the reinforcement can follow every appropriate behavior (continuous reinforcement schedule) or only a portion of the appropriate behaviors (intermittent reinforcement). Continuous reinforcement results in a quick increase in the rate of the reinforced behavior, and intermittent reinforcement results in maintenance of the behavior change when the behavior is no longer being reinforced.

When a behavior that has been followed by a reinforcer in the past no longer is reinforced, *extinction* has occurred. Often the immediate result of extinction is a temporary increase in the previously reinforced behavior. If a teacher who has attended to a child's temper tantrums begins to ignore the temper tantrums, the child is likely to increase the frequency and duration of tantrum behavior; however, if the teacher continues to ignore the tantrums (and there are no other reinforcers that follow the tantrums, like peer attention), the tantrums should decrease in frequency.

*Negative reinforcement*, like *positive reinforcement*, is a procedure for increasing the rate of a desired behavior. In negative reinforcement, some unpleasant event (stimulus) is terminated following the desired behavior. For example, a teacher tells students that children who complete their assignments at 85% accuracy will be relieved of their homework assignment.

*Punishment* is a process in which the consequences of a behavior reduce the future rate of that behavior. There are three types of punishment procedures. In the application of an unpleasant consequence, a behavior is followed by some unpleasant stimulus, such as extra work, a verbal reprimand, or physical punishment. In response cost, a teacher removes a reinforcer contingent on a specified behavior. Children may lose 3 minutes of recess each time they receive a check next to their names on the board. In *time out*, the child is denied the opportunity to participate in positive reinforcement for a specified period of time, contingent on a specified undesired behavior. Requiring a child to sit on a bench at recess when playing roughly or to sit on a mat during art are examples of time out.

When a child has learned to say "red" only to colors in the red spectrum, the response of saying "red" is under the *stimulus control* of the color red. This control is established by reinforcing the correct response and/or punishing the incorrect response. The reinforcer may be praise or a star. The punisher may be "no" or an X on the paper. When the child learns to respond differently to red and not red, this shows *discrimination learning*. The child who goes to the cookie box when Mother is occupied on the telephone has also mastered a discrimination learning task. Going to the cookie box is reinforced with a cookie when Mother is on the phone. When Mother is not on the phone, she either prevents the child from getting a cookie or reprimands the child.

*Shaping* involves reinforcing improvement in behavior. For example, a child may work only three math problems during a 30-minute period. The teacher would like the child to work 15 problems. (It is assumed the teacher has determined that the problems are at the appropriate level of difficulty for the child.) If reinforcement were contingent on the child working 15 problems, reinforcement would not occur. The teacher establishes a series of steps between the current level of performance and the goal behavior and applies differential reinforcement at each step. Only if the child performs the behavior at or above the behavioral criterion at the operative step in the hierarchy does the child receive the reinforcer. When the child is consistently successful at one step, the next step is operative, and the child's behavior must meet or exceed the criterion for reinforcement at that step. A related procedure is *task analysis*, which involves specifying the prerequisite behaviors to successful performance of a given behavior. Many instructional tasks are composed of several smaller steps that occur in a specific order. Often the difficulty of the task is the reason a child is having difficulty mastering the task. A *skill hierarchy* breaks a complex skill, such as two-digit multiplication, into sequential steps in which each step is a prerequisite for the next higher step in the hierarchy. Skill hierarchies exist in all areas of human learning, including reading, penmanship, dressing, and eating. Task analysis is a useful tool for selecting what skill to teach. Shaping procedures involve the application of reinforcement and extinction to teaching the selected skill.

*Prompting* involves the use of additional cues to increase the probability the child will respond appropriately to the discriminative stimulus. These extra cues increase the saliency of the discriminative stimuli and are phased out as soon as the behavior is under control of the discriminative stimulus. Prompts may be visual, verbal, or physical. The first-grade teacher who places pictures with letters of the alphabet is using visual prompts to increase the probability that the child will make the correct letter-sound association. The phasing out of prompts involves gradually decreasing the saliency of the prompt.

*Modeling* involves having a teacher or peer demonstrate the desired behavior to a child. Models can be live or filmed. When models are present at the time the child imitates the modeled behavior, the model serves as a special type of visual prompt. The effects of modeling extend beyond the direct and immediate imitation of specific behaviors. Children can learn complex sequences of behavior (e.g., participating in a game or ordering a meal in a restaurant) through observation. Furthermore, modeling effects do not depend on the child or the model receiving reinforcement for the imitated behaviors. An impulsive child who is paired with a more reflective child to work on puzzles and games may later adopt a more reflective problem-solving approach.

In recent years behavior analysts have attempted to modify cognitions (i.e., thoughts, attitudes, and perceptions) that are thought to influence overt behavior (Meyers & Craighead, 1985). For example, an impulsive child may be instructed to imitate a model who talks out loud while solving a problem. The model provides the child with an example of helpful *self-instructional talk* (Meichenbaum & Goodman, 1971).

## Steps in Behavior Analysis

In applying the preceding principles, the behavior analyst follows a six step process.

1. Identify the target behaviors. Rather than being sat-

isfied with the problem definition "Lucy is lazy," the analyst states the behavior in specific, observable, behavioral terms. Lazy does not tell us what Lucy does or does not do, and two people might have different ideas about what lazy means. Is Lucy daydreaming or is she turning in messy work? Unless the target behaviors are defined specifically and behaviorally, the existing antecedents and consequences of the behavior cannot be determined, and reinforcement and punishment cannot be administered consistently.

Once the problem, or undesired behavior, is stated in behavioral terms, the desired replacement behavior is stated. If the problem behavior is daydreaming, the desired behavior might be working on the task. The replacement behavior is incompatible with the undesired behavior. That is, Lucy cannot be daydreaming and working on the task at the same time.

2. Count the target behaviors. Since the undesired and replacement behaviors are incompatible, only one needs to be counted. Counting behaviors is necessary to evaluate the effectiveness of the behavior change intervention. This preintervention count is referred to as the baseline. It is preferable to count the target behavior continuously from the baseline until the intervention has been in effect for long enough to determine its effectiveness. A follow-up count following the intervention determines the durability of the behavior change. There are several different ways to count behavior. In a frequency count, each incidence of the target behavior is counted or tallied. The count may occur during a part of the day only. Frequency counts are appropriate for discrete behaviors that either occur infrequently (e.g., hitting) or for a short duration (e.g., calling out answers in class). In a duration count, the percentage of time that a behavior occurs is estimated. Duration counts are best suited for behaviors that occur infrequently and have a duration of more than a few seconds. Owing to the difficulty of actually timing the amount of time a child is engaged in a behavior such as being off-task, a time sampling procedure is usually used to estimate the percentage of time the behavior occurs. The teacher may set a timer to go off at five randomly set intervals during a 30-minute work period or record whether the child was on-task or off-task each time the timer rang. If the child was on task at four out of five rings, the teacher estimates that the child was on task 80% of the time.

The results of the count are charted on a graph similar to the one in the following figure.

3. Assess the antecedents and consequences of both the desired and undesired behaviors. The purpose of this step is to determine the consequences and antecedents that may be maintaining the undesired behavior and to identify possible reinforcers for increasing the desired behavior and conditions under which the desired behavior is more likely to occur. The analyst determines what happens after the child engages in the undesirable behavior. How does the teacher respond? What is the reaction of

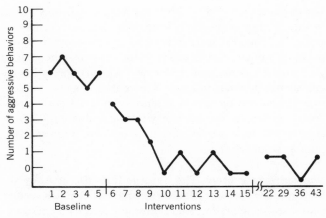

Frequency of aggressive behavior during approximately 30 minutes of outdoor play.

peers? What is the effect of the undesirable behavior on the child's assignment? The analyst determines the conditions under which the undesired behavior is most likely to occur (antecedents). Are there certain task characteristics (i.e., presentation of materials, subject matter, amount of structure, length or difficulty of the assignment, response requirements), setting characteristics (i.e., independent seatwork, group discussion, certain persons nearby), or other conditions (i.e., time of day, medication levels) that are associated with the undesired behavior? The same investigation of consequences and antecedents surrounding the desired behavior is accomplished at this step. This assessment of antecedent and consequent events may uncover unintended reinforcers that are contingent on the undesired behavior (e.g., the child gets the play materials when pushing a peer, the teacher attends to whining behavior, or the child avoids the task by turning in incomplete work) as well as insufficient reinforcers or even punishers following the desired behavior (e.g., the child gets extra work after completing in-class assignments or the child receives no positive peer attention when he or she asks politely to play).

4. Based on the analysis at step 3, create a plan for changing antecedent and consequent events to result in an increase in the desired behavior and a decrease in the undesired behavior. Any of the learning principles previously discussed may be applied at this step. Prompts may be added, reinforcement and punishment contingencies changed, shaping and extinction procedures implemented.

5. Implement the planned intervention. During implementation, counting of the target behaviors continues.

6. Evaluate the effectiveness of the intervention. Using the data obtained from the counting to compare the baseline performance with performance during the intervention, the intervention may be continued as is, modified, or terminated. If the intervention is having the desired outcome, the analyst will want to plan to gradually withdraw

teacher-administered reinforcers (going from continuous to intermittent schedules), gradually phase out prompts, and select the next most important target behavior to improve or increase the difficulty of the reinforced behavior. To increase the probability the desired behavior will generalize to other settings, the intervention may be applied in different settings. If the intervention is not having the desired outcome, the analyst will reexamine hypotheses created at stage 3, resulting in a modified intervention plan at stages 4 and 5.

*Illustrative case study.* The hypothetical case of Andy illustrates the six steps of behavior analysis. Andy, a seven-year-old second grader, was aggressive on the playground, and his teacher asked the consultant for assistance in reducing Andy's aggressiveness.

1. Identify the target behaviors. The consultant helped the teacher state the problem behavior in behavioral terms by asking questions like "What would Andy be doing if I saw him act aggressively?" The specific undesired behaviors were hitting, pushing, grabbing, kicking, and threatening to hurt a child. Using questions like, "What would you like Andy to do instead of hitting, grabbing, etc?", the consultant helped the teacher define the desired behavior as participating nonaggressively.

2. Count the target behaviors. Because Andy's aggressive behavior tended to occur during outdoor play, the counting occurred during outdoor play. Because the aggressive behaviors occurred frequently and did not last over time, a frequency count was used. Aggressive behaviors were counted for five consecutive days to obtain a baseline (Figure 1).

3. Assess antecedents and consequences. Informal and formal observations of Andy indicated that aggressive behaviors were associated with the following antecedent events: unstructured play and teacher far away. Andy was more likely to participate when play was structured and the teacher was nearby. When Andy was aggressive, the following consequences were likely to occur: the teacher talked with him, he was sent to the principal's office (about one-third of the time), and he got to play with the equipment of his choice (the children he bullied gave in to him). When Andy participated without being aggressive, he received no teacher or principal attention and the other children rejected him.

4. As a result of the assessment at step 3, the following plan was selected. Andy was encouraged to play more structured games and the teacher stayed close to Andy during outdoor play. When Andy behaved aggressively, he was given one warning signal, a whistle. If he continued to play aggressively, he was given a second signal to go sit on a bench for 5 minutes. He received no verbal attention from the teacher or principal when he played aggressively. When Andy participated nonaggressively, he earned the privilege of being equipment monitor, respon-

sible for bringing and returning all playground equipment. The teacher and principal praised Andy for participating nonaggressively, and his classmates were primed to react positively to Andy by the promise of a group reward, contingent on Andy's meeting the weekly goal for playing nonaggressively. The group reward was 10 extra minutes of recess time.

5. Implement the planned intervention. The intervention plan was explained to Andy and to the class before it was implemented.

6. Evaluate the effectiveness of the intervention. Figure 1 shows the results of the frequency count of aggressive behaviors during baseline and intervention. Owing to the decrease in aggressive behaviors, the plan was continued for 2 weeks. After the 2 weeks, the teacher gradually introduced less structure, supervised play less closely, and offered praise less frequently. The teacher counted the aggressive behaviors again on four occasions after the initial intervention was terminated. Based on results at these follow-up counts, the teacher removed the group contingency (day 22) and Andy was only occasionally permitted to be equipment monitor (day 26).

## REFERENCES

Alberto, P. A., & Troutman, A. C. (1982). *Applied behavior analysis for teachers.* Columbus, OH: Merrill.

Becker, W. C. (1971). *Parents are teachers.* Champaign, IL: Research Press.

Meichenbaum, D. N., & Goodman, J. (1971). Training impulsive children to talk to themselves: A means of developing self-control. *Journal of Abnormal Psychology, 77,* 115–126.

Meyers, A. W., & Craighead, W. E. (1985). *Cognitive behavior therapy with children.* New York: Plenum.

JAN N. HUGHES
*Texas A&M University*

**BEHAVIORAL ASSESSMENT**
**BEHAVIORAL OBJECTIVES**
**BEHAVIOR MODIFICATION**
**TASK ANALYSIS**

# APPLIED PSYCHOLINGUISTICS

*Applied Psycholinguistics* is an international journal that publishes papers on the psychological processes underlying language and the acquisition of language. This journal, established in 1980 by Dr. Sheldon Rosenberg of the University of Illinois at Chicago Circle and published by Cambridge University Press, has an international and interdisciplinary readership.

The journal offers innovative papers across the entire spectrum of psycholinguistic research including psycholinguistic processing, language acquisition, language disorders in children and adults, development of speech perception and production, bilingualism and second language learning, and acquisition and use of sign language. It also covers studies of language and cognition, pragmatics and discourse processing, assessment of communicative competence and linguistic maturity, reading and writing disorders, the development of literacy, and language disorders associated with autism, mental retardation, emotional disturbance, environmental deprivation, specific learning disabilities, and hearing impairment.

In addition to research reports, position papers, and problem-oriented reviews of important topics as well as short notes, discussions of previously published papers, book reviews, and methodological notes are considered for publication. The journal occasionally publishes the proceedings of symposiums and special issues devoted to single topics. For example, during 1985 and 1986, the journal published two theme issues on "The Psycholinguistics of Writing" and "Language Loss." These issues presented research reports on the development of writing in preschool or school-age children and adults in both native and foreign languages, and on dysgraphia and other writing disorders, either developmental or acquired. Also included were papers on the loss or reorganization of an individual's native language as a second language is learned; the loss of a language through disuse; the loss of a language from dementia or aphasia; lexical and rule loss as a language undergoes continued development, as in Creolization, or as a language declines, as in language death; and the loss of infants' prelinguistic auditory-perceptual or motor capabilities as a first language is acquired.

For further information about the journal, contact The Editorial Office, *Applied Psycholinguistics*, Harvard Graduate School of Education, Larsen Hall, 7th Floor, Cambridge, MA 02138.

PHILIP M. PRINZ
*Pennsylvania State University*

# APPLIED SPECIAL EDUCATION

Approximately 4.5 million children are currently receiving special education services in public school programs in the United States (Ysseldyke & Algozzine, 1983). Special needs of exceptional learners require the application of special education in differing settings and amounts. Applied special education services are available as either *direct or indirect programming*. In direct services, special education practitioners work directly with students to aid school success. Personnel involved in direct application of special education services include teachers, speech and language clinicians, psychologists, physical therapists, and occupational therapists. Indirect services involve as-

sistance from special education practitioners to general education personnel involved with special education students enrolled in regular education programs (Blackhurst & Berdine, 1981). Many of the special education students receiving indirect services are provided consultation and limited direct service by the same professionals who provide direct applied special education services.

School personnel are required by law to prepare an individualized educational plan for each child receiving either indirect or direct applied special education services. Long- and short-term objectives and goals are developed for each student, and the plan specifies which professionals will deliver services and in what amounts. Adjunct, or related, services are also specified on the plan. The individualized educational plan must be reviewed at least once a year or whenever a change in program or placement is made.

Students may receive special education services in several settings. In many instances, special education service is provided as an adjunct to regular class instruction. Students spend the majority of their day in mainstream classes but receive services in resource or part-time rooms under the direction of special education personnel. Other students may be enrolled primarily in special education classes but spend some time in general education classrooms. These may include art, music, physical education, and academic classes. Applied special education services may also be delivered in full-time settings in regular schools or special centers. Residential or institutional settings may be warranted to meet unique needs of the learner for either academic, behavioral, or physical problems. Special education services are applied according to the principle of least restrictive environment, which places a student in the setting that is least restrictive to his or her individual needs. The services may range from regular classes to more restrictive settings in hospitals, institutions, or center schools.

**REFERENCES**

Blackhurst, A. E., & Berdine, W. H. (1981). *An introduction to special education*. Boston: Little, Brown.

Ysseldyke, J. E., & Algozzine, B. (1983). *Introduction to special education*. Boston: Houghton Mifflin.

CRAIG D. SMITH
*Georgia College*

**INDIVIDUAL EDUCATION PLAN**
**LEAST RESTRICTIVE ENVIRONMENT**
**RESOURCE ROOM**

# APRAXIA

Apraxia refers to a series of conditions in which the individual is unable to execute purposive movement in the absence of gross impairment to the sensory and motor systems of the central nervous system (CNS). The parietal lobes (either unilateral or bilateral) of the cerebrum, which are responsible for sensory and motor activity, may be involved, as may be the pathways conveying information to or from the centers for movement. The corpus callosum (commisural tracts allowing for communication between the two hemispheres) and tracts implicating centers for communication (Wernicke's area) are believed to be involved in the processing of verbal commands and the conveyance of direction to the motor areas of the brain. With gross CNS abnormality (such as that which may arise with cerebrovascular accident or lesions resulting from developmental disabilities such as cerebral palsy), the inability to effect purposive movement is often the result of damage to neural tissue subserving movement and sensory reception from the affected area. In cases where hemiplegia or paralysis is evident, apraxia is not applied. These disorders, which result in the compromise of movement as a result of injury to primary motor or sensory tracts, are not regarded as apraxias.

Clinical presentation can be divided into five main forms. Since these have varying underlying substrata, all forms of apraxia manifest themselves in the breakdown of execution of precise motor functioning, thus limiting functional proficiency in a number of ways. Prior to Liepmann's contribution to the understanding of the motor component of apraxia (Hecan, 1981), emphasis on the language component of these disorders maintained preeminence and was closely tied to concepts of aphasia. More contemporary practitioners (Ayres, 1975; Silberzahn, 1983) regard apraxia as a disorder of sensory integration interfering with the ability to plan and execute motor tasks that should be automatized.

In ideomotor apraxia the individual who is capable of comprehending a verbally presented command (one who is not aphasic or does not have any other receptive incapacity) has difficulty in the execution of the command. Commands may range from the direction to perform simple gestures, such as "make a fist, wave good-bye" to the execution of more instrumental responses such as simulating the use of a tool in its absence. The simulation might include hammering a nail into wood, brushing one's teeth, etc. Imitation of such "gestures" presented by a model may or may not be equally impaired.

In ideomotor apraxia, the individual is observed to fail in his or her ability to complete simple, isolated commands to complete a motor response on verbal or imitative instruction. A second form of this disorder is ideational apraxia. This manifests itself in the individual's inability to form a plan of action for more complex chains of behavior and results in the execution of a multistep task. In this form, simple gestures may remain intact, although the individual can not combine a series of isolated actions in appetitive fashion to complete the task. A demonstration of this form of apraxia becomes evident when the in-

dividual is presented with the tools needed to complete the action and has difficulty in assembling the sequence in appropriate order. For example, if provided with toothpaste, toothbrush, and a cup for rinsing the mouth, the apractic individual may attempt to make contact between the cup and toothbrush, or pour water over the toothbrush rather than combine the appropriate elements in the generally accepted sequence for toothbrushing. Individually, the tools may be employed appropriately, but in execution of the multistep plan, failure to combine individual links in the chain becomes evident. Upon imitation by a model, the task may be completed in appropriate sequence if the number of elements in the sequence is not too long or complex. A clear distinction between ideomotor and ideational apraxia is yet to be achieved, with some investigators considering ideational apraxia to be a more severe form of ideomotor apraxia (Benson & Geschwind, 1973).

Constructional apraxia, a third clinical subtype, manifests itself as a defect in establishing, through graphomotor representation or component reconstruction, accurate spatial relations of a model. Although the individual with this form of apraxia is capable of executing the individual discrete responses in reconstructing a model, a spatial disorientation becomes evident. The instructions given to the individual may be either visually or verbally presented, but once again in the latter case, it must be certain that the individual is capable of comprehending the commands presented. To assess the possibility of a constructional apraxia, block design tasks may be helpful. In such an approach, the individual is required to replicate a visually presented geometric design using a series of blocks, which, when assembled with proper juxtaposition, result in an accurate reproduction. The apractic may evade the spatial boundaries of the model in the reconstruction by aligning the blocks in an alternate orientation, or by rotating or reversing subcomponents. Object assembly tasks may similarly be employed, although they are by presentation more "representational in nature and more sensitive to visual recognition" (McFie, 1975, p. 41). Assessment of constructional apraxia through a writing task may be assisted by application of the Bender Motor Gestalt Test (Bender, 1938). Evidence of impairment of spatial relations may be seen in model replication with frequent reversal, integration, and rotational errors.

Brain (1941) reported on a fourth subtype of defect in executing purposive motor activity with regard to dressing skills. The clinical presentation of what Brain regarded as dressing apraxia involved the inability of the individual to organize activity for the purpose of donning a common article of clothing. Given a jacket either partially or completely turned inside out, difficulty in organizing the series of activities necessary to dress becomes evident. The apractic may rotate the garment in space, roll it up into a ball, and, in general, appear confused in his or her ability to dress. Although this is a rare and specific form of apraxia, the apparent deficit in the ability to execute a multistep task is not unlike that observed in the ideational form of the disorder. A second subtype of dressing apraxia involves the apractic's disregard for one side of the body. The individual may dress and groom only one side of the body while totally neglecting care of the other. Although these are both forms of dressing apraxia, the underlying causes are believed to be different.

Speech differentiation requires the most precise and subtle of neuromuscular coordination of any of an individual's motor skills. The complexity of oropharyngeal musculature coordination therefore finds itself the target of dyscontrol, as does any other motor system of the body (Rosenbek, et al., 1984). In oral apraxia (also referred to as buccofacial apraxia), "the articulatory action has lost its usual selectivity, and as a result the patient cannot immediately assume the correct positions of tongue and lip" (Luria, 1973, p. 187); consequently, the individual is not capable of articulate speech without laboring and significant practice. The extreme to which this can be observed in some oral apractics may be seen in their inability to physically localize their tongue within their mouths on verbal instruction to do so. Thus, the apractic who is requested to place the tongue to the left side of the mouth may only be able to do so with great concentration, if at all. The apparent automatization of place of oropharyngeal structure is apparently disturbed, resulting in what may at times be confused with dysarthria. The latter, however, connotes a disorder distinct from oral apraxia with divergent substrate, generally involving cranial nerve involvement.

While these specific subtypes may be delineated by having the apractic perform a series of motor tasks, a more generalized developmental apraxia may be ascertained through observation with less rigorous testing. The child with developmental apraxia is observed to have an overall immaturity and clumsiness in carrying out motor skills. The classroom teacher may observe that motor tasks that appear to be routine to other children are accomplished by the apractic child with great expenditure of effort and marginal precision. These tasks may include gross or fine motor components as well as oral or occulomotor proficiency. The apractic is often identified during the early school or preschool years. While splinter skills or components of chained sequences may be present, difficulties in dressing, drawing, cutting, pasting, and learning to write may be evident. Difficulties in executing these skills and adaptive behaviors that are emerging and becoming more refined at this time in development may be the first indications that sensory motor integration is impaired. The young apractic may have not developed a sensorimotor awareness of body parts and their use in more complex skills (Silberzahn, 1983) through everyday experience, and must therefore acquire this experience to attain greater efficiency in motor actions.

Many times, assessment of *intellectual abilities* will reveal a discrepancy between verbal and performance skills, and yield a lower full-scale IQ than may be expected given the perceived level of the child's conceptual abilities. Performance on the Wechsler Intelligence Scale for Children (WISC) has been shown to result in high verbal and low performance scores for children with sensorimotor compromise (Brain, 1977). This discrepancy may be regarded as indicative of a learning disability, which it connotes if the delay in motor proficiency is of sufficient magnitude.

The treatment of apraxia involves an educative and habilitative process, through which the child receives more experience in developing motor routines and a generally increased familiarity with his or her body and its potential for action. Gross motor activities involving active joint movement with concomitant proprioceptive feedback is necessary, in addition to the development of specific motor responses and an expanded motor repertoire. In general, the apractic should have the opportunity to engage in a variety of activities involving tactile, vestibular, and proprioceptive input (Silberzahn, 1983).

Thus apraxia, in general, relates to the difficulty in differentiating a response subserved by the sensory and motor systems of the central nervous system in the absence of gross and symptomatic involvement of the brain. Its treatment requires learning automatized motor patterns to promote organization of the sensorimotor system and effective response differentiation.

## REFERENCES

Ayres, A. J. (1975). Sensorimotor foundations of academic ability. In W. M. Cruickshank & D. P. Hallahan (Eds.), *Perceptual and learning abilities in children, Vol. 2.* (pp. 300–358) Syracuse, NY: Syracuse University Press.

Bender, L. A. (1938). *A visual motor Gestalt test and its clinical use.* New York: American Orthopsychiatric Association.

Benson, D. F., & Geschwind, N. (1973). The aphasias and related disturbances. In A. B. Baker & L. H. Baker (Eds.), *Clinical neurology 1*(8), 1–26. New York: Harper & Row.

Brain, W. R. (1941). Visual disorientation with special reference to lesions of the right cerebral hemisphere. *Brain, 64,* 43.

Brain, W. R. (1977). *Brain's diseases of the nervous system* (8th ed.). New York: Oxford University Press.

Brown, J. W. (1972). *Aphasia, apraxia, and agnosia.* Springfield IL: Thomas.

Hecan, H. (1981). Apraxias. In S. B. Filskov & T. J. Boll (Eds.), *Handbook of clinical neuropsychology* (pp. 257–286). New York: Wiley.

Luria, A. R. (1973). *Higher cortical functions in man.* New York: Basic Books.

McFie, J. (1975). *Assessment of organic intellectual impairment.* NY: Academic.

Rosenbek, J. C., McNeil, M. R., & Aronson, A. E. (1984). *Apraxia of speech: physiology-acoustic-linguistic-management.* San Diego: College Hill Press.

Silberzahn, M. (1983). Sensory integrative theory. In H. L. Hopkins & H. D. Smith (Eds.), *Willard and Spackman's occupational therapy* (6th ed.). Philadelphia: Lippincott.

ELLIS I. BAROWSKY
*Hunter College, City University
of New York*

## MOTOR LEARNING
## STEREOTYPIC MOVEMENT DISORDERS

## APTITUDE TESTING

The term aptitude test has been traditionally employed to refer to tests designed to assess the level of development attained by an individual on relatively homogenous and clearly defined segments of ability such as spatial visualization, numerical aptitude, or perceptual speed. Aptitude tests measure the effects of learning under the relatively uncontrolled and unknown conditions of daily living. In this sense, they differ from achievement tests, which measure the effects of a relatively standardized set of experiences encountered in an educational program. The two types of tests differ in use as well. Achievement tests generally represent a terminal evaluation of an individual's status on the completion of training. Aptitude tests serve to predict subsequent performance. They are employed to estimate the extent to which an individual will profit from a specific course of training, or to predict the quality of his or her achievement in a new situation.

The term special aptitude originated at a time when the major emphasis in testing was placed on general intelligence. Traditional intelligence tests were designed primarily to yield a single global measure of the individual's general level of cognitive development such as an IQ. Although they were comprised of a heterogeneous grouping of subtests, both practical and theoretical analysis soon recognized that intelligence tests were limited in their coverage of abilities. This development led to the construction of separate tests for the measurement of a few widely accepted aptitudes not included in the intelligence batteries. Since traditional intelligence tests oversample from abstract functions involving the use of verbal or numerical symbols, a particular need was felt for tests covering the more concrete or practical abilities. Thus began the area of assessment known as aptitude testing. The earliest tests developed were those measuring mechanical aptitude, but soon tests to measure clerical, musical, and artistic aptitude were developed. These special aptitudes were regarded as supplementary to the IQ in a description of an individual, and were usually administered in conjunction with a standard intelligence battery.

A strong impetus to the construction of special aptitude tests was provided by the problems of matching job requirements with the specific pattern of abilities that characterize each individual, a task commonly faced by psychologists in career counseling or in the classification of industrial and military personnel. Intelligence tests were not designed for this purpose. Aside from the limited representation of certain aptitudes discussed earlier, their subtests or item groups were often too unreliable to justify the sort of intra-individual analysis required for classification purposes. To respond to this need, the testing field turned to the development of multiple aptitude batteries.

Like intelligence tests, multiple aptitude batteries measure a number of abilities, but instead of a total score, they provide a profile of scores, one for each aptitude; thus they provide a suitable instrument for making intra-individual analysis. In addition, the abilities measured by multiple aptitude batteries are often different than those measured by intelligence batteries. Aptitude batteries tend to include more concrete skills with less emphasis on verbal skills than intelligence tests.

Multiple aptitude batteries represent a relatively recent development in the testing field. Nearly all have appeared since 1945. Much of the test research and development began in the armed forces during World War II, when the Air Force designed special batteries to select training candidates to be pilots, bombadiers, radio operators, and range finders. The armed services still sponsor a considerable amount of research in this area, but a number of multiple aptitude batteries have been developed for civilian use in educational and vocational counseling and in personnel selection and classification.

The application of factor analysis to the study of trait organization provided the theoretical basis for the construction of multiple aptitude batteries. Factor analysis identified, sorted, and defined the abilities that were loosely grouped under the definition of intelligence. The tests that best measured the factors identified in factor analysis were then included in the multiple aptitude battery. The Chicago Test of Primary Mental Abilities (1941) represents the first attempt to construct a battery based on factor analysis using the pioneer factor analytic work of Thurstone. Most multiple aptitude batteries developed since that time have employed the use of factor analysis in construction.

About a dozen multiple aptitude batteries have been developed for use in education, counseling, and personnel classification. These instruments vary widely in approach, technical quality, and amount of available validation data. Many have been designed explicitly for counseling purposes in which classification decisions are preeminent. In a counseling situation, the profile of test scores is used to aid the counselee in choosing among several possible fields of educational or occupational specialization. In business and industry, data gained from the administration of multiple aptitude test batteries may be used for institutional decisions regarding the assignment of personnel to different jobs. In education, multiple aptitude batteries such as the SRA Primary Mental Abilities Test (1962), are used to guide admission of students to different educational curricula. The armed services use aptitude data to assign specific job classifications to personnel after screening with a more general instrument. The Air Force pioneered this practice, but all branches of the armed services now use the Armed Services Vocational Aptitude Battery (ASVAB) (1976).

A number of multiple aptitude batteries have been designed for use with high-school students to aid in the transition from high school to work or postsecondary training. The most widely used of these tests is the Differential Aptitude Test (1947, 1962, 1972) (DAT). Based on the factor analytic work of Thurstone, the DAT is used in the educational and vocational counseling of students in grades 8 through 12. It provides a profile of scores on eight subtests: Verbal Reasoning, Numerical Ability, Abstract Reasoning, Clerical Speed and Accuracy, Mechanical Reasoning, Spatial Relations, Spelling, and Language Usage. Using the student's profile in conjunction with an *interest inventory*, a counselor can use a computer or case book to predict the student's success in postsecondary education, or generate a list of potential careers. The Comprehensive Ability Battery (1977) and the Guilford-Zimmerman Aptitude Survey (1956) are other multiple aptitude batteries that are often used with this population.

The General Aptitude Test Battery (GATB) was developed by the U.S. Employment Services (USES) for use by employment counselors in state employment service offices. The GATB is comprised of 12 tests that combine to yield nine factor scores: Intelligence, Verbal Aptitude, Numerical Aptitude, Spatial Aptitude, Form Perception, Clerical Perception, Motor Coordination, Finger Dexterity, and Manual Dexterity. The profile of these subtest scores can then be compared with profiles corresponding to a huge number of job categories. An alternative form is available for nonreading adults.

Unlike the multiple aptitude batteries, special aptitude tests typically measure a single aptitude. Certain areas such as vision, hearing, motor dexterity, and artistic talents are often judged to be too specialized to justify inclusion in standard aptitude batteries, yet often these abilities are vital to a certain task. Special aptitude tests were designed to measure such abilities. They are often administered in conjunction with an aptitude battery, either to assess a skill not included in the battery or to further probe a skill or interest. Special aptitude tests may also be custom-made for a particular job, constructed using a simulation of the requisites of the job, such as the Minnesota Clerical Test, the Meier Art Judgment Test, or the Seashore Measure of Musical Talents. Despite wide use in education, counseling, and industry, the development of aptitude tests has been slow. Many of the aptitude tests currently in use were developed in the 1940s and 1950s.

## REFERENCES

Anastasi, A. (1982). *Psychological testing*, (5th ed.). New York: Macmillan.

Bayroff, A. G., & Fuchs, E. F. (1968). The armed forces vocational aptitude battery. *Proceedings of the 76th annual convention of the American Psychological Association, 3*, 635–636.

Bemis, S. E. (1968). Occupational validity of the General Aptitude Test Battery. *Journal of Applied Psychology, 52*, 240–244.

Bennett, G. K., Seashore, H. G., & Wesman, A. G. (1974). *Fifth edition manual for Differential Aptitude Tests, Forms S and T*. New York: Psychological Corporation.

Buros, O. K. (1978). *The eighth mental measurements yearbook*. Highland Park, NJ: Gryphon Press.

*Counseling from profiles: A case book for the Differential Aptitude Tests* (2nd ed.) (1977). New York: Psychological Corporation.

Ghiselli, E. E. (1973). The validity of aptitude tests in personnel selection. *Personnel Psychology, 26*, 461–477.

Green, D. R. (Ed.) (1974). *The aptitude–achievement distinction: Proceedings of the Second CTB/McGraw-Hill Conference on Issues in Educational Measurement*. New York: McGraw-Hill.

Guilford, J. P., & Zimmerman, W. S. (1956). *The Guilford–Zimmerman Aptitude Survey*. New York: McGraw-Hill.

Meier, N. C. (1942). *Art in human affairs*. New York: McGraw-Hill.

*Minnesota Clerical Test* (1959). New York: Psychological Corporation.

Schutz, R. E. (1972). S.R.A. Primary Mental Abilities. *Seventh mental measurements yearbook*, Vol. 11 (pp. 1066–1068).

Seashore, C. E. (1938). *Psychology of music*, New York, McGraw-Hill.

Sheridan Psychological Services, Orange, CA. Hakstian, A. R., & Cattell, R. B. (1977). *The Comprehensive Ability Battery*. Champaign, IL: Institute for Personality and Ability Testing.

Thurstone, L. L. (1938). Primary mental abilities. *Psychometric Monographs*, No. 1.

U.S. Department of Labor, Employment, and Training Administration (1980). *Manual, USES General Aptitude Test Battery*. Washington, DC: U.S. Government Printing Office.

LIZANNE DESTEFANO
*University of Illinois,
Urbana-Champaign*

**ACHIEVEMENT TESTS**
**ASSESSMENT**
**CRITERION REFERENCE TESTING**
**VOCATIONAL TRAINING OF HANDICAPPED**

## APTITUDE-TREATMENT INTERACTION

Aptitude-treatment interaction refers to an educational phenomenon in which students who are dissimilar with regard to a particular aptitude perform differently under alternate instructional conditions. The alternate instructional conditions are specifically designed to reflect the students' aptitude differences. Thus, if a significant performance difference between the groups results under alternate instructional conditions, an aptitude by treatment interaction has occurred.

Aptitude-treatment interactions have been discussed at length by Bracht (1970), who defines an aptitude-treatment interaction as "a significant disordinal interaction between alternate treatments and personological variables" (p. 627). A personological variable is any measure of an individual characteristic such as learning style, intelligence, achievement anxiety, or locus of control. Disordinal interactions refer to performance differences between groups that denote the significantly better performance of one group under one set of conditions and the significantly better performance of the second group under alternate conditions. Figure 1 graphically displays a disordinal aptitude-treatment interaction.

Figure 1 depicts hypothetical data for two groups of students who differ on a particular aptitude, one group being high and the other being low. Alternate treatments, matched to the students' aptitude, were provided. Students with low aptitude performed better under treatment number 1. Students with high aptitude performed better under treatment number 2. The data confirm the occurrence of an aptitude-treatment interaction and support the use of different instructional approaches for these two groups of students.

Figures 2 and 3, respectively, display hypothetical experimental outcomes that are not indicative of an aptitude-treatment interaction.

In Figure 2, both groups of students, despite the aptitude difference, performed better under treatment number 1. In Figure 3, treatment number 1 was again superior for both groups of students. However, the differences for the low-aptitude students under treatment conditions number 1 and number 2 were not significant. The aptitude difference does not suggest the use of different treatments for the two groups; other factors may dictate the use of one or the other treatment for both groups. In this instance,

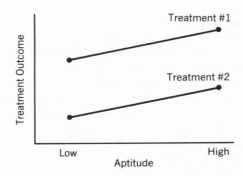

Figure 2. Hypothetical experimental outcome that is not indicative of an aptitude-treatment interaction.

the aptitude dimension did not clarify the choice between treatments.

Interest in aptitude-treatment interactions is fueled by the widely espoused commitment to individualization of instruction and the quest for teaching adaptations that enhance individual student performance. Appreciation for individual differences is a relatively recent development (Snow, 1977). Snow believes that the "recognition that individual differences in aptitude not only predict learning outcomes but also often interact with instructional treatment variations" (p. 11). This concept makes adaptive instruction a possibility. Teachers have long recognized individual differences and have accommodated such differences in a myriad of ways. Nowhere is the concern for individual differences greater than in special education. The Individual Educational Program requirement of PL 94–142 has mandated individualized educational planning for all exceptional children. Adaptation and accommodation to individual learner needs and characteristics is at the heart of the special education instructional process. Corno and Snow (1986), in a discussion of adapted teaching, view adaptations as involving either direct aptitude development or circumvention of inaptitude. In special education, the adage "teach to the strengths and remediate the weaknesses" prevails. Teachers generally seek intact or relatively strong abilities as avenues for instruction. Accompanying remediation is most often fo-

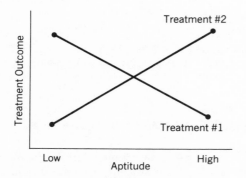

Figure 1. Disordinal aptitude-treatment interaction.

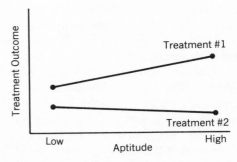

Figure 3. Hypothetical experimental outcome that is not indicative of an aptitude-treatment interaction.

cused on specific skill or knowledge deficits that impede academic performance or independent functioning. Unfortunately, the commitment among educators, particularly teachers of the exceptional, to individualized instruction in practice is not matched by a strong commitment to educational research. "While it is clear that teachers adapt their behavior to students' individual differences at virtually all levels of education, what is less clear is the underlying logic and intentionality that governs these adaptations" (Corno & Snow, 1986, p. 614).

The systematic experimental investigation of teaching adaptations in relation to student characteristics is the focus of aptitude-treatment interaction research. However, the research to date underscores the difficulties associated with investigations of this kind. Bracht's review of 90 aptitude-treatment interaction studies yielded only five in which disordinal interactions were found. However, Bracht's review did help to clarify the nature of the aptitude and treatment variables and to identify the variables that increase the probability of significant aptitude-treatment interactions. Bracht's review included five studies that involved handicapped learners; none of the studies yielded significant interactions. Bracht notes that the subjects in these five studies bore categorical labels such as mentally retarded and emotionally disturbed. Such broad categories tend to mask the considerable heterogeneity that exists within the groups—a factor that works against the probability of aptitude-treatment interactions. In another review, Ysseldyke (1973) discussed five aptitude-treatment interaction studies involving handicapped learners grouped for instruction according to modality differences. Auditory and/or visual functioning were the modalities under consideration. Instruction matched to modality strengths or preferences failed to yield evidence of significant interactions across a variety of academic outcome measures (e.g., reading achievement and word recognition skills) in any of these studies.

Another review of research specifically involving modality-instructional matching has been reported by Arter and Jenkins (1977). Preset criteria limited the number of studies reviewed in depth to 14. In all of the studies, the students were assigned to a modality group based on a statistical difference in modality functioning (modality assessments had adequate test-retest reliability and validity). Alternate instructional methods had a clear modality emphasis and outcome measures were constant across the groups. Only one study (Bursuk, 1971) demonstrated a significant modality-instruction interaction. This study involved tenth-grade below-average readers who were given instruction in listening and reading comprehension (reading comprehension lessons were given to the visual modality preference group only) over an entire school semester. The authors point out the specificity and control of subjects, treatments, and outcome measures that distinguish the Bursuk study from the remaining 13 research reports.

The meager results from studies specifically designed to demonstrate the interaction between modalities and instruction have not been a deterrent to practitioners. Despite the lack of supportive research, instruction based on the modality concept has been widely implemented. The instructional approach involved children who were tested to determine modality preferences and instruction provided via the preferred modality. It also involved training of perceptual and perceptual-motor skills to enhance the child's readiness for later academic instruction. An extensive body of literature relates to the efficacy of perceptual-motor training. Kavale and Mattson (1983) applied the technique of meta-analysis to 180 efficacy studies. Meta-analysis permits the integration of the results from a large number of independent research studies to reveal the presence of treatment effects that might be obscured in traditional research reviews with a narrative format. The authors found that perceptual-motor interventions were not effective in improving academic, cognitive, or perceptual-motor variables. The results of this review are consistent with the conclusions drawn by others in earlier reviews of perceptual-motor training (Hallahan & Cruickshank, 1973; Myers & Hammill, 1976). The negative or negligible results of efficacy studies should not be surprising in light of the paucity of aptitude-treatment interactions found in studies designed to demonstrate the efficacy of the modality-instructional match. The modality model of instruction is founded on aptitude-treatment interaction theory, but the applicability of aptitude-treatment interaction theory to modality-based instruction has yet to be demonstrated and validated.

Aptitude-treatment interaction research is by no means confined to special education or to investigations of modality-based instruction. Aptitude-treatment interaction research has been conducted in other academic areas such as math (Holton, 1982) and reading (Blanton, 1971). The results generally have been disappointing.

Even though the number of research studies that have successfully demonstrated aptitude-treatment interactions is extremely limited, the research has provided considerable insight into the complexities of the interaction phenomenon and the conditions that favor the occurrence of aptitude-treatment interactions. Bracht (1970) found that disordinal interactions were related to the degree of control over treatment tasks, the factorial makeup of the specific personological variables, and the nature of the dependent outcome variables. Controlled treatments, factorially simple personological variables, and specific, rather than complex, outcome variables favor aptitude-treatment interaction. Snow (1977) stresses the "essential importance of detailed description of specific instructional variables and specific groups of people" (p. 12) to aptitude-treatment interaction research. In retrospect, the few research reports that documented significant aptitude by treatment interactions displayed the prerequisite degree of control and specificity of critical variables that seem essential for aptitude-treatment interactions to occur.

In discussing the relationship of aptitude-treatment interaction research to emerging instructional theory, Snow (1977) cautions educators not to expect general theories of instruction to evolve from aptitude-treatment interaction investigations. The research findings to date suggest that each aptitude-treatment interaction, when found, will be valid only in a specific context. Each finding will pertain to a particular group of students under particular instructional conditions. Generalizations, if made at all, will be limited. Educators should not anticipate general educational theories with potential for broad application to emerge from aptitude-treatment interaction research. Those who initiate "blanket treatments" (Snow, 1984) on the premise of aptitude-treatment interactions are likely to be disappointed, as were the proponents of perceptual-motor training. Rather, aptitude-treatment interaction theory implies ongoing evaluation of student and instructional variables and a constant readiness to adjust to meet changing conditions.

## REFERENCES

Arter, J. A., & Jenkins, J. R. (1977). Examining the benefits of modality considerations in special education. *Journal of Special Education, 11*(3), 281–298.

Berliner, C. D., & Cohen, L. S. (1973). Trait-treatment interaction and learning. In F. N. Kerlinger (Ed.), *Review of research in education* (Vol. 1). Ithasca, IL: Peacock.

Blanton, B. (1971). Modalities and reading. *Reading Teacher, 25*(2), 210–212.

Bracht, G. H. (1970). Experimental factors related to aptitude-treatment interactions. *Review of Educational Research, 40*(5), 627–645.

Bursuk, L. A. (1971). Sensory mode of lesson presentation as a factor in the reading comprehension improvement of adolescent retarded readers. (ERIC Document Reproduction Service No. ED 047 435).

Corno, L., & Snow, R. E. (1986). Adapting teaching to individual differences among learners. In M. C. Wittrock (Ed.), *Handbook of research on teaching* (3rd ed.). New York: Macmillan.

Hallahan, D. P., & Cruickshank, W. M. (1973). *Psychoeducational foundations of learning disabilities*. Englewood Cliffs, NJ: Prentice-Hall.

Holton, B. (1982). Attribute-treatment-interaction research in mathematics education. *School Science & Mathematics, 82*(7), 593–601.

Kavale, K., & Mattson, P. D. (1983). "One jumped off the balance beam": Meta-analysis of perceptual-motor training. *Journal of Learning Disabilities, 16*(3), 141–188.

Myers, P. I., & Hammill, D. D. (1976). *Methods for learning disorders* (2nd ed.). New York: Wiley.

Snow, R. E. (1977). Individual differences and instructional theory. *Educational Researcher, 6*(10), 11–15.

Snow, R. E. (1984). Placing children in special education: Some comments. *Educational Researchers, 13*(3), 12–14.

Ysseldyke, J. E. (1973). Diagnostic-prescriptive teaching: The search for aptitude-treatment interactions. In L. Mann & D. A. Sabatino (Eds.), *The first review of special education*. Philadelphia: JSE.

LIBBY GOODMAN
*Pennsylvania State University*

DIAGNOSTIC-PRESCRIPTIVE TEACHING
DIRECT INSTRUCTION
TEACHER EFFECTIVENESS

## ARCHITECTURAL BARRIERS

Recent efforts to fully integrate disabled individuals into the societal mainstream have demanded the elimination of physical barriers that impede access to facilities and the surrounding environment. Common barriers to facility or service accessibility confronted by handicapped citizens include constricted entranceways, ill-equipped public facilities (e.g., restrooms and parking areas), limited passageways, poor room spacing and layout, inadequate lighting, and limitations in the availability of supplementary mediums for providing public information (e.g., braille directions, visual warning or evacuation alarms).

Prior to the 1960s, the vast majority of buildings and thoroughfares were designed for the "ideal user" (i.e., an able-bodied young adult). However, over the past two decades, the National Center for Law and the Handicapped (1978) and the U.S. Department of Housing and Urban Development (1983) have reported that the confluence of federal and state legislation, judicial pronouncements, and publicly accepted standards of accessibility have brought about significant and permanent changes in the architectural design of structures and thoroughfares. These changes have prompted the removal of barriers that inhibit the accessibility (e.g., mobility and orientation) of physically and sensorily impaired citizens.

The American National Standards Institute (ANSI) specifications, originally adopted in 1961 and updated in the 1970s, establish barrier-free criteria for buildings, entraceways, and thoroughfares. These standards are designed to eliminate all architectural barriers that have historically impeded the access of the following populations:

*Nonambulatory Disabled*: People with physical impairments that confine them to wheelchairs.

*Semiambulatory Disabled*. People with physical impairments that cause them to walk with insecurity or difficulty and require the assistance of crutches, walkers, or braces.

*Coordination Disabled*. Those with impairments of

muscle control result in faulty coordination and that create an increased potential for personal injury.

*Sight Disabled.* Those with impairments that affect vision, either totally or partially, to the extent that an individual functioning in the environment is insecure or liable to injury.

*Hearing Disabled.* People with impairments that affect hearing, either totally or partially, to the extent that an individual functioning in the environment is insecure or liable to injury.

Modifications that may be required to eliminate architectural barriers in facilities and along public accessways include, but are not limited to, the construction of ramps, wheelchair lifts, and curbing cutouts; the improvement of transfer areas and enlarged spaces for parking facilities; the enhancement of public facilities such as restrooms, telephones, physical education facilities, and dining areas; and the improvement of passageways, entrances (e.g., doors, doorways), room designs (e.g., spacing and layout), facility lighting, and public/user information systems.

Recent efforts to financially assist local and state educational agencies in the removal of architectural barriers have been authorized by the U.S. Congress (1983) through the appropriation of funds under Section 1406 of the Education of the Handicapped Act Amendments of 1983 (PL 98-199).

## REFERENCES

National Center for Law and the Handicapped. (1978, July/August). *Moving toward a barrier free society*: Amicus. South Bend, IN: Amicus.

U.S. Department of Housing and Urban Development. (1983). *Access to the environment*. Washington, DC: U.S. Government Printing Office.

GEORGE JAMES HAGERTY
*Stonehill College*

## ACCESSIBILITY OF BUILDINGS
## ARCHITECTURE AND THE HANDICAPPED

## ARCHITECTURE AND THE HANDICAPPED

It has been estimated that approximately 10% of the population has some degree of physical handicap (Moe, 1977). These physical handicaps are of three general types: visual, hearing, and physical/orthopedic. Of these individuals 22 million persons in the United States have some limitation of mobility, with approximately 400,000 confined to wheelchairs. In addition, there are 5½ million individuals who are visually handicapped and 8 million deaf or hearing-impaired persons (Sorensen, 1979).

Apart from the visually handicapped/blind, hearing impaired/deaf, and physically/orthopedically impaired, are those individuals who have health impairments involving cardiopulmonary disorders or neuromuscular diseases. These disorders may permit some mobility but may result in diminished stamina, poor coordination, or limited grasping and manipulative capacity.

Architectural considerations vary and are dependent on whether the handicap is physical, visual, or aural. In fact, such considerations can involve competing requirements that necessitate the establishment of unique environments for the physically handicapped in comparison with the visually handicapped. For example, a physically handicapped person confined to a wheelchair may function best in spaces that are open and large. In contrast, individuals who are blind may do better in smaller spaces where key elements of the sensory environment are within close range. Similarly, an environment that reflects noises may be advantageous for the blind but a disadvantage to the hearing impaired, who have difficulty in attenuating to multiple acoustical cues.

There are a number of general factors to be considered in designing or adapting environments:

1. Many handicapped persons may be smaller or weaker than average; therefore, slopes, reach distances, and forces necessary to open and close objects should be reduced.

2. A number of individuals who use mobility-assist devices (e.g., wheelchairs) may have secondary disabilities that involve difficulty in strength, grasping, etc.

3. Most persons blind at birth, or shortly after birth, know braille, while those adventitiously blind often do not know braille.

4. Tactile signals and signs should be few in number and their location carefully considered to ensure uniformity of placement throughout a building.

5. Audible signals should be in the lower frequencies, because persons lose the capacity to hear higher frequencies with increasing age.

6. Many deaf and blind persons can hear and see in favorable environments such as acoustically "dead" surroundings for the deaf and well-lit and magnified print environments for the blind.

7. Visual and aural signals are best to provide redundancy of cues and to accommodate deaf or blind persons (Sorensen, 1979, p. 2).

Through the use of mobility training programs provided through special education classes or rehabilitation efforts, the blind are able to go virtually anywhere. While guide dogs are used by a small proportion of the blind population, most blind people are initially guided through a building and later follow a memorized route. As might be expected, the primary impediments for the blind are unanticipated hazards such as people or objects moving across their paths or objects placed temporarily in a familiar area. Some specific building modifications that can be of assistance to the blind include:

Providing steps and stairs that are not open and do not have square, extended nosings on each step.

Using sound-reflecting walls since such walls allow the blind to better use their sense of hearing as a guide (moreover, sounds reflected from surfaces assist in orienting the blind to their position in an area).

Changing the construction materials in walking surfaces to denote entrances, restrooms, stairs, and other potentially hazardous areas.

Identifying doors leading to dangerous areas by door knobs that are distinctive from that of hardware used throughout the remainder of a building.

Placing all signs and letters/numbers at a consistent height, usually between 5 feet and 5 feet, 6 inches from the floor, so that the blind will know where to find them.

Of all those having auditory deficits, few are totally deaf. Even with a large hearing loss, many of those who are legally deaf can hear and comprehend if the environment is devoid of ambient noises. Modifications that can be of assistance to the deaf include:

Warning and direction devices equipped with visual indicators, as well as audible signals.

Telephones equipped with amplifiers for the hard of hearing and telephone typewriters for those who cannot use a standard phone even with amplification.

Clear signs so the deaf do not have to ask for directions since some deaf individuals have a difficult time talking and being understood.

Those individuals who have physical disabilities can be divided into those who are ambulant (able to walk with canes, crutches, or braces) and the chair-bound. The architectural requirements for these two groups, while similar, differ in some respects.

The ambulant disabled frequently have difficulty in stooping or bending. Consequently, modifications may include:

Placing handles, controls, switches, etc., within the reach of a standing person so stooping is unnecessary.

Placing ramps with a maximum gradient of slope of 1:12.

Using steps and stairs with nonprotruding nosings so individuals with restricted joint movement or braces will not catch their toes as they climb.

Placing hand rails on both sides of steps and stairs that extend beyond the first and last steps.

Chairbound individuals evidencing high degrees of independence use collapsible adult-size wheelchairs. Apart from the greater space needed for wheelchair movement, the chair-bound individual may need:

Grab bars to transfer via the front of the wheelchair to the shower, bed, and so on.

Space alongside a chair or bed.

The placement of countertops, control devices, and so on within the low to middle range of a standing person's areas of reach.

Much of the impetus for the modification of buildings and facilities for the physically handicapped is attributable to the Architectural Barriers Act of 1968 (PL 90-480) and its subsequent amendments. The act specifies that buildings financed with federal funds must be designed and constructed to be accessible to the physically handicapped. In addition, the Rehabilitation Act of 1973 (PL 93-112) created the Architectural and Transportation Barriers Compliance Board, which has as its mission, in part, to:

Ensure compliance with the Architectural Barriers Act, as amended.

Examine alternative approaches to barriers that confront handicapped individuals in public settings.

Determine the measures that federal, state, and local governments should take to eliminate barriers.

Many states, by state statute, require that accessibility for the physically handicapped be provided in newly constructed, privately funded buildings that are open to the public. All states require that publicly funded buildings be accessible to the handicapped. A number of states require that when extensive remodeling is undertaken, such remodeling will include making the building accessible.

Funds for state education agencies have been appropriated for the removal of architectural barriers in schools. This one-time, nonrecurring appropriation was authorized by Section 607 of the Education for All Handicapped Children Act (PL 94-142) as amended by Section 5 of the Education of the Handicapped Act amendments of 1983, PL 98-199. These grant funds have not yet been disbursed to state education agencies.

## REFERENCES

Harkness, S. P., & Groom, J. N. (1976). *Building without barriers for the disabled.* New York: Whitney Library of Design.

Moe, C. (1977). *Planning for the removal of architectural barriers for the handicapped.* Monticello, IL: Council of Planning Librarians.

Sorensen, R. J. (1979). *Design for accessibility.* New York: Mc-Graw-Hill.

PATRICIA ANN ABRAMSON
*Hudson Public Schools,
Hudson, Wisconsin*

## ACCESSIBILITY OF BUILDINGS
## MOBILITY TRAINING

## ARENA, JOHN (1929–    )

John Arena received his BA in education and psychology in 1951, and MA in special education in 1959, from San Francisco State College. He then went on to postgraduate training and work at the University of California, Berkeley. Arena taught in the regular classroom and served as an administrator and teacher of the multiply handicapped and learning disabled. He later founded a school for dyslexic children.

As the publisher of Academic Therapy Publications since 1965, Arena has acted as a springboard for the translation of educational themes into operational terms. Publications dealing with the identification, diagnosis, and remediation of learning disabilities have taken complex concepts and clarified them for usable classroom applications, a process that Arena calls a top priority. The journal *Academic Therapy* falls into the "practical, concrete realm," focusing on helping the teacher to more effectively and efficiently teach children. Editor of some 15 books, editorial advisor to the *Journal of Special Education,* and consultant to the *Bulletin of the Orton Society,* Arena also lectures at Dominican College of San Rafael, California.

ELAINE FLETCHER-JANZEN
*Texas A&M University*

## ARGENTINA, SPECIAL EDUCATION
## SERVICES FOR YOUNG CHILDREN IN

Among the countries of Latin America, Argentina has a well-established record of providing educational services to its citizens. Mandatory school attendance was established in 1884 and Argentina has the highest literacy rate (84%) in Latin America (UNESCO, 1984). The National Directorate of Special Education is responsible for the spe-cial instruction of mentally, physically, and socially handicapped students. Services are provided from preschool through adulthood.

Early intervention services for children from birth to age 3 were scarce in Argentina and poorly organized (UNESCO, 1981). There was a need for early educational intervention services for children and their families prior to enrolling a child in a nursery school or special center. As a result, services were developed for early stimulation and education. These services are divided by handicapping condition and are provided in infant consultation units. For children with slight to moderate mental handicaps, services focus on sensory and motor stimulation, socialization skills, and speech development. Parents are involved in these activities so that follow through can be done at home. For children with physical handicaps (blind, partially sighted, deaf or hard of hearing), the education is divided into two stages. The first stage is early neurological and sensory stimulation; it is continued until the child has reached a developmental level of 18 months (UNESCO, 1981). The next stage involves stimulation of sensorimotor activities, language development, and the development of self-care and socialization skills. Guidance and educational services also are given to the families.

The primary goal of these intervention programs is to raise the child's level of developmental functioning so that he or she can enter a prenursery special education program. Along with outreach to parents is the involvement and continuing education of special education teachers. There is a central registry of handicapped children so that they may be referred to the appropriate resources. Primary prevention programs are initiated via the media, with special programs for or articles on handicapped children. Public meetings on issues relating to handicapped students constitute an ongoing effort at general education as to the needs of handicapped children.

### REFERENCES

UNESCO. (1981). *Handicapped children: Early detection, intervention and education in selected case studies from Argentina, Canada, Denmark, Jamaica, Jordan, Nigeria, Sri Lanka, Thailand, and the United Kingdom* (Report No. ED/MD/63). Paris: Author.

UNESCO. (1984). Wastage in primary education from 1970 to 1980. *Prospects, 14,* 348–367.

KAREN F. WYCHE
*Hunter College, City University
of New York*

## LATIN AMERICA, SPECIAL EDUCATION IN

## ARITHMETIC INSTRUCTION

The Direct Instructional System for Teaching Arithmetic and Reading (DISTAR) is the foremost example of the directive teaching process. It is a highly structured, systematic program for teaching disadvantaged preschool and primary grade children. The method emphasizes structure, programmed learning, drill, and repetition. Basic skills and concepts are presented in a way that requires mastery of each step in the programmed sequence before proceeding to subsequent steps. A major goal of the DISTAR program is to reduce the correlation between IQ and achievement by ensuring that prerequisite skills are learned, designing motivational strategies to keep the student engaged in the learning activity, and accelerating the learning rate of the student mastering the learning task (Bereiter, 1976). The Bereiter–Engelmann model was designed to alleviate the language and conceptual deficits often displayed by disadvantaged children.

Baine (1978) points out that highly efficient instructional techniques are required to teach handicapped youngsters while accommodating individual needs within group instruction. He found the Distar materials to be well-suited for the purpose. The Engelmann–Becker model emphasized small-group instruction, using daily sequenced lessons in reading, arithmetic, and language. The objectives of the DISTAR program, which address language and reading development as well as arithmetic computation and concept skills, include knowledge of letters, numbers, forms, perceptual discrimination, relational concepts, grouping, ordering, reasoning and problem solving, and social skills. The arithmetic curriculum includes addition, subtraction, multiplication, division, measurement, and word problems.

Distar was the curriculum of Bereiter and Engelmann's (1966) Academic Preschool; it was designed to help low socioeconomic class children progress academically. The DISTAR teacher has aides to help with the delivery of instruction. Small-group lessons of 35 to 40 minutes employ techniques of positive reinforcement, correction procedures, and teaching to mastery. Criterion-referenced tests are administered periodically and are the basis for regrouping and staff training.

Teachers in the Academic Preschool in Champaigne, Illinois, followed scripts in their interaction with students. The scripts were specified sequential programs of instruction. Teachers bombarded students with rapid-fire verbal interface involving a great deal of drill exercise. Children were expected to respond in like manner; this led to the tag "pressure cooker teaching." The underlying assumption was that the academic failure of the disadvantaged or middle-class child was due to a failure of instruction, and that if accelerated learning schedules were instituted, results of enriched instruction would be maintained.

To build on gains attained in preschool programs, several Follow Through programs were designed. They rely on the highly structured DISTAR materials for arithmetic, reading, and language. Structured programs described in the DISTAR literature involve students through third grade. These programs represent a cross-section of the country. The East Las Vegas Follow Through project incorporates a variety of basal reading and mathematics series along with the highly structured DISTAR system of instruction. In each subject, teachers work with small groups of students 90 minutes daily providing special correction procedures and frequent opportunity for student oral and written responses. Diagnostic assessment is frequent. Children with limited English are provided instruction in their native language. There is a strong parent program in establishing a bilingual language and home-reading program.

The Uvalde, Texas, Direct Instruction program incorporates problem-solving skills for disadvantaged students so that at the end of three years students can compete with peers from higher socioeconomic levels. The design of this program allows students who already possess prerequisite skills to move ahead at accelerated rates. A classroom teacher, with the help of a paraprofessional, uses the Direct Instruction materials that include DISTAR language, reading, mathematics, and spelling mastery skills. Homogeneous groups are made up of 5 to 10 students. Those who need extra help are tutored by adults and peers. Criterion-referenced progress tests are administered every 2 weeks by trained diagnosticians. Instruction is monitored; to ensure quality, in-service instruction is provided continually throughout the year. There is an active parent group that supports the program. Since almost 70% of the students are Hispanic, DISTAR materials are in Spanish. The bilingual instruction is designed to encourage students to function in English as soon as possible.

The focus of the Cherokee, North Carolina, DISTAR program is planned learning that incorporates preserving the Cherokee language and customs. Students are instructed in language and folklore by a full-time Cherokee aide each week. They also make pottery, baskets, beadwork, and fingerweaving in the traditional ways. When the students have completed the three levels of the DISTAR program, they move into the regular program of the school's upper elementary grades, regardless of their age.

The DeKalb County Follow Through program in Smithville, Tennessee, addresses the needs of disadvantaged rural children. The program incorporates the DISTAR materials and methods: positive reinforcement, group responses, individual turns, teaching to mastery, and immediate correction of errors. The reading curriculum includes decoding and comprehension (Level I), reading for understanding (Level II), and comprehension and information acquisition skills (Level III). The arithmetic curriculum includes addition and subtraction (Level I), multiplication, complex addition and subtraction, and fractions (Level II), and column addition, long division, complex multiplication, and story problems (Level III). One teacher and two or three aides are assigned a maximum of 25 students in groups of 10 (those who learn at a rapid rate) or 5 (those who learn at a slower rate) for 35 minutes daily in each content area. Biweekly criterion-referenced tests are administered to monitor progress. Health and other support services, staff development, and parent involvement are also components of the DeKalb County program.

The Flippin, Arkansas, Follow Through program also relies on the structured DISTAR program. Flippin is a rural, mainly white, low-to-medium-income community. The goal of the Flippin Follow Through program is to build on Head Start gains. The DISTAR instructional system is the core of the program. On completion of the three programmed levels that comprise the DISTAR system, regardless of grade level, students move into the regular programs of the Flippin schools. Arithmetic is taught by a problem-solving approach, progressing from basic addition and subtraction to multiplication and fractions, renaming, long division, column addition, measurement, and story problems. One teacher and at least one aide staff each K-3 classroom. They are expected to incorporate all of the following instructional techniques: teaching to mastery, group response, positive reinforcement, immediate correction of errors, individual turns, and rapid pacing. DISTAR instruction occurs in the morning. Criterion-referenced tests are administered biweekly in arithmetic, reading, and language. The Flippin program also features health services, a strong parent support program, and continuous in-service training.

The Nichols Avenue Follow Through program in Washington, DC, also relies on the DISTAR program of highly structured, carefully sequenced instructional tasks that are designed to enhance skill mastery. In addition to DISTAR instruction, physical education, art, and science are taught by district resource teachers. Instruction to small groups of six to ten occurs for 30 to 35 minutes daily in each content area. Criterion-referenced tests are administered every 9 weeks and result in placement of students in the most appropriate learning environment. In-service training for teachers and a parent support group are other components of the Nichols Avenue program. Other Follow Through programs that incorporate the DISTAR materials and procedures include the following: Public School 137 in Brooklyn, New York; The Bandini Center, San Diego, California; and Williamsburg County Schools in Kingstree, South Carolina.

Conclusions of evaluation studies regarding the effectiveness of the DISTAR approach are mixed. Generally reported were possible advantages in arithmetic computation achievement and disadvantages regarding word meaning, paragraph meaning, and arithmetic concept skills development. Elkind (1970) questioned the efficiency, economy, and learning benefits of formal instructional programs at the preschool level, particularly for middle-class children. Positive results were reported by Bereiter and Engelmann (1976, 1973, 1966a) and Schwartz (1974). Studies that reported no significant differences in effectiveness of the DISTAR program include Ogletree (1976), Ogletree and Ogletree (1976), and Mahan

(1971). Kaufman (1972, 1974) reported mixed results—no difference in developing oral language ability but positive results in spelling, word-study skills, and arithmetic computation. Qualitative evaluations that surveyed teachers' opinions of the DISTAR program generally reported positive attitudes, particularly concerning slow learners and learning-disabled students (Fleischner & Garnett, 1980; Mayes, 1977; DiPasalegne & Ogletree, 1976; Moodie & Hoen, 1972; Moodie, 1973; Guinet, 1971).

## REFERENCES

Baine, D. (1978). Direct instructional techniques for young handicapped children. *Elements: Translating Theory into Practice,* 9(8), 6–8.

Becker, W. C., & Engelmann, S. (1976). Analysis of achievement data on six cohorts of low-income children from 20 school districts in the University of Oregon direct instruction Follow Through model. *Research in Education,* March 1978.

Bereiter, C. (1976). IQ differences and social policy. In N. F. Ashline, T. R. Pezullo, & C. I. Norris (Eds.), *Education, inequality, and national policy* (pp. 137–155). Lexington, MA: Lexington.

Bereiter, C., & Engelmann, S. (1966). *Teaching disadvantaged children in the preschool.* Englewood Cliffs, NJ: Prentice-Hall.

Bereiter, C., & Engelmann, S. (1966a). Effectiveness of direct verbal instruction on IQ performance and achievement in reading and arithmetic. *Research in Education,* Nov. 1969.

DiPasalegne, R. W., & Ogletree, E. J. (1976). An assessment of DISTAR by Chicago innercity teachers. *Research in Education,* April 1978.

Elkind, D. (1970). The case for the academic preschool: Fact or fiction. *Young Children, 25*(3), 132–140.

Fleischner, J., & Garnett, K. (1980). Arithmetic learning disabilities: A literature review. *Research in Education,* May 1982.

Guinet, L. (1971). Evaluation of DISTAR materials in three junior learning assistance classes. *Research in Education,* March 1972.

Kaufman, M. (1972). The effect of the DISTAR instructional system on first and second grade achievement: An evaluation of the 1971–1972 Title I program of Winthrop, Massachusetts. *Research in Education,* April 1973.

Kaufman, M. (1974). The effect of the DISTAR instructional system: An evaluation of the 1972–1973 Title I program of Winthrop, Massachusetts. *Research in Education,* Dec. 1975.

Mayes, B. (1977). What do reading teachers teach in first grade classes? A study of questions teachers ask. *Research in Education,* Jan. 1979.

Moodie, A. G. (1973). An evaluation of the DISTAR Language I program at Seymour Elementary School. *Research in Education,* July 1974.

Moodie, A. G., & Hoen, R. (1972). Evaluation of DISTAR programs in learning assistance classes of Vancouver 1971–1972. *Research in Education,* Oct. 1973.

Ogletree, E. J. (1976). A comparative study of the effectiveness of DISTAR and eclectic reading methods for innercity children. *Research in Education,* April 1978.

Ogletree, E. J., & Ogletree, G. S. (1976). Teachers' opinions of the DISTAR reading program. *Research in Education,* April 1978.

Schwarz, J. I. (1974). Effects of a structured pedagogy on children's language. *Research in Education*, June 1975.

FREDRICKA K. REISMAN
*Drexel University*

**ARITHMETIC REMEDIATION**
**DIRECT INSTRUCTION**
**DISTAR**
**MATHEMATICS, LEARNING DISABILITIES IN**

## ARITHMETIC REMEDIATION

Remediation in arithmetic has evolved into an instructional system comprised of goals and objectives; tests at various levels and of kinds that assess the objectives; instructional activities that represent curriculum at the concrete, pictorial, and abstract levels; and summative evaluations. Instructional goals are based on the general mathematics goals of a school district or similar educational agency. These goals usually emerge from curriculum groups of teachers, supervisors, administrators, and content specialists from outside the school district. In some cases, goals are determined by available textbooks. Objectives are translations of the goals into observable performance statements.

According to the National Council of Supervisors of Mathematics (NCSM, 1979), the goal of the mathematics curriculum should be to ensure that each student is able to

1. Solve problems
2. Apply mathematics to everyday situations
3. Determine if results are reasonable
4. Estimate
5. Compute
6. Use geometry
7. Measure
8. Read, interpret, and construct tables, charts, and graphs
9. Use mathematics to predict
10. Understand the role of computers

Objectives used to assess each of the NCSM goals might be to

1. Generate a list of possible solutions for finding the difference between two integers
2. Purchase items from a store and use the correct amount of money
3. State whether a series of answers make sense
4. State whether a quantity is reasonable for a specified purpose
5. Add with renaming
6. Find the circumference of a circle
7. Find the volume of a container
8. Interpret a graph showing income of teachers compared to inflation rates over time
9. Use a graph to predict direction of a group of stocks over time
10. Describe the use of the computer as a mathematics tutor

Diagnostic assessments may include survey tests, concept tests, interviews, attitude scales, and learning style inventories. Survey tests tap broad ranges of mathematics competence and serve to present an overview of students strengths and weaknesses. Survey tests also are referred to as screening tests, where there are relatively few items for each of a great number of objectives. Survey tests have the following characteristics:

1. They may be group or individually administered
2. Test items are usually sequenced from easy to difficult
3. They are usually not timed
4. They may be machine scored.
5. Test results indicate further areas of investigation in terms of student strengths and weaknesses.

Concept tests may be used for diagnosing in more depth weaknesses identified in the survey test. Concept tests tap objectives with a greater number of items than survey tests. There may be five items on the concept test as compared with two on the survey test for each objective. Furthermore, a greater number of objectives are assessed on a concept test. Examples of concept tests include the *Diagnostic Test of Arithmetic Strategies, KeyMath Diagnostic Arithmetic Test*, and *Individual Assessment Battery: Standardized Form.*

Interviews are crucial to diagnostic assessment, which is the foundation for designing, developing, implementing, and evaluating remedial programs in mathematics. Interviews occur after the paper-pencil assessments and may accompany additional diagnosis at concrete and pictorial levels. Interviews provide a structure for probing how and what a student is thinking. The following types of data may emerge from interviews: (1) what the student is thinking; (2) the student's thought processes, e.g., whether the thinking is concrete or simplistic, whether cause-effect relations are apparent; (3) the problem-solving strategies being used by the student; (4) the mode of representation that appears most comfortable for the student: concrete, pictorial, or abstract; (5) how the student's performance compares with age peers as well as with other things that the student can do, e.g., science, writing, art, music, sports, and social interaction. Interviews may be organized around topics such as whole numbers, fractions, geometry, measurement, and mathematical applications. The purpose of the interview is to collect data in a manner that is more thorough than from written tests. It is important to probe during an interview and to avoid correcting errors and instructing. If the student gets stuck, rephrase questions and move to a lower but related objective. The interview should allow the diagnostic teacher to identify error patterns, understand the student's thinking in regard to isolated errors, and observe whether the student's performance differs on the same objective with concrete models, or pictorial and abstract representations. Data from interviews should clarify performance on written assessments. The following matrix serves as a structure for selecting interview activities in terms of mode of representation of probe items:

The following are guidelines for conducting an interview:

1. Establish rapport to get to know the student and allow the student to relax.
2. Explain the purpose of the meeting as well as what you wish to learn. Ask the student whether he or she has any questions about the meeting.
3. Probe and learn about the student's strengths and weaknesses; do not teach.
4. Check to determine whether the student can perform prerequisite as well as corequisite skills. Prerequisites are subskills or components of a task; corequisites are parallel tasks. Multiplication and division may be considered corequisites by the time the student is in grade five; addition is prerequisite to multiplication, while subtraction is prerequisite to division.
5. Look for generic patterns of performance that may be trouble spots. Most errors in arithmetic are not random but represent patterns of misunderstanding.
6. Ask questions that serve different purposes to help identify different styles of thinking. Include divergent and convergent types such as "How many different ways can you use these materials to help you find an answer?" or "What is your favorite color?"

Attitude scales provide information about the student's interest in, fear of, or enjoyment of arithmetic. Often those students who do not do well in mathematics have high anxiety toward the subject and do not like mathematics. Thus since attitude often interacts with performance, it is necessary to gather information about the student's attitude as part of the diagnostic process. The following are some instruments that assess attitude toward mathematics: (1) Aiken Mathematics Attitude Scale (Aiken, 1972);

(2) Dutton Mathematics Attitude Scale (Dutton, 1956); and (3) Mott Mathematics Student Survey (Mott, 1984).

Learning style inventories provide another view of how the student learns best. This type of inventory may assess preferences by the student such as grouping (e.g., small group, large group, or individual), or preferences concerning instruction (e.g., teacher explanations, peer tutoring, or self-instruction).

Cawley (1985), Reisman and Kauffman (1980), and Reisman (1981), presented a number of remedial instructional strategies. These include the following:

1. Present small amounts of a sequence to be learned in an organized format
2. Use visual or auditory cues that highlight what is to be learned
3. Use separating and underlining as cues
4. Emphasize patterns
5. Teach rehearsal strategies such as repetition, verbal elaboration, systematic scanning, and grouping material to be remembered
6. Reinforce attention to a relevant dimension
7. Point out relevant relationship
8. Emphasize differences in distinctive features of stimuli
9. Control irrelevant stimuli
10. Replace incidental learning tasks with structured intentional learning tasks
11. Reduce complexity of task
12. Use consistent vocabulary
13. Use a model whose competency in the task has been established
14. Encourage deferred judgment during problem solving
15. Use peer-team learning
16. Provide immediate knowledge of results
17. Plan for transfer in learning
18. Use short, simple sentences when giving directions
19. Use concrete examples of spatial and quantitative relationships
20. Use prompting

Summative evaluation should include broad objectives that allow students to demonstrate their ability to compare, summarize, classify, interpret, judge, imagine, hypothesize, and engage in decision making. Remediation is an integrated system of assessment and instruction. The concept of remediation described here goes beyond the diagnose-prescribe model that focuses on fixing with a remedy, to preventive model that implies doing it right the first time.

## REFERENCES

Aiken, L. R. (1972, March). Research on attitudes toward mathematics. *Arithmetic Teacher, 19*(3), 229–234.

Brown, J. S., & Burton, R. R. (1978). Diagnostic models for procedural bugs in basic mathematical skills. *Cognitive Science, 2,* 155–192.

Cawley, J. F. (1985). *Cognitive strategies and mathematics for the learning disabled.* Rockville, MD: Aspen.

Dutton, W. H. (1956). Attitudes of junior high school pupils toward arithmetic. *School Review, 64,* 18–22.

Mott, T. (1984). *Mott Mathematics Student Survey.* Unpublished doctoral dissertation, University of Pittsburgh.

Reisman, F. K. (1981). *Teaching mathematics: Methods and content.* Boston: Houghton Mifflin.

Reisman, F. K. (1982). *A guide to the diagnostic teaching of arithmetic.* Columbus, OH: Merrill.

Reisman, F. K., & Kauffman, S. H. (1980). *Teaching mathematics to children with special needs.* Columbus, OH: Merrill.

Suydam, M. N. (1979, February). The case for a comprehensive mathematics curriculum. *Arithmetic Teacher, 26,* 10–13.

FREDRICKA K. REISMAN
*Drexel University*

**ARITHMETIC INSTRUCTION**
**MATHEMATICS, LEARNING DISABILITIES IN**

## ARMITAGE, THOMAS RHODES (1824–1890)

Thomas Rhodes Armitage, an English physician forced by failing sight to leave the practice of medicine, founded the British and Foreign Blind Association in 1868. This organization, which became the Royal National Institute for the Blind, had as its major purposes the establishment of an effective educational program for the blind and the elimination of the existing confusion over printing systems for the blind.

Armitage established the Royal Normal College and Academy of Music to provide vocational preparation for blind students. Eighty percent of its graduates became self-supporting, a unique accomplishment in that time. After conducting an extensive study of printing systems for the blind, Armitage and his association became the leading English proponents of braille. They were instrumental in the ultimate adoption of that system throughout Britain.

## REFERENCES

Armitage, T. R. (1886). *Education and employment for the blind* (2nd ed.). London: Harrison.

Ross, I. (1951). *Journey into light.* New York: Appleton-Century-Crofts.

PAUL IRVINE
*Katonah, New York*

## ARMSTRONG v. KLINE (1979)

*Armstrong* v. *Kline* was filed on behalf of handicapped children seeking special education services during the summer term. The plaintiffs argued that handicapped children needed continuous, year-round programming in order to receive an appropriate education. The state countered that summer school was beyond the needs of these children and was not made available to nonhandicapped children free of charge and therefore was not required. In finding that some handicapped children are in need of year-round services, the court used the reasoning that "the normal child, if he or she has had a loss, regains lost skills in a few weeks, but for some handicapped children, the interruption in schooling by the summer recess may result in a substantial loss of skills previously learned."

The court was referring principally to the severely handicapped, concluding that they would most likely require summer sessions. Of particular importance is that the court's finding seems to shift the burden of proof from the parents (to show need) to the school district (to show a lack of necessity for year-round programming). These rulings have been upheld in the appeals process thus far. The court did not issue a blanket requirement for summer sessions for all handicapped children, but rather required a determination to be made on the basis of the needs of the individual child.

CECIL R. REYNOLDS
*Texas A&M University*

**SUMMER SCHOOL FOR THE HANDICAPPED**

## ARMY GROUP EXAMINATIONS

The Group Examination Alpha, better known as the Army Alpha, was the first group test of intelligence for adults. The examination was one of a battery of tests developed as a result of the armed forces's need during World War I to have an objective means of classifying vast numbers of recruits for military service.

The original examination, consisting of 13 subtests, was developed between June and September 1917 by the Committee on the Psychological Examining of Recruits. The committee was chaired by R. M. Yerkes and included W. V. Bingham, H. H. Goddard, A. S. Otis, T. H. Haines, L M. Terman, F. L. Wells, and G. M. Whipple. Although experience among measurement experts with group examination procedures was rare, the committee relied heavily on A. S. Otis's group adaptation to the Binet scales for content and standards for administration (Yoakum & Yerkes, 1920). The committee worked continuously for almost a month developing, selecting, and adapting methods for the test content, and another month thoroughly testing the efficacy methods in military stations across the United States. The resulting version of the test consisted of eight subtests: (1) oral directions, (2) disarranged sentences, (3) arithmetic reasoning, (4) information, (5) Otis synonyms and antonyms, (6) practical judgment, (7) number series complete, and (8) analogies. There were five alternative forms provided and the average administration time was 40 to 50 minutes for groups of up to 500 recruits (Linden & Linden, 1968).

Between April 1 and December 1, 1918, Army Alpha was administered to approximately 1,250,000 military recruits. Contributing to its reliability and concurrent validity, the Army Alpha correlated with other ability measures as follows:

0.50 to 0.70 with officer ratings

0.80 to 0.90 with Stanford–Binet

0.72 with Trabue B and LC completion test combined

0.80 with Beta

0.94 with composite of Alpha, Beta, and Stanford-Binet.

## Army Beta

The Army Alpha had more than adequately addressed the need for an instrument with which large numbers of individuals could be evaluated in a short period of time, but another problem quickly emerged. Army psychologists did not know what to do about the approximately 30% of the draftees who either could not read English or read so slowly that they could not perform on the Army Alpha. The Army Group Examination Beta, or Army Beta, was prepared to meet this need. The development of an instrument that could be group-administered without a heavy emphasis on reading or understanding verbal language presented special problems. These problems were mainly eliminated through the use of demonstration charts and pantomime to convey instructions (Yoakum & Yerkes, 1920).

The final version of the examination consisted of seven subtests: (1) maze test, (2) cube analysis, (3) X-O series, (4) digit symbol, (5) number checking, (6) pictorial completion, and (7) geometrical completion. The Beta also took approximately 50 minutes to administer and yielded the same type of numerical scores as the Alpha. Although the ability scores obtained on the Beta were somewhat less accurate than on the Alpha for the higher range of intelligence, the data obtained revealed the following correlations:

0.80 with the Alpha

0.73 with the Stanford–Binet

0.91 with the Stanford–Binet, Alpha, and Beta

The general administration procedure for the Army examinations soon became routine. Groups of draftees (100 to 500) reported to a special building to take the mental test(s). Based on whether the draftees could speak and/or write English, they were assigned to take either the Army Alpha for literates or Army Beta for illiterates or foreign-born recruits. Depending on the individual's performance on one of these tests, a decision was made regarding classification in the military or on the need for further testing to ascertain mental capacity for military service. Individuals failing the Alpha exam were automatically administered the Beta exam to factor out the possible role of reading and oral language in their poor performance. Anyone failing the Alpha exam and the Beta exam initially was given one of three individual performance examinations. Thus, no individual was designated as mentally incompetant solely based on performance on the group examinations.

The Army Alpha and the Army Beta yielded numerical scores of ability ranging from 0 to 212, which for military classification purposes were translated into the letter grades A, B, C, D, or E. Classifications were assigned as in the following examples:

| Intelligence Grade | Probable Classification | Definition | Score (Alpha) |
|---|---|---|---|
| A | High officer type | Very superior | 135–212 |
| B | Commissioned/ Noncommissioned officer | Superior | 105–134 |
| ⋮ | | | |
| D− | Considered fit for regular duty; rarely suited for tasks requiring special skill or alertness | Very inferior | 0–14 |

The scores on the Alpha showed a high correlation with the individual's social status. The data also seemed to indicate a high correlation between an individual's Alpha score and level of occupational responsibility (Yoakum & Yerkes, 1920). These data were at least partially responsible for the soon to be widespread use of tests to predict vocational success, but as Matarazzo (1972) points out in reporting this data, there was a failure to highlight the considerable overlap in the scores obtained by individuals in the various occupational groups. More important, the vast amounts of data generated from the Army Alpha exams provided glimpses of the full range of adult abilities, confirming Galton's assumption that intelligence test scores are normally distributed in the population at large. Additionally, these data were largely responsible for the practice of using a fixed mental age for calculating adult intelligence.

The practical utility of the entire battery is expounded in terms of the number of men discharged from military service before the country wasted vast amounts of money, effort, and time training them. Yoakum and Yerkes (1920) report that between April and November 1918, 45,653 draftees were found deficient to serve in the military. From a measurement or psychometric perspective, the subtests and techniques developed and used for the army group examinations paved the way for the tremendous growth of group and individual testing in education and industry. Subtests developed for the army examinations are very much in evidence on most current tests of intelligence. For example, the most widely used individual tests of intelligence today, the Wechsler scales, are composed of subtests that are in many respects identical to the subtests on the Army Alpha and Beta. This is not surprising: the author of these scales, David Wechsler, participated in the army testing program during World War I.

The influence of the army group examinations is not all positive. Anastasi (1976) reminds us that often tests modeled after the army examinations failed to acknowledge and account for the limitations of the technical properties of the group examination methods. This failure resulted in much of the negative sentiment toward ability testing in the United States. That sentiment threatened the demise of psychological testing. Thus the army examinations may have done as much to retard as to advance the progress of psychological tests. The ease and efficiency of these group techniques also created a preference for impersonal testing as opposed to the more clinical, individual testing methods promoted by pioneers such as Binet (Matarazzo, 1972).

## REFERENCES

Anastasi, A. (1976). *Psychological testing* (4th ed.). New York: MacMillan.

Linden, K. W., & Linden, J. D. (1968). *Modern mental measurement: A historical perspective.* Boston: Houghton-Mifflin.

Matarazzo, J. D. (1972). *Wechsler's measurement and appraisal of adult intelligence* (5th ed.). Baltimore: Williams & Wilkins.

Yoakum, C. S., & Yerkes, R. M. (1920). *Army mental tests.* New York: Holt.

JULIA A. HICKMAN
*University of Texas, Austin*

INTELLIGENCE TESTS
MEASUREMENT

## ARTHRITIS, JUVENILE

Juvenile rheumatoid arthritis (JRA) is a systemic disease that causes inflammation of one and usually more joints.

The manifestations of JRA vary considerably among patients. The most common symptoms include joint swelling, warmth, tenderness, and pain, which may lead to stiffness, contractures, and retardation of growth. This disease is usually accompanied by fever bursts, rash, and visceral symptoms.

This form of arthritis is the most common connective tissue disease in children and is the most prevalent of the arthritic diseases. It has been estimated that around 250,000 Americans suffer from JRA with an incidence of 1.1 cases per year 1000 school-age children (Varni & Jay, 1984). The disease affects more girls than boys. It is similar to adult rheumatoid arthritis except that it typically appears before puberty and is more likely to stay in remission.

The causes of JRA are unknown. While infection, autoimmune disorders, trauma, psychological stress, and heredity have been considered, little evidence has been found to support any of these ideas. As there are no known causes, there are also no known cures. The most common treatment is the administration of large doses of aspirin. Other common drug treatments include gold salts, antimalarial drugs, corticosteroids, and penicillamine. Special exercises and sometimes periods of rest may also be employed. Different kinds of heat may be applied to reduce stiffness and pain, and a variety of other pain-control measures have been tried. Splints are often used to prevent deformity and enhance function. Surgery, including total joint replacement, may sometimes be necessary and can be beneficial.

There are basically three forms of JRA: systemic, polyarticular, and pauciarticular. The systemic form accounts for approximately 20% of the population with JRA. High fevers, rashes, stomach pains, and severe anemia are usually present in this type. Pauciarticular accounts for 30 to 40% of the cases. It begins by affecting only a few joints, usually the large ones (knees, ankles, or elbows). Polyarticular is the most common type, accounting for 40–50% of children with JRA. This type affects several joints (five or more), usually small joints of the fingers and hands (Arthritis Foundation, 1983).

The long-term effects of JRA vary greatly depending on the type as well as the individual. There is no way to know the outcome of the disease in its early stages. However, the overall prognosis for children with JRA is good. Most will be able to go through adulthood without any severe physical limitations. Only about 25% will suffer any significant disability (Jay, Helm, & Wray, 1982). In some cases the disease will go into permanent remission but structural damages and functional limitations will remain. In other cases the disease may continue to be active throughout the individual's life.

In addition to physical considerations, certain psychological aspects of JRA are also important. McAnarney, Pless, Satterwhite, and Friedman (1974) found that children who have JRA but no disabilities have more emotional problems than disabled arthritics. They also found that parents of the nondisabled children had a poorer understanding of the disease and were less likely to acknowledge its impact on the child's behavior, schooling, and social relations. Litt, Cuskey, and Rosenburg (1982) found that good self-image and greater autonomy coincided with higher compliance in treatment.

Wilkinson (1981) studied the emotional and social behavior of adolescents with chronic rheumatoid arthritis. She found that one of the major complaints among these adolescents was people's tendency to treat them as younger than their age because of their smaller size. She also reported a high anxiety level because of restricted mobility and fears about an uncertain future.

Schaller (1982) has stressed the need to avoid an image of chronic invalidism. It is important to account for the limitations experienced by individuals with JRA; however, when not specifically restricted by the disease, they should be expected to perform as well as their peers.

The way children are treated by others affects their self-image; therefore, those working with these children should help them to avoid feelings of inferiority. Wilkinson (1981) reported that the adolescents in her study expressed a desire for more social contacts with able-bodied individuals and a desire to be in regular rather than special classes.

In the classroom as well as at home, children should not be unnecessarily restricted from activities. They should be encouraged to find alternatives when they cannot participate in regular play. Periodically calling on the child to do an activity requiring movement may help relieve stiffness whenever the child is not in pain. Beales, Keen, and Holt (1983) have stressed the importance of being aware of the child's perception of pain. Children may be less likely to interpret internal sensations as pain and therefore may fail to recognize it as a warning sign. Often, even when children know they are in pain they may not complain and may even try to conceal it. Some visible signs that may help determine the presence of pain are walking with a stiff gait, taking short steps, tense muscles, and inability to perform certain tasks.

Another important consideration is JRA's erratic and unpredictable changes from day to day and even throughout the day. Usually the most severe stiffness occurs in the morning. Finally, it is very important for people supervising individuals with JRA to know the signs of aspirin overdose: rapid or deep breathing, ringing in the ears, decrease in hearing, drowsiness, nausea, vomiting, irritability, and unusual behavior.

### REFERENCES

Arthritis Foundation. (1983). *Arthritis in children and When your student has childhood arthritis*. Atlanta, GA: Patient Services Department.

Beales, J. G., Keen, J. H., & Holt, P. L. (1983). The child's per-

ception of the disease and the experience of pain in juvenile arthritis. *Journal of Rheumatology, 10*(1), 61–65.

Jay, S., Helm, S., & Wray, B. B. (1982). Juvenile rheumatoid arthritis. *American Family Physician, 26*(2), 139–147.

Litt, I. F., Cuskey, W. R., & Rosenberg, A. (1982). Role of self-esteem and autonomy in determining medication compliance among adolescents with juvenile rheumatoid arthritis. *Pediatrics, 69*(1), 15–17.

McAnarney, E. R., Pless, I. B., Satterwhite, B., & Friedman, S. B. (1974). Psychological problems of children with chronic juvenile arthritis. *Pediatrics, 53*, 523–528.

Schaller, J. G. (1982). Juvenile rheumatoid arthritis. *Pediatric Annals, 11*(4), 375–382.

Varni, J. W., & Jay, S. M. (1984). Biobehavioral factors in juvenile rheumatoid arthritis: Implications for research and practice. *Clinical Psychology Review, 4*, 543–560.

Wilkinson, V. A. (1981). Juvenile chronic arthritis in adolescence: Facing the reality. *International Rehabilitation Medicine, 3*, 11–176.

DAN HATT
NURI PUIG
LOGAN WRIGHT
*University of Oklahoma*

**ARTHRITIS, JUVENILE**
**PHYSICAL HANDICAPS**

## ARTICULATION DISORDERS

The term articulation refers to the movements of the articulators in the production of the speech sounds making up our language. There are approximately 40 speech sounds or phonemes categorized as either vowels or consonants. Children learn these sounds gradually in a fairly predictable sequence. Speech-language pathologists are particularly interested in the developmental sequence of consonant acquisition because consonants are more important to intelligibility than vowels. Some of the earliest acquired consonants are m, n, h, and p. Some of the later acquired consonants are s, sh, th, and z.

When an articulation error occurs, production of the phoneme is imprecise in one of several ways. Sometimes, the intended phoneme is replaced by another phoneme and referred to as a sound substitution. An example would be the word *rabbit* produced as *wabbit*. In other instances, misproduction results in a phoneme being substituted by a sound other than one normally found in the language. For example, a person may produce an s sound with a lateral emission of breath (central emission is normal) resulting in a lateral lisp. This type of error is usually referred to as a distortion since the sound is still distinguishable as the target sound but is imprecise. Sometimes sounds within words are deleted so that a word like *boat* is pronounced as *bow*. These errors are referred to as sound omissions.

The main criterion that is used in the diagnosis of an articulation disorder is intelligibility of speech. That is, the less intelligible a person's speech, the more likely that the person has an articulation disorder. Children usually are not considered to have articulation disorders unless they have several sound errors. Since many young children normally have misarticulations at an early age, they are not considered to have articulation disorders unless the intelligibility of the speech is considerably less than that encountered in other children of the same age.

Some articulation errors are accompanied by physical abnormalities like cleft palate, mental retardation, or brain damage. The physical abnormalities are usually contributing factors to misarticulation. A large group of misarticulating children have no apparent physical causes for the articulation errors. These children are referred to as having a functional articulation disorder. Some have poor dentition, poor speech sound discrimination, low intelligence, poor gross and fine motor skills, etc. Researchers, however, have found no relation between these factors and misarticulation (Winitz, 1969).

There are a number of articulation treatment techniques employed by speech-language pathologists in the remediation of misarticulation (Van Riper, 1969). These methodologies can be classified into two major categories, motor and cognitive-language. The motor methodologies usually include some form of speech sound discrimination training. Some other techniques are sound stimulation ("say sun"), phonetic placement (describing where the articulators are supposed to be for a specific sound), and facilitating context (finding a phonetic context that helps a child say a sound correctly).

The cognitive-language approaches teach the sounds within communicative contexts. For example, the child who omits final consonants will say the words *bow* and *boat* as *bow*. The child's misarticulation will then result in miscommunication. Creating situations where misproduction contributes to miscommunication is often motivating enough to improve articulation.

## REFERENCES

Darley, F., & Spriestersbach, D. (1978). *Diagnostic methods in speech pathology* (2nd ed.). New York: Harper & Row.

Ingram, D. (1976). *Phonological disability in children*. New York: Elsevier.

Van Riper, C. (1978). *Speech correction: Principles and methods* (6th ed.). Englewood Cliffs, NJ: Prentice-Hall.

Winitz, H. (1969). *Articulatory acquisition*. New York: Appleton-Century-Crofts.

FREDERICK F. WEINER
*Pennsylvania State University*

## SPEECH AND LANGUAGE HANDICAPS

## ART THERAPY

Art therapy is a relatively new technique developed by Margaret Naumberg (1917), who applied her experience as an art teacher and psychologist to treating children with behavior problems. Naumberg used the art of children as a tool to guide therapy. The techniques of art therapy are based on the knowledge that every person has the capacity to project his or her inner feelings into visual form.

Naumberg's first book was published in 1947; it describes the application of psychoanalytical principles to the use of art therapy (Detre, 1983). Naumberg is also credited with developing active teaching methods to facilitate artistic expression, i.e., the scribble technique and rhythmic exercises to enhance creativity and guide imagination.

Naumberg studied and worked with Maria Montessori and was partly influenced by the European painters, Matisse, Braque, and Picasso. The influences of Freud and Jung enabled her to apply the principles of psychology and psychiatry to art work; this led to the interpretation of drawings. This technique was then put to use in treating people with emotional problems.

There are two approaches to art therapy. The psychoanalytical approach, which was developed by Naumberg, uses art work to symbolize the unconscious. However, in 1958 Edith Kramer began using art therapy as a way of helping individuals to express current life experiences and to solve life problems (Dalley, 1984). Tukianen (1980) divided art therapy into three separate modalities. These are the supportive, active, and psychoanalytical elements. The supportive modality is aimed at social rehabilitation; the active form concentrates on ego development; and the analytical form uses patients' drawings as a diagnostic tool. All patients who participate in art therapy are required to draw. It is claimed that these techniques are useful in preventing suicide and in diagnosing depression and schizophrenia in adults.

Art therapy has also been used in special education. Art therapy has been helpful in treating children with learning disabilities (Mullin, 1974) as well as children who are mentally retarded. Mullin found that children who are mentally limited or too depressed to make even simple drawings can use pictures from magazines to stimulate their thought processes. Children are encouraged to communicate to one another through art work, which has been found to be helpful in reducing emotional stress. Salant (1974) used art therapy with preschool children to help them with their problems. The art therapist, a teacher, and a parent work together in helping children develop through their art work. Art therapy is based on the idea that man's most fundamental thoughts and feelings can be transferred from the unconscious into images rather than words (Dalley, 1984).

The work pioneered by Naumberg is now being used in schools, hospitals, and institutions. Art therapists must have advanced training (Rubin, 1984) and practical experience with supervision, working directly with patients from early childhood through adulthood.

## REFERENCES

Dalley, T. (1984). *Art as therapy. The introduction to the use of art as a therapeutic technique.* London: Tavistock.

Detre, K. C. (1983). Roots of art therapy. *American Journal of Art Therapy, 22,* 111–123.

Mullin, J. B. (1974). The expressive therapies in special education, *American Journal of Art Therapy, 13,* 54–58.

Naumberg, M. (1917). *A direct method of education* (Bulletin #4). New York: Bureau of Educational Experiments.

Rubin, J. A. (1984). *The art of art therapy.* New York: Brunner/Mazel.

Salant, E. G. (1975). Preventive art therapy with a preschool child. *American Journal of Art Therapy, 14,* 67–70.

Tukianen, K. (1980). Art therapy. *American Journal of Art Therapy, 32,* 300–314.

STEVEN GUMERMAN
*Temple University*

## PSYCHOANALYSIS AND SPECIAL EDUCATION PSYCHOTHERAPY WITH THE HANDICAPPED THERAPEUTIC RECREATION

## ASPHYXIA

Asphyxia is a medical emergency requiring immediate intervention to prevent infant mortality and morbidity (Golden & Peters, 1985). Asphyxia occurs with inadequate oxygenation and cellular perfusion. This article deals specifically with asphyxia that occurs during the time of birth or shortly thereafter. Many terms are associated with oxygen deprivation during this period; pertinent information can be found in different sources under the headings of neonatal asphyxia, asphyxia neonatorium, perinatal asphyxia, intrapartum asphyxia, and hypoxic ischemic encephalopathy (HIE). Asphyxia has been hard to define accurately, which has caused difficulty in research on its effects and prognosis for recovery. The classical definition of asphyxia has been a low Apgar score with more emphasis on the 5- or even 10-minute scores than on the 1-minute (Fitzhardinge & Pape, 1981). As low Apgar scores are not necessarily associated with asphyxia, however, this definition is not always accurate and is a poor predictor for neurological outcome. Predicting outcome is very difficult. Even infants with 0 Apgar scores at birth have survived after efficient intervention with no serious handicaps (Rosen, 1985). Incidence of damage is generally overestimated when compared with actual findings (Brann, 1985). HIE, whose description follows, is predictive of later deficits.

Four basic mechanisms underlie asphyxia during the immediate perinatal period: (1) interruption of umbilical blood flow; (2) failure of placental exchange because of premature separation of the placenta from the uterus; (3) inadequate perfusion or oxygenation of the maternal side of the placenta as in severe hypotension; and (4) infant failure to inflate the lungs and complete transition to extrauterine life. In early stages, asphyxia may reverse spontaneously if the cause is removed, but later stages require varying degrees of medical intervention because of circulatory and neurological changes (Fitzhardinge & Pape, 1981).

Asphyxia is a progressive yet potentially reversible process with severity and duration of the insult affecting later outcome. Severe asphyxia can result in death within 10 minutes without proper intervention (Fitzhardinge & Pape, 1981). Delayed intervention may exacerbate cellular injury in all organ systems, contributing to a poor outcome. The brain is the most vulnerable system and mediates the most pronounced effects on later life. Asphyxia not only affects the brain directly, but also impairs the autoregulation centers controlling cerebral blood flow, which may cause intraventricular hemorrhage with resultant complications (Golden & Peters, 1985). Premature infants appear to be particularly susceptible to this complication.

Cerebral palsy (CP) is the most frequent complication of asphyxia. Even then, risk is high only when the Apgar score is low (<3) for prolonged periods (>10 to 15 minutes) (Freeman, 1985). The incidence of CP may be as high as 38% in infants with Apgar scores of 0 to 3 at 20 minutes, and often occurs in conjunction with mental retardation and seizures. Asphyxia does not seem to be associated with severe mental retardation in the absence of CP (Paneth & Stark, 1983).

HIE may result from severe asphyxia. Children diagnosed with HIE show signs of neurologic dysfunction within 1 week, and often within 12 hours, after birth. The major signs of dysfunction include seizures, altered states of consciousness, and abnormalities in tone, posture, reflexes, and respiration. Infants who exhibit seizures have a 30 to 75% likelihood of long-term sequelae. Mortality is high among infants who had definite neurologic abnormality at discharge. Full-term infants with a history of asphyxia and an abnormal neurologic exam during the first week of life show a 7% incidence of early death and a 28% incidence of neurological handicaps. The most common deficits seen in severely affected children include spastic quadriplegia (a form of CP), severe mental retardation, seizures, hearing deficits, and microcephaly. Treatment for HIE is improving but research is difficult. Identification of infants at risk for neurological handicaps is becoming increasingly important as early intervention techniques improve (Brann, 1985).

Overall, the majority of asphyxiated infants suffer no detectable neurologic or intellectual sequelae. Prognosis is good even in relatively serious cases if neurologic examination is normal by 1 week of age. As would be expected, prognosis is poor when the asphyxia is long and severe or subsequent abnormal clinical features appear (Paneth & Stark, 1983). Much about asphyxia and its sequelae is still not well understood. However, adequate prenatal care, careful monitoring during labor and delivery with prompt obstetrical intervention, and immediate intervention after delivery by professionals skilled in resuscitation all contribute to lowering the incidence of asphyxia and lessening its long-term effects (Phibbs, 1981).

### REFERENCES

Brann, A., Jr. (1985). Factors during neonatal life that influence brain disorders. In J. Freeman (Ed.), *Prenatal and perinatal factors associated with brain disorders* (NIH Pub #85-1149, pp. 263–358). Bethesda, MD: National Institutes of Health.

Fitzhardinge, P. M., & Pape, K. E. (1981). Follow-up studies of the high risk newborn. In G. Avery (Ed.), *Neonatalogy: Pathophysiology and management of the newborn* (2nd. ed., pp. 350–367). Philadelphia: Lippincott.

Freeman, J. (1985). Summary. In J. Freeman (Ed.), *Prenatal and perinatal factors associated with brain disorders* (NIH Pub #85-1149, pp. 13–32). Bethesda, MD: National Institutes of Health.

Golden, S., & Peters, D. (1985). Delivery room care. In G. Merenstein & S. Gardner (Eds.), *Handbook of neonatal intensive care* (pp. 31–54). St. Louis: Mosby.

Paneth, N., & Stark, R. I. (1983). Cerebral palsy and mental retardation in relation to indicators of perinatal asphyxia. *American Journal of Obstetrics & Gynecology, 146,* 960–966.

Phibbs, R. H. (1981). Delivery room management of the newborn. In G. Avery (Ed.), *Neonatalogy: Pathophysiology and management of the newborn* (2nd ed., pp. 350–367). Philadelphia: Lippincott.

Rosen, M. G. (1985). Factors during labor and delivery that influence brain disorders. In J. Freeman (Ed.), *Prenatal and perinatal factors associated with brain disorders* (NIH Pub #85-1149, pp. 13–32). Bethesda, MD: National Institutes of Health.

BRENDA M. POPE
*New Hanover Memorial
Hospital, Wilmington,
North Carolina*

APGAR RATING SCALE
CEREBRAL PALSY
LOW BIRTH WEIGHT INFANTS
PREMATURITY/PRETERM

## ASSESSMENT

The need for assessment of students' abilities was recognized long before Congress passed the Education of All Handicapped Children Act, PL 94-142. Thomas Jefferson saw the virtues of identifying gifted students and allotting financial aid to those who needed it in order to ensure that these students further their education (Cronbach, 1984). While the need for special services for exceptional children has been long recognized, little was done on a uniform basis in the United States until the passing of PL 94-142.

An important question should be asked: Why assess? Taylor (1984) answers this query by considering the stages assessment should take and explaining why. The first stage of assessment is to screen and identify those students with potential problems. This stage may be formal, as with group testing, or informal, as when conducting behavioral observations. The next reason for assessment is to determine and evaluate the appropriate teaching programs and strategies for a particular student. At this point it is possible to implement strategies in the classroom before making a formal referral. This stage also allows for information about previously successful strategies to be incorporated into teaching programs.

The third stage involves determining the current level of functioning and the educational needs of the student. Possible strategies for remediation and the student's strengths and weaknesses should be identified at this point. In the next stage, assessment is used to make decisions about placement within special education and student classification; i.e., what would be the least restrictive environment for the student? The last step is to develop individual educational programs (IEP) for the student using the information obtained in the assessment process.

This is not to imply that all students with educational problems must go through all of these stages of assessment. If a problem can be remediated within the regular classroom, then it is pointless to continue assessment. Evaluations should be done completely and carefully to ascertain exactly what the student needs and how to meet those needs in the best possible way.

A number of important historical events played a part in determining how the special needs of exceptional children are currently evaluated. These events have been outlined in a number of sources (Cronbach, 1984; Graham & Lily, 1984; Nitko, 1983; Nunnally, 1970; Sattler, 1982; Wisland, 1977). Several significant milestones are summarized here.

*1837.* A French physician, Sequin, established the first school to educate children who are mentally retarded. He was one of the first to advocate the idea that the mentally retarded could be educated. He also developed the Sequin Form Board, which was later adopted by others for assessing intelligence.

*1856.* The Chicago public schools implemented the use of written exams for promotion of elementary students and for admission to high school.

*1861.* In England, payment by results policy was instituted as arithmetic, reading, and writing tests were used to determine the government's funding of the schools.

*1869*. Francis Galton, considered to be the founder of individual psychology, made the first systematic and statistical investigation of individual differences and mental inheritance. By using subjects of all intellectual levels, including those at the extremes, he showed that psychological traits are normally distributed.

*1890*. James McKeen Cattell helped establish the foundations of mental measurements in the United States. He was also the first person to introduce the term mental test.

*1904*. A two-factor theory of intelligence was introduced by Charles Spearman. His theory maintained that an individual's capacity consists of a general factor of intelligence (g) and other specific factors or special abilities (s).

*1905*. In France, a means of systematically evaluating the needs of individual students within the educational system was needed, as concepts had been unclearly defined causing great variation from school to school. To meet this need, Alfred Binet and Theophile Simon developed the first practically applied, individually administered test of intelligence, the 1905 Binet-Simon scale.

*1908*. The first professionally developed standardized test of educational achievement was introduced by C. W. Stone.

*1912*. William Stern first suggested the concept of a mental quotient determined by the mental age and the chronological age of an individual (MA/CA). This idea of an intelligence quotient was adopted by Binet.

*1914*. The first commercially available standardized achievement test, the Courtis Standardized Research Test in Arithmetic, was published by Lewis Terman.

*1916*. The Stanford Revision of the Binet-Simon Scale of Intelligence was introduced by Lewis Terman.

*1917*. The first commercially available group intelligence test, the Absolute Point Scale, was developed by Arthur Sintor Otis.

*1921*. The Psychological Corporation was founded by L. M. Terman, G. M. Ruch, and T. L. Kelley.

*1936*. E. F. Lindquist designed the Iowa Every Pupil Test of Basic Skills, which was later renamed the Iowa Test of Basic Skills.

*1938*. The Bender Visual Motor Gestalt Test was introduced. It was purported to measure perceptual-motor abilities as well as psychological and personality components.

*1939*. David Wechsler introduced a new individually administered test of intelligence, the Wechsler-Bellevue Intelligence Scale.

*1963*. The theory of fluid intelligence, which is of a physiological base, and crystallized intelligence, which is influenced by educational factors, was proposed by Raymond B. Cattell.

*1969*. Arthur R. Jensen began publication of his controversial articles on the heritability of intelligence.

*1975*. Congress passed PL 94-142, the Education of All Handicapped Children Act, imposing guidelines and criteria that must be met by the educational systems to service all eligible students.

Test publishing has become a flourishing and lucrative industry since World War I. With this growth has come some substantial advantages, the most significant of these being the increased emphasis on test standardization and the provision of norms for purposes of comparison of individuals with the populations within which they exist. This has been pervasive in all areas of assessment used with exceptional children in the education system.

Consideration of more than just a student's intellectual capacity has also become prevalent as other aspects of the individual and his or her capabilities are assessed in conjunction with this area. Other areas that are relevant to evaluation for special education are the student's current level of academic functioning, the level of adaptive behavior, and, in some cases, the evaluation of personality and behavioral factors. All of these areas play an integral part in the assessment of exceptional students.

Intellectual assessment has played a key role since the beginning of interest in special children. There have been many changes within the intellectual assessment field as well. With the growth of the test publishing industry, instruments used to assess intelligence have increased in number. Along with this increase have come changes in the content of the instruments as well as the way the concept of intelligence has been defined. While the Binet-Simon Intelligence Scale purported to measure an overall concept of intelligence, later instruments attempted to further refine this construct. Witness, for example, the subscores of the Wechsler scales, which give not only a full-scale score but also verbal and performance scores. The McCarthy Scales of Children's Abilities yield not only a general cognitive index but also information about a student's abilities in verbal, perceptual-performance, quantitative, memory, and motor development areas. More recently, the Kaufman Assessment Battery for Children has drawn from past research to develop an instrument that yields not only a global mental processing composite score but also scores pertaining to the processing of information presented sequentially and simultaneously. With these changes has come the advancement of not only how the concept of intelligence is evaluated, but also how intelligence test results relate to intervention in special education.

Tests of educational achievement are also an important aspect of the evaluation of the special education needs of children. There are numerous tests that have been developed to assess a child's level of academic functioning compared with other students of the same age or grade. The content of such measures is usually related to actual academic curricula. There are instruments available that assess many academic areas within one test, while others merely concentrate on one specific area. The number of available instruments of these various types is multitudinous and they have been compiled in various tests elsewhere (Compton, 1984). The relevance of such tests when assessing the needs of exceptional children is evident. Information gained from such measures can lead to more effective educational planning for individual students. These instruments allow for the careful scrutinization of students' strengths and weaknesses in academic areas to establish those who are in need of remediation.

Adaptive behavior may also be an integral part of the assessment of exceptional students. It is essential that this area be assessed for the classification of the mentally retarded as the American Association on Mental Deficiency (AAMD) defines mental retardation as not only low intellectual functioning but also subaverage functioning in adaptive behavior (Sattler, 1982). Other educational classifications such as emotionally disturbed and behavior disordered also make it necessary to evaluate this area of functioning. As with intelligence and achievement, there are a number of instruments available to use to assess adaptive behavior levels. Some examples are the AAMD Adaptive Behavior Scales and the Vineland Adaptive Behavior Scales. These allow specific behavior deficits or strengths to be evaluated; such information is imperative for designing proper behavior management or training programs within educational settings.

The evaluation of personality and emotional disorders also has benefited from the growth of the test publishing industry. While such tests play a role in the educational system, it is to a much lesser extent than those previously mentioned. The relevance of using such measures depends on the type of problem a particular student has. This type of instrument is most likely to be used in evaluating those students who may be classified as emotionally disturbed. While the other areas (intelligence, adaptive behavior, and academic achievement) are more likely to be assessed using instruments that are objective in nature, this is not necessarily true of personality instruments. It is acceptable to use those that are more subjective such as the Children's Apperception Test, as well as those that purport to be more objective such as the Personality Inventory for Children. Either of these types, or a combination of the two, may yield useful information about a student and his or her problems. This information may then be used to determine the type of educational environment most suitable for the student.

All of these types of assessments are an important part of special education evaluation. They can all give useful information about the students and their specific needs within the educational setting.

## REFERENCES

Compton, C. (1984). *A guide to 75 tests for special education* Belmont, CA: Lake.

Cronbach, L. J. (1984). *Essentials of psychological testing* (4th ed.). New York: Harper & Row.

Graham, J. R., & Lily, R. S. (1984). *Psychological testing*. Englewood Cliffs, NJ: Prentice-Hall.

Nitk, A. J. (1983). *Educational tests and measurement: An introduction*. New York: Harcourt Brace Jovanovich.

Nunnally, J. C., Jr. (1970). *Introduction to psychological measurement*. New York: McGraw-Hill.

Sattler, J. M. (1982). *Assessment of children's intelligence special abilities* (2nd ed.). Boston: Allyn & Bacon.

Taylor, R. L. (1984). *Assessment of exceptional students: educational and psychological procedures*. Englewood Cliffs, NJ: Prentice-Hall.

Wisland, M. V. (1977). *Psychological diagnosis of exceptional children* (2nd ed.). Springfield, IL: Thomas.

CAROL S. SCHMITT
*Eastern Kentucky University*

**ACHIEVEMENT TESTS**
**"g" FACTOR THEORY**
**INTELLIGENCE TESTING**
**KAUFMAN ASSESSMENT BATTERY FOR CHILDREN**
**WECHSLER ADULT INTELLIGENCE SCALE-REVISED**
**WECHSLER INTELLIGENCE SCALE FOR CHILDREN-REVISED**

## ASSESSMENT, CURRICULUM BASED

See CURRICULUM-BASED ASSESSMENT.

## ASSIMILATION

Assimilation is one of two complementary processes of adaptation to the environment in Jean Piaget's theory of intellectual development; its counterpart is accommodation. Assimilation involves incorporating external elements (objects or events) into existing cognitive or sensorimotor schemes; incoming information is interpreted or adjusted in a manner consistent with current cognitive structures.

In contrast, accommodation involves changing the structures that assimilate information (Brainerd, 1978).

The distinction between assimilation and accommodation can be illustrated by a physiological example: digestion of food (Ginsburg & Opper, 1969). Acids (or the body's current schemes or structures) transform the food into a form that can be used; thus elements of the external world are assimilated. Accommodation occurs in this example when, in order to deal with a foreign substance, stomach muscles contract, acids are released by certain organs, etc. Physical structures (the stomach and other organs) accommodate to an external element (food).

Assimilation involves both constraints on the nature and range of a child's interactions with the environment and the seeking out of new stimuli that can be assimilated into existing schemes (Gelman & Baillargeon, 1983). Piaget discusses three forms of assimilation: functional assimilation; which involves a basic tendency to use an existing structure such as a sucking reflex; recognitory assimilation, which involves recognizing particular situations in which the scheme should be applied; and generalizing assimilation, which involves a tendency to generalize a scheme to new objects and situations (Ginsburg & Opper, 1969).

## REFERENCES

Brainerd, C. J. (1978). *Piaget's theory of intelligence.* Englewood Cliffs, NJ: Prentice-Hall.

Gelman, R., & Baillargeon, R. (1983). A review of some Piagetian concepts. In P. H. Mussen (Ed.), *Handbook of child psychology: Vol. III. Cognitive development* (pp. 167–230). New York: Wiley.

Ginsburg, H., & Opper, S. (1969). *Piaget's theory of intellectual development: An introduction.* Englewood Cliffs, NJ: Prentice-Hall.

LINDA J. STEVENS
*University of Minnesota*

ACCOMMODATION
PIAGET, JEAN

# ASSISTIVE DEVICES

The term assistive device has been applied to a wide range of highly specialized mechanical, electronic, and computer-based consumer tools that are now commonly used in rehabilitation and special education settings. The assistive device is typically designed to perform a particular prosthetic or orthotic function, but it is not a prosthesis or an orthosis in the traditional medical sense (Webster, Cook, Tompkins, & Vanderheiden, 1985). For example, an artificial arm that is operated by electric impulses generated by the user's nervous system (a myoelectric prosthesis) is not considered an assistive device in the same sense that a robotic arm is. The arm is completely separate from the user's body and can be operated by a number of alternative control mechanisms. While it may be configured or applied with a specific individual's needs in mind, it is essentially modular and noncustomized in nature. The myoelectric arm must be carefully designed and fitted to the individual using it (Caldwell, Buck, Lovely, & Scott, 1985; Apostolos, 1985).

Sensory aids such as hearing aids and tools for vision-impaired individuals are often considered assistive devices as well. In function, these are closer to the generally applied robotic arm than to the individually designed and fitted myoelectric arm.

The gray area of technological application between individualized medical uses and "off-the-shelf" technologies for rehabilitation and special education is the domain of communication aids, computer access devices, and aids to daily living that fall in neither category and share the functional categorization of assistive devices. The term was most likely coined by the Assistive Device Center of California State University in 1978 and has been imitated in recent years by similarly focused efforts internationally (MacDonald & Baillie, 1984; Coleman, Cook, & Meyers, 1982).

A communication aid is used with a person having limited or total inability to speak, usually from lack of motor control. This condition may be a result of congenital anomaly, accident, or a temporary condition.

Speechlessness may or may not be accompanied by cognitive language impairment; frequently nonspeaking students are multiply handicapped. Such students have needs in two of three areas: speech, mobility, and self-care. There is no typical candidate for a communication aid. The student may have cerebral palsy, mental retardation, or any of a number of disabilities that severely limit conversation, writing, and interaction with instructional or vocational materials. The communication device serves a prosthetic function, replacing natural speech, writing, and drawing with output in the form of audible speech (synthetic or recorded), written text, or graphics (Randal, 1983).

The terms nonvocal or nonverbal have been used to describe the student requiring an augmentative speech device. Such terms are not satisfactory because the student may have vocalizations, some intelligible speech that is functional, and even intact verbal skills including reading and writing. The term allolingual has been suggested by Baker (1982), but it has not found widespread acceptance. The most acceptable current term to describe students having no functional speech and those using augmentative communication systems is nonspeaking. Augmentative communication systems may incorporate any existing speech as one mode of communication.

The multiply physically handicapped student requires access not only to speaking and writing, but also to devices in the environment: appliances, lights, doors, alarm systems, telephones, and transportation systems. In this area, assistive devices provide control of such necessary implements through the same mechanism or control interface that the individual may use to obtain control of his or her communication aid. For example, a recent research and development project paired rehabilitation engineers with a communication aid manufacturer to provide wheelchair control to a severely handicapped student with cerebral palsy. The student used a head-operated photo sensitive device to point to linguistic units on a communication aid and to control her wheelchair (Trefler, Romich & Russel, 1985).

The third area of assistive device application is in providing access to the large body of educational materials and vocational opportunities afforded by the computer. Many assistive devices, from simple mechanical keyguards to sophisticated high-technology devices such as keyboard emulators and infared data transmitters, have been designed solely for this purpose and are now readily available.

## REFERENCES

Apostolos, M. K. (1985). An application of aesthetics in the use of a robotic arm. *Proceedings of the Eighth Annual Conference on Rehabilitation Technology*. Memphis, TN: Rehabilitation Engineering Society of North America.

Baker, B. (1982). Is a rose a rose? *Communication Outlook, 4*(2), 3–18.

Caldwell, R. R., Buck, C. S., Lovely, D. F., & Scott, R. N. (1985). A myoelectric b/e prosthesis system for young children. *Proceedings of the Eighth Annual Conference on Rehabilitation Technology*. Memphis, TN: Rehabilitation Engineering Society of North America.

Coleman, C. L., Cook, A. M., & Meyers, L. (1982). *Final report: D.O.E. grant numbers 6007902261, field-initiated research project-enhancing the educational potential of non-oral children through matching communication device capabilities to children's needs*. Sacramento, CA: Assistive Device Center, California State University.

MacDonald, B. J., & Baillie, E. (1984). *Abstracts: Third international conference on augmentative and alternative communication*. Boston: Massachusetts Institute of Technology.

Randal, J. (1983). *Health technology case study 26: Assistive devices for severe speech impairments*. Washington, DC: U.S. Congress, Office of Technology Assessment, OTA-HCS-26.

Trefler, E., Romich, B., & Russel, N. (1985). Modular technology for the severely physically disabled—the Lainey system. *Proceedings of the Eighth Annual Conference on Rehabilitation Technology*. Memphis, TN: Rehabilitation Engineering Society of North America.

Webster, J. G., Cook, A. M., Tompkins, W. J., & Vanderheiden, G. C. (1985). *Electronic devices for rehabilitation*. New York: Wiley.

MARY BRADY
*Pennsylvania Special Education
Assistive Device Center,
Elizabethtown, Pennsylvania*

AUGMENTATIVE COMMUNICATION SYSTEMS
COMMUNICATION BOARDS
ELECTRONIC COMMUNICATION AIDS

## ASSOCIATION FOR CHILDHOOD EDUCATION INTERNATIONAL (ACEI)

Founded in 1931, the Association for Childhood Education International's membership includes teachers, parents, and other individuals concerned with improving educational practices for children from infancy through early adolescence. Members participate in local and state group activities, including meetings, workshops, and regional conferences. The association organizes an annual conference and travel/study tours abroad. The membership promotes the rights, education, and well-being of all children in the home, school, and community. Improved standards for teacher preparation and others involved with the care and development of children are among the association's goals. Professional growth of educators and active cooperation of all agencies and individuals concerned with children provide another focus for activities. Public information regarding the needs and rights of children is disseminated in order to stimulate community awareness. The association provides information services for members, individuals, other organizations, and government agencies. A library is maintained at association headquarters. The collection includes volumes on childhood and elementary education. Association offices are located at 11141 Georgia Avenue, Suite 200, Wheaton, MD 20902.

PHILIP R. JONES
*Virginia Polytechnic Institute
and State University*

## ASSOCIATION FOR CHILDREN AND ADULTS WITH LEARNING DISABILITIES (ACLD)

The Association for Children and Adults with Learning Disabilities (ACLD) was organized as a nonprofit organization in 1964 by parents of children with learning disabilities. The name of the organization as adopted initially (Association for Children with Learning Disabilities) was proposed by Samuel Kirk. The purpose of the organization is to advance the education and general welfare of children and adults of normal or potentially normal intelligence who have learning disabilities of a perceptual, conceptual, or coordinative nature, or related problems (Article I, Section 2(a), ACLD Bylaws). The ACLD has affiliates in all 50 states, the District of Columbia, and West Germany. The ACLD membership, including more than 800 local chapters, consists of over 60,000 parents, professionals from various disciplines, learning-disabled adults, and other interested persons.

The ACLD national office is located at 4156 Library Road, Pittsburgh, PA 15234. This office provides information and referral services and has a resource center of publications and films. The ACLD and its state affiliates may work directly with school systems in planning and implementing early identification programs and improved regular and special education. The ACLD holds annual international and state conferences. The official ACLD newsletter, *Newsbriefs*, is published five times annually.

SHIRLEY A. JONES
*Virginia Polytechnic Institute
and State University*

## ASSOCIATION FOR PERSONS WITH SEVERE HANDICAPS, (TASH)

Formerly the American Association for the Education of the Severely/Profoundly Handicapped (AAESPH) the Association for Persons with Severe Handicaps (TASH) has as its primary objective to assist in creating, disseminating, and implementing programs useful for the education and independent lifestyles of persons who are severely handicapped. Formed in 1975 as a membership-supported nonprofit organization, TASH addresses issues relevant from birth through adulthood. Current membership includes professionals, paraprofessionals, parents, and medical and legal personnel. Chartered chapters existed in 18 states and 1 province during 1985, with additional chapters developing in the United States and Canada.

The Association publishes a monthly newsletter and quarterly journal and convenes an annual meeting in early December. Other publications and bibliographies covering such topics as vocational training, behavior modification, curricula, working with families, and parenting are disseminated to members and interested groups. The association endeavors to promote public policy, legislation, and appropriations benefiting severely handicapped youths and adults. The Association also works with the media concerning the presentation and portrayal of persons with disabilities. The offices of TASH are located at 7010 Roosevelt Way, NE, Seattle, WA 98115.

PHILIP R. JONES
*Virginia Polytechnic Institute
and State University*

## ASSOCIATION FOR SPECIAL EDUCATION TECHNOLOGY (ASET)

The growth of technology has been geometric in the past two decades and the use of technology has become per-vasive throughout special education. Largely in response to the explosion of technology, the Association for Special Education Technology (ASET) was formed in 1973. The ASET is intended to stimulate the development of new technologies for special education, to foster cooperation among special educators and educational technologists, and to assist in the dissemination of information concerning applications of new technologies to special education problems. In 1978 ASET founded the *Journal of Special Education Technology* as the official ASET journal; its purpose is the dissemination of information concerning technology in special education. Information regarding ASET and its journal may be obtained from ASET, UMC 68, Utah State University, Logan, Utah 84322.

CECIL R. REYNOLDS
*Texas A&M University*

## ASSOCIATION FOR THE ADVANCEMENT OF BEHAVIOR THERAPY (AABT)

In 1966 the Association for Advancement of the Behavioral Therapies was founded. In 1968 it was renamed the Association for Advancement of Behavior Therapy (AABT). The AABT is headquartered in New York City. It consists of 3300 members divided into 20 foreign and state groups. Membership is predominantly held by psychiatrists and psychologists, although 5% of its members include dentists, social workers, medical engineers, physiotherapists, and other professionals interested in the problems, issues, and development of the area of behavior modification with an emphasis on clinical applications.

Among its activities, the AABT sponsors training programs and lectures aimed at professionals and semiprofessionals, contacts behavior therapists for referrals, provides communication accessibility among behavior therapists interested in similar areas of research or specific problems, and maintains a speaker's bureau. Affiliates of AABT conduct training meetings, workshops, seminars, case demonstrations, and discussion groups. The AABT holds committees on continuing and public education.

The AABT publications include a mini-journal entitled *The Behavior Therapist* (published 10 times per year), *Behavior Therapy* (5 per year), *The Behavioral Assessment Journal* (quarterly), the *Membership Directory* (biennial), and the *AVU Directory* and *Training Directory*. Further, the AABT bestows the annual President's New Researcher Award. The annual convention is held in November.

MARY LEON PEERY
*Texas A&M University*

## ASSOCIATION FOR THE GIFTED

Founded in 1958, the Association for the Gifted is one of the 13 divisions of the Council for Exceptional Children. As of October, 1985, membership exceeded 2000. The five goals of this organization are (1) to promote an understanding about gifted and talented students and their educational needs among educators, parents, and the lay public; (2) to communicate information about the latest issues and trends in the field of gifted education; (3) to advocate policies that promote supportive legislation and funding for the gifted and talented at the federal, state, and local levels; (4) to disseminate information on education of the gifted to all interested parties; and (5) to expand the existing knowledge base about gifted students and their needs.

This association distributes two publications to its membership. One, *The Journal for the Education of the Gifted*, is a forum for theoretical, descriptive, and research articles that analyze and communicate knowledge about the gifted and talented. The second publication, *TAG-UPDATE*, is the association's newsletter.

Membership inquiries should be made to the Association for the Gifted, 1920 Association Drive, Reston, VA 22091. Members of The Association for the Gifted are required to join the Council for Exceptional Children. A special student category of membership is available for those who qualify for this discounted membership fee.

MARY K. TALLENT
*Texas Tech University*

## ASSOCIATION OF BLACK PSYCHOLOGISTS

The Association of Black Psychologists (ABPsi) was founded in San Francisco in 1968 when a number of black psychologists across the country united to broach the serious problems facing black psychologists and the larger black community. The founding members set about building an organization through which they could confront the long-neglected needs of black professionals. They also hoped to have a positive impact on the mental health of the black community through programs, services, training, and advocacy. From the original group, the membership of ABPsi had grown to over 600 members in 1985. The members address issues of a psychological nature that have adverse effects on the black community.

The goals of the organization are to:

1. Enhance the psychological well-being of black people in America
2. Promote constructive understanding of black people through positive approaches to research
3. Develop an approach to psychology that is consistent with the experiences of black people
4. Define mental health in consonance with newly established psychological concepts and standards regarding black people
5. Develop internal support systems for black psychologists and students of psychology
6. Develop policies for local, state, and national decision making that have impact on the mental health of the black community
7. Promote values and a lifestyle that supports black survival and well-being
8. Support established black organizations and aid in the development of new independent black institutions to enhance blacks' psychological, educational, cultural, and economic situation.

The main offices of the Association of Black Psychologists can be reached at P.O. Box 2929, Washington, DC 20013.

NADINE M. LAMBERT
*University of California,
Berkeley*

## ASSOCIATIVE LEARNING

Associative learning, as demonstrated in the classical conditioning experiments of Pavlov (1927), is based on the concept that events or ideas that are experienced at the same time tend to become associated with each other. When a new (conditioned) stimulus is presented with an old (unconditioned) stimulus, the conditioned stimulus assumes the capability of eliciting a (conditioned) response almost identical to the original (unconditioned) response. The conditioned stimulus should be presented about half a second before the unconditioned stimulus for maximum effectiveness.

Associative learning is routinely applied when students recognize words, spell, and recall math facts. A number of remedial techniques are also based on the associative principle. Multisensory approaches to reading, which presume the formation of associative bonds across sensory modalities, have been successful in remediating deficits in mildly and severely reading-disabled children and in retarded students (Sutaria, 1982). Visual imagery training, in which children learn to associate mental pictures with printed text, has been shown to improve learning-disabled students' reading comprehension (Clark, Warner, Alley, Deshler & Shumaker, 1981).

Retarded children, for whom associative skills are often an area of relative strength, have improved their memory performance when taught to pair words according to their conceptual similarity (Lathey & Tobias, 1981). Associative learning is a fundamental principle of teaching, and children's associative learning skills can be corrected and compensated for by using a variety of techniques.

## REFERENCES

Clark, F., Warner, M., Alley, G., Deshler, D., Shumaker, J., Vetter, A., & Nolan, R. (1981). *Visual imagery and self questioning*. Washington, DC: Bureau of Education for the Handicapped (ERIC Document Reproduction Service No. ED 217 655).

Lathey, J. W., & Tobias, S. (1981, April). *Associative and conceptual training of retarded and normal children*. Paper presented at the annual meeting of the American Educational Research Association, Los Angeles (ERIC Document Reproduction Service No. ED 206 139).

Pavlov, I. P. (1927). *Conditioned reflexes*. London: Oxford University Press.

Sutaria, S. (1982). *Multisensory approach to teaching of reading to learning disabled students*. Paper presented at the annual meeting of the World Congress on Reading, Dublin, Ireland (ERIC Document Reproduction Service No. ED 246 600).

GARY BERKOWITZ
*Temple University*

# CONDITIONING
# REVISUALIZATION

# ASTHMA

Asthma is one of the most common lung diseases of childhood. It is a difficulty in breathing caused by obstruction to the flow of air in the bronchial tubes because of swelling of the lining membranes, contraction of the surrounding musculature, and plugging of the tubes by mucus. This is inevitably accompanied by wheezing. Other symptoms are sometimes present such as a persistent cough and shortness of breath. The distress of asthma attacks is sometimes worsened by simple activities like laughing or lying down (Asthma and Allergy Foundation of America, 1980).

Asthma affects about 2 million children under 17 and as many as 4 to 7% of children in the United States may at some time suffer from asthma (Evans, 1981). It accounts for 20 to 25% of school absences owing to chronic diseases. Asthma may appear at any age but it generally appears in the first 20 years of life. The frequency of onset diminishes rapidly after 40 years. In children there is an estimated ratio of 2:1 for boys over girls, but as asthmatics mature and approach adulthood, the sex ratio becomes essentially equal. There is little doubt that some asthma has a genetic basis but such is difficult to prove in a given case. Some symptoms diminish systematically with age. This is referred to as "growing out of asthma." The reason

for this more or less spontaneous cure is not understood, but one should not consider it a total cure, since the symptoms may reappear later. Asthmatic patients may have at least minimal airway obstruction throughout their lives.

Asthma can be precipitated by a variety of triggers such as environmental pollution, exercise (especially when breathing cold air), viral infections, aspirin and related substances, emotional factors and allergens (the most common being pollen), animals or feathers, molds and fungus, insects, occupational dust, chemicals, house dust, and foods. To confirm the diagnosis of asthma, three steps can be followed: (1) provoke bronchio constriction by having the patient inhale stimuli thought to produce smooth muscle hyperactivity; (2) give bronchodilations to check on the reversibility of the attack; and (3) establish the chronicity and intermittency of attacks (Greer, Harm, & Marion, 1983).

Asthma can be classified on a continuum, with intrinsic or perennial asthma (a type of asthma that presents symptoms all year round) at one end and extrinsic or seasonal asthma (which tends to be aggravated during certain seasons, especially the fall) at the other (Greer, Marion, & Harm, 1985). Treatment for asthma must be continuously evaluated because of its variability. Medical treatment falls into two categories: the first is immunotherapy, which is the process of desensitizing the child's allergies by injecting the child with progressively increasing amounts of the allergen. Effectiveness of this treatment is limited by compliance to the administration of allergen shots. The second category is pharmacologic therapy. The most common drug prescribed is theophyllene, which is a bronchodilator that reduces the frequency and the severity of attacks. If this or other medication fails to control the attacks, then corticosteroids are used, but, because of their serious side effects, they should not be used unless all other forms of treatment fail.

Psychological factors are usually not sufficient by themselves to cause asthma. For this and other reasons psychotherapy is not used as a way to control the disease. It has, however, proven effective with psychological problems resulting from the disorder. Broncho constriction in asthmatic patients can result in anxiety in both patients and their parents. Relaxation techniques, biofeedback, and systematic desensitization have also proven effective in managing some cases. Parentectomy (Kapotes, 1977), the removal of patients from the home environment that appears to trigger the attack, is sometimes recommended. Recently, a number of comprehensive self-management programs for asthma have been developed. These are designed to provide patients with the skills to assume responsibility for controlling the affliction. Such programs as the *Living with Asthma* project (Greer, Backial, & Leung, 1984; Greer, Allman, & Leung, 1984; Greer, et al., 1984) evolved from the treatment and rehabilitation program established at CARIH. Patients are provided with information about the mechanics of breathing, the changes that occur during attacks, triggers of attacks, and the medication to control them. When an asthmatic knows his or her condition is due to allergies, then an effective way to control attacks is to avoid the allergens that he or she is sensitive to (Flod, Franz, & Yalant, 1976).

Asthmatic children in educational settings face the problem that teachers may be unfamiliar with the condition and frightened by attacks. It is very important that teachers have meetings with the parents, the child, and the physician to learn about the child's condition and to become familiar with procedures to be followed in case of an attack. Physical education teachers can usually respect a child's knowledge of his or her condition even though exercise can trigger attacks. Preexercise medication can sometimes be useful in preventing attacks. School absenteeism could be reduced by realizing that, through medication, attacks can be controlled. If asthma is under control, a child should be capable of participating in all educational activities.

## REFERENCES

American Lung Association. (1981). There are solutions for the student with asthma. *American Lung Association Publication Item 0083.*

Asthma and Allergy Foundation of America. (1980). Handbook for the asthmatic. *Asthma and Allergy Foundation of America Publication.*

Evans, H. E. (1981). What happens when a child has asthma. *American Lung Association Publication.*

Flod, N. E., Franz, M. L., & Yalant, S. P. (1976). Recent advances in bronchial asthma. *American Journal of Diseases of Children, 130,* 890–899.

Greer, T. L., Backiel, M., & Leung, P. (1984). *Living with asthma: Manual for teaching self-management skills to children.* Washington, DC: U.S. Department of Health and Human Services.

Greer, T. L., Marion, R. J., & Harm, D. L. (1985). Childhood asthma. In V. B. Hasselt, P. S. Strain, & M. Henson (Eds.), *Handbook of developmental and physical disabilities.* New York: Pergamon.

Greer, T. L., Ullman, S., & Leung, P. (1984). *Living with asthma: Manual for teaching adults the self-management of childhood asthma.* Washington, DC: U.S. Department of Health and Human Services.

Kapotes, C. (1977). Emotional factors in chronic asthma. *Journal of Asthma Research, 15,* 5–14.

ANA YERALDINA BENEKE
LOGAN WRIGHT
*University of Oklahoma*

## ALLERGIC DISORDERS
## BIOFEEDBACK

## ASTIGMATISM

Astigmatism is a refractive error that causes reduced visual acuity and a lack of sharply focused, clear vision. In astigmatism, the curve of the cornea is irregular. Because of this irregularity, some light rays may come to focus in front of the retina, some on the retina, and some at the theoretical point behind it. The result is distorted or blurred vision and headache or eye fatigue after intensive close work (Barraga, 1983).

Astigmatism does not seem to be clearly related to difficulties in learning to read. In some cases it has even been associated with better than average reading (Lerner, 1985). The special educator should be aware of the symptoms of astigmatism (Rouse & Ryan, 1984): headaches; discomfort in tasks that demand visual interpretation; problems seeing far as well as near; red eyes; distortion in size, shape, or inclination of objects; frowning and squinting at desk tasks; and nausea in younger or lower-functioning students. Astigmatism is generally correctable with eyeglasses or contact lenses, which should be worn full-time by affected students. These students may be helped in the classroom by being moved closer to the front of the room and by a reduction in the amount of time spent on near tasks.

## REFERENCES

Barraga, N. (1983). *Visual handicaps and learning* (revised ed.). Austin, TX: Exceptional Resources.

Lerner, J. (1985). *Learning disabilities: Theories, diagnoses, and teaching strategies.* Boston: Houghton Mifflin.

Rouse, M. W., & Ryan, J. B. (1984). Teacher's guide to vision problems. *Reading Teacher, 38*(3), 306–317.

ANNE M. BAUER
*University of Cincinnati*

## VISUAL ACUITY
## VISUAL TRAINING

## ASYMMETRICAL TONIC NECK REFLEX (ATNR)

Asymmetrical tonic neck reflex (ATNR) is one of a group of postural central nervous system reflexes that in the normal child is inhibited and incorporated into more sophisticated motor skills. The ATNR can be demonstrated easily in normal infants to about 40 weeks by placing the child on the back and turning the head to the left or right. As the face is turned to the left, the left arm extends and the right arm flexes, bringing the right hand flexed to the skull side of the head simultaneous with flexion of the leg on that and the opposite side. In the normal child with no pathology, this reflex is gradually inhibited; thus, children of 24 to 36 months can reach for toys in front of them; look to the side and still bring a cracker or spoon to the mouth when the head is in midposition; and cross the midline.

Later on, the child can sustain weight on the arms and knees, and rotation of the head will not result in collapse or support on the skull side arm.

The child who has central nervous system damage above the level of the midbrain (usually considered to be in the basal ganglia, cerebral cortex, or both) will demonstrate a persistent ATNR well beyond the age of 1 year, with accompanying profound damage into adult life. The child with severe ATNR finds self-feeding impossible. Persistence of ATNR can interfere with sitting and standing balance and dressing and writing, and make voluntary motion difficult or impossible.

Some help can be provided to children with delayed inhibition of ATNR by positioning and adaptive motor responses in physical and occupational therapy. Proper classroom seating can help moderately to severely involved children learn to diminish uninhibited reflexive responses when they are relaxed and listening. Excitement, anxiety, and stress may override the child's ability to inhibit the reflexive movement, making controlled, purposeful movement difficult or impossible for the more severely involved young adult with persistent uninhibited ATNR.

## REFERENCES

Ayers, A. J. (1979). *Sensory integration and the child.* Los Angeles: Western Psychological Services.

Banus, B. S., Kent, C., Norton, Y., Sudiennick, D., & Becker, M. (1979). *The developmental therapist.* Thorofare, NJ: Slack.

Chusid, J. G. (1978). *Correlative neuroanatomy and functional neurology* (16th ed.). Los Angeles: Lang Medical Publications.

Fiorentino, M. R. (1965). *Reflex testing methods for evaluating central nervous system development.* A monograph in American Lectures in Orthopedic Surgery, Publication Number 543. Springfield, IL: Thomas.

RACHAEL J. STEVENSON
*Bedford, Ohio*

## CENTRAL NERVOUS SYSTEM

## ATARAX

Atarax (hydroxyzine hydrochloride) may be used for symptomatic relief of anxiety and tension associated with psychoneurosis and as an adjunct in organic disease states in which anxiety is manifested. It also may be used as a sedative; the most common manifestation of overdosage is extreme sedation. Other uses include treatment of pruritis owed to allergic conditions such as chronic urticaria and dermatoses. Although not a cortical depressant, its action may be due to suppression of activity in certain key regions of the subcortical area of the central nervous system. Adverse reactions may include dryness of mouth and drowsiness, with the possibility of tremor, involuntary motor activity, and convulsions reported in cases where higher than recommended doses have been used.

A brand name of Roeris Pharmaceuticals, it is available in tablets of 10, 25, 50, and 100 milligrams, and as a syrup. The recommended dosage for children under 6 years of age is 50 mg daily in divided doses, and for children over 6 years of age 50 to 100 mg daily in divided doses. When used as a sedative, dosage is recommended to be 0.6 mg/kg (milligram per kilogram of body weight) at all childhood ages, and 50 to 100 mg for adults.

## REFERENCE

*Physicians' desk reference* (1984) (pp. 1675–1676). Oradell, NJ: Medical Economics.

LAWRENCE C. HARTLAGE
*Evans, Georgia*

## BENADRYL
## DRUG THERAPY

## ATAXIA

Ataxia is a type of cerebral palsy caused by the loss of cerebellar control. It is characterized by an unbalanced gait. An ataxic gait is often referred to as a drunken gait, as it resembles the walk of someone who is intoxicated.

According to Batshaw and Perret (1981), "The cerebellum coordinates the action of the voluntary muscles and times their contractions so that movements are performed smoothly and accurately" (p. 163). That is, the cerebellum senses where the limb is in space (based on input to the cerebellum), estimates where the target is, integrates the information, and then carries out the infinitesimal corrections necessary to compensate for inaccuracies in motor output, thereby maintaining fluid movement.

A child whose primary diagnosis is ataxia has poor righting and equilibrium reactions, and a staggering, lurching, irregular, and broad-based gait (Brown, 1973). According to Connor, Williamson, and Siepp (1978), the child has difficulty sustaining posture, as well as shifting posture in a coordinated manner. He or she often stumbles and falls. This postural instability may make the child overly cautious. The child may stiffen his or her trunk abnormally in order to increase stability. When walking, the child may visually fix on an object in the environment in an effort to maintain postural control. According to Walsch (1963), when an older child attempts purposeful reaching, he or she often overshoots the mark because of the presence of a distal, wavering tremor. Nystagmus is often present.

It is important that physical therapy begin as early as

possible. According to Connor, Williamson, and Siepp (1978), early intervention should concentrate on the development of proximal control and stability. Repetition and reinforcement of movement is necessary so that responses become reliable. Activities that increase tremors or stiffening must be avoided. However, since children with ataxia demonstrate variations in their movement behavior, individual program planning is necessary.

## REFERENCES

Batshaw, M. L., & Perret, Y. M. (1981). *Children with handicaps: a medical primer*. Baltimore, MD: Brookes.

Bobath, B., & Bobath, K. (1976). *Motor development in the different types of cerebral palsy*. London: Heinemann Medical.

Brown, J. E. (1973). Disease of the cerebellum. In A. B. Baker & L. H. Baker (Eds.), *Clinical neurology, Vol. II*. New York: Harper & Row.

Connor, F. P., Williamson, G. G., & Siepp, J. M. (1978). *Program guide for infants and toddlers with neuromotor and other developmental disabilities*. New York: Teachers College Press.

Swaiman, K. F., & Right, F. S. (Eds.) (1982). *The practice of pediatric neurology* (2nd ed.). St. Louis, MO: Mosby.

Walsch, G. (1963). *Cerebellum, posture, and cerebral palsy* (Clinics in Developmental Medicine, No. 8). London: Heinemann Medical Books.

CAROLE REITER GOTHELF
*Hunter College, City University of New York*

**CEREBRAL PALSY**
**CEREBELLAR DISORDERS**

## ATHETOSIS

Athetosis is a central nervous system disorder characterized by slow, writhing movements, most notable in the extremities. These involuntary muscle movements have been described also as wormlike or snakelike. The actual movements consist of alternating flexion–extension and supination–pronation of the limbs, and are usually associated with increased, though variable, muscle tone (Chow, Durard, Feldman, & Mills 1979).

Athetosis is a form of cerebral palsy (CP), accounting for approximately 15 to 30% of children with that diagnosis; however, the overall incidence rate is declining, probably because of improved neonatal intensive care (Batshaw & Perret, 1981). The condition, also known as choreo-athetoid CP, often occurs in conjunction with other forms of CP, especially spasticity. As a form of cerebral palsy, athetosis is one of a group of nonprogressive neuromotor disorders caused by earlier brain damage. Unlike other common forms of CP, the athetoid type presents a problem of controlling movement and posture rather than

a difficulty in initiating voluntary movement. The uncontrolled, purposeless, involuntary movements associated with athetosis are not evidenced during sleep. Although the precise nature of the central nervous system insult is often indeterminable, among known causes may be various prenatal factors (e.g., anoxia, blood group incompatibilities, excessive radiation dosage during gestation, physical injuries, various maternal infections); perinatal factors (e.g., prematurity, head trauma, asphyxia, kernicterus); and postnatal factors (e.g., head trauma, hemorrhage, infections of the brain or cranial linings). In the United States, one to two children per thousand may be affected by CP, including athetosis or mixed cerebral palsy with athetosis. It is believed that in the more pure athetoid type of CP, the site of lesion is generally in the basal ganglia or extrapyramidal track (Vaughan, McKay, & Behrman, 1979).

Secondary problems important to the special educator frequently accompany athetosis. Early difficulties may be observed in sucking, feeding, chewing, and swallowing. Special techniques to deal with these problems may come from speech/language pathologists, occupational therapists, physical therapists, or physicians. Speech articulation is often impaired and drooling may be present. In addition, hearing loss, epilepsy, and mental retardation may exist simultaneously. However, careful assessment of cognitive functioning is essential because both speech and motor skills are affected.

Little, if any, in the way of curative action is successful with cerebral palsy. Early intervention, special education, and vocational rehabilitation will be important, but the exact nature of the treatment approach will depend largely on the presence, nature, and degree of concomitant disorders. As many of 70% of children with the athetoid type of CP may function in the mentally retarded range, so educational and habilitative services must take into account the child's developmental limitations. Because facial muscles are involved in athetosis, vision disorders, especially of the eye-muscle imbalance type, may be present in more than 40% of the affected group (Black, 1980). Hearing loss is also common, though less so than vision problems, necessitating early and continuous audiometric evaluations and the possible provision of amplification devices. Physical therapy, including bracing and splinting to help maintain balance and to control involuntary movements, may be indicated in many cases. Orthopedic surgery and neurosurgery, though sometimes helpful with other forms of CP, have not yet shown promise for children with athetosis (Gornall, Hitchcock, & Kirkland, 1975).

## REFERENCES

Batshaw, M. L., & Perret, Y. M. (1981). *Children with handicaps: A medical primer*. Baltimore, MD: Brookes.

Black, P. D. (1980). Ocular defects in children with cerebral palsy. *British Medical Journal, 281,* 487.

Chow, M. P., Durand, B. A., Feldman, M. N., & Mills, M. A. (1979). *Handbook of pediatric primary care.* New York: Wiley.

Gornall, P., Hitchcock, E., & Kirkland, I. S. (1975). Stereotaxic neurosurgery in the management of cerebral palsy. *Developmental Medicine and Child Neurology, 17,* 279.

Vaughan, V. C., McKay, R. J., & Behrman, R. E. (1979). *Nelson textbook of pediatrics.* Philadelphia: Saunders.

JOHN D. WILSON
*Elwyn Institutes,*
*Elwyn, Pennsylvania*

**CEREBRAL PALSY**
**CENTRAL NERVOUS SYSTEM**

# ATTENTION DEFICIT DISORDER-HYPERACTIVITY (ADD-H)

Attention deficit disorder-hyperactivity (ADD-H) is a behavioral disorder believed to comprise anywhere from 3 to 8% of the elementary school population in the United States (Barkley, 1981), with boys receiving this diagnosis 10 times more frequently than girls (American Psychiatric Association, 1980). Therefore, it is not surprising that ADD-H is the most common problem referred to child guidance clinics. Clinical reports have often described children with ADD-H as overactive, inattentive, impulsive, difficult to discipline, and unable to inhibit their activity in response to situational demands (Ross & Ross, 1982). Secondary characteristics such as aggression, motor incoordination, academic failure, and poor peer relationships are also pathognomonic of the disorder. Loney (1980) has underscored that hyperactivity (hyperactivity and ADD-H are sometimes used interchangeably in the present review depending on how they are referred to in previous literature) and its core problem, attention, do not exist in isolation in children, and that much of the literature in this area has focused on the "four As" of ADD-H—activity, attention, aggression, and achievement. In fact, in view of the recent research indicating that hyperactivity is more of a cognitive than a motoric problem, the American Psychiatric Association (1980) recently relabeled this syndrome as attention deficit disorder. There also has been recognition that there may be at least four overlapping, yet separable, syndromes related to ADD-H, specifically, attention deficit disorder with hyperactivity, aggression, conduct disorder, and learning disability.

Over the past several years, the concept of ADD-H and the terms used to describe the disorder have undergone a series of revisions. These revisions have reflected important changes in the conceptualization of the diagnosis among clinical researchers. For example, the first investigators to recognize the syndrome (Ebaugh, 1923; Hohman, 1922) reported a population of children who were antisocial, impulsive, and overactive, yet of normal intelligence. It was believed that these characteristics were a sequel to lethargic encephalitis. At a later point, Strauss and Lehtinen (1955) compared "brain-injured" children to a population of non-brain-injured mentally retarded children. They described the behavior of the brain-injured group as erratic, uncontrollable, and overactive. It was later concluded that any child manifesting such symptoms was probably neurologically impaired, and this led to the term minimal brain damaged (MBD). There were a number of disagreements among the psychiatric community because of the dearth of clear evidence demonstrating a link between organic impairment and hyperactivity. Thus it was recommended that the label dysfunction replace the term damaged, primarily owing to the belief that behavioral symptoms alone could not be used to imply neurological impairment.

With the emergence of the revised nomenclature (*Diagnostic and Statistical Manual,* 2nd ed.) of the American Psychiatric Association (1968), the term MBD was relabeled hyperkinetic reaction of childhood. This syndrome focused primarily on the behavioral characteristics of overactivity and restlessness. However, as previously noted, research over the past decade has shifted the focus of hyperactivity to a disorder of attention. Hence the term and description of hyperactivity was again changed, this time to attention deficit disorder (*Diagnostic and Statistical Manual,* 3rd ed. [DSM III]; American Psychiatric Association, 1980), in accordance with research suggesting that these children's inability to sustain and regulate attention is more relevant than their overactivity (Douglas & Peters, 1979). Further, the DSM III has recognized a dichotomy between those children solely with attentional problems (ADD) and those with attentional problems and overactivity (ADD-H). (For the present review, ADD-H is being used to refer to both ADD and ADD-H groups.) Specifically, in accordance with the DSM III, the essential features of the attention deficit disorder are inability to sustain attention and effort; impulsivity, and for some ADD children, overactivity. The Table presents the specific diagnostic criteria for ADD-H as set forth by the American Psychiatric Association (1980).

A host of etiologies for ADD-H have been posited throughout the years, including neurological abberrations (Werry, et al., 1972), food additives (Feingold, 1975), and environmental stressors (Barkley, 1981). Nonetheless, few of these theories have received convincing empirical support, leading many scholars in this field to conclude that there are as many causes for ADD-H as there are ADD-H children themselves.

Perhaps the changing diagnostic nosology and the variability of prevalence rates for this pervasive childhood disorder have been a function of inadequate assessment techniques in child psychology, psychiatry, and special education. The past several years have witnessed a number of new assessment instruments for identifying ADD-

Diagnostic and Statistical Manual III Diagnostic Criteria for Attention Deficit Disorder

---

A. Inattention. At least three of the following:
1. Often fails to finish things he or she starts
2. Often does not seem to listen
3. Easily distracted
4. Has difficulty concentrating on school work or other tasks requiring sustained attention
5. Has difficulty sticking to a play activity.

B. Impulsivity. At least three of the following:
1. Often acts before thinking
2. Shifts excessively from one activity to another
3. Has difficulty organizing work (not because of cognitive impairment)
4. Needs a lot of supervision
5. Frequently calls out in class
6. Has difficulty awaiting turn in games or group situations.

C. Hyperactivity. At least two of the following:
1. Runs about or climbs on things excessively
2. Has difficulty sitting still or fidgets excessively
3. Has difficulty staying seated
4. Moves about excessively during sleep
5. Is always on the go or acts driven.

D. Onset before the age of seven.

E. Duration of at least 6 months.

F. Not due to schizophrenia, affective disorder, or severe or profound mental retardation.

---

*Source:* American Psychiatric Association (1980).

H children. Rating scales, which are relatively simple to use and can be completed without interfering with the child's activities, have been used extensively in the assessment of ADD-H children. Teacher ratings have proven to be the most frequently used rating scales in diagnosing these children because of their facility in administration, scoring, and reliability (Sprague, 1979). The Conners' Teacher Rating Scale (Conners, 1969) has been the most widely used, although a major difficulty with this instrument, as with other teacher ratings, is that a diagnosis based solely on a score yielded from the Conners' will primarily identify only those children with aggressive behavior and conduct difficulties. Such rating scales may often eliminate those children solely with attentional problems (ADD). In recent years, however, there has been a trend to develop instruments to assess the attentional difficulties that are now emphasized as part of the recent diagnostic criteria in the DSM III (Ullmann, Sleator, & Sprague, 1984).

Although parent ratings typically have proven more variable than teacher ratings (Sandoval, 1977) and less sensitive to pharmacological interventions (Barkley, 1977), parents' impressions are often of clinical importance and must be considered as part of the diagnostic process. Parent ratings of noncompliance have been found to be highly related to measures of compliance to parental commands, suggesting that child noncompliance is the chief concern of parents seeking professional assistance for children suffering from this disorder. Peer and self-ratings have been used infrequently to date with ADD-H children, although their potential utility as diagnostic tools remains highly viable (Wynne & Brown, 1984).

Direct observational methods (in which observers typically count the occurrence of stipulated behaviors) have been employed frequently in research involving ADD-H children and have been found to distinguish ADD-H children from their normal peers (Routh & Schroeder, 1976), particularly in those situations that are highly structured (Schleifer, et al., 1975). However, one basic problem with observational studies is that many of them have not distinguished ADD-H from conduct-disordered children. The difficulty in differentiating these two disorders has been a critical diagnostic issue in the field of hyperactivity for some time (Quay, 1979), since acting-out and behavioral difficulties are such pervasive associated features in ADD-H children.

Recently, Atkins, Pelham, and Licht (1985) have advocated that practitioners and researchers use a multivariate assessment approach in the diagnosis of ADD-H children. As Sprague (1979) has concluded, ADD-H is not a unitary behavioral dimension, but a complex constellation of a number of related symptoms. Thus, rating scales, observational techniques, and laboratory measures may assess various behavioral and cognitive dimensions in one child. For example, episodic outbursts might be reflected in the teacher's global rating of the child, but they may not have occurred during the period of observation and hence would not be recorded. Thus, in identifying these children, it is imperative that diagnostic data be accumulated from a multitude of sources including teachers, parents, diagnosticians, and even ADD-H children themselves.

Various treatment programs for ADD-H children have been widely investigated. They range from fluorescent lighting (Sprague, 1979) to dietary regimens (Feingold, 1975); although the use of stimulant drugs in the short-term management of these children has been one of the best-documented therapies in child psychiatry (Gittelman, 1983). The use of stimulant medication has been remarkably effective in ameliorating the poor attention, social behavior, and other troublesome symptomatology of ADD-H children. Much to the disappointment of many practitioners, however, psychostimulants have not been found to enhance academic achievement, prevent the development of antisocial behavioral patterns, or alter the natural history of the disorder. For this reason, there has been an active attempt to identify suitable alternatives to medication.

The most frequently used nonpharmacological therapy for ADD-H has been contingency management (Sprague, 1983). Although the use of operant techniques has offered practitioners some hope in the successful management of the disorder, there has been some evidence to suggest that behavioral changes do not endure over time (Mash & Dalby, 1979); there also has been concern that partial reinforcement actually increases poor attention and impulsivity by attracting the child away from the task at hand and toward the reinforcer (Douglas & Parry, 1983; Parry & Douglas, 1983). Thus, in response to the rather disappointing results of long-term stimulant drug outcome (Weiss, 1983), and concerns regarding the side effects of both stimulant drugs and operant techniques (Douglas, 1980), recent research has attempted to train these children to use various methods of self-control as opposed to control by outside agents (Douglas, et al., 1976). Although some investigators have been guardedly optimistic regarding the use of these cognitive therapies with ADD-H children (Brown, Wynne, & Medenis, 1985), many researchers have failed to confirm the efficacy of cognitive techniques with this population (Abikoff, in press). Since no single treatment has been documented to be overwhelmingly successful with these children, recent research has addressed the integration of medication and specific therapies. These studies have generally indicated that cognitive therapy in combination with stimulant medications is more efficacious than stimulants used alone (Hinshaw, Henker, & Whalen, 1984). Similarly, others have found that behavior therapy, when combined with stimulants, is superior to the effects of stimulants alone (Sprague, 1983). Thus, the multitreatment studies offer a glimmer of hope on the empirical horizon in our challenging efforts to treat this disorder.

The clinical myth that ADD-H bears a benign prognosis at adolescence and adulthood simply has not been supported in several follow-up studies (Weiss, 1983). Much to the disappointment of many practitioners, research has provided strong empirical support that although ADD-H symptomatology dissipates to some extent with age, cognitive and behavioral difficulties persist in a large percentage of patients at adolescence. Antisocial and acting-out behavior remain a problem in about one-third of adolescents previously diagnosed as ADD-H. Contrary to what some have believed, however, drug and alcohol abuse are generally not significant problems to adolescent ADD-H youngsters, even if these youths were treated with stimulants for many years as children. Academically, ADD-H adolescents are approximately two grade levels behind their normal peers in important areas such as reading and arithmetic. Thus, learning disabilities are often a common outcome for these adolescents. It is of no surprise also that poor peer relationships, low self-esteem, and demoralization persist into the ADD-H youngster's adolescent years (Brown, Borden, & Clingerman, 1985). In fact, what is particularly distressing to many clinicians has been the rather guarded prognosis of ADD-H youths despite the longevity and intensity of traditional treatment interventions, including stimulant medication. Although the use of combined therapies has improved outcome to some ex-

tent (Satterfield, Hoppe, & Schell, 1982), contrary to the popular clinical lore that ADD-H dissipates during the pubescent years, ADD-H still remains a disorder to be dealt with during adolescence and even adulthood (Weiss, 1983).

## REFERENCES

Abikoff, H. (in press). Efficacy of cognitive training interventions in hyperactive children: A critical review. *Clinical Psychology Review*.

American Psychiatric Association. (1968). *Diagnostic and statistical manual of mental disorders* (2nd ed.). Washington, DC.

American Psychiatric Association. (1980). *Diagnostic and statistical manual of mental disorders*. (3rd ed.). Washington, DC.

Atkins, M. S., Pelham, W. E., Licht, M. H. (1985). A comparison of object classroom measures and teacher ratings of attention deficit disorder. *Journal of Abnormal Child Psychology, 13,* 155–167.

Barkley, R. A. (1977). The effects of methylphenidate on various types of activity level and attention in hyperkinetic children. *Journal of Abnormal Child Psychology, 5,* 351–369.

Barkley, R. A. (1981). *Hyperactive children*. New York: Guilford.

Brown, R. T., Borden, K. A., & Clingerman, S. R. (1985). Pharmacotherapy in ADD adolescents with special attention to multimodality treatments. *Psychopharmacology Bulletin, 21,* 192–211.

Brown, R. T., Wynne, M. E., & Medenis, R. (1985). Methylphenidate and cognitive therapy: A comparison of treatment approaches with hyperactive boys. *Journal of Abnormal Child Psychology, 13,* 69–87.

Conners, C. K. (1969). A teacher rating scale for use in drug studies with children. *American Journal of Psychiatry, 126,* 152–156.

Douglas, V. I. (1980). Higher mental processes in hyperactive children: Implications for training. In R. M. Knights & D. J. Bakker (Eds.), *Rehabilitation, treatment, and management of learning disorders* (pp. 65–91). Baltimore, MD: University Park Press.

Douglas, V. I., & Parry, P. (1983). Effects of reward on delayed reaction time task performance of hyperactive children. *Journal of Abnormal Child Psychology, 2,* 313–326.

Douglas, V. I., Parry, P., Marton, P., & Garson, C. (1976). Assessment of a cognitive training program for hyperactive children. *Journal of Abnormal Child Psychology, 4,* 389–410.

Douglas, V. I., & Peters, K. G. (1979). Toward a clearer definition of the attentional deficit in hyperactive children. In G. A. Hale & M. Lewis (Eds.), *Attention and the development of cognitive skills* (pp. 173–247). New York: Plenum.

Ebaugh, F. G. (1923). Neuropsychiatric sequelae of acute epidemic encephalitis in children. *American Journal of Diseases of Children, 25,* 89–97.

Feingold, B. F. (1975). *Why your child is hyperactive*. New York: Random House.

Gittelman, R. (1983). Hyperkinetic syndrome: Treatment issues and principles. In M. Rutter (Ed.), *Developmental neuropsychiatry* (pp. 437–449). New York: Guilford.

Hinshaw, S. P., Henker, B., & Whalen, C. (1984). Cognitive-behavioral and pharmacologic interventions for hyperactive boys: Comparative and combined effects. *Journal of Consulting and Clinical Psychology, 52,* 739–749.

Hohman, L. B. (1922). Post-encephalitic behavior disorders in children. *Johns Hopkins Hospital Bulletin, 33,* 372–375.

Loney, J. (1980). Hyperkinesis comes of age: What do we know and where should we go? *American Journal of Orthopsychiatry, 50,* 28–42.

Mash, E. J., & Dalby, J. T. (1979). Behavioral interventions for hyperactivity. In R. L. Trites (Ed.), *Hyperactivity in children: Etiology, measurement and treatment implications* (pp. 161–216). Baltimore, MD: University Park Press.

Parry, P., & Douglas, V. I. (1983). Effects of reinforcement on concept identification in hyperactive children. *Journal of Abnormal Child Psychology, 2,* 327–340.

Quay, H. C. (1979). Classification. In H. Quay & J. S. Werry (Eds.), *Psychopathological disorders of childhood* (pp. 1–42). New York: Wiley.

Ross, D. M., & Ross, S. A. (1982). *Hyperactivity: Current issues, research, and theory* (2nd ed.). New York: Wiley Press.

Routh, D. K., & Schroeder, C. S. (1976). Standard playroom measures as indices of hyperactivity. *Journal of Abnormal Child Psychology, 4,* 199–207.

Sandoval, J. (1977). Measurement of the hyperactive syndrome in children. *Review of Educational Research, 47,* 293–318.

Satterfield, J. H., Hoppe, C. M., & Schell, A. M. (1982). A prospective study of delinquency in 110 adolescent boys with attention deficit disorder and 88 normal adolescent boys. *American Journal of Psychiatry, 139,* 795–798.

Schleifer, M., Weiss, G., Cohen, N., Elman, M., Cvejic, H., & Kruger, E. (1975). Hyperactivity in preschoolers and the effect of methylphenidate. *American Journal of Orthopsychiatry, 45,* 38–50.

Sprague, R. L. (1979). Assessment of intervention. In R. L. Trites (Ed.), *Hyperactivity in children: Etiology, measurement, and treatment implications* (pp. 217–229). Baltimore, MD: University Park Press.

Sprague, R. L. (1983). Behavior modification and educational techniques. In M. Rutter (Ed.), *Developmental neuropsychiatry* (pp. 404–421). New York: Guilford.

Strauss, A. A., Lehtinen, L. E. (1955). *Psychopathology of the brain injured child, Vol. 1.* New York: Grune & Stratton.

Ullman, R. K., Sleator, E. K., & Sprague, R. L. (1984). A new rating scale for diagnosis and monitoring of ADD children. *Psychopharmacology Bulletin, 20,* 160–164.

Weiss, G. (1983). Long-term outcome: Findings, concepts, and practical implications. In M. Rutter (Ed.), *Developmental neuropsychiatry* (pp. 422–436). New York: Guilford.

Werry, J. S., Minde, K., Guzman, A., Weiss, G., Dogan, K., & Hoy, E. (1972). Studies on the hyperactive child—VII: Neurological status compared with neurotic and abnormal children. *American Journal of Orthopsychiatry, 42,* 441–451.

Wynne, M. E., & Brown, R. T. (1984). Assessment of high incidence learning disorders: Isolating measures with high discriminant ability. *School Psychology Review, 13,* 231–237.

RONALD T. BROWN
*Emory University School
of Medicine*

ATTENTION SPAN
CONNER'S PARENT RATING SCALE
CONNER'S TEACHER RATING SCALE
FEINGOLD DIET
HYPERACTIVITY
RITALIN

## ATTENTION SPAN

Adequate attention span requires optimal arousal, selection of task-relevant information, maintenance of attention long enough to get a task done, and central processing of the task (Posner & Boies, 1971). Arousal is assessed by heart rate, respiration, or other indicators of autonomic arousal, and there is a level that is optimal for learning. At very low levels of arousal, learning is inefficient and attention to environmental stimuli is diffuse; at very high levels, attention is narrowed but learning becomes inefficient, particularly for complex tasks. Teachers can increase arousal by increasing the novelty of classroom activities, by asking students questions to generate curiosity (Berlyne, 1960), by rotating students in and out of the "action zone" (the T-shaped front-row-and-center region of the classroom) (Piontrowski & Calfee, 1979), or by directing questions to students outside the action zone.

Selective attention is assessed most frequently by use of incidental learning tasks. The child is instructed to recall a specific set of items (e.g., pictures of animals), but other incidental items (e.g., household items) are actually paired with the target (central) items during presentation. After being given tests of recall for central items, the child is tested for recall of the central-incidental pairs. The assumption is that only items that are attended to will be recalled. Recall for central items increases steadily from preschool age through adolescence, while memory for incidental items remains stable. The correlation between central and incidental recall becomes increasingly negative between ages 6 and 13 in normal children, indicating an increasing ability to screen out distractions with age. Adolescents and adults appear to screen out distractors by rehearsing central stimuli (Hagen & Stanovich, 1977). Hallahan, et al. have found selective attention problems to be common in children with learning problems. They also found that these children can be trained to improve their attention to central stimuli by using task-relevant self-talk and by being reinforced for recall of central items (Hallahan & Reeve, 1980).

Maintenance of attention can be assessed by observation, by interviewing, or by self-monitoring. In observational methods, eye contact with assigned task materials, with the teacher during instruction, or during task-relevant interaction with peers, is scored as engaged (on-task); other activities are scored as nonengaged (Piontrowski & Calfee, 1979). Observed engaged time is related to achievement; for example, Leach reports that 58% of the variance in primary mathematics achievement is accounted for by academic engaged time (Leach & Dolan, 1985). Observed on-task attention increases from ages 5 to 11 (Higgins & Turnure, 1984), although students may become more adept at appearing to maintain attention with development (Hudgins, 1967). Self-monitoring of "paying attention" improved observed engaged time among second graders, and reinforcement for self-monitoring accuracy improved engaged time more than self-monitoring alone (Rooney, Hallahan, & Lloyd, 1984).

## REFERENCES

Berlyne, D. (1960). *Conflict, arousal, and curiosity.* New York: McGraw-Hill.

Hagen, J. W., & Stanovich, K. E. (1977). Memory: strategies of acquisition. In R. V. Kail & J. W. Hagen (Eds.), *Perspectives on the development of memory and cognition.* Hillsdale, NJ: Erlbaum.

Hallahan, D. P., & Reeve, R. E. (1980). Selective attention and distractibility. In B. K. Keogh (Ed.), *Advances in special education, Vol. 1.* Greenwich, CT: JAI Press.

Higgins, A. T., & Turnure, J. E. (1984). Distractibility and concentration of attention in children's development. *Child Development, 55,* 1799–1810.

Hudgins, B. B. (1967). Attending and thinking in the classroom. *Psychology in the Schools, 66,* 29–32.

Leach, D. J., & Dolan, N. K. (1985). Helping teachers increase student academic engagement rate: The evaluation of a minimal feedback procedure. *Behavior Modification, 9,* 55–71.

Piontrowski, D., & Calfee, R. (1979). Attention in the classroom. In G. A. Hale & M. Lewis (Eds.), *Attention and cognitive development* (pp. 297–329). New York: Plenum.

Posner, M. I., & Boies, S. J. (1971). Components of attention. *Psychological Review, 78,* 391–408.

Rooney, K. J., Hallahan, D. P., & Lloyd, J. W. (1984). Self-recording of attention by learning disabled students in the regular classroom. *Journal of Learning Disabilities, 17,* 360–364.

JOHN MACDONALD
*Eastern Kentucky University*

**ATTENTION DEFICIT DISORDER**
**HYPERACTIVITY**
**HYPERKINESIS**

# ATTITUDES OF HANDICAPPED STUDENTS

Attitudes are learned beliefs that develop over time. They are feelings that develop from experiences with others and the environment, and they influence the way people behave toward, feel about, and accept others. In addition, the attitudes of others will affect the way we view ourselves and our capabilities. People with a positive self-attitude or self-concept will have a much better chance of achieving success than people with a negative self-concept

(Smith, Price, & Marsh, 1986). Unfortunately, handicapped students tend to have a lower self-concept than nonhandicapped students.

There are many reasons for the handicapped having lower self-attitudes, and they may vary from individual to individual. Generally, the handicapped encounter so many negative experiences that it is difficult for them to develop a positive self-attitude. A major negative experience is academic failure. While limited amounts of failure may inspire many children to overcome obstacles, it is difficult for handicapped students' self-concepts to be immune from repeated failures. Furthermore, the handicapped experience many negative reactions from others, and these reactions cannot be hidden. These negative experiences can result in a lack of confidence in abilities and a lower self-attitude. The handicapped's lack of confidence can lead to behavior problems, or to withdrawn, overly anxious, immature behaviors. These behaviors can further limit a student's academic progress, interactions with others, and self-attitude.

Since self-attitudes are essential for academic and social success, it is imperative that the handicapped develop positive self-attitudes. To establish positive attitudes in handicapped students, young children should develop a sense of self-importance, and older students should be encouraged to balance their failures with an appreciation of their specific talents and abilities (Polloway, Payne, Patton, & Payne, 1985).

## REFERENCES

Polloway, E. A., Payne, J. S., Patton, J. R., & Payne, R. A. (1985). *Strategies for teaching retarded and other special needs learners* (3rd ed.). Columbus, OH: Merrill.

Smith, T. E. C., Price, B. J., & Marsh, G. E., II (1986). *Mildly handicapped children and adults.* St. Paul, MN: West.

LARRY J. WHEELER
*Southwest Texas State University*

**LEARNED HELPLESSNESS**
**SELF-CONCEPT**

# ATTITUDES TOWARD THE HANDICAPPED

With the passage of P.L. 94-142 and Section 504, the visibility of disabled children and adults has increased in mainstream American society. This has precipitated a need for the examination of attitudes, reactions, and behaviors toward the disabled to foster their integration into a society that has traditionally excluded them (Hazzard, 1983).

Siller (1976) points out that attitudes and reactions to the handicapped are wide ranging and complex. They are based on variables considered related to and important to attitudinal formation (e.g., family background, culture, and personality). Age, sex, and other demographic variables appear to be significant determinants in the manner in which attitudes toward the disabled are expressed rather than in their formation. Generally, Siller (1976) found that women may have attitudes similar to those of men, but they are more likely to express them in ways influenced by their sex role. Voetz (1980) found girls to be more nurturing and accepting than boys on psychological indices and more likely to respond in a socially desirable direction (Hazzard, 1983). Gottlieb and Gottlieb (1977) did not find this to be true. Siller (1976) found that adolescents of both sexes tend to be more rejecting than older or younger persons. Coie and Pennington (1976) and Hazzard (1983) support the notion that children's knowledge about and understanding of disabilities increase with age.

Personal contact with the disabled may either substantially improve or worsen attitudes, depending on the quality of the previous interaction. Voeltz (1980) and Fenrick and Petersen (1984) found that nonhandicapped children with the most contact with handicapped peers held the least negative attitudes and were the most accepting of their handicapped peers. Others (Cook & Wollersheim, 1976; Gottlieb, Cohen, & Goldstein, 1974) reported no difference according to the amount of contact.

The importance of developing positive attitudes toward the handicapped is critical to the success of the least restrictive environment mandate of P.L. 94-142. As more handicapped children are both mainstreamed into regular classes (as in the case of the mildly handicapped) or placed within the elementary/secondary school setting (as with the more severely handicapped), attention must be placed on assisting regular teachers in accommodating these children in the general school program and on to fostering positive attitudes in nonhandicapped students. Reynolds, Martin-Reynolds, and Mark (1982) report that the most important ingredient in making mainstreaming work is teacher attitude. Some studies have indicated that it is difficult for regular classroom teachers to accept the handicapped in their classrooms (Alexander & Strain, 1978; Macmillan, Jones, & Meyers, 1976). This may be due to teachers' feeling inadequately prepared to serve the needs of handicapped children rather than any general negative attitude toward disability. Guerin and Szatlock (1974) and Harasiymiw and Horn (1975) found teacher attitude to be positively affected by experiences in in-service programs (Reynolds, Martin-Reynolds, & Mark, 1982).

Attitudes of children toward the handicapped have also been positively affected through a variety of programs aimed at increasing contact with the disabled and offering quality of interaction. Fenrick and Petersen (1984) successfully used a peer tutoring program designed to lessen negative attitudes toward moderately and severely handicapped students. Rynders, et al. (1980) also found that junior high school students had increased positive perceptions of their teammates who had Down's syndrome after an extended time period of bowling together.

Investigations by Gottlieb (1978) and others on the social effects of the integration of mildly handicapped children into classroom settings with nonhandicapped peers are inconclusive (Voeltz, 1980). Furthermore, it may be inaccurate to generalize data involving mildly handicapped children to the social integration of severely handicapped children (Voeltz, 1980). One may assume with confidence that negative attitudes toward the disabled represent a real barrier to their filling appropriate roles in society (Siller, 1976). Positive teacher intervention efforts and structured, long-term contact with handicapped peers (Fenrick & Petersen, 1984) may serve as viable means to breaking down barriers.

## REFERENCES

Alexander, C., & Strain, P. S. (1978). A review of educators attitudes towards handicapped children and the concept of mainstreaming. *Psychology in the Schools, 15,* 390–396.

Coie, J., & Pennington, B. (1976). Children's perceptions of deviance and disorder. *Child Development, 47,* 407–413.

Cook, J., & Wollersheim, J. (1976). The effect of labeling of special education students on the perceptions of contact versus noncontact normal peers. *Journal of Special Education, 10,* 187–198.

Fenrick, N. J., & Petersen, T. K. (1984). Developing positive changes in attitude towards moderately/severely handicapped students through a peer tutoring program. *Education and Training of the Mentally Retarded, 19*(2), 83–91.

Gottlieb, J., Cohen, L., & Goldstein, L. (1974). Social contact and personal adjustment as variables relating to attitudes toward EMR children. *Training School Bulletin, 71,* 9–16.

Gottlieb, J., & Gottlieb, B. (1977). Stereotype attitude and behavioral intentions toward handicapped children. *American Journal of Mental Deficiertcy, 82,* 65–71.

Hazzard, A. (1983). Children's experience with, knowledge of, and attitude toward disabled persons. *Journal of Special Education, 17*(2), 131–139.

MacMillan, D. L., Jones, R. L., & Meyers, C. E. (1976). Mainstreaming the mildly retarded: Some questions, cautions, and guidelines. *Mental Retardation, 14,* 11–13.

Reynolds, B. J., Martin-Reynolds, J., Mark, F. D. (1982). Elementary teachers' attitudes toward mainstreaming educable mentally retarded students. *Education and Training of the Mentally Retarded, 17*(3), 171–177.

Rynders, J. E., Johnson, R. T., Johnson, D. W., & Schmidt, B. (1980). Producing positive interaction among Down syndrome and nonhandicapped teenagers through cooperative goal structuring. *American Journal of Mental Deficiency, 85,* 268–273.

Siller, J. (1976). Attitudes towards disability. In H. Rusalem & D. Malikin (Eds.), *Contemporary vocational rehabilitation* (pp. 63–79). New York: New York University Press.

Voeltz, L. M. (1980). Children's attitudes toward handicapped peers. *American Journal of Mental Deficiency, 84*(5), 455–464.

MARSHA H. LUPI
*Hunter College, City University
of New York*

## ATTRIBUTIONAL RETRAINING

Many handicapped pupils perceive themselves to be incompetent in a variety of school-related activities. While these self-perceptions may accurately reflect limited skills in these areas, they may also affect youngsters' willingness to engage in learning tasks. When presented with school tasks, even tasks in which they have evidenced recent success, many pupils will state that they cannot do the work and as a consequence will not even try. To address the learning needs of their pupils, special education teachers need to focus on their pupils' cognitive and motivational characteristics. An intervention procedure entitled attributional retraining has been used to influence pupils' self-perceptions and their subsequent motivation to learn.

Attribution retraining may be defined as a systematic set of procedures designed to influence individuals' perceptions concerning the causes of their performance on tasks. Many of the procedures are derived from research in the area of cognitive behavior modification. In attributional retraining the focus is on modifying learners' thoughts concerning why they have succeeded or failed on a task. Although attributional retraining procedures have been used in treatment programs for a variety of problems including alcoholism, anxiety, depression, and diet management, the focus on this presentation will be on the use of these procedures with youngsters who evidence severe learning problems.

Most of the attributional retraining programs focus on the role of effort on student achievement. This emphasis is due, in part, to the fact that pupils can choose to change their levels of effort. In addition, high achieving pupils tend to attribute successes to their ability and effort and ascribe their failures to lack of effort. When students perceive that increased effort will result in success, they persist; this, in turn, enhances their performance. In contrast, children who have learning problems frequently attribute their failures to lack of ability, and fail to persist on academic tasks.

One of the first attributional retraining studies was conducted by Dweck (1975). In this investigation, children identified as learned helpless were asked to solve arithmetic problems. One group of pupils was given math tasks in which they continually succeeded; another group was given tasks that they occasionally failed at. When pupils did not correctly respond on an arithmetic task, they were were given attributional feedback indicating that they should have tried harder. All the youngsters in the study were subsequently given difficult math problems. Pupils who received the attributional feedback maintained or improved their performances after failure, whereas the per-

formances of children who continually succeeded deteriorated if they failed on a math problem. Chapin and Dyck (1976) and Fowler and Peterson (1981) subsequently reported that persistence on academic tasks was jointly affected by reinforcement procedures and attribution retraining. Fowler and Peterson also reported that reinforcement/attribution retraining that involved direct attributional feedback to pupils was more effective in increasing reading persistence than other treatment procedures. Recently, educational researchers have reported that attribution training procedures may influence students' use of learning strategies (Johnson & Winograd, 1985; Palmer & Goetz, 1984). Attribution training may affect both pupils' achievement outcomes and how they learn.

Related to thee attributional retraining research, DeCharms (1976) developed a two-part program to help teachers enhance personal causation of elementary-aged children. The project was designed to influence pupils' goal planning and ultimately produce a person who is in control of his or her achievements. The experiment involved two groups: one consisted of motivation-trained teachers using an experimental curriculum; a control group had untrained teachers and the regular curriculum. The first step involved a personal causation training course for all teachers in the experimental group, followed by a year-long immplementation of a number of classroom exercises. Personal causation training did appear to affect pupils' self-confidence and their academic achievement scores. Four years later, a semistructured interview revealed higher personal goals and responsibility orientation for those children in the trained group over those in the untrained group. Five years later, it was found that more pupils from the trained group had graduated. While there were a variety of components to the training program, one of the crucial elements was teaching the pupils that they had control over their achievement outcomes.

Although additional research is needed to determine how and when to most effectively use attributional retraining procedures, it appears that teachers' direct attributional feedback to children does influence pupils' willingness to learn and their school achievement. Teachers' systematic feedback to their pupils that effort is important in determining their successes or failures may affect youngsters' persistence on school tasks and ultimately their achievement.

### REFERENCES

Chapin, M., & Dyck, D. G. (1976). Persistence in children's reading behavior as a function of N length and attribution retraining. *Journal of Abnormal Psychology, 85*, 511–515.

Decharms, R. (1976). *Enhancing motivation: Change in the classroom.* New York: Irvington.

Dweck, C. S. (1975). The role of expectations and attributions in the alleviation of learned helplessness. *Journal of Personality and Social Psychology, 31*, 674–685.

Fowler, J. W., & Peterson, P. L. (1981). Increasing reading persistence and altering attributional style of learned helpless children. *Journal of Educational Psychology, 73,* 251–260.

Johnson, P. H., & Winograd, P. N. (1985). Passive failure in reading. Unpublished manuscript.

Palmer, D. J., & Goetz, E. T. (in press). Selection and use of study strategies: The role of the studier's beliefs about self and strategies. In C. Weinstein, E. Goetz & P. Alexander (Eds.) *Learning and study strategies: Issues and assessments, instructions and evaluations.* New York: Academic.

Douglas J. Palmer
Norma Guerra
*Texas A&M University*

## LEARNED HELPLESSNESS MOTIVATION

# ATTRIBUTIONS

Attribution theorists assert that individuals seek causes for events in their environment and that these perceived causes influence subsequent behavior. The individual is seen as a naive psychologist searching for theories and cause and effect relationships that explain his or her behavior as well as the behavior of others. The father of modern attribution theory, Fritz Heider (1958), has argued that individuals' subjective experiences are essential for understanding how they perceive the world. Furthermore, Heider proposed that these causal ascriptions subsequently influence a person's behavior.

Weiner (1972, 1979) has extensively examined attributions for achievement outcomes. Within academic settings, content, ability, effort, task difficulty, and chance are among the most commonly investigated of individuals' attributions (Weiner, 1979). Weiner (1974) proposes that attributions for success and failure can be classified within a two-dimensional taxonomy: locus of control (internal or external) and stability (fixed or variable). Attributions of ability and effort are classified as internal, while luck and task difficulty are considered external. On the stability dimension, ability and task difficulty are viewed as fixed, and effort and luck are seen as variable.

Pupils systematically use a variety of achievement-related information to derive attributions for their school performance. The primary types of information that individuals use when deciding which factors caused their performance include their current performance outcome, their history of performance on similar tasks, and the performance of others on the same or similar tasks. For example, if a pupil with a history of learning difficulties in math just answered some arithmetic problems correctly, as did 95% of the other pupils in the class, that pupil is most likely to attribute success to an easy task. In contrast, if the pupil does poorly on a school task in which he or she has had a history of failure, yet most of the student's classmates or friends appear to understand, the pupil may attribute failure to a lack of competence. These illustrative vignettes reflect the attributional antecedents and attributions that differentiate many handicapped and nonhandicapped pupils. By definition, many special education pupils experience a history of failure prior to being referred and ultimately placed in special education classes. It is this background of failure, current achievement problems, and the recognition that other pupils are doing well on classroom assignments that leads to perceptions of lack of competence. In turn, these perceptions concerning lack of ability influence pupils' expectancy for future performance and their willingness to try new tasks and persist on difficult ones.

Recently there has been considerable interest generated concerning the consequences of repeated academic failure and its effect on the motivation and achievement of special education children. The repeated academic failure experienced by these students may cause them to doubt their abilities and reduce their persistence and effort when exposed to novel or familiar tasks. Researchers have found that learning-disabled (LD) children are less likely than nonhandicapped children to attribute their failures to insufficient effort and more likely to attribute their failures to their own inabilities. LD pupils also have exhibited less persistence on achievement tasks than nonhandicapped pupils. Investigators have found that LD pupils' tendency to attribute failure to ability is negatively related to persistence. It has also been reported that when LD children succeed at a task, they are less likely to attribute the success to their abilities and more likely to attribute the success to luck or ease of the task. These children appear to blame themselves when they fail and not give themselves credit when they succeed. Low levels of persistence and effort often result in additional failures, and the special education student, more frequently subjected to these difficulties, is caught in a vicious downward spiral of motivation and performance (Licht & Kistner, 1986).

## REFERENCES

Heider, F. (1958). *The psychology of interpersonal relations.* New York: Wiley.

Licht, B. G., & Kistner, J. A. (1986). Motivational problems of learning disabled children: Individual differences and their implications for treatment. In J. K. Torgesen & B. W. L. Wong (Eds.), *Learning disabilities: Some new perspectives.* Orlando, FL: Academic.

Weiner, B. (1972). *Theories of motivation: From mechanism to cognition.* Chicago: Rand McNally.

Weiner, B. (1974). *Achievement motivation and attribution theory.* Morristown, NJ: General Learning.

Weiner, B. (1979). A theory of motivation for some classroom experiences. *Journal of Educational Psychology, 71,* 3–25.

Douglas J. Palmer
Michael L. Stowe
*Texas A&M University*

## ACHIEVEMENT MOTIVATION

# ATYPICAL CHILD SYNDROME

A syndrome is a cluster of physical or behavioral characteristics that have been observed in a group of people and that are used to define a condition that these people share. Atypical child syndrome is a term borrowed from the medical profession and is no longer in common usage. The current term referring to this group is exceptional children. An exceptional child is one who deviates from the norm and could be categorized on the basis of a set of physical and/or behavioral characteristics. There are a variety of specific disorders in the area of special education that use the term syndrome as a part of the classification. Hunter's syndrome, Down's syndrome, Turner's syndrome, Lesch-Neyhan syndrome, Cornelin deLange syndrome, Sturge-Weber syndrome, and Klinefelter's syndrome are but a few that are discussed in the special education literature.

A wide range of handicaps contribute to the atypical child's condition. That condition may range from mild to severe, physical to mental, educational to social, or any combination of those conditions. What is difficult is to fit an individual into a category, as each individual has a different combination and severity of disability. Handicapped classifications are set up according to the characteristics of the children that deviate from the average or normal child and should be used to help educational programs meet the individual's needs. Kirk (1972) describes five categories: (1) communication disorders (learning disabilities and speech handicaps); (2) mental deviations (gifted and retarded); (3) sensory handicaps (auditory and visual); (4) neurological, orthopedic, or other health problems; and (5) behavior disorders. Although these categories have been used by psychology, sociology, physiology, and the medical profession, they will be briefly addressed from the educational standpoint.

Learning disabilities is a recently developed classification for those individuals that have language difficulties, visual or auditory-perceptual problems, and memory or other cognitive disabilities. Usually the child has an average or above average IQ, although development will be hindered owing to the cognitive disability. Many times the learning problems contribute to behavior problems resulting from academic failure, unobtainable expectations, frustrations, etc. Although definitions have related these dysfunctions to the central nervous system (Clements, 1966), remediation is dealt with through educational intervention with a focus on academic, social, and emotional adjustment.

Mental retardation involves below average intellectual functioning with social and behavioral deficits. Grossman (1973) describes five levels of individuals with retardation, all of whom have IQs below 85 and engage in behaviors inappropriate for their age group. Individuals with borderline retardation (from 85 to 70 IQ) are fre-quently referred to as slow learners. Individuals with mild retardation (the educable mentally retarded) range from 69 to 55 IQs and have some potential to master basic academic skills. These individuals can live as independent or semiindependent adults. Moderately or trainable mentally retarded individuals with IQs of 54 to 40 have potential for learning self-help, social, and communication skills and simple occupational tasks. Severely mentally retarded individuals range from 39 to 25 IQs and need continual monitoring. They may be taught simple self-help skills, work tasks, and some type of communication system. The profoundly retarded, with IQs below 25, are totally dependent and require close supervision. Some may be able to perform self-help skills. Educational programs for the mentally retarded have made great gains. Depending on severity, educational programs range from self-contained classrooms to special schools and employ a great many management and instructional techniques (Snell, 1978). The goal is to teach these individuals skills to help them become as independent as possible.

Sensory handicaps range greatly from minimal visual defects and hard of hearing to blindness and deafness. Education can range from no special programming, to special part-time instruction from an itinerant teacher, to special schools. Focus in the public schools is on auditory and visual perception training.

Bleck and Nagel (1975) offer an excellent handbook for teachers of the physically handicapped. Basically, these individuals are disabled in motor abilities that do not affect educational achievement, although there may be some difficulties in social and emotional adjustment. The school needs to adapt the physical environment to accommodate wheelchairs, braces, etc. Teachers with neurologically impaired students need to be aware of complications, such as seizures.

Behavior disorders interfere with a child's growth and the development of relationships with others. Hewett and Jenkins (1945) define three types of behavior disorders involving those having unsocialized aggression (participating with peers in misdemeanors and crime) or over-inhibition (overdependent and withdrawn). All involve social maladjustments and emotional disturbances. Although they are dealt with through the mental health fields, education has taken on prevention and treatment. The intervention, whether through resource rooms, itinerant teachers, special classes, special or residential schools, or hospitals, includes psychodynamics, behavior modification, and developmental, ecological, or psychoeducational strategies (Kirk, 1972).

## REFERENCES

Bleck, E. G., & Nagel, D. A. (1975). *Physically handicapped children: A medical atlas for teachers*. New York: Grune & Stratton.

Clements, D. D. (1966). *Minimal brain dysfunction in children*

(Public Health Service Publication N. 415). Washington, DC: Department of Health, Education, and Welfare.

Fliegler, I. A., & Bish, C. E. (1959, December). Summary of research on the academically talented student. *Review of Educational Research, 29*, 408–450.

Hewett, L. E., & Jenkins, R. L. (1945). *Fundamental patterns of maladjustment: The dynamics of their origin.* Springfield, IL: state of Illinois.

Gloss, G. H., & Jones, R. L. (1968). *Correlates of school district provisions for gifted children: A statewide study.* Paper presented at the annual meeting of the Council for Exceptional Children, New York.

Grossman, H. J. (Ed.). (1973). Manual on terminology and classification in mental retardation. *American Journal of Mental Deficiency* (Special issue. Series No. 2).

Kirk, S. A., (1972). *Educational exceptional children.* Boston: Houghton Mifflin.

Snell, M. E. (1978). *Systematic instruction of the moderately and severely handicapped.* Columbus, OH: Merrill.

Donna Filips
*Steger, Illinois*

**EVALUATION**
**LEARNING DISABILITIES**
**MENTAL RETARDATION**

## AUDIOGRAM

An audiogram is a graphic representation of the threshold of hearing for each ear, measured at discrete frequencies using pure-tone signals, and transduced through an earphone for determining air conduction (AC) and through a bone vibrator for determining bone conduction (BC) thresholds. The audiogram form and symbols plotted on the audiogram, representing hearing thresholds, have been standardized (ANSI S3.21-1978) and are shown in the Figure.

The abscissa of the audiogram shows frequency in hertz (Hz) from 125 to 8000 Hz. The ordinate shows hearing level (HL) in decibels (dB) from −10 to 110 dB. 0-dB HL

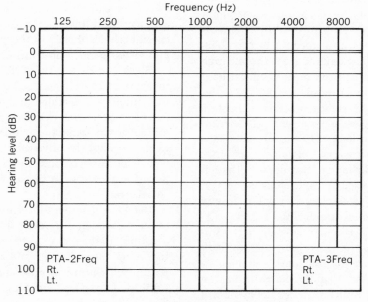

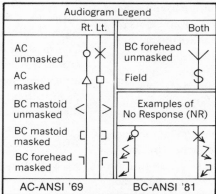

Audiogram Form and Symbols.

for each frequency represents the statistical average of normal hearing. If an individual has normal hearing, all pure-tone thresholds would be plotted on the 0-dB HL line. Thresholds <0-dB HL would mean better hearing than normal and thresholds >0-dB HL would mean poorer hearing than normal, or the amount of hearing loss. AC hearing thresholds between −10 and 20 are considered within a normal range, while thresholds from 25 to 40 indicate a mild hearing loss; 41 to 55 dB, a moderate one; 56 to 70, moderate to severe; 71 to 90 severe, and greater than 91 dB, profound.

Air-conduction thresholds are obtained through earphones so that sound is conducted to the inner ear by the air in the ear canal and recorded as "O" for the right and "X" for the left ear. Bone-conduction thresholds are obtained through a bone vibrator, usually placed on the mastoid behind the ear so that sound is conducted to the inner ear by the cranial bones and recorded as "<" for the right and ">" for the left ear. When the possibility exists that a pure-tone presented to one ear may be heard in the other ear, a narrow-band masking sound is directed to the non-test ear to eliminate it from responding to the pure-tone presented to the test ear. AC and BC thresholds obtained with masking have different symbols than those obtained unmasked.

Once thresholds have been obtained, the AC thresholds for each ear are connected with a solid line and BC thresholds are connected with a dotted line. Sometimes audiologists color code their symbols so that all right ear thresholds are plotted in red and left ear in blue.

## REFERENCES

American National Standards Institute. (1969, 1973). *Specifications for audiometers S3.6*. New York.

American National Standards Institute. (1978). *Methods for manual pure-tone audiometry S3.21*. New York.

Yantis, P. A. (1985). Puretone air-conduction testing. In J. Katz (Ed.), *Handbook of clinical audiology* (3rd ed.) (pp. 153–169). Baltimore, MD: Williams & Wilkins.

THOMAS A. FRANK
*Pennsylvania State University*

**AUDIOMETRY**
**AUDITORY ABNORMALITIES**

# AUDIOLOGY

Audiology is the study of hearing and hearing disorders, including assessment procedures, hearing conservation, and the habilitation and rehabilitation of individuals having hearing impairment. The field of audiology can be differentiated into specialty areas.

Clinical audiology is concerned with assessing the degree, type, and site of lesion of hearing loss, and determining appropriate rehabilitation procedures. Emphasis is placed on testing/diagnostic procedures, interpretation of results, and counseling. Pediatric audiology is like clinical audiology, except emphasis is placed on special procedures for assessment of hearing in infants and young children. Experimental audiology concerns itself with investigations designed to advance testing/diagnostic procedures and increase knowledge of normal and abnormal auditory systems. Educational audiology provides appropriate therapies to preschool and school-age children having educationally significant hearing impairments. Industrial audiology deals with the effects of noise on humans, hearing conservation programs, noise control, interpretation of state and federal programs, and noise standards. Rehabilitative audiology has as its primary goal providing therapies for children and adults with hearing impairment. Therapies include speech reading, auditory training, and speech-language therapy.

## REFERENCES

Martin, F. N. (1981). *Introduction to audiology* (2nd ed.). Englewood Cliffs, NJ: Prentice-Hall.

Newby, H. A., & Popelka, G. R. (1985). *Audiology* (5th ed.). Englewood Cliffs, NJ: Prentice-Hall.

THOMAS A. FRANK
*Pennsylvania State University*

**AUDIOMETRY**
**AUDITORY ABNORMALITIES**

# AUDIOMETRY

Audiometry is the collection of techniques and procedures used for measuring hearing. Traditionally, measurements are done with a calibrated electronic instrument called an audiometer. Generally, three types of audiometry, called pure-tone, speech, and impedance/admittance audiometry, are done during an audiometric evaluation.

Pure-tone audiometry is the measurement of the threshold of hearing for air- and bone-conducted pure tones. Air-conducted pure tones are transmitted through an earphone so that sound is conducted to the inner ear by the air in the ear canal as part of the pathway. Bone-conducted pure tones are transmitted by a bone vibrator usually placed on the mastoid process behind the outer ear so that sound is conducted to the inner ear by the cranial bones. The American National Standards Institute (ANSI) has specified the methods for manual pure-tone audiometry (ANSI, S3.21-1978). As a result of pure-tone audiometry, the severity and type of hearing loss can be classified for each ear.

Speech audiometry is concerned with determining the threshold of hearing for speech and with measuring speech discrimination ability. The threshold of speech can be measured by determining the lowest hearing level that causes an individual to just be aware of or detect speech known as a speech awareness threshold (SAT) or speech detection threshold (SDT). Another speech threshold measure, spondee threshold (ST), is found by determining the lowest level at which an individual can just hear and understand bisyllabic words spoken in spondaic stress 50% of the time. If speech stimuli other than bisyllabic words are used (e.g., body parts), this measure is known as a speech reception threshold (SRT). Speech discrimination testing is done to determine the percentage of words (usually monosyllabic) correctly identified when the words are presented loud enough to be heard at normal conversational level. This measure is also known as word or speech recognition or identification; it can be used to judge social adequacy, for hearing-aid fitting, and for diagnostic site-of-lesion testing.

Impedance/admittance audiometry is done on a special instrument. It is not truly a measurement of hearing but rather a test battery to obtain diagnostic information about eardrum mobility (tympanogram) and middle- and inner-ear function (acoustic reflex tests). The results of impedance/admittance testing can be used alone for diagnostic purposes; however, when used in conjunction with pure-tone and speech audiometry results, the type, degree, site-of-lesion, and in some cases the underlying pathology of the hearing loss can be determined.

**REFERENCES**

American National Standards Institute. (1978). *Methods for manual pure-tone threshold audiometry S3.21-1978*. New York.

Dirks, D. D. (1985). Bone-conduction testing. In J. Katz (Ed.), *Handbook of clinical audiology* (3rd ed.) (pp. 202–223). Baltimore, MD: Williams & Wilkins.

Feldman, A. S., & Wilber, L. A. (1976). *Acoustic impedance and admittance—The measurement of middle ear function*. Baltimore, MD: Williams & Wilkins.

THOMAS A. FRANK
*Pennsylvania State University*

AUDIOLOGY
AUDITORY ABNORMALITIES

## AUDITORY ABNORMALITIES

Auditory abnormalities are disorders or dysfunctions of the ear that affect the hearing mechanism or sense of hearing. Auditory abnormalities can occur in just one part of the ear or in several parts of the ear simultaneously.

A congenital abnormality of the outer ear is called a microtia. If a patient has a microtia and an intact ear canal, he or she usually does not have a hearing loss. A smaller than normal ear canal, common in Down's syndrome, is known as a stenotic canal; it usually does not cause hearing impairment. An absent ear canal, or an ear canal that "dead-ends," is known as an atresia; it causes a moderate to severe conductive hearing loss. An overabundance of wax (cerumen) in the ear canal can cause a mild to moderate conductive loss if it is impacted.

The most common auditory abnormality in children is the presence of fluid in the middle-ear space, usually due to Eustachian tube dysfunction; however, there are many causes of middle-ear fluid. Middle-ear fluid is especially prevalent in children having cranio-facial disorders (Down's, cleft palate, etc.). Usually, middle-ear fluid causes a mild to moderate educationally significant conductive hearing loss because movement of the eardrum and middle-ear bones are restricted. A hole in the eardrum, known as a perforation or rupture, can cause a mild to severe conductive hearing loss, depending on its location and size. A fixation of the stapes in the oval window of the inner ear is a condition known as otosclerosis; this usually produces a progressive, mild to severe conductive hearing loss. If the joint between the incus and stapes becomes disarticulated, usually by a blow to the head, a moderate to severe conduction hearing loss occurs. There are many middle-ear congenital middle-ear abnormalities, including absent, fixed, or distorted middle-ear bone malformations. Generally, auditory abnormalities that involved the outer or middle ear and produced conductive hearing losses are amenable to drug therapy or surgical correction to restore hearing.

There are many auditory abnormalities that can affect the function of the inner ear and that may be part of an overall syndrome involving other sensory systems, skeletal formation, internal organs, or the nervous system. Generally, inner-ear abnormalities affect the sensory hair cells in the Organ of Corti, causing a sensorineural hearing loss that can range from mild to profound and that can be unilateral (one ear) or bilateral (both ears). In children, about 50% of educationally significant inner-ear hearing losses are inherited and about 50% are acquired. If a child is born with an absent inner ear (cochlea), the condition is known as an inner-ear aplasia. Common genetic causes of inner-ear hearing loss are syndromes such as Ushers or Waardenburgs and interfamily marriages. Common acquired causes are due to prematurity, meningitis, and birth injury. An inner-ear hearing loss owed to aging is called presbycusis. One from excessive noise exposure is called acoustic trauma or noise-induced.

Auditory abnormalities can also occur from a problem with the auditory nerve (VIII cranial nerve), a brainstem disorder or a temporal lobe dysfunction. A tumor growing on the acoustic nerve or in the brain-stem region usually causes poor speech discrimination ability but does not always cause a loss of hearing sensitivity. A temporal lobe dysfunction usually produces poor understanding for speech on the ear contralateral to the lesion. Many children have trouble processing speech, especially in reference to auditory sequential memory or hearing speech in a noisy background. These children are usually diagnosed as having a central auditory processing problem. The exact site of lesion is not known; however, temporal lobe and association areas of the brain are suspected.

An auditory abnormality in any part of the ear can cause tinnitus, which is any sound perceived in the head. In most cases, it is a symptom of an inner-ear hearing loss. Abnormalities of the outer, middle, and inner ear can cause a feeling of fullness; however, most often this is a symptom of a middle-ear abnormality. Dizziness is another symptom of hearing loss, often from a dysfunction in the inner ear, but it can also occur from an outer- or middle-ear abnormality.

## REFERENCES

Ginsberg, I. A., & White, T. P. (1985). Otologic considerations in audiology. In J. Katz (Ed.), *Handbook of clinical audiology* (3rd ed.) (pp. 15–38). Baltimore, MD: Williams & Wilkins.

Jaffe, B. F. (1977). *Hearing loss in children*. Baltimore, MD: University Park Press.

Jerger, S., & Jerger, J. (1981). *Auditory disorders: A manual for clinical evaluation*. Boston: Little, Brown.

Northern, J. L., & Downs, M. P. (1984). *Hearing in children* (3rd ed.). Baltimore, MD: Williams & Wilkins.

Schuknecht, H. F. (1974). *Pathology of the ear*. Cambridge, MA: Harvard University Press.

Zimmerman, R. L. (1985). Neurologic considerations for audiologists. In J. Katz (Ed.), *Handbook of clinical audiology* (3rd ed.) (pp. 39–53). Baltimore, MD: Williams & Wilkins.

THOMAS A. FRANK
*Pennsylvania State University*

**AUDIOMETRY**
**AUDIOGRAM**

# AUDITORY DISCRIMINATION

Auditory discrimination is the process of an individual's ability to recognize, interpret, and distinguish among auditory stimuli and to respond appropriately. Most often, auditory discrimination is thought to involve the ability to differentiate speech sounds leading to an understanding of the speech message. However, auditory discrimination also involves an individual's ability to differentiate nonspeech sounds of varying intensities, frequencies, and durations. In part, the study of psychoacoustics is devoted to understanding human perception of acoustic stimuli.

Applied to speech, auditory discrimination is the process that enables an individual to recognize, interpret, and distinguish differences among all of the phonemes that make up speech segments. In a broader sense, it is the ability to distinguish and understand speech. Auditory discrimination also involves the process of selecting relevant from nonrelevant stimuli in the environment. This process is called auditory figure-ground, auditory differentiation, auditory selective listening, competing message integration, and listening in noise.

Auditory discrimination can be tested in several ways using a variety of specially designed tests in quiet or noisy backgrounds using an open- or closed-set response. Some auditory discrimination tests employ a rhyming word format so that the individual has to hear a pivotal phoneme to distinguish between two words or to identify the stimulus word from rhyming word alternatives. Some auditory discrimination tests require the listener to hear key words in a sentence or phrase.

Generally, auditory discrimination is tested by presenting a list of monosyllabic words through an earphone or loudspeaker at various sound pressures or hearing levels corresponding to a normal conversational levels, most comfortable levels, or sensational levels above an individual's speech threshold. The monosyllabic word lists can be presented by tape or by monitored live voice. Usually the word lists are phonetically balanced, meaning that the phonetic elements of the words on the list are balanced in relation to their occurrence in normal speech. An auditory discrimination score is the percentage of words correctly identified. A normal discrimination score is usually considered to be 86 to 100% and in some cases 80 to 100%. A discrimination loss is the difference between an individual's score compared with a normal score under the same conditions; it can be classified as to severity from mild to profound. Auditory discrimination tests can also be scored by determining the number of phonemes correctly and incorrectly identified.

## REFERENCES

Konkle, D. F., & Rintelmann, W. F. (1983). *Principles of speech audiometry*. Baltimore, MD: University Park Press.

Levitt, H. (1978). The acoustics of speech production. In M. Ross & T. G. Giolas (Eds.), *Auditory management of the hearing impaired child* (pp. 45–115). Baltimore, MD: University Park Press.

THOMAS A. FRANK
*Pennsylvania State University*

**AUDITORY PERCEPTION**
**AUDITORY PROCESSING**

## AUDITORY PERCEPTION

Many children with specific language/learning deficits have been described as having auditory perceptual dysfunction (Aten & Davis, 1968; Bakker, 1967; Lowe & Campbell, 1965). Clinically, the term auditory perceptual impairment is often applied by exclusion. That is, once it has been determined that the child's language/learning problem cannot be attributed to mental retardation, hearing loss, frank neurological signs, severe emotional disturbance, paralysis of the speech musculature, or infantile autism, it is hypothesized that the child might have difficulty processing speech and language through the auditory mode and thus might have auditory perceptual deficits (Benton, 1964).

In 1973, Tallal and Piercy (1973a) began to address the following question: What are the relevant stages of auditory processing that might be prerequisite to speech perception? Based on a model of auditory perception developed from studies of animal behavior and physiology, Tallal developed a hierarchical model of stages of auditory processing and a method for assessing each stage (Tallal & Piercy, 1973b). The model begins with detection of a single auditory event. Each auditory event is characterized by a specific frequency, intensity, and duration. Next, detection of two versus one event is assessed with the critical variable being the time between the offset of the first event and the onset of the second; this function is called temporal resolution. Once two events can be perceived, it is possible to discriminate the characteristics of the two stimuli; i.e., whether they are the same or different. If different, do they differ in frequency, intensity and/or time? Once two stimuli are discriminated and identified as different, it is possible to determine their temporal order: which one came first and which one followed. For both discrimination and temporal order judgments, the magnitude of difference between the stimuli and rate of presentation will effect this ability. Finally, once all of these stages of processing have been accomplished with two stimuli, the same stages can occur with three or more stimuli. The number of stimuli that can be processed, stored, and recalled is referred to as memory span. Although this is a serial stage model, for the purpose of assessment, it does not rule out the possibility that many of these stages may occur in parallel.

Tallal and colleagues have demonstrated specific deficits at these various stages of processing and related them to specific deficits in both perceiving and producing speech sounds that characterize children with specific language and reading disorders (Tallal & Piercy, 1973b; Tallal, Stark, & Mellits, 1985). For example, developmentally dysphasic children have been shown to have a severe deficit in the rate at which two or more auditory stimuli can be processed (Tallal & Piercy, 1973b). This rate processing deficit has been shown to interfere with auditory memory

span (Tallal & Piercy, 1973b). Perhaps more significantly, a direct link between this specific rate processing deficit and an inability to perceive and produce rapidly changing temporal cues that characterize certain speech sounds (i.e., /ba/, /da/, /ga/, /pa/, /ta/, /ka/) has been demonstrated (Tallal & Piercy, 1974; Stark & Tallal, 1979).

In conclusion, auditory perception comprises a hierarchical series of steps between the detection (or hearing) of sound at the periphery (the ear) to discriminating, sequencing, storing, and recalling the rapidly changing spectra that characterize the speech stream centrally (at the cortical level). Patients with language/learning problems may have specific deficits at any stage in this complex process. It is important to evaluate basic auditory perception separately from speech/language perception to pinpoint deficits.

### REFERENCES

Aten, J., & Davis, J. (1968). Disturbances in the perception of auditory sequence in children with minimal cerebral dysfunction. *Journal of Speech & Hearing Research, 11,* 236–245.

Bakker, D. J. (1967). Temporal order, meaningfulness, and reading ability. *Perceptual & Motor Skills, 24,* 1027–1030.

Benton, A. L. (1964). Developmental aphasia and brain damage. *Cortex, 1,* 40–52.

Lowe, A. D., & Campbell, R. A. (1965). Temporal discrimination in aphasic and normal children. *Journal of Speech & Hearing Research, 8,* 313–314.

Stark, R., & Tallal, P. (1979). Analysis of stop-consonant production errors in developmentally dysphasic children. *Journal of the Acoustical Society of America, 66,* 1703–1712.

Tallal, P., & Piercy, M. (1973a). Defects of non-verbal auditory perception in children with developmental aphasia. *Nature, 241,* 468–469.

Tallal, P., & Piercy, M. (1973b). Developmental aphasia: Impaired rate of non-verbal processing as a function of sensory modality. *Neuropsychologia, 11,* 389–398.

Tallal, P., & Piercy, M. (1974). Developmental aphasia: Rate of auditory processing and selective impairment of consonant perception. *Neuropsychologia, 12,* 83–93.

Tallal, P., Stark, R., & Mellits, D. (1985). Identification of language impaired children on the basis of rapid perception and production skills. *Brain & Language, 25,* 314–322.

PAULA TALLAL
*University of California, San Diego*

AUDITORY ABNORMALITIES
AUDITORY DISCRIMINATION
AUDITORY PROCESSING

## AUDITORY PROCESSING

Children in the school environment are required to acquire information auditorally. They must be able to sit and listen for long periods of time, cope with noisy environments, and comprehend information presented orally by the teacher. The ability to do this has been labeled auditory processing.

The term auditory processing includes two somewhat different notions. It is, first of all, the physical act of receiving a sound from the environment and transmitting it from the outer ear, through the VIIIth nerve and into the auditory pathways of the brain itself. The second notion is that an individual notices the signal and interprets it. Auditory processing, then, is "the ability to collect, transmit, decode, and integrate acoustic signals that arrive at the ear and continue on through the central auditory pathways to the temporal lobe in the auditory cortex of the central nervous system" (Bess & McConnell, 1981, p. 210).

A number of skills have been included under this definition. Among these are the following:

1. *Discrimination*. The ability to differentiate among sounds not having the same intensity, duration, or frequency.
2. *Localization*. The ability to determine the source of a sound.
3. *Auditory Attention*. The ability to attend to sound, particularly speech, over long periods of time.
4. *Auditory Figure Ground*. The ability to discriminate a speaker's voice from background noise.
5. *Auditory Discrimination*. The ability to differentiate among words and sounds that are similar.
6. *Auditory Closure*. The ability to understand a word or message when part of the signal is missing.
7. *Auditory Blending*. The ability to synthesize phonemes into words.
8. *Auditory Analysis*. The ability to identify phonemes or morphemes within words.
9. *Auditory Association*. The ability to identify a sound with its source.
10. *Auditory Memory; Sequential Memory*. The ability to store and recall auditory stimuli in exact order (Keith, 1981).

Kitchen and Hill (1977) have identified several behavioral characteristics that might indicate there is an auditory processing disorder. These include normal hearing with or without an auditory discrimination breakdown; a peripheral hearing loss that is not of sufficient degree to be causing the learning difficulties being experienced by the child; problems in the areas of reading, writing, and spelling; difficulty in monitoring one's own voice; and overreaction to loud noises.

It must be noted that no direct cause and effect relationship has been found between auditory processing skills and language development, reading, or other academic skills (Rees, 1981). It is true that many children who have learning problems do poorly on tests of auditory processing. However, many children with no learning problems also perform poorly on these tests. It is important, therefore, to be cautious in coming to any conclusions about the relationship between auditory processing and learning. Other terms used to describe auditory processing include central auditory functioning, central auditory ability, and central auditory perception.

In summary, auditory processing is the system whereby the human organism takes in an auditory signal, transmits it to the brain, then perceives it and interprets it. A number of skills have been associated with auditory processing. Among them are discrimination, attention, blending, and analysis. Certain behavioral characteristics such as reading problems and difficulty in monitoring one's own voice might be an indication of an auditory processing problem. However, no direct cause and effect relationship has been found between auditory processing and learning.

### REFERENCES

Bess, F. H., & McConnell, F. E. (1981). *Audiology, education, and the hearing-impaired child*. St. Louis: Mosby.

Keith, R. W. (1981). Tests of central auditory function. In R. J. Roeser & M. P. Downs (Eds.), *Auditory disorders in school children* (pp. 159–176). New York: Thieme-Stratton.

Kitchen, L. M., & Hill, M. J. (1977, April). *The audiologist in the educational setting*. Publication of the Special Study Institute 12, co-sponsored by Oakland Schools and the Michigan Department of Education, Special Education Services.

Rees, N. S. (1981). Saying more than we know: Is auditory processing a meaningful concept? In R. W. Keith (Ed.), *Central auditory and language disorders in children* (pp. 94–120). San Diego, CA: College Hill.

CAROLYN L. BULLARD
*Lewis and Clark College*

**AUDITORY DISCRIMINATION**
**CENTRAL AUDITORY DYSFUNCTION**
**LEARNING DISABILITIES**

## AUDITORY—VISUAL INTEGRATION

Auditory—visual perceptual integration is poorly understood; therefore, it is seldom measured and described in the psychoeducational diagnostic process. Instead, beginning in the 1920s with German psychology, and later (1930s) in clinical work, the focus fell almost solely on visual—motor perceptual development. Indeed, psychology in general, and Gestalt psychology in particular, drew heavily from the easily administered, easily scored visual motor tests. Bender's (1938) *Visual-Motor Gestalt Test*, an extension of Wertheimer's (1923) laboratory instrument, soon became the most commonly administered psycholog-ical test. Early on, these easily administered tests showed substantial correlations with intelligence (Armstrong & Hauck, 1960) as a diagnostic test for brain damage (Shaw & Cruickshank, 1956), academic achievement (Koppitz, 1958), emotional difficulties (Clawson, 1959), and percep-tual development (Koppitz, 1962).

Auditory perception, which in many respects appears to be a sensory–perceptual corollary of visual perception, remains relatively unexplored. The reason may be that the auditory perceptual structures are less well under-stood than visual perception, and more difficult to ascer-tain. For example, it is difficult to identify precisely where auditory sensorial function stops, perception begins, au-ditory perception ends, and receptive language begins.

The result has been that psychologists and special ed-ucators have generally limited the theoretical scope to an explanation of auditory–visual perceptual integration as an operational construct important to human learning. However, that fact also conveys a certain ambience, as remedial educators have been tenacious about the impor-tance of auditory–visual integration within the reading process. They believe that reading would be a slow, awk-ward instructional process in the absence of integrating perceptual symbolic information from the primary sensory channels. Many reading experts are convinced that per-ceptual integration is critical to early learning of letters and letter phonemic symbolism. For example, the visual perceptual system may neurally code a "B" and a "D" as distinct symbols based on luminancy differences. A "B" uses a different neuronal subsystem than a "D" because it draws on lateral inhibition and activation associated with on-center neurons; "D" draws on off-center neurons. Symbolic clarity in the visual perceptual realm may be influenced by these factors, all of which have been well investigated: extent and organization of retinal area ac-tivities; transformation of receptive-field organization; and estimates of size of receptive field.

In reading, as in most visual tasks, the eye gathers in-formation during the pauses between saccadic movements. Ultimately, stimulus letters are recognized; that is, an ap-propriate subvocal or auditory response (saying a letter) occurs. The recognition (perceptual) memory can hold at least three letters for a period of about 1 second, until they have been rehearsed.

A scan component is needed to transform the visual information in very short-term visual perceptual memory into motoric information, and then auditory information. Actually, the visual scan component has at least three dis-tinguishable functions: deciding which areas of the visual field contain information; directing processing capacity to the locations selected by the prescan ("attention"); and converting the visual input from the selected locations into the forms of motor memory units and ultimately auditory information.

In principle, although not in detail, the auditory scan is exactly analogous to the visual scan. The auditory scan selects some contents of auditory memory (e.g., the sound representation of one letter) and converts them into motor information. A street address is remembered by placing it into auditory–perceptual memory. By means of this short-term loop, information can be retained in auditory short-term memory. Subvocal rehearsal, the subvocal output of the rehearsal component, is entered into the auditory short-term memory just as though it had been a vocal out-put. Once that occurs, visual imagery results. The impor-tance of visual–auditory or auditory–visual perceptual in-tegration becomes paramount when confronting remedial reading difficulties. Critchley (1964) noted that children with so-called congenital word blindness failed to develop visual perceptual memory, while their auditory perceptual memory was unaffected.

A great deal of literature from the mid and late 1960s suggests a close interrelationship between the short-term storage mechanisms of vision and audition. Conrad (1959) has shown that subjects frequently make substitution er-rors when recalling lists of visually presented letters in which the letter substituted (e.g., ANQT) sounds similar to the correct letter (e.g., ANQE). Although these letters are highly dissimilar in appearance, they sound similar when spoken aloud. Thus, visual material, Conrad sug-gests, must have been translated and encoded in auditory storage.

Murray (1968) reports extensive studies of short-term storage for visual and auditory items. His results show how the similarity of sounds affected recall of the list (acoustic similarity). In Murray's experiment, conditions enabling the auditory system to assist in the coding and storing of incoming information tend to produce superior performances; this may indicate that the auditory mech-anism is generally superior to the visual mechanism in this respect. Such a superiority has also been demon-strated by Murdock (1968).

Wickelgren (1965) has demonstrated that the presence of acoustic elements in visually presented material can influence the accuracy of recall. Subjects listened to four random letters. Next, eight letters were visually presented and copied by the subject. Finally, a test of the first four aural letters was administered. Even though the inter-polated material had to be copied rather than spoken, if the eight letters were similar in sound to the aural letters, performance on auditory recall was poorer than when the visual letters were quite dissimilar in sound.

Ross (1969) developed a logical test of the audio–visual interaction in short-term storage by measuring the reten-tion of simple symbols (+ and −) either organized in pat-terns (e.g., − + + − + − + −) or unpatterned (e.g., + − + + − + − − +). Blanton and Odom (1968) found a su-periority in seeing and hearing children over deaf children in terms of the span of digits that could be recalled. How-ever, this result may reflect greater experience with num-bers on the part of the normal children.

In short, an integration of information from the visual and auditory perceptual channel seems to be occurring. How else, in fact, could a person read graphics, or listen to others read, and write the graphic symbol being received aurally? Reading is a dual process that, except for the handicapped learner who may be missing one of the sensory channels or have perceptual deficits, is an integrated function.

Of all the perceptual functions, perceptual integration is the most poorly understood. The result is that applied tests do not exist for the practitioner. One study illustrative of research in the area is by Birch and Belmont (1965), who administered a series of cards with three patterns of dots. The examiner first tapped out a pattern. The subject was to listen to the tapped pattern and then look at three sets of dot patterns. One set represented the tapped pattern, the others did not. The examiner than required the subject to point to the appropriate pattern, for instance, the pattern representing the previously tapped sound. Those children who had the greatest difficulty on this task were the most difficult to teach under remedial conditions of reading instruction. These subjects were found to be unable to deal effectively with tasks requiring judgments of auditory–visual equivalence. Thus, the ability to treat visual and auditory patterned information as equivalent differentiated the good reader from the poor reader.

In summary, auditory–visual integration would appear to be the internal stimulation of the opposite modality, for instance, visual perceptual information is received and a signal system translates the meaning to the auditory perceptual modality. Information on the assumed trait is limited, and awaits much research. It does seem likely that this function holds promise as a predictor of what modality may be used as a unisensory or multisensory receiving mechanism in planning an intervention.

## REFERENCES

Armstrong, R. G., & Hauck, P. A. (1960). Correlates of the Bender-Gestalt scores in children. *Journal of Psychological Studies, 11*, 153–158.

Bender, L. (1938). *Visual Motor Gestalt Test and its Clinical Use.* American Ortho Psychiatry Association Research Monograph 3.

Birch, H. G., & Belmont, L. (1965). Auditory-visual integration in brain damaged and normal children. *Journal of Developmental Medicine and Child Neurology, 7*, 135–144.

Blanton, R. L., & Odom, P. B. (1968). Some possible interferences and facilitation effects of pronounciability. *Journal of Verbal Learning Behavior, 7*, 844–846.

Clawson, A. (1959). The Bender-Gestalt Visual Motor Gestalt Test as an index of emotional disturbance in children. *Journal of Project Technology, 23*, 198–206.

Conrad, R. (1959). Errors of immediate memory. *British Journal of Psychology, 50*, 349–359.

Critchley, M. (1965). *The dyslexic child.* London: Heineman.

Koppitz, E. M. (1958). The Bender Gestalt Test and learning disturbances in young children. *Journal of Clinical Psychology, 14*, 292–295.

Koppitz, E. M. (1962). Diagnosing brain damage in young children with the Bender Gestalt Test. *Journal of Consultative Psychology, 26*, 541–546.

Murdock, B. B., Jr. (1968). Modality effects in short-term memory: Storage or retrieval? *Journal of Experimental Psychology, 78*, 70–86.

Murray, D. J. (1968). Articulation and acoustic confusability in short-term memory. *Journal of Experimental Psychology, 78*, 679–684.

Ross, B. M. (1969). Sequential visual memory and the limited magic of the number seven. *Journal of Experimental Psychology, 80*, 339–347.

Shaw, M. C., & Cruickshank, W. M. (1956). The use of the Bender-Gestalt Test with epileptic children. *Journal of Clinical Psychology, 12*, 192–193.

Wertheimer, M. (1923). Untersuchanger zur Lehre von der Gestalt. II. *Psychol. forsch, 5*, 301–350.

Wickelgren, W. A. (1965). Acoustic similarity and intrusion errors in short-term memory. *Journal of Experimental Psychology, 70*, 102–108.

DAVID A. SABATINO
*West Virginia College
of Graduate Studies*

**AUDITORY PERCEPTION**
**AUDITORY PROCESSING**
**VISUAL PERCEPTION AND DISCRIMINATION**

## AUGMENTATIVE COMMUNICATION SYSTEMS

Augmentative communication systems are methods of communication that are used as a supplement to vocal speech. These systems are used with handicapped persons who are unable to use speech as their primary communication method. They are used as permanent alternative substitutes for oral speech or as supplemental communication methods when oral speech is difficult to understand or delayed in development (Harris & Vanderheiden, 1980).

Augmentative communication systems are used with many types of handicapped persons to enhance communication and the development of language skills. A child or adult who is developmentally ready to communicate but is unable to do so because of physical or other handicapping conditions is at risk for developing poor social interaction and language skills. Even when it seems likely that oral speech may eventually develop, augmentative communication systems are used to prevent delayed communication development. Several studies have shown that the use of augmentative communication systems can sometimes lead to improved oral communication skills (Silverman, McNaughton, & Kates, 1978).

There are two categories of augmentative communication systems: unaided and aided. Unaided communication systems use only the physical body for communication. Sign language, gestures, vocalizations, and facial expressions are unaided communication methods. Aided communication methods require additional tools or equipment to convey a message. Typewriters, communication boards, pen and paper, and microcomputers can all be used as aided communication methods. Although aided communication systems are physically cumbersome, they have the advantage of being easily understood by most listeners. Unaided systems usually require familiarity with the nonspeaking person for the communication system to be understood.

Effective augmentative communication systems should promote social and communicative interactions. To enhance interaction across many social situations, more than one type of augmentative communication system may be needed. The handicapped person should be able to use a variety of augmentative communication methods and apply them appropriately. A handicapped person might rely on a large microcomputer for lengthy conversations, school work, and phone calls through a modem. Because a large microcomputer is not portable, the same person may have a communication board to take shopping or to go outside. In addition, head nods, simple gestures, and vocalizations might be used for rapid communication with friends and family who are familiar with the person. Through using all available augmentative communication methods, social interaction can be enhanced and communication can become effective.

## REFERENCES

Harris, D., & Vanderheiden, G. (1980). Enhancing the development of communicative interaction. In R. E. Schiefelbusch (Ed.), *Nonspeech language and communication: Analysis and intervention*. Baltimore, MD: University Park Press.

Silverman, H., McNaughton, S., & Kates, B. (1978). *Handbook of Blissymbolics*. Toronto, Ontario: Blissymbolics Communication Institute.

SHARON L. GLENNEN
*Pennsylvania State University*

## ALTERNATIVE COMMUNICATION METHODS IN SPECIAL EDUCATION
## BLISSYMBOLS

# AUSTRALIA, SPECIAL EDUCATION IN

Australian special education in the latter half of the twentieth century has been characterized by rapid growth and extensive heterogeneity among states in the areas of service delivery systems, proportion of children served, integration, and professional training opportunities. The results of a national survey indicate that the prevalence rates of various handicapping conditions in Australia are broadly comparable to those found elsewhere (Ward, 1982).

The extreme variability in the organization of special education services among states is compounded by the important contributions of nonstate agencies. In certain areas, voluntary agencies rather than state programs have been the primary sources of education for the disabled for years. These voluntary groups and associations, which still make an extensive contribution to special education in Australia, are tangible evidence of community concern and support. Some have been able to attract funding, to use it effectively, and to develop exemplary programs.

With the assistance of new and substantial government funding, the integration of special education students and regular education students is being carried out on a large scale in Australia, and services for the profoundly retarded are being developed. Nonetheless, special schools maintain an important role in the continuum of services and places in these schools are in demand. There remains a need for services for the emotionally disturbed and full-time education for children in residential settings (Ward, 1982).

Interest in gifted and talented education gathered momentum in Australia in the late 1970s. Issues such as identification, programming practices, and teacher training were addressed, and special-interest high schools were formed in some states and territories. Each state now has an Association for the Gifted and Talented and the future outlook is optimistic in this area (Croome, 1982).

Australia has made considerable advances in the training of special educators. Prior to 1970, few training opportunities were available for teachers of special students. Recent government interest and funding, however, have led to a rapid increase in training opportunities and a wide variety of programs is currently available at universities throughout Australia. Australian tertiary institutions form the basis of an integrated approach to special education training at both preservice and in-service levels (Andrews & Atkinson, 1976).

## REFERENCES

Andrews, R. J., & Atkinson, J. K. (1976). The training of special educators in Australian tertiary institutions. *Exceptional Child, 23,* 175–197.

Croome, A. B. (1982). Gifted and talented education in Australia. *Roeper Review, 4*(4), 38–40.

Ward, J. (1982). Special education in Australia. *Exceptional Child, 29,* 137–148.

GREG VALCANTE
*University of Florida*

# NEW ZEALAND, SPECIAL EDUCATION IN

# AUTISM

Autism is generally regarded as the most severe of a group of developmental disorders arising early in childhood. Although isolated written case reports exist from as early as the 1800s, the first systematic description of the disorder was published by Leo Kanner in 1943. Kanner felt that autism was the earliest form of schizophrenia, and his choice of the term "autistic" to describe the children's poor relatedness followed Bleuler's (1911) earlier use of the term as one of the hallmarks of adult schizophrenia. Rutter (1978) and others have pointed out how the use of that term has contributed to the confusion surrounding this perplexing disorder.

Although some have argued that autism is not a disorder distinct from other developmental disorders involving language and/or mental retardation, a careful review of the literature (Rutter & Schopler, 1985) appears not to support this view. Rather, four diagnostic criteria form the basis for this disorder: early onset, present at least by the age of 3 years, and often noted from shortly after birth; failure of the child to form social relationships, even taking into account any delays in this area attributed to the mental retardation that usually accompanies autism; deviant as well as delayed development of communications skills and the failure to use language effectively as a tool in social relationships; and stereotyped, repetitive patterns of behavior involving rigid habits and routines that must not be violated and a refusal to engage in unfamiliar or new activities. The syndrome so defined represents the most current thinking about the diagnosis of autism and differs somewhat from the definition proposed by Kanner (1943), which is sometimes known as Kanner's syndrome or classic autism. The disorder can readily be distinguished from childhood schizophrenia by the absence of the delusions and hallucinations and the much later onset of childhood schizophrenia.

Studies in the United States (Schopler, et al., 1980; Schopler, Reichler, & Renner, 1985) and in Europe (Wing & Gould, 1979) have produced a considerable body of epidemiological data about autism. The rate of incidence is usually put at 4 to 5 per 10,000 births, although the use of broader diagnostic criteria may raise the incidence to as many as 20 per 10,000. The disorder affects about four times as many boys as girls. Some have noted that affected girls tend to have a somewhat poorer outcome (Lotter, 1978). Perhaps one-quarter of the population suffers from a seizure disorder that develops by adolescence (Deykin & McMahon, 1978), and the development of seizures early in life (e.g., before age three) is a poor prognostic sign.

Both the issues of the children's intelligence and parental socioeconomic status (SES) have been a source of controversy about autistic children. Kanner (1943) originally felt that the children all had at least average intellectual ability; he noted that some children even demonstrated prodigious abilities in certain circumscribed areas, usually involving memory, but also in some cases involving musical or artistic skills, sense of direction, or calculation ability. Despite the existence of these "peak skills" in some areas, three-fourths of the children have been shown to be mentally retarded, with no more than 10% having "average" scores (Rutter, 1979). Those children who have no language and/or an IQ of 50 or less have a poorer prognosis than others.

Kanner's original sample of 11 autistic children (as well as several other subsequent samples reported by other authors) also contained a disproportionate number of families from upper SES levels. This observation had been used to substantiate the position that autism might be a disorder of psychogenic origin. However, a large-scale (e.g., 500 families) study of this phenomenon (Schopler, Andrews, & Strupp, 1979) has indicated that only about 20% of the sample came from the two upper SES classes. The families in the sample were represented in both race and sex in approximately the same proportion as they are in the statewide population from which the sample was drawn. A number of sampling and selection biases appear to have contributed to the impression that autism is an upper-SES disorder.

Although Kanner himself was uncertain about the exact causes of autism, mental-health professionals of his era commonly assumed that the disorder was due to psychological factors, especially parental pathology. Perhaps the most famous proponent of the parental-pathology hypothesis was Bettelheim (1950), who maintained that autistic children withdraw and do not relate in response to the perceived coldness and pathology of their family environment. It was felt that the best treatment regimen involved separation of the child and parents. Parents received therapy to help them stop evoking this behavior from their children while the children were encouraged to express their feelings and conflicts in a permissive play-oriented setting. This view of parents and this treatment approach was first challenged by Rimland (1964) and later by others (Cantwell, Baker, & Rutter, 1978) who have shown that families of autistic children do not show more pathology than other families. In fact, scapegoating and prejudice by mental-health professionals have impeded parental efforts to find help for their children (Schopler, 1971). The movement away from the psychogenic theory of autism is reflected in the reclassification of autism by the government, in 1977, as a developmental disability, and by the American Psychiatric Association in its 1980 *Diagnostic and Statistical Manual* (DSM-III) as a "pervasive developmental disorder."

In recent years, one focus of research has been on identifying biochemical, genetic, or other *medical causes* of autism. Although it is still not clear whether autism is a unitary disease process, as Kanner (1943) supposed, as the syndrome is investigated, a wide array of organic factors that are associated with the disorder is being identified.

This makes it increasingly unlikely that a specific process underlies all autistic disturbances. Autism has been at times associated with prenatal or perinatal complications, maternal rubella during pregnancy, celiac disease, tuberous sclerosis, possible deficiencies in purine metabolism, and genetic conditions such as fragile-X syndrome (Rutter & Schopler, 1985). None of these factors, however, accounts for more than a very small percentage of the total number of cases, and most physical examinations and current studies of brain structure and metabolic functioning of autistic people show no abnormalities. Thus, even if autism is not a unitary process, we are not sure if the various factors identified are somehow functionally related in a final common pathway to autism. Whatever the organic basis of the disorder, it is very subtle and not easily understood. Although biomedical research into the causes of autism holds much promise for the future, medical treatment per se for autism is of limited value except in situations where the administration of medication may be helpful in treating conditions such as epilepsy or extreme hyperactivity.

A variety of other treatments have been proposed and attempted with autistic children. Traditional approaches such as analytically oriented "talking therapy" and play therapy are not successful because only a few autistic children have the language skills to be able to participate. Even when sufficient language exists, autistic people have difficulties in relating to others; that precludes the formation of the therapist–client relationship so critical in traditional therapeutic methods. More recent approaches (called megavitamin therapy) have involved the administration of large doses of water-soluble vitamins such as vitamin $B_6$, the use of diets low in refined sugar and/or additives, and the use of stimulants such as fenfluramine. While encouraging individual case reports support the use of each of these methods, few controlled studies exist to demonstrate their utility with a wide range of autistic children. Given the diversity of etiological agents thought to cause autism, it seems unlikely that any of these approaches will be effective for a broad sample of children.

The most effective forms of treatment to date have involved the development of behavioral and educational management strategies for autistic children and their parents. Originally, behavioral treatment was applied to children in special residential schools or hospital units where the children were separated from their families in order to create a more controlled, predictable environment. While the application of contingencies did produce some marked short-term improvements in behavior and in important areas such as language, follow-up studies suggested that gains could not be sustained outside the residential setting unless extensive parent training was given (Lovaas, et al., 1973). In addition, the removal of the child from the natural environment of home tended to increase the guilt many parents felt and added to their perceptions of themselves as inept and inadequate.

The first program to combine the elements of individualized assessment, a structured *outpatient education* and family involvement program geared to the needs of each individual family, is the TEACCH program (Treatment and Education of Autistic and related Communications-handicapped CHildren) in North Carolina (Schopler & Reichler, 1971; Schopler & Olley, 1982). The assessment process is built around the Psychoeducational Profile, or PEP (Schopler, Reichler, & Lansing, 1978), an instrument especially designed to use with this population. The PEP is composed of items within the intellectual reach of most autistic children that tap an array of skill areas while avoiding reliance on rigid administration formats and/or high-level language skills. The resulting skills profile is fully shared with parents, who have observed most of the assessment. The profile can readily be translated into an individual education plan (IEP). The IEP forms the basis for the child's home treatment program and a parallel structured educational experience in a public school classroom. In the home-training program, parents are given teaching tasks to carry out at home in daily work sessions with their child. In visits to one of the TEACCH treatment centers, they demonstrate their work with the child in front of a one-way mirror while staff members observe. The staff in turn designs subsequent home programs and demonstrates these with the parents observing. In this way both parents and professionals use their special knowledge of the child as cotherapists to foster development. Similarly, in the classroom specially trained teaching staff, parents, and center staff combine their perspectives on the child's needs to design an individual educational approach for that child. Following basic research in the area (Schopler, Brehm, Kinsbourne, & Reichler, 1971), classes are kept small, usually with no more than five to seven students, and the classroom day is well-organized and structured. A variety of teaching techniques may be used, including simultaneous communications (sign language) in the teaching of communication skills, perceptual and motor skills activities, and group learning tasks, as well as more traditional behavior modification approaches.

The most recent area of education interest concerns the adolescent and adult autistic person. Since few opportunities exist for education, employment, or recreation after the mandatory program of public school, there is a great need to extend the range of services to include these people. The TEACCH program, among others, is working to provide appropriate assessment and vocational and daily living skills training for older autistic persons and their families. Parents and professionals are also working together to promote research and treatment for autistic people of all ages in an organization known as the National Society for Autistic Children (NSAC). This organization has been especially important as a resource of information and support for all who work with this population.

It is clear that educational approaches such as those

described have resulted in a reduction of some of the symptoms of autism and the increased likelihood that the children and their families will live successfully together for a longer period of time. However, as Lotter (1978) and others have noted, the prognosis for most autistic children remains guarded. The best predictors of later outcome are the presence of "communicative" language and an IQ above 50. Only about 10% of autistic children will eventually be able to make adjustments allowing them to live and work and make decisions about their personal lives outside of a supervised setting such as a group home or other residential placement. Very few marry, although some do learn to enjoy heterosexual companionship. Symptoms generally become a bit less severe in adulthood, but the basic defect in relatedness remains the single most significant impediment to establishing a fully independent style of living for even the most able autistic people.

## REFERENCES

Bettelheim, B. (1950). *Love is not enough*, Glencoe, IL: Free Press.

Bleuler, E. (1911). Dementia praecox oder Gruppe der Schizophrenien (J. Zinkin, translator). New York: International University Press.

Cantwell, D., Baker, L., & Rutter, M. (1978). Family factors. In M. Rutter & E. Schopler (Eds.), *Autism: A reappraisal of concepts and treatment*. New York: Plenum.

Deykin, E., & McMahon, D. (1978). The incidence of seizures among children with autistic symptoms. *American Journal of Psychiatry, 136*, 1310–1312.

Kanner, L. (1943). Autistic disturbances of affective contact. *Nervous Child, 2*, 217–230.

Lotter, V. (1978). Follow-up studies. In M. Rutter & E. Schopler (Eds.), *Autism: A reappraisal of concepts and treatment*. New York: Plenum.

Lovaas, I., Koegel, R., Simmons, J., & Long, J. (1973). Some generalization and follow-up measures on autistic children in behavior therapy. *Journal of Applied Behavior Analysis, 6*, 131–166.

Rimland, B. (1964). *Infantile autism*. New York: Appleton-Century-Crofts.

Rutter, M. (1978). Diagnosis and definition of childhood autism. *Journal of Autism and Developmental Disorders, 8*, 139–161.

Rutter, M. (1979). Language, cognition and autism. In R. Katzman (Ed.), *Congenital and acquired cognitive disorders*. New York: Raven.

Rutter, M., & Schopler, E. (1985). Autism and pervasive developmental disorders; Concepts and diagnostic issues. Paper prepared for NIMH Research Workshop.

Schopler, E. (1971). Parents of psychotic children as scapegoats. *Journal of Contemporary Psychotherapy, 4*, 17–22.

Schopler, E., Andrews, C., & Strupp, K. (1979). Do autistic children come from upper-middle-class parents? *Journal of Autism and Developmental Disorders, 9*, 139–151.

Schopler, E., & Olley, J. (1982). Comprehensive educational services for autistic children: The TEACCH model. In C. R. Reynolds & T. R. Gutkin (Eds.), *Handbook of School Psychology*. New York: Wiley.

Schopler, E., & Reichler, R. (1971). Parents as co-therapists in the treatment of psychotic children. *Journal of Autism and Childhood Schizophrenia, 1*, 87–102.

Schopler, E., Reichler, R., DeVellis, R., & Daly, K. (1980). Toward objective classification of childhood autism: Childhood Autism Rating Scale (CARS). *Journal of Autism and Developmental Disorders, 10*, 91–103.

Schopler, E., Reichler, R., & Lansing, M. (1978). *Individualized assessment and treatment for autistic and developmentally disabled children: The Psychoeducational Profile. Vol. I.* Baltimore, MD: University Park Press.

Schopler, E., Reichler, R. J., & Renner, B. R. (1985). The Childhood Autism Rating Scale (CARS) for diagnostic screening and classification of autism. New York: Irvington.

Wing, L., & Gould, J. (1979). Severe impairments of social interaction and associated abnormalities in children: Epidemiology and classification. *Journal of Autism and Developmental Disorders, 9*, 11–30.

ERIC SCHOPLER
*University of North Carolina,
Chapel Hill*

JERRY L. SLOAN
*Wilmington Psychiatric
Associates, Wilmington,
North Carolina*

**AUTISTIC BEHAVIOR**
**NATIONAL SOCIETY FOR CHILDREN AND ADULTS WITH AUTISM**

## AUTISTIC BEHAVIOR

Autistic behavior is the name for those activities and characteristics frequently associated with the developmental disorder known variously as autism, early infantile autism, or Kanner's (1943) syndrome. Although autism is a specific syndrome having well-defined diagnostic criteria, a wide variety of behaviors are said to be autistic. Further, many of the behaviors are occasionally exhibited by children with other developmental syndromes and disorders such as mental retardation, cerebral palsy, and serious disorders of receptive and/or expressive language. A particular pattern of symptoms, including an early age of onset as well as social and language peculiarities, characterizes the syndrome known as autism and distinguishes it from all other childhood psychotic disorders. Thus, the mere presence of behaviors called autistic in a child's repertoire does not guarantee that autism is the appropriate diagnosis for that child. Further, it is very unusual for any child diagnosed as autistic to show all of the behaviors that have been associated with autism.

One of the first attempts to compile the range of behaviors observed among autistic children was made by Creak (1964) and her colleagues in Great Britain. Similar sets of observations have been reported since that time by others. The observations may be summarized as follows:

1. Unusual and/or self-stimulatory behaviors such as rocking to and fro, flicking fingers in front of the eyes, flapping arms or hands rapidly at particular frequencies, adopting unusual postures, or toe walking.

2. Reluctance to use the distance receptors of vision and hearing. This translates into an avoidance of eye contact and inattention to auditory and visual cues and information. By contrast there is often an excessive and age-inappropriate reliance on near receptors such as taste, touch, and smell for exploration. The threshold for pain may also be unusually high.

3. A preoccupation with certain objects or the operations of objects, often without respect to their intended function. For example, a child may be fascinated by an empty record turntable spinning or may play with a toy truck only by turning it on its side to spin its wheels.

4. The absence of speech or, where speech exists, delays and/or peculiarities such as the use of jargon, the repetition of phrases or whole passages (echolalia), the reversal or misuse of personal pronouns, and idiosyncratic use of words (neologisms).

5. Unusual anxieties, often unrelated to actual environmental circumstances. For instance, a child may become unusually upset if furniture is rearranged in a room, but may remain calm and seemingly unconcerned while involved in an auto accident or while performing dangerous activities such as climbing or balancing at great heights.

6. An unwillingness to have familiar routines changed or delayed and a reluctance to participate in new activities or to process unexpected events. Thus a child may insist on walking exactly the same route to school daily, may wish to constantly possess a particular toy, or consume only certain foods. Any changes or interruptions of these routines produce extreme anxiety.

7. A pattern of uneven intellectual development characterized by general mental retardation with "islands" of near normal, normal, or even supranormal functioning. A child may not be able to answer simple questions (why, when, where, etc.), but the same child may perform complex mathematical calculations or read large and unfamiliar words, though this skill is usually not accompanied by adequate comprehension.

Several authors have attempted to provide rating scales as an aid in formulating a diagnosis to quantify the types and amounts of autistic behavior a child shows while being observed. Three scales in fairly widespread use are the BRIAAC (Ruttenberg, et al., 1966), the CARS (Schopler, et al., 1985), and the BOS (Freeman, et al., 1984). Such scales may be useful in planning educational or behavioral intervention programs because they focus on particular problem behaviors and they usually reliably dis-

ciminate among samples of normal, retarded, and autistic people. However, they are less useful in establishing individual diagnoses because they only tap behaviors observed within the relatively brief observation period. They tend to be of greatest use in the most severe cases of autism, where mental retardation is also likely to be quite marked. Nevertheless, the scales are very useful in the overall process of diagnosis and intervention.

## REFERENCES

Creak, M. (1964). Schizophrenic syndrome in childhood: Further progress report of a working party. *Developmental Medicine and Child Neurology, 6*, 530–535.

Freeman, B., Ritvo, E., & Schroth, P. (1984). Behavior assessment of the syndrome of autism: Behavior Observation System. *Journal of the American Academy of Child Psychiatry, 23*, 588–594.

Kanner, L. (1943). Autistic disturbances of affective contact. *Nervous Child, 2*, 217–250.

Ruttenberg, B., Dratman, M., Fraknoi, J., & Wenar, C. (1966). An instrument for evaluating autistic children. *Journal of the American Academy of Child Psychiatry, 5*, 453–478.

Schopler, E., Reichler, R., & Renner, B. (1985). *Childhood Autism Rating Scale (CARS)*. New York: Irvington.

JERRY L. SLOAN
*Wilmington Psychiatric
Associates, Wilmington,
North Carolina*

## AUTISM
## NATIONAL SOCIETY FOR CHILDREN AND ADULTS WITH AUTISM

## AUTISTIC CHILDREN

See AUTISM.

## AUTOMATICITY

Automaticity is an aspect of perceptual and motor processing that occurs outside of conscious awareness. Factors such as stimulus novelty and response practice have been found to be related to automaticity in cognitive functioning (Neiser, 1976). When aroused by a novel or difficult stimulus, extensive cognitive processing occurs, forcing the event into conscious awareness. However, an habitual response elicited by an expected stimulus may be performed at an automatic level requiring little or no attention.

Since humans have a limited attention capacity, automatic functions add to the efficiency of the information processing system (Kutas & Hillyard, 1980). Many simple perceptual processes are innately automatic, while even complex activities such as reading can become automatic with sufficient practice. In fact, Hancock and Byrd (1984) state that reading efficiency is dependent on the extent to which decoding skills become automatized, and Garnett and Fleischner (1980) have related automatization to basic math facts acquisition.

Learning disabilities, and mental retardation, have been discussed in terms of deficient automatization processes. Learning-disabled children have been found to take longer to produce acquired math facts than their non-disabled peers (Garnett & Fleischner, 1980). Their inability to perform this well-drilled task at an automatic level suggests that learning-disabled children's thinking processes are more circuitous and attention demanding. Severely disabled readers have been found to have difficulty processing letters within words, while less impaired readers, who have automatized letter recognition, read whole words in a controlled, attention-demanding manner (Hancock & Byrd, 1984).

Other researchers have suggested that automatic functions may be available to learning-disabled and retarded students, but that other factors impede their effects. Thus, retarded children have been found to perform as well as their nonretarded peers on a measure of perceptual memory automatization (Stein, Laskowski, & Trancone, 1982). The retarded children, however, had more difficulty organizing new skills, thereby preventing the automitization of more complex processes. In another study, learning-disabled children were found to produce the correct definitions of familiar words at a rate equal to that of non-disabled children, but showed a rapid decline in rate and accuracy when unfamiliar words were introduced (Ceci, 1983). As more purposeful processing was required, the learning-disabled students failed to decode the words, and instead substituted words that could be processed at an automatic level.

## REFERENCES

Ceci, S. J. (1983). Automatic and purposeful semantic processing characteristics of normal and language/learning disabled children. *Developmental Psychology, 19*(3), 427–439.

Garnett, K., & Fleischner, J. (1980). *Automatization and basic fact performance of normal and learning disabled children* (Technical Report No. 10). Washington, DC: Office of Special Education (ERIC Document Reproduction Service No. ED 210 839).

Hancock, A. C., & Byrd, D. (1984, April). *Automatic processing in normal and learning disabled children.* Paper presented at the annual meeting of the Southwestern Psychological Association, New Orleans (ERIC Document Reproduction Service No. ED 246 414).

Kutas, M., & Hillyard, S. A. (1980). Reading senseless sentences: Brain potentials reflect sementic incongruity. *Science, 207,* 203–204.

Neiser, U. (1976). *Cognition and reality.* San Francisco: Freeman.

Stein, D. K., Laskowski, M. A., & Trancone, J. (1982). *Automatic memory processes in mentally retarded persons.* Paper presented at the annual meeting of the American Psychological Association, Washington, DC (ERIC Document Reproduction Service No. ED 227 604).

GARY BERKOWITZ
*Temple University*

**COGNITIVE STRATEGIES
CONDITIONING
TRANSFER OF LEARNING**


# AUTOMUTISM

See ELECTIVE MUTISM.


# AUTONOMIC REACTIVITY

The autonomic nervous system consists of the sympathetic nervous system and the parasympathetic nervous system. The sympathetic nervous system increases heart rate, adrenal secretions, sweating, and other responses that prepare the body for vigorous activity. The parasympathetic nervous system increases salivation, digestion, and other vegetative responses while antagonizing many effects of the sympathetic nervous system.

The sympathetic system can be activated by sudden sensory stimuli or by emotional experiences. The response to a stimulus depends on one's interpretation of the stimulus and not on just the stimulus itself. Shock believed to be escapable increases heart rate; shock believed to be inescapable decreases it (Malcuit, 1973). A task given to fifth-grade boys as a test increased heart rate; a similar task given to them as a game decreased it (Darley & Katz, 1973).

The sympathetic nervous system is apparently most reactive in early childhood, when gauged by variability of heart rate (Shields, 1983). Sympathetic reactivity is fairly stable over time and may be related to personality traits. Many people with an antisocial personality have a weak sympathetic response to frightening stimuli. Some authors link high sympathetic responsiveness with impulsiveness and distractibility (Shields, 1983).

## REFERENCES

Darley, S. A., & Katz, K. (1973). Heart rate changes in children as a function of test versus game instructions and test anxiety. *Child Development, 44,* 784–789.

Malcuit, G. (1973). Cardiac responses in aversive situation with and without avoidance possibility. *Psychophysiology, 10,* 295–306.

Shields, S. A. (1983). Development of autonomic nervous system responsivity in children: A review of the literature. *International Journal of Behavioral Development, 6*, 291–319.

JAMES W. KALAT
*North Carolina State University*

CENTRAL NERVOUS SYSTEM
LEARNED HELPLESSNESS

# AVERSIVE CONTROL

The use of aversive stimuli to control behavior is one of the most controversial techniques employed by teachers, researchers, psychologists, therapists, and others. The effectiveness of this procedure is defined by its effect on behavior: it suppresses the behavior that it follows. This definition is similar to that for punishment. Indeed, aversive control is one form of punishment.

The controversy surrounding the use of aversive control is illustrated by Wood and Lakin (1982). They indicate that, although most states approve of the use of moderate corporal punishment, it is specifically forbidden by statutes in others (e.g., Maine and Massachusetts).

The use of aversive consequences for behavior control generally is viewed as a technique to be used only when other techniques have not been successful. Snell (1983) indicates that:

> Aversive conditioning using strong primary aversion (such as electric shock and slapping) to eliminate behavior is very defensible in two general instances: when the behavior is so dangerous or self-destructive that positive reinforcement and extinction are not feasible and when all other intervention methods (reinforce competing response, extinction, milder punishment forms) have been applied competently and have been documented as unsuccessful. (p. 140)

Despite the reservations that have been expressed regarding the use of aversives, aversives have been used to control behavior, particularly self-injurious behavior (SIB). Lemon juice (Sajwaj, Libet, & Agras, 1974), noxious odors (Baumeister & Baumeister, 1978), and electric shock (McConaghy, Armstrong, & Blaszcynski, 1981) are examples of aversive methods that have been used.

At times and under certain conditions, aversive procedures have been found to be the treatment of choice. However, aversive control should be reduced or eliminated when the desired behavior change has occurred or when the target behavior responds to less severe techniques. Suppression, and not elimination, of targeted behavior may result from using this technique. Unexpected and unintended results often occur whenever a punishment procedure is used; it is possible that similar side effects may occur when aversive control is used.

The use of aversives to control behavior raises many ethical questions. The basic rationale for the use of aversives is that other methods have failed, the child is at risk, and the aversive to be used is not as harmful as the behavior that is targeted for change.

## REFERENCES

Baumeister, A., & Baumeister, A. (1978). Suppression of repetitive self-injurious behavior by contingent inhalation of aromatic ammonia. *Journal of Autism & Childhood Schizophrenia, 8*, 71–77.

McConaghy, N., Armstrong, M., & Blaszczynski, A. (1981). Controlled comparison of aversive therapy and covert sensitization in compulsive homosexuality. *Behavior Research & Therapy, 19*, 425–434.

Sajwaj, T., Libet, J., & Agras, S. (1974). Lemon juice therapy: The control of life threatening rumination in a six-month old infant. *Journal of Applied Behavior Analysis, 1*, 557–566.

Snell, M. (Ed.). (1983). *Systematic instruction of the moderately and severely handicapped* (2nd ed.). Columbus, OH: Merrill.

Wood, F. H., & Lakin, K. C. (Eds.), (1982). *Punishment and aversive stimulation in special education: Legal, theoretical and practical issues in their use with emotionally disturbed children and youth.* Reston, VA: Council for Exceptional Children.

PHILIP E. LYON
*College of St. Rose*

BEHAVIOR MODIFICATION
OPERANT CONDITIONING
PUNISHMENT

# AVERSIVE STIMULUS

An aversive stimulus, whether unconditioned (e.g., bright lights) or conditioned (e.g., a frown or gesture) is "an unpleasant object or event" (Sulzer-Azaroff & Mayer, 1986) that can be used to decrease or increase a behavior. When presented as a consequence of, or contingent on, a specific behavior, it may be used to reduce or eliminate the rate of that behavior. However, when an aversive stimulus is removed contingent on the emission of a behavior, it may increase the rate of that behavior. In any case, an aversive stimulus is typically referred to as a punisher.

The application of aversive stimuli to effectively reduce or eliminate severe self-destructive behaviors and/or severe chronic behaviors has been demonstrated by several researchers including Lovaas and Simmons (1969) and Risley (1968). However, the many disadvantages of applying aversive stimuli to reduce behaviors (e.g., withdrawal, aggression, generalization, imitation, negative self-statements; Sulzer-Azaroff & Mayer, 1986) seem to outweigh the advantages. Aversive stimuli to reduce behaviors should be reserved for serious destructive behaviors and employed only when other less aversive procedures have been tried. A more detailed presentation of the use of aversive stimuli may be found in Sulzer-Azaroff & Mayer (1986).

### REFERENCES

Lovaas, O. I., & Simmons, J. O. (1969). Manipulation of self destruction in three retarded children. *Journal of Applied Behavior Analysis, 2,* 143–157.

Risley, T. (1968). The effects and side effects of punishing the autistic behaviors of a deviant child. *Journal of Applied Behavior Analysis, 1,* 21–35.

Sulzer-Azaroff, B., & Mayer, G. R. (1986). *Achieving educational excellence using behavior strategies.* New York: Holt, Rinehart, & Winston.

ALLISON LEWIS
LOUIS J. LANUNZIATA
*University of North Carolina,
Wilmington*

**BEHAVIOR MODIFICATION
PUNISHMENT**

## AVEYRON, WILD BOY OF

See WILD BOY OF AVEYRON.

## AYLLON, TEODORO (1929– )

Teodoro Ayllon obtained his PhD in clinical psychology in 1959 at the University of Houston. His special areas of interest are in behavior and condition therapy and applied behavior analysis. His major field of interest is in clinical psychology. He has done extensive research in behavioral analysis and management and has published articles and books concerning this subject.

Some of his principal contributions include "Eliminating Discipline Problems by Strengthening Academic Performance," "The Elimination of Discipline Problems Through a Combined School-Home Motivational System," and "Behavioral Management of School Phobias." In these articles, Ayllon discusses a procedure in which discipline problems and school phobias can be remedied by having parents support the child with positive reinforcement to increase motivation to go to school and improve performance.

He continues his research in clinical psychology and behavioral management and remains involved in the field of psychology. Ayllon's work has been recognized with honors. He is presently a professor of psychology and special education in the psychology department at Georgia State University.

### REFERENCES

Ayllon, T. (1974). Eliminating discipline problems by strengthening academic performance. *Journal of Applied Behavior Analysis, 7,* 71–76.

Ayllon, T., Garber, S., & Pisor, K. (1975). The elimination of discipline problems through a combined school-home motivational system. *Journal of Behavior Therapy, 6,* 616–626.

Ayllon, T., Smith, D., & Rogers, M. (1970). Behavioral management of school phobia. *Journal of Behavioral Therapy & Experimental Psychiatry, 1,* 125–138.

REBECCA BAILEY
*Texas A&M University*

## AYRES, A. JEAN (1920– )

A. Jean Ayres received her BS (1945) and MS (1954) in occupational therapy. In 1961 she earned her PhD in educational psychology from the University of Southern California. From 1964 to 1966, she was a postdoctoral trainee at the Brain Research Institute, University of California, Los Angeles. She worked as an occupational therapist from 1946 to 1955 in several California rehabilitation centers, and taught or conducted research at the University of Southern California in the departments of Occupational Therapy and Special Education between 1955 and 1984. She had a private practice in occupational therapy from 1977 to 1984.

Ayres has published over 50 articles, tests, and films. The majority of her work has dealt with occupational therapy, especially as related to perceptual and sensory integrative dysfunction and neuromuscular integration. Ayres (1972) emphasized the normalization of the sensory

A. Jean Ayres

integration process in the brain stem, but not to the exclusion of cortical integrative processes. Ayres' approach to learning and behavior disorders is distinguished by use of a neurological as opposed to educational or psychodynamic model to assist in understanding the problems. Ayres' research found that students with certain identifiable types of sensory integrative dysfunctions, and who received occupational therapy specifically for the integrative dysfunction, showed greater gains in academic scores than those who received an equal amount of time in academic work. Perhaps her greatest contribution is as the progenitor of sensory-integrative therapy as a treatment for learning disorders, a therapeutic approach in widespread use among occupational therapists.

Ayres developed the Southern California Sensory Integration Tests and the Sensory Integration and Praxis Tests. She was named to the 1971 edition of *Outstanding Educators of America*. She has also received the Eleanor Clarke Slagle Lectureship and the Award of Merit, the highest awards from the American Occupational Therapy Association. She is a charter member of the honorary Academy of Research of that organization.

## REFERENCES

Ayres, A. J. (in press). *Sensory Integration and Praxis Tests*. Los Angeles, CA: Western Psychological Services.

Ayres, A. J. (1972). Improving academic scores through sensory integration. *Journal of Learning Disabilities, 5,* 338–343.

E. VALERIE HEWITT
*Texas A&M University*

**OCCUPATIONAL THERAPY**
**SENSORY-INTEGRATIVE THERAPY**

# B

## BABINSKI REFLEX

The Babinski reflex is a superficial reflex occurring normally during infancy but abnormally after the first year or when locomotion begins. The Babinski reflex is elicited by firmly stroking the lateral aspect of the sole of the foot, moving forward from the heel to the fifth toe. Another reflex elicited in the same manner is the plantar reflex, which occurs normally throughout life (Behrman & Vaughan, 1983).

The Babinski response consists of extension of the great toe and fanning of the other toes. The plantar reflex response consists of flexion of the toes (Menkes, 1984). The presence of Babinski's reflex after the first year is an indication of spinal cord lesions and requires further neurological evaluation (Whaley & Wong, 1983).

### REFERENCES

Behrman, R. E., & Vaughan, V. C. (Eds.). (1983). *Nelson textbook of pediatrics* (12th ed.). Philadelphia: Saunders.

Menkes, J. H. (1984). Neurologic evaluation of the newborn infant. In M. E. Avery & H. W. Taeusch (Eds.), *Schaffer's diseases of the newborn* (5th ed., pp. 652–661). Philadelphia: Saunders.

Whaley, L. F., & Wong, D. L. (1983). *Nursing care of infants and children* (2nd ed.). St. Louis: Mosby.

ELIZABETH R. BAUERSCHMIDT
*University of North Carolina,
Wilmington*

## APGAR RATING SCALE
## DEVELOPMENTAL MILESTONES

## BABY DOE

The term *Baby Doe* has come to signify the issue of denying life-sustaining treatment to infants born with permanent handicaps combined with life-threatening but surgically correctable conditions. These infants are the focus of a debate that tests the limits of medical certainty in diagnosis and raises profound ethical and legal issues.

A major stimulus to the ethical and legal debate on foregoing life-sustaining treatment for newborns was provided by Duff and Campbell (1973). Their article describes how and why nontreatment was chosen for 43 out of 299 infants during a 30-month period in the intensive care nursery at Yale New Haven Hospital.

The term *Infant Doe* was first used on April 9, 1982, when a baby boy with Down's syndrome and esophageal atresia (a defect that prevents normal feeding) was born in Bloomington, Indiana. His parents refused to give consent for surgery to correct the tracheoesophageal defect. The courts refused to intervene and Infant Doe died 6 days later. The Reagan administration responded by informing hospitals that Section 504 of the Rehabilitation Act of 1973, which prevents discrimination against individuals with handicaps in programs receiving federal funds, protects imperiled newborns. The administration issued an Interim Final Regulation in March 1983 that articulated this policy of nondiscrimination and established procedures to implement it. This regulation was overturned by a federal court because of the administration's failure to follow established notice and comment on procedures in promulgating it.

In July 1983 the Reagan administration issued a second similar proposed rule. It stated that treatment of an infant with a handicap was mandatory unless treatment was "medically contraindicated." It ruled that the denial of treatment on the basis of a potentially disabling or handicapping condition constituted unlawful discrimination. It was also specified that this regulation was not intended to mandate futile therapies that would only prolong an infant's process of dying.

On October 11, 1983, "Baby Jane Doe" was born in Port Jefferson, New York. She was born with mylomeningocele, hydrocephaly, microcephaly, bilateral upper extremity spaticity, a prolapsed rectum, and a malformed brain stem. Her parents chose a course of conservative treatment as an alternative to surgery. Based on anonymous information, the Department of Health and Human Services filed a complaint with the state Child protection Agency. The July, 1983 ruling made it clear that the federal government was ready to step in if the decision of a state agency was considered insufficient. This case focused attention on the question of the federal government's right to intrude into the private realm of family decision making.

In 1983, the President's Commission for the Study of Ethical Problems in Medicine and Biomedical Research issued, as part of its report, a statement on the decision to forgo life-sustaining treatment in critically ill newborns. It contrasted the presumption that parents are the appropriate decision makers for their infants with the *parens patriae* power of the state. That is, while laws concerning the family protect a substantial range of discretion for parents, the state may supervise parental decisions before they become operative to ensure that the choices made are not neglectful or abusive to the child. It concluded that public policy should resist state intervention into family decisions unless serious issues are at stake and the intervention is likely to achieve better outcomes. Additionally, the commission suggested that infants with handicaps be treated no less vigorously than their nonhandicapped peers. However, it also suggested that futile therapies that merely delay death without offering a reasonable probability of saving a baby's life should be avoided. Finally, in ambiguous cases, where the course of action that would benefit the infant is not chosen by the parents, authorized persons acting for the state as *parens patriae* must step in.

On April 15, 1985, the Department of Health and Human Services issued the final rule and model guidelines that encouraged hospitals to establish infant care review committees (ICRCs). This was part of the child abuse and neglect prevention and treatment program included in the Child Abuse Amendments of 1984 (PL 98-457). This legislation attempts to protect the rights of infants with disabilities and limit governmental intervention into the practice of medicine and parental responsibilities. The purpose of the ICRCs is to educate hospital personnel and families of infants with disabilities and life-threatening conditions, to recommend guidelines concerning the withholding from infants of medically indicated treatment (including appropriate hydration, nutrition, and medication), and to offer counsel and review in cases involving infants with disabling and life-threatening conditions. This legislation states three circumstances under which treatment is not considered medically indicated: the infant is chronically and irreversibly comatose, the treatment would prolong dying but not be effective in ameliorating life-threatening conditions, and the treatment itself would be futile and inhumane. However, when even one of these three circumstances exists (and therefore failure to provide treatment would not be considered withholding medically indicated treatment), the infant must be provided with appropriate hydration, nutrition, and medication. Additionally, the law states that the withholding of treatment must not be based on subjective opinions about the future quality of life of such a person but is to be based on the treating physicians' "reasonable medical judgment." These guidelines are advisory and not mandatory in any way.

## REFERENCES

Duff, R. S., & Campbell, A. G. M. (1973). Moral and ethical dilemmas in the special-care nursery. *New England Journal of Medicine, 289*, 890–894.

*Federal Register*. (1985, April 15). Child abuse and neglect prevention and treatment program; final rule. Model guidelines for health care providers to establish infant care review committees. *50*, 14878–14901.

President's Commission for the Study of Ethical Problems in Medicine and Biomedical and Behavioral Research. (1983). *A report on the ethical, medical and legal issues in treatment decisions*. Washington, DC: Author.

Rhoden, N. K., & Arras, J. D. (1985). Withhholding treatment from Baby Doe: From discrimination to child abuse. *Milbank Memorial Fund Quarterly/Health and Society, 63*, 27–50.

Vitiello, M. (1984). The Baby Jane Doe litigation and Section 504: An exercise in raw executive power. *Connecticut Law Review, 17*, 95–164.

CAROLE REITER GOTHELF
*Hunter College, City University
of New York*

PARENTS OF THE HANDICAPPED
LEGISLATION REGARDING THE HANDICAPPED

## BACKWARD READERS

Backward readers is an archaic term that was commonly used in the first quarter of the twentieth century; its use gradually declined. The term still appears in the literature occasionally and as late as 1970 was one of the 50 most frequently appearing technical terms in psychological reports prepared by school psychologists. It is used far less frequently by teachers and psychologists in contemporary special education settings.

In its broadest usage, backward reader referred to anyone with a significant reading problem. The term was derived from the tendency of young children with reading problems to reverse letters and words. Many children will read *was* for *saw* and frequently confuse d, b, p, and q during the early stages of learning to read. If such reversals persist past the age of nine, they are highly significant as indicators of dyslexia. Such reversals have also been termed strephosymbolia. Applied in a technically correct sense, backward readers should only be used to refer to children who have reversal problems, though this specific meaning has been largely lost over the years. When encountering the term in evaluations, reports, or school records, it is a good idea to query the individual using the term to clarify the specific meaning intended. Backward readers has been found to be a frequently misinterpreted term in both educational and clinical settings.

CECIL R. REYNOLDS
*Texas A&M University*

DYSLEXIA
READING DISORDERS
STREPHOSYMBOLIA

# BAER, DONALD M. (1931–    )

Donald M. Baer received his BA degree in liberal arts from the University of Chicago in 1950 and his PhD in experimental psychology in 1957. He is currently with the department of human development of the University of Kansas at Lawrence.

He is most noted for his work with retarded children and reinforcement of appropriate behavioral imitativeness. He has explored environmental situations in which retarded individuals can be taught imitation and language through the use of behavioral reinforcement and shaping techniques. He found that after reinforcement for appropriate imitation, generalization to similar situations was enhanced. Baer's current research is in the learning process as related to personal and social adaptation in young children.

## REFERENCES

Baer, D. M. et. al (1967). The development of imitation by reinforcing behavioral similarity to a model. *Journal of the Experimental Analysis of Behavior, 10*, 405–416.

Bijou, S. W., & Baer, D. M. (1978). *Behavior analysis of child development*. Englewood Cliffs, NJ: Prentice-Hall.

RICK GONZALES
*Texas A&M University*

# BANDURA, ALBERT (1925–    )

Albert Bandura earned his BA at the University of British Columbia in 1949 and his MA and PhD (1952) from the University of Iowa. Influenced by K. L. Spence and the Hullian research tradition, Bandura is recognized as one of the founders of social learning theory. Since 1953, he has served as professor of psychology and as department chairman at Stanford University.

Well known for his work on modeling and self-regulation, Bandura proposes that human thought, affect, and behavior are strongly influenced by vicarious learning. His cognitive-behavioral approach has led to innovations in behavior therapy, where modeling is used to promote the development of psychological competencies. Overall, Bandura feels psychology, through its research, bears an obligation to society for the betterment of humanity.

Bandura's major publications include *Adolescent Aggression, Social Learning and Personality Development, Aggression: A Social Learning Analysis, Principles of Behavior Modification, Psychological Modeling, Social Learning Theory*, and *Social Foundation of Thought and Action: A Social Cognitive Theory*. In addition, he has published over 100 journal articles and works.

President of the American Psychological Association (APA) in 1974, Bandura has also served as chairman of the Board of Directors for APA, trustee for the American

Albert Bandura

Psychological Foundation, and president and chairman of the Western Psychological Association. His consultantships include series editor on social learning theory for Prentice-Hall since 1970.

## REFERENCES

Bandura, A. (1969). *Principles of behavior modification.* New York: Holt, Rinehart, & Winston.

Bandura, A. (1971). *Psychological modeling, conflicting theories.* Chicago: Aldine-Atherton.

Bandura, A. (1973). *Aggression: A social learning analysis.* Englewood Cliffs, NJ: Prentice-Hall.

Bandura, A. (1977). *Social learning theory.* Englewood Cliffs, NJ: Prentice-Hall.

Bandura, A. (1986). *Social foundations of thought and action: A social cognitive theory.* Englewood Cliffs, NJ: Prentice-Hall.

Bandura, A., & Walters, R. H. (1959). *Adolescent aggression.* New York: Ronald.

Bandura, A., & Walters, R. H. (1963). *Social learning and personality development.* New York: Holt, Rinehart, & Winston.

MARY LEON PEERY
*Texas A&M University*

**SOCIAL LEARNING THEORY**

# BANNATYNE, ALEXANDER D. (1925–    )

Alexander Bannatyne received his BA in education and philosophy at Auckland University in New Zealand in 1949. He obtained his PhD in psychology at the Institute of Psychiatry at the University of London in 1953. As a professor, he taught on learning disabilities to doctoral students at the University of Illinois, 1966 to 1969.

Bannatyne's major areas of work are in dealing with learning-disabled children and their reading, writing, and spelling abilities. Bannatyne believes that to understand abnormal, one must be knowledgeable about what is normal. Only through presentation of the abnormal in con-

Alexander D. Bannatyne

junction with a knowledge of the normal can we work out what has gone wrong; only then do we have standards against which to measure degrees and types of abnormalities (Bannatyne 1971). Bannatyne did studies on the relationships among learned and unlearned handedness, spelling ability, mirror imaging, motor functioning, balance, memory for designs, and auditory vocal sequencing in terms of hemispheric activity and dominance. He found that three types of brain functions may exist: (1) an efficient balanced brain associated with unlearned handedness, balancing ability, and competent spelling; (2) a less verbally efficient right hemisphere dominant brain that seems to give mirror imaging, spatial competence, and left-handedness; and (3) a brain that is visuospatially inept even though it is not given to the drawing of mirror images.

Some of his major works include *Language, Reading, and Learning Disabilities, Bannatyne System: Reading, Writing and Spelling, Body Image*, and *How Children Can Learn to Live Rewarding Lives*.

## REFERENCES

Bannatyne, A. D. (1971). *Language, reading, and learning disabilities* Springfield, IL: Thomas.

Bannatyne, A. D. (1973a). *Body image: Communication program.* Lafayette, LA: Learning System.

Bannatyne, A. D. (1973b). *How children can learn to live rewarding lives*. Springfield, IL: Thomas.

Bannatyne, A. D. (1973c). *Reading: An auditory-vocal proceso.* San Rafael, CA: Academic Therapy.

Bannatyne, A. D. (1975). *Bannatyne system: Reading, writing, and spelling*. Lafayette, LA: Learning System.

ELIZABETH JONES
*Texas A&M University*

## BARDON, JACK I. (1925–　　)

Jack I. Bardon earned his BA is psychology at Cleveland College of Western Reserve University in 1949, with a minor in education. He continued his professional education at the University of Pennsylvania, earning the MA in psychology in 1951 and a PhD in clinical psychology in 1956. From 1952 until 1958, Bardon was a school psychologist in the Princeton, New Jersey, schools and served as coordinator of special education services from 1958 to 1960. In 1960 he became director of the Rutgers University doctoral program in school psychology with the academic rank of associate professor. He won promotion to professor in 1963 and became head of the department in 1968.

It was during his tenure at Rutgers that Bardon began to have impact nationally on the delivery of school psychological services to handicapped children. His program in school psychology at Rutgers was one of the early, pioneering programs in the field and, along with the University of Texas program, had a major influence on the development of doctoral school psychology. The Rutgers program reflected Bardon's own principal, driving interest: to determine how the body of knowledge and the methods and techniques of psychology can be applied to the improvement of schooling generally, and to meeting the special needs of exceptional children in schools specifically. Bardon was instrumental in developing the primary role definitions of school psychologists (Bardon, 1982; Bardon & Bennett, 1974). Recently, Bardon has been involved in work to help differentiate school psychology from other disciplines (Bardon, 1983). His work has benefited special education and regular education by improving the ability of school psychologists to provide services to children at all levels.

Bardon left Rutgers in 1976 to accept a professorship at the University of North Carolina at Greensboro, where he became an Excellence Foundation Professor in 1983. Bardon has served the professions involved with exceptional children both well and broadly. He was editor of the *Journal of School Psychology* from 1968 through 1971, and serves on the editorial board of seven journals in the field. He was on the board of directors of the American Orthopsychiatric Association from 1981 to 1984; was president

Jack I. Bardon

of the division of school psychology of the American Psychological Association in 1969; and, in 1968, was on the board of directors of the National Register of Health Service Providers in Psychology. Bardon continues to have a widely felt influence on the organization and delivery of school psychological services.

## REFERENCES

Bardon, J. I. (1982). The psychology of school psychology. In C. R. Reynolds & T. B. Gutkin (Eds.), *The handbook of school psychology*. New York: Wiley.

Bardon, J. I. (1983). Psychology applied to education: A specialty in search of an identity. *American Psychologist, 38*, 185–196.

Bardon, J. I., & Bennett, V. C. (1974). *School psychology*. Englewood Cliffs, NJ: Prentice-Hall.

CECIL R. REYNOLDS
*Texas A&M University*

**AMERICAN ORTHOPSYCHIATRIC ASSOCIATION**
**BENNETT, VIRGINIA C.**
**PHILLIPS, BEEMAN N.**

## BARRAGA, NATALIE C. (1915–      )

Natalie C. Barraga obtained her BA in home economics from North Texas State University in 1938; her MEd from the University of Texas, Austin, in 1957; and her EdD in special education for the visually handicapped from George Peabody College for Teachers in 1963. Barraga's entry into the study of the visually handicapped originated from a prior interest in child development and a concern for her daughter, who had a severe visual impairment. Years of teaching focused her objectives on those learners who had low vision. She experimented with ways to help students learn and read visually when they had a desire to do so.

Natalie C. Barraga

Barraga's research documented that the use of vision (when impairment is present) is learned and not determined by acuity measurements, and that functional academic visual tasks could be taught with a sequential progressive learning program. She developed visual assessment tools and published a systematic instructional program, *Development of Efficiency in Visual Functioning*.

Professor emerita at the University of Texas at Austin, Barraga has published several books, monographs, assessment instruments, and articles. She has lectured extensively overseas, and maintains an interest in promoting interdisciplinary communication and an international exchange of information, especially with third World countries.

ELAINE FLETCHER-JANZEN
*Texas A&M University*

## BARRIER-FREE EDUCATION

The delivery of special education services to all handicapped children in the least restrictive environment means that school buildings and facilities must be designed or altered to make those services accessible. Barrier-free design standards typically give technical specifications that cover building entrances and exits, parking, curbs, stairs, elevators, lavatories, drinking fountains, hazard warnings, and building elements and fixtures. In both new construction and modifications of existing facilities, buildings may be subject to a variety of definitions and design standards (Redden, 1979). The American National Standards Institute (ANSI) criteria are cited in the regulations for Section 504 of the Rehabilitation Act of 1973 as the minimum access standard to assure compliance with nondiscrimination provisions. The new design standards set forth in the Uniform Federal Accessibility Standards (UFAS, 1984) generally are consistent with federal standards now in effect, major model building codes, and most state and local codes; they are based on ANSI A117.1-1980. The 1984 UFAS criteria are geared to adult dimensions and anthropometrics. Some states, however, have developed design guidelines for special education facilities that consider the total learning environment for children with all types of handicaps (Abend, et al., 1979).

Certain important terms that are widely used in the laws and literature pertaining to requirements for accessibility should be distinguished. The term accessible describes facilities or elements of a facility that comply with applicable design standards and that can be approached, entered, and used by physically handicapped individuals (UFAS, 1984). Physically handicapped means an individual who has a physical impairment, which may include an impaired sensory, manual, or speaking ability that may functionally limit access to and use of a building or facility (UFAS, 1984). A barrier-free environment requires the removal of all architectural barriers to accessibility (Redden, 1979). It should be noted that the regulations for Section 504 (which are applicable to recipients of funds from the U.S. Department of Education or Health and Human Services) do not require barrier-free environments. Section 504 requires "program accessibility"—that is, a recipient's program or activity, when viewed in its entirety, must be readily accessible to and usable by handicapped persons. Access to each facility is not required. While the program accessibility standard can be achieved by a number of effective methods, including structural changes, priority must be given to methods that provide the most integrated setting appropriate. Under Section 504, it is not permissible to isolate handicapped students in a single accessible building.

In 1983, Congress appropriated funds to implement Section 607 of the Education of the Handicapped Act. The program under Section 607 provides grants to state educational agencies to assist them in making subgrants to local educational agencies and intermediate educational units to remove architectual barriers by altering existing buildings and equipment. This formula grant program is subject to requirements under the Architectural Barriers Act of 1968 and the 1984 Uniform Federal Accessibility Standards.

## REFERENCES

Abend, A. C., Bedner, M. J., Froehlinger, V. J., & Stenzler, Y. (1979). *Facilities for special educational services: A guide for planning new and renovated schools.* Reston, VA: Council for Exceptional Children.

Redden, M. R. (Ed.). (1979). Assuring access for the handicapped. San Francisco: Jossey-Bass.

Uniform Federal Accessibility Standards. (1984, August 7). 49 F.R. 31528-31621.

SHIRLEY A. JONES
*Virginia Polytechnic Institute
and State University*

## ACCESSIBILITY OF BUILDINGS
## ACCESSIBILITY OF PROGRAMS

# BARRIERS, ARCHITECTURAL

See ARCHITECTURAL BARRIERS.

# BARSCH, RAY H. (1917–      )

Ray H. Barsch earned his BA in special education in 1950 and MEd in school psychology in 1952 from the University of Wisconsin, Milwaukee. He went on to receive his PhD in educational psychology from Northwestern University in 1959 under the direction of Claude Mathis, Paul Witty, and Helmer Myklebust.

Barsch is principally known for his development of a curriculum called movigenics, a theory of movement developed from "the study of origin and development of patterns of movement in man and the relationship of those movements to his learning efficiency." He regards movigenics as "orientation—a cognitive map to guide practitioners toward a goal of practical synthesis" (Barsch, 1976).

As an ardent supporter of interdisciplinary approaches to assessment and teaching in special education, Barsch defines learning disabilities as a concept that focuses on learning rather that "a frantic but seldom fruitful effort to delineate a uniform and specific set of characteristics" (Barsch, 1976).

Since 1970 Barsch has been a professor in the department of special education at California State University, Northridge, and in the division for continuing education at the University of Santa Clara. Among other positions and consultantships, Barsch directed teacher preparation programs in the department of counseling and behavioral studies at the University of Wisconsin (1963–1966) and the Easter Seal Development Center in Milwaukee, Wisconsin (1950–1964).

From the early 1970s to the early 1980s, Barsch was a professor in the School of Education at the California State University, Northridge. He also directed the Ray Barsch Center for Learning, where he specialized in one-on-one therapy for children with specific learning problems and counseled parents. Barsch presently continues his work by supervising the development of the Special Education Teacher Program in Ventura, California, and the training of graduate students in various evaluation and therapy techniques.

Recipient of many awards, Barsch received the International Milestone Award of the International Federation of Learning Disabilities at its world congress in the Netherlands in 1974.

## REFERENCE

Barsch, R. H. (1976). *Achieving perceptual motor efficiency: A space oriented approach to learning* (Vol. 1). Seattle, WA: Special Child.

ELAINE FLETCHER-JANZEN
*Texas A&M University*

# BASAL READERS

Basal reader programs are comprehensive, meaningfully sequenced collections of stories, frequently arranged in groups according to a central theme or topic. Smith and Johnson (1980) described these programs as being based on the belief that a controlled vocabulary of high-frequency words, coupled with the presentation of easily decodable pattern words, facilitates learning to read and the improvement of reading skills.

Basal reader programs are intended to be used to instruct children from the stage of nonreading, through the acquisition of developing skills, to the level of mature, flexible reading. Typically, these programs include various correlated and supplementary materials including teachers' manuals, workbooks, skills sheets, activity boxes, criterion-referenced monitoring systems, and even computer software management programs. This self-contained aspect of basal reader programs is intended to provide all that is necessary for a core reading program. Teachers are carefully guided through instructional directed reading activities as outlined in the accompanying manuals. The structure of these lesson plans, explained by both Stauffer (1969) and Harris (1970), follows the sequence of prereading preparation, guided silent reading, oral rereading and comprehension assessment, skill development activities, and enrichment. In addition, teachers are usually provided with suggestions for choosing related books and other materials to use in conjunction with the basal reader.

Of course, the reading books themselves constitute the essential materials in any basal program. Usually there is a set of readiness materials for use with children at the beginning stages of reading instruction. These are followed by readers considered to be at the preprimer and primer levels of difficulty. The readers contain a limited number of frequently repeated words that assist in the development of a basic sight vocabulary. These basic reading books are followed by progressively more difficult readers extending through all the elementary grades and frequently into the middle and junior high grades as well. Many of these higher level basal readers consist of comprehensive literary anthologies and, according to Ringler and Weber (1984), may include a variety of narrative types such as realistic fiction, fantasy, science fiction, folklore, poetry, and plays.

## REFERENCES

Harris, A. J. (1970). *How to increase reading ability* (5th ed.). New York: McKay.

Ringler, L. H., & Weber, C. K. (1984). *A language-thinking approach to reading.* New York: Harcourt Brace Jovanovich.

Smith, R. J., & Johnson, D. D. (1980). *Teaching children to read* (2nd ed.). Reading, MA: Addison-Wesley.

Stauffer, R. G. (1969). *Directing reading maturity as a cognitive process.* New York: Harper & Row.

JOHN M. EELLS
*Souderton Area School District,
Souderton, Pennsylvania*

**READING DISORDERS**
**READING REMEDIATION**

## BASELINE DATA

A baseline measurement occurs prior to the beginning of an intervention. It involves precise counting of the target behavior (i.e., dependent variable) during whatever current conditions exist. A common misconception is that baseline data can only be gathered in the absence of any intervention. This is not true. Baselines are measures of behavior under current conditions. If these conditions are not ones in which there is no intervention, then this information should be stated in the program outline. If there is an informal intervention that currently is ongoing (e.g., telling a child to "stop"), then this response should continue. If one were to attempt to stop intervening with a behavior and then take baseline data, that person would be defeating the purpose of the baseline procedure because removing the intervention procedure acts as an intervention itself. Data gathered during this time would be intervention data and different from those that were representative of the behavior during the condition in which the behavior became important enough to the practitioner to attempt intervention aided by data collection.

Baselines are meant to be representative measures of the target behavior. As such they should also be reliable and valid. Reliability should be scored by having two persons simultaneously record the data and by comparing those data records using different calculation procedures (e.g., Kappa), dependent on which recording technique was used (e.g., momentary time sampling) and the properties of the data. Validity, in its simplest form, requires that a measure be that which was purported. If after writing the behavioral definition of the target behavior the definition was compared to the behavior to determine whether the behavior written was that which the student exhibited, the primary form of validation would be completed. If the definition is given to another person and he or she is asked whether the written definition was observable in the student's behavior, and if that person found it to be so, the second form of validation would be completed.

Baseline data should be stable prior to the initiation of intervention. Stability is said to have occurred when there is an absence of directionality or trend in the data and when there is restricted variation in the pattern of the data. Trend is said to occur when there are three or more data points patterned in a specific direction. This is also referred to as celeration and is illustrated by data that accelerate or decelerate. Baseline data that are either accelerating or decelerating are generally not useful as preintervention data. The trend in the data suggests that there is already something that is influencing the target behavior. However, when the trend is countertherapeutic (i.e., moving in the undesired direction), the need for protracted baseline data collection is negated. Therefore, if the trend of the baseline data is therapeutic, continuation of the baseline is indicated until such time as the behavior becomes acceptable or until it levels off and becomes stable. If the data are countertherapeutic, this is not necessary and intervention can be begun in 5 to 10 sessions or days.

Variability in the data during baseline in the absence of a significant trend must be measured by examining its degree to determine its effect on the baseline. Baseline data should be stable so that the practitioner can say with reasonable certainty that the target behavior occurred in a specific condition prior to intervention. Stability is measured as the degree of variability about the mean. In research and teaching with humans we would look for +/− 50% variability about the baseline mean (Alberto & Troutman, 1982). For example, if we gathered 10 days of baseline data and then summed each day's score and divided by 10 we would have the mean of the baseline. If this mean were 40%, then all data should fall between 60% and 20% during the baseline as that is the range established by the +/− 50% rule. A single (or perhaps 2) data point(s) falling outside this range could be judged to be an oddity; it should not hamper the identification of these data as stable. However, more than this number would indicate a lack of stability and a longer baseline would be required. Baseline stability or countertherapeutic trend is a basic requirement prior to the initiation of intervention programming.

## REFERENCE

Alberto, P. A., & Troutman, A. C. (1982). *Applied behavior analysis for teachers.* Columbus, OH: Merrill.

LYLE E. BARTON
*Kent State University*

**APPLIED BEHAVIOR ANALYSIS**
**BEHAVIOR MODIFICATION**

## BASE RATE

A base rate is a baseline measurement of a target behavior's rate of responding. This measurement is useful when the student's behavior of interest is one for which frequency recording is the appropriate recording strategy and for which rate of responding is the appropriate datum. The latter case is true when the response frequency dependent on duration of observation is important. For example, should the target behavior be either units of "X" assembled in a workshop or incidences of aggressive behavior, frequency would be an appropriate recording strategy. If, in addition, the issue of importance is this number within a specified time frame, then rate of response becomes the appropriate datum. If this period of observation tends to vary, then rate of response is the only appropriate datum. Therefore, the special education practitioner would record the frequency of student response and then divide the frequency by the number of minutes (or hours)

of observation. The resultant figure (e.g., 1.56, 0.75, 0.05) would be indicative of the relative frequency of responding per unit of measurement (e.g., minutes, hours) and would be reported as rate per minute (rpm) or rate per hour (rph).

To determine the base rate, these data would be gathered over a period of days or sessions and would be examined to meet the criterion for stability for any baseline data; that is, the data must be stable (have limited variability) or countertherapeutic. Stability is said to occur when the data vary no more than +/− 50% of the baseline mean (Alberto & Troutman, 1982). A countertherapeutic trend is said to occur when the data are not stable but moving in the opposite direction. Base-rate data are usually reported as a mean figure (e.g., "the mean base rate was . . ."), however, these data may be reported as including the range and the usual data display via a graph.

## REFERENCES

Alberto, P. A., & Troutman, A. C. (1982). *Applied behavior analysis for teachers.* Columbus, OH: Merrill.

LYLE E. BARTON
*Kent State University*

**APPLIED BEHAVIOR ANALYSIS**
**BEHAVIOR MODIFICATION**

## BASIC ACHIEVEMENT SKILLS INDIVIDUAL SCREENER (BASIS)

The Basic Achievement Skills Individual Screener (BASIS, Psychological Corporation, 1983) is an individually administered achievement test designed to assess a student's skills in the areas of reading, mathematics, and spelling. There are three subtests covering these subjects that are norm- and criterion-referenced. In addition to the subtests, there is an optional writing subtest that is scored by comparing an examinee's performance to "average" sample passages for grades 3 to 8. The BASIS is appropriate for use with children in grades 1 through 12, and with post-high school students to a limited extent, e.g., to assess adult basic educational skills.

As is appropriate in the development of an achievement test, considerable attention was given to the content validity of the scale. Huebner (1984) noted that the match between the task demands for the subtests closely parallels what a child would be expected to do in the classroom setting. For example, a modified cloze procedure is used to test reading comprehension, and spelling is assessed by a standard dictation procedure. Both of these activities are common in the classroom.

The BASIS was standardized on a representative sample, based on geographic region, socioeconomic status, school system enrollment, ethnicity, and public vs. private schools, of 3064 children in grades 1 through 12 and an additional 232 post-high school students. Based on this sampling, the norms are equal or superior to other screening-type measures of academic achievement. Reliability data for both internal consistency and sort-term test-retest stability are adequate for an individually administered, screening-type measure. All KR-20's were .85 or above, with the vast majority hovering around the .95 range. The stability coefficients were all above .80 for the three samples that were retested at grades 2, 5, and 8.

## REFERENCES

Huebner, E. S. (1984). Test review: Basic Achievement Skills Individual Screener (BASIS). *Journal of Psychoeducational Assessment, 2*, 173–176.

Psychological Corporation (1983). *Basic Achievement Skills Individual Screener (BASIS)*. New York: Psychological Corporation.

JACK A. CUMMINGS
*Indiana University*

## BASIC SKILLS TRAINING

## BASIC EDUCATIONAL SKILLS INVENTORY

See BASIC SCHOOL SKILLS INVENTORY—DIAGNOSTIC.

## BASIC SCHOOL SKILLS INVENTORY–DIAGNOSTIC (BSSI-D)

The Basic School Skills Inventory–Diagnostic (BSSI-D) (Hammill & Leigh, 1983) is a classroom-based assessment device intended for use by teachers or other school personnel to assist with the determination of instructional needs of young children (ages four through six) and older handicapped or underachieving children. The scale originated with teachers' descriptions of characteristics of children "ready" and "not ready" for school. The subscales include daily living skills (e.g., independent school behaviors); spoken language; reading; writing; mathematics; and classroom behavior.

Percentiles, standard scores for subtests (mean 10 and standard deviation of 3), and a composite of the six subtests referred to as a Skill Quotient (mean of 100 and standard deviation of 15) are provided. The standardization sample (*N* = 376) included boys and girls residing in urban and rural communities. The sample is in close agreement with the 1980 Census, although middle- to upper-socioeconomic groups and blacks are slightly un-

derrepresented. The internal consistency of the scales range from .81 to .97. Criterion-related validity was examined through correlations between the BSSI-D and teacher ratings of readiness and school achievement. While statistically significant, the validity coefficients are low, ranging from .22 (writing) to .38 (spoken language). Another source of validity is suggested by developmental changes in skills. The authors report a study that successfully differentiated between normal and learning-disabled children (*N* = 12). The intercorrelations between subtests suggest a unified construct of "readiness."

## REFERENCE

Hammill, D. D., & Leigh, J. E. (1983). *Basic School Skills Inventory-Diagnostic*. Austin, TX: Pro Ed.

DAVID W. BARNETT
*University of Cincinnati*

## PRESCHOOL ASSESSMENT
## PRESCHOOL SCREENING

## BASIC SKILLS TRAINING

Historically, the term "basic skills" refers to the traditional disciplines of reading, writing, and arithmetic that are stressed in the early years of formal education. These areas of study are those that are seen as necessary for an individual to become a contributing member of society. Without at least a rudimentary proficiency in these basic areas, individuals experience difficulty in developing independence and self-esteem.

The exceptional child or adult, however, may require a completely different type of basic skill training than the traditional disciplines deemed necessary for normal functioning within society. Depending on the severity of the handicapping condition, basic skills for special education may vary little or greatly from those of regular students and adults. Basic skills training for exceptional children could best be termed those activities and subject areas that provide for each child's individual learning abilities (allowing for his or her weaknesses) in such a way that deviation from the norm is as limited as possible. This training allows children to accomplish what Blake (1981) refers to as "cultural tasks," in which needs are met through means that are acceptable to society.

Specifically, basic skills for the exceptional child might include those skills noted by Berdine and Blackhurst (1981): training in attention skills, increased memory capacity, the ability to transfer and generalize recently learned skills, and language. By using these as basics in special education, regardless of the curriculum content, the individual is prepared to receive and apply knowledge within his or her personal limits.

## REFERENCES

Berdine, W. H., & Blackhurst, A. E. (1981). *An introduction to special education.* Boston: Little, Brown.

Blake, K. A. (1981). *Educating exceptional pupils: An introduction to contemporary practices.* Reading, MA: Addison-Wesley.

JAMES H. MILLER
*University of New Orleans*

## BASIC EDUCATIONAL SKILLS INVENTORY—
### DIAGNOSTIC
## FUNCTIONAL DOMAINS
## FUNCTIONAL INSTRUCTION

## BATEMAN, BARBARA (1933–        )

Barbara Bateman received her BA (1954) in psychology from the University of Washington, her MA (1958) from San Francisco State College, and her PhD in special education (1962) from the University of Illinois. In the early years of her professional career, she taught mentally retarded and emotionally disturbed blind children at Washington State Hospital and a variety of exceptional children in the Oregon public schools. Bateman continued in the field teaching at the university level and became professor of education at the University of Oregon in 1969.

She has always been a strong advocate of direct instruction, and has urged the field of education to accept the direct instructional philosophy, methods, and materials in publications such as *Essentials of Teaching* (1971) and *Teaching Reading to Learning Disabled and Other Hard-to-Teach Children* (1979). In the 1970s, Bateman's interests broadened to the legal aspects of special education; she received her JD from the University of Oregon Law School in 1976, and has published on law and special

**Barbara Bateman**

education, including *So You're Going to Hearing: Preparing for a P.L. 94-142 Hearing* (1980).

## REFERENCES

Bateman, B. (1971). *Essentials of teaching.* Sioux Falls, SD: Adapt Press.

Bateman, B. (1979). Teaching reading to learning disabled and other hard-to-teach children. In L. Resnick & P. Weaver (Eds.), *Theory and practice of early reading.* Hillsdale, NJ: Erlbaum.

Bateman, B. (1980). *So you're going to Hearing: Preparing for a P.L. 94-142 hearing.* Northbrook, Ill.: Hubbard.

STAFF

## BATTELLE DEVELOPMENTAL INVENTORY (BDI)

The Battelle Developmental Inventory (BDI) was developed by the Battelle Memorial Institute (1984). It is an expansion, update, and renorming of an earlier Battelle scale, the Children's Early Education Developmental Inventory. Both scales were developed under funding from grants to the Battelle Memorial Institute from the federal Bureau of Education for the Handicapped, now known as Special Educational Programs. Developed and normed for use from birth to age 8 years, the BDI is intended to assess developmental strengths and weaknesses in five major domains. A briefer screening version may also be used.

The five primary domains assessed by the full BDI include personal-social, adaptive, motor, communication, and cognitive. The complete scale consists of 341 items; the screening scale employs 96 of these items. The administration of the BDI requires formal standardized testing with the child, interviews with a primary caregiver (defined as a parent, teacher, or other significant person), and observations of the child, estimated in the manual to take about 1 hour. The administration of the full battery yields 30 profile scores including adult interaction, expression of feelings or affect, self-concept, peer interaction, coping, and social role, giving a personal-social total; attention, eating, dressing, personal responsibility, and toileting, giving an adaptive total; muscle control, body coordination, locomotion, gross motor score, fine muscle, perceptual motor, and fine motor score, giving a motor total; receptive and expressive, giving a communications total; and perceptual discrimination, memory, reasoning, academic skills, and conceptual development, giving a cognitive total.

Four major purposes for the BDI are outlined in the examiner's manual. These purposes include (1) the assessment and identification of handicapped children; (2) assessment of the nonhandicapped child; (3) planning and providing instruction; and (4) assessment of the effects of various programs on the progress of handicapped children. These are highly desirable and extremely ambitious goals for any battery of tasks. Despite having such laudable goals and many positive features, including special, adaptive testing procedures for the handicapped, the BDI falls short on all of its goals. For example, the entire amount of material on planning and providing instruction, one of the four purposes of the BDI, covers less than eight pages. Internal consistency data are not reported and were considered inappropriate (a strong argument against the use of the scales is the same argument presented by the authors for not presenting internal consistency reliability data). There are no groupings of items on the BDI, including the various profile scores, that measure any unitary constructs of children's behavior or development. Many other scales have easily found such groupings and test users should be highly suspicious of tests that do not report these data. Strangely, standard errors of measurement are reported calculated on the basis of a procedure that has little to do with the accuracy or precision of measurement; it is an estimation procedure used when less precise data are available than what was present on the BDI. Test-retest reliability data are based on raw scores, which spuriously inflated these values. Minimal validity data are present and what is present is only moderate in its support of the BDI. At this time, the BDI should be considered a research tool only and should not be used in classification or programming decisions.

**REFERENCE**

Battelle Memorial Institute. (1984). *Battelle development inventory*. Allen, TX: DLM Teaching Resources.

CECIL R. REYNOLDS
*Texas A&M University*

# BATTERED CHILD SYNDROME

In 1962, pediatrician C. Henry Kempe published an article entitled "The Battered Child Syndrome." This marked the first official recognition by the medical establishment of the problem of child abuse. Kempe's article focused on abuse as a deliberate, violent attack on a child by a malicious adult and criticized the medical profession for failing to diagnose and report such cases. Child abuse is a broad term currently used to describe incidents of violent attack, neglect, or sexual abuse that may result in psychological and behavioral disturbances as well as physical or even life-threatening injury. Ellerstein (1981) states that between 1 and 3% of children in the United States are abused. Figures vary depending on laws governing reporting and definitions of child abuse. About 4000 children die each year as a result of abuse.

Researchers have investigated several factors associated with child abuse. Various models, each emphasizing the importance of particular factors, have been formulated to explain the phenomenon. The psychopathological model focuses on the personality characteristics of the perpetrator. Attributes such as personal history of abuse, low self-esteem, and inability to cope with frustration are seen as important contributing factors (Gil, 1970). In the sociological model, environmental factors such as poverty, acceptance of corporal punishment, and overcrowding in the home receive emphasis (Gil, 1970). The cognitive-behavioral model takes into account style of responding to stress and the belief systems of abusive parents (Green, 1984). A broader model encompassing the preceding elements and accounting for the significance of interactions between parents and children is referred to as the ecological model (Roscoe et al., 1985).

Investigators have found that some children are more likely than others to become victims of child abuse. Children at increased risk for abuse often come from larger than average families, have low birth weights or were premature as infants, and fail to form attachment bonds with a caregiver. Also, males are more likely to be abused, as are handicapped, retarded, and otherwise different or difficult children (Newberger, 1982).

Kempe's early article on the battered child syndrome achieved considerable public notoriety and drew the attention of legislators, resulting in the passage of mandatory reporting of child abuse in all 50 states. Physicians and other health professionals are legally required to report suspected child abuse. Additionally, most states require other professionals having contact with children to report suspected cases of abuse. These professionals include teachers, social workers, and child-care workers.

**REFERENCES**

Ellerstein, N. S. (Ed.). (1981). *Child abuse and neglect: A medical reference*. New York: Wiley.

Gil, D. (1975). Unraveling child abuse. *American Journal of Orthopsychiatry, 45*, 345–356.

Green, A. (1984). Child maltreatment: Recent studies and future directions. *Journal of the American Academy of Child Psychiatry, 23*, 675–678.

Kempe, C. H. (1962). The battered child syndrome. *Journal of the American Medical Association, 181*, 17–24.

Newberger, E. H. (Ed.). (1982). *Child abuse*. Boston: Little, Brown.

Roscoe, B., Callahan, J., & Peterson, K. (1985). Who is responsible? Adolescents' acceptance of theoretical child abuse models. *Adolescence, 20*, 188–197.

BERNICE ARRICALE
*Hunter College, City University
of New York*

**CHILD ABUSE**
**CHILD CARE AGENCIES**
**CHILD CARETAKER**

## BAUMEISTER, ALFRED A. (1934–    )

Born in Fairbanks, Alaska, Alfred A. Baumeister received his BA from the University of Alaska (1957) and his MA (1959) and PhD (1961) in psychology from George Peabody College. He is presently a professor at Vanderbilt University and George Peabody College, and directs the John F. Kennedy Center for Research on Education and Human Development at Vanderbilt University.

Baumeister has presented over 150 papers and published over 200 original investigations, literature reviews, and theoretical reports, many of which are concerned with learning and memory processes among mentally retarded children. He found that there are quantitative and structural differences in the short-term information processing capabilities of retarded and nonretarded subjects (Baumeister, Runcie, & Gardepe, 1984). Another major effort has been directed at understanding the treatment of aberrant behavior such as stereotyped movements and self-injurious actions.

Baumeister has been active in the improvement of psychological services to the mentally retarded. He has written about the role of the psychologist in public institutions (Baumeister & Hillsinger, 1984) and has served as a consultant to several state and federal agencies. He is a member of the Psychology Review Committee for the Joint Committee of the Accreditation of Hospitals.

Baumeister has been president of both the American Academy on Mental Retardation and the Division of Mental Retardation of the American Psychological Association. For several years, he served as a witness before the U.S. House and Senate appropriations subcommittees. He has received awards for research contributions from the American Association on Mental Deficiency (1979) and the American Academy on Mental Retardation (1986).

### REFERENCES

Baumeister, A. A., & Hillsinger, L. B. (1984). The role of psychologists in public institutions for the mentally retarded revisited. *Professional Psychology, 15*, 134–141.

Baumeister, A. A., Runcie, D., & Gardepe, J. (1984). Processing of information in iconic memory: Differences between normal and retarded subjects. *Journal of Abnormal Psychology, 93*, 433–447.

E. VALERIE HEWITT
*Texas A&M University*

## BAYLEY SCALES OF INFANT DEVELOPMENT (BSID)

The Bayley Scales of Infant Development (BSID) were copyrighted in 1969. The final publication is the result of a 35-year research effort assessing infant development. There are three complementary parts to the BSID. The mental scale measures sensory perceptual activities, object constancy, memory and learning, communication, classification, and generalization. The motor scale measures body control, large muscle coordination, and finger and hand manipulations. The infant behavior record contains rating scales for 24 items assessing social orientation, goal directedness, general emotional tone, activity, cooperativeness, fearfulness, etc.

The BSID were standardized on a stratified sample of more than 1200 children. Control variables included age, sex, urban–rural residence, and education. Norms are available for 14 age groups from 2 to 30 months. A manual supplement has been published to facilitate training on the BSID. In addition, a training film/videotape is available.

The BSID consists of sensitive, well-normed measures that permit the early identification of retarded mental or motor development. Treatment or corrective action may be taken based on early diagnosis.

### REFERENCE

Bayley, N. (1969). *The Bayley Scales of Infant Development*. New York: Psychological Corporation.

THOMAS F. HOPKINS
*Center for Behavioral
Psychotherapy, White Plains,
New York*

**Alfred A. Baumeister**

# BECHTEREV (BEKHTIAREV) VLADIMIR M. (1857–1927)

Vladimir M. Bechterev was born in Viatka province, Russia. He was a noted physiologist and neuropathologist and the founder of the School of Reflexology. He was also the founder of the first Russian experimental psychological laboratory at the University of Kazan. Bechterev obtained his PhD at the Military Medical Academy in St. Petersburg (Petrograd, now Leningrad) in 1881. He continued postgraduate studies at the universities of Leipzig, Berlin, and Paris. At Leipzig he became familiar with the work of Wilhelm Wundt, considered to be the founder of experimental psychology. In 1885 Bechterev became professor at the University of Kazan and in 1893, professor at the Military Medical Academy. The same year he began to publish a journal, *Neurological Review*. Bechterev was also interested in the education of exceptional children. His work in this area is referred to as pedagogical reflexology. In 1911 he addressed the International Congress of Pedology in Brussels, Belgium. His pioneering work contributed immensely toward the future development of Soviet defectology.

Bechterev made an important contribution to the knowledge of anatomy and physiology of the nervous system. He conducted research on localization function of the brain and became famous for his work on nerve currents. He also identified the layer of fibers in the cerebral cortex known as Bechterev's fibers.

Bechterev was a prolific writer who produced over 135 publications and papers, including *General Principles of Reflexology* (1918) and *Objective Psychology* (1913).

## REFERENCES

Bechterev, V. M. (1913). *Objective psychologie oder psycho-reflex-ologia*. Leipzig/Berlin: Verlag Teubner.

Bechterev, V. M. (1918). *Obshtchie osnovi reflexologii* (General principles of reflexology). St. Petersburg:

Debus, A. G. (Ed.). (1968). *World who's who in science*. Chicago: Marquis.

Prokhorov, A. M. (Ed.). (1970). *Bolshaya Sovetskay Entsyklopedia* (Major Soviet encyclopedia) (3rd ed.). Moscow: Soviet Encyclopedia Publishing.

IVAN Z. HOLOWINSKY
*Rutgers University*

# BECKER, WESLEY C. (1928–      )

A native of Rochester, New York, Wesley C. Becker received his BA (1951), MA (1953), and PhD (1955) from Stanford University in psychology, statistics, and learning theory. Currently, he is associate dean, Division of Counseling and Educational Psychology, in the College of Education at the University of Oregon.

Originally a child clinical psychologist, Becker's initial research interest was in how behavior problems and personality characteristics develop as a function of parental child-rearing practices. This developed into an interest in applications of behavior analysis to changing parent and child behaviors. His book, *Parents Are Teachers*, has been published in German, Portuguese, and Spanish. Becker's interest shifted to applications of behavior analysis to teachers and problem students (Becker, 1986; Becker, Engelmann & Thomas, 1975). In the late 1960s, he became interested in effective instructional practices, especially as they applied to hard to teach children. This is still his major interest, but he has become more active in disseminating research findings on effective instructional practices (Becker, 1984).

Becker has been a member of Phi Beta Kappa and a consultant to the Australian Association for Direct Instruction. He has been included in *Who's Who in America*.

## REFERENCES

Becker, W. C. (1971). *Parents are teachers*. Champaign IL: Research.

Becker, W. C. (1984, March 18–23). *Direct instruction—A twenty year review*. Paper presented at the 16th annual Banff International Conference on Behavioral Science Honoring B. F. Skinner's 80th birthday.

Becker, W. C. (1986). *Applied psychology for teachers: A behavioral cognitive approach*. Chicago: Science Research Associates.

Becker, W. C., Engelmann, S., & Thomas, D. R. (1975). *Teaching 1: Classroom management*. Palo Alto, CA: Science Research Associates.

E. VALERIE HEWITT
*Texas A&M University*

# BEERS, CLIFFORD W. (1876–1943)

Clifford W. Beers founded the mental hygiene movement following 3 years as a patient in mental hospitals in Connecticut in the early part of the twentieth century. Because of the abuses that he suffered, he left the hospital determined to reform the system, to see harsh custodial care replaced with medical treatment. His book, *A Mind that Found Itself*, published in 1908, gives a vivid account of his experiences, and at the time created a public outcry against inhumane treatment of mental patients.

A gifted speaker and organizer, Beers obtained the support of eminent psychiatrists and other prominent people to form the Connecticut Society for Mental Hygiene in 1908, the National Committee for Mental Hygiene in

1909, and the International Committee for Mental Hygiene in 1930.

Beers's influence on the mental hygiene movement has been a lasting one, both through the work of the outstanding people he enlisted in the movement, and the continued popularity of *A Mind That Found Itself*, still in print after more than three-quarters of a century.

### REFERENCE

Beers, C. W. (1981). *A mind that found itself* (5th ed.). Pittsburgh: University of Pittsburgh Press.

PAUL IRVINE
*Katonah, New York*

## BEHAVIOR, DESTRUCTIVE

See DESTRUCTIVE BEHAVIORS.

## BEHAVIORAL ASSESSMENT

Behavioral assessment is distinguished from other types of assessment by the assumptions on which it is based and the purposes for which it is designed (Nelson & Hayes, 1979). It has been used in the assessment of problems as varied as social withdrawal, insomnia, learning disabilities, and seizure disorders (Mash & Terdal, 1981). Behavior domains assessed include cognitive and affective as well as motor behaviors (Cone, 1979). Techniques include interviewing, observation, checklists, psychophysiological and mechanical measurement, self-monitoring, and behavioral products. An argument has even been made for the inclusion of intelligence tests in behavioral assessment (Nelson, 1980).

Assessment is performed to generate treatment plans. This means that the quality of assessment is judged by the effectiveness of the intervention plans that it generates (treatment utility). Internal consistency, stability, interrater agreement, criterion-related validity, content validity, and construct validity are all necessary to establish treatment utility, and thus are as important as traditional assessment.

Although prior history and biological status affect the kinds of behaviors a person does or does not demonstrate, the occurrence of behaviors and their continuation are a function of immediate environmental events. In other words, behavior is purposeful within an environment. Because of this association between environment and behavior, behavioral assessment takes place in the natural setting in which the behavior occurs. In assessing bedtime tantrums, for example, child and parent behavior at bedtime may be observed by a professional on a home visit or by the parents themselves.

There is an emphasis on assessing publicly observable events such as specific motor behaviors or statements made by a client. This emphasis exists to reduce the need for inference (and possible bias) by the clinician. Besides the technical advantage of producing data of assessable reliability, it has the additional advantage of allowing clients, clinicians, parents, and other change agents to see directly the effects of treatment. Covert events (thoughts and feelings) can be incorporated by having clients observe and report their own internal behavior, or by teaching clients to perform a specific cognitive behavior and observing changes in behavior products or other overt behavior (Kendall & Braswell, 1985).

Identifying behaviors targeted for change is done by interviewing the person making a referral, generally the client or a person responsible for the client's welfare. Selection of target behaviors must be made with serious consideration of the ethics of changing behaviors (Harris & Kapche, 1978). It is generally easier for the client to identify behaviors that should be reduced than behaviors to be increased; however, replacement behaviors may be inappropriate unless treatment plans explicitly include increasing specific appropriate behaviors. The target may be to change the frequency (rate), form (topography), duration, intensity, setting, or latency of a behavior (the amount of time between a cue for a behavior and the onset of the behavior). These characteristics may be more or less salient in a specific problem and must be assessed. For example, temper tantrums generally have both frequency and duration as salient features: the rate of tantrums may be reduced from 10 per day to 1 per day, but duration may increase from 10 minutes each episode to 4 hours if duration is not targeted.

Controlling events are events that precede the behavior signaling its occurrence (antecedents), and that follow the occurrence of the behavior and have either the effect of strengthening or weakening the behavior (consequences). Different characteristics of a single target behavior may be under different controls. For example, tantrum behavior may be precipitated by the presentation of a frustrating task and the demand to perform it, but duration may be maintained by staff attention. Controlling events can be identified if changes in the occurrence of controlling events are made and the target behavior changes.

Skill deficits may preclude a desirable behavior from being performed. Techniques of task analysis (Resnick, Wang, & Kaplan, 1973) decompose behaviors into the simple parts that are necessary for performing the behavior. The client is assessed for performance of these prerequisite behaviors, thus yielding information that can be used to train the more complex skill. Among other methods, information from criterion-referenced tests can be useful for this purpose.

To evaluate intervention effects, data about the target behaviors must be collected prior to the start of an intervention, during a baseline period, as well as after the intervention has begun. Because a behavioral intervention may have inadvertent side effects, it is important for the clinician to hypothesize these and to assess them as well as intended treatment effects. For example, a plan may be to reduce a child's inappropriate talking out in class; the clinician should consider that talking out in class discussions and talking out on the playground may reduce also. Behavior change is evaluated using experimental designs that attempt to remove the threats to validity encountered in single-subject research (Barlow & Hersen, 1984).

Three of the most commonly used behavioral assessment techniques are interviewing, observation, and behavior products. Techniques that are occasionally used include self-monitoring, psychophysiological assessment, checklists and questionnaires, sociometry, and psychoeducational assessment. Interviewing may be the only assessment method available when the behavior is covert, occurs at a low rate, or occurs in a setting in which it is not feasible to observe. Also, the selection and definition of target behaviors must take place in an interview with the client or with someone responsible for the client's welfare. The clinician must decide who will be most informative regarding the client's behavior, and must consider interviewing several persons if any one person's knowledge of the problem is incomplete. Behavioral interviews proceed from an initial phase of problem identification, in which the clinician attempts to elicit all problems of concern to the interviewee, to problem specification, in which the problem behaviors are sufficiently specified so that the clinician and interviewee would agree on occurrences of the behavior if it were observed. Then comes the problem analysis phase, in which the clinician and interviewee attempt to identify controlling events and skill deficits. In consultation and some forms of direct service, the interview also may be used to generate plans for intervention. A fifth phase of interviewing involves evaluating the effectiveness of an intervention. Of these five phases, the most important for successful problem solution appears to be problem specification. The success of this phase depends on the clinician's ability to ask questions eliciting specific descriptions of behavior and controlling events while at the same time maintaining rapport (Haynes, 1978; Tombari & Bergan, 1978).

Observations serve two main purposes in behavioral assessment: to assess characteristics of target behaviors as they change following intervention, and to identify the controlling events of a behavior. In addition, observations can be used to identify goals for behavior change by identifying group norms for behavior. For example, a teacher may want to increase a child's participation in class discussions, but 100% would be too much. Observations reveal that classmates spend 4% of class time participating in discussions; therefore, reaching this level may be a suitable goal. Observation methods vary according to the rate of the behavior, the characteristics being assessed, the training and experience of the observer, and the observer's purpose. Behaviors that are low-rate (e.g., less than one occurrence an hour) will usually need to be recorded by participant observers (e.g., parents, staff) and be tallied on a daily or weekly basis to yield a measure of behavior frequency. Duration and latency of behaviors will need to be timed. Intensity can be rated by an observer, and topography can be described in a verbal narrative. Identifying controlling events requires being able to track immediately preceding and following events. These events, if observers are trained to look for them, can be recorded in an anecdotal record, a narrative report of each occurrence of a behavior. A houseparent, reporting an incident of running away, can note the time and setting of the occurrence, immediately preceding events, the chain of running-away behaviors, the duration of the incident, and likely consequent events.

Sampling is required in observation of high-rate behaviors because it is not convenient or possible to observe target behaviors continuously. In time sampling, a decision must first be made about the length of an observation session (e.g., 20 minutes). This will depend on the rate of the behavior; the session should be long enough to observe many occurrences. A second decision concerns dividing the observation session into smaller units (intervals), deciding on the length of each interval and the interval sampling method to be used. Interval length needs to be short (e.g., 3 seconds) for high-rate behaviors, but can be long (e.g., 1 hour) for low-rate behaviors. The shorter the interval length, the closer the agreement between time sampling and continuous monitoring, but the more tedious observation becomes. In whole-interval sampling, a behavior is recorded only if it has been occurring during the entire interval. In partial-interval sampling, a behavior is recorded if it occurred at any time during the interval. Compared with continuous monitoring, whole-interval sampling consistently underestimates time, while partial-interval sampling overestimates time (Powell, 1984). A method of sampling that provides an unbiased estimate of frequency is momentary time sampling. In this method, an observation is made at the precise onset of an interval. If the behavior is occurring at the moment, it is recorded. Each method generates a summary score indicating the proportion of intervals in which the behavior occurred. If intervals are short (much shorter than average behavior duration), an estimate of behavior duration can be made if one counts consecutive intervals in which the behavior occurred.

Behavior products, such as a math worksheet completed by a student or number of pounds gained by a person with an eating disorder, are less reactive than interviews, observations, self-monitoring, or client-completed check-lists (Webb et al., 1966). Such measures are most often used as measures of behavior change in addition to more reactive measures. Although in many instances producing little information about controlling events, some products may produce clues about such events. For example, examination of a child's math worksheet may reveal consistent misapplications of a math rule (Brown & Burton, 1978); or an examination of absentee records may reveal that a child's nonattendance tends to occur following weekends and holidays.

## REFERENCES

Barlow, D. H., & Hersen, M. (1984). *Single case experimental designs*. New York: Pergamon.

Brown, J. S., & Burton, R. R. (1978). Diagnostic models for procedural bugs in basic mathematical skills. *Cognitive Science, 2*, 155–192.

Cone, J. D. (1979). Confounded comparisons in triple response mode assessment research. *Behavioral Assessment, 1*, 85–95.

Harris, A., & Kapche, R. (1978). Behavior modification in schools: Ethical issues and suggested guidelines. *Journal of School Psychology, 16*, 25–33.

Haynes, S. N. (1978). *Principles of behavioral assessment*. New York: Gardner.

Kendall, P. C., & Braswell, L. (1985). *Cognitive-impulsive therapy for impulsive children*. New York: Guilford.

Mash, E. J., & Terdal, L. G. (Eds.). (1981). *Behavioral assessment of childhood disorders* (pp. 441–482). New York: Guilford.

Nelson, R. O. (1980). The use of intelligence tests within behavioral assessment. *Behavioral Assessment, 2*, 417–425.

Nelson, R. O., & Hayes, S. C. (1979). Some current dimensions of behavioral assessment. *Behavioral Assessment, 1*, 1–16.

Powell, J. (1984). On the misrepresentation of behavioral realities by a widely practiced direct observation procedure: Partial interval (one-zero) sampling. *Behavioral Assessment, 6*, 209–220.

Resnick, L. B., Wang, M. C., & Kaplan, J. (1973). Task analysis in curriculum design: A hierarchically sequenced introductory math curriculum. *Journal of Applied Behavior Analysis, 6*, 679–709.

Tombari, M. L., & Bergan, J. R. (1978). Consultant cues and teacher verbalizations, judgments, and expectancies concerning children's adjustment problems. *Journal of School Psychology, 16*, 212–219.

Webb, E. J., Campbell, D. T., Schwartz, R. D., & Sechrest, L. (1966). *Unobtrusive measures: Nonreactive research in the social sciences*. Chicago: Rand McNally.

JOHN MACDONALD
*Eastern Kentucky University*

BEHAVIOR CHARTING
BEHAVIORAL CONSULTATION
BEHAVIOR MODIFICATION

## BEHAVIORAL CONSULTATION

Over the last three decades, consultation has become an increasingly important tool in the provision of psychological services to children and youths in educational settings (Meecham & Peckham, 1978; Ramage, 1979). School-based consultation may be rendered from a variety of theoretical perspectives. These include mental health consultation, which is linked to psychodynamic theories of personality (Caplan, 1970), organization development consultation (Schmuck, 1982), which has its origins in social psychological theory strongly influenced by the Lewinian perspective, and behavioral consultation, which is linked to behavioral theory (Bandura, 1977; Skinner, 1953). The following discussion describes the behavioral approach to consultation services.

There are no characteristics that uniquely define consultation. Consequently, there are no features that uniquely characterize behavioral consultation. Nonetheless, there are features that tend to be associated with consultation services. Perhaps the most widely shared attribute of consultation activities is that they generally involve indirect service (Bergan, 1977). Typically, service is rendered by a consultant (e.g., psychologist) to a consultee (e.g., teacher), who in turn provides services to one or more clients (e.g., students). The indirect approach to service characteristic of consultation is generally regarded as a major advantage of this form of service delivery. A consultant providing services to a number of consultees can bring expertise to many more clients than could be served by a direct-service approach. There is a multiplier effect in which the skills of the consultant can be brought to bear on client problems without the extensive time commitment required when the consultant provides direct services to the client.

A second attribute of consultation is that it is generally a problem-solving venture in which the consultant provides expert advice related to a problem presented by the consultee (Bergan, 1977). The consultant usually elicits a description of the problem from the consultee, assists in the development of a plan to solve the problem, and participates in an evaluation to determine the extent to which the problem has been solved.

A third feature of consultation is that it is typically assumed to involve a collegial relationship between the consultant and the consultee (Bergan, 1977). This means that the consultant has no direct authority over the consultee and the consultee has no direct authority over the consultant. Rather, each has an area of professional responsibility with respect to the services provided to the client. The consultant serves as an adviser. The consultee uses consultant advice in making and implementing decisions aimed at solving the problem(s) presented in consultation.

The three attributes discussed in the preceding paragraphs are not unique to behavioral consultation. Yet, they are a part of consultation rendered from a behavioral perspective. What distinguishes behavioral consultation from other varieties of consultation is the use of a behavioral perspective in providing consultation services (Bergan, 1977; Feld, Bergan, & Stone, in press). The behavioral viewpoint affects consultation in three important ways. First, it dictates that problems presented in consultation be conceptualized from a behavioral perspective. Second, it calls for the use of behavioral principles in designing interventions to solve problems. Third, it assumes an empirical approach to determining the effectiveness of consultation interventions.

Consultation services are generally rendered in a series of stages, each of which is designed to address a particular aspect of the problem-solving endeavor. Four stages are generally recognized in consultation (Bergan, 1977; Dorr, 1979; Goodwin & Coates, 1976; Tombari & Davis, 1979). The are (1) problem identification, (2) problem analysis, (3) plan implementation, and (4) problem evaluation.

Problem identification sets the direction that consultation will take. Within the behavioral perspective, a problem is defined in terms of a discrepancy between observed behavior and desired behavior. The problem is to eliminate the discrepancy. Determining the existence of a discrepancy between observed and desired behavior requires that the concerns communicated by the consultee be expressed in behavioral terms. During problem identification, the consultant assists the consultee to describe current client functioning and desired functioning in terms of current behaviors and desired behaviors. Data are generally collected to document the status of current behavior. A problem exists if the data reveal a difference between current and desired behavior that the consultee regards as a significant discrepancy.

Problem analysis follows problem identification. During this stage of consultation, the factors that may be influencing client behaviors of concern are identified and a plan is formulated to effect desired changes in behaviors. Behavioral principles are heavily relied on in determining influences on behavior. Problem analysis generally begins with the specification of antecedent and consequent environmental conditions that may be affecting behavior. However, client skills and behavioral patterns may also be the subject of analysis (Piersel, 1985). After hypothesized influences on client behavior have been identified, a plan is formulated to change client behavior. The consultant is generally responsible for specifying the strategies that may be used to achieve behavior change. However, the consultee often plays a major role in identifying specific tactics that may be useful in implementing a plan. For example, a consultant may determine that positive reinforcement may be useful in increasing a particular behavior of concern to the consultee. The consultee may then identify the type of reinforcement to be used with the behavior.

After a suitable plan has been formulated, it is imple-

mented. Implementation is generally the responsibility of the consultee. However, the consultee may direct an implementation effort in which others actually carry out the plan. For instance, a teacher may direct a peer tutoring program designed to increase the reading skills of a group of children. The principal role of the consultant during implementation is one of monitoring what is occurring and of assisting the consultee to make minor revisions in the plan in those instances in which the plan is not working as expected.

The final stage in consultation is problem evaluation. During this phase of consultation, the consultant and the consultee determine the extent to which the goals of consultation have been achieved and the extent to which the plan implemented to attain goals has been effective. Evaluation data guide the course of consultation. If the goals of consultation have been achieved, a new problem may be identified or services may terminate. If the goals of consultation have not been achieved, consultation generally returns to problem analysis.

Behavioral consultation has been most widely applied in solving learning and/or adjustment problems manifested by children and youths in educational settings (Bergan, 1977). In the typical case, services are directed toward one client (e.g., a student). However, there have been many applications involving groups. For example, consultation may be used to modify the behavior of all of the children in a class (Bergan, 1977). It has also been suggested that behavioral consultation could be useful for organization development including all of the individuals associated with an educational setting (Piersel, 1985). However, applications of behavioral consultation for this purpose are lacking.

Piersel (1985) has outlined procedures for using behavioral consultation in special education programs. He points out that consultation is ideally suited to meeting the goal of providing students eligible for special services with a program that reflects the least restrictive alternative environment for rendering services. Piersel indicates that consultation should begin with an attempt to solve problems manifested by the child in the regular classroom environment. When evidence is gathered indicating that a solution cannot be achieved in the classroom, placement in a special program is considered. It is at this point that assessment and case conferences with the family and other professionals occur.

There is a large body of research documenting the effectiveness of behavioral consultation (Feld, Bergan, & Stone, in press). Research on the effectiveness of behavioral consultation is of two types. The first involves studies of the application of behavioral principles in consultation to achieve changes in behavior. Research of this kind has shown the behavioral approach to be effective in remediating a large variety of behavioral and academic problems (Bergan & Tombari, 1976; Conoley & Conoley, 1982; Medway, 1979; Medway & Forman, 1980).

The second body of research on the effectiveness of the behavioral approach compares the effectiveness of behavioral consultation with that of other forms of service. Although many of the comparative studies have methodological flaws (Medway, 1979), the overall body of literature comparing behavioral consultation with other forms of service shows support for the behavioral approach (Medway, 1979).

## REFERENCES

Bandura, A. (1977). *Social learning*. Englewood Cliff, NJ: Prentice-Hall.

Bergan, J. R. (1977). *Behavioral consultation*. Columbus, OH: Merrill.

Bergan, J. R., & Tombari, M. L. (1976). Consultant skill and efficiency and the implementation of outcomes of consultation. *Journal of School Psychology, 14*, 3–13.

Caplan, G. (1970). *The theory and practice of mental health consultation*. New York: Basic Books.

Conoley, J. C., & Conoley, C. W. (1982). The effects of two conditions of client-centered consultation on student teacher problem descriptions and remedial plans. *Journal of School Psychology, 20*, 323–328.

Dorr, D. (1979). Psychological consulting in the schools. In J. J. Platt & R. J. Wicks (Eds.), *The psychological consultant*. New York: Grune & Stratton.

Feld, J. D., Bergan, J. R., & Stone, C. A. (in press). Behavioral approaches to school based consultation: Current status and future directions. In C. A. Maher (Ed.), *Behavioral approaches to providing educational services in schools*. Hillsdale, NJ: Erlbaum.

Goodwin, D. L., & Coates, T. J. (1976). *Helping students help themselves*. Engelwood Cliffs, NJ: Prentice-Hall.

Meacham, M. L., & Peckham, P. D. (1978). School psychologists at three-quarters century: Congruence between training, practice, preferred role and competence. *Journal of School Psychology, 16*, 195–206.

Medway, F. J. (1979). How effective is school consultation: A review of recent research. *Journal of School Psychology, 17*, 275–282.

Medway, F. J., & Forman, S. G. (1980). Psychologists' and teachers' reactions to mental health and behavioral school consultation. *Journal of School Psychology, 18*, 338–348.

Piersel, W. C. (1985). Behavioral consultation: An approach to problem solving in educational settings. In J. R. Bergan (Ed.), *School psychology in contemporary society*. Columbus, OH: Merrill.

Ramage, J. C. (1979). National survey of school psychologists: Update. *School Psychology Digest, 8*, 153–161.

Schmuck, R. A. (1982). Organizational development in the schools. In C. R. Reynolds & T. B. Gutkin (Eds.), *The handbook of school psychology*. New York: Wiley.

Skinner, B. F. (1953). *Science and human behavior*. New York: Macmillan.

Tombari, M. L., & Davis, R. A. (1979). Behavioral consultation. In G. D. Phye & D. J. Reschly (Eds.), *School psychology: Perspectives and issues*. New York: Academic.

JOHN R. BERGAN
*University of Arizona*

**BEHAVIOR ASSESSMENT**
**CONSULTATION**
**CONSULTATION, MENTAL HEALTH**

## BEHAVIORAL DEFICIT

The terminology associated with behavioral deficit has become confused as a result of various incomplete usages. The original usage was associated with the 1961 American Association on Mental Retardation inclusion of adaptive behavior in their definition of mental retardation. Adaptive behavior implies that many educational, psychological, sociological, and biological influences interact on the child, affecting function and performance. Principally, it is a term designed to offset the dependence the public schools, mental health agencies, and social welfare institutions had placed on measured intelligence.

Those who disagreed with this view, advanced the deviance model, which suggested that unacceptable learning and behavioral problems were surface symptoms, unexplained by gross generalizations, one of which was the IQ score. Deviance was specified as specific behaviors, usually identified on test items, subtest performance, or perceptual-motor or language-sensitive instruments. Thus the child was no longer viewed as being deviant, but rather as having a behavioral deficit(s).

The original concept was closely associated with developmental disabilities. Work in the late 1950s, and early 1960s with handicapped children resulted in a description of developmental lag, placing the emphasis for the disability on irregular test protocols and subtest patterns clinically thought to reflect possible neurological insult. The search had begun by psychoeducational researchers to specify the nature of these so-called behavioral deficits through the use of test and subtest patterns. In 1966, S. D. Clements placed into motion, through the committee he chaired on minimal neurological impairment, the search for neurological damage as an explanation of specific learning disabilities.

Learning disabilities as a handicapped condition, based on the search for a specific behavioral deficit, began in earnest. Even the language in the definition of learning disabilities, in keeping with the pathology-symptom diagnostic model associated with the other categories of handicapping conditions, attested to perceptual cognitive deficits, a diagnostic factor still required by most states in applying the label of learning disabilities. Tests designed to measure visual and auditory perceptual, perceptual-motor, and other cognitive abilities began to flood the market. The term specific added to learning disabilities accentuated that a deficit in one or more of the psychological processes was accountable for the condition.

Kirk (1972) noted that, "Hence, the term specific learning disabilities refers to severe handicaps in central processes, which inhibit the child's normal development in such specific areas as talking, thinking, perceiving, reading, writing, and spelling" (p. 162). Dunn (1973), in response, added the work major to specific learning disabilities. In his definition he combined the words *specific basic learning* process, which involved perception, conception, or expression associated with the areas of oral and written language and mathematics. In 1974, Gleason and Haring provided the first general behavioral definition of learning disabilities and in so doing used the term behavioral deficit as the principal construct associated with the concept learning disabilities. "We define a learning disability as a behavioral deficit almost always associated with academic performance and that can be remediated by precise, individualized instructional programming" (p. 226).

Initially, no other two tests were used as widely, generated more research, or were more closely identified with pioneer work in learning disabilities than the Illinois Test of Psycholinguistic Abilities (ITPA) (Kirk, MacCarthy, & Kirk, 1968) and the Developmental Test of Visual Perception (1964), offered by Frostig, LeFever, and Wittlesey. The ITPA reportedly measured 12 behavioral areas and recorded them on a profile. The profile then served as a graphic representation of various auditory and visual perceptual and language-associated behaviors. A behavioral deficit could easily be observed. The Frostig, et al. test measured five perceptual motor and associated skills and reported them on a profile. The purpose of the profile was to promote remedial prescriptive instruction of the behavioral deficit. Controversy began immediately and has continued over the application of remediation to a behavioral deficit as opposed to a strength. The late 1970s and early 1980s have seen a new birth of interest in neurological and cognitive function, with several new test batteries on the market, most of which are designed to specify behavioral deficits.

There are two major issues that surround the construct of behavioral deficits. The first is the possibility or utility of cognitive skills being broken into specific component parts. It should be remembered that all assumed cognitive behaviors are named, usually after a test or subtest designed to measure them. They are not occurrences in nature that are directly observable. The second issue is the reliability of most tests designed to ascertain or describe a basic behavior and therefore illustrate a behavioral deficit. As the reliability decreases, so does the validity.

A behavioral deficit then is a concept suggesting that human abilities are not all the same, and in some cases fall to a deficit level. Operationally defining a deficit has not been well done through the use of tests or subtests in terms of when a deficit statistically or clinically exists. Therefore, while the concept itself has driven several major thrusts (both diagnostic and treatment), including the term developmental disability to some degree, and theoretically is responsible for describing learning disability, it remains an incomplete term, less than fully developed by those who use it on a clinical basis.

## REFERENCES

Clements, S. D. (1966). *Task force I: Minimal brain dysfunction in children. Monograph No. 3.* Washington, DC: U.S. Government Printing Office.

Dunn, L. M. (Ed.). (1973). *Exceptional children in the schools: Special education in transition.* New York: Holt.

Frostig, M., Lefever, D., & Wittlesey, J. (1964). *The Marianne Frostig Developmental Test of Visual Perception.* Palo Alto, CA: Consulting Psychology.

Gleason, C., & Haring, N. (1974). Learning disabilities. In N. G. Haring (Ed.), *Behavior of exceptional children* (pp. 245–295). Columbus, OH: Merrill.

Kirk, S. A. (1972). *Educating exceptional children* (2nd ed.). Boston: Houghton Mifflin.

Kirk, S. A., McCarthy, J., & Kirk, W. (1968). *Illinois Test of Psycholinguistic Abilities.* Urbana, IL: University of Illinois Press.

Koppitz, E. M. (1971). *The Bender Gestalt Test for young children.* New York: Grune & Stratton.

DAVID A. SABATINO
*West Virginia College of
Graduate Studies*

ABILITY TRAINING
BEHAVIORAL OBJECTIVES

# BEHAVIORAL DISORDERS

*Behavioral Disorders* is the official journal of the Council for Children with Behavioral Disorders (CCBD) of the Council for Exceptional Children. Founded in 1975, *Behavioral Disorders* serves as a resource for those professionals interested in the education and treatment of behaviorally disordered children and youth.

The journal, with a quarterly distribution to the 6,200 members of CCBD and 575 individual and institutional subscribers, was developed under the editorships of Albert Fink of Indiana University (1975–1978), Denzil Edge of the University of Louisville (1978–1981), and Robert B. Rutherford, Jr., of Arizona State University (1981–1987) into a forum for the publication of manuscripts derived from documented thought and empirical evidence. These data-based articles are presented in several forms: experimental research (either original or replications), research and practice reviews and analyses, program or procedure descriptions, and scholarly reviews of texts, films, and other media. The editorial process of the journal is designed to thoroughly and professionally analyze submitted manuscripts in terms of originality, relevance of topic, importance of the findings or concepts, content organization, and documentation.

Historically, *Behavioral Disorders* evolved from an early dependence on cosponsored thematic issues and reliance on solicited manuscripts to an open journal relying on unsolicited manuscripts submitted by professionals in the field. *Behavioral Disorders* has contributed significantly to the professional literature on behavioral disorders of children and youths.

ROBERT B. RUTHERFORD, JR.
*Arizona State University*

# BEHAVIORAL OBJECTIVES

In the broadest sense, an objective is a statement of an aim or desired outcome. In an educational sense, an instructional objective may be a quantifiable and/or an observable academic or social achievement that specifies the enabling steps necessary to accomplish the objective in a stated period of time. All instructional or behavioral objectives must have observable or measurable outcomes. The difference between an instructional and a behavioral objective is the result to be achieved. The latter may be broader in scope and not confined to an educational effort; it may rather include a wide range of specified behavioral outcomes, for example, speech, language, perceptual development, motor training, and social skill development.

Behavioral objectives and instructional (teaching) objectives are frequently used interchangeably. While each impacts on the other, these two sets of objectives address two different performances. A behavioral objective focuses on any visible activity displayed by a learner (student). It has at its core the terminal behavior, or what the learner can demonstrate has been learned. An instructional objective may include the desired learner outcomes; it will specify the criteria acceptable for success in attaining that outcome, but it focuses on what will be taught and how it will be taught.

The purpose for developing behavioral objectives is to increase teaching efficiency by having educators and behavioral scientists determine what it is that will be learned, how it will be taught, what materials will be used, and the length of time within which it should be learned against a predetermined criteria or standard. Behavioral objectives become targets to which teachers can direct their instruction. In the process of instruction, their use requires educators to determine whether outcomes or observations of performance are being effectively and efficiently provided and creating an exactness for what is learned and how it is taught. Thus, a teaching methodology may be used for a specified amount of time under conditions that will permit the educator to judge the amount of progress being made. Mager (1962) notes, "An instructor will function in a fog of his own making until he knows what he wants his students to be able to do at the end of the instruction" (p. 2).

One of the most common points of confusion is between a course description (or what a course is about) and behavioral objectives (those specific, measurable, or observable performances a student will demonstrate at the completion of a course). Behavioral objectives must contain statements of concrete, measurable, or observable performances. In contrast, nonbehavioral goals are broad, abstract statements; they are not derived from previous observations or performance test data. They do not consider the skills necessary to enter into a next level of work. Nonbehavioral objectives are based on philosophy, ideology, and attitude, not the proficiency of task to be taught.

Popham and Baker (1970) note five different considerations necessary in the preparation and use of behavioral objectives. They are

1. *Systematic instructional decision making.* The use of behavioral objectives and the measured outcome to determine the most efficient method of instruction and how effective a specified method was in achieving an objective.

2. *Behavioral and/or educational objectives.* Determine what is to be accomplished, in what time period, and how it is to be accomplished.

3. *Selection of appropriate educational objectives.* Selecting significant and meaningful objectives is not easy; indeed, the task tends to be elusive and difficult. Educators must choose between the content (e.g., a math score, reading score from a formal or informal test, new words to be learned) and behaviors that are reasoned to influence the process of learning (e.g., time on task). Many times the two intersect and both become important elements in achieving a goal.

4. *Establishing performance standards.* One of the most difficult tasks is to set the criteria that denote whether a behavioral objective has been achieved successfully. There are no absolutes or clear rules for achieving that purpose. Some guidelines exist, such as the 80/80 criterion, which states that 80% of what has been taught must be demonstrated as a succssfully learned outcome at an 80% minimal level of performance. Thus, if 10 words were taught, on measurement eight words must be learned before the next list of words is taught. Many educators use the 80% criterion as a minimal standard for instructional or subject matter content objectives. A large percentage of these same practitioners believe that a 90% criterion is useful with behavioral objectives. The estab-

lishment of performance standards addresses the sophistication or precision of the objective. While performance standards may largely be intuitive, a performance standard frequently addresses the knowledge the educator has of the learner.

5. *The curriculum rationale.* Educators spend their professional lives developing and implementing the curriculum. Countless hours are spent discussing curriculum questions each school year through school-district, building-level, and grade-level curriculum committees; in addition, thousands of curriculum guides exist in the United States. Combine those teacher-made curricula and guides with the innumerable commercially printed materials, and it would appear the curricular-planning process is complete. It is not. Despite all these efforts, 20 to 30% of schoolchildren fail academically or socially each year. Why?

A simple and very clear explanation is that most curricula are targeted at theoretical learners who are ready to learn and have no disabilities. An educator using a general curricular guide or commercial material is exclusively concerned with determining the objectives for the eudcational system, and not any one typical or atypical youth in that system. There are basically two kinds of decisions that educators must make. First, they must decide what the objectives (the ends) of the instructional system should be; second, they must decide on the procedures (the means) for accomplishing those objectives. This is, the curricular rationale for using behavioral or instructional objectives. This point becomes critical when individualization of instruction is sought. The use of behavioral objectives suggests the teacher is selecting and evaluating instructional procedures to accomplish those objectives. Thus teachers are engaged in instructional decision making. Herein resides the critical difference between using a curriculum and an instructional objectives process. Instructional objectives require stated levels of success, and measured and/or observable outcomes. In short, they are empirical solutions requiring data. Curricular structures are generally value-based.

How then are behavioral objectives established? Usually by determining a behavioral characteristic such as inattentiveness, or a score on a test, or a set of facts or things to be learned, e.g., words or numbers. Behavioral objectives specify what it is to be learned and place a comfortable floor beneath the learner by dropping below what the learner can do initially and ending with what the learner can comfortably learn in a given period of time. A sound behavioral objective does not test the learner's limit, unless designed to do so for good reason.

A behavioral objective is one activity in a series of, or sequence of, activities to be learned. That sequence can become the curriculum. The principal reason for having many small, tightly sequenced steps in the curriculum is that learner performance is examined frequently. More important, the learner is provided with corrective feedback after every trial. That point is critical. What the learner knows does not fall to an assumption that cannot be proven. Behavioral or instructional objectives, once sequenced, become important interlocking steps. Because the ability of children to learn varies widely, particularly when materials change, each objective permits the individual student the necessary time on tasks.

The three major advantages of a behavioral objective are

1. Students are not compared with others, but with themselves and the speed with which they may learn a given task comfortably.

2. Each tightly sequenced step is validated in the curricular process; all assumptions about learning rate or about what has been learned are rejected.

3. There is a starting point, something the student knows, and a stopping point, a task within the comfort level to be learned.

A curriculum based on a series of behavioral objectives is a scientific approximation of the art of teaching. For that reason, P.L. 94-142 (1975) required that an individual educational program (IEP) be written for every handicapped child served under this legislation. An IEP is a behavioral objective and/or an instructional objective that requires a specific diagnostic process (with a multidisciplinary team) and a preparation procedure. It ensures the availability of data for accountability.

## REFERENCES

Mager, R. F. (1962). *Preparing instructional objectives.* Palo Alto, CA: Fearon.

Popham, W. J., & Baker, E. (1970). *Establishing instructional goals.* Englewood Cliffs, NJ: Prentice-Hall.

DAVID A. SABATINO
*West Virginia College
of Graduate Studies*

## AGE APPROPRIATE CURRICULUM TEACHING STRATEGIES

## BEHAVIORAL OBSERVATION

Behavior observation is at the core of behavioral assessment. Behavior observation is a procedure for categorizing motor and verbal behavior into an organized permanent record. A behavior observation system meets three criteria (Jones, Reid, & Patterson, 1974). These include "recording of behavioral events in their natural settings at the time they occur, not retrospectively; the use of trained impartial observer-coders, and descriptions of behaviors which (sic) require little if any inference by observers to code the events" (p. 46). Excluded from this definition are narrative recordings, anecdotal records, checklists and rating scales, and procedures that require a person to observe and record his or her own behavior.

Behavior observations occur in diverse settings and for numerous purposes. In educational settings, behavior observations are used for purposes of diagnosing individual students, planning an intervention to modify a pupil's behavior, evaluating interventions, consulting with teachers, and conducting research.

Although specific observational procedures and instruments vary in many important ways, they all require selectivity. The observation instrument structures the observer's attention to those selected aspects of behavior and the setting that are presumed to be most relevant to the purposes of the observation. Behavior occurs in a continuous stream, yet the observer must categorize behavior into objectively defined behavioral codes and encode it into an organized, permanent record. Care in defining what is to be observed is critical to measurable results. Narrative recordings and checklists can assist in selecting the most significant behavioral codes as well as the contextual, or environmental, events thought to be associated with the selected behaviors. Data on these antecedent and consequent events are useful in designing a plan for modifying the behaviors of concern.

To minimize observer subjectivity, the selected behaviors are defined as objectively as possible. "Aggressive behavior" is not as objective a definition as "hits, shoves, grabs, and tackles." Although "aggressive behavior" can serve as useful shorthand in coding behavior, the clear specification of the behaviors encompassed by this term gives the observer an objective definition of aggression. When the behavioral codes are objectively defined, any two trained observers should agree on the presence or absence of a behavior. Behavior observations can occur in natural settings (e.g., classroom, peer group, or home) or in simulated or role playing settings.

Observational instruments vary in their degree of formality from homemade teacher-used instruments to published instruments requiring highly trained observers. Three major types of observational procedures are frequency recordings, duration recordings, and interval recordings (Barton & Ascione, 1984). In frequency recordings, the number of times a behavior occurs within the observational period is recorded. Frequency recordings are best suited to behaviors that have a discrete beginning and end, that last approximately the same amount of time each time they occur, and that do not occur so frequently that separating each occurrence becomes difficult. Hand raises, inappropriate noises, bed-wetting, and hitting are examples of frequency target behaviors. The Figure shows the results of a frequency recording of a disruptive student's behavior. Each block represents 1 minute, and each observational period lasts 15 minutes. The totals at the end of each row are the frequencies of that target behavior

Observer: Cathy Snow (consultant)
Date: November 5, 1985
Student: Julie
Circumstance: Math seatwork

| Behavior | | | | | | | | | | | | | | | | Total |
|---|---|---|---|---|---|---|---|---|---|---|---|---|---|---|---|---|
| Noise | II | I | I | III | | I | III | I | I | II | IIII | II | III | I | I | 26 |
| Physical contact | | | I | | II | | | I | I | | | III | | | I | 9 |
| Out of seat | | | | | | | I | | | | | | | I | I | 3 |

Frequency recording sheet.

in a 15-minute period. Observations should continue over several days to obtain a reliable measure.

A duration recording is a direct measure of the amount of time an individual engages in the target behavior. Duration recordings are most appropriate for behaviors that have a clear beginning and ending and that last for more than a few seconds. If a child gets out of his or her seat and stays out of the seat for periods of time ranging from 1 to 6 minutes, a duration count would indicate the percentage of time the child was out of the seat during the observational period.

In interval recordings, the occurrence or nonoccurrence of selected behaviors during a series of equal time intervals is recorded. Interval recording is recommended when several behaviors need to be observed, when behaviors occur at a high rate, or when behaviors do not have clear-cut beginnings and ends. There are several variations of interval recording procedures. Typically, some sort of signaling device (e.g., an audio timer or beeps on a prerecorded cassette) cues the observer to make a recording. The observer records which target behavior occurred during the preceding interval (usually 10 seconds).

Frequency, duration, and interval recordings can be adapted to a format that allows recording of selected antecedents and consequences of the behavioral codes. At the same time the observed child's behavior is coded, the antecedent and consequent circumstances are coded. Barton and Ascione (1984) provide examples of these different observational instruments.

Observational procedures are measurement procedures, and their reliability and validity need to be established. An important part of establishing reliability is determining the extent to which two observers agree in their use of the instrument while observing the same behavior and context. Validity issues include the relationship of the behavioral code to the referral problem (face validity) and the normality of the observed behavior. One way of determining whether a child's behavior in particular settings (e.g., a classroom) is atypical is to observe other children in the same settings. If the observer alternates between observing the target child and observing other children in a classroom, the observer will have a composite observation of the typical child to compare with the referred child. Haynes (1978) discusses reliability, validity, and other methodological issues in observations.

## REFERENCES

Barton, C. J., & Ascione, F. R. (1984). Direct observation. In T. H. Ollendick & M. Hersen (Eds.), *Child behavioral assessment* (pp. 166–194). New York: Pergamon.

Haynes, S. N. (1978). *Principles of behavioral assessment.* New York: Gardner.

Jones, R. R., Reid, J. B., & Patterson, G. B. (1974). Naturalistic observation in clinical assessment. In P. McReynolds (Ed.), *Advances in psychological assessment.* San Francisco: Jossey-Bass.

JAN N. HUGHES
*Texas A&M University*

APPLIED BEHAVIOR ANALYSIS
BEHAVIOR THERAPY

# BEHAVIOR ANALYSIS, APPLIED

See APPLIED BEHAVIOR ANALYSIS.

# BEHAVIOR CHARTING

Behavior charting is a term commonly used as an equivalent to describe a graphic representation of behavioral data. Graphing behavioral data allows the special edu-

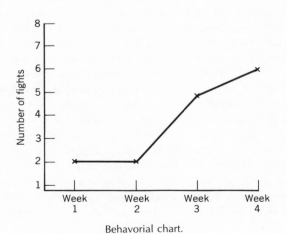

Behavorial chart.

cator to see changes easily in target behaviors (behaviors that are to be increased or decreased in frequency or duration). The ordinate, or vertical line, of the graph is labeled with the behavioral measurement scale (see Figure). This could be the number of occurrences of off-task behavior, the number of fights a child has, or the percentage of time that a child follows instructions. The abscissa, or horizontal line, is labeled with the unit of time. This could be treatment sessions, days, weeks, minutes, or other intervals over which changes in behavior can be measured (Sulzer-Azaroff & Mayer, 1977). A graph of a child's fighting behavior is shown in the accompanying Figure. As can be seen from the figure, this particular child's incidences of fighting are getting more frequent with time. This behavioral chart will allow the special educator to evaluate the effectiveness of any treatment that may eventually be implemented.

## REFERENCE

Sulzer-Azaroff, B., & Mayer, G. R. (1977). *Applying behavior-analysis procedures with children and youth.* New York: Holt, Rinehart and Winston.

RANDY W. KAMPHAUS
*Eastern Kentucky University*

APPLIED BEHAVIOR ANALYSIS

# BEHAVIOR DISORDERS

The terms behaviorally disordered, emotionally disturbed, emotionally handicapped, and socially maladjusted are used synonymously by practitioners in special education. One of the reasons that different terms are used interchangeably is that various states use a variety of terms in their legal language to describe students who are drawing undue attention to themselves in matters of personal/social behaviors.

Special education has in the last 50 years developed a repertoire of interchangeable terms. While the terms may be interchangeable, the meanings of these terms are not always the same. Behavioral disorder implies that a student's social/personal regulative and adjustive mechanisms are poorly defined and generally faulty, given a specific social or environmental condition. The relativity of the term behavioral disorders begins with the displaying situationally and socially of unacceptable behaviors. There are sharp contrasts in what may reflect acceptable behaviors in such settings as urban, rural, large school, small school, etc. In addition, young teacher, old teacher, autocratic or democratic philosophy of the principal, type of community, etc. affect acceptable behaviors. In short, immediate cultural-linguistic circumstances of the child and community are all relative factors.

The concept of social relativity comes into play when we see actual cases of students with well-defined social values seemingly respecting those values, but then rejecting them to embrace the culture and mores of the urban gang, or, the reverse situation. The point is that adjustment capabilities are devastated by the perceptions and distortions of the student in regard to the social order, and, in turn, of the social order in regard to the student. Additionally, the judgments of peers and adults concerning the fitness of a person in regard to the social order is not a constant, but influenced by age, sex, status, and ethnicity, and a number of other variables. When there is drug usage, violent behavior, verbal aggressiveness, a wide range of asocial, dysocial, and antisocial, antischool behaviors, status crimes, and even criminally punishable offenses, these may be judged to be disordered.

When do we say a student is failing to make a satisfactory adjustment? The words satisfactory adjustment should signal a recognition that such an expression requires a socially relative value judgment. What goes into that value judgment rests on many factors, including the proximity to the rules being broken and whose rules are being broken.

Revolutionary thinking in regard to all handicapped persons, and in particular the mentally ill, developed in the wake of the French Revolution. The great French psychiatrist Phillipe Pinel was the first to separate criminals from the insane. The lag in services, if not consideration for the mentally ill, resided in a collection of many superstitions. Emotional difficulties have been attributed to every conceivable cause: biological, physiological, sociological, religious, psychological, and genetic, to name just a few.

There can be little question that Freud and his observations, records, and theories raised the level of excitement in the field and stimulated an international response to theoretical explanation and treatment. The cost for such predominance by one person was that the early to mid-twentieth century was dominated by his thinking, and two camps were formed: the Freudians and the neo-Freudians. The influence of this one man was so powerful that he still influences, if not overwhelms, classic psychoanalytic thinking. Freud's theories were his direct contribution to child psychiatry. He believed his theories were supported by his observations from treatment. He proposed that psychological development must proceed through four sequentially related childhood psychosexual stages. Any inhibition of development critical to those stages would fixate the emotional structures needed for adult adjustment and result in stunted emotional development. Fixation in some stage would result in faulty emotional defense mechanisms, permitting the person to be flooded by anxieties. Neurosis was, according to Freudian psychology, the presence of more anxiety than the emotional defense structures can cope with comfortably. Psychosis was

the loss of reality owing to the operational incapacitation of the mental defense structures.

Freud's emphasis on childhood, and the growth and development of the mind as a parallel to the biological development of organs, bones, and muscle, was a major contribution for the wrong reasons. These biologically metaphoric hypotheses of emotional development did provide a universal understanding of the importance of child-rearing practices, and a set of constructs that permitted an explanation of emotional disturbance scientifically was appealing. A mixed blessing is that Freud's theories far outran any data that any science could produce. Constructs such as the three major components of the mind—the id, ego, and super ego—are without substantiation.

The neo-Freudians of the post-World War II period extended Freud's biologically based metaphors to include socioenvironmental consideration. The slow, deliberate treatment processes associated with psychoanalytic theory soon gave way to the so-called client-centered theories that drew on principles of self-worth and self-actualization, and were then extended into public school counseling and classroom environments.

By the late 1950s, in response to Clifford Beer's book, *The Mind that Found Itself*, the two world wars, and the spectacular results achieved by the Veterans' Administration in treating emotionally disturbed soldiers, a national emphasis was placed on curing mental illness. However, emotional disturbance is not an acute disease. It is a chronic long-term adjustment disorder, found especially in children.

The 1960s were, however, a period when three significant phases occurred. The national mood in favor of treating mental illness took on a strong mental health dimension aimed at the public schools. There was a gradual development of classes for emotionally disturbed children in the public schools, and many of these classes were transferred from residential facilities in the beginning. The most promising factor was a change in the attitude of community and public policy makers toward treatment for emotionally disturbed children in the public schools by the public schools. However, the growth of programs was slow and awkward, and in contrast to programs and services for other handicapped populations (e.g., the mentally retarded), programs and services for the emotionally disturbed were practically nonexistent. However, state after state began to require teaching credentials and legislate monies for programs. The issues, once again, were why people are emotionally disturbed, how many are emotionally disturbed, and what can be done for them?

The public schools wanted a quick fix. Wolpe (1976) provided educators with behavior therapy. The behavior therapy and behavior modification content for controlling, regulating, and shaping acceptable behaviors in populations of norm-violating, chronically disruptive children was well timed. It opened the door to mechanical practices, based on simple principles that most any teacher could comprehend with little formal training. No longer was it necessary to comprehend the theories associated with the structure of the mind. It was a simple case of identifying, through observation, those student behaviors that were in deviation of the code or norm for the classroom or corridor, or that drew unfavorable attention to the student. Those behaviors became the target for treatment and the term behavioral disorders came into vogue.

None of the older terminologies were replaced; in 1977, Epstein, Cullinan, and Sabatino attempted to survey the use of the definition behavior disorders among states. The District of Columbia and 45 states replied. The component most prevalent in state definitions was disorder of emotion/behavior; the least common component was prognosis.

These researchers (Epstein, Cullinan, & Sabatino, 1977) identified two definitive types of definitions:

> First, numerous authoritative individuals or groups have defined behavior disorders; these statements generally reflect the theoretical positions and professional experiences of their authors and are often intended to structure an exposition of behavior disorders or to provoke thoughtful exploration of a particular position. Another (the second) kind of definition functions primarily to guide the delivery of resources or services to behaviorally disordered children—for example, a state educational agency's definition. (p. 418)

Fifteen definitional components were identified and reported in the data from the study.

Three components, disorders of emotion/behavior, interpersonal problems, and learning/achievement problems, appeared to be separate major areas of child functioning in which problems could occur. Disorders of emotion/behavior was found in all definitions, but the language of the definitions hardly indicated widespread agreement across states. For example, 15 definitions used the word emotion and/or a related reference to interpersonal or mental condition, excluding reference to behavior problems; 18 definitions used behavior and/or alluded to various overt behavior problems, with no mention of difficulties of emotion; 16 definitions referred to both types of problems. Among those definitions that referred to emotional or behavioral disorders, a wide variation in terms and emphases was evident. A majority of state definitions included the components interpersonal problems and learning/achievement problems. A wide range of terms were employed, representing quite different viewpoints that in turn emphasized treatment forms and even expected results.

The components deviation from norm, chronicity, severity, etiology, prognosis, and exclusions functioned as qualifiers in the majority of definitions. The fact that deviation from norm appeared in almost half of the definitions indicated awareness that emotional or behavioral

disorders must not only consider the home, school, and social environment, but any discrepancy between a particular child's functioning and that of other pupils of that age in a particular environment. Absent from the definitions were specific statements addressing normal behavioral and emotional patterns. This means the boundaries of diagnosing these behavioral patterns do not have many boundaries wherein the deviation from norm components can be consistently considered. Severity and chronicity components appeared in well over one-third of the definitions. These were apparently intended to distinguish the mild from severe: those in need of in-class support and/or in-school therapy from those who require institutionalization.

The intent of the etiology component may have been to assure that children receiving special education for the behaviorally disordered were truly behaviorally disordered, i.e., that their disturbed functioning arose from some of the classical causes of a behavioral disorder such as organic damage, parental pathology, family breakdown, cultural deprivation, etc. Across the eight definitions that contained this component, however, divergent and even contradictory etiologies were emphasized. Prognosis apparently was included to provide special education primarily to the mildly behaviorally disordered in contrast to the more severely involved. This component is at odds with severity, a principal identification factor in behavioral disorders that affords a reduced likelihood of favorable response to treatment. Over one-third of the definitions contained an exclusions component, which stated that a child should not be identified as behaviorally disordered, regardless of emotional and behavioral problems, if he or she manifests concomitant handicaps. The most common of these handicaps are mental retardation, sensory disabilities, orthopedic disabilities, brain damage, delinquency, social maladjustment, and drug abuse.

Special education needed and certification components require that before formal identification is accomplished, certain individuals or groups designated as official labelers have to verify that a pupil is behaviorally disordered. Specific assessment procedures were not recommended by many states. In fact, diagnostic procedures were rarely addressed.

Behavioral disorders is a practical term, favored currently by many educators instead of more clinical or medically oriented (psychological/psychiatric) terminology. The reason is that all children and youths display a wide range of behaviors, the majority of which are normal. That is, children learn to respond by displaying an acceptable repertoire of behaviors to social cues. Children need the latitude to select a behavior in the learning process and try it; if acceptability or appropriate behaviors are displayed, normal adjustment is assumed to be manifest. A behavioral disorder exists when chronic, or inappropriate persistence is practiced. Certainly, home conditions, intelligence, appropriate modeling, and all important classroom management can inhibit or inadvertently reinforce many unwanted behaviors.

Behavioral disorders are transitory, temporal responses, many of which disappear with age and changes in environmental conditions. Therefore, definitions of behavioral disorders must distinguish between those that are referencing age-specific developmental periods and those that persist over time. There is the stigma and social learning significance of a pejorative label that serves no other purpose but to classify a child diagnostically. Generally, social interaction and self-concept research has shown these labels to set negative self-fulfilling prophecies into motion. Behavioral disorder is not meant to be anything more than a vague categorical descriptor of a handicapping condition for legal and educational purposes. The importance of this definition educationally is that it promotes defining precisely those targeted behaviors that are in need of modification. The term suggests that the educator must observe what is drawing unfavorable attention to the child, or delaying social and academic learning, and prepare specific behavioral objectives to combat the problem.

Behavioral disorders is a useful construct for the current state of knowledge that guides current special educational practices. It contains many improvements over earlier classification systems. It is not, however, a replacement for sophisticated statistical and clinical nomenclatures such as those found in the third edition of the *Diagnostic and Statistical Manual of Mental Disorders* (1980; DSM III) prepared by the American Psychiatric Association. A number of subclassification systems exist within the broad category of behavioral disorders. Most of these attempt to suggest, if not prescribe, the general course of diagnosis and treatment. The DSM III is a psychiatrically derived classification system for use with children and adults with emotional disorders. It is the standard classification system within mental health facilities in the United States, though it has far less official influence in public education. In the DSM III, disorders are grouped into five major divisions: intellectual, behavioral, emotional, physical, and developmental. The eight subclassifications reflecting level of behavior are (1) superior—unusually effective functioning in social relations, occupational functioning, and use of leisure time; (2) very good—better than average functioning in social relations, occupational functioning, and use of leisure time; (3) good—no more than slight impairment in either social or occupational functioning; (4) fair—moderate impairment in either social relations or occupational functioning, or some impairment in both; (5) poor—marked impairment in either social relations or occupational functioning, or moderate impairment in both; (6) very poor—marked impairment in both social relations and occupational functioning; (7) grossly impaired—gross impairment in virtually all areas of functioning; and (8) unspecified.

Indeed, there are children and youths whose behavioral learning is inadequately or poorly taught, or badly linked to social cues, but there are also those whose emotional structures are faulty to the degree that public school focus on a specific behavior, or set of behaviors, would not be profitable, at least not without intense clinical support.

Behaviorally disordered children may constitute one of the major national issues confronting the schools and society. Observation, diagnosis, and intervention strategies are poorly defined nationally. There is evidence that aggressive children are often detected. Unfortunately, there is also evidence that withdrawn children may not be recognized. The validity of treatment, indeed the value of any one approach may be questioned. Services too frequently are based on eliminating a problem student, not on teaching appropriate behaviors. Behavioral disorders as a loose configuration of symptoms may be the least developed special educational practice at this time. These disorders have the capability of being larger in incidence than any other, and most costly in both resources needed and loss of productivity.

Finally, behavioral disorders are difficult to distinguish from learning disabilities. Frequently, the terms are used together. Certainly, children do react to the frustration of school failure by displaying inappropriate behaviors. There is no question that the symptoms of restlessness, aggressiveness, conflict, and other manifestations of behavioral disorders influence academic learning. Algozzine and Korinck (1985) note a national expansion, if not explosion, in learning disabilities, and fewer behavioral disorders (about 10% of the school-age population). Why? Probably because behavioral disorders remain an unsavory, mixed-bag issue, poorly understood by the schools and community and therefore threatening. Behavioral disorders, unlike learning disabilities, is not yet a concept whose time has come.

## REFERENCES

Algozzine, B., & Korinck, L. (1985). Where is special education for students with high prevalence handicaps going? *Exceptional Children, 51,* 388–394.

American Psychiatric Association. (1980). *Diagnostic and statistical manual of mental disorders* (3rd ed.). Washington, DC: Author.

Epstein, M. H., Cullinan, D., & Sabatino, D. A., 1977. State definitions of behavior disorders. *Journal of Special Education, 11,* 417–425.

DAVID A. SABATINO
*West Virginia College
of Graduate Studies*

## DIAGNOSTIC AND STATISTICAL MANUAL OF MENTAL DISORDERS (DSM III) EMOTIONAL DISORDERS

# BEHAVIORISM

The root of behaviorism is the term behavior, which may be defined as the set or universe of things an organism can do, or more simply, what an organism does. Typically, behavior is a term used in the fields of psychology or sociology to describe human or animal activity, but it is important to note that the term can be, and is, applied to a wide range of other things, including plants, simple microorganisms, machines, and even subatomic particles. The critical attribute is that the activities or functions of the organism must be observable and therefore capable of being measured. Just as it is possible to speak of the behavior of single organisms of varying complexity and composition, it is also possible to examine the behavior of organisms in groups. The empirical emphasis of the term behavior is especially prominent in the United States, where the term is associated with a particular school of psychology known as behaviorism. Behaviorism has its philosophical roots in the radical empiricist traditions of early thinkers such as John Locke and David Hume in Europe and in the twentieth-century movement known as logical positivism. The common thread philosophically is that behavior may be (and, for some, must be) understood purely as a lawful phenomenon in itself, without reference to intervening variables such as will, mind, volition, or motivation, which purport to explain why behavior occurs.

Early in the the twentieth century, the young discipline of psychology was quite concerned with such concepts as will and mind, notably in the work of introspectionists such as Titchner. However, when Pavlov and his colleagues demonstrated that learning was a process whose parameters could be empirically specified and whose results could be reliably predicted, psychologists such as John Watson saw that human behavior could be studied in a simpler, more elegant way, as other sciences were being studied. Watson articulated his position as follows: "Psychology, as the behaviorist views it, is a purely objective, experimental branch of science which needs introspection as little as do the sciences of chemistry and physics. . . ." (1913, p. 176). Watson's fervent rejection of the idea of introspection, mental states, or any other nonempirical behavior analysis has earned him general recognition as the founder of behaviorism.

It remained for later thinkers, notably Edward L. Thorndike and B. F. Skinner, to refine and clearly articulate behaviorism. Watson had emphasized stimulus conditions (following Pavlov's respondent conditioning principles) in his work; the most famous example was his introduction of the fear of a white rat in a young boy (Watson & Rayner, 1920). Thorndike (1935), through is Law of Effect, and Skinner (1953), through his Principle of Reinforcement, argued that the consequences of response determine much of what we learn. Skinner in particular has written extensively of the many ways in which this operant conditioning can be observed and applied in our daily affairs. Like Watson before him, Skinner adamantly rejects the need for a psychology of the mind or any other attempt to understand behavior in subjective terms. For Skinner, behavior is conditioned by external events, and as such it can be controlled, predicted, and studied by empirical methods. The wide range of studies of both human and animal learning (Kazdin, 1975; Kimble, 1961) as a function of behavioral methods demonstrate how powerful the principles of behaviorism can be when effectively applied.

More recently, behaviorists cautiously have begun to re-examine the role of mental processes in determining behavior. Members of this new school of thought, sometimes called cognitive behaviorism, include psychologists such as Albert Bandura (1977) and Donald Meichenbaum (1977). Reconsideration of the role of mental process in behavior has come about for two reasons. First, certain kinds of learning, such as modeling, occur in the absence of typical observable consequences. It is thought that in some cases a form of self-reinforcement (or perhaps self-punishment) through language is responsible for strengthening the behavior (Bandura, 1977). Others (e.g., Meichenbaum, 1977) have noted that traditional behavioral learning paradigms have been too simplistic to account for the wide array of individual differences in behavior, especially among humans. Even unyielding behavioral analyses such as Skinner's make use of variables such as reinforcement history, which imply some sort of cognitive process in mediating across gaps in time.

The influence of behavioristic thought in psychology is undeniable. The emphasis on empirical research conditions that seemed so strident and incongruous in Watson's time is now taught as the basis of good research, and the importance of both Pavlovian and Skinnerian conditioning has been observed even in popular literature. Behavioristic methods of treatment occupy a prominent place in the study of psychopathology, and behavioral principles are being applied in industrial/organizational settings. As the school of thought broadens its consideration of variables involved in behavior, it holds even brighter promise as 'a tool for understanding what we do and why we do it.

## REFERENCES

Bandura, A. (1977). Self-efficacy: Toward a unifying theory of behavioral change. *Psychological Review, 84,* 191–215.

Kazdin, A. (1975). *Behavior modification in applied settings.* Homewood, IL: Dorsey.

Kimble, G. A. (1961). *Hilgard and Marquis' conditioning and learning,* (2nd ed.). New York: Appleton-Century-Crofts.

Meichenbaum, D. (1977). *Cognitive behavior modification: An integrative approach.* NY: Plenum.

Skinner, B. F. (1953). *Science and human behavior.* NY: Free Press.

Thorndike, E. L. (1935). *The psychology of wants, interests and attitudes.* New York: Appleton-Century.

Watson, J. (1913). Psychology as the behaviorist views it. *Psychological Review, 20*, 1958–1977.

Watson, J., & Rayner, R. (1920). Conditioning emotional responses. *Journal of Experimental Psychology, 3*, 1–14.

JERRY L. SLOAN
*Wilmington Psychiatric
Associates, Wilmington,
North Carolina*

BEHAVIOR MODIFICATION
PSYCHOANALYSIS
SOCIAL LEARNING THEORY

# BEHAVIOR MODELING

Modeling is a training intervention that was popularized by social learning theory and the works of Albert Bandura (Bandura, 1971). When using this procedure, the practitioner physically demonstrates or shows a visual representation (e.g., photo sequence, videotape, movie) of the production of the behavior. In essence, the practitioner shows the student the appropriate way to respond. The demonstration often includes secondary informational sources such as feedback about the model's success and the environmental and contextual cues that led the model to behave in the particular fashion demonstrated.

The effectiveness of this procedure can be enhanced through attention to several variables. Of primary consideration are the characteristics of the person providing the model. In some cases the person who demonstrates the behavior could be another student. This would be appropriate when the other student is (1) competent to do the behavior; (2) someone the student can identify with (i.e., someone similar to himself or herself); (3) someone held in high esteem by the target student; (4) able to demonstrate the appropriate behavior clearly; (5) able to demonstrate novel responses that the target student has not yet learned to do; and (6) reinforced for the performance of the target behavior.

Student factors are also important to the modeling process. First, the student must be sufficiently motivated to become an active participant in the modeling process. An absence of sufficient motivation will negate the qualities of the model and the modeling event. Second, the attention of the student must be keyed to the relevant properties of the modeled behavior. Third, the student must have sufficient motor abilities to replicate the modeled behavior. Finally, the ability of the student to remember and recall the modeled act will greatly affect the general and functional utility of the modeled behavior. This retention is based on two processes: imagination and verbalization. In the first case, when stimuli are consistently paired, the occurrence of one of the paired stimuli will signal the other. In the second case, labeling of an event (a verbal process whether vocalized or not) lends saliency to the event.

Factors related to the instructional variables can also affect the effectiveness of modeling. Reinforcement for the modeled behavior must be sufficient in quantity and quality to bring about student participation. For example, Lovaas (1967) has shown that children imitate precisely when they are rewarded for precise replication of modeled behaviors. However, when children are reinforced nondifferentially (i.e., for approximations of the response), they produce poorly matched responses. Modeled behavior is most effectively acquired and maintained when the modeled behaviors are familiar and functional to the target student. Overt rehearsals of the modeled response can considerably enhance the acquisition and maintenance of the modeled behavior.

Modeling, therefore, is a useful instructional procedure. As a technology for instruction, it requires that its users follow specific procedures to produce maximum results. These procedures are neither esoteric nor difficult to follow. Because modeling is thought to be a "least restrictive" instructional prompting procedure, and because it is usable in most environments, it should be considered to be an instructional procedure of choice under most circumstances.

## REFERENCES

Bandura, A. (1971). Analysis of modeling processes. In A. Bandura (Ed.), *Psychological modeling: Conflicting theories.* Chicago: Aldine-Atherton.

Lovaas, O. I. (1967). A behavior therapy approach to the treatment of childhood schizophrenia. In J. P. Hill (Ed.), *Minnesota symposia on child psychology* (Vol. 1). Minneapolis: University of Minnesota Press.

LYLE E. BARTON
*Kent State University*

COGNITIVE BEHAVIOR THERAPY
SOCIAL LEARNING THEORY
THEORY OF ACTIVITY

# BEHAVIOR MODIFICATION

Behavior modification is generally regarded as a term that encompasses the various methods derived from learning theory that are used to alter the response patterns of humans and other animals. The term has been used in this way by Bandura (1969); he and other behaviorists such as Skinner (1965) have enumerated a wide variety of learning principles that have been translated into methods for learning or changing behavior.

Although behavior modification is sometimes considered as a unitary position in discussions of certain issues in psychology, the techniques involved are derived from several different theoretical approaches to learning. Each approach tends to emphasize environmental determinants, as opposed to person-based determinants, of individual differences among organisms in the way in which they learn behavior. On the other hand, each approach also emphasizes the importance of determining the specific environmental variables that influence the behavior of an individual.

One such approach (Wolpe, 1982) is based on classical or respondent conditioning, which was studied extensively early in the twentieth century by Ivan Pavlov, the Russian psychologist, and John Watson, the American sometimes known as the father of behaviorism. In this type of learning, a neutral stimulus is paired in time with another stimulus (called the unconditioned stimulus) already able to elicit a particular response, usually unlearned, from an organism's repertoire. Through repeated pairings, this neutral stimulus also acquires the capability of eliciting the original (or unconditioned) response; this neutral stimulus is called the conditioned stimulus. For example, Watson and Rayner (1920) performed a classic study in which a neutral stimulus (a white rat) took on fear-inducing properties for a young boy when it was presented to the child paired with a sudden loud noise (an unconditioned stimulus) that startled and frightened the child (the unconditioned response). Soon the child began attempting to avoid the white rat because of its newly acquired association with the loud noise. Classical conditioning is apparently important in establishing subtle types of learning such as attitudes, basic emotional states such as love, fear and trust, and other similar behaviors acquired over long periods of time.

A second major approach to behavior modification (Skinner, 1965) is based on operant or instrumental conditioning. The basis of this approach is the so-called law of effect articulated by Thorndike (1935). He proposed that responses followed by pleasurable consequences would be strengthened, whereas responses followed by unpleasant consequences would be weakened. This formulation was refined and greatly expanded by others, notably Skinner, who had demonstrated that consequences (Thorndike would have called them effects) are important in learning a wide variety of behaviors. Most of these behaviors involve some activity or operation (hence the term operant conditioning) in the form of a skill the organism learns. An important derivative of operant conditioning has been described by Premack (1965). He showed that the opportunity to perform a desirable activity may be used as a consequence to reinforce or strengthen the performance of a less preferred activity. Thus a person may be willing to do something relatively unpleasant (perhaps balancing a checkbook or reading a boring book) if this activity is followed soon thereafter by a pleasurable activity (perhaps a movie or a golf outing).

The modification of behavior using the outlined principles of operant conditioning is sometimes called applied behavior analysis. Usually this involves detailed empirical specification of the behavior to be changed (or to be learned), careful observation of the contributing conditioning elements, and the development of a strategy (changing antecedent stimulus conditions, response consequences, or both) to achieve the desired results. It is important to note that the use of behavior modification techniques does not require the use of terms such as normal or abnormal to describe the behavior being examined. In fact, the learning theorists who have contributed to the development of behavior modification techniques assume that behavior is learned according to principles that operate nearly identically in all situations, even though a given observer may have a higher or lower value to place on a particular learned behavior. As a result, descriptive terms such as abnormal are frequently rejected because their use tempts us to infer that different laws of learning have governed the behavior so described.

## REFERENCES

Bandura, A. (1969). *Principles of behavior modification*. New York: Holt, Rinehart, & Winston.

Premack, D. (1965). Reinforcement therapy. In D. Levine (Ed.), *Nebraska symposium on motivation*. Lincoln: University of Nebraska Press.

Skinner, B. F. (1965). *Science and human behavior*. New York: Free Press.

Thorndike, E. L. (1935). *The psychology of wants, interests and attitudes*. New York: Appleton, Century.

Watson, J., & Rayner, R. (1920). Conditioning emotional response. *Journal of Experimental Psychology, 3*, 1–14.

Wolpe, J. (1982). *The practice of behavior therapy* (3rd ed.). New York: Pergamon.

JERRY L. SLOAN
*Wilmington Psychiatric
Associates, Wilmington,
North Carolina*

APPLIED BEHAVIOR ANALYSIS
OPERANT CONDITIONING

# BEHAVIOR PROBLEM CHECKLIST

The Behavior Problem Checklist, developed by Quay and Peterson (1967, 1979), is a Likert-type rating scale that measures the degree to which 55 frequently occurring problem behaviors are present in children from kindergarten through sixth grade. The 55 target behaviors were selected as those most frequently occurring in a review of 427 child-guidance clinic cases. Each item is rated on a three-point scale to indicate the severity of the problem.

Parents and teachers may serve as respondents. Administration time is approximately 10 minutes.

Factor analytic studies of the Behavior Problem Checklist have been conducted with several special child populations: public school children, institutionalized juvenile delinquents, students in classes for the emotionally disturbed, and outpatients at a child guidance clinic. Based on the findings of these studies, four subscales have been developed: (1) conduct problem (psychopathy, undersocialized aggression); (2) personality problem (neuroticism, anxiety disorders); (3) inadequacy-immaturity; and (4) socialized delinquency (sociopathy, socialized aggression). Quay and Peterson (1979) have used teachers' ratings to report means and standard deviations for both normal and clinical groups on each of the four subscales. Raw scores can be used to obtain a subscale profile for an individual child. Norms are not available for parent ratings. Quay and Peterson (1967) report interrater reliability coefficients ranging from 0.23 to 0.77. Test-retest reliabilities range from 0.21 to 0.52.

The Behavior Problem Checklist is one of the most extensively researched behavior questionnaires. It has been used in both clinical and research settings to evaluate the behavior problems of children (Humphreys & Ciminero, 1979; Spivack & Swift, 1973).

## REFERENCES

Humphreys, L. E., & Ciminero, A. R. (1979). Parent report measures of child behavior: A review. *Journal of Clinical Child Psychology, 8,* 56–63.

Quay, H. C., & Peterson, D. R. (1967). *Manual for the Behavior Problem Checklist.* Champaign, IL: Children's Research Center, University of Illinois.

Quay, H. C., & Peterson, D. R. (1979). *Behavior Problem Checklist.* Miami, FL: Authors.

Spivack, G., & Swift, M. (1973). The classroom behavior of children: A critical review of teacher-administered rating scales. *Journal of Special Education, 7,* 55–89.

LIZANNE DESTEFANO
*University of Illinois,
Urbana-Champaign*

**BEHAVIOR ASSESSMENT**
**BEHAVIORAL CHARTING**
**BEHAVIORAL CONSULTATION**

## BEHAVIOR PROBLEM CHECKLIST, REVISED

The Revised Behavior Problem Checklist (RBPC) is a widely researched rating scale for the clinical evaluation of deviant behavior. The RBPC (Quay & Peterson, 1983) consists of four major scales: conduct disorder (22 items), socialized aggression (17 items), attention problems–im-

maturity (16 items), and anxiety–withdrawal (11 items). Two additional scales are psychotic behavior (6 items) and motor tension–excess (5 items). Twelve items are intended for future research with young children. Although the checklist was developed primarily by teacher ratings, other raters, including parents, have been used.

Estimates of internal consistency reliability ranged from .68 to .95. Interrater reliabilities ranged from .52 to .85. Test-retest reliabilities (two-month interval) ranged from .49 to .83 ($N = 149$). Support for validity includes a substantial relationship between the RBPC and the Behavior Problem Checklist (BPC), discrimination between normal children and clinical groups, and support from numerous studies for many facets of validity.

The authors do not provide representative norms based on Census data; local norms are suggested. However, norms are provided on 1071 unselected children (grades K–12). The authors point out that inner-city minorities are not represented. Comparisons with specific samples can be made (e.g., inpatient, LD).

## REFERENCES

Lahey, B. B., & Piacentini, J. C. (1985). An evaluation of the Quay-Peterson Revised Behavior Problem Checklist. *Journal of School Psychology, 23,* 285–289.

Quay, H. C. (1983). A dimensional approach to behavior disorder: The Revised Behavior Problem Checklist. *School Psychology Review, 12,* 244–249.

Quay, H. C., & Peterson, D. R. (1983). *Interim manual for the Revised Behavior Problem Checklist.* Coral Gables, FL: University of Miami.

DAVID W. BARNETT
*University of Cincinnati*

## BEHAVIOR THERAPY

Behavior therapy encompasses a broad range of philosophical, theoretical, and procedural approaches to the "alleviation of human suffering and the enhancement of human functioning" (Davison & Stuart, 1975, p. 755). An approach to assessment, therapy, ethics, and professional issues, it has been used successfully with a variety of populations (adults, children, adolescents, mentally retarded, etc.) in diverse settings (schools, hospitals, psychiatric facilities, mental health centers, etc.) and for various problems (anxiety, depression, addictive disorders, social skills deficits, psychotic behaviors, marital dysfunction, academic skills, parent-child problems, etc.). There are probably few human behaviors that have not been addressed by behavior therapists.

A number of terms with somewhat different origins and connotations have been used almost interchangeably to denote the field. These terms include behavior therapy, behavior modification, applied behavior analysis, social learning theory, cognitive-behavior therapy, clinical behavior therapy, and multimodal behavior therapy. Attempts to clarify or standardize the meaning of the various terms based on the populations served (e.g., individual or group), techniques used (e.g., systematic desensitization, contingency management), methodologies (e.g., single-subject designs), or theoretical bases (e.g., classical conditioning, operant conditioning) have failed to gain wide acceptance (Franzini & Tilker, 1972; Wilson, 1978).

Several formal definitions of behavior therapy have been proposed. For example, Wolpe (1982) defined behavior therapy as "the use of experimentally established principles and paradigms of learning to overcome unadaptive habits" (p. 1). Whereas Wolpe's definition emphasizes a theoretical basis of behavior therapy, other definitions stress the methods of inquiry used by behavior therapists. For example, Ross, in his presidential address to the Association for Advancement of Behavior Therapy, defined behavior therapy as "the empirically controlled application of the science of human behavior to the alleviation of psychological distress and the modification of maladaptive behavior" (Ross, 1985, p. 196). This definition reflects the growing acceptance of methodological behaviorism, which focuses on the methods used in obtaining psychological information. Such a definition, however, does not delineate behavior therapy from other construct systems that might also use empirical methods of inquiry.

The difficulty of arriving at a single definition of behavior therapy was well summarized by Kazdin and Wilson (1978):

> Contemporary behavior therapy is marked by a diversity of views, a broad range of heterogeneous procedures with different theoretical rationales, and open debate about conceptual bases, methodological requirements, and evidence of efficacy. In short, there is no clearly agreed upon or commonly accepted definition of behavior therapy. (p. 1)

This lack of consensus reflects both the continuous development of behavior therapy and the various models within the behavioral construct system.

At least four major models within behavior therapy can be identified: (1) applied behavior analysis, (2) neobehavioristic mediational model, (3) social learning theory, and (4) cognitive-behavior therapy (Agras, Kazdin, & Wilson, 1979). The models differ on the bases of historical tradition, fundamental principles, and therapeutic procedures.

Applied behavior analysis draws heavily from the Skinner tradition of operant conditioning. Behavior is assumed to be under the control of environmental stimuli. These controlling stimuli include the consequences of behavior as well as the antecedent events that are associated with differential consequences. Intervention involves the manipulation of the controlling environmental stimuli in order to modify overt behavior. Therapeutic procedures are based on principles derived from operant conditioning such as reinforcement, punishment, extinction, and stimulus control. The token economy, in which appropriate behaviors earn tokens that later can be exchanged for desired activities, consumable goods, and privileges, is a procedure representative of applied behavior analysis.

The neobehavioristic mediational model is based primarily on the principles of classical conditioning derived from the learning theories of Pavlov, Hull, and Mowrer (Wolpe, 1982). The model emphasizes the role of anxiety as a conditioned emotional response. For example, the anxiety response can be elicited by previously neutral stimuli as a result of pairing those neutral stimuli with noxious stimuli. Therapeutic procedures such as systematic desensitization and flooding are designed to reduce the anxiety underlying behavioral disorders by exposing the individual to the conditioned, feared stimulus in the absence of the noxious stimulus.

According to the third model, social learning theory (Bandura, 1977), three interacting systems regulate behavior. The first system is external stimulus control, which regulates behavior either through the association of stimuli, as in classical conditioning, or through antecedent stimuli reliably predicting differential consequences of behavior. Response feedback, primarily in the form of reinforcing consequences, provides a second regulatory system. Finally, cognitive processes mediate the effect of external events by influencing which events are attended to and how those events are perceived and interpreted. An important cognitive mediator of behavior change is self-efficacy, the expectation that the behavior required to produce an outcome can be performed. Social learning theory further posits that human functioning is a result of the reciprocal interaction among behavior, the environment, and a person's cognitions (Bandura, 1981). That is, not only does the environment influence behavior, but a person's behavior also influences the environment. Modeling of the desired behavior by the therapist, either with or without the client's subsequent performance, is a therapeutic procedure derived from social learning theory's emphasis on cognitive processes such as the capacity to learn through observation.

The most recent development in behavior therapy is the emergence of cognitive-behavior therapy (Beck, 1976; Mahoney, 1974). According to this model, it is the perception of events rather than the events themselves that most influence behavior. Further, adaptive and maladaptive patterns are acquired through cognitive processes. Thus irrational beliefs, errors of logic, faulty self-talk, dysfunctional attributions, and mental representations of one's self and one's world contribute to behavioral and emotional disorders. Cognitive restructuring, in which clients are taught to examine and change faulty cognitions, is a representative procedure used in cognitive-behavior therapy.

Despite the diversity of models in the behavioral construct system and the inability to provide a single defi-nition of behavior therapy, a number of characteristics and assumptions of behavior therapy can be delineated (Agras et al., 1979; Haynes, 1984; Kazdin & Hersen, 1980). No one of these characteristics is definitive of the field, nor does any one necessarily differentiate behavior therapy from other systems. Nevertheless, taken together, they represent the common core of behavior therapy.

One set of characteristics concern methods of inquiry:

1. There is a commitment to empiricism and scientific methodology as the primary basis for developing and evaluating concepts and therapeutic techniques.
2. There is a commitment to an explicit, testable, and falsifiable conceptual foundation.
3. Therapeutic procedures and hypotheses with suffi-cient precision to make evaluation, replication, and generalization possible are specified.
4. There are close ties to the experimental findings of the science of psychology.
5. There is a low level of inference about data so as to minimize biases.

These epistemological principles imply that behavior ther-apy will continue to evolve as new knowledge is gained from empirical findings.

A second set of characteristics concerns the assump-tions about behavior and behavioral disorders.

1. There is a deterministic model of behavior in which environmental antecedents and consequences are assumed to have the greatest impact on behavior. Recently, interactional models have been introduced in which behavior, the environment, and the person (most notably cognitive events and physiological conditions) are all presumed to influence one an-other.
2. There is an emphasis on current determinants of be-havior as opposed to historical determinants (i.e., early childhood experiences).
3. The same principles that govern normal behavior also govern abnormal behavior. That is, no quali-tative difference separates normal from abnormal behavior.
4. There are multiple determinants of behavior. The determinants of behavioral disorders may vary from individual to individual, and from one disorder to another.
5. Both the disease model of abnormal behavior and the implication that dysfunctional behavior is a sign or symptom of an underlying illness are rejected. In-stead, dysfunctional behavior is construed as a "problem in living" or as learned, maladaptive be-havior. Thus the dysfunctional behavior itself is tar-geted for behavior change.

6. Psychological disorders can be expressed in behav-ioral, cognitive, and affective modes. These modes can covary to differing degrees owing to situational factors and individual differences.
7. There is the relative specificity of behavior to the situation in which it occurs as opposed to the belief that behavior is consistent across situations.

A third set of characteristics concerns the methods of behavior change:

1. Therapeutic procedures are derived from experi-mental-clinical psychology.
2. Therapy is conceptualized as an opportunity to un-learn maladaptive behaviors and to learn adaptive behaviors.
3. The importance of tailoring therapy to the individ-ual based on an assessment of the idiosyncratic de-terminants of the individual's dysfunctional behav-ior is emphasized.
4. The importance of the therapist-client interaction as one source of behavior change is emphasized.
5. There is an ongoing evaluation of intervention re-sults in order to modify procedures as needed.
6. Intervention results are generalized from the inter-vention setting to the client's natural environment.

In conclusion, behavior therapy is a multifaceted and diverse system linked by a common core of assumptions. It is a viable system that has withstood numerous criti-cisms to emerge as a major approach within the psycho-logical treatment field.

## REFERENCES

Agras, W. S., Kazdin, A. E., & Wilson, G. T. (1979). *Behavior therapy: Toward an applied clinical science.* San Francisco: Freeman.

Bandura, A. (1977). *Social learning theory.* Englewood Cliffs, NJ: Prentice-Hall.

Bandura, A. (1981). In search of pure unidirectional determi-nants. *Behavior Therapy, 12,* 30–40.

Beck, A. T. (1976). *Cognitive therapy and the emotional disorders.* New York: International Universities Press.

Davison, G. C., & Stuart, R. B. (1975). Behavior therapy and civil liberties. *American Psychologist, 30,* 755–763.

Franzini, L. R., & Tilker, H. A. (1972). On the terminological confusion between behavior therapy and behavior modifica-tion. *Behavior Therapy, 3,* 279–282.

Haynes, S. N. (1984). Behavioral assessment of adults. In M. Her-sen & G. Goldstein (Eds.), *Handbook of psychological assess-ment.* New York: Pergamon.

Kazdin, A. E., & Hersen, M. (1980). The current status of behavior therapy. *Behavior Modification, 4,* 283–302.

Kazdin, A. E., & Wilson, G. T. (1978). *Evaluation of behavior ther-apy: Issues, evidence, and research strategies.* Cambridge, MA: Ballinger.

Mahoney, M. J. (1974). *Cognition and behavior modification.* Cambridge, MA: Ballinger.

Ross, A. O. (1985). To form a more perfect union: It is time to stop standing still. *Behavior Therapy, 16,* 195–204.

Wilson, G. T. (1978). On the much discussed nature of the term "behavior therapy." *Behavior Therapy, 9,* 89–98.

Wolpe, J. (1982). *The practice of behavior therapy* (3rd ed.). New York: Pergamon.

JEFFREY L. PHILLIPS
*University of North Carolina,
Wilmington*

**APPLIED BEHAVIOR ANALYSIS**
**BEHAVIOR MODIFICATION**
**DESENSITIZATION**
**SOCIAL LEARNING THEORY**

## BEHAVIOR THERAPY

*Behavior Therapy* is the journal of the Association for Advancement of Behavior Therapy. The journal is an interdisciplinary publication primarily for original research of an experimental and clinical nature that deals with theories, practices, and evaluation of behavior therapy or behavior modification. The major emphasis of the journal is on empirical research but methodological and theoretical papers are also published. The format for publication includes articles, brief reports of approximately eight pages, invited book reviews, case studies, and clinical replication series. Manuscripts having an assessment focus should be submitted to *Behavioral Assessment,* a companion journal. *Behavior Therapy* is published in five issues (January, March, June, September, and November) and edited by David H. Barlow, PhD, Department of Psychology, State University of New York at Albany, Albany, NY 12222.

CRAIG D. SMITH
*Georgia College*

## BELGIUM, SPECIAL EDUCATION IN

Special education has existed in Belgium since the early nineteenth century, but it developed mostly during the 1960s. It is currently organized, on the Law of the 6th July 1970, which provides special education for youngsters between 3 and 21 (exceptions can be made for pupils below 3 or between 21 and 25) who are capable of receiving education but unable to attend a regular school.

Special education has been divided into eight types of teaching, according to the educational needs of the mildly retarded (type 1); the moderately or severely retarded (type 2); the emotionally disturbed (type 3); the physically handicapped (type 4); the health impaired (type 5); the visually impaired (type 6); the hearing impaired (type 7); and the specific learning disabled (type 8). It should be noted that the labels relate to the types of teaching, and not to the pupils themselves, although the practitioners do not always respect this differentiation.

The different types of teaching are divided into three levels: the kindergarten (3 to 6/8 years old); primary (6/8 to 13/15 years old); and secondary (13/15 to 21 years old), except for type 1, which is not organized at the kindergarten level, and type 8, which is organized at neither the kindergarten nor at the secondary level. The secondary level includes, for its part, different forms of teaching according to their long-term goals: form 1, social adaptation and preparation for living in a sheltered environment; form 2, vocational and social adaptation teaching in preparation for living and working in a sheltered environment; form 3, vocational teaching adapted to pupils who are able to live and work in a normal environment; and form 4, teaching with the same goals as regular secondary education, but with a methodology adapted to the handicapped.

Admission to special schools requires an official document delivered either by a center after a multidisciplinary exam (for types 1, 2, 3, 4, and 8) or by a physician (for types 5, 6, and 7); this document indicates the type and level of special education corresponding to the child's educational needs.

The change of class or level is decided by the multidisciplinary school staff, which is assisted by the psycho–medico–social (PMS) center. Orientation or reorientation toward regular education or toward another type of special teaching are entrusted to the PMS center. In case of conflicts among the different parties involved (parents, principals, and school or medical inspectors), the Advisory Committee of Special Education (the president of which is the main inspector) gives a recommendation. After having given a second recommendation, the committee can refer to a youth judge if necessary.

The different ways of obtaining special education are full-time, part-time (usually not organized), homebound, by correspondence, or by integrated education. Integrated education enables the pupils to attend several classes in a regular school while receiving help and support from the special school where they remain enrolled and attend classes. This integration is realized individually, in accordance with the recommendations of the multidisciplinary school staff and the PMS center, and in agreement with the parents, the inspector, and the Department of Special Education.

The psycho–medico–social guidance of the pupils is ensured by specialized PMS centers, which are independent from the schools. These centers specifically help in the choice of educational objectives, taking into account the reports of previous exams; when necessary, they do complimentary exams. They give their recommendations about school or vocational orientation or reorientation, and deal with hearings about the social and vocational integration of pupils.

The staff of a special school include (besides the head and the teaching staff) the educational staff, the medical and paramedical staff (physicians, speech therapists, physical therapists, nurses), and the social, psychological, and administrative staff. The staff is assigned to the school depending on the number of pupils and the types of special teaching. Up to now, the training of this staff has been identical to the training of the staff in charge of regular education. Specific complimentary training is organized, but it is not compulsory.

The recent trends in special education show that serious efforts remain to be made in several areas: the parents of handicapped pupils should be more fully integrated as educational partners by participating more actively in the choice of educational priorities and objectives and in the maintenance of the acquired skills and their generalization outside the school environment; severely handicapped pupils (severely and profoundly mentally retarded, multiply handicapped, seriously emotionally disturbed) should receive more individualized care; the individualization of methods and educational programs should continue to be worked on; the methodology for choosing appropriate behavioral objectives and the planning of the educational intervention and implementation of it should be defined (in this respect, the importance of the behavioral model has to be more widely acknowledged by the educational staff); a special effort must be made for integrating mentally handicapped and behaviorally disturbed pupils; and more appropriate initial and permanent training of professionals (especially teachers) should be implemented to reconcile practice and research.

GHISLAIN MAGEROTTE
*Mons State University*

# BELL, ALEXANDER GRAHAM (1847–1922)

Alexander Graham Bell, inventor of the telephone, educator, and spokesperson for the deaf, was born and educated in Scotland. Emigrating first to Canada and then to the United States, Bell, whose father and grandfather were authorities in the field of speech, and who had himself specialized in the anatomy of the vocal apparatus, opened a school in Boston for the training of teachers of the deaf in 1872; he became a professor at Boston University and married one of his students, Mabel Hubbard, who was deaf, as was his mother.

Widely acclaimed for his numerous inventions, Bell used his vast influence to foster his major interest, the teaching of the deaf. An avid proponent of oral methods of teaching the deaf, Bell became the acknowledged leader of the oral movement in the United States. He also campaigned tirelessly for the establishment of day schools for the deaf to provide an alternative to residential school placement. Bell was a founder of the American Association to Promote the Teaching of Speech to the Deaf, later renamed the Alexander Graham Bell Association for the Deaf, and of the *Volta Bureau*, which he established for the dissemination of knowledge about the deaf.

## REFERENCE

Bruce, R. V. (1973). *Alexander Graham Bell and the conquest of solitude*. Boston: Little, Brown.

PAUL IRVINE
*Katonah, New York*

# BELL, TERREL H. (1921–      )

Terrel H. Bell received his BA from Southern Idaho College of Education in 1946. He then received his MS from the University of Idaho in 1954. In 1961 he received his Ph.D in educational administration from the University of Utah. Since that time Bell has been the recipient of 21 honorary doctorates conferred by various universities and colleges throughout the United States.

Since serving from 1942 to 1946 in World War II with the U.S. Marines, Bell has served as a superintendent of schools in Idaho, Wyoming, and Utah. From 1974 to 1976 Bell was U.S. commissioner of education and from 1981 to 1984 he was appointed by the President and confirmed by the U.S. Senate as secretary of the U.S. Department of Education. Since that appointment, Bell has been professor of educational administration at the University of Utah.

Bell's numerous honors and awards include the Department of Defense Distinguished Public Service Medal awarded by Secretary of Defense Caspar Weinberger in 1984. Bell has authored numerous books and publications. He appointed the members, wrote the national charter, and provided support and leadership for the work of the National Commission on Excellence on Education. The commission report, "A Nation at Risk," was quoted nationwide in newspapers and television. Twelve national forums were sponsored to disseminate the commission report and stimulate support. Over 12 million copies of "A Nation at Risk" have been printed, reprinted, and widely disseminated.

## REFERENCES

Bell, T. H. (1956). *The prodigal pedagogue*. New York: Exposition.

Bell, T. H. (1960). *A philosophy of education for the space age*. New York: Exposition.

Bell, T. H. (1972). *Your child's intellect: A parent's guide to home based preschool education*. Salt Lake City, Utah: Olympus.

Bell, T. H. (1974). *Active parent concern*. Englewood Cliffs, NJ: Prentice-Hall.

Bell, T. H. (1984). *Excellence.* Salt Lake City, Utah: Deseret Book.

ROBERTA C. STOKES
*Texas A&M University*

## BELLEVUE PSYCHIATRIC HOSPITAL

The history of psychiatric care at Bellevue Hospital Center and the history of psychiatric care in the United States are closely interwoven. Bellevue has been at the vanguard of treatment for the mentally ill since the eighteenth century, pioneering methods of identifying and categorizing patients, training psychiatrists and psychiatric nurses, and developing out-patient as well as in-patient courses of treatment.

The Public Workhouse and House of Correction, which opened in 1736, ultimately became Bellevue Hospital. It contained a six-bed unit designed to provide care for "the infirm, the aged, the unruly, and the maniac." By 1826, a total of 82 of the 184 patients were listed as insane. In 1879 a pavilion for the insane was erected within hospital grounds. The concept of including the care and treatment of psychiatric patients in a general hospital rather than entirely apart from the treatment of the physically ailing was revolutionary.

In 1902 the Department of Bellevue and Allied Hospitals appointed a resident physician, two assistants, and trained nurses to provide medical attention for psychiatric patients, thereby providing the framework for the development of a modern psychiatric service. During the early 1900s, the primary function of the department of psychiatry at Bellevue was to "afford temporary care and treatment for those patients who are to be transferred to the state hospital for mental diseases within 10 days." Perhaps a more important function than maintaining patients on remand was to "provide care for another group of patients which had hitherto been neglected, patients whose psychoses are of such a character that they are not suitable for commitment to a hospital for the insane nor are they acceptable in a general hospital, e.g., cases of mild mental disorders, psychoneuroses, epilepsy, deliria, transitory attacks of confusion or excitement." Simultaneously, in an effort to discourage long-term hospitalization, the department of psychiatry at Bellevue established mental health clinics and the practice of ongoing contact with patients' families.

The Children's Inpatient Psychiatric Service began at Bellevue in 1920. Separate male and female adolescent wards were maintained providing for 30 patients each. In 1935 the New York City Board of Education established a special school for emotionally disturbed children at Bellevue. Now designated as P.S. 106, the school continues to function at Bellevue.

In establishing itself as a psychiatric prison ward, Bellevue has contributed to forensic medicine via the Psychiatric Clinic of the Court of General Sessions, established in 1931. This psychiatric prison ward encouraged the development of rigid safeguards for the rights of all psychiatric patients, including prisoners.

Among many firsts at Bellevue, in 1936 Karl Murdock Bowman was the first physician in the country to use insulin shock therapy for treatment of mental illness. In 1939 David Wechsler developed the Wechsler-Bellevue Scale of Intelligence, later called the Wechsler Adult Intelligence Scale, a test still widely used today. Wechsler went on to develop a number of intelligence tests often used with handicapped children including the Wechsler Intelligence Scale for Children and the Wechsler Pre-School Scale of Intelligence. Loretta Bender, a pioneer in work with autistic children and youths, worked at Bellevue during the 1950s and 1960s. In 1984, when its facilities in the New Bellevue Hospital at 27th Street and East River Drive in New York City were completed, Bellevue's psychiatric department was united for the first time with the rest of Bellevue. Psychiatry was truly integrated into a full-service hospital setting.

### REFERENCES

Bellevue Hospital Center. *Bellevue hospital center.* New York: Author.
New York City Health and Hospitals Corporation. (1984). *The nation's largest municipal health care system: directory of services.* New York: Author.
Walsh, James (Ed.). (1982). *Bellevue.* New York: Bellevue Hospital Center.

CATHERINE HALL RIKHYE
*Hunter College, City University
of New York*

## BENADRYL

Benadryl (diphenhydramine hydrochloride) is used for perennial or seasonal (hay fever) allergic rhinitis, motion sickness, and allergic conjunctivitis owed to inhalant allergens and foods. An antihistamine, it has anticholinergic (drying) and sedative side effects. In isolated cases, it has been used as a sedative for treatment of hyperactivity. Adverse reactions include diminished mental alertness in both adults and children, with occasional excitation in the young child. Overdose with this or other antihistamines may cause hallucinations, convulsions, and death.

A brand name of Parke-Davis Company, it is available in capsules of 25 and 50 ms; as an elixir for oral use; and in injectable syringes. Dosage for children (over 20 pounds) is 12.5 to 25 mg three to four times daily, with maximum daily dosage not in excess of 300 mg. For adults, dosage is 25 to 50 mg three to four times daily.

## REFERENCE

*Physicians' desk reference.* (1984). (pp. 1447–1448). Oradell, NJ: Medical Economics.

LAWRENCE C. HARTLAGE
*Evans, Georgia*

## ATARAX
## COMPAZINE
## DRUG THERAPY
## NAVANE

## BENDER, LAURETTA (1897–     )

Born in Butte, Montana, in 1897, Lauretta Bender obtained her BS and MA degrees from the University of Chicago in 1922 and 1923, respectively. She obtained her MD degree at the State University of Iowa in 1926 and returned to Chicago (Billings Hospital) for her internship (1927–1928) and residency in neurology (1928). A residency in psychiatry at Boston's Psychopathic Hospital preceded another psychiatric residency, in 1929–1930, at Johns Hopkins' Phipps Clinic. She also received postgraduate training in neuroanatomy, physiology, and pathology at the University of Amsterdam on a Rockefeller grant in 1926–1927.

Bender has held numerous appointments, including assistant instructor of neuropathology at Iowa (1923–1926) and several psychiatric positions in the New York City area. These include senior psychiatrist at Bellevue Hospital (1930–1956), director of the Child Guidance Clinic at the New York City Infirmary (1954–1960), principal research scientist of Child Psychiatry at New York State Department of Mental Hygiene (1956–1960), director of Psychiatric Research at the Children's Unit of Creedmor State Hospital (1960–1969), and attending psychiatrist at the New York Psychiatric Institute (1969–1973). She has held teaching positions at New York University, Adelphi College Graduate School, and Columbia University. She is currently retired and living in Maryland.

Bender has received numerous awards and is a fellow of the American Medical Association, American Psychiatric Association, American Neurological Association, and American Orthopsychiatric Association.

With over 100 chapters and articles, Bender is widely published in the fields of child psychiatry, neurology, and psychology. She is best known for her Visual Motor Gestalt Test (1937), several books, including *Psychopathological Disorders of Children with Organic Brain Disease* (1956), and studies of learning disabilities (1970). Her theory of the role of brain pathology in the development of childhood schizophrenia is less known but also important. In addition, she developed the Face-Hand Test, which examines double simultaneous tactile sensation (face and hand). A variation of this test, the Fink-Green-Bender Test, has been used to discriminate between children with neurologic and schizophrenic disorders.

## REFERENCES

Bender, C. (1937). *A visual motor gestalt test and its clinical use.* New York: American Orthopsychiatric Association.

Bender, C. (1956). *Psychopathological disorders of children with organic brain disease.* Springfield, IL: C. Thomas.

Bender, C. (1970). Use of the visual motor gestalt test in diagnosing learning disability. *Journal of Special Education, 4,* 29–39.

ANTONIO E. PUENTE
*University of North Carolina,
Wilmington*

## BENDER GESTALT

## BENDER GESTALT

The Bender Gestalt is a brief, nonverbal, perceptual-motor assessment instrument. Originally developed by Lauretta

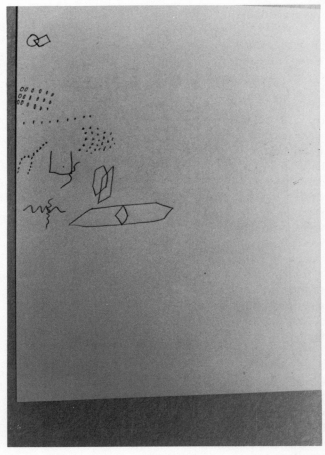

Figure 1. Bender drawings of a high IQ but depressed nine-year-old boy referred for being "shy, withdrawn, and unhappy."

Figure 2. Bender drawings of a hostile, aggressive thirteen-year-old boy referred for a "learning disability." Note the unusual refusal to draw one of the figures.

Bender (1938) as a measure of visual-motor maturation in children, the test has become one of the most widely used assessment techniques for individuals of all ages. The Bender has, for example, been used with adults as a projective personality technique, and with children as an indicator of school readiness, emotional problems, and learning difficulties. However, it has been most widely used as a screening measure for brain dysfunction in both adults and children. (Figures 1 and 2.)

The test consists of nine figures, each of which is printed on a separate 4-inch by 6-inch card. Cards are presented one at a time and subjects are instructed to copy each figure as accurately as possible. Variations on this basic procedure include having subjects reproduce the figures from memory, embedding the figures in distracting backgrounds, and placing time limits on performance (Dana, Field, & Bolton, 1983). The test is typically administered individually, however, group administration procedures have also been developed (Koppitz, 1975). Although Bender did not provide a formal scoring method for the test, a number of objective scoring systems have since been devised (Lacks, 1984). The Developmental Bender Test Scoring System (Koppitz, 1963) has become the preferred scoring method for children's protocols. Designed for use

with children between ages 5 and 10, the system identifies 30 scoring items (errors in the drawings; for example, rotations, distortions in shape, and failure to integrate the components of the design). Each item is worth one point and enters into a composite developmental score that may then be compared with age-appropriate norms provided by Koppitz (1975). A review of 31 studies revealed high interrater reliability for the developmental system (correlations ranged from .79 to .99; 81% of the correlations were at .89 or above). Despite the availability of objective scoring techniques, many practitioners prefer a global, intuitive interpretation based on clinical judgment (Dana, Field, & Bolton, 1983).

## REFERENCES

Bender, L. (1938). *A visual motor Gestalt test and its clinical use.* New York: American Orthopsychiatric Association.

Dana, R. H., Field, K., & Bolton, B. (1983). Variations of the Bender-Gestalt-Test: Implications for training and practice. *Journal of Personality Assessment, 47*(1), 76–84.

Koppitz, E. M. (1963). *The Bender Gestalt Test for young children.* New York: Grune & Stratton.

Koppitz, E. M. (1975). *The Bender Gestalt Test for young children. Vol. 2: Research and application. 1963–1973.* New York: Grune & Stratton.

Lacks, P. (1984). *Bender Gestalt screening for brain dysfunction.* New York: Wiley.

ROBERT G. BRUBAKER
*Eastern Kentucky University*

VISUAL MOTOR PROBLEMS
VISUAL PERCEPTION AND INTEGRATION

# BENNETT, VIRGINIA C. (1916– )

Virginia C. Bennett, a former nurse, studied elementary education at Rutgers University, earning a BA in this field in 1956. She subsequently was awarded an MEd in educational psychology (1961) and the EdD in school psychology (1963), both from Rutgers University, where she was on the faculty from 1963 until her retirement in 1983. During the years 1960 to 1963, Bennett was a W. S. Grant Foundation fellow.

Bennett has worked in school psychology as both a practitioner and a trainer of school psychologists since 1963. Her primary interest has been identification of children with learning problems, with emphasis on the remediation process, for those identified, through planning programs for teachers to implement within the regular classroom setting. She pioneered the mainstreaming of children identified for special educational resources in her practice in the New Jersey schools. With her doctoral students, she planned and implemented a program for the early identification (screening) of kindergarten children in the pub-

Virginia C. Bennett

lic schools of Trenton, New Jersey, a school district with a high proportion of minority group and Hispanic children.

Although always interested in the problems of schoolchildren, and always convinced that the public schools are the most effective milieu for dealing with those problems, Bennett's interests throughout 25 years as a school psychologist and a trainer in a highly urban state have focused in recent years on the problems of poor black children and youths, as well as on those of the increasing numbers of Hispanic children in the schools. These latter interests are exemplified in her publication of work with school-age parents and in the development of a doctoral program geared to the application of psychological knowledge and skills to the solution of educational problems.

Bennett has long been recognized for her leadership in school psychology, where she is perhaps best known for her work with Bardon (Bardon & Bennett, 1974; Bennett & Bardon, 1976). With Bardon, she pioneered the development of professional preparation programs for school psychologists. In 1977 the Division of School Psychology of the American Psychological Association recognized her with the Distinguished Service Award. Bennett is now professor emeritus at Rutgers–The State University.

REFERENCES

Bardon, J. I., & Bennett, V. C. (1974). *School psychology*. Englewood Cliffs, NJ: Prentice-Hall.

Bennett, V. C., & Bardon, J. I. (1976). Applied research can be useful. *Journal of School Psychology, 14*, 67–73.

CECIL R. REYNOLDS
*Texas A&M University*

## BENZEDRINE

Benzedrine is a psychostimulant that acts on the central nervous system. It was the subject of widespread abuse and distribution under the slang term "bennies" until the 1970s. Its previous legitimate uses included, at times, the treatment of hyperactivity and obesity. It is no longer in use in the treatment of childhood or adolescent disorders.

STAFF

**ATTENTION DEFICIT DISORDER
DEXEDRINE**

## BEREITER, CARL (1930–       )

Carl Bereiter received his BA (1951) and MA (1952) in comparative literature and his PhD (1959) in education from the University of Wisconsin. He was a research associate at Vassar College (1959–1961) and then joined the faculty at the University of Illinois (1961–1967). Since 1967, Bereiter has been a professor at the Ontario Institute for Studies in Education.

In the early 1960s, Bereiter and Siegfried Engelmann taught reading, mathematics, and logical skills to young disadvantaged children. Out of this effort came the method they called direct instruction, an approach that was often misperceived as behavioristic rather than rational analysis of difficulties of understanding.

Most of Bereiter's recent work has been in collaboration with Marlene Scardamalia. Through research on composing and comprehension processes, they have identified an immature strategy that seems to reflect a general way of coping superficially with academic tasks. This discovery led to Bereiter's broadening his studies to intentional learning: how it develops, how it is influenced by school practices, and how a higher level of intentional control over learning can be fostered in students.

REFERENCES

Bereiter, C., & Engelmann, S. (1966). *Teaching disadvantaged children in the preschool*. Engelwood Cliffs, NJ: Prentice-Hall.

Bereiter, C., & Scardamalia, M. (1985). Cognitive coping strategies and the problem of "inert" knowledge. In S. S. Chipman, J. W. Segal, & R. Glaser (Eds.), *Thinking and learning skills: Research and open questions* (Vol. 2, pp. 65–80). Hillsdale, NJ: Erlbaum.

STAFF

## BETTELHEIM, BRUNO (1903–       )

Bruno Bettelheim received his MD degree from the University of Vienna in 1938. He also studied under Sigmund Freud and has been strongly influenced by Freudian thought. Bettelheim is a psychiatrist who has gained his fame from work with emotionally disturbed children, particularly those with autism.

During his long association with the University of Chicago, Bettelheim acted as principal of the University of Chicago's Sonia Shankman Orthogeneic School, a residential treatment center for severely emotionally disturbed children. The philosophy and operation of the Shankman School are described in Bettelheim's book *Love Is Not Enough* (1950), and four case studies of the treatment there are covered in his *Truants from Life* (1955).

Bettelheim sought in his treatment of severely disturbed children to create a particular social environment, a society with its own definite set of mores, closely paralleling those of society at large. He believes that social norms and standards are important to the treatment of emotionally disturbed children just as they are important in normal populations.

He has published many books, including *Children of the Dream* (1969) and *The Empty Fortress* (1967). He is currently living in Potola Valley, California.

## REFERENCES

Bettelheim, B. (1950). *Love is not enough: The treatment of emotionally disturbed children*. Glencoe IL: Free Press.

Bettelheim, B. (1955). *Truants from life: The rehabilitation of emotionally disturbed children*. Glencoe IL: Free Press.

Bettelheim, B., (1967). *The empty fortress: Infantile autism and the birth of the self*. London: Collier-Macmillan.

Bettelheim, B., (1969). *Children of the dream*. New York: Macmillan.

REBECCA BAILEY
*Texas A&M University*

## BIALER, IRVING (1919–        )

Irving Bialer received his BA (1943) from Brooklyn College and his PhD (1960) in clinical psychology from George Peabody College, with a minor in education of exceptional children. His major field of interest is in clinical psychology; mental retardation and clinical child psychology are two special areas of interest.

His publications have dealt with issues of assessment and diagnosis in the areas of mental retardation and neurological impairment, personality and motivational development in retarded individuals, and drug-related treatments for behavior problems in neuropsychiatrically impaired children. He has over 30 publications to his credit, including books, articles, and book chapters. Some of his most significant publications include a chapter in *Social-Cultural Aspects of Mental Retardation*, discussing the relationship of mental retardation to emotional disturbance and physical disability, and *The Psychology of Mental Retardation: Issues and Approaches* (coedited with Manny Sternlicht), which focuses on the theoretical, practical issues and approaches to dealing with the psychology of mentally retarded people. Bialer and R. L. Cromwell wrote an article entitled "Failure as Motivation with Mentally Retarded Children," which was published in the *American Journal of Mental Deficiency*.

Bialer has held many academic positions in psychology and special education and has been a consulting editor to the *American Journal of Mental Deficiency* as well as the journal's book review editor from 1971 to 1981.

## REFERENCES

Bialer, I. (1970). Relationship of mental retardation to emotional disturbance and physical disability. In H. C. Haywood (Ed.), *Social-cultural aspects of mental retardation* (pp. 607–660). New York: Appleton-Century-Crofts.

Bialer, I., & Cromwell, R. L. (1965). Failure as motivation with mentally retarded children. *American Journal of Mental Deficiency, 69*, 680–684.

Bialer, I., & Sternlicht, M. (Eds.). (1970). *The psychology of mental retardation: Issues and approaches*. New York: Psychological Dimensions.

REBECCA BAILEY
*Texas A&M University*

## BIBLIOTHERAPY

Bibliotherapy is an approach to helping pupils understand themselves and their feelings and to providing in-classroom counseling to meet their emotional and social needs (Lerner, 1985). Readings and other media materials in which the characters learn to cope and deal effectively with problems similar to those which are, or will be, encountered by the students are used. The materials range from student selected readings to teacher chosen books, magazines, or articles designed to emphasize or illustrate a particular point or issue (Ysseldyke & Algozzine, 1984). Bibliotherapy may be used in either a remedial (dealing with current pupil distress) or preventive (anticipating future problems children may face) form, for children with physical, emotional, social, learning, or other handicaps (McKinnon & Kiraly, 1984).

As with psychotherapy, bibliotherapy includes three main components: identification, catharsis, and insight. Identification with characters, situations, or elements of a story enables the reader to view his or her problem from a new and different perspective and thus gain hope and tension release (catharsis). Such tension reduction allows the student to gain insight into his or her motiviations and actions and allows for positive change in attitude and behavior. This process is structured and guided by the teacher through the use of classroom discussion, example, and illustration (Lenkowsky & Lenkowsky, 1980).

Bibliotherapy offers many advantages for special education. It is effective in the reduction and management of the stress that often accompanies and impairs learning, development, and adjustment in handicapped children (Humphrey & Humphrey, 1985). It may be used individually or with small groups or classes of children. Bibliotherapy can be modified to the needs of children at any age and little formal training or experience is required for teachers to become proficient bibliotherapists. There is a large body of literature available that presents the problems, feelings, and situations faced by handicapped children and adolescents. In addition, research application demonstrates the potential for bibliotherapy to be a powerful agent for behavior change (Lombana, 1982).

## REFERENCES

Humphrey, J. H., & Humphrey, J. N. (1985). *Controlling stress in children*. Springfield, IL: Thomas.

Lenkowsky, B., & Lenkowsky, R. (1980). Bibliotherapy for the learning disabled adolescent. In C. H. Thomas & J. L. Thomas (Eds.), *Meeting the needs of the handicapped: A resource for teachers and librarians*. Phoenix, AZ: Oryx.

Lerner, J. (1985). *Learning disabilities* (4th ed.). Boston: Houghton Mifflin.

Lombana, J. H. (1982). *Guidance for handicapped students*. Springfield, IL: Thomas.

McKinnon, A. J., & Kiraly, J. (1984). *Pupil behavior, self-control and social skills in the classroom*. Springfield, IL: Thomas.

Ysseldyke, J. E., & Algozzine, B. (1984). *Introduction to special education*. Boston: Houghton Mifflin.

RONALD S. LENKOWSKY
*Hunter College, City University
of New York*

**COUNSELING THE HANDICAPPED
SOCIAL SKILLS**

## BIJOU, SIDNEY W. (1908–    )

Born in Baltimore, Maryland, Sidney W. Bijou received his BS in business administration from the University of Florida in 1933. He received his MS (1937) from Columbia University and his PhD (1941), both in psychology, from the University of Iowa. Professor emeritus at the University of Illinois, Bijou has been an adjunct professor of special education and psychology at the University of Arizona.

Although he was the coauthor of the *Wide Range Achievement Test* (Bijou & Jastak, 1941), his major interest is in the behavioral analysis of child development (Bijou, 1976; Bijou & Baer, 1965, 1978). He also coauthored a book on the behavior analysis and modification of children (Bijou & Ruiz, 1981). One of his major contentions is that the child and the environment are always interacting and maintaining a symbiotic relationship. He emphasizes the commonality of a general goal for children, normal and retarded, in early childhood education, regardless of age or degree of handicapping condition, while stressing individualization of education and treatment.

Sidney W. Bijou

Bijou has been a National Institute of Mental Health senior fellow, a Fullbright-Hays fellow, president of the Midwestern Association of Behavior Analysis, and president of the American Psychological Association's Division of Developmental Psychology. He has also received the Research Award from the American Association of Mental Deficiency, and the G. Stanley Hall Award in child development from the American Psychological Association.

## REFERENCES

Bijou, S. W. (1976). *Child development: The basic stage of early childhood*. Englewood Cliffs, NJ: Prentice-Hall.

Bijou, S. W., & Baer, D. M. (1965). *Child development: Universal stage of infancy* (Vol. 2). New York: Appleton-Century-Crofts.

Bijou, S. W., & Baer, D. M. (1978). *Behavior analysis of child development*. Englewood Cliffs, NJ: Prentice-Hall.

Bijou, S. W., & Jastak, J. F. (1941). *Wide range achievement test*. New York: Psychological Corporation.

Bijou, S. W., & Ruiz, R. (Eds.). (1981). *Behavior modification: Contributions to education*. Hillsdale, NJ: Erlbaum.

E. VALERIE HEWITT
*Texas A&M University*

## BILINGUAL SPECIAL EDUCATION

Bilingual special education is an educational alternative within the continuum of services provided for handicapped students whose dominant language is other than English and who consequently require instruction through the medium of their primary or home language. The objectives of bilingual special education are a combination of those for bilingual education and special education as spelled out in respective legislation.

Title VII of the Elementary and Secondary Education Act, known as the Bilingual Education Act, aims to equalize educational opportunity for all children whose English proficiency is limited (LEP). Its objective is to ensure that LEP students' academic achievement shall not be adversely affected by their poor command of English.

Public Law 94-142, the Education for All Handicapped Children Act, is based on the constitutional principles of equal protection and due process. It guarantees for all culturally and linguistically different handicapped children the right to assessment procedures that are nonbiased and in the child's primary language, to assessment by a multidisciplinary team, and, for parents and guardians, correspondence and other communications in their native language. The educational objective of special education is to provide individually designed educational programs (IEPs) to meet the unique needs of each student such that the student may achieve at levels commensurate with his or her ability.

While there is no legislative indication that bilingual special education is a distinct educational service. Carpenter (1983) notes that "the legal bases for such service emerge from the application of special education regulations to IEP contents" (p. 34). It is the IEP that is generally employed to specify the linguistic educational services required and the extent of those services.

Despite the recognized legal basis for bilingual special education, it has only recently been defined. As a result, a range of important issues and problems have emerged as the focus for discussion and research. These include issues of assessment, personnel, curriculum and methodology, ethnolinguistic variability, and parental involvement.

*Assessment.* Historically, LEP students have been overrepresented in special education programs, particularly in the categories of mental retardation, speech/language impairment, and learning disabilities (Carpenter, 1983; Cummins, 1984). This continues to be the case despite corrective litigation and legislation. The LEP student is particularly at risk for inappropriate placement primarily because of inadequate testing instruments that are heavily verbally laden and that reflect Anglo middle-class cultural values. Efforts to resolve this issue have focused on translating existing tests or creating new ones, developing local norms for already standardized tests, providing trained native-speaking evaluation professionals, and using translators or interpreters. In addition, the fundamental assumptions of IQ testing in general have been questioned, resulting in the creation of culture-fair tests. While sizable advances have been made where the evaluation of LEP Spanish-speaking students is concerned, the availability of tests for other than Spanish-speaking students is severely limited. Before such instruments can be gen-

erated, there is a need for more research to establish developmental norms for minority groups for a whole range of different behaviors (Toronto & Mares-Merrill, 1983).

*Language.* Crucial to the appropriate assessment of LEP students is the ability to distinguish between linguistic deficits, those implying central nervous system (CNS) damage to the language and other cognitive centers of the brain, and linguistic differences, those that are the result of normal difficulties in the process of acquiring a second language. Miller (1984) has pointed out that many of the handicapping conditions attributed to LEP students are related to language. Unfortunately, no standardized yardstick exists for telling the difference between language deficits and language difficulties for children whose mother tongue is not English. However, Miller (1984) suggests that existing knowledge concerning language development in general and second language acquisition in particular offers some guidelines. Since language learning, whether of a mother tongue ($L_1$) or a second ($L_2$) or subsequent language ($L_3$, $L_4$, etc.), employs the same underlying CNS mechanisms, one may not be language impaired in the second (or subsequent) language without also demonstrating dysfunction in the primary language. It follows that any assessment of a potentially handicapped LEP student must be conducted in the primary language before an adequate determination can be made concerning the nature of the learning difficulty.

*Personnel.* Personnel issues are concerned with the availability and training of bilingual special educators. The demand for trained bilingual special educators far exceeds the current supply nationwide (Baca, 1980). Several universities, for example, in the states of California, New Mexico, New York, and Texas, have instituted degree programs to train bilingual special educators, and many *Local Educational Agencies* nationwide carry out extensive in-service programs. One of the questions resulting from efforts to provide training for bilingual special educators has been whether there needs to be a separate specialization and new courses expressly designed for this area. A review of programs involved in the preparation of bilingual special educators reveals that they appear to require the same training as nonbilingual special educators with some additions, notably, courses such as foundations of bilingual education, principles and practices of bilingual education, linguistics, psycholinguistics, sociolinguistics, first and second language development, multicultural education, English as a second language, assessment of first and second language functioning, diagnosis of language problems, and research in bilingual special education. Furthermore, a full command of English and the target language is deemed essential.

*Curriculum and Methodology.* The greater part of the literature on the culturally and linguistically different handicapped child has focused on issues of assessment. Little attention has been given to curriculum and methodology. Many school districts continue to place LEP handicapped students in English monolingual learning environments or keep them in bilingual classes (Erickson & Iglesias, 1986). These practices are frequently justified on the basis of the unavailability of trained bilingual special education personnel, on the low numbers of LEP children requiring special services, or on the linguistic variance of the student body, making it impractical to set up separate classes. Consequently, the instructional alternative offered to these children may be English as a second language. On the other hand, Carpenter (1983) reports that advocates for bilingual special education support the use of a combination of models and techniques employed in both bilingual and special education. However, questions concerning appropriate and effective curriculum and methodology for bilingual special education are still open to research.

*Ethnolinguistic Variability.* Limited English proficiency minority students, even those who share a similar language and culture, are a highly heterogeneous population. A tendency exists to assume that all members of a particular ethnic or linguistic group hold not only the same set of values but also speak the same version of the language. In fact, Plata (1982) notes that variability within ethnic groups has been found to be large and may depend on factors such as length of residence in the United States, level of education, child-rearing beliefs and practices, socioeconomic status, geographic location, and values and attitudes toward the new culture and its language. Language patterns also vary depending on sociolinguistic patterns such as age and sex of speaker, individual being addressed, and the context and content of the interaction. While ethnolinguistic variability would appear to create insurmountable instructional difficulties, research exists (such as the Significant Bilingual Instructional Features descriptive study of classes serving Puerto Rican, Cuban, Mexican, Navajo, and Cantonese-speaking Chinese students in six sites across the United States) that describes and explains successful bilingual instruction for LEP students (Tikunoff, 1985). Studies such as this one provide successful models that may be applied to bilingual special education settings.

*Parent Involvement.* Despite legal provisions for parental involvement in the referral, evaluation, and placement process for LEP handicapped children, minority parents continue to be minimally involved in the process (Carpenter, 1983). Several reasons have been proposed in the literature, most revolving around issues of cross-cultural, cross-linguistic communication. Parents may themselves be limited in English proficiency and find it extremely difficult to participate. They may bring to the process cultural values calling for respect of educational institutions and their representatives. Consequently, they may lack the assertiveness of the Anglo parent when dealing with school-related issues concerning their child. Moreover, the complexity of the legal process as frequently presented to them, even through an interpreter, may be daunting (Condon, Yates-Peters, & Sueiro-Ross, 1979). In addition, the educational jargon and particularly the jargon of special education is not only unfamiliar to parents but the appropriate equivalent in the target language may not be known to the bilingual professional or to the interpreter. As a result, the large variation existing in the target language translations of various terms renders them incomprehensible. One notable effort to standardize such terms in Spanish is the *Bilingual Special Education Dictionary* (Figueroa, Ruiz, & Díaz-Guerrero, 1983). It provides comprehensible Spanish versions of special education terms with clear examples illuminating some of the more abstract concepts. As of this writing, no other bilingual special education standardized dictionary is widely available, although state and local educational agencies make available translations of regulations in other languages.

## REFERENCES

Baca, L. (1980). *Policy options for insuring the delivery of an appropriate education to handicapped children who are of limited english proficiency.* Reston, VA: Council for Exceptional Children.

Carpenter, L. J. (1983, August). *Bilingual special education: An overview of issues.* Los Alamitos, CA: National Center for Bilingual Research.

Condon, E. C., Yates-Peters, J., & Sueiro-Ross, C. (1979). *Special education and the Hispanic child: Cultural perspectives.* Philadelphia: Temple University—Teacher Corps Mid-Atlantic Network.

Cummins, J. (1984). *Bilingualism and special education: Issues in assessment and pedagogy.* San Diego, CA: College-Hill.

Erickson, J. G., & Iglesias, A. (1986). Assessment of communication disorders in non-English proficient children. In O. I. Taylor (Ed.), *Nature of communication disorders in culturally and linguistically diverse populations.* San Diego, CA: College-Hill.

Figueroa, R. A., Ruiz, N. T., & Díaz-Guerrero, R. (1983). *The bilingual special education dictionary,* Oakland, CA: National Hispanic University Press.

Miller, N. (1984). Language problems and bilingual children. In N. Miller (Ed.), *Bilingualism and language disability: Assessment and remediation.* San Diego, CA: College-Hill.

Plata, M. (1982). *Assessment, placement and programming of bilingual exceptional pupils: A practical approach,* Reston, VA: Council for Exceptional Children.

Tikunoff, W. J. (1985). *Applying significant bilingual instructional features in the classroom,* Rosslyn, VA: National Clearinghouse for Bilingual Education.

Toronto, A. S., & Mares-Merrill, S. (1983). Developing local normed assessment instruments. In D. R. Omark & J. G. Ericbson (Eds.), *The bilingual exceptional child*, San Diego, CA: College-Hill.

H. ROBERTA ARRIGO
*Hunter College, City University
of New York*

**CULTURAL BIAS IN TESTING
RACIAL DISCRIMINATION IN SPECIAL EDUCATION**

## BILL OF RIGHTS FOR THE DISABLED

The Bill of Rights for the Disabled is a codification by the United Cerebral Palsy Association of rights that have been won for the handicapped in court cases and before legislatures during the 1960s and 1970s. These rights are as follows:

1. The right to prevention, early diagnosis, and proper care.
2. The right to a barrier-free environment and accessible transportation.
3. The right to an appropriate public education.
4. The right to necessary assistance, given in a way that promotes independence.
5. The right to a choice of lifestyles and residential alternatives.
6. The right to an income for a lifestyle comparable to that of the able-bodied.
7. The right to training and employment as qualified.
8. The right to petition social institutions for just and humane treatment.
9. The right to self-esteem.

STAFF

## BINET, ALFRED (1857–1911)

Alfred Binet, the founder of French experimental psychology, became director of the Laboratory of Physiological Psychology at the Sorbonne in Paris in 1895. In the same year, he and a colleague founded the first French journal of psychology, *Année psychologique*. He was cofounder of the Société Libre pour l'Étude Psychologique de l'Enfant, which after his death became the Société Alfred Binet.

Binet's investigations took him outside the laboratory. He observed children in schools and camps and used questionnaires and interviews to collect data. In 1904 the minister of public instruction appointed him to a commission created to formulate methods for identifying mentally retarded children in the public schools so that these children could be given a special school program. Out of Binet's work with this commission came the first scale for measuring intelligence, based on the idea of classifying children according to individual differences in performance of tasks requiring thinking and reasoning. On the assumption that intelligence increases with age, he employed the concept of mental age. Results were expressed both as mental age and by a score obtained by subtracting mental age from chronological age. The German psychologist William Stern proposed an improved way of expressing the test results: dividing mental age by chronological age, yielding an intelligence quotient.

The scale was first published by Binet and Theodore Simon in 1905 and was revised in 1908 and 1911. It was translated into English by H. H. Goddard in the United States. In 1916 L. M. Terman at Stanford University published his *Stanford Revision of the Binet Scales*. For half a century dozens of translations and revisions of Binet's scales dominated the field of intelligence testing; they are still extensively used.

Alfred Binet had a variety of other interests in the field of psychology. One of his earliest works was a book on hypnosis. In addition, he developed, with Simon, a classification of mental disorders. He also used pictures and inkblots to study thought processes, foreshadowing later projective techniques.

### REFERENCES

Varon, E. J. (1935). The development of Alfred Binet's psychology. *Psychological Monographs* (No. 207). Princeton, NJ: Psychological Review.

Watson, R. I. (1963). *The great psychologists*. New York: Lippincott.

PAUL IRVINE
*Katonah, New York*

## BIOCHEMICAL IRREGULARITIES

It has been long recognized that a large number of metabolic diseases have characteristic clinical, pathological, and biochemical irregularities that can be attributed to the congenital deficiency of a specific enzyme. This inadequacy is in turn owed to the presence of a particular abnormal gene. The identification and consequent understanding of such biochemical problems began in the early part of the twentieth century with the first demonstration of Mendelian inheritance in humans. A. E. Garrod (Roberts, 1967) derived the basic concept of these disorders through studies on the rare condition known as alcaptonuria (Garrod, 1909). His classical investigation of this abnormality has provided an elegant and simple model for the interpretation of a great variety of different inherited diseases subsequently discovered.

Alcaptonuria is a condition in which large quantities of homogentisic acid are excreted into the urine, which turns black on standing. Under normal conditions, the amino acid tyrosine is converted through a series of enzymatic reactions to fumarate and acetoacetate (La Du, 1966). Garrod noted that when homogentisic acid, a normal intermediary metabolite of tyrosine, was fed to alcaptonuric subjects, it was excreted quantitatively in urine, whereas when given to normal subjects it appeared to be readily metabolized. Additionally, the administration of tyrosine or proteins containing it to alcaptonurics augmented the excretion of homogentisic acid.

The other striking feature of alcaptonuria to which Garrod drew attention was its familial distribution. After studying the characteristic pedigrees of these subjects, he concluded that they implied a hereditary or genetic basis for the condition. Garrod pointed out that the homogentisic acid must be derived from tyrosine and that the essential feature of alcaptonuria was a block in the metabolism of this substance, whereby breakdown could proceed only as far as homogentisic acid.

Eventually Garrod described a number of metabolic peculiarities of this kind and called them inborn errors of metabolism. He viewed the inborn errors as conditions in which the specific enzyme deficiency effectively blocked at a particular point a sequence of reactions that form part of the normal course of metabolism. As a result, metabolites immediately preceding the block would accumulate and metabolites subsequent to the block would not be formed (Harris, 1975). The various biochemical, clinical, and pathological manifestations of the condition could be regarded as secondary consequences of this primary metabolic defect. These secondary changes might be complex and widespread and would depend in general on the nature and the biochemical effects of the metabolites that tended to accumulate or whose formation was restricted (Harper, Rodwell, & Mayes, 1977).

It is now understood that the end products of gene action are proteins, either structural cell components, elements of extracellular matrices, or enzymes. Since genes are potentially mutable units, a change in a gene will disturb the synthesis of the specific protein for which it is responsible. This results in the formation of a different protein (or no protein at all), which alters the process or processes that depend on it. When the protein is absent or deficient, the normal process is impaired. The expression of such a mutation is a phenotypic effect of more or less consequence to the individual. Such defects in cellular enzyme formation are most often characterized by abnormal protein, carbohydrate, or fat metabolism.

All biochemical processes are under genetic control and each consists of a complex sequence of reactions. Part (a) of the following Figure schematically represents a portion of a normal metabolic pathway. A substrate, the substance on which an enzyme acts, is converted into a product through the activity of a specific enzyme. A metabolic pathway consists of many such reactions or steps, each being dependent on the previous reaction and each catalyzed by a specific enzyme (Jenkins, 1983). Part (b) of the figure illustrates how a change in a gene that interferes with the synthesis of an essential enzyme interrupts this process. A block in the normal pathway may produce an accumulation of the substances preceding the block, such as the monosaccharide (simple sugar) galactose in galactosemia or the amino acid phenylalanine in phenylketonuria. In other cases, the block may create a deficiency

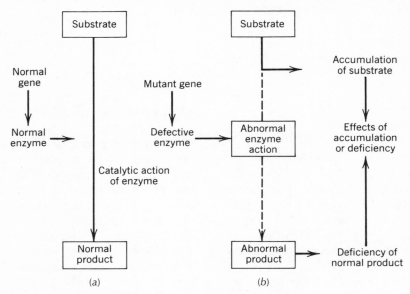

Alternative metabolic pathways. (a) formation of a normal product. (b) accumulation of substrate or deficiency of product as a result of an abnormal metabolic pathway (adapted from Whaley and Wong, 1983).

in the normal product, such as the pigment melanin in albinism or the hormone thyroxine in familial cretinism. Sometimes alternative metabolic pathways are used that result in an increase in the products of these processes such as phenylketones in phenylketonuria. The effects of defective gene action are often observable in the individual as diseases.

There are many inherited disorders caused by an inborn error of metabolism that involves either the accumulation or degradation of metabolic processes. For the most part, they are rare diseases, and the mode of transmission is almost always autosomal recessive genes. This may be best understood by considering the double-dose effect as it relates to the concept that one gene is responsible for one enzyme. If a specific gene controls the formation of an essential enzyme, and each individual has two such genes (the normal homozygote), then the enzyme is produced in normal amounts. The heterozygote, who has only one gene with a normal effect, is still capable of producing the enzyme in sufficient amounts to carry out the metabolic function under normal circumstances. However, the abnormal homozygote, who inherits a defective gene from each parent, has no functional enzyme and is, thus, clinically affected. It is becoming increasingly possible to detect and, therefore, to screen for a large variety of such inborn errors of metabolism. This should lead to the detection of the presence of the disease in the heterozygote (who is a carrier), the newborn, and the fetus before birth, thus allowing for proper genetic counseling of the parents and successful treatment of affected individuals (Goodenough, 1978).

**REFERENCES**

Garrod, A. E. (1909). *Inborn errors of metabolism*. New York: Oxford University Press.

Goodenough, U. (1978). *Genetics* (2nd ed.). New York: Holt, Rinehart, & Winston.

Harper, H. A., Rodwell, V. W., & Mayes, P. A. (1977). *Review of physiological chemistry* (16th ed.). Los Altos, CA: Lange Medical.

Harris, H. (1975). *The principles of human biochemical genetics* (2nd ed.). New York: American Elsevier.

Jenkins, J. B. (1983). *Human genetics*. New York: Benjamin/Cummings.

La Du, B. N. (1966). Alcaptonuria. In J. B. Stanbury, J. B. Wyngaarden, & D. S. Fredickson (Eds.), *The metabolic basis of inherited diseases*. New York: McGraw-Hill.

Roberts, J. A. F. (1967). *An introduction to medical genetics* (4th ed.). New York: Oxford University Press.

Whaley, L. F., & Wong, D. L. (1983). *Nursing care of infants and children* (2nd ed.). St. Louis: Mosby.

TIMOTHY A. BALLARD
*University of North Carolina,
Wilmington*

CONGENITAL DISORDERS
CRETINISM
INBORN ERRORS OF METABOLISM
PHENYLKETONURIA

## BIOFEEDBACK

Biofeedback is a highly structured form of therapy that provides immediate feedback about involuntary biological functions such as heart rate, blood pressure, or brain waves. The feedback generally uses visual and auditory devices to show the subject what is happening to normally autonomic bodily functions as the patient attempts to influence them.

The classical animal experiments conducted by Neal Miller and his colleagues in the 1960s demonstrated that involuntary actions such as heart rate, blood pressure, and salivation could be altered by making rewards and punishments contingent on changes in these involuntary responses. This research suggested that people could be taught to control a number of physiological responses formerly thought to be involuntary (Miller, 1978).

In the field of special education, the effectiveness of biofeedback has been exaggerated, but a few procedures do seem to offer promise. The two most frequently used types of biofeedback with learning-disabled and gifted populations are passive and active. During passive electromyographic (EMG) biofeedback, the subject is asked to maintain a signal indicating a low level of tension or other required response. During active electromyographic biofeedback, the subject is asked to produce different levels of tension and or other required responses and to perform differential relaxation. For example, in biofeedback treatment of migraine headaches, patients are taught to warm their hands through temperature feedback. This hand warming is associated with increased blood flow to the hands which in turn leads to a lessening of arterial pressure in the brain (Blanchard et al., 1978).

Electromyographic biofeedback has been used as an intervention strategy for hyperactivity (Braud, Lupin, & Braud, 1975; Christie, Dewitt, Kaltenbach, & Reed, 1984; Omizo & Michael, 1982; Rivera & Omizo, 1980). Braud et al. (1975) studied the effects of biofeedback on muscular activity and tension in a hyperactive boy. When the child's forehead muscle group exceeded a certain point, a tone sounded and the child was instructed to "keep the tone off" by sitting and relaxing. Muscular tension and activity decreased both within and across training sessions. It was found that continued practice using laboratory techniques was needed to maintain treatment results. Without parent and school cooperation, the treatment effects deteriorated.

Omizo and Michael (1982) demonstrated through the use of biofeedback-induced relaxation training increased attention to task and reduced impulsivity among hyperactive boys, but no effect on locus of control; this is also supported by the findings of Rivera and Omizo (1980). The basic treatment package asked the boys, seated in a reclining position, to induce the biofeedback unit to register a pattern of low activity while relaxation tapes were played for them.

Bhatara, Arnold, Lorance, & Gupta (1979) reviewed the literature on EMG biofeedback and concluded that there is insufficient evidence to support the clinical utility of EMG feedback in hyperactive children. Biofeedback is seen as a promising technique in this area but the problems found in the research to date must be solved.

There must be more tightly controlled designs to rule out the influence of task-motivated suggestions and expectant attitudes. There must be adequate follow-ups carried out on larger populations. Researchers must question the influence of suggestion, motivation, and emotion. Finally, most of the successful results with biofeedback techniques are closely related to relaxation therapies. Thus it would be fruitful to combine biofeedback with older proven therapies.

Progressive muscle relaxation and EMG biofeedback training were used to study the treatment effects on anxiety for 30 gifted children (Roome & Romney, 1985). The biofeedback group was connected to an Inner Tell EMG and told to experiment with various mental images to reduce the meter reading. The progressive muscle relaxation group listened to tapes in a chair. The results indicated neither treatment to be more effective than the other. Both groups showed a significant reduction in stated anxiety and a shift toward internal locus of control as compared with the control group. This study, like so many others (Zimet, 1979), is contradictory and the results are inconclusive owing to the limited number of sessions and lack of follow-up testing. There is still no conclusive evidence that a person's ability to learn self-control through biofeedback can be predicted from locus of control orientation. The instructional set, not biofeedback itself, appears to be the pivotal variable.

A relatively recent area of investigation is the use of urodynamic biofeedback with children with myelomeningocele (spina bifida), the most common congenital central nervous system defect. Neurogenic urinary and fecal incontinence is prevalent in the majority of these children. The impact of the physical and psychosocial difficulties associated with chronic incontinence in spina bifida children can cause great distress (Hunt, 1981).

Rectosphincteric biofeedback was used to reduce the number of accidents in eight spina bifida children with chronic fecal incontinence. Six of the eight children reduced the number of accidents and two children became continent (Varni, 1983). Wald (1981) used a similar procedure and found four of eight children had a good clinical response, defined as the disappearance of fecal soiling or a greater than 75% reduction in the frequency of soiling. The results of these studies are encouraging.

In the Killam, Jeffries, and Varni (1985) study using urodynamic biofeedback training, six of eight children demonstrated improved self-regulation of detrusor or sphincter functioning, but only one child demonstrated improvements in urinary incontinence. Unexpectedly, chronic neurogenic fecal incontinence was reduced in four children owing to placement of the surface electrodes in the perianal position.

Much research will be necessary before biofeedback can be advocated as a viable general treatment, although there is evidence that this approach can help in the remediation of some physical problems that once could be treated only by such somatic approaches as medication or surgery (Shapiro & Surwit, 1976).

## REFERENCES

Bhatara, V., Arnold, L. E., Lorance, T., & Gupta, D. (1979). Muscle relaxation therapy in hyperkinesis: Is it effective? *Journal of Learning Disabilities, 11*, 182–186.

Blanchard, E. B., Theobald, D. E., Williamson, D. A., Silver, B. V., & Brown, D. A. (1978). Temperature biofeedback in the treatment of migraine headaches. *Archives of General Psychiatry, 35*, 581–588.

Braud, L. W., Lupin, M. N., & Braud, W. G. (1975). The use of electromyographic biofeedback in the control of hyperactivity. *Journal of Learning Disabilities, 8*, 420–425.

Christie, D. J., Dewitt, R. A., Kaltenbach, P., & Reed, D. (1984). Using EMG biofeedback to signal hyperactive children when to relax. *Exceptional Children, 50*, 547–548.

Hunt, G. M. (1981). Spina bifida: Implications for 100 children at school. *Developmental Medicine & Child Neurology, 23*, 160–172.

Killam, P. E., Jeffries, J. S., & Varni, J. W. (1985). Urodynamic biofeedback treatment of urinary incontinence in children with myelomeningocele. *Biofeedback & Self-Regulation, 10*, 161–171.

Miller, N. E. (1978). Biofeedback and visceral learning. *Annual Review of Psychology, 29*, 373–404.

Omizo, M. M., & Michael, W. B. (1982). Biofeedback-induced relaxation training and impulsivity attention to task, and locus of control among hyperactive boys. *Journal of Learning Disabilities, 15*, 414–416.

Rivera, E., & Omizo, M. M. (1980). An investigation of the effects of relaxation training on attention to task and impulsivity among male hyperactive children. *Exceptional Child, 27*, 41–51.

Roome, J. R., & Romney, D. M. (1985). Reducing anxiety in gifted children by inducing relaxation. *Roeper Review, 7*, 177–179.

Shapiro, D., & Surwit, R. S. (1976). Learned control of physiological function and disease. In H. Leitenberg (Ed.), *Handbook of behavior modification and behavior therapy* (pp. 74–123). Englewood Cliffs, NJ: Prentice-Hall.

Varni, J. W. (1983). *Clinical behavioral pediatrics: An interdisciplinary biobehavioral approach.* New York: Pergamon.

Wald, A. (1981). Use of biofeedback of treatment of fecal incontinence in patients with myelomeningocele. *Pediatrics, 68*, 45–49.

Zimet, G. D. (1979). Locus of control and biofeedback: A review of the literature. *Perceptual & Motor Skills, 49*, 871–877.

DEBORAH A. SHANLEY
*Medgar Evans College, City
University of New York*

**HYPERACTIVITY
SPINA BIFIDA**

# BIOGENIC MODELS

Biogenic, or organic, models present causes of human actions in terms of the biological substrate that underlies behavior. Thus to predict, explain, and control behavior, the various activities of the nervous system and other bodily organs must be understood and manipulated. Implicit in this model is the notion that effective therapies will primarily involve biological manipulations such as drugs or surgery. This approach can be contrasted with psychogenic models that emphasize psychological constructs as explanatory mechanisms of behavior (Bootzin, 1984).

Contemporary models of behavior are rarely in absolutely biological or psychological terms, but when a model is primarily biogenic in nature there are important implications for the user's conceptual framework in understanding behavior and implementing behavioral change programs. Biogenic models place the locus of the cause of problem behavior squarely within the individual's biological deficits and give only minimal roles to other parts of the ecosystem such as family or school. Most contemporary biogenic models are reductionistic and pin their ultimate hopes on an understanding of the relationships among biological, biochemical, and behavioral phenomena. Alterations, which are observed in cognitions or social relations, can be viewed as symptoms of physiological actions. Although our current understanding of biological factors may not allow for biochemical cures for all behavioral problems, the ultimate direction of the biogenic approach lies in biomedical interventions (Engel, 1977).

Critics of the biogenic model have difficulty denying that in a physical sense all behavior can ultimately be traced to biological processes. They do contend, however, that reductionist approaches may not always be the most fruitful guides to practice in education. Biogenic models tend to blame the victim by emphasizing changing the organism and not the environment or situation in which the individual exists (Albee, 1980). It is often the case that concepts of the biogenic model are confused with those of the medical or disease model. Engel (1977), however, proposed a disease model that replaced a biomedical with a biopsychosocial approach to the understanding of disordered behavior.

The organic (biogenic) model represents one of the major historical threads in the understanding of the etiology of abnormal behavior. This model has been advanced at least since the time of the Greek physician Hippocrates (Brown, 1986), and is still seen in such concepts as minimal brain dysfunction (Bootzin, 1984). Indeed, for thousands of years, it was the only viable alternative to magical or supernatural explanations of exceptional behavior. It should be noted, however, that biogenic models have not always resulted in more humane treatment or exacting scientific research into the nature of behavior disorders. For example, the warehousing of patients in the late nineteenth- and early twentieth-century psychiatric hospitals was the result in part of a belief that dealing with mental disease was hopeless until science found a biological cure (Erickson & Hyerstay, 1980).

Biogenic models may be of value to the classroom special education teacher as the basis for planning interventions. Reed (1979) noted the role of neuropsychological diagnoses in developing educational techniques that take into account deficits in brain function. In a rejoinder, Balow (1979) pointed out that such biogenic models were of limited use to the classroom teacher because of their lack of relevance for educational practice and their unclear specification of the link between specific biological dysfunctions and differential educational planning.

## REFERENCES

Albee, G. (1980). A competency model to replace the deficit model. In M. Gibbs, J. Lachenmeyer, & J. Sigal (Eds.), *Community psychology: Theoretical and empirical approaches* (pp. 213–238). New York: Gardner.

Balow, B. (1979). Biological defects and special education: An empiricist's view. *Journal of Special Education, 13*, 35–40.

Bootzin, R. (1984). *Abnormal psychology: Current perspectives* (4th ed.). New York: Random House.

Brown, R. T. (1986). Etiology and development of exceptionality. In R. T. Brown, & C. R. Reynolds (Eds.), *Psychological perspectives on childhood exceptionality: A handbook.* (pp. 181–229). New York: Wiley.

Engel, G. (1977). A need for a new medical model: A challenge for biomedicine. *Science, 96*, 129–136.

Erickson, R., & Hyerstay, B. (1980). Historical perspectives on treatment of the mentally ill. In M. Gibbs, J. Lachenmeyer, & J. Sigal (Eds.), *Community psychology: Theoretical and empirical approaches.* (pp. 29–64). New York: Gardner.

Reed, H. (1979). Biological defects in special education: An issue in personnel preparation. *Journal of Special Education, 13*, 9–33.

LEE ANDERSON JACKSON, JR.
*University of North Carolina,
Wilmington*

**BIOLOGICAL BASIS OF EMOTIONAL DISTURBANCE**

BIOLOGICAL BASIS OF LEARNING AND MEMORY
MEDICAL MODEL, DEFENSE OF

## BIOLOGICAL BASIS OF EMOTIONAL DISORDERS

Biological factors contribute to emotional disorders in various ways. A genetic predisposition has been strongly implicated for schizophrenia, depression, and manic-depressive illness. There is at least moderate evidence of a genetic contribution to childhood autism, obsessive-compulsive disorder, panic disorder, and other conditions.

Whether because of genetics, improper nutrition, or other sources, certain areas of the nervous system can misfunction in ways that lead to behavioral abnormalities. For example, individuals who are subject to panic disorder have an overresponsive sympathetic nervous system. Even at rest, they have an elevated heart rate and blood epinephrine level compared with controls (Nesse et al., 1984). They may respond with anxiety, agitation, and palpitations to injections that produce only mild signs of arousal in other people (Charney, Heninger, & Breier, 1984; Liebowitz, et al., 1984).

Many types of emotional disorders have been linked to abnormalities affecting one or more synaptic transmitter systems in the brain. One example is depression. Most antidepressant drugs prolong the activity of the monoamine transmitters (dopamine, norepinephrine, and serotonin) in the brain. One interpretation of the effect of antidepressant drugs has been that they counteract an initial deficiency in the activity at monoamine synapses. That interpretation may be incorrect, however; a prolonged increase in the abundance of synaptic transmitter molecules at a synapse leads to a compensatory decline in the later release of that transmitter and to a decline in the number of receptors sensitive to that transmitter. Because of the multitude of effects, it is uncertain whether the antidepressant drugs help to repair an initial overactivity or underactivity of the monoamine synapses. Nevertheless, it is likely that some disorder of those synapses is responsible for many manifestations of depression.

Another probable example of a behavioral disorder linked to abnormalities at synapses is Gilles de la Tourette's syndrome. This uncommon condition affects mostly boys and has its onset in childhood. The symptoms include tics, repetitive movements, repetitive sounds, and learning disabilities (Golden, 1977). Although the cause is not known, the usual treatment is haloperidol and other drugs that block dopamine synapses in the brain.

The biological basis of an emotional disorder need not be a permanent chemical disorder of the brain, however, and drugs are not always the best remedy even for a biological disorder. Many cases of depression have been linked to inadequate or poorly timed sleep. Occasionally,

individuals suffer from winter depressions as a result of inadequate sunlight. Uncorrected visual problems may lead to headaches. Many adolescents experience moodiness and aggressive outbursts that may be triggered by hormonal changes. A lack of exercise may predispose the body to overreact to stress. Malnutrition can aggravate psychological disorders as well. In certain cases, emotional disorders can be alleviated by altering sleep, diet, exercise, and other habits without resorting to tranquilizers, antidepressant drugs, or other medical interventions. For further information, see Kalat (1984), Pincus and Tucker (1985), or Snyder (1980).

### REFERENCES

Charney, D. S., Heninger, G. R., & Breier, A. (1984). Noradrenergic function in panic anxiety. *Archives of General Psychiatry, 41*, 751–763.

Golden, G. S. (1977). Tourette syndrome. *American Journal of Diseases of Children, 131*, 531–534.

Kalat, J. W. (1984). *Biological psychology* (2nd ed.). Belmont, CA: Wadsworth.

Liebowitz, M. R., Fyer, A. J., Gorman, J. M., Dillon, D., Appleby, I. L., Levy, G., Anderson, S., Levitt, M., Palij, M., Davies, S. O., & Klein, D. F. (1984). Lactate provocation of panic attacks: Vol I. Clinical and behavioral findings. *Archives of General Psychiatry, 41*, 764–770.

Nesse, R. M., Cameron, O. G., Curtis, G. C., McCann, D. S., & Huber-Smith, M. J. (1984). Adrenergic function in patients with panic anxiety. *Archives of General Psychiatry, 41*, 771–776.

Pincus, J. H., & Tucker, G. J. (1985). *Behavioral neurology* (3rd ed.). New York: Oxford University Press.

Snyder, S. H. (1980). *Biological aspects of mental disorder*. New York: Oxford University Press.

JAMES W. KALAT
*North Carolina State University*

DIAGNOSTIC AND STATISTICAL MANUAL OF MENTAL DISORDERS (DSM III)
EMOTIONAL DISORDERS

## BIOLOGICAL BASIS OF LEARNING AND MEMORY

To understand the biological basis of learning and memory, two largely independent questions must be dealt with: (1) How does a pattern of experience alter the future properties of cells and synapses in the nervous system? (2) How do populations of altered cells work together to produce adaptive behavior?

Striking progress has been made toward answering the first question. According to studies of invertebrates, short-term increases in behavior can be induced by chemical changes that block the flow of potassium across the presynaptic membrane of certain neurons. Longer lasting changes in behavior require the synthesis of proteins in the neurons to be changed (Kandel & Schwartz, 1982). Protein synthesis also appears to be necessary for learning by vertebrates, especially for long-term retention (Davis & Squire, 1984).

Certain of the brain changes associated with learning or the ability to learn are large enough to be visible under a light microscope. Enhanced learning ability is associated with a proliferation of glial cells and increased branching of dendrites (Uphouse, 1980). Impaired learning is associated with the opposite anatomical changes. The extent of branching of dendrites is highly correlated with the number of synapses found in the brain.

Investigators have not determined how the changed neurons operate together to produce the overall changes in behavior identified as learning. They have, however, identified areas of the mammalian brain that are necessary for certain aspects of learning. The famous neurological patient H. M. had most of his hippocampus removed as a treatment for severe epilepsy. He can recall very few events that have occurred since that operation, although he has been able to learn new skills such as reading material written in mirror fashion and working the Tower of Hanoi puzzle (Cohen & Squire, 1980; Milner, Corkin, & Teuber, 1968). Experiments with animals have indicated that amnesia is most severe if damage to the hippocampus is combined with damage to the amygdala. Damage to those two areas impairs animals' ability to store sensory information and respond to it a few minutes later (Zola-Morgan & Squire, 1985). Various other patterns of learning and memory loss occur after damage to the frontal lobes of the cerebral cortex and to numerous subcortical structures.

Moscovitch (1985) has pointed out that human infants, like adults with damage to the hippocampus or frontal cortex, learn from experience but seldom show evidence of recalling a specific incident. It may be no coincidence, he notes, that the hippocampus and frontal cortex are among the last structures of the brain to reach full maturity. The normal amnesia of infancy may, therefore, be due to the same mechanisms as the amnesia of brain-damaged adults.

Impaired learning and memory among children and adolescents are not generally caused by discretely localized brain damage. Exposure to alcohol and other toxins in utero can greatly impair brain development, as can phenylketonuria, severe malnutrition, or a chronic lack of social stimulation in early childhood. Head injury leading to a temporary loss of consciousness is a commonly overlooked source of minor, diffuse brain damage.

## REFERENCES

Cohen, N. J., & Squire, L. R. (1980). Preserved learning and retention of pattern-analyzing skill in amnesia: Dissociation of knowing how and knowing that. *Science, 210,* 207–211.

Davis, H. P., & Squire, L. R. (1984). Protein synthesis and memory: A review. *Psychological Bulletin, 96,* 518–559.

Kandel, E. R., & Schwartz, J. H. (1982). Molecular biology of learning: Modulation of transmitter release. *Science, 218,* 433–443.

Milner, B., Corkin, S., & Teuber, H. L. (1968). Further analysis of the hippocampal ammesic syndrome: 14-year follow-up study of H. M. *Neuropsychologia, 6,* 215–234.

Moscovitch, M. (1985). Memory from infancy to old age: Implications for theories of normal and pathological memory. *Annals of the New York Academy of Sciences, 444,* 78–96.

Uphouse, L. (1980). Reevaluation of mechanisms that mediate brain differences between enriched and impoverished animals. *Psychological Bulletin, 88,* 215–232.

Zola-Morgan, S., & Squire, L. R. (1985). Medial temporal lesions in monkeys impair memory on a variety of tasks sensitive to human amnesia. *Behavioral Neuroscience, 99,* 22–34.

JAMES W. KALAT
*North Carolina State University*

# BIOLOGICAL FACTORS AND SOCIAL CLASS

Biological factors seem to relate to social class in two distinguishable ways. First, they may predispose to membership in a given social class. Great controversy exists concerning genetic influences on intelligence, mental disorders, and other characteristics that correlate with social class. Historically, the eugenics movement argued for eugenic marriages and involuntary sterilization as ways to "race betterment" and to the reduction of the number of those seen as doomed by poor genetic endowment to low social class membership (Block & Dworkin, 1976). Second, people in various socioeconomic status (SES) groups may be differentially subject to environmentally based biological insults. Thus, low SES may impair biological functioning (e.g., Birch & Gussow, 1970).

## Biological Predispositions to Social Class

Herrnstein (1971, 1973) argued that our society is and will increasingly become a meritocracy, in which social status derives from genetically based intelligence. His position may be summarized in a logical syllogism in which the premises that people's intelligence, as measured by IQ tests, is partly inherited, and that social standing in our society depends partly on intelligence, lead to the conclusion that social standing in our society reflects inherited (biological) factors. Herrnstein cited a variety of data in support of the two premises. Further, he suggested that as our society becomes more egalitarian, individual differences in intelligence would be based even more on genetic differences. As a result, social classes will come even more to rest on genetic differences, and the genetically weaker lower classes will increasingly be unable to compete for success (Herrnstein, 1973).

Herrnstein's position evoked a storm of criticism. Critics contended that IQ tests may not measure actual intelligence; that studies vary widely in estimating genetic influences on intelligence; and that many studies have serious methodological flaws. Thus, heretability of IQ is actually unknown and may be much lower than Herrnstein proposed. Critics also stated that the correlation between IQ and social status may rest largely on the correlation between IQ and education; that improvement in environmental conditions might raise overall intelligence to an extent that no group would be left out; that Herrnstein did not accurately summarize past research; and that many factors other than IQ, including motivation and personality, contribute to success.

Herrnstein overstated his position; many of the previously mentioned criticisms are well taken. Unfortunately, arguments similar to those of Herrnstein's, but without supporting data, were used by the eugenics movement, making the issue emotional and political rather than scientific (Block & Dworkin, 1976).

Biological factors, including genetic ones, are often involved in serious mental disorders such as schizophrenia. The often found relationship between serious mental disorders and lower socioeconomic group membership may be partially explained by the "drift" hypothesis: such disorders may reduce affected individuals' economic earnings to the extent that they drift toward poverty. Onset of a serious mental disorder prior to the establishment of a career is indeed correlated with lower socioeconomic achievement (Kessler, Price, & Wertman, 1985), and biological factors frequently contribute to early onset.

## Social Class and Biological Insults

Low social class status and poverty conditions have important effects on human growth and development. In a summary of research, Birch and Gussow (1970) reported that low social class was associated with a variety of deleterious physical effects, which in turn impaired intellectual and other functioning in school and other settings.

Some of their findings may briefly be summarized: (1) Incidence of obstetric and perinatal complications in general and of prematurity and low birth weight in particular is higher in low-SES groups, particularly among blacks. (2) Prematurity and other perinatal complications interact with social class; middle- or high-SES environments can compensate for the potentially adverse effects of such complications, whereas low-SES environments exacerbate them. (3) Prematurity, again particularly in lower SES levels, is associated with specific learning and behavioral problems that interfere with school performance over and above effects on IQ. (4) Malnutrition is more common among lower SES pregnant women and children. Recent research (e.g., Brody & Brody, 1976) generally supports Birch and Gussow's (1970) summary, but it also emphasizes the role of interactions between predisposing biolog-

ically based causes of handicapping conditions and subsequent home environment (e.g., Sameroff & Chandler, 1975).

The relationship between low social class and biologically based impairments led Birch and Gussow (1970) to propose that a cycle of poverty transmitted environmentally based biological inadequacies from one generation to another. The factors include poor maternal health, poor nutrition and growth, infant and child malnutrition, illness, and poor medical care. Such factors increase the risk of school failure and subsequent underemployment resulting in poverty. This in turn increases the risk to mothers and children in the next generation. For a summary of research on SES-related factors that may adversely affect biological functioning see Brown (1986).

## REFERENCES

Birch, H. G., & Gussow, J. D. (1970). *Disadvantaged children: Health, nutrition, and school failure.* New York: Harcourt, Brace, & World.

Block, N. J., & Dworkin, G. (Eds.). (1976). *The IQ controversy.* New York: Pantheon.

Brody, E. B., & Brody, N. (1976). *Intelligence: Nature, determinants, and consequences.* New York: Academic.

Brown, R. T. (1986). Etiology and development of exceptionality. In R. T. Brown & C. R. Reynolds (Eds.), *Psychological perspectives on childhood exceptionality* (pp. 181–229). New York: Wiley.

Herrnstein, R. J. (1971, Sept.) IQ. *Atlantic Monthly,* 43–64.

Herrnstein, R. J. (1973). *IQ in the meritocracy.* Boston: Little, Brown.

Kessler, R., Price, R., & Wertman, C. (1985). Social factors in psychopathology: Stress, social support and coping processes. *Annual Review of Psychology, 36,* 531–572.

Sameroff, A. J., & Chandler. M. J. (1975). Reproductive risk and the continuum of caretaking casualty. In F. D. Horowitz, M. Hetherington, S. Scarr-Salapatek, & G. Siegel (Eds.), *Review of child development research. Vol. 4* (pp. 187–244). Chicago: University of Chicago Press.

ROBERT T. BROWN
LEE ANDERSON JACKSON, JR.
*University of North Carolina,
Wilmington*

**EARLY EXPERIENCE AND CRITICAL PERIODS
ETIOLOGY
LOW BIRTH WEIGHT INFANTS
PREMATURITY/PRETERM**

## BIRCH, HERBERT G. (1918–1973)

Herbert G. Birch was born in New York City on April 21, 1918. He graduated from New York University (NYU) in 1939, and received the PhD degree in psychology in 1944.

In 1960 Birch received the MD degree from the New York College of Medicine. He served as a research associate at the Yerkes Laboratories for Primate Biology from 1944 to 1946, as an instructor in psychology at NYU the next year, and as an assistant and associate professor at the City College of New York from 1947 to 1955. For the following 2 years, Birch was research associate at Bellevue Medical Center in New York City. From the time he received the MD degree in 1960 until his death, he was a member of the faculty of the Albert Einstein College of Medicine in New York City, first as an associate research professor and then as a full professor of pediatrics and director of the Center for Normal and Aberrant Behavioral Development. Concurrently, he was professor of psychology and education at the Ferkauf Graduate School of Humanities and Social Sciences, Yeshiva University.

An internationally known researcher in child development and brain injury, Birch was the author of 200 articles and coauthor of six books, the latter including *Brain Damage in Children* (1964), *Disadvantaged Children: Health, Nutrition, and School Failure* (1970), and *Children with Cerebral Dysfunction* (1971). He served in an editorial capacity for a number of journals, including the *Journal of Special Education*, the *American Journal of Mental Deficiency*, the *American Journal of Child Psychology and Human Development*, and the *International Journal of Mental Health*. In 1971 he received the Kennedy International Award for Scientific Research for outstanding scientific research contributing to the understanding and alleviation of mental retardation.

Birch died at his home in Suffern, New York, on February 4, 1973. In his eulogy, Dr. Leon Eisenberg said of Birch, "Those who knew Herbert Birch recognized that they were in the presence of authentic genius. His knowledge was encyclopedic; his intellect, prodigious; his productivity, unmatched." In May 1973, Birch was posthumously granted the Research Award of the American Association on Mental Deficiency.

## REFERENCES

Birch, H. G. (Ed.). (1964). *Brain damage in children*. Baltimore, MD: Williams & Wilkins.

Birch, H. G., & Diller, K. (1971). *Children with cerebral dysfunction*. New York: Grune & Stratton.

Brich, H. G., & Gussow, J. D. (1970). *Disadvantaged children: Health, nutrition and school failure*. New York: Grune & Stratton.

Eisenberg, L. (1971). Herbert Birch 1918–1973. *International Journal of Mental Health, 1*, 80–81.

PAUL IRVINE
*Katonah, New York*

Herbert G. Birch

# BIRCH, JACK W. (1915–    )

A native of Glassport, Pennsylvania, Jack W. Birch received a BS with a major in English and science and a minor in special education from California State College, Pennsylvania, in 1937. He received an MEd from Pennsylvania State University in 1941, and a PhD in psychology from the University of Pittsburgh in 1951. Birch has taught classes for educable mentally retarded children and was a psychologist and supervisor of special education. He is emeritus professor of education at the University of Pittsburgh where he specialized in special education and rehabilitation. Currently he is Belle Van Zuijlen Professor at the University of Utrecht in Holland.

Birch published over 120 articles and books. The topics include research about the mentally retarded, gifted, talented, speech handicapped, blind, deaf, and physically handicapped. Birch (1978) reviewed the process of mainstreaming in a national sample of school systems. He concluded that schools must expand individualized education and he made recommendations on how to implement mainstreaming effectively. He cited four essential conditions that must be met if mainstreaming is to work: (1) regular educators must receive orientation to what adaptations, if any, the inclusion of handicapped pupils require; (2) all teachers must learn to use the specialized instructional materials exceptional children may need; (3) an overt arrangement must let regular classroom teachers find help from special education teachers for pupils; and (4) regular class teachers must get immediate assistance (with no loss of face) if a crisis in class or individual management occurs.

For his contributions to special education and rehabilitation, Birch received an award from the Pennsylvania Federation for the Council for Exceptional Children. He also earned an award for service from the National Accreditation Council, Services to the Blind and Visually Handicapped. Birch was elected president of the Council for Exceptional Children and of the Foundation for Exceptional Children.

## REFERENCE

Birch, J. W. (1978). Mainstreaming that works in elementary and secondary schools. *Journal of Teacher Education, 29*, 18–21.

E. VALERIE HEWITT
*Texas A&M University*

## BIRTH INJURIES

Birth injuries are the traumatic injuries to the brain, skull, spinal cord, peripheral nerves, and muscle of the newborn that occasionally occur during the birth process. These injuries include cephalohematoma, skull fracture, central nervous system hemorrhage, spinal cord injury, peripheral nerve injury, bony injury, abdominal injury, cerebral palsy, and seizure disorders. The frequency of these birth injuries has greatly decreased with the declining use of high and midforceps, better monitoring during labor, and decreased vaginal breech deliveries (Brann, 1985).

Cephalohematoma usually refers to a benign traumatic lesion to the skull in which blood pools under the periosteum and is confined by suture boundaries. But 10 to 25% of all cephalohematomas are associated with an underlying skull fracture. These fractures rarely pose major problems but if depressed can result in compression of the skull (Menkes, 1984).

Central nervous system hemorrhage may be caused by mechanical trauma to the infant's brain during the birth process. The hemorrhage may occur in the subarachnoid space, the subdural space, or the dural space, or it may be intracerebral. The most common type of traumatic central nervous system hemorrhage is the subarachnoid hemorrhage resulting from tears in the meninges. Usually this is a benign condition unless it is associated with perinatal hypoxia or meningitis (Oxorn, 1986).

Subdural hemorrhage, now uncommon, may result in hydrocephalus and seizures. Intracerebral hemorrhage, one of the rarest types of traumatic central nervous system hemorrhage in the newborn, may result in increased intracranial pressure, hemiparesis, and convulsions. Hemorrhage into the dural space is also rare, but it usually results in massive hemorrhage and early neonatal death (Brann, 1985).

Traumatic spinal cord injuries are unusual. The most common sites of damage are the lower cervical and upper thoracic regions. These injuries can lead to stillbirth, respiratory failure, paralysis, or spasticity (Oxorn, 1986).

Peripheral nerve injuries can involve trauma to the brachial plexus, the phrenic nerve, the facial nerve, or the radial nerves. The nerve injuries are usually caused by traction or direct compression of the nerve itself. Trauma to the brachial plexus may cause muscle atrophy, contractures, and impaired limb growth (Menkes, 1984).

Trauma to the phrenic nerve may cause diaphragm paralysis and mimic congenital pulmonary or heart disease, resulting in long-term ventilatory support. Damage to the facial nerve results in weakness of the muscles to the affected side of the face, causing failure on the affected side of the mouth to move and the eyelid to close. Radial nerve injury may result in wrist drop and the inability to extend the fingers and the thumb (Menkes, 1984).

Traumatic bony injuries include fractures of the clavicle, humerus, and femur. Fracture of the clavicle is the most common bony injury; it usually occurs in association with shoulder dystocia. Fractures of the humerus and femur are rare and result from traumatic delivery (Oxorn, 1986).

Traumatic abdominal injuries are uncommon but they can have serious consequences. The traumatic abdominal injuries include hepatic or splenic rupture; they result from traumatic delivery. These injuries are usually life-threatening conditions (Oxorn, 1986).

Cerebral palsy is a chronic nonprogressive disorder of the pyramidal motor system resulting in lack of voluntary muscle control and coordination. The cause is uncertain but cerebral anoxia during the perinatal period has been associated with the resulting cerebral damage (Rosen, 1985).

There are several types of cerebral palsy: spastic, dyskinetic, ataxic, and mixed-type. Spastic cerebral palsy, the most common clinical type, is characterized by hypertonicity, uneven muscle tone, persistent primitive reflexes, lack of normal postural control, and incomplete spastic paralysis (Whaley & Wong, 1983).

Dyskinetic cerebral palsy is characterized by slow, writhing movements that involve the entire body. There is also high-frequency deafness associated with this type of cerebral palsy. Ataxic cerebral palsy is manifested by irregular muscle action and failure of muscle coordination. Mixed-type cerebral palsy is manifested by a combination of spasticity and atethosis, the slow writhing movements (Whaley & Wong, 1983).

Disabilities associated with cerebral palsy include mental retardation, seizure disorders, impaired behavioral and interpersonal relationships, and impairment of other senses. Approximately two-thirds of those diagnosed with cerebral palsy are also mentally retarded. About 50% of those with cerebral palsy have some type of seizure disorder. Those with impaired behavioral relationships usually have poor attention spans and hyperactive behavior. Impairment of the other senses include both visual and hearing defects (Batshaw & Perret, 1981). Cerebral palsy is a lifelong affliction. Most of those with the disorder live to adulthood but only 10% become self-supporting. The other 90% need support both medically and socially (Batshaw & Perret, 1981).

Seizure disorders may result from many causes, including perinatal asphyxia, intracranial hemorrhage, infection, congenital defects, metabolic disorders, drug withdrawal, inherited defects, and kernicterus. Perinatal asphyxia is the most frequent cause of seizures in the pre- and full-term infant. Perinatal asphyxia as the cause of neonatal seizures has the poorest prognosis. Approximately 60% of those infants with seizures caused by perinatal asphyxia have permanent neurologic sequelae and lifelong seizure disorders (Brann, 1985).

## REFERENCES

Batshaw, R. L., & Perret, Y. M. (1981). *Children with handicaps: A medical primer*. Baltimore, MD: Brookes.

Brann, A. W. (1985). Factors during neonatal life that influence brain disorders. In J. M. Freeman (Ed.), *Prenatal and perinatal factors associated with brain disorders* (NIH Publication No. 85-1149, pp. 263–358). Bethesda, MD: U.S. Department of Health and Human Services.

Menkes, J. H. (1984). Neurologic evaluation of the newborn infant. In M. E. Avery & H. W. Taeusch (Eds.), *Schaffer's diseases of the newborn* (5th ed., pp. 652–661). Philadelphia: Saunders.

Oxorn, H. (1986). *Human labor and birth* (5th ed.). Norwalk, CT: Appleton-Century-Crofts.

Rosen, M. G. (1985). Factors during labor and delivery that influence brain disorders. In J. M. Freeman (Ed.), *Prenatal and perinatal factors associated with brain disorders* (NIH Publication No. 85-1149, pp. 359–440). Bethesda, MD: U.S. Department of Health and Human Services.

Whaley, L. F., & Wong, D. L. (1983). *Nursing care of infants and children* (2nd ed.). St. Louis: Mosby.

ELIZABETH R. BAUERSCHMIDT
*University of North Carolina,
Wilmington*

ABSENCE SEIZURES
BRAIN DAMAGE
CEREBRAL PALSY
GRAND MAL SEIZURES

# BIRTH ORDER

Birth order refers to a child's ordinal position in the family. The results of research into the effects of birth order on such variables as personality, mental illness, intelligence, achievement, and occupational status are equivocal; but a wide variety of claims have been made regarding the consequences of ordinal position. Some of the reported relationships for personality and intellectual functioning will be presented along with serious challenges and possible explanations.

The study of birth order can be traced at least as far back as *English Men of Science* (1874), in which Galton reported that firstborns were considerably overrepresented among the scientists of his day. Alfred Adler (1958), also convinced of the influence of family position on development, wrote:

> Wherever I have studied adults, I have found impressions left on them from their early childhood and lasting forever. The position in the family leaves an indelible stamp upon the style of life. (p. 154)

Interest in birth order follows from recognition that family experience has a major impact on human development. The family is the child's first social unit, and ordinal position may significantly affect a child's environment and the dynamic interactions that are played out over childhood.

Each ordinal position is believed to be subject to different patterns of interaction; as a result, children within the same family have different social-learning experiences (Adler, 1958; Forer, 1976). The nature and consistency of these experiences may result in distinctive behavioral traits. For example, the amount of time that parents have available for a particular child is a function of birth order. Parents spend almost twice as much time in direct contact with firstborns as they do with succeeding children (White, Kaban, & Attanucci, 1979). Further, the older child in a family is accorded more opportunities to practice language skills and take responsibility for and teach younger siblings (Harris, 1973; Smith, 1984).

Harris (1973) describes the firstborn as being adult-civilized—the parents are more actively involved in nurturing and guiding this child. As subsequent children are added to the family, the parents spend less and less time in direct care, and older siblings assume more responsibility for child care. Younger children in the family are more likely to be peer-civilized. Therefore, the firstborn or only child would be expected to identify more closely with the parents and hold more traditional values than later-born children (Schacter, 1959; Sutton-Smith & Rosenburg, 1970).

Since different patterns of interaction accompany each ordinal position, children from the same family have different social-learning experiences. Differential patterns of reinforcement for certain behavior patterns may foster characteristic behavior traits such as greater leadership and independence among firstborn children and more dependence in later-borns (Schacter, 1959). Thus a social theory of personality development is proposed that emphasizes the interpersonal relationships that stem from the perceived ordinal position of a child.

Various personality profiles, though sometimes overlapping and inconsistent, have been suggested for each ordinal position. The proposed profiles follow.

**Firstborn.** Firstborns tend to exhibit higher standards of moral honesty, higher need for achievement, earlier social maturation, better work habits, and higher need for recognition and approval (Forer, 1976; Harris, 1973). Firstborns are also higher in leadership, independence, and sensitivity to stress (Sutton-Smith & Rosenberg, 1970).

**Secondborn.** Secondborns typically have good social skills, seek out group activities, and maintain better relationships in life than do firstborns. They also show more dependency behavior and seek more adult help and approval (Forer, 1976; McGurk & Lewis, 1972).

**Middleborn.** Middleborns, like secondborns, show better interpersonal skills and tend to express greater sensitivity to the feelings and needs of others (Falbo, 1981; Miller & Maruyama, 1976). Middle children generally have the fewest behavior problems, enjoy a healthier adjustment to life, and as adults experience less anxiety in new or threatening situations (Touliatos & Lindholm, 1980; Yannakis, 1976). They also show more concern for peer norms and consequently accept peer advice more readily (Harris, 1973).

**Lastborn.** The youngest child is more likely to be more dependent and peer oriented (Schacter, 1959). This birth order also has been associated with higher propensity to use of alcohol and cigarettes (Ernst & Angst, 1983).

**Onlyborn.** Only children have a tendency to be leaders rather than joiners and show considerable affinity for independent behavior (Falbo, 1981). Schacter (1959) reports that only children experience more fear and anxiety during adolescence and adulthood than laterborn children. Conventional wisdom that singletons are selfish, lonely, and uncooperative is clearly unsupported (Falbo, 1984).

Many factors may affect a child's perception of ordinal position and associated family dynamics. Sex of siblings and spacing are important, as is the status of adopted children and stepchildren. For example, Adler (1958) has suggested that the male child with all female siblings may place more emphasis on his masculinity. A secondborn might assume the responsibilities of a firstborn who is developmentally delayed. With adopted children or stepchildren, previous family interactional patterns may have consequences for adjustments to new ordinal positions. Forer (1976) believes that the child's adjustment will be better the younger he or she is at the time of transition, and the closer the match between former and current ordinal positions.

However, a sizable body of conflicting data and opinion casts serious doubt on the value of the birth order variable for understanding personality (Ernst & Angst, 1983; Schooler, 1972; Stagner & Katzoff, 1936). Ernst and Angst (1983) concluded their extensive analysis of birth order and personality by saying:

Birth order and sibship size do not have a strong impact on personality. The present investigation points instead to a broken home, an unfriendly educational style, and a premature disruption of relations with parents as concomitants of neuroticism, and to higher income and social class . . . and an undisturbed home as concomitants of higher achievement.

They do not deny that birth order may be significant for some individuals, but maintain that it has been overrated and pales in significance in comparison with other social variables.

The well-known confluence model of Zajono and Markus (1976) is important because it makes predictions concerning the relationship of birth order and intellectual ability. Their model suggests that the average intellectual environment (AIE) of the family predicts the intelligence of each child, where AIE is equal to the total intellectual level of the family divided by the number of family members. According to the model, in a family with two children spaced only a few years apart, the second child is expected to have a lower IQ. In a family where the spacing between first- and second-born exceeds 7 years, the prediction would be reversed. In addition to spacing, the model also considers the unique advantage of firstborns who learn from teaching their siblings. The model also predicts that children from father-absent families and twins should have lowered IQs, as will later-borns from larger families.

Unfortunately, the confluence model does not account for the consistently found inverse relationship between family size and intellectual performance. The impact of sibship size, though slight, is more accentuated as socioeconomic status declines and more pronounced on verbal than quantitative measures (Steelman, 1985). More important, it now appears that reported birth order effects are actually artifacts of sibship size or socioeconomic status; the birth order relationship is essentially random (Steelman, 1985). The only child represents an exception (scoring lower than predicted) to this inverse relationship.

Page and Grandon (1979) offer the admixture theory as an alternative interpretation of the reported correlations of birth order with intellectual functioning. They suggest that social class, race, and family size interact to determine birth order effects. Furthermore, their analysis indicates that social class and race are the dominant factors, while family size and birth order are actually negligible in their effects.

Serious doubt has been cast on the significance of birth order for both the intellectual and personality-social domains. The profiles associated with various ordinal positions must now be viewed with skepticism. Birth order at certain times and in some cultures has likely been a highly significant developmental variable. Where primogeniture has been important, the life experiences of firstborn males were vastly different from those of other siblings and were no doubt instrumental in promoting their success. Such extreme differences in expectations, socialization, and educational and economic opportunities no longer occur systematically in our society. It is therefore not likely that particular traits can be dependably related to birth order. At the very least, one should exercise extreme caution in interpreting birth order data. Birth order may have systematic effects on development, but the nature of extant research suggests that this variable is of little or no consequence in predicting either personality or intellectual functioning.

## REFERENCES

Adler, A. (1958). *What life should mean to you.* New York: Capricorn.

Ernst, C., & Angst, J. (1983). *Birth order: Its influence on personality.* Berlin: Springer-Verlag.

Falbo, T. (1981). Relationships between birth category, achievement, and interpersonal orientation. *Journal of Personality & Social Psychology, 41,* 121–131.

Falbo, T. (Ed.). (1984). *The single child family.* New York: Guilford.

Forer, L. K. (1976). *The birth order factor.* New York: McKay.

Galton, F. (1874). *English men of science.* London: Macmillan.

Harris, I. D. (1973). Differences in cognitive style and birth order. In J. C. Westman (Ed.), *Individual differences in children* (pp. 199–210). New York: Wiley.

McGurk, H., & Lewis, M. (1972). Birth order: A phenomenon in search of an explanation. *Developmental Psychology, 7,* 366.

Miller, N., & Maruyama, G. (1976). Ordinal position and peer popularity. *Journal of Personality & Social Psychology, 33,* 123–131.

Page, E. B., & Grandon, G. M. (1979). Family configuration and mental ability: Two theories contrasted with U.S. data. *American Educational Research Journal, 16,* 257–272.

Rogers, J. L. (1984). Confluence effects: Not here, not now! *Developmental Psychology, 20,* 321–331.

Schacter, S. (1959). *The psychology of affiliation.* Stanford, CA: Stanford University Press.

Schooler, C. (1972). Birth order effects: Not here, not now. *Psychological Bulletin, 78,* 161–175.

Smith, T. (1984). School grades and responsibility for younger siblings: An empirical study of the teaching function. *American Sociological Review, 49,* 248–261.

Stagner, R., & Katzoff, E. T. (1936). Personality as related to birth order and family size. *Journal of Applied Psychology, 20,* 340–346.

Steelman, L. C. (1985). A tale of two variables: A review of the intellectual consequences of sibship size and birth order. *Review of Educational Research, 55,* 353–386.

Sutton-Smith, B., & Rosenberg, B. G. (1970). *The sibling.* New York: Holt, Rinehart, & Winston.

Touliatos, J., & Lindholm, B. W. (1980). Birth order, family size, and children's mental health. *Psychological Reports, 46,* 1097–1098.

White, B. L., Kaban, B. T., & Attanucci, J. S. (1979). *The origins of human competence.* Lexington, MA: Heath.

Yiannakis, A. (1976). Birth order and preference for dangerous sports among males. *Research Quarterly, 47,* 62–67.

Zajonc, R. B., & Markus, G. B. (1975). Birth order and intellectual development. *Psychological Review, 82,* 74–88.

JAMES M. APPLEFIELD
*University of North Carolina,*
*Wilmington*

PERSONALITY ASSESSMENT
SOCIOECONOMIC STATUS
TEMPERAMENT

## BIRTH TRAUMA

According to Freudian psychodynamic theory, early traumatic and painful events produce memories that, when repressed into the unconscious, may affect later life. Otto Rank (1929) elaborated on the proposition that birth is itself traumatic: It suddenly and painfully thrusts the infant from the warm secure womb into a cold, hostile, and frustrating world. When frustrated later in life, people may in some ways behave as though they wished to return to the womb.

More recently, Leboyer (1975) has argued that birth should be as gentle as possible for both mother and infant. In his birthing technique, the shock of birth is reduced by, among other things, keeping light and noise levels in the delivery room low. At birth, the newborn is placed on the mother's breast, massaged to decrease initial crying, and placed in a warm bath. The father attends and assists in handling the newborn.

Although some physicians initially suggested that Leboyer's method put both newborn and mother at risk, research indicates that the procedure is safe. Relative to those conventionally delivered, Leboyer infants evidence normal physiological functioning (Kliot & Silverstein, 1984) and no differences in either maternal or infant morbidity or infant behavior (Nelson et al., 1980). At present, with the exception of shorter active labors among mothers expecting a Leboyer delivery (Nelson et al., 1980), advantages of the method appear more psychological than physiological (Grover, 1984). Indeed, evidence of long-term consequences of both conventional and Leboyer births are notably lacking, and the concept of birth trauma, particularly the Rankian version, is largely in disrepute.

## REFERENCES

Grover, J. W. (1984). Leboyer and obstetric practice. *New York State Journal of Medicine, 84,* 158–159.

Kliot, D., & Silverstein, L. (1984). Changing maternal and newborn care. *New York State Journal of Medicine, 84,* 169–174.

Leboyer, F. (1975). *Birth without violence.* New York: Knopf.

Nelson, N. M., Enkin, M. W., Saigal, S., Bennett, K. J., Milner, R., & Sackett, D. L. (1980). A randomized clinical trial of the Leboyer approach to childbirth. *New England Journal of Medicine, 302,* 655–60.

Rank, O. (1929). *The trauma of birth.* New York: Harcourt, Brace.

ROBERT T. BROWN
SHIRLEY PARKER WELLS
*University of North Carolina,
Wilmington*

## BIRTH INJURIES

## BLATT, BURTON (1927–1985)

Burton Blatt, widely known as a leader in the movement for deinstitutionalization of people with mental retardation, began his professional career as a special class teacher in the public schools of New York City. After earning the doctorate in special education at Pennsylvania State University in 1956, he served on the faculties of Southern Connecticut State College and Boston University before joining the faculty of Syracuse University in 1969, where he served as dean of the School of Education from 1976 until his death in 1985.

In 1971 he formed the Center on Human Policy at Syracuse University, devoted to the study and promotion of open settings for people with mental retardation and other disabilities. His work was characterized by an inspirational humanism that contributed greatly to his effectiveness as a leader.

### REFERENCES

Blatt, B. (1984). Biography in autobiography. In B. Blatt & R. J. Morris (Eds.), *Perspectives in special education: Personal orientations* (pp. 263–307). Glenview, IL: Scott, Foresman.

Blatt, B., & Kaplan, F. (1966). *Christmas in purgatory: A photographic essay on mental retardation* (2nd ed.). Boston: Allyn & Bacon.

Semmel, M. I. (1985). In memoriam: Burton Blatt, 1927–1985. *Exceptional Children, 52,* 102.

PAUL IRVINE
*Katonah, New York*

## BLIND

Blind is a term used to refer to those students who have either no vision or, at most, light perception (the ability to tell light from dark) but no light projection (the ability to identify the direction from which light comes) (Faye, 1970; Colenbrander, 1977). Educationally, one who is

blind learns primarily through tactual, auditory, and kinesthetic experiences, without the use of vision. The legal term for blindness is corrected visual acuity of 20/200 or less in the better eye and/or field of vision of 20 degrees or less (Goble, 1984). Individuals classified as blind under this legal definition receive certain benefits such as special educational materials and an extra income tax deduction.

The degree to which blindness or any type of visual impairment affects development depends on the type of visual loss, the severity of the loss, the age of onset, intellectual abilities, and environmental experiences. Lack of vision results in delays or limitations in motor, cognitive, and social development.

Blind children are limited in their ability to get about. Without visual input, the blind infant is not motivated to reach and move toward interesting objects in the environment. As soon as the blind infant finds it exciting to hear sounds, he or she will begin to reach and move toward the objects in the environment that produce sound. This does not occur for several months, since hearing sound does not motivate movement toward objects as soon as seeing objects (Fraiberg, 1977). As a result of the limitation in mobility, an older blind student cannot change his or her surroundings and activities as freely as a sighted one. Blind students, therefore, are dependent on assistance from others; this affects their attitudes and social relationships (Lowenfeld, 1981).

Cognitively, blind children are restricted in their range and variety of experiences. They cannot perceive objects in the environment that are beyond their grasp, including those that are too large or too small, or those that are moving. Blind children who use their tactual sense cannot directly observe such objects as the sun, the moon, and the clouds. Large buildings, mountains, and rivers cannot be observed as a whole. Other examples of objects that are inaccessible are flies, ants, butterflies, and spider webs: they are too fragile. Other objects such as burning wood or boiling water, cannot be touched under certain circumstances. Hearing, while it gives clues such as distance and direction, does not give a concrete idea of an object. If a blind child hears a bird, he or she can learn its sound and identify its location, but cannot perceive its shape, size, or other physical characteristics (Lowenfeld, 1981).

Socially, blind children are limited in interaction with the environment. They cannot see facial expressions of parents, teachers, and peers; they cannot model appropriate social behavior through imitation; and sometimes they are unaware of the presence of others unless a sound is made. While touch provides direct information, it is often socially unacceptable (Division for the Visually Handicapped, Council for Exceptional Children, 1982).

Historically, academically oriented blind and low-vision students have been mainstreamed successfully into regular classes. They obtain their specialized skills in a variety of placement options. These include

1. *Itinerant Program.* The blind or low-vision student is enrolled in the regular class in the neighborhood school and an itinerant teacher who travels from school to school provides direct instruction and serves as a consultant to the regular teachers several times a week.

2. *Resource Room Program.* The blind or low-vision student is enrolled in the regular class in a school within the district or town and a resource room teacher is housed in the school and is readily available to work with the student on a daily basis at regularly scheduled times and when needed.

3. *Special Class.* The blind or low-vision student is enrolled in a self-contained class in a public or private school setting for most of the day. Usually, those students with multiple impairments in addition to a visual handicap are placed in this type of setting.

4. *Residential School.* The blind or low-vision student enrolled in this placement usually has additional disabilities and/or cannot be cared for adequately at home. Sometimes blind students attend residential schools for short periods of time to develop intensive skills in such areas as orientation and mobility, vocational training, and technology (Cartwright, Cartwright, & Ward, 1981).

The unique curriculum for blind students includes reading and writing braille; typing; listening skills using human and synthetic speech; map and chart reading; domestic skills; orientation and mobility; career education; and instruction in the use of special aids and equipment such as the Cranmer abacus, talking calculators, cassette tape recorders, electronic reading machines, and other hardware and software adaptations that access computers (Heward & Orlansky, 1984).

Major resources relevant to blind students include:

American Association of Education and Rehabilitation for Blind and Visually Impaired, Alexandria, VA

American Council of the Blind, Washington, DC

American Foundation for the Blind, New York City

American Printing House for the Blind, Louisville, KY

Division for the Visually Handicapped, Council for Exceptional Children, Reston, VA

Howe Press, Perkins School for the Blind, Watertown, MA

National Association for Parents of the Visually Impaired, Austin, TX

National Federation of the Blind, Baltimore, MD

National Library Service, Division for the Blind and Physically Handicapped, Washington, DC

Recording for the Blind, Inc., Princeton, NJ.

## REFERENCES

Cartwright, G. P., Cartwright, C. A., & Ward, M. (1981). *Educating special learners.* Belmont, CA: Wadsworth.

Colenbrander, A. (1977). Dimensions of visual performance. *Archives of American Academy of Ophthalmology, 83,* 332–337.

Division for the Visually Handicapped, Council for Exceptional Children. (1982). *Visual impairments fact sheet.* Reston, VA: ERIC Clearinghouse on Handicapped and Gifted Children.

Faye, E. E. (1970). *The low vision patient.* New York: Grune & Stratton.

Fraiberg, S. (1977). *Insights from the blind.* New York: Basic Books.

Goble, J. L. (1984). *Visual disorders in the handicapped child.* New York: Marcel Dekker.

Heward, W. L., & Orlansky, M. D. (1984). *Exceptional children.* Columbus, OH: Merrill.

Lowenfeld, B. (1981). *Berthold Lowenfeld on blindness and blind people.* NY: American Foundation for the Blind.

ROSANNE K. SILBERMAN
*Hunter College, City University of New York*

**AMERICAN PRINTING HOUSE FOR THE BLIND**
**BLINDISMS**
**BRAILLE**
**ELECTRONIC TRAVEL AIDS**

## BLIND INFANTS

An increase in the birth of blind infants can be related to four major factors: (1) prematurity; (2) family history of a visual defect; (3) infection during pregnancy; and (4) difficult or assisted labor (Ellingham et al., 1976). With increasing medical advances in saving premature infants, the incidence of retinopathy of prematurity (previously termed retrolental fibroplasia) is rising (Morse & Trief, 1985). In fact, it is estimated that by 1990 there will be somewhere between 12,000 and 19,000 visually impaired preschoolers (up to 5 years of age) (Hill et al., 1984).

The increase of visually impaired infants demands focused attention toward early intervention efforts. Unfortunately, many of the infants born prematurely are also born with deafness, mental retardation, and blindness (Morse & Trief, 1985). Programs for both normally developing blind infants and multiply handicapped infants require intervention in areas including motor, sensory, communication, and conceptual development. Parent involvement is a critical component in the early intervention of blind infants (Moore, 1984). As an example, Ferrell (1985) developed a training handbook for parents of visually impaired and multiply handicapped children, describing several intervention strategies. Research is clearly needed in this area because much of what we know about the development of blind infants is currently based on research efforts from the 1960s (Fraiberg, 1977).

## REFERENCES

Ellingham, T., Silva, P., Buckfield, P., & Clarkson, J. (1976). Neonatal at risk factors, visual defects and the preschool child: A report from the Queen Mary Hospital multidisciplinary child development study. *New Zealand Medical Journal, 83*, 74–77.

Ferrell, K. (1985). *Reach out and teach: Meeting the training needs of parents of visually and multiply handicapped young children.* New York: American Foundation for the Blind.

Fraiberg, S. (1977). *Insights from the blind.* New York: Basic Books.

Hill, E., Rosen, S., Correa, V., & Langley, M. B. (1984). Preschool orientation and mobility: An expanded definition. *Education of the Visually Handicapped, 16*, 58–72.

Moore, S. (1984). The need for programs and services for visually handicapped infants. *Education of the Visually Handicapped, 16*, 48–57.

Morse, A., & Trief, E. (1985). Diagnosis and evaluation of visual dysfunction in premature infants with low birth weight. *Journal of Visual Impairment and Blindness, 79*, 248–251.

VIVIAN I. CORREA
*University of Florida*

## BLIND
## VISUAL IMPAIRMENT

# BLINDISMS

Blindisms is a term used to describe a group of simple or complex repetitive behaviors that involve both small movements of various parts of the body, such as eye rubbing, head turning, and hand flapping, and large body movements such as rocking or swaying (Warren, 1984). This term is actually a misnomer, since these behaviors occur in other types of children as well, including those who are autistic, retarded, and even normal. More appropriate terms that do not single out blind children are stereotypic behaviors or mannerisms.

One of the most common mannerisms in blind children is pressing on one or both eyes. Pressure on the eyeball results in a pleasurable sensation to the child, i.e., the child may find it entertaining and relaxing. The most active eye pressers are children with retinal disorders (Scott, Jan, & Freeman, 1985). Children who are continual eye pressers tend to have deeply depressed eyes and black circles around their eyes; this detracts from their overall appearance. Another common mannerism, not considered by parents to be unusual when it first develops, is rocking. Whereas sighted children find other pleasurable activities

to replace rocking, blind children tend to persevere in this activity.

Mannerisms frequently occurring in children with low vision, particularly those with rubella, are light gazing at the sun or fluorescent lights and waving of fingers in front of their eyes against the lights. Many become so involved in these behaviors that it is extremely difficult to direct their attention to more appropriate activities within the environment (Scott, Jan, & Freeman, 1985).

There are several theories regarding the causes of stereotypic behaviors in blind children. One of them is that these behaviors are efforts to increase the level of sensory stimulation (Burlingham, 1967; Curson, 1979; Scott et al., 1985). It has also been suggested that stereotypic repetitive behaviors are pleasurable because of the motor discharge (Burlingham, 1965). Another theory related to cause of stereotypic behaviors is that the behaviors are a result of social rather than sensory deprivation (Warren, 1984). However, according to Webster (1983), one cannot separate the sensory stimulation factor from the social stimulation factor in the case of blind infants. Williams (1978) has indicated that mobility plays a role in inhibiting stereotypic behavior patterns, and that lack of early mobility causes these behaviors to perpetuate.

Stereotypic behaviors tend to increase in both sighted and blind children when they are under stress. However, these repetitive patterns are fewer, and more intensely practiced, in blind children (Warren, 1984). They continue because they become self-reinforcing and therefore self-sustaining (Eichel, 1979). Research studies have shown that behavior modification approaches can reduce or eliminate some stereotypic behaviors in visually handicapped children (Caetano & Kaufman, 1975; Miller & Miller, 1976; Williams, 1978).

Parents and teachers are advised to work together to help blind and low-vision children develop positive exploratory and mobile behaviors. These efforts will enable this population to become more socially accepted by their peers, to attend more to the outside environment, and to prevent possible physiologic damage caused by excessive eye poking or rubbing, or head banging (Warren, 1984).

## REFERENCES

Burlingham, D. (1965). Some problems of ego development in blind children. *Psychoanalytic Study of the Child, 20*, 194–208.

Burlingham, D. (1967). Developmental considerations in the occupations of the blind. *Psychoanalytic Study of the Child, 22*, 187–198.

Caetano, A. P., & Kaufman, J. M. (1975). Reduction of rocking mannerisms in two blind children. *Education of the Visually Handicapped, 7*, 101–105.

Curson, A. (1979). The blind nursery school child. *Psychoanalytic Study of the Child, 34*, 51–83.

Eichel, V. J. (1979). A taxonomy for mannerisms of blind children. *Journal of Visual Impairment and Blindness, 72*, 125–130.

Jan, J. E., Freeman, R. D., & Scott, E. P. (1977). *Visual impairment in children and adolescents.* New York: Grune & Stratton.

Miller, B. S., & Miller, W. H. (1976). Extinguishing "blindisms": A paradigm for intervention. *Education of the Visually Handicapped, 8,* 6–15.

Scott, E. P., Jan, J. E., & Freeman, R. D. (1985). *Can't your child see?* Austin, TX: Pro-Ed.

Smith, M. A., Chethik, M., & Adelson, E. (1969). Differential assessments of "blindisms." *American Journal of Orthopsychiatry, 39,* 807–817.

Warren, D. H. (1984). *Blindness and early childhood development.* New York: American Foundation for the Blind.

Webster, R. (1983). What—no blindisms in African blind children? *Imfama, 7,* 16–18.

Williams, C. E. (1978). Strategies of intervention with the profoundly retarded visually-handicapped child: A brief report of a study of stereotypy. *Occasional Papers of the British Psychological Society, 2,* 68–72.

ROSANNE K. SILBERMAN
*Hunter College, City University
of New York*

**BLIND
SELF-STIMULATION
VISUAL IMPAIRMENT
VISUAL TRAINING**

## BLIND LEARNING APTITUDE TEST (BLAT)

The Blind Learning Aptitude Test (BLAT) was developed in 1969 by T. Ernest Newland as a nonverbal, individually administered multiple aptitude battery for use with blind and partially sighted children and adolescents. The age range of BLAT is from 6 to 20 years, but it is most often recommended for use between the ages of 6 and 12. The test was designed to objectively measure learning process rather than learning product in blind children by minimizing the influence of experiences to which the sighted child is subjected. In fact, the majority of the items were taken from tests designed to minimize cultural bias. The BLAT items are presented in an embossed format involving dots and lines similar to those used in braille, however, no knowledge of braille is required to complete the test. The 61 tactile stimulus items measure abilities such as discrimination, generalization, and sequencing. Standardized on a sample of 961 blind students in a number of residential and day schools for the blind across the United States, the author reports reliability coefficients ranging from 0.86 to 0.93. The BLAT yields a learning aptitude test quotient with a mean of 100 and a standard deviation of 15 points, making it similar to the IQ. The BLAT also yields a learning aptitude age, which is defined as the midpoint of an age range for a given score. Although it

was welcomed as an alternative to traditional tests for the blind on its development in 1969, the BLAT is not widely used in education or research today.

### REFERENCES

Buros, O. K. (1978). *The eighth mental measurements yearbook.* Highland Park, NJ: Publisher: Buros Foundation.

Hecht, P. J., & Newland, T. E. (1965). Learning potential and learning achievement of educationally blind third–eighth graders in a residential school. *International Journal of Education of the Blind, 15,* 33.

Newland, T. E. (1971). *Manual for the Blind Learning Aptitude Test: Experimental edition.* Urbana, IL: Author.

LIZANNE DESTEFANO
*University of Illinois,
Ubana-Champaign*

**BLIND
VISUAL IMPAIRMENT
VISUAL PERCEPTION AND DISCRIMINATION**

## BLISSYMBOLS

Blissymbols, or Blissymbolics, is a graphic symbol system that was originally created by Charles K. Bliss in 1942 (Bliss, 1965). Blissymbols consist of 100 meaningful picture symbols that are combined in a logical manner for communication. Not simply a set of symbols, Blissymbolics is a language that has its own linguistic rule system. Blissymbolics was originally developed to be a language that could be easily learned and understood for international communication. In 1971, Blissymbols were first used as an augmentative communication symbol system for nonspeaking handicapped persons at the Ontario Crippled Children's Center in Toronto, Canada (Silverman, McNaughton, & Kates, 1978). Currently, Blissymbolics is one of many picture graphic symbol systems that have been developed for use with augmentative communication systems.

In Blissymbolics, the symbols are designed to depict the semantic concepts they represent. The meaning of the symbol can be pictographic, ideographic, or arbitrary (Figure 1). Pictographic symbols physically look like the concept they represent. Ideographic symbols represent feelings or ideas about a concept. Arbitrary symbols are

House   Woman        Happy   Sad           Plural  Action
   Pictographic          Ideographic              Arbitrary

Figure 1.   Categories of Blissymbol concept representation.

usually used only as semantic grammatical markers. Some symbols are mixed, with one or more categories of meaning combined.

By combining the basic 100 symbols together, many word concepts can be communicated. For example, the symbols for *happy* and *thing* are combined to create *toy*, a thing that can make someone happy (Figure 2).

**thing marker**    **Happy**    **Toy**

Figure 2.   Combining Blissymbols to create new word concepts.

Blissymbolics uses semantic indicators to convey complex linguistic concepts such as plurality, action, number, and tense. In addition, the meaning of a symbol can change through changes in symbol size, orientation, position, or by adding pointers. The Blissymbolics Communication Institute (BCI), in Toronto, Canada, has developed an international standardized vocabulary of Blissymbols that is published in a user's dictionary (Hehner, 1980). New symbols are added after they are approved by BCI. Symbols that are newly created but are not approved should be designated with the combined symbol until they are approved (Figure 3).

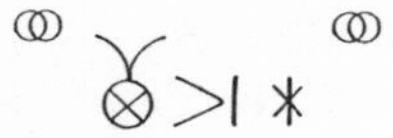

**Spaceship**
(combine) flying plane to (the) stars (combine)

Figure 3.   Use of the combined symbol to create new words.

Many studies have documented the effectiveness of using Blissymbolics with nonspeaking, physically handicapped persons (Silverman, McNaughton, & Kates, 1978). In addition, they have been used with the mentally retarded, the hearing impaired, and adults with aphasia. Blissymbols are best suited for persons who are unable to use traditional written language as an alternative communication method but are capable of learning large vocabularies.

**REFERENCES**

Bliss, C. K. (1965). *Semantography-Blissymbolics*. Sydney, Australia: Semantography.

Hehner, B. (1980). *Blissymbols for use*. Toronto, Canada: Blissymbolics Communication Institute.

Silverman, F., McNaughton, S., & Kates, B. (1978). *Handbook of Blissymbolics*. Toronto, Canada: Blissymbolics Communications Institute.

SHARON L. GLENNEN
*Pennsylvania State University*

**ALTERNATIVE COMMUNICATION METHODS IN SPECIAL EDUCATION**
**AUGMENTATIVE COMMUNICATION SYSTEMS**

## BLOOM, BENJAMIN S. (1913–    )

Benjamin S. Bloom, currently a Charles H. Swift distinguished service professor emeritus of education at the University of Chicago, earned his PhD in 1942 from the University of Chicago. He is noted for his work with taxonomies of educational objectives, the impact of environment and heredity on intelligence, and mastery learning.

Bloom's *Taxonomy of Educational Objectives* (1956) classifies cognitive behaviors in a hierarchy of domains: knowledge, comprehension, application, analysis, synthesis, and evaluation. The taxonomy provides a framework for viewing the educational process, classifies goals of the educational system, and specifies objectives for learning experiences.

Prior to Bloom's (1964) book, *Stability and Change in Human Characteristics*, it was assumed that learning occurred in a regular, ascending line. His research refuted that belief by showing that intelligence is a developing function and that the stability of measured intelligence increases with age. Correlational data and the absolute scale of intelligence development showed that, in terms of intelligence measured at age 17, about 50% of the development of IQ takes place before age 4 while 80% of the development of adult IQ takes place by age 8. Thus educators began to focus more on the early years of development since Bloom found that changes in the relevant environmental factors have the greatest effect on a specific characteristic in its most rapid period of change.

Bloom also has attempted to identify highly favorable learning conditions that can be made available to most learners. He has found that mastery learning, which includes detailed trial tests and a variety of feedback correctives, can be used with groups of students to improve their levels of learning (Brandt, 1979). The process of trial test/feedback correctives helps students to discover their learning errors and to correct them.

**REFERENCES**

Bloom, B. S. (Ed.). (1956). *Taxonomy of educational objectives. The classification of educational goals—Handbook I, cognitive domain*. New York: McKay.

Bloom, B. S. (1964). *Stability and change in human characteristics.* New York: Wiley.

Brandt, R. (1979). A conversation with Benjamin Bloom. *Educational Leadership, 37*(2), 157–161.

ANN E. LUPKOWSKI
*Texas A&M University*

## BOBATH METHOD

Karel Bobath, a neuropsychiatrist, and Berta Bobath, a physiotherapist, developed an assessment and treatment program in England based on central nervous system (CNS) functioning. Their approach focuses on the whole child and is referred to as neurodevelopmental treatment (NDT).

Central nervous system functioning is regarded as the basis of all motor functioning. It provides the individual with the ability to perform all posture and movement tasks, from the most simple to the most highly integrated complex ones. The individual is able to maintain the head and trunk in a mid-line or balanced position while pursuing a motor task because of the working of the CNS.

If for some reason—as in cerebral palsy, other developmentally delaying conditions of childhood, or stroke—the working of the CNS is impaired, a therapist trained to use the NDT method would work with the person to improve the quality of tone and movement. Problems related to tone, posture, and fluidity of movement are the focus of the therapy.

Treatment has two basic goals: (1) the inhibition of primitive and postural reflexes that are abnormally present, and (2) the facilitation of insufficiently developed normal postural reactions. All therapy is developmentally oriented and is determined by the unique, specific needs of the individual.

Through therapy the individual experiences the feeling of more normal movement patterns and works to maintain these new, more efficient motor patterns. The treatment is dynamic in that there is interaction as the therapist makes constant changes in handling to match the individual's postural and movement responses.

It is the normal postural reflex mechanism that provides the basis for the individual to exhibit normal postural tone and variety in movement patterns. Through the process of co-contraction, the trunk and head (proximal parts) are stabilized, thus allowing for more finitely graded motor activity to be performed by the arms, hands, legs, and feet (distal parts). It is important for the individual to develop a more normal postural reflex mechanism so that efficient, purposeful actions can increase. The righting and equilibrium reactions are the bases of the normal postural reflex mechanism.

A major emphasis of NDT when employed with children is that parents and teachers be taught appropriate handling techniques by the therapist with the physician's approval. For carryover and integration of new skills to occur, the same handling procedures used by the therapist should be used at home and in the classroom.

### REFERENCES

Bobath, K. (1980). *A neurophysiological basis for the treatment of cerebral palsy.* Philadelphia: Lippincott.

Levitt, S. (1982). *Treatment of cerebral palsy and motor delay.* Oxford, England: Blackwell Scientific.

Morrison, D., Pothier, P., & Horr, K. (1978). *Sensory-motor dysfunction and therapy in infancy and early childhood,* Springfield, IL: Thomas.

Scherzer, A., & Tscharnuter, I. *Early diagnosis and therapy in cerebral palsy.* New York: Marcel Dekker.

MARY K. DYKES
*University of Florida*

CEREBRAL PALSY
OCCUPATIONAL THERAPY
PHYSICAL THERAPY

## BODER TEST OF READING-SPELLING PATTERNS

The Boder Test of Reading-Spelling Patterns (the Boder Test) is subtitled "A diagnostic test for subtypes of reading disability," a designation that reflects the medical orientation of the test's senior author and the need for a typology of dyslexia. Boder and Jarrico (1982), in devising the Boder Test, relied on several assumptions about children and about reading.

The first assumption is that each dyslexic reader has a distinctive pattern of cognitive strengths and weaknesses across the two primary factors of the reading process: the visual gestalt and the auditory analytic functions. In Boder's scheme, the former underlies the development of a sight vocabulary and the latter the development of phonic word analysis or word attack. The Boder Test thus gives the following as its operational definition of developmental dyslexia:

> A reading disability in which the reading and spelling performance gives evidence of cognitive deficits in either the visual gestalt function or auditory analytic function, or both. A corollary of this definition is that when the reading-spelling pattern of poor readers gives no evidence of such cognitive deficits, the reading disability is regarded as nonspecific rather than dyslexic. (Boder & Jarrico, 1982, p. 5)

Accordingly, the Boder Test is intended to allow for differential diagnosis of developmental dyslexia by analyzing together a child's reading and spelling performances as interdependent functions. The manual describes what is offered as "a systematic sequence of simple reading and spelling tasks . . ." giving "an essentially qualitative analysis of the ability to learn to read and spell, for which quantitative criteria are provided" (Boder & Jarrico, 1982, p. 5).

Four subgroups of reading disability are then identified: (1) *dysphonetic dyslexics*, children with strong visual-gestalt reading functions and weak phonic analysis; (2) *dyseidetic dyslexics*, children with strong phonic analysis functions and weak visual gestalt areas; (3) *mixed dysphonetic-dyseidetic*, children who are weak in visual gestalt and phonic analysis; and (4) *nonspecific reading disability*, children strong in visual gestalt and phonic analysis function but not reading well. According to Boder and Jarrico (1982, p. 6), these patterns exist only among reading-disabled children, for "strengths and deficits in the gestalt and analytic functions of dyslexic children are manifested in three characteristic reading-spelling patterns not found among good readers who are at or above grade level in both reading and spelling." Significant reading retardation is defined in the Boder Test as reading two or more years below normal expectancy for grade level or mental age, although it is noted that performance one year below may be diagnostically significant. The authors further assert (p. 9) that the "test can make a reliable early diagnosis of a reading disability and identify the child's preferred modality, either visual or auditory, in learning how to read."

The test proper consists of an oral reading test (word recognition) and a written spelling test. The spelling words are determined from the results of the reading test. The test is individually administered in not more than about 30 minutes. According to the manual, the test may be administered by teachers, reading specialists, psychologists, physicians, and speech therapists.

The reading test consists of 13 "graded" word lists of 20 words each; half of each list contains words that are phonetically regular and half words that are not phonetic. Word lists are presented twice, in timed (1 second) and untimed (10 seconds) conditions. Reading level is determined to be the grade level corresponding to the highest graded word list at which the students read 50% or more of the words correctly. A more precise reading level is obtained by giving 2 months of additional credit for each word read correctly from the flash presentation above this basal level. Two other scores are yielded by the Boder Test, reading age (reading level $-5$) and reading quotient (RA/CA) $\times$ 100; if the child's overall mental ability is substantially above or below average, this quotient is to be corrected for MA by use of the following formula: RQ $=$ (2RA/(MA $+$ CA)) $\times$ 100 or, by using RQ $=$ (3RA/(MA $+$ CA $+$ Grade Age)) $\times$ 100. A set of rules is provided based on the RQ and the pattern of spelling errors to allow classification of each child as normal, dysphonetic, dyseidetic, mixed, or nonspecific in reading skill.

Although the Boder Test is the product of much clinical experience with children and reflects great insight into abnormal reading processes, the technical development of the Boder Test was inadequate to support its use in other than research settings. The use of antiquated quotients for scaling, the failure to collect normative data, and significant problems with the development of reliability and validity data all argue strongly against use of the scale. Boder's model of reading disabilities may still be useful in the conceptualization and treatment of children's reading difficulties, particularly in learning disabilities placements where differentiated instruction is possible, although the visual learner—auditory learner aspects of the approach are antiquated and have not been supported over the years (Reynolds, 1981). The use of the Boder Test in the diagnosis or evaluation of dyslexia or other reading difficulties is insupportable at this time and other means of implementing Boder's model of dyslexia should be pursued.

**REFERENCES**

Boder, E., & Jarrico, S. (1982). *Boder Test of reading-spelling patterns*. New York: Grune & Stratton.
Reynolds, C. R. (1981). Neuropsychological basis of intelligence. In G. Hynd & J. Obrzunt (Eds.), *Neuropsychological assessment and the school aged child: Issues and procedures*. New York: Grune & Stratton.

CECIL R. REYNOLDS
*Texas A&M University*

**GRADE EQUIVALENTS**
**RATIO IQ**
**READING DISORDERS**

# BODY IMAGE

Body image as defined by Galloway and Bean is "the individual's awareness and knowledge of the physical and spatial characteristics" of his or her own body (1974, p. 126). Included in this definition is the idea of knowing body parts and the relationships among body parts. Thus, laterality and directionality stem from body image (Marshall, 1975). In addition, body image is often considered a component of self-concept.

The body awareness and knowledge of an exceptional child may be distorted because of sensory, perceptual, or cognitive dysfunctions inherent in the handicapping condition. Visual or hearing impairments, for example, may deprive a developing child of sensory information necessary for a complete and functional body image. Children with learning disabilities may have problems with body image that influence their learning and development (Cruickshank, 1977). Mentally retarded children, when compared with normal children, have been found to express body images of larger size and less detail and symmetry (Wysocki & Wysocki, 1973).

Typically, body image is assessed by a student's drawing of a person; problems in body image are suspected when a student evidences laterality and directionality confusion. When such basic problems are encountered, the educational plan may include developmental approaches typically associated with preschool education and physical motor development.

Beyond a definition of body image emphasizing body awareness and knowledge, a more popular definition includes the feelings that accompany a person's body knowledge. Conceptualized in this light, body image is a precursor to self-concept (Morse, 1975). Thus, accurate body image is not only necessary for foundations basic to learning, but also essential for self-concept development and, ultimately, self-acceptance.

## REFERENCES

Cruickshank, W. M. (1977). *Learning disabilities in home, school, and community.* Syracuse: Syracuse University Press.

Galloway, H. F., & Bean, M. F. (1974). The effects of action songs on the development of body-image and body-part identification in hearing-impaired preschool children. *Journal of Music Therapy, 11,* 125–134.

Marshall, E. D. (1975). Teaching materials for children with learning disabilities. In W. M. Cruickshank & D. P. Hallahan (Eds.), *Perceptual and learning disabilities in children Vol. 1* (pp. 279–307). Syracuse: Syracuse University Press.

Morse, W. C. (1975). The learning disabled child and considerations of life space. In W. M. Cruickshank & D. P. Hallahan (Eds.), *Perceptual and learning disabilities in children Vol. 1* (pp. 337–353). Syracuse: Syracuse University Press.

Wysocki, B. A., & Wysocki, A. C. (1973). The body-image of normal and retarded children. *Journal of Clinical Psychology, 29*(1), 7–10.

STEVEN R. TIMMERMANS
*Mary Free Bed Hospital and
Rehabilitation Center, Grand
Rapids, Michigan*

## DRAW-A-PERSON MENTAL STATUS EXAMS

## BODY TYPES

Typology is the attempt to take complex observations of people and reduce them to a few salient characteristics or classifications in order to make human behavior more understandable and predictable. Classifying or typing people according to their body build, and using these classifications for predicting other phenomena such as personality or disease acquisition, is deeply rooted in the history of western civilization. The Greek physician Hippocrates, before the time of Christ, categorized people according to body types and claimed that certain diseases were associated with each type. It was believed, for example, that short, thick people were more likely to have a stroke, whereas, tall, thin people were liable to contract tuberculosis. More recently, Kretschmer (1925), using a similar classification of body type, hypothesized a relationship between body build and mental illness: long, lean people were more likely to succumb to schizophrenia while short, blocky individuals were apt to become manic-depressives.

The most recent and notable attempt to classify people according to bodily characteristics and their associated personality types was conducted by the American psychologist and physician William Sheldon. A system was developed to measure and classify the human body along three dimensions (Sheldon, 1940); this provided an individual's somatotype. A person receives a score ranging from one to seven on each of three bodily characteristics: endomorphy, mesomorphy, and ectomorphy. Endomorphy refers to a soft and rounded appearance. The extreme endomorph would be rated as 7-1-1 on the three components; the associated personality type would be considered viscerotonic, meaning a love of comfort and relaxation, sociability, and extroversion. The typical sterotype would be the jolly, gregarious fat person.

The second bodily characteristic, mesomorphy, refers to a strong muscular anatomy. At the extreme it would be rated as 1-7-1. Somatotonia is the related personality. This denotes a physically active individual who is assertive and adventuresome. The stereotype is a loud, aggressive athlete.

Ectomorphy is the third bodily characteristic. It gets rated as 1-1-7 at the extreme and refers to the thin, delicate person. Cerebrotonia is the associated personality type. This includes individuals who are restrained, private, and intellectually intense. The stereotype would be that of a shy, introverted scholar. The three bodily characteristics can vary along a seven-point scale, creating the possibility of many diffeeent combinations of these types with a hypothetically average person rated at 4-4-4.

Originally, Sheldon's theory hypothesized a relatively direct relationship between body type and behavior. Once the body build is created through genetic, biochemical, and physiological processes, certain behavior tends to follow. Even though there is some support for a correlation between body type and behavior (Shasby & Kingsley, 1978; Sheldon, Lewis, & Tenney, 1969; Walker, 1963), current authors (Cortes & Gatti, 1972; Glueck & Glueck, 1956; McCandless, 1961) have modified the genetic and physiological explanation by emphasizing a reciprocal relationship between people with different body types and the social-cultural milieu. Certain body types may arouse negative or positive social reactions in others; this fosters differential personality development (McCandless, 1961). In support of this social learning explanation, several studies (Brodsky, 1954; Lerner & Korn, 1972; Staffieri, 1967) have verified the existence of a body build-behavior stereotype. People with certain physiques create stereotype expectations in others of how they will behave.

## REFERENCES

Brodsky, C. (1954). *A study of norms for body form-behavior relationships*. Washington, DC: Catholic University of America.

Cortes, J., & Gatti, F. (1972). *Delinquency and crime: A biopsychosocial approach*. New York: Seminar.

Glueck, S., & Glueck, E. (1956). *Physique and delinquency*. New York: Harper.

Kretschmer, E. (1925). *Physique and character* (W. J. H. Sprott, Trans.). London: Routledge & Kegan.

Lerner, R. M., & Korn, S. J. (1972). The development of body-build stereotypes in males. *Child Development, 43*, 908–920.

McCandless, B. (1961). *Children and adolescents*. New York: Holt, Rinehart, & Winston.

Shasby, G., & Kingsley, R. F. (1978). A study of behavior and body type in troubled youth. *Journal of School Health, 48*, 103–107.

Sheldon, W. H. (1940). *The varieties of human physique: An introduction to constitutional psychology*. New York: Harper & Brothers.

Sheldon, W. H., Lewis, N. D. C., & Tenney, A. M. (1969). Psychotic patterns and physical constitution: A thirty-year follow-up of thirty-eight-hundred psychiatric patients in New York State. In D. V. Siva Sanker (Ed.), *Schizophrenia: Current concepts and research*. New York: PJD.

Staffieri, J. (1967). A study of social stereotype of body image in children. *Journal of Personality & Social Psychology, 7*, 101–104.

Walker, R. (1963). Body build and behavior in young children. *Child Development, 34*, 1–23.

JOHN O'NEILL
*Hunter College, City University
of New York*

**HEREDITY**
**PHYSICAL ANOMALIES**

## BOEHM TEST OF BASIC CONCEPTS

The Boehm Test of Basic Concepts (BTBC) (Boehm, 1971) was designed as a teaching and screening instrument to assess children's mastery of 50 basic language concepts considered necessary for school success in the beginning academic years. The BTBC is intended for individual or group administration in kindergarten through second grade.

The purpose of the BTBC is twofold: to identify individual children with low levels of concept mastery, and to reveal specific concepts that large numbers of children have not yet acquired. Two parallel or alternate forms are available.

No formal training is required to administer, score, and interpret the BTBC. However, standardized administration procedures must be followed. Interpretation requires the teacher to consider the performance of individual children and the performance of the group as a whole in order to institute appropriate concept remediation procedures.

The BTBC can be recommended for use as a screening instrument to assess mastery of basic concepts in beginning schoolchildren. The inherent usefulness of such an instrument to the early primary classroom teacher and the simple administration procedure are the BTBC's strengths. Problems exist with the test's ceiling and item gradient and with the relative lack of sophistication of the stimulus pictures. However, children in special education have particular difficulty with basic language concepts such as next, alike, same, above, and so on, and the BTBC may be especially useful with these children, particularly in the early grades.

## REFERENCE

Boehm, A. (1971). *Boehm Test of Basic Concepts*, San Antonio, TX: Psychological Corporation.

STAFF

## BONET, JUAN P. (1579–1629?)

Juan Pablo Bonet, a Spanish philologist, instructed deaf students in language and articulation, and taught them a manual alphabet and system of signs that he had developed. He wrote the first book on the education of the deaf, *Simplification of the Letters of the Alphabet and Method of Teaching Deaf-Mutes to Speak*. This work, which appeared in 1620, provided a basis for the developments relating to the education of the deaf in Europe and Great Britain during the eighteenth century (Lane, 1984).

## REFERENCE

Lane, H. (1984). *When the mind hears*. New York: Random House.

PAUL IRVINE
*Katonah, New York*

# BORDERLINE PERSONALITY DISORDER

Borderline personality disorder is a diagnostic classification included in the most recent version of the *Diagnostic and Statistical Manual of Mental Disorders* (DSM III; American Psychiatric Association, 1980). In the past, various borderline disorders were described in ambiguous terms as mild (or latent) forms of schizophrenia (falling somewhere between psychosis and neurosis). With the publication of the DSM III, the disorder received official recognition as a distinct diagnostic entity, closer in form to the affective disorders than schizophrenia (Archer, 1985); however, questions have recently been raised about the reliability and validity of the borderline diagnosis (Widiger, 1982).

The diagnosis of borderline personality disorder requires the presence of at least five of the following: impulsive or unpredictable behavior, unstable interpersonal relationships, difficulty in controlling anger or inappropriate anger, identity disturbance, unstable mood (including depression, anxiety, and irritability), physically self-damaging acts, chronic feelings of boredom, and intolerance of being alone. As is the case with other personality disorders, the borderline disorder represents a chronic, pervasive pattern of behavior that emerges during late childhood/adolescence and interferes with social and occupational functioning for much of the individual's adult life. Despite the presence of symptoms during adolescence, the DSM III recommends that this diagnosis be reserved for individuals 18 years of age and older. For those under 18, the diagnosis of identity disorder, characterized by a similar clinical picture (e.g., mild depression, anxiety, self-doubt, negative/oppositional behavior), is preferred. Identity disorder reflects an inability to establish an acceptable sense of self and includes uncertainty about such issues as career goals, sexual orientation or behavior, moral values, friends, and long-term goals. Contrary to DSM III recommendations, however, the borderline diagnosis is often used with children and adolescents (Bradley, 1981), a practice that has recently received some empirical support (Archer et al., 1985).

## REFERENCES

American Psychiatric Association. (1980). *Diagnostic and statistical manual of mental disorders* (3rd ed.). Washington, DC: Author.

Archer, R. P. Ball, J. D., & Hunter, J. A. (1985). MMPI characteristics of borderline psychopathology in adolescent inpatients. *Journal of Personality Assessment, 49*, 47–55.

Bradley, S. J. (1981). The borderline diagnosis in children and adolescents. *Child Psychiatry & Human Development, 12*(2), 121–127.

Widiger, T. A. (1982). Psychological tests and the borderline diagnosis. *Journal of Personality Assessment, 46*, 227–238.

ROBERT G. BRUBAKER
*Eastern Kentucky University*

CHILDHOOD PSYCHOSIS
CHILDHOOD SCHIZOPHRENIA
DIAGNOSTIC AND STATISTICAL MANUAL OF MENTAL
  DISORDERS (DSM III)

# BOWER, ELI M. (1917–    )

Eli M. Bower obtained his BS from New York University in 1937 and his MA from Columbia University in 1947. He continued his education at Stanford University, receiving his EdD in counseling psychology in 1954. He was president of the American Orthopsychiatry Association at the University of California, Berkeley.

His major areas of study include orthopsychiatry, enhancing growth and learning for the disabled, and engaging children with games in the school setting. Orthopsychiatry was founded in 1924 by joining together mental health professionals and parents of disabled children. The technical definition of orthopsychiatry is the science that concerns itself with the study and treatment of behavior disorders, especially of young people. Bower's concerns in this area lie with behavioral and social problems and their daily resolutions (Bower 1971). Bower (1974) also feels that games should be encouraged as teaching devices, allowing children the freedom to be involved while learning to relate to the real world. Games may be a new idea as an academic subject and for the socialization of children. Bower (1974) also deals with the question of whether children with learning disabilities can be helped early enough in an economical, effective, and institutionally acceptable manner to change their course of school development.

Some of Bower's major works include *Games in Education and Development, Early Identification of Emotion-*

Eli M. Bower

*ally Handicapped Children in School*, and *Orthopsychiatry and Education*.

## REFERENCES

Bower, E. M. (1971). *Orthopsychiatry and education*. Detroit: Wayne State University Press.

Bower, E. M. (1974). *Early identification of emotionally handicapped children in school*. Springfield, IL: Thomas.

Bower, E. M., & Shears, L. M. (1974). *Games in education and development*. Springfield, IL: Thomas.

ELIZABETH JONES
*Texas A&M University*

## BRACKEN BASIC CONCEPT SCALE (BBCS)

The Bracken Basic Concept Scale (BBCS; Bracken, 1984) assesses understanding of basic conceptual terms in 11 different categories: colors, letter identification, numbers/counting, comparisons, shapes, direction/position, social/emotional, size, texture/material, quantity, and time/sequence. The diagnostic battery consists of 258 items, with varying numbers of items per subtest. A four-picture format with black and white line drawings is presented in an easel arrangement. The battery is to be administered individually to children between the ages of 2½ and 8, and requires either a pointing or verbal response, as the child chooses. It requires 20 to 30 minutes to administer. The screening version has two alternative forms of 30 items each, to be administered individually or in groups to children in kindergarten and first grade. It requires 5 to 10 minutes to administer, and has a workbook format with two items (eight pictures) per page.

The first five subtest scores of the diagnostic battery can be combined to yield a school readiness composite. Based on this score, basals and ceilings for the other six subtests can be established. Scores can be converted to standard scores, percentile ranks, stanines, and concept ages.

The diagnostic battery was standardized on 1109 children selected to be representative of the general population in terms of ethnic group, geographic region, and parents' educational level. The number of children per age group is not given in the manual. Test-retest reliability was measured using 27 children, with correlations ranging from 0.67 to 0.98, varying by subtest. Content validity is discussed at length in the manual. Studies comparing the BBCS to other tests of concepts and vocabulary have reported correlations ranging from 0.68 (Token Test) to 0.88 (Boehm Test of Basic Concepts; Peabody Picture Vocabulary Test, Revised).

## REFERENCE

Bracken, B. A. (1984). *Bracken Basic Concept Scale*. Columbus, OH: Merrill.

MARGO E. WILSON
*Lexington, Kentucky*

## BRAIDWOOD, THOMAS (1715–1806)

Thomas Braidwood, a Scottish teacher, established Great Britain's first school for the deaf in Edinburgh in 1760. Unaware of the methods of teaching the deaf that had been developed on Europe by Heinicke, Epée, and others, Braidwood developed his own techniques, through which his students learned to speak and lip read, and to read and write. Once he had established the effectiveness of his methods, Braidwood published a proposal for the provision of public funds for the education of those deaf students whose families could not afford to pay for schooling, and for the training of teachers in his methods. When public funding was not granted, Braidwood declared that the system would remain his property, and swore to secrecy the family members and others at the school who had learned his techniques (Bender, 1970).

Braidwood moved his school to Hackney, near London, in 1783. Because of his obsession with secrecy, it was not until after Braidwood's death that the details of his methods became known. The writings of his nephew, Joseph Watson, who assisted him at Hackney and later established England's first school for the indigent deaf, showed that Braidwood had developed an elaborate oral method of instruction that generally paralleled the development of the oral approach elsewhere. Braidwood's great contribution was the initiation of education for the deaf in Great Britain (Bender, 1970).

## REFERENCE

Bender, R. (1970). *The conquest of deafness*. Cleveland: Case Western Reserve University.

PAUL IRVINE
*Katonah, New York*

## BRAILLE

Braille is a tactile system that blind people use to read and write. The basis of braille is a rectangular "cell" consisting of six raised dots, two vertical rows of three dots each. The official code, Standard English Braille (Grade

2), consists of alphabet letters, numbers, punctuation, composition signs, and 189 contractions and short-form words, both of which are abbreviations of whole words to increase the speed of reading and writing braille. The Nemeth Braille code is used to transcribe mathematics and science; other codes are used to transcribe foreign languages and musical notation.

The first tactually perceptible code was developed in the early nineteenth century by Charles Barbier, a French army officer; its purpose was to send and receive messages at night. Louis Braille modified Barbier's code and published his system in 1829, while he was a professor at the Paris School for the Blind. Although Braille was permitted to teach his system outside of school hours, it was not officially accepted by the school until 1854, two years after he died. In the United States, the first school to adopt Braille's code was the Missouri School for the Blind, in 1869.

Reading and writing braille is taught to blind students by educators specifically trained to teach these skills to visually handicapped pupils placed in a variety of settings, including resource room or itinerant programs within the public school, or a residential school for the blind. The majority of good braille readers use two hands. A skilled two-handed reader usually begins reading a line of braille by placing both hands at the beginning of the line; when the middle of the line is reached, the right hand continues across the line, while the left hand moves in the opposite direction and locates the beginning of the next line. After the entire first line has been read by the right hand, the left hand reads the first several words on the next line, while the right hand moves quickly back to meet the left hand (Mangold, 1982). Important mechanical skills needed by braille readers include light finger touch, finger curvature, smooth independent hand movements, and page turning.

A major disadvantage of braille reading is that its average speed is two to three times slower than that of print reading. An average speed of 90 words per minute has been reported as typical for readers in the upper elementary grades (Harley, Henderson, & Truan, 1979). Braille books are also large and cumbersome, and they require large amounts of storage space. However, Mellor (1979) reports that braille as a medium for reading and recording information is superior to other mediums for providing random access to a page; skimming a page; labeling; filing; writing memorandums; reading tables and diagrams; reading technical or difficult material; allowing the reader to be an active participant in reading; and providing deafblind individuals with their only means of reading.

Young blind children learn to write braille using a Perkins Brailler, a six-keyed device that has similarities to a typewriter. Once blind students become proficient in reading braille and in using the Brailler, they are taught to use the slate and stylus, a more complex procedure in which braille dots are punched out one at a time by hand, from right to left. While the Brailler is easier to use, the slate and stylus is smaller, easier to carry, and more useful for taking short notes.

There have been several innovations in braille reading, writing, and production. One of them is an electronic braille device that can send and retrieve information to and from a computer. This device can store information on audio cassette tapes and present it in a braille display of 20 or more characters in a single line of movable pins representing braille dots. The blind individual presses on a keyboard similar to the Brailler and the information is converted to a digital code that is recorded on the tape in a cassette. The encoded information moves the six pins up and down so that the reader can read the configurations on the one-line display. When the reader gets to the end of the line, he or she touches a switch, which then presents the next line of braille stored on the cassette. Blind students can write and edit their papers with ease using one of these machines. (Olson, 1981; Ruconich, 1984). The electronic braille device reduces considerably the storage space needed for braille materials since an ordinary 60-minute audio cassette tape can store the equivalent of 400 pages of bulky paper braille. It is marketed by several commercial companies.

Another recent invention is an electronic braille printer that enables a person to produce hard-copy braille in either six- or eight-dot computer code. It also provides an onboard Grade 1 translator. Using translation software, the user can produce Grade 2, Nemeth, or music braille codes in six-dot computer braille code mode.

Another innovation is a paperless braille device that provides access to the screen of a computer by directly reading the computer's memory. It enables the blind person to access information on a full screen in increments of up to 20 characters while maintaining orientation to screen format through the use of auditory and tactile cues.

While the cost of such electronic braille devices is currently extremely high, their benefits are overwhelmingly positive in enabling blind individuals to access the available technology. As a result, more and more of this equipment will become available for use by blind students in special education programs yearly.

## REFERENCES

Harley, R. K., Henderson, F. M., & Truan, M. B. (1979). *The teaching of braille reading.* Springfield, IL: Thomas.

Mangold, S. (1982). Teaching reading via braille. In S. Mangold (Ed.), *A teachers' guide to the special educational needs of blind and visually handicapped children.* New York: American Foundation for the Blind.

Mellor, C. M. (1979). Technical innovations for braille reading, writing, and production. *Journal of Visual Impairment and Blindness, 73,* 339–341.

Olson, M. R. (1981). *Guidelines and games for teaching efficient braille reading.* New York: American Foundation for the Blind.

Ruconich, S. (1984). Evaluating microcomputer access technology for use by visually impaired students. *Education of the Visually Handicapped, 15,* 119–125.

ROSANNE K. SILBERMAN
*Hunter College, City University
of New York*

**BLIND**
**VERSABRAILLE**

## BRAILLE, LOUIS (1809–1852)

Louis Braille, blinded in an accident at the age of three, developed his system of reading and writing for the blind while serving as a teacher at the Institution National des Jeunes Aveugles, the school for the blind in Paris. Dissatisfied with earlier approaches that were cumbersome and difficult to read, Braille developed a code employing one or more raised dots in a cell three dots high and two wide. An accomplished musician, he also worked out an application of his system to musical notation. Ironically, his school did not accept his system and actually forbade its use. Braille feared that his invention would die with him, but it survived, although it did not immediately flourish. It was not until 1916 that braille was officially adopted by the schools for the blind in the United States. A universal braille code for the English-speaking world was adopted in 1932.

### REFERENCE

Kugelmass, J. (1951). *Louis Braille: Windows for the blind.* New York: Messner.

PAUL IRVINE
*Katonah, New York*

## BRAIN DAMAGE

The expression brain damage denotes a condition where extragenetic influences arrest or impair the normal structure, growth, development and functioning of brain tissue (Cruickshank, 1980). Damage to the brain can be either congenital or acquired after birth, with acquired damage resulting most frequently from trauma (Rourke, Bakker, Fisk, & Strang, 1983). The severity of dysfunction and prognosis for recovery following trauma depend on many variables, including the nature, location, and extent of the injury, the developmental level, and demographic factors such as age and sex (Rourke et al., 1983).

Brain damage does not always impair learning ability; conversely, impaired learning ability is not always caused by brain damage. Thus it is interesting that explanations of learning impairment often suggest underlying brain dysfunction. In many cases, brain dysfunction is inferred from behavior in the absence of any hard neurological signs. Speculative diagnoses such as minimal brain damage (MBD) neither clarify the cause of the learning impairment nor specify rehabilitation strategies (Rutter, 1983). Such diagnostic labels minimize the importance of individual differences. Even classification of children into large diagnostic groups such as retarded or learning disabled probably generates more confusion than clarification and does not provide sufficient focus to aid in remediation.

Brain damage is but one of many important variables that influence behavior. To understand a child's learning problems, nonneurological factors must be investigated carefully. Even in a case of documented brain injury, learning impairment may reflect an impoverished home environment, problems in emotional adjustment, poor motivation, systemic health problems, developmental lags, and genetic predispositions (Figure 1).

Brain damage may be the most important factor in a given case, but the label brain damage offers no clarification unless the nature, location, and extent of the damage are understood. There is also considerable danger in labeling a child brain damaged. To do so implies permanence, encourages drug treatment, minimizes the importance of education or remediation, and shifts responsibility to physicians (Gaddes, 1980). Given such a label, important and remediable strengths may be ignored.

Clinical neuropsychological assessment of a child involves the elucidation of brain-behavior relationships in a developing human organism; consequently, this is a unique area of inquiry with problems quite different from those encountered in investigating the mature brain (Rourke et al., 1983). The developing brain undergoes rapid changes, and brain damage during childhood may impair future development of certain cognitive and behavioral capacities.

The brain of a child shows a capacity for development and recovery of function following brain injury. It has been

| Organic | Genetic |
| | Neurological |
| | Systemic |
| Individual | Cognitive |
| | Emotional |
| | Cultural |
| | Achievement |
| Social/ | Family |
| Situational | Social |
| | Academic |

Figure 1. Factors that influence behavior.

argued (the Kennard principle) that early brain damage produces less dramatic behavioral effects and better prospects for recovery than damage in later life. This claim is only partially correct. The prognosis of early brain damage depends on many variables, including the type, location, and extent of the injury (Rourke et al., 1983). Most brain-injured children show some capacity for development of functions or recovery of functions, although it is difficult to predict the extent, rate, and degree of improvement because it depends on a number of neurological and psychological factors (Rourke et al., 1983).

Early brain damage may produce permanent dysfunction, delayed onset of dysfunction, or no dysfunction, depending on the maturational status of the system (Teuber & Rudel, 1962). For example, the effect of brain damage initially may be mild until functions subserved by damaged tissue become crucial for behavioral performance during development.

The term growing into a deficit has been used to emphasize the importance of the maturational status of the brain area at the time of damage (Rourke et al., 1983). Rourke (1983) argues that attentional deficits are a special problem for the young brain-damaged child, while older brain-damaged children show cognitive deficits. Rourke contends the young brain-injured child also has cognitive deficits, but they may not be apparent because of the generalized effects of attentional deficits. As attentional deficits resolve, the previously masked cognitive deficits become evident. Part of the process of recovery may involve the brain-injured child's learning to solve old problems in new ways by reorganizing functional elements of the behavioral repertoire (Luria, 1973). Thus one important premise of neuropsychology is that if the nature and extent of the deficit can be identified early in life, effective remediation can be instituted to minimize the consequences of brain damage on future learning.

In summary, consequences of brain lesions must be assessed in light of the dynamic nature of the developing brain and its emerging anatomical and functional asymmetries. Only by looking at these factors can we hope to understand the apparent paradox that the immature brain is simultaneously characterized by both a greater vulnerability to cerebral impairment and an apparently enhanced potential for recovery of function (Chelune & Edwards, 1981).

There are few common behavior patterns characterizing brain damage. However, most changes suggest a loss of the normal inhibitory influence of the cortex on behavior (Rutter, 1983). There is also frequently a deficit in attention that can lead to perseveration, hyperactivity, and impaired sensory processing (Cruickshank, Bentzen, Ratzeburg & Tannhauser 1961; Gordon, White, & Diller, 1972; Haskell, Barrett, & Taylor, 1977).

Attention deficit disorders or hyperactivity represent early and common consequences of brain injury. Such behaviors may reflect a deficit in planning and regulation of behavior, a deficit in memory, or loss of inhibitory control on the brain stem reticular system. In cases where a major behavioral component of the dysfunction is attention deficits, other deficits may not be observable or may not be easily measured.

Deficits affecting primarily the diencephalon often produce impaired memory consolidation. Individuals with such deficits may be able to attend to a task but they do not benefit from their experiences. As with attentional deficits, memory deficits can be pervasive and lead to more generalized deficits unless effectively remediated.

Higher level functions involve more complex cortical processing of information. The left hemisphere processes verbal material and deals with material in a discrete manner. The right hemisphere deals with nonverbal and new material in a more global manner. Functions can be divided further in each hemisphere; thus cortical damage can have dramatically different effects on behavior and learning depending on the brain area damaged. Cognitive functions relate primarily to cortical processing and include a broad range of behaviors. Early deficits in acquired brain damage may be generalized, but most pronounced recovery is noted in sensory and motor function and speech comprehension. Often recovery of language is given precedence and other functions may suffer. Left hemisphere damage is likely to impair syntactical functions, although with increasing severity, more general language processing may be involved. Furthermore, right-sided sensory and motor deficits may be observed as well as processing of verbally labeled material. Right hemisphere impairment results in deficits in visuo-spatial functions and spatial memory. Recovery of these functions is likely to lag behind language. Developmental changes appear to shift from right hemisphere global functions to left hemisphere linguistic functions. Rourke (1983) postulates that the left hemisphere functions in an automated manner, thus freeing the right hemisphere to deal with novelty, complexity, and intermodal integration.

Brain damage not only attenuates intellectual functions but also increases the chance of problems in emotional adjustment (Rutter, 1981). While brain damage can cause emotional lability, emotional problems are usually secondary or reactive to intellectual impairment, physical handicaps, or altered peer relations. The emotional consequences of brain injury are substantially influenced by the child's level of preinjury functioning as well as postinjury social support systems. Social learning is a complex cognitive function that involves learning social cues and gestures and modifying social behavior. Head-injured children are most likely to retain characterological deficits that limit full remediation (Lezak, 1976).

Neuropsychological assessment in the schools is a topic that has received much support during the last decade. Literature in the fields of special education, school psychology, and, recently, child neuropsychology has espoused understanding neuropsychological principles when assessing and planning educational intervention for children who are experiencing significant learning or behavioral problems in school (Hynd & Obrzut, 1981; Rourke et al., 1983).

Since impaired learning may reflect the influence of multiple factors, an initial step in understanding the nature of learning impairment is to explore carefully the various potential contributing factors in each case. Once these factors are identified they can be prioritized in terms of their assumed significance (Long, 1985). In this way a framework is established for diagnosing the significance of brain-damage effects in each individual case.

An adequate evaluation involves assessing intelligence (verbal and nonverbal), memory, academic achievement, and emotional adjustment. In some cases more specific neuropsychological functions also must be tested (Figure 2). In addition, consideration must be given to social/environmental factors and their contribution to overall performance. The assessment must produce a valid and reliable picture of the individual's strengths and weaknesses, and allow inferences about underlying brain functions to be made. It is important to differentiate between behavioral problems that reflect structural lesions and behaviors having no direct relationship to the brain's continuity.

Determining the nature (e.g., acute vs. chronic) and extent of brain damage of the child presents a much more difficult task for the neuropsychologist than the diagnosis of adult brain injury. The major difficulty concerns the role of age and development in children. Children change quickly in the kinds of skills we can expect them to acquire, and all children with the same chronological age are not at the same developmental level. It is necessary to take developmental factors into account. A basic rule in assessing children is to use multiple tests so that patterns and changes can be seen. The resulting profile then can be used to determine whether the hypothesis of delayed development is tenable (Golden & Anderson, 1979).

Assessment of intellectual and academic strengths and weaknesses for remedial or rehabilitative purposes, such as constructing an individual educational program (IEP), is maximally useful only when certain requirements are met (Hartlage, 1981). First, a majority of the child's educationally related cognitive abilities and methods of higher order information processing skills must be assessed in a quantifiable, replicable, and valid manner. Second, the assessment should be translated into a relevant and valid educational plan. Third, the assessment procedures should be reasonably efficient in terms of time and effort needed to administer and interpret them. In essence, the neuropsychological assessment process should be designed to test the specific referral problem and to provide the information needed to devise an appropriate program for the child in question (Hartlage, 1981).

Comprehensive neuropsychological batteries developed for use with children such as the Reitan-Indiana Neuropsychological Battery and the Luria-Nebraska Neuropsychological Battery-Children's Revision add significantly to the evaluation and remedial planning process (Berg et al., 1984; Lezak, 1976). The major drawback to the use of these batteries is the great deal of time and training required for administration and interpretation (Hartlage, 1981; Reynolds, 1981).

Hartlage (1981) suggests an alternative approach in the application of neuropsychological principles to the interpretation of developmental, behavioral, and test data that can provide a systematic framework for understanding patterns of learning strengths and weaknesses and for making direct translations of the findings into intervention strategies that are uniquely relevant to the child's cerebral organization. By knowing the neuropsychological implications of common psychoeducational tests, such as the Wechsler Intelligence Scale for Children—Revised (WISC–R), Bender-Gestalt, Wide Range Achievement Test, and Peabody Picture Vocabulary Test, the neuropsychologist can determine which additional tests, if any, are needed to complete an adequate neuropsychological diagnostic profile (Hartlage, 1981). Detection with an accurate description of dysfunction leads to a remediation program to enhance the child's acquisition of skills using the child's intact areas and capitalizing on the child's neuropsychological strengths.

There are basically two approaches to the development of educational intervention based on psychoeducational test data: the strength model and the deficit model (Clark & Reynolds, 1984; Hartlage & Telzrow, 1984; Reynolds, 1981). The deficit model is the one most familiar to educators. This model is based on the premise that greater use of an impaired function will increase competency in that area (Hartlage & Telzrow, 1984) or restore dysfunctional neurological systems to their normal capacity (Clark & Reynolds, 1984). When neurological or genetic bases exist for the child's problem, the deficit approach to remediation is doomed to failure since it attempts to identify damaged or dysfunctional areas of the brain and focuses training specifically on those areas.

An academic intervention plan that focuses on deficits is not only ineffective, it is also more frustrating for the child, teacher, and parents (Hartlage & Telzrow, 1984). According to Reynolds (1981), this approach could be harmful to the child in that there is a high likelihood for

Basic sensory and motor functions
Perceptual and perceptual-motor functions
Attention
Language abilities
Intelligence
Problem-solving and abstract reasoning
Memory
Emotional adjustment

Figure 2. Essential areas of neuropsychological assessment.

failure and subsequent loss of self-esteem. To date there is limited empirical evidence to suggest any significant gains in academic or general behavioral functioning as a result of these efforts (Clark & Reynolds, 1984).

Remediation based on strengths has received little emphasis in educational settings primarily because eligibility for special education services is tied directly to the identification of deficits and treatments to restore those deficits (Hartlage & Telzrow, 1984). Reynolds (1981) has proposed the adoption of a habilitative or a strength model for the remediation of learning or behavioral problems. This approach involves designing instructional strategies that are based on or capitalize on the cognitive and neuropsychological strengths that are sufficiently intact so as to enable the child to successfully complete steps in an educational program (Clark & Reynolds, 1984; Reynolds, 1981). The strength model has been found to be effective in rehabilitation programs for adults, and preliminary research (Reynolds, 1981) shows great promise in its application with children.

To develop an individualized remediation strategy, careful attention must be given to the level of functioning and the role that various brain systems play in such functions. Luria's model of hierarchical systems is a convenient conceptual framework. The foundation for learning is based, at the lowest level, on attention. While the whole brain is involved in attention, in most cases the brain stem is of primary importance and brain-stem lesions can disrupt attention significantly. The child must be able to select salient cues and attend to them in order to learn effectively. When attention deficits are present, other intervention strategies may be ineffective. Attention deficits can be managed to some extent by (1) restricting distractors in the environment, (2) presenting more potent stimuli, and (3) dividing study into shorter periods of time. If these strategies are unsuccessful, consideration should be given to referral to pediatric neurology for psychopharmacological treatment.

Like attention, memory is related to total brain function and memory stores are located throughout the central cerebrum. However, the diencephalon and limbic system are particularly important for memory consolidation (storage of information). Deficits in memory obviously impair learning and severely limit acquisition of information. Intervention can be enhanced by (1) aiding the child in strategies for processing information by presenting it in discrete units, (2) increasing incentives, as most are strongly linked to memory consolidation, (3) sustaining practice, and (4) using multimodal sensory input. In memory rehabilitation in children, it is important to understand areas of weakness and assist in resorting to alternative methods of input and storage.

Remediation strategies must take into account strengths and deficits in higher level or cortical processing. With a comprehensive assessment, including neuropsychological assessment, not only modality but material specific weaknesses can be identified and remediation can be established to bypass such weaknesses.

Intervention and remediation in brain-impaired children involve standard procedures with adjustment in manner or mode of presentation. These children need sustained study on material where they receive effective feedback, and where material is interesting and presented on their level. Computer systems are an ideal tool for special education with such children, as they can provide individualized courses of study. Such systems should be viewed as an adjunct rather than a replacement for the educator.

## REFERENCES

Berg, R. A., Bolter, J. F., Chien, L. T., Williams, S. J., Lancster, W., & Cummins, J. (1984). Comparative diagnostic accuracy of the Halstead-Reitan and Luria-Nebraska neuropsychology adult and children's batteries. *International Journal of Clinical Neuropsychology, 6,* 200–204.

Chelune, G. J., & Edwards, P. (1981). Early brain lesions: Ontogenetic-environmental consideration. *Journal of Consulting & Clinical Psychology, 49,* 777–790.

Clark, J. H., & Reynolds, C. R. (1984, August). *Habilitation or rehabilitation: Strength versus deficit.* Paper presented at the meeting of the American Psychological Association, Toronto, Canada.

Cruickshank, W. M. (Ed.). (1980). *Psychology of exceptional children and youth.* Englewood Cliffs, NJ: Prentice-Hall.

Cruickshank, W. E., Bentzen, F. A., Ratzeburg, E. H., & Tannhauser, M. T. (1961). *A teaching method for brain-injured and hyperactive children: A demonstration-pilot study.* Syracuse, NY: Syracuse University Press.

Gaddes, W. H. (1980). *Learning disabilities and brain function: A neuropsychological approach.* New York: Springer-Verlag.

Golden, C. J., & Anderson, S. (1979). *Learning disabilities and brain dysfunction: An introduction for educators and parents.* Springfield, IL: Thomas.

Gordon, R., White, D., & Diller, L. (1972). Performance of neurologically impaired preschool children with educational material. *Exceptional Child, 38,* 428–437.

Hartlage, L. C. (1981). Neuropsychological assessment techniques. In C. R. Reynolds & T. Gutkin (Eds.), *Handbook & School Psychology* (pp. 296–320). New York: Wiley.

Hartlage, L. C., & Telzrow, C. F. (1984). Neuropsychological basis of educational assessment and programming. In P. E. Logue & J. M. Schear (Eds.), *Clinical neuropsychology: A multidisciplinary approach* (pp. 297–313). Springfield, IL: Thomas.

Haskell, S. H., Barrett, E. K., & Taylor, H. (1977). *The education of motor and neurologically handicapped children.* New York: Wiley.

Hynd, G. W., & Obrzut, J. E. (1981). *Neuropsychological assessment and the school-age child.* New York: Grune & Stratton.

Lezak, M. D. (1976). *Neuropsychological assessment.* New York: Oxford University Press.

Long, C. J. (1985). Neuropsychology in private practice: Its changing focus. *Psychotherapy in Private Practice, 3,* 45–55.

Luria, A. R. (1973). *The working brain: An introduction to neuropsychology.* New York: Basic Books.

Otto, W., McMenemy, R. A., & Smith, R. (1973). *Corrective and remedial teaching.* Boston: Houghton Mifflin.

Reitan, R. M., & Davison, L. A. (1974). *Clinical neuropsychology: Current status and applications.* New York: Wiley.

Reynolds, C. R. (1981). Neuropsychological assessment and the habilitation of learning: Considerations in the search for the aptitude × treatment interaction. *School Psychology Review, 10,* 343–349.

Rourke, B. P. (1983). Reading and spelling disabilities: A developmental neuropsychological perspective. In U. Kirk (Ed.), *Neuropsychology of language, reading and spelling* (pp. 209–234). New York: Academic.

Rourke, B. P., Bakker, D. J., Fisk, J. L., & Strang, J. D. (1983). *Child neuropsychology: An introduction to theory, research, and clinical practice.* New York: Guilford.

Rutter, M. (1981). Psychological sequelae of brain damage in children. *American Journal of Psychiatry, 138,* 1533–1544.

Rutter, M. (1983). *Developmental Neurospsychiatry.* New York: Guilford.

Stevens, M. M. (1982). Post concussion syndrome. *Journal of Neurosurgical Nursing, 14,* 239–244.

Teuber, H. L., & Rudel, R. (1962). Behavior after cerebral lesions in children and adults. *Developmental Medicine & Child Neurology, 4,* 3–20.

CHARLES J. LONG
TINA L. BROWN
*University of Tennessee,
Memphis*
*Memphis State University*

**NEUROPSYCHOLOGY**

# BRAIN DISORDERS (DEGENERATIVE MOTOR DYSFUNCTION)

Degenerative disorders of the central nervous system are a group of diseases of unspecified etiology leading to progressive deterioration and, eventually, death. Many of these disorders demonstrate a familial pattern and for some there is evidence of heritability (Slager, 1970). Specific degenerative disorders are characterized by their unique clinical and pathological features associated with age of onset and type and progression of symptoms (Alpers & Mancoll, 1971; Slager, 1970).

Major degenerative brain disorders such as Alzheimer's disease, Pick's disease, and Creutzfeldt-Jakob disease have their onset during the middle to late adult years. The same is typically true of the major motor neuron disease, amyotrophic lateral sclerosis, and Huntington's chorea, a major, degenerative disease of the basal ganglia. The remainder of this chapter will describe briefly several degenerative disorders that affect children and hence have relevance for special education.

Several genetically determined disorders are associated with progressive cerebral degeneration in children. Major types are the lipid storage disease, the leukodystrophies, and progressive degeneration of the gray matter (Sandifer, 1967). Tay-Sachs disease, a major example of cerebral lipidosis that is confined to children of Jewish descent, is an infantile variety of cerebromacular degeneration (Walton, 1971). Symptoms, which emerge during early infancy and result in death during the second or third year of life, include spastic paralysis, epilepsy, dementia, and optic atrophy leading to blindness (Sandifer, 1967). Alper's disease is an example of a disorder characterized by gray matter degeneration. Onset of symptoms occurs during infancy or early childhood. Symptoms include mental deficiency, cerebral palsy, ataxia, blindness, and epilepsy (Slager, 1970). Death typically occurs within a few months to several years (Sandifer, 1967). Hallervorden-Spatz disease encompasses a group of degenerative disorders that affect boys more than girls (Sandifer, 1967). Symptoms occur between the ages of 8 and 10 and include spastic paralysis, choreo-athetosis, and slowly developing dementia (Sandifer, 1967). Demyelinating leukodystrophies are disorders associated with progressive paralysis and increased mental impairment (Conway, 1977). One example in metachromatic leukodystrophy, inherited as an autosomal recessive trait. Apparently normal development up until about 2 years is followed by onset of symptoms that include ataxia, impairment in swallowing and speaking, tonic seizures, and mental regression (Conway, 1977). Other examples of the demyelinating leukodystrophies include Krabbe's disease, Grienfield's disease, and Alexander's disease (Conway, 1977).

Spinocerebellar ataxias are a group of degenerative disorders involving the cerebellum and associated pathways. Friedreich's ataxia is an autosomal recessive disorder with symptoms developing between ages 7 and 15 (Conway, 1977). Early symptoms include ataxia, gait disturbances, and poor coordination, including frequent falling (Rosenberg, 1979). Other cerebellar signs, including nystagmus, dysarthria, and sensory impairments distally may be evident. Other forms of progressive ataxia affecting children include Ramsay Hunt syndrome, hereditary cerebellar ataxia, and Louis-Bar syndrome (Conway, 1977).

Demyelinating encephalopathies are a group of progressive degenerative disorders resulting in death. One example is Leigh's disease (subacute necrotizing encephalopathy), an autosomal recessive condition with onset occurring during infancy. Characteristics of this disorder include hypotonia, ataxia, and spasticity. Respiratory or feeding problems may be associated with this condition, resulting in failure to thrive (Conway, 1977; Slager, 1970). Schilder's disease is another example of the demyelinating encephalopathies. The progressive deterioration associated with this condition may result in significant behavioral disturbance in children during the middle years of childhood (Conway, 1977). More advanced symptoms of Schilder's disease include ataxia, cortical blindness, seizures, and deafness.

Some authors include among the degenerative diseases of the nervous systems neurocutaneous syndromes such as neurofibromatosis and tuberous sclerosis (Rosenberg, 1979; Walton, 1971). Such disorders may be expressed with wide degrees of severity, hence individual monitoring is essential. In summary, degenerative disorders of the nervous system are progressive, frequently hereditary conditions that produce significant mental, motor, and behavioral impairments that frequently result in death. Because of the genetic component associated with the transmission of many of these conditions, genetic counseling may be advisable for parents who have one affected child. Special education and related services may be required for children with degenerative disorders who survive to school age. The assistance of a variety of social service agencies may be of value to the families of afflicted children for counseling and group and individual support.

**REFERENCES**

Alpers, B. J., & Mancoll, E. L. (1971). *Clinical neurology* (6th ed.). Philadelphia: Davis.

Conway, B. L. (1977). *Pediatric neurologic nursing*. St. Louis: Mosby.

Rosenberg, R. N. (1979). Inherited degenerative diseases of the nervous system. In P. B. Beeson, W. McDermott, & J. B. Wyngaarden (Eds.), *Cecil textbook of medicine* (15th ed., pp. 764–772). Philadelphia: Saunders.

Sandifer, P. H. (1967). *Neurology in orthopaedics*. London: Butterworths.

Slager, U. T. (1970). *Basic neuropathology*. Baltimore, MD: Williams & Wilkins.

Walton, J. N. (1971). *Essentials of neurology* (3rd ed.). Philadelphia: Lippincott.

CATHY F. TELZROW
*Cuyahoga Special Education
Service Center, Maple
Heights, Ohio*

**COGENITAL DISORDERS**
**GAIT DISTURBANCES**
**HEREDITY**
**PHYSICAL ANOMALIES**
**NEUROPSYCHOLOGY**

# BRAIN GROWTH PERIODIZATION

Brain growth periodization refers to the rapid unequal development of the central nervous system (CNS) in general and the brain in particular. Following the moment of conception, neuronal cells begin an accelerated developmental course of division and reorganization (Gardner, 1969). This process involves the sequence of neuronal cell proliferation, migration, differentiation, axonal growth, formation of synapses, process of elimination, and, finally, myelination. Complexity of this emerging system is immense, and it grows within the context of plasticity and modifiability that exists throughout prenatal, perinatal, and early postnatal development (Moore, 1985).

The formation of the neural plate, which is marked by rapid neuronal cell proliferation, is evident within 16 days following conception. This plate then folds over into a tube shape. After a month, it closes toward the front and rear. The majority of cells attach themselves to the front of the tube and eventually form the brain.

Cell differentiation occurs at variable rates, as dictated by the location of cells within the CNS, where the cortical areas change rapidly and other areas mature more slowly. Next, the axonal growth and dendritic formations of the cells expand to make synaptic connections to one another. This highly ordered circuitry, which links up the brain electrochemically, is controlled by genetic programming and is largely influenced by the environment. One function of the synapses is related to specificity of action, which changes relative to location in the CNS (Sidman & Rakic, 1982). The primary sensory and motor structures are examples of highly specific functioning areas.

Genetic programming initiates the processes of brain growth, but environmental influences modify its form and function. Myelination can be thought of as insulating the neuronal cells to increase the conductivity of sending or receiving electrochemical messages. Early influences of nutrition and mother's health and lifestyle impinge on prenatal development; social, cultural, and economic factors further refine brain growth through postnatal life (Avery, 1985; Freeman, 1985).

Epstein (1978) has postulated that periodic growth spurts of the brain occur at predictable ages, and that rapid growth periods are associated with increases in mental age. Further, complementary curricula employed during rapid growth periods would maximize the individual's biological capacities to facilitate learning. Although the theory is logical, research has not yet decided its empirical efficacy. Current research is warranted to move from correlational to causal explanations.

The observation of a growing and changing system that is adapting to environmental influences before and after birth complicates the prediction of any pathological outcome (i.e., early insult resulting in later specific learning disorders). Special educators should be aware of the periodic growth of the brain in the framework of a dynamic interaction between genetics and environment. Recognition of this complex process promotes understanding of students' individual differences and necessitates the development of unique perspectives for intervention.

## REFERENCES

Avery, G. (1985). Effects of social, cultural and economic factors on brain development. In J. M. Freeman (Ed.), *Prenatal and perinatal factors associated with brain damage* (Publication No. 85–1149) (pp. 163–176). Washington, DC: National Institutes of Health.

Epstein, H. T. (1978). Growth spurts during brain development: Implications for educational policy and practice. In J. S. Chall & A. F. Mirsky (Eds.), *Education & the brain* (pp. 343–370). Chicago: University of Chicago Press.

Freeman, J. M. (1985). *Prenatal and perinatal factors associated with brain damage* (Publication No. 85–1149). Washington, DC: National Institutes of Health.

Gardner, E. (1968). *Fundamentals of neurology.* Philadelphia: Saunders.

Moore, R. Y. (1985). Normal development of the nervous system. In J. M. Freeman (Ed.), *Prenatal and perinatal factors associated with brain damage* (Publication No. 85–1149) (pp. 33–51). Washington, DC: National Institutes of Health.

Sidman, R. L., & Rakic, P. (1982). Development of the human central nervous system. In W. Haymaker, & R. D. Adams (Eds.), *Histology and histopathology of the nervous system* (pp. 3–145). Springfield, MA: Thomas.

SCOTT W. SAUTTER
*Peabody College,*
*Vanderbilt University*

BRAIN DAMAGE
BRAIN DISORDERS (DEGENERATIVE MOTOR
   DYSFUNCTION)
NEUROLOGICAL ORGANIZATION

## BRAIN INJURY

See BRAIN DAMAGE, see BIRTH INJURIES.

## BRAIN ORGANIZATION

See NEUROLOGICAL ORGANIZATION.

## BRAIN STEM AUDIOMETRY

Brain stem audiometry is an electrophysiologic measurement of hearing function currently known as auditory brain stem response (ABR) audiometry. As a diagnostic procedure, brain stem audiometry is used for the assessment of a peripheral hearing function (especially for high-risk infants, the retarded, and those individuals who are unable to respond appropriately to traditional tests) and to determine the neurological integrity of the auditory nerve and brain stem (especially for adults suspected of having an auditory nerve or brain stem tumor or other neural pathology). Brain stem audiometry can be done when the patient is lightly sedated, asleep, or awake.

Brain stem audiometry is possible because the neural reaction of the brain stem is time-locked to an acoustic stimulus while higher level ongoing brain stem neural activity is random. Consequently, with the use of an averaging computer, the time-locked brain stem neural response to an acoustic stimulus can be extracted from the random ongoing higher level brain stem neural activity.

A brain stem audiometer contains an averaging computer that triggers stimulus-generating instrumentation that transduces an acoustic stimulus through an earphone, loudspeaker, or bone vibrator. The patient is fitted with an active surface electrode along the midline of the head (usually at the vertex) and reference surface electrodes (usually on each mastoid or earlobe). The output of the electrodes are amplified, filtered, and directed to the averaging computer, which is programmed to present many repetitions of the same stimulus and average the response of the neural activity for each stimulus for a period of about 10 milliseconds following the onset of the stimulus. The resultant pattern, known as the ABR waveform, is characterized by six to seven identifiable peaks having different latencies and amplitudes. Each peak is thought to originate from a neural generator starting with the auditory nerve through the brain stem. Peak I and especially Peak V are the most robust in reference to stimulus level and procedural variables.

If brain stem audiometry is done to determine the existence of a peripheral hearing impairment, an ABR waveform is obtained to high level auditory stimuli and to the same stimuli at lower levels until an ABR waveform cannot be determined for each ear. Then the latency of Peaks I and V at each stimulus level (intensity) are usually plotted on an intensity-latency graph referenced to age-appropriate norms. This procedure allows for determining the degree and type of peripheral hearing loss. When used to determine neurological integrity, an ABR waveform is usually obtained for one or two high-level auditory stimuli for each ear. The amplitude and latency of the ABR peaks are analyzed individually and compared across ear and to norms to determine whether a pathologic condition exists.

## REFERENCES

Davis, H. (1976). Principles of electric response audiometry. *Annals of Otology, Rhinology, & Laryngology, 85*(28), 1–96.

Fria, T. (1980). The auditory brain stem response: Background and clinical applications. *Maico Monographs in Contemporary Audiology, 2,* 1–44.

Glasscock, M. E., Jackson, G. G., & Josey, A. F. (1981). *Brainstem electric response audiometry.* New York: Thieme-Stratton.

Jacobson, J. T. (1983). Auditory evoked potentials. *Seminars in Hearing* (Vol. 4). New York: Thieme-Stratton.

THOMAS A. FRANK
*Pennsylvania State University*

## AUDIOLOGY
## AUDIOMETRY

# BRAIN TUMORS

Brain tumors are the most frequent type of childhood cancer, after leukemia. Over half of the brain tumors in childhood occur in the area of the cerebellum and brain stem; the rest occur higher in the brain, primarily in the cerebrum. Presenting symptoms for children with cerebellar tumors include early morning headaches, nausea and vomiting, vision problems, and loss of balance. Children with tumors located higher in the brain may experience more focal symptoms such as weakness on one side of the body or vision problems. For any child with a brain tumor, these symptoms are often accompanied by changes in mood and academic performance. These findings can easily lead parents or teachers to assume that the child is developing a school phobia.

Many brain tumors are treated successfully with various combinations of surgery, radiation, and chemotherapy. Depending on the type and location of the tumor, and the treatment, most children are able to resume schooling (at least on a limited basis) within a few months following treatment. Teachers need to be aware of the treatment regimen and possible side effects for a child recovering from a brain tumor. For a period of 2 to 4 months following surgery, mood and behavior changes are frequently observed, presumably a result of cranial irradiation and the psychological impact of having been diagnosed with a severe illness (Katz, 1980; Mulhern, Crisco, & Kun, 1983). Some of these children will receive chemotherapy for 1 to 3 years following surgery. Most children experience at least one of the following side effects: hair loss (usually reversible), nausea, behavioral changes, and painful mouth sores. Cortisone, taken to reduce the traumatic effects of surgery, also may cause changes in mood and physical appearance.

A decline in academic performance following surgery (compared with their previous performance) can be expected for most of these children (Hirsch et al., 1979; Walther & Gutjahr, 1982). After returning to school, children may improve gradually in school performance. Other children experience a continued decline in academic performance as a result of the various treatment side effects.

A continued decline also could signal a recurrence of the tumor. Regular communication with the child's primary physician is important to obtain information regarding the medical treatment and, in turn, to inform the physician about the child's functioning at school.

As these children resume school, they need regular, detailed assessment of their abilities and deficits. A complete neuropsychological assessment should be obtained every few years. There have not been enough studies to predict what specific deficits will occur; however, available data suggest that most children recovering from brain tumors suffer from at least one of the following: (1) poor coordination, (2) poor memory, (3) difficulty in acquiring and integrating new concepts, (4) a decline in overall IQ (ranging from only a few to 20 or more points), (5) emotional problems, especially somatic worries and low self-esteem (Mulhern, Crisco & Kun, 1983). Most of these children will require either special education placement and a learning program that emphasizes gradual acquisition and practice of basic skills or placement in a regular classroom with the ready availability of additional resources. Parents can play a significant role in helping the child to perform at a maximal level.

Students who had previously done well in school often are frustrated by their inability to work as quickly and efficiently as before. Teachers need to offer reassurance and encouragement, as well as extra time to learn and practice new material. Some students with impaired efficiency can continue to learn and use new information, but they may require more time than usually allowed on a timed exam to demonstrate their true levels of ability.

## REFERENCES

Hirsch, J. F., Renier, D., Czernichow, R., Benveniste, L., & Pierre-Kahn, A. (1979). Medulloblastoma in childhood. Survival and functional results. *Acta Neurochirurgica, 48,* 1–15.

Katz, E. R. (1980). Illness impact and social reintegration. In J. Kellerman (Ed.), *Psychological aspects of childhood cancer* (pp. 14–46). Springfield, IL: Thomas.

Mulhern, R. K., Crisco, J. J., & Kun, L. E. (1983). Neuropsychological sequelae of childhood brain tumors: A review. *Journal of Clinical Child Psychology, 12*(1), 66–73.

Walther, B., & Gutjahr, P. (1982). Development after treatment of cerebellar medulloblastoma in childhood. In D. Voth, P. Gutjahr, & C. Langmaid (Eds.), *Tumours of the central nervous system in infancy and childhood* (pp. 389–398). Berlin: Springer-Verlag.

SAMUEL LEBARON
PAUL M. ZELTZER
*University of Texas Health Science Center, San Antonio*

## BRAIN DISORDERS (DEGENERATIVE MOTOR DYSFUNCTIONS)
## CHEMOTHERAPY

## BRAZELTON, THOMAS B. (1918–      )

A native of Waco, Texas, Thomas B. Brazelton received his BA from Princeton University in 1940. He received his MD from Columbia College of Physicians and Surgeons in 1943. He is currently with the department of pediatrics, Harvard Medical School.

Brazelton has researched early attachment of infants to their primary caregivers and done cross-cultural research on child-rearing practices in Kenya, Guatamala, Mexico, and Greece. He has compared the interactional behaviors of African and American mothers in age-appropriate teaching tasks (Dixon, et al., 1984). Both groups demonstrated positive interactions, but their techniques were different. Brazelton sees this as important in terms of culture-specific values, expectations for children, and goals for and assumptions of the teaching process.

Brazelton developed the Brazelton Behavioral Assessment Scale (Brazelton, 1973). This is a behavioral evaluation of a newborn infant that measures interactions between an infant and social or potentially social stimuli, the infant's various reflexes, and its physiologic response to stress. Other work involving infants includes the study of the social interaction rhythms of infants. Lester, Hoffman, and Brazelton (1985) found that term infants were more likely to lead interactions with their mothers than preterm infants. This finding may help explain later reported differences in a child's development.

Brazelton received an award from the Child Study Association of America for his work with infants. He has also received a medal of outstanding service to children from *Parents' Magazine*. The *American Journal of Nursing* gave him an award for his film on the Brazelton Behavioral Assessment Scale. He continues to influence millions of American parents with his successful television show "What Every Baby Knows."

### REFERENCES

Brazelton, T. B. (1973). *Neonatal behavioral assessment scale.* Philadelphia: Lippincott.

Dixon, S. D., LeVine, R. A., Richman, A., & Brazelton, T. B. (1984). Mother-child interaction around a teaching task: An African-American comparison. *Child Development, 55*(4), 1252–1264.

Lester, B. M., Hoffman, J., & Brazelton, T. B. (1985). The rhythmic structures of mother—Infant interaction in term and preterm infants. *Child Development, 56*(1), 15–27.

E. VALERIE HEWITT
*Texas A&M University*

Laura Dewey Bridgman

School for the Blind at the age of 7. The director of the institution, Samuel Gridley Howe, developed an educational program for Bridgman and she quickly learned to read from raised letters and to communicate with manual signs. She related well to people and developed into a cheerful, intelligent woman who used her talents to teach other deaf-blind students at Perkins.

Bridgman was the first deaf-blind person to become well educated, andher achievement received wide attention. Charles Dickens visited her and published an account of their meeting. That publication led Helen Keller's mother to appeal to Howe to find a teacher for Helen; the teacher he recommended was Anne Sullivan Macy, who, as a student at Perkins had lived in the same house as Bridgman. What Bridgman accomplished was later repeated by Helen Keller and other similarly handicapped persons. But Bridgman was the first to demonstrate that proper education could enable a deaf-blind person to lead a happy and productive life.

### REFERENCE

Ross, I. (1951). *Journey into light.* New York: Appleton-Century-Crofts.

PAUL IRVINE
*Katonah, New York*

## BRIDGMAN, LAURA DEWEY (1829–1899)

Laura Dewey Bridgman, deaf and blind from the age of 2, entered the Perkins Institution and Massachusetts

## BRIGANCE DIAGNOSTIC INVENTORIES

Brigance (1981) states that the purpose of the Brigance inventories is to "assess preacademic, academic, and vocational skills and to provide a systematic performance record to help teachers define instructional objectives and plan individualized educational programs." The major areas tested by the Brigance inventories are reading, writing, spelling, mathematics, language, and motor skills. The inventories evaluate over 500 skill sequences in grades preschool through 12.

The Brigance inventories are a broad and comprehensive set of four informal and individually administered criterion-referenced tasks. They are easily administered by classroom teachers, special education teachers, psychologists, and administrators. Although time limits are not enforced, it takes from 15 to 90 minutes to administer an inventory. An additional 15 to 30 minutes is required for scoring. Scores available on subtests include grade and age. Recordkeeping is designed for continuous and ongoing assessment through the use of color coding, charts, and graphs.

The Brigance inventories are not yet normed. Field testing has been conducted in Canada and in 30 states. Because the inventories are not administered in a standardized manner, test-retest reliability may be difficult to establish. Grade-level scores should not be used to measure student progress as they may be slightly elevated and are generally misleading (see entry on Grade Equivalents).

There are four inventories: (1) the Diagnostic Inventory of Early Development (yellow binder), which addresses grades preschool through 2 and measures preambulatory motor skills, gross and fine motor skills, self-help, prespeech, general knowledge, readiness, reading, writing, and mathematics; (2) the Diagnostic Inventory of Basic Skills (blue binder), which addresses grades Kindergarten through 6 and measures readiness, reading, word recognition, fluency, analysis, vocabulary, handwriting, grammar, spelling, mathematics, computation, measurement, and geometry; (3) the Diagnostic Inventory of Essential Skills (red binder), which addresses grades 4 through 12 and measures reading, word recognition, oral reading, comprehension, analysis, reference, writing, spelling, mathematics, computation, fractions, decimals, percents, and measurements; and (4) the Diagnostic Comprehensive Inventory of Basic Skills (green binder), which addresses Kindergarten through 9 and measures all skills in the Diagnostic Inventory of Basic Skills (blue binder) and speech, listening skills, metrics, and reading comprehension. The inventories are published by Curriculum Associates, Inc., 5 Esquire Road, North Billenia, MA 01862.

MARIBETH MONTGOMERY KASIK
*Governors State University*

**CRITERION-REFERENCED TESTING
GRADE EQUIVALENTS**

# BRISTOL SOCIAL ADJUSTMENT GUIDES AND PROFILE

Recent trends in public policy and professional practice show a growing preference for behaviorally versus analytically based definitions of children's social and emotional maladjustment. This preference is manifest in the rapid development of behavioral criteria for the identification and classification of emotional disturbance in the fields of special education (Miller & Epstein, 1979) and clinical child psychology and psychiatry (Achenbach, 1980; American Psychiatric Association, 1980). Educators and clinicians are particularly encouraged by the advantages associated with standardized rating scales and checklists that are keyed to observable and potentially alterable behaviors. More popular scales and checklists afford relatively unobtrusive evaluations of child behavior in natural social settings such as the classroom or home (compared with the rather obtrusive and unnatural setting of the isolated clinical examination session). These evaluations are made by contextually knowledgeable persons such as teachers and parents. One of the leading behavior rating scales, the Bristol Social Adjustment Guides (BSAG, Stott, 1972, 1985), has gained international interest largely owing to its behaviorally oriented item content and inclusion in large-scale normative studies involving over 25,000 American, Canadian, and British schoolchildren.

The revised BSAG is designed for teacher observation of children 5 through 15 years old. It is comprised of 110 verbal items that teachers may employ to describe children's ongoing behavior in school environs. Each verbal indicator is presented with reference to some specific social or learning situation in which the child's adjustment to self, peers, or adults may be observed. For example, within the social context of talking with teacher, the BSAG provides problem behavior indicators such as "can't get a word out of her," "overtalkative, tires teacher with constant chatter," and "chats only when alone with teacher." The indicators, drawn originally from the language of schoolteachers, are phenomenologically focused and devoid of clinical terminology and, therefore, eliminate or reduce the necessity for respondent teachers to make inferences regarding the meaning of child behavior or the nature of internal, mediating psychological processes such as thoughts or feelings. Teachers rate each indicator as either present (by underlining) or absent (not underlining), thus constituting a two-point scale for each item. Included also is a complementary set of 43 "healthy" behavior items that teachers may use alternatively in describing children's typical styles of personal and interpersonal coping (e.g., in talking with teacher, a child's behavior may be described as "forward, opens conversations").

The 110 indicators are collected into several mutually

exclusive groups, including six core syndromes and two associated groupings of problem behavior. The item grouping was accomplished through a nonparametric clustering strategy (described by Stott, Marston, & Neill, 1975) that merged phenotypically similar behaviors as a function of their simultaneous incidence in the normative population. The six core syndromes include (1) unforthcomingness (containing 13 indicators), representing a set of timid, unassertive, and socially ineffective behaviors; (2) withdrawal (9 indicators), describing isolationism, uncommunicativeness, and apparent indifference toward other people; (3) depression (10 indicators), an inability or unwillingness to seek out or respond to environmental stimuli, sometimes viewed as lethargy or passive resistance; (4) inconsequence (22 indicators), characterizing impulse-ridden, impetuous, or hyperactive behavior carried out without consideration of possible adverse consequences; (5) hostility (17 indicators), defining a variety of provocative and often aggressive actions through which children attempt to break off unsatisfying relationships with others, particularly adults; and (6) peer maladaptiveness (12 indicators), referring to intrusive and instigative behaviors performed without regard for the rights of other children or directed to violate peer value systems.

The two associated problem behavior groupings are (1) nonsyndromic underreaction, comprising a collection of nine generally passive and constricted malbehaviors, too varied to be regarded as a homogeneous syndrome but, nevertheless, confirmatory of syndromic maladjustment as indicated by unforthcomingness, withdrawal, or depression; and (2) nonsyndromic overreaction, containing 12 generally antagonistic and interfering behaviors similarly viewed as supportive of specific syndromic maladjustment as suggested by inconsequence, hostility, or peer maladaptation. The remaining 6 of the 110 indicators form a neurological scale of apparently unmotivated behaviors such as tics and unwilled hand motion.

The BSAG further combines the several syndromes and groupings to form two overall adjustment scales. Scores for unforthcomingness, withdrawal, depression, and the nonsyndromic underreactive grouping are combined to produce underreaction scale scores (termed Unract), whereas scores for inconsequence, hostility, peer maladaptiveness, and the associated overreactive grouping are summed to yield an overreaction scale score (Ovract). These overall scales are applied as initial indicators of the existence and gravity of children's maladaptivity.

The independent factorial integrity of the BSAG's overall adjustment scales and the unique variation and factorial independence of the several core syndromes have been examined through principal components and principal axes factor analyses with various populations (Hale, 1978; McDermott, 1980b, 1981a, 1981b, 1982a, 1982b, 1984; McDermott & Watkins, 1981). These studies consistently support the practice of using the Unract and Ovract scales as indexes of overall adjustment and the in-

dividual core syndromes as bases for differential description of children's social and emotional disturbances. Additionally, the use of the BSAG's adjustment scales and core syndromes for the identification and classification of childhood exceptionality has been established through a program of retrospective, concurrent, and predictive criterion validation studies (Davis, Butler, & Goldstein, 1972; Hale & McDermott, 1984; Hale & Zuckerman, 1981; McDermott, 1980a; McDermott & Hale, 1982; Stott, 1978, 1979; Stott & Wilson, 1977; Stott et al., 1975) in special education, child psychopathology, pediatric epidemiology, and criminology.

To enhance application of the BSAG in school and clinical practice, the Bristol Social Adjustment Profile (BSAP; McDermott, 1983) was introduced. Illustrated in the Figure, the BSAP enables easy conversion of BSAG raw scores for Unract, Ovract and the six core syndromes to standardized $T$ scores having a mean of 50 and standard deviation of 10. To apply, the specialist observes whether either the overall Unract or Ovract adjustment scale $T$ score equals or exceeds 70. The 70 $T$ score is widely regarded as an appropriate cutting value for determining general maladjustment versus adjustment (Quay & Peterson, 1983; McDermott & Watkins, 1985; Trites & Laprade, 1983; Trites, Dugas, Lynch, & Ferguson, 1979). Once maladjustment is confirmed by elevation on either Unract or Ovract, the specialist examines $T$-score elevations on the various core syndromes to determine the exact pattern of maladjustment manifested.

More recently, the BSAG and BSAP have been incorporated into a comprehensive microcomputer-based assessment system called the McDermott Multidimensional Assessment of Children (M.MAC; McDermott & Watkins, 1985). The M.MAC automatically converts BSAG raw scores to $T$ scores based on combined norms for boys and girls, separate norms for boys and girls, or special norms entered by the specialist for particular regions, minority groups, or clinical subpopulations. The BSAP is applied to differentiate variations of social-emotional adjustment ("good adjustment" for $T$ scores below 60 and "adequate adjustment" for those between 60 and 69) and levels of maladjustment ("mild" for $T$ scores between 70 and 79, "moderate" between 80 and 89, "severe" between 90 and 99, and "extreme" above 99). Moreover, the M.MAC microcomputer system permits one to alter maladjustment cutting values and to enter BSAG ratings obtained from two independent teachers, to observe the profile similarity of the teachers' evaluations, and to merge teachers' ratings for a more reliable and generalizable assessment of child adjustment.

When the BSAG is used with M.MAC, a child's performance across the overall adjustment scales and core syndromes is used to determine the child's similarity to each of the major adjustment and maladjustment types identifiable in the general child population. Thus detected maladjustment is typed as either a conduct disorder, anx-

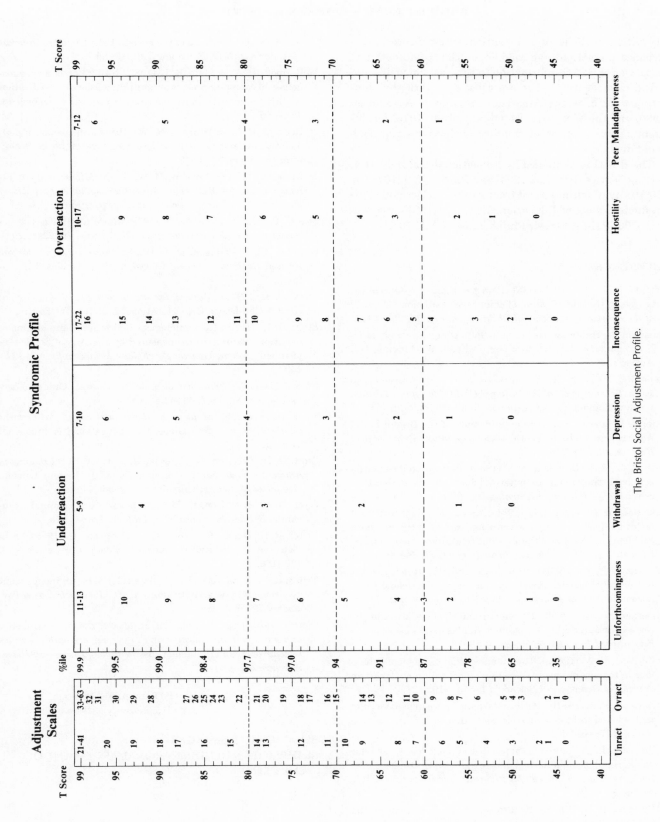

The Bristol Social Adjustment Profile.

iety-withdrawal disorder, attention-deficit disorder, disturbance of emotions and conduct, or some combination of these. Use of BSAG information in this fashion yields empirical classifications that are consistent with the standard set forth by the American Psychiatric Association (1980) and the World Health Organization (1978) for differential classification of childhood behavioral and emotional disorders.

The BSAG is published by Educational and Industrial Testing Service, P.O. Box 7234, San Diego, CA 92107. The BSAP is available at no cost from Paul A. McDermott, PhD Graduate School of Education, University of Pennsylvania, 3700 Walnut Street, Philadelphia, PA 19104.

## REFERENCES

Achenbach, T. M. (1980). DSM-III in the light of empirical research on the classification of child psychopathology. *Journal of the American Academy of Child Psychiatry, 19*, 395–412.

American Psychiatric Association. (1980). *Diagnostic and statistical manual of mental disorders* (3rd ed.). Washington, DC: Author.

Davis, R., Butler, N. R., & Goldstein, N. (1972). *From birth to seven: Second report of the National Child Development Study*. London: Longmann and National Children's Bureau.

Hale, R. L. (1978). A factor analytic study of the Bristol Social Adjustment Guides in a rural school population. *Psychological Reports, 42*, 215–218.

Hale, R. L., & McDermott, P. A. (1984). Pattern analysis of an actuarial strategy for computerized diagnosis of childhood exceptionality. *Journal of Learning Disabilities, 17*, 30–37.

Hale, R. L., & Zuckerman, C. (1981). Application of confirmatory factor analysis to verify the contruct validity of the Behavior Problem Checklist and the Bristol Social Adjustment Guides. *Educational & Psychological Measurement, 41*, 843–850.

McDermott, P. A. (1980a). Prevalence and constituency of behavioral disturbance taxonomies in the regular school population. *Journal of Abnormal Child Psychology, 8*, 523–536.

McDermott, P. A. (1980b). Principal components analysis of the revised Bristol Social Adjustment Guides. *British Journal of Educational Psychology, 50*, 223–228.

McDermott, P. A. (1981a). The manifestation of problem behaviour in ten age groups of Canadian school children. *Canadian Journal of Behavioural Science, 13*, 310–319.

McDermott, P. A. (1981b). Patterns of disturbance in behaviorally maladjusted children and adolescents. *Journal of Clinical Psychology, 37*, 867–874.

McDermott, P. A. (1982a). Generality of disordered behavior across populations of normal and deviant school children: Factorial relations analyses. *Multivariate Behavioral Research, 17*, 69–85.

McDermott, P. A. (1982b). Syndromes of maladaptation among elementary school boys and girls. *Psychology in the Schools, 19*, 281–286.

McDermott, P. A. (1983). A syndromic typology for analyzing school children's disturbed social behavior. *School Psychology Review, 12*, 250–259.

McDermott, P. A. (1984). Child behavior disorders by age and sex based on item factoring of the revised Bristol Guides. *Journal of Abnormal Child Psychology, 12*, 15–35.

McDermott, P. A., & Hale, R. L. (1982). Validation of a systems-actuarial computer process for multidimensional classification of child psychopathology. *Journal of Clinical Psychology, 38*, 477–486.

McDermott, P. A., & Watkins, M. W. (1981). Dimensions of maladaptive behavior among kindergarten level children. *Behavioral Disorders, 7*, 11–17.

McDermott, P. A., & Watkins, M. W. (1985). *Microcomptuer systems manual for McDermott Multidimensional Assessment of Children*. New York: Psychological Corporation.

Miller, T. L., & Epstein, M. H. (1979). State terminology of behavioral disorders. *Psychology in the Schools, 16*, 224–229.

Quay, H. C., & Peterson, D. R. (1983). *Interim manual for the Revised Behavior Problem Checklist*. Coral Gables, FL: Authors.

Stott, D. H. (1972). *Manual for the Bristol Social Adjustment Guides*. San Diego, CA: Educational & Industrial Testing.

Stott, D. H. (1978). Epidemiological indicators of the origins of behavior disturbance as measured by the Bristol Social Adjustment Guides. *Genetic Psychology Monographs, 97*, 127–159.

Stott, D. H. (1979). The Bristol Social Adjustment Guides. *Therapeutic Education, 7*, 34–44.

Stott, D. H. (1985). *Manual for the Bristol Social Adjustment Guides* (rev. ed.). San Diego, CA: Educational & Industrial Testing.

Stott, D. H., Marston, N. C., & Neill, S. J. (1975). *Taxonomy of behaviour disturbance*. Toronto, Canada: Mussen. London: Hodder & Stoughton/University of London Press.

Stott, D. H., & Wilson, D. M. (1977). The adult criminal as juvenile. *British Journal of Criminology, 17*, 47–57.

Trites, R. L., Dugas, E., Lynch, G., & Ferguson, H. (1979). Prevalence of hyperactivity. *Journal of Pediatric Psychology, 4*, 179–188.

Trites, R. L., & Laprade, K. (1983). Evidence for an independent syndrome of hyperactivity. *Journal of Child Psychology & Psychiatry, 24*, 573–586.

World Health Organization. (1978). *Mental disorders: Glossary and guide to their classification in accordance with the ninth revision of the International Classification of Diseases*. Geneva, Switzerland: Author.

PAUL A. McDERMOTT
*University of Pennsylvania*

**BEHAVIORAL ASSESSMENT**
**McDERMOTT MULTIDIMENSIONAL ASSESSMENT OF CHILDREN**

# BRITTLE BONE DISEASE (OSTEOGENESIS IMPERFECTA)

Osteogenesis imperfecta appears in several forms, one that is nearly always fatal to the neonate (osteogenesis imperfecta congenita), and a later appearing variation (osteogenesis imperfecta tarda) in which the affected individual may live a normal life (Behrman & Vaughan, 1983). The congenital variety results from an autosomal recessive gene; the later appearing from an autosomal dominant gene.

The later appearing type (OI Type I) is present in 1 out of 30,000 births. Bone fractures are present at birth about 10% of the time and scoliosis is seen in about 20% of affected adults. There is a distinct blue coloring and bulging appearance of the white portion of the eyes (sclera). One-third of this group will show hearing impairment after age 10; earlier onset is uncommon. "Occurrence of neonatal fractures does not predict more deformity or more handicap" (Behrman & Vaughan, 1983).

In the second type (OI Type II), the condition is generally fatal. Half of the infants survive the birth process but expire soon afterward, usually to respiratory difficulties associated with the skeletal anomalies. The limbs are usually severely deformed. There is no effective treatment for Type II.

Management of the disorder centers around proper support and support of skeletal growth. Parents must learn first aid for fractures. The youngster must learn to engage in activities that minimize the risk of fracture without becoming inactive. Nutrition and genetic counseling are essential, as is a careful monitoring of the hearing loss (Bennett, 1981).

## REFERENCES

Behrman, R., & Vaughan, V. (1983). *Nelson textbook of pediatrics* (12th ed.). Philadelphia: Saunders.

Bennett, P. (1981). *Diseases, The nurse's reference library series.* Philadelphia, Pennsylvania: Informed Communications Book Division.

JOHN E. PORCELLA
*Rhinebeck Country School,
Rhinebeck, New York*

## OSTEOPOROSIS

# BROCA, PIERRE PAUL (1824–1880)

Pierre Paul Broca, a French surgeon and physical anthropologist noted for his studies of the brain and skull, was a member of the Academy of Medicine in Paris and professor of surgical pathology and clinical surgery. Through postmortem examinations he learned that damage to the third convolution of the left frontal lobe of the brain (Broca's convolution) was associated with loss of the ability to speak; this was the first demonstration of a connection between a specific bodily activity and a specific area of the brain. His announcement of this finding in 1861 led to a vast amount of research on cerebral localization.

Broca was a key figure in the development of physical anthropology in France. He founded a laboratory, a school, a journal, and a society for the study of anthropology. He originated techniques and invented instruments for studying the skull, and helped to establish that the Neanderthal man discovered in his time was a primitive ancestor of modern man.

## REFERENCE

Talbott, J. H. (1970). *A biographical history of medicine: Excerpts and essays on the men and their work.* New York: Grune & Stratton.

PAUL IRVINE
*Katonah, New York*

# BRONFENBRENNER, URI (1917–    )

Uri Bronfenbrenner was born in Moscow, Russia, in 1917, and came to the United States at an early age. He received his BA degree from Cornell in 1938, his EdM from Harvard in 1940, and his PhD from the University of Michigan in 1942. After World War II, Bronfenbrenner returned to the University of Michigan as assistant professor. In 1948 he joined the faculty of Cornell as professor of psychology, child development, and family relationships.

Bronfenbrenner has written widely in developmental psychology. He is perhaps best known for his ecological approach to developmental psychology. The ecological environment, according to Bronfenbrenner, is like a set of nested Russian dolls in which one doll contains another which contains another and so forth. He recognizes three levels of ecological environment in psychological development. "At the innermost level is the immediate setting containing the developing person. This can be the home, the classroom, or . . . the laboratory" (Bronfenbrenner, 1979).

The next level involves influences beyond the immediate setting and the relationships among them. The school and peer group are examples of this second level. Bronfenbrenner (1979) says that a "child's ability to learn to read . . . may depend no less on how he is taught than on the existence and nature of ties between the school and the home." The third level involves influences from events in settings in which the child is not directly involved. Our industrialized society, in which both parents are employed, has a direct influence on how children of such parents develop. Bronfenbrenner is also known for his comparison of education in the United States and the Soviet Union.

## REFERENCES

Bronfenbrenner, U. (1972). *Two worlds of childhood: U.S. and U.S.S.R.* New York: Simon & Schuster.

Bronfenbrenner, U. (1979). *The ecology of human development: Experiments by nature and design.* Cambridge, MA: Harvard University Press.

STAFF

**Lou Brown**

## BROWN, ANN L. (1943–      )

Ann L. Brown was educated at the University of London, receiving her BA in psychology with first-class honors in 1964 and her PhD in psychology in 1967. She is currently professor of psychology at the University of Illinois, doing research in areas of cognitive psychology, particularly reading and metacognition.

Brown served as associate editor for *Child Development* between 1976 and 1979. She also has served as consulting editor for the *Journal of Experimental Psychology, Developmental Psychology, American Journal of Mental Deficiency*, and the *American Journal of Psychology*. She is currently on the editorial board of the Harvard University Press Cognitive Science Series and on the MIT Press Learning and Development and Conceptual Change Series. She is also a member of the governing board of the Cognitive Science Society.

Brown works in several areas of cognition and is considered a leader in the area of metacognition. She distinguishes between knowledge (cognition) and the understandings of that knowledge (metacognition). A particularly significant work is "Knowing When, Where and How to Remember: A Problem in Metacognition" (1978).

### REFERENCE

Brown, A. L. (1978). Knowing when, where and how to remember: A problem in metacognition. In R. Glaser (Ed.), *Advances in instructional psychology*. Hillsdale, NJ: Erlbaum.

RICK GONZALES
*Texas A&M University*

## BROWN, LOU (1939–      )

Lou Brown received his BA (1963) in social studies education and his MA (1965) in clinical psychology from East Carolina University. He received his PhD (1969) in special education from Florida State University. Since 1969 he has been a professor in the Department of Rehabilitation Psychology and Special education at the University of Wisconsin, Madison.

In the field of special education, his efforts have focused on the development of service delivery models and longitudinal curricula that prepare people with severe intel- lectual disabilities to live, work, and play in integrated environments. His dream is that some day all people with severe intellectual disabilities will live in decent family-style homes, will perform real work in the real world for real money, will enjoy rich and varied recreation/leisure environments and activities, and will avail themselves of all community environments.

Some consider him a member of a radical fringe, probably because his earlier segregationist attitudes and negative beliefs about people who are severely disabled have changed dramatically. He now strongly advocates that people with severe handicaps can become productive members of integrated society. Thus he rejects institutions, special schools, sheltered workshops, activity centers, group homes, and other manifestations of segregation as economically, programmatically, and existentially untenable.

He and his students and associates are working to involve people with severe handicaps in the real world of work by matching an individual with a handicap to a job that satisfies everyone, including the employer (Brown et al., 1985b). He further advocates what has been termed the composite person; that is, joining two people with different abilities and disabilities so as to complete at least one part of a job performed by a nondisabled worker in an integrated work place.

Finally, Brown believes that most school and vocational training programs teach useless skills and counterproductive attitudes instead of how to function in actual integrated communities. Most of his recent written works represent attempts to prepare the lowest functioning people in society for integrated work (Brown et al., 1985a).

### REFERENCES

Brown, L., Shiraga, B., York, J., Kessler, K., Strohm, B., Rogan, P., Sweet, M., Zanella, K., Van Deventer, P., & Loomis, R. (1985a). Integrated work opportunities for adults with severe handicaps: The extended training option. *Journal of the Association for Persons with Severe Handicaps*, pp. 262–269.

Brown, L., Shiraga, B., York, J., U. Solner, A., Z. Albright, K., Rogan, P., McCarthy, E., & Loomis, R. (1985b). *Educational programs for students with severe intellectual disabilities.* Madison, WI: Madison Metropolitan School District.

E. VALERIE HEWITT
*Texas A&M University*

## BROWN, ROBERT T. (1940–    )

Born in 1940 in Greenwich, Connecticut, Robert T. Brown obtained his BA degree from Hamilton College in 1961 and his PhD in experimental psychology from Yale University in 1966. At Yale he worked with Allan R. Wagner and Frank A. Logan before conducting his dissertation research under the supervision of William Kessen. After a USPHS postdoctoral fellowship at the University of Sussex, he was on the faculty of the College of William and Mary and then the University of North Carolina, Chapel Hill. He is now professor of psychology at the University of North Carolina, Wilmington.

**Robert T. Brown**

His research on the effects of rearing environments on problem solving in rats and on imprinting in chicks and ducklings has influenced theories of early experience and critical periods. In addition to being a consulting editor of the *Encyclopedia of Special Education*, he coedited two books of relevance to special education, *Perspectives on Bias in Mental Testing* (Reynolds & Brown, 1984) and *Psychological Perspectives on Childhood Exceptionality: A Handbook* (Brown & Reynolds, 1986). He coedits, with Cecil R. Reynolds the Plenum Perspectives on Individual Differences, a series of professional books.

### REFERENCES

Brown, R. T., & Reynolds, C. R. (Eds.). (1986). *Psychological perspectives on childhood exceptionality: A handbook.* New York: Wiley.

Reynolds, C. R., & Brown, R. T. (Eds.). (1984). *Perspectives on bias in mental testing.* New York: Plenum.

CECIL R. REYNOLDS
*Texas A&M University*

## BROWN SCHOOLS

The Brown Schools were established in 1940. There are three locations one in San Marcos, Texas, and two in Austin, Texas. The Brown Schools also own and operate many other facilities for the handicapped throughout the United States. The school serves students as a treatment center for children who suffer from emotional disorders, brain damage, learning disabilities, and developmental delays or retardation. The school program is coeducational with ungraded classes ranging from K–12. The center is primarily a residential treatment facility. The school curriculum features general academic programs, prevocational training, language and speech therapies, counseling, reading programs, remediation, and tutorial instruction.

The Brown Schools provide modern professional services to implement individual treatment programs. The individualization of the treatment programs provide for continuous modification, reevaluations and reassessments according to the needs of each client. Professional services including psychiatry, psychology, education, nursing, prevocational training, social work, and recreation therapy. The services of the Brown Schools are available for children, adolescents, and adults, and provide programs on a 24-hour basis. The Brown Schools can be reached at P.O. Box 4008, Austin, Texas 78765.

### REFERENCE

Sargent, J. K. (1982). *The directory for exceptional children* (9th ed.). Boston: Porter Sargent.

PAUL C. RICHARDSON
*Elwyn Institutes,*
*Elwyn, Pennsylvania*

## BROWN v. BOARD OF EDUCATION

In 1954, *Brown* v. *Board of Education* was brought to the Supreme Court by a Kansas City black family, the Browns. It was joined by other cases from South Carolina, Virginia, and Delaware (Alexander, Corns, & McCann, 1969; Zirkel, 1978). The plaintiffs, black students from various states, were seeking admission to public schools that had been restricted to white students. Black students had been denied admission to attend these schools under the "separate but equal" doctrine that had been adopted in a previous court case (Bolmeier, 1973). Under this doctrine, schools claimed that black students were being treated equally through the provision of equal facilities, even though these facilities were separate. The plaintiffs claimed that, by being denied equal facilities, they were also being deprived of their right to an equal education.

The *Brown* v. *Board of Education* 347 U.S. 483 decision (1954) was unanimously in favor of the plaintiffs. The Court declared that separate educational facilities were unequal because they violated the black students' right to an equal education under the Fourteenth Amendment of the Constitution, which guarantees equal protection of the law to all American citizens. As delivered by Justice Warren, the Brown decision follows (Fellman, 1976):

> Today . . . [education] is a principal instrument in awakening the child to cultural values, in preparing him for later professional training, and in helping him to adjust normally to his environment. In these days, it is doubtful that any child may reasonably be expected to succeed in life if he is denied the opportunity of an education. Such an opportunity, where the state has undertaken to provide it, is a right which must be made available to all on equal terms. (p. 137)

Because of the complexities of this case, the U.S. attorney general and the attorneys general of the different states involved in the case were recalled for a second deliberation in 1955. The 1954 decision was sustained and the Court ordered that immediate steps were to be taken to eliminate segregation in public schools, with local school authorities given the responsibility of implementing the Court order.

Today, this Court decision is regarded as a landmark in the history of the U.S. educational system because it set a direction for future Court decisions that emphasized that children cannot be discriminated against on the basis of race, sex, or national origin. Although this decision had no direct bearing on special education at the time, it established a nondiscriminatory policy that was later applied to such individuals as the mentally retarded, the learning disabled, and the emotionally handicapped. As such, these individuals are now guaranteed equal educational opportunities.

## REFERENCES

Alexander, K., Corns, R., & McCann, W. (1969). *Public school law: Cases and materials*. St. Paul, MN: West.

Bolmeier, E. C. (1973). *Landmark decisions on public school issues*. Charlottesville, VA: Michie.

Felman, D. (1976). *The Supreme Court and education* (3rd ed.). New York: Teachers College, Columbia University.

Zirkel, P. A. (1978). *Supreme Court decisions affecting education*. Bloomington, IN: Phi Delta Kappa.

EMILIA C. LOPEZ
*Fordham University*

CULTURE FAIR TESTS
DISPROPORTIONALITY
SOCIOECONOMIC STATUS

# BRUININKS-OSERETSKY TEST OF MOTOR PROFICIENCY

The Bruininks-Oseretsky Test of Motor Proficiency (Bruininks, 1978) is an individually administered test of gross and fine motor functioning of children from $4\frac{1}{2}$ to $14\frac{1}{2}$ years of age. It is the latest revision of the Oseretsky tests of motor proficiency published in Russia in 1903 (later translated into English by Edgar Doll in 1946). The complete battery comprises 46 items subdivided into 8 subtests. In addition to subtest scores, composite scores are available for the gross motor subtests, the fine motor subtests, and the total battery. The complete form takes from 45 to 60 minutes to administer. There is also a 14-item short form, requiring 15 to 20 minutes, which provides a single index of general motor proficiency.

Subtest and composite scores can be expressed in terms of age-based standard scores, percentile ranks, and stanines. Age equivalents are available for each subtest. The battery was standardized on a sample of 765 children between the ages of $4\frac{1}{2}$ and $14\frac{1}{2}$. The sample was stratified by age, sex, race, community size, and geographic region according to the 1970 Census. Test-retest reliability ranges from .56 to .86. Validity was investigated using factor analysis of items, age differentiation, and comparative studies with retarded and learning-disabled children.

## REFERENCES

Bruininks, R. H. (1978). *Bruininks-Oseretsky Test of Motor Proficiency*. Circle Pines, MN: American Guidance Service.

Doll, E. A. (1946). *The Oseretsky Tests of Motor Proficiency*. Minneapolis, MN: American Guidance Service.

LIZANNE DESTEFANO
*University of Illinois,
Urbana-Champaign*

# BRUNER, JEROME (1915–     )

Bruner obtained his BA from Duke University in 1937 and PhD in psychology from Harvard in 1941. He immediately went to work in Washington D.C. for the war effort in the areas of political intelligence and psychological warfare.

Bruner was appointed Professor of Psychology at Harvard University (1945–72) and Cambridge University in England (1972–79) and served as Director of the Center for Cognitive Studies at Harvard (1960–72). He presently serves as Director of the New York Institute for the Humanities and is the George Herbert Mead Professor at the New School for Social Research.

Bruner's principal areas of research have been in the knowledge acquisition processes: perception, memory, learning, thought, and literary and scientific creation. As a strong mentalist, Bruner assisted American Psychology towards a more cognitive basis; for example, the publication of *A Study of Thinking* (1956) centered on problem solving and thinking and was supported by Jean Piaget.

As a strong functionalist, Bruner participated in curriculum design and reform. For example, the *Process of Education*, (1960) was a controversial study of the underlying structure of science curriculum and focus for the learner, and *Man: A Course of Study* combined psychological ideas about pedagogy with science curriculum in different media.

Bruner's interests in child development and public policy led to his involvement in the planning and establishment of the Head Start Program in the United States. A general theme of bridging the gap between the sciences and humanities or scientific knowledge and daily living, is present throughout Bruner's work. He is currently engaged in the study of narrative modes of thought and the functional acquisition of language, which he hopes will assist a "divided psychology regenerate a new and more interesting whole."

Author of some 200 essays, reviews, and articles and 15 books, Bruner has also served on two presidential commissions and received many awards and honorary degrees.

### REFERENCES

Bruner, J. S., Goodnow, J. J., & Austin, G. A. (1956). *A study of thinking*. NY: John Wiley.

Bruner, J. S. (1961). *The process of education*. Cambridge, Mass.: Harvard University Press.

ELAINE FLETCHER-JANZEN
*Texas A&M University*

## BRUXISM AND THE HANDICAPPED STUDENT

Bruxism can be defined as "the nonfunctional gnashing and grinding of teeth occurring during the day or night" (Richmond, et al., 1984). The adverse effects of bruxism include severe dental wear, damage to the alveolar bone, temporomandibular joint disorders, and hypertrophy of masticatory muscles, as well as occasional infection. It can also result in significant pain, permanent damage to the structures of the mouth and jaw, and lost teeth (Richmond et al., 1984; Rugh & Robbins, 1982). Dental wear is the most commonly used measure to determine the extent of bruxism.

Estimates of the frequency of bruxism in the nonretarded population have ranged between 5% (Reding et al., 1966) to a high of 21% (Wigdorowicz-Makowerowa et al., 1977), with no significant differences between sexes (Bober, 1982) or age groups (Lindqvist, 1971).

Investigators have reported more dental wear as a consequence of bruxism in severely mentally retarded children than in nonretarded children (Lindqvist & Heijbel, 1974). An informal survey by Blount et al. (1982) indicated that 21.5% of a profoundly retarded group engaged in bruxism. The study of Richmond et al. of some 433 mentally retarded individuals in a state institution revealed a rate of 41 to 59% in this group based on a questionnaire used with direct-care staff who were asked to observe the residents. Higher rates were reported for deaf retarded individuals. Older patients were more likely to grind teeth and wear into the dentin than younger ones.

A variety of explanations for bruxism have been advanced. The etiology of bruxism has been approached along lines of local, psychological, and systemic causes. An example of a local cause is occlusive abnormalities. Glaros and Rao (1977) believe that stress is a major cause. Systemic explanations include heredity factors and endocrinal or neurological dysfunction. It has been suggested (Lindqvist & Heijbel, 1974) that bruxism may be a form of stereotypy among retarded populations. It has also been suggested (Richmond et al., 1984) that it can be considered a form of self-injurious behavior.

While such methods as deep muscle relaxation and massed practice have been found to assist individuals of normal intelligence, these methods require a certain level of cognitive ability to be successfully deployed and may not be suited for bruxists who have cognitive difficulties or retardation. Behavioral methods to reduce bruxism have been favored in recent years (Rugh & Robbins, 1982). Thus positive reinforcement has been used to reduce its incidence in retarded individuals (i.e., to reinforce nonbruxist behaviors) and to encourage incompatible behaviors such as keeping the mouth open. Problems with positive reinforcers include the fact that social and tactile reinforcers usually do not have strong effects with severely retarded individuals. Edibles result in further chewing, thus reinforcing behaviors that are not compatible with efforts to reduce bruxism.

Hence behavioral treatment has sometimes been of an aversive nature (e.g., using a contingent sound blast). Such treatment, however, involves expensive equipment. Blount et al. (1982) were able to use a much simpler method, known as icing, with two profoundly retarded women. They greatly reduced their bruxism and successfully generalized their improvements beyond the training sessions. In icing there is a brief contingent application of ice to cheeks or chin as an aversive stimulus. Another, similar method of aversive control of bruxism in a mentally retarded nonverbal child in a class for trainable mentally retarded children was accomplished by Kramer (1981). The method involved the use of a contingent verbal "no" accompanied by the teacher's finger to the child's jaw.

## REFERENCES

Blount, R. L., Drabman, R. S., Wilson, N., & Stewart, D. (1982). Reducing severe diurnal bruxism in two profoundly retarded females. *Journal of Applied Behavior Analysis, 15*, 565–571.

Bober, H. (1982). Cause and treatment of bruxism and bruxomania. *Dental Abstracts, 3*, 658–659.

Glaros, A. G., & Rao, S. M. (1977). Bruxism: A critical review. *Psychological Bulletin, 84*, 767–781.

Heller, R. F., & Strang, H. R. (1973). Controlling bruxism through automated aversive conditioning. *Behavior Research & Therapy, 11*, 327–328.

Kramer, J. J. (1981). Aversive control of bruxism in a mentally retarded child: A case study. *Psychological Reports, 49*, 815–818.

Lindqvist, B. (1971). Bruxism in children. *Odontologisk Revy, 22*, 413–424.

Lindqvist, B., & Heijbel, J. (1974). Bruxism in children with brain damage. *Acta Odontologica Scandinavica, 32*, 313–319.

Reding, G. R., Rubright, W. C., & Zimmerman, S. O. (1966). Incidence of bruxism. *Journal of Dental Research, 45*, 1198–1204.

Richmond, G., Rugh, J. D., Dolfi, R., & Wasilewsky, J. W. (1984). Survey of bruxism in an institutionalized retarded population. *American Journal of Mental Deficiency, 88*, 418–421.

Rugh, J. D., & Robbins, W. J. (1982). Oral habit disorders. In B. Ingersoll (Ed.), *Behavioral aspects in dentistry* (pp. 179–202). New York: Appleton-Century-Crofts.

Wigdorowicsz-Makowerowa, N., Grodzki, C., & Maslanka, T. (1977). Frequency and etiopathogenes of bruxism (on the basis of prophylactic examinations of 1000 middle-aged men). *Czaopismo-Stomatologiczne, 25*, 1109–1112.

DAVID C. MANN
*St. Francis Hospital,
Pittsburgh, Pennsylvania*

**DENTISTRY AND THE HANDICAPPED CHILD
SELF-INJURIOUS BEHAVIOR**

# BUCKLEY AMENDMENT

The Buckley amendment is the commonly known name for the Family Educational Rights and Privacy Act (FERPA, 1976). The general purpose of this legislation is protection of student records from unauthorized inspection and/or disclosure (Jacobson, 1976). As such, the Buckley amendment provides that parents and eligible students have rights of access to any educational records directly relating to the student if the institutions housing those records receive federal funds under any program administered by the Department of Education. The law also extends to individuals the right to challenge at a hearing those records believed to be inaccurate, misleading, or otherwise inappropriate, and to control the disclosure of any information contained in the files.

The law stipulates the parent of a student and eligible students have the right to review and inspect the education records kept by the agency or institution where the student is or has attended. Parent is defined as "a parent, guardian, or individual acting as a parent of a student in the absence of a parent." Eligible student is defined as "a student who has attained 18 years of age or is attending an institution of postsecondary education" (FERPA, 1976, p. 24671). Specifically, the law requires that the educational facilities allow the individuals designated to review and inspect educational records or copies of those records within 45 days of a formal request. They must further provide appropriate explanations and interpretations of the records to ensure that parents understand the information contained within. The institution is also forbidden to destroy records once there is an active request for inspection.

The right to inspect records is limited in a number of areas at the postsecondary level (FERPA, 1976, p. 24672). Also, certain limitations to access are inherent as to what is defined in the law as "education records." In general, education records include all information held by the educational institution that directly relates to the student. The term, however, does not apply to certain information held by teachers, administrators, or law enforcement personnel as long as it is not shared with any other personnel with the exception of substitutes or law enforcement personnel in the same jurisdiction. The term also excludes records maintained by physicians, psychiatrists, psychologists, etc., that are not disclosed to others not providing the treatment. This calls for particular concern and commitment on the part of certain persons working in the schools (Bersoff, 1982; Reynolds, Gutkin, Elliot & Witt, 1984).

In conjunction with the right to inspect and review records, the Buckley amendment also affords parents and eligible students the right to amend education records they deem inaccurate, misleading, or violating the privacy or other rights of students (FERPA, 1976, p. 24672). Within a "reasonable period of time" (which is not clearly defined in the law), the institution must inform the parents whether they intend to honor the request for amendment. If the institution decides not to amend the records as requested, they are obligated to inform the parents of the refusal and of the parents' right to an impartial hearing. If, as a result of the hearing, the institution maintains that the information is in some way inaccurate, misleading, or in some way violating students' rights, it must amend the education record and provide written notification to the complainant. If, however, the institution decides that the education record is not inaccurate, it should inform the parents in writing and subsequently allow the parents the opportunity to add to the education record a written statement affirming parental objection to the information contained therein. This addition must be maintained as long as the record itself and is subject to the same guidelines as the main record if disclosed to a third party.

The second primary right afforded parents and eligible students under the Buckley amendment is the right to determine when and if a student's education records may be released to a third party. That is, the parents must provide written consent to the educational institution before the institution may disclose any personally identifiable information from the education records of a student. Personally identifiable information is specifically defined as the name of the student, the student's parent, or other family member; the address of the student; a personal identifier such as the student's Social Security number or student number; a list of personal characteristics that would make the student's identity easily traceable; or other information that would make the student's identity easily traceable (FERPA, 1976, p. 24671).

It is required that the consent form include, at a minimum, the nature of the educational records to be disclosed, the purpose of the disclosure, and the party to which the records are released. Also, if the parents or eligible student desire it, a copy of the information disclosed must be provided.

There are several conditions under which prior consent is not required for the release of personally identifiable educational records. Generally, educational institutions and agencies may release educational records to other school officials without consent when the parties to whom the records are released have legitimate educational interests. Although the institution must include criteria for determining what are school officials and what are legitimate educational interests in their annual policies and procedures (1976), there is no clarification of the terms in the law.

Other exceptions to the prior consent requirement occur when:

The student is seeking enrollment in another educational institution

There exists a state statute requiring local officials to report certain information to appropriate authorities

Releasing education records to organizations studying student testing methods, releasing educational records to certain accrediting organizations

Releasing records to parents of dependent students attending a postsecondary institution

Releasing records to the appropriate persons in an emergency to protect the health and/or safety of the students or others

The disclosure of personally identifiable information that is classified as directory information by the educational agency is also exempt from the prior consent guidelines. In this case, the institution or agency is only legally required to inform individuals via public notice of the information that is considered directory information, the right of the parent or eligible student to refuse the classification for the student in question, and the length of time given to refuse in written form the classification.

Enforcement of the rights provided for in the Buckley amendment are handled by the Educational Rights and Privacy Act Office in Washington, DC. The office generally intervenes when there is a complaint filed against an educational institution by a parent or eligible student asserting that their rights have been violated. Persons contending their rights have been violated must submit their complaint to the office in writing. On receipt of the complaint, the office must notify in writing the complainant and educational institution that the complaint has been received. The notification must include the nature of the complaint and the institution must be given the opportunity to return a written response to the allegations. The office investigates the alleged violations, securing additional verbal and/or written responses from both parties. Following the investigation, the complainant and educational institution receive written notification of the office's findings. If the institution has been found to be out of compliance, the office provides specific steps for them to follow to remedy the situation. If the agency fails to voluntarily comply within the time specified in the steps for complaince, the matter is submitted to a review board, which appoints a hearing committee or hearing panel (FERPA 1976, p. 24675) to hear the case. The panel conducts a fact-finding hearing and its decision is submitted to the Secretary of Health, Education, and Welfare. The Secretary can accept, modify, or reverse the decision of the panel, in which case it is presented to the educational institution. If the secretary rules that the institution is out of compliance, the institution may receive no federal funds until such time that it comes into compliance.

Portions of the Buckley amendment were incorporated into the Education of All Handicapped Children's Act (PL 94-142, 1975). Under this act, parents are guaranteed the right to inspect and review all records pertaining to identification, education, placement, and access to a free, appropriate public education for their handicapped children (Bersoff, 1982). Further specified in PL 94-142 are definitions of terms in the Buckley amendment such as "consent" and "personally identifiable information."

Some have suggested that although educational agencies are required to inform parents in writing of their rights, in actuality parents may not be able to actively participate for a number of reasons. Roit and Pfohl (1984), for example, investigating materials given to parents informing them of their rights guaranteed under PL 94-142, found that printed materials distributed by educational institutions are often unattractive and at a higher level of readability than many parents can comprehend. When evaluating the use of an act that supposedly protects parents and students rights, pragmatic issues such as these must be investigated. The ways in which FERPA regulates the functioning of certain educational personnel (e.g., school psychologists) are covered in numerous sources (e.g., Bersoff, 1982; Reynolds et al., 1984). Individual state compliance has also been addressed (Jacobson, 1976).

## REFERENCES

Bersoff, D. (1982). The legal regulation of school psychology. In C. R. Reynolds and T. B. Gutkin, *The handbook of school psychology*. New York: Wiley.

FERPA(Family Educational Rights and Privacy Act of 1976), 245-248, 451-465

Jacobson, A. V. (1976). The 1974 Family Rights and Privacy Act. *Journal of Kansas Bar Association*, 185–193.

Public Law 94-142, *The Education of All Handicapped Children Act*. November 29, 1975.

Reynolds, C. R., Gutkin, T. B., Elliot, S. N., Witt, J. C. (1984). *School psychology: Essentials of theory and practice*. New York: Wiley.

Roit, M. C., & Pfohl, W. (1984). The readability of P.L. 94-142 parent materials: Are parents truly informed? *Exceptional Children, 50*(6), 496–507.

JULIA A. HICKMAN
*University of Texas, Austin*

**CONFIDENTIALITY OF INFORMATION
PARENTS OF THE HANDICAPPED**

# BUREAU OF EDUCATION
# FOR THE HANDICAPPED (BEH)

The Bureau of Education for the Handicapped (BEH) was created in 1966 to administer all U.S. Office of Education programs designed for the handicapped. During the late 1960s and early 1970s, BEH administered newly created federal programs for the handicapped, including regional resource centers that provided testing to determine the special education needs of handicapped children. It also administered service centers for the deaf-blind; offered technical assistance on programs for the gifted and talented; provided funds for recruiting and training special education personnel; created experimental preschool and early education programs that could serve as models for school districts; and mounted research projects concerning the handicapped. Eventually, BEH's responsibility was extended to include the provision of technical assistance, compliance monitoring, and evaluation of state education agency and local school district implementation of PL 93-380, the Education Amendments of 1974, and PL 94-142, the Education of All Handicapped Children Act of 1975. The BEH was succeeded in name but not in authority and responsiblity by the Office of Special Education when the U.S. Department of Education was created in 1980. For a more detailed description of federal legislation and the role of BEH, see Weintraub, Abeson, Ballard, and LaVor (1976).

## REFERENCE

Weintraub, F. J., Abeson, A., Ballard, J., & LaVor, M. L. (1976). *Public policy and the education of exceptional children*. Reston, VA: Council for Exceptional Children.

ROLAND K. YOSHIDA
*Fordham University*

# BUREAU OF INDIAN AFFAIRS (BIA)

The Bureau of Indian Affairs (BIA) is an operating component of the U.S. Department of the Interior. The mission of the agency is to encourage Indian and Alaskan native people to manage their own affairs under the trust relationship to the federal government, and to facilitate full development of their human and natural resources (U.S. Government Printing Office, 1985). To carry out that mission, the bureau supports programs providing education, job training, and economic and natural resource development to Indian tribes and individuals (U.S. Government Printing Office, 1986, p. I–N58).

The BIA directly operates schools on or near Indian reservations, and operates other such schools via contract. The BIA also provides supplementary educational services, through tribal organizations, to Indian children in public schools. The U.S. Department of Education also administers programs, mostly through local educational agencies, that provide supplementary services for Indian children.

Special provisions of the Education of the Handicapped Act (EHA) apply to BIA. Under Section 611(f)(1) of the EHA, the secretary of education is authorized to make payments to BIA under the Part B state grant program, not to exceed 1% of the total available for all states, "according to the need for such assistance for the education of handicapped children on reservations serviced by elementary and secondary schools operated for Indian children by the Department of the Interior." The secretary of the interior must submit an application to the secretary of education and meet other requirements in order to receive Part B funds.

The BIA's responsibilities under the EHA are like those of a state education agency. The BIA submits a state plan application for grant funds. It is responsible for ensuring that the programmatic and procedural requirements of PL 94–142 are met. The BIA has monitoring and supervisory responsibility over programs run by its grantees.

Tribal and other agencies apply to BIA for Part B funds. Grant awards are made by BIA based on the need and justification, as demonstrated in the application, for supplemental funding over and above that provided through BIA's basic support program (the Indian School Equalization Program). The BIA agencies, like other public agencies, are subject to the excess cost requirements of PL 94–142. The BIA may retain up to the greater of 5% of its grant award or $350,000 for administrative costs associated with carrying out the law.

In December 1984, 5364 Indian children were identified as handicapped by BIA. Of that number, 57% (3057) were classified as learning disabled and another 23% (1250) as speech impaired. The remaining 20% were distributed through all conditions except deaf-blind. During school year 1982–1983, 82% of the children were in regular classes, 12% in separate classes, and 6% in separate schools (U.S. Department of Education, 1985).

Handicapped Indian children not in BIA-operated schools (i.e., those in public and other non-BIA schools) are included in the count of children made by a state. (They are not separately identified as Indians, so their number is unknown). They are not to be included in the BIA count. Similarly, a state may not count for purposes of state grant reimbursement handicapped children served in BIA-operated schools in the state.

The BIA has received a Part B grant of close to a full 1% of the appropriated amount in recent years. The 1985 grant amount was $11,239,095. If BIA used the full 5% allowable for administrative costs (in fact, they generally use less), the Part B state grant average share per child for BIA children would be $1991. The Part B state grant average share per child for the 50 states in 1985 was $275. BIA-operated school agencies, however, do not have the same relationship to state and local taxing authorities as do conventional local educational agencies.

## REFERENCES

U.S. Department of Education. (1985). *Seventh annual report to Congress on the implementation of the Education of the Handicapped Act.* Washington, DC: Author.

U.S. Government Printing Office (1985). *Catalog of federal domestic assistance.* Washington, DC: Author.

U.S. Government Printing Office (1986). *Appendix to the budget of the United States government, fiscal year 1987.* Washington, DC: Author.

JAMES R. RICCIUTI
*United States Office of
Management and Budget*

CULTURAL BIAS IN TESTING
SPECIAL EDUCATION, LEGAL REGULATIONS OF

## BURKS' BEHAVIOR RATING SCALES (BBRS)

The Burks' Behavior Rating Scales (BBRS), Preschool and Kindergarten Form and Grades One–Nine Form, are rating inventories used to identify the type and severity of problem behaviors exhibited by referred children ages 2 to 15. The scales may be completed by parents, teachers, or any responsible person who knows the rated child well. Raters use a five-point scale ranging from 1 ("You have not noticed this behavior at all") to 5 ("You have noticed this behavior to a very large degree") to render quantitative judgments about the severity of observed negative behaviors.

Individual items are clustered together to form 19 (18 for the Preschool and Kindergarten Form) factor-analytically derived behavior categories bearing diagnostic labels such as excessive withdrawal, excessive dependency, poor coordination, poor academics, poor impulse control, poor reality contact, or excessive aggressiveness. Items are summed for each behavior category (usually by someone other than the rater) and transferred to a profile sheet. The profile sheet orders each category score along a continuum indicating the degree of significance of the presence of each negative behavior. Significance ratings can be used in differential diagnosis and in prioritizing intervention needs. Comparison of score profiles obtained from various raters can help broaden the scope of understanding and interpretation of the child's behavior patterns. The BBRS manual includes a lengthy discussion of the possible meanings of category scores and intervention suggestions for each problem behavior area. The BBRS has received favorable reviews as a clinical tool to aid in behavior assessment (Lerner, 1985) and is widely used to obtain parents' and teachers' evaluations of problem behavior areas.

## REFERENCES

Burks, H. F. (1977). *Burks' Behavior Rating Scales.* Los Angeles: Western Psychological Services.

Lerner, J. V. (1985). Review of the Burks' Behavior Rating Scales. In D. J. Keyser & R. C. Sweetland (Eds.), *Test critiques. Vol. II* (pp. 108–112). Kansas City, MO: Test Corporation of America.

GEORGE MCCLOSKEY
*American Guidance Service,
Circle Pines, Minnesota*

BEHAVIOR PROBLEM CHECKLIST, REVISED
CHILD BEHAVIOR CHECKLIST

## BUROS, OSCAR K. (1905–1978)

Oscar K. Buros is remembered internationally as the foremost proponent of critical analyses of educational and psychological tests. Buros attended the State Normal School in Superior, Wisconsin from 1922 to 1924 and completed his undergraduate education at the University of Minnesota in 1925. Buros received his graduate degree from the Teachers College, Columbia University. He accepted a faculty appointment at Rutgers University in 1932 and was a member of that faculty until his retirement in 1965. During World War II, he was in charge of testing for the

U.S. Army's specialized training program, and later an adviser on the assessment of leadership at West Point.

He married Luella Gubrud who, an accomplished artist in her own right, later shared with him the responsibilites for the famous *Buros Mental Measurements Yearbook* (MMY) series. It was she who saw the last edition through to its completion following his death on March 19, 1978. Buros published the first *MMY* in 1938. Seven other *Yearbooks* followed, as well as the *Mental Measurements Yearbook* monographs series (1968, 1970, and 1975a–i) and the *Tests in Print* series (1961, 1974).

He was the recipient of many professional honors and awards. Some of these were citations in 1953 from both the American Educational Research Association and the American Psychological Association for excellence in contributions to measurement; a senior Fulbright lectureship in statistics at Makerere University College, Uganda, 1956–1957; the 1965 Phi Delta Kappa research award; and in 1973 both an honorary Doctor of Science degree from Upsala College and the Distinguished Service to Measurement Award from the Educational Testing Service. Buros was a fellow of the American Statistical Association and the American Psychological Association. Rutgers University's Graduate School of Applied and Professional Psychology established a professorship in Buros's honor in 1985.

In 1979, the Buros Institute of Mental Measurements was moved to the University of Nebraska-Lincoln. The institute has continued the Buros tradition by publishing *Tests in Print III* (Mitchell, 1983) and the *Ninth Mental Measurements Yearbook* (Mitchell, 1985).

### REFERENCES

Buros, O. K. (1938). *The 1938 mental measurements yearbook.* Highland Park, NJ: Gryphon.

Buros, O. K. (1961). *Tests in print.* Highland Park, NJ: Gryphon.

Buros, O. K. (1968). *Reading tests and reviews I.* Highland Park, NJ: Gryphon.

Buros, O. K. (1970). *Personality tests and reviews I.* Highland Park, NJ: Gryphon.

Buros, O. K. (1974). *Tests in print II.* Highland Park, NJ: Gryphon.

Buros, O. K. (1975a). *Personality tests and reviews II.* Highland Park, NJ: Gryphon.

Buros, O. K. (1975b). *Reading tests and reviews II.* Highland Park, NJ: Gryphon.

Buros, O. K. (1975c). *Intelligence tests and reviews II.* Highland Park, NJ: Gryphon.

Buros, O. K. (1975d). *English tests and reviews.* Highland Park, NJ: Gryphon.

Buros, O. K. (1975e). *Foreign language tests and reviews.* Highland Park, NJ: Gryphon.

Buros, O. K. (1975f). *Mathematics tests and reviews.* Highland Park, NJ: Gryphon.

Buros, O. K. (1975g). *Science tests and reviews.* Highland Park, NJ: Gryphon.

Buros, O. K. (1975h). *Social studies tests and reviews.* Highland Park, NJ: Gryphon.

Buros, O. K. (1975i). *Vocational tests and reviews.* Highland Park, NJ: Gryphon.

Mitchell, J. V. Jr. (1983). *Tests in print III.* Lincoln, NE: Buros Institute of Mental Measurements.

Mitchell, J. V. Jr. (1985). *The ninth mental measurements yearbook.* Lincoln, NE: Buros Institute of Mental Measurements.

JANE CLOSE CONOLEY
*University of Nebraska, Lincoln*

## TESTS IN PRINT

# BUROS MENTAL MEASUREMENTS YEARBOOK

There are nine *Mental Measurements Yearbooks* (MMYs) (Buros 1938, 1940, 1949, 1953, 1959, 1965, 1972, 1978; Mitchell, 1985). The yearbooks provide test users with factual information on all known tests published separately in the English-speaking countries of the world. In addition, the books contain test reviews written by professional people representing a variety of viewpoints. The volumes are also sources of comprehensive bibliographies for specific tests, and references relevant to the tests.

The purpose of all the *MMYs* is to provide a forum in which tests can be reviewed candidly to facilitate intelligent consumer choice and use of tests. The most recent *MMY* (Mitchell, 1985) contains descriptive information on 1409 new or revised tests, 1266 test reviews, extensive listings of test references and reviewer references, several indexes including indexes of test titles, classified subject areas, publishers, scores, and names of test authors and reviewers.

The books are published by the Buros Institute of Mental Measurements, located since 1979 at the University of Nebraska, Lincoln, Department of Educational Psychology. The institute, established originally by Oscar K. Buros, has published over 20 volumes (edited by Buros) relating to test description and review.

### REFERENCES

Buros, O. K. (1938). *The 1938 mental measurements yearbook.* Highland Park, NJ: Gryphon.

Buros, O. K. (1940). *The 1940 mental measurements yearbook.* Highland Park, NJ: Gryphon.

Buros, O. K. (1949). *The third mental measurements yearbook.* Highland Park, NJ: Gryphon.

Buros, O. K. (1953). *The fourth mental measurements yearbook.* Highland Park, NJ: Gryphon.

Buros, O. K. (1959). *The fifth mental measurements yearbook.* Highland Park, NJ: Gryphon.

Buros, O. K. (1965). *The sixth mental measurements yearbook.* Highland Park, NJ: Gryphon.

Buros, O. K. (1972). *The seventh mental measurements yearbook.* Highland Park, NJ: Gryphon.

Buros, O. K. (1978). *The eighth mental measurements yearbook.* Highland Park, NJ: Gryphon.

Mitchell, J. V., Jr. (1985). *The ninth mental measurements yearbook.* Lincoln, NE: Buros Institute of Mental Measurements.

JANE CLOSE CONOLEY
*University of Nebraska, Lincoln*

## BUROS, OSCAR K.
## TESTS IN PRINT

# BURT, SIR CYRIL (1883–1971)

Sir Cyril Burt became the first psychologist in the world to be employed by a school system when he was appointed to the position of psychologist with the London County Council in 1913. Burt's career centered around the application of psychology to the study and education of children. He made pioneering investigations in the areas of mental retardation, delinquency, and the genetics of intelligence, and conducted studies that served as models of the application of the scientific method to the study of human characteristics. Burt developed numerous tests for use by school psychologists and published his influential *Factors of the Mind* in 1941. He was co-editor of the *British Journal of Statistical Psychology*.

From 1931 until his retirement in 1950, Burt was professor of psychology at University College, London, where he devoted most of his attention to the training of psychologists and the continuation of his research and writing. He was knighted in 1946.

Sadly, Burt's work and reputation are marred by recent findings that he deliberately fabricated data in some of his best known studies. These acts of fraud cast doubt on his research findings, but do not erase his great contributions to psychology as a clinician, theoretician, and teacher (Hearnshaw, 1979).

## REFERENCES

Burt, C. (1941). *The factors of the mind: An introduction to factor analysis in psychology.* New York: Macmillan.

Hearnshaw, L. S. (1979). *Cyril Burt, psychologist.* Ithaca, NY: Cornell University Press.

PAUL IRVINE
*Katonah, New York*

# C

## CAFÉ AU LAIT SPOTS

Café au lait spots are areas of patchy pigmentation of skin, usually light brown in color. They are so-named because of their resemblance in color to coffee with cream. They are of diagnostic significance because they may indicate the presence of serious disease such as neurofibromatosis, polyostotic fibrous dysplasia, or tuberous sclerosis (*Blakiston's*, 1979; Johnson, 1979). Café au lait spots may be found in normal individuals.

When six or more café au lait spots are present and they are larger than 1.5 cm in diameter, neurofibromatosis is suspected (Johnson, 1979). Neurofibromatosis, also known as Von Recklinghausen's disease, is a genetic disorder inherited as an autosomal dominant trait (Batshaw & Perret, 1981). In addition to the presence of café au lait spots, which exist at birth and hence aid in the diagnosis of this condition, other symptoms include multiple skin-colored tumors or nodules and freckles of the axillae (armpits), which represent the Crowe's sign of neurofibromatosis.

Neurofibromatosis may have numerous neurological, psychological, and educational implications. Tumors or neurofibromas typically develop prior to puberty. These tumors may be associated with the spinal or cranial nerves and hence may result in sensory deficits such as visual or hearing impairment. Enlargement and deformation of the bones and scoliosis (curvature of the spine) may occur. Hypertension may be present in young victims of this condition. There is reported to be an increased incidence of mental retardation (Johnson, 1979) and school problems associated with neurofibromatosis (Batshaw & Perret, 1981). In severe cases, the presence of multiple contiguous tumors produces elephantiasis neuromatosa, a cosmetically disfiguring condition. While skin tumors may be removed, there is some evidence these may recur and multiply (*Fact Sheet*, 1983).

In addition to neurofibromatosis, café au lait spots also have been observed in other neurocutaneous syndromes such as tuberous sclerosis (Bourneville's disease) (Rosenberg, 1979). Also inherited as an autosomal dominant trait, tuberous sclerosis is characterized by nevi or moles on the face, epilepsy, and mental retardation (Rosenberg, 1979). The course of tuberous sclerosis begins with the onset of epilepsy and declining mental ability during the first decade, with development of facial lesions around the cheeks and nose several years later (Rosenberg, 1979).

Café au lait spots occurring in the size and number as noted previously are considered diagnostically significant in neurofibromatosis. Ninety percent of afflicted individuals are reported to exhibit them at birth (Johnson, 1979). Because their presence is associated with serious medical conditions such as neurofibromatosis and tuberous sclerosis, identification of numerous café au lait spots in children without medical diagnoses warrants referral to a physician. Educational management of children who have been diagnosed as having neurofibromatosis or tuberous sclerosis should be conducted on an individual basis because the severity and expression of symptoms vary widely.

### REFERENCES

Batshaw, M. L., & Perret, Y. M. (1981). *Children with handicaps: A medical primer*. Baltimore, MD: Brookes.

*Blakiston's Gould medical dictionary* (4th ed.) (1979). New York: McGraw-Hill.

*Fact Sheet: Neurofibromatosis*. (1983). Bethesda, MD: National Institute of Neurological and Communicative Disorders and Stroke.

Johnson, M. (1979). Certain cutaneous diseases with significant systemic manifestations. In P. B. Beeson, W. McDermott, & J. B. Wyngaarden (Eds.), *Cecil textbook of medicine* (15th ed.) (pp. 2266–2312). Philadelphia: Saunders.

Rosenberg, R. N. (1979). Inherited degenerative diseases of the nervous system. In P. B. Beeson, W. McDermott, & J. B. Wyngaarden (Eds.), *Cecil textbook of medicine* (15th ed.) (pp. 764–772). Philadelphia: Saunders.

CATHY F. TELZROW
*Cuyahoga Special Education
Service Center, Maple
Heights, Ohio*

MINOR PHYSICAL ANOMALIES
NEUROFIBROMATOSIS

## CALDWELL, BETTYE M. (1924–    )

Bettye M. Caldwell received her BA (1945) from Baylor University, her MA (1946) from the University of Iowa,

Bettye M. Caldwell

and her PhD (1951) in psychology from Washington University. Caldwell's career, which has spanned more than 30 years, reflects her interest in early childhood education and development. Currently, she is a Donaghey Distinguished Professor of Education at the University of Arkansas at Little Rock.

Since the late 1960s, when Caldwell was a member of the National Advisory Committee for Research and Evaluation for Project Head Start, she has maintained an interest in the impact of research on social policy. She has devoted her efforts to early intervention programs for very young handicapped children, demonstration daycare centers, and training parents and others who work with young children. By studying the impact of day care on factors such as intellectual and social development and mother-child attachment, Caldwell has shown that day care can have a significant, positive impact on children, especially those from disadvantaged backgrounds (Caldwell, 1977).

A leader in her field, Caldwell has been president of the National Association for the Education of Young Children (1982–1984) and editor of the journal *Child Development* (1968–1971). She has served on the editorial board and the board of directors for other journals and organizations. She also has earned international notice, serving as a U.S. delegate to the U.S.S.R. and the People's Republic of China to study early education programs in those countries.

**REFERENCES**

Bradley, R. H., & Caldwell, B. M. (1984). 174 Children: A study of the relation between home environment and mental development in the first five years. In A. Gottfried (Ed.), *Home environment and early cognitive development* (pp. 5–56). New York: Academic.

Caldwell, B. M. (1977). Child development and social policy. In M. Scott & S. Grimmett (Eds.), *Current issues in child development*. Washington, DC: National Association for the Education of Young Children.

ANN E. LUPKOWSKI
*Texas A&M University*

## CAMP, BONNIE (1931–    )

Bonnie Camp received her BA from Mississippi State College for Women in 1948, and her MA and PhD in clinical psychology from Indiana University in 1954. She went on to receive her MD in 1965 from the University of Colorado School of Medicine and pediatric training from the University of Colorado Health Sciences Center.

While employed as a pediatrician in the Denver Health and Hospitals Neighborhood Health Center, Camp organized a tutorial reading program for children with severe reading delay in the center's catchment area using community aides, older students, and volunteers. The program was eventually extended to schools through the Denver School District.

Camp is best known for her development of the Think Aloud Program (Camp & Bash, 1978). Think Aloud is a cognitive behavior modification program designed to improve social and cognitive problem-solving skills in young children. It was conceived as a training program to decrease impulsivity, encourage consideration of alternatives, and plan a course of action. It emphasizes the use of cognitive modeling as a teaching tool whereby teachers model their own strategies for thinking through problems.

Camp is currently the interim director of the JFK Child Development Center at the University of Colorado Health Sciences Center and professor of pediatrics and psychiatry at the University of Colorado School of Medicine. She has received the National Institute of Mental Health Research Career Development Award and has served on many national advisory committees.

**REFERENCE**

Camp, B. W., & Bash, M. A. (1978). The "Think Aloud" classroom program. Denver: University of Colorado Medical School.

STAFF

## CAMPBELL, SIR FRANCIS JOSEPH (1832–1914)

Francis J. Campbell was born on a farm in Tennessee on October 9, 1832. Blinded in an accident at the age of 3, he was educated at the newly opened Tennessee State Institution for the Blind, where he later served as a teacher of music while studying at the University of Tennessee. Following a period as a student at Harvard University and then as a teacher of the blind in Wisconsin, he became an instructor at Perkins Institution and Massachusetts Asylum for the Blind, where he served for 11 years as head of the music department.

A talented pianist, Campbell left Perkins to continue his music education in Europe and to study methods of teaching the blind. While in London he met Thomas

Sir Francis Joseph Campbell

Rhodes Armitage, a blind physician who had just completed joining together Britain's numerous organizations for the blind into a federation that ultimately became known as the Royal National Institute for the Blind.

Campbell's account of the large number of students at Perkins whom he had helped prepare for successful careers as professional musicians led Armitage to establish a music school to train blind children, with Campbell as headmaster. Starting in 1872 with two students, the school ultimately became the Royal Normal College and Academy of Music, with an enrollment, by 1885, of 170 students. Campbell's original faculty included a number of teachers from Perkins, and through the years he maintained a continuing exchange of teachers with Perkins and other schools in the United States. As a result, the Royal Normal College and Academy of Music probably had more influence on American teaching methods than any other foreign school. The institution, under Campbell, combined general education and physical training with careful vocational preparation, job placement, and follow-up after graduation. Between 80 and 90% of the graduates became self-supporting, mostly as musicians, teachers, and technicians trained in piano tuning and repair. This unprecedented achievement stimulated an emphasis on vocational preparation in schools for the blind throughout the world.

Campbell believed strongly in the value of physical exercise, and took great pride in his own physical prowess—he once scaled the formidable Mont Blanc, a feat that he considered one of the crowning achievements of his life. He viewed physical training as an essential ingredient in any educational program preparing the blind for active and productive lives and developed an extensive physical education program that greatly influenced other schools for the blind.

In recognition of his work on behalf of the blind, Campbell was knighted by King Edward VII in 1909. Campbell retired as headmaster in 1912. He died on June 30, 1914.

## REFERENCES

Koestler, F. A. (1976). *The unseen minority: A social history of blindness in America.* New York: McKay.

Ross, I. (1951). *Journey into light.* New York: Appleton-Century-Crofts.

PAUL IRVINE
*Katonah, New York*

## CAMPHILL COMMUNITY MOVEMENT

The Camphill Community (movement) was founded by Karl Koenig (1902–1966) after he fled the Nazi powers of central Europe in 1939. The name Camphill refers to the group's first house in Aberdeen, Scotland.

The Camphill Community is based on the writings of Rudolph Steiner (1861–1925). It works for a full understanding of people's spiritual being, eternal purpose, and earthly tasks. The goals of Steiner's work (known as anthroposophy) include allowing all human beings, handicapped or not, to develop to their potential and to find a productive place in society. The fostering and development of individual human dignity is of paramount importance.

Camphill villages are currently found in 11 countries, with 5 in the United States. Despite minor differences, village life centers around the family, community, and productive, meaningful work. The family typically consists of parents, children, and a number of mentally handicapped individuals living and working together, free from labels and distinctions. Mutual responsibility is stressed; no salaries are paid but individuals have their needs met by the community.

The Camphill Special School, Glenmoore Pennsylvania, currently serves 72 children from elementary through high school age. Its program complements the philosophies of the larger Camphill Community and provides the "structure, rhythm, regularity, and consistency" needed for curative education. Each child works from an individual education program based on an adaptation of the Waldorf School movement. The education of the whole child is stressed; specific therapies (painting, speech, medicine, music) are provided depending on need. Older students are prepared vocationally for life after graduation through training in groundskeeping, woodwork, and household activities.

A 4-year training seminar is currently offered in the Beaver Run, Pennsylvania school. It is designed to train the individual in curative education using the Waldorf curriculum, as well as in all aspects of community living in the Camphill tradition.

Persons interested in joining or learning more about the Camphill communities are encouraged to contact them directly.

Camphill Special Schools
Beaver Run
Glenmore, PA 19343

Camphill Village USA
Copake, NY 12516

Camphill Village USA
Kimberton Hills
PO Box 155
Kimberton, PA 19442

Camphill Village Minnesota
Route 3
PO Box 249
Sauk Centre, MN 56378

JOHN E. PORCELLA
Rhinebeck Country School,
Rhinebeck, New York

# CAMPING FOR THE HANDICAPPED

Camping for the handicapped is divided into two types—individual and organized camping. The camping areas used for individualized camping are either in developed or wilderness states. Developed campsites are usually near conveniences that facilitate their use by handicapped campers, e.g., they offer amenities such as tent pads, electrical and water outlets, and restroom facilities. Their nature paths are wide and smooth to facilitate travel for children and youths who are wheelchair-bound or impaired in motor functioning (Sessoms, 1984).

Wilderness campgrounds have cruder facilities and fewer activity programs for the handicapped than developed camping areas. Most are designed for a low level of human use. They lack conveniences such as smooth paths and picnic facilities. As a rule, they are considered closed to the physically handicapped, though there are no limitations to all other persons.

Organized camping has been defined as the merging of outdoor recreation and education in a campsite setting (Sessoms, 1984). Organized camping is carried out on day and residential bases. Activities at organized camps for the handicapped range from general activities (such as sports and games, hobbies, arts and crafts, and drama) to special-purpose activities such as computer training and weight control. Such camps are also likely to emphasize education and rehabilitation (Wiseman, 1982). Major emphases in organized camps are to foster socialization skills, the acceptance of responsibilities, and the learning of leisure skills, and to facilitate living in communal atmospheres.

Organized camping programs for the handicapped are sponsored by the following types of agencies: (1) private or commercial campers agencies, whose fees come from their clients; (2) quasipublic agencies, some of whose funds come from donations and endowments, while the balance is paid by the participants, e.g., Easter Seals and American Red Cross camps; and (3) public-camping programs supported and sponsored by either local or municipal parks and recreation systems, or by organizations serving the handicapped and parent groups.

Four different types of organized camping programs for the handicapped may be distinguished. One type is camps that are located within communities where campers participate on a daily basis; these have accessible toilets, play, and eating areas. Another type is resident camps for the handicapped. These have cabins, dining halls, staff quarters, and indoor and outdoor recreation facilities. Their sessions last from 1 to 8 weeks. A third type is combination resident and daycamping opportunities that permit some campers to attend daily while others remain overnight. Finally, there are special purpose camps that promote a single concept or activity such as a specific sport or religion (Wiseman, 1982).

Since 1975, some programs have adopted noncategorical approaches, i.e., involving all handicapped campers in a normalized integrated camp program. Handicapped campers are evaluated for an integrated camping program on the basis of their level of functioning in camp activities. The handicapped camper is placed in integrative, halfway, or special groups in such integrated camps depending on his or her capabilities.

In integrative camping, handicapped campers participate in all activities together with able-bodied campers. Handicapped campers in the halfway group may have the potential for regular group participation but still lack some ability to fully engage in activities. Usually, they engage in the same activities as the regular group and share the same facilities, but they do so separately (Sessoms, 1984).

Handicapped campers in the special group require a segregated and supervised program because of the severity and complexity of their condition. All camping activities are modified to the capabilities and interests of this group.

## REFERENCES

American Camping Association standards for persons with special needs (Part IIC). (1980). Martinsville, IN: Bradford Woods.

Choosing a summer camp. (1985). Exceptional Children, 14(3), 37–39.

Physical Education for the Handicapped. (1982). Involving impaired and handicapped persons in regular camp programs. Washington, DC: IRUC.

Sessoms, H. (1984). Leisure services (3rd ed.). Englewood Cliffs, NJ: Prentice-Hall.

Wiseman, D. (1982). A practical approach to adapted physical education. Reading, MA: Addison-Wesley.

THOMAS BURKE
Hunter College, City University
of New York

**EQUINE THERAPY**
**RECREATIONAL THERAPY**

# CANADA, SPECIAL EDUCATION IN

A unique combination of factors—historic, geographic, and cultural—influence special education in Canada. Canada is home to approximately 25 million people. It is a large country with low overall population density. Canada is divided into 10 provinces and two territories. From west to east, the provinces are British Columbia, Alberta, Saskatchewan, Manitoba, Ontario, Quebec, New Brunswick, Prince Edward Island, Nova Scotia, and Newfoundland. The two territories are the Yukon and Northwest Territories.

In Canada, under the provisions of the British North American Act and the recently approved Constitution, education is the responsibility of the provinces rather than the federal government. This means that policies and legislation governing the conduct of special education must be enacted in each province, and funding must be provided by revenues of that province. The result is that special education in each province is shaped by the needs of the population, demographic patterns, financial resources, and values of the people of that province. There is much more variation in Canada than in a country in which legislation and funding for special education emanate from a central federal authority, as in the United States. This also makes it difficult to describe special education in Canada in general terms.

Geographic factors contribute to inefficiencies and expenses in transportation and service delivery. An additional factor that influences all educational services in Canada, including special education, is the coexistence of two distinct official languages within one country. The majority of the population of Quebec is French-speaking, and almost 40% of the population of New Brunswick, which borders Quebec, is also French speaking. In the other provinces, the majority of the population has English as its first language. However, there are small numbers of French-speaking residents in each province and territory of Canada. In the northern parts of the provinces and the two northern territories, large segments of the population are native Indians and Inuit for whom English is a second language, and for whom there exists a wide range of dialects and first languages. There are also many children of new Canadian families who do not speak English when they enter Canadian schools. With Canada's two official languages, and policies that encourage a multicultural society, there are many educational problems related to differences among the languages of home, school, and community.

In most provinces, the trend historically has been development from a large urban school district outward. Special education services were first developed in large cities, and then more slowly in smaller districts. *Report on Legislation and Services for Exceptional Children in Canada* (Ballance & Kendall, 1969) indicated a high degree of variation in services within a province (from urban to rural school districts) and from province to province. In

1969 only about half the provinces had a special education branch within the Department of Education and only about 3% of the school population had been identified as receiving special education services. This number reflected only those who had been placed in segregated settings, and did not include students receiving remediation in their classrooms or in an integrated program of any type.

The years from 1969 to 1972 were a period of rapid growth in special education in Canada. There were significant changes in educational legislation and official policy formulations in seven provinces (Alberta, British Columbia, Manitoba, Newfoundland, Ontario, Quebec, and Saskatchewan). There was a definite commitment to change on the part of the three Maritime Provinces (New Brunswick, Nova Scotia, and Prince Edward Island). However, only Saskatchewan adopted a mandatory basis for special education for exceptional children at that time. The other provinces continued to rely on the development of special services as part of their general legislative mandate to provide education for all children within the provincial jurisdiction. Another trend that emerged during this period was a concern with alternatives to special class placement and a commitment to the integration of exceptional children into regular classes.

The widespread discussion about special education in Canada in the early 1970s produced two other documents that have helped to shape special education. In 1971 *Standards for Educators of Exceptional Children* was issued (Hardy, Minto, Perkins, & Quance, 1971); it is frequently referred to as the SEECC report. The authors of the report recommended a model and minimum standards for the training of teachers of exceptional children. These recommendations have been translated into regulations by each provincial Department of Education working in conjunction with the faculties of education at the major universities in that province. A committee of the Council for Exceptional Children in Canada released a set of principles to govern legislation for services for children with special needs (Treherne, Dice, Grigg, & Sanche, 1974). These principles have influenced subsequent legislation to varying degrees in every province in the country in the past decade.

In the mid-1980s it is estimated that 12% of the school-age population requires special education. It remains difficult to obtain accurate estimates of the numbers receiving and requiring services for a variety of reasons (Csapo & Goguen, 1980). The delivery models that have been adopted in Canadian provinces have largely been designed in the United States to meet U.S. needs. Such adoption reflects the natural influences of a bordering country. These models advocate provision of a range of administrative arrangements for service delivery from full segregation to full integration. Striving for as much integration of exceptional children with the rest of the school population as possible is a major goal. Each province publishes a manual of legislation, regulations, policies, and guidelines for special education that can be obtained from the provincial Department of Education. To obtain a detailed, accurate picture of gifted and special education in the provinces of Canada, it would be necessary to consult these provincial documents.

Bunch (1984) has argued that three shortcomings can be found in current attempts to provide appropriate education for all exceptional children in Canada. He cites the lack of mandated special education services for all children in four of the provinces and the two territories, and the failure to identify many pupils with mild to moderate learning and behavioral problems. The third problem is lack of resources (money, trained personnel, etc.) to provide optimal services at an adequate level in all regions of the country. However, with Canada's emphasis on minority rights and individual freedoms, Canadians in all parts of the country are striving to provide special education and the opportunity for a full life to all handicapped and exceptional individuals.

## REFERENCES

Ballance, K. E., & Kendall, D. C. (1969). *Report on legislation and services for exceptional children in Canada*. Toronto, Ontario: Council for Exceptional Children in Canada.

Bunch, G. O. (1984). Special education in Canada: An overview. In D. D. Hammill, N. R. Bartel, & G. O. Bunch (Eds.), *Teaching children with learning and behavior problems* (Canadian ed.). Toronto, Ontario: Allyn & Bacon.

Csapo, M., & Goguen, L. (Eds.). (1980). *Special education across Canada*. Vancouver, British Columbia: Centre for Human Development and Research.

Hardy, M., McLeod, J., Minto, H., Perkins, S., & Quance, W. (1971). *Standards for educators of exceptional children in Canada*. Toronto, Ontario: Crainford.

Treherne, D., Dice, T. L., Griggs, E. E., & Sanche, R. P. (1974). *A matter of principle: Standards governing legislation for services for children with special needs*. Regina, Saskatchewan: Council for Exceptional Children in Canada.

NANCY L. HUTCHINSON
BERNICE Y. L. WONG
*Simon Fraser University*

**HUMANISTIC SPECIAL EDUCATION**
**POLITICS AND SPECIAL EDUCATION**

## CANCER, CHILDHOOD

Cancer is actually a group of diseases. It originates from a single malignant cell that has potentially unlimited growth. In cancer, the malignant cells invade noncancerous parts of the body in a systematic way, changing normal cells so that they lose control of their own growth processes and themselves become cancerous. This process is called

metastasis. Injury or destruction of normal cells is a consequence (Pendergrass, Chard, & Hartmann, 1985). As the growth of cancer proceeds, cells sometimes break away from the original concentration of malignant cells to be carried to other parts of the body, which then also become cancerous. Cancerous symptoms appear because of the injury to or destruction of normal cells. The symptoms are frequently subtle, particularly during initial stages.

Cancer is a leading cause of mortality in children between the ages of 1 and 15 years, exceeded only by accidents as a cause of death in this age group. The incidence is 130 cases for each 1 million children who are under the age of 15. Approximately 40% of these cases will be leukemia.

The medical treatment of cancer involves radiation, chemotherapy, and—rarely in children—surgery. The treatment often causes weight loss, fatigue, nausea, and emotional distress, among other significant problems (Link, 1982). The physical discomfort suffered by the child and the resulting irritability require extremely sensitive attitudes on the part of teachers. Additionally, the disease, both in its manifestations and the time required to treat it, may result in lost time from school or instruction (Bigge & Sirvis, 1986).

Children who have cancer are likely to be referred for instruction and related services of a special education nature when they are unable to deal with the demands of regular school work. Under the guidelines established by PL 94-142, they would receive these under the category of health impairments (*Federal Register*, 1977, p. 42478).

## REFERENCES

Bigge, J., & Sirvis, B. (1986). Physical and health impairments. In N. G. Haring & L. McCormick (Eds.), *Exceptional children and youth* (4th ed.). Columbus, OH: Merrill.

Link, M. P. (1982). Cancer in childhood. In E. E. Bleck & D. A. Nagel (Eds.), *Physically handicapped children: A medical atlas for teachers* (2nd ed., pp. 121–144). New York: Grune & Stratton.

Pendergrass, T. W., Chard, R. L., & Hartmann, J. R. (1985). Leukemia. In N. Hobbs & J. M. Perrin (Eds.), *Issues in the care of children with chronic illness* (pp. 324–343). San Francisco: Jossey-Bass.

DON BRASWELL
*Research Foundation, City University of New York*

**CHEMOTHERAPY**

## CANTRELL, ROBERT P. (1938–    )

Robert P. Cantrell received his BA (1960) and MA (1962) in psychology from Baylor University. He received his

Robert P. Cantrell

PhD in 1969 from George Peabody College for Teachers with a major in experimental child psychology and a minor in special education. Since 1980, he has been an adjunct professor in the department of special education, Kent State University, an adjunct professor in the department of specialized instructional programs, Cleveland State University, the codirector of the Institute for Ecological Study of Children and Youth, and the director of research, Positive Education Program, Cleveland, Ohio.

Early experiences as a psychologist on a special education diagnostic team taught him that teachers of special children demand practical solutions to their special teaching problems. Partly from these experiences, he became an advocate of a heuristic, ecological system of problem solving (Cantrell & Cantrell, 1977). Although many professionals learn over time to develop solutions to these practical problems, he recognized that there are inadequate means by which we transmit this knowledge of effective intervention strategies to the next generation of professionals.

Cantrell expects his future research to emphasize pinpointing the key elements in repartitions ecological patterns for behavior-disordered children. He hopes to identify intervention strategies that produce the most efficient and effective changes in the ecologies of which behavior-disordered children are an integral part (Cantrell & Cantrell, 1980).

## REFERENCES

Cantrell, R. P., & Cantrell, M. L. (1977). Evaluation of a heuristic approach to solving children's problems. *Peabody Journal of Education, 54*(3), 168–173.

Cantrell, R. P., & Cantrell, M. L. (1980). Ecological problem solving: A decision-making heuristic for prevention-intervention education strategies. In J. Hogg & P. Mittler (Eds.), *Advances in mental handicap research* (Vol. 1). New York: Wiley.

E. VALERIE HEWITT
*Texas A&M University*

## CARDIAC DISORDERS

Congenital cardiac disorders, with their subsequent physical impairments, constitute some of the most common and serious childhood illnesses. Congenital cardiac disorders are those in which defects in the structure of the heart and/or great vessels alter the normal flow of blood through the cardiorespiratory system. Whaley and Wong (1983) report the incidence of congenital heart disease to occur in approximately 8/1000 to 10/1000 live births. They also report that congenital anomalies are the major cause of death outside of prematurity. However, with the evolution of palliative and varied surgical techniques, the percentage of those infants who survive cardiac malformations/lesions in the neonatal period has dramatically increased; therefore, serious complex defects currently account for a large number of individuals passing through infancy and childhood into full maturity (Nelson, Behrman, & Vaughn, 1983). Surgically corrected congenital defects constitute the largest group of those surviving until adulthood.

The cause of congenital cardiac anomalies is still relatively unknown at this time; however multifactorial patterns have been associated with an increased incidence of the disease. The following prenatal factors have been identified as having causal relationships of varying degrees: maternal rubella infection and other viruses such as cytomegalovirus, coxsackle virus B, and nerpesvirus nomines B (Nelson, Behrman, & Vaughn, 1983; Nora, 1971); poor maternal nutrition (Reeder, Mastroianni, & Martin, 1983); alcohol, dextroamphelamine, lithium chloride, progesterine/estrogen, and warafin, which are suspected teratogenic agents, as well as maternal overexposure to radiation (Taybi, 1971).

Genetic factors have also been associated with an increased incidence of cardiac disorders. Those parents who already have a child with a cardiac defect have a higher incidence of a second child with a cardiac malformation than parents with an unaffected child (King, 1975). Although this incidence is higher than the general population, it is still quite low (2 to 5%) (King, 1975, p. 87; Nelson, et al., 1983, p. 1121). Other factors predisposing children to congenital heart disease are parents who have congenital cardiac disease themselves or chromosomal aberrations such as Down's syndrome and/or other noncardiac anomalies. Rowe and Uchida (1961) found that between 30 and 40% of all children with Down's syndrome have heart defects of some kind.

The general signs and symptoms associated with congenital cardiac defects in children have been outlined by Miller (1985): (1) dyspnea, especially on exertion; (2) feeding difficulties or a general failure to thrive; (3) stridor or choking spells; (4) increased heart and respiratory rate (tachypnea) with retractions when the ribs show with each breath; (5) numerous respiratory tract infections; (6) in older children, delayed or poor physical and/or mental development with a decreased exercise tolerance; (7) cyanosis, posturing (particularly a squatting position and clubbing of fingers and toes); (8) heart murmurs; and (9) dyaphoresis.

Cardiac lesions have been classified into two broad categories: acyanotic and cyanotic. "Acyanotic defects are those in which the blood flows from the arterial (left, oxygenated) side of the heart to the venous (right, deoxygenated) side as a result of a connection between the two sides and/or from a pressure gradient (left-to-right shunt)" (Carroll-Johnson & Neal, 1985, p. 605). Most acyanotic disorders are asymptomatic. There are six acyanotic defects demonstrating the left to right shunting of blood. The blood flows from the left ventricle to the right ventricle, where it mixes with venous blood with ventricular-septal defects (VSD). Watson (1968) has cited ventricular-septal defects as the most common cause of cardiac mortality. Atrial-septal defects (ASD) have blood flowing from the left atrium to the right atrium, then through the right ventricle before moving into the pulmonary artery and pulmonary circulation. Patent ductus arteriosus (PDA) is signified when the ductus arteriosus, which normally closes after birth, remains patent, thus recirculating blood repeatedly through the lungs, and, in essence, overoxygenating the blood. The fourth acyanotic lesion is a coarctation of the aorta. Narrowing of the aorta in this lesion manifests itself with an increased blood pressure in the upper extremities with a reciprocal decrease in pressure in the systemic circulation. Aortic stenosis is the narrowing or general inflexibility of the aortic valve, which increases the workload of the left ventricle with subsequent left ventricular hypertrophy resulting. Pulmonary stenosis in a like manner is the narrowing of the pulmonary valve. However, this narrowing results in decreased blood flow to the lungs and an increase in right ventricular pressure.

There are four cyanotic defects, with the outstanding clinical feature being cyanosis. The tetralogy of Fallot, with its four associated defects, has been described by Sacksteder, Gildea, and Dassy (1978, p. 267) as "(1) a large membranous ventricular septal defect; (2) right ventricular outflow obstruction; (3) right ventricular hypertrophy; and (4) dextroposition or overriding of the aorta." The outstanding clinical feature is cyanosis, along with associated features such as clubbing of nailbeds and squatting posture.

In addition to the tetralogy of Fallot, transposition of the great arteries is another cyanotic disorder. In this instance, the aorta arises from the right ventricle and the pulmonary artery from the left ventricle. Hence, two parallel and separate circulatory systems exist, one pulmonary and one systemic. This condition is incompatible with life unless coexisting lesions allow a mixture of blood to sustain life until the heart can be surgically repaired (Sacksteder, Gildea, and Dassy, 1978, p. 266).

The type of medical intervention or surgical treatment required for congenital heart disease depends on the type or severity of the cardiac lesion. The majority of children with mild congenital heart disease require no treatment. Children with severe heart defects may develop congestive heart failure, which is frequently treated with a cardiac glycoside (digoxin) and furesmide (lasix). Selective palliative surgical procedures may be done to improve oxygenation temporarily until the child grows. Total correction of the heart defect is usually postponed until the benefits of surgery outweigh the risks, or until the child is between the ages of 3 and 5 years (Rowe, 1978).

Parents of children with congenital heart defects are encouraged to treat their children normally. In all but the most severe cases, a normal life can be expected. Restriction of the child's activities is rarely suggested, but it is often implemented as a control measure by parents. Discipline problems are common, and sibling rivalry is seen frequently because of the attention given the child with the cardiac disorder by parents, health care workers, and educators. The best means of avoiding overprotection of the child is to have a functional knowledge of the child's unique disorder. Overprotection frequently results in increased anxiety in the child and interferes with a normal lifestyle. Parents are recommended to manage their child's heart condition by providing a well-balanced diet, prevention of anemia, and the usual childhood immunizations.

Those children whose lesions are moderate to severe need not severely restrict their activities. Nelson, Behrman, and Vaughn (1983, p. 1167) suggest merely tailoring the child's activities to his or her ability to participate; however, rough competitive contact sports should be avoided. Generally, the child will establish his or her own limits. Nelson et. al (1983) also suggests that transportation to and from school may help school performance by eliminating excessive fatigue.

Additional, but imperative, guidelines for all children with cardiac lesions include treating bacterial infections vigorously but not prophylactically to prevent infective endocarditis. Specifically, cyanotic children should be alert for dehydration and iron deficiencies, which may interfere with activity tolerance. As maturity is achieved, women should be counseled regarding the risks of childbearing and the use of contraceptives.

## REFERENCES

Carroll-Johnson, R. M., & Neal, M. C. (Eds.). (1985). *American Journal of Nursing, 1985 nursing boards review* (pp. 605–607). Pacific Palisades, CA: Nurseco.

King, O. M. (Ed.). (1975). *Care of the cardiac surgical patient.* St. Louis: Mosby.

Miller, A. (Ed.). (1985). *Mosby's comprehensive review of nursing* (11th ed.) (pp. 400–405). St. Louis: Mosby.

Nelson, W. E., Behrman, R. E., & Vaughn, V. C. (Eds.) (1983). *Textbook of pediatrics* (12th ed.) (pp. 1121–1167). Philadelphia: Saunders.

Nora, J. J. (1971). Etiologic factors in congenital heart diseases. In S. Kaplin (Ed.), *Pediatric clinics of North America* (Vol. *18*, pp. 1059–1074). Philadelphia: Saunders.

Reeder, S. J., Mastroianni, L., & Martin, L. (Eds.). (1983). *Maternity nursing* (15th ed.). Philadelphia: Lippincott.

Rowe, R. D. (1978). Patent ductus arteriosus. In J. Keith, R. Rowe, & R. Vlad (Eds.), *Heart disease in infancy and children* (3rd ed.). New York: Macmillan.

Rowe, R. D., & Uchida, I. A. (1961). Cardiac malformation in mongolism: A prospective study of 184 mongoloid children. *American Journal of Medicine, 31*, pp. 726–735.

Sacksteder, S., Gildea, J. H., & Dassy, C. (1978, Feb.). Common congenital cardiac defects. *American Journal of Nursing*, 266–272.

Taybi, H. (1971). Roentgen evaluation of cardiomegaly in the newborn period and early infancy. In S. Kaplin (Ed.), *Pediatric clinics of North America, 18*(4) (pp. 1031–1058). Philadelphia: Saunders.

Watson, H. (Ed.). (1968). *Pediatric cardiology*. London: Lloyd-Luke.

Whaley, L. F., & Wong, D. L. (1983). The child with heart disease. In L. F. Whaley & D. L. Wong (Eds.), *Nursing care of infants and children* (2nd ed.) (pp. 1279–1337). St. Louis: Mosby.

MARY CLARE WILLIAMS
*Ramey, Pennsylvania*

**PHYSICAL HANDICAPS**
**PHYSICAL EDUCATION OF THE HANDICAPPED**


# CAREER EDUCATION FOR THE HANDICAPPED

Career education is a comprehensive educational program aimed beyond work. It includes the whole person, who functions in a society in a variety of roles such as citizen, family member, student, and advocate (Kokaska, 1980). Career education is often thought of as an introduction to vocational education. In context, it is much broader than vocational education. This comprehensive and functional orientation in career education has received wide acceptance as a major curricular emphasis in special education (Clark, 1980).

Career education is divided into three phases: elementary career awareness, junior high or middle school career exploration, and high school and postsecondary career preparation (Phelps & Lutz, 1977). Career awareness can begin in the earliest years of schooling using the young child's curiosity for the adult world. It focuses on the various ways people work. At this level, children are exposed to a wide variety of vocations, the work ethic, and self-awareness. Phelps and Lutz (1977) characterize this phase as relying heavily on basic academic skills. Each successive phase shifts from a classroom orientation and basic skills to simulations and practical natural experiences. Yet each phase of the career education sequence emphasizes communication skills, language, computation, and socialization.

The next phase of career education, career exploration, provides opportunities to explore the world of work with simulated and hands-on experiences. Students learn work values and personal values through activities that give them a taste of the work environment. Career preparation often begins at the high school level in vocational programs or as a preparation for postsecondary training in a university, vocational-technical school, or on-the-job training program. Kokaska (1980) added career placement as a fourth phase, but also emphasized that each phase can and does continue throughout life. A handicapped person can be working at one job while continuing education and exploring another field of possible employment.

There are three major elements within each phase of career education: the school, the family, and community experiences. Career education creates and uses educational experiences in the community, business and industry, the family, and the school for each phase and level in career education sequence. The list of potential sources of assistance and experiences is extensive (Brolin & Kokaska, 1979). This functional, community-based educational emphasis forms the foundation for programs for severely handicapped individuals (Wilcox & Bellamy, 1982).

The infusion of career education into the curriculum creates a systematic curriculum organized through the postsecondary levels that emphasizes process rather than content Miller and Schloss (1982) believe that the integrated curriculum enhances the likelihood that instructional goals will be achieved and maintained.

A major question in designing curriculum in career education programs is, "What skills are essential to the individual to make him a more effective person?" (Brolin & Kokaska, 1979, p. 106). Boyan (1980) poses two questions in developing career education curriculum, "Where will the student live when he or she finishes schooling?" and "Where will he or she work?" From these questions the following curriculum outline is generated for the moderately handicapped:

Personal hygiene and grooming

Care and selection of clothing

Health and safety practices

Cooking, meal planning, and related kitchen skills

Home management and housekeeping

Socialization skills (manners and interpersonal relations)

Eating habits

Use of the telephone

Leisure-time skills

Physical training and sensory-motor integration (including regular exercise)

Language
Reading and writing for survival
Math/money skills
Time telling
Mobility in the community
Shopping
Use of community resources and public facilities
Family life education
Specific occupational skills

Brolin and Kokaska (1979) identified 22 career education competencies in three major clusters: daily living skills, personal/social skills, and occupational guidance and preparation. It is reported that these competencies represent the major goals and outcomes that should be completed by students if they are to be successful in community life.

Career education is a concept that provides an alternative curricular orientation for educating handicapped students. While encompassing all of the basic skills, social skills, and content areas, it provides a functional, practical, and still holistic orientation to developing curriculum and instruction for handicapped students. It is much more than the mere preparation for vocational training. Career education is general curriculum development orientation that holds great promise for not only secondary aged and postsecondary handicapped students, but all handicapped individuals.

## REFERENCES

Boyan, C. (1980). Curriculum considerations in career education for moderately handicapped. In G. M. Clark & W. J. White (Eds.), *Career education for the handicapped: Current perspectives for teachers.* Boothwyn, PA: Educational Resources Center.

Brolin, D. E., & Kokaska, C. J. (1979). *Career education for handicapped children and youth.* Columbus, OH: Merrill.

Clark, G. M. (1980). Career education: A concept. In G. M. Clark & W. J. White (Eds.), *Career education for the handicapped: Current perspectives for teachers.* Boothwyn, PA: Educational Resources Center.

Kokaska, C. J. (1980). A curriculum model for career education. In G. M. Clark & W. J. White (Eds.), *Career education for the handicapped: Current perspectives for teachers.* Boothwyn, PA: Educational Resources Center.

Miller, S. R., & Schloss, P. (1982). *Career-vocational education for handicapped youth.* Rockville, MD: Aspen.

Phelps, L. A., & Lutz, R. J. (1977). *Career exploration and preparation for the special needs learner.* Boston: Allyn & Bacon.

Wilcox, B., & Bellamy, G. (Eds.). (1982). *Design of high school programs for severely handicapped students.* Baltimore, MD: Brookes.

DANIEL R. PAULSON
*University of Wisconsin, Stout*

REHABILITATION
VOCATIONAL EVALUATION

## CARNINE, DOUGLAS W. (1947–    )

A native of Sullivan, Illinois, Douglas Carnine received his BS in psychology from the University of Illinois, Urbana, in 1969, his MA in special education from the University of Oregon, Eugene, in 1971, and his PhD in educational psychology from the University of Utah, Salt Lake City, in 1974. At the University of Illinois, he became a member of Phi Beta Kappa and was a National Science Foundation fellow.

**Douglas W. Carnine**

As an undergraduate student, Carnine began working with Wesley Becker to conduct research on classroom management. Later, he helped Siegfried Engelmann to develop DISTAR arithmetic and to implement the direct instruction model of teaching in 10 school districts in eight states (Silbert, Carnine, & Stein, 1981). These experiences led to Carnine's belief that curriculum, staff development, and administrative leadership all must be addressed in any program that intends to improve schools.

Recently, Carnine has turned away from the idea of administrators taking the lead in introducing school effectiveness programs toward helping them focus on teaching variables (Engelmann & Carnine, 1982). Discouraged over the heavy demands placed on a teacher's time, Carnine is currently investigating the effects of technology on the quality of instructional programs and improving teacher effectiveness (Carnine, 1983).

## REFERENCES

Carnine, D. (1983). Direct institutional: In search of instructional solutions for educational problems. In D. Carnine, & D. Elkind (Eds.), *Interdisciplinary voices in learning disabilities and remedial education* (pp. 1–66). Austin, TX: Pro-Ed.

Engelmann, S., & Carnine, D. W. (1982). *Theory of instruction.* New York: Irvington.

Silbert, J., Carnine, D., & Stein, M. (1981). *Direct instruction mathematics.* Columbus, OH: Merrill.

E. VALERIE HEWITT
*Texas A&M University*

# CARROW ELICITED LANGUAGE INVENTORY (CELI)

The Carron Elicited Language Inventory (CELI) (Carrow, 1974) is a diagnostic test of expressive language containing 52 model utterances that a child is asked to imitate. The sentences were selected to include basic sentence types, specific grammatical morphemes, and selected transformational rules. The grammatical morphemes include nouns, plurals, verbs, adjectives, adverbs, pronouns, articles, negatives, prepositions, demonstratives, conjunctions, and contractions. The child's imitations of the model sentences are audiorecorded and then scored for error types such as substitutions, omissions, additions, transpositions, or reversals. The scoring and analysis forms provide detailed scoring sections and a separate verb protocol.

The CELI was standardized on a sample of 475 white middle-class children residing in the Southwest. Normative data for mean total error scores and mean subcategory error scores are provided at one-year intervals for ages 3 to 7 years, 11 months. Percentile and stanine scores are also provided. High test-retest reliability correlations are reported.

A major assumption underlying the CELI is that a child's imitations of model sentences will closely resemble his or her proficiency in spontaneous speech. However, studies by Kuczaj and Maratsos (1975), Haniff and Seigel (1981), Prutting, Gallagher, and Mulac (1975), Connell and Myles-Zitzer (1982), McDade, Simpson, and Lamb (1982), and Stephens (1976) indicate that the sentence imitation task may not be a valid measure of spontaneous language, underestimating the spontaneous language performance of some children (usually language-disordered children), and overestimating the spontaneous language performance of others (usually children with normal language development). Strengths of the CELI include ease of administration and greater depth than most tests of expressive language.

## REFERENCES

Carrow, E. *Carrow Elicited Language Inventory* (1974). Boston: Teaching Resources Corporation.

Connell, P. J., & Myles-Zitzer, C. (1982). An analysis of elicited imitation as a language evaluation procedure. *Journal of Speech and Hearing Disabilities, 47,* 390–396.

Haniff, M. H., & Seigel, G. M. (1981). The effect of context on verbal elicited imitation. *Journal of Speech and Hearing Disabilities, 46,* 27–30.

Kuczaj, S., & Maratsos, M. (1975). What children *can* say before they *will. Merrill-Palmer Quarterly, 21,* 89–112.

McDade, H. L., Simpson, M. A., & Lamb, D. E. (1982). The use of elicited imitation as a measure of expressive grammar: A question of validity. *Journal of Speech and Hearing Disabilities, 47,* 19–24.

Prutting, C. A., Gallagher, T. M., & Mulac, A. (1975). The expressive portion of the NSST compared to a spontaneous language sample. *Journal of Speech and Hearing Disabilities, 40,* 40–48.

Stephens, M. I. (1976). Elicited imitation of selected features of two American English dialects in head start children. *Journal of Speech and Hearing Disabilities, 19,* 493–508.

MARGO E. WILSON
*Lexington, Kentucky*

# CARTWRIGHT, G. PHILLIP (1937–     )

G. Phillip Cartwright received his BS (1960) in psychology and MS (1962) in special education from the University of Illinois. He received his PhD (1966) in special education and educational research from the University of Pittsburgh. Currently, he is professor and head of the Division of Special Education and Communication Disorders, Pennsylvania State University.

In the 1960s, Cartwright became convinced that the American education system was not providing an adequate education for handicapped children. He attempted to implement the then heretical idea of training regular educators to identify handicapped youngsters in their early years and to help those youngsters to succeed in a regular classroom. Cartwright also proposed that the training of both regular and special education teachers be modified to include learning the use of alternative train-

**G. Phillip Cartwright**

ing approaches (Cartwright, 1977). One such approach is the use of computer technology in the process of training teachers. With this philosophy, Cartwright developed a series of computer-assisted instruction (CAI) courses. Now that his beliefs are no longer considered heretical, but practical, Cartwright continues to work in the field of computer-assisted instruction (Cartwright, 1984; Cartwright, Cartwright, & Robine, 1972).

Cartwright was chosen for a research fellowship in England. He also has been listed in *American Men and Women in Science*, *Who's Who in the East*, and *Leaders in Education*.

### REFERENCES

Cartwright, G. P. (1977). Educational technology. In S. Tarver & R. Kneedler (Eds.), *Changing perspectives in education*. Columbus, OH: Merrill.

Cartwright, G. P. (1984). Computer applications in special education. In D. F. Walker & R. D. Hess (Eds.), *Instructional software: Principles and perspectives for design and use*. Belmont, CA: Wadsworth.

Cartwright, G. P., Cartwright, C. A., & Robine, G. C. (1972). CAI course in the early identification of handicapped children. *Exceptional Children, 38*, 453–459.

E. VALERIE HEWITT
*Texas A&M University*

## CASCADE MODEL OF SPECIAL EDUCATION SERVICES

The Cascade Model of Special Education Services is a conceptualization of the range of placement and service options available for handicapped children. The placement options are presented in hierarchical form and range from the least restrictive placement in the regular education classroom to the most restrictive placement in hospital or institutional settings. The Cascade Model was first proposed by Reynolds in 1962 and an amended version was proposed by Deno in 1970. Both proposals predated the passage of the Education of All Handicapped Children Act of 1975 (PL 94-142), a time when placement and service options for the handicapped were scarce. Reynolds and Birch (1977) characterized the pre-PL 94-142 administrative arrangements as a two-box system in which parallel but separate educational programs for regular and special education were in operation within school buildings. Interaction and movement of children between the two systems was difficult at best, and more often, nonexistent. The Cascade Model helped create understanding of and support for a better system that "facilitates tailoring of treatment to individual needs rather than a system for sorting out children so they will fit conditions designed according to group standards not necessarily suitable for the particular case" (Deno, 1970, p. 235).

The Cascade Model visually appears as a triangular form that contains two essential elements: the degree of placement specialization and the relative number of children in the various placement options. The base of the triangle coincides with regular classroom placement, the preferred placement for the largest number of handicapped students. Progressively more specialized placements are included as the triangle extends toward the apex. The decreasing width of the triangle reflects the decreasing numbers of children to be placed in progressively more restrictive environments. Deno's Cascade Model was widely cited and reproduced; it has become a fundamental concept for the field of special education. (See Figure 1 for an example of the Cascade Model.)

The basic concepts of specialization embodied in the Cascade Model were subsequently incorporated into federal and state laws as the least restrictive environment principle (Peterson, Zabel, Smith, & White, 1983). Variations of the Cascade Model have been presented by other authors (Cartwright, Cartwright, & Ward, 1985). However, the basic elements of degree of restrictiveness and relative numbers of children in the different placement options have been retained.

Despite its popularity and utility, the Cascade Model has been criticized. Reynolds and Birch (1977) view the original Cascade Model as "too place oriented" because of its "clearest focus on administrative structures and places." They offer an alternative conceptualization of the Cascade Model in which instructional diversity is emphasized. (See Figure 2.)

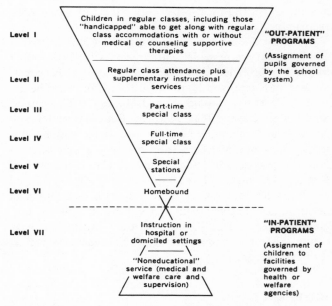

Figure 1. The cascade system of special education service. The tapered design indicates the considerable difference in the numbers involved at the different levels and calls attention to the fact that the system serves as a diagnostic filter. The most specialized facilities are likely to be needed by the fewest children on a long-term basis. This organizational model can be applied to the development of special education services for all types of disabilities.

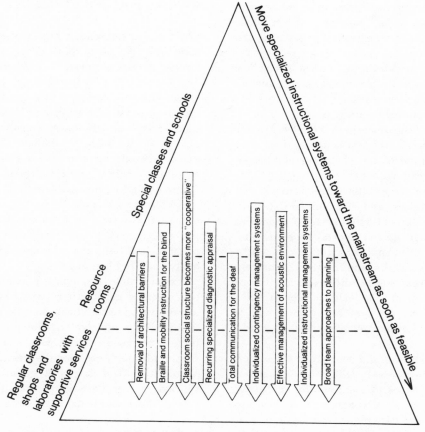

Figure 2. Changes occurring in the cascade (fewer specialized places; more diverse "regular" places)

The Instructional Cascade envisions the regular education classroom as the primary and optimal setting for the delivery of specialized services to handicapped children. Children are seen as moving among the levels of the cascade for educational purposes. Ideally, a child would be moved to a more restrictive setting only for compelling educational reasons and would be moved back as quickly as possible. The model shows that specialized instructional procedures are possible in regular classroom settings. The Instructional Cascade reflects the growing support for integration of the handicapped into regular education programs.

## REFERENCES

Cartwright, G. P., Cartwright, C. A., & Ward, M. E. (1985). *Educating special learners* (2nd ed.). Belmont, CA: Wadsworth.

Deno, E. (1970). Special education as developmental capital. *Exceptional Children, 37*(3), 229–237.

Peterson, R. L., Zabel, R. H., Smith, C. R., & White, M. A. (1983). Cascade of services model and emotionally disabled students. *Exceptional Children, 49*(5), 404–408.

Reynolds, M. C. (1962). A framework for considering some issues in special education. *Exceptional Children, 28*(7), 367–370.

Reynolds, M. C., & Birch, J. W. (1977). *Teaching exceptional children in all America's schools*. Reston, VA: Council for Exceptional Children.

LIBBY GOODMAN
*Pennsylvania State University*

**LEAST RESTRICTIVE ENVIRONMENT**
*See* PHILOSOPHY OF EDUCATION FOR THE HANDICAPPED; SPECIAL CLASS

# CASE HISTORY

Case histories serve several purposes: to provide information about rare disorders, individual differences in treatment responsiveness, or the natural course for a disorder (Kratochwill, 1985); to provide information necessary to plan and monitor appropriate treatment; to provide data needed by external agencies; to illuminate pitfalls to be avoided; and to provide information for scientific, administrative, and instructional purposes.

Identification information in a complete case history should include client's name, date of birth, sex, ethnicity, dominant language, marital status, guardians' names if a minor, residence, phone number, persons to notify in an emergency, medical status, and current program status (e.g., grade or placement if an educational setting); this information should be in an easily located part of the record. Historical data, as determined relevant for client welfare by a multidisciplinary committee, should include developmental, health, and educational history; work history if an adult; and significant family events.

Specific statements of the concerns of the referral agent should be included. The client's status at the time of referral should include information about current health, including current medications; sensory or perceptual abilities; motor abilities; language skills; current adaptive behavior; intellectual abilities and academic skills; other cognitive data, such as current belief systems or attributions as may be pertinent to the referral problem; emotional behavior; social skills and behavior; family status; and vocational aptitudes, skills, and interests. A description of the client's current status with respect to the referring problem should always be included. The preintervention frequency of the problem behavior should be recorded to establish treatment effectiveness at a later time.

The case history should contain not only the treatment goals for a client, but the process by which those goals were determined, including dates of meetings for discussing goals, those who were present, alternative plans discussed, costs and benefits of alternative plans, and the final treatment plan agreed on. Records should also be maintained of the course of treatment implementation, including the goal to which the treatment session was directed, what was done during the session, and the clinician's notes about difficulties or unexpected results.

To establish intervention effectiveness, a record must be maintained of changes in the client's behavior or level of skill. Data from observations, self-monitoring, or other methods can be collected and recorded and effectiveness assessed by means of single-subject designs (Barlow & Hersen, 1984). These techniques have the advantage of demonstrating that specific treatments have been tried and have been effective or noneffective; of being sensitive to subtle changes in behavior; and of allowing the comparison of several alternative treatments.

## REFERENCES

Barlow, D. H., & Hersen, M. (1984). *Single-case experimental designs: Strategies for studying behavior change.* (2nd ed.). New York: Pergamon.

Kratochwill, T. R. (1985). Case study research in school psychology. *School Psychology Review, 14,* 204–215.

JOHN MACDONALD
*Eastern Kentucky University*

**MEDICAL HISTORY**
**MENTAL STATUS EXAM**

## CASPAR HAUSER CHILDREN

Children raised under highly deprived conditions are sometimes described, particularly in older literature, as Caspar Hauser children. In 1828, when about 17 years of age, Caspar Hauser appeared in rags in Nuremberg. He could write his name primitively, but was poorly coordinated and appeared retarded. Under the care of a local teacher, he learned some speech and social graces. He was able to recall that he lived alone for years in a dark room and was cared for by someone who never spoke or was seen. His story, originally written by Anselm von Feuerbach, is summarized by Shattuck (1980).

Unfortunately, as with most such cases, interpretation of Caspar Hauser's progress is difficult because of lack of knowledge about his early environment, how he had lived prior to isolation, and whether, for example, had previously acquired language.

Considerable development occurs in many areas after severe early deprivation, particularly when individuals are recovered in childhood. Normal language development is less likely, and prolonged deprivation cannot be completely reversed (Clarke & Clarke, 1976; Skuse, 1984). Genie, although occasionally described as a modern-day Victor (the Wild Boy of Aveyron), would better be described as a modern-day Caspar Hauser since she was raised in a severely deprived environment.

## REFERENCES

Clarke, A. M., & Clarke, A. D. B. (Eds.). (1976). *Early experience: Myth and evidence.* New York: Free Press.

Shattuck, R. (1980). *The forbidden experiment: The story of the wild boy of Aveyron.* New York: Farrar Straus Giroux.

Skuse, D. (1984). Extreme deprivation in early childhood—II. Theoretical issues and a comparative review. *Journal of Child Psychology & Psychiatry, 25,* 543–572.

ROBERT T. BROWN
*University of North Carolina,
Wilmington*

**EARLY EXPERIENCE AND CRITICAL PERIODS**
**FERAL CHILDREN**
**GENIE**
**WILD BOY OF AVEYRON**

## CATALOG OF FEDERAL DOMESTIC ASSISTANCE

The *Catalog of Federal Domestic Assistance* is a compendium of all programs, projects, and activities of the federal government that provide benefits or assistance to the public (U.S. Government Printing Office, 1985). The catalog provides basic descriptive information on each program or activity, such as the purposes of the program, eligible applicants, total funds available, examples and dollar range of prior awards, and person to contact. The catalog covers programs providing both financial and nonfinancial forms of assistance (e.g., information, technical assistance, transfer of real property). It is updated and published twice a year by the General Services Administration, an agency of the federal government.

Programs are organized by sponsoring agency, but are also indexed across all agencies by subject area, by the type of entity or individual eligible to apply for assistance, and even by application deadline. The indexes make the catalog a useful reference guide for someone trying to locate potential sources of assistance for a particular project or in a specific subject area (e.g., mental retardation, early childhood education).

The catalog is distributed free of charge on a limited basis to state and local officials. It can also be purchased from the U.S. Government Printing Office.

**REFERENCE**

U.S. Government Printing Office. (1985). *Catalog of federal domestic assistance.* Washington, DC: Author

JAMES R. RICCIUTI
*United States Office of
Management and Budget*

# CATARACTS

A cataract is an imperfection in the clarity or a clouding of the lens of the eye. It will be experienced by a majority of people who live to an old age (Eden, 1978). Surgically removing the affected lens is the only treatment.

Eden (1978) defines three types of cataracts. Senile cataracts are those that occur as part of the normal aging process. Cell layers form around the lens as people grow older; this is similar to rings forming in the trunks of trees. The lens becomes opaque and loses its resiliency. Secondary cataracts are those that result from some other trauma or disease. For example, persons with diabetes often develop cataracts. Secondary cataracts can also result from excessive radiation, electrical shock, and the side effects of some drugs. Excessive use of cortisone, for example, has been related to the development of lens opacity. Congenital cataracts are those that are present from birth. This type of cataract is very rare. Illnesses during pregnancy such as German measles (rubella) can cause congenital cataracts (Harley & Lawrence, 1977).

It was once thought that cataracts had to be "ripe" before the lens could be removed. For example, *Melloni's Illustrated Medical Dictionary* (Dox, Melloni, & Eisner, 1979) defines a mature cataract as one in which the entire lens substance has become opaque and thus easy to sep-

arate from its capsule. However, Eden (1978) reports that such ripening is not necessary before surgery is possible.

Some cataracts get progressively worse; others do not. Some cataracts involve only the periphery of the lens; others may be more centrally located (Harley & Lawrence, 1977). Therefore, the symptoms can vary a great deal from patient to patient, and, although surgery is the only cure, it is often not necessary.

Post operative treatment of cataract removal involves the use of regular glasses or contact lenses, or the insertion of artificial plastic lenses in the eye itself. Such treatments are effective in restoring vision to the affected eye.

**REFERENCES**

Dox, I., Melloni, B. J., & Eisner, G. (1979). *Melloni's illustrated medical dictionary.* Baltimore, MD: Williams & Wilkins.

Eden, J. (1978). *The eye book.* New York: Viking.

Harley, R. K., & Lawrence, G. A. (1977). *Visual impairment in the schools.* Springfield, IL: Thomas.

THOMAS E. ALLEN
*Gallaudet College*

**AMBLIOPIA
BLIND**

# CATEGORICAL EDUCATION

Categorical education is the practice of separating handicapped children into subgroups representing different types of disability. Each subgroup bears a specific categorical designation and its members are reviewed as a cohesive group for instructional purposes. The traditional categorical group structure presumes that there is significant homogeneity of student characteristics within each subgroup and that there is significant heterogeneity among the groups. That is, the members of one group share common qualities that can distinguish them from the members of all other groups. The assumptions of homogeneity within categories and heterogeneity among categories are not well founded (Iano, 1972; Hallahan & Kauffman, 1977; Kirk & Elkins, 1975; Leland, 1977), particularly for the mildly handicapped.

Various categorical labels have been used to designate the separate subgroups of handicapped children. Different labels were frequently used to apply to essentially the same children (e.g., perceptually impaired, minimally brain damaged, and minimal cerebral dysfunction are terms that have been subsumed under the term learning disabilities). Dementia, feeblemindedness, and idiot are terms that have given way to the general label of mental retardation. The Education for All Handicapped Children Act of 1975 (PL 94-142) stipulates 11 handicapping conditions: mentally retarded, hard of hearing, deaf, speech impaired, deaf-blind, learning disabled, visually handicapped, seriously emotionally disturbed, orthopedically handicapped, other health impaired, and multihandicapped. These categories have become the prototype for the nation and are reflected in state and local plans for the education of handicapped children. Gifted children were not included in PL 94-142 because this legislation addressed only handicapping conditions. Only the broader concept of exceptionality encompasses atypical children who are set apart by abilities as well as those who are afflicted with disabilities.

Although the categories of disabilities recognized by states and school districts may be more consistent as a result of PL 94-142, the specific criteria actually used to identify handicapped children vary greatly from state to state and among local school districts. The variability in identification and placement criteria has created the phenomenon that the same child can be placed in different categories in different states or school systems. Under a categorical system, the child invariably is labeled with a disability designation. The process of labeling has been studied and the negative consequences of labeling for the child, family, and school community have been discussed at length. Discussions of the pros and cons of categorical labels are available in numerous works (Hewitt & Forness, 1977; Kirk & Gallagher, 1979; Lilly, 1979).

In 1972, the Project on Classification of Exceptional Children, under the leadership of Nicholas Hobbs, undertook a systematic review of the classification and labeling of children. Ultimately, the task force steered a middle course between proponents and opponents of labeling and set forth recommendations for improving classification and labeling practices. Five sets of recommendations addressed the harmful effects of classification and labeling; they dealt with

> (a) improvements in the classification systems, (b) some constraints on the use of psychological tests, (c) improvements in procedures for early identification of children of developmental risk, (d) safeguards in the use of records, and (e) attention to due process in classifying and placing exceptional children. (Hobbs, 1975, pp. 232–233)

A growing disaffection with traditional categorical education has led to the development of alternative practices. Critics of traditional categorical labels such as mentally retarded, learning disabled, or socially emotionally disturbed emphasize that such labels are of little use to the teacher who must plan appropriate instructional programs. Behaviorally based designations that group children on the basis of educationally relevant variables (Lovitt, 1967; Quay, 1968) and common remedial instructional needs (Hallahan & Kauffman, 1977) are recommended as an effective alternative.

## REFERENCES

Hallahan, D. P., & Kauffman, J. M. (1977). Labels, categories, behaviors: ED, LD, and EMR reconsidered. *Journal of Special Education, 11* (2), 139–149.

Hewett, F. M., & Forness, S. R. (1977). *Education of exceptional learners*. Boston: Allyn Bacon.

Hobbs, N. (1975). *The future of children*. San Francisco: Jossey-Bass.

Iano, R. P. (1972). Shall we disband special classes? *Journal of Special Education, 6* (2), 167–177.

Kirk, S. A., & Gallagher, J. J. (1979). *Educating exceptional children*. Boston: Houghton Mifflin.

Kirk, S. A., & Elkins, J. (1975). Characteristics of children enrolled in the child service demonstration centers. *Journal of Learning Disabilities, 8* (10), 630–637.

Leland, H. (1977). Mental retardation and adaptive behavior. *Journal of Special Education, 6* (1), 71–80.

Lilly, M. S. (1979). *Children with exceptional needs*. New York: Holt, Rinehart & Winston.

Lovitt, T. (1967). Assessment of children with learning disabilities. *Exceptional Children, 34* (4), 233–239.

Quay, H. C. (1968). The facets of educational exceptionality: A conceptual framework for assessment, grouping, and instruction. *Exceptional Children, 35* (1), 25–32.

LIBBY GOODMAN
*Pennsylvania State University*

## CASCADE MODEL OF SPECIAL EDUCATION SERVICES

## CATECHOLAMINES

Epinephrine (adrenaline) and norepinephrine (noradrenaline) are hormones of the sympathetic division of the autonomic nervous system. Epinephrine was the first hormone to be isolated, and by 1897 Abel had separated it from the adrenal gland and found it to be represented by the formula C17 H15 No4. By 1905, the Japanese chemist Takamine treated Abel's abstract and named the product adrenaline, with the formula C9 H13 No3 (Krantz & Carr, 1961). Norepinephrine was not identified until 1942; it derives its name from the German expression Nitrogen ohne radikal, referring to the fact that the molecule is identical to that of epinephrine except for missing the methyl group on the nitrogen atom.

Epinephrine produces a variety of metabolic effects useful in an emergency: increased epinephrine levels result in what is often called the "fight, flight, or fright" reaction (West & Todd, 1963). Epinephrine stimulates the effector cells of the pilomotor nerves to cause hair erection, and also causes pupillary dilation, giving rise to the picture of a fright reaction. By also causing a rapid rise in blood pressure and an increase in the rate and amplitude of respiration, it prepares for more effective fright or flight from danger. The metabolic behavioral effects of epinephrine and norepinephrine are in some ways opposite, in that while epinephrine is associated with tachycardia (rapid heartbeat), norepinephrine is associated with brachycardia (slow heart action) (Eranko, 1955). In children, normal levels in plasma are 3–6 m/l for norepinephrine, and >1 m/l for epinephrine (Cone, 1968).

## REFERENCES

Cone, T. E. (1968). The adrenal medulla. In R. Cooke & S. Levin (Eds.), *The biologic basis of pediatric practice* (pp. 1171–1177). New York: McGraw-Hill.

Eranko, O. (1955). Distribution of adrenaline and noradrenaline in the adrenal medulla. *Nature, 88,* 175.

Krantz, R. C., & Carr, C. J. (1961). The *pharmacologic principles of medical practice* (5th ed.). Baltimore, MD: Williams & Wilkins.

West, E. S., & Todd, W. R. (1963). *Textbook of biochemistry* (3rd ed.). New York: Macmillan.

LAWRENCE C. HARTLAGE
*Evans, Georgia*

## EPINEPHRINE

## CAT SCAN

Computerized axial tomography (CAT) scanning is an imaging technique (Binder, Haughton, & Ho, 1979) that permits visualization of many of the important landmarks and structures of the brain (see Figure 1). This is a recent technique that did not become commercially available until 1973 (Hounsfield, 1973). The importance of this breakthrough in diagnostic neuroradiology is exemplified by the fact that the 1979 Nobel Prize in Medicine was awarded to the scientists G. N. Hounsfield and A. M. Cormack, who established the theoretical physics and radiographic basis for CAT scanning. The fascinating history behind these monumental breakthroughs is reviewed in the text by Oldendorf (1980).

CAT scanning is accomplished by passing a narrow X-ray beam directed toward a detector on the other side through the patient's head (or body). The detector is sensitive to the number of X-ray beam particles that pass through the tissue; this in turn is related to the density of the tissue (e.g., the greater the density the fewer the X-ray particles that pass through). The X-ray beam is passed through the head (or body) in numerous planes so as to examine the same point from multiple directions, thus allowing a specification of density for any given point on the surface of a plane. Next, each density point is color-coded depending on the degree of density; these various density points are used to computer generate an "image" of the tissue being examined (see Figure 2).

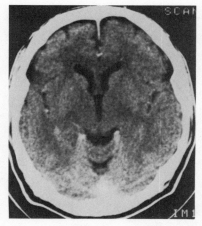

Figure 1. CAT scan image of the brain in horizontal plane. The two upside down L-shaped dark areas represent the anterior horns of the lateral ventricles. The light area just adjacent and lateral to these structures is the caudate nucleus. The centrally located dark area just below the anterior horns in this figure represents the third ventricle. On either side of the third ventricle is the thalamus. The angular slightly darker area that runs from the outside top of the candate nucleus down and adjacent to the outside of the thalamus is the internal capsule. Lateral to the internal capsule is the putamen-globus pallidus complex.

CAT scanning has numerous useful applications. The CAT image approximates an actual anatomic specimen taken in a similar plane; thus significant structural abnormalities can be detected. This is particularly true in cases of cerebral trauma, vascular infarctions, congenital and neoplastic disorders, and degenerative brain diseases (see Figure 3). For children with developmental disorders, CAT scanning may reveal any major structural anomalies of the brain, but it has not been found to be routinely diagnostic in children in which the only problem is a learning disability (Denkla, LeMay, & Chapman, 1985). These observations suggest that, in general, there is no gross

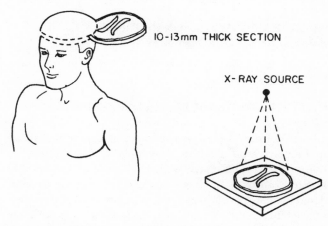

Figure 2. Diagrammatic representation of the position of the view of the CAT image.

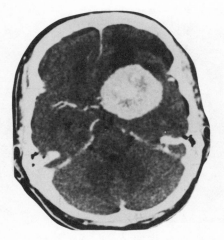 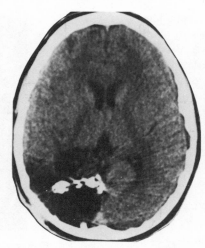 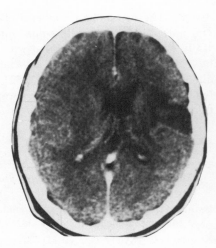

Figure 3. Representative CAT scan depiciting different types of organic pathology. Left: tumor (menin-gioma). Middle: gunshot wound. Right: stroke (dark area on right side).

anatomic derangement associated with learning disorders.

### REFERENCES

Binder, G. A., Haughton, V. M., & Ho, K-C. (1979). *Computed tomography of the brain in axial, coronal and sagittal planes* Boston: Little, Brown.

Denkla, M. B., LeMay, M., & Chapman, C. A. (1985). Few Ct scan abnormalities found ever in neurologically impaired learning disabled children. *Journal of Learning Disabilities, 18,* 132–135.

Hounsfield, G. N. (1973). Computerized transverse axial scanning (tomography). I. Description of system. *British Journal of Radiology, 46,* 1016–1022.

Oldendorf, W. H. (1980). *The quest for an image of brain.* New York: Raven Press.

ERIN D. BIGLER
*Austin Neurological Clinic*
*University of Texas, Austin*

## NUCLEAR MAGNETIC RESONANCE (NMR) X-RAY SCANNING TECHNIQUES

## CATTELL, JAMES MCKEEN (1860–1944)

James McKeen Cattell was educated at Lafayette College in Pennsylvania and the University of Leipzig in Germany. He worked under Wilhelm Wundt at Leipzig and at Sir Francis Galton's psychological laboratory in London. He held the world's first professorship in psychology, at the University of Pennsylvania, and later was professor of psychology and head of the department of psychology at Columbia University (Woodworth, 1944).

A devoted researcher, Cattell conducted significant investigations in areas such as reaction time, perception, association, and individual differences. He developed numerous tests and coined the term mental tests. He studied the backgrounds and characteristics of eminent scientists, and published the widely used directory *Biographical Dictionary of American Men of Science.* To promote the practical application of psychology, he founded the Psychological Corporation and served as its president for many years. He also edited a number of influential journals, including the *American Journal of Psychology, Psychological Review,* and *Science.* Cattell, through his students, research, and writing and editing, was a major figure in the development of psychology as a profession in the United States (Watson, 1968).

### REFERENCES

Watson, R. I. (1968). *The great psychologists.* New York: Lippincott.

Woodworth, R. S. (1944). James McKeen Cattell, 1860–1944. *Psychological Review, 51,* 201–209.

PAUL IRVINE
*Katonah, New York*

## CAWLEY'S PROJECT MATH

Project MATH (Mathematics Activities for Teaching the Handicapped) is a comprehensive developmental mathematics program for children with special needs. The program was developed by Dr. John Cawley and his associates at the University of Connecticut under a federal grant operated from 1970 to 1975. The project was entitled "A Program Project Research and Demonstration Effort in Arithmetic Among the Mentally Handicapped"; it is available commercially.

The teaching model used in the curriculum is called the *Interactive Unit* (IU). This teaching model allows for the presentation of information to the learner in four different ways and also allows the learner to respond to questions or information in four different ways. There are 16 possible interactions that can take place between the teacher and the learner for any concept being taught. No interaction is considered to be cognitively superior to another. The interactive unit teaching model offers several advantages for the instructor. Chief among these advantages is that the model allows an instructor to teach around a disability. Learners who have difficulty in reading or writing may be taught by any of the remaining nine interaction possibilities. The instructor components of the IU are state, construct, present, and graphically symbolize. The learner components are state, construct, identify, and graphically symbolize.

The goal of the curriculum is to give a balanced emphasis to the development of skills, concepts, and social growth. The content of the math strands addressed are patterns, numbers, operations, measurements, fractions, and geometry. There are multiple lessons and support materials for concepts taught in each strand. A math concept inventory accompanies each level of the curriculum. This inventory is essentially a criterion-referenced test used to make initial placement decisions in the curriculum and to measure growth.

The verbal problem solving component of the curriculum is unique in that problem solving is introduced at the lowest level of the curriculum (Level I) and is carried out in an increasingly complex manner in the remaining levels. Problem solving is viewed as the ultimate objective of the mathematics curriculum. Unlike most mathematics programs, reading is not an essential prerequisite for entry into the verbal problem-solving exercises; the need for computational skills is also minimized. The focus of the verbal problem-solving component is on the processing of information necessary for the solution, not on the practice of computational skills. Levels I and II use sets of pictures, cards, and prepared scripts to guide a teacher and learner through the problem-solving activities. In Level III, reading is required for the first time. The use of extraneous information and language plays a major role in the problem-solving activities.

The final component of the Cawley's Project MATH curriculum consists of *Social Utilization Units*. These units are real-life extensions of the verbal problem-solving exercises; they require teams of learners to use mathematics to solve real-life problems. The units also stress social responsibility in that each member of the team is responsible for performing a task or gathering information so that the team's problem can be solved.

Two years of field testing, from 1972 to 1974, was undertaken. It involved 1917 children instructed by 116 teachers in seven states. In addition to the curricular development thrust of the project, a large number of research studies were undertaken and published, primarily in the area of verbal problem solving. Cawley has continued to build on the Project MATH materials and to expand the basic model so that it can be used by a wide variety of special educators. One added component to the model is the emphasis on error analysis and the teaching of nontraditional algorithms.

## REFERENCES

Cawley, J. F. (Ed.). (1984). *Developmental teaching of mathematics for the learning disabled*. Rockville, MD: Aspen Systems.

Cawley, J. F. (Ed.). (1985). *Secondary school mathematics for the learning disabled*. Rockville, MD: Aspen Systems.

Cawley, J. F., Goodstein, H. A., Fitzmaurice, A. M., Lepore, A., Sedlak, R. A., & Althaus, V. (1976, 1977). *Project MATH: Mathematics activities for teaching the handicapped: Levels I–IV*. Tulsa, OK: Educational Progress Corporation.

Goodstein, H. A. (1981). Are the errors we see the true errors? Error analysis in verbal problem solving. *Topics in Learning and Learning Disabilities, 1*(3), 31–45.

ROBERT A. SEDLAK
*University of Wisconsin, Stout*

## MATHEMATICS, LEARNING DISABILITIES IN

## CENTILE SCORES

See PERCENTILE SCORES.

## CENTRAL AUDITORY DYSFUNCTION

Central auditory dysfunction is a term used to describe a broad spectrum of difficulties that may arise when an individual attempts to process an auditory signal. This disorder occurs even in people without hearing problems. The term implies an underlying notion that when an individual exhibits certain difficulties in correctly interpreting an auditory signal, there is some type of damage in the brain.

During the past decade, a number of tests were devised to evaluate the integrity of the central auditory processing mechanism. These measures were used to evaluate the auditory processing of adults with anatomical lesions. Generally, these tests presented a speech signal that reduced redundancy and made listening more difficult. It was found in a series of correlational studies that the performance of adults with known lesions was poorer than that of normal adults (Berlin & Lowe, 1972). It was then assumed that children who also performed poorly on similar tests suffered from some type of central auditory dysfunction (Keith, 1981b). In the last 10 or 15 years, there have been attempts to determine whether children with language disorders also have central auditory dysfunction. If they did, the question pertains to the relationship between the two and what remedial strategies could be used successfully. Language acquisition, language disorders of various types, and learning disabilities have all been considered to be directly related directly related to various types of central auditory dysfunction.

Two basic types of tests are given to evaluate the central auditory functioning of an individual. The first test is designed to evaluate the auditory neuromaturational level of the individual. Keith (1981a) suggests that these tests meet the following criteria: They should (1) not be loaded with language comprehension items; (2) not require linguistic manipulation of the signal; (3) not require, or at least minimize, cross-modal input or response; (4) use nonlinguistic signals; and (5) be primarily a speech imitative task using nonmeaningful material or speech material so familiar that comprehension plays no role in the process. The following tests are suggested by Keith:

1. *Auditory Localization.* Generally children are able to localize at a very early age so any normal child past infancy should be able to localize without difficulty.

2. *Binaural Synthesis.* An example of this test is the Rapidly Alternating Speech Perception Test, where sentences are switched rapidly from one ear to the other. If the child has difficulty with this test, it is assumed that there may be a lesion located in the brain stem.

3. *Binaural Separation.* The Staggered Spondaic Word Test is used to determine whether the child shows ear dominance or whether the left ear score increases with age. Dichotic listening tests are also included in this category to determine whether children are establishing hemispheric dominance. A failure to do so may imply a neurological basis for a learning, reading, or language problem.

4. *Resistance to Distortion.* Three types of tests are generally used in this category: speech in noise, filtered speech, and time-compressed speech. Individuals with normal central auditory functioning generally have no difficulty with these tasks, but when there is a specific lesion or other auditory abnormality, the individual will have difficulty in understanding speech with reduced redundancy.

Keith notes that these tests are only to be used after language has emerged. He also notes that the tests have substantial maturational effects up until about age 12. Research has indicated that there are children with no apparent language or learning difficulties who perform poorly on these tests. Likewise, there are children with such difficulties who have no problems with the tests. Keith cautions that while these tests might give some indication of the neurologic status of a child, they do not indicate specific language, learning, or reading deficits. Furthermore, they do not in themselves suggest any particular remediation strategy.

The second type of tests can be categorized as auditory-language tests. These tests are heavily loaded both cognitively and linguistically. Examples are tests in which the child must point to a series of pictures in the order in which the words for them are heard. It is to be noted that this task is not simply a single-factor auditory-perceptual test, but requires memory and comprehension. Another example of an auditory-language test is one that asks the child to listen to a word with a phoneme missing, and then identify the missing phoneme. This is a complex language-mediated task requiring the child to analyze a distorted signal. Another frequently administered test, the Goldman-Fristoe-Woodcock Test of Auditory Discrimination Noise Subtest, contains a similarly difficult task. The child must use visual perception, auditory-visual association, and an auditory-visual-motor response with a vocabulary that may not be familiar.

While noting that a number of children with language problems do poorly on tests of central auditory functioning, Rees (1981) observes that it is not at all clear whether the deficits actually produce the language disorders or whether they are simply behavioral correlates of these and other disabilities. She further criticizes these tests stating that "no one has developed an intelligible account of how these central auditory processing skills or the lack of them, relate to language acquisition or academic learning" (p. 118). She considers the tests that are heavily loaded with linguistic and cognitive material to be tests designed more to evaluate an individual child's metalinguistic ability (the ability to analyze and talk about language) than to measure directly the child's ability to learn language. While these tasks may be good indicators of the individual child's ability to function successfully in school, she questions whether they have a fundamental relationship with central auditory processing. Rees notes that in some ways all the phenomena that have been clustered under the rubric of central auditory functioning have only one thing in common—they all involve data taken in through the ear.

In summary, central auditory dysfunction refers to problems individuals may exhibit in processing an auditory signal even when they have no hearing problem. When adults with known brain lesions were asked to perform specific tasks related to auditory functioning, it was found that they exhibited specific problems. Some children with learning problems performed similarly on tests of auditory processing. It was presumed they also might have some kind of brain damage. Two types of tests are given to test auditory functioning. The first evaluates auditory maturational level, the second tests language-related auditory functions. It is not clear whether there is a cause and effect relationship between auditory functioning and learning disorders.

## REFERENCES

Berlin, C., & Lowe, S. S. (1972). Temporary and dichotic factors in central auditory testing. In J. Katz (Ed.), *Handbook of clinical audiology*. Baltimore, MD: Williams & Wilkins.

Keith, R. W. (1981a). *Central auditory and language disorders in children*. San Diego, CA: College Hill.

Keith, R. W. (1981b). Tests of central auditory function. In R. J. Roesser & M. P. Downs (Eds.), *Auditory disorders in school children* (pp. 159–173). New York: Thieme-Stratton.

Rees, N. S. (1981). Saying more than we know: Is auditory processing disorder a meaningful concept? In R. W. Keith (Ed.), *Central auditory and language disorders in children* (pp. 94–120). San Diego, CA: College Hill.

CAROLYN BULLARD
*Lewis & Clark College*

**AUDITORY ABNORMALITIES**
**AUDITORY DISCRIMINATION**
**AUDITORY PERCEPTION**
**AUDITORY VISUAL INTEGRATION**

## CENTRAL NERVOUS SYSTEM

The central nervous system (CNS) refers to the brain, including the cerebral cortex, cranial nerves, cerebellum, spinal cord, and other subcortical structures contained within the cranial vault. It consists of more than 12 billion neurons and approximately 10 times that number of glial cells. The cerebral cortex represents the CNS structure underlying most adaptive behavior, including sensation, perception, judgment, intellective functioning, and purposeful movement. Divided into two cerebral hemispheres, the respective cerebral cortices tend to be differentiated in terms of functions. As with other CNS structures that develop embryologically from the prosencephalon, the cerebral hemispheres have contralateral representation, i.e., the left side of the cortex controls the right side of the body, and vice versa. Each cerebral hemisphere is divided into anterior and posterior regions by the central sulcus or fissure of Rolando. Those cortical areas just anterior to the Rolandic fissure are specialized for motor functions, with motor enervation proceeding from superior areas of the motor strip, which control lower extremity movement, downward to more inferior areas, which control movement of the face. Just posterior to the Rolandic fissure is the sensory area, which controls such phenomena as sensitivity to stimulation for body areas corresponding to those enervated by the motor strip.

In addition to lateralized representation of motor and sensory functions, the cerebral cortex areas are also specialized for processing given types of information, and for processing information in given ways. In essentially all right-handed and in most left-handed individuals, the left cerebral hemisphere is more efficient in processing verbal or linguistic types of information, with the right hemisphere more specialized for the processing of spatial types of information. This specialization of function can be demonstrated in normal individuals by injecting fast-acting barbiturate types of drugs such as sodium amytal into a selected cerebral hemisphere. Following such an injection to the left cerebral hemisphere, for example, individuals will normally experience a brief period of aphasia, during which they are both unable to comprehend spoken language and to formulate verbalizations. Within a few minutes, all verbal functions return to preinjection levels. Similar temporary impairment of spatial function is demonstrated on right hemisphere injection (Hartlage & Flanigin, 1982).

In addition to specialization for type and process of cognitive information processing, the cerebral hemispheres also mediate differentiated emotional functions. Damage, deprivation of blood supply, unilateral electroconvulsive treatment, and depressant medication all have been shown to result in different emotional responses for each cerebral hemisphere. Insult to the right cerebral hemisphere produces what has been called the "la belle indifference syndrome," characterized by poor monitoring of behavior and euphoria. Insult to the left hemisphere produces the "catastrophic reaction," characterized by depression (Robertson & Inglis, 1973; Schwartz, Davidson, & Maer, 1975; Tucker, 1981).

Anatomically, the cerebral hemispheres are divided into four lobes. The frontal lobes are separated posteriorly from the parietal lobes by the central sulcus, and from the temporal lobes by the Sylvan fissure, which also separates the superiorly located parietal lobes from the temporal lobes. The occipital notch, at the posterior end of the parietal lobes, divides the parietal lobes from the occipital lobes. An approach to further subclassification of the cerebral hemispheres is the cytoarchitectural system of Brodmann, in which discrete areas of the cerebral cortices are divided into 52 Brodmann areas (Krieg, 1957) and are referred to and identified by numbers corresponding to those locations. For example, "Brodmann's area 8" corresponds to the frontal eye fields.

There is good evidence that in most individuals the cerebral hemispheres are not symmetrical (Geschwind & Levitsky, 1968; Von Bonin, 1962). This asymmetry has been related to differences in facility with processing certain types of information and other psychological characteristics (Lansdell & Smith, 1975; Levy, 1974; Reynolds, 1981). This hemispheric asymmetry has been postulated as being etiologic in certain mental disorders such as schizophrenia (Gruzelier, 1984; Newlin, Carpenter, & Golden, 1981), autism (Colby & Parkinson, 1977; Dawson, Warrenburg, & Fuller, 1982), and a number of other maladaptive behaviors (Sandel & Alcorn, 1980).

Separating the right and left cerebral hemispheres is the corpus callosum, which contains many fibers that convey impulses between the hemispheres. Right-handed individuals have a somewhat smaller corpus callosum than do individuals who are left handed or with mixed hand dominance. This phenomenon may be related to greater hemispheric specialization in strongly right-handed individuals (Witelson, 1985). Differential specialization has been suggested as a possible explanation of such conditions as dyslexia, on the basis that the lack of specialization in the language hemisphere may preclude the refinement of sophisticated processes involved in reading (Witelson, 1977).

Although much adaptive behavior is attributed to the cerebral hemispheres, other portions of the central nervous system mediate behaviors of crucial importance to the individual. The 12 cranial nerves (olfactory, optic, oculomotor, trochlear, trigeminal, abducens, facial, acoustic, glossopharyngeal, vagus, accessory, and hypoglossal) control such functions as smell, visual acuity, eye movement, facial sensation and movement, and hearing.

The cerebellum, located posteriorly and partially under the occipital lobe, with connections to many portions of the cerebral cortex, is involved with balance and with coordination of some motor activities (because some areas of the cerebellum are uniquely sensitive to the effects of alcohol, law enforcement officers often check some aspects of cerebellar function when screening drivers suspected of intoxication). A number of brain areas often referred to as subcortical (e.g., amygdala, hippocampus, thalamus) because of their location under the cortex, have been identified as playing important roles in such behaviors as emotion, memory, movement, and the integration of information from diverse cortical areas (Riklan & Levita, 1965). The medulla, that portion of the central nervous system that bridges with the spinal cord, is more involved with lower sensory and motor functions than with higher cognitive abilities.

Although some areas of the CNS have been shown to be crucial for the performance of given tasks, the CNS functions in an interrelated way for the execution of most complex tasks. Damage to the CNS will almost always result in a complex disorder requiring special educational services.

## REFERENCES

Colby, K. M., & Parkinson, C. (1977). Handedness in autistic children. *Journal of Autism and Childhood Schizophrenia, 7,* 3–9.

Dawson, G., Warrenburg, S., & Fuller, D. (1982). Cerebral lateralization in individuals diagnosed as autistic in early childhood. *Brain and Language, 15,* 353–368.

Geschwind, N., & Levitsky, W. (1968). Human brain: Left-right asymmetries in temporal speech region. *Science, 161,* 186–187.

Gruzelier, J. H. (1984). Hemispheric imbalances in schizophrenia. *International Journal of Psychophysiology, 1,* 227–240.

Hartlage, L. C., & Flanigin, H. (1982, Oct.). *An abbreviated intracarotical amytal testing procedure.* Paper presented at the annual meeting of the National Academy of Neuropsychologists, Atlanta, GA.

Krieg, W. J. S. (1957). *Brain mechanisms in diachrome* (2d ed.). Evanston, IL: Brain Books.

Lansdell, H., & Smith, F. J. (1975). Asymmetrical cerebral function for two WAIS factors and their recovery after brain injury. *Journal of Consulting and Clinical Psychology, 43,* 931.

Levy, H. (1974). Psychological implications of bilateral asymmetry. In S. J. Dimond & J. G. Beaumont (Eds.), *Hemispheric function in the Human Brain.* London: Elek Science.

Newlin, D. B., Carpenter, B., & Golden, C. (1981). Hemispheric asymmetries in schizophrenia. *Biological Psychiatry, 16,* 561–581.

Reynolds, C. R. (1981). The neuropsychological basis of intelligence. In G. Hynd & J. Obrzut (Eds.), *Neuropsychological assessment of the school aged child: Issues and procedures.* New York: Grune & Stratton.

Riklan, M., & Levita, E. (1965). Laterality of subcortical involvement and psychological functions. *Psychological Bulletin, 64,* 217–224.

Robertson, A. D., & Inglis, J. (1973). Cerebral asymmetry and electroconvulsive therapy. *Proceedings of the 81st Annual Convention of the American Psychological Association, 8,* 431–432.

Sandel, A., & Alcorn, J. (1980). Individual hemispherity and maladaptive behaviors. *Journal of Abnormal Psychology, 9,* 514–517.

Schwartz, G. E., Davidson, R. J., & Maer, F. (1975). Right hemisphere lateralization for emotion in the human brain: Interactions with cognition. *Science, 190,* 286–288.

Tucker, D. M. (1981). Lateral brain function emotion, and conceptualization. *Psychological Bulletin, 89,* 19–46.

Von Bonin, G. (1962). Anatomical asymmetries of the cerebral hemispheres. In V. B. Mountcastle (Ed.), *Interhemispheric relations and cerebral dominance* (pp. 1–6). Baltimore, MD: Johns Hopkins Press.

Witelson, S. (1977). Developmental dyslexia: Two right hemispheres and none left. *Science, 195,* 309–311.

Witelson, S. F. (1985). The brain connection: The corpus callosum is larger in left handers. *Science, 229,* 665–668.

LAWRENCE C. HARTLAGE
*Evans, Georgia*

**APHASIA**
**BRAIN ORGANIZATION**
**CEREBRAL DOMINANCE**
**CEREBRAL FUNCTION**
**LEFT BRAIN-RIGHT BRAIN**

# CENTRAL PROCESSING DYSFUNCTIONS IN CHILDREN

The world is a colorful, noisy, and interesting place. To learn and respond to the world around them, infants, children, adolescents, and adults receive information about their world through the senses of vision, hearing, smell, touch, and bodily movement.

The brain serves as a center for (1) receiving incoming sensations from the eyes, ears, skin, muscles, and internal organs; (2) analyzing and organizing sensory information; (3) interpreting or giving meaning to the sensory information that is being received; (4) generating messages to send to all parts of the body for purposes of responding; and (5) storing information for later use (Chalfant & Scheffelin, 1969).

When the brain does not function properly in receiving, analyzing, and storing sensory information or sending messages to the bodily parts, a dysfunction is said to exist. Because the brain is part of the central nervous system, which processes sensory information, a breakdown in this system is often referred to as a central processing dysfunction.

Central processing dysfunctions can be caused by damage to the brain, but brain damage is not always the cause. There are many cases in which individuals behave as if they had a central processing dysfunction, but show no evidence of brain damage. All of the causes of central processing dysfunctions are not yet known.

There are three major systems in which a central processing dysfunction might occur: the visual processing system, the auditory processing system, and the haptic processing system. Symptoms of dysfunctions in these systems follow.

With visual processing dysfunctions, a student may have normal visual acuity but have difficulty processing and obtaining meaning from visual information. Some of the major characteristics of visual processing dysfunctions are difficulty in (1) attending to or focusing on what is seen; (2) seeing the difference between printed numbers, letters, and words; (3) learning spatial relationships such as left-right, up-down, far-near; (4) distinguishing a figure or object from the background within which it is embedded; (5) reorganizing a whole when one or more of its parts are missing, as in constructing a puzzle; (6) remembering what has been seen; and (7) responding quickly to visual stimuli. Visual processing dysfunctions may result in academic learning disabilities in reading, writing, and arithmetic (Kirk & Chalfant, 1984).

In auditory processing dysfunctions, a student may have normal hearing, but have difficulty in processing what is heard. Auditory processing dysfunctions are characterized by difficulty in (1) listening or attending to sound; (2) locating the origin or source of sound; (3) hearing the differences or similarities between pitch, loudness, rhythm, melody, rate, or duration of sounds; (4) listening to a teacher's instructions (figure) through the interferences of classroom noises (background); (5) reorganizing a spoken word when only part of the word is heard, e.g., telepho—; (6) remembering what has been heard; and (7) associating sounds to experiences such as "ding-dong" to a bell. Dysfunctions in auditory processing may result in learning disabilities in understanding spoken language, expressing oneself through oral language, forming concepts, and developing abstract thinking skills (Kirk & Chalfant, 1984).

In the haptic processing system, the term haptic processing refers to the information received from both touch and movement. Dysfunctions in the haptic system will result in difficulty in performing fine motor tasks such as writing, manipulating tools and equipment, or learning motor performance skills. There are two subsystems for haptic processing (Gibson, 1965). The first subsystem is the tactile or cutaneous one. If a dysfunction exists in the tactile system, difficulties may be experienced in (1) being sensitive to the presence of pressure or textures on the skin; (2) reorganizing objects through the sense of touch; (3) perceiving information about surface areas, sizes, shapes, boundaries, angles, etc.; and (4) being sensitive to pressure or aware of pain. Children with difficulties in the tactile system will have difficulty performing any task that requires the coordinated use of fingers such as learning to button or use a knife, fork, or spoon, or writing.

The second subsystem is the kinesthetic one. Bodily movement such as the movement of fingers, toes, arms, legs, head, lower jaw, tongue, and trunk, provides information about the body itself. Movement also provides information about direction and the location of objects in the environment in relation to the body itself. Muscular efforts such as lifting, pulling, and pushing objects give information about the weight of objects and gravity. Dysfunctions in the kinesthetic system result in difficulty in learning movement patterns such as crawling, walking, eating, dressing, undressing, writing, and riding a bicycle, or those needed for competing in sports activities (Kirk & Chalfant, 1984).

In summary, central processing dysfunctions can have a wide range of impact on a child or student. Young children often will be delayed in developing an understanding of and the use of oral language, visual-motor coordination, and/or cognitive abilities such as attention, discrimination, memory, conceptualization, and problem-solving skills. Students of school age may present academic disabilities in reading, writing, spelling, or arithmetic. As a result of failure over a long period of time, the expectations of children and students to succeed diminishes until they expect to fail. The result is little confidence in their ability, unwillingness to try, and low self-esteem (Pysh, 1982).

## REFERENCES

Chalfant, J. C., & Scheffelin, M. A. (1969). *Central processing dysfunction in children: A review of research* (NINDS Monograph No. 9). Washington, DC: U.S. Department of Health, Education, and Welfare.

Gibson, J. J. (1965). *The senses considered as perceptual systems.* Boston: Houghton Mifflin.

Kirk, S. A., & Chalfant, J. C. (1984). *Academic and developmental learning disabilities.* Denver: Love.

Pysh, M. V. (1982). *Learning disabled and normal achieving children's attributions and reactions to success and failure.* Unpublished doctoral dissertation, Northwestern University, Evanston, IL.

JAMES C. CHALFANT
*University of Arizonia*

**BRAIN DAMAGE**
**LEARNING DISABILITIES**
**LEARNING DISABILITIES, PROBLEMS IN DEFINITION OF**
**LEARNING STYLES**

# CENTRAL TENDENCY

Measures of central tendency are used to describe the typical or average score in a sample or population of scores. Many measures of central tendency exist, but the three most popularly used in the behavioral sciences are the mean, the median, and the mode.

The mean is the most widely used measure of central tendency. It is the arithmetic average of a given set of scores. For example, given the set of scores 87, 96, 98, 110, 113, 114, 119, the mean is 105.29, the sum of the seven scores divided by the number of scores, seven.

The median of a set of scores is the score that divides the set into two groups with each group containing the same number of scores. To compute the median, first rank the set of scores from smallest to largest. When the number of scores is odd and there are no ties, the median is the middle score. For example, the median of the above scores is 110. When the number of scores is even, with no ties, the median is the average of the two middle scores. Thus, the median score of 87, 96, 98, 110, 113, 114, 119, 120 is 110 + 113/2 = 111.50.

The mode is the score that occurs most frequently in a set of scores. For the scores 87, 96, 98, 98, 98, 110, 113, 114, 119, the mode is 98. When there are two modes, the distribution of scores is said to be bimodal. All three measures may be used when the data are quantitative. The median and mode are used with ranked data, whereas only the mode is applicable to nominal data.

The mean is the preferred measure of central tendency when the variable measured is quantitative and the distribution is relatively symmetric. It is relatively stable and reflects the value of every score in the distribution and, unlike the median and the mode, it is amenable to arithmetic and algebraic manipulations. These qualities make the mean useful not only for describing the average of a set of scores, but also for making inferences about population means. We can infer the value of the population mean from the sample mean, and also make inferences about the differences between population means for the same or different groups of individuals on one or more variables. When the distribution of scores is skewed, or the variable being measured is qualitative, the mean is not the preferred measure of central tendency.

For skewed distributions, the median is used. This is because the median is not affected by the scores falling above and below it. For example, the median of the scores 109, 108, 107, 106, 60 is 107; it more accurately reflects the typical score than the mean of 98. Inferences about the population median may also be concluded (see Marascuilo & McSweeney, 1977).

When the distribution is symmetric and unimodal, the median, mean, and mode are the same. When the distribution is skewed, however, the median and mean are unequal with median > mean in negatively skewed distributions and mean > median in positively skewed distributions.

## REFERENCES

Glass, G. V., & Hopkins, K. D. (1984). *Statistical methods in education and psychology* (2nd ed.). Englewood Cliffs, NJ: Prentice-Hall.

Hays, W. L. (1981). *Statistics* (3rd ed.). New York: Holt, Rinehart and Winston.

Kirk, R. E. (1984). *Elementary statistics* (2nd ed.). Monterey, CA: Brooks/Cole.

MacGillivray, H. L. (1985). Mean, median, mode, and skewness. In S. Kotz, N. L. Johnson, & C. B. Read, *Encyclopedia of the statistical sciences, Vol. 5,* New York: Wiley.

Marascuilo, L. A., & McSweeney, M. (1977). *Nonparametric and distribution-free methods for the social sciences.* Monterey, CA: Brooks/Cole.

GWYNETH M. BOODOO
*Texas A&M University*

**STANDARD DEVIATION**

# CEREBELLAR DISORDERS

The cerebellum is an oval-shaped portion of the brain under the occipital lobe of the cerebrum and behind the brain stem. It has a right and left hemisphere and a central section. The cerebellum integrates information vital to the control of posture and voluntary movement. The cerebellum is responsible for maintaining equilibrium and trunk balance; regulating muscle tension, spinal nerve reflexes, posture, and balance of the limbs; and regulating fine movements initiated by the frontal lobes.

Persons with cerebellar dysfunction may show any or

all of the following deficits: wide-based clumsy gait; tremor on attempted motion; clumsy, rapid alternating movements; inability to control the range of voluntary movements with overshooting the goal most common; low muscle tone; and scanning speech with inappropriate accenting of syllables. Rapid alternating eye movements (nystagmus) may be observed as a component of closely associated vestibular involvement.

Tumors of the cerebellum, heavy metal poisoning, repeated high fever or head trauma, and hypothyroidism can affect the cerebellum directly. Since the cerebellum receives postural and movement information from many parts of the brain, integrates them and sends information out to motor coordinating areas, the function of the cerebellum may be impaired by a wide range of neurological conditions. Multiple sclerosis, blood clots, and congenital anomalies of other parts of the brain can influence the cerebellum via input/output tracts as well. The spinocerebellar diseases are a family of degenerative hereditary diseases that affect (to varying degrees) the cerebellum, spinal cord, brain stem, and other parts of the nervous system. Most of these diseases have their onset in childhood, are slowly progressive, and have no known specific inheritance patterns, cause, or treatment, although in some individual family studies clinical findings and inheritance patterns are consistent. It is believed that inherited biochemical abnormalities are causal, and some have been identified. Some diseases in this category with early onset, rapid progression, and strong familial tendencies are Marie's ataxia, Roussy-Levy syndrome, and Friedreich's ataxia. Although progression results in clumsiness, poor balance, later use of a wheelchair for safety, slurred speech, and loss of skilled hand function, there is usually no related impairment to intelligence.

Friedreich's ataxia is a hereditary disease of unknown origin with symptoms of frequent falling, clumsiness, and incoordination (ataxia) beginning between age 5 and 25. Slurred speech, swallowing difficulty, contractures, deformities, and weakness typically result in the need to use a wheelchair within 5 to 10 years. The lack of intellectual impairment is often in considerable contrast to the severity of the physical impairments, a circumstance that represents a challenge to educators to provide stimulating instruction within the limitations presented by the child's deteriorating physical condition. Occupational, physical, and speech therapists can provide useful adaptive support techniques to the child's teachers and family so that optimal function can continue as long as possible. Clinical experience has shown that these children are vulnerable because of their insight into the progressive nature of their disease. Anxiety, anger, and depression may occur, and such feelings may be exacerbated by observing the struggles and deaths of elder siblings. The impact on family life when several siblings have Friedreich's ataxia is profound. Since the average onset age is 13 years, a family may have a number of children before the eldest has symptoms and is diagnosed. Clinical experience suggests that early admission of all symptomatic family members to special education programs where supportive related services are available can help normalize adaptive responses and provide maximum comfort, safety, deformity prevention, and learning opportunities while prolonging activity. Estimates suggest that with proper management there may be 10 to 20 years of productivity following onset. Death frequently is due to progressive heart failure, medical complications, or effects of inactivity rather than the disease itself.

Dr. John C. Eccles (1973), a recognized authority on the cerebellum, believes that the relative simplicity of neuronal design, together with its well-defined action in control of movement, will result in the cerebellum becoming one of the first parts of the brain where linkage between structure and function can be documented. The rapid growth of specific knowledge about cerebellar diseases suggests that differential diagnosis by a skilled neurologist together with genetic studies when indicated are imperative in children with cerebellar disorders, as there are treatable conditions that may present symptoms similar to the degenerative disorders.

## REFERENCES

Berkow, R. (Ed.). (1982). *The Merck manual of diagnosis and therapy* (14th ed.). Rahway, NJ: Merck, Sharp & Dohme.

Eccles, J. C. (1973). *The understanding of the brain*. New York: McGraw-Hill.

Stolov, W. C., & Clowers, M. R. (Eds.) (1981). *Handbook of severe disability* (stock #017-090-00054-2). Washington, DC: U.S. Government Printing Office.

RACHAEL J. STEVENSON
*Bedford, Ohio*

**ATAXIA**
**BRAIN ORGANIZATION**
**FRIEDREICH'S ATAXIA**

## CEREBRAL DOMINANCE

Cerebral dominance refers to the asymmetrical lateralization of language and perceptual functions in the human brain. Cerebral dominance, or hemispheric specialization, was initially applied to language functions that are served by the left hemisphere in most individuals. However, the term was later expanded to include cognitive functions of nonverbal reasoning and visual-spatial information processing that are associated with the right hemisphere. In short, functions associated with the left hemisphere involve processing linguistic, analytical, and sequential information while the right hemisphere is responsible for processing nonlinguistic or spatial information in a holistic fashion (see Witelson, 1976).

Early reference to cerebral dominance can be traced back to Dax in 1836 and Broca in 1861; they found that damage to the left hemisphere results in disorders of speech and language. They believed that the left hemisphere is the dominant side for most people in that it controls the functions of language (Gaddes, 1980). The notion of cerebral dominance was further delineated by the writings of Jackson, who postulated that the left hemisphere is the dominant or the leading side and right hemisphere is the automatic and minor side (Dean, 1984). The emphasis in determining cerebral dominance for language was also noted by Orton (1937). He speculated that delayed or incomplete lateralization for linguistic functions by the left hemisphere results in the types of language disorders often seen in children.

Methods for assessing specializations of each hemisphere have employed invasive techniques such as direct electrical stimulation of the brain, hemispheric anesthetization, and split-brain studies. *Noninvasive procedures* have involved dichotic listening and split-visual field research.

Research using direct electric stimulation of the brain was pioneered by Penfield (Penfield & Roberts, 1959). This technique was developed to map the centers of the brain that controlled specific functions prior to surgical procedures. Since the brain does not contain pain receptors, the patient was conscious when a small electrical current was applied to the surface of the brain to determine areas of the brain associated with such functions as vision, hearing, olfaction, or haptic sensations. Applications of electrical stimulation to areas believed to control speech would be verified by the patient's inability to talk. These "aphasic arrests" would occur only when areas of the brain associated with speech were electrically stimulated. In this way, hypotheses about other functions of the brain could also be verified if responses associated with those functions were absent during stimulation.

Another invasive technique to study brain functioning has been to anesthetize one hemisphere by injecting sodium amytal in the carotid artery located on either the right or left side of the patient's neck. This procedure, known as the Wada test, quickly anesthetized that side of the brain. For example, if the left side or the side dominant for language was infused, the individual would become speechless while the drug was in effect, while the functions of the right hemisphere would remain intact. Wada and Rasmussen (1960) hypothesized that the left hemisphere is dominant for processing verbal information and the right hemisphere for nonverbal information. To demonstrate this, Wada and his associate injected sodium amytal into the left hemisphere and asked the patient to sing "Happy Birthday"; the patient was able to hum the tune without producing the words. When the right hemisphere was anesthetized and the patient was required to perform the same task, the patient was only able to recite the words of "Happy Birthday" in a monotone without producing a tune. Using this procedure, Milner (1974) found that 95% of right-handed and 70% of left-handed individuals are left hemisphere dominant for language.

Split-brain surgery or commissurotomy is another invasive technique used to study cerebral dominance. A commissurotomy is a surgical procedure used to stop the spread of seizure activity from a focal point in one hemisphere to the other hemisphere via the corpus callosum. This procedure involves the severing of the corpus callosum, a large band of nerve fibers that connects the left and right hemispheres, thereby preventing any communication between the hemispheres.

Much research was conducted by Speery in the 1950s. Researchers were able to localize functions of language, motoric control of the same or opposite sides of the body, and visual discrimination (Hacaen, 1981). In one study that examined visual perception, Levy and her associates (Levy, Trevarthen, & Speery, 1972) used stimulus figures in which the left half of one face was joined with the right half of another. The patient was required to gaze at a dot on the center of the screen before a figure was flashed on the screen. The presentation was such that each half of the face would be projected to only one hemisphere. When the patient was asked to respond by pointing to the correct picture from available alternatives, the left sides of faces, which are processed by the right hemisphere, were correctly chosen more often than the right sides regardless of the hand used for pointing. However, when the patient was required to verbally identify the picture, the face on the right side (left hemisphere) was chosen, although the number of errors made by this response mode was much higher. These results were subsequently replicated using other stimuli, suggesting that the right hemisphere is superior in processing nonverbal visual stimuli.

A noninvasive technique in the study of brain-behavior relationships has been dichotic listening. This procedure involves the simultaneous presentation of verbal or nonverbal information to each ear. Similar but different information is presented to each ear and the subject's task is to identify or recall what was heard. This technique was initially developed by Broadbent (1954) to study auditory attention and later adapted by Kimura (1961) to study cerebral lateralization. Studying normal individuals, Kimura found that subjects were more able to identify correctly verbal information when it was presented to the right ear (left hemisphere). If the information was nonverbal, however, a left-ear advantage (right hemisphere) was found. Kimura also showed that if patients having neurological disorders were found to be left hemisphere dominant for language (via the Wada test), a right-ear advantage was noted for verbal information. Similarly, if the patient was right hemisphere dominant for language, a left-ear advantage (right hemisphere) was found for verbal information. These findings suggested that superiority for each ear varies with the specialization in function for the opposite hemisphere.

Studies that have examined language lateralization for dyslexic children using a dichotic listening paradigm have found mixed results. Dyslexic or reading-disabled children are usually characterized by a two-year lag in reading achievement despite average intelligence and an absence of any sensory-motor, neurological or emotional difficulties (Hynd & Cohen, 1983). Some studies (e.g., Witelson & Rabinovitch, 1972) have reported that dyslexic children show a left-ear advantage for verbal information. Other researchers (e.g., Leong, 1976) have demonstrated a right-ear advantage for verbal information for both dyslexic and normal readers. Differential findings may be partially due to differences in methodology and criteria of subject selection.

Another noninvasive technique in studying cerebral dominance has been split-visual field research. This involves a tachistoscopic presentation of verbal or spatial information to either the right-half or left-half visual fields. The visual pathways are such that information perceived in the left-visual field is processed by the right hemisphere while right-visual field information is processed by the left hemisphere. Studies have demonstrated that while word recognition levels were lower for the dyslexic children when compared with normal readers, both readers showed a right-visual field superiority for words (Marcel & Rajan, 1975). However, when pictures were presented to either visual field, Witelson (1976) reported that while normal readers had a significant left visual-field advantage, this difference was not significant for a dyslexic group. These results suggest that while dyslexic readers, like normal readers, have a left-hemisphere representation for language, the dyslexic group appears to lack right-hemisphere specialization for visual-spatial information.

In sum, invasive and noninvasive techniques have made significant contributions in mapping functions of the brain. However, our knowledge of hemispheric specializations is far from complete. Given the inter-individual differences in cognitive processing, the brain's ability to compensate for damage, and developmental factors, the assessment of hemispheric specializations remains a complex endeavor.

## REFERENCES

Broadbent, D. E. (1954). The role of auditory localization in attention and memory. *Journal of Experimental Psychology, 47,* 191–196.

Dean, R. S. (1984). Functional lateralization of the brain. *Journal of Special Education, 18,* 239–256.

Gaddes, W. H. (1980). *Learning disabilities and brain function: A neuropsychological approach.* New York: Springer-Verlag.

Hacaen, H. (1981). Apraxias. In S. B. Filskov & T. J. Boll (Eds.), *Handbook of clinical neuropsychology.* New York: Wiley.

Hynd, G., & Cohen, M. (1983). *Dyslexia: Neuropsychological theory, research, and clinical differentiation.* New York: Grune & Stratton.

Jackson, J. H. (1874). On the duality of the brain. *Medical Press Circulator, 1,* 19, 41, 63.

Kimura, D. (1961). Cerebral dominance and the perception of verbal stimuli. *Canadian Journal of Psychology, 15,* 166–171.

Leong, C. K. (1976). Lateralization in severely disabled readers in relation to functional cerebral development and synthesis of information. In R. M. Knights & D. J. Bakker (Eds.), *Neuropsychology of learning disorders: Theoretical approaches.* Baltimore, MD: University Park Press.

Levy, J., Trevarthen, C., & Speery, R. W. (1972). Perception of bilateral chimeric figures following hemispheric disconnection. *Brain, 95,* 61–78.

Marcel, T., & Rajan, P. (1975). Lateral specialization of recognition of words and faces in good and poor readers. *Neuropsychologia, 13,* 489–497.

Milner, B. (1974). Hemispheric specialization scope and limits. In F. O. Schmitt & F. G. Warden (Eds.), *The neurosciences: Third study programme.* Cambridge, MA: MIT Press.

Orton, S. T. (1937). *Reading, writing, and speech problems in children.* New York: Norton.

Penfield, W., & Roberts, L. (1959). *Speech and brain mechanisms.* Princeton, NJ: Princeton University Press.

Wada, J. A., & Rasmussen, T. (1960). Intracarotid injection of sodium amytal for lateralization of cerebral speech dominance: Experimental and clinical observations. *Journal of Neurosurgery, 17,* 266–282.

Witelson, S. F. (1976). Abnormal right hemisphere specialization in developmental dyslexia. In R. M. Knights & D. F. Bakker (Eds.), *Neuropsychology of learning disorders: Theoretical approaches.* Baltimore, MD: University Park Press.

Witelson, S. F. & Rabinovitch, M. S. (1972). Hemispheric speech lateralization in children with auditory-linguistic deficits. *Cortex 8,* 412–426.

GURMAL RATTAN
*Indiana University of Pennsylvania*

RAYMOND S. DEAN
*Ball State University*
*Indiana University School of Medicine*

# CEREBRAL FUNCTION, LATERALIZATION OF

The human brain is divided longitudinally into two distinct hemispheres. Research over the past century has confirmed early speculations (Broca, 1861; Dax, 1865) that each of these cerebral hemispheres serve specialized functions (Dean, 1984). Although anatomical differences have been identified between hemispheres at birth, more complex patterns of functional specialization may well continue to develop throughout childhood (Dean, 1985).

Our present understanding of the lateralization of functions in the cerebral cortex owes much to the early efforts of investigations of the late nineteenth century (e.g.,

Broca, 1861; Dax, 1865; Jackson, 1874). Based on case studies of patients with confirmed brain damage, a number of researchers (e.g., Broca, 1861) argued in favor of the localization of individual functions (e.g., speech) to specific structures of the brain. Moreover, it was generally reported during this time that with damage to the left cerebral hemisphere, one could expect impaired language functions (Broca, 1861; Dax, 1865). These early underpinnings of the notion of lateralization were further extended by Jackson (1874), who suggested that a lateralization of functions corresponds to the two hemispheres of the brain. Jackson (1874) argued that the left cerebral hemisphere is responsible for language-related functions, while the right hemisphere is the more automatic side, responsible for sensation and perception. The notion of hemispheric dominance grew out of such early arguments, which equated language lateralization in the left hemisphere with control functions. Although rather naive some hundred years later, the idea of hemispheric dominance continues in the literature. Clearly, these early case studies, which attempted to draw conclusions concerning the neuropsychology of normal individuals based on observations of patients with brain damage, were limited. However, the scientific interest stimulated by these reports in tandem with increasingly sophisticated approaches in research is responsible for the wealth of our present knowledge about the functioning of the brain.

While the differences in hemispheric functioning are acknowledged by most neuroscientists, the specific mechanism underlying these differences continues to be debated. At this point, it is not clear whether functional lateralization is related to differences in processing (e.g., Geschwind & Levitsky, 1968), storage (e.g., Dean, 1984), or attention (e.g., Kinsbourne, 1975). However, most researchers have found the arguments attributing observed differences to processing predisposition for the individual hemispheres compelling. From this point of view, the differences in functioning for the sides of the brain are due to biological differences in processing information that implicate the left hemisphere in language-related tasks and the right side in nonverbal elements (Dean, in press).

Although communication between hemispheres is acknowledged, specific functional differences may be attributed to the individual hemispheres. Indeed, it is rather well established that the left hemisphere of the brain best processes information in a sequential, temporal, and analytic fashion. This may be likened to a verbal-sequential mode of thought in which information is represented, processed, and encoded with the aid of linguistic units (Dean, 1983; Paivio, 1971).

A second mode of thought may be seen to correspond to the functions of the right hemisphere. This mode is most clearly oriented toward processing visual information in a concrete, simultaneous, or holistic fashion (e.g., Sperry, 1974). Rather primitive when compared with the left, the right hemisphere seems predisposed to represent, reor-

ganize, and encode visual-spatial elements (e.g., Dimond & Beaumont, 1974). Indeed, the use of imagery seems to be the most idiosyncratic expression of its processing (Seamon & Gazzaniga, 1973).

Hemispheric lateralization has been argued to be an interactive process in which the mode is dependent on the degree of cognitive reformulation, constraints of attention, and actual hemispheric differences in function (Dean, 1984; Gordon, 1974; Paivio; 1971). It has been suggested that normal individuals can employ different strategies that make differential use of one hemisphere or the other regardless of the form of the original stimulus (Dean, 1984). Clearly, information presented in a visual fashion may be encoded almost entirely in semantic terms (Conrad, 1964). So, too, it has been shown that verbal stimuli may be encoded and recalled as visual memory traces (Bower, 1970; Dean, 1983). As Dean (1984) points out, "even young learners can generate visual or verbal encoding strategies which correspond to hemispheric specific abilities regardless of the form of the original stimulus array" (p. 249). This point of view acknowledges independent cognitive processes served by each hemisphere while it stresses the importance of interhemispheric communication. It seems, therefore, that the verbal-nonverbal or left-right hemispheric differences may well be an exaggeration of reality. That is, cerebral lateralization may be more heuristically attributed to modes of processing information than to lateralization for specific stimuli. Therefore, the total task demands for the process of a given bit of information are necessary prior to assuming hemispheric lateralization.

The lateralization of functions is dependent in part on the degree to which cognitive processing is necessary for interpretation and encoding (e.g., Gordon, 1974). Indeed, few differences have been found between hemispheres for lower level information processing. For example, in the discrimination of sensory elements such as brightness, color, pressure, sharpness, pitch, and contour, little lateralization exists in processing (e.g., Dean, 1984; Rabinowicz, 1976). However, when learners are required to form generalizations, categorize, reorder, or integrate, or when they are called on to abstract common elements, clear hemispheric differences emerge. As would be expected, cerebral lateralization is dependent on the amount of interpretation or prior knowledge that the subject must draw on in dealing with the incoming information. Such cognitive processing enhances the degree to which functionally lateralized abilities are relied on (e.g., Moscovitch, 1979).

Although less than complete agreement exists among neuroscientists, it would seem that functional lateralization of cerebral hemispheres of the brain corresponds to the developmental pattern of consolidation that occurs from birth and progresses through adolescence (Dean, 1985). Dean (1984) argues that the rate of lateralization in the child varies with the specific function being examined. In keeping with this hypothesis, Krashen (1973) has offered data favoring a progressive decrease in the role played by the right cerebral hemisphere in verbal-analytic tasks with the child's increasing neurological development. The progressive lateralization of cerebral functions seems concomitant with the rate and variable progression in the maturation of the commissure-association cortex (Sperry, 1969).

Gender differences have been reported for the lateralization of cerebral functions. The force of the data in this area suggests less secure hemispheric specialization for females than for males (e.g., Witelson, 1976). Although anatomical gender differences exist (e.g., MacLusky & Naftolin, 1981), the functional differences found for males and females seem more heuristically attributed to organizational factors than differences in structure (e.g., Kolata, 1979). A convincing argument may be made for a genetic-hormonal cultural locus for observed gender differences (Dean, 1984).

In sum, the functioning of the left hemisphere seems predisposed to process information in a sequential, temporal, or analytic fashion; as such, language is an excellent tool for such forms of cognition. The right hemisphere, in contrast, is best prepared to function in a more simultaneous, holistic, or nonverbal fashion, with spatial reasoning and imagery being the most consistently reported mode of thought. This pattern corresponds with a large body of research in both cognitive psychology and the neurosciences. A good deal of interhemispheric communication should be recognized and functional lateralization is exhibited only as the individual must employ higher order cognitive skills in an attempt to comprehend or learn the incoming information.

## REFERENCES

Bower, G. H. (1970). Analysis of a mnemonic device. *American Scientist, 58,* 496–510.

Broca, P. (1861). Nouvelle observation d'aphemie produite par une lesion de la moite posterieure des deuxieme et troiseme circonvolutions frontales. *Bulletin de la Society Anatomique de Paris, 36,* 398–407.

Conrad, R. (1964). Accoustic confusions in immediate memory. *British Journal of Psychology, 55,* 75–83.

Dax, G. (1865). Lesions de la moitie gauche de l'encephale coincident avec l'oubli des signes de la pensee. *Gazette Hebdomadaire de Medicine et de Chirurgie, 2,* 259–262.

Dean, R. S. (1983, Feb.). *Dual processing of prose and cerebral laterality.* Paper presented at the annual meeting of the International Neuropsychological Society, Mexico City, Mexico.

Dean, R. S. (1984). Functional lateralization of the brain. *Journal of Special Education, 18*(3), 239–256.

Dean, R. S. (1985). Foundation and rationale for neuropsychological bases of individual differences. In L. C. Hartlage & C. F. Telzrow (Eds.), *The neuropsychology of individual differences: A developmental perspective.* New York: Plenum.

Dimond, S., & Beaumont, J. (1974). *Hemisphere function in the human brain.* London: Elek Scientific Books.

Geschwind, N., & Levitsky, W. (1968). Human brain: Left-right asymmetries in temporal speech region. *Science, 161,* 186–187.

Gordon, H. W. (1974). Auditory specialization of the right and left hemispheres. In M. Kinsbourne & W. L. Smith (Eds.), *Hemispheric disconnection and cerebral function.* Springfield, IL: Thomas.

Jackson, J. H. (1874). On the duality of the brain. In J. Taylor (Ed.), *Selected writings of John Hughlings Jackson, Vol. 2.* London: Hodder & Stoughton.

Kinsbourne, M. (1975). Cerebral dominance, learning, and cognition. In H. R. Myklebust (Ed.), *Progress in learning disabilities.* New York: Grune & Stratton.

Kolata, G. B. (1979). Sex hormones and brain development. *Science, 205,* 985–987.

Krashen, S. D. (1973). Lateralization, language learning, and the critical period: Some new evidence. *Language Learning, 23,* 63–74.

MacLusky, N. J., & Naftolin, F. (1981). Sexual differentiation of the central nervous system. *Science, 211,* 1294–1302.

Moscovitch, M. (1979). Information processing and the cerebral hemispheres. In M. S. Gazzaniga (Ed.), *Handbook of behavioral neurobiology, Vol. 2: Neuropsychology.* New York: Plenum.

Paivio, A. (1971). *Imagery and verbal processes.* New York: Holt, Rinehart, & Winston.

Rabinowicz, B. H. (1976). *A non-lateralized auditory process in speech perception.* Unpublished master's thesis, University of Toronto.

Seamon, J. G., & Gazzaniga, M. D. (1973). Coding strategies and cerebral laterality effects. *Cognitive Psychology, 5,* 249–256.

Sperry, R. W. (1969). A modified concept of consciousness. *Psychological Review, 76,* 532–536.

Sperry, R. W. (1974). Lateral specialization in the surgically separated hemispheres. In F. O. Schmitt & F. G. Worden (Eds.), *The neurosciences: Third study program,* New York: Wiley.

Witelson, S. F. (1976). Early hemisphere specialization and interhemisphere plasticity: An empirical and theoretical review. In S. Segalowitz & F. Gruber (Eds.), *Language and development and neurologic theory.* New York: Academic.

RAYMOND S. DEAN
*Ball State University*
*Indiana University School*
*of Medicine*

**HEMISPHERIC ASYMMETRY**
**HEMISPHERIC FUNCTIONS**
**LATERALITY**
**LEFT BRAIN-RIGHT BRAIN**
**NEUROPSYCHOLOGY**

## CEREBRAL INFARCTION

Cerebral infarction refers to the death of brain tissues resulting from a sudden onset of a circulation disorder that often leads to a neurological deficit. Infarction is caused by conditions of anoxia, hypoglycemia, or ischemia (Toole, 1984; Toole & Patel, 1974). Anoxic infarction results from a lack of oxygen to the brain, whereas hypoglycemic infarction occurs when an insufficient level of blood glucose exists for a prolonged period of time despite normal circulation. The most prevalent of the infarctions, however, is ischemic infarction, which results from a sudden interruption of blood supply owed to an obstruction in an artery. Cerebral infarction can occur in any of the cerebral blood vessels of the carotid (anterior portion of the brain) or vertebral basilar (posterior portion of the brain) systems. It may be confused with symptomology resulting from cerebral hemorrhage, tumor, or other space-occupying lesions. Because ishcemic infarctions are the most common, they will be the focus of the remaining discussion.

Transient ischemic attack (TIA) refers to a temporary obstruction of blood vessels; this is frequently caused by platelet-fibrin emboli or blood clots. An embolus is an aggregate of blood particles and tissue overgrowth (thrombus), fatty deposits, clumps of bacteria, or obstructive gas bubbles that block the blood vessels. Other causes of TIAs are acute high blood pressure and vasospasm or spasmodic constriction of blood vessels.

Transient ischemic attacks always have a sudden onset and peak in intensity within 2 to 5 minutes. Symptoms quickly disappear, within 30 minutes, but if symptoms persist past 24 hours, the diagnosis changes to a complete stroke or a cardiac vascular accident. The extent to which TIAs result in temporary or permanent neurological damage in unclear. Symptoms of carotid TIA include monocular blindness or blurring of vision in a previously normal eye; aphasic reactions such as difficulty with writing, reading, arithmetic, receptive and expressive language; and contralateral weakness and numbness of the face, arm, and leg, which may occur either simultaneously or separately. Weakness is characterized by heaviness or clumsiness of the extremities, while numbness can be described as a numbing sensation or a pins or needles sensation. These sensations do not spread or "march" to the various anatomical parts, but occur simultaneously. Vertebral basilar TIAs, however, have the following symptomology: vertigo (spinning movement of the environment); intermittent diplopia (double vision); visual blurring of both eyes; espisodic ataxia (gait problems); and spells in which sudden loss of strength in the lower extremities causes the patient to fall to the ground without loss of consciousness.

Transient ischemic attacks may occur sporadically or regularly, either in a short time span or over several months or years. More than one-third of the patients with diagnosed TIAs sustain a complete stroke within one year, while more than one-half of these patients eventually sustain a major stroke during their lifetime. Patients with TIAs may suffer mild cognitive impairments, especially on delayed recall tasks (Lezak, 1983). Patients suspected of having a TIA can have the diagnosis confirmed by an angiography, which enables a radiological visualization of the blood vessels.

Medical therapy usually involves a regimen of drugs that have the properties of inhibiting the formation or aggregration of red blood cells and the narrowing of arteries. Such drugs consist of aspirin, Anturane, Persantine, and Conmadin (Lubic & Palkovitz, 1979).

## REFERENCES

Lezak, M. D. (1983). *Neuropsychological assessment* (2nd ed.). New York: Oxford University Press.

Lubic, L. G., & Palkovitz, H. P. (1979). *Discussions in patient management: Stroke.* New York: Medical Examination.

Toole, J. F. (1984). *Cerebrovascular disorders* (3rd ed.). New York: Raven.

Toole, J. F., & Patel, A. N. (1974). *Cerebrovascular disorders* (2nd ed.). New York: McGraw-Hill.

GURMAL RATTAN
*Indiana University of
Pennsylvania*

RAYMOND S. DEAN
*Ball State University
Indiana University School
of Medicine*

## ANOXIA

## CEREBRAL LESION, CHRONIC

A chronic cerebral lesion is one that has been in existence beyond what might be considered to be the amount of time required for recovery of lost function.

Chronic cerebral lesions, much like acute cerebral lesions, are likely to influence behavior in ways related to their location and extent or size. Unlike acute cerebral lesions, however, chronic cerebral lesions may have greater effects on behavior than effects related to their location and extent. Increased effects on behavior can result from two conditions. The primary behavioral loss can be due to the interruption of developmental schemata, whereby a child who sustains a chronic cerebral lesion at an early age may be precluded from development of the normal repertoire of behaviors dependent on the integrity of the area of lesion. Since the normal sequence of ontogenetic recapitulation of phylogenetic phenomena is interrupted, not only is there limitation of the behavior dependent on the specific area of cerebral tissue that sustains a lesion, but also of the subsequent behaviors dependent on the development of that initial behavior. The secondary loss from a chronic cerebral lesion results from a disuse atrophy phenomenon, whereby deterioration of muscle tissue or degeneration of neurotransmitter receptor sites, resulting secondary to the lesion, inhibits the development, performance, or acquisition of given behavioral skills.

Chronic cerebral lesions, especially those acquired after the developmental sequence is completed, may have lesser behavioral effects than those of acute lesions, in that the individual over time may acquire compensatory skills that help overcome some of the behavioral limitations imposed by the lesion.

Although chronic cerebral lesions can have onset at any age, many such lesions of congenital or prenatal onset result in death or profound developmental handicap. Onset age appears to be related to the severity of the handicap imposed by the lesion. Although it has been traditional to believe that the effects of chronic brain lesions are less severe in children because of presumed greater plasticity in the organization of their central nervous systems (Lyons & Matheny, 1984), there is accumulating evidence that a chronic cerebral lesion acquired early in childhood may have more severely debilitating effects (Cermak, 1985; Levin, Benton, & Grossman, 1982). There is also evidence that such lesions limit the development of memory and intellectual ability to a greater extent with early age onset than with later age onset (Levin, Eisenberg, Wigg, & Kobayashi, 1982). Further, there is evidence to suggest a greater likelihood of emotional problems resulting from chronic cerebral lesions at an early age (Rutter, 1981). These problems may interact with cognitive problems, depending on the age at which the lesion was acquired (Lyons & Matheny, 1984). The selective results of unilateral cerebral lesions on such specific aspects of behavior as language development, previously thought to be less specific when acquired at an early age, have been found to be similar in early childhood onset to those of later age onset (Aram et al., 1985). Even for those children who appear to show good recovery from early onset chronic cerebral lesions, there is a strong likelihood that special educational placement may be necessary (Lehr, 1984). The etiology of the chronic cerebral lesion, whether from head injury, brain tumor, or radiation therapy, appears to be unrelated to the neuropsychological outcome (Bruce, 1982).

Although recent developments in neurochemistry suggest that neurochemical adaptations at surviving synapses may mediate behavioral changes over time, which would account for frequent observations that behavioral consequences of chronic cerebral lesions change as time following the injury increases (Marshall, 1984), there is no generally accepted explanation for why this change over time should occur.

## REFERENCES

Aram, D. M., Ekelman, B. L., Rose, D. F., & Whitaker, H. A. (1985). Verbal and cognitive sequelae following unilateral lesions acquired in early childhood. *Journal of Clinical and Experimental Neuropsychology, 7,* 55–78.

Bruce, D. A. (1982). Comment. *Neurosurgery, 11,* 672–673.

Cermak, L. A. (1985, Feb.). The effects of age at onset and causal agent of brain injury on later adaptive functioning in children. Paper presented at the International Neuropsychological Society, San Diego. Abstract in *Proceedings*, p. 10.

Lehr, E. (1984, Aug.). Good recovery from severe head injury in children and adolescents. Paper presented at American Psychological Association meeting, Toronto, Ontario.

Levin, H. S., Benton, A. L., & Grossman, R. G. (1982). *Neurobehavioral consequences of closed head injury.* New York: Oxford University Press.

Levin, H. S., Eisenberg, H. M., Wigg, N. R., & Kobayashi, K. (1982). Memory and intellectual ability after head injury in children and adolescents. *Neurosurgery, 11,* 668–672.

Lyons, M. J., & Matheny, A. P. (1984). Cognitive and personality differences between identical twins following skull fracture. *Journal of Pediatric Psychology, 9,* 485–494.

Marshall, J. F. (1984). Brain function: Neural adaptations and recovery from injury. *Annual Review of Psychology, 35,* 277–308.

Rutter, M. (1981). Psychological sequelae of brain damage in children. *American Journal of Psychiatry, 138,* 1533–1544.

LAWRENCE C. HARTLAGE
*Evans, Georgia*

**BIRTH INJURIES**
**BRAIN DAMAGE**
**CEREBRAL INFARCTION**
**HEAD INJURY**

## CEREBRAL PALSY (CP)

Cerebral palsy (CP), sometimes called congenital spastic paralysis, is characterized by varying degrees of disturbance of voluntary movements caused by damage to the brain. Cerebral refers to the brain and palsy refers to weakness or lack of control. Cerebral palsy was originally called Little's disease after the English surgeon William John Little, who first described it. Later, Winthrop Phelps, an orthopedic surgeon, coined the term cerebral palsy and brought it into common usage as a result of his extensive work with this population in the United States.

There is agreement among experts in the field that cerebral palsy is a complex of characteristics attributed to brain injury. It has been defined by the United Cerebral Palsy Research and Educational Foundation as having the following elements: (1) being caused by injury to the brain; (2) causing motor disturbance, including paralysis, weakness, and uncoordination; (3) consisting of a cluster of symptoms; (4) usually originating in childhood; and (5) perhaps including learning difficulties, psychological problems, sensory defects, convulsions, and behavioral disorders of organic origin. In addition to these elements, cerebral palsy is nonprogressive, static, and unamenable to treatment.

There are two major types of CP: spastic, characterized by sudden, violent, involuntary muscular contractions, and athetosic, characterized by ceaseless, involuntary, slow, sinuous, writhing movements. The physical symptoms of CP can be so mild that they are detected only with difficulty, or they can be so profound that the affected individual is almost complete physically incapacitated. It is not unusual for a cerebral palsied individual to function normally intellectually. However, this intelligence is often masked (at least to the lay person) by uncontrolled physical characteristics, involuntary movements of the body and extremities, speech disorders, and drooling. Cerebral palsy is not a disease, and it is not curable.

The incidence of cerebral palsy varies; a conservative estimate of its occurrence is 1.5 to 2.0 cases per 1000 live births. It has been estimated that the incidence may be higher in areas where there is inadequate prenatal care and accompanying prematurity. While CP occurs at every socioeconomic level, it is more prevalent among lower socioeconomic groups. Children born in poverty situations have a greater chance of incurring brain damage from factors such as malnutrition, poor prenatal and postnatal care, and environmental hazards during infancy. Cerebral palsy occurs slightly more frequently in males than in females, and more white than black children are affected. Cerebral palsy makes up the largest category of physical disabilities, representing 30 to 40% of all children in programs for the physically disabled.

In most cases, cerebral palsy is congenital (approximately 85% of all cases), meaning damage to the brain occurs during pregnancy or at birth. However, infectious diseases or severe head injuries can cause cerebral palsy at any time in life. Postnatal causes are said to be acquired, whereas those present at birth are congenital. It is generally agreed that CP cannot be inherited.

Prenatal causes of CP include German measles in the mother, pH incompatibility, maternal anoxia, use of drugs, and metabolic disorders such as maternal diabetes. Faulty growth of the fetal brain may occur if the mother is malnourished during pregnancy. In addition, maternal exposure to the toxic substances in X-rays may also damage the brain of the fetus. Perinatal (birth process) causes include prolonged labor, breech delivery, anoxia, and prematurity. High fever, poisonings, and other related factors may cause harm immediately following birth. After birth (postnatal) causes include anoxia, direct trauma to the brain, and infection. Poisonings also may contribute to brain damage during the postnatal period. In some cases, severe and consistent child beating has caused CP.

It is estimated that as many as three-quarters of all persons with CP have additional disabilities such as retardation, seizures, auditory and visual handicaps, or communication disorders. Approximately 50 to 60% of CP children are retarded. Mental retardation has been difficult to diagnose in the population since intelligence tests were standardized on children with adequate speech, language, and motor abilities. Seizures are associated with approx-

imately 25 to 35% of individuals with cerebral palsy and are much more prevalent with spastic CP persons. Strabismus (squinting) occurs in approximately 30 to 35% of cerebral-palsied individuals. Some athetotic CPs experience farsightedness while spastic CPs are nearsighted. Visual field reduction also can occur in some tyeps of CP (Capute, 1975).

Speech and/or language problems can range from normal speech and reception processing and expression to that which is nonfunctional. Speech in the two major types of CP has been characterized by Berry and Eisenson (1956) as (1) spastic speech, e.g., "slow, labored rate, lack of vocal inflection, gutteral or breathy quality of voice, uncontrolled volume, and, most important, grave articulatory problems which reflect the inability to secure graded, synchronous movement of the tongue, lips, and jaw"; and (2) athetoid speech, e.g., "varying gradations of a pattern of irregular, shallow, and noisy breathing; whispered or hoarse phonation, and articulatory problems varying from the extremes of complete mutism or extreme dysarthria (impaired articulation) to a slight awkwardness in lingual movement."

Speech disorders are found in 70% of cerebral-palsied children. It has been reported that speech defects are found in 88% of persons with athetosis, 85% of those with ataxia, and 52% of those who are spastic. Most of the speech problems are caused by problems controlling the muscles used to make speech sounds.

Minear (1965) developed a classification scheme for cerebral-palsied individuals based on motor characteristics as well as the area of the body where the problem is located. The six types within the motor component were adopted by the American Academy for Cerebral Palsy and have been described by others (Bleck, 1975; Denhoff, 1976; Healy, 1983). The six types include spasticity, athetosis, ataxia, rigidity, tremor, and mixed.

Spasticity is the most common type of CP, occurring in approximately 40 to 60% of the total. Stiffness of the muscles in spastic children occurs when the injury is on the brain surface or when it involves those nerves leading from the surface through the substance of the brain and onto the spinal cord. The spastic type is characterized by a loss of voluntary motor control. When the child initiates voluntary movement, it is likely to be jerky, with lack of control in the body extremities. This disability may affect any or all limbs. Involvement in the upper extremities may include varying degrees of flexing of the arms and fingers, depending on the severity of the disability. When lower extremities are involved, there may be a scissoring movement of the legs, caused by muscle contractions.

Athetosis is the second largest group in the CP population, occurring in approximately 15 to 20% of the total. This type is caused by injury to the brain's motor switchboard. Athetoid children are characterized by involuntary jerky, writhing movements, especially in the fingers and wrists. The head is often drawn back with the neck extended and mouth open. There are generally two types of athetosis: tension and nontension. The tension athetoid's muscles are always tense; this reduces contorted movement of limbs. The nontension athetoid has contorted movements without muscle tightness. Unlike the spastic child, all movements cease during sleep. The movements occur only in a conscious state; when emotionality increases, athetosis movements become intensified. Athetoids are usually higher in intelligence than spastic CP victims.

Ataxia is less prevalent than spasticity and athetosis. Together with tremor and rigidity, it makes up approximately 8% of the total CP population. The injury is in the cerebellum. Ataxic children are characterized by a lack of coordination and sense of balance. The eyes are often uncoordinated and the child may stumble and fall frequently.

Rigidity and tremor types of CP are extremely rare. Rigidity is unlike the other types in that the lower level of muscles stiffen and a rigid posture is maintained. The rigid type is usually severely retarded with a high incidence of convulsions. In tremor, there is involuntary movement in one extremity, usually one hand or arm. The motion may vary in its consistency and pattern. In intention tremor, the involuntary movement happens only when the child attempts an activity while in constant tremor. The involuntary movement is continuous.

Mixed is another variation of CP. It is a combination of the other five types with one type predominating. Approximately 30% of individuals with CP have more than one type.

The movement or motor component of the clinical classification system is composed of two types, pyramidal and extrapyramidal. The pyramidal type refers to the spastic cerebral-palsied group because the usual nerve cell involved in this disorder is shaped like a pyramid. Extrapyramidal refers to all other types of CP, athetosis, rigidity, tremor, ataxia, and mixed, in which the area of the brain affected is composed of conglomerates of nerve cells (Capute, 1975).

In addition to describing CP by type of neuromuscular or motor involvement, Denhoff (1976) also characterized this multihandicapped population by the body parts that are affected. This is also known as topographical classification, with (generally) seven types. With hemiplegia, one half, either the right side or left side, of the body is involved. Of cerebral-palsied individuals 30 to 40% fall into this category. The legs are involved to a greater extent than the arms with diplegia. Of all cerebral-palsied children 10 to 20% are diplegic. Quadriplegia involves all four limbs accounts for 15 to 20% of the total CP population. With paraplegia, occurring in 10 to 20% of all cerebral cases, only the legs are involved. Monoplegia involves only one limb and triplegia involves three limbs. These two types rarely occur. With double hemiplegia, both halves of the body are involved, but unlike quadriplegia, the two sides are affected differently. This type, too, rarely occurs.

Also CP can be classified by the severity of the motor involvement. Deaver (1966) described the CP child based on the mild, moderate, and severe classification scheme. Even though the descriptions were formulated several years ago, they are still useful today because of the explicitness of the activity level included in each category. In the mild category, no treatment is needed. The individual has no speech problem, is able to care for himself or herself, and can walk without the aid of appliances. In the moderate category, treatment is needed for speech problems and/or difficulties in ambulation and self-care. Braces and other equipment are needed. In the severe category, treatment is needed, but the degree of involvement is at a level wherein the prognosis for speech, self-care, and ambulation is poor.

Educational programs for children with cerebral palsy in the public schools gained momentum in the early 1970s with the emphasis on deinstitutionalization and normalization. Prior to this, many of these children, with multiple handicaps and not adequately diagnosed, remained in institutions for the mentally retarded.

It is generally agreed by experts in the field that treatment and educational considerations are extremely important and more complicated since cerebral-palsied children are multihandicapped. Not only must special equipment and facilities be provided to accommodate their physical disabilities, but additional special education techniques are needed to accommodate other handicaps (mental retardation, learning disabilities, auditory and visual disabilities).

When planning and implementing educational programs for cerebral-palsied individuals, a cadre of persons working in a multidisciplinary approach must be used. Many educators and physicians (Capute, 1975; Gearheart, 1980; Healy, 1983) have delineated the specific roles of the individuals who must work together in the education of cerebral-palsied children. The degree of CP and physical characteristics will determine the extent of participation by the physician. The physician may prescribe drugs for the patient to relax and to control the convulsions as well as treat overall health problems. Braces and other mechanical devices that provide support and allow children to walk are usually prescribed by medical doctors. The physical therapist works to facilitate motor development, to prevent or slow orthopedic problems, and to improve posture and positioning so that the child may benefit from other intervention activities. The occupational therapist uses creative, educational, and recreational activities to enhance self-help skills and teach parents to handle the child's daily living activities. The speech pathologist will monitor the child's progress in speech and language and provide therapy if the child is able to benefit from it. The speech therapist also may work with parents and other educational personnel on how to stimulate language development. An audiologist, learning disabilities specialist, and teacher of the mentally retarded may be needed to provide some direct and indirect services to the primary teacher when required.

A variety of specialized equipment is available to teachers, including adapted typewriters, pencil holders, book holders, page turners, and special desks to make cerebral-palsied individuals more self-sufficient.

The success achieved by the cerebral-palsied child depends largely on the extent of his or her physical and mental disability. While some cerebral-palsied people will need constant care in a protected environment, many can lead relatively normal lives and become productive citizens if given the opportunity.

## REFERENCES

Berry, M. F., & Eisenson, (1956). *Speech disorders.* New York: Appleton-Century-Crofts.

Bleck, E. E. (1975). Cerebral palsy. In E. E. Bleck & D. A. Nagel (Eds.), *Physically handicapped children: A Medical atlas for teachers.* New York: Grune & Stratton.

Capute, A. J. (1978). Cerebral palsy and associated dysfunctions. In R. H. Haslam & P. G. Valletutti (Eds.), *Medical problems in the classroom.* Baltimore, MD: University Park Press.

Cruickshank, W. M. (1976). *Cerebral palsy: A developmental disability.* Syracuse, NY: Syracuse University Press.

Deaver, G. G. (1955). Cerebral palsy: Methods of evaluation and treatment. *Institute of physical medicine & rehabilitation, 9.*

Denhoff, E. (1978). Medical aspects. In W. M. Cruickshank (Ed.), *Cerebral palsy: A developmental disability* (3rd ed.). Syracuse, NY: Syracuse University Press.

Gearheart, B. R. (1980). *Special education for the 80s.* St. Louis: Mosby.

Healy, A. (1983). Cerebral palsy. In J. A. Blackman (Ed.), *Medical aspects of developmental disabilities in children—birth to three.* Iowa City, IA: University of Iowa Press.

Minear, W. L. (1956). A classification of cerebral palsy. *Pediatrics, 18,* 841–852.

CECELIA STEPPE-JONES
*North Carolina Central University*

**HABILITATION OF HANDICAPPED
HIGH INCIDENCE HANDICAPS CONDITIONS
MULTIPLE HANDICAPPING CONDITIONS
PHYSICAL HANDICAPS**

# CERTIFICATION/LICENSURE ISSUES

With only a few exceptions, the issues and standards involving special education programs do not differ from those that apply to teacher education programs nationwide. These issues include teacher testing, the use of teaching personnel having college degrees but lacking teacher preparation courses, standards used to approve teacher education programs, and state certification requirements.

A number of states have moved toward, or implemented, the use of tests as part of the certification process. Some states require a test of basic skills prior to entering a teacher education program (e.g., California, Missouri), while other states require teachers to achieve a passing score on a content area test. It has been suggested that such tests will have a significant impact on the qualifications of individuals desiring to become teachers, particularly minority populations (Feistritzer, 1983). Feistritzer (1983) has suggested that the number of minority candidates entering teacher preparation programs has declined by approximately 90%. For special education programs that serve a disproportionately large number of minority students and have tried to aggressively recruit minority persons to teach, such a decline may have serious consequences.

An issue that has importance to special education is that of appropriate certification in the actual field of teaching. While most teachers are certified to teach in some field, not all teachers have been trained and certified to teach in the field to which they are assigned. For example, large numbers of special education teachers are not certified in special education or are not teaching the types of handicapped children and youths for which they hold a special education certificate. Thus teachers who are qualified to teach nonhandicapped children in elementary schools may be teaching learning-disabled, emotionally disturbed, or some other type of handicapped children. While emergency, temporary, or provisional certificates permit regular education teachers to teach handicapped learners, there is some question as to whether this constitutes the most appropriate and effective instruction for these students. The validity of a system that allows not fully prepared teachers to work with handicapped students appears questionable.

Many teacher-training programs are competency-based and result in program graduates receiving generic teaching licenses or endorsements. While this affords local school districts considerable flexibility for serving students, there is concern that distinct differences exist among differing handicapping conditions that cannot be met through the preparation of a generic teacher. While the needs of some handicapped students can be served using generic teaching personnel, the use of resource rooms for mildly/moderately handicapped learners (learning disabled, etc.) often results in placement with a noncategorically certified teacher rather than a teacher who holds a categorical (learning disabled, etc.) certificate.

Certification and licensure are also affected by supply and demand. In the past, special education teachers have been in short supply and the use of temporary or provisional certificates, as noted earlier, became common. This led to the development of teacher preparation programs that prepare teachers to meet temporary endorsement requirements as well as to meet full certification requirements. In many respects, programs become defined by the certification standards they parallel and are not being designed to promote excellence. Teachers, or prospective teachers, tend to enroll in programs that most expeditiously meet the minimum standards necessary for them to maintain or gain employment. For this reason, preparation programs in competitive situations (i.e., with other institutions of higher education) may feel compelled to meet minimum training requirements, which, in turn, become maximum training requirements.

An additional issue is the use of special education personnel in areas of exceptionality, at age levels, and in program models for which they are not qualified by training, experience, or certification. Because of shortages of fully qualified personnel in some areas, school districts have employed teachers to work with students having handicaps who are at an age for which the teacher was not trained. This may result, for example, in a teacher who has training, experience, and certification in working with young, learning-disabled students working with adolescent, emotionally disturbed students. Such practices are presumed not to be in the best interests of the students involved.

Teachers who have received degrees from one state institution and are certified/licensed in that state can have difficulty in obtaining certification when desiring to teach in another state. Certification departments in each state evaluate the qualifications and comparability of out-of-state programs of study to determine whether they meet state standards. Thus individuals who may be qualified to teach in one state may be unable to teach in another state where reciprocity agreements do not exist. These individuals must either begin another program, "correct" deficiencies, or stay out of teaching. Through this process, many school districts lose a valuable supply of teachers who may have considerable experience and may be forced to employ less qualified or experienced teachers (e.g., provisionally certified).

## REFERENCES

Council for Exceptional Children. (1983). Code of ethics and standards for professional practice. *Exceptional Children, 50*, 205–218.

Feistritzer, C. E. (1983). *The condition of teaching.* Lawrenceville, NJ: Princeton University Press.

Maple, C. C. (1983). Is special education certification a guarantee of teaching excellence? *Exceptional Children, 49*, 308–313.

PATRICIA ANN ABRAMSON
*Hudson Public Schools,
Hudson, Wisconsin*

## SPECIAL EDUCATION, LEGAL REGULATION OF
## PROFESSIONAL STANDARDS FOR SPECIAL EDUCATORS
## PERSONNEL TRAINING IN SPECIAL EDUCATION

## CHALFANT, JAMES C. (1932– )

A native of Fremont, Ohio, James C. Chalfant earned his BS (1954), his MS (1958), and his EdD (1965) from the University of Illinois. Currently, he is head of the Division of Special Education and Rehabilitation, University of Arizona.

Early in his career, Chalfant worked on an integrated training program for children with Down's syndrome. The program was of intensive behavior shaping related to self-help skills and the development of language, motor, and social skills (Chalfant, Silikovitz, & Tawney, 1977). The state of Illinois made the program available to all who taught children with Down's syndrome. Chalfant also helped develop teacher assistance teams in several states. These teams would be available in a school to help an individual teacher manage a situation for which the teacher would need additional help that was, for various reasons, unavailable (Chalfant & Pysh, 1982).

The Office of Special Education Programs, U.S. Department of Education, asked Chalfant to work on a task force that focuses on issues and practices in identifying learning-disabled students. The objective is to summarize alternative practices for identification of these students for state departments of education and to provide suggestions for evaluating and modifying current practices, as requested.

Chalfant received a Presidential Citation for Outstanding Service from President Lyndon B. Johnson while working with the Division of Handicapped Children and Youth, U.S. Office of Education. He was also given the Award of Honor as "the international educator who has most influenced the field of learning disabilities in South Africa" from the South African Association for Children with Learning Disabilities.

## REFERENCES

Chalfant, J. C., & Pysh, M. V. (1982). *Teacher assistance teams: A procedure for supporting classroom teachers* (Filmstrip; Audio Cassette; Handout). New Rochelle, NY: Pem Press, Pathescope Educational Media.

Chalfant, J. C., Silikovitz, R. G., & Tawney, J. W. (1977). *Systematic instruction for retarded children: The Illinois program.* Danville, IL: Interstate.

E. VALERIE HEWITT
*Texas A&M University*

## CHALL, JEANNE S. (1921– )

Jeanne S. Chall earned her BA from the City College of New York in 1941. She went on to do her graduate work at Ohio State University, receiving her PhD in 1952. Chall

Jeanne S. Chall

taught at the City College of the City University of New York for 15 years. She joined the faculty at Harvard in 1965 and is currently professor of education and director of the reading laboratory in the Harvard Graduate School of Education.

Chall has long been active in the fields of education, reading, and language-related learning disabilities. She has served on numerous national committees and has also served as a consultant to various government education agencies. She is a member of the editorial boards of various journals in fields of reading, education, and educational psychology, including *Reading Research Quarterly* and the *Journal of Educational Psychology*. She has authored two major reading texts, one now in its second edition (Chall, 1967, 1983a, 1983b). In earlier work, Chall authored two columns on the readability of instructional materials. Chall has published diagnostic instruments to aid in the diagnosis of reading and other language-related disorders. The most notable of these is the *Roswell-Chall Diagnostic Reading Test of Word Analysis Skills* (1978).

In addition to her diagnostic instruments, Chall's major contributions to the field of special education have been in her research in reading and learning disabilities and in teacher training in these closely related areas. She has received many honors for her outstanding achievements. In 1979, Chall was elected to the Reading Hall of Fame and the National Academy of Education. In 1982, Chall received both the American Educational Research Association Award for Distinguished Contributions to Research in Education, and the American Psychological Association Edward L. Thorndike Award for Educational Psychology. Currently, Chall continues to pursue her research interests in reading and language development and in diagnostic testing of reading disorders.

## REFERENCES

Chall, J. S. (1967). *Learning to read: The great debate*. New York: McGraw-Hill.

Chall, J. S. (1983a). *Learning to read: The great debate* (2nd Ed.). New York: McGraw-Hill.

Chall, J. S. (1983b). *Stages of reading development*. New York: McGraw-Hill.

Roswell, F. G., & Chall, J. S. (1978). *Roswell-Chall diagnostic test of word analysis skills, revised and extended*. La Jolla, CA: Essay Press.

KATHRYN A. SULLIVAN
*Texas A&M University*

## CHARACTER DISORDER

Character disorder or personality disorder (as it is now more commonly called) refers to a group of mental illnesses that are deeply embedded in the personality, pervasive in their influence on the individual's behavior, and likely to persist over a long period of time. With the publication of the third edition of the *Diagnostic and Statistical Manual of Mental Disorders* (*DSM-III*), personality disorders have been recognized to be of central importance in the classification of mental illness (Millon, 1981). In the past, the term "character" has been applied to these disorders to signify their enduring, lasting, or relatively permanent nature, as in "character trait" or "characteristic" of a person.

Theodore Millon, a leading authority in this area of psychopathology, stresses inflexibility, interpersonal ineffectiveness, and poor stability under stress as characteristics that distinguish these disorders from normal personality (Millon, 1981). His views are echoed in the DSM-III: "Personality traits are enduring patterns of perceiving, relating to, and thinking. . . . It is only when *personality traits* are inflexible and maladaptive and cause either significant impairment in social or occupational functioning or subjective distress that they constitute *Personality Disorders*" (American Psychiatric Association, 1980, p. 305).

Problems in social relationships and disturbances of mood (anger, anxiety, or depression) are frequently associated with personality disorders. The character-disordered individual consistently behaves in a manner that is inappropriate or ineffective, yet he or she may not recognize this behavior as the source of the problem or as undesirable in any way. Personality disorders are usually recognizable in childhood or adolescence, but the behavior persists and becomes the individual's typical or usual manner of functioning throughout most of the lifespan.

Because these conditions frequently do not result in the individual feeling distress or discomfort, voluntary requests for treatment are relatively uncommon. The person may be referred for treatment by a parent, judge, or other authority who recognizes the disruptive nature of the individual's behavior. Treatment is usually long and difficult, often directed more at society's need to manage these individuals than the individual's desire for change (Reid,

1983). Since cure would involve change in basic aspects of the patient's personality, less ambitious changes resulting in smoother social and vocational functioning are usually more practical. Institutionalization may be necessary for individuals who are dangerous to themselves or others. The complexity and expense of treating antisocial personality (a common character disorder) has been well described by Goldstone (1976).

DSM-III describes 12 types of personality disorders: paranoid, schizoid, schizotypal, histrionic, narcissistic, antisocial, borderline, avoidant, dependent, compulsive, passive-aggressive, and a classification for atypical, mixed, or other personality disorders. Some of these classifications have a long history in the professional literature; others have appeared more recently. For example, the antisocial personality disorder or psychopathic personality has been recognized and researched for many years. Cleckley's *The Mask of Sanity* (1976) offers the classic treatment of this disorder. On the other hand, borderline personality disorder is a term of recent origin, having first appeared in the 1980 edition of DSM-III.

## REFERENCES

American Psychiatric Association (1980). *Diagnostic and statistical manual of mental disorders* (3rd ed.). Washington, DC: Author.

Cleckley, H. (1976). *The mask of sanity* (5th ed.). St. Louis: Mosby.

Goldstone, S. (1976). The treatment of antisocial behavior. In B. B. Wolman (Ed.), *The therapist's handbook* (pp. 410–429). New York: Van Nostrand Reinhold.

Millon, T. (1981). *Disorders of personality DSM-III: Axis II*. New York: Wiley.

Reid, W. H. (1983). *Treatment of the DSM-III psychiatric disorders*. New York: Brunner/Mazel.

ROBERT R. REILLEY
*Texas A&M University*

## DIAGNOSTIC AND STATISTICAL MANUAL OF MENTAL DISORDERS (DSM-III)
## EMOTIONAL DISORDERS
## PERSONALITY ASSESSMENT

## CHEMICALLY DEPENDENT YOUTHS

Chemically dependent youths are children and adolescents who want and need continued use of a psychoactive substance to sustain or maintain a chronic state of euphoria or intoxication. Alcohol and drug use by young people must be viewed not in isolation but in concert with that period of life known as adolescence. Substance use and addiction have profound effects on development and have serious implications for the future functioning of the abuser (Cohen, 1983).

The period of life commonly referred to as adolescence generally runs from 12 to 22 years of age. Adolescents are often described by age groupings: early (12 to 15), middle (15 to 18), and late (18 to 22). Although these divisions are convenient, they do not adequately describe the complex period of adolescence. More important are the biological, emotional, social, academic, and intellectual changes that young people undergo as they move from childhood to adulthood. Because these phases vary widely across adolescents and even within the same adolescent, no one variable, including age, is sufficient. The complex interplay of these dynamic phases in youth and the distinct stages of movement from drug use to chemical dependency best explain chemical dependency. Newman and Newman (1975) note that the physical development that accompanies puberty leads to a heightened awareness of body sensations. Drugs, especially marijuana and the hallucinogens, accentuate pleasurable bodily sensations and may be used by adolescents in an attempt to increase the sense of physical arousal. Cohen (1984) warns that adolescence, a period of critical psychosocial development when adaptive responses are being learned, is much more vulnerable to the loss of learning time than is adulthood.

Two types of chemical dependency occur, physical and psychological. Some substances induce tolerance and create a physical craving and addiction cycle, whereas others create a psychological dependency in which the user experiences changes in mood. Further, some compounds create both a physical and psychological dependency. In the latter case, chemically dependent youths may undergo detoxification to treat the physical craving and resultant withdrawal symptoms, but may continue to experience a craving or felt need to use again. This process sets up a cycle of dependency, detoxification, and return to use that accounts for the recidivism rate among addicted youths.

Psychological dependence is characterized by a drive to continue taking a drug when the user feels the effects of the drug are needed to maintain his or her sense of well being at an optimal level. The complex interaction of drug effects, personality, and stage of development constitute the degree of psychic craving or compulsion the user may experience. Drug-seeking behavior or compulsive drug use develops when the user comes to believe that the drug can produce pleasure and deter discomfort such that continuous or periodic administration of the drug is required. This mental state is the most powerful of all the factors involved in chronic intoxication with psychoactive drugs (Adesso, 1985).

Physiological dependence is characterized by reliance of body tissue on the continued presence of a drug within the user's system. Its presence is unknown to the user as long as the drug continues to be taken and is of no immediate consequence until the drug is withdrawn or no longer available. The magnitude of the dependence and the severity of the withdrawal symptoms vary directly with the type, amount, frequency, and duration of the drug use. Physiological dependence manifests itself as severe and immediate physical pain and discomfort, commonly referred to as withdrawal symptoms or abstinence syndrome. Symptoms may include fever, chills, gastrointestinal cramps, watery eyes, runny nose, and muscle cramping or spasms. They are frequently accompanied by psychological dependence. For drugs like alcohol, barbiturates, narcotic analgesics (morphine, Percodan, heroin) and cocaine, withdrawal symptoms and accompanying psychological dependence are so uncomfortable and threatening that they motivate young drug users to continue to seek and administer the drug. For drugs like stimulants (speed), and to a lesser degree marijuana and hallucinogenics (LSD, mescaline, psilocybin, peyote), the primary disturbance is psychological rather than physiological. But it should be noted that although the symptoms are not as severe as with physiological withdrawal, the user does experience discomfort of a mental or emotional nature (Bardo & Risner, 1985).

Different drug compounds act on different youths in different ways, both psychologically and physiologically. A 13-year-old pubescent male who is smoking two to three joints of high-grade (THC potent) marijuana daily over a 5- to 6-month period is likely to develop a psychological compulsion while not experiencing physical withdrawal symptoms on cessation. However, evidence suggests that THC lowers levels of the male hormone testosterone in the young male's system, retarding development of secondary sexual characteristics. Additionally, an amotivational syndrome from chronic cannabis intoxication results in lethargy, restlessness, and increased irritability (Cohen, 1984). Conversely, the same male drinking 1 to 3 ounces of alcohol (beer, wine, or hard liquor) over the same period of time will most likely experience both psychological and physiological withdrawal symptoms. Although medical complications may be more severe in the latter case, emotional, social, and intellectual complications occur in both.

Kandel (1984) proposes that culturally determined developmental stages of drug behavior are observed in adolescents. Initiation, progression, and regression in drug behavior are related to factors like prior delinquent behavior, high levels of drug-using peer affiliations, and parental models who use or abuse alcohol and drugs. The role of genetics in the development of substance abuse is also a major area of concern (Crabbe et al., 1985). Extensive research, primarily using animal models, indicates a strong predisposition to addiction in the offspring of addicted parents, particularly those using alcohol and sedative compounds. In sum, environment, psychosocial variables, and genetics are important concepts for consideration in adolescent substance abuse.

A single episode of intoxication does not produce either physical or psychological dependency. Several stages occur in the move from no use to dependency. The initial reason to try any drug depends more on the value the youth places on its use than on its pharmacological properties. Curiosity and availability, key factors at this stage, are influenced by the social factors of peer pressure and acceptance, adult role models, and family norms or values. The majority of youthful experimenters do not proceed through all stages to dependence because of the drug effects themselves not being valued and the fact that most peer-group norms do not support continued use (Kandel, et al., 1978).

Experimental use may proceed to casual or occasional use, frequently referred to as socio-recreational use. This pattern usually involves imitation of adult role models who drink during social gatherings or use other drugs as mood enhancers. The youthful user may use drugs while at a party once or twice a month, or while attending a movie or listening to music with friends. Such use tends to be spontaneous and in a social context where drugs are readily available. Reasons for use are primarily social in that friends use and approve of use. Also, the drugs enhance self-confidence and social interaction during the identity phase of adolescence. The youthful user does not avidly seek drugs at this stage but will participate with a group if drugs are available.

The third stage, regular use, is distinguished from sociorecreational use by several features. The user at this stage actively seeks drugs, and is rarely seen in a social context without being intoxicated. Psychological dependence occurs. The user perceives that he or she functions better in social gatherings while intoxicated. Regular use also may involve physiological dependence if the user develops tolerance to a drug and experiences physical discomfort with cessation. The pharmacological properties of the drug become critical at this point. Whether the user proceeds into the final stage, dependency, is partly a function of what the drug does for the user's personality and the user's stage in adolescence.

The final stage is physical and/or psychological reliance on the drug to produce the user's desired effect. Heavy or compulsive use implies daily intoxication, although the user may indulge in binge-type use. Although only a minority of users become chemically dependent youths, the central factor is the degree to which use dominates the life of the adolescent. Intoxication may avoid other critical issues of adolescence (e.g., responsibilities of school and family, stress, lack of self-confidence) or mask the pain and discomfort of other pathological personality or mental disorders. Psychological and physical dependence are critical at this stage because regardless of reasons for continued use, the youthful user will have to continue to take the drug in order to avoid the newly acquired set of symptoms and difficulties associated with chemical dependency (Kandel, 1984).

## REFERENCES

Adesso, V. J. (1985). Cognitive factors in alcohol and drug use. In M. Galizio & S. A. Maisto (Eds.), *Determinants of substance abuse* (pp. 179–208) New York: Plenum.

Bardo, M. T., & Risner, M. E. (1985). Biochemical substrates of drug abuse. In M. Galizio & S. A. Maisto (Eds.), *Determinants of substance abuse* (pp. 65–99). New York: Plenum

Cohen, S. (1983). *The alcoholism problems.* New York: Haworth.

Cohen, S. (1984). Adolescence and drug abuse: Biological consequences. In D. J. Lettieri & J. P. Ludford (Eds.), *Drug Abuse and the American adolescent* (pp. 104–109). Rockville, MD: National Institute on Drug Abuse.

Crabbe, J. C., McSwigan, J. D., & Belknap, J. K. (1985). The role of genetics in substance abuse. In M. Galizio & S. A. Maisto (Eds.), *Determinants of substance abuse* (pp. 13–54). New York: Plenum.

Kandel, D. B. (1980). Developmental stages in adolescent drug involvement. In D. J. Lettieri, M. Sayers, & H. W. Pearson (Eds.), *Drug abuse and the American adolescent* (pp. 120–127). Rockville, MD: National Institute on Drug Abuse.

Kandel, D. B. (1984). Drug use by youth: An overview. In D. J. Lettieri & J. P. Ludford (Eds.), *Drug abuse and the American adolescent* (pp. 1–24) Rockville, MD: National Institute on Drug Abuse.

Kandel, D. B., Kessler, R. C., & Margulies, R. (1978). Adolescent initiation into stages of drug use: A developmental analysis. In D. B. Kandel (Ed.), *Longitudinal research in drug use: Empirical findings and methodological issues* (pp. 73–99) Washington, DC: Hemisphere.

Newman, B. M., & Newman, P. R. (1975). *Development through life: A psychosocial approach.* Homewood, IL: Dorsey.

L. Worth Bolton
*Cape Fear Substance Abuse Center, Wilmington, North Carolina*

**ALCOHOL AND DRUG ABUSE PATTERNS**
**DRUG ABUSE**
**SUBSTANCE ABUSE**

# CHEMOTHERAPY

The treatment of cancer in children usually includes chemotherapy, which consists of drugs that are administered to the child intravenously, intramuscularly, or orally on a repeated schedule (e.g., every 10 days or every month). The purpose of chemotherapy is to poison the cancer cells. Unfortunately, it also is toxic to healthy cells of the body. As a result, many children receiving chemotherapy experience unpleasant side effects.

Two common side effects of chemotherapy are nausea and vomiting. Children differ in the extent to which they have these symptoms. Furthermore, the degree of nausea and vomiting for a given child may vary widely from one course of chemotherapy to the next, even when there are no changes in chemotherapy. Many children feel intensely ill during the days they receive chemotherapy and for a few days afterward. Other children are able to carry on with play and other normal activities to varying degrees (Zeltzer, LeBaron, & Zeltzer, 1984).

Another possible side effect is a temporary susceptibility to bacterial infection or excessive bleeding. During such a period, physicians usually will advise the child not to participate in any contact sports or activities (e.g., gymnastics) that might increase the risk of bleeding. Because children on chemotherapy also are sometimes at risk for severe illness with certain viral infections, doctors often advise these children to stay home from school for a period of time if there is an outbreak of chicken pox. However, for the majority of time the child is receiving chemotherapy, the doctor usually will permit the child to engage in all normal school activities, including sports.

Another problem related to chemotherapy is that total hair loss may occur. Baldness is the most troublesome side effect of chemotherapy for many children. Bald children may feel so embarrassed that they refuse to go to school. Many children cope with this problem by wearing a cap, kerchief, or wig; others explain to their friends the reason for the baldness. Fortunately, in almost all cases, the hair grows back once chemotherapy is completed.

What are the effects of chemotherapy on the child's behavior and academic performance? Many of these children are absent from school at regular intervals because of medical appointments and chemotherapy side effects. Some children also stay home because of embarrassment over hair loss and fear of being rejected by peers. A further reason for school absence is a fear of failure because of the large amount of school material missed (Deasy-Spinetta, 1981; Deasy-Spinetta & Spinetta, 1980; Katz, Kellerman, Rigler, Williams, & Siegle, 1977).

For some children, radiation to the head produces cognitive deficits, especially when combined with injections of chemotherapy into the spinal canal. Many children with cancer show little or no evidence of cognitive deficits, but these are problems that can occur gradually and may be long-lasting. During the acute phase of radiation therapy, there often is transient swelling of the brain, which could produce additional temporary cognitive deficits.

There are several ways educators can be helpful to the student who is receiving chemotherapy. A teacher or counselor needs to contact the student's parents to discuss ways in which the student's educational needs can be met. For example, if the student is in the hospital, a few books and short assignments could be sent. If the child is likely to be at home for some time, homebound education may be indicated. A student who would not otherwise qualify for special education can qualify on the basis of the illness and can benefit greatly from both home and hospital teacher visits combined with regular school attendance.

With the permission of the child's parents, it usually is helpful to contact the student's physician to learn about the doctor's expectations regarding the student's capabilities during the period of treatment. The teacher also can ask the student how he or she feels about returning to school. A discussion of the student's needs and feelings with classmates can give the class an opportunity to discuss their misconceptions and worries about the student, as well as to ask questions. Children who are unable to return to school for a period of time usually appreciate receiving cards, drawings, or letters from classmates at school.

Educators need to be aware that hospitalization or confinement to bed at home because of nausea and vomiting does not necessarily preclude school work. On the contrary, involvement in school work, at least at a minimal level, can have therapeutic value. By attending school a few hours a day, having a homebound teacher, or doing some school work in the hospital, children can be distracted from unpleasant physical symptoms or worries. Some adolescents who receive chemotherapy in the morning prefer to come to school in the afternoon rather than to spend the rest of the day at home feeling sick. If the student experiences some nausea, he or she may need to leave the class abruptly. If these considerations are discussed in advance, then involvement in school can be therapeutic for the many children and may reduce the severity of nausea and vomiting.

Teachers can be most helpful to children receiving chemotherapy by maintaining a flexible attitude and realistic expectations. Most children receiving chemotherapy can maintain a normal educational load. However, specific expectations regarding homework and exams need to be flexible because of the intermittent nature of treatment-related problems. Frequent consultation with the student and parent will help to define reasonable and appropriate educational goals.

## REFERENCES

Deasy-Spinetta, P. (1981). The school and the child with cancer. In J. J. Spinetta & P. Deasy-Spinetta (Eds.), *Living with childhood cancer* (pp. 153–168). St. Louis: Mosby.

Deasy-Spinetta, P. M., & Spinetta, J. J. (1980). The child with cancer in school: Teachers' appraisal. *American Journal of Pediatric Hematology/Oncology, 2*, 89–94.

Katz, E. R., Kellerman, J., Rigler, D., Williams, K., & Siegle, S. E. (1977). School intervention with pediatric cancer patients. *Journal of Pediatric Psychology, 2*, 72–76.

Zeltzer, L. K., LeBaron, S., & Zeltzer, P. M. (1984). The adolescent with cancer. In R. Blum (Ed.), *Chronic illness and disabilities in childhood and adolescence* (pp. 375–395). Orlando, FL: Grune & Stratton.

SAMUEL LEBARON
LONNIE K. ZELTZER
*University of Texas Health
Science Center, San Antonio*

**CANCER, CHILDHOOD
HOMEBOUND INSTRUCTION**

## CHESS, STELLA (1914–      )

Stella Chess was born and educated in New York City. She received her BA from Smith College in 1935 and MD from New York University School of Medicine in 1939. She served several internships and completed psychoanalytic training in 1946 at New York Medical College, where she also became an instructor and associate professor of child psychiatry. In 1966 Chess moved to a full professorship at New York University Medical Center.

**Stella Chess**

Chess may be best known for her collaboration (1956–1967) with her husband, Alexander Thomas, and Herbert Birch on a longitudinal study on the individual characteristics of children. This study found early differentiable temperament factors that persist and strongly influence later behavior. Chess was involved in other longitudinal studies, including studies of infant behavior patterns and child care practices of Puerto Rican families in New York City (1956–1964); children with congenital rubella (1967–1970); and the behavioral development of multihandicapped children (1977–1981).

In 1974 Chess was awarded the Family Life Book Award of Child Study of America for her book *How to Help Your Child Get the Most Out of School* (1974). She also received the Agnes Purall McGavin Award for Outstanding Contributions to the Prevention of Mental Health Disorders in Children from the American Psychological Association in 1983.

ELAINE FLETCHER-JANZEN
*Texas A&M University*

## CHILD ABUSE

The age-old phenomenon of child maltreatment has only recently attracted the attention of mental health professionals. Psychiatric and psychological exploration of child battering has lagged two decades behind the pioneering efforts of pediatricians and radiologists in establishing medical diagnostic criteria for physical abuse in children. Between 1963 and 1965, the passage of laws by all 50 states requiring medical reporting of child abuse ultimately subjected the abusing parents to legal process; these laws were also the catalyst for the formation of child protective services throughout the nation. The first psychological studies of abusing parents were carried out during this period.

Child abuse is currently regarded as the leading cause of death in children and a major public health problem. The proliferation of child abuse and neglect might bear some relationship to the alarming general increase of violence in our society demonstrated by the rising incidence of violent crimes, delinquency, suicide, and lethal accidents. In the last 10 years, child abuse has become a major focus of research and clinical study. A concerted effort is being made by federal, state, and local governments to develop programs for the study, prevention, and treatment of child abuse.

Owing to its complexity and far-reaching consequences, the problem of child abuse has attracted the attention of professionals from widely divergent backgrounds. Contributions to this area have come from the fields of pediatrics, psychiatry, psychology, social work, sociology, nursing, education, law, and law enforcement. Such multidisciplinary involvement has been essential in tracking down cases, locating medical treatment, and arranging for protective intervention and long-term planning with families. At the same time, it has become a source of confusion as a result of the differing roles, frames of reference, and terminology of each specialty. Exclusively cultural, socioeconomic, psychodynamic, and behavioral interpretations of the child abuse syndrome have failed to present the full picture.

The definition of child abuse has been continually expanding in recent years. In a classic paper, "The Battered Child Syndrome," (Kempe et al. (1962) described child abuse as the infliction of serious injury on young children by parents or caretakers. The injuries, which included fractures, subdural hematoma, and multiple soft tissue injuries, often resulted in permanent disability and death. Fontana's concept of the "maltreatment syndrome" (1964) viewed child abuse as one end of a spectrum of maltreatment that also included emotional deprivation, neglect, and malnutrition. Helfer (1975) recognized the prevalence of minor injuries resulting from abuse and suspected that abuse might be implicated in 10% of all childhood accidents treated in emergency rooms. Gil (1974) extended the concept of child abuse to include any action that prevents a child from achieving his physical and psychological potential.

Child protective services are specialized agencies ex-

isting under public welfare auspices; they are responsible for receiving and investigating all reports of child abuse or maltreatment for the purpose of preventing further abuse, providing services necessary to safeguard the child's well-being, and strengthening the family unit. These agencies are responsible for maintaining service until the conditions of maltreatment are remedied. They also have the mandate to invoke the authority of the juvenile or family court to secure the protection and treatment of children whose parents are unable or unwilling to use their services.

The wide variety of behavior and personality traits observed in abusing parents suggests that a specific abusive personality does not exist. Rather, individuals with a certain psychological makeup operating in combination with the burden of a painfully perceived childhood and immediate environmental stress might be likely to abuse the offspring who most readily elicits the unhappy childhood imagery of the past.

While environmental stress has often been suggested as a prominent etiological factor in child abuse, the precise definition of this relationship has eluded most investigators. One author has attributed child abuse almost exclusively to socioeconomic determinants (Gil, 1968, 1970), but most researchers agree that environmental stress is only the catalyst, in many instances, for an abuse-prone personality.

The stress argument has at least in part been predicated on the high percentage of low socioeconomic status (SES), multiple problem families in child abuse registers throughout the country. It is probable that reporting procedures themselves have led to the greater emphasis on socioeconomic determinants. Any controlled study that matches for SES is compelled to look beyond such variables as family income for the origins of child abuse. The conclusion that Spinetta and Rigler (1972) reach in their review of the literature is far more likely—that environmental stress is neither necessary nor sufficient for child abuse but that it does, in some instances, interact with other factors such as parent personality variables and child behaviors to potentiate child battering.

Environmental stress includes current events that widen the discrepancy between the limited capacity of the parents and increased child-rearing pressures. The stress may consist of a diminution of child-rearing resources owing to a spouse's illness or desertion, or to the unavailability of an earlier caretaker such as a neighbor or some other family member.

Environmental stress also includes the actual or threatened loss of a key relationship that provides the parent with emotional security and dependency gratification. This may occur when the spouse becomes physically or emotionally unavailable or when ties with parents or important relatives are severed owing to estrangement, illness, or death. Additional child-rearing pressures such as the birth or illness of another child, or the assumption of temporary care of other children, create environmental stress that may also lead to child abuse.

Justice and Duncan (1975) described the contribution of work-related pressures to environmental stress in situations of child abuse. They cited four types of work-related situations: unemployed fathers caring for children at home; working mothers with domestic obligations; overworked husbands who neglect their wives; and traumatic job experiences resulting in undischarged tension. Justice and Justice (1979) were able to document the importance of stress in terms of excessive life changes in child-abusing families by means of the *Social Readjustment Rating Scale* developed by Holmes and Rahe (1967).

The greatest area of agreement in the field of child abuse has pertained to the history and background of the abusive parents themselves. These individuals have usually experienced abuse, deprivation, rejection, and inadequate mothering during childhood. As children they were subjected to unrealistic expectations and premature demands by their parents. Parents with these characteristics are said to have "abuse-prone" personality traits.

The psychodynamics in a given case of child abuse are largely determined by the abuse-prone personality traits of the parent. The relationship between the abusing parent and his or her child is distorted by the cumulative impact of the parent's own traumatic experiences as a child reared in a punitive, unloving environment. Individuals who abuse their children cannot envision any parent-child relationship as a mutually gratifying experience. The task of parenting mobilizes identifications with the parent-aggressor, child-victim dyad of the past. The key psychodynamic elements in child abuse are role reversal, excessive use of denial and projection as defenses, rapidly shifting identifications, and displacement of aggression from frustrating objects onto the child.

Role reversal occurs when the unfulfilled abusing parent seeks dependency gratification, which is unavailable from his or her spouse or family, from the "parentified" child. It is based on an identification with the child-victim. The child's inability to gratify the father or mother causes the youngster to be unconsciously perceived as the rejecting mother. This intensifies the parent's feelings of rejection and worthlessness, which further threaten his or her narcissistic equilibrium. These painful feelings are denied and projected onto the child, who then becomes the recipient of the parent's self-directed aggression.

Any plan for the prevention or treatment of child abuse must be designed to create a safe environment for the child and to modify the potentiating factors underlying abuse. Therefore, an effective treatment program must deal specifically with the parental abuse proneness, those characteristics of the child that make him or her vulnerable for scapegoating, and the environmental stresses that trigger the abusive interaction.

A wide range of psychotherapeutic and educational techniques have proven successful in reducing the symptoms and problems of abused children. In general, these children present with ego deficits and cognitive impairment to such a degree that an emphasis on ego integration, reality testing, containment of drives and impulses, and strengthening of higher level defenses (similar to those techniques applied to borderline and psychotic children) proves necessary.

The ideal objective in studying and treating child abuse on a nationwide scale is, as with any major public health problem, the development of a strategy for prevention. Thus far, early case findings and protective intervention in abusing families have been the primary areas of interest for workers in this field. As more basic knowledge is accumulated about the child-abuse syndrome, through clinical experience and research, one can envision a logical shift in focus from treatment and rehabilitation (secondary prevention) to primary intervention.

## REFERENCES

Fontana, V. (1964). *The maltreated child.* Springfield, IL: Thomas.

Gil, D. (1968). Incidence of child abuse and demographic characteristics of persons involved. In R. E. Helfer & C. H. Kempe (Eds.), *The battered child.* Chicago: University of Chicago Press.

Gil, D. (1970). *Violence against children.* Cambridge, MA: Harvard University Press.

Gil, D. (1974). *A holistic perspective on child abuse and its prevention.* Paper presented at the Conference on Research on Child Abuse, National Institute of Child Health and Human Development, Washington D.C.

Helfer, R. E. (1975). *The diagnostic process and treatment programs.* Washington, DC: U.S. Department of Health, Education and Welfare, National Center for Child Abuse and Neglect.

Holmes, T., & Rahe, R. (1967). The social readjustment rating scale. *Journal of Psychosomatic Medicine, 11,* 213–218.

Justice, B., & Duncan, D. (1975). *Child abuse as a work-related problem.* Paper presented at American Public Health Association, Chicago.

Justice, B., & Justice, R. (1979). *The broken taboo: Sex in the family.* New York: Human Science Press.

Kempe, C. H., Silverman, F., Steele, B., Droegemueller, W., & Silver, H. (1962). The battered child syndrome. *Journal of the American Medical Association, 181,* 17–24.

Spinetta, J., & Rigler, D. (1972). The child abusing parent: A psychological review. *Psychological Bulletin, 77,* 296–304.

CHARLES P. BARNARD
*University of Wisconsin, Stout*

## BATTERED CHILD SYNDROME
## CHILD CARE AGENCIES

# CHILD ANXIETY SCALE (CAS)

The Child Anxiety Scale (CAS) is a 20-item self-report inventory of anxiety for young children. The CAS was published in 1980 by the Institute for Personality and Ability Testing.

Items for the CAS were selected based on their relationship to items on a "second-order anxiety factor" of the Early School Personality Questionnaire (ESPQ). Of 320 items tried out, the 20 items correlating most highly with this factor were selected.

The norms for the CAS were derived from a standardization study involving 2105 cases (1097 boys and 1008 girls). The test manual does not do an adequate job of describing the standardization sample. The manual also admits that the geographic representation of the sample did not mimic the national population. The authors tested for significant score differences by region by randomly selecting 30 cases from each region and testing for differences with an ANOVA (Analysis of Variance procedure). The results were insignificant but this may be due to a lack of statistical power because of small sample sizes rather than a lack of real differences. The match of the CAS sample to U.S. Census statistics by socioeconomic status or ethnic group is not shown. In light of other evidence, one cannot help but assume that the sample was selected on a convenience basis as much as on the basis of important stratification variables.

Results of a test-retest study were favorable with coefficients ranging from .82 at grade 1 to .92 at grade 3. Estimates of internal consistency were somewhat lower.

A variety of types of validity evidence are reported in the manual. First, the correlations between each of the 20 items and the ESPQ are reported. These range from .17 to .49. In addition, a study was conducted correlating CAS scores with parent mobility but a significant relationship was not found. In addition, the CAS scores of children in single versus dual parent families were compared and no significant differences between the groups were reported. Taken together, the results of these validity studies appear mixed at best and unimpressive at worst.

In summary, as a brief measure of children's anxiety the CAS shows some potential but suffers from problems with a poor standardization sample and poor evidence of validity.

## REFERENCE

Gillis, J. S. (1980). *Child Anxiety Scale*. Champaign, IL: Institute for Personality and Ability Testing.

RANDY W. KAMPHAUS
*Eastern Kentucky University*

## REVISED CHILDREN'S MANIFEST ANXIETY SCALE

# CHILD BEHAVIOR CHECKLIST

The Child Behavior Checklist (CBCL) (Achenbach & Edelbrock, 1983) was developed to provide "standardized descriptions" of problems and social competencies of children from 4 to 16. The CBCL contains 118 behavior problem items. The social competence items (20) relate broadly to skills, interests, and peers. The average completion time for parents is reported to be 15 to 17 minutes.

The CBCL is used with the Revised Child Behavior Profile. Analysis of the CBCL on a sample of clinically referred children ($N = 2300$) resulted in empirical scales grouped into internalizing and externalizing syndromes and narrow band scales that vary by age and sex (e.g., schizoid or anxious, depressed, uncommunicative, obsessive-compulsive, somatic complaints, social withdrawal, hyperactive, aggressive, and delinquent for boys 6 to 11). Scores for social competence (activities, social, and school) and total behavior problems are available. Normative information ($N = 1300$) was derived from interviews of randomly selected parents in the Washington, DC, area (Achenbach & Edelbrock, 1981). Normalized T scores with a mean of 50 and standard deviation of 10 are provided.

Extensive reliability and validity data are reported. The median test-retest correlation was .89 (1-week interval), the median correlation between mothers' and fathers' scores was .66. Criterion-related validity was examined through the ability of the scales to distinguish between referred (for mental health services) and nonreferred children.

## REFERENCES

Achenbach, T. J., & Edelbrock, C. (1981). Behavior problems and competencies reported by parents of normal and disturbed children aged 4 through 16. *Monographs of the Society for Research in Child Development, 46* (serial No. 188).

Achenbach, T. J., & Edelbrock, C. (1983). *Manual for the Child Behavior Checklist and Revised Child Behavior Profile*. Burlington, VT: University of Vermont.

DAVID W. BARNETT
*University of Cincinnati*

# CHILD CARE AGENCIES

Child care agencies are public or private agencies or institutions that provide noneducational habitational services. They range from daycare centers to residential correctional institutions. The most common child care agency is the foster home or group home. Children who are placed in child care agencies are usually wards of the state. Most placements are made in cases of neglect or abuse. A number of child care agencies serve as alternative placements to secure correctional facilities for delinquent youths. The advantages of a child care agency over larger institutional care are the level of community involvement, individual attention, familylike environment, and easier adjustment to a less restrictive environment. Child care agencies are licensed by the state and are usually supervised by the social services divisions of the state, county, or city. The child care agency may have an educational component or may use local public schools for educational services.

DANIEL R. PAULSON
*University of Wisconsin, Stout*

ADOPTEES
ADVOCACY FOR HANDICAPPED CHILDREN
COMMUNITY-BASED INSTRUCTION
COMMUNITY-BASED SERVICES
FOSTER HOMES FOR THE HANDICAPPED

## CHILD CARETAKER

Any individual or agency that provides services (either direct or indirect) to children can be considered a child caretaker. Consequently, within special education there are numerous individuals and agencies that can be considered child caretakers (e.g., medical and mental health specialists, parents, school personnel, and social workers). However, the two most common caretakers for most children are the family and the school. Of these two, the family is considered the primary caretaker.

Within the family, there are many members who can be regarded as child caretakers. Grandparents, aunts, uncles, and even siblings may assume some of the responsibilities for the child's care. It is usually the parents, however, who have the major responsibility for the child's care and upbringing. They provide their children with the necessities of life (e.g., clothes, food, shelter, and love). They also have the primary responsibility for their child's early socialization (Smith, Price, & Marsh, 1986), and exert a significant influence on his/her social and intellectual development (Simpson, 1982). The parents are also the ones who seek services from other caretakers in those areas in which they lack expertise. Depending on the type and severity of their child's disability, parents of exceptional children may seek services from a variety of caretakers.

The other principal child caretaker, and the one from which the parents of exceptional children seek services, is the school. Schools contain many individuals who provide services to all children, including exceptional children. For example, administrators, counselors, librarians, and teachers provide services to children, and, as such, may be regarded as child caretakers. In addition to these individuals, there are a number of other personnel within the schools who also provide services to exceptional children (e.g., school psychologists, speech therapists, physical therapists, occupational therapists, and behavior specialists), depending on the services the child may require. Although many individuals within the schools may be regarded as caretakers, it is usually the child's teacher who is considered the primary caretaker. As caretakers, teachers provide many direct and indirect services to children. In addition to the traditional services they provide as caretakers, parents and special educators also should be willing to work together to enhance the child's development and serve as advocates for the special needs of exceptional children. Advocacy may be required at times to maximize the delivery of services (McGregor, 1982). These additional responsibilities will help the parents and special educator to become more effective child caretakers.

### REFERENCES

McGregor, D. J. (1982). Readers respond: The advocacy dilemma. *Exceptional Children, 49,* 14–15.

Simpson, R. L. (1982). *Conferencing parents of exceptional children.* Rockville, MD: Aspen.

Smith, T. E. C., Price, B. J., & Marsh, G. E., II. (1986). *Mildly handicapped children and adults.* St. Paul, MN: West.

LARRY J. WHEELER
*Southwest Texas State
University*

FAMILY RESPONSE TO A HANDICAPPED CHILD
TEACHER EFFECTIVENESS

## CHILD DEVELOPMENT

Published six times a year by the University of Chicago Press, *Child Development* is a professional journal sponsored by the Society for Research in Child Development. As an interdisciplinary group, the Society for Research in Child Development uses the *Child Development* journal to publish manuscripts from all academic and professional disciplines that study developmental processes. The articles range from empirical and theoretical to reviews of previous research. The scholarly papers that appear in *Child Development* focus on the growth and development of children from conception through adolescence, including the development of language, thinking and reasoning, moral judgment, social skills, and family relationships.

The distribution of the journal, while primarily North American, is international. The editorial board is made of world renowned scholars. *Child Development*, clearly the most comprehensive journal in this field, is read by psychologists, pediatricians, anthropologists, social workers, and others who wish to obtain information related to research in child development.

MICHAEL J. ASH
JOSE LUIS TORRES
*Texas A&M University*

## CHILD FIND

Two federal enactments have stimulated a renewed interest in, and efforts toward, locating handicapped children. These so-called child find efforts have been given increased importance under both PL 93-380, the Educational Amendments of 1974, and the Education for All Handicapped Children Act of 1975, as amended by PL 98-199. Public Law 93-380 introduced the requirements that states institute systematic procedures in order to locate all handicapped children from birth to age 21. Of central concern in this mandated effort was the location of children not enrolled in school programs. There was a two-stage logic behind this emphasis on locating handicapped children from birth to age 5. First, the determination of an accurate child count would provide a data base on which to plan appropriate intervention programs. Second, the data produced relating to preschool handicapped children might well document the extent of need for additional early intervention programs.

The second act of concern is the Education of the Handicapped Act, as amended by PL 98-199. This extensive piece of legislation includes such features as the requirement for a free appropriate public education in the least restrictive environment, due process procedures, nondiscriminatory testing, individualized education programs, and parent participation. In addition, the law requires states to establish a goal of providing services to all handicapped children from birth and to locate unserved handicapped children below age 6 if the requirements of the act are in conflict with a state law or practice or a court order regarding the education of 3-, 4-, and 5-year-old children.

JAMES BUTTON
*United States Department
of Education*

**EARLY IDENTIFICATION OF HANDICAPPED CHILDREN
EDUCATION FOR ALL HANDICAPPED CHILDREN ACT OF
1975**

## CHILD GUIDANCE CLINIC

Child guidance clinics are the result of the blending of several historical forces. The feminist movement was instrumental in opening the way for the *Century of the Child* (Key, 1909). This was precipitated by a new interest in child psychology that occurred at the turn of the century. Concern for children was also evidenced at this time in the passage of child labor laws. Also, as compulsory education gained momentum, problem children could no longer be hidden away at home and school-related problems became more prominent. In fact, the first clinic created for children (Lightner Witmer, at the University of Pennsylvania in 1896) was primarily concerned with the adaptation of children to the school situation. In 1891, America's earliest child psychologist of renown, G. Stanley Hall, designed the first journal devoted to child psychology; it served as a record of educational literature, institutions, and progress.

A second major force in the development of child clinics was the mental hygiene movement that was stimulated by the publication of *The Mind That Found Itself* (Beers, 1908). Beers and his associates set out to disprove the age-old dictum that suggested once insane, insane forever. This proved to be a significant step in the direction of acknowledging that if mental hygiene held value for adults, the same must hold true for children.

Another significant force was the influence of the psychiatrists that came to be known as the Boston Group. They viewed mental disorders as maladjustments of the personality rather than as diseases of the nervous system. Adolf Meyer (1928), a member of this group, believed that all possible factors should be considered, including original endowment, personality traits, home influences, habits, bodily ailments, and environmental stresses. Meyer is also believed to be the initiator of psychiatric social work as his wife visited the homes of his patients to determine emotional histories and information about their personalities and other illnesses. Meyer's wife was also concerned with preparing families for the return of the patient to the home setting. This interest in families and the childhood experiences of adult patients established a precedent for similar interest in the families and experiences of child patients.

By 1921 there were a number of clinics for children that were attached to mental hospitals, social agencies, schools, and colleges. Child guidance clinics were formally organized under that name in 1922 by the National Committee for Mental Hygiene and the Commonwealth Fund. These early clinics emphasized a team approach to the diagnosis and treatment of children's problems. A social worker and psychologist (under the supervision of a psychiatrist) constituted the treatment team. Thus, the interdisciplinary team concept was initiated, and it was revolutionary for its time. While interdisciplinary teams today have considerable overlap in role and function, the early teams were regimented so that the psychologist did the necessary testing, the social worker dealt with the parents (typically just the mother), and the psychiatrist worked with the child.

The Philadelphia Child Guidance Clinic was one of these early clinics; it has survived the years and seems reflective of the changes that have evolved. This is the clinic that is identified strongly with one of the major orientations to working with families: primarily structural family therapy as developed by Salvador Minuchin (1974). As Minuchin was an employee of the Philadelphia-based clinic, so were other influential persons in the development of family therapy such as Jay Haley, Harry Aponte, and Braulio Montalvo. This clinic also demonstrates the great overlap of functioning by various disciplines; social workers, psychologists, and psychiatrists all share equally in the delivery of services. In fact, a project supervised by Haley and Minuchin in the early 1970s focused on the training of lay people as significant helpers with troubled families. The Philadelphia Child Guidance Clinic, with its emphasis on one-way mirrors, live supervision, and video taping has also distinguished itself as a significant training institution. While not on the same scale as the Philadelphia clinic, many other clinics have followed the lead and developed themselves as centers of treatment and training. Certainly, the early child guidance clinics initiated the development of a far more elaborate treatment delivery system, but their influence still seems easily distinguishable as one considers the many community mental health centers that feature the multidisciplinary treatment teams that are now considered standard practice.

## REFERENCES

Beers, C. (1908). *The mind that found itself*. New York: Longmans, Green.

Key, E. (1909). *The century of the child*. New York: Putnam.

Meyer, A. (1928). Presidential address: 35 years of psychiatry in the United States and our present outlook. *American Journal of Psychiatry*, LXXXV, 1–32.

Minuchin, S. (1974). *Families and family therapy*. Cambridge, MA: Harvard University Press.

CHARLES P. BARNARD
*University of Wisconsin, Stout*

**CHILD CARE AGENCIES**
**CHILD PSYCHIATRY**
**CHILD PSYCHOLOGY**

## CHILDHOOD APHASIA

Childhood aphasia, a label used in the pediatric and neurologic literature to describe disorders of speech and language in children, covers various disorders of communication. It is applied to children who have impairment of previously normal language and to children who failed in the normal acquisition of language.

The term aphasia derives from adult pathology in which an acute or progressive lesion produces a characteristic language disorder; it is "a clinical term that denotes the loss or impairment of language following brain damage and therefore, by definition, aphasia is a neurologic disorder" (Benson, 1979). When the brain has reached maturity, all the cerebral areas have their specialized activities. The language function is localized in the left hemisphere in right-handed people but also in the majority of left-handed persons. The cerebral hemispheres are not symmetrical anatomically or functionally. The asymmetry is already present in the fetus, but it becomes more marked in adult life. The planum temporale (superior temporal cortex) is larger on the left side of the brain and corresponds to an auditory association area which, in the adult, is included in the receptive area for language, called Wernicke's area. The left hemisphere is preponderant for language but its activities result from relations with different areas of the same hemisphere and also with the right hemisphere, which participates in language function.

An exhaustive study of cerebral lateralization, cerebral dominance, and asymmetrical functions in the nervous system has been recently reviewed by Geschwind and Galaburda (1985). Many classifications of the adult aphasias are known. Benson (1979) describes in detail eight different types of acquired aphasia that are based on the possibility of the patient expressing himself or herself in a fluent way or not, of understanding spoken language or not, of repeating, reading, and writing. In the adult there are mainly two groups of aphasia. The first, in which the patient is more affected in the comprehension of oral language, is called receptive, sensory, or Wernicke's aphasia. The patient is able to speak fluently but speech may have no connection with the questions asked. The pathology involves the posterior-superior portion of the first temporal gyrus (Wernicke's area). In the second group, the aphasic patient has great difficulties with speech but is able to write or to show the answers indicating that comprehension is correct. This is expressive, motor, or Broca's aphasia. The underlying pathology affects mainly the prerolandic region of the brain (frontal operculum or Broca's area).

Acquired aphasia in children is defined as impairment of previously normal language. Even in similar pathologic processes, as in adults, the clinical symptoms of aphasia in children depend on the degree of language development prior to cerebral insult. Childhood aphasia is characterized by an absence of spontaneous expressive language (oral, written, and gestural), producing a clinical syndrome of nonfluent speech or mutism (Wright, 1982). In all cases, the lexicon is reduced and the syntax is simplified; there is no logorrhea and even the lesion is temporal.

Recovery is more frequent and rapid than in the adult, but when children regain language they rarely return to the premorbid level. Guttmann (1942) showed that disorders of language are mainly a reduction of the verbal expression of speech (thus, mainly a motor disorder). The prognosis is good unless there are simultaneous expressive and comprehension disorders.

Basser (1962) supported hemispheric equipotentiality because pre- or perinatal hemiplegia does not produce language impairment if the lesion is left or right; there is a possible transfer to the other hemisphere of the processes responsible for language when the damage is early, before language development. But if language is already acquired at the time of the hemiplegia, there is a persistent language deficit. Alajouanine and Lhermitte (1965) studied acquired aphasia in 32 children ages 6 to 15 years. The lesion was always in the left hemisphere, either traumatic or vascular. In all cases, they observed a reduction in expression in oral language, written language, or gestures; spontaneous language was nearly absent. Lenneberg (1967) suggested that up to age 11, language function could be assumed by the right hemisphere. However, Hecaen (1976) showed that 88% of acquired aphasias in children are due to left hemisphere lesions, while only 33% have right hemisphere lesions. Woods and Teuber (1978) confirmed that less than 10% of acquired aphasia results from right hemisphere lesions; if left-handedness is excluded, only 5% are due to right hemispheric lesions. Recovery, more frequent than in adults, is less evident if there are bilateral lesions. Recovery is better and more likely to occur with early lesions, before age 8. The recovery is never complete in comparison with normal controls, even when the child is no longer aphasic. In children with an injury prior to 12 months, there is no deficit in language, but the verbal IQ is significantly lower than that of sibling controls, showing that hemispheric specialization for language is very early. If the injury to the left hemisphere is made after 1 year, there is a persistent aphasic deficit as well as impaired cognitive function (Woods & Carey, 1979).

A syndrome of aphasia with convulsive disorders has been described in childhood by Landau and Kleffner (1957). This syndrome occurs in children who have had normal language development. It may begin between 18 months of age and 13 years, but the peak is reached between 3 and 7 years. The affected children may develop acutely or progressively (over days to months) a severe impairment of verbal comprehension as well as a loss of expressive language. At times, they appear deaf. The deficit has been ascribed to a verbal auditory agnosia (Rapin et al., 1977). The aphasic disorder may fluctuate with complete recovery and relapse. Intelligence remains normal. Outcome is variable with complete recovery or persistence of a mild or moderate deficit. Epileptic fits usually precede the language disorder, but they are not always present even though the electroencephalogram (EEG) always shows paroxysmal epileptic activity. The clinical fits usually disappear before 15 years and the EEG also becomes normal. No organic lesion has been shown in this syndrome.

Developmental language disorders or dysphasias are seen in children who have never acquired normal language function. They have been described under various terms: congenital or developmental aphasias, specific language disorders, and dysphasias. From the literature it appears that the capability for human language is partially an innate cognitive skill (Mayeux & Kandel, 1985). The process of acquisition of normal language function (Rapin, 1982; Wright, 1982) starts at birth. Infants with normal hearing are sensitive to sounds and react to them; they progressively become able to discriminate the acoustically subtle phonetic cues crucial for the comprehension of human language. This sensitivity is lost as language is acquired. Children learn to associate meaningful visual precepts (visual memory) with discriminable auditory ones (auditory memory), and to demonstrate this by pointing to objects on verbal command. Therefore, language acquisition is not a passive operation based on imitation. The child will only start to repeat syllables and words when he or she is able to segment speech sounds and elemental units of meaningful language extracted from the casual conversation all around. Auditory comprehension precedes speaking. An infant understands the meaning of a word before vocalizing it and initially learns to comprehend the spoken symbol of a word (decoding). When the child comprehends the word, he or she is able to express the language symbol (encoding) (Wright, 1982). Children progressively acquire the rules of grammar and form sentences by age 4. It will take a child much longer to perfect articulatory skills and to learn to produce highly complex sentences. The addition of new words throughout the vocabulary continues throughout life. The process of acquisition follows a progression related to the overall maturation and development of the infant, but it also requires normal functioning and control of the structures involved in sound production.

The acquisition of language by children in all cultures follows a similar series of stages. Some children progress through these stages faster than others, but the average age for each stage is the same for all cultures, with peaks of development at certain age. At 3 to 6 months, an infant is able to do cooing, then babbling at 6 to 9 months. At 9 to 12 months, the baby imitates sounds and says the first intelligible words. By 14 months, the first word is given in a specific sense, usually "mommy" and "daddy." By 18 months, the vocabulary has 10 to 15 words. At 2 years, the child is able to make some sentences containing two or three words. At 3 years, speech contains questions and statements, as well as some emotional tone. Questions are of importance as they show the interest of the child in the surrounding world. At 4 years, complex sentences of a few words are used and the child knows his or her first and last names.

Developmental language disorders traditionally have been divided into two groups. The first is disorders of receptive language, in which impaired comprehension is the essential feature; however, one may find some degree of verbal language and articulation dysfunction. The second group is expressive language disorders, characterized by delayed talking; poverty of words (especially in naming); and agrammatical spontaneous speech but normal comprehension, provided the child has no deafness, no mental retardation, no cerebral palsy and is not psychiatrically disturbed and did not suffer from environmental deprivation. As this type of classification has not satisfied clinicians or linguists, other subgroups have been proposed (Aram & Nation, 1975; Bishop & Rosenbloom, in press; Rapin, 1982, 1985). The classification presented by Rapin (1985) takes into account the input–central processing–output stages of language operation as well as the level of language most severely affected; it is based on the various levels of acquisition of language. The levels are phonology (concerned with sounds used as linguistic symbols), grammar (syntax and morphology, or the arrangement of words into meaningful sentences), semantics (the representation of meaning in language), pragmatics (how language is used).

In verbal auditory agnosia (word deafness), one is incapable of decoding the sounds around him or her (phonologic level, first necessary step to comprehension of language). The child does not understand phonemes or verbal words; therefore, he or she cannot reproduce them, is mute, or utters single words with phonologic distortion. The syntax is poor. These children learn gestural language and can express themselves through drawings. Their comprehension of symbols and cognitive functions is good and is expressed through games. They will benefit from teaching techniques for deaf children.

In semantic-pragmatic syndrome, the child has an impaired comprehension of the meaning and intent of communication but has good phonology and syntax. The child has a fluent language and often reproduces what is said, but is echolalic for even well-constructed sentences. As the deficit affects comprehension and use of language, the syndrome will be mainly observed with sophisticated questions. If these are put in a simply way, the child can answer yes or no, showing the deficit is not a cognitive one. These children have good auditory memory and are able to repeat long sentences, but their spontaneous speech often lacks precision. As pragmatics is affected in this syndrome, the subject cannot read facial expression or recognize tone of voice, so speech can be unadapted to the situation, creating difficulties in social contacts and behavioral problems. These children also can learn to read, but they do not totally understand what they read.

In semantic-syntactic-organizing syndrome, the deficit lies at two levels: syntax, necessary to organize words into meaningful sentences, and semantics, which is concerned with the meaning of sentences. Therefore, children are dysfluent using incorrect words in an inadequate order. The repetition of words is better than spontaneous speech.

Mixed receptive-expressive (phonologic-syntactic) syndrome is the most frequently seen syndrome of the developmental dysphasias. Comprehension is always better than expression, and can even be normal. The children are dysfluent, have a reduced vocabulary, and an elementary syntax. The phonology is also impaired, producing some distortions of poorly articulated words. Speech may be telegraphic.

In severe expressive syndrome (verbal apraxial), children with normal comprehension have a deficiency in coding language symbols into words. Their speech is extremely poor; often the children are mute. They learn to read and sign.

Phonological programming deficit syndrome is a subgroup of severe expressive syndrome. Children have a good comprehension, are fluent, and are able to speak in sentences. Phonologic disorder produces distorted pronunciation with substitutions or omissions in words; speech is uncomprehensible to other than family members.

The classifications used in developmental language disorders are still descriptive and the anatomic clinical correlations are less well understood than in adult or childhood acquired language disorders. The mechanisms involved are not only dependent on the left hemisphere, they have still to be elucidated.

## REFERENCES

Alajouanine, T., & Lhermitte, F. (1965). Acquired aphasia in children. *Brain, 88,* 653–662.

Aram, D. M., & Nation, J. E. (1975). Patterns of language behavior in children with developmental language disorders. *Journal of Speech & Hearing Research, 18,* 229–241.

Basser, L. S. (1962). Hemiplegia of early onset and the faculty of speech with special reference to the effects of hemispherectomy. *Brain, 85,* 427–460.

Benson, D. F. (1979). Aphasia. In K. M. Heilman & E. Valenstein (Eds.), *Clinical neuropsychology.* New York: Oxford University Press. 22–58.

Bishop, D. V. M., & Rosenbloom, L. (in press). Childhood language disorders: Classification and overview. In W. Yule, M. Rutter, & M. Bax (Eds.), *Language development and disorders. Clinics in developmental medicine.* Blackwell Scientific & Lippincott.

Geshwind, N., & Galaburda, A. M. (1985). Cerebral lateralization. Biological mechanisms, associations and pathology. *Archives of Neurology, 42-I,* 428–459; 42–II; 521–552; 42–III, 634–654.

Guttmann, E., (1942). Aphasia in children. *Brain, 65,* 205.

Hecaen, H. (1976). Acquired aphasia in children and the ontogenesis of hemispheric functional specialization. *Brian & Language, 3,* 114–134.

Landau, W. M., & Kleffner, F. R. (1957). Syndrome of acquired aphasia with convulsive disorder in children. *Neurology, 7*, 523–530.

Lenneberg, E. H. (1967). *Biological foundations of language.* New York: Wiley.

Mayeux, R., & Kandel, E. R. (1985). Natural language, disorders of language, and other localizable disorders of cognitive functioning. In E. R. Kandel & J. H. Schwartz (Eds.), *Principles of Neural Science.* New York: Elsevier.

Rapin, I. (1982). *Children with brain dysfunction: Neurology, cognition, language and behavior.* New York: Raven.

Rapin, I. (1985). Communication disorders in children. In H. Szliwowski & J. Bormans (Eds.), *Progrès en neurologie pédiatrique.* Brussels: Prodim.

Rapin, I., Mattis, S., Rowan, A. J., & Golden, G. G. (1977). Verbal auditory agnosia in children. *Developmental Medicine & Child Neurology, 19*, 192–207.

Woods, B. T., & Carey, S. (1979). Language deficits after apparent clinical recovery from childhood aphasia. *Annals of Neurology, 6*, 405–409.

Woods, B. T., & Teuber, H. L. (1978). Changing patterns of childhood aphasia. *Annals of Neurology, 3*, 273–280.

Wright, F. S. (1982). Disorders of speech and language. In K. F. Swaiman & F. S. Wright (Eds.), *The Practice of pediatric neurology.* St. Louis: Mosby.

HENRI B. SZLIWOWSKI
CATHERINE WETZBURGER
*Hôspital Erasme, Université
Libre de Bruxelles, Brussels,
Belgium*

APHASIA
DEVELOPMENTAL APHASIA
LEFT BRAIN, RIGHT BRAIN
MUTISM


# CHILDHOOD NEUROSIS

See PSYCHONEUROTIC DISORDERS.


# CHILDHOOD PSYCHOSIS

Researchers in child psychology and psychiatry agree that there exist identifiable clinical syndromes where children are out of touch with reality, withdraw from the social world around them, and show unusual and bizarre behaviors. These psychotic children present great challenges to their caretakers: parents who try to provide for the psychotic child's needs and integration into the family system; teachers who try to educate the child and provide basic social skills training; and mental health professionals who try to treat the child clinically.

Consider the following case that the author supervised at a community mental health center. A 9-year-old boy was referred by foster parents following a sudden onset of bizarre destructive behavior and hallucinations. He thought monsters lurked behind doors, heard voices, and displayed bizarre speech during psychotic episodes. This child had been placed in several different foster homes since being abused and neglected as an infant. Two of his siblings were being legally adopted by one set of foster parents, but this child's behavior had led them to decide not to adopt him. He showed poor social skills, was intrusive with others (i.e., did not keep his hands to himself), and had a short attention span. He tolerated stress poorly and would sometimes lash out at others in a violent manner when frustrated. Several psychiatric hospitalizations had only temporarily stabilized self-control and reality orientation. This child was psychotic.

Other clinical cases make the important point that highly unusual and even bizarre behavior does not necessarily imply that a child is psychotic. During the clinical evaluation, for example, one 8-year-old boy freely launched into colorful descriptions of monsters and secret fantasy worlds. His conversation was marked by bizarre verbalizations with little distinction between reality and illusion. He mixed grandiose and paranoid ideas with characters of fantasy and real significant others from his life. Taken out of context, these verbalizations might be construed to reflect an active psychotic delusional state. However, on other occasions, the child was able to perceive reality accurately and to describe his delusions as a fantasy game. This child was not psychotic, but used fantasy as a retreat from high conflict and turmoil in his life. His family history did suggest that he was at risk for developing a psychotic state under stress since his mother had been diagnosed as schizophrenic.

Incidence of childhood psychosis is estimated at a maximum of 6 in 10,000 children (Werry, 1972), with a more probable estimate of 1 in 1,000 children (Quay & Werry, 1979). Unfortunately, methodological difficulties impede accurate estimates of incidence. However, research consistently shows that more boys than girls are diagnosed for each of the psychotic disorders. Estimated differences vary considerably, but it appears that at least twice as many boys are diagnosed as psychotic (Wing, 1968).

Early interest in psychotic states in children appeared near the turn of the twentieth century in the writings of Kraepelin and Bleuler, who introduced the terms dementia Praecox (early insanity) and schizophrenia (split mind), respectively. Both of these pioneers felt that the onset of many of their adult patients' psychotic disorders had been in their childhood. Thus childhood psychosis was seen as essentially identical symptomatically to adult schizophrenia. The concept of childhood psychoses gained greater acceptance as a result of articles by Potter (1933), Bender (1942), and Bradley and Bowen (1941) on childhood schizophrenia; Kanner (1943) on early infantile autism; Rank (1949) on atypical child psychosis; and Mahler (1952) on symbiotic psychosis. These early writings were uniformly based on medical model or disease conception of mental abnormality and were marked by conceptual ambiguity and a lack of specific diagnostic criteria (Wing, 1968).

The evolution of theoretical syndromes points to three general types of childhood psychosis: (1) childhood schizophrenia, (2) early infantile autism, and (3) atypical or symbiotic psychosis.

Interest in childhood schizophrenia followed Potter's (1933) paper. The schizophrenic child was seen as someone who was disinterested in the environment, manifested disturbed thought processes and frequently poor verbal skills, had difficulty in forming emotional attachments to others, and showed bizarre behaviors with a tendency to perseverate in various activities. This view of childhood schizophrenia was modeled after adult schizophrenia.

Research on childhood autism was pioneered by Kanner (1943), who described autistic children as generally having a limited ability to relate to other people beginning in infancy, a language disturbance making it difficult to communicate with others, and conspicuous and obsessive behavior for repetition and maintaining sameness.

Symbiotic psychosis is a rare subtype described by Mahler (1952) as a disturbance owed to intense resistance by the child to becoming psychologically independent of the mother. The number of cases reported is small. The syndrome may be due to repeated early traumatic events and also may stem from a constitutional predisposition to fail to see the mother as a separate object (Mahler, 1965). The onset of this syndrome occurs between 2½ and 5 years of age, preceded by fairly normal development during the first 2 years of life. The onset of symptoms can be set off by such events as illness of a mother, birth of a sibling, or the beginning of school. The following Figure shows the general distribution of cases (not necessarily according to Mahler's theory) of childhood psychoses given on age of onset.

The child manifests the behaviors of extreme separation anxiety, emotional withdrawal, and distortions of reality similar to autism. Threats of separation create panic. Frustration tolerance is low, and even minor disruptions in routine create panic. There is a craving for sameness. This type of environmental disinterestedness diminishes contact with reality. This syndrome produces hypoactivity or hyperactivity, peculiar thoughts and abnormal speech, and aggressive behavior such as biting and hitting. The central symptom is profound anxiety to the point of panic over the possibility of separation from the mother. When this bond is threatened, the symbiotic child may show excessive screaming and temper tantrums. These episodes may be followed by disturbed thinking and the expression of bizarre ideas. Following the onset of the psychotic state, the child may show regression in previ-

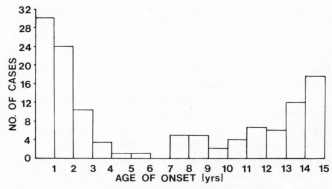

Distribution of cases of childhood psychosis given by age of onset (first detection)

ously acquired habits such as toilet training and disturbances in other behaviors such as eating and sleeping.

The *Diagnostic and Statistical Manual of Mental Disorders* (DSM III; American Psychiatric Association, 1980) attempted to integrate the various approaches to childhood psychosis. This was not an easy task because of the complexity of the subject matter and the distinct points of view on such disorders as childhood schizophrenia. The resulting classification system is organized under the concept of pervasive developmental disorders, with separate subcategories for infantile autism and childhood onset pervasive developmental disorder. This latter category is very general and appears to reflect early research on childhood schizophrenia represented by the work of Lauretta Bender; it excludes work on symbiotic psychosis by Mahler. A separate less specifically defined category, atypical pervasive developmental disorder, allows the clinician to use diagnostic flexibility in describing the individual case, including a symbiotic psychotic child. The clinician can draw on the diagnostic criteria for adult schizophrenia in determining the appropriateness of this category for a child. The DSM III represents the most current thinking of the mental health profession on these disorders, and contains specific criteria for each psychotic disorder.

## Treatment Approaches

*Psychotherapy.* Individual psychotherapy has been widely used in the treatment of childhood psychosis. Treatment approaches differ depending on the clinician's theory of the causes of the disorder, but they have in common an attempt to resolve psychic turmoil. Psychoanalytic-based approaches focus on the individual child and the presumed intrapsychic conflicts created by a fractured mother-child relationship (Mahler, 1965). Other approaches focus more on interpersonal skills and involve other family members in the treatment (Reiser, 1963).

Research on the effectiveness of psychotherapy with psychotic children has produced differing estimates of improvement. Most writers agree that it often helps to improve symptoms, but there is disagreement on how much it contributes beyond an untreated recovery rate. Some reported recovery rates have been astoundingly high, but the research is difficult to evaluate because of differing criteria used to measure success and lack of untreated control groups.

*Milieu and Educational Therapy.* This approach manipulates the total environment in a residential setting. It addresses impairments to all areas of functioning and employs multiple treatments (individual, educational, and group therapy). Children referred for these programs are usually the most disturbed; this may partly explain why clinical improvement occurs in a high percentage of cases. Milieu therapy often focuses on improving adaptive self-care skills and improving reality orientation to facilitate better relatedness to others. Research on the effectiveness of such programs is difficult to evaluate owing to lack of experimental controls, diverse groups of psychotic children, and small sample sizes. However, more structured programs appear to be more effective (Schopler, 1974).

*Behavior Therapy.* Principles of learning theory have been successfully applied to treating the symptoms of psychotic children, especially autism (Ferster, 1961). The application of behavioral contingencies has helped child care workers and parents to shape the behavior of disturbed children in positive ways, but research suggests that the effects are not easily generalizable across settings.

*Organic Treatments.* A wide variety of physical treatments have been attempted. Electroconvulsive shock therapy, sensory deprivation, vitamin therapy, hallucinogenic drugs (LSD), and antipsychotic drugs all have been used. Campbell (1973) concluded that little success can be attributed to any of these treatments though antipsychotic drugs are effective in alleviating the worst of some symptoms such as aggressiveness and hallucinations.

In summary, biological, genetic, and family factors combine to produce psychotic disturbance in children. A small percentage of children appear to be at risk of developing psychotic symptoms owed to these etiological factors when exposed to extreme environmental stress. Although a variety of treatments may produce some positive changes, long-term prognosis is generally poor for psychotic children. A high percentage continue to show psychotic symptoms or minimal social adjustment over time. With onset before age 10, the prognosis appears to be particularly poor. When a therapist and/or parent demonstrates a high degree of emotional involvement over time, the prognosis improves.

## REFERENCES

American Psychiatric Association. (1980). *Diagnostic and statistical manual of mental disorders* (3rd ed.). Washington, DC: Author.

Bender, L. (1942). Schizophrenia in childhood. *Nervous Child, 1*, 138–140.

Bradley, C., & Bowen, M. (1941). Behavior characteristics of schizophrenic children. *Psychiatric Quarterly, 15*, 296–315.

Campbell, M. (1973). Biological interventions in psychoses of childhood. *Journal of Autism & Childhood Schizophrenia, 3*, 347–373.

Ferster, C. (1961). Positive reinforcement and behavioral deficits of autistic children. *Child Development, 32*, 437–456.

Kanner, L. (1943). Autistic disturbances of affective contact. *Nervous Child, 2*, 217–250.

Mahler, M. (1952). On child psychosis in schizophrenia: Autistic and symbiotic infantile psychosis. *Psychoanalytic Study of the Child, 7*, 286–305.

Mahler, M. (1965). On early infantile psychosis: The symbiotic and autistic syndromes. *Journal of the American Academy of Psychiatry, 4*, 554–568.

Potter, H. W. (1933). Schizophrenia in children. *American Journal of Psychiatry, 12*, 1253–1270.

Quay, H. C., & Werry, J. S. (1979). *Psychopathological disorders of childhood* (2nd ed.). New York: Wiley.

Rank, B. (1949). Adaptation of the psychoanalytic technique in the treatment of young children with atypical development. *American Journal of Orthopsychiatry, 19*, 130–139.

Reiser, D. (1963). Psychosis of infancy and early childhood. *New England Journal of Medicine, 269*, 790–798, 844–850.

Schopler, E. (1974). Changes of direction with psychotic children. In A. Davids (Ed.), *Child personality and psychopathology: Current topics* (Vol. 1). New York: Wiley.

Werry, J. S. (1972). Childhood psychosis. In H. D. Quay & J. S. Werry (Eds.), *Psychopathological disorders of childhood*. New York: Wiley.

Wing, J. (1968). Review of B. Bettelheim, *The empty fortress. British Journal of Psychiatry, 114*, 788–791.

WILLIAM G. AUSTIN
*Cape Fear Psychological Services, Wilmington, North Carolina*

**BORDERLINE PERSONALITY DISORDER**
**DEPRESSION**
**EMOTIONAL DISORDERS**
**MENTAL STATUS EXAMS**
**PSYCHONEUROTIC DISORDERS**

## CHILDHOOD SCHIZOPHRENIA

The term childhood schizophrenia is one that is, at present, the subject of considerable dispute among authorities in the fields of child psychiatry and psychology. The dispute has mainly to do with the boundaries of this term and the validity of the concept of a childhood onset schizophrenic disorder. As a result of the uncertainty and differences of opinion, firm conclusions have not been reached, and the variation in interpretation of the term childhood schizophrenia has made compilation of a data base problematic.

A large part of the current confusion about childhood schiozphrenia results from changes in the definition of the term itself. As Walk (1964) has noted, most authors prior to 1930 tended to diagnose schizophreniclike disorders in children much as they would have diagnosed them in adults. Typical of this literature is De Sanctis's (1906) use of the term *dementia precocissimia*, which apparently was a variant of Kraepelin's concept of *dementia praecox* in adults.

By about 1935, several major clinics had been established in the United States for the study and treatment of severe children's disorders. The directors of these clinics (Bender, 1947; Kanner, 1943; Potter, 1933) all published descriptions of their samples of children and follow-up studies delineating the children's progress. Throughout the period 1930 to 1960, the terms infantile psychosis, autism, and childhood schizophrenia tended to be used interchangeably, although Kanner and his colleagues (Kanner, 1949; Kanner & Eisenberg, 1955) tended to define autism as a separate category that was seen as the earliest form of schizophrenia. Most of these early authors also agreed that schizophrenic disorders closely resembling the adult disorder could occur in childhood, although adult symptoms such as delusions and hallucinations did not occur before about age six. Creak (1961) provided a working definition of childhood schizophrenia that included nine basic characteristics. However, this definition included a substantial overlap into both the autistic and schizophrenic syndromes. Early analytic writers such as Bettelheim (1950) and Szurek (1956) also tended to lump a wide variety of disorders under the rubric of childhood psychosis. In contrast to earlier authorities who were uncertain about etiology, psychoanalytic writers felt that the etiology of the disorder was always psychogenic.

By the end of the period 1965 to 1980, it became clear that some important and distinct subpopulations were emerging. Barbara Fish and her colleagues (Fish et al., 1968) developed a classification system based on language and the ability to integrate basic functions in infancy, and Rutter (1978) presented his findings from long-term studies at Maudsley Hospital in London. In addition, Kolvin (1971), Vrono (1974), and others had published epidemiological data that demonstrated that two major peaks occurred in the distribution of cases across age. The first, at about 2 to 3 years, consisted of cases of autism and autisticlike disorders. The second, occurring in early adolescence, consisted of cases resembling adult schizophrenia with delusions, hallucinations, and a thought disorder of form or content. It was also clear that a mixed or residual group with unclear symptoms existed, and most writers clearly acknowledged that some crossover cases existed that did not follow the age of onset distinction. This tripartite division of severe childhood disorders is the basis

of the third edition of the *Diagnostic and Statistical Manual of Mental Disorders* (DSM-III) (American Psychiatric Association, 1980) classification of pervasive developmental disorders.

In DSM-III, childhood schizophrenia is not set apart as a separate category, but is diagnosed using the adult criteria for schizophrenia. These include

1. Deterioration from a previous level of functioning in work, social relations, or self-care.
2. Psychological disturbances such as thought disorders of content (delusions) or form (loose associations), perceptual disturbances (hallucinations), blunted or flattened affect, loss of sense of self, and loss of goal direction or volition. The patient is also usually withdrawn and may show disturbances of motor behavior.
3. Onset, usually, in adolescence or early adulthood (always by age 45).
4. No organic etiology or cause.
5. Affective disorders (such as mania or depression) that are less prominent than the schizophrenia.
6. Duration of illness of at least six months.

DSM-III suggests that this approach is controversial. Part of the problem involves the inherent difficulty in identifying delusions, hallucinations, and thought disorders in children whose language abilities are very limited. Another shortcoming involves the inability to diagnose organic disorders in children, especially at an early age. Finally, a number of authors (e.g., Fish & Ritvo, 1979) have noted the crossover of children from one category to another. This crossover does not occur often in samples of more retarded children, who tend to show more autistic symptoms, but it occurs often enough among samples with average intelligence to prompt concern about the diagnostic criteria.

Demographic data using the DSM-III criteria for schizophrenia in children are virtually nonexistent except insofar as they may be inferred from data obtained for adults. The overall incidence of schizophrenia is thought to be about 1% of the population, with an equal sex distribution and a higher incidence rate in lower socioeconomic classes. It also appears to have a higher incidence in some families, but the concordance rate, even in monozygotic twins, is not perfect, implying intervening environmental and/or biological factors. The lower limit for the age of onset using the DSM-III criteria appears to be 8 or 9 years, but there are isolated reports of much earlier onset. As Rutter (1974) notes, the differences in age of onset between autism and schizophrenia and the low incidence of any severe disorder between ages three and early adolescence suggest that both autism and schizophrenia are etiologically distinct and valid syndromes. Unfortunately, little of substance can be said regarding the prognosis or etiology of schizophrenia in children or adults. Whereas autism has been linked to a number of organic and/or genetic conditions, the changing definition of childhood schizophrenia has prevented the compilation of a large enough data base to permit inferences about etiology. The same general state of affairs exists concerning prognosis, although in adults, schizophrenia is thought to have a very poor outcome and a high relapse rate, as noted in DSM-III.

As noted previously, early in this century it was common to lump all severe childhood disorders together diagnostically; it was assumed that these were earlier forms of adult schizophrenia. In the last 20 years, however, it has become clear that distinctions should be made among these disorders. The most important differential diagnoses are between schizophrenia and disorders such as autism, mental retardation, and pervasive developmental disorders or disintegrative diseases of organic origin such as Heller's syndrome. Some of these disorders are documented in DSM-III and some are not, but delineation of the differences among them may illuminate the nature of schizophrenia in children.

Both schizophrenia and mental retardation may coexist in the same individual, and DSM-III is careful to point out that some of the social isolation and odd behavior seen in retarded children, especially at a very early age, may be mistaken for symptoms of schizophrenia. In general, however, among the retarded one may expect to find a steady, unremitting course to the disorder, whereas schizophrenics will usually show a prolonged period of normal development. In addition, many retarded persons have physical (particularly facial) stigmata that permit their identification into basic syndromes, but the presence of such stigmata is rare in child schizophrenia of later onset. Goldfarb (1967) has noted stigmata present in early onset psychoses and Bender (1947) also noted their presence among psychotic children, but it is not clear how their samples correspond to current DSM-III categories. Hallmarks of schizophrenia such as delusions and hallucinations are rarely found in individuals who are diagnosed only as retarded. It is generally possible to distinguish between retardation and schizophrenia when careful psychological testing is done to establish the subject's mental age as a baseline for judging the appropriateness of language and social behavior.

By far the most effort has been expended to differentiate schizophrenia from infantile autism. Kanner (1943) initially described autism as the earliest form of schizophrenia, but it has become clear that there are marked differences between the two disorders. First, Rutter (1974) points out that there is a great difference in the distribution of the age of onset between the two disorders, with a peak at 2 to 3 years for the onset of autism and a much later peak in adolescence for schizophrenia. In addition, the course of the two disorders differs sharply, with schizophrenic children having a period of normal development followed by an uneven course, whereas autistic children show deviant development from birth and a consistent course. The symptoms themselves differ: schizophrenic symptoms such as delusions and hallucinations are rare in autism, whereas the autistic child's need for sameness and frequent seizures (in about 25% of cases) are not usual features of schizophrenia. Although most major studies of schizophrenia show a familial loading for schizophrenia and an equal sex distribution, schizophrenia is rare in the families of autistic children and autism occurs more frequently in boys than girls by a ratio of about 4:1 (Rutter, 1985). In most cases (a few exceptions have been reported) children who are diagnosed as autistic do not resemble schizophrenics as adults (Kanner & Eisenberg, 1955).

Some authorities have noted that distinguishing between autism and other disorders is particularly difficult when the child is of average intelligence and does not show many of the characteristic language and behavior peculiarities of the younger and/or more limited autistic child. Asperger (1944) proposed that these children constitute a separate diagnostic group characterized by normal intellect, restricted and obsessive interests in certain subjects or activities, and constricted emotional and social responses. However, this description also applies to many children who have been diagnosed as autistic at an earlier age, especially those with better intelligence and/or language skills.

Schopler (1985) has pointed out that until some behavior distinction between higher level autism and so-called Asperger's syndrome can be demonstrated, confusion might be reduced if Asperger's syndrome were not regarded as a distinct diagnostic category. Most cases could adequately be classified as autistic or as schizoid disorders of adolescence (Rutter & Schopler, 1985). Both high-level autism and the adolescent schizoid disorder differ from schizophrenia, however, since the former disorders do not have hallucinations as a major feature and have an earlier age of onset with a fairly even course marked by the failure to develop normal social relationships.

Heller (1930) described a disorder in which an initial period of 3 to 4 years of apparently normal development is followed by a gradual and widespread disintegration of behavior involving areas as diverse as receptive and expressive language and bowel and bladder training. Social impairment and a general loss of interest in the outside world follow. Other disorders such as tuberous sclerosis may, in the early stages, show some features similar to schizophrenia. However, the early onset age of these latter disorders and the broad deterioration (including social skill areas such as toileting), accompanied in some cases by seizures and other physical problems, are the distinguishing features for differential diagnosis. The etiology is thought to be organic.

Because of the heterogeneity of the cases that have been labeled as schizophrenia, a wide variety of treatments have been employed, as has been the case with autism.

Insofar as schizophrenic children may have more intact intellectual/language skills than children with other severe disorders, the traditional play, insight-oriented, and "talking" therapies might be expected to be more effective. Unfortunately, no good studies documenting the utility of this approach are available, again owing in part to differences in diagnostic terminology over the years. Similarly, since drugs such as the phenothiazines have demonstrated value with adult schizophrenic populations, one might expect them to be effective with younger patients diagnosed with schizophrenic symptoms. Campbell (1975), Fish (Fish et al., 1968), and others have noted the favorable effects of such drugs with children, but it is again not clear how their samples fit into the DSM-III scheme. It is noteworthy that most antipsychotic drugs are apparently not especially effective in reducing the symptoms of autism, except in isolated cases (Rutter & Schopler, 1985). The most common form of treatment today involves parental support, counseling, and special psychoeducational strategies, much as with autistic children. In fact, many classes for severely disturbed or psychotic children contain a mix of autistic, schizophrenic, and other types of children. Whether the use of DSM-III nosology will lead to enhanced and differentiated treatment for these diagnostic groups remains to be seen.

## REFERENCES

American Psychiatric Association (1980). *Diagnostic and Statistical Manual of Mental Disorders* (3rd ed.). Washington, DC: author.

Asperger, H. (1944). Die autistischen psychopathen im kindersalter. *Archives Fur Psychiatrie und Nervenkrankheiten, 117,* 76–136.

Bender, L. (1947). Childhood schizophrenia. Clinical study of one hundred schizophrenic children. *American Journal of Orthopsychiatry, 17,* 40–56.

Bettelheim, B. (1950). *Love is not enough.* Glencoe, IL: Free Press.

Campbell, M. (1975). Pharmacotherapy in early infantile autism. *Biological Psychiatry, 10,* 399–423.

Creak, M. (1961). Schizophrenia syndrome in childhood: Progress report of a working party. *Cerebral Palsy Bulletin, 3,* 501–504.

DeSanctis, S. (1906). On some varieties of dementia praecox. Translated and reprinted in J. G. Howells, *Modern perspectives in international child psychiatry.*

Fish, B., & Ritvo, E. (1979). Psychoses of childhood. In J. Noshpitz (Ed.), *Basic handbook of child psychiatry.* New York: Basic Books.

Fish, B., Shapiro, T., & Campbell, M. (1968). A classification of schizophrenic children under five years. *American Journal of Psychiatry, 124,* 1415–1423.

Goldfarb, W. (1967). Factors in the development of schizophrenic children: An approach to subclassification. In J. Romano (Ed.), *The origins of schizophrenia.* New York: Excerpta Media Foundation.

Heller, T. (1930). About dementia infantilis. Reprinted in J. Howells (Ed.), *Modern perspectives in international child psychiatry.* Edinburgh: Oliver & Boyd.

Kanner, L. (1943). Autistic disturbances of affective contact. *Nervous Child, 2,* 219–230.

Kanner, L. (1949). Problems of nosology and psychodynamics of early infantile autism. *American Journal of Orthopsychiatry, 19,* 416–426.

Kanner, L., & Eisenberg, L. (1955). Notes on the follow-up studies of autistic children. In P. Hoch & J. Zubin (Eds.), *Psychopathology of childhood.* New York: Grune & Stratton.

Kolvin, I. (1971). Psychoses in childhood—A comparative study. In M. Rutter (Ed.), *Infantile autism: Concepts, characteristics and treatment.* London: Churchill-Livingstone.

Potter, H. (1933). Schizophrenia in children. *American Journal of Psychiatry, 12,* 1253–1270.

Rutter, M. (1974). The development of infantile autism. *Psychological Medicine, 4,* 147–163.

Rutter, M. (1978). Diagnosis and definition. In M. Rutter & E. Schopler (Eds.), *Autism: A reappraisal of concepts and treatment.* New York: Plenum.

Rutter, M. (1985). Infantile autism and other pervasive developmental disorders. In M. Rutter & L. Hersov (Eds.), *Child and adolescent psychiatry: Modern approaches.* Oxford: Blackwell Scientific.

Rutter, M., & Schopler, E. (1985). Autism and pervasive developmental disorders: Concepts and diagnostic issues. Paper prepared for National Institute of Mental Health Research Workshop, Washington, DC.

Schopler, E. (1985). Convergence of learning disability, higher-level autism, and Asperger's syndrome. *Journal of Autism and Developmental Disabilities, 15*(4), 359.

Szurek, S. (1956). Childhood schizophrenia symposium 1955: Psychotic episodes and psychotic maldevelopment. *American Journal of Orthopsychiatry, 25,* 519–543.

Vrono, M. (1974). Schizophrenia in childhood and adolescence. *International Journal of Mental Health, 2,* 7–116.

Walk, A. (1964). The pre-history of child psychiatry. *British Journal of Psychiatry, 110,* 754–767.

ERIC SCHOPLER
*University of North Carolina,*
*Chapel Hill*

JERRY L. SLOAN
*Wilmington Psychiatric*
*Associates, Wilmington,*
*North Carolina*

AUTISM
CHILDHOOD PSYCHOSIS
PSYCHONEUROTIC DISORDERS

## CHILD PSYCHIATRY

Child psychiatry is a subdiscipline of psychiatry, a branch of medicine focusing on human emotional development and pathology. As a subspeciality, child psychiatry is approximately 75 years old, with Freud's treatment of a young boy in 1909 marking its genesis (Jones, 1959). The practitioner of child psychiatry must have comprehensive training both in general psychiatry and child development. This includes a firm understanding of trends in cognitive, language, and motor development. Training in neurology is also essential in understanding which developmental delays may be attributed to organic as opposed to psychogenic etiology.

Initial involvement of the child psychiatrist is focused on the mentally retarded and an assessment of them for the purpose of deciding on entrance to state schools and hospitals for the mentally retarded. This may have been influenced by European trends in determining which children were able to benefit from a public education and which were ineligible as a result of deficient mental abilities (Wolman, 1972). This focus has been greatly expanded to areas of treatment and prevention, with assessment being regarded as the role of a multidisciplinary team.

While the earliest child psychiatrists often acted in a unitary fashion, more contemporary approaches have included psychiatrists as team members. This has also been reflected in their involvement in a larger variety of agencies than traditionally noted. Earlier trends in child psychiatry have placed the psychiatrist in medically oriented facilities such as hospitals, state homes for the retarded, and pediatric services. Recent trends have included child psychiatric services in child-guidance clinics, community mental health facilities, and, with the introduction of PL 94-142, in community-based schools.

Along with this shift in orientation, child psychiatrists have attained more of a consultant status; they are no longer seen as the sole practitioner for the young child. Their presence is observed throughout the progression from the mainstream classroom to the residential facility, as noted in Deno's Cascade Model. For example, if the child with special needs is educated within the mainstream class, resource room, or special education class, the child psychiatrist may consult to assist in determining developmental needs requiring medical attention. This assessment is made in conjunction with other members of the multidisciplinary team. As the placement shifts to a more restrictive milieu, as with residential placement, the multidisciplinary team remains the functional unit for developing the individual education plan (IEP), with the child psychiatrist maintaining a consultant and team-member status and contributing from his or her area of expertise.

Another domain of child psychiatry includes participation on recommendations of Committees for the Handicapped (COH) and school-based guidance and support teams. Within his or her area of expertise, this new consultant to the educational system contributes in a unique manner, evaluating the child for possible psychophar-macological intervention to assist in the learning process. With the advent of medications focusing on attentional deficit disorders, disruptive behaviors, and childhood depression syndromes, new tools interface the educational and the medical approaches with child development and treatment. This requires the special knowledge that the child psychiatrist is trained to possess. Transcending traditional training in dynamic psychotherapy, the knowledge of more contemporary behavioral management techniques has also become part of the armamentarium of this profession, thus allowing for additional assistance in structuring the child's environment for facilitating growth. In conjunction with significant school personnel and the family, the child psychiatrist may assist in developing treatment plans geared to maximize the child's educational experience. To carry out this role, the practitioner must have a sound foundation of knowledge about child development, assessment of personality and its pathology, therapeutic intervention, and prevention (Noshpitz, 1979).

## REFERENCES

Jones, E. (Ed.). (1959). *Sigmund Freud: collected papers* (5 vols). New York: Basic Books.

Noshpitz, J. D. (1979). *Basic handbook of child psychiatry* (4 vols.). New York: Basic Books.

Wolman, B. B. (Ed.) (1972). *Manual of child psychopathology*. New York: McGraw-Hill.

ELLIS I. BAROWSKY
*Hunter College, City University
of New York*

**CASCADE MODEL OF SPECIAL EDUCATION SERVICES
MENTAL STATUS EXAMS
MULTIDISCIPLINARY TEAMS**

## CHILD PSYCHOLOGY

Child psychology is concerned with answering two basic questions: How do children change as they develop, and what are the determinants of these developmental changes? (Hetherington & Parke, 1979). Modern child psychology is particularly concerned with understanding the processes that produce and account for age-related changes in children. Child psychology is concerned with development from conception to adolescence.

Historically, modern child psychology can be traced to the work of G. Stanley Hall, president of Clark University and one of the founders of the American Psychological Association (Kessen, 1965). In 1893 Hall published *The Contents of Children's Minds,* the first systematic study of large groups of children using a questionnaire method to obtain information about children's and adolescents' behaviors, attitudes, and interests. During the early years of this century, research in child psychology was primarily atheoretical and focused on the description of age changes in physical, psychological, and behavioral characteristics. Child psychologists in the past several decades, however, have been primarily interested in studying the basic processes underlying development. Some of the earliest researchers and theorists who had great impact on the expansion of the field of child psychology were Binet, who developed the first test of intelligence, Gesell, who investigated perceptual-motor abilities in young children, Freud, who proposed a theory of personality development, and Piaget, who published an influential theory of children's cognitive development.

Biologists and geneticists have made important contributions to an understanding of some of the processes and mechanisms related to development (Rosenthal, 1970). Behavior geneticists have been concerned with the mechanisms by which genetic factors contribute to a wide range of individual differences observed in human behavior across the entire life span. Research suggests that genetic factors play a role in the development of many physical and physiological characteristics, in intelligence, sociability, emotional responsiveness, and in some types of psychopathology.

Developmental changes in sensory capacities, visual-perceptual abilities, and fine and gross motor skills are major areas of study by child psychologists during the period of infancy. Among the specific areas studied are sound discrimination, visual stimulus preferences, and depth perception. Another important focus of child psychologists during infancy has been the effects of early experiences on their cognitive, motor, and social-emotional development. Among the issues addressed are the timing of experiences (i.e., early versus later experiences; the existence of critical periods) and concerns with the plasticity of development (i.e., can previously acquired behavior patterns be modified by later experience?; Bower, 1977).

Child psychologists recognize the influence of heredity on setting the foundation for the course of development. These genetic factors interact with the child's learning experiences to determine actual developmental outcomes. Learning processes (e.g., conditioning mechanisms, imitation), are therefore an important area of study by child psychologists.

During the past two decades, five areas of development have received considerable attention by child psychologists. These areas are emotional development, language development, cognitive development, moral development, and the development of sex role behaviors (Mussen, 1970).

In the area of emotional development, research has focused on the manner in which positive and negative emotions originate and how the expression of emotions changes with age (Yarrow, 1979). Another area that has attracted considerable interest is the development of at-tachment, in which infants show a specific desire to be near particular caretakers in their environment. Related to this issue is the study of the development of fears in the young child, particularly the fear of strangers. Child psychologists also have been interested in the ways that children learn to label and recognize their own and other people's emotions.

Language development represents one of the most significant achievements of childhood because of its importance in communication, thinking, and learning. Child psychologists differ on their views of the mechanisms underlying the development of language. Some argue that language is innate while others contend that language can be accounted for by traditional learning principles. A third view, which is held by most current theorists, is that both genetic and learning factors play a role in language development (Dale, 1976).

Research in children's cognitive development has dominated the field of child psychology. The area of cognition pertains to the mental activity and behavior through which knowledge is acquired and processed, including learning, perception, memory, and thinking. The psychological processes that underlie cognitive development are of particular interest to the child psychologist, including the operations involved in receiving, attending to, discriminating, transforming, storing, and recalling information.

Piaget (1952) developed the most comprehensive and influential theory of cognitive development. His theory emphasized developmental changes in the organization and structure of intelligence, and how differencess in those structures are reflected in the learning of children at different ages. Another component of Piaget's theory involved his approach to the development of social cognition, i.e., the way in which children perceive, understand, and think about themselves, other people, and social interactions. Piaget's provocative theory probably has stimulated more research by contemporary child psychologists than any other theory.

In addition to investigating the basic processes by which children learn, researchers also have investigated how children retain information and recognize, recall, and use it when needed. A distinction is made between two types of memory: short term and long term. Developmental changes in various strategies used by children to facilitate memory such as rehearsal, mental imagery, and organization, also have been investigated by child psychologists.

Child psychologists have noted individual differences in the cognitive styles that children use to process information. One of the most frequently studied dimensions of cognitive style is reflectivity-impulsivity. Reflectivity-impulsivity is associated with a number of intellectual, social, and personality factors.

Cognitive problem-solving abilities, as reflected in the concept of intelligence, have attracted the attention of psychologists for nearly a century. Child psychologists have addressed such issues as whether intelligence is a unitary, generalized ability, or a group of relatively separate abilities. In addition, the modifiability of intelligence has attracted much research attention in recent years (Lewis, 1976). There have been debates between those groups who argue that intelligence is genetically determined and, therefore, not alterable, and those who suggest that intelligence is more dependent on learning experiences. Similarly, the development and use of intelligence tests has generated considerable controversy within the field, with some investigators arguing that such tests are culturally biased toward white middle-class experiences. Intelligence tests, based on the concept of global intelligence, yield a single IQ score and continue to be widely used by practicing psychologists in clinical and academic settings. Tests of intellectual ability generally have been shown to be good predictors of achievement in academic settings.

The development of sex roles also has been an area of study in child psychology. Sex-role typing is the process by which children acquire the values and behaviors that are regarded as appropriate to either males or females in a specific culture. Characteristics of masculinity and femininity appear to be developed very early in life and are stable over time. Research indicates that the development of sex roles and sex differences in behavior is a complex phenomenon that involves the interaction of biological, social, and cognitive factors (Maccoby & Jacklin, 1974).

One component of the socialization process of children that has been of particular interest to child psychologists is the development of moral values and moral behaviors. Psychological research has focused on three basic aspects of morality: (1) cognitive factors including knowledge of ethical rules and judgments about whether various acts are right or wrong; (2) behavioral factors involving negative acts such as cheating, lying, resisting temptation, and controlling aggression, and behaviors involved in prosocial acts such as sharing, cooperation, altruism, and helping; and (3) emotional factors of morality such as feelings of guilt following a transgression (Hoffman, 1979).

Children are intimately involved in a number of social systems including the family, peer group, and school. Child psychologists have investigated the influence of these social systems on various aspects of the development of children (Hartup, 1979).

There is a long history of interest by child psychologists in the family's role in the socialization process. Of particular interest has been the relationship between child-rearing attitudes and practices and children's cognitive, personality, and social development. Contemporary issues pertaining to the family that have been investigated by child psychologists include the effects of child abuse, divorce, single-parent families, and maternal employment on the child's development.

Relationships with age mates are another important influence on the development of children. Age-related changes in peer interactions and the role of play behaviors have been the focus of much research. The influence of peers as models for negative and prosocial behaviors, and factors affecting peer group acceptance, also have been investigated.

Finally, child psychologists have studied the influence of the school as a socializing agent with children. In particular, the effects of teachers on children's academic achievement as well as social and emotional development has been examined. One area of interest has been an investigation of the impact of teacher expectations on children's performance in the classroom.

The major research interests in child psychology have changed over the course of time, often in response to social and historical pressures. Much of the knowledge that has accumulated in this field has been used to meet the needs of children in today's society and improve their well being through the implementation of various programs and services. In recent years, child psychologists have become increasingly interested and influential in the formulation of social policies affecting children (Seitz, 1979).

## REFERENCES

Bower, T. G. R. (1977). *A primer of infant development*. San Francisco: Freeman.

Dale, P. S. (1977). *Language development: Structure and function* (2nd ed.). New York: Holt, Rinehart, & Winston.

Hartup, W. W. (1979). The social worlds of childhood. *American Psychologist, 34,* 944–950.

Hetherington, E. M., & Parke, R. D. (1979). *Child psychology: A contemporary viewpoint* (2nd ed.). New York: McGraw-Hill.

Hoffman, M. L. (1979). Development of moral thought, feeling, and behavior. *American Psychologist, 34,* 958–966.

Kessen, W. (1965). *The child*. New York: Wiley.

Lewis, M. (Ed.). (1976). *Origins of intelligence*. New York: Plenum.

Maccoby, E. E., & Jacklin, C. N. (1974). *The psychology of sex differences*. Stanford, Stanford University Press.

Mussen, P. H. (Ed.). (1970). *Carmichael's handbook of child psychology*. New York: Wiley.

Piaget, J. (1952). *The origins of intelligence in children*. New York: International Universities Press.

Rosenthal, D. (1970). *Genetic theory and abnormal behavior*. New York: McGraw-Hill.

Seitz, V. (1979). Psychology and social policy for children. *American Psychologist, 34,* 1007–1008.

Yarrow, L. J. (1979). Emotional development. *American Psychologist, 34,* 951–957.

Lawrence J. Siegel
*University of Texas Medical Branch, Galveston*

**CHILD PSYCHIATRY**
**CLINICAL PSYCHOLOGY**
**PEDIATRIC PSYCHOLOGIST**

# CHILDREN OF A LESSER GOD

*Children of a Lesser God* is a play by Mark Medoff that was a hit on the Broadway stage in 1980. It is about the meeting, courtship, and marriage of James Leeds, a speech teacher at a state school for the deaf, and Sarah Norman, a maid at the school who has been deaf from birth and who refuses to lip read or speak. Sarah wishes to be left alone in her silent world; James insists that she learn to lip read and speak if she is to achieve first-class citizenship in the hearing, speaking world. He repeats aloud everything he and Sarah sign in an attempt to teach Sarah to lip read. The two cannot reconcile their differences, and, in the end, they separate. James asks Sarah to return, but it is left unclear whether or not the marriage will be successful.

Mark Medoff, the author of *Children of a Lesser God*, found sign language an interesting theatrical device, and used deafness as a symbol for the problems inherent in all human communication. He wrote the play for Phyllis Frelich, a founding member of the National Theater of the Deaf, in response to her difficulty in finding roles. The play was developed based on situations suggested by Medoff and improvised by Frelich and her husband Robert Steinberg, who originally played the role of James in workshop and regional productions of the play.

## REFERENCES

Guernsey, O. L., Jr. (Ed.) (1980). *The best plays of 1979–1980.* New York: Dodd, Mead.

Kakutani, M. (1980, April 1). Deaf since birth, Phyllis Frelich became an actress and now a star. *New York Times, III* 7:1.

Medoff, M. (1980). *Children of a Lesser God.* New York: Dramatists Play Service.

CATHERINE O. BRUCE
*Hunter College, City University of New York*

DEAF
DEAF EDUCATION
SIGN LANGUAGE

# CHILDREN OF THE HANDICAPPED

Parents have the responsibility of providing care, love, and social training for their children. It is commonly assumed that many of a child's developmental abilities (e.g., expressive language, reasoning, social and emotional) will be enhanced through formal and informal activities initiated by parents. This may not be assumed for children of handicapped individuals who may grow up in environments where stimulation in communication areas and training in the socialization processes are less accessible. However, this does not mean that a child of a handicapped person will be deficient in cognitive and affective development. It may mean that the child will have to adapt to different methods of learning and rely more on relatives, teachers, and others who can provide the necessary stimulation. Individual differences in intelligence, physical abilities, and temperament will play an important role in how well children adapt to the environment and how growth and development proceed when confronted with obstacles. The type of disability of the parent, the parent's intellectual ability, and the parent's motivation to rear children properly are also crucial factors.

A great deal of literature has emerged regarding the effects of deaf parents' speech on their children's speech and langauge development. Some studies note that children of deaf parents have developed normal speech and language (Lenneberg, 1967; Mayberry, 1976), while other studies report that these children have not developed normal speech because of the manual sign procedures used in the home (Sachs, Bard, & Johnson, 1981; Sachs & Johnson, 1976).

Evidence indicates that children of parents who are intellectually handicapped (Rosenberg & McTate, 1982; Schilling, Schinke, Blythe, & Barth, 1982) and emotionally disturbed (Goodman, 1984) have a tendency toward physical abuse and neglect of their children and may be delinquent in providing the kind of stimulation necessary for normal growth and development. Children of mildly handicapped parents and parents with some forms of acquired handicaps are generally born with the capacity for normal development. Early attention to these deficits and delays will ensure more wholesome human and physical environments. Because of inadequate knowledge of good parenting skills, parents of handicapped children may make errors in judgment and fail to provide proper care.

To minimize the probability that children of handicapped parents will experience developmental deficits, emphasis must be placed on adequate parenting and improving the quality of the child-rearing environment. This can be done through parent training that emphasizes effective parenting skills. This training will not only eliminate developmental disabilities in some children, but also make handicapped individuals more responsible and effective parents.

## REFERENCES

Goodman, S. (1984). Children of emotionally disturbed mothers: Problems and alternatives. *Children Today, 13,* 6–9.

Lenneberg, E. (1967). *Biological foundations of language.* New York: Wiley.

Mayberry, R. (1976). An assessment of some oral and manual language skills of hearing children of deaf parents. *American Annals of the Deaf, 121,* 507–512.

Rosenberg, S., & McTate, G.A. (1982). Intellectually handicapped mothers: Problems and Prospects. *Children Today, 11,* 24–26.

Sachs, J., Bard, B., & Johnson, M. (1981). Language learning with restricted input: Case studies of two hearing children of deaf parents. *Applied Psycholinguistics, 2,* 33–54.

Sachs, J., & Johnson, M. (1976). Language development in a hearing child of deaf parents. In W. von Raffler-Engel & Y. Lebrun (Eds.), *Baby talk and infant speech*. Lisse, Netherlands: Swets & Zeitlinger.

Schilling, R. F., Schinke, S. P., Blythe, B. J., & Barth, R. P. (1982). Child maltreatment and mentally retarded parents: Is there a relationship? *Mental Retardation, 20,* 201–209.

CECELIA STEPPE-JONES<br>
North Carolina Central<br>
University

**FAMILY RESPONSE TO A HANDICAPPED CHILD**

## CHILDREN'S ADAPTIVE BEHAVIOR SCALE

The Children's Adaptive Behavior Scale (CABS) (Richmond & Kicklighter, 1980), for children 5 through 10 years of age, was designed to evaluate skills in a social environment broader than the classroom. Unlike most adaptive behavior scales that are administered to a child's parents, guardians, or teachers, the CABS consists of tasks and questions administered directly to the child. The administration of the CABS usually takes between 20 and 30 minutes. The CABS measures adaptive behavior in five domains: language development, independent functioning, family role performance, economic vocational activity, and socialization. Scores on the five domains are summed to yield a total adaptive behavior score.

Raw scores on each of the CABS five domains can be transformed to approximate age equivalents. Norms for the CABS are based on the performance of a standardization sample of 250 mildly retarded children in South Carolina and Georgia public schools. The CABS manual includes a suggestion that school systems using the CABS may wish to establish local norms.

The CABS manual and Kicklighter, Bailey, and Richmond (1980) summarize technical data for the CABS. Internal consistency reliability coefficients range from .63 to .83 and test-retest reliability coefficients range from .98 to .99. The correlation between the CABS total raw scores and WISC-R Full Scale IQ is .51; the correlation between the CABS and AAMD Adaptive Behavior Scale total raw score is .42.

### REFERENCES

Kicklighter, R. H., Bailey, B. S., & Richmond, B. O. (1980). A direct measure adaptive behavior. *School Psychology Review, 9,* 168–173.

Richmond, B. O., & Kicklighter, R. H. (1980). *Children's Adaptive Behavior Scale.* Atlanta, GA: Humanics Limited.

PATTI L. HARRISON<br>
University of Alabama

**ADAPTIVE BEHAVIOR**
**VINELAND ADAPTIVE BEHAVIOR SCALE**

## CHILDREN'S DEFENSE FUND (CDF)

The Children's Defense Fund (CDF) is an advocacy organization for poor, minority, and handicapped children. Efforts are undertaken on behalf of large numbers of children as opposed to individual children. Relevant to special education, the organization has addressed exclusion of children from school as well as the labeling and treatment of children with special needs (Staff, 1974). The CDF maintains a lobbying organization, pursuing an annual legislative agenda in the U.S. Congress; works with state and local child advocates, providing information, technical assistance, and support; monitors the development and implementation of federal and state policies; and litigates selected cases (Children's Defense Fund, undated).

The CDF also develops information on key issues affecting children. It has published books and handbooks of interest to special education, including *94-142 and 504: Numbers that Add Up to Educational Rights for Handicapped Children, How to Help Handicapped Children Get an Education,* and *A Children's Defense Budget: An Analysis of the President's FY 1986 Budget and Children.* A monthly newsletter, *CDF Reports,* is also published.

The CDF was founded in 1973. Until 1978 CDF was known as the Children's Defense Fund of the Washington Research Project. It is a private organization, with its main office in Washington and state offices in Mississippi and Ohio.

### REFERENCES

Children's Defense Fund. (Undated brochure). *About the Children's Defense Fund.* Washington, DC: Author.

Staff. (1974). An interview with Marian Edelman Wright. *Harvard Educational Review, 44,* 53–73.

DOUGLAS L. FRIEDMAN<br>
Fordham University

## CHILDREN'S EARLY EDUCATION DEVELOPMENTAL INVENTORY

See BATTELLE DEVELOPMENTAL INVENTORY.

## CHILDREN'S MANIFEST ANXIETY SCALE (CMAS)

Originally published in 1956 by Castaneda, McCandless, and Palermo as a downward extension of Taylor's Manifest Anxiety Scale for adults (Taylor, 1951), the Children's Manifest Anxiety Scale (CMAS) was substantively revised in 1978 (Reynolds & Richmond). The *Revised Children's*

*Anxiety Scale* (RCMAS) was published in 1985 (Reynolds & Richmond). Since its first publication, more than 150 articles using the CMAS or the RCMAS have been published in various scholarly journals. These scales have been used in studies of the effects of anxiety on children's learning, behavior in the classroom, and response to a variety of treatment programs, and in descriptive studies of anxiety and its relationship to behavior, gender, ethnicity, age, socioeconomic status, and other variables.

Designed to measure anxiety of long-standing duration (i.e., trait as opposed to state or situational anxiety), the RCMAS has four empirically derived subscales titled: Concentration/Social, Worry and Oversensitivity, Physiological Anxiety, and Lie or Social Desirability. Standard scores are provided for a total anxiety score and for each subscale. Reliability data are good with most studies reporting internal consistency estimates in the .80s across age (5 to 19 years), gender, and race (black, white, and Hispanic). Extensive validity data are provided in the test manual (Reynolds & Richmond, 1985).

The RCMAS is used principally by school, child clinical, and pediatric psychologists in the screening and diagnosis of various anxiety-related emotional disorders in children, and by researchers interested in children's anxiety. Learning-disabled and other groups of children in special education programs have been shown to display higher than normal levels of anxiety on the RCMAS (Paget & Reynolds, 1984), while students in programs for the intellectually gifted demonstrate lower than average anxiety levels when compared with the normal population (Scholwinski & Reynolds, 1985).

## REFERENCES

Castaneda, A., McCandless, B., & Palermo, D. (1956). The children's form of the Manifest Anxiety Scale. *Child Development, 27,* 327–332.

Paget, K. D., & Reynolds, C. R. Dimensions, levels, and reliabilities on the Revised Children's Anxiety Scale with learning disabled children. *Journal of Learning Disabilities, 17,* 137–141.

Reynolds, C. R., & Richmond, B. O. (1978). What I think and feel: A revised measure of children's manifest anxiety. *Journal of Abnormal Psychology, 43,* 281–283.

Reynolds, C. R., & Richmond, B. O. (1985). *Revised Children's Manifest Anxiety Scale.* Los Angeles: Western Psychological Services.

Scholwinski, E. & Reynolds, C. R. (1985). Dimensions of anxiety among high IQ children. *Gifted Child Quarterly, 29,* 125–130.

Taylor, J. A. (1951). The relationship of anxiety to the conditioned eyelid response. *Journal of Experimental Psychology, 41,* 18–92.

CECIL R. REYNOLDS
*Texas A&M University*

**ANXIETY**

# CHILD SERVICE DEMONSTRATION CENTERS (CSDC)

Child Service Demonstration Centers (CSDCs) (1971–1980) were federally funded operations that, in their totality, represented the largest single national commitment specifically made to the education of the learning disabled (Mann et al., 1984).

Their beginnings are to be found in several pieces of legislation. PL 88-164, passed in 1963, which predated the introduction of the modern term learning disabilities (LD), provided assistance to learning-disabled children in a bill directed at the educational needs of handicapped children under the rubric of "crippled and other health impaired." Then, under PL 91-230, passed in 1969, the U.S. commissioner of education was enjoined by Congress "to seek to make equitable geographic distribution of training programs, and train personnel throughout the nation, and . . . to encourage the establishment of a model training center in each of the states." This was to be done by making grants or contracts available to public schools, state educational agencies, nonprofit organizations, and colleges and universities. Such model centers for the learning disabled were then authorized, and ultimately created, under PL 91-230, Title VI-G.

This law made possible Child Service Demonstration Centers to serve learning-disabled students. Under the law, the to-be-created centers were to (1) provide testing and educational evaluation to identify learning-disabled students; (2) develop and conduct model programs designed to meet their special educational needs; (3) assist appropriate educational agencies, organizations, and institutions "in making such model programs available to other children with learning disabilities"; and (4) disseminate new methods or techniques for overcoming learning disabilities and evaluate their effectiveness.

From 1971 to 1980, 97 CSDCs were created in all, with each of the 50 states being served by at least one during that time. The majority operated under the auspices of state educational agencies (SEAs). A good number also operated out of universities, and sometimes out of local educational agencies (LEAs), often on the basis of their serving as agencies of the states. The private sector was only minimally represented.

Many of the CSDCs were to carry out state as well as federal mandates. Often they were supported by state and local funds and resources that allowed them to augment their efforts far beyond the limits allowed by their relatively meager funds. Thus the hopes of the federal government that state and local education agencies would contribute to the support of the CSDCs with their own funds were realized.

The federal government had high hopes for the CSDCs. They were expected to assume major responsibility for trailblazing in the creation of service models, programs, and technologies; the identification, diagnosis, and remediation of learning disabilities; and the training of regular as well as special education teachers, specialists, and administrators. They were also expected to play a major role in research on the learning disabled. Furthermore, they were cast as both transformation instigators and partners for state educational agencies. In these roles they were expected to help the state agencies to plan and implement statewide learning disabilities programs and services; indeed, the initial CSDCs were granted to state educational agencies to further this expectation.

While every state had at least one project, as did the Commonwealth of Puerto Rico, some states had multiple centers operating at the same time under their state educational departments (e.g., California, New York). Most centers operated for 3 years; reapplication and competition for further funding was needed for subsequent years. The strategy was that the first year would involve planning, the second year the actual operation of the center, and the third year replication and dissemination. Some states, however, put projects together to create longitudinal efforts of some duration.

During their tenure, the CSDCs served a mix of urban, suburban, and rural areas. Most of the services were rendered, however, to rural children. This was in large part the result of the federal government's insistence that unserved and underserved learning-disabled students, who were in greatest abundance in rural areas at the time, be given priority in the provision of services.

For much the same reason, the racial composition of the learning-disabled students served by the CSDCs included a disproportionate number of minority students. Two projects were directed to American Indians and two to Puerto Rican students, while many of the urban and rural centers were oriented to the needs of black students. This is an interesting point in light of the fact that some advocacy groups at the time were claiming that learning disabilities were a white middle-class syndrome, with minority students being consigned to classes for the mentally retarded or having their academic problems neglected.

The CSDCs emphasized elementary school-aged children since the LD movement is generally oriented to this stage of education. There were some preschool and secondary efforts as well. Interest and efforts in the latter accelerated during the later years of funding as the federal government increased its emphasis on secondary school programming.

The CSDCs were in the vanguard of mainstreaming and the provision of special education services in the least restrictive environment. They also did much to relate special education services for learning-disabled pupils to those of general education. In these respects they clearly fulfilled the federal government's expectations. Their major service delivery models were those of resource rooms, consulting teachers, and regular classrooms.

The assessment and diagnostic efforts of the CSDCs were traditional. They were strictly secondary to the service and training functions assumed by the centers. Furthermore, they eventually resulted in controversies that still percolate in education. Although the CSDCs were expected to identify appropriately handicapped children who had specific learning disabilities, as per federal definitions, their screening and identification efforts were such as to assign children to their services on the basis of academic failure and other school problems rather than on the basis of any precise learning disability criteria. It was on such bases that a position was taken by some critics that the concept of learning disabilities, as a defensible independent diagnostic entity apart from and different from school failure, could not be sustained.

The intervention models stressed by the CSDCs were strongly academic, as might be expected since students receiving services from the CSDCs usually had been referred because of academic problems. Remedial reading was the treatment of choice, on similar grounds. Perceptual motor training, including ITPA-based interventions, held the second highest priority, particularly in the early projects, when perceptual motor training was still the vogue. Surprisingly, the behavioral movement that so dominated special education during much of the CSDCs' sway does not appear to have greatly influenced most of the CSDCs, though some had strong behavioral emphases. While only several projects have averred ecological orientations, there was an ecological shift over the course of CSDC operations. Earlier projects were committed to overcoming learning disabilities through direct intervention, while later ones were more likely to emphasize helping learning-disabled students to adjust to academic and school environments and assisting schools in their accommodations to the special needs of learning-disabled students.

One of the major efforts made by CSDCs was in respect to training. Some of this was at the college and university level. Most, often representing an introduction to LD concepts and practices, was of an in-service nature directed at regular as well as special education teachers, administrators, paraprofessionals, and parents.

The CSDCs' efforts at replication were considerable. Most of the replications were at the local level, with far fewer at the state level. Impressive is the fact that there were 16 national replications. The CSDCs generated an extraordinary number of screening, remedial, and curricular materials and training manuals for teachers and parents. Because these were in the public domain, many were adapted by schools subsequent to the CSDCs' close, though often without awareness of their origins.

While there were some exemplary research efforts, the CSDCs remained essentially service agencies and, generally speaking, did not assume the research leadership originally expected of them. This was not surprising since neither their funding, personnel capabilities, nor the nature of local conditions were such as to encourage earnest research. The Learning Disability Institutes, funded in

1977, were created in response the federal government's recognition of these facts and a desire to seek wider research efforts from other sources.

Public Law 91-239 also authorized the creation of the Leadership Training Institute (LTI) at the University of Arizona (1971–1974). The institute was supposed to assist the CSDCs in addition to carrying out its own research and training missions. It was later replaced by the National Learning Disabilities Assistance Project (1975–1979), which was entirely devoted to providing support functions for the CSDCs.

The federal government clearly expected the CSDCs to have a major national impact on LD practices. That they did not fulfill such expectations can be attributed to a variety of causes. One was the fact that their allocation of funds was far below original authorizations. Another was that individual centers came on line too slowly and irregularly, thus any collaborative thrust on their part was weakened. Still another reason was that they did not affect state educational policies as had been hoped, the states usually pursuing their own LD agendas rather than those of the federal government or of the CSDCs. Furthermore, the demands made on the CSDCs regularly changed as a consequence of changes in federal direction and because of disagreements among recognized LD specialists as to the nature of learning disabilities and the goals of intervention. Finally, most of the projects were funded for only 3 years, and several were funded for 2 or less, hardly time to create forceful and enduring efforts. Nevertheless, they did sensitize many areas of the nation and its schools to the needs of learning-disabled children and provided them with guidance, training, programs, materials, and direct services during a period when the field of learning disabilities was still emerging as an area of educational concern in the United States. Undoubtedly, they also shaped current concepts and services.

The CSDCs were subject to a number of external evaluations. A study of the CSDCs' intervention efforts was carried out by Kirk and Elkin in 1975. In 1976 a major yearlong effort was made by the American Institute of Research to examine the operations of the CSDCs. In 1979 Ysseldyke et al. began their studies of the CSDCs' assessment approaches (Thurlow & Ysseldyke, 1979). At the final closing of the CSDCs, Mann et al. published several summative articles reviewing the status and contributions of the CSDCs (Boyer et al., 1982; Mann et al., 1983; Mann et al., 1984).

## REFERENCES

Boyer, C. W., Mann, L., Davis, C. H., Metz, C. M., & Wolford, B. (1982). The Child Service Demonstration Centers: Retrospect of an age. *Academic Therapy, 18,* 171–177.

Kirk, S. A., & Elkin, V. (1975). Characteristics of children enrolled in the Child Service Demonstration Centers. *Journal of Learning Disabilities, 16,* 63–68.

Mann, L., Davis, C. H., Boyer, C. W., Metz, C. M., & Wolford, B. (1983). LD or not LD, that was the question: A retrospective analysis of the Child Service Demonstration Centers' compliance with the federal definition of learning disabilities. *Journal of Learning Disabilities, 16,* 14–17.

Mann, L., Cartwright, G. P., Kenowitz, L. A., Boyer, C. W., Metz, C. M., & Wolford, B. (1984). The Child Service Demonstration Centers: A summary report. *Exceptional Children, 50,* 532–540.

Thurlow, M. L., & Ysseldyke, J. E. (1979). Current assessment and decision making practices in model LD programs. *Learning Disability Quarterly, 4,* 15–24.

JONI J. GLEASON
*University of West Florida*

## DIAGNOSIS IN SPECIAL EDUCATION LEARNING DISABILITIES

## CHILD STUDY JOURNAL

The *Child Study Journal* is a quarterly publication of the faculty of applied and professional studies, State University of New York, Buffalo. Published in March, June, September, and December, it serves as a medium for theory and research on child and adolescent development. Particular attention is given to articles devoted to the educational and psychological aspects of human development.

Manuscripts are published in conformity with American Psychological Association style, and are requested in duplicate. The editorial address is *Child Study Journal,* Donald E. Carter, Editor, Brown Hall 312 J, Department of Behavioral and Humanistic Studies, State University of New York at Buffalo, 1300 Elmwood Avenue, Buffalo, NY 14222.

LAWRENCE C. HARTLAGE
*Evans, Georgia*

## CHILD VARIANCE PROJECT

The Conceptual Project in Child Variance was undertaken from 1970 to 1972 at the University of Michigan under the direction of William C. Rhodes. It was funded as a special project by the (then) Bureau of Education for the Handicapped to "order and organize the vast but scattered literature on emotional disturbance and other types of variance in children" and to "serve as a prototype for combining the functions of graduate training and professional research" (Rhodes & Tracy, 1974, p. 1). The product of this prodigious undertaking is a series of five volumes in which the literature on explanations of variance, intervention with variant children, and service provision are integrated and synthesized.

The first volume, *Conceptual Models*, has had a significant impact on subsequent treatments of childhood emotional disturbance and the education of disturbed children. The volume is comprised of papers in which explanatory models from five perspectives are presented. These models include biological, behavioral, psychodynamic, sociological, and ecological accounts of deviance. A paper on countertheoretical perspectives is included, as is a paper by Rhodes establishing a framework for understanding and synthesizing these diverse accounts.

The organization of the second volume, *Interventions*, derives from the first. In it, intervention with variant children is considered from biophysical, behavioral, psychodynamic, environmental, and countertheoretical perspectives. (The paper on environmental intervention explores approaches derived from both the sociological and ecological perspectives.) Of course, the rapid and multifaceted advance in the treatment of disturbed children in the decade since the publication of this volume has limited its usefulness. Nonetheless, the logic of its organization has endured. The idea that intervention must be understood in the context of the explanatory system has influenced scholars and teacher trainers to this day.

In the third volume, *Service Delivery Systems*, the development of contemporary services for deviant children provided by educational, correctional, mental health, and social welfare systems and religious institutions is analyzed from a historical perspective. The current services provided by these systems in a representative American community are examined and evaluated through a series of case studies. The fourth volume, *The Future*, is a treatise by Rhodes on the somewhat profound cultural and philosophical changes that must be realized for our society to fulfill its caretaking role. The fifth volume, *Exercise Book*, presents a series of exercises through which the sometimes complex and abstract content of the previous volumes may be brought to life for students.

Although the project has not yet realized the ultimate and far-reaching goals set forth by Rhodes in *The Future*, its impact on our thinking about emotional disturbance, the education of emotionally disturbed children, and the training of teachers of the emotionally disturbed has been significant and enduring. The organization of explanatory theory and its application to the understanding of intervention approaches are legacies of the Child Variance Project. Furthermore, its emphasis on the understanding of problems in their broadest context provided impetus to the subsequent development of ecological theory and intervention approaches.

## REFERENCES

Rhodes, W. C. (1975). *A study of child variance. Exercise book*. Ann Arbor: University of Michigan Press.

Rhodes, W. C., & Tracy, M. L. (1974). Preface. In W. C. Rhodes & M. L. Tracy (Eds.), *A study of child variance. Vol. 2. Interventions* (pp. 1–15). Ann Arbor, MI: University of Michigan Press.

Rhodes, W. C., & Tracy, M. W. (Eds.). (1974). *A study of child variance. Vol. 1. Conceptual models*. Ann Arbor, MI: University of Michigan Press.

Rhodes, W. C., & Tracy, M. L. (1974). *A study of child variance. Vol. 2. Interventions*. Ann Arbor, MI: University of Michigan Press.

Rhodes, W. C., & Tracy, M. W. (Eds.). (1974). *A study of child variance. Vol. 3. Service delivery systems*. Ann Arbor, MI: University of Michigan Press.

Rhodes, W. C., & Tracy, M. L. (1974). *A study of child variance. Vol. 4. The future*. Ann Arbor, MI: University of Michigan Press.

PAUL T. SINDELAR
*Florida State University*

**AFFECTIVE EDUCATION**
**EMOTIONAL DISORDERS**

# CHINA, SPECIAL EDUCATION IN

A discussion of special education in China can easily begin with a political fact: the lands and peoples considered to be within the historic boundaries of China are now administered by three different governments. The communist government, which won control of the Chinese mainland in 1949, administers most of the country, whereas the nationalist government, which was recognized throughout China from 1911 to 1949, now administers the province of Taiwan. Finally, Hong Kong is a British crown colony that is scheduled to revert to China in 1997. Each of these areas has a distinct educational policy. Therefore, generalizations are not possible, and each system should be considered separately.

On the Chinese mainland, official policy toward students with special learning problems places responsibility for their education squarely in the lap of the body politic. Families and communities are called on to care for the disabled and ensure that they are educated and contributing to society in some fashion suited to their abilities. Students are expected to help their crippled classmates to school, for example, and teachers are expected to spend extra time after class helping slower learners. The state does operate a few special schools for the sensorially handicapped in urban areas, and it endorses special extracurricular programs for the gifted, most of which are also in the major cities. But with 80% of the Chinese population living in rural areas, the vast majority of the handicapped and learning disabled are employed in agricultural work not requiring literacy or much formal training (Hittman, 1977).

This official policy has the double advantage of being both ideologically correct and economically suitable. After years of disruption of the educational system, first with war and then with the ideological reforms of the Cultural Revolution, revamping general education nationwide is an enormous task in itself. State responsibility for special education may well expand once China advances technologically and economically, but in the meantime, families and communities must find ways to serve locally those with special learning problems.

The educational system in Hong Kong is very complicated. After the British established control over Hong Kong in the late nineteenth century, a modified version of the British private school system was introduced. Rather than supplanting the Chinese system, however, the colonial system coexisted (and continues to coexist) with it. Almost all services for students in need of special education are delivered through the Chinese school system, private residential schools, and community-based facilities. Until recently, most special education services were provided through religious and private philanthropic organizations. A sevenfold population growth occurred in Hong Kong during the 30 years following World War II, however, and the pressures this brought to bear on the resources of the area forced the government to modify the noninterventionist position it had long maintained with respect to education and social welfare. Its highest priorities were to grapple with the serious shortages of housing, hospitals, and schools.

The educational goal of providing 6 years of universal primary schooling was not achieved until 1971. Even so, the need for a centralized unit for special education was recognized early on, and the Special Education Section of the Education Department was established in 1960. The section's mandate was formally outlined in two successive 5-year plans that began in 1966. Its role is to monitor and advise on programs of special education. In addition, it provides facilities, placement, and remedial services, teacher training, and braille printing services. In cooperation with the Social Welfare Department and the Medical and Health Department, the Education Department now provides over 30 special schools and dozens of special classes for a variety of disabilities. To the greatest extent possible, the curriculum in the special facilities follows that of regular classes. There is, however, a significantly smaller student-teacher ratio in special education, from a low of 10 to 1 for the deaf and hearing impaired to a high of 25 to 1 for the physically impaired (Rowe, 1971). In spite of such provisions, the main policy thrust of the Education Department is normalization and integration of special education students into the regular school system and into the community as a whole. The government is aware that with the current social trend toward nuclear families in Hong Kong, this policy may exert increasing stress on fam-

ilies of the handicapped. It is therefore trying to provide enough support services within the community to families to care for the disabled without resorting to institutionalization.

Preschool special education is an important part of this strategy. By starting handicapped children in school when they are 4 years old, the government hopes that they will be ready to join grade 1 classes at age 6 and continue in the regular system. Related to this is the importance placed on the improvement of diagnostic and remedial services. A developmental screening program sponsored by the government operates in all maternal and child health clinics, and parents are encouraged to have their children assessed before they are 5 years old. Screening in the primary school is also conducted for sight, hearing, and speech defects, and for behavioral or learning disabilities. The screening programs are intended to identify and treat minor handicaps before they develop into major learning disabilities, again allowing children to function successfully within the regular school system.

Where mainstreaming is not possible, the government prefers to work through private individuals and religious or volunteer organizations rather than provide public services outright. Strachan (1979) reports that fully 70% of the rehabilitative services in Hong Kong are provided through the private sector.

Some of the problems in special education that Hong Kong is striving to overcome are pedagogical in nature: the shortage of trained personnel, insufficient special equipment, inappropriate instructional methods and texts, and competition for places in the regular schools. These problems have begun to ease somewhat over the past decade.

Other problems, more deeply rooted and perhaps more difficult to solve, are more social in nature. The housing shortage deserves special mention because it has required unnecessary institutionalization. It is estimated that one third of the in-patient disabled could be discharged if there were somewhere for them to go. Where housing exists, physical access to buildings and transportation systems are inadequate. In response to these problems, the government has established halfway houses for the mentally ill, specially designed nursing homes and boardinghouses for the handicapped, and a number of specially equipped minibuses for the severely disabled.

Employment for the adult handicapped remains a problem. Vocational education is available, and in 1982 the Labor Department established a centralized employment service for the handicapped similar to that available to the general population. There is, however, a reluctance to hire the handicapped that the administration is trying to resolve through public education.

In nationalist China the policy toward the education of those with special needs was first officially voiced in the republican era. The opportunity for learning was extended to all on an equal basis in the original Chinese constitution of 1911, and the right of students with special needs to an appropriate education was explicitly recognized in the constitution of 1947. It was not made clear at that time who exactly was included in the special education population, but the physically handicapped, the sensorially deficient, and the mentally retarded were commonly regarded as candidates for special programs. Regulations concerning the expansion and improvement of special education were formulated in 1970. They spelled out the following seven categories of disability: mental retardation, visual impairments, hearing impairments, speech disorders, orthopedic handicaps, chronic diseases and physical "delicacy," and emotional and behavioral disorders (Kuo & Ferng, 1971). A 1977 amendment added learning disorders as a category of handicap.

In an effort to identify systematically all children needing special education, a national prevalence study on exceptional children was carried out from 1974 to 1976. Teachers were required to locate out-of-school children and visit their homes. Children referred for possible handicapping conditions then underwent medical and psychiatric screening. Over 34,000 children both in and out of school were identified and diagnosed as a result of this widespread effort (Kuo, 1979). Four kinds of programs are available to special education students: regular classes plus special services; part- or full-time special classes; special schools; and instruction by itinerant teachers in hospitals, custodial institutions, or at home. Placement must suit the handicap, which is determined by a diagnostic team of doctors, school psychologists, special educators, and school administrators. Equally important, placement must suit the family situation and expectations of the parents. Students must be reevaluated periodically, and efforts made to place them in as normal an educational environment as possible.

One of the benefits nationalist China has derived from their special education system is improved school attendance nationwide, particularly at the secondary level where the attendance rate grew from 62.2% in 1967–1968 to 91.01% in 1976–1977 (Kuo, 1979). Other improvements are expected, but there are three obstacles slowing the process. The first is a widely held view of special services to the handicapped as a philanthropic endeavor better addressed by social welfare organizations than by the education system. This works against integration in the regular schools. Compounding the problem is the fact that in nationalist China, the reputation and public ranking of each school is determined by the performance of its students on national examinations. Special education students are often considered educationally subnormal and thus a liability to the status of the school. Finally, there is only a low level of funding allocated to special education. Although nationalist China is more advanced than the mainland in its process of economic development (the communists have admitted to being behind by about 20 years), the nationalists must still make difficult choices in the

allocation of educational resources. Improvement of general and higher education has been given strong priority in these choices so far.

It is worth noting that it is in nationalist China, where the western vision of special education has been implemented most fully, that some of the toughest questions have been posed. For example, are western techniques appropriate for Chinese manifestations of certain disabilities? Chiu (1979) found that group counseling for emotionally disturbed schoolchildren resulted in no reduction of social anxiety and no improvement in personal and social adjustment. As another example, lip reading, which is widely considered a skill worth developing in the deaf in the West, has been promoted in Taiwan but not without great debate. Mandarin, used by all students in the educational system in Taiwan, is a highly homonymous language. Sounds can have up to five tones and even if you consider only one tone of a sound, it can have dozens of meanings (e.g., the second tone yi is the sound associated with over 20 distinct characters). Clearly, this will complicate the use of lip reading in Taiwan and other areas where tonal languages are spoken.

Another set of questions has been raised regarding the adoption of special education for the gifted in China. Scholarship has traditionally been highly valued in the Chinese culture. For centuries, only those who passed through a series of examinations were permitted to hold civil office and advance through the elaborate governmental bureaucracy. With the demise of the imperial system, that value was carried on in the official educational policy of the republic. It was explicitly noted in the constitution of 1911 that special training should be provided for the gifted. Implementation of this policy (as with so many others of the time) was held up by a long succession of international wars and internecine disruptions. In 1970, however, the first of a series of special efforts for the gifted began. Ability grouping was introduced in junior high schools in nationalist China. Unfortunately, this experiment was a disappointment for many reasons. First, classes were very large—50 to 60 pupils per teacher on average—and the teachers were not given any special training in the education of the gifted, so the classes were conducted much like those in the general program. Also, selection for the program resulted in much wider heterogeneity than might be expected. One criterion was performance on IQ tests that had been developed in the West. The suitability of such tests for the Chinese has been seriously questioned. Another criterion was teacher recommendation; this was sometimes granted for reasons related to family status and social relations rather than ability alone (Kuo, 1981).

Although teacher training and curricular materials for the gifted have improved since then (Wu & Schaffer, 1981), the very notion of special education for the gifted within the public education system is often met with skepticism. In all three administrative areas of China, schools are ranked according to their educational effectiveness, and entrance to the best schools depends on student scores on highly competitive national examinations. In other words, the educational system itself is structured so that the students are placed and educated according to their ability; the most able are admitted to the most prestigious and challenging institutions and programs. Given this kind of systemwide competitive academic promotion, just how necessary are special programs for the academically gifted?

One last question: To what extent are disabilities themselves culturally bound? It has been reported (Kuo, 1981) that reading disabilities as generally characterized in the West are found with remarkable infrequency in nationalist China. It has been hypothesized that in roman and other phonetic scripts, the sound is derived first from the orthography; then meaning is derived from the mentally decoded sound. Chinese orthography, on the other hand, first evokes meaning; then a sound is attributed to it. (This helps account for the fact that one written script has served to convey meaning for seven major Sinitic language families and Japanese, an Altaic language, besides.) Is it possible that this has protected the Chinese from reading disabilities? Such questions may never be answered fully, but they prod fertile debate, serve as cautions against generalizing across cultures, and offer insight into the way we view special education in the United States.

## REFERENCES

Hittman, S. (1977, April). *Special education in the People's Republic of China*. Paper presented at the 55th annual international convention of the Council for Exceptional Children, Atlanta, GA. (ERIC Document Reproduction Service No. ED 139 206)

Kuo, W. F. (1979, January). *Legislation for handicapped children in the ROC*. Paper presented at the Special Education in Transition International Symposium on Special Education, Taipei, Taiwan. (ERIC Document Reproduction Service No. ED 182 876)

Kuo, W. F. (1981). Preliminary study of reading disability in the Republic of China. In L. Tarnopol & M. Tarnopol (Eds.), *Comparative reading and learning difficulties*. Lexington, MA: Heath.

Kuo, W. F. (1981, August). *Special classes for the gifted and talented: A review of research in the Republic of China*. Paper presented at the World Conference on Gifted and Talented Children, Quebec, Canada. (ERIC Document Reproduction Service No. ED 212 119)

Kuo, W. F., & Ferng, J. J. (1971, February). *Special education programs in Taiwan, Republic of China*. Paper presented at the Pan Pacific Conference on the Education of Exceptional Children, Honolulu, Hawaii. (ERIC Document Reproduction Service No. ED 049 571)

Rowe, E. (1971, February). *Special education in Hong Kong*. Paper presented at the Pan Pacific Conference on the Education of Exceptional Children, Honolulu, Hawaii. (ERIC Document Reproduction Service No. ED 049 578)

Strachan, I. R. (1978). *Integrating the disabled within the community: The Hong Kong approach*. Paper presented at the second European Conference of Rehabilitation International; Disability in the Family, Brighton, England. (ERIC Document Reproduction Service No. ED 177 756)

Wu, T. W., & Schaffer, E. C. (1981, August). *Gifted and talented education in the Republic of China*. Paper presented at the fourth World Conference on Gifted and Talented, Montreal, Quebec, Canada. (ERIC Document Reproduction Service No. ED 214 323)

JANET S. BRAND
*Hunter College, City University
of New York*

## JAPAN, SPECIAL EDUCATION IN

## CHLAMYDIA TRACHOMATIS INFECTIONS

Chlamydia trachomatis is the most prevalent sexually transmitted infection in the United States today. The annual incidence is estimated to be as high as 3 million (Washington, Gove, Schachter, & Sweet, 1985). Of sexually active adolescents who were examined, about 22% had a chlamydia infection (Fraser, Rettig, & Kaplan, 1983).

Chlamydia is spread by intimate and/or sexual contact, and affects both women and homosexual/heterosexual men in all socioeconomic classes. The disease is especially alarming because it is often silent, having no symptoms. Up to 70% of women and 25% of men with chlamydia may be relatively asymptomatic (Washington et al., 1985).

The bacteria can cause painful urination and pelvic, urinary, eye, and respiratory infections in both sexes. Additional symptoms in women may include vaginal discharge, lower abdominal pain or sensitivity, abnormal Pap smear (often described as heavy or moderate inflammation), vaginal bleeding between periods even when taking birth-control pills regularly, and uterine infection. Symptoms in men may include penile discomfort and/or discharge.

If silent or not correctly diagnosed and treated, the disease can lead to such serious complications as pelvic inflammatory disease, ectopic (tubal) pregnancy, infertility, and, possibly, cervical cancer in women and urethritis and sterility in men. Though common, the disease may not be recognized among the mentally handicapped, often thought of as asexual by many medical or social work personnel. Mentally retarded adolescents, and young adults in particular, should receive education in the recognition of chlamydia and other venereal diseases.

Chlamydia infections are curable with a full 21-day treatment with tetracycline. A 7-day treatment may be effective for men, but not for women. Sulfisoxazole and erythromycin are also effective, but penicillin is not.

## REFERENCES

Fraser, J., Rettig, P., & Kaplan, D. (1983). Prevalence of cervical chlamydia trachomatis and Neisseria gonorrheae in female adolescents. *Pediatrics, 71,* 333–336.

Washington, E., Gove, S., Schachter, J., & Sweet, R. (1985). Oral contraceptives, chlamydia trachomatis infection, and pelvic inflammatory disease. *Journal of the American Medical Association, 253,* 2246–2250.

C. Sue Lamb
Ginga L. Colcough
*University of North Carolina,
Wilmington*

## HERPES

# CHLORPROMAZINE

Chlorpromazine (CPZ) is the generic name for Thorazine, a phenothiazine used in the treatment of psychoses and other psychiatric disorders. Though CPZ was synthesized by Charpentier in 1950 during research intended to produce an antipsychotic medication, the endeavor began in 1949 with a French surgeon Laborit, who was seeking a medication to reduce shock during surgery (Leavitt, 1982). Chlorpromazine is used primarily in the treatment of schizophrenia, but also has been used at low dosages to treat nausea and seasickness.

Though the actions of CPZ on the central nervous system (CNS) are not completely understood, it tends to produce the following behavioral changes: decreases apparent agitation, decreases perceptions of anxiety, decreases reports of hallucinatory experiences, produces mild to moderate sedating effects that appear to be both dosage and clinical condition dependent, and decreases spontaneous motor activity.

Because CPZ and all phenothiazines appear to block dopamine receptors in the CNS, a number of motor-related adverse effects are noted, especially during initial usage, chronic usage, or at high dosages. Three general reactions may be observed: dystonic reactions (most often with children, especially during acute infections or while dehydrated; these include spasms of neck muscles, rigidity with extension of back muscles, jaw tics, difficulty in swallowing or talking, and facial spasms with tongue protrusion, and may be accompanied by sweating or pallor); feelings of motor restlessness (e.g., agitation, inability to sit still, tapping of feet, insomnia, strong desire to move about without reported anxiety; often occurs within 2 to 3 days of initiating treatment); parkinsonlike symptoms (most frequent with elderly persons; include masked facial appearance, increased salivation/drooling, motor slowing, including slowed speech, swallowing difficulties, and cogwheel rigidity) (McEvoy, 1985). In addition, blurred vision

and dry mouth are reported during early stages of treatment. A persistent motor syndrome called tardive dyskinesia, characterized by rhythmic involuntary movements of facial and oral musculature and occasionally the limbs, may develop in conjunction with CPZ administration. The elderly, especially females, on high dosages are reported as most at risk for this condition.

## REFERENCES

Leavitt, F. (1982). *Drugs and behavior.* New York: Wiley.

McEvoy, G. K. (1985). *American hospital formulary service: Drug information 85.* Bethesda, MD: American Society of Hospital Pharmacists.

Robert F. Sawicki
*Lake Erie Institute of
Rehabilitation, Lake Erie,
Pennsylvania*

## PHENOTHIAZINES
## STELAZINE

# CHOLINESTERASE

Neurons are the basic information processing and transmitting elements of the central nervous system. The transmission of impulses across these nerve cells is a biochemical process. As such, a neurochemical process is the foundation of all human behavior.

Impulses travel from one neuron to another across a biochemical junction (synapse). Specifically, when an impulse reaches the terminal button of a neuron, it releases a transmitter substance called acetylcholine (ACh), which causes a temporary change in the membrane of the receiving neuron. If there is sufficient chemical stimulation, the second neuron will subsequently fire. Following the alteration of the membrane potential, the enzyme *cholinesterase* (ChE) neutralizes (destroys) the transmitter substance and thus restores the synapse to a resting state. In this way a single impulse is transmitted through the nervous system.

Neuroscientists have long hypothesized that this biochemical process underlies learning and memory functioning in the brain (Hillgard & Bower, 1975). While a clear relationship has not been established between cholinesterase activity and memory functioning, a number of investigators have consistently found a cholinergic deficit in dementia patients (e.g., Perry et al., 1978). Based on postmortem examination, these investigators found reduced cholinesterase levels in those areas of the brain typically associated with memory (e.g., the hippocampus). Thus, it appears that a reduction in cholinesterase activity may be related to memory dysfunctions. Research efforts are presently under way that examine the relationship between increased cholinergic activity and memory and learning functions.

## REFERENCES

Hillgard, E. R., & Bower, G. H. (1975). *Theories of learning*. Englewood Cliffs, NJ: Prentice-Hall.

Perry, E. K., Tomlinson, B. E., Blessed, G., Bergmann, K., Gibson, P. H., & Perry, R. H. (1978). Correlation of cholinergic abnormalities with senile plaques and mental test scores in senile dementia. *British Medical Journal, 2,* 1457–1459.

JEFFREY W. GRAY
*Ball State University*

RAYMOND S. DEAN
*Ball State University*
*Indiana University School*
*of Medicine*

## NEUROLOGICAL ORGANIZATION
## SYNAPSES

## CHOMSKY, AVRAM NOAM (1928—    )

Avram Noam Chomsky was born in Philadelphia on December 7, 1928. He obtained his BA at the University of Pennsylvania in 1949 and his MA in 1951. At the university, Chomsky studied linguistics, mathematics, and philosophy. Between 1951 and 1955, he was a junior fellow of the Society of Fellows at Harvard University, where he conducted research for his PhD degree. His PhD was awarded in 1955 at the University of Pennsylvania. Since 1955, Chomsky has been teaching at the Massachusetts Institute of Technology, where he is currently professor of modern languages and linguistics.

He is famous for the construction of a system of generative programs developed out of his interest in modern logic and mathematics. The main argument of his theory is that grammatical rules for any given language are, in general, similar in all languages. Chomsky also believes that the structure of language is biologically determined and "species specific" for humans.

He is a recipient of numerous honorary degrees, including ones from the University of Chicago and London, and he is an internationally recognized authority in psycholinguistics. Chomsky delivered the Beckman lectures at the University of California at Berkeley in 1967, the John Locke lecture at the University of Oxford in 1969, and the Shearman memorial lectures at the University of London the same year. He is a fellow of the Harvard Cognitive Studies Center and a member of numerous scientific associations, including the American Academy of Arts and Sciences. Chomsky is the author of many publications, among them *Syntactic Structures* (1957), *Cartesion Linguistics* (1966), *Language and Mind* (1968), and *Logical Structure of Linguistic Theory* (1975).

## REFERENCES

Chomsky, A. N. (1957). *Syntactic structures*. 'S-Gravenhage: Mouton.

Chomsky, A. N. (1966). *Cartesion linguistics: A Chapter in the history of rationalist thought*. New York: Harper & Row.

Chomsky, A. N. (1968). *Language and mind*. New York: Harcourt, Brace & World.

Chomsky, A. N. (1975). *Logical structure of linguistic theory*. New York: Plenum.

Lyons, J. (1970). *Noam Chomsky*. New York: Viking. *Who's Who* (1985). New York: St. Martin's.

IVAN Z. HOLOWINSKY
*Rutgers University*

## CHOREA

Choreiform movement is a term used to describe a disorder characterized by quick, sudden, random, purposeless, jerky, irregular, spasmodic movement. Choreiform movement can occur in any body part and often is observed in shoulders, arms, and hands, or in the tongue and face as grimaces. Clark (1975) reports a hemichorea may occur on one side of the body with vascular lesions of the basal ganglia of the brain. There are a number of diseases in which choreiform movement is a part of the descriptive syndrome, including hysterical chorea, which is a kind of conversion hysteria with the movement disorder a primary symptom (Hensyl, 1982).

Two major kinds of chorea are of primary interest to school personnel because of their possible school-age onsets and their markedly different outlook for recovery or prognosis. Sydenham's chorea (also known as chorea minor, rheumatic chorea, or St. Vitus's dance) is a disease of the central nervous system that usually occurs following streptococcal inflammation. Its slow start, often several months after the initial infection, begins with choreiform movements involving all muscles except those of the eyes. There are seldom any specific laboratory findings. There is no specific treatment except for sedation and protection from injury, together with prophylactic follow-up for identified residual infection. Recovery is slow and spontaneous, usually within 3 to 6 months, with no permanent damage to the central nervous system. Medical follow-up is recommended, and return to regular school is encouraged as soon as the transitory motor symptoms permit. The disease is reported to be more common in girls, with onset most frequent in summer and early fall (Berkow, 1982).

The second major type of chorea is Huntington's chorea (also known as chorea degenerative, progressive, or hereditary). The age of insidious onset of Huntington's chorea is reported by most sources to be between 30 and 50 years (Barr, 1979; Chusid, 1976; Clark, 1975). However, a subtype of this disease has been described with onset in childhood, with initial symptoms of stiffness (rigidity), slowed movement (bradykinesia), and later choreiform movement (Berkow, 1982). The disease is characterized by progressive choreiform movement, progressive mental deterioration, and marked personality changes. Swallowing becomes difficult, walking impossible, and dementia profound with progression. Death usually follows within 10 to 15 years. Treatment is symptomatic for motor symptoms. There is no known treatment for the dementia.

Huntington's chorea is transmitted as an autosomal dominant trait, which means that half of the children of an affected parent are at risk for developing the disease. Those who do not have the disease do not transmit it. In cases where the family history is not known, affected individuals with onset after childbearing years may transmit the disease to offspring before their own onset. Research has been directed toward a chemical identification of those with the disease, but at present the only conclusive evidence is family history, and *all* potential known carriers are advised not to have children. Chusid (1976) suggests that most American cases have been traced to two brothers who emigrated from England.

Clinical experience suggests that the subtypes with early childhood onset appears to progress more rapidly to early death. The presence of several children with the disorder in one family is a devastating experience. The serious implications of Huntington's chorea should serve to reinforce the importance of differential diagnosis of choreiform movement disorders by a skilled neurologist with appropriate medical follow-up. Supportive special education services should be provided.

## REFERENCES

Barr, M. L. (1979). *The human nervous system* (3rd ed.). Hagerstown, MD: Harper & Row.

Berkow, R. (Ed.). (1982). *The Merck manual of diagnosis and therapy.* (14th ed.). Rahway, NJ: Merck, Sharp & Dohme.

Chusid, J. G. (1976). *Correlative neuroanatomy and functional neurology.* (16th ed.). Los Angeles: Lang Medical.

Clark, R. G. (1975). *Manter and Gatz's essentials of clinical neuroanatomy and neurophysiology.* (5th ed.). Philadelphia: Davis.

Hensyl, W. R. (1982). *Stedman's medical dictionary* (24th ed.); Baltimore, MD: Williams & Wilkin.

Stolov, W. C., & Clowers, M. R. (Eds.). (1981). *Handbook of severe disability* (stock #017-090-00054-2). Washington, DC: U.S. Government Printing Office.

RACHAEL J. STEVENSON
*Bedford, Ohio*

**HEREDITY**
**GENETIC COUNSELING**
**HUNTINGTON'S CHOREA**

# CHORIONIC VILLUS SAMPLING (CVS)

Chorionic villus sampling (CVS), sometimes called chorion-villus biopsy, is a relatively new technique that allows diagnosis of chromosomal abnormalities, many inborn errors of metabolism, and other disorders, in the first trimester of pregnancy. Conducted before organogenesis is complete, it cannot detect reliably disorders such as neural tube defects; they may be assessed with later maternal serum alpha-fetoprotein (AFP) screening.

Still experimental, CVS has clear advantages over amniocentesis as a technique for antenatal (prenatal) diagnosis. It can be performed optimally at 9 weeks of pregnancy as opposed to 16 to 18 weeks, and results, including chromosomal analyses, are available in about a week after testing, as opposed to the 2 to 4 weeks for amniocentesis (*Lancet*, 1986). Thus genetic counseling can be provided early in pregnancy in cases where disorders are identified, avoiding some of the ethical and emotional concomitants of later abortion.

In CVS, 10–50 mg of placental tissue are removed. Enzyme assay and DNA analysis are performed directly on this tissue; chromosomal analysis is generally done on cultures of the CVS tissue. Most CVS assays are done transcervically, with a small percentage conducted abdominally (*Lancet*, 1986).

Risk of CVS is not established, although the likelihood of it infecting the embryo appears low. Of particular concern is the suggestion of greater risk of test-induced abortion following CVS than following amniocentesis (Clarke, 1985), although at least one study has found no difference between the two techniques (Jahoda, Vosters, Sacks, & Galjaard, 1985). A number of questions, particularly regarding safety, remain unanswered (*Lancet*, 1986). Widespread availability of CVS will depend on the outcome of large-sample controlled studies of risk and accuracy. Research reports are appearing frequently, and coordinated evaluation studies in Europe, Canada, and the United States began in 1985 (Clarke, 1985).

## REFERENCES

Clarke, M. (1985). Fetal diagnosis trial. *Nature, 315,* 269.

Jahoda, M. G., Vosters, R. P. L., Sacks, E. S., & Galjaard, H. (1985). Safety of chorionic villus sampling. *Lancet, 2,* 941–942.

Staff. (1986). The potential of chorionic villus sampling. *Lancet, 1,* 76.

ROBERT T. BROWN
*University of North Carolina, Wilmington*

BRENDA M. POPE
*New Hanover Memorial Hospital, Wilmington, North Carolina*

**AMNIOCENTESIS**

## CHROMOSOMAL ABNORMALITIES

The normal human chromosome complement includes 22 pairs of autosomes identical in both sexes and one pair of heterochromosomes or sex chromosomes, XX in the female and XY in the male. The autosome pairs are numbered according to their size, from 1 to 22 (1 being the largest and 22 the smallest); the X chromosome is medium sized while the Y-chromosome is very small. It was demonstrated by Lejeune, Gautier, and Turpin (1959) that a chromosome anomaly is consistently associated with mongolism. Since 1959, many other diseases linked with a chromosomal aberration have been described. Moreover, a new medical specialty, cytogenetics, has emerged, devoted to the study of chromosomes. Many books and thousands of papers have been written, attesting to interest in chromosome pathology in humans. Systematic newborn surveys, summarized by Hook and Hamerton (1977), have shown that 1 baby out of 160 shows a chromosome anomaly at birth, affecting either the autosomes or the sex chromosomes; often the anomaly is associated with congenital malformations and mental retardation. Recently, techniques have been refined so that new syndromes have been discovered, making the figure of 1 out of 160 seem underestimated. How and when do chromosome anomalies happen? What are the most frequent observable chromosome syndromes? How do they affect the physical and mental status of the carriers? What are the possibilities of prevention? These are some of the questions to be discussed in the following paragraphs.

After the birth of a malformed baby, the parents try to remember what could have gone wrong during pregnancy to explain the pathology of the child. However, as far as chromosome anomalies are concerned, this has no interest, for chromosome anomalies observed in the newborn occur *before* (or very early after) conception, when the mother does not know she is pregnant. Conception is achieved when the male sexual cell (or gamete), the spermatozoon, penetrates the female gamete, the ovum, and their nuclei fuse. Before this event, gametes of both sexes must proceed to maturation through a complicated process known as meiosis. The aim of meiosis is simple: to keep the chromosome number of the species constant and bring to the offspring half of its genetic information from the father and half from the mother. In human gametes, only 23 chromosomes, one of each pair, are found. The union of two gametes with 23 chromosomes gives back a new organism showing again 46 chromosomes and resembling both parents. The meiotic separation of the chromosomes of each pair occurs following "disjunction." However, sometimes a pair of chromosomes fails to separate and a nondisjunction is observed. For example (Figure 1), if pair 21 is concerned and nondisjunction occurs, a gamete with two chromosomes 21 and another without any 21 will be formed. After fecundation by a normal gamete with one chromosome 21, one zygote with three chromosomes 21 will be formed (trisomy 21), and one with only one (monosomy 21). The resulting fetuses will not be normal. The trisomic 21 will be a mongol and the monosomic 21 will not live and will be eliminated through a spontaneous abortion. Nondisjunctions happen fairly often in humans (Boué et al. 1975), but most aneuploid zygotes are aborted. Only about 10% escape elimination and give birth to an abnormal child. In some cases, nondisjunction occurs just after conception, in the early embryo showing only two or a few cells (called blastomeres). This is a *mitotic* nondisjunction and not a meiotic one. If one blastomere is affected, but not the other(s), the affected one will give rise to trisomic and monosomic lineages (Figure 2), while normal cells will derive from the other(s). The presence of two or more cell lines with different chromosome numbers in the same organism is called mosaicism; one normal cell line in a mosaic may alleviate the symptomatology. Trisomy 21/normal mosaics are less mentally handicapped than standard trisomics 21; trisomy 18/normal mosaics live longer than standard trisomics 18, etc. The demon-

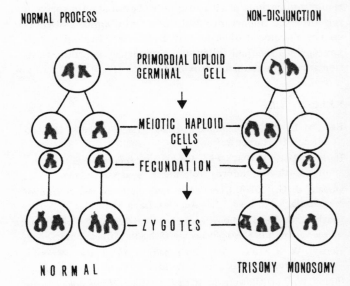

NORMAL PROCESS                                    NON-DISJUNCTION

PRIMORDIAL DIPLOID
GERMINAL     CELL

MEIOTIC HAPLOID
CELLS

FECUNDATION

ZYGOTES

NORMAL                                    TRISOMY  MONOSOMY

Figure 1.  Origin of constitutional monosomies and trisomies. The fate of one pair of chromosomes is followed through meiosis. On the left, the normal process leads to the formation of haploid cells with only one chromosome of the pair (normal disjunction). After fecundation, normal zygotes are produced. On the right, the chromosomes fail to separate (nondisjunction). One of the daughter cells inherits the two chromosomes, the other has no chromosomes at all. After fecundation by a normal gamete, one zygote will be trisomic and the other monosomic. The accident is *prezygotic* (before fecundation).

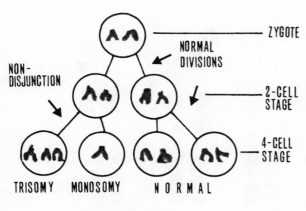

## MOSAICISM

Figure 2. Origin of mosaicism. The zygote is normal and one pair of chromosomes are followed through successive divisions. The first division leads to two normal cells (stage two). On the right, a new normal division gives rise again to two normal cells. On the left, due to a *mitotic* nondisjunction, a trisomic and a monosomic cell are produced. Thus, at the four-cell stage, the embryo shows three different chromosome numbers. Each of these cells will be at the origin of cell populations with different karyo-types and all these lines will form the fetus: This is mosaicism. The accident is *postzygotic* (after fecundation).

stration of the presence of a mosaic is best obtained when more than one tissue is studied in culture.

Nondisjunction is not the only cause of chromosome anomalies: translocation is another cause. There are several types of translocations. The most simple is the fixation of a part of a chromosome (the donor) on another chromosome (the receiver); the donor becomes smaller than its complete homologue of the same pair; the receiver, on the contrary, is larger, and this morphological characteristic allows easy detection (Figure 3). If a person is a carrier of both the small donor and the enlarged receiver, the genetic information is complete and the translocation is *balanced*. But two chromosomes of different pairs may exchange some segments; this is called a reciprocal translocation. Or two whole chromosomes may fuse (tandem translocation), usually with the loss of the centromeric function of one of them (if there is no loss, the newly formed chromosome is dicentric; this causes division anomalies). A particular type of translocation is the fusion of two V-shaped acrocentric chromosomes (13, 14, 15, 21, and 22), either by the short arms or the centromeres. The resulting fused chromosome is X-shaped, and the carrier of such a rearrangement has 45 chromosomes instead of 46. As this sort of centromeric fusion was first described at the beginning of the century by Robertson, who was studying speciation in insects, it is sometimes referred to as Robertsonian fusion.

What are the clinical consequences of a translocation? In the balanced state, there are usually no anomalies for the carrier. But they are dramatic for part of the offspring following the formation of unbalanced gametes, after meiotic processes. An example is given by the centromeric fusion 13/21. The balanced carrier is normal and fertile. During meiosis, the attached 13/21 pairs with the free 13 and 21. Then disjunction happens at random and gametes with different genotypes occur: one with the free 13 and the free 21, the other with the 13/21 alone. Both are balanced and the first is completely normal. After fecundation with a normal gamete of the opposite sex, normal zygotes will be formed. But the translocated 13/21 can be included in a gamete together with the free 21. After fecundation of a normal gamete with one chromosome 21, a trisomic 21 zygote will develop. At the same time, a gamete with only one 13 is formed. If it is fecundated, a monosomy 21 will affect the embryo, with subsequent abortion. Thus the normal carrier of a translocation 13/21 is at risk for having either a trisomic 21 child, mentally handicapped child or a spontaneous abortion. Indeed, any balanced translocation may lead to unbalanced gametes; in that sense, the anomalies observed in the offspring are inherited. Translocation in one of the parents is one of the major indications of prenatal diagnosis; conversely, recurrent abortions are an indication for the study of the chromosomes of the couple.

There are other types of chromosome anomalies, less frequent but with evident clinical consequences. *Deletions* are the loss of a part of a chromosome (a well-known example is the cri du chat syndrome, which is due to a deletion of the short arms of chromosome 5). *Rings* are a special form of deletion, with the loss of the terminal portion of both arms, the telomeres, and fusion of the free ends. *Inversions* result in genes which are not in their usual sequence. *Isochromosomes* are observed after the horizontal cleavage of the centromere instead of the normal vertical one. Moreover, an ovum can be fertilized by two spermatozoa and give rise to a triploid zygote. On the whole, these anomalies are rare in newborns or handicapped persons, but more often observed in abortusses, cancer cells, or cells in culture submitted to experimental conditions. More frequent still is a new class of chromosome anomalies recently identified: the fragile sites. If cells are cultivated in special media, one or more chromosomes of the affected patients may exhibit a remarkable constriction known as a fragile site. One of the sites is located at the end of the long arms of the X-chromosome at the level of the q27 band. The fragile X can be transmitted through apparently normal mothers (normal because, besides the fragile X, they have a normal X) to half of their sons, who will be mentally retarded with a characteristic facies and macro-orchidism after puberty.

Chromosomes are the conveyers of the genes, which are the determinants of the hereditary characters through the activation of specific biochemical processes. The number of genes in human beings is not known, but it is estimated to be between 10,000 and 100,000, located on the 46 chro-

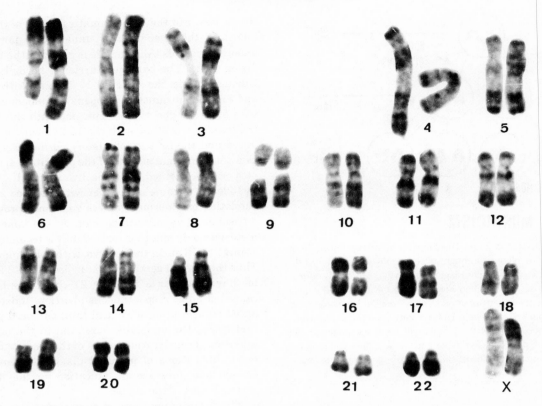

Figure 3. Balanced translocation between a chromosome 1 and a chromosome 4 (arrows; R-banding). The karyotype was studied following the birth of a malformed child and two spontaneous abortions.

mosomes. Thus when a chromosome anomaly is observed with the optic microscope, it concerns a very large number of submicroscopic genes. When a trisomy is present, this means tens, if not hundreds, of genes represented three times instead of two. This excess of genes is responsible for the symptomatology. When a deletion occurs, many genes are lost with deleterious consequences; very likely, some biochemical pathways are incomplete. On the contrary, when the chromosome anomaly is a balanced translocation, all genes are present and the carrier is not affected. However, small undetected deletions may be present even in apparently balanced translocation carriers and associated with a pathological condition. This is more frequent when the rearrangement is observed in the offspring of parents with a normal karyotype (*de novo* translocation). Moreover, when the genes are not in their original sequence, their expression may be affected (position effect), and some of the anomalies observed in balanced translocations can be explained this way, at least theoretically. The same chromosome anomalies are associated with the same symptoms. Thus the thorough description of all malformations is important to clinicians. Some signs are so specific that the trained practitioner is able to diagnose correctly a chromosome anomaly even without karyotype studies. The most frequent chromosome anomalies and their main symptoms are summarized in the Table (de Grouchy & Turleau, 1982). A chromosome anomaly is suspected when the patient shows many malformations (polymalformations), often with a peculiar face and developmental or mental retardation.

Sex chromosome anomalies deserve a special comment. As clearly indicated by their name, sex chromosomes are primarily involved in sex determinism. The presence of a Y chromosome is linked with the differentiation of the embryonic gonad into a testis; in the absence of a Y chromosome, the primitive gonad becomes an ovary. Moreover, in the mammalian XX female, only one chromosome is active (Lyon, 1961). Despite the fact that the females have 2 Xs and the males only X, the genetic active material in both sexes is the same (research in progress shows that a few genes escape inactivation). Female nuclei show a peculiar condensation, the sex chromatin or Barr body, formed by the inactivated X chromosome. Males with 47 chromosomes, an XXY sex complement, and a Barr body in their cells have *Klinefelter's syndrome*. The supernumerary X is inactivated as in females and they exhibit a sex chromatin, as normal women do. Indeed, female patients with three X chromosomes show two Barr bodies. In any cell, whatever the number of Xs, only one is active. Should such large supernumerary chromosomes not be inactivated, like the autosomes, many more anomalies would be observed, mainly in the reproductive organs (see Table). However, some, but not all, 47 XXY males show mild mental retardation; a few may be affected with a

Most Frequent Human Chromosomal Aberrations

| Disease | Frequency at Birth | Main Symptoms | Mental Status | Life Expectancy |
|---------|--------------------|---------------|---------------|-----------------|
| *trisomy 21* (47, +21) | 1/1000 | Characteristic facies (mongolism); hypotony; 25% of cases with heart malformation | Mental retardation | Children reaching age 5 may live until 50 (25% die before 1 year) |
| *trisomy 18* (47, +18) | 1/4500–1/8000 | Small face; fingers folded; great toe extended; severe congenital heart malformation in 85% of cases; 90% of affected children are girls | Failure to thrive | A few weeks |
| *trisomy 13* (47, +13) | 1/4500–1/8000 | Polymalformations with characteristic facies (absence of or very small eyeballs; cleft lip and palate) | Difficult to test; severely affected | A few days |
| cri du chat (46, 5 p-) | 1/20,000 | Lunar facies; characteristic cry (like kittens) | Severe mental retardation | Normal or at least until adult age |
| Klinefelter syndrome (47, XXY) | 1/1000 males | Eunuchoidism after puberty; small testis with azoospermia | Normal to mild mental retardation | Normal |
| Turner syndrome (45, X) | 1/10,000 females | Small stature (less than 145 cm at adulthood); absence of ovaries; infantile genitalia; at birth, edema of feet and hands | Normal | Normal |
| 47, XYY males | 1/1000 males | No specific symptomatology | Normal to behavioral anomalies | Normal |

more severe mental handicap (IQ 70-55), or present with criminal behavior because of immaturity (Akesson, 1983). Females with 45 chromosomes and only one X show *Turner's syndrome*. In a study of 45 women with Turner's syndrome, Nielsen et al. (1977) found no difference in intelligence between the affected patients, their normal sisters, or a series of control cases. The presence of a supernumerary Y chromosome in 47 XYY males has been more controversial (Hamerton, 1976). The lay press spoke of a crime chromosome after the finding by Jacobs et al. (1965) of nine patients with a 47 XYY complement out of 35 male inmates in the Scottish maximum Security Hospital at Castairs near Edinburgh. All nine patients had aggressive behavior and mild mental retardation. From the many studies conducted since then, it can be summarized that an association is present between the two Ys and height (patients are usually taller than 180 cm) and some behavioral disturbances (impulsivity, absence of self-control, aggressiveness), but many 47 XYY men enjoy a normal life without any knowledge of their chromosome anomaly. Therefore, even the term YY *syndrome* seems inappropriate, a syndrome being the sum of several symptoms; XYY condition or XYY constitution are preferred. Interestingly, the children of 47 XYY patients usually have normal chromosomes. Theoretically, half of their sons should show a 47 XYY karyotype. Since this is not the case, the concept of gamete selection has been proposed: the normal gametes (those with only one Y) have a greater

chance to achieve conception. The same holds for 47 XXX females.

The natural causes of chromosome anomalies are still largely unknown. Experimental conditions are associated with an increase in chromosome anomalies: ionizing radiation, chemical compounds including many drugs, and viruses are responsible for a wide range of chromosome damages. However, no anomalies such as trisomies or translocations observed in abortusses or newborns have been obtained repeatedly. Genetic causes have been investigated, for in animals or plants some genes are known to affect nondisjunction. In humans, no such genes are known and there are not more chromosome anomalies in children of consanguineous marriages. Moreover, most of the deviant karyotypes reported in newborns are accidental, the parents themselves showing normal chromosomes. Nevertheless, one association seems certain: the effect of aging in the female. It has been known for a long time that trisomy 21 in the child is correlated with the mother's age. In one way or another, age favors nondisjunction; this seems true for pairs other than the 21 in humans. It is, however, not clear whether aging of the ovum itself, and not only aging of the mother, is responsible for nondisjunction.

This lack of understanding of the causes of chromosome anomalies in man seems disappointing, but many studies have been undertaken in different directions to solve this problem. At birth, we only see the tip of the iceberg, namely the fetuses that have survived to their aneuploidy. It would be more interesting to know what happens at conception. Research in this direction is expanding; test tube babies (in vitro fecundation) offer a good experimental model. Many embryo transfers are followed by abortion, and many eggs do not reach the blastocyst stage. Techniques developed to study the chromosomes of very early embryos (Angell et al., 1983) show that the high abortion rate is associated with chromosome anomalies. In the same way, methods allowing the study of the chromosomes of spermatozoa bring a new insight to the cause and frequency of early abortions (Rudak et al., 1978). In a more practical approach, prenatal diagnosis during the first trimester is available (Fraccaro et al., 1985); this gives more physical and psychological comfort to pregnant mothers at risk. A final achievement, however, is in view. The refinement of banding techniques associated with the advancements of molecular biology brings the hope that in the near future the gene map of the human will be known. Mechanisms of chromosome anomalies will then be understood from an etiological point of view or from a curative one. Undoubtedly, the burden of chromosomal abnormalities will be alleviated for future generations.

## REFERENCES

Akesson, H. O. (1983). Psychiatric disorders in males with supernumerary X chromosomes (Vol. 1). Göteborg, Sweden: Psychiatric Department, Lillhagen's Hospital.

Angell, R. R., Aitken, R. J., Van Look, P. F. A., Lumsden, M. A., & Templeton, A. A. (1983). Chromosome abnormalities in human embryos after in vitro fertilization. *Nature, 303,* 336–338.

De Grouchy, J., Turleau, C. (1982). Atlas des maladies chromosomiques (2nd ed.). Paris: Expansion Scientifique Française.

Fraccaro, M., Simoni, G., & Brambati, B. (1985). *First trimester diagnosis* (Vol. 1). Berlin: Springer-Verlag.

Hamerton, J. L. (1976). Human population cytogenetics: Dilemmas and problems. *American Journal of Human Genetics, 28,* 107–122.

Hook, E. B., & Hamerton, J. L. (1977). The frequency of chromosome abnormalities detected in consecutive newborn studies—differences between studies—results by sex and by severity of phenotypic involvement. In E. B. Hook & I. A. Porter (Eds.), *Population Cytogenetic Studies in Human* (pp. 63–79). New York: Academic Press.

Jacobs, P. A., Brunton, M., Melville, M. M., Brittain, R. P., & MacLemont, W. F. (1965). Aggressive behavior, mental subnormality and the XYY male. *Nature, 208,* 1351–1352.

Lejeune, J., Gautier, M., & Turpin, R. (1959). Les chromosomes humains en culture de tissus. *C.R. Acad. Sci., 248,* 602–603.

Lyon, M. F. (1961). Gene action in the X-chromosome of the mouse. *Nature, 190,* 372–373.

Nielsen, J., Nyborg, H., & Dahl, G. (1977). Turner's syndrome. Acta Jutl. XLV (Vol. 1). *Medicine Series 21,* Arhus University Press.

Rudak, E., Jacobs, P. A., & Yanagimachi, R. (1978). Direct an-

alysis of the chromosome constitution of human spermatozoa. *Nature, 274,* 911–913.

L. KOULISCHER
*Institut de Morphologie
Pathologique, Belgium*

CONGENITAL DISORDERS
CRI DU CHAT SYNDROME
GENETIC COUNSELING
KLINEFELTER'S SYNDROME
TURNER'S SYNDROME

## CHROMOSOMES, HUMAN, ANOMALIES AND CYTOGENETIC ABNORMALITIES

Chromosomal (cytogenetic) abnormalities are the most frequent cause of congenital (present at birth) malformations, affecting some 1 in 200 newborns (Moore, 1982). Their importance is reflected in the fact that they account for at least 10 to 15% of individuals with mental retardation severe enough to require institutionalization (Moore, 1982; Pueschel, 1983) and for about 8 to 10% of newborn and early infant deaths (Sperling, 1984). Further, some 30% of spontaneously aborted embryos/fetuses had a chromosomal abnormality, an incidence 50 times higher than that in live births, meaning that incidence in all pregnancies must be about 5% (Sperling, 1984).

Because chromosomal abnormalities involve disruption in the action of many genes, most are associated with severe and varied effects (Brown, 1986). These frequently, but not always, involve general and specific intellective deficits, particular facial anomalies and cardiovascular, digestive, and pulmonary defects. Further, people with a chromosomal abnormalities usually have such characteristic phenotypes (physical appearance and physiological and behavioral functioning) that they frequently look more like unrelated persons with the same chromosomal abnormality than like their own siblings (Moore, 1982). The common characteristics that differentiate individuals with one abnormality from normal people or those with a different abnormality are called syndromes. Some two dozen chromosomally based syndromes have been identified. Although some, particularly the familiar Down's, Klinefelter's, and Turner's syndromes are relatively common, others are so rare that only 50 or so cases have been reported (Smith, 1982).

This entry will address general issues about abnormalities, provide background information for more specialized reading, and address similarities and differences among currently identified syndromes. As is the case with other genetically based disorders and congenital and perinatal abnormalities, new research routinely leads to significant changes in knowledge.

Vogel and Motulsky (1979, p. 18) elegantly describe human cytogenetics as "a successful late arrival." Although the chromosome theory of inheritance had been proposed in 1902, cytogenetics really began in 1956 with the discovery that the diploid number of human chromosomes was 46 instead of the commonly accepted 48. To give an idea of past attitudes toward the handicapped and their behavior, the diploid number 48 had been found by Painter (1923) in studies of spermatogenesis in testes of three inmates of the Texas State Insane Asylum who had been castrated because of, among other things, their excessive masturbation. When in 1959 researchers discovered chromosomal bases for three common and well-established human syndromes (Down's, Klinefelter's, and Turner's), human cytogenetics really came into its own. Since then, a variety of chromosomally based syndromes have been discovered on the basis of now routine cytogenic analysis of spontaneously aborted fetuses, early death newborns and infants, and individuals with physical and behavioral abnormalities. A number of children traditionally labeled by diagnosticians as "syndromish in appearance" (something looks wrong but no etiology is known) now are identified as having a chromosomal abnormality. In most cases, the description of the physical and behavioral characteristics of the syndrome has followed, rather than preceded, chromosomal analysis. Further, subsequent studies have identified multiple chromosomal bases for syndromes such as Down's, Klinefelter's, and Turner's that help to account for high variability among and even within affected individuals. A variety of technical advances account for much of our knowledge about these abnormalities (Sperling, 1984; Vogel & Motulsky, 1979).

## Normal and Abnormal Karyotypes

Normal humans have 23 pairs of chromosomes in all body cells, 22 pairs of autosomes, and one pair of sex chromosomes. Females normally have two long X sex chromosomes and males one long X and one shorter Y sex chromosomes. Chromosomes (colored bodies) are visible only early in mitosis, when cell samples are subjected to certain stains. A karyotype is a picture of chromosomes arranged by pair. The 22 autosomal pairs are arranged from the longest (1) to the shortest (22), followed by the sex chromosomes. A karyotype, showing chromosomal bands, of a normal human male is shown in Figure 1. Figure 2 shows a typical chromosome pair; the short arm is termed "p" and the long arm, "q"; the two arms are held together at the centromere, or primary constriction. Cohen and Nadler (1983) suggest the useful mnemonic of associating "p" with petite. Chromosomes are grouped into three types: metacentric (e.g., numbers 1 and 3), where the arms are nearly equal in length; submetacentric (e.g., numbers 4 and 5), where the "p" arm is distinctly shorter than the

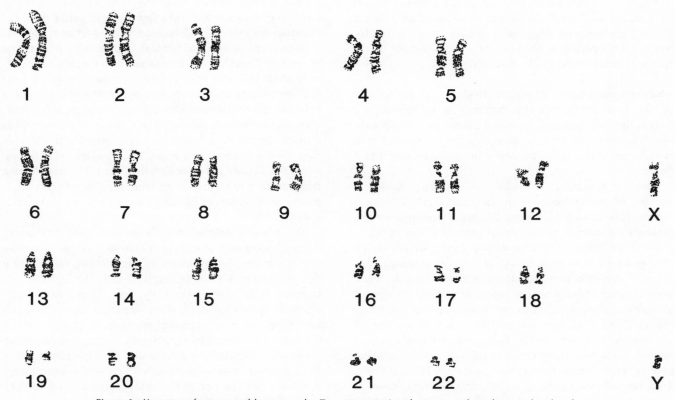

Figure 1. Karyotype for a normal human male. Twenty-two pairs of autosomes have been ordered and numbered according to convention from largest to smallest. Sex chromosomes are labeled X and Y.

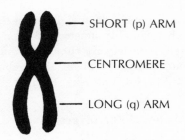

SHORT (p) ARM

CENTROMERE

LONG (q) ARM

Figure 2. Standard nomenclature for describing parts of a chromosome, after Cohen and Nadler (1983).

"q"; and acrocentric (e.g., numbers 14 and 21), which have a secondary constriction and abbreviated and apparently genetically inactive satellite "p" arms.

***Normal Cell Division.*** During mitosis, the process of duplication of body cells, each of the 46 chromosomes divides and one member of each migrates to a pole of the cells. When the cell divides, each offspring cell contains the same 23 pairs of chromosomes. Thus mitosis is a process of chromosome duplication. In meiosis, the process of production of germ cells (sperm and eggs), each of the 23 chromosome pairs divides and one member of each pair migrates to a pole of the cell. When the cell divides, each offspring has 23 chromosomes. Thus each germ cell has 23 chromosomes. Meiosis is a process of chromosome reduction. Women's eggs will all have 22 autosomes and an X chromosome; men's sperm all have 22 autosomes and can have either an X or Y. In sexual recombination, when a sperm penetrates an egg, the resulting zygote normally has the appropriate 46 chromosomes. Thus gender of offspring is determined by the father's sperm.

***Abnormal Karyotypes.*** Abnormalities can be: (1) an abnormal total number of chromosomes in an individual's body cells; (2) structural aberrations resulting from breakage in one or more chromosomes; or (3) populations of cells of different chromosome numbers in the same individual (mosaicism).

Aneuploidies refers to deviations, greater or fewer, in number of chromosomes from the normal 46. The most common aneuploidy is trisomy 21, which accounts for the greatest number of chromosomal abnormalities in spontaneous abortions as well as in live births. Trisomies on most pairs are prenatally lethal. Similarly, monosomy, absence of one of a pair, resulting in fewer that 46 chromosomes, is virtually always prenatally lethal, except for Turner's syndrome, in which one X chromosome is missing (45,X). Even then, only one in 150 to 200 45,X embryos survives to full-term birth. The most common cause of aneuploidy is nondisjunction, the failure of a chromosome pair to split during formation of germ cells in meiosis. Thus one offspring germ cell will have a "double dose" of one chromosome and the other will have none. Anaphase lag can also produce monosomy.

Mosaicism results from nondisjunction occurring mitotically in a cell in an embryo in an early stage of development. As a result, if the embryo survives and continues to develop, it will have both normal and abnormal, generally trisomic, cell populations. Because of the presence of normal cells, individuals with mosaicism will generally show less severe symptoms than those with the pure syndrome.

The basis for nondisjunction is not known, but is presumed to be manifested biochemically. In nondisjunction Down's syndrome, approximately 80% of the cases result from maternal and 20% from paternal nondisjunction (Sperling, 1984). Since all autosomal trisomies (not just Down's syndrome) increase dramatically with maternal age, research focuses on factors that correlate with aging, including potential problems with aging oocytes themselves. Hypothesized links with irradiation, chemical agents, methods of birth control, and endocrine factors have not been fully confirmed, but some evidence suggests they play a role (Hassold & Jacobs, 1984).

Chromosomes may break, with material being either lost or attached to another chromosome. The most common structural aberrations are translocations, which result when two chromosomes break and parts of one are transferred to another. A reciprocal translocation occurs when two nonhomologous chromosomes exchange pieces. Individuals with such translocation chromosomes themselves have an appropriate balance of chromosomes and are phenotypically normal. Since they are carriers of a translocation chromosome, their offspring may suffer from duplication-deficiency syndromes, notably partial trisomies.

Important because of clinical implications are centric fusions, or Robertsonian translocations. Centric fusion occurs when two acrocentric chromosomes each break near the centromere and rejoin. Generally, the short arms of both and the centromere of one are lost. Again, individuals may be unaffected, although they have one fewer than normal chromosome, but they are carriers. Their offspring may have a trisomy syndrome. Monosomies are also possible, but appear to be prenatally lethal. The best known translocation is Down's syndrome, resulting from centric fusion of chromosome 21 with chromosome 14 or, less frequently, 15.

Several other structural aberrations also may occur. Simple loss of part of a chromosome may result in a deletion syndrome. Isochromosomes occur when instead of a chromosome pair dividing longitudinally through the centromere, it divides horizontally, producing two chromosomes with identical arms. Fertilization will produce a cell with three "p" or "q" arms and only one of the other. When the segment between two breaks in a chromosome becomes inverted, reversing the gene order, an inversion results. Ring chromosomes occur when both ends of a chromosome break off and the tips of the centric segment rejoin. The resulting circular chromosome is unstable and has material from both ends deleted.

*Standard Nomenclature.* Normal and abnormal human karyotypes are described using a standard system, general aspects and examples of which are given here. More detailed descriptions are in Cohen and Nadler (1983), Smith (1982), Vogel and Motulsky (1979), and most human genetics textbooks.

As shown in Table 1, the order of information is (1) total number of chromosomes; (2) sex chromosomes; and (3) any abnormalities. Extra or missing chromosomes are indicated by "+" and "−", respectively, before the affected chromosome's number; extra or missing parts are indicated by "+" and "−", respectively, after the affected part. Structural aberrations are indicated by a standard abbreviation followed, parenthetically, by the number of the affected chromosome(s). Then, also parenthetically, the affected arm(s) and, if known, the chromosomal band numbers, are stated. Mosaics are indicated by a (/) mark separating descriptions of the two cell populations.

## Abnormalities and Their Characteristics

Although chromosomal syndromes vary widely in their effects, the various types share some characteristics. Because much genetic material has been either added or is missing, many are lethal and most of the rest involve multiple and severe complications. However, as normal individuals vary in their physical and behavioral characteristics, so do those affected by chromosomal abnormalities. Not all will show even all of the major effects.

The description and characteristics of major cytogenic abnormalities occurring in live births are in Tables 2 and 3. It is important that different sources vary in their estimates of incidence and specification of major characteristics. In a number of cases, subsequent cases have led to changes in what were initially thought to be defining characteristics. For example, Cat-eye syndrome (trisomy 22p) was named for the striking coloboma of the iris seen originally. However, it has occurred only in a minority of the 40 cases that had been reported at the time of Smith's summary (1982).

*Chromosomal Aneuploidies.* The most common abnormalities are aneuploidies, involving an added or missing chromosome (Table 2). Multiple forms of some may occur. By far the most common is Down's syndrome (trisomy 21), but several others have been reported. Early death is common in all, and in some types virtually all die in early infancy. Although each has individual characteristics, all involve brain damage generally resulting in moderate to severe mental retardation, congenital heart disease, and malformed ears. Specific facial, limb, and digit abnormalities are also common. All increase dramaticaly in incidence with maternal age (Vogel & Motulsky, 1979).

Turner's and Klinefelter's syndromes have clear phenotypic characteristics and were described before the development of modern cytogenic techniques. Both are associated with absence of puberty and sterility. Unfortunately, as pointed out by Brown (1986), textbook authors have frequently described sex-chromosome aneuploidies in chapters on mental retardation. However, standard forms are associated with low average intelligence (IQ ≈ 90), not mental retardation, although incidence of mental retardation is higher than among the normal population. Many affected individuals will complete high school and college. Mosaic Turner females and Klinefelter males will be less affected. Klinefelter males and Poly-X females with extra X chromosomes above trisomy for sex chromosomes are much more adversely affected and likely to be retarded.

Klinefelter and Poly-X syndromes increase with maternal age (Hassold & Jacobs, 1984). However, incidence of neither Turner's nor XYY syndrome correlates with maternal age, consistent with largely paternal origin (Hassold & Jacobs, 1984; Simpson, 1982).

*Abnormal Parts of Chromosomes.* Several partial trisomy syndromes, involving extra chromosomal material, and deletion syndromes are known, as shown in Table 3. Mental retardation of some degree is common to all. Low birth weight and specific facial and digital anomalies are also frequent.

Of particular current interest is Fragile X syndrome, resulting from a constriction in the X chromosome, which cytogenic studies reveal to be relatively common. Associated with mental retardation in affected males, it appears to be second only to Down's syndrome as a cytogenic cause of mental retardation.

## Implications for Special Educators

As cytogenic analyses become more standard, increasing numbers of children will be identified as having some chromosomal disorder. Many minor ones will have few im-

### Table 1. Examples of Karyotype Nomenclature

| Karyotype | Description |
|---|---|
| 46,XX; 46,XY | Normal female and male |
| 47,XX,+21 | Female with trisomy 21 (Down's syndrome) |
| 46,XY/47,XY+21 | Male with mosaic trisomy 21 (Down's syndrome) |
| 46XY,+t(14q21q) | Male with Down's syndrome owed to centric-fusion type translocation between chromosomes 14 and 21 |
| 46,XX,del(5p) or 46,XX,5p− | Female with cri du chat owed to deletion of part of short arm of chromosome 5 |
| 46,XY,fra X(q27) | Male with fragile X syndrome, involving constriction at distal end of long arm of chromosome |

Table 2. Chromosomal Aneuploidies and Characteristics

| Syndrome | Incidence (live births) | Source | Characteristics |
|---|---|---|---|
| *Autosomal Trisomies* | | | |
| Trisomy 8 | Very rare | Mosaicism (mainly) | Variable height; MR (M → S); CHD; poor coordination; prominent forehead; deep-set eyes; digital abnormalities |
| Trisomy 9 | Very rare | Mosaicism (mainly) | LBW; MR (S); CHD; low-set malformed ears; joint contractures; majority die in infancy |
| Trisomy 13 (Patau syndrome) | 1:7000 to 20,000 | Nondisjunction | LBW; MR (S); CHD; apnea; seizures; bilateral cleft lip and/or palette; failure to thrive; majority die in infancy |
| Trisomy 18 (Edwards syndrome) | 1:8000 | Nondisjunction | Three times more frequent in females; LBW; MR (S); failure to thrive; CHD; prominent occiput, majority die in infancy |
| Trisomy 21 (Down's syndrome) | 1:650–800 | Nondisjunction—94% Mosaicism—2.4% Translocation—3.3% | MR (M → Mod); CHD; hypotonia; flat occiput; epicanthic fold; large tongue; above average infant death rate |
| Trisomy 22 | Very rare | Nondisjunction (?) | MR; growth retardation; microcephaly; CHD; cleft palate; digit abnormalities; majority die in infancy |
| *Sex Chromosome Aneuiploidies* | | | |
| Turner's syndrome | 1:10,000 | Various | Short stature; sterility; short webbed neck; broad, flat chest; IQ $\approx$ 90. |
| (45,X) | 57% of cases | Missing paternal X | |
| (45,X/46XX, others) | 12% of cases | Mosaicism | |
| (45,X/46,XY) | 4% of cases | Mosaicism | |
| (other) | 27% of cases | Inversion and deletion | |
| Klinefelter's syndrome | 1:1000 | Various | Sterility; hypogonadism; decreased facial and pubic hair; IQ $\approx$ 90; behavior problems |
| (47,XXY) | 82% of cases | Nondisjunction | |
| (48,XXXY) | 3% of cases | Nondisjunction | More problems with added X chromosomes |
| (49,XXXXY) | <1% of cases | Nondisjunction | |
| (47,XXY/46,XY) | 8% of cases | Mosaicism | |
| (Others) | 6% of cases | | |
| Poly X Syndrome | 1:1000 | Nondisjunction | No characteristic features; some delayed speech and motor development; more problems with added X chromosomes |
| (47,XXX) | 98 + % of cases | | |
| (48,XXXX) | Rare | | |
| 47,XYY syndrome | 1:1000 | Nondisjunction | Variable features; tall; impulsive behavior; IQ $\approx$ 90 |

MR = mental retardation (S = severe; Mod = moderate, M = mild); CHD = congenital heart disease; LBW = low birth weight. Information from Cohen and Nadler (1983), Gerald and Meryash (1983), and Smith (1982).

Table 3. Syndromes Involving Abnormal Part of Chromosomes

| Syndrome | Incidence | Source | Characteristics |
|---|---|---|---|
| *Autosomal Partial Trisomies* | | | |
| Trisomy 9p | Rare | Translocation (?) | MR (S); delayed growth and puberty; delayed language; digital abnormalities |
| Partial trisomy 10q | Rare | Translocation (?) | LBW; MR (S); flat occiput; digital abnormalities; CHD; 50% die in infancy |
| Trisomy 20p | Rare | Translocation (?) | MR (M → Mod); hypotonia; facial abnormalities; digital deformities |
| Cat-eye syndrome (trisomy 22p) | Rare | Translocation (?) | MR (M); emotional retardation; normal growth; CHD; coloboma of iris; other eye defects |
| *Autosomal Partial Deletion* | | | |
| 4p- | Rare(?) | Partial deletion | LBW; MR (S); beaked nose; microcephaly; cleft palate; hypotonia; seizures; early death |
| Cri du chat (5p-) | Rare | Partial deletion | LBW; MR (S); catlike cry; hypotonia; epicanthal folds; microcephaly |
| 9p- | Rare | Partial deletion | Normal growth; MR (S); micronathia; trignocephaly; wide-spaced nipples |
| 11p- (Andiria-Wilms Tumor Association) | Rare | Partial deletion | MR (Mod → S); growth deficiency; microcephaly; eye defects: micronathia; andiria; Wilms tumor |
| 13p- | Rare | Partial deletion | LBW; MR (S); failure to thrive; microcephaly; CHD; facial and digital abnormalities |
| 18p- | Rare | Partial deletion | Variability in effect; LBW; MR (variable); epicanthal folds; large, floppy ears |
| 18q- | Rare | Partial deletion | LBW; MR (S); seizures; CHD; microcephaly; limb, digital, and genital abnormalities |
| 21q- | Rare | Partial deletion | MR; hypertonia; growth retardation; microcephaly; micrognathia; large ears |
| 22q- | Rare | Partial deletion | MR; hypotonia; microcephaly; epicanthal folds; digital abnormalities |
| *Constriction Syndrome* | | | |
| Fragile X | 1:1000 males | Constriction at distal end of long arm of X chromosome | Long face; prominent chin; MR (M → S); developmental delay; language problems; specific learning problems |

MR = mental retardation (S = severe; Mod = moderate; M = mild); CHD = cogenital heart disease; LBW = low birth weight. Information from Cohen and Nadler (1983), Gerald and Meryash (1983), and Smith (1982).

plications for teachers. Others will be associated with general and specific intellectual deficits, coordination problems, and emotional disorders. Special educators and others in education generally may need to become familiar with the syndrome and standard nomenclature. Further, research will doubtless render some current knowledge incorrect and we must be ready to accept new information. It should be kept in mind that syndromes can induce stereotypes, and that affected children should be treated on the basis of their individual characteristics, not the general ones of a syndrome.

## REFERENCES

Brown, R. T. (1986). Etiology and development of exceptionality. In R. T. Brown & C. R. Reynolds (Eds.), *Psychological per-spectives on childhood exceptionality: A handbook* (pp. 181–229). New York: Wiley.

Cohen, M. M., & Nadler, H. L. (1983). Chromosomes and their abnormalities. In R. E. Behrman & V. C. Vaughn, III (Eds.), *Nelson textbook of pediatrics* (12th ed., pp. 288–310). Philadelphia: Saunders.

Gerald, P. S., & Meryash, D. L. (1983). Chromosomal disorders other than Down syndrome. In M. D. Levine, W. B. Carey, A. C. Crocker, & R. T. Gross (Eds.), *Developmental-behavioral pediatrics* (pp. 346–353). Philadelphia: Saunders.

Hassold, T. J., & Jacobs, P. A. (1984). Trisomy in man. *Annual Review of Genetics, 18*, 69–97.

Moore, K. L. (1982). *The developing human* (3rd ed.). Philadelphia: Saunders.

Painter, T. S. (1923). Studies in mammalian spermatogenesis. II. The spermatogenesis of man. *Journal of Experimental Zoology, 37*, 291–321.

Pueschel, S. M. (1983). The child with Down syndrome. In M. D. Levine, W. B. Carey, A. C. Crocker, & R. T. Gross (Eds.), *Developmental-behavioral pediatrics* (pp. 353–362). Philadelphia: Saunders.

Scarr, S., & Kidd, K. K. (1983). Developmental behavior genetics. In P. W. Mussen, M. M. Haith, & J. J. Campos (Eds.), *Handbook of child psychology: Infancy and developmental psychobiology* (4th ed., Vol. 2, pp. 345–433). New York: Wiley.

Simpson, J. L. (1982). Abnormal sexual differentiation in humans. *Annual Review of Genetics, 16,* 193–224.

Smith, D. W. (1982). *Recognizable patterns of human malformation* (2nd ed.). Philadelphia: Saunders.

Sperling, K. (1984). Frequency and origin of chromosome abnormalities in man. In G. Obe (Ed.), *Mutations in man* (pp. 128–146). Berlin and New York: Springer-Verlag.

Vogel, F., & Motulsky, A. G. (1979). *Human genetics.* Berlin and New York: Springer-Verlag.

ROBERT T. BROWN
*University of North Carolina,*
*Wilmington*

CHROMOSOMAL ABNORMALITIES
CRI DU CHAT
DOWN'S SYNDROME
ETIOLOGY
FRAGILE X SYNDROME
KLINEFELTER'S SYNDROME
TURNER'S SYNDROME
XYY SYNDROME

# CHRONIC ILLNESS IN CHILDREN

There are many chronic illnesses that children may suffer from. They include some but not all of the conditions regarded as being within the traditional scope of special education. Among important chronic illnesses are asthma, cystic fibrosis, diabetes, epilepsy, leukemia, juvenile rheumatoid arthritis, muscular dystrophy, sickle cell anemia, and thalassemia.

Each group within the broad constituencies of chronic illness by itself may not constitute a large number of children, but together they represent a large group. Thus, Gortmaker (1985) and Pless and Roghmann (1975) have estimated that some 10 to 15% of children have chronic health impairments of some sort. While many of these impairments are mild, others are severe and debilitating. Hobbs, Perrin, and Ireys (1985) estimate that at least 1 million children have severe diseases and that many of these diseases are chronic. This number expands if Hobbes et al. include children who might otherwise be considered physically handicapped, e.g., children with spina bifida, and others who have suffered severe and catastrophic trauma from injuries.

Many of the children who suffer from chronic illness, e.g, asthma or diabetes, have their health needs reasonably well met within the mainstream of society (by medical practitioners and public health agencies). The more severe of these illnesses, however, require more persistent, pervasive, and demanding care. The severity of a child's medical condition does not directly relate to the type and severity of the problem encountered. Some children with severe medical conditions may have little difficulty in participating within the mainstream of everyday living, including at school. Others with relatively mild physical or physiological disturbances may have their lives severely affected by their problems.

Educationally, some chronically ill children will be served under PL 94-142, either because their conditions are directly diagnosed as constituting handicaps requiring special education services, or because the consequences of their illnesses or injuries result in handicapping conditions that require such services. They are often served under the rubric of "other health impaired."

Where a chronically ill child's health condition, rather than the problems or limitations posed by a handicap, is a main consideration, and the child is not able to effectively participate in special education services within school settings, the child is likely to receive special education services via instruction in the home. In this situation, medical services are likely to be emphasized in their service delivery models.

Despite the fact that some chronically ill children are being effectively served under current special education laws and regulations, there are those who believe that the parents and policy makers who were the prime movers in the creation of state and federal programs for the education of the handicapped largely overlooked the needs of chronically ill children (Walker & Jacobs, 1985). Hobbes, Perrin, and Ireys claim that chronically ill children and youths have "shared in relatively little of the sustained attention given to children with other handicapping conditions, such as mentally retardation" (1985, pp. 4–5).

## REFERENCES

Gortmaker, S. L. (1985). Demography of chronic childhood diseases. In N. Hobbes & J. M. Perrin (Eds.), *Issues in the care of children with chronic illness: A sourcebook on problems, services and policies.* San Francisco: Jossey-Bass.

Hobbs, N., Perrin, J. M., & Ireys, H. T. (1985). *Chronically ill children and their families.* San Francisco: Jossey-Bass.

Pless, I. B., & Pinkerton, P. (1975). *Chronic childhood disorder: Promoting patterns of adjustment.* Chicago: Year Book Medical.

Pless, I. B., & Roghmann, K. J. (1971). Chronic illness and its consequences: Some observations based on three epidemiological surveys. *Journal of Pediatrics, 79,* 351–359.

Walker, D. K., & Jacobs, F. (1985). Public school programs for chronically ill children. In N. Hobbes & J. M. Perrin (Eds.),

*Issues in the care of children with chronic illness: A sourcebook on problems, services and policies.* San Francisco: Jossey-Bass.

DOUGLAS L. MANN
*V. A. Medical Center, Medical University of South Carolina*

## ASTHMA
## DIABETES
## OTHER HEALTH IMPAIRED

## CHURCH WORK WITH THE HANDICAPPED

During the early development of Christianity, the influence of Christ's healing works and the Apostle Paul's writings shaped the Christian attitude toward handicapped persons. However, as Christianity spread across Europe, especially during the Middle Ages, Christian attitudes varied. Religious teaching led to persecution (witnessed in the Inquisition), isolation (lest a clean person be tainted), and protection (many monasteries tended to the handicapped) (Hewett & Forness, 1977; Scheerenberger, 1982). It was during this time (1377 AD) that the first asylum (Hospital of St. Mary of Bethlehem, known as Bedlam) was founded. In the early part of the seventeenth century, St. Vincent dePaul initiated a program for "idiots." In the eighteenth century William Tuke, a Quaker, established a program for the humane treatment of the mentally retarded and the mentally ill (Scheerenberger, 1982). Also in the eighteenth century, the charitable work that had been the purview of the church began to receive attention from governments (Hewett & Forness, 1977). Religious organizations such as the St. Vincent dePaul Society, and much later the YMCA and YWCA, provided services, but their roles were diminished. Kowalski (1978) believes that today the government has nearly totally replaced the church as a provider of services to the handicapped.

According to Parks (1975), the doing of good works is viewed as one path to Christian salvation. It is this belief that has marked the history of church work with the handicapped. Recent changes can best be characterized as moving from provider of services to facilitator of integration. For example, the World Council of Churches (National Council of Churches, 1978) stated that the disabled ought to be full members of the church. The United Presbyterian Church in the United States (1979) committed the church to full integration and mandated physical adaptations for accessibility. In 1978 the U.S. Catholic bishops declared that the role of the church was to function as an advocate for handicapped persons (U.S. Catholic Conference, 1978).

In addition to the hundreds of religious schools that provide special education and residential services for handicapped children, and the hundreds of hospitals and medical care facilities that are church supported, there are a large number of organizations dedicated to service/advocacy for the handicapped. The following is a list of some of these organizations.

1. Board of Missions, Ministry of the Deaf, Lutheran Church–Missouri Synod
2. Department of Urban Ministries, Board of Missions, United Methodist Church
3. Ephphatha Missions for the Deaf and Blind
4. Episcopal Conference of the Deaf
5. International Catholic Deaf Association
6. National Congress of Jewish Deaf
7. Xavier Society for the Blind
8. National Apostolate with Mentally Retarded Persons
9. Advisory Committee on Ministry with Handicapped Persons, United States Catholic Conference
10. Task Force on Church and Disability, World Council of Churches

### REFERENCES

Hewett, F. M., & Forness, S. R. (1977). *Education of exceptional learners.* Boston: Allyn & Bacon.

Kowalski, A. P. (1978). The church and the handicapped. *America, 138*(9), 426–427.

National Council of Churches (1978). *The handicapped and the wholeness of the family of God.* New York: Author.

189th General Assembly of the United Presbyterian Church (1979). Overture 16: On responding to the concerns of the handicapped. *Church and Society, 69,* 22–34.

Parks, L. D. (1975). Barriers to normality for the handicapped adult in the United States. *Rehabilitation Literature, 36,* 108–111.

Scheerenberger, R. C. (1982). Treatment from ancient times to the present. In P. T. Cegelka & H. J. Prehm (Eds.), *Mental retardation: From categories to people* (pp. 44–75). Columbus, OH: Merrill.

Stine, E. (1979). The disabled, the new community and the world. *Church and Society, 69,*(3), 10–19.

United States Catholic Conference (1978). *Pastoral statement of the U.S. Catholic bishops on handicapped people.* Washington, DC: USCC Publications.

JAMES K. MCAFEE
*Pennsylvania State University*

## CITIZEN ADVOCACY GROUP

See ADVOCACY GROUP, CITIZEN.

# CIVIL RIGHTS OF THE HANDICAPPED

A handicapped person has certain rights guaranteed by law that relate to education, employment, health care, senior citizen activities, welfare, and any other or private services, programs, or activities that receive federal assistance.

Diamond (1979) has summarized the need for services and the specific rights of handicapped individuals from a personal perspective. She reports that handicapped persons have a right to private and public education at the elementary, secondary, and postsecondary levels. In addition to the education curriculum, supportive or rehabilitative services should be made available. When requiring a service, e.g., when dining out or shopping, the same courtesies should be extended to handicapped individuals as to others.

People with disabilities have the right to travel assisted or unassisted on airplanes, trains, buses, and taxi cabs. Persons with disabilities have a right to gain entrance to public facilities without being inconvenienced, and buildings should be free of architectural barriers. Handicapped individuals have a right to receive equal treatment by doctors and hospitals. This will require that medical personnel acquire understanding and knowledge of disabilities. Handicapped persons have a right to apply for any license (e.g., marriage, fishing) made available to nonhandicapped individuals without additional requirements or embarrassment. It is unlawful to discriminate against the handicapped regarding employment practices. It is also unlawful for the owner of commercial property to refuse to sell, rent, lease, or in any way discriminate because of a disability. As important as the services needed is the right to feel assured that the members of society will look on the handicapped as responsible people capable of making a contribution to society.

It is the responsibility of the Office for Civil Rights in the Department of Education and the Office for Civil Rights in the Department of Health and Human Services to enforce federal laws prohibiting discrimination against persons on the basis of race, color, national origin, sex, age, or handicap in federally assisted programs or activities, and to investigate discrimination complaints brought by individuals under these statutes.

**REFERENCE**

Diamond, S. (1979). Developmentally disabled persons: Their rights and their needs for services. In R. Wiegerink & J. Pelosi (Eds.), *Developmental disabilities: The DD movement* (pp. 15–25). Baltimore, MD: Brookes.

CECILIA STEPPE-JONES
*North Carolina Central
University*

## ACCESSIBILITY OF BUILDINGS

ACCESSIBILITY OF PROGRAMS
ATTITUDES TOWARDS THE HANDICAPPED
SOCIAL BEHAVIOR OF THE HANDICAPPED

## CLASS-ACTION SUITS

Class actions are lawsuits in which a class of persons is represented by one or more of its members. In federal and in most state courts, groups of persons who have similar interests in the law and fact of the lawsuit can sue or be sued through a representative who acts on their behalf. A class action offers the following: the benefits of a clear resolution of a specific issue; the convenience of a useful method to assert legal rights in cases that have common interest where small individual claims might otherwise preclude judicial relief; and the saving of time, money, and effort by eliminating repetitious lawsuits (Redden & Vernon, 1980).

General requirements of a class action follow: the representative class must be large, although no specific number has been determined, so that it would be impractical to name each individual as a party to be brought before the court; the court must be able to clearly recognize the group as a class by virtue of its well-defined interests; and members of the class must raise the same questions of law and fact. The existence of an ascertainable class is evidenced by its certification by the court, which is necessary for the maintenance of a class action. All persons who will be affected by a judgment in a class action must be notified that such an action has commenced; each is provided an opportunity to present his or her side of the case. The court's ruling in a class-action suit applies to all members of that class unless a member has requested an option indicating that he or she does not wish to be bound by the specified court action (Payne & Patton, 1980; Redden & Vernon, 1980).

Court rulings in class-action suits have stimulated both litigation and legislation on behalf of handicapped individuals. During the 1950s courts were confronted with class actions concerning the civil rights of handicapped children and adults. The majority of the actions were focused on the public's responsibility to provide education and treatment for handicapped citizens. The legal doctrines which courts have relied in substantiating the right to an education for the handicapped stem, in part, from the Supreme Court ruling in *Brown v. Board of Education*. The Supreme Court ruled in this landmark decision that all children are constitutionally entitled to an equal educational opportunity (Abeson & Bolick, 1974; Kirp, 1976). Subsequent class-action suits addressed the enforcement of the ruling in *Brown v. Board of Education* (Martin, 1980). Handicapped children were no longer denied a public education, however, many issues remained unresolved, and new issues surfaced in the courts, as well. For example, several state laws still regarded the severely handicapped as uneducable and thereby excluded this group from public schools. Questions regarding racial overrepresentation in special programs were also subjects of extensive litigation (Kirp, 1976).

The major legislation that governs our present delivery of services to exceptional children, PL 94-142 (1975), precipitated litigation that was more diverse and more individualized, thereby decreasing the numbers of representative classes. With the advent of PL 94-142, class-action suits declined and individual legal claims were filed in matters of due process, Individual Education Plan (IEP) challenges, placement, and related services. In the years since 1983, issues that had not previously been addressed have been presented in the courts; for example, payment of attorney fees and damages and a renewed interest in placement (Lufler, 1984).

## REFERENCES

Abeson, A., & Bolick, N. (1974). *A continuing summary of pending and completed litigation regarding the education of handicapped children*, Reston, VA: Council for Exceptional Children.

Kirp D. (1976). *Trends in education: The special child goes to court.* Columbus, OH: University Council for Educational Administration.

Lufler, H. (1984). Chapter 4—Pupils. In P. K. Piele (Ed.), *The yearbook of school law*. Topeka, KA: National Organization on Legal Problems of Education.

Martin, R. (1980). *Educating handicapped children the legal mandate*. Champaign, IL: Research Press.

Patten J., & Patton J. (1981). *Mental retardation*. Columbus, OH: Merrill.

Redden, K. & Vernon, E. (1980). *Modern legal glossary*. Charlottesville, V.A. Michie.

FRANCES T. HARRINGTON
*Radford University*

**BROWN v. BOARD OF EDUCATION**
**LARRY P.**
**EDUCATION FOR ALL HANDICAPPED CHILDREN ACT OF 1975**

# CLASSROOM MANAGEMENT

Broadly conceived, classroom management refers to the orderly organization of materials and activities and the development of acceptable student behavior within the school learning environment. Although a deceptively simple concept, any consideration of the purposes and techniques of classroom management suggests numerous other educational concerns. Classroom management techniques must be in harmony with the school's perception of the nature and purpose of instruction and must satisfy a significant number of ethical and legal concerns. Similarly, the school's organizational structure must be constructed in a manner that will allow meeting the psychoeducational assumptions implicit in any selected alternative. For these reasons, classroom management techniques must be selected with regard to many considerations. Few authors advocate a single approach as optimal for all settings.

Although classroom management can be broadly conceived, the usual topic of interest is the behavior of students and, specifically, discipline in the classroom. Clearly, the control of student behavior receives far more emphasis than other potential events that could be associated with classroom management. Public opinion consistently notes school discipline, often described as student control, to be a major problem in schools. In addition, a 1981 survey of teachers conducted by the National Education Association found 90% of the respondents indicating negative instructional outcomes as a result of student misbehavior. Cruickshank (1981) found similar results in that the control of students was seen to be one of the five most important issues identified by teachers throughout the course of a 15-year longitudinal study. Clearly then, classroom management is now virtually synonymous with discipline. Why discipline is a problem in contemporary U.S. schools is not fully understood. However, Charles (1985) and Jones and Tanner (1981) offer an analysis of the origin of the problem.

Given the widespread concern for discipline in the schools, it is not surprising that many models of classroom management have emerged. Since most of the efforts of classroom management techniques are devoted to redirecting atypical behavior, most currently advocated procedures were derived from intervention strategies used in laboratory or clinical settings. Relatively few of the available procedures were initially developed within the classroom, although there are exceptions (e.g., Cantor & Cantor, 1976; Kounin, 1977). In conceptualizing variations in individuals, Rhodes and Tracy (1972) enumerated several general models that emphasize a perspective on the causes and alteration of behavior.

Almost all current approaches to classroom management are derived from one of the following perceptions. The *biophysical model* emphasizes the role of biology as a determinant of behavior. Interventions drawn from this model emphasize the control of environmental stimuli to a limited extent, and tend to rely more on the effects of diets, the elimination of environmental hazards to biological processes, genetic counseling, and the use of psychotropic drugs. The *sociological model* emphasizes the context of the school in society. This approach stresses the role of society in determining the nature of behaviors in need of control and the social forces operating to promote or inhibit specific behaviors. Classroom management techniques drawn from this viewpoint tend to emphasize the influence of, for example, community and peer group on individual behavior. The *behavioral model* emphasizes, in particular, the immediate consequences of behavior for its role in the subsequent occurrence or lack of occurrence of behavior. Classroom management strategies drawn from this influence generally emphasize the role of the teacher (or other significant individuals) in the provision of consequences to particular behaviors. Control is sought by the careful manipulation of consequences. The *ecological model* emphasizes the context of behavior, noting that behavior never occurs in isolation and that naturally occurring events coerce specific types of behavior, e.g., a chair promotes sitting behavior, close proximity may promote speaking behavior. Finally, *the psychodynamic model* represents many alternative viewpoints that conceptualize the individual as possessing a dynamic intrapsychic life. The personality emerging from these inner forces becomes the basis for behavior. Personality formation and its ultimate effect on behavior is interpreted differently across the many models. However, virtually all psychodynamic models see the basis for behavioral change as the personal realization of the causes of one's behavior.

All of the above models have had significant influence on the development of techniques for classroom management. The sociological and ecological models, though theoretically suggesting great promise, have generally not spawned specific procedures widely placed into practice. The biophysical model has largely remained the purview of physicians. Both the psychodynamic and the behavioral models have, however, demonstrated immense appeal to educators and have generated many variations in approach. Of the two, the behavioral model is now the more dominant in the special education literature. Early conceptualizations that relied on the teacher's control of contingencies have been augmented in recent years through the widespread use of modeling techniques (e.g., Bandura, 1969), cognitive behavior modification (e.g., Meichenbaum, 1977), group contingency programs (e.g., Litow & Pumroy, 1975), and other advances. Significant problems in transfer of training and generalization of learned behaviors remain obstacles to the use of the approach. An excellent overview of representative classroom management techniques can be found in Charles (1985) and Walker and Shea (1984).

## REFERENCES

Bandura, A. (1969). *Principles of behavior modification.* New York: Holt.

Cantor, L., & Cantor, M. (1976). *Assertive discipline: A take charge approach for today's educator.* Seal Beach, CA: Cantor and Associates.

Charles, C. M. (1985). *Building classroom discipline: From models to practice* (2nd ed.). New York: Longman.

Cruickshank, D. (1981). What we know about teachers' problems. *Educational Leadership, 38,* 402–405.

Jones, R. S., & Tanner, L. N. (1981). Classroom discipline: The unclaimed legacy. *Phi Delta Kappan, 62,* 494–497.

Kounin, J. (1977). *Discipline and group management in classrooms.* New York: Holt.

Litow, L., & Pumroy, D. K. (1975). A brief review of classroom group-oriented contingencies. *Journal of Applied Behavior Analysis, 8,* 341–347.

Meichenbaum, D. (1977). *Cognitive-behavior modification: An integrative approach.* New York: Plenum.

Rhodes, W. L., & Tracy, M. L. (Eds.). (1972). *A study of child variance: Conceptual models.* Ann Arbor, MI: University of Michigan.

Walker, J. E., & Shea, T. M. (1984). *Behavior management: A practical approach for educators.* (3rd ed.). St. Louis: Times Mirror/Mosby.

TED L. MILLER
*University of Tennessee,*
*Chattanooga*

**APPLIED BEHAVIOR ANALYSIS**
**BEHAVIOR ASSESSMENT**
**DISCIPLINE**

## CLAUSEN, JOHS (1913–     )

Johs Clausen was born in Bergen, Norway. He is a psychophysiologist and researcher in mental retardation. In 1939 he obtained his MA at the University of Oslo and in 1956 his PhD at the Faculty of Medicine, University of Oslo. Between 1949 and 1951, Clausen was a research fellow at Columbia University. He participated in the Columbia Greystone Project and the New York State Brain Research Project. He was also a research fellow with the Norwegian Research Council from 1953 to 1955; an associate scientist at the New York Psychiatric Institute from 1955 to 1966; and research psychologist, chief of psychological research, and research administrator at the Training School at Vineland (American Institute of Mental Studies). Clausen conducted research on ability structures and autonomic nervous functions in mentally retarded individuals. From 1966 to 1984, Clausen was chief research scientist, department of psychology, New York State Institute for Basic Research in Mental Retardation. He is a member of the American Psychological Association, Eastern Psychological Association, American Association for the Advancement of Science, American Association on Mental Deficiency, Society for Physiological Research, New York Academy of Science, and the American Academy on Mental Retardation. Clausen is the author of *Ability Structure and Subgroups in Mental Retardation* as well as more than 55 scientific studies.

REFERENCE

Clausen, J. (1966). *Ability structure and subgroups in mental retardation*. Washington, DC: Spartan Books.

IVAN Z. HOLOWINSKY
*Rutgers University*

## CLEFT LIP/PALATE

The phenomenon of cleft lip and palate is a rather frequent one all over the world: 0.1% of all neonates are born with a more or less severe cleft, ranging from a cleft uvula or a partly cleft upper lip to a two-sided complete cleft of upper lip, jaw, and hard and soft palate. Normally, three main groups are discerned: cleft lip only (CL), cleft palate only (CP), and cleft lip and palate combined (CLP). Cleft lip and palate malformations are congenital and originate in the fourth to seventh week (CL) and in the seventh to twelfth week (CP) of embryonic development. Although in some cases viral, medical, and X-ray influences may play a role in causing these malformations, they are generally believed to have a hereditary basis. The chance of cleft lip and palate increases accordingly as the occurrence of clefts in a family are more frequent and more severe, and with the closeness of the relationship (mother or father). The occurrence of clefts is more frequent in boys than in girls and, moreover, types of clefts are not equally divided between the sexes.

Problems arising from being born with a cleft lip and palate are highly dependent on the part of the world in which the baby is born. In Third World countries, where no surgery is done on cleft lip and palate children, the main problem is survival and nourishment. In highly developed countries, the problems for cleft lip and palate children mainly concern communication and socialization. But even in these countries, a large differentiation can be found in the treatment of cleft lip and palate children depending on the scientific ideas and theories of the treating medical team. However, for all newborn babies with cleft lip and palate, the first problem encountered is the feeding, because of the difficulties in sucking and swallowing. In Third World countries, infants depend entirely on breast feeding: if the baby is kept in a somewhat deviant feeding position (almost vertically sitting on the mother's lap or nearly horizontally held against the body of the mother), breast feeding is generally considered to be successful. Breast feeding is advisable in highly developed countries as well, because apart from other advantages, it is highly beneficial to the mother-child bond. In case of insurmountable breast feeding problems, feeding by means of special spoons and cups is preferred to bottles with long nipples (so-called lamb's nipples). Sometimes the infant will be provided with an obturator, a small plastic plate covering the cleft in the palate. This may help normal sucking, but it must be frequently renewed and readjusted because of the growing of the infant's mouth.

In most countries where surgery is applied, the child passes through a whole program of treatment and rehabilitation during the first years of life, often starting with healing of the lip followed by closure of the soft palate some months later, and sometimes the hard palate as well. The schedule and type of treatment depends to a large extent on the philosophy of the medical team: for example, the plastic surgeon will stress the aesthetic and visible aspects, the orthodontist the dental aspects, the speech pathologist the importance of the development of language and speech, etc. Nevertheless, it will be clear that the best results are achieved by an interdisciplinary team of experts in close cooperation, all aiming to establish normal appearance, normal dental function, and good language and communication skills. The whole rehabilitation program is normally spread over more than 15 years.

As for the intellectual abilities of cleft lip and palate children, many prejudices have to be disproved. Visible congenital deformations, especially of the head, are often wrongly associated with poor mental capacities. In recent research, cleft lip and palate children were found to have at least average general intelligence, with no intellectual differences between boys and girls. The lowest scoring group are children with cleft palate only (CP), the group with no visible abnormalities.

As for the speech and language development and related verbal expression abilities of cleft lip and palate children, a clear retardation is found compared with normal children. One of the causes might be hearing problems, since cleft lip and palate children have increased chances of inflammation of the middle ear combined with hearing impairment. Nevertheless, these possible hearing losses are not considered to be the main cause of the speech and language retardation. Nor are the pronunciation problems that result from the abnormalities of the speech production mechanism, although a thorough speech training program will nearly always be necessary. No one-to-one relationship can be found between the severity of the malformation or the proportions of the cleft and the degree of retardation in language and speech development. More and more the psychosocial development of the child is believed to be a ground for speech and language problems too.

Because interaction between parent and child is the cradle of the development of communication, it is clear that acceptance of the infant and his or her problems is a must. The birth of a child with a cleft lip and palate will undoubtedly cause the parents a mental shock. The emotional problems of the parents, their anxieties and concerns, require immediate professional counseling to create safe and adjusted surroundings for the child. Well-balanced interaction between parents and infant provides the possibility for the cleft palate child to develop normal linguistic, communicative, and social skills.

**REFERENCES**

Brookshire, B. L., Lynch, J. I., & Fox, D. R. (1984). *A parent-child cleft palate curriculum.* Tigard, OR: C. C. Publications.

Bzoch, K. R. (Ed.). (1979). *Communicative disorders related to cleft lip and palate* (2nd. ed.). Boston: Little, Brown.

Grabb, W. C., Rosenstein, S. W., & Bzoch, K. R. (Eds.). (1971). *Cleft lip and palate.* Boston: Little, Brown.

Heineman-de Boer, J. A. (1985). Cleft palate children and intelligence. Lisse, Netherlands: Swets & Zeitlinger.

F. J. KOOPMANS-VAN BEINUM
*Amsterdam, The Netherlands*

**PHYSICAL ANOMALIES**
**LANGUAGE DISORDERS, EXPRESSIVE**
**LANGUAGE DEFICIENCIES AND DEFICITS**

## CLELAND, CHARLES C. (1924–       )

Charles Cleland received his BS in political science in 1950, and his MS in educational psychology in 1951, from Southern Illinois University. Cleland's doctoral work in educational psychology and general and industrial management at the University of Texas, Austin (1957), presented a theme that has been reflected in most of his work.

After a year as chief psychologist at the Lincoln State School (Illinois), Cleland returned to Texas to the Austin State School. In 1959 he was promoted to superintendent of the Abilene State School, where he stayed for four years until joining the faculty in the educational psychology department at the University of Texas, Austin.

Since that time, Cleland has been a professor of special education and educational psychology, teaching courses primarily in the areas of mental retardation, residential

**Charles C. Cleland**

care, and management of service facilities. Although Cleland does not view himself as researcher (personal communication, June 26, 1985), his 250 articles, chapters in books, monographs, and books on a wide variety of subjects may prove otherwise. His principal publications include *Mental Retardation: Developmental Approach, Exceptionalities Through the Lifespan*, and *Mental Retardation Approaches to Institutional Change.*

**REFERENCES**

Cleland, C. C. (1978). *Mental retardation: A developmental approach.* Englewood Cliffs, NJ: Prentice-Hall.

Cleland, C. C., & Schwartz, J. D. (1969). *Mental retardation approaches to institutional change.* New York: Grune & Stratton.

Cleland, C. C., & Schwartz, J. D. (1982). *Exceptionalities through the lifespan.* New York: Macmillan.

ELAINE FLETCHER-JANZEN
*Texas A&M University*

## CLERC, LAURENT (1785–1869)

Laurent Clerc, deaf from the age of one, was educated at the Institution Nationale des Sourdes Muets in Paris; following graduation served as a teacher there. He traveled to the United States with Thomas Hopkins Gallaudet to open the nation's first school for the deaf, now the American School for the Deaf, at Hartford, Connecticut, in 1817. Schooled in the teaching methods of Epée and Sicard, Clerc was the school's first teacher and was responsible for the training of new teachers.

Clerc was the first educated deaf person to be seen in the United States. He exemplified the potential of education for the deaf, and was influential in the movement to establish public responsibility for the education of the deaf.

**REFERENCES**

Lane, H. (1984). *When the mind hears.* New York: Random House.

Turner, W. W. (1871). Laurent Clerc. *American Annals of the Deaf, 15,* 14–25.

PAUL IRVINE
*Katonah, New York*

## CLINICAL EVALUATION OF LANGUAGE FUNCTIONS (CELF)

The Clinical Evaluation of Language Functions (CELF) (Semel & Wiig, 1980) is a diagnostic battery designed to assess selected language functions in the areas of syntax, semantics, memory, word finding and retrieval, and phonology (supplementary subtests). These areas are assessed both as production (expressive) and processing (receptive) skills. The 11 subtests and two supplementary subtests are criterion-referenced to identify a child's strengths and weaknesses against criteria based on the performances of normal and language-disordered children and adolescents. Also included are criteria for deciding when further assessment in a given area is warranted, formats for analyzing error responses, and suggested tasks for informally testing the same factors probed in each subtest (extension testing).

The test was originally standardized on a group of 139 children and adolescents grades Kindergarten to 12, only 50 of whom were considered normal in the areas of language and academic performance. Test-retest reliability varies by subtest, ranging from .56 to .98, but it was based only on a group of second-graders. Validity was examined through correlations with several other tests of language, with correlations in the moderate range. The publisher has provided four updates for the test, and scores can now be reported by age or grade equivalence, standard score, and percentile rank, and can be interpreted using means and standard deviations. Additionally, Update 2 reported a new standardization sample of 1378 students, all considered normal.

Strengths of the test include ease of administration, breadth of areas of assessment, and inclusion of items making the test appropriate for older children (through 12th grade). Weaknesses include the need to consult the more recent updates to derive a variety of interpretations of raw scores, minimal evidence of test reliability and validity (Spekman & Roth, 1984), and lack of a theoretical basis for the selection of test items and subtest areas (Muma, 1984).

### REFERENCES

Darley, F. L. (Ed.). (1979). *Evaluation of appraisal techniques in speech and language pathology.* Reading, MA: Addison-Wesley.

Muma, J. R. (1984). Semel and Wiig's CELF: Construct validity? *Journal of Speech and Hearing Disorders 49,* 101–103.

Semel, E. M., & Wiig E. H. (1980). *Clinical evaluation of language functions.* Columbus, OH: Merrill.

Spekman, N. J., & Roth, F. P. (1984). Clinical evaluation of Language Functions (CELF) Diagnostic Battery: An analysis and critique. *Journal of Speech and Hearing Disorders 49,* 97–100.

MARGO E. WILSON
*Lexington, Kentucky*

## CLINICAL INTERVIEW

Assessment interviews are conducted to identify and define current problems, to collect information concerning why current problems exist, or to make a diagnostic decision. The focus can be on information the client provides directly (content interviews), or on information that the client's behavior provides (process interviews, also known as mental status exams), or both. Manuals for conducting process interviews with children include Beiser's (1962), Goodman & Sours' (1967), and Greenspan's (1981). Content interviews have been emphasized in the literature on behavioral assessment of adult disorders (e.g., Haynes, 1978); prior to 1975, however, there were few references to content interviews with children. Since then, a number of studies have demonstrated that children can directly provide reliable information (e.g., Abu-Saad & Holzemer, 1981; Herjanic & Campbell, 1977), particularly when describing publicly observable events.

As with any assessment instrument, the quality of an interview depends on getting accurate information with the least amount of error. Three major sources of error are present in the interview: the interviewer, the interviewee, and the interview setting. One obvious interviewer error is the failure to ask for necessary information. It is unlikely that information that is not specifically asked for will be obtained; thus the information needed from an interview should be well planned. Some interviews are highly structured (e.g., the Vineland Adaptive Behavior Scales); others use rough organizing frameworks such as BASIC ID (Lazarus, 1973) or S-O-R-K-C (Kanfer & Saslow, 1969); the interview also may be organized ad hoc by the clinician. Several structured interviews for the assessment of child psychopathology exist (e.g., Edelbrock & Costello, 1984; Orvaschel, Sholomskas, & Weissman, 1980). The specific plan an interviewer uses will depend on the interviewer's purpose and theoretical model. The interviewer, however, must be careful not to lead the client's responses; only information to which the client has access should be asked for, and it should be clear to the client that no one response is favored by the interviewer. A second information-gathering error is the failure to recognize and clarify ambiguous responses. This source of error can be reduced by asking questions that clarify contradictory information.

A great deal of information can be given during interviews; thus, the storage and retrieval system used by the clinician is a third potential source of error. Audio or video recording ensures that all information given is stored, but recordings are cumbersome to review, may have adverse effects on rapport, and are not readily available in some settings. Notetaking is more efficient and can be more easily organized, but notetaking can also detract from rapport with some clients. Notetaking also has the effect of implicitly reinforcing clients for giving specific types of information, an advantage if this is information that the clinician needs. The interviewer may decide to neither record nor take notes; but the interviewer then needs to rely more heavily on specific memory strategies, e.g., making frequent summary statements of known information, and later writing notes.

An interviewer may use tactics that initially result in accurate information, but the information quality will deteriorate throughout the interview if the interviewer does not maintain a relationship in which the client continues to want to give accurate information. Maintaining warmth, empathy, genuineness and person reinforcement may help maintain rapport. The interviewer must remain alert to changes in affect and change tactics to maintain an appropriate relationship.

Sources of interviewee error fall into categories of effects of developmental deficits, client perceptions of the nature and consequences of the interview, and fatigue. To the extent that the effects of these sources of error are under some control by the interviewer, they represent interviewer errors of control. Clinicians should be alert to signs of fatigue and other physiological effects; interview sessions should be a short as possible and conducted at times when the client is rested and least distractible. Children and developmentally delayed adults have deficits in their knowledge of vocabulary and conversational conventions (Conti & Camras, 1984; Dickson, 1981), in their understanding of what a listener needs to know (Flavell et al., 1968), and in the facility with which they can meet the cognitive demands of answering questions (Shatz, 1977). These sources of error can be partly controlled by ensuring that vocabulary used by the interviewer is familiar to the client, by keeping cognitive demands low (e.g., by asking for single bits of information at once rather than multiple bits), and by clearly explaining what information the interviewer knows and what information is needed. There is evidence that closed-ended or multiple-response format questions (e.g., "When the other kids call you that name, do you feel angry, sad, or something else?") obtain more reliable responses from developmentally younger persons than open-ended questions (e.g., "How do you feel when they call you that name?"), and some evidence that open-ended questions produce more refusals and less complete information than closed-ended ones (Ammons, 1950; Miller & Bigi, 1979). However, there is a tendency for developmentally delayed adults and children to give acquiescent responses to yes-no questions, and to give the last choice in multiple-response formats (Sigelman et al., 1981). There is a also a tendency for normal children under six to assume that they understand ambiguous questions and not ask clarifying questions (Robinson & Robinson, 1984). These deficits imply that when interviewing young children and developmentally delayed older persons, clinicians need to ask closed-ended questions, but avoid yes-no formats; clinicians should also be alert to a possible response bias. Sigelman et al. (1981) found a picture-choice format to be the most reliable, but nonverbal formats for interviewing may not always be available.

The interviewee's expectations about the interview and about what will be done with the information obtained is also likely to affect validity. Clinicians should ensure that clients understand what will happen during the interview, why the interview is being conducted, and how the information will be used, and should elicit any concerns the client has about the interview. In interpreting data, the clinician should consider the likelihood that the client may have been giving biased responses because of the demands of the setting; for example, when interviewing a client in a dormitory about involvement in an incident of stealing, it is likely that the client will give biased information, particularly if the client believes such information will be shared with houseparents. Bias owed to ecological demand characteristics can be reduced if the interview is designed so that the client believes the interview will be ecologically helpful. If the clinician begins the interview by asking whether there are problems in the setting that the client would like to have ameliorated, the client is more likely to be cooperative in sharing information.

The interview setting influences the interview, and can therefore be a source of error. Interviewer and interviewee should generally be alone unless the presence of other persons is expected to enhance the quality of the interview (e.g., a young child may be very fearful unless mother is present). The clinician needs to consider how the presence of other persons may affect the demand characteristics of the interview when interpreting the results. The client's prior experience with the clinician may also bias results; this problem is minimal in situations in which interviewer and interviewee have never met. The location of the interview may also affect the information that is elicited; interviewing a child in a classroom, for example, may generate a client expectation that the interviewer is a teacher; on the other hand, the setting can be used to prompt information that may not be normally accessible. It's possible, for example, that a child will give more reliable information about what has occurred in a classroom when the child is interviewed alone in the classroom. The setting for the interview should be carefully planned by the clinician.

## REFERENCES

Abu-Saad, H., & Holzemer, W. L. (1981). Measuring children's self-assessment of pain. *Issues in Comprehensive Pediatric Nursing, 5,* 337–349.

Ammons, R. B. (1950). Reactions in a projective doll-play interview of white males two to six years of age to differences in skin color and facial features. *Journal of Genetic Psychology, 76,* 323–341.

Beiser, H. R. (1962). Psychiatric diagnostic interviews with children. *Journal of the American Academy of Child Psychiatry, 1,* 656–670.

Conti, D. J., & Camras, L. A. (1984). Children's understanding of conversational principles. *Journal of Experimental Child Psychology, 38,* 456–463.

Dickson, W. P. (1981). Introduction: Toward an interdisciplinary conception of children's communication abilities. In W. P.

Dickson (Ed.), *Children's oral communication abilities* (pp. 1–10). New York: Academic.

Edelbrock, C., & Costello, A. J. (1984). *A review of structured psychiatric interviews for children.* Unpublished manuscript.

Flavell, J. H., Botkin, P. T., Fry, C. L., Wright, J. W., & Jarvis, P. E. (1968). *The development of role-taking and communication skills in children.* New York: Wiley.

Goodman, J., & Sours, J. (1967). *The child mental status examination.* New York: Basic Books.

Greenspan, S. I. (1981). *The clinical interview of the child.* New York: McGraw-Hill.

Haynes, S. N. (1978). The behavioral interview. In S. N. Haynes (Ed.), *Principles of behavioral assessment.* New York: Gardner Press.

Herjanic, B., & Campbell, W. (1977). Differentiating psychiatrically disturbed children on the basis of a structured interview. *Journal of Abnormal Child Psychology, 5,* 127–134.

Kanfer, F. H., & Saslow, G. (1969). Behavioral diagnosis. In C. M. Franks (Ed.). *Behavior theory: appraisal and status.* New York: McGraw-Hill.

Lazarus, A. (1973). Multimodal behavior therapy: Treating the BASIC ID. *Journal of Nervous and Mental Disease, 156,* 404–411.

Miller, P. H., & Bigi, L. (1979). The development of children's understanding of attention. *Merrill-Palmer Quarterly, 25,* 235–250.

Orvaschel, H., Sholomskas, D., & Weissman, M. M. (1980). *The assessment of psychopathology and behavioral problems in children: A review of epidemiological and clinical research (1967–1979).* Rockville, MD: National Institute of Mental Health, Division of Biometry and Epidemiology (DHHS Publication No. (ADM)80-1037).

Robinson, E. J., & Robinson, W. P. (1984). Realizing you don't understand: A further study. *Journal of Child Psychology and Psychiatry, 25,* 621–627.

Shatz, M. (1977). The relationship between cognitive processes and the development of communication skills. *Nebraska Symposium on Motivation, 25,* 1–42.

Sigelman, C. K., Schoenrock, C. J., Winer, J. L., Spanhel, C. L., Hromas, S. G., Martin, P. W., Budd, E. C., & Bensberg, G. J. (1981). In R. H. Bruininks, C. E. Meyers, B. B. Sigford, & K. C. Lakin (Eds.), *Deinstitutionalization and community adjustment of mentally retarded people.* Washington, DC: American Association on Mental Deficiency.

JOHN MACDONALD
*Eastern Kentucky University*

ASSESSMENT
MENTAL STATUS EXAMS

# CLINICAL PSYCHOLOGY

The diversity of the field of clinical psychology as it has evolved almost a century following its conception makes it difficult to provide a concise description of this subspecialty of psychology. A useful, albeit far from comprehensive, definition of the scope of clinical psychology is provided by Goldenberg (1973):

> The subspecialty of Clinical Psychology may be defined as that branch of psychology which deals with the search for and application of psychological principles aimed at understanding the uniqueness of the individual client or patient, reducing his personal distress, and helping him to function more meaningfully and effectively. (p. 3)

Lightner Witmer is credited with being the first person to use the term clinical psychology in his reference to the clinical application of psychological principles and theories. Witmer established the first psychological clinic at the University of Pennsylvania in 1896 for the purpose of studying children with physical disabilities and mental retardation to assist them in their school achievement. In addition, he proposed that the psychology clinic serve as a training facility for educators and psychologists.

During the next several decades, the major role of clinical psychologists was to provide psychological testing, primarily intellectual assessment, to children with learning problems. They worked mainly in university-based clinics. By World War II, clinical psychologists had become involved in psychiatric hospitals and specialized settings for the mentally retarded and physically handicapped.

World War II was one of the most important forces in the development of clinical psychology as it was a unique opportunity for the expansion and systematic training of clinical psychologists. Services needed because of the large number of men returning to Veterans Administration hospitals with numerous psychiatric problems provided the impetus for the funding and growth of training programs in clinical psychology.

In 1949 the first conference on training clinical psychologists was held in Boulder, Colorado. This conference endorsed the training of clinical psychologists within a scientist-professional model, placing an equal emphasis on proficiency in research and professional practice. A PhD in psychology from a university-based graduate program and a supervised, year-long internship was regarded as the standard of training (Raimy, 1950). While the majority of clinical psychologists continue to be trained according to the guidelines set forth at the Boulder conference, alternative training models have appeared during the past decade. These new programs (doctor of psychology program and autonomous professional schools of psychology) emphasize training in the professional skills necessary for the delivery of a wide range of psychological services (Peterson, 1968). Because of their recent development, it is difficult, at this time, to evaluate the impact of these new training programs on the field of clinical psychology.

Contemporary clinical psychologists are considerably broader in their roles and functions than their predecessors of 40 years ago. In addition, the settings in which they are employed and the scope of the problems with which they work is diverse, reflecting the ever expanding nature of the field. Among the settings in which clinical psychologists practice are psychiatric hospitals and clinics, general hospitals, child guidance clinics, community mental health centers, private practice offices, schools and universities, courts, adult and juvenile correction facilities, rehabilitation centers, and business and industry.

Clinical psychologists work with problems that vary across the lifespan, from infancy to advanced age. The problems they address include social and interpersonal difficulties, sexual dysfunctions, marital discord, developmental disorders and learning problems, substance abuse, child-rearing problems, organic brain impairments, vocational problems, and difficulties in coping with stressful experiences.

The activities in which clinical psychologists engage can be subsumed under the headings of assessment and psychodiagnostic testing, treatment, research, teaching, consultation, program evaluation, and administration. Psychological testing has been deemphasized in recent years. Today, the most frequent activity of clinical psychologists is treatment (Bernstein & Nietzel, 1980). The locus of treatment or intervention may be an individual, a group of persons with similar problems, the family, or the larger community. In recent years, the prevention of psychological problems also has gained greater importance in the activities of clinical psychologists. While there are a variety of schools or systems of therapy to which clinical psychologists subscribe, they can generally be grouped within one of three broad theoretical orientations: (1) psychodynamic, (2) behavioral, and (3) existential-humanistic (Korchin, 1976).

### REFERENCES

Bernstein, D. A., & Nietzel, M. T. (1980). *Introduction to clinical psychology.* New York: McGraw-Hill.

Goldenberg, H. (1973). *Contemporary clinical psychology.* Monterey, CA: Brooks/Cole.

Korchin, S. J. (1976). *Modern clinical psychology: Principles of intervention in the clinic and community.* New York: Basic.

Peterson, D. R. (1968). The doctor of psychology program at the University of Illinois. *American Psychologist, 23,* 511–516.

Raimy, V. C. (Ed.). (1950). *Training in clinical psychology.* New York: Prentice-Hall.

LAWRENCE J. SIEGEL
*University of Texas Medical Branch, Galveston*

## DIAGNOSTIC AND STATISTICAL MANUAL OF MENTAL DISORDERS (DSM-III) MENTAL STATUS EXAMS

## CLINICAL TEACHING

Clinical teaching is teaching that is prescriptive (diagnosis → prescription → remediation), with the intent of matching the student's strengths and weaknesses to a specific type of instruction. Clinical teaching is therefore often called diagnostic-prescriptive teaching. It is a continuous test-teach-test process. This process was influenced by Johnson and Myklebust (1967), Smith (1968, 1974), Learner (1985), and many others. Teaching strategies in clinical teaching include task analysis and applied behavior analysis.

Learner (1985) views the clinical teaching process as a five-stage repetitive cycle of decision making that consists of assessment, planning, implementation, evaluation, and modification of the assessment. She further adds that the clinical teacher considers the student's ecological, home, social, and cultural environments.

Smith (1983) offers eight steps in the clinical teaching process: (1) the clinical teacher should objectively observe and analyze the student's classroom abilities; (2) the teacher should objectively observe and analyze the nature of the student's successes and difficulties on different types of tasks; (3) the teacher should scrutinize the characteristics of alternative tasks and settings; (4) compare and contrast how information gained from step (3) might interact with the observations in steps (2) and (1) so as to result in more favorable achievement; (5) the teacher should consult with the student whenever possible, present the choices for modification, and together decide which ones to try; (6) the teacher should set short-term goals, make the modifications; and (7) teach; (8) evaluate progress after a reasonable time interval; if successful, continue teaching similar but higher level objectives; if unsuccessful retrace steps 1–7 (p. 361).

### REFERENCES

Johnson, D., & Mykelbust, H. (1967). Learning disabilities: Educational principles and practices. New York: Grune & Stratton.

Learner, J. (1985). Learning disabilities: Theories, diagnosis, and teaching strategies (4th ed.). Boston: Houghton Mifflin.

Smith, C. R. (1983). Learning disabilities: The intervention of learner, task and setting. Boston: Little, Brown.

Smith, R. M. (1968, 1974). Clinical teaching: Methods of instruction for the retarded. New York: McGraw-Hill.

MARIBETH MONTGOMERY KASIK
*Governors State University*

## CLOZE TECHNIQUE

The cloze technique is a procedure that is used for both the assessment and instruction of reading comprehension skills. Based on the psychological construct of closure, the technique was first developed by Taylor (1953), who believed that a person reading a narrative or expository selection psychologically endeavors to complete a pattern of thought and language that is left incomplete. With the cloze technique, such a language pattern is typically a reading passage from which words have been deleted. Typically, in a reading selection of approximately 250 words, e.g., every tenth lexical word would be deleted and it would be the reader's task to fill in the missing words.

According to Rye (1982), the cloze technique may be more appropriately considered a construction procedure, whereby the reader uses both linguistic knowledge and past experience to complete sentences in appropriate ways. Experience and language are used to choose the correct grammatical class of words.

Cloze exercises may be developed from basal reader texts, trade books, content area materials, and any other reading selections that are appropriate for a given population of readers. Often, the cloze procedure has been used as a device for the assessment of reading comprehension. As described by Smith and Johnson (1980), it may involve the use of a variety of cloze passages taken from the same reading material. For example, three different passages of approximately 100 words in length may be taken from the beginning, middle, and end of a selection. Then, certain words are deleted, e.g., every fifth or tenth lexical word. The reader's task is to read the passage and write in the missing word on a blank. Ekwall (1985) elaborated on this procedure by stating that the first and last sentences of the selection should be left intact, with every fifth word omitted to be replaced with a blank of 10 spaces in length. Again, the reader is required to read the selection and fill in blank spaces with a word that would seem to fit.

Cloze exercises can be used with either individual students or groups of students. As an assessment tool, there is usually no time limit for the completion of a cloze exercise. The evaluation or scoring of a cloze passage is usually based on a percentage of blank spaces that have been completed correctly. Furthermore, according to Smith and Johnson (1980), only the exact deleted word should be counted as correct. If a student is able to complete approximately 45 to 50% of the omitted spaces correctly, the reading material is judged to be at the reader's instructional level. If 60% or more of the blanks have been filled in correctly, the selection is probably at the reader's independent reading level. If fewer than 45% of the blanks are completed correctly, the material is at the reader's frustration reading level.

In addition to being used as a diagnostic measure, the cloze technique can also be used to improve reading comprehension in an instructional setting. In this manner, the technique can be used as a prereading activity to determine the reader's ability to deal with certain material, and as a postreading activity to develop certain comprehension skills and to practice various comprehension strategies, e.g., the use of context clues in understanding what has been read.

The cloze technique, therefore, based on the construct of perception and closure as defined by the gestalt psychologists, assumes the ability of a fluent reader to predict or anticipate what is coming next in a reading passage. This requires the use of various reading skills, including context clues, knowledge of linguistic patterns, and the ability to comprehend in general what is being read. As Rye (1982) describes, the activity involves a sampling of information from a contextual setting and the formation of hypotheses, a prediction of what will appear subsequently in the selection both linguistically and conceptually. The value of the cloze technique as both a diagnostic and instructional device lies in its demand on the reader's comprehension abilities and a variety of language skills.

## REFERENCES

Ekwall, E. E. (1985). *Locating and correcting reading difficulties* (4th ed.). Columbus, OH: Merrill.

Miller, W. H. (1974). *Reading diagnosis kit.* New York: Center for Applied Research in Education.

Rye, J. (1982). *Cloze procedure and the teaching of reading.* Exeter, NH: Heinemann.

Smith, R. J., & Johnson, D. D. (1980). *Teaching children to read* (2nd ed.). Reading, MA: Addison-Wesley.

Taylor, W. L. (1953). Cloze procedure: A new tool for measuring readability. *Journalism Quarterly, 30,* 415–433.

JOHN M. EELLS
*Souderton Area School District,
Souderton, Pennsylvania*

**READING DISORDERS**
**READING REMEDIATION**

# COGENTIN

Cogentin is the proprietary name of benztropine mesylate, a skeletal muscle relaxant used in the treatment of Parkinson's disease (Modell, 1985). Cogentin acts on the basal ganglia of the brain. By restoring more normal chemical balance in the basal ganglia, specific movement disorders associated with parkinsonism are relieved. Cogentin reduces tremors, gait disturbances, and rigidity in afflicted individuals (Long, 1982). Common side effects, especially during initial drug use, include blurred vision, nervousness, constipation, and dryness of the mouth. On rare occasions more serious side effects may occur, including confusion, hallucinations, nausea, and vomiting (Long, 1982). Common cold and cough remedies may interact unfavorably with Cogentin. The drug is not recommended for use in children under 3 years of age, and should be used with caution in older children (Long, 1983; *Physician's Desk Reference*, 1983).

### REFERENCES

Long, J. W. (1982). *The essential guide to prescription drugs*. New York: Harper & Row.

Modell, W. (Ed.). (1985). *Drugs in current use and new drugs* (31st ed.). New York: Springer.

*Physician's desk reference* (37th ed.). (1983). Oradell, NJ: Medical Economics.

CATHY F. TELZROW
*Cuyahoga Specific Education
Service Center, Maple
Heights, Ohio*

**DRUG THERAPY
MEDICATION**

## COGNITIVE BEHAVIOR THERAPY

The term cognitive behavior therapy refers to a diverse assemblage of theoretical and applied orientations that share three underlying assumptions. First, a person's behavior is mediated by cognitive events (i.e., thoughts, images, expectancies, and beliefs). Second, is a corollary to the first; it states that a change in mediating events results in a change in behavior. Third, a person is an active participant in his or her own learning. The third assumption recognizes the reciprocal relationships among a person's thoughts, behavior, and environment and runs counter to the behaviorist's unidirectional view of the individual as a passive recipient of environmental influences.

During the reign of behaviorism in American psychology, cognitions were banned from investigation because the earlier methods used in their investigation were methodologically unsound and because cognitions, which are not directly observable, were considered inappropriate subject matter for the scientific study of psychology. During the 1960s, an explosion of research into such cognitive processes as attention, memory, problem solving, imagery, self-referent speech, beliefs, attributions, and motivation heralded a cognitive revolution in American psychology. Behaviorists impressed with the rigor of experimental cognitive psychologists and alert to the limitations of traditional behaviorism increasingly considered the role of cognitive variables in the development of behavior and in the treatment of maladaptive behavior. Because Bandura's research in observational learning was couched in a learning theory framework, it provided a timely bridge between the cognitivists and behaviorists. Bandura's explanations for modeling became more cognitive as he introduced such cognitive constructs as attention, retention, and expectancies to explain observational learning. Bandura's view of the reciprocal relationships among cognitions, behavior, and environment remains a basic tenet of cognitive behavior therapy. The widely discussed *controversy* between the cognitivists and the behaviorists that was prevalent in the 1960s and early 1970s has now quieted. The compatibility of the two perspectives has been recognized and the advantages of the joint consideration of cognitions and behaviors in modifying behaviors has been demonstrated.

A variety of therapies derived from research in cognitive psychology and taking advantage of the broadened behavioral perspective were developed and subjected to empirical test. These therapies attempt to modify thinking processes as a mechanism for effecting cognitive and behavioral changes. Particular therapeutic approaches that are closely identified with cognitive behavior therapy include modeling, self-instructional training, problem-solving training, rational emotive therapy, cognitive therapy, self-control training, and cognitive skills training. Because self-instructional training and problem-solving training illustrate the dual focus on cognitions and behavior, have been researched in schools, and are particularly well suited to classroom application, they will be briefly described in this entry.

In self-instructional training, the child is taught to regulate his or her behavior through self-talk. The child is taught to ask and to answer covertly questions that guide his or her own performance. The questions are of four types:

1. Questions about the nature of the problem (OK. Now what is it I have to do? I have to find the two cars that are twins.)
2. Plans, or self-instructions for solving the task (How can I do it? I could look at each car carefully, looking at the hood first, and then the front wheels, until I get to the end.)
3. Self-monitoring (Am I using my plan?)
4. Self-evaluation. (How did I do? I did fine because I looked at each car carefully and I found the twins.)

The particular self-statements vary according to the type of task.

The steps in teaching children to use self-speech to guide problem-solving behavior are derived from research in the developmental sequence by which language regulates one's behavior. First, an adult talks out loud while solving a task, and the child observes (modeling). Next, the child performs the same task while the adult verbally instructs the child. Next, the child performs the task while instructing himself or herself out loud. Then the child performs the task while whispering. Finally, the child performs the task while talking silently to himself or herself, with no lip movements.

Research in self-instructional talk has demonstrated that it helps impulsive children to think before acting (Meichenbaum & Goodman, 1971). While treated children have improved on novel problem-solving tasks and academic performance (Camp, Blom, Hebert, & Van Doorninck, 1977; Douglas, Parry, Marton, & Garson, 1976; Meichenbaum & Goodman, 1971), results of treatment on classroom behavior have been inconclusive (Camp, 1980; Camp et al., 1977).

Problem-solving training is similar to self-instructional training in that the child is taught to think through problems following a systematic problem-solving process. In a series of studies, Spivack and Shure (Spivack, Platt, & Shure, 1976; Spivack & Shure, 1974) taught preschool children the following interpersonal cognitive problem-solving skills: problem identification, means-end thinking, alternative thinking, and consequential thinking. Means-end thinking includes the ability to plan, step-by-step, ways to reach an interpersonal goal. Alternative thinking includes the ability to generate different plans for solving a given interpersonal problem. Consequential thinking is the ability to anticipate and evaluate consequences of a given interpersonal solution. These skills are taught in game-type interactions involving pictures, puppets, and stories depicting interpersonal problem situations. Research on problem-solving training has demonstrated improvement on teacher ratings, academic performance, and behavior observations (Shure, 1981).

## REFERENCES

Camp, B. W. (1980). Two psychoeducational treatment programs for young aggressive boys. In C. K. Walen & B. Henker (Eds.), *Hyperactive children—The social psychology of identification and treatment.* New York: Academic.

Camp, B. W., Blom, G. E., Hebert, F., & Van Doorninck, W. J. (1977). "Think Aloud": A program for developing self-control in young aggressive boys. *Journal of Abnormal Child Psychology, 5,* 157–169.

Douglas, V. I., Parry, P., Marton, P., & Garson. C. (1976). *Journal of Abnormal Child Psychology, 4,* 389–410.

Meichenbaum, D. H., & Goodman, J. (1971). Training impulsive children to talk to themselves: A means of developing self-control. *Journal of Abnormal Psychology, 77,* 115–126.

Shure, M. B. (1981). Social competence as a problem-solving skill. In J. D. Wine & M. D. Smyne (Eds.), *Social competence* (pp. 158–185). New York: Guilford Press.

Spivack, G., Platt, J. J., & Shure, M. B. (1976). *The problem-solving approach to adjustment.* San Francisco: Jossey-Bass.

Spivack, G., & Shure, M. B. (1974). *Social adjustment of young children: A cognitive approach to solving real-life problems.* San Francisco: Jossey-Bass.

JAN N. HUGHES
*Texas A&M University*

## COGNITIVE RETRAINING

## COGNITIVE STRATEGIES
## SELF CONTROL CURRICULUM

## COGNITIVE DEVELOPMENT

Cognitive development consists of numerous overlapping conceptual and theoretical processes involving changes that occur in mental capacity and facility between birth and death. Cognition, the product of cognitive development, refers to mental processes by which individuals acquire knowledge. Moreover, cognition is the process of acquiring a conscious awareness that helps us to "know" and "understand" in a wide spectrum of activities such as remembering, learning, thinking, and attending. As a human phenomenon, cognition is comprised of unobservable events, their subsequent comprehension, and resultant response (Flavell, 1982). These covert behaviors characterize the activities of human thought processes.

In an effort to present general parameters of childhood cognitive development as it pertains to special education, several cognitive perspectives must be addressed. The human is an active problem solver who attempts to discriminate, extract, and analyze information; subsequently, directed planful action undergoes developmental change. Three contemporary theoretical orientations are consistent with the theme of the child as an active problem solver: Piaget's theory of cognitive development; information-processing approaches, and social learning theory.

One of the most influential descriptors of how development occurs is Piaget's theory of cognitive development (Piaget, 1970). In his work, cognitive structures are represented in the symbolic medium of formal logic, where each structure is regarded as a broad system of logical operations that mediates and unites a whole range of more specific intellectual behaviors and characteristics. Even though research with large samples of infants have confirmed Piaget's theories, certain aspects of his developmental accounts have come under scrutiny (Flavell, 1980; Gelman, 1978) and warrant revision or reinterpretation. Nevertheless, the Piagetian approach remains an important scientific paradigm on human intellectual development. The formative phases of the domain of study known as cognitive development are rooted in Piaget's theoretical formulations.

Piaget defines intelligence as a basic life function through which an individual adapts to the environment. In Piaget's view, children do not simply receive information from the environment, they actively seek and achieve knowledge through their own efforts. This interaction, from Piaget's biological perspective, is viewed as adaptation. Organisms adapt by using their newly acquired information by processing and gaining understanding of the environment. Thus adaptation and construction of reality depend on a child's level of cognitive development.

Piaget views cognitive development as a process of the development of cognitive structures and intellectual functions. He uses the term schema to describe mental structures used by the individual to represent, organize, and interpret experience. Therefore, a schema is defined as a pattern of thought or action by which an individual constructs an "understanding" of some aspect of the environment. Three types of intellectual structures have been defined by Piaget: sensorimotor (organized behavior patterns used to represent or respond to objects or experiences), symbolic (internal cognitive images used to represent past experiences), and operational (internal cognitive images that organize thoughts logically).

According to Piaget's theory, cognitive development depends on maturation (genetically transmitted) and the child's interactions with the environment. Contingent on normal maturation are the organism's ability to adapt to environmental changes and demands. Thus, with maturation, assimilation, and accommodation (Piaget, 1970), the human organism tries to interpret new experiences in terms of existing information.

Analogously, through accommodation, the child modifies an existing schema to suit a novel experience. Hence, Piaget describes intellectual growth as an active process whereby children are repeatedly assimilating new experiences and accommodating their cognitive structures to their new experiences. The cognitive operations of adaptation and organization facilitate children's ability to construct a progressively better understanding of the world. A child's formulation of self and external world depend on the knowledge base acquired up to the particular point in time at which a response is necessary. Consequently, the greater immaturity of the child's cognitive system, the more limited the interpretation of environmental events.

Age ranges designated for each of Piaget's four stages are average estimates; nonetheless, the sequential emergence of hierarchical "stages" are believed to be absolutely constant or invariant. Piaget felt that earlier developmental stages are not skipped en route to later stages. Accomplishments for each stage are said to accumulate; i.e., skills achieved in earlier stages are not lost with the advent of latent stages.

## Sensorimotor Stage

During the sensorimotor stage of development, birth to about 2 years of age, cognitive development originates with ability to organize and coordinate bodily sensations and perceptions with the child's own physical movements and actions. Throughout sensorimotor development, an infant progresses from instinctual reflexive actions at birth to symbolic reflexive actions toward the end of the second year.

Initial means of coordinating sensation and action are accomplished through instinctual reflexive behaviors such as sucking and rooting. These behaviors are exhibited during substage 1 simple reflexes (ages birth to 1 month).

Substage 2, first habits and primary circular reactions, is comprised of first acquired adaptations. For example, when orally stimulated by a bottle during the first substage (simple reflexes), an infant might suck; conversely, during the second substage, repetitions of sucking may commence when no bottle is present.

During substage 3 (4 to 8 months), secondary circular reactions, behaviors are also repetitious and pleasurable; however, they focus on events and objects in the external environment that occur by chance.

Throughout substage 4 (8 to 12 months), coordination of secondary schemata, cognitive thought is comprised of intentional combining previously unrelated stimuli, producing simple feats, solving simple problems, and imitating the behavior of others. Piaget suggests that throughout substage 4, an infant is applying known cognitive structures to new situations to produce coordinated, goal-directed, and independent imitative actions with his or her own body or environment.

Substage 5 (12 to 18 months), tertiary circular reactions, is evidenced by exploratory trial and error schematas in which the infant purposely discovers new procedures to solve problems or reproduce interesting outcomes. Piaget refers to this period as the developmental starting point for human curiosity and interest in novelty.

Finally, during the last sensorimotor substage (18 to 24 months), internalization of cognitive structures begins to develop. Mental functioning shifts from a purely sensorimotor plane to a symbolic plane in which infants develop the ability to use primitive symbols.

## Object Permanence

Object permanence, considered one of the infant's most significant cognitive development achievements during the sensorimotor stage, is the idea that people, places, and things continue to exist when they are no longer visible or detectable through the senses. According to Piaget, the object concept first appears during substage 4, coordination of secondary schemata. During substage 5, tertiary circular reactions, an infant searches for and locates hidden objects in novel and familiar locations; nonetheless, this occurs only if movement of the objects is visible. In the final sensorimotor substage, object permanence is complete; invisible movement of objects can be followed in the imagination by means of mental representations. Thus the infant searches for and finds objects that have been hidden through visible displacements.

Contrary to Piaget, Bower's (1982) research suggests that infants understand object permanence earlier, during primary circular reactions, even though they will not search for objects during this substage. Evidence of object permanence in Bower's research is indicated by the infant's surprise or anticipation of perceived object location. Bower suggests that errors in spatial reasoning, rather than absence of the object concept, account for younger infants' failure to search in Piagetian tasks.

## Preoperational Stage

In the preoperational stage (ages 2 to 7 years), a period when symbolic schemata predominates, a young child's symbolic system expands such that use of language and perceptual images moves well beyond abilities at the end of the sensorimotor period. The preoperational stage consists of two phases: the preconceptual period (ages 2 to 4 years) and the intuitive period (ages 5 to 7 years).

According to Piaget, deficits in logical reasoning are evident throughout the preconceptual period. For example, egocentrism, the most salient feature of preconceptual thought, is evidenced by an inability to distinguish easily between a child's own perspective and that of someone else. Another deficit exhibited during the preconceptual period is animism; the young child believes that inanimate objects have human qualities and are capable of human action. During the preconceptual period, pretend play develops to a level in which children are capable of creating fantasy worlds, inventing imaginary playmates, participating in role playing, and using play as a vehicle for coping with emotional crises.

The second phase of the preoperational stage, the intuitive period, is an extension of preconceptual thought where the use of symbolic thought improves. Perceptually based logic appears in class inclusion problems such as "a string of beads that has both blocks and beads," whereby the child focuses on one feature only. According to Piaget, the child has a hard time thinking about the subset.

To aid in the use of symbolic thought, two main systematic capabilities are necessary during the preoperational period: centration and irreversibility. Fundamentally, centration is a child's tendency to focus on a single aspect of a problem while ignoring other information that helps the child to answer correctly. Irreversibility is the inability to reverse or to undo an action mentally.

Recent research (Flavell, Everett, Croft, & Flavell, 1981; Mossler, Marvin, & Greenberg, 1976) suggests that preoperational children are less egocentric, take another's point of view, and can conserve, contrary to what Piaget found. Gelman (1978) found that preschoolers are capable of causal reasoning. Additional research (Beilin, 1980) indicates that conservation problems can be taught to preoperational children by methods such as identity training; i.e., objects or substances transformed in a conservation task are still the same regardless of their new appearance. Finally, the work of Acredolo and Acredolo (1979) suggests that reversibility and compensation are not absolutely necessary for conservation.

## Concrete Operations Stage

Piaget's concrete operations stage, a period between ages 7 and 11 years, is a stage during which the child's thinking crystallizes into a coherent organization of cognitive operations. Cognitive deficits most evident in the preoperational stage completely fade during the concrete operations stage.

Cognitive operations shift to a more refined system of thought that leads to levels that facilitate previously unattainable competencies. During concrete operations development, children often display horizontal decalage meaning the child can solve some conservation problems but not others. For example, conservation skills such as reversibility develop such that the child can mentally reverse flow of action and thereby realize that a column of water can look the same when poured back into its original container. Ability to classify and reverse enables linguistic humor to develop. Another shift is the move from egocentrism to relativism. The child can now decenter, or operate with two or more aspects of a problem simultaneously.

## Formal Operations Stage

The formal operations stage, the final stage of Piaget's cognitive development theory, is characterized by the ability to reason abstractly and hypothetically. Abstract quality of thought can be seen primarily in the adolescent's use of verbal propositions in problem solving. For example, the concrete thinker (sensorimotor stage) needs to see concrete elements A, B, and C to be able to make the logical inference that if A>B and B>C, then A>C. Conversely, formal thinkers can solve the previous problem merely by having it presented as a verbal puzzle.

Although the transition to formal operations takes place gradually over several years, systematic and abstract thinking builds a foundation for considering morality, justice, beliefs, and values. Socially, the formal thinker no longer need rely on concrete experiences with people to form complex judgments about them.

## Formal Thought in Adolescence

Since Piaget's classic experiments, many researchers have delved into the nature of adolescent thought. Their objective has been to specify the characteristics that distinguish this form of reasoning and problem solving from other more primitive forms.

One important characteristic of formal thought involves seeking explanations rather than mere descriptions of what has been observed. Another characteristic of formal thought involves the ability to remove oneself from the immediate context of a problem in order to get an additional perspective. One of the most socially significant characteristics of formal thought is the metacognitive ability to thinking about thinking; i.e., the ability to reflect on the thought process itself. In sum, formal thought is characterized by a relative freedom from the immediate constraints of a problem, which results in flexibility.

## Late Adolescence and Adulthood

During this stage the most pronounced changes in cognitive development have taken place. Nonetheless, small but observable changes are still evident later in life. Young adults, from Erikson's (1963) theory of psychosocial development, experience a crisis of identity versus role confusion. Moreover, sex and romance influence the role of young adults.

Cognitive development continues to refine in its development as the young adult attempts to conceptualize a lifelong role in society by selecting an occupation. This mature realism about one's occupation is seen as a process that remains throughout one's life, sometimes leading to midlife career changes.

## Information-Processing Approach to Cognitive Development

As a model of human cognitive development, information processing explains decision making, knowing, and remembering as processes. In this approach to the study of cognitive development, the mind is conceived of as a complex congnitive system, analogous in some ways to a computer. In essence, human cognition becomes what the computer must know in order to produce behavior y. Information from the environment is abstracted from sensory systems and "flows" through a variety of proposed information-processing components. Information is transformed and analyzed at each step; feedback and feedforward loops among the components influence these transformations and analyses. Planning and purposeful thinking are derived by executive functions. The executive system contains sets of elementary information-processing rules that construct, execute, and monitor the flow of information to achieve objectives.

Most of the information-processing research builds directly on Piaget's contributions to the understanding of cognitive development. Contrary to Piaget's structural explanation underlying the thought structure of logic in thought processes and operational reversibility, information processing accounts for and identifies specific mental processes by which cognition is processed. Some researchers, such as Pascual-Leone (1980) and Case (1978), have modified Piagetian theory to take into account information-processing considerations (also called neo-Piagetian theories). One such approach is Siegler's (1981) rule-assessment approach. In essence, Siegler's work examines a child's problem-solving skills within a domain at different ages. A child's pattern of responses across problems helps to determine which of information-processing rules the child is using.

Several other information-processing perspectives have examined cognitive development. For example, researchers have found that young children have limited attention and persistence at tasks (Wellman, Ritter, & Flavell, 1975) and that their curiosity interferes with systematic problem solving. Thus, contrary to Piagetian theory, very young children may fail to solve many problems because they are unable to sustain their attention long enough to gather the necessary information. By about age 5 children become more persistent in their attempts to solve problems. Hence younger children may know to look first at relevant stimuli and label them; whereas, older children are better at selectively attending without special training.

## Social Learning Theory

Social learning theorists (e.g., Bandura, 1977b) suggest that cognitive development is much more than a result of some combination of individual characteristics and environmental influences. They view all three as existing within a mutually interdependent network; they exist as a set of reciprocal determinants. Thus cognitions, beliefs, and expectations influence behavior and vice versa. Behavior partially determines the nature of the environment, whereas cognitions determine the psychological definitions of the environment.

Learning takes place either directly (through association of behaviors and consequences) or through modeling. The direct consequences of behavior, or reinforcements, are not conceptualized in the more traditional fashion that ignores awareness of the contingencies on the part of the child. Hence consequences of behavior explicitly carry information and function to provoke the individual into formulating and testing hypotheses. Thus reinforcement influences whether or not a response will elicit cognitions or thoughts about stimulus associations.

Learning is thought to be acquired through modeling. All new behaviors are observed along with their consequences. Inherent symbolic abilities facilitate abstraction and representation of information and provide an efficient means for retaining that information. From a social learning perspective, the anticipation of reinforcement may serve as a stimulus to direct attention to a model's behavior; hence, reinforcement may facilitate learning.

In summary, social learning theory places a great deal of emphasis on symbolic and self-regulatory processes. Cognitive development is important to the extent that changes in cognitive functioning influence changes in those processes. In children, development becomes more refined with experience and actual manipulation; consequently, children are better able to represent efficiently and retain observational experiences. Additionally, symbolic processes, attentional processes, and motivational processes change with observational learning.

## Implications for Special Education

Traditional stages of cognitive development apply to the handicapped and the nonhandicapped alike. Handicapping conditions, however, may result in irregularities or delays in cognitive development, particularly in profoundly mentally retarded or multiply impaired persons. Some profoundly mentally retarded handicapped never progress into the higher stages of cognitive development such as preoperational or operational thought. Other handicapped children acquire skills by rote or through carefully structured instruction, but have difficulty in applying them to new situations (Brown, Campione, & Murphy, 1977).

Most mildly and moderately retarded children do progress through Piaget's lower stages of cognitive development; however, their rate of skill acquisition is much slower. As the child gets older, the gap between the age at which specific skills are expected to be learned and the age at which they are actually learned increases. The retarded child also performs cognitive tasks with less efficiency than the nonretarded child (Campione & Brown, 1978).

Learning-disabled (LD) people represent the largest percentage of the handicapped population (U.S. Office of Special Education, 1984); they evidence a broad array of cognitive dysfunctions. These deficits emerge when academic learning lags with age. Children who are learning disabled may not exhibit specific cognitive problems early in development; however, skills acquired during Piaget's preoperational stage (intuitive thinking) are learned at a slower pace. Thus, problems in areas such as mathematics, reading, and memory are more prevalent.

During the primary years, LD children have problems with seriation and classification tasks that are essential for mathematics. They cannot sort objects by size, match objects, or grasp the concept of counting and addition. In reading, LD children evidence word recognition errors (omissions, insertions, substitutions, reversals, and transpositions) and comprehension errors (inability to recall facts, sequences, or main ideas).

Word recognition difficulties suggest that LD children are unable to make a word or a letter stand for or represent something else. These are preconceptual skills (ages 2 to 7) of cognitive development in which symbolic thought develops. Problems with centration may inhibit reading comprehension.

Learning-disabled students generally have problems with recalling auditory and visual stimuli. They also have problems with tasks requiring production or generation of specific learning or memorization strategies that influence the efficient organization of input for retrieval and recall. Bauer (1979) found that poor readers perform poorly on memory tasks that require complex organizational and retrieval strategies. Kauffman and Hallahan (1979) suggest that LD students fail to engage in strategies that enhance attention and recall. These deficits are evident when applied to academic tasks.

Cognitive development may be viewed from numerous perspectives and subsequently applied to academic problems encountered in the field of special education. The information-processing approach to cognitive development is still in the embryonic stage. It is best described as a complement to, rather than a replacement for, Piaget's earlier framework. Growth and extension of the cognitive development literature continues and quite often fills in some of the gaps in Piaget's model; hence, advances in empirical findings will eventually aid in the development of successful school-based interventions.

## REFERENCES

Acredolo, L., & Acredolo, L. T. (1979). Identity, compensation, and conservation. *Child Development, 50*, 524–535.

Bauer, R. H. (1979). Memory, acquisition, and category clustering in learning disabled children. *Journal of Experimental Child Psychology, 217*, 365–383.

Beilin, H. (1980). Piaget's theory: Refinement, revision, or rejection? In R. Kluwe & H. Spada (Eds.), *Developmental models of thinking.* New York: Academic.

Bower, T. G. R. (1982). *Development in infancy.* San Francisco: Freeman.

Brown, A., Campione, J., & Murphy, M. (1977). Maintenance and generalization of training meta-mnemonic awareness of educable retarded children. *Journal of Experimental Child Psychology, 24*, 191–211.

Campione, J. C., & Brown, A. (1978). Toward a theory of intelligence: Contributions from research with retarded children. *Intelligence, 2*, 279–304.

Case, R. S. (1978). Intellectual development from birth to adulthood: A neo-Piagetian interpretation. In R. W. Siegler (Ed.), *Children's thinking: What develops?* Hillsdale, NJ: Erlbaum.

Erikson, E. H. (1963). *Childhood and society* (2nd ed.). New York: Norton.

Flavell, J. (1980, Fall). A tribute to Piaget. *Society for Research in Child Development Newsletter.*

Flavell, J. (1982). On cognitive development. *Child Development, 53*, 1–10.

Flavell, J., Everett, B. A., Croft, K., & Flavell, E. R. (1981). Young children's knowledge about visual perception: Further evidence for the Level 1-Level 2 distinction. *Developmental Psychology, 15*, 95–120.

Gelman, R. (1978). Cognitive development. *Annual Review of Psychology, 29*, 297–332.

Kauffman, J. M., & Hallahan, D. P. (1979). Learning disabled and hyperactivity. In B. B. Lahey & A. E. Kazdin (Eds.), *Advances in clinical child psychology* (Vol. 2). New York: Plenum.

Mossler, D. G., Marvin, R. S., & Greenberg, M. T. (1976). Conceptual perspective taking in 2- to 6-year-old children. *Developmental Psychology, 12*, 85–86.

Moynahan, E. D. (1973). The development of knowledge concerning the effect of categorization upon free recall. *Child Development, 44*, 238–246.

Pascual-Leone, J. (1980). Constructive problems for constructive theories: The current relevance of Piaget's work and a critique of information-processing simulation psychology. In R. H. Kluwe & H. Spada (Eds.), *Developmental models of thinking.* New York: Academic.

Piaget, J. (1970). Piaget's theory. In P. H. Mussen (Ed.), *Carmichael's manual of child psychology* (Vol. 1). New York: Wiley.

Siegler, R. S. (1981). Developmental sequences within and between concepts. *Monographs for the Society for Research in Child Development, 46* (Serial No. 189).

U.S. Office of Special Education. (1984). *Sixth annual report to Congress on the implementation of Public Law 94-142: The Education for All Handicapped Children Act.* Washington, DC: U.S. Department of Education.

Wellman, H. M., Ritter, K., & Flavell, J. (1975). Deliberate memory in the delayed reactions of very young children. *Developmental Psychology, 11*, 780–787.

JOSE LUIS TORRES
MICHAEL J. ASH
*Texas A&M University*

COGNITIVE STRATEGIES
COGNITIVE STYLES
INFORMATION PROCESSING
INTELLIGENCE
PIAGET, JEAN
SOCIAL LEARNING THEORY

# COGNITIVE IMPAIRMENT AND METAL POLLUTANTS

It is well known that children who are exposed to high doses of lead and other metal pollutants may suffer permanent neurological sequelae and cognitive impairments (Moon, Marlow, Stellern, & Errera, 1985). The causes of metal pollution are often associated with substandard living conditions: e.g., living in dilapidated substandard housing with peeling lead-based paints or plaster, living with household dust carrying metal pollutants, and living in proximity to heavy traffic or factories with noxious emissions. Inadequate nutrition also contributes to the effects of metal pollution.

Some of the physical difficulties associated with metal pollution are loss of appetite, chronic abdominal pain, headache, and anemia. Reported behavior difficulties associated with high levels of such poisoning are decreased learning performance, deficient attention, irritability, and clumsiness. Investigators have implicated metal toxicity in nonadaptive behavior as manifested in classroom situations (Marlowe, Moon, Errera, Cossairt, McNeil, & Peak, in press), associated with learning-disabled children

(Marlowe, Errera, Cossairt, & Welch, in press) and with emotional disturbances in children (Marlowe, Errera, & Jacoby, 1983).

The assessment of metal concentrations in humans is easily carried out through various bodily analyses, e.g., of blood, teeth, and hair. The study of hair is both easy and noninvasive: samples are subjected to the study of atomic absorption spectroscopy (Laker, 1982). Trace elements such as metals accumulate in hair at concentrations that are usually higher than in the blood serum. Hair thus can provide a record of a child's nutrient and mineral status. A method appropriate to classroom use to help teachers identify children who are potentially suffering from metal pollution is the Metal Exposure Questionnaire (Marlowe et al., 1983). This provides quantitative information about the possibility that a schoolchild is suffering significantly from metal pollutants.

Many of studies of metal pollutant effects suffer from methodological errors. One of the more significant of these is that while investigators study the effects of one toxic metal, they often fail to take into account the effects of other toxic metals on a child's behavior (Moon et al., 1985).

While there is clear evidence indicating that high doses of metal pollution are physically and cognitively deleterious, there is less certainty as to whether low doses of such metals have significant effects. A number of studies have suggested that they do. Low levels of arsenic, cadmium, mercury, aluminum, and lead have been implicated in cognitive, perceptual, and behavioral childhood developmental deficits (Marlowe, Errera, J., Stellern, & Beck, 1983; Winneke et al, 1983). Some investigators also have hypothesized that metal combinations have interactive effects, thereby increasing the total toxicity in a child (Moon et al., 1985).

Among the more comprehensive reviews of literature concerning the behavioral effects of metal pollutants is that of Rimland and Larson (1983), who summarized studies of the relationship between incidence of learning disabilities and long-term, low-level metal exposure as measured through hair analysis. They found a total of nine studies. In five of the studies, learning-disabled subjects were found to have significantly more lead and/or cadmium than their controls. In the four remaining studies, the learning-disabled students were found to be somewhat higher in lead, cadmium, and/or aluminum concentrations.

The potential widespread nature of metal pollutants' toxic effects has been demonstrated by Moon, Marlowe, Stellern, & Errera (1985). These investigators, studying a randomly selected sample of elementary school children, found significant relationships between low metal concentrations and diminished performance on a variety of cognitive and academic tasks. They also discovered interactive effects. Thus, both increases in arsenic and its interaction with lead were significantly related to decreased reading and spelling achievement. Increases in aluminum and the interaction of aluminum with lead were associated with decreased visual motor performance.

## REFERENCES

Laker, M. (1982). On determining trace element levels in man: The uses of blood and hair. *Lancet, 12*, 260–263.

Marlowe, M., Errera, J., Cossairt, A., & Welch, K. (in press). Hair mineral content as a predictor of learning disabilities. *Journal of Learning Disabilities*.

Marlowe, M., Errera, J., & Jacoby, J. (1983). Increased lead and cadmium levels in emotionally disturbed children. *Journal of Orthomollecular Psychiatry, 12*, 260–267.

Marlowe, M., Moon, C., Errera, J., Cossairt, A., McNeil, A., & Peak, R. (in press). Main and interaction effects of metallic toxins on classroom behavior. *Journal of Abnormal Child Psychology*.

Moon, C., Marlowe, M., Stellern, J., & Errera, J. (1985). Main and interaction effects of metallic pollutants on cognitive functioning. *Journal of Learning Disabilities, 18*, 217–220.

Rimland, B., & Larson, G. E. (1983). Hair mineral analysis and behavior: An analysis of 51 studies. *Journal of Learning Disabilities, 16*, 279–285.

Winneke, G., Kramer, U., Brockhaus, U., Evers, U., Kujanek, G., Lechner, H., & Janke, W. (1983). Neuropsychological studies in children with elevated tooth-lead concentrations. *International Archives of Occupational Environmental Health, 51*, 231–252.

LESTER MANN
*Hunter College, City University of New York*

## LEAD POISONING
## POVERTY, RELATIONSHIP TO SPECIAL EDUCATION

## COGNITIVE RETRAINING

Cognitive retraining involves remediation of acquired cognitive dysfunction arising from brain injury, cerebrovascular accidents, or other less common neurological disorders. Referred to by different terms, cognitive retraining is synonymous with cognitive redevelopment, cognitive remediation, neurological retraining, and cognitive rehabilitation. In each case, the goal is to produce functional changes in verbal (e.g., verbal problem solving) and/or nonverbal (e.g., visual-spatial reasoning) skills or abilities. The approach attempts to strengthen premorbid patterns of mental functioning or the design of compensatory strategies to circumvent permanently impaired functions (i.e., return is unlikely). Cognitive retraining may involve remediation of deficits, capitalization on individual strengths, or the training of compensatory approaches. With dysfunction differing from one individual to the next, the therapist may design a program integrating more than one of these approaches. Indeed, rarely will a brain-dam-

aged patient be presented with a specific area of impairment that is not reflected in other areas of cognitive functioning (e.g., abstract reasoning and memory).

As a precursor to such cognitive therapy, a complete neuropsychological assessment is often conducted to detail the patient's functional strengths and weaknesses. Moreover, neuropsychological assessment often relies on standardized observations of behavior that show a direct correspondence to the functional integrity of the brain. In this way, the examination provides a comprehensive picture of the patient's cognitive abilities; this is useful in planning retraining and rehabilitation in general. Neuropsychological assessment provides an objective baseline from which success in treatment may be documented.

Cognitive retraining is a recent endeavor and therefore many of its methods continue to be developed. Most approaches involve controlling materials and strategies in therapy such that optimal conditions exist to facilitate task performance (Diller & Gordon, 1981). The cognitive therapist seeks to move the patient in small enough steps to the final goal so that the opportunity for failure is rare. Although retraining packages have been developed, the majority of cognitive retraining involves a task analysis approach to the specific disorder (Dean, 1982). Task analysis involves (1) assessing the patient's modality specific cognitive functioning; (2) defining content elements necessary (terms, rules, and the like) to achieve the objective of therapy; (3) identifying the level of cognitive functioning and modality (visual memorization, etc.) necessary to master content; (4) specifying relationships between content and cognitive functions for the patient; (5) using small steps and correction feedback in retraining procedures; and (6) chaining small components together to encompass the final goal (Dean, 1982). Specific approaches may vary from teaching specific verbal strategies as compensation for spatial deficits to relearning phonetic skills necessary in reading.

From the above description, it should be clear that the present state of the art of cognitive retraining remains at a clinical level. Thus, most retraining procedures are applied without benefit of a consistent research base. In fact, the research that does address the effectiveness of cognitive training procedures is limited by a lack of control for spontaneous recovery. That is to say, following brain damage, a degree of functional recovery occurs without intervention. Clearly this recovery must be accounted for in evaluating the effectiveness of any retraining procedure (Dean, in press).

## REFERENCES

Dean, R. S. (1982). Neuropsychology and the rehabilitation process. *Bulletin of the National Academy of Neuropsychologists*, 161–162.

Dean, R. S. (in press). Neuropsychological assessment. In J. D. Cavenar & S. B. Guze (Eds.), *Psychiatry*. Philadelphia, Lippincott.

Diller, L., & Gordon, W. A. (1981). Rehabilitation and clinical neuropsychology. In S. B. Filskov & T. J. Boll (Eds.), *Handbook of clinical neuropsychology* (pp. 702–703). New York: Wiley.

RAYMOND S. DEAN
*Ball State University*
*Indiana University School*
*of Medicine*

COGNITIVE STRATEGIES
NEUROPSYCHOLOGY

# COGNITIVE STRATEGIES

Cognitive strategies are cognitive processes that we use to monitor, control, and manage our cognitive functioning. They mediate both learning and performance. While cognitive strategies have been studied under various names for a long time, credit should probably go to Bruner, Goodnow, and Austin (1956) for first using the construct in the modern-day sense of the term. During recent years, there has been considerable interest in the training and remediation of such strategies.

All of us, whether child, adult, gifted, or mentally retarded, constantly use cognitive strategies to control and direct our thinking and behavior. Word attack skills are strategic in nature, as are the carrying processes used in arithmetic. The ways students take notes or check test responses for accuracy are determined strategically. The manner in which an individual deports himself or herself during a job interview is strategically controlled.

While a variety of cognitive theories have influenced work on cognitive strategies, information processing theories have been the most influential of all. Defining cognitive strategies from an information processing point of view, Young has pointed out that most tasks and problems can be carried out and solved in a variety of different ways and that individuals "have at their command a number of different strategies from which to choose for these purposes . . . there is an analogy between strategies and the subroutines used by computer programers to organize [their programs]" (1978, pp. 357–358).

Cognitive strategies are theoretically distinguished from cognitive capacities (abilities) and knowledge (information). They are regarded as cognitive techniques that guide the ways our capacities are exercised and our knowledge is used. Strategies are learned both informally and formally. Most important from the standpoint of special education is that they are susceptible to training and improvement.

Apropos of this susceptibility is the distinction that has been made between fixed and modifiable cognitive characterisics (Baron, 1978). Fixed cognitive characteristics (i.e., cognitive capacities or abilities such as intelligence and memory) are difficult to influence environmentally or to change to any significant degree. Modifiable cognitive characteristics, such as cognitive strategies, however, are usually amenable to change and may be significantly improved by education and remediation. While fixed cognitive characteristics ultimately set limits on the development and expression of all cognitive processes, including cognitive strategy, some cognitive researchers believe that effective use of cognitive strategies can overcome "hard wired" cognitive limitations to a great degree: that students with mental retardation, for example, can approach normal cognitive achievement in certain areas if they are taught how to use strategies properly. One of the most important of intervention studies with the mentally retarded was carried out in the area of strategic training by Belmont and Butterfield (1975). These investigators found that with strategic training, mentally retarded learners were able to function on levels equivalent to those of non-retarded individuals in particular tasks.

Some cognitive strategies are general and can be applied across a broad spectrum of activities; e.g., checking one's work for accuracy on completion is a general strategy that is useful in most tasks. Other strategies are only applicable to specific situations, e.g., applying the processes of single-column addition.

There are short-term cognitive strategies and there are long-term ones. A student will apply certain strategies when taking a particular multiple choice quiz; these strategies serve a short-term purpose. The same student may develop a plan for gaining entry to professional school; in such a case, long-term strategies will be involved.

Cognitive strategies are sometimes used with full awareness of their application. At other times they operate automatically and with little or no consciousness of their use. We are usually most conscious of using them and laborious in their application when we are first learning them or when we attempt to correct or improve on them. As a rule, the more automatically cognitive strategies operate, and the less aware we are of their operations, the smoother and more effortless they will be. They are also likely to be more effective from the standpoint of freeing up our cognitive apparatuses to work on other aspects of a task or problem. Thus a concert pianist's efforts at interpreting music is at first consciously strategic in nature. The pianist plays with conscious intent to give the music certain nuances while practicing it. During the concert, however, such strategies, while still directing the pianist's playing, work at lower levels of awareness or entirely in an automatic fashion. Indeed, a high degree of awareness of any strategic intentions on the pianist's part would make it impossible to sustain smooth playing, particularly during passages of high velocity.

The particular cognitive strategies that an individual acquires and uses depend on that individual's experiences and instruction. They also depend on the individual's abilities and maturity. An adult will usually use more sophisticated and effective strategies than a 10-year-old child. A gifted child uses more complex strategies and has access to a wider range of strategies than does a retarded child. A deaf child will be limited in the use of certain strategies because of limited language capabilities but may learn to use still others more effectively than hearing children (Mann & Sabatino, 1985).

Not all cognitive strategies have the same degree of effectiveness. Some are effective for an appropriate age level or handicap but not for others; e.g., a first grader uses counting strategies that are effective for that age but may actually have negative effects if used in later grades. A child with learning disabilities may be ineffective at strategies that a good learner uses with ease.

Some strategies may even be harmful. A child who is a social isolate may use strategic approaches to other children that are intended to make friends but instead result in rejection. A child who is having trouble with advanced mathematics keeps using calculation strategies that are cumbersome and that interfere with understanding. If remedial cognitive strategy training is to succeed with such children, it will often require the unlearning of "bad" strategies prior to the acquisition of good ones.

Furthermore, it is not enough to know how to use a particular strategy well. It also is required that the user be skilled in its application and know when the strategy is appropriate or when another strategy should be used instead. Regular practice under varied conditions appears essential for most new strategies to become effective. Mentally retarded students will almost always be found to be deficient in their use of cognitive strategies and to require a great deal of rehearsal to master new strategies (Baron, 1978).

Success in school may ultimately depend on the number of effective strategies that a student can appropriately employ. Children with good abilities may fail academically because they do not know enough effective strategies to deal with their school work, or because they rely on inadequate or inappropriate strategies, or because they fail to effectively use the good strategies at their disposal. On the other hand, children with limited abilities may succeed academically because they have learned to use cognitive strategies to compensate for and minimize the impact of their deficiencies.

A number of classification systems have been suggested for cognitive strategies. Baron (1978) has suggested that we categorize them in three ways: (1) central strategies that are basic to the development of others strategies; (2) general strategies applicable to a variety of situations; and (3) specific strategies pertaining to particular types of applications.

Newell (1979) has addressed the classification of strategies using an analogy of an inverted cone of strategic skills. At the bottom of the cone are a large number of strategies that apply only to certain problems or situations, e.g., a carrying strategy for two-column addition.

Such narrow strategies may be powerful and, if properly used, should effectively solve the problems to which they are applied. They are, however, limited to specific types of problems or work only under particular conditions.

As we move up Newell's inverted cone to its tip we find more generalizable but less effective strategies; there is a tradeoff between generalizability and effectiveness. At the very tip of the cone we find a few highly general strategies that are applicable to almost any problem or situation but that are weak and by themselves unable to solve any specific problem. Checking one's school work to see that it is accurate is an example of a general beneficial cognitive strategy, but it has weak effects and by itself can solve no specific problem. In between lie a variety of intermediate-level strategies that vary in specificity and power. It has been suggested that the most useful approach to cognitive strategy training from a general remedial standpoint might be to address such intermediate level strategies (Brown & Palincsar, 1982). Thus scanning written pages in a systematic left to right fashion is a strategy that has some specificity, i.e., it applies to reading; it also has some generality in that it applies to a wide range of reading.

In determining what type of strategies to use with special education students, the cognitive trainer is confronted with decisions as to optimal training programs. Teachers engaged in the cognitive training of learning-disabled children might well stick to specific and intermediate-level strategies that are directly applicable to particular types of school work. Psychologists might be interested in more general types of cognitive strategic training such as is involved in problem solving, test taking, etc.

A distinction has been made between blind and informed cognitive strategy training. Blind training programs are ones in which the subjects do not know the purpose of the training they are receiving. Informed cognitive strategy training not only trains the pupils strategically but helps them to understand the purpose of the training and the benefits to be derived from it. There is evidence that both types of training programs can be effective. However, students trained under informed conditions are likely to use their strategies more effectively and to continue to use them after their formal training is over (Kendall, Borowski, & Cavanaugh, 1980).

A number of researchers have offered recommendations to guide cognitive strategy training with handicapped students (Belmont & Butterfield, 1979; Brown & Palincsar, 1982; Borkowski & Cavanaugh, 1980). Some investigators have advised that teachers of handicapped students may wish to use cognitive strategy curricula (Borkowski & Cavanaugh, 1979; Winschel & Lawrence, 1975).

The study of cognitive strategies has been persistent throughout the past decade and a half, with considerable interest being shown in values of cognitive strategic training for the amelioration of learning problems. One of the most useful of introductions to the topic is to be found in *Teaching Exceptional Children to Use Cognitive Strategies*

(Kaufman, 1980), a special issue of *Exceptional Child Quarterly* wherein a variety of experts provide both theoretical insights and practical information concerning the use of strategies with handicapped students.

The most active interest in cognitive strategies currently is in metacognition, which represents a supraordinate realm of executive cognitive strategies that monitor and regulate lower level strategies, and in cognitive behavioral interventions, which involve strategic training. In their book *Foundations of Cognitive Process*, Mann and Sabatino (1985) clarify the relationships among these different realms of strategic functioning.

## REFERENCES

Baron, J. (1978). Intelligence and general strategies. In G. Underwood (Ed.), *Strategies of information processing* (pp. 403–450). London: Academic.

Belmont, J. M., & Butterfield, E. C. (1979). Learning strategies as determinants of memory deficiencies. *Cognitive Psychology, 2,* 411–420.

Borkowski, J. G., & Cavanaugh, J. C. (1979). Maintenance and generalization of skills and strategies by the retarded. In W. R. Ellis (Ed.), *Handbook of mental deficiency* (2nd ed.). Hillsdale, NJ: Erlbaum.

Borkowski, J. G., & Kornarski, E. A. (1981). Educational implications of efforts to change intelligence. *Journal of Special Education, 15,* 289–306.

Brown, A. C. & Palincsar, A. S. (1982). Inducing strategic learning from texts by means of informed, self control training. *Topics in Learning & Learning Disabilities. 2,* 1–17.

Bruner, J. S., Goodnow, J. J., & Austin, G. A. (1956). A study of thinking. New York: Wiley.

Kaufman, J. M. (Ed.). (1980). Teaching exceptional children to use cognitive strategies. *Exceptional Education Quarterly, 1.*

Kendall, C. R., Borkowski, J. G., & Cavanaugh, J. C. (1980). Metamemory and the transfer of an interrogative strategy by EMR children. *Intelligence, 4,* 255–270.

Mann, L., & Sabatino, D. A. (1985). *Foundations of cognitive processes in remedial and special education.* Rockville, MD: Aspen.

Newell, A. (1979). One final word. In D. T. Tuma & F. Reid (Eds.), *Problem solving and education: Issues in teaching and research.* Hillsdale, NJ: Erlbaum.

Winschel, J. F., & Lawrence, E. A. (1975). Short-term memory: Curricular implications for the mentally retarded. *Journal of Special Education, 9,* 395–408.

Young, R. M. (1978). Strategies and the structure of a cognitive skill. In G. Underwood (Ed.), *Strategies of information processing* (pp. 357–401). London: Academic.

Zigler, E., & Balla, D. (1971). Luria's verbal deficiency theory of mental retardation and performance on sameness, symmetry and opposition tasks: A critique. *American Journal of Mental Deficiency, 74,* 400??

JONI J. GLEASON
*University of West Florida*

## COGNITIVE STYLE

INFORMATION PROCESSING
METACOGNITION

## COGNITIVE STYLES

Cognitive styles are constructs that help to explain the ways that personality variables affect cognition. Kogan has defined them as reflecting "individual variations in *modes* of attending, perceiving, remembering and thinking" (1980, p. 64). Two individuals who score identically on intelligence and other cognitive aptitude or achievement tests and are the same in information processing capabilities may nevertheless differ significantly in school work, success on the job, and other behaviors because they differ in their cognitive styles (Mann & Sabatino, 1985).

The study of cognitive styles began in earnest following World War II, urged on by concern about the psychiatric casualties of that war and postwar interest in personal self-development and psychotherapy. Personality assessment had become exceedingly popular. Thus interest developed respecting the ways that personality variables affect cognitive variables. Studies of what came to be known as cognitive styles emerged.

Interest in cognitive styles first appeared most prominently in the work of George Klein et al. at the Menninger clinic. While the original work was conceptualized in terms of perceptual attitudes (perceptual types of tests being used as the most prominent way of assessing cognitive styles), later research emphasized the cognitive aspects of the research and the term cognitive controls became the dominant descriptor applied to work seeking to determine how personality factors interact with and influence cognitive skills.

Many definitions of cognitive styles have been offered. They generally agree that cognitive styles should be thought of as personality characteristics or traits that are related to other personality characteristics. Furthermore, while cognitive styles cannot always be distinguished or separated from cognitive skills, they are distinct from cognitive contents.

A considerable number of different types of cognitive styles have been distinguished through research. Some are similar, but others are clearly different in their implications for cognitive functioning. It is not unusual to study children and adults from the standpoint of several different cognitive styles.

While the assessment of cognitive styles of schoolchildren is usually done through paper and pencil questionnaires and tests, problem-solving tasks and perceptual types of apparatus are also used. Among the most ingenious of the latter has been tilting-room chair test (Goldstein & Blackman, 1977). In this test, the subjects sit in a chair that is suspended in a small room. Both the chair and the room may be tilted either left or right in varying degrees. In one version, the Room-Adjustment Test (RAT), the room is tilted 56 degrees and the chair 22 degrees. There are eight trials; in four of these trials the room and chair are tilted in the same direction; in the other four they are tilted in opposite directions. The object of the test is to determine the degree of effectiveness with which the subject can direct the examiner to reorient the room to an upright position under these circumstances. In the Body Adjustment Test (BAT), the room remains tilted and the subject directs the examiner to move him or her to an upright position. The degree to which the subjects succeed on these orientation tasks was originally used to assess an individual's ability at field articulation and later to assess an individual's degree of field independence-dependence.

The scores assigned an individual on the basis of performance on cognitive-style assessments are usually used to place the subject somewhere on a bipolar continuum whose poles represent opposing stylistic types, e.g., leveling-sharpening, scanning-focusing. The more the individual's score is oriented toward one pole or another, the more he or she is characterized as being typified by the particular cognitive style associated with that pole. In the case of some cognitive styles, however, an individual will be characterized as belonging to one of several cognitive-style categories, according to the means by which questions were answered or problems solved. This category is presumed to identify the way that an individual characteristically perceives, thinks, solves problems, etc. An example of this is provided by conceptual styles tasks that categorize children as to whether they tend to be analytic, categorical, or relational in their thinking.

Though there has been disagreement on the issue, Kogan has suggested that cognitive styles can be classified on the basis of whether the results obtained are judgmental, i.e., have positive or negative implications attached to particular styles and their scores. Thus certain cognitive styles clearly suggest good or poor cognitive performance, e.g., Witkin's field dependence-independence continuum. Other cognitive styles, however, only indirectly imply cognitive strength or weakness, while still others appear to be truly stylistic, i.e., inputing neither cognitive strength nor weakness but rather suggesting different ways of thinking. Still other cognitive styles can be interpreted either in terms of cognitive strengths and weaknesses or in purely stylistic terms, depending on the circumstances of usage and interpretation.

While the study of cognitive styles began with adult populations, it gradually moved over to juvenile populations as well, including those of children with learning problems and handicaps. This has been more for research rather than diagnostic purposes. The two most popular of cognitive-style study approaches to schoolchildren and special education students are those of field independence-dependence and conceptual tempo. Blackman and Goldstein (1982) have suggested that a major reason for their popularity is the easy availability of instruments to assess them. Another reason seems to be that they appear to be

cognitive styles that may have particular relevance to school work.

There have been many studies suggesting that field-independent students are better and more self-dependent learners than field-dependent ones; that they are better decoders in reading than field-dependent students; and that they are better at math and science as well. Field-independent students have been found to do better in "discovery" types of learning situations; while field-dependent students are benefited by structured learning situations. Gifted children are more likely to be field independent than mentally retarded ones (Mann & Sabatino, 1985). Learning-disabled pupils are more likely to be field dependent than normal readers.

In respect to conceptual tempo, this cognitive-style dimension characterizes children on the basis of their placement on a reflection-impulsivity dimension, according to their performance on problem-solving tests, etc. As might be expected, reflective children are usually better students, while impulsive ones are more likely to read inaccurately and to manifest behavior problems.

In recent years interest in hemispheric differences have led to the postulation that different cognitive styles are associated with the two halves of the brain (Kane, 1984), and that individuals will have preferences in respect to the types of cognition they employ depending on whether they are left brain or right brain oriented.

While the research into cognitive styles has been very active, and results are regularly found indicating that cognitive styles are significantly related to school and academic variables that are important to both normal and handicapped children, the sum and substance of this research does not appear to support a position that knowledge of a handicapped child's particular cognitive style, in and of itself, is particularly helpful in respect to predicting school achievement (Swanson, 1980) or in guiding day-to-day instruction or management. Socioeconomic and general cognitive factors play roles of far greater importance in the school lives of special education students. Indeed, many of the significant differences found in the school performances of special education students who differ in cognitive style appear to be the result of consequences of investigators confounding their variables.

The most popular variant or offshoot of cognitive styles currently are identified as learning styles. Since learning styles tend to be educationally oriented, they have received a great deal of attention in educational circles. Learning style constructs, which emphasize learning preferences rather than personality characteristics, have taken much of the attention away from other types of cognitive styles among researchers concerned with school and academic achievement.

## REFERENCES

Blackman, S., & Goldstein, K. M. (1982). Cognitive styles and learning disabilities. *Journal of Learning Disabilities, 15,* 106–113.

Goldstein, K. M., & Blackman, S. (1977). *Cognitive styles: Five approaches to theory and research*. New York: Wiley.

Kane, M. (1984). Cognitive styles of thinking and learning. Part one. *Academic Therapy, 19*, 527–536.

Kogan, N. (1980). Cognitive styles and reading performance. *Bulletin of the Orton Society, 39*, 63–77.

Mann, L., & Sabatino, D. A. (1985). *Foundations of cognitive processes in remedial and special education*. Rockville, MD: Aspen.

Swanson, L. (1980). Cognitive style, locus of control, and school achievement in learning disabled females. *Journal of Clinical Psychology, 36*, 964–967.

EMILY WAHLEN
LESTER MANN
*Hunter College, City University of New York*

LEARNING STYLES
PERSONALITY TESTS
SPERRY, R.
SPLIT BRAIN RESEARCH
TEMPERAMENT

## COLITIS

Ulcerative colitis is a chronic inflammatory disease of the colon (large intestine). It is a progressive disease, spreading to include part or all of the colon and rectum. It is characterized by alternating remissions and relapses. The disease is usually more severe in children than adults, carrying an increased risk of malignancy because of the greater severity and duration of the disease (Dixon & Walker, 1984). A disease closely related to ulcerative colitis is Crohn's disease, which involves the small intestine as well as the large. Symptomatology and progression in Crohn's closely resembles that in ulcerative colitis.

The cause of ulcerative colitis is unknown. Symptoms of the disease include diarrhea with blood and mucous, abdominal pain preceding defecation, anemia, and rectal urgency. Weight loss is apparent in some children owing to reduced caloric intake or to limitation of food eaten to avoid discomforts of the disease (Dixon & Walker, 1984).

Treatment of colitis varies with severity and extent of the disease. The goal of treatment for children is to bring about remission to allow normal growth and development. Medical therapy includes use of corticosteroids to control inflammation and sulfasalazine to control flare-ups. Undesirable side effects of the two precipitate cautious use with children. Corticosteroids interfere with growth, increase susceptibility to infection, and cause temporary alterations in physical appearance. Sulfasalazine can cause headaches, nausea, vomiting, anorexia, and rash.

If the disease does not respond to medical therapy, or if it involves complications, surgery is required. Part or all of the colon is removed and then resected together or attached to the abdominal wall. If attached to the abdominal wall, a stoma is formed to allow excretion of waste products into an external collecting apparatus. With surgery, the effects of the disease disappear.

Children and their families need a great deal of emotional support and understanding in dealing with the manifestations of the disease and the effects of treatment. Children need special understanding and encouragement when dealing with side effects of steroid treatment or adjusting to the use of an external collecting apparatus. Advances in development of collection apparatus now make it possible for most children to participate in many activities and sports. Most individuals with colitis live a normal life under prolonged medical care.

## REFERENCES

Bokey, E. L., & Shell, R. (1985). *Stomal therapy: A guide for nurses, practitioners and patients*. Sydney, Australia: Pergamon.

Dixon, M. L., & Walker, W. A. (1984). Ulcerative colitis and Crohn's disease. In S. S. Gellis & B. M. Kagan (Eds.), *Current pediatric therapy* (pp. 195–198). Philadelphia: Saunders.

Goodman, M. J., & Sparberg, M. (1978). *Ulcerative colitis*. New York: Wiley.

Goulston, S. J., & McGovern, V. J. (1981). *Fundamentals of colitis*. Oxford, England: Pergamon.

Hanauer, S. B. (1984). Ulcerative colitis. In R. E. Rakel (Ed.), *Conn's current therapy* (pp. 410–415). Philadelphia: Saunders.

CHRISTINE A. ESPIN
*University of Minnesota*

FAMILY RESPONSE TO A HANDICAPPED CHILD
PHYSICAL HANDICAPS

## COLLABORATIVE PERINATAL PROJECT

The main purpose of the Collaborative Perinatal Project is to evaluate factors in pregnancy that may relate to cerebral palsy and other abnormalities of the central nervous system. The project is sponsored by the National Institute of Neurological and Communicative Disorders and Strokes. Over 50,000 pregnant women were recruited (from January 1959 to December 1965) for the largest prospective study of its kind. Although readers of the study are urged to regard conclusions as tentative, it is generally agreed that this massive undertaking adds substantially to what is known about the general epidemiology of birth defects.

Data collected at the 14 university-affiliated hospitals include information on the mother's social and medical background; coexisting diseases; complications of pregnancy; current drug/medication use; and previous use of drugs (extending beyond the mother's last menstrual period). Each participant was interviewed at least monthly throughout pregnancy, at scheduled intervals during the infant's first 2 years, and annually until the child reached 8 years. Records on each child until the age of 8 years include birth and developmental history, diseases, noted congenital defects, and information on siblings and father. Infants received daily examinations for the first 7 days of life (and weekly for prolonged postnatal hospitalizations), with an extensive, standard pediatric exam at age one. Of the mortality rate (4.4% or 2227 stillborn or died before age 4), 81% came to autopsy.

A tangential purpose of this project is the epidemiological investigation of the possible teratogenic role of drugs (or those drugs that cause malformations): in other words, the relationship between drugs taken during pregnancy and malformations in offspring. Although frequent hypotheses are suggested, only a few such relationships are accepted universally as causal. Potent teratogens (e.g., thalidomide) are identified relatively easily. Less potent drugs with less dramatic outcomes are equally important but more difficult to isolate and detect. The Collaborative Perinatal Project provides the opportunity to use a battery of epidemiological and statistical method to screen a variety of drugs against a variety of malformation outcomes.

The study (1) provides quantitative information, much not previously available, on relationships among birth defects; (2) confirms and elaborates on, in quantitative terms, factors such as single umbilical artery and birth defects; (3) raises, in quantitative terms, hypotheses concerning risk factors, some previously suspected but without quantitative information and some not previously suspected; and (4) concludes that birth defects are rarely attributable to a single cause and that many malformation outcomes appear to have multiple risk factors that are interrelated.

Heinonen et al. (1977) were commissioned by the National Institutes of Health to document all findings. Their text contains detailed information on methods, malformations, drugs used, etc. Additional information is obtained by writing to the Perinatal Research Bureau, National Institute of Neurological and Communicative Disorders and Strokes, National Institutes of Health, Bethesda, MD 20014.

**REFERENCE**

Heinonen, O. P., Slone, D., & Shapiro, J. (1977). *Birth defects and drugs in pregnancy*. Littleton, MA: Publishing Sciences Group.

C. MILDRED TASHMAN
*College of Saint Rose*

**CONGENITAL DISORDERS**
**LOW BIRTH WEIGHT INFANTS**
**PREMATURITY/PRETERM**

# COLLECTIVE BARGAINING AND SPECIAL EDUCATION

During the early 1970s, collective bargaining between teacher unions and school boards increased substantially in comparison with previous years (Cresswell & Murphy, 1975). By the beginning of the 1980s, it became clear that collective bargaining was also being extended to issues affecting educational policy. While the issue has not been intensively studied, and practices vary widely in school systems with enrollments over 15,000, collective bargaining agreements have been found to affect not only teacher assignment, but student assignment and curriculum policy. Negotiated agreements have been found to progress through three different stages, the first pertaining to teacher placement, the second student placement, and the third curriculum issues.

In the area of special education, the early work of Mitchell et al. (1971) found that the interests of special education teachers tended not to be reflected in such bargaining agreements, either in the area of working conditions or educational policy. However, the more recent work of Goldschmidt et al. (1984) found that teachers' interests in both areas were reflected in collective negotiations. Collective negotiations have progressively affected special education with regard to teacher placement, student placement, and curriculum. Agreements focus on concerns of special educators as well as regular teachers and administrators with responsibilities for students with special needs. They also reflect federal, state, and local policies relative to such students.

Provisions of negotiated agreements relative to special education focus on student placement in self-contained classes as well as mainstreamed classes and establish student/teacher ratios by setting limits on the size of special education classes. Special education teachers have obtained rights to be involved not only in placement decisions but also in setting educational policy in so far as agreements regulate curriculum and/or teaching methods for students with special needs.

Class size provisions establish either guidelines or formulas for computing maximum class size, often by assigning weights to different categories of needs. While many agreements allow no departures from size limits, others allow some flexibility where there is mutual agreement by teachers, union, and administrators. Often, agreements provide for balancing enrollment in classes that exceed specified size by shifting students from one class to another, or for providing some form of compensation for teachers whose classes exceed the maximum allowed by the contract. The majority of agreements incorporate class size limits specified in state laws.

With respect to the placement of handicapped students, negotiated agreements affect both special and regular classes. Many agreements place exact or implied limits on the number of handicapped students as well as the types of handicapped students that can be assigned to special or regular classes. Teachers' rights to make recommendations on placement decisions for handicapped students have been increasingly recognized. Agreements may specify the ranges of achievement required for placement in specific classes or permit the teacher to decide whether the student is capable of satisfactory performance. Often, provisions permit regular teachers to refer students who require special services.

Collective bargaining agreements affect handicapped students by regulating teacher working conditions in other areas. They also affect curricula relative to special needs students. In the national sample of bargaining agreements of school systems with enrollments of 15,000 or more, studied by Goldschmidt et al. (1984), 60% were found to affect teacher working conditions not only by providing them with decision-making prerogatives in the area of student placement (18%), but also by regulating teacher participation on committees to study the problems of special education (23%); by providing teacher compensation or release time for completing individualized education programs (IEPs) or attending parent conferences (18%); and by offering salary increments for teaching students with special needs (20%).

In addition, 15% provide for in-service or other training at board expense to improve training for special education teachers, and 10% provide for training and/or recertification of regular teachers at school board expense. Of the sample, 27% specified the content of in-service training programs, 38% required that teachers be involved in developing the content of such programs, and 24% delimited the number and scheduling of in-service programs.

With respect to curricula, agreements specify what classes are to be provided for particular categories of handicapped students and the materials to be used. They also cover testing and evaluation instruments, evaluation forms, audiovisual hardware and software to be provided, as well as books, workbooks, etc. To staff these classes andprovide the specified curricula, agreements identify the types of specialists to be provided, including psychologists, speech and hearing clinicians, therapists, counselors, etc.

In summary, collective bargaining agreements have been found to affect teacher and student placement, as well as curricula, and to reflect state, federal, and judicial mandates in the area of special education. The Education for All Handicapped Children Act of 1975 (PL 94-142), and the judicial precedents on which the law was based, has exerted a significant impact on these agreements. State authorities incorporated the principles of these enactments within state laws, and collective bargaining agreements at local school district level have incorporated state enactments. Because these agreements, on the whole, contain effective and expeditious enforcement provisions (e.g., third-party binding arbitration), they have been found to promote implementation of both state and federal laws and judicial mandates.

## REFERENCES

Cresswell, A. M., & Murphy, M. J. (1976). *Education and collective bargaining*. Berkeley, CA: McCutchan.

Goldschmidt, S. M., et al. (1984). *The extent and nature of educational policy bargaining*. Eugene, OR: University of Oregon, Center for Educational Policy and Management.

Mitchell, D. E., et al. (1981). The impact of collective bargaining on school management and policy. *American Journal of Education, 89*(2).

NANCY BORDIER
*Hunter College, City University
of New York*

POLITICS AND SPECIAL EDUCATION
SUPERVISION IN SPECIAL EDUCATION
TEACHER EFFECTIVENESS

# COLLEGE PROGRAMS FOR DISABLED COLLEGE STUDENTS

Following the end of World War II, the majority of colleges and universities in the United States became more sensitive to the needs of students who would have been financially disabled without the original G.I. bill. This same sensitivity, however, on the part of colleges and universities for those who were physically, socially, and/or academically handicapped did not manifest itself to any major degree until the 1970s.

In April 1978 the Association on Handicapped Student Service Programs in Post-Secondary Education (AHSSPPE) came into existence. This organization, along with others, provided professional support for full implementation of the Architectural Barriers Act of 1968 as upgraded and expanded on by Section 504 of the Vocational Rehabilitation Act of 1973, which became operational in April of 1977. The net effect of this act was to ensure the access and use of public schools (elementary through college) by the physically disabled through assurance that the schools would be constructed to accommodate the handicapped person.

Similarly, by the late 1970s a few colleges and universities began formal programs to serve college-bound students who had academic deficits resulting from either some innate and formal learning (language) disability and/or environmentally induced one. Those higher education institutions having programs for this population were identified in part by research projects sponsored by the National Association of College Admission Counselors (NACAC) (Mangrum, 1984). Two agencies that contributed to the development of the NACAC directory of college programs were the Post Secondary School Committee of the Association for Children with Learning Disabilities (ACLD) and the Loyola Academy of Wilmette, Illinois. Other references that identify colleges and universities having academic support services are Liscio's *A Guide to Colleges for Learning Disabled Students*; Mangrum and Strichart's *College and the Learning Disabled Student*; the *FCLD's Guide for Parents of Children with Learning Disabilities*; and *Peterson's Guide to Colleges with Programs for Learning Disabled Students*. These references suggest that the prospective user ask certain questions, as identified by Liscio (1984):

1. Is there a special program for learning-disabled students?
2. How many full-time learning-disabled students are enrolled in the program?
3. Is there a brochure or writen description of the program available?
4. Do learning-disabled students in special programs take regular college courses?
5. Are special courses required of learning-disabled students? Do they carry college credit? Can credit be used toward graduation?
6. Are there additional tuition or fee requirements for learning-disabled students? (p. 12)

Additionally, the prospective users of these references and others like them, following a personal on-site examination of the institution and its services as listed, will probably determine that the primary thrust or intent of the institution's services falls into one of two categories: (1) assistance and support that is not necessarily remedial, and (2) assistance and support that is intended to be remedial. The former is specifically characterized by the use of books on tape (the same service used by blind students); oral presentations instead of written exams; cassette tapes in lieu of written papers; readers for reading textbooks and exams; and notetakers. These services allow the language-handicapped student to cope and to graduate in spite of unremediated reading and spelling deficits.

The college-aged learning-disabled student who is looking for a school to attend will find that the majority of two- and four-year higher education institutions (both public and private) that offer support services will be of the type just depicted; for example, those that provide assistance and support that is not necessarily intended to be remedial. The student who wishes to become language independent, academically as well as socially, might want to consider the other major type of service.

Those institutions that intend to remediate the student's language handicap and his or her accompanying social and psychological deficits, will be characterized by instruction that is designed to remediate the student's reading, spelling, written expression, and arithmetic deficits. The kind of instruction that would be most commonly used would directly reteach the basic or requisite information that must be known to read, spell, write, and carry out mathematical operations. Other probable aspects of this second service posture would be the use of tutors who have been trained to carry out direct remediation of the students academic deficits and formal support programs that deal directly with the student's social habilitation and

psychological needs. Both types of schools offer their learning-disabled students the opportunity to take exams in a private setting without time constraints; use tape recorders to record lectures; take a reduced load as necessary; and partake in the institution's traditional student support services. Beyond the traditional academic assistance and/or remediation, most institutions of higher learning also offer counseling and testing support services.

## REFERENCES

*The FCLD guide for parents of children with learning disabilities.* (1984). New York: Foundation for Children with Learning Disabilities.

Kavale, K., & Forness, S. (1985). *The science of learning disabilities.* San Diego, CA: College Hill.

Liscio, M. A. (1984). *A guide to colleges for learning disabled students.* Orlando, FL: Academic.

Mangrum, C. T., & Strichart, S. S. (1984). *College and the learning disabled student.* Orlando, FL: Grune & Stratton.

Nash, R. T. (1985). Remediation courses, Project Success, University of Wisconsin-Oshkosh. Unpublished raw data.

*Peterson's guide to colleges with programs for learning disabled students.* (1985). Princeton, NJ: Peterson's Guide.

ROBERT T. NASH
*University of Wisconsin,
Oshkosh*

## CONTINUING EDUCATION FOR THE HANDICAPPED

## COLOR BLINDNESS

The inability to perceive or discriminate colors is known as color blindness. There are four main types of color blindness, each containing a number of subtypes. The most rare type is known as *achromotopsia*. In this condition, the subject sees no color; everything is perceived as black, white, or shades of gray. This condition can result from a degenerative process. In the absence of such pathology, the condition is due to an autosomal recessive gene and is extremely rare.

The more common types of color vision disturbances are closely related to retinal physiology, specifically, to the structure and function of the cones. Since the cones are not evenly distributed in the retina, color vision in the visual field is somewhat variable. Color perception is not possible in the periphery of the visual field and diminishes as the object moves away from the point of fixation (Wald, 1968). The perception of color is dependent on not only the presence of different types of cone cells, but of complex chemical pigments thought to respond selectively to the different wavelengths of light.

*Protanopia* refers to the condition in which the individual has difficulty in distinguishing red. *Deuteranopia* is the condition in which the individual has difficulty in distinguishing green. *Tritanopia* is the condition in which the individual cannot distinguish blue; it is a severe and rare form of colorblindness, affecting less than .1% of the population. Tritanopia is considered to be an autosomal dominant trait.

Red-green color disturbances occur in both protanopia and deuteranopia. The former is more severe and less common than the latter. Both are sex-linked (X) recessive traits, explaining their nearly exclusive presence in males. The prevalence of protanopia is about 1:100; deuteranopia about 1:20 (Linksz, 1964).

Determination of the condition is easily made using pseudoisochromatic plates (Isihara test) that present colored patterns or numbers to the individual. The normal person sees one pattern or number; those with color disturbances see the stimulus differently (Thuline, 1972).

Color blindness is not generally considered to be a significant handicap. Some authors (Cooley, 1977) feel that the tests are far too sensitive and that some persons have been needlessly denied employment. The classroom teacher, especially in the early grades, should expect to find at least one color-blind male in the classroom. Tasks involving color discrimination must be eliminated. The literature is replete with retinal changes owed to phenothiazine (Mellaril, Thorazine) administration (Apt, 1960; Weekly et al., 1960). Color vision anomalies may occur if a youngster is under phenothiazine therapy.

## REFERENCES

Apt, R. (1960). Complications of phenothiazine tranquilizers ocular side effects. *Survey Ophthalmology 5,* 550.

Cooley, D. (Ed.) (1977). *Family medical guide.* New York: Better Homes and Gardens.

Linksz, A. (1964). *An essay on color vision and clinical color vision tests.* New York: Grune & Stratton.

Thuline, H. (1972). Color blindness in children: The importance and feasibility of early recognition, *Clinical Pediatrics. 11*(5). 295–299.

Wald, G. (1968). The receptors of human color vision. *Science Magazine, 145,* 1007.

Weekly, R., Potts, A., Rebotem, J., & May, R. (1960). Pigmentary retinopathy in patients receiving high doses of a new phenothiazene. *Archives of Ophthalmology 64,* 65.

JOHN E. PORCELLA
*Rhinebeck Country School,
Rhinebeck, New York*

**MELLARIL**
**THORAZINE**
**VISUAL PERCEPTION AND DISCRIMINATION**
**VISUALLY IMPAIRED**

# COLUMBIA MENTAL MATURITY SCALE

The Columbia Mental Maturity Scale (CMMS; Burgemeister, Blum, & Lorge, 1972) is a multiple choice for-

mated measure of general reasoning ability (p. 7). The CMMS assesses reasoning, which is best described as nonverbal, through the presentation of a series of 6-by-18-inch stimulus cards, each with an array of four or five options. The administration procedures are simple. The examiner merely asks the examinee to find "which one is different." The examinee then selects the one option that is perceptually or conceptually different from the remaining choices.

The CMMS, appropriate for children between the ages of 3 years, 6 months and 9 years, 11 months, requires approximately 15 to 20 minutes to administer; of the 92 items, the examinee is administered 51 to 65, depending on his or her age. While the CMMS produces a total test standard score (age deviation score) with the parameters of an IQ ($\bar{X} = 100$, SD $= 16$), the test should not be viewed as a measure of general intelligence. Intelligence is comprised of many components in addition to general reasoning abilities (e.g., verbal comprehension, verbal fluency, memory, spatial and perceptual aptitude, speed, quantity).

The technical adequacy of the CMMS is appropriate for a screening test. The CMMS Examiner's Manual reports corrected split-half reliability coefficients for the total test in a range from .85 (ages 8 and 9) to .91 (ages $4\frac{1}{2}$ and $5\frac{1}{2}$). The manual also reports a median test-retest reliability coefficient of .85 for a 7- to 10-day test-retest interim. The CMMS correlates in the mid .60 range with the Otis-Lennon Mental Ability Test and the Stanford-Binets, and in the .31 to .61 range with various achievement skills as assessed by the Stanford Achievement Test. The CMMS was standardized on a fairly representative sample of 2600 children reflecting the 1968 U.S. population characteristics, including geographic region, age, sex, race, and parental occupation.

The CMMS is not as widely used as its attributes and utility warrant. It is a good "ice breaker" in the assessment of shy children, and also provides a good diagnostic contrast when the examiner wishes to compare a child's nonverbal reasoning with his or her verbal reception, reasoning, and expression.

## REFERENCE

Burgemeister, B. B., Blum, L. H., & Lorge, I. (1972). *Columbia Mental Maturity Scale* (3rd ed.). New York: Harcourt Brace Jovanovich.

BRUCE BRACKEN
LINDSAY S. GROSS
*University of Wisconsin,
Milwaukee*

# COMMUNICATION AIDS, ELECTRONIC

See ELECTRONIC COMMUNICATION AIDS.

# COMMUNICATION BOARDS

Communication boards are simple, nonelectronic, augmentative communication systems used by nonspeaking persons. They are usually made individually according to the skills and needs of the nonspeaking user. The advantages of communication boards are their flexibility and low cost. Any symbol system ranging from objects and pictures to written alphabet letters can be used as message symbols. The communication board can be accessed by direct selection, through scanning, or by an encoding process. As the nonspeaking person's skills change over time, the communication board can be easily adapted to reflect those changes.

The major disadvantage of communication boards is the lack of spoken or written output from the system. The listener who interacts with a nonspeaking communication board user must be able to physically see the communication board to receive a message. For long messages, the listener must remember each symbol selected and mentally sequence the symbols back together to understand the message. Communication boards are used frequently with handicapped children and adults who have limited vocabularies. In addition, they are often used as a secondary backup communication device for nonspeaking persons who rely primarily on sophisticated electronic augmentative systems.

## REFERENCES

Musselwhite, C. R., & St. Louis, K. O. (1982). *Communication programming for the severely handicapped: Vocal and nonvocal strategies*. Houston, TX: College-Hill Press.

Schiefelbusch, R. L. (1980). *Nonspeech language and communication: Analysis and intervention*. Baltimore, MD: University Park Press.

SHARON L. GLENNEN
*Pennsylvania State University*

AUGMENTATIVE COMMUNICATION DEVICES
COMPUTER USE WITH THE HANDICAPPED
ROBOTICS

# COMMUNICATION DISORDERS

Communication disorders are studied through the diagnosis and treatment of individuals with speech, language, and hearing problems, including problems with articulation, language, voice, fluency, and hearing. The most common terms applied to this discipline are speech pathology and audiology or communication disorders and sciences. The speech-language pathologist and audiologist are concerned with habilitating or rehabilitating children or adults with speech, language, or hearing problems. Speech-language pathologists deal with a wide variety of problems, ranging from working with a child with a misarticulated *s* sound to treating an adult who has suffered a stroke and has lost all speech and language abilities. The audiologist is concerned with the diagnosis, measurement, and study of hearing and hearing loss. The audiologist may prescribe the use of a hearing aid, aural rehabilitation through lip reading and auditory training, and use of sign language, or the use of other devices that assist communication purposes.

*Disorders of articulation* or *phonological disorders* involve problems in the production of the sounds of a language. The disorder may be the result of a maturational, learning, or organic problem (e.g., cleft of the palate), or an impairment of the neurological system (e.g., dysarthria). Sounds are distorted, omitted, or substituted for by other sounds. Sometimes a speaker will add an extra sound to a word. Misarticulation may reduce the intelligibility of speech, draw attention to itself, and impair the communication process. Misarticulations can result from impairment of the auditory (hearing) mechanism. In children with moderate to severe hearing loss, 21% of the consonants and 12% of vowels are misarticulated.

*Voice disorders* result from misuse or abuse of the larynx or improper or faulty valving of the air stream by the vocal folds. Also contributing to voice disorders is the inability of the soft palate to appropriately couple the nasal cavities to the rest of the vocal tract. Inappropriate valving of the air stream may lead to excessive air flow through the larynx, resulting in a breathy voice quality. Faulty valving of the air stream, known as laryngeal hypofunction, may result from vocal fold paralysis or a growth on the vocal folds preventing them from approximating. A lot of laryngeal tension coupled with air escaping through the glottis may lead to the perception of a hoarse voice quality or a rough voice. This may be associated with mucous on the vocal folds or laryngeal growths. A harsh voice quality is associated with lower than normal pitch and a hard glottal attack (explosive release of subglottal pressure), along with the perception of noise in the acoustic spectrum.

Voice disorders also include inappropriate use of pitch and loudness. Excessively high pitch may be associated with excessive laryngeal tension and may be seen in severely hearing-impaired individuals who are unable to monitor their own voice quality. Low pitch may be associated with virilization of the female larynx owed to excessive intake of androgenous hormones, or it may be associated with vocal abuse in preadolescent children with the development of laryngeal neoplasms. Weak voice quality or reduced loudness is associated with the inability to valve the air stream and generate sufficient subglottal pressure—a growth may interfere with laryngeal valving or one or both of the vocal folds may be paralyzed. Excessive loudness is associated with laryngeal hyperfunction. It is also observed in individuals with a bone conduction hearing loss. These individuals are unable to hear themselves speak and increase their vocal effort to do so.

Proper use of the velopharyngeal port is necessary in

directing air out the oral cavity and in building up pressure within the oral cavity for the production of certain consonant sounds. The inability to achieve appropriate velopharyngeal closure will introduce excessive nasal resonance into the speech acoustic spectrum. Certain groups of individuals exhibit excessive nasal resonance; these are speakers with cleft of the palate, individuals with dysarthria, and, in some cases, individuals with moderate to severe hearing loss. At the other extreme, complete velopharyngeal closure will produce the perception of hyponasality or the lack of nasal resonance. This may occur with a severe cold, where the nasopharnyx is completely blocked owing to the swelling of the nasal and pharyngeal mucosa.

The most frequent disorder treated by speech pathologists is stuttering. It is known as a *fluency disorder* and its cause is unknown. Some theorists suggest that stuttering is learned; others suggest that it is the result of psychological conflict. Some researchers suggest that stuttering results from biological factors such as a lack of cerebral dominance or mixed dominance; auditory dysfunction; a lack of coordination among the respiratory, phonation, and articulatory subsystems of speech; or a breakdown in the neurological control of the speech mechanism.

Less than 1% the population have been identified as stutterers. Also, more males stutter than females. Generally, the incidence of stutterers decreases with age. Little is known about the prevalence of stuttering in older adults.

The most often cited characteristics of stuttering are part-word repetitions, where sounds or syllables are repeated; prolongations, where the duration of the initial syllable of a word is increased; hesitations, where a silent or tense pause is usually judged as an instance of stuttering when a listener thinks that a speaker is unable to initiate phonation; and interjection, an attempt to initiate phonation when stuttering is anticipated.

Both children and adults can be *language impaired*. Some children are slow to acquire most aspects of language; for example, two-word utterances typically occur at 18 months in a normal developing child, but they may occur at 40 months in a language-delayed child. Children described as mentally retarded fall into this language-delayed or language-deviant group. Autistic children may also exhibit language impairment. They fail to respond normally to other individuals, fail to use objects appropriately, and may not react in a normal way (failure of reaction) to sensory stimuli. They also fail to develop normal communication skills. Rather than exhibiting spontaneous imitation of others' speech, autistic children show a high frequency of unsolicited imitative behavior. In other instances of language disorders, some children begin to develop language normally during the first years of life, but after an illness or head trauma, language learning is delayed or ceases. The most common term used to describe

this condition is acquired aphasia, a condition more prevalent in adults than in children. The specific language difficulties associated with this disorder depend on the age at which the insult took place. Before 3 years of age, the child usually becomes uncommunicative and does not respond to the speech of others. Improvement in language acquisition can prove to be rapid. With the injury occurring after 3 years of age, language comprehension and production may be reduced but they are not absent. There are word-finding difficulties, with recovery being slower and residual problems being present years later.

Adults who exhibit language disorders typically do so as the result of damage to the brain. Aphasia is a language disorder involving the comprehension and expression of language. The damage generally occurs in the left hemisphere. There are different types of aphasia. They involve deficits of spoken language, omission of function words where speech sounds telegraphic, loss of substantive words, and auditory comprehension deficits. The patient with aphasia may often suffer from limb paralysis, vision problems, and a reduction in intellectual capacity. The second cause of language disorders in adults is senile dementia or Alzheimer's disease. Senile dementia is not a part of normal aging. It is progressive and is associated with deterioration of memory, intellectual function, and communicative ability. Word meaning and the ability to generate meaningful utterances degenerate with the person's overall intellectual functioning.

The science of hearing is called audiology and those who practice the discipline are called audiologists. Hearing loss is one of the most common handicapping conditions in both children and adults. Approximately 15 million Americans have a hearing loss that interferes with communication. Annually, 3000 to 5000 infants are born with a profound hearing loss.

*Hearing disorders* include a reduction in the sensitivity to sound and the inability of the ear to differentiate among sounds. Hearing impairment may result from the inability of the ear to conduct sound, to analyze sound, or a combination of both. The hearing disorder may be genetic, or may be acquired before or after birth. A moderate to profound hearing loss acquired during the first year of life will have devastating effects on the communicative ability of the child. If the hearing loss is acquired after the first year, the individual can more readily learn to communicate with professional help. The important factor is the early detection of the hearing loss and an early intervention program.

The auditory mechanism is the primary sense through which speech and language are acquired. There is no agreement as to the severity of hearing loss that will cause speech and language problems. There is some indication that speech and language problems begin to occur with a hearing loss of greater than 40 dB. Deaf children with a hearing loss of at least 70 dB commonly have problems in articulation, voice, timing, and rhythm.

## REFERENCES

Bloodstein, O. (1979). *Speech pathology: An introduction*. Boston: Houghton Mifflin.

Boone, D. R. (1985). Disorders of language in adults. In P. H. Skinner & R. L. Shelton (Eds.), *Speech language and hearing: Normal processes and disorders* (pp. 372–396). New York: Wiley.

Boone, D. R. (1983). Voice disorders. In T. J. Hixon, L. D. Shriberg, & J. H. Saxman (Eds.), *Introduction to communication disorders* (pp. 311–351). Englewood Cliffs, NJ: Prentice-Hall.

Curlee, R. F. (1985). Disorders of fluency. In P. H. Skinner & R. L. Shelton (Eds.), *Speech language and hearing: Normal processes and disorders* (pp. 307–331). New York: Wiley.

Northern, J. L., & Lemme, M. (1982). Hearing and auditory disorders. In G. H. Shames & E. H. Wiig (Eds.), *Human communication disorders: An introduction* (pp. 299–329). Columbus, OH: Merrill.

Shelton, R. L. (1985). Disorders of articulation. In P. H. Skinner & R. L. Shelton (Eds.), *Speech language and hearing: Normal processes and disorders* (pp. 216–266). New York: Wiley.

Shelton, R. L. (1985). Disorders of phonation. In P. H. Skinner & R. L. Shelton (Eds.), *Speech language and hearing: Normal processes and disorders* (pp. 269–304). New York: Wiley.

Wiig, E. H. (1982). Language disabilities in the school-age child. In G. H. Shames & E. H. Wiig (Eds.), *Human communication disorders: An introduction* (pp. 258–293). Columbus, OH: Merrill.

HARVEY R. GILBERT
*Pennsylvania State University*

APHASIA
AUDIOLOGY
AUDITORY ABNORMALITIES
LANGUAGE DEFICIENCIES AND DEFICITS
LANGUAGE DISORDERS
LANGUAGE DISORDERS, EXPRESSIVE
SPEECH AND LANGUAGE DISORDERS

## COMMUNICATION METHODS IN SPECIAL EDUCATION, ALTERNATIVE

See ALTERNATIVE COMMUNICATION METHODS IN SPECIAL EDUCATION.

## COMMUNICATION SPECIALIST

A communication specialist is any one of a number of professionals who deal with aspects of both normal and disordered human communication. Such an individual may have expertise in communication theory, small group communication, organizational communication, or rhetoric. This individual may call himself or herself a linguist, a psycholinguist, a sociolinguist, a cultural linguist, or a rhetorician. The specialist is concerned with the influence of such diverse disciplines as linguistics, psychology, and sociology on human communication in general and language and speech in particular. In addition, these professionals study the development of normal communication theories and processes.

The study of disordered communication can also be considered in the realm of the communication specialist. The individual typically has expertise in communication disorders, education of the hearing impaired, or neurolinguistics. Speech and language disorders in children and adults can be studied from an organic (anatomic and physiologic) or functional (psychological, learning) perspective. The specialist in disordered communication may be concerned with such problems as language delay in children from multiple articulation errors or delay in (or loss of) the acquisition of morphologic, syntactic, or semantic rules of language. The communication specialist will also be concerned with language disorders owed to neurologic factors (e.g., brain damage).

HARVEY R. GILBERT
*Pennsylvania State University*

COMMUNICATION DISORDERS
SPEECH AND LANGUAGE HANDICAPS
SPEECH LANGUAGE PATHOLOGIST

## COMMUNITY-BASED INSTRUCTION

Community-based instruction refers to the opportunity for students to have direct interaction with resources in the community while participating in educational programs. With the current emphasis on education in the least restrictive environment for all students with handicaps, community-based instruction has been implemented in many special education programs, especially in those that serve students with moderate to severe handicaps. For students with moderate and severe handicaps to perform adequately in normalized postschool environments, skills must be taught in locations where they will naturally occur (Brown et al., 1983).

Community-based instruction may be implemented using a number of models (Brown et al., 1983). These include consecutive instruction, whereby skills are taught in a simulated setting within the school facility until a certain skill level is reached; instruction in nonschool settings then follows. Concurrent instruction can occur where instruction takes place in both school and nonschool settings at daily or weekly intervals. Nonschool instruction can be implemented with direct training in nonschool (community) settings only students must have current access or have contact with the setting in the future.

Community-based instruction may involve training in a number of areas. Ordering, purchasing, and eating food in a restaurant may be taught. Use of consumer services such as public transportation, banks, and laundromats may be emphasized during training. Recreation skills may be taught in natural community sites including parks, community gymnasiums, aerobics/fitness centers, and video arcades. Students may be taught to use stores and shops such as grocery stores, pharmacies, and department stores. Vocational skills may be taught in community vocational sites. Selection of community-based training sites can be determined by examining the current and future needs of particular students in community-referenced activities (Wehman, Renzaglia, & Bates, 1985). Certain skills such as street crossing, appropriate social interaction with nonhandicapped peers and adults, and nonvocal or vocal communication may be taught in more than one community-based training activity.

A number of advantages in using community-based instruction with students who have moderate to severe handicaps have been cited by professionals in the field of special education. If training takes place in heterogeneous, nonschool environments, student adaptive functioning will be more likely in current and subsequent community settings. Transfer and generalization of community skills will be more likely to occur when taught in natural rather than simulated settings (Brown et al., 1979; Brown et al., 1976). In addition, handicapped students participating in community-based instruction will have frequent access to nonhandicapped peers who may serve as role models. In turn, the awareness by nonhandicapped people of their peers with handicaps will be enhanced. This will enable the nonhandicapped peers to be cognizant of the abilities of individuals with handicaps, thus promoting a smoother transition to postschool environments on the part of handicapped individuals. Parent and teacher expectations of student abilities may be increased when community-based instruction occurs. Finally, the opportunity for students to sample the reinforcing aspects of activities in the community can be an advantage in achieving acquisition of functional skills (Wehman & Hill, 1982; Wehman et al., 1985).

A number of factors need to be taken into account when considering community-based instruction. These include staffing, transportation, scheduling, costs, necessary curriculum changes, and modifications for severely physical handicapped students (Hamre-Nietupski et al., 1982). Considerations such as these require careful planning on the part of teachers and administrators to facilitate adequate community-based programming.

## REFERENCES

Brown, L., Branston, M. B., Hamre-Nietupski, S., Pumpian, I., Certo, N., & Gruenwald, L. (1979). A strategy for developing chronological age-appropriate and functional curricular con-

tent for severely handicapped adolescents and young adults. *Journal of Special Education, 13,* 81–90.

Brown, L., Nietupski, M., & Hamre-Nietupski, S. (1976). Criterion of ultimate functioning. In M. A. Thomas (Ed.), *Hey, don't forget me!* Reston, VA: Council for Exceptional Children.

Brown, L., Nisbet, J., Ford, A., Sweet, M., Shiraga, B., York, J., & Loomis, R. (1983). The critical need for nonschool instruction in educational programs for severely handicapped students. *Journal of the Association for Persons with Severe Handicaps, 8*(3), 71–77.

Hamre-Nietupski, S., Nietupski, J., Bates, P., & Maurer, S. (1982). Implementing a community-based educational model for moderately and severely handicapped students: Common problems and suggested solutions. *Journal of the Association for Persons with Severe Handicaps, 7*(4), 38–43.

Wehman, P., & Hill, J. (1982). Preparing severely handicapped youth for less restrictive environments. *Journal of the Association for Persons with Severe Handicaps, 7*(1), 33–39.

Wehman, P., Renzaglia, A., & Bates, P. (1985). *Functional living skills for moderately and severely handicapped individuals.* Austin, TX: Pro-Ed.

CORNELIA LIVELY
*University of Illinois,
Urbana-Champaign*

COMPETENCY EDUCATION
NON-SHELTERED EMPLOYMENT
SHELTERED WORKSHOPS
VOCATIONAL TRAINING OF HANDICAPPED

# COMMUNITY-BASED JOB TRAINING FOR STUDENTS WITH AUTISM AND DEVELOPMENTAL DISABILITIES

In the past few years, the need to better prepare persons with disabilities for life after high school has become recognized by federal and local agencies and has been well documented in the professional literature. Now, targeted as a national priority, the development of programs to facilitate the transition from school to adult living has received substantial funding and attention. A major component of this transition movement involves vocational preparation of handicapped students.

Traditionally, vocational training efforts have centered on nonhandicapped and mildly handicapped students, with little or no related instruction being provided to persons having more severe handicaps. In fact, sheltered workshops and day treatment centers have served as the primary vehicles for the delivery of adult services for persons who are developmentally disabled, with few other placement alternatives (Schutz & Rusch, 1982). However, as the first generation of students served by the Education for All Handicapped Children Act (PL 94-142) has begun to graduate from school, it has become clear that additional educational and vocational programs are required so that these individuals may also become employed.

The purpose of community-based job training is to prepare students for employment through the provision of instruction in actual job tasks at work sites within the local community. Research has shown that, because students with developmental disabilities often have difficulty transferring skills learned in one situation to another (Koegel, Rincover, & Egel, 1982), it is advantageous to assess and to teach job skills in the settings in which they will ultimately have to be performed (Berkell, 1985). Through the provision of vocational training in job sites within the community, teachers can facilitate student mastery of specific job skills, as well as the development of interpersonal job-related skills required to maintain various employment positions.

There are five major phases involved in community-based job training: (1) student evaluation, (2) job development, (3) instruction at the work site, (4) supervision reduction, and (5) client follow-up. Each of these phases must be addressed by the vocational trainer regardless of the student's ability level.

Vocational training should begin with an assessment of a person's interests and aptitudes for different jobs. This involves the realistic assessment of learner needs and characteristics. Many of the vocational evaluation instruments commonly used by special educators and vocational rehabilitation counselors are useful for assessing mildly and moderately handicapped youths, but they provide less useful information when used with individuals with severe learning problems. For persons with developmental disabilities, assessment is most appropriately conducted through on-the-job evaluation, work samples, and interview techniques.

Vocational evaluation is both a student-centered and work-related assessment process. Prior to beginning a community-based job training program, the teacher must survey the local job market to become aware of the types of jobs available and plan the curriculum to prepare students for these types of work.

In order to match the student to a particular job, the evaluator requires information not only about student preferences, abilities, and behaviors, but also about the demands of the job and the behavioral characteristics required of workers on the job. Job analysis is the systematic study of an occupation in terms of what the worker does in relation to data, people, and things; the methodology and techniques employed; the machines, tools, equipment, and work aids used; the materials, products, subject matter, or services that result; and the traits required of the worker (McCray, 1982). This procedure is especially useful as a means of identifying essential job tasks; it provides much instructionally relevant information.

A comprehensive approach to vocational preparation involves both job skill development and the development of work-related skills. Job skills training generally focuses on use of equipment, production rate, and quality of the product produced. Work-related behaviors include self-care and grooming, communication skills, interpersonal social skills, leisure skills for break times, and travel skills.

Direct skill training and ongoing assessment are the major instructional requirements of a community-based job training program (Rusch & Mithaug, 1980). Instruction that is systematic and behavioral in nature tends to be most effective in vocational training.

The type and amount of supervision required by a student at a work site is often contingent on the nature of the handicapping condition and the complexity of the job task. Some autistic and developmentally disabled students may need ongoing supervision for an indefinite period of time, while others will require only a minimum of supervision following their initial training.

One key to increasing independence on the job is to fade, or reduce, supervision and assistance to the student as soon as possible in order to avoid the development of dependency on the teacher. Rotating supervisors during the training sessions is also beneficial in reducing such dependency, as well as in increasing generalization from the teacher to an actual job supervisor.

In contrast to job training programs for mildly handicapped persons, students with autism and developmental disabilities may require systematically planned job retention and follow-up services for many years following graduation from school. Methods of determining follow-up intervention strategies include periodic employee evaluations and progress reports, parent/guardian questionnaires, on-site visits, and telephone contacts with employers and family members or group home staff (Moon, Goodall, Barcus, & Brooke, 1985).

A problem or potential problem may be discovered through the use of such ongoing follow-up assessment procedures. When the client is in a new job situation, it is also helpful to request that the employer contact the job trainer with any concerns as soon as they arise. As the client and the employer become more comfortable with each other, the need for contact with the job trainer will become less frequent.

Preparation of students with developmental disabilities for productive employment has become a major educational concern. Issues regarding the selection of instructional locations and the types of assessment and training methods used in vocational preparation programs have received increased attention in the past decade. Research has shown that, because students with autism and developmental disabilities often have difficulty in transferring skills learned from one situation to another, it is advantageous to teach job skills in community-based settings rather than in the classroom. By providing vocational training in the job sites within the community, teachers can help students to master the necessary competencies for specific jobs and to learn job-related skills necessary to maintain various employment positions.

## REFERENCES

Koegel, R. L., Rincover, A., & Egel, A. I. (1982). *Educating and understanding autistic children*. San Diego, CA: College Hill.

Moon, S., Goodall, P., Barcus, M., & Brooke, V. (Eds.). (1985). *The supported work model of competitive employment for citizens with severe handicaps: A guide for job trainers*. Richmond, VA: Rehabilitation and Training Center, Virginia Commonwealth University.

Rusch, F. R., & Mithaug, D. E. (1980). *Vocational training for mentally retarded adults: A behavior analytic approach*. Champaign, IL: Research.

Schutz, R. P., & Rusch, F. R. (1982). Competitive employment: Toward employment integration for mentally retarded persons. In K. P. Lynch, W. E. Kiernan, & J. A. Stark (Eds.), *Prevocational and vocational education for special needs youth: A blueprint for the 1980's* (pp. 133–160). Baltimore, MD: Brookes.

Stodden, R. A., Casale, J., & Schwartz, S. E. (1977). Work evaluation and the mentally retarded: Review and recommendations. *Mental Retardation, 15*, 25–27.

DIANNE E. BERKELL
*C.W. Post Campus, Long Island University*

**SHELTERED WORKSHOPS**
**UNEMPLOYMENT OF THE HANDICAPPED**
**VOCATIONAL REHABILITATION**

# COMMUNITY-BASED SERVICES

The concept of normalization has led to the current trend of serving individuals who might have been institutionalized in the community. These handicapped individuals must be provided with support services to help them successfully adjust to community life. To achieve the goal of normalization, the handicapped should be involved in developmental activities that are closely associated with those of nonhandicapped individuals. These activities should center around integration into the normal life of the community. To the maximum extent possible, each handicapped individual's developmental activities should focus on the following life cycle. During infancy and early childhood, skill development should be related to sensorimotor skills, communication, self-help, and socialization. During the stages of childhood and early adolescence, there should be application of basic academic skills in daily life activities; application of appropriate reasoning and judgment in mastery of the environment; and participation in interpersonal relationships. During late adolescence and adulthood, vocational and social activities should be the major areas of focus (Grossman, 1977). Intagliata, Kraus, and Willer (1980) conducted a study to determine the impact of deinstitutionalization on the community-based service system. Basic observations reported in this study include the following:

Agencies served a large portion of formerly institutionalized individuals

Agencies served individuals with low intellectual levels

Formerly institutionalized individuals required needed services to be more intensive

Special programs were needed to provide appropriate services for the lower functioning individuals

Pollard, Hall, & Kiernan (1979) state that there are many services available to the handicapped from various separate systems such as health, education, rehabilitation, recreation, employment, and housing. However, when these systems are working separately, there is little chance for them to solve the varied problems of the handicapped. There is a great need for these human services to work together to provide comprehensive community services. According to Schalock (1985), comprehensive community-based services for the handicapped include community living alternatives, habilitation programs, and support programs. Community living alternatives range from the highest level of independence, independent living, to congregate living, home care, supervised living, staffed apartments, and group homes, to the lowest level of independence, community institutional facilities. The habilitation programs in education range from the highest level of community integration, mainstreamed classes in public schools, to resource rooms, day training programs, and residential programs, to the lowest level of community integration, homebound instruction. The habilitation programs in employment range from the highest level of productivity, competitive employment, to transitional employment, sheltered workshop, and work activity, to the lowest level of activity, day training programs. The last category of comprehensive community services, support services, includes health and mental health care, legal services, home assistance (respite care), early identification/intervention, and transportation. In addition, the importance of the following points in designing and providing community living and habilitation alternatives are crucial:

Natural environments are the preferred service settings

Generic services should be used as much as possible

Assistance to the client should be provided only at the level actually needed to promote independence and self-sufficiency

Training should focus on increasing the client's independence, productivity, and community integration

Everyone has potential for growth regardless of his or her current functioning level (Schalock, 1985 p. 38)

Scheerenberger (1981) conducted a study of all superintendents of public residential facilities throughout the

United States. All superintendents completed the questionnaire. The results indicated that the community variables that resulted in problems causing community placement failures included inadequacies in appropriate living settings, behavioral management programs, specialized services, and adult programs. Community services for the mildly and moderately retarded that were considered to be effective were transportation, medical services, educational opportunities, and advocacy. On the other hand, these same services for the severely and profoundly retarded were found to be less than adequate.

## REFERENCES

Grossman, H. J. (Eds.). (1977). *Manual on terminology and classification in mental retardation* (Special Publication No. 2). Washington, DC: American Association on Mental Deficiency.

Intagliata, J., Kraus, S., & Willer, B. (1980). The impact of deinstitutionalization on a community-based service system. *Mental Retardation, 18,* 302–308.

Pollard, A., Hall, H., & Kiernan, C. (1979). Community services planning. In P. R. Magrab & J. O. Elder (Eds.), *Planning services to handicapped persons: Community, education, health.* Baltimore, MD: Brookes.

Schalock, R. L. (1985). Comprehensive community services: A plea for interagency collaboration. In R. H. Bruininks & K. C. Lakin (Eds.), *Living and learning in the least restrictive environment.* Baltimore, MD: Brookes.

Scheerenberger, R. C. (1981). Deinstitutionalization: Trends and difficulties. In R. H. Bruininks, C. E. Meyers, B. B. Sigford, & K. C. Lakin (Eds.), *Deinstitutionalization and community adjustment of mentally retarded people.* Washington, DC: American Association on Mental Deficiency.

JANICE HARPER
*North Carolina Central
University*

**DEINSTITUTIONALIZATION
NORMALIZATION
REHABILITATION**

# COMMUNITY PLACEMENT

The term community placement is generally used to denote those living, working, and recreational/leisure arrangements found in community environments as opposed to institutions. It refers to those environments in which persons with disabilities work, live, and recreate within a community. Community placement has received increased attention as the most appropriate and desirable treatment setting for persons with disabilities (Lakin et al., 1982). As early as 1969 Wolfensberger stressed the importance of community services and facilities as a viable alternative to institutionalization. Others quickly recommended that such a movement be guided by the prin-

ciple of normalization (Wolfensberger, 1972). The deinstitutionalization movement has created a need for a variety of community placement options. Community placement not only permits easier access to those experiences that lead to a more normal lifestyle, but also may sensitize nonhandicapped persons to those with handicapping conditions.

State-of-the-art community placement facilities share several common aspects. They are community-based, small in size, supervised by a social or private agency, and based on the principles of normalization and human management (Mamula & Newman, 1973). Training to allow persons increased access to, and participation in, existing community activities is a desirable characteristic. The physical location of the community placement should facilitate access to all community services enjoyed by persons without handicaps. These services would include access to parks, medical services, shopping facilities, federal and state support services, and other community services (e.g., post offices, banks).

The array of services provided in the community typically includes vocational opportunities, residential options, and recreational/leisure activities. Community vocational opportunities should include competitive employment (Hill & Wehman, 1983), long-term supported employment (Wehman & Kregel, 1985), small enterprise-contract shops (Wald & Rhodes, 1984), and mobile work crews (Wald & Rhodes, 1984).

Educational opportunities available in the community should consist of classes in age-appropriate regular education buildings (Brown, Ford et al., 1983). Curricular priorities should stress functional life skills with training conducted in the natural environments in which behaviors will ultimately be performed (Brown, Nisbet et al., 1983). Residential options in the community range from natural homes or foster care (one to six persons) to group homes and domiciliary care facilities. The appropriateness of each option is determined by the individual needs of the residents.

The full range of recreational/leisure opportunities that are available to persons without handicaps should also be available to persons with handicaps. These should include recreational facilities (YMCA, YWCA, health clubs, etc.), sporting events (town leagues), and spectator sports. Other opportunities should include movies, concerts, and theater. In summary, it is important that whatever the recreational/leisure opportunities available in the community for persons without handicaps also be available to those with handicaps.

## REFERENCES

Brown, L., Ford, A., Nisbet, J., Sweet, M., Donnellan, A., & Gruenewald, L. (1983). Opportunities available when severely handicapped students attend chronological age appropriate regular schools. *Journal of the Association for Persons with Severe Handicaps, 8*(1), 16–24.

Brown, L., Nisbet, J., Ford, A., Sweet, M., Shiraga, B., York, J.,

& Loomis, R. (1983). The critical need for nonschool instruction in educational programs for severely handicapped students. *Journal of the Association for Persons with Severe Handicaps.* 8(3), 71–78.

Hill, M., & Wehman, P., (1983). Cost benefit analysis of placing moderately and severely handicapped individuals into competitive employment. *Journal of the Association for the Severely Handicapped.* 8(1), 30–38.

Lakin, K. C., Krantz, G. C., Bruiniks, R. H., Clumpner, J. L., & Hill, B. K. (1982). One hundred years of data on populations of public residential facilities for mentally retarded people. *American Journal of Mental Deficiency, 87,* 1–8.

Mamula, R. A., & Newman, N. (1973). *Community placement of the mentally retarded.* Springfield, IL: Thomas.

Rhodes, L. E., & Valenta, L. (1985). Industry-based supported employment: An enclave approach. *Journal of the Association for Persons with Severe Handicaps.* 10(1), 12–20.

Wald, B. A., & Rhodes, L. E. (1984). *Developing model vocational programs in rural settings for adults with severe retardation: The mobile crew model.* Paper presented at the meeting of the Association for Persons with Severe Handicaps, Chicago, IL.

Wehman, P., & Kregel, J. (1985). A supported work approach to competitive employment of individuals with moderate and severe handicaps. *Journal of the Association for Persons with Severe Handicaps, 10*(1), 3–12.

Wolfensberger, W. (1969). Twenty predictions about the future of residential services in mental retardation. *Mental Retardation, 6*(7), 51–54.

Wolfensberger, W. (1972). *The principle of normalization in human services.* Toronto, Ontario: National Institute on Mental Retardation.

SUE ANN MORROW
*EDGE, Inc., Bradshaw, Michigan*

LONNY W. MORROW
*Northeast Missouri State University*

**COMMUNITY-BASED SERVICES**
**COMMUNITY RESIDENTIAL PROGRAMS**
**DEINSTITUTIONALIZATION**

# COMMUNITY RESIDENTIAL PROGRAMS

There is an array of community residential options available. Foster homes, also known as personal care homes or family care homes (McCoin, 1983), are private homes rented or owned by a family with one or more persons with disabilities living as family members (Hill & Lakin, 1984). The number of residents rarely exceeds six (Miller & Intagliata, 1984). These residences are licensed by a state agency or a local facility (e.g., a hospital). Foster homes are available for both children and adults. They tend to be homelike, with the person with the disability being "one of the family."

Group homes are residences with staff to provide care and supervision of one or more persons with disabilities (Hill & Lakian, 1984). Financial support comes from a variety of sources, including churches, states, private non-profit organizations, and private for-profit organizations (Miller & Intagliata, 1984). It is not uncommon to find group homes staffed with house parents (a man and a woman who live in the residence, with one having an additional outside job) and one or two additional staff members for the hours when the majority of residents are home. The number of residents living in groups varies from home to home. Most of the research conducted has involved group homes serving under 20 residents (Miller & Intagliata, 1984).

Semiindependent living facilities are facilities having separate units or apartments with staff members living in one unit or apartment; however, staff members live in the same building to provide support services to those in need. Services might include assistance with budgeting or managing money, housework, or laundry. Currently, these facilities are mainly supported by nonprofit organizations (Hill, Lakin, & Bruininks, 1984).

Domicilary care facilities are community-based facilities whose primary function is to provide shelter and protection to the residents. There are no training or rehabilitation activities conducted (Miller & Intagliata, 1984). Since there is a lack of emphasis on training or rehabilitation, these types of facilities are deemed most appropriate for persons with high levels of independent living skills who need little or no additional training, or for those persons who, because of severe medical or physical needs or age, would not benefit from additional skill training (Miller & Intagliata, 1984). The number of residents in these facilities ranges from 5 to 200. Most of these facilities are operated by individual proprietors (Hill et al., 1984).

Although there are a variety of names given to domiciliary care facilities, there are generally two broad categories. Board and care facilities are also known as boarding homes and adult homes. As a general rule, these facilities provide a room and meals to the residents. Some also provide limited supervision. The major source of support for most residents is Social Security. (Miller & Intagliata, 1984). Health care facilities are also known as convalescent care homes, nursing homes, skilled nursing facilities, intermediate care facilities, and health-related facilities (Miller & Intagliata, 1984). In addition to providing a room and meals, these facilities also provide some level of nursing care to the residents. Generally, these facilities are funded through Medicare and Medicaid.

Halfway houses are short-term residential options available to persons leaving institutional settings (Katz, 1968). The setting is supervised with emphasis on facilitating the person's reentry into the community. The number of residents ranges from 12 to 25.

**REFERENCES**

Hill, B. K., & Lakin, K. C. (1984). *Classification of residential facilities for mentally retarded people* (Brief No. 24). Minneapolis, MN: Center for Residential and Community Services, University of Minnesota, Department of Educational Psychology.

Hill, B. K., Lakin, K. C., & Bruininks, R. H. (1984). Trends in residential services for people who are mentally retarded 1977–1982. *Journal of the Association for Persons with Severe Handicaps, 9*(4), 243–251.

Katz, E. (1968). *The retarded adult in the community.* Springfield, IL: Thomas.

McCoin, J. M. (1983). Adult foster homes: *Their managers and residents.* New York: Human Sciences.

Miller, B., & Intagliata, T. (1984). *Promises and realities for mentally retarded citizens: Life in the community.* Baltimore, MD: University Park Press.

SUE ANN MORROW
*EDGE Inc., Bradshaw,
Michigan*

LONNY W. MORROW
*Northeast Missouri State
University*

## INDEPENDENT LIVING RESIDENTIAL FACILITIES

## COMPAZINE

Compazine (prochlorperazine) is used for the short-term treatment of generalized nonpsychotic anxiety, the control of severe nausea and vomiting, and the management of the manifestations of psychotic disorders. Compazine may impair mental or physical abilities, especially during the first few days of therapy. Adverse reactions can include drowsiness, dizziness, blurred vision, restlesness, agitation, jitteriness, insomnia, and motor dysfunctions such as muscle spasms, pseudo-parkinsonism, and tardive dyskinesia. Overdose can produce coma.

A brand name of Smith Kline and French, Compazine is available in tablets of 5, 10, and 25 mg, in sustained release capsules of 10, 15, and 30 mg in injectible ampuls, and in suppositories of $2\frac{1}{2}$, 5, and 25 mg. Dosage may vary, ranging from $2\frac{1}{2}$ mg, according to the symptom being treated. It is given one or two times per day for severe nausea and vomiting in young children to a maximum of 25 mg per day in children 6 to 12 years of age being treated for psychosis.

### REFERENCE

*Physicians' desk reference.* (1984). (pp. 1874–1877). Oradell, NJ: Medical Economics.

LAWRENCE C. HARTLAGE
*Evans, Georgia*

**ATARAX**
**BENADRYL**
**NAVANE**

## COMPENSATORY EDUCATION

Compensatory education usually refers to supplemental educational services provided through federal, state, or local programs to educationally disadvantaged children in schools with concentrations of children from low-income families.

The largest such program is that authorized by Chapter 1 of the Education Consolidation and Improvement Act, formerly known as Title I of the Elementary and Secondary Education Act. Federal grants are made through state education agencies to local school districts based on the number of children from families in poverty. About 14,000 school districts, or about 90% of all districts, receive Chapter 1 funds.

Local educational agencies then allocate funds to schools based on poverty and educational criteria. Schools provide services to children based not on family income, but on extent of educational deprivation. This determination is made at the local level within broad federal guidelines. In general, schools with the greatest concentrations of children from poor families and children most in need of services receive priority in program delivery.

In the most recent year for which data are available (1983–1984), 4.8 million children received compensatory education through the federal program (Carpenter & Hopper, 1985). Additional children receive services from state and local compensatory education programs, and some Chapter 1 participants receive additional services from such programs. For the federal program, about 55% of participants are white, 27% black, 14% Hispanic, and 4% other (White, 1984). Service provision at the elementary level is emphasized: in 1983–1984, 7% of participants were in kindergarten or below, 69% of participants were in grades 1 to 6, and 24% were in grades 7 to 12. This distribution has been relatively constant over time (Carpenter & Hopper, 1985). Participants are concentrated in lower achievement quartiles; as the achievement quartile increases, percent participation in Chapter 1 decreases (White, 1984).

The law allows for a wide range of services to be provided: instructional services, purchase of materials and equipment, teacher training, construction, and social and health services. However, about 80% of funds are spent on instructional services (White, 1984), with particular emphasis on reading and math. About three-fourths of participants receive compensatory reading and almost one-half receive compensatory math, with language arts the next most common service (Carpenter & Hopper, 1985). Almost two-thirds of districts pull students out of regular classrooms to provide services in classes that are likely to be smaller and more personnel-intensive than regular classes. Title I average class size was about 10 children, with a 4.5 to 1 student to instructor ratio (White, 1984).

Chapter 1 programs resemble special education programs for learning-disabled children in several ways. They attempt to address a similar symptom: low or lower than expected achievement. There is a special concentration on attacking difficulties with reading and mathematics skills. Children are often removed from regular classrooms for part of the school day for more personnel-intensive services in smaller classes. That is not to suggest that children served, educational needs, or instructional content of programs for learning-disabled children and compensatory education are identical, or that learning-disabled children are interchangeable with children receiving compensatory education. They are not. But in terms of difficulty addressed, administrative design, or general approach to service delivery, there are important similarities.

Given the Chapter 1 eligibility criterion of educational disadvantagement, nothing prohibits a handicapped child who receives special education and related services from also being served as an educationally deprived child through compensatory education. Anecdotal evidence suggests this may not be common for a number of reasons. First, the situation would be relevant to a limited number of handicapped children, e.g., a speech-impaired child in a Chapter 1 school who is also educationally disadvantaged. Second, participation in two separate special programs could involve removing a child from the regular class twice each day or numerous times each week. This may not be advisable. Third, resources available to provide special programs are not unlimited.

Evaluation of the federal compensatory education program has improved over the years. The reader is encouraged to interpret the results of the most recent major federal longitudinal study (Carter, 1983). Findings from a large new federal study required by law are due in early 1987. This will be of particular interest to those in special education because the study includes the first school-based comparison of compensatory education, special education, bilingual education, and regular education programs.

It is also important to remember the many compensatory education programs run by state and local educational agencies complement and extend Chapter 1. Information on children served, services provided, and evaluation results of these programs is available from state and local education agencies.

### REFERENCES

Carpenter, M., & Hopper, P. (1985). *Synthesis of state Chapter 1 data: Draft summary report.* Washington, DC: Advanced Technology.

Carter, L. (1983). *A study of compensatory and elementary education: The sustaining effects study final report.* Washington, DC: System Development Corporation.

Riddle, W. (1985). *Elementary and Secondary Education Act: A condensed history of the original law and major amendments.* Washington, DC: Congressional Research Service.

White, B. F. (1984). *Compensatory education.* Washington, DC: Office of Management and Budget.

JAMES R. RICCIUTI
*United States Office of
Management and Budget*

**BILINGUAL SPECIAL EDUCATION**
**MIGRANT HANDICAPPED**
**SOCIOECONOMIC STATUS**

## COMPETENCY EDUCATION

Implementation of educational curricula in secondary special education programs requires a shift from traditional content-based curricula to more process-based approaches. Moore and Gysbers (1972) cautioned against viewing students as needing to be brought up to a grade level by the end of the school year, thereby creating passive-dependent students who may evidence apathy, irresponsibility, or rebellious behavior. A process-oriented approach, which relates curriculum directly to the outside world and focuses on each student's unique learning and motivational methods, is recommended for exceptional learners.

Competency education emphasizes developing skills; acquiring knowledge and information (or content) becomes secondary. In curriculum development and planning, the programming concerns revolve around what skills, or competencies, are essential to the student in order to make him or her a more effective person and community member. In competency-based education, the content of a curriculum is selected for its utility in bringing about and exercising those skills. The competencies become the goals, and the curriculum becomes the vehicle by which the goal of skill development may be realized (Cole, 1972).

A competency-based curriculum can assure that each student acquires competencies deemed essential to function adequately as a consumer, a producer, a learner, and a citizen. This means that some exceptional students may need to go beyond the traditional period of time allotted in a secondary program if they are to adequately gain desired competencies. The responsibility is fixed on the educational system to ensure that the student gains those skills, or competencies, essential for adequate community adjustment (Brolin, 1976). It is frequently proposed that a secondary-level educational curriculum that best meets the life career development needs of special education students should revolve around career education concepts that emphasize three primary curriculum areas and one support area. The three curriculum areas are daily living skills; occupational guidance and preparation; and personal-social skills. A fourth curriculum area that lends itself to competency-based educational programming and is supportive to the other three is academic skills. As many as 22 major competencies have been identified as important to acquire at the secondary level under one of these major areas (Brolin, 1974).

### REFERENCES

Brolin, D. (1976). *Vocation preparation of the retarded citizen.* Columbus, OH: Merrill.

Brolin, D., & Kokaska, C. (1974). Critical issues in the job placement of the educable mentally retarded. *Rehabilitation Literature, 10*(2), 16–18.

Cole, H. P. (1972). *Process education: The new direction for elementary-secondary schools.* Englewood Cliffs, NJ: Educational Technology.

Moore, E. J., & Gysbers, N. C. (1972). Career development: A new focus. *Educational Leadership, 30,* 108.

CRAIG D. SMITH
*Georgia College*

VOCATIONAL EVALUATION
VOCATIONAL TRAINING OF HANDICAPPED

## COMPETENCY TEST

A competency test is an assessment of an individual's attainment of skills that are believed to be minimally necessary to function in society. Competency tests enjoy widespread social and political support and are mandated in most, if not all, states as a precondition for grade-to-grade promotion, graduation, and/or receipt of a high-school diploma (Pipho, 1978). The simplicity of the definition belies the complexity of the competency test issue, and the difficulty in developing adequate and effective competency measures.

There is no discernible consensus as to what competency tests should measure or how competencies (once identified) should be assessed. The variability in test content found in competency tests is evidence of the inherent lack of clarity of the definitions and specifications of competency tests (Haney & Madaus, 1978). Test items vary from basic school skills to life skills; test formats vary from traditional pencil and paper tests to performance in applied settings. Although observation and evaluation of actual performance would be ideal, as a practical matter this approach is too costly and difficult for most school districts to undertake. The traditional school skills of reading, writing, and math are heavily represented (Pipho, 1978). Also, competency tests tend to employ familiar formats such as multiple choice, true–false, or short-answer questions (Haney & Madaus, 1978). In practice, the competency tests converge on one point, the assessment of minimal levels of attainment rather than the broader goals of education (Haney & Madaus, 1978).

As with any achievement test (a competency test is an achievement test), content validity is a critical concern. McClung (1977) has suggested that minimum competency tests must demonstrate curriculum validity by measuring topics actually covered in the school curriculum and must demonstrate instructional validity by ensuring that the curricular topics to be tested have actually been taught. The legitimacy of minimum competency tests has been challenged on this specific issue (Flygare, 1981). The in-

ability of school officials to demonstrate adequate content match between minimum competency tests and curriculum content resulted in a court-ordered issuance of high-school diplomas to students who had failed the minimum competency test requirements.

The predictive validity of minimum competency tests is also at issue. The use of competency tests rests on the assumption that performance on such tests predicts later life success, even though research shows that school achievement is generally not a strong predictor of success in adult life (Jencks et al., 1978). The predictive power of minimum competency tests has yet to be demonstrated.

Performance standards are another problematic issue of competency tests. Glass's (1978) review of current methods for establishing pass-fail cutoffs led him to conclude that "methods for establishing mastery levels on competency tests were arbitrary and could yield potentially dangerous results." Milder critics concede that the process of establishing performance standards is subjective and vulnerable to social and political influences.

The public believes competency tests are a means to improve our educational system and the performance of the students who pass through it. If competency tests are to become an enduring feature of education and are to be used as the basis for decisions of promotion and/or graduation, the technical problems involved in their development and use must be addressed and resolved.

## REFERENCES

Flygare, T. J. (1981). Graduation competency testing fails in Georgia. *Phi Delta Kappan, 63*(2), 134–135.

Glass, G. V. (1978). Minimum competency and incompetency in Florida. *Phi Delta Kappan, 59*(9), 602–605.

Haney, W., & Madaus, G. F. (1978). Making sense of the competency testing movement. *Harvard Educational Review, 48*(4), 462–484.

Jencks, C., Smith, M., Acland, H., Bane, M., Cohen, D., Gintis, H., Heyns, B., & Michelson, S. (1978). *Inequality: A reassessment of the effects of family and schooling in America.* New York: Basic Books.

McClung, M. (1977). Competency testing: Potential for discrimination. *Clearinghouse Review, 2,* 439–448.

Pipho, C. (1978). Minimum competency testing in 1978: A look at state standards. *Phi Delta Kappan, 59*(9), 585–588.

LIBBY GOODMAN
*Pennsylvania State University*

ACHIEVEMENT TESTS
MINIMUM COMPETENCY TESTING

## COMPETENCY TESTING FOR TEACHERS

Competency testing for teachers is an educational and political practice that has been implemented in a few states within the last decade and is under consideration in other states. While all states in the United States have certification requirements for teachers, many states have delegated decision making and testing to teacher training institutions within the states. In other states the decision has returned to state agencies in the form of competency tests administered at the completion of teacher training (Lines, 1985). Some states, notably Arkansas, intend to test already certified teachers to continue or withdraw certification. In Texas, prospective teacher trainees will be tested prior to entry into teacher education programs for minimum competency in basic arithmetic, writing, and reading skills beginning in 1986. In South Carolina, a competency test is used to set salary level.

Generally, competency testing for prospective or active teachers is oriented toward basic skills content and knowledge of pedagogy. Texas has begun the development of competency tests in over 90 subject areas for secondary teachers. The most widely used test is the *National Teacher Examination* (NTE), developed by the Educational Testing Service (ETS), which has stated that the test should be used only to test entering teachers on academic knowledge. The ETS does not set cutoff scores for passing, so each state must decide on a passing score. The issue of validity of the NTE and other such tests is a major one in competency testing of teachers. Validity is a major concern in the legal cases developing around such testing.

The validity issues in teacher competency testing have not been seriously challenged with respect to content validity for prospective teachers, usually because the content being tested is fairly low in difficulty in the areas of arithmetic, spelling, grammar usage, and reading comprehension. Louisiana requires the use of an NTE pedagogical test as well as a basic skills test. Supreme Court decisions, notably *United States vs. South Carolina* (1976), have affirmed that a test such as the NTE may be used even though it does not have predictive validity of later job performance. The only validity reported for the NTE has been for performance in teacher training. Also, the same decision affirmed that the test may be used as the basis for salary determination. Lines (1984) has discussed a related case in Alabama, in which the school district using the NTE must show evidence for concurrent validity for its hiring and termination decisions whenever a disproportionate proportion of a minority group is affected.

Kauchak (1984) reported on the effects of the use of the NTE for certification in Louisiana after 1978. He concluded that the test has greatly reduced the number of new black teachers in Louisiana. Only 23% of the prospective black teachers have taken the NTE since the testing program began. The percentage of blacks attempting the test declined from 31% in 1978 to 13% in 1982. This reduction in the number of black teachers has been a major issue in competency testing for teachers, especially in the southern states.

The predictive validity of minimum competency knowledge tests for teachers has generally been demonstrated to be near zero. That is, the tests do not predict effective teaching in the classroom in future years. While some lawsuits have been based on this lack of validation, the South Carolina decision indicates that states may apply such a test without requiring predictive validity. The court uses the standard that it is reasonable that teachers possess knowledge such as that measured in such tests at the time of certification. Whether such a test will hold up for continued certification of already practicing teachers is uncertain.

## REFERENCES

Kauchak, D. (1984). Testing teachers in Louisiana: A closer look. *Phi Delta Kappan, 65*, 626–628.

Lines, P. M. (1985). Testing the teacher: Are there legal pitfalls? *Phi Delta Kappan, 66*, 618–622.

VICTOR L. WILLSON
*Texas A&M University*

CRITERION-REFERENCED TESTING
TEACHER EFFECTIVENESS

# COMPULSORY ATTENDANCE (AND THE HANDICAPPED)

Compulsory school attendance laws have been in effect in nearly every state and in most other parts of the western world for the bulk of the twentieth century. These laws require the parents or legal guardians of all children to send them to school or to provide an equivalent education. The ages of children for whom school attendance is compulsory varies as well, but includes children between the ages of 7 and 16 years in the vast majority of states. The courts have exempted some religious groups from the enforcement of compulsory attendance laws, notably the Amish nationwide and in some states the Mennonites. The states differ greatly in what constitutes a legal school under their compulsory attendance laws. Some states recognize only state certified and supervised schools (public or private), while some allow children to attend noncertified church-supported schools. Others are even more liberal and allow home schooling accomplished by lay parents. Compulsory attendance laws have been the subject of much litigation since their initial enactment.

Many consider compulsory attendance laws to be an infringement on various rights granted to the general populace in the first 10 amendments to the U.S. Constitution (the Bill of Rights). However, the courts have held, with minor religious exceptions, that the state has a compelling interest in the welfare of all children within its jurisdiction and that the provision for education under compulsory circumstances is an acceptable part of this compelling interest and is a legal extension of the police powers of the state. The full extent of the state's compelling interest in education has yet to be defined in adequate detail by the courts, but it is related to the provision of an education that allows individuals to become contributing members of society, preventing them from becoming burdens on the state.

Prior to the passage of the Education for All Handicapped Children Act of 1975 (PL 94-142), which required the states to make available to all handicapped children a free, appropriate, public education, few states enforced their compulsory attendance laws where handicapped children were involved. Many school districts throughout the country would not allow many handicapped children to attend, and in many such instances, encouraged parents to keep these children at home. Many states remain lax in the enforcement of compulsory attendance statutes with regard to the handicapped. With the growing problem of delinquency in the United States, there has been a recent trend away from strict enforcement of truancy laws.

In most states, the handicapped are included in the compulsory attendance laws and the failure (or refusal) of the parents or legal guardians to present these children for school attendance is likely actionable on civil and/or criminal bases in most states. However, school officials or child welfare workers will, in the typical case, have to take the lead in seeking the enforcement of compulsory attendance laws for handicapped children. It is clear, however, that unless specifically exempted by the wording of the state statute, handicapped children are required to attend school. What constitutes a school or an equivalent educational program may be different for the handicapped than the nonhandicapped given the broad authority granted to multidisciplinary teams to diagnose and prescribe educational plans in PL 94-142.

CECIL R. REYNOLDS
*Texas A&M University*

## EDUCATION FOR ALL HANDICAPPED CHILDREN ACT OF 1975

## COMPUTER-ASSISTED INSTRUCTION

Computer-assisted instruction (CAI) refers to educational software that can be run by students with little or no teacher assistance. In CAI, the computer presents information, asks questions, and verifies responses in much the same way a teacher does. Unlike traditional means of instruction, however, CAI allows students to work at their own levels and paces. This mode of instruction can be beneficial to handicapped students who have difficulty in working at the same pace as their nonhandicapped peers. Because CAI can be geared toward students' needs, interests, and expertise, it is generally considered to increase students' motivation to learn.

There are six types of computer-assisted instruction:

informational, drill and practice, tutorial, instructional gaming, simulation, and problem solving. The various types of CAI represent a continuum of instructional formats, ranging from the highly structured to the unstructured (Levy & Lahm, 1984).

*Informational CAI* presents text and graphics only and provides minimal interaction between the student and the computer program. The purpose of this type of CAI is to provide information that may be prerequisite to the acquisition of concepts and skills.

*Drill and practice programs* provide students with practice using materials they have already encountered. Because these programs cover various levels of many subject areas, they can be used for both remediation and acceleration. Good drill and practice programs include immediate corrective feedback to reinforce the acquisition of content; they also allow students to jump ahead when they encounter material they have already mastered.

*Tutorials* provide new information. Typically, a program presents a body of information and then questions the student accordingly. Good tutorials have the power of branching (the capability to assess the user's mastery of a concept and then go to an appropriate level of content presentation). If the student masters a concept, the program goes to the next step of instruction; if the student does not achieve mastery, the program goes to a remedial sequence.

*Educational games* should not be confused with arcade-type games. Educational games provide intellectual challenge, stimulate curiosity, and serve as a source of motivation. Well-designed computer games include variable-difficulty levels, multiple-level goals, hidden information, and randomness. Instructional games can be used individually or with small groups. Often, games are used for review or as a reward for a particular accomplishment.

*Simulations* are among the most powerful learning tools. They are based on the discovery approach to learning (i.e., learning by doing). Simulations provide situations that are analogous to real-life situations, but they control limiting factors that exist in the real situation such as danger, expense, time, and space. Some of the more popular simulations involve students in situations where they see the results of their attempts to solve difficult problems; for example, the meltdown of a nuclear reactor, going West in a covered wagon, or docking a spacecraft with an orbiting satellite (McClellan, 1984).

*Problem-solving CAI* focuses on the process of finding an answer to a problem rather than the answer itself. One of the best-known problem-solving packages is Logo. Logo is a procedure-oriented language that provides students with concrete ways to think about problems systematically. Students divide problems into smaller ones by writing small procedures for each problem. The language is based on the learning theories of Jean Piaget and was developed in 1968 as a part of the National Science Foundation project (Papert, 1980). Learning to program in Logo transforms learning to a self-directed, active task.

In the past few years, as researchers have begun to explore the potential applications of artificial intelligence, they have pointed out some of the *shortcomings of* CAI. For example, with traditional CAI, students cannot ask questions. Further, CAI programs usually cannot handle unanticipated answers. Often, CAI programs do not have any information base of a particular subject; they simply offer questions and answers that have been preprogrammed. Researchers are now looking at ways of improving CAI by giving it the capability of responding to the idiosyncrasies of each student's learning style. In the future, educators can look forward to programs that combine the best features of traditional CAI with new developments in artificial intelligence. These programs are expected to include a problem-solving model appropriate for the target domain of knowledge; a tutoring or teaching model; and a model of the student, including individual student characteristics such as knowledge about the content to be learned (Roberts, 1984). Intelligent computer-assisted instruction programs will allow users to communicate with the computer in natural English sentences. Programs will be able to accommodate random student questions on a given topic. Intelligent computer-assisted instruction will be more teacherlike in that programs will keep track of what the student knows and needs to know. The program will also have the capability of understanding when and how to provide a student with information and when to ask a question (McGrath, 1984).

### REFERENCES

Levy, S. A., & Lahm, E. A. (1984). Microcomputers in special education curriculum. In E. McClellan (Ed.), *Microcomputer applications in special education* (pp. 21–43). Reston, VA: Council for Exceptional Children.

McClellan, E. (1984). Introduction to microcomputers. In E. McClellan (Ed.), *Microcomputer applications in special education* (pp. 1–21). Reston, VA: Council for Exceptional Children.

McGrath, D. (1984). Artificial intelligence: A tutorial for educators. *Electronic Learning, 4,* 39–43.

Papert, S. (1980). *Mindstorms.* New York: Basic Books.

Roberts, F. C. (1984, June). *An overview of intelligent CAI systems.* Paper presented at the Special Education Technology Research and Development Symposium, Washington, DC.

ELIZABETH MCCLELLAN
*Council for Exceptional*
*Children, Reston, Virginia*

**COMPUTER LITERACY**
**COMPUTER-MANAGED INSTRUCTION**
**COMPUTER USE WITH THE HANDICAPPED**

## COMPUTERIZED AXIAL TOMOGRAPHY

See CAT SCAN.

## COMPUTER LITERACY

Because the state of the art of computer technology is constantly changing, so too is the definition of computer literacy. In the past, computer literacy was virtually synonymous with learning to write computer programs. Typically, computer novices gained an understanding of the machines by writing programs in BASIC (Beginner's All-Purpose Symbolic Instructional Code). Recently, however, the major thrust in computer literacy has shifted away from programming toward the applications of computer technology in various settings, particularly the home, school, and office. The primary reason for this shift has been the increased availability of good software and inexpensive hardware.

The problem of defining computer literacy is compounded by the fact that individuals with different educational levels have differing computer needs. Meeting these needs requires varying levels of expertise. For example, for the high-school student, computer literacy encompasses the following areas: basic knowledge of how to operate a computer; an understanding of how computers are used in work and for leisure; an appreciation of the ethical, social, and economic ramifications of computer usage; and an ability to use computers for instruction, information collection and retrieval, word processing, decision making, and problem solving (Computer Competency, 1983).

For teachers, computer literacy means being knowledgeable about the capabilities of hardware and software and understanding how computers can enhance students' educational experiences. For those who work with handicapped students, computer literacy also implies an understanding of the ways in which technology can be used to improve services to special needs learners. Specifically, to be computer literate, special educators should acquire the following competencies:

1. Understand the fundamental operation and care of computers and software.

2. Become fluent in the basic terminology of computer technology.

3. Be able to apply computer technology to improve instruction.

4. Be able to use computers for management of instruction.

5. Understand how microprocessor-based technology can compensate for motoric, sensory, and cognitive disabilities.

6. Become proficient in evaluating software and hardware.

7. Be able to use an authoring system or language to develop instructional programs.

8. Understand the principles of telecommunication, especially as they apply to the improvement of instruction and learning.

Educators continue to debate the inclusion of computer programming as a component of computer literacy. Many educators, particularly those who work with young children and/or gifted and talented children, believe that teaching students to write programs can help them to develop problem-solving skills that can be applied to real-life experiences. For example, Papert (1980) mentions that the language Logo was designed by Piagetian psychologists to help children "think about thinking" (i.e., to understand the steps they go through in solving a problem).

For teachers and teacher educators, however, the development of authoring systems and languages has reduced the need for learning an all-purpose language such as BASIC. An authoring system is a highly structured template that allows computer users with a minimal understanding of computer technology to develop computer-assisted tutorials and drill and practice routines. Proficiency in high-level languages such as PASCAL or "C" would be left to educators who are interested in designing state-of-the-art instructional and management software (Cartwright, 1984).

## REFERENCES

Cartwright, G. P. (1984). Technology competencies for special education doctoral students. *Teacher Education and Special Education, 7*, 82–87.

Computer Competency. (1983, May). *Chronicle of higher education* (p. 5).

Papert, S. (1980). *Mindstorms*. New York: Basic Books.

ELIZABETH MCCLELLAN
*Council for Exceptional*
*Children, Reston, Virginia*

## COMPUTER-ASSISTED INSTRUCTION
## COMPUTER USE WITH THE HANDICAPPED

# COMPUTER-MANAGED INSTRUCTION

Computer-managed instruction (CMI) refers to a category of computer programs that are used by educators to organize and manage data related to instruction. In the early days of microcomputers in the schools, CMI was limited to packages that helped teachers monitor students' grades or those that allowed administrators to keep track of students' schedules and records. In the past few years, however, sophisticated CMI packages have been created that not only facilitate recordkeeping but also aid in the diagnosis of students' strengths and weaknesses. In special education in particular, CMI is used to analyze test data, determine goals and objectives based on the data, generate individualized educational plans (IEPs) monitor student progress, and generate reports (McClellan, 1984).

Since 1975, when PL 94-142 was passed, the responsibilities of special education teachers and administrators

have increased dramatically. Broader child-find programs have increased the number of children receiving special education services. Individualized educational programs are prepared annually. With larger numbers of students and increased individualization, the number of personnel who provide special education and related services has also grown. All of this growth calls for increased paperwork on the part of the teacher and administrator. Fortunately, computer programs have been developed to manage the paperwork.

The ERIC Clearinghouse on Handicapped and Gifted Children (1980) has published a list of tasks that computers can perform to assist in the management of instruction. These tasks include the following:

1. Generate IEPs from a large data base
2. Generate report cards
3. Generate quarterly student reports
4. Score tests
5. Recommend appropriate activities for students
6. Locate learning materials
7. Describe diagnostic materials
8. Report on student due-process status
9. Remind when notices are due or should be sent out
10. Report on student achievement and evaluation status
11. Store information on health history

In addition, software has been developed for the following administrative functions:

1. Reimburse computation according to state and federal formulas
2. Screen, assess, place, and review counts of students
3. Generate standardized reports
4. Report on compliance with PL 94-142
5. Cross-reference child counts by class, school, teacher, and handicap
6. Record testing and reports
7. Send personalized mailings to parents and service providers
8. Provide lists of incomplete information on student records
9. Audit trails for program placement and review

The key to the successful implementation of computer-managed instruction is not with single-purpose computer programs but with integrated packages. Software developers have created sophisticated, and often expensive, packages that can be customized to meet the specific needs of the teacher, administrator, or school system. These programs usually call for the creation of large data bases that integrate classroom and administrative information. Information stored in these master files might include student tracking data, assessment and diagnostic information, IEP goals and objectives, and classroom performance data. Integrated packages can also include instructional sequences and performance data (Lahm & Levy, 1984). The computer's capacity to analyze data rapidly and to present them in ways that are easily used suggests a tremendous potential for reducing the amount of time and paper work required to generate reports. More important, however, teachers and administrators can use the data compiled and analyzed by computer-managed instruction packages as a basis for making decisions that affect teaching and learning.

## REFERENCES

ERIC Clearinghouse on Handicapped and Gifted Children. (1980). *Computers for special education management: Progress, potential, and pitfalls.* Reston, VA: Council for Exceptional Children.

Lahm, E. A., & Levy, S. A. (1984). Microcomputers in special education management. In E. McClellan (Ed.), *Microcomputer applications in special education* (pp. 44–59). Reston, VA: Council for Exceptional Children.

McClellan, E. (1984). Introduction to microcomputers. In E. McClellan (Ed.), *Microcomputer applications in special education* (pp. 1–21). Reston, VA: Council for Exceptional Children.

ELIZABETH MCCLELLAN
*Council for Exceptional
Children, Reston, Virginia*

## COMPUTER LITERACY
## COMPUTER USE WITH THE HANDICAPPED

# COMPUTERS IN HUMAN BEHAVIOR

*Computers in Human Behavior* is a scholarly journal devoted to research that attempts to articulate the relationship between psychology, the science of human behavior, and technological advances in computer science. Articles are concerned with advances in research design and the technology of research, but also with the effects of computers on the topics chosen for study by psychologists. Changes in clinical practice, ethics, and standards related to computers are also examined. Articles appearing in the journal have also included studies of the equivalence of testing conditions (computerized vs. standard administration) and computerized interpretation of tests. The latter two areas are of interest to special educators as several articles have addressed placement decisions and educational diagnosis using computer programs to interpret

tests. *Computers in Human Behavior* is a Pergamon Press journal; it began publication in 1985.

CECIL R. REYNOLDS
*Texas A&M University*

# COMPUTER USE WITH HANDICAPPED

For handicapped persons, computers have three main functions: compensation for disabilities, management, and instructional delivery.

In terms of compensation for disabilities, one of the most exciting aspects of computer technology is the use of augmentative devices for communication and control. Computers, particularly microcomputers, help users overcome communication problems associated with limited mobility and sensory impairment. To increase the speed and accuracy of using computers, engineers and educators have developed special input and output devices. Innovative input devices include voice recognition, the mouse, joysticks and game paddles, mechanical keyboard aids such as guards, mouths, and headsticks, and splints. Examples of computer output devices are synthetic speech, Blissymbols, tactile display (Opticon), braille, and portable printers (Brady, 1982).

For individuals with cerebral palsy, amyotrophic lateral sclerosis, or severe paralysis, one of the biggest problems of computer usage is the multiple simultaneous key strokes required to run many pieces of standard software. To take advantage of the computer's capacity to control the environment, a person with limited mobility must have an adaptive firmware card. The card is a device that enables a person with limited mobility to run software by activating a single switch (Schwedja & Vanderheiden, 1982). Single switches and expanded keyboards require only slight movement, such as the blinking of an eye.

Access to standard software allows handicapped individuals to use the computer for information management. The four primary areas of information management are word processing, data base management, financial management, and telecommunication. Word processing packages allow users to draft, edit, and print text with relative ease. Changing margins and moving sentences or paragraphs are a matter of a few key strokes. Learning-disabled students can use word processing packages to overcome some of the problems associated with writing (Arms, 1984). Data base management programs are used to store, sort, and retrieve large amounts of information. In special education, administrators and teachers use data base management programs to file information such as students' names, addresses, birth dates, disabilities, and test scores. Financial management programs such as spreadsheets allow users to create, monitor, and change budgets. Other programs help with checkbook balancing and income tax preparation.

With the use of a modem (modulator/demodulator) and a telephone, computer users have access to virtually limitless sources of information. Users who subscribe to electronic networks such as SpecialNet can send messages to other users' electronic mailboxes, or they can review messages on electronic bulletin boards. Subscribers to information utility services (e.g., The Source and CompuServe) can access stock market reports, make travel reservations, obtain up-to-the-minute weather reports, or search through large bibliographic data bases for information on a given topic.

Word processing, data base management, financial management, and telecommunications packages have reached a high level of sophistication. Users can now take the information from one program and load it into another. If, for example, a user wanted to include a budget in a manuscript, he or she could load the information from a spreadsheet program into the text of a word processing package. Or, a homebound individual could compose text on the word processor and send it to a teacher or other interested party by loading it into the telecommunication software. When these programs are designed to work in concert, they are called integrated software (McClellan, 1984).

In addition to the functions that allow the computer to aid in communication and information management, the computer has certain characteristics that enhance the delivery of instruction. Interaction means that the computer can perform many of the functions that are typically performed by the teacher such as providing immediate feedback. Software can be designed so that rates of response and level of difficulty can be varied according to the student. One of the characteristics that tends to motivate students is branching capability (i.e., the capability of moving from one part of a program to another). Branching allows learners to decide whether they need to repeat material or move on to new material. Moreover, the computer is tireless; it does not become irritated when asked to repeat information or activities.

## REFERENCES

Arms, V. M. (1984). A dyslexic can compose a computer. *Educational Technology, 24,* 39–41.

Brady, M. (1982). The Trace Center International Hardware/Software Registry: Programs for handicapped students. *Journal of Special Education Technology, 5,* 16–21.

McClellan, E. (1984). Introduction to microcomputers. In E. McClellan (Ed.), *Microcomputer applications in special education* (pp. 1–21). Reston, VA: Council for Exceptional Children.

Schwejda, P. & Vanderheiden, G. (1982). Adaptive-firmware card for the Apple II. *Byte, 7,* 276–314.

ELIZABETH MCCLELLAN
*Council for Exceptional
Children, Reston, Virginia*

## COMPUTER LITERACY
## COMPUTER MANAGED INSTRUCTION

## CONCEPT FORMATION

The term concept is used to describe one of the ways the human mind organizes the tremendous amounts of data with which it is bombarded. As Ausubel (1968) points out:

> Anyone who pauses long enough to give the problem some serious thought cannot escape the conclusion that man lives in a world of concepts, rather than a world of objects, events, and situations. . . . Reality, figuratively speaking, is experienced through a conceptual or categorical filter (p. 505).

A concept would appear to be a mental construct that serves to group together similar entities. Having knowledge of a concept means having at least knowledge of the common elements that define inclusion or exclusion of an entity from a category. The presence of a concept is tested by observing which objects are placed in the same category or are acted on similarly. The individual carrying out such an activity may or may not have any idea what the concept is that he or she is using for categorization, nor what the common elements may be.

There are often confusions between the ideas of concept and language. It is not an uncommon approach to define a concept as "something about an idea expressed in words of our language" (Platt, 1963, p. 21). However, it is clear that animals as well as humans have comcepts (Humphrey, 1984). A dog does not react to an unfamiliar cat each time it sees one as if it were a unique object. Rather, it behaves toward the cat based on its past experiences with other cats. The dog, then, must have some concept of cats.

The relationship between a concept and language is a problematical one, however. Gagne (1970), for example, has argued that there are two types of concepts, concrete ones such as "dog," which are based on direct empirical experience, and those such as "uncle" or "democracy" which cannot exist without language. It is further argued by some that the way language organizes and categorizes information actually effects the way one perceives incoming data. For example, different languages break up the color spectrum differently. A number of studies have been conducted to determine whether individuals from different cultures actually perceive colors differently, based on their language.

Two general approaches for concept formation have been described (Martorella, 1972). The first is inductive, the second deductive. Concepts learned inductively start with a group of facts, data, or concepts that are already understood. Through the use of certain intellectual skills, new, more abstract concepts are developed. For example, to assist a child in learning the rule that "e" in a VCVe word usually makes the vowel long, the child could compare two lists of similar words, one containing the final "e," the other not. The deductive approach, on the other hand, begins by presenting the more abstract principle. The learner develops an understanding of the principle through repeated mental operations on examples pertinent to the concept. In this case, a child would be presented with the rule about the final "e" first, and then would be shown a number of examples. Research has not yet determined that teaching using either type of model is clearly superior. There is, in fact, some indication in cognitive style research that the success of one method over the other is at least to some degree dependent on a person's individual learning style (Witkin, Moore, Goodenough, & Cox, 1977).

Vygotsky (1962) made a similar distinction between two types of conceptual learning. He described two methods for learning concepts depending on whether the concept is spontaneous or scientific. Spontaneous concepts are learned from day-to-day concrete exposure to specific examples of the concept. An example of this type of concept would be that of "dog." The individual learns what a dog is by living with a dog and by seeing pictures of many different kinds of dogs. However, a term like exploitation is probably learned through a mediated situation in a formal learning environment. The individual is presented with only the beginning schematics of the term's meaning. A fuller understanding is gained over time with examples not directly experienced by the learner, but learned through discussion and reading.

In a sense, the development of spontaneous concepts is an upward process, the development of scientific ones a downward one. Concepts learned through an upward process start with a number of concrete examples, with the learner developing a general notion of the essence of "dogginess." Concepts learned through a downward process tend to start with definitions, with the learner gradually determining which specific instances are examples of the general notion.

Behaviorists have attempted to explain the development of concepts in strict stimulus-response terms. Vygotsky and others have objected to this explanation on the grounds that while the mental processes described by behaviorists are necessary, they are not sufficient for explaining how external phenomena become categorized into conceptual frameworks. These thinkers find the stimulus-response paradigm an inadequate explanation for how the brain arrives at the essence of concepts such as dogginess or exploitation.

Festinger (1957), in describing the process of concept formation, borrowed from the Piagetian notion of equilibrium. Festinger stated that if an organism has two cognitions that are perceived as being dissonant with one another, there is a tendency to attempt a modification of the cognitive structures to reduce the dissonance. This process, he states, creates new concepts. For example, if a child calls all animals doggie but notices others call some

of those cats, the child will in time modify his or her notion of what characteristics identify members of the class of dogs.

DeCecco (1968) has proposed the following general model for teaching concepts:

1. Describe what performance is expected after the concept is taught.
2. For complex concepts, reduce the number of attributes to be taught; emphasize dominant attributes.
3. Provide clear verbal associations.
4. Give positive and negative examples of the concept.
5. Present the examples either in close succession or simultaneously.
6. Present a new positive example, asking the student to identify it.
7. Verify the student's understanding of the concept.
8. Ask the student to define the concept.
9. Provide opportunities for the student to practice the concept with appropriate reinforcement (p. 58).

There was considerable interest in the process of concept formation during the late 1960s and early 1970s, when new mathematics and social studies curricula were being developed. The back-to-basics movement led to a declining interest in this field of inquiry. Recently, with the introduction of problem solving into the curriculum, a renewed interest in concept formation has developed. The hope is that, particularly for students with special needs, understanding how concept formation occurs will guide teachers in helping their students become more effective learners.

## REFERENCES

Ausubel, D. P. (1968). *Educational psychology: A cognitive view*. New York: Holt, Rinehart, & Winston.

DeCecco, J. P. (1968). *The psychology of learning and instruction*. Englewood Cliffs, NJ: Prentice-Hall.

Festinger, L. (1964). The motivating factor of cognitive dissonance. In R. C. Harper, et al. (Eds.), *The cognitive processes*. Englewood Cliffs, NJ: Prentice-Hall.

Gagne, R. M. (1970). *The conditions of learning* (2nd ed.). New York: Holt, Rinehart, & Winston.

Humphrey, N. (1984). *Consciousness regained: Chapters in the development of the mind*. Oxford, England: Oxford University Press.

Martorella, P. H. (1972). *Concept learning: Designs for instruction*. Scranton, PA: Intext Educational.

Platt, M. M. (1963). Concepts and the curriculum. *Social Education, 27*, 21.

Vygotsky, L. S. (1962). *Thought and language*. Cambridge, MA: MIT Press.

Witkin, H. A., Moore, C. A., Goodenough, D. R., & Cox, P. W. (1977). Field-dependent and field-independent cognitive styles and their educational implications. *Review of Educational Research, 47,* 1–64.

CAROLYN BULLARD
*Lewis & Clark College*

## ABSTRACT THINKING, IMPAIRMENT IN THOUGHT DISORDERS VYGOTSKY, L. S.

## CONCEPT OF ACTIVITY

See THEORY OF ACTIVITY.

## CONCRETE OPERATIONS

Concrete operations is the third of four invariant stages of Piaget's theory of cognitive development. According to Piaget, the distinctive features of children's thought occurring during the period of concrete operations are logic and objectivity that includes the ability to perform mental manipulations directly related to objects and events. These manipulations, which emerge between the ages of approximately 7 to 11 years, are termed operations by Piaget. To qualify as an operation, an action must be internalizable, reversible, and part of an overall system of actions. By internalizable Piaget meant that a child can think about the action "without losing their original character of actions" (1953, p. 8). An example of internalization during the concrete operations stage is the performance of mental arithmetic. Essential to understanding number and size relationships are transitivity and associativity. Transitivity, the basis for seriation, is the ability to arrange a series of events or objects in a continuum such as "less than," "greater than," "fewer than," or "more than." Associativity is demonstrated by understanding that parts of a whole may be combined in different ways without effecting a change on the whole.

Reversibility is another ability that characterizes a child's thought during the concrete operations stage. The child is able to reverse actions mentally; e.g., the child learns that the number of fingers on a hand counted sequentially from thumb to little finger is the same as counted from little finger to thumb, or the child imagines the effect weights will have when placed on or taken off a scale. Actions cannot be isolated manipulations. Instead, they are part of a coherent system of thinking. Concrete operational children develop a capacity to think about concept classes in equivalent and hierarchic forms; for example, oranges and bananas are both fruit, fruit is food, but all food is not fruit.

The classic measure of whether a particular child is capable of concrete operational thinking is provided by the task of conservation. There are more than 1000 published studies on conservation (Yussen & Santrock, 1982). In a classic study, a child is seated before two same size beakers equally filled with water and a taller empty beaker. The experimenter pours one of the beakers into the tall empty one and asks the child if the amounts in the tall beaker and the unpoured beaker are the same or different. The conserver, i.e., the concrete operational thinker, knows that the amount of liquid has not changed and that if it were poured back into the original container (internalization of a reversible action) it would be the same.

In recent years, several aspects of Piaget's theory of cognitive development have been challenged. As early as 1964, Jerome Bruner showed that children who should not be able to conserve, according to Piaget, could do so if the transformation of the object (pouring the beaker of water) were hidden from view. Since then, there has been considerable debate as to the accuracy of Piaget's four-stage model. It now seems clear that many specifics of Piaget's theory such as the age of onset of concrete operations, are in doubt. Nonetheless, the elegance and insight that Piaget brought to the study of children's thinking was immense.

### REFERENCES

Bruner, J. S. (1964). The course of cognitive growth. *American Psychologists, 19,* 1–15.

Piaget, J. (1953). *Logic and psychology.* Manchester, England: Manchester University.

Yussen, S. R., & Santrock, J. W. (1982). *Child development: An introduction.* Dubuque, IA: Brown.

MICHAEL ASH
JOSE LUIS TORRES
*Texas A&M University*

## COGNITIVE DEVELOPMENT

## CONDITIONING

Conditioning is a general term that describes a strengthening (through a predictive relationship) of an association between a stimulus and a response or between two stimuli. With conditioning, responses become increasingly likely to occur under appropriate circumstances. In operant conditioning, the probability of a response that has been followed by reinforcement increases. In Pavlovian (or respondent or classical) conditioning, the probability of a response to an initially neutral stimulus increases when that neutral stimulus is followed by one that reliably elicits a response in reflex fashion. Pavlovian conditioning is named after the great Russian physiologist Ivan Pavlov (1927), whose research established the basic phenomena associated with this type of conditioning. However, the phenomenon itself had been discovered and described some years earlier by an American psychologist, E. B. Twitmeyer.

## Basic Aspects for Pavlovian Conditioning

The paradigm for Pavlovian conditioning is

$$CS \rightarrow UCS \rightarrow UCR \quad \text{(before conditioning)}$$

$$CS \rightarrow CR \quad \text{(after conditioning)}$$

Pairing of an initially neutral conditional stimulus (CS) with an unconditional stimulus (UCS) that reliably elicits a response (UCR) leads to a conditional response (CR) occurring to the CS. Frequently, but not always, the CR is similar to the UCR in form. For example, Pavlov would sound a bell (CS) and then give a dog food (UCS) that elicited salivation (UCR). After several pairings of the bell with food, the bell itself elicited salivation. Using the paradigm

$$\underset{\text{(bell)}}{CS} \rightarrow \underset{\text{(food)}}{UCS} \rightarrow \underset{\substack{\text{(sali-}\\ \text{vation)}}}{UCR} \quad \text{(before conditioning)}$$

$$\underset{\text{(bell)}}{CS} \rightarrow \underset{\substack{\text{(sali-}\\ \text{vation)}}}{CR} \quad \text{(after conditioning)}$$

we can see that through pairing, a response can occur to a stimulus that never occurred to it before.

Watson (1916) made Pavlovian conditioning the basic form of learning in his formulation of behaviorism. In 1920 Watson and Rayner published a classic article on conditioning of an emotional response in a human infant. While one experimenter held a white rat (CS) toward 11-month-old Albert, the other experimenter hit a bar with a hammer, making a very loud noise (UCR) that elicited crying (UCS) from Albert. After only five pairings, the rat itself elicited crying (CR).

The basic aspects of conditioning can be briefly described:

*Acquisition.* With repeated trials, strength of the CR increases to some maximum level.

*Extinction.* Presentation of the CS without the UCS leads to a decrease in intensity of the CR until no response is observed.

*Spontaneous Recovery.* Presenting the CS after some delay following extinction may reevoke a CR, although it will be of relatively low intensity.

*Reacquisition.* Repairing of the CS and UCS generally leads to more rapid reconditioning than original conditioning.

*Generalization.* After conditioning, a CR will tend to occur, but at lower intensity, to similar stimuli.

*Discrimination.* Presentation of one CS ($CS_1$) followed by a UCS and of another ($CS_2$) not followed by a UCS will generally result in the subject developing a discrimination such that it produces a CR to $CS_1$ but not $CS_2$.

## Some Important Issues

*The nature of the CR.* Pavlov proposed that the CS came to take the place of the UCS—stimulus substitution— in a mechanical process. Thus, the CR should be similar in form to the UCR. However, although dogs salivate to both bells and food, they do not try to eat the bell. Indeed, they look at and move toward the food dish, behaviors that suggest that conditioning produces a CR that anticipates the UCS (Zener, 1937). Recent research (Rescorla, 1966; Siegel, 1975) suggests that in at least some cases, conditioning indeed leads to the CS eliciting a CR that reflects expectancy of the UCS. For example, Siegel gave rats a series of insulin injections in which the hypodermic needle was the CS, the insulin was the UCS, and insulin-elicited hypoglycemia was the UCS. In response to a CS-only test, the rats showed hyperglycemia, as though they were compensating for the anticipated UCS, insulin. The influential Rescorla and Wagner (1972) model proposes that conditioning will occur only when the CS provides information ("expectancy") about the UCS.

*Biological constraints on learning.* Although early theorists felt that all stimuli and responses should be equally conditionable, research shows that they are not. In their now classic study, Garcia and Koelling (1966) gave rats either "sweet water" or "bright-noisy water" (water paired with flashing lights and noise) and then either shocked them or made them ill. Of rats given sweet water, only those made ill subsequently avoided drinking the water; of rats given bright-noisy water, only those shocked subsequently avoided drinking. Similar results appear to hold in humans (Seligman, 1970). The specificity of "cue-consequence relations" is a topic of current interest. The implication is that some types of associations have particularly important adaptive value, and have been selected through evolution.

Consideration of biological factors helps to resolve the controversial question of whether or not young infants demonstrate classical conditioning. Although the existence of such conditioning had been generally accepted, Sameroff (1971) concluded that positive studies either could not be replicated or suffered from methodological problems, and that conditioning in newborns had not clearly been demonstrated. Sameroff and Cavenaugh (1979) later suggested that studies published since the initial review, which successfully demonstrated conditioning, had used CS and UCS pairings of biological relevance to the newborn. Indeed, by pairing biologically relevant stimuli, Blass, Ganchrow, and Steiner (1984) have obtained conditioning in infants of 2 to 48 hours of age. Tactile stimulation (CS) was followed by presentation of sucrose solution (UCS) that elicited sucking (UCR). Newborns sucked during CS in conditioning and showed extinction of sucking during subsequent CS-only trials. Further, seven of eight experimental infants cried during extinction trials at a time when the sucrose had been presented, suggesting an affective component of the conditioning.

*Long-delay learning.* Initially, research indicated that the CS and UCS had to be closely linked in time for conditioning to occur. However, in some circumstances, particularly where the UCS elicits illness, an association may be formed with a novel taste or olfactory CS encountered over 12 hours earlier (Revusky & Garcia, 1970). Thus, under circumstances such as food poisoning, a CR can occur to a stimulus removed in time from the UCS. Recently, some have suggested that aversions to food that develop in cancer patients undergoing chemotherapy may be classically conditioned since most chemotherapeutic agents induce intense symptoms of food poisoning (Braveman & Bronstein, 1985).

*Higher-order conditioning.* The potential role of Pavlovian conditioning is greatly extended by higher-order conditioning, originally described by Pavlov and recently studied in detail by Rescorla (1980). In such conditioning, a first CS ($CS_1$) is paired with a UCS to establish a CR to $CS_1$. Then, a second CS ($CS_2$) is paired only with $CS_1$, leading to the response conditioned to $CS_1$ now occurring to $CS_2$. Thus, once a response has been conditioned to a CS, other CSs may be tied to it that are not themselves directly associated with the UCS but are remote from it. If the original link between $CS_1$ and the UCS is broken, as in extinction, the higher-order CRs also diminish.

## Applications to Children's Development

*Development of emotions.* Since the time of Watson, Pavlovian conditioning has played an important role in accounting for the association of positive and negative emotional reactions with particular stimuli. Watson and Rayner demonstrated how conditioning could lead to negative emotions such as fear. Indeed, conditioning is viewed as a major process underlying the development of severe fears or phobias.

As conditioning may induce phobias, so it may be used to reduce them. As early as 1924, Jones "counterconditioned" a severe fear of rabbits in a child, Peter, by pairing a rabbit with pleasurable stimuli such as peer play and ice cream cones. By the end of the process, Peter no longer feared rabbits and, indeed, was petting them. This procedure, now called desensitization, is one of the most effective means of treating phobias in children and adults. Conditioning may also produce positive emotional responses, as shown, for example, in children's excitement at the sight of a favored food, person, or toy.

*Development of meaning.* Conditioning is one process thought to underlie the attachment of meaning to words (Mowrer, 1954). Pairing a word (CS) with the object (UCS) signified by the word will result in responses elicited by the object becoming attached to the word as a CR. Thus, pairing the word *doll* with an actual doll leads to responses elicited by the doll becoming associated with *doll*. Although a conditioning model cannot deal with all meaning, particularly that involving abstract concepts, it does provide a framework for understanding how reactions to stimuli can become attached to symbols for them. If an object comes to elicit an emotional response, then the word for the object may also elicit that response. If a child who has been painfully knocked to the ground by a large dog now fears all large dogs, he or she may show fear at the phrase *large dog*. On the other hand, a child who likes ice cream cones might well show positive anticipation to the phrase *ice cream cone*.

Also important is the related concept of mediated or semantic generalization. Once a CR occurs to a word, it will occur to words similar in meaning if the individual has developed a concept involving that word. Thus, if conditioned to respond to the word *shoe*, an individual will respond more to *boot*, or other words similar in meaning, than to *shoot*, a word similar in physical characteristics. Already apparent by at least age eight semantic generalization becomes stronger with age (Osgood, 1953).

## Implications for Educators

Those dealing with children need to be sensitive to the fact that they and the situation they are in are paired with what they say and do to the children. So is the situation paired with peers' reactions to children. Thus, teachers who use aversive means of classroom management may condition children to be anxious about them and their classrooms. Similarly, children who are ridiculed in class or on the playground or who experience much failure and little success may become conditioned to fear school itself and teachers generally. In extreme, a school phobia may result.

We should also be aware that children will arrive at school with conditioned likes and dislikes and emotional responses. Some may have been specifically food poisoned or have had gastric distress after eating and may have strong aversions to certain foods. Others may have strong fears. However controversial it may be, those in special education should consider the roles of conditioning when predicting the effects of mainstreaming on handicapped children. Those children who succeed socially and academically will have a positive conditioning experience, whereas those who are not accepted and/or fail academically may suffer from negative conditioning and develop conditioned responses associated with anxiety and fear of failure.

## REFERENCES

Blass, E. M., Ganchrow, J. R., & Steiner, J. E. (1984). Classical conditioning in new born humans 2–48 hours of age. *Infant Behavior and Development, 7,* 223–235.

Braveman, N. S., & Bronstein, P. (Eds.). (1985). Experimental assessments and clinical applications of conditioned food aversions. *Annuals of the New York Academy of Sciences, 443.*

Garcia, J., & Koelling, R. A. (1966). Relation of cue to consequence in avoidance learning. *Psychonomic Science, 4,* 123–124.

Jones, M. C. (1924). A laboratory study of fear: The case of Peter. *Pedagogical Seminary and Journal of Genetic Psychology, 31,* 308–315.

Mowrer, O. H. (1954). The psychologist looks at language. *American Psychologist, 9,* 660–694.

Osgood, C. E. (1953). *Method and theory in experimental psychology.* New York: Oxford University Press.

Pavlov, I. P. (1927) *Conditioned reflexes* (translated by G. V. Anrep). New York: Oxford University Press.

Rescorla, R. A. (1966). Predictability and number of pairings in Pavlovian fear conditioning. *Psychonomic Science, 4,* 383–384.

Rescorla, R. A. (1980). *Pavlovian second-order conditioning.* Hillsdale, NJ: Erlbaum.

Rescorla, R. A., & Wagner, A. R. (1972). A theory of Pavlovian conditioning: Variations in the effectiveness of reinforcement and nonreinforcement. In A. H. Black & W. F. Prokasy (Eds.), *Classical conditioning II: Current research and theory.* New York: Appleton-Century-Crofts.

Revusky, S. H., & Garcia, J. (1970). Learned associations over long delays. In G. H. Bower & J. T. Spence (Eds.), *The psychology of learning and motivation, Vol 4.* New York: Academic.

Sameroff, A. J. (1971). Can conditioned responses be established in the newborn infant? *Developmental Psychology, 5,* 1–12.

Sameroff, A. J., & Cavenaugh, P. J. (1979). Learning in infancy: A developmental perspective. In J. D. Osofsky (Ed.), *Handbook of infant development* (pp. 344–392). New York: Wiley.

Seligman, M. E. P. (1970). On the generality of the laws of learning. *Psychological Review, 77,* 406–418.

Siegel, S. (1975). Conditioning insulin effects. *Journal of Comparative and Physiological Psychology, 89,* 189–199.

Watson, J. B. (1916). The place of the conditioned reflex in psychology. *Psychological Review, 23,* 89–116.

Watson, J. B., & Rayner, R. (1920). Conditioned emotional reactions. *Journal of Experimental Psychology, 3,* 1–14.

Zener, K. (1937). The significance of behavior accompanying conditioned salivary secretion for theories of the conditioned reflex. *American Journal of Psychology, 50,* 384–403.

ROBERT T. BROWN
*University of North Carolina,
Wilmington*

## BEHAVIOR MODIFICATION
## OPERANT CONDITIONING

# CONDUCT DISORDER

A conduct disorder has been identified as "antisocial behavior resulting from mental conflicts" (Harriman, 1975). It is a disorder of conduct characterized by acting out, aggression, and disruptive behavior. Von Isser, Quay, and Love (1980) state that characteristics of conduct disorders are "overt aggression, both verbal and physical; disruptiveness; negativism; irresponsibility; and defiance of authority—all of which are at variance with the behavioral expectations of the school." Quay (1979) equates conduct disorder with the term unsocialized aggression. The essential feature of a conduct disorder according to the third edition of the *Diagnostic and Statistical Manual of Mental Disorders* (DSM III, 1980) is "a repetitive and persistent pattern of conduct in which either the basic rights of others or major age-appropriate societal norms or rules are violated" (p. 45). The DSM III identifies the following types of conduct disorders:

Undersocialized, aggressive (312.00)

Undersocialized, nonaggressive (312.10)

Socialized, aggressive (312.23)

Socialized, nonaggressive (312.21)

Atypical (312.90)

Safer (1980) reports approximately 30 to 40% of disruptive secondary school students began first grade exhibiting serious conduct disorders, and that these problems continued throughout their education. He also reports the prevalence of persistent and serious conduct disorders among 6% of all students. Causes of conduct disorders may be child abuse, labeling, parental neglect, violence on television, racial tension, socioeconomic status, emotional disturbance, frustration, or trauma.

Frequently found characteristics of conduct disorders (Quay, 1979; Reckless & Dintz, 1972) include fighting, hitting, temper tantrums, destructiveness of property, impertinence, disruptiveness, refusal to take direction, irritability, losing temper easily, attention-seeking, showing off, domination of others, bullying, threatening, hyperactivity, dishonesty, irresponsibility, stealing, loyalty to delinquent friends, belonging to a gang, staying out late, truancy, disorderly conduct, incorrigibility, and intoxication.

Students exhibiting conduct disorders are frequently referred to special education classes for behavior disorders and emotional disturbances. They are often labeled juvenile delinquents and are subject to suspension from school. Some conduct disorders are treated effectively through the use of applied behavior analysis, behavior modification, and token economy.

## REFERENCES

American Psychiatric Association (1980). *Diagnostic and statistical manual of mental disorders* (3rd ed.). Washington, DC: American Psychiatric Association.

Quay, H. C. (1979). Classification. In H. C. Quay & J. S. Werry (Eds.), *Psychological disorders of childhood* (2nd ed.). New York: Wiley.

Reckless, W. C., & Dinitz, S. (1972). *The prevention of delinquency: An experiment.* Columbus, OH: Ohio State University Press.

Safer, D. J. (1982). *School programs for disruptive adolescents.* Baltimore, MD: University Park Press.

Von Isser, A., Quay, H. C., & Love, C. T. (1980). Interrelationships among three measures of deviant behavior. *Exceptional Children, 46,* 272–276.

MARIBETH MONTGOMERY KASIK
*Governors State University*

**ANTISOCIAL BEHAVIOR**
**ANTISOCIAL PERSONALITY**
**EMOTIONAL DISORDERS**

# CONDUCTIVE HEARING LOSS

Auditory functioning can be altered at several levels: the ear, the auditory nerve, or the brain. In the ear, there are two types of anatomical structures—those concerned with the mechanical transmission of sound (a physical process) and those concerned with the transformation of the sound waves into nervous impulses (a biological process). Conductive hearing loss (CHL) applies to the condition resulting from an alteration of the former in opposition to sensory-neural hearing loss, which results from pathology of the latter. The combination of CHL with sensory-neural hearing loss is called mixed hearing loss. For more details about terms and causes of the different types, see Davis and Silverman (1960).

The mechanical transmission of the sound vibrations obeys the laws of acoustics. It is effected by the external and middle ear, the fluids of the inner ear, and the combined displacements of the cochlea's basilar and tectorial membranes. These bring the vibrations to bear on the sensory cells of the organ of Corti, the hair cells. There the conduction process ends; the hair cells are the transducers that transform the acoustic phenomenon into a biochemical and bioelectrical event. The CHL alone is never greater than 60 dB hearing loss, for higher intensity sounds reach the inner ear directly through the skull (von Békésy, 1948). In small children, it is often superimposed on sensoryneural hearing loss, thereby producing an additional deficiency.

Interference with the conduction process most commonly occurs at the level of external or middle ear structures.

One of the most frequent causes of temporary CHL is the external obstruction of the external ear canal (the auditory meatus) by cerumen, a waxlike secretion. Obstruction by foreign bodies is also relatively frequent, especially in children. Various malformations of the external ear can affect hearing, the most serious being nondevelopment of the external auditory meatus.

The tympanic membrane, or eardrum, located between the external and middle ear, is linked with the malleus, incus, and stapes. With these ossicles it constitutes the tympano-ossicular chain, which transmits the sound arriving through the external ear to the oval window, an orifice in the bony wall separating middle and inner ear. Numerous pathological processes can affect these structures and thus produce conductive hearing loss. The eardrum can be swollen by inflammation, stiffened by sclerosis, or perforated. The ossicles may be partly or totally absent or malformed. The mobility of the chain may be reduced by fixation of the stapes in the oval window owing to abnormal bone proliferation at that level. This occurs in otosclerosis (otospongiosis), a frequent condition in adults and a rare one in children.

The accumulation of fluid in the ear occurs in several different forms of otitis media. One of them, serous otitis media, is a frequent chronic or semichronic disease of small children up to 5 or 6 years of age. It is often associated with obstruction of the eustachian tube. These conditions can usually be alleviated or cured relatively easily by medical and/or surgical treatment. However, since the CHL caused by them is mild or moderate, it is often ignored or neglected: This could have serious consequences in later life. Animal studies by Webster and Webster (1979) have shown that temporary moderate auditory restriction in the rat produces changes in the auditory brain stem nuclei. Studies reviewed by Ruben (1984) indicate that language-related skills may be durably impaired, even after restoration of normal hearing, in children who had prolonged CHL during the early years of life. This is because the early years are a particularly sensitive period for language development.

Because CHL affects only the mechanical part of the auditory channel, it produces a decrease in the sound pressure level reaching the inner ear, but no qualitative deformation of that sound. Therefore, a hearing aid that amplifies the sound waves, inasmuch as it does not itself introduce distortions, is capable of restoring a practically normal hearing sensation. While most causes of CHL can be efficiently corrected by medical and/or surgical treatment, the latter may have to be delayed, especially in children where plastic reconstruction surgery can only be done at a certain age level. For these patients, as well as for those where medico-surgical therapy has failed, is contraindicated, is impossible for practical reasons, or is refused by the patient, a well-adapted hearing aid is an excellent solution.

While CHL alone does not prevent spoken language development, it may severely slow down its progression and affect speech skills if undiagnosed or inadequately treated. In the latter case, speech and hearing therapy, following the appropriate medical and/or surgical treatment and/or hearing aid fitting, may be required. Special education may also be necessary as a temporary measure for those children whose speech and language deficiencies prevent them from holding their own in a school for those who hear normally. The great majority of children with CHL, however, can follow their whole curriculum in a mainstream situation, for instance, in ordinary schools with normally hearing children.

## REFERENCES

Davis, H., & Silverman, S. R. (1960). *Hearing and deafness.* New York: Holt, Rinehart and Winston.

Ruben, R. J. (1984). An inquiry into the minimal amount of auditory deprivation which results in a cognitive effect in man. *Acta Oto-Laryngological.* (Suppl. 414) 157–164.

von G. Békésy, (1948). Vibration of the head in a sound field and its role in hearing by bone conduction. *Journal of the Acoustical Society of America, 20,* 749–760.

Webster, D. B., & Webster, M. (1979). Effects of neonatal conductive hearing loss on brain stem auditory nuclei. *Annals of Otology, Rhinology and Laryngology, 88,* 684–688.

OLIVIER PÉRIER
*Université Libre de Bruxelles,*
*Centre Comprendre et Parler,*
*Belgium*

**DEAF**
**DEAF EDUCATION**
**DEPRIVATION, BIONEURAL RESULTS OF**

# CONFIDENTIALITY OF INFORMATION

One major right guaranteed all citizens under the U.S. Constitution is the right to privacy. Included within this privilege is the right to have certain information held confidential. Recent legislation specifically addresses the right to confidentiality of information as it applies to disabled individuals and students, including special education students (Overcast & Sales, 1982; Reynolds, Gutkin, Elliot, & Witt, 1984). Two basic forms of information are covered in the legislation: information held by educational or residential institutions; and certain information discussed by individuals with certain school officials.

Only since the 1970s have the legal rights of disabled individuals and parents of students, including handicapped students, been viewed as in need of regulation. Historically, parents and students had virtually no rights to monitor the information held in institutional files. Often this information was readily accessible to individuals not directly concerned with the educational welfare of the individual in question. In the event that important educational decisions were based on this information in the files, parents, for example, were afforded little if any input into the decisions made. Nor were parents aware of what, where, and when information regarding their children was released to others (Overcast & Sales, 1982).

The Buckley amendment (FERPA, 1976) was enacted in direct response to this practice by educational institu-

tions or agencies that appeared to be in violation of their clients' constitutional rights. It now stands as the major legal document that provides parents and eligible students with the right to: review and inspect educational records; amend inaccurate records; and control disclosure of personally identifiable information in educational records. More specific to handicapped children, parts of this document are reiterated in the Education for All Handicapped Children's Act (PL 94-142, 1975). This act specifically extends parents of handicapped children the right to control or participate in major educational decisions directly affecting their child. Under this law, as in the Buckley amendment, consent must be given before certain filed information can be revealed to individuals outside the educational institution. In addition, under PL 94-142, parents must be able to inspect and amend all information in their child's file.

In addition to these legal documents that ensure the right to have recorded information held confidential, there are also certain guidelines intended to protect the confidentiality of information disclosed by students to certain educational personnel (e.g., counselors, school psychologists). The issue of what and how much information is confidential is not entirely clear. In general, professionals (e.g., psychologists) are bound by their particular ethical standards to protect the confidentiality of information revealed to them in private sessions. This information can usually be revealed without the individual's consent unless there is evidence that the information would result in harm or danger to the patient or others (Reynolds et al., 1984, p. 259). When this information is revealed to school personnel, there seems to be even more ambiguity regarding what is to be held confidential. Overcast and Sales (1982) state:

> It is simply not clear how much confidentiality a student may expect in dealing with school personnel. It depends on the nature of the communication, to whom the communication is directed, and the particular status of the state law. (p. 1089)

## REFERENCES

Overcast, T. D., & Sales, B. D. (1982). The legal rights of students in the elementary and secondary public schools. In C. R. Reynolds & T. B. Gutkin (Eds.), *The handbook of school psychology.* New York: Wiley.

Reynolds, C. R., Gutkin, T. B., Elliot, S. N., & Witt, J. C. (1984). *School psychology: Essentials of theory and practice.* New York: Wiley.

JULIA A. HICKMAN
*University of Texas, Austin*

**BUCKLEY AMENDMENT**
**EDUCATION FOR ALL HANDICAPPED CHILDREN ACT OF 1975**

# CONGENITAL DISORDERS

Two concepts are joined together in the expression congenital disorders, making it pertinent to begin this entry with a short comment on each. Congenital stands for present at birth. This definition does not imply any causal relationship. Nevertheless, for a long time, the terms congenital and hereditary have been confused. Indeed, some congenital disorders may be hereditary, but in many others heredity is not involved. Thus the clear recognition of the absence of any familial factor allows many couples to be reassured concerning the possible recurrence of congenital disorders.

Disorder (malformation or anomaly are also used) means any defect when compared with the normal. Earlier, mainly visible anomalies were detected; today, disorders are described at any level, on the surface or inside the organism, with the aid of sophisticated technical procedures. Therefore, according to Warkany (1971), "Congenital malformations are structural defects present at birth. They may be gross or microscopic, on the surface of the body or within it, familial or sporadic, hereditary or nonhereditary, single or multiple." Only the molecular level must be added to this definition to include all congenital disorders.

Estimations of the incidence of congenital disorders vary from report to report, depending heavily on the mode of ascertainment: external examination only at birth, X-rays, microscopic analyses of tissues, functional tests, inclusion or exclusion of stillbirths, distinction between major and minor defects, and even the personal interest of the examiner in charge at the birth of the child. Thus in a Belgian study, significantly more congenital heart anomalies were observed in two maternity wards participating in a concerted action project of the European Economic Community, probably because the neonatologist pediatricians had special training in cardiology (Borlée-Grimée, De Wals, & Vinçotte-Mols, 1985). Nevertheless, a mean figure could be 2 to 3%. This may seem very high, but it is well established that stillbirths show more congenital anomalies than live births, and that at least 50% of abortions of the first trimester show severe chromosome defects that are likely linked with expulsion (Boué & Boué, 1975). Therefore, the figure of 2 to 3% represents only a small proportion of all malformed embryos. Moreover, all disorders are included, from severe congenital heart malformations incompatible with life, to the partial fusion of two small toes. On the other hand, it is important to point out that congenital disorders are not so exceptional in our species and fortunately, not all are associated with a severe handicap. To our knowledge, there is no particular definition of major and minor anomalies; the interpretation is usually left to reporting authors.

There are many causes of congenital disorders. It is possible to distinguish three broad categories: (1) disorders genetically transmitted following classical Mendelian modes (McKusick, 1983), (2) disorders owed to anomalies of the genetic material but usually not transmitted (e.g., chromosome anomalies), and (3) disorders owed to environmental factors. Many can be recognized at birth by at least one characteristic symptom and some others are detected only later in life.

Dominant heredity is most frequently observed in the case of minor anomalies that do not impair normal life (e.g., supernumerary or fused fingers or toes). A dominant congenital defect is theoretically transmitted to half the offspring, and may be followed through many generations. Sometimes, one generation seems skipped over, or, on the contrary, more severely affected: this is due to variations in penetration or expressivity of the gene. However, severe congenital disorders can be transmitted through a dominant mode. This is the case in Huntington's chorea, a disease of the nervous system (for a recent review, see Robert, 1985). Strictly speaking, Huntington's chorea is a congenital disorder, the gene responsible for it being present at birth. However, carriers of the mutation enjoy a normal life until 30 or 40 years of age and in reproduction transmit the gene to half their offspring. The onset of the disease is observed with a progressive neurological symptomatology (involuntary movements), and often a psychiatric component (depression sometimes ending in suicide). Death usually follows 10 to 15 years after the onset of symptoms.

Recessive heredity is characterized by the birth of affected children to normal parents. Indeed, the father and the mother are heterozygous for a common mutant gene, and 25% of their offspring are homozygous and affected. Hundreds of examples are found in McKusick's catalog of Mendelian diseases in man (1983). When the disorder is severe, people with the disease usually do not reproduce and the genes are eliminated: the reservoir of the disease is thus found in the heterozygous carriers. Many recessive disorders are rare: consanguineous marriages are a well-known favoring factor, as is a common ethnic background (e.g., Tay-Sachs disease is more frequent in Ashkenazi Jews, sickle-cell anemia in blacks, thalassemia in Mediterranean populations). However, this is not a general rule, and unrelated parents from different ethnic backgrounds may be heterozygous for a common recessive gene (a well-known example is mucoviscidosis). When a recessive disorder is suspected, the diagnosis must first be firmly established with the use of appropriate techniques: X-rays, laboratory tests, pathologic and molecular studies. Genetic counseling then becomes possible.

Congenital disorders may be sex-linked, either dominant or recessive. In the first case, females and males are affected, in the second only males. Some common congenital malformations such as cleft lip and palate, clubfoot, spina bifida cystica, anencephaly, and pyloric stenosis are not transmitted through simple Mendelian inheritance, but nevertheless show a clear familial aggregation (Carter, 1976). In these cases, a particular genetic mechanism, called polygenism, is involved. In short, the anomaly is determined by more than one gene, all acting in the same direction and possibly interacting with environmental factors. Beyond a given threshold, the malformation is present. For instance, let us suppose a birth defect associated with the presence of five specific genes acting together in a specific environment. The intact father may possess four of them and the intact mother three. Unpredictably, they can transmit to one of their children five or more deleterious genes. Of course, they may also have non-affected children. The risk is not of the monogenic type; i.e., 50%, 25%, or sex-linked. Empirical tables have been proposed after tabulating direct observations. For example, in a determined population, the risk of having a child with a cleft lip is 1 in 1000 births. A couple who already has one affected child will have a risk increase of 40 times (4%; Carter, 1976).If one of the two parents is affected, the risk before any pregnancy is around 3%. If one of the parents is affected and one child is also affected, the risk is 11%. A major cause of congenital anomalies, usually associated with mental retardation, is chromosome anomalies. The malformations are undoubtedly of genetic origin, owed to anomalies of genetic material, but even if they are genetic and congenital, they are usually not hereditary.

A number of congenital disorders are due to environmental factors. The term environmental must, however, be understood in a broad sense: everything that alters the normal parameters of the body, the body being considered a conglomerate of cells. Clearly, this means that environmental factors can originate from the surrounding area in which the patient lives (e.g., radiation, viruses, drugs), or inside his or her own body (e.g., diabetes, hypothyroidism). This creates abnormal environmental conditions for the cells and, if the patient is a pregnant woman, for the fetus.

In experiments with animals, many agents are known to cause congenital disorders when they are administered to pregnant females (Warkany, 1971). The systematic study of these effects is called teratology. A catalog of teratogenic agents is regularly published and kept up to date (Shepard, 1983). Many drugs are known to be associated with fetal malformations. Pregnant women are usually warned to seek medical advice before taking any medication. Nevertheless, some compounds, although carefully tested before marketing, escape detection and are responsible for the birth of malformed babies. The case of thalidomide is well known. This sedative drug, used also by pregnant women for nausea and vomiting, was found to induce severe anomalies in the human fetus when ingested between the 35th and the 50th day after the last menstrual period (the 23rd to 38th day after conception). Rat and mouse embryos did not seem to suffer from thalidomide administered to pregnant females. However, when the relationship between human malformations and thalidomide was established, the effect of the drug was studied again on macaques. They showed the same sensibility as man. Rabbits also suffered, but to a lesser degree. This demonstrates the importance of selecting a good experimental model. All teratogenic agents cannot be reviewed here; only a few will be discussed.

Ionizing radiations have a well-known teratogenic effect. However fear of congenital malformations in the fetus must not stop pregnant women from having examinations needed for their health (and thus for their baby's health). The teratogenic effect is dose-dependent; it also depends on the site of irradiation and the advancement of the pregnancy. As all this has been extensively demonstrated, it is best to advise the radiologist about a pregnancy or to perform a pregnancy test in case of doubt. Some viruses, but not all, also present with teratogenic activity. The example of rubella is well known; however, the risk is not the same throughout pregnancy. The maximum fetal sensitivity is during the first trimester. Alcohol ingestion may be harmful and cause fetal alcohol syndrome. Heavy smoking is also responsible for fetal damage and low birth weight. Diseases of the mother may affect the fetus if not corrected. Diabetes causes the birth of large infants, higher mortality at birth, and a tendency to hypoglycemia and respiratory distress after delivery (Delaney & Ptacek, 1970). Moreover, some authors are convinced that congenital malformations are more frequent in children of diabetic mothers or at least that some diabetic mothers are more at risk than others. However, if the ingestion of some drugs is known to be teratogenic, the absence of other elements, like vitamins, is harmful. Nutritional deficiencies as a cause of congenital malformations in experimental animals are well documented (Warkany, 1971). These situations are seldom encountered under normal human living conditions, but they explain why a vitamin supplement is advised for pregnant women.

The prevention of congenital malformations has many aspects. An important and simple means of prevention is regular medical surveillance during pregnancy. Another mode of prevention is to avoid any known teratogenic agent and to have balanced nutritional intake. If the birth of a child with severe congenital disorders is followed by death, necropsy is of paramount importance to determine the recurrence risk for the parents. However, sophisticated means of surveillance have been developed for the at-risk mother to be. Prenatal diagnosis is offered, including chromosome analysis of the fetus, research on abnormal genes at the molecular level with recombinant DNA techniques, blood sampling or biopsy of the fetus, follow-up of the anatomical growth of the fetus with ultrasound, various biochemical dosages in the amniotic fluid, and direct viral research on fetal tissues. For some defects, no known treatment is possible, and interruption of pregnancy may appear as the most appropriate solution. For others, treatment is possible either directly with the fetus or just after birth. Thus if a curable congenital heart malformation is diagnosed before birth, the mother can be delivered in a hospital specializing in the correction of such an anomaly.

Neonatal screening is important in some metabolic or endocrine disorders. For instance, hypothyroidism at birth is responsible for future mental retardation of the child, known as cretinism. Nevertheless, after delivery, hypothyroidic children are potentially normal, the maternal thyroid having supplemented the fetus. Immediate substitution treatment allows normal intellectual development. Hypothyroidism can be diagnosed just after birth by the increase of the hormone stimulating the thyroid activity (the thyreostimulating hormone [TSH]) in the blood. Testing is possible on a few drops of blood taken in the perinatal period, and the affected babies, duly treated, enjoy normal development (Delange et al., 1979). Many other disorders can be detected by neonatal screening (Bickel et al., 1980), and progress in this area is promising. This compensates for the high incidence of congenital disorders at birth.

## REFERENCES

Bickel, H., Guthrie, R., & Hammersen, G. (1980). *Neonatal screening for inborn errors of metabolism* (Vol. 1). Berlin: Springer-Verlag.

Borlée-Grimée, I., De Wals, P., & Vinçotte-Mols, M. (1985). Problems in the ascertainment of congenital heart disease. Review of 308 cases registered in Hainaut from 1979 to 1982. In P. De Wals, J. A. C. Weatherall, & M. F. Lechat (Eds.), *Registration of congenital anomalies in Eurocat Centers* 1979–1983. Louvain-la-Neuve, Cabay.

Boué, J., Boué, A., & Lazar, P. (1975). The epidemiology of human spontaneous abortions with chromosome anomalies. In R. J. Blondau (Ed.), *Aging gametes*. Basel, Switzerland: Karger.

Carter, C. O. (1976). Genetics of common single malformations. *British Medical Bulletin, 32*, 21–26.

Delange, F., Beckers, C., Höfer, R., König, M. P., Monaco, F., & Varrone, S. (1979). Neonatal screening for congenital hypothyroidism in Europe. *Acta Endocrinologica, 90* (Suppl. 223), 1–27.

Delaney, J. J., & Ptacek, J. (1970). Three decades of experience with diabetic pregnancies. *American Journal of Obstetrics & Gynecology, 106*, 550.

McKusick, V. (1983). *Mendelian inheritance in man* (6th ed.). Baltimore, MD: Johns Hopkins University Press.

Robert, J. M. (1985). La chorée de Huntington: Histoire naturelle de la maladie. *Journal de Genetique Humaine, 33*, 83–90.

Shepard, T. H. (1983). *Catalog of teratogenic agents* (4th ed.). Baltimore, MD: Johns Hopkins University Press.

Warkany, J. (1971). *Congenital malformations* (Vol. 1). Chicago: Year Book Medical.

L. KOULISCHER
*Institut de Morphologie
Pathologique, Belgium*

**GENETIC COUNSELING
GENETIC VARIATIONS
HEREDITY**


# CONGENITAL WORD BLINDNESS, HISTORY OF

This term refers to "a condition in which, with normal vision and therefore seeing the letters and words distinctly, an individual is no longer able to interpret written or printed language" (Hinshelwood, 1917, p. 2). The term was the title of a book written by Hinshelwood (1917) in which he described case studies and intervention techniques with individuals who evidenced word blindness. Hinshelwood's clients showed such disability subsequent to strokes or brain damage induced by chronic alcoholism. He extended the use of this term to children who showed the same reading disability. However, "congenital word blindness" was originally used by Morgan (1896), whose paper was one of the first to document a clear case of severe reading disability in a 14-year-old boy of apparent brightness. The boy knew all his letters and could write and read them singly. However, except for some common sight words such as the, and, of, and that, he could not read any word, even words that he encountered daily, such as the name of his father's house. The boy's parents provided him with tutors and sent him to schools to teach him to read, but despite concerted teaching efforts, the boy's reading disability persisted.

Morgan and Hinshelwood were ophthalmologists. They were intrigued by their clients and observed and recorded the details of severe reading disabilities. They both used the term congenital word blindness to describe adults and children with clear, pronounced reading disabilities. Specifically, Hinshelwood (1917) hypothesized that children with congenital word blindness sustained a brain defect in the left hemisphere, where he thought visual word and letter memories were stored. According to Hinshelwood, the inability to read was attributed to deficient visual memory, for he believed good readers recognize or remember words by activating a visual picture rather than by analyzing individual letters in the words. Additionally, both he and Morgan considered such a brain defect to be congenital (Smith, 1983).

Hinshelwood believed that intensive practice and the development of the brain's visual memory would enable individuals with congenital word blindness to reach reading proficiency (Mercer, 1983). Specifically, he suggested a three-stage approach to the remediation of deficits: teaching the individual letters for storage in the supposed visual-memory center of the brain; teaching word recognition by spelling the printed words aloud so as to use the individual's good auditory memory for letter sounds; and enabling storage of the reading words using oral and written practice. It has been suggested that Hinshelwood's emphasis on visual memory and generally visual interpretations of reading disability had a significant impact on subsequent visual-perceptual theories of learning disabilities (Smith, 1983).

## REFERENCES

Hinshelwood, J. (1917). *Congenital word blindness*. London: Lewis.

Mercer, C. D. (1983). *Students with learning disabilities* (2nd ed.). Columbus, OH: Charles E. Merrill.

Morgan, W. P. (1896). A case of congenital word blindness. *British Medical Journal, 2*, 1378.

Smith, C. R. (1983). *Learning disabilities: The interaction of learner, task and setting*. Boston: Little, Brown.

BERNICE Y. L. WONG
*Simon Fraser University*

## DYSLEXIA
## READING DISORDERS

## CONNERS' PARENT-RATING SCALE

The Conners *Parent-Symptom Questionnaire (PSQ)* (see, Conners' Teacher-Rating Scale) (Goyette, Conners, & Ulrich, 1978) has been the most widely used parent-rating scale in the assessment of hyperactive children. The version most frequently used is a 48-item scale whose factors have been analyzed into five groupings: conduct problems, learning disability (inattention), psychosomatic problems, impulsivity-hyperactivity, and anxiety. Although only four questions bear on the hyperactivity factor, 10 questions are used to compose the hyperactivity index.

Each of the items from the Conners PSQ (e.g., "excitable, impulsive," "cries easily or often," "restless in the squirmy sense," "destructive") is rated on a four-point continuum from "not at all" (scored 0) to "very much" (scored 3). Scores for each factor of the PSQ are computed by summing the points across all items comprising that factor and by dividing by the number of items in that factor. Whereas a mean score of 1.5 on the hyperactivity index has generally been accepted as the lower limit for establishing a diagnosis of hyperactivity, some investigators have insisted on a score of two standard deviations above the mean for the child's age to make such a diagnosis (Barkley, 1981).

Some researchers have suggested that the PSQ is not as reliable and sensitive in designating children as hyperactive as the Conners Teacher Scale (Barkley, 1981; Sleator & von Neumann, 1974). Moreover, Barkley (1981) has found that the total score of the PSQ and the hyperkinesis index do not correlate significantly with laboratory measures of attention and activity. However, ratings on the PSQ do correlate with measures of noncompliance to parental commands, suggesting that child noncompliance may be the primary concern of parents responding to the hyperactivity index of the questionnaire (Barkley, 1981).

The scores from each of the factors of the PSQ have been found to be highly related to children's sex and age; boys are rated as more problematic than girls. Further, parental ratings differ by sex, with mothers' ratings being more severe than fathers' (Barkley, 1981). The PSQ and its factor scores have been found to be sensitive to the effects of stimulant drug therapy (Brown, Wynne, & Slimmer, 1984) and behavior management programs (Barkley, 1981). Children scoring higher on the PSQ have been found to be at greater risk for academic failure and have responded more favorably to pharmacotherapy than their peers having lower scores (Barkley, 1981).

Normative data for the PSQ are available (Goyette, et al., 1978) and test-retest reliabilities over short periods of time have been found to be satisfactory. Studies employing discriminant analyses to predict diagnostic categories have also indicated favorable construct validity of the PSQ with the scale correctly classifying 77% of neurotic children, 70% of clinic referred children, 74% of hyperactive children, and 83% of normal children from its factor scores (Barkley, 1981).

### REFERENCES

Barkley, R. A. (1981). *Hyperactive children: A handbook for diagnosis and treatment*. New York: Guilford.

Brown, R. T., Wynne, M. E., & Slimmer, L. W. (1984). Attention deficit disorder and the effect of methylphenidate on attention, behavioral, and cardiovascular functioning. *Journal of Clinical Psychiatry, 45*(11), 473–476.

Goyette, C. H., Conners, C. K., & Ulrich, R. F. (1978). Normative data in revised Conners Parent and Teacher Rating Scales. *Journal of Abnormal Child Psychology, 6*, 221–236.

Sleator, E. K. & von Neumann, A. W. (1974). Methylphenidate in the treatment of hyperkinetic children. *Clinical Pediatrics, 13*, 19–24.

Sprague, R. L. & Sleator, E. K. (1977). Methylphenidate in hyperkinetic children: Difference in dose effects on learning and social behavior. *Science, 198*, 1274–1276.

RONALD T. BROWN
*Emory University School
of Medicine*

## ATTENTION-DEFICIT DISORDER
## HYPERKINESIS

## CONNERS' TEACHER-RATING SCALE

The Conners Teacher Rating Scale (Conners, 1969) has been used widely in the identification of hyperactive children and has been demonstrated to be sensitive to stimulant medications (Werry, Sprague, & Cohen, 1975) and other psychotropic drugs. The original 39-item teacher questionnaire was later factor analyzed by Conners; it resulted in the *Abbreviated Teacher Rating Scale (ATRS)*, a 10-item instrument sometimes referred to as the hyperkinesis index. This version of the Conners rating scale was included in the Early Clinical Drug Evaluation Unit (a branch of the National Institute of Mental Health) recommendations for use in selecting and monitoring hyperactivity.

The items from the abbreviated Conners scale (e.g., "sits fiddling with small objects," "hums and makes other noises," "restless or overactive," "excitable") are rated on a 4-point continuum from "not at all" (scored 0) to "very much" (scored 3). For the 10-item scale, the possible scores range from 0 to 30. Sprague et al. (Sprague, Cohen, & Werry, 1974) recommended a cutoff (minimum score) of 15 (two standard deviations above the overall mean score) in the selection of children for research studies and treatment programs.

Previously the abbreviated version of the scale had proven useful for the research and clinical community as it repeatedly had been demonstrated to be both reliable and valid (Sandoval, 1977) for assessing special populations; it was also quick to administer and score. However, since the adoption of the new diagnostic label "attention deficit disorder (ADD)," which replaces hyperactivity in the most recent version of the American Psychiatric Association's *Diagnostic and Statistical Manual of Mental Disorders* (DSM III), the Conners scale has been assailed. Although the Conners scale does continue to be efficient at selecting children with hyperactivity and conduct disorders, it has failed to select those children whose primary difficulty is inattention, a key diagnostic feature in the revised DSM III (Ullmann, Sleator, & Sprague, 1985). Based on their recent research findings, Ullmann et al. (1985) advocated that both the 39-item teacher scale and the abbreviated form be abandoned as research tools. At the time the Conners scale was developed in the early 1970s, it was an innovative advance in the researcher's diagnostic armamentarium. Nonetheless, progress since that time has made necessary the development of new rating scales to reflect the recent diagnostic features of ADD (Ullmann, Sleator, & Sprague, 1984).

## REFERENCES

American Psychiatric Association. (1980). *Diagnostic and statistical manual of mental disorders* (3rd ed.). Washington, D.C.: APA.

Conners, C. K. (1969). A teacher rating scale for use in drug studies with children. *American Journal of Psychiatry, 126,* 804–888.

Sandoval, J. (1977). The measurement of the hyperactive syndrome in children. *Review of Educational Research, 47,* 293–318.

Sprague, R. L., Cohen, M. N., & Werry, J. S. (1974). *Normative data on the Conners' Teacher Rating and Abbreviated Scale.* Champaign: University of Illinois, Institute for Child Behavior and Development.

Ullmann, R. K., Sleator, E. K., & Sprague, R. L. (1984). A new rating scale for diagnosis and monitoring and ADD children. *Psychopharmacology Bulletin, 20,* 160–164.

Ullmann, R. K., Sleator, E. K., & Sprague, R. L. (1985). A change of mind: Conners' Abbreviated Rating Scales reconsidered. *Journal of Abnormal Child Psychology 13,* 553–565.

Werry, J. S., Sprague, R. L., & Cohen, M. N. (1975). Conners' Teacher Rating Scale for use in drug studies with children— An empirical study. *Journal of Abnormal Child Psychology, 3,* 217–227.

RONALD T. BROWN
*Emory University School
of Medicine*

## ATTENTION DEFICIT DISORDER

*HYPERKINESIS*

# CONSCIENCE, LACK OF IN HANDICAPPED

Society is particularly concerned that children develop the skills to regulate their own behavior or, stated differently, internalize moral principles. Situations often arise that pose a conflict between the individual desires of the person and the requirements of society. These circumstances call for the exercise of self-control as the person suppresses self-interested behavior in favor of actions that serve the needs of others. Two areas of research bear directly on this problem—altruism and resistance to temptation.

## Altruism

Altruism refers to behavior that is carried out to benefit another in the absence of threat or expected reward. Altruism entails self-control since the helper must weigh the costs of helping (e.g., material loss or physical danger) against the benefits (e.g., self-satisfaction) of helping (Kanfer, 1979). Research with children has relied on several measures of altruism, including donating possessions to a charity or another child, willingness to rescue someone in trouble, peer ratings, and naturalistic observations of helping and sharing.

Most children show an increase in sharing during the period of middle childhood. This change parallels children's decreasing egocentrism and increasingly sophisticated moral reasoning abilities. However, the relationship among these variables is not clearly understood. At least with children of average IQ, general level of cognitive development is unrelated to various measures of altruism (Rushton & Wiener, 1975). There does appear to be a weak relationship between generosity and level of moral reasoning among 7- to 11-year-old children, but it is not known if moral reasoning directly affects moral behavior (Rushton, 1975). Most studies fail to find a relationship between sex and altruism, but when differences are noted they tend to show females as more altruistic (Krebs, 1970). Finally, investigators have found a substantial degree of behavioral specificity across situations that offer an opportunity for altruistic behavior. For example, a child may donate a toy to a needy stranger but fail to volunteer time to help a peer. The correlation across measures is about .30 and may reflect the weak effect of an underlying personality variable or experimental or psychometric artifacts (Rushton, 1976).

One research finding that is unequivocal is that the altruistic behavior of children can be modified. Numerous studies have shown that children will imitate an altruistic model (Harris, 1971). In fact, the influence of a model was shown in one study to extend up to 4 months, even though posttesting was conducted under very different circumstances (Ruston, 1975). These results have obvious implications for child-rearing practices.

## Resistance to Temptation

Resistance to temptation is another example of self-control. Here the child is required to exercise self-restraint in the absence of immediate surveillance. Several studies have examined variables that promote this form of self-control. From a developmental perspective, the emergence of language is important in that it allows the child to regulate his or her behavior by stating rules of conduct (Kanfer & Phillips, 1970). The ability to verbalize rules may be necessary but usually is not sufficient for resisting temptation.

Children who score high on resistance to temptation often make use of cognitive strategies (i.e., self-control techniques). A body of work by Kanfer (Hartig & Kanfer, 1973; Kanfer & Zich, 1974) and Mischel (Mischel, Ebbesen, & Zeiss, 1972; Mischel & Patterson, 1978) has shown that resistance to temptation is enhanced when children distract themselves (e.g., sing songs or thinking of a "fun activity"), repeatedly state a rule (e.g., "I'm a good girl if I don't look at the hampster"), or engage in mental transformations (e.g., "The pretzel is really just a log of wood"). The fact that older children are more successful in such situations is in part attributed to a greater facility in the use of language and a larger repertoire of cognitive strategies.

Researchers have just recently begun to extend these findings to retarded individuals. It has been noted that mildly retarded adolescents prefer immediate rewards even though by waiting they could receive twice as many of those rewards (Franzini, Litrownik, & Magy, 1978). In one study with moderately retarded adolescents, training in self-instruction ("I am gonna get more money if I wait to get paid . . . I sure am a good worker") reinforced practice and the provision of successful models led to a fivefold increase in the delay of gratification (Franzini, Litrownik, & Magy, 1980).

The importance of verbal controlling strategies in resistance to temptation is underscored by a study comparing Down's syndrome children to nonretarded children matched for level of cognitive development. On the average, the retarded children were less able to resist temptation than were the nonretarded children, a finding consistent with the Franzini et al. (1980) study. Interestingly, those Down's syndrome children that were most successful were observed to spontaneously engage in verbal and nonverbal behaviors that served to distract them from the desired object (Kopp, Krakow, & Johnson, 1983).

In considering the research in both the areas of altruism and resistance to temptation, a clear directive for teachers and parents is evident. In order to enhance self-control one should not think in terms of building the child's character. Instead, the child should be taught specific verbal and nonverbal behavioral skills that can be used for self-regulation in tempting situations.

## REFERENCES

Franzini, L. R., Litrownik, A. J., & Magy, M. A. (1978). Immediate and delayed reward preferences of TMR adolescents. *American Journal of Mental Deficiency, 82*, 406–409.

Franzini, L. R., Litrownik, A. J., & Magy, M. A. (1980). Training trainable mentally retarded adolescents in delay behavior. *Mental Retardation, 18*, 45–47.

Harris, M. (1971). Models, norms and sharing. *Psychological Reports, 29*, 147–153.

Hartig, M., & Kanfer, F. H. (1973). The role of verbal self-instructions in children's resistance to temptation. *Journal of Personality & Social Psychology, 25*, 259–267.

Kanfer, F. H. (1979). Personal control, social control, and altruism: Can society survive the age of individualism? *American Psychologist, 34*, 231–239.

Kanfer, F. H., & Phillips, J. S. (1970). *Learning foundations of behavior therapy.* New York: Wiley.

Kanfer, F. H., & Zich, J. (1974). Self-control training: The effects of external control on children's resistance to temptation. *Developmental Psychology, 10*, 108–115.

Kopp, C. B., Krakow, J. B., & Johnson, K. L. (1983). Strategy production by young Down syndrome children. *American Journal of Mental Deficiency, 88*, 164–169.

Krebs, D. L. (1970). Altruism: An examination of the concept and a review of the literature. *Psychological Bulletin, 73*, 258–302.

Mischel, W., Ebbesen, E. B., & Zeiss, A. R. (1972). Cognitive and attentional mechanisms in delay of gratification. *Journal of Personality & Social Psychology, 21*, 204–218.

Mischel, W., & Patterson, C. J. (1978). Effective plans for self-control. In W. A. Collins (Ed.), *Minnesota symposia on child psychology* (Vol. 2). Hillsdale, NJ: Erlbaum.

Rushton, J. P. (1975). Generosity in children: Immediate and long term effects of modeling, preaching, and moral judgment. *Journal of Personality & Social Psychology, 31*, 459–466.

Rushton, J. P. (1976). Socialization and the altruistic behavior of children. *Psychological Bulletin, 83*, 898–913.

Rushton, J. P., & Wiener, J. (1975). Altruism and cognitive development in children. *British Journal of Social & Clinical Psychology, 14*, 341–349.

Laurence C. Grimm
*University of Illinois, Chicago*

IMPULSE CONTROL
MORAL REASONING
SELF-CONTROL CURRICULUM

## CONSENT, INFORMED

Increased parental involvement through informed consent is a primary feature of PL 94-142, the Education for All Handicapped Children Act of 1975. The intent of the informed consent requirement is to change the relationship between schools and parents from one of the schools as the primary authority in determining the appropriate education for handicapped students to one of shared decision making. Prior to the passage of PL 94-142, some schools consulted with parents and told them about their children's special education placement and some did not, carrying the doctrine of *in loco parentis* to an intolerable extreme. However, court decisions and decrees have stated that the consequences of possible labeling, segregation, and exclusion of handicapped children from other children, and changes in their curriculum, may infringe on their constitutional rights of life, liberty, or property, and that individuals who may be subject to such deprivation must consent to any process with these possible results.

To protect students from arbitrary changes in placement, PL 94-142, Sections 121a.500, 504, and 505 (*Federal Register*, 1977) present the requirements for securing informed consent from parents. Parental consent must be received before conducting a preplacement evaluation and before placing a child in a program providing special education and related services. Some school systems have requested parental consent for individualized educational programs and reevaluations of students; however, in meeting Section 121a.504, such permission is not legally mandated but still seems to be good practice. If the parents refuse to give their consent to evaluation or placement, the school system may request a due process hearing to obtain the authority to proceed with the assessment and placement process without parental consent.

Bersoff (1978) argues that informed consent is more of a stated principle than a well-defined and agreed on concept. However, consensus exists that the principle of informed consent has three characteristics: knowledge, voluntariness, and capacity. First, PL 94-142, Section 121a.500(a) requires that parents be "fully informed of all information relevant to the activity for which consent is sought." Bersoff (1978, 1982) argues that it is impossible for schools to present every technical detail of the evaluations to be performed or to anticipate every benefit and hazard that could arise from the evaluation or special education placement. Section 121.505 provides guidelines on what needs to be provided at a minimum to parents such as a description of the actions to be taken by the school district and the rationale for those actions. In addition, the regulations make it clear that school personnel must make a good faith effort to communicate with parents; they must provide the notice in the parents' native language and must ensure that parents understand the content of the notice.

Second, consent is given voluntarily in the absence of any coercion, misrepresentation, or duress; consent is not permanently binding and can be withdrawn at any time. Finally, the law presumes that parents are competent to make decisions about their children's educational programs. If school districts believe that particular parents cannot make such decisions, they should then initiate procedures for the appointment of a substitute decision maker, typically in the form of a guardian ad litem. The American Educational Research Association, American Psychological Association, and the National Council on Measurement in Education have agreed on and endorsed a definition of informed consent that, although specific to the taking of educational and psychological tests, presents general principles applicable to nearly any special education circumstance. In the *Standards for Educational and Psychological Testing* (Committee to Revise the Standards, 1985), these organizations define informed consent as:

> The granting of consent by the test taker to be tested on the basis of full information concerning the purpose of the testing, the persons who may receive the test scores, the use to which the test scores may be put, and other such information as may be material to the consent process. (pp. 91–92)

Full disclosure of information necessary to the decision-making process and a full understanding of the information seem to be the key to obtaining informed consent.

Bersoff (1978, 1982), Overcast and Sales (1982), and Kotin (1978) suggest various procedures for securing informed consent and corresponding criteria and assessment techniques to determine the extent to which the informed consent principle has been implemented. Current practice in special education varies greatly from school district to school district. However, careful attention to obtaining informed consent is not just good professional practice, it is a requirement of federal law.

## REFERENCES

Bersoff, D. N. (1978). Procedural safeguards. In L. G. Morra (Ed.), *Developing criteria for the evaluation of due process procedural safeguards provisions of Public Law 94-142* (pp. 63–142). Washington, DC: U.S. Office of Education.

Bersoff, D. N. (1982). The legal regulation of school psychology. In C. R. Reynolds & T. B. Gutkin (Eds.), *The handbook of school psychology*. New York: Wiley.

Committee to Revise the Standards. (1985). *Standards for educational and psychological testing*. Washington, DC: American Psychological Association.

Kotin, L. (1978). Recommended criteria and assessment techniques for the evaluation by LEAs of their compliance with the notice and consent requirements of PL 94-142. In L. G. Morra (Ed.), *Developing criteria for the evaluation of due process procedural safeguards provisions of Public Law 94-142* (pp. 143–178). Washington, DC: U.S. Office of Education.

Overcast, T. D., & Sales, B. D. (1982). The legal rights of students in the schools. In C. R. Reynolds & T. B. Gutkin (Eds.), *The handbook of school psychology*. New York: Wiley.

U.S. Department of Health, Education, and Welfare. (1977). Education of handicapped children: Implementation of Part B of the Education of Handicapped Act. *Federal Register, 42*(163), 42474–42518.

ROLAND K. YOSHIDA
*Fordham University*

## EDUCATION FOR ALL HANDICAPPED CHILDREN ACT OF 1975

# CONSENT AGREEMENT

See CONSENT DECREE.

# CONSENT DECREE

A consent decree is a legal mandate or court order issued by a judiciary authority that has jurisdiction over the particular civil matter resolved in the decree. It is a legally enforceable order of that court. Consent decrees derive from the agreement of the adversarial parties to a civil lawsuit to end their disagreement provided that certain acts are performed by one or both parties and agreed to in order to avoid continuing litigation. The agreement is drawn up by the two parties, signed by the appropriate legal representatives, and submitted to the court for review. If the court decides the agreement is fair and entered into with appropriate understanding and representation by both parties, the court will then mandate and enforce the decree by court order.

Many special education cases are decided by consent agreements that become enforceable court decrees. Among the best known and most influential are *Diana* and *Guadalupe*. Consent decrees are binding only on the parties to the decree, however, and do not make case law or set legal precedent.

CECIL R. REYNOLDS
*Texas A&M University*

# DIANA v. STATE BOARD OF EDUCATION

# CONSTITUTIONAL LAW (IN SPECIAL EDUCATION)

Judicial interpretations of the Constitution and its amendments have played a major role in the comparatively recent efforts to obtain and maintain appropriate special education programs and services for handicapped children and youth and their families. The groundwork for this role was laid in the 1954 Supreme Court decision in *Brown v. Board of Education*; the decision made clear that separate education facilities for children of different races are inherently not equal (Lippman & Goldberg, 1973). This decision affirmed that, because of the importance of education today, education "is a right which must be available to all on equal terms" (*Brown v. Board*, 347 U.S. 483). Citing this decision almost 20 years later, attorneys in two class-action suits built their arguments for landmark special education cases that were resolved in federal district courts: *PARC v. Board* (*PARC v. Commonwealth*, 334 F.

Supp. 1257, E.D. Pa., 1971), which made clear that mentally retarded children in Pennsylvania are entitled to free education programs appropriate for their needs; and *Mills v. Board* (*Mills v. Board of Education, District of Columbia*, 348 F. Supp. 866, 1972), which extended free and appropriate education to all handicapped children in the District of Columbia.

Both the *PARC* and *Mills* cases have been cited in subsequent litigation involving similar and related principles that eventually were incorporated into federal legislation. Of particular importance to special education are the Rehabilitation Act of 1973, which requires access to programs and facilities, and the Education of All Handicapped Children Act of 1975 (PL 94-142). Public law 94-142, and more recently the Education of the Handicapped Act Amendments of 1983 (PL 98-199), embody the principles of zero project, nondiscriminatory testing, individualized and appropriate education planning and programming, least restrictive alternative as preferred educational placement, and procedural due process. All of these principles can be found in the guarantees of the Fifth and Fourteenth amendments to the Constitution (Turnbull & Fiedler, 1985) which state:

No person shall . . . be deprived of life, liberty, or property, without due process of law. (Constitution of the United States, Amendment V, 1791)

No State shall make or enforce any law which shall abridge the privileges or immunities of citizens of the United States; nor shall any State deprive any person of life, liberty or property without due process of law, nor deny to any person within its jurisdiction the equal protection of the laws. (Constitution of the United States, Amendment XIV, 1868)

For a detailed discussion of litigation in special education and its reliance on constitutional guarantees and interpretations of the Supreme Court, see Turnbull and Fiedler (1984).

## REFERENCES

Ballard, J., Ramirez, B. A., & Weintraub, F. J. (1982). *Special education in America: Its legal and governmental foundations.* Reston, VA: Council for Exceptional Children.

Lippman, L., & Goldberg, I. (1973). *Right to education: Anatomy of the Pennsylvania case and its implications for exceptional children.* New York: Teachers College Press.

Turnbull, J. R., III, & Fiedler, C. R. (1984). *Judicial interpretation of the Education for All Handicapped Children Act.* Reston, VA: Council for Exceptional Children.

Weintraub, F. J., Abeson, A., Ballard, J., & LaVor, M. L. (1977). *Public policy and the education of exceptional children.* Reston, VA: Council for Exceptional Children.

Weintraub, F. J., & Ramirez, B. A. (1985). *Progress in the edu-*

*cation of the handicapped and analysis of PL 98-199*. Reston, VA: Council for Exceptional Children.

MARJORIE E. WARD
*The Ohio State University*

**BROWN *v.* BOARD OF EDUCATION
LARRY P.
MILLS *v.* BOARD OF EDUCATION
PASE *v.* HANNON
THE PENNSYLVANIA ASSOCIATION FOR RETARDED
   CITIZENS *v.* PENNSYLVANIA**

# CONSULTATION

Consultation refers to a professional relationship in which a specialist attempts to improve the functioning of another professional. Although there are many models of school consultation, each with different sets of assumptions, techniques, and goals, Bergan and Tombari's definition (1976) is general enough to encompass the idiosyncrasies of these various models. "Consultation refers to services rendered by a consultant (e.g., school psychologist) to a consultee (e.g., teacher) who functions as a change agent with respect to the learning or adjustment of a client (e.g., a child) or a group of clients" (p. 4).

Consultation in school settings is an indirect model of providing broadly defined mental health services to children. The consultant attempts to effect a change in children's behavior and learning by attempting to change the teacher's (or administrator's) attitudes, perceptions, and behaviors. One of the rationales for consultation is the economy of resources it offers. By improving teacher and administrator functioning, the psychologist can affect many more children than possible in the traditional counseling and testing models of service delivery.

Certain key elements distinguish consultation from other professional activities. First, consultation is a professional-to-professional relationship that is focused on helping the consultee to do a job. Consultation is a voluntary relationship; thus the consultee is free to accept or reject the consultant's help and recommendations. In turn, the consultee is expected to contribute to the problem-solving process and is responsible for implementing action plans that result from the consultation. Finally, the consultant respects the confidential nature of the relationship.

One professional activity that shares similarities with consultation is supervision; however, consultation differs from supervision in several important ways. Because the supervisor is administratively responsible for the supervisee's work, the supervisee is obligated to accept the supervisor's advice. A supervisor is usually a senior professional in the same discipline as the supervisee, whereas the consultant is usually trained in a discipline different

from that of the consultee. Thus supervision involves a hierarchical obligatory relationship, while consultation involves a egalatarian voluntary relationship.

Consultation has both remedial and preventive goals, but different consultation models emphasize one or the other goals. Thus when consulting with a teacher, the consultant attempts to improve both the learning and adjustment of the child about whom the teacher is concerned and the teacher's ability to cope effectively with similar children in the future. This latter, preventive goal of consultation allows psychologists to broaden their impact beyond the target child.

The goals of consultation listed by Conoley and Conoley (1982) are relevant to several consultation models and include (1) providing an objective point of view; (2) increasing problem-solving skills; (3) increasing coping skills; (4) increasing freedom of choice; (5) increasing commitment to choices made; and (6) increasing available resources.

The different models of school consultation do not have identical conceptual bases. For example, behavioral consultation is based on social learning theory, and the technology of applied behavioral analysis is used to change students' and teachers' behaviors. Process consultation is based on social, psychological, and general systems theory and assumes interpersonal and group processes affect educational outcomes. There are certain assumptions, or concepts, that are common to the various models. Two shared assumptions are that children's classroom behaviors and learning are determined by variables in the child and in the classroom setting and that the consultant must work jointly with the consultee to solve problems.

Considerable attention in the consultation literature is given to the task of entry as a consultant into an organization. Entry tasks include (1) obtaining approval for consultation from administrators; (2) establishing a shared set of expectations with administrators and teachers regarding consultation's purposes, the roles and responsibilities of the consultant and consultees, confidentiality, and the types of problems to be discussed in consultation; and (3) establishing the consultant as a credible and trustworthy resource person. If teachers are accustomed to receiving recommendations from psychologists, and the psychologist-consultant does not carefully lay the groundwork for the consultative relationship, the teacher and the psychologist will find themselves working at cross purposes, based on their differing expectations for the interaction.

Consultation involves two jobs: working on the content, or specific problem brought to consultation, and working on the process of helping the consultee improve his or her job-related performance. It is important for the consultant to have specialized knowledge that is relevant to the consultation content (e.g., the particular behavior, learning, or programmatic concern). Indeed, the reason the consultee asked for the consultant's help is that the consultee believes the consultant has such relevant knowledge. Knowledge bases the psychologist-consultant might draw from in teacher consultation include child development, theories of learning, childhood psychopathology, tests and measurements, diagnosis of learning and behavior, group processes, individual instructional programming, and treatment of childhood learning and behavioral disorders.

In addition to content skills, the consultant must have skills necessary for establishing and maintaining rapport with the consultee and for facilitating the consultee's professional growth. Thus the consultant (1) seeks clarification, encouraging consultees to see problems from new or broader perspectives; (2) supports the consultee while he or she is grappling with the problem, boosting consultee motivation and self-confidence; (3) asks questions that require consultees to validate information; (4) probes for feelings to help consultees accept their emotional reactions to children; (5) provides choices to increase consultee freedom to choose and commitment to choices made; and (6) confronts consultees either directly or indirectly to increase consultee objectivity. An example of an indirect confrontation is telling a female teacher who is inappropriately "mothering" a young girl that the girl is expecting the teacher to do too much for her and the girl needs to learn that the teacher cannot be her mother. An example of a direct confrontation is telling a male teacher that he seems to be apologizing to his students when he assumes an authoritative role, and that perhaps students are misbehaving because they are picking up on his discomfort in the authoritarian role.

Five models of school consultation are described with respect to their primary purpose and the roles and skills required of the consultant. Psychoeducational consultation is the type of consultation most frequently practiced in schools. After the psychologist has evaluated a child, the psychologist interprets the evaluation results to the teacher, presents recommendations to the teacher, and engages the teacher in a discussion of these recommendations so that the teacher will be able to choose and implement one or more recommendations. The primary purpose is remedial. The consultant's primary role is to diagnose the problem and recommend treatment.

Behavioral consultation is based on social learning theory. The behavioral consultant applies the technology of applied behavior analysis to the task of changing student and teacher behavior. The consultant observes the child as well as the teacher in the classroom to identify and count target behaviors, determine antecedents and consequences of those target behaviors, and recommend changes expected to result in a change in target behaviors. Because the teacher is ultimately responsible for making any changes that are recommended by the consultant, the consultant needs to establish a collaborative working relationship with the teacher. The primary goal in behavioral consultation is remedial; however, the consultant expects consultees will improve their skills in applied behavior analysis and will apply their new skills to similar problems in the future.

In educational consultation, the consultant presents new information or teaches new skills to consultees by conducting in-service workshops. The effective consultant-trainer carefully assesses educational needs of the workshop audience as well as the expectations of the administrators, and provides training that matches those needs and expectations.

The mental health consultant's primary purpose is to improve the consultee's ability to effectively cope with similar problems in the future without the consultant's continued help. The particular problem discussed in consultation acts as leverage for changing the consultee's behavior. A secondary goal is to change the child's behavior. Because the focus is on the consultee, the consultant's process skills are especially important. The mental health consultant uses clinical interviewing skills to determine the reason a teacher is experiencing difficulty and employs different consultation approaches depending on the presumed reason for the consultee's difficulty. When the consultee's problem is presumed to be a lack of objectivity, the consultant uses specialized skills that require specialized training in consultation techniques. The consultant attempts to minimize the teacher's displacement of personal problems onto the work setting.

In program consultation, the consultant is requested by the administration to design or to evaluate a specific program such as a gifted education program, a race relations program, or a truancy program. The consultant must have experience and skills relevant to the particular program. The consultant issues a written report that contains recommendations for the school to implement.

Process consultation, like program consultation, is initiated by an administrator. It attempts to effect a change in the system rather than in the individual teacher or child. Process consultation is based on social psychological and general systems theory. The process consultant attempts to improve interpersonal and group processes used by administrators, teachers, parents, and students to reach educational objectives. Thus the consultant will involve the administrators and teachers in a mutual problem-solving effort aimed at diagnosing and changing such human processes as communication, leadership, decision making, and trust. The process consultant does not deal directly with the subject matter of the interactions of an organization. Rather, the consultant provides help with the methods of communication, problem solving, planning, and decision making (Schmuck, 1976).

Consultation is a term that encompasses a diverse set of models for delivering psychological services to a school (or other organization). The common thread is that the psychologist attempts to affect change in clients of the organization (e.g., students) by influencing the behaviors of persons who have a responsibility for client care.

## REFERENCES

Bergan, J. R., & Tombari, M. L. (1976). Consultant skill and efficiency and the implementation and outcomes of consultation. *Journal of School Psychology, 14*(1), 3–14.

Conoley, J. C., & Conoley, C. W. (1982). *School consultation: A guide to practice and training*. New York: Pergamon.

Schmuck, R. A. (1976). *Process consultation and organization development*. Reading, MA: Addison-Wesley.

JAN N. HUGHES
*Texas A&M University*

CONSULTATION, MENTAL HEALTH
MULTIDISCIPLINARY TEAMS
PREREFERRAL INTERVENTIONS
PRESCHOOL SCREENING
PROFESSIONAL SCHOOL PSYCHOLOGY

## CONSULTATION, MENTAL HEALTH

Mental health consultation is an indirect mode of providing mental health services to clients served by some agency. The mental health consultant attempts to improve the psychological adjustment of persons in the community (i.e., students, parishioners, probationers, or patients) by consulting with professional caregivers in the community (i.e., teachers, clergymen, probation officers, or doctors). Gerald Caplan's seminal book, *The Theory and Practice of Mental Health Consultation* (1970), summarized his most important writings on the subject and offered the first comprehensive coverage of this mode of providing mental health services. Caplan defined mental health consultation as "a process of interaction between two professional persons—the consultant, who is a specialist, and the consultee, who invokes the consultant's help in regard to a current work problem with which he is having some difficulty and which he has decided is within the other's area of specialized competence" (p. 19). Other persons have broadened this definition to include consultation with more than one consultee and consultation with nonprofessionals (Altrocchi, 1972).

The mental health consultant may be a psychiatrist, psychologist, or social worker, and the consultee may be any person whose ministrations to lay persons in the community have mental health implications. Mental health consultation is more prevalent in schools than in other settings. Reasons for its prevalence in schools include the opportunity provided in schools to affect the mental health of large numbers of children through consultation with a small number of teachers, the recognition of the importance of schooling on children's mental health, the presence of psychologists in schools, and the demonstrated relevance of psychological theories and knowledge to educational goals and practices. Consistent with the focus of this work, the following discussion of consultation will be specific to mental health consultation in schools.

There are several key elements in the previous definition of consultation that distinguish consultation from other professional activities. First, the consultee (teacher,

principal, other administrator) invokes the consultant's help. Because consultation is a professional-to-professional interaction, the consultee is responsible for determining whether the assistance of the consultant would be helpful.

Second, the consultee retains responsibility for the problem. Thus, when teachers or administrators ask for a consultant's help, they do not diminish their responsibility for instructing the child or administering the program. Because the consultee retains responsibility for the problem and its handling, the consultee is an active participant in a joint problem-solving process. Responsibility for problem formulation and solution is shared between the consultant and consultee. Thus, consultation is different from referral of a child to a psychologist who then assumes sole responsibility for diagnosing the problem and prescribing treatment. In the referral model, the treatment may or may not be the teacher's responsibility to implement. By contrast, any recommendations that result from the consultation process are the responsibility of the consultee to implement. Moreover, the consultee is free to accept or to reject the consultant's advice, and the consultee may terminate the relationship at any point. The consultant has no authority over the consultee except the authority of the consultant's good ideas.

Consultation is a confidential relationship. By the time a teacher seeks a consultant's help, he or she may feel discouraged. Teachers would be reluctant to reveal their perceived failures in consultation if the relationship were not confidential. The active role of the teacher-consultee requires the teacher to communicate openly and honestly, with no fear that the consultant will disclose aspects of the communication to third parties. The active role is necessary because the consultant depends on the teacher's wealth of information regarding the problem, including past efforts to solve it. Furthermore, the teacher's values, beliefs, role constraints, resources for solving the problem, instructional methods, interactional style, knowledge base, and skills are important variables for the consultant to consider in jointly designing a plan for solving the problem brought to consultation. If the consultation plan is not compatible with the unique characteristics of the teacher's work situation, either it will not be implemented as intended or it will result in a disruption of the teacher's functioning. The confidential nature of the consultation relationship enables the consultee to play the active role required in consultation.

Consultation is a collaborative relationship. The consultant's role is that of a facilitator. Although consultation includes giving expert advice, the consultant's primary method of assisting teachers includes offering observations, asking questions that clarify the problem or place the problem in a new perspective, suggesting information that needs to be obtained in order to understand the problem, serving as a springboard for the teacher's own ideas, and sharing pertinent knowledge from such fields as child development, learning theory, group processes, behavior analysis, child psychopathology, tests and measurements, or family systems theory.

The problems discussed in consultation are work-related problems. The consultant does not help the consultee solve personal problems. Although personal problems influence work performance, the professional-to-professional nature of consultation requires a focus on work-related concerns. When personal problems are brought up by the teacher, the consultant conveys an accepting attitude but refocuses the discussion on the teacher's professional functioning.

Caplan categorized mental health consultation as to the kind of problem dealt with (a case or an administrative problem) and as to the focus (the client or program on the one hand or the consultee on the other). This resulted in four categories of consultation.

In *client-centered case* consultation, the focus is on a child's problems. The goal of change in the teacher is secondary to the goal of formulating the problem. A written report to the teacher summarizes the diagnostic findings and recommendations for the teacher's handling of the problem.

In *consultee-centered case* consultation, the focus is on the student; however, the consultant's primary goal is change in the teacher's knowledge, skills, self-confidence, or objectivity. The problem case is a leverage point for effecting a change in the teacher that will enable the teacher to work more effectively, not only with the particular child who is the focus of consultation, but also with similar children in the future. This expected ripple effect in consultation extends the impact of consultation to an indefinite number of children. Because a change in the teacher is the primary goal, the consultant spends considerable time with the teacher, helping the teacher gain new perspectives, insights, knowledge, and skills that will generalize to similar problems in the future. Rather than offering an expert formulation of the problem and strategy for change, the consultant engages the teacher as a peer professional in a problem-solving process, facilitating the teacher's ability to solve the problem independently. As assumption in consultee-centered case consultation is that the teacher will generalize new learnings to future cases if the teacher accepts responsibility for the problem formulation and action plans in consultation. In this type of consultation, the task of assessing the child's problem is secondary to the task of assessing the nature of the teacher's work difficulty, which may involve a lack of knowledge, skills, self-confidence, or professional objectivity. The consultant's expertise is directed primarily to the task of helping the teacher remedy whichever of these shortcomings is present. It is this type of consultation about which the most has been written, and it is this type of consultation that has become nearly synonymous with the term mental health consultation.

In *program-centered administrative* consultation, the focus is on a particular program for which the administrator-consultee has responsibility. The primary goal is the assessment of obstacles to achieving goals of a particular program. After a site visit and interviews with persons in the school, a written report summarizing the consultant's findings and recommendations is prepared. As in client-centered case consultation, the goal of educating administrators to handle similar problems in the future is secondary.

In *consultee-centered administrative* consultation, the focus is on the administrator's skills in areas such as group processes, leadership, and interpersonal relationships. This model of consultation is frequently referred to as organizational development consultation. It assumes that change in social structures and human processes within a school will result in the greatest positive impact on the mental health of students and teachers.

Typically, the consultant has no line authority over consultees. Two sources of influence over consultees available to consultants are expert and referent power (Meyers, Parsons, & Martin, 1979.) Expert power is the influence the consultant has with a consultee based on the consultee's attribution of expertise to the consultant. Teachers seek out a consultant's help because they believe the consultant has special expert knowledge relevant to the problem for which consultation is sought. Referent power is influence the consultant has with consultees based on the consultee's identification with the consultant. When a consultee admires the consultant and identifies with the consultant's values, attitudes, and behaviors, the consultant is attributed referent power. Much of the consultation literature focuses on methods of building rapport, or referent power. While not using the term referent power, Caplan recommends such identification techniques as emphasizing the peer-professional relationship, "onedownsmanship," empathic listening, conveying respect for the consultee, accepting the consultee, emphasizing commonalities, being approachable, and engaging in informal social contacts with consultees.

Although consultation is different from teaching, the consultant has an educational role. As teacher, the consultant instructs, shares information, translates psychological theories into educationally relevant practices, models approaches, offers ideas, and interprets data. As facilitator, the consultant provides a model of professional objectivity, guides teachers in problem solving, encourages, helps consultees deal with affect that may decrease their ability to deal effectively with a problem, and helps consultees avoid displacement of personal problems in the work setting. The consultant also facilitates communication among different organizational units within the school (i.e., regular and special education teachers, grade level teachers, and administrators).

Empirical evidence derived from over 60 studies on the effectiveness of consultation services in alleviating special problems brought to consultation is positive (Mannino & Shore, 1975; Medway, 1979). Fewer studies on the preventive goals of consultation have been published; however, the results of these studies are positive (Gutkin & Curtis, 1982).

## REFERENCES

Altrocchi, J. (1972). Mental health consultation. In S. Golann & C. Eisdorfer (Eds.), *Handbook of community mental health* (pp. 477–507). New York: Appleton-Century-Crofts.

Caplan, G. (1970). *The theory and practice of mental health consultation*. New York: Basic Books.

Gutkin, T. B., & Curtis, M. J. (1982). School-based consultation: Theory and techniques. In C. R. Reynolds & T. B. Gutkin (Eds.), *The handbook of school psychology* (pp. 796–828). New York: Wiley.

Mannino, F. V., & Shore, M. F. (1975). Effecting change through consultation. In F. V. Mannino, B. W. MacLennan, & M. F. Shore (Eds.), *The practice of mental health consultation*. New York: Gardner.

Medway, F. J. (1979). How effective is school consultation: A review of recent research. *Journal of School Psychology, 17,* 275–282.

Meyers, J., Parsons, R. D., & Martin R. (1979). *Mental health consultation in the schools*. San Francisco: Jossey-Bass.

JAN N. HUGHES
*Texas A&M University*

CONSULTATION
PSYCHOLOGY IN THE SCHOOLS
SCHOOL PSYCHOLOGY

# CONTINGENCY CONTRACTING

A contingency contract is a written agreement between parties that details specific behaviors that are expected and the various reinforcers or punishers that are associated with compliance or noncompliance with the terms of the contract. Contingency contracts have been used successfully with a wide variety of subjects to help manage diverse behaviors; they have become exceptionally popular management alternatives in special education.

Stuart (1971) has delineated five components that should be incorporated into an ideal contract. First, an exact explanation of the behaviors, rewards, punishers, and privileges must be provided. For example, if a teacher wanted a student to remain in his or her seat in exchange for extra time at the microcomputer, the time of in-seat behavior that must be exhibited before a specified amount of time at the computer can be earned must be detailed. Closely related to the first point is the second requirement: that all behaviors must be observable and measurable and that all terms must be specified. For example, once computer time has been earned, one should be able to refer to the contract to learn when the time may be claimed. Also, in-seat behavior can be operationally defined and measured accurately. However, a behavior such as "attending" is more nebulous and would be difficult to measure reli-

ably enough for use in a contract. Third, contingencies for failure to meet with the terms of the contract should be specified for both parties. Just as a child must suffer the consequences if he or she does not perform as required, the manager must also be willing to suffer consequences (e.g., double reinforcement for the subject) if his or her part of the agreement is not fulfilled. Fourth, a bonus clause for consistent performance may be included if the subject or the manager feels it may be beneficial. This addition would help to stress the positive aspects of the contract. Finally, either the contract or the manager should provide a means of monitoring the effectiveness of the contract. By providing for this feedback, the contract can help to induce more positive comments on the part of the involved parties when each is in compliance with contract terms. Kazdin (1975) notes that well-developed contingency contracts offer a number of advantages over traditional management strategies: subject input into the contract can enhance performance and motivation; subject negotiation of contingencies will result in the contingencies being truly reinforcing; contracts can be flexible; contracts specify both behaviors and contingencies; and the logistics of contract implementation can help to structure interactions between parties and thus lead to more successful and lasting changes.

An interesting example of the effectiveness of a contract system was recently presented by Kelley and Stokes (1982). The subjects in their study were seven individuals who were being paid $2.35 an hour to attend a combination academic (GED preparation) and vocational training program. During baseline conditions the pay was based purely on attendance. During contract conditions, however, the subjects were paid contingent on their academic performance. Contracts were individually negotiated weekly by each subject and the teacher and reasonable performance minimums were accepted by each party. A withdrawal design was used, and the results clearly demonstrated that the contracting conditions were superior to the baseline conditions when academic performance was considered. Similarly, Bristol and Sloane (1974) used contracting in an attempt to increase the study time of undergraduate students enrolled in an introductory psychology course. Their results showed that the contracts were effective at increasing study time. However, while only the grades of the poorer students were affected, contracting did prove to be a viable alternative for helping these students to structure their study time and improve their performance.

Contingency contracting holds great promise as a useful management tool for special educators. Since contracts by nature enhance communication by specifying expectations on the part of both parties, compliance with the terms and performance can be easily measured and contingencies can be enforced. As with any behavioral strategy, however, consistent application of the procedures is mandatory. For further specific information on contracting, the reader is referred to the *Journal of Applied Be-*

*havior Analysis*. For information on implementation and examples of contracts, see Kerr and Nelson (1983).

## REFERENCES

Bristol, M. M., & Sloane, H. (1974). Effects of contingency contracting on study rate and test performance. *Journal of Applied Behavior Analysis, 7*, 271–285.

Kazdin, A. E. (1975). *Behavior modification in applied settings.* Homewood, IL: Dorsey.

Kelley, M. L., & Stokes, T. (1982). Contingency contracting with disadvantaged youths: Improving classroom performance. *Journal of Applied Behavior Analysis, 15*, 447–454.

Kerr, M. M., & Nelson, C. M. (1983). *Strategies for managing behavior problems in the classroom.* Columbus, OH: Merrill.

Stuart, R. B. (1971). Behavioral contracting within the families of delinquents. *Journal of Behavior Therapy and Experimental Psychiatry, 2*, 1–11.

ANDREW R. BRULLE
*Eastern Illinois University*

APPLIED BEHAVIOR ANALYSIS
BEHAVIOR MODIFICATION

# CONTINGENCY MANAGEMENT

Contingency management refers to the controlling of the various contingencies of reinforcement by an individual in an attempt to modify behavior. These contingencies of reinforcement were described by Skinner (1974); they refer to a change in the environment of a subject after a behavior is exhibited. Skinner (1974) proposed that the action that followed a behavioral episode would either strengthen or weaken the probability that the behavior would occur again.

If something is added to the environment that results in an increased probability of occurrence (i.e., the behavior occurs more often), this contingency of reinforcement is termed positive reinforcement. If, on the other hand, the behavior occurs less often, the contingency of reinforcement is called an aversive punisher. If something is subtracted from the environment following the emission of a behavior that results in a decrease in the rate or duration, the contingency is a response cost punisher. However, if the subtraction results in an increase in the behavioral occurrence, it is called negative reinforcer.

Teachers and researchers in the field of special education have been managing these contingencies of reinforcement in a variety of settings and with numerous subjects for years; they have demonstrated conclusively that many individuals in classrooms can be effective contingency managers. Various factors that influence the effectiveness of the contingency manager include the reinforcing properties of the contingency (i.e., whether the subject "likes" or "dislikes" it), other contingencies that are op-

erating in the subject's environment, and the schedule of reinforcement or punishment.

One strategy for learning the reinforcing properties of various contingencies is to administer a questionnaire to each member of the class asking them to rate how much they like each entry. As will become abundantly evident, the reinforcing properties of various contingencies are totally individualized. While a contingency manager may be able to glean some ideas for reinforcers or punishers from a questionnaire or an interview, the only method to learn with certainty about the effects of various contingencies is experimentation. Additionally, the practitioner will have to observe closely the subject's environment to learn what other contingencies are operating.

Schedules of reinforcement also play a major role in the effectiveness of contingency management. While the effects of various schedules have been described elsewhere (e.g., Sulzer-Azaroff & Mayer, 1977), a few general rules follow: when teaching new behaviors, continuous (after every occurrence of the behavior) schedules are best; punishment schedules that are continuous result in a rapid decrease in behavioral rate/duration; for the maintenance of a rate/duration, an intermittent (the contingency is administered after a certain [as determined by the manager] amount of time has elapsed) schedule is most effective (Kazdin, 1975).

An example of contingency management that illustrates many of the above principles was recently presented by Barton, Brulle, and Repp (1985). In this study the researchers delivered positive reinforcers if, after a certain amount of time (determined individually on a daily basis), the subject had not engaged in an inappropriate behavior and had exhibited appropriate behaviors. If the subject did emit an inappropriate response, this behavior was immediately consequated with a mild punisher. This combination of positive reinforcement delivered on a precise schedule with mild punishers proved to be effective in decreasing the rate of inappropriate behaviors and increasing the rate of appropriate ones.

The science of contingency management is exceptionally broad and encompasses, in general, the field of applied behavior analysis. The interested reader is referred to some of the many fine behavioral texts (e.g., Kerr & Nelson, 1983; Sulzer-Azaroff & Mayer, 1977) for more detailed, yet general, discussions of applications. For detailed explanations of specific contingencies and/or schedules, see the *Journal of Applied Behavior Analysis* or the *Journal of the Experimental Analysis of Behavior*.

## REFERENCES

Barton, L. E., Brulle, A. R., & Repp, A. C. (1985). Reducing stereotypic behavior by using DRO and momentary restraint. *Journal of Mental Deficiency Research, 29*, 71–79.

Kazdin, A. E. (1975). *Behavior modification in applied settings.* Homewood, IL: Dorsey Press.

Kerr, M., & Nelson, C. (1983). *Strategies for managing behavior problems in the classroom.* Columbus, OH: Merrill.

Skinner, B. F. (1974). *About behaviorism*. New York: Knopf.

Sulzer-Azaroff, B., & Mayer, G. R. (1977). *Applied behavior analysis procedures with children and youth*. New York: Holt, Reinhart & Winston.

ANDREW R. BRULLE
*Eastern Illinois University*

**APPLIED BEHAVIOR ANALYSIS**
**BEHAVIOR MODIFICATION**

## CONTINUING EDUCATION FOR THE HANDICAPPED

Comparatively little is known about the continuing education needs or practices of handicapped persons. For the most part, it is presumed that handicapped persons take advantage of typical continuing and adult education programs afforded to nonhandicapped persons. Because the bulk of school-age, mildly/moderately handicapped persons are handicapped by virtue of their educational deficiencies, it is expected that these individuals blend into society on exit from the education program (Telford & Sawrey, 1977). Thus continuing education programs are seldom tailored to the unique needs of handicapped individuals.

The types of continuing education available to handicapped learners is dependent on the community in which an individual resides and the resources available. In general, however, programs of continuing education can include academic education, creative arts, economic education, basic and literacy education, home and family life education, human relations training, recreation education, and occupational education.

For those individuals exhibiting more severe handicapping conditions or requiring a unique form of assistance, continuing education consists of specific training/education in independent living, communication skills, or vocational employment. This type of continuing education is offered through public and private vocational rehabilitation facilities as well as social service organizations. For the most part, these programs of continuing education are supported by public funds intended to promote greater self-sufficiency and independence.

PATRICIA ANN ABRAMSON
*Hudson Public Schools,*
*Hudson, Wisconsin*

**ADULT BASIC EDUCATION**
**ADULT PROGRAMS FOR THE DISABLED**
**VOCATIONAL REHABILITATION**

## CONTINUUM OF SPECIAL EDUCATION SERVICES

In education, as in psychology, there are some generally accepted procedures and settings for treating children's problems. Central to most educational treatment regimens are special classes where reduced teacher-student ratios allow for more individualized instruction. An examination of special education in a typical school system in the United States reveals an incremental continuum or ordered array of special education classes designed to serve the individual needs of nearly all children. Many special educators now agree that a range or continuum of placement alternatives must exist for exceptional students (Deno, 1973; Lerner, Dawson, & Horvath, 1980). A continuum of special education services and several critical defining dimensions are illustrated in the Figure. This depiction of a continuum of special education was influenced by Deno's (1970) model of special education placement alternatives and Blackhurst and Berdine's (1981) analysis of special education services. Before examining this conceptualization of special education placements, however, a discussion of the "special" components of special education is in order.

At least four aspects are unique about special education: specialized educators, special curricular content, special instructional methods, and special instructional materials. Prior to the mainstreaming trend that resulted from PL 94-142, these four services were almost always provided to children within the context of special classes or schools. These classes and schools are commonly categorized along a continuum reflecting their degree of separation from the mainstream. Resource rooms, self-contained classes, special day schools, and residential treatment centers reflect this continuum, with resource rooms being a relatively less restrictive environment (LRE) than residential centers. The determination of the least restrictive environment should be done in the context of a student's needs. Thus, for many exceptional children, full-time placement in a regular classroom may be considered the least restrictive environment, whereas for other children placement in a special education resource or self-contained class may be viewed as the least restrictive environment. The goal is to place a child in the least restrictive environment relative to the severity of his or her handicapping condition. Therefore, even with the current trend toward mainstream programs, many exceptional children will receive some, if not all, of their education in one or more of the special environments outside of regular classes.

An examination of the Figure indicates that the continuum of special education services can be conceptualized into at least six discrete, logistical units (i.e., regular class, resource room, self-contained class, special day school, homebound/hospitalized, and residential center), which, in some cases, have been broken down further to highlight

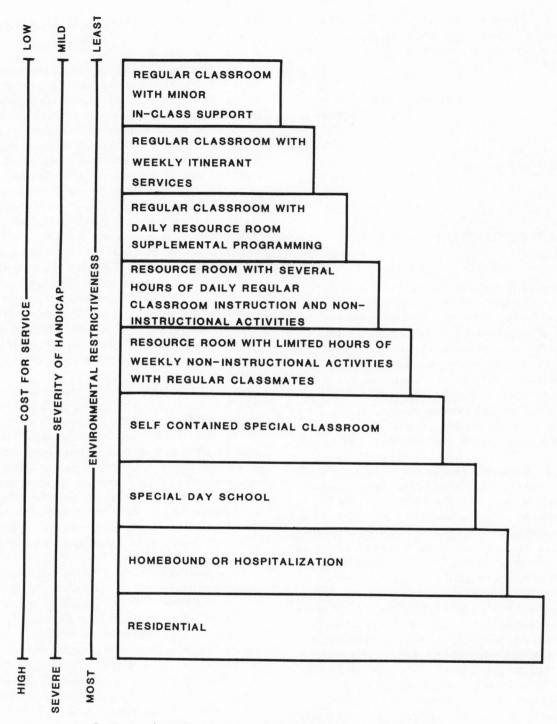

Continuum of special education services with three major qualitative dimensions.

that supplemental services from other specialists or programs can result in an even wider continuum of services. The nine types of special education services enumerated in the Figure are a representative, rather than definitive, representation of most school systems. Three critical dimensions that further define this continuum of special education services are included in the Figure and have been labeled Environmental Restrictiveness, Severity of Handicap, and Cost of Service. Each of these dimensions has been qualitatively anchored with reference to regular education classes. Thus, as placements get further away from the mainstream, they become increasingly more restrictive and costly, and are generally designed to handle more severe, pervasive handicaps.

Ideally, placement decisions should be based on an analysis of an individual's needs and a system's methods for treating such needs. In practice, however, there is a strong tendency to place children based almost entirely on their classification (i.e., learning disabled are placed in resource programs, behavior disordered and mentally retarded and are placed in self-contained or even more restrictive placements). This trend in placement decision making is changing and can be further facilitated by routinely assessing basic factors such as parents, regular teacher, specialists, the target child, and setting. Individualized educational programming calls for flexible use of settings and support personnel. It seems logical that when support personnel are skillful and motivated, the possibility of successfully educating a child in the mainstream is high. Conversely, when support is poor, even a mildly handicapped child may not benefit from placement in the mainstream.

In summary, the amount of special attention is probably the most critical variable with respect to the particular type of class in which a child is placed. In a typical resource room arrangement, the exceptional child is enrolled in a regular program but is provided with additional educational and emotional support in one or maybe two areas of weakness (e.g., mathematics, reading, and social skills). The resource class would most likely be organized in a small group or tutorial fashion. In the self-contained special class arrangement, exceptional children are usually physically segregated from other groups of children and receive all academic instruction from special educators, but on a limited basis throughout the day they share in other activities such as sports, dining, and assemblies with nonhandicapped peers.

Some school systems have organized special day schools for different groups of exceptional children, especially the emotionally disturbed, physically handicapped, trainable mentally retarded, and multiply handicapped. In general, these special schools are located some distance from the regular schools; this segregates children and staff and limited interaction with nonhandicapped peers takes place. Homebound or hospital services are provided primarily for children with serious health complications and/or multihandicapped preschoolers. Finally, there are residential schools or institutions for children with various severe handicapping conditions. Children live at the school and thus are able to receive intensive, daily educational, psychological, and medical services. Recently, researchers have begun to investigate the effectiveness of services for exceptional children in the mainstream and at virtually all other points on the continuum of special education. Readers interested in the effectiveness of special education programs are referred to Carlberg and Kavale (1980), O'-Connor, Stuck, and Wyne (1979), and Sindelar and Deno (1978).

## REFERENCES

Blackhurst, A. E., & Berdine, W. H. (1981). Basic concepts of special education. In A. E. Blackhurst & W. H. Berdine (Eds.), *An introduction to special education*. Boston: Little.

Carlberg, C., & Kavale, K. (1980). The efficacy of special versus regular class placement for exceptional children: A meta-analysis. *Journal of Special Education, 14*(3), 295–309.

Deno, E. (1970). Special education as development capital. *Exceptional Children, 37*, 229–237.

Deno, E. (1973). *Instructional alternatives for exceptional children*. Reston, VA: Council for Exceptional Children.

Lerner, J., Dawson, D., & Horvath, L. (1980). *Cases in learning and behavior problems*. Boston: Houghton Mifflin.

O'Connor, P. D., Stuck, G. B., & Wyne, M. D. (1979). Effects of a short-term intervention resource-room program on task orientation and achievement. *Journal of Special Education, 13*(4), 375–385.

Sindelar, P. T., & Deno, S. L. (1978). The effectiveness of resource programming. *Journal of Special Education, 12*(1), 17–28.

STEPHEN N. ELLIOTT
*Louisiana State University*

**CASCADE MODEL OF SPECIAL EDUCATION**
**DENO, EVELYN**
**LEAST RESTRICTIVE ENVIRONMENT**
**MAINSTREAMING**

## CONTRACT PROCUREMENT

Contract procurement is a term used in vocational rehabilitation facilities, sheltered workshops, and work activities centers. The term is simply defined; however, the concept and process are more complex. The word contract refers to jobs that are used in the cited facilities to teach work habit skills or trade skills, or provide activities that result in reimbursement to persons with disabilities. The term procurement refers to the act of attaining contracts. The term contract procurement, as it relates to programs for the disabled, refers to the process of attaining work from businesses to be done by persons with disabilities. Subcontracts and prime manufacturing are two categories of contracts.

Subcontracts are jobs that are attained from businesses and that involve no purchases of materials or equipment. An example would be assembling circuit boards for microcomputers. Company A manufactures the parts to be assembled on the circuit boards. They purchase the boards and the boxes for shipping, and send a truck once a week to pick up the assembled and packaged product. The contract involves only labor; on completion of the contract, all surplus parts are returned to Company A.

Prime manufacturing contracts necessitate the purchase and inventory of materials to create a product. Attaining work is a sales function. In the process of selling the abilities of a work program, not only the equipment available but the manpower require legal protection. For example, Company A subcontracts the assembly of circuit boards to Work Program B. All assembly and packaging is done at Work Program B's site. However, Company A gets a special order for microcomputers with an additional resistor on the circuit boards that are already assembled into the microcomputers and boxed. The deadline is such that delivery and pickup of changes is too costly between Company A and Work Program B. Consequently, a labor force must be procured and attained by Company A if their business is to complete the work. They must open the boxes and add the resistor to each microcomputer circuit board, then repackage the unit.

Understanding that sales is a key concept in contract procurement is important. Often work programs fail to understand that attaining work is a process of identifying, attaining, working, and delivering. Some programs still use nonsales people to attain work and deliver a product, thus causing contract procurement for persons with disabilities to be thought of as cheap, subsidized labor.

The process of attaining work is subdivided into time and motion studies, and submitting a bid for subcontract or setting a price for prime manufacturing. Time and motion refers to setting up the work in the most efficient manner and then timing the steps in completing the work. The federal Department of Labor publications explain the rules for time and motion studies. A bid should include the following information: labor rate, overhead, materials, handling and waste, freight, and profit.

The bid also should include any conditions that may need to be included in the subcontract that concern the workshop regulations.

JEFF HEINZEN
*Indianhead Enterprise,*
*Menomonie, Wisconsin*

## HABILITATION
## REHABILITATION

## CONTROL GROUPS

Control groups are aggregates of subjects who do not receive the treatment of interest in an experimental or quasi-experimental intervention. They are used in research and program evaluation to provide baselines against which to measure the impact of an experimental manipulation and as a means to rule out alternative explanations of "treatment" effects. Control groups are useful particularly in field settings, where there may be a number of plausible rival accounts for the meaning of the researcher's observations. Whether the study is an elaborate investigation or the simple introduction of classroom innovation, control groups are often crucial to the interpretation of results.

The logic of the use of control groups centers around the ability to equate subjects in the "treatment" (experimental) and control groups on all factors except the treatment of interest. Many studies are limited because the assignment of subjects to experimental and control groups

is such that the assumption of equivalence is not tenable. In addition, the nature of the research setting may result in the contamination of the control groups by such factors as rivalries with the experimental group or imitation of the treatment by the control group (Cook & Campbell, 1979).

Control groups often involve a no-treatment control, where members engage in their activities with no intervention by the experimenter. Cook, Leviton, and Shadish (1985) note that rather than a no-treatment control group, it might be preferable to use a control that allows for comparison between the treatment of interest and another intervention. This might particularly be the case where practitioners are concerned with the relative efficacy of approaches or where ethical constraints prohibit withdrawal or denial of treatment.

Particularly in the case of quasiexperimental designs, where random assignment of subjects is not possible, a number of control groups are often used to rule out different competing interpretations. For example, members of a placebo control group receive an irrelevant treatment that gives an amount of time and attention similar to that of the experimental group (Cook & Campbell, 1979).

It is commonplace to introduce innovative programs in special education. By following proper control group design, one can judge the effectiveness of "reforms as experiments" and make policy decisions on a more rational basis (Campbell, 1969).

### REFERENCES

Campbell, D. T. (1969). Reforms as experiments. *American Psychologist, 24,* 409–429.

Cook, T. D., & Campbell, D. T. (1979). *Quasiexperimentation: Design and analysis issues for field settings.* Chicago: Rand McNally.

Cook, T. D., Leviton, L. C., & Shadish, W. R. (1985). Program evaluation. In G. Lindzey & E. Aronson (Eds.), *Handbook of social psychology. Vol. 1* (3rd ed., pp. 699–777). New York: Random House.

LEE ANDERSON JACKSON, JR.
*University of North Carolina,*
*Wilmington*

## MEASUREMENT
## RESEARCH IN SPECIAL EDUCATION

## CONVERGENT AND DIVERGENT THINKING

Emerging from Guilford's structure of intellect model of human intelligence, the concepts of convergent and divergent thinking are often applied to the education of gifted children. Both are viewed as high-level cognitive operations that individuals use when making decisions (Guilford, 1966, 1984).

Convergent thinking requires a narrowing process by which an individual develops classification rules that explain the relationships among objects and concepts. Essential to this process is the invocation of recall and recognition strategies. As such, the products of convergent thinking tend to be in the form of single "correct" answers. Critics have argued that typical school instruction demands an inappropriate proportion of convergent thinking at the expense of more creative (divergent) processes (Steffin, 1983).

Divergent thinking involves a broad scanning operation, enabling an individual to generate multiple possible solutions. It has received a major share of research attention in creativity, problem solving, and critical thinking (Steffin, 1983).

Guilford (1984) has discussed three aspects of divergent thinking. One aspect, fluency, relates to the breadth of associations available to an individual regarding a particular stimulus. A second, flexibility, is defined as the simultaneous consideration of multiple classes of information. In contrast to convergent processes, flexibility allows the individual to develop novel combinations. The third aspect, elaboration, is an integrative process that results in the formation of a broad theory. Here the thinker, demonstrating insight, is able to make predictions based on incomplete information.

Several studies have shown that young children's divergent productions can be increased by the use of open-ended questions in class discussions (Pucket-Cliatt, Shaw, & Sherwood, 1980; Thomas & Holcomb, 1981). These studies have also suggested that teachers can become increasingly comfortable using open-ended questions and that they can decrease their reliance on rote memory activities.

Steffin (1983) suggests that microcomputers offer new opportunities for fostering divergent thinking. Increasingly sophisticated computer simulations, with their capacity for user-controlled interaction and variability in presentation, can teach students to develop algorithms that can be generalized across learning situations.

While learning-disabled (Jaben, 1983) and language-deficient (Burrows & Wolf, 1983) children have shown gains in creativity following training in divergent thinking, the observation and development of creative thinking in gifted students continues to dominate the research literature at the present time.

## REFERENCES

Burrows, D., & Wolf, B. (1983). Creativity and the dyslexic child: A classroom view. *Annals of Dyslexia, 33,* 269–274.

Guilford, J. P. (1966). Basic problems in teaching for creativity. In C. W. Taylor & F. E. Williams (Eds.), *Instructional media and creativity.* New York: Wiley.

Guilford, J. P. (1984). Varieties of divergent production. *Journal of Creative Behavior, 18,* 1–10.

Jaben, T. H. (1983). The effects of creativity training on learning disabled students' creative written expression. *Journal of Learning Disabilities, 16,* 264–265.

Pucket-Cliatt, M. J., Shaw, J. M., & Sherwood, J. M. (1980). Effects of training on the divergent thinking abilities of kindergarten children. *Child Development, 51,* 1061–1064.

Steffin, S. A. (1983). Fighting against convergent thinking. *Childhood Education, 59,* 255–258.

Thomas, E., & Holcomb, C. (1981). Nurturing productive thinking in able students. *Journal of General Psychology, 104,* 67–79.

GARY BERKOWITZ
*Temple University*

CREATIVE PROBLEM SOLVING
TEACHER EXPECTANCIES
TEACHING STRATEGIES

# CONVULSIONS, FEBRILE

See FEBRILE CONVULSIONS.

# CONVULSIVE DISORDERS

See EPILEPSY.

# COPROLALIA

Coprolalia is a condition characterized by an irresistible urge to utter obscene words and phrases. Obscenities are interspersed randomly within a dialogue, interrupting the normal flow of conversation. The cursing is usually uttered during a break between sentences and in a loud, sharp tone in contrast to normal voice. The frequency of obscene utterances has a tendency to vary from low to high frequencies for extended periods of time. Coprolalic episodes are positively associated with periods of anxiety and anticipation.

Coprolalia is most often associated with Gilles de la Tourette's syndrome (TS) and is evident in some patients following a stroke. As with other tics associated with TS, coprolalia can be controlled by TS patients for brief intervals. Lees, Robertson, Trimble, and Murray (1984) report that TS patients exhibiting coprolalia attempt to substitute euphemisms or somewhat disguised neologisms for obscenities. Early estimates of the prevalence of coprolalia in Tourette syndrome patients were approximately 60%, but more recently have been revised to approximately 33% (Lees et al., 1984).

Both medical and behavioral treatments have been

used successfully to control coprolalic expressions. Erenberg, Cruse, and Rothner (1985) report that the preferred medical treatment is the use of haloperidol, a drug used in treating hyperkinetic and manic disorders. Comings and Comings (1985) recommend starting with low doses of haloperidol (.05 mg daily for 1 week) and increasing the dosage by .05 mg at weekly intervals until a 70 to 90% reduction of symptoms occurs. Because of the sedative side effects of haloperidol, stimulant drugs may be given simultaneously. Price, Lockman, Pauls, Cohen, and Kidd (1986) report, however, that stimulant drugs appear to be associated positively with increases in the frequency of tics.

Behavioral treatments have included the use of self-management and negative practice techniques. Friedman (1980), for instance, had a patient substitute socially acceptable utterances for obscenities whenever she had the urge to curse. Evans and Evans (1983) decreased the rate of utterances of an expletive using a self-counting procedure. The patient simply recorded each frequency of his use of the target expletive. Storms (1985) had patients practice their tics until they were tired, had them rest, and then repeated the practice.

Medical and behavioral treatments of coprolalia have been used in combination with each other as well as in isolation. Storms (1985), for instance, used doses of haloperidol in combination with negative practice to reduce the frequency of tics.

## REFERENCES

Comings, D. E., & Comings, B. G. (1985). Tourette syndrome: Clinical and psychological aspects. *Human Genetics, 37,* 435–450.

Erenberg, G., Cruse, R. P., & Rothner, A. D. (1985). Gilles de la Tourette's syndrome: Effects of stimulant drugs. *Neurology, 35,* 1346–1348.

Evans, W. H., & Evans, S. S. (1983). Self-counting in the treatment of Gilles de la Tourette syndrome. *Journal of Precision Teaching, 4,* 14–17.

Friedman, S. (1980). Self-control in the treatment of Gilles de la Tourette's syndrome: Case study with 18-month follow-up. *Journal of Consulting & Clinical Psychology, 48,* 400–402.

Lees, A. J., Robertson, M., Trimble, M. R., & Murray, N. M. F. (1984). A clinical study of Gilles de la Tourette syndrome in the United Kingdom. *Journal of Neurology, Neurosurgery, & Psychiatry, 47,* 1–8.

Price, R. A., Leckman, J. F., Pauls, D. L., Cohen, D. J., & Kidd, K. K. (1986). Gilles de la Tourette syndrome: Tics and central nervous system stimulants in twins and non-twins. *Neurology, 36,* 232–237.

Storms, L. (1985). Massed negative practice as a behavioral treatment for Gilles de la Tourette's syndrome. *American Journal of Psychotherapy, 39,* 277–281.

LAWRENCE J. O'SHEA
*University of Florida*

TOURETTE'S SYNDROME
STIMULANT DRUGS
TICS

# CORE SCHOOL

The term core refers to an educational concept that first emerged in the United States in the 1930s and 1940s. The core school tries to provide a common background for all students and engineer a course of study that combines basic topics from school subjects that are usually taught separately. The intention of this concept was to make education more meaningful for students. Most popular in the 1950s, its popularity has declined in recent years, but it is still operational (Manning, 1971).

The core concept has two basic components: time and philosophy (Oliver, 1965). Time is usually administered through a "block time class," for example, two or more class periods are joined together in order to study a wide range of related subjects. The philosophy of core involves the breaking down of strict boundaries between disciplines. Thus, students may study a topic from literary, historical, mathematical, and artistic viewpoints concurrently rather than as separate topics in isolated classes (Manning, 1971; Oliver, 1965).

Beyond these two basic components, cores are identified as having the following characteristics (Hass, 1970; Manning, 1971; Oliver, 1965):

1. They are problem centered.
2. Learning is done through firsthand experiences by the learner.
3. Students are involved in the planning, teaching, and evaluation processes.
4. Students are provided with opportunities for total growth by way of lifelike environments.
5. The instruction is more personal, allowing for individual guidance.
6. There are opportunities for integrated knowledge across subject lines.

The core concept, when practiced, will probably be more student-oriented than may occur in other settings. The organization and overlapping of classes can be especially beneficial to the special education student needing structure and concentrated study. Student-oriented classes provide motivation for paying attention and becoming an active participant in the learning process.

## REFERENCES

Hass, G., Wiles, K., & Bondi, J. (1970). *Reading in curriculum* (2nd ed.). Boston: Allyn & Bacon.

Manning, D. (1971). *Toward a humanistic curriculum.* New York: Harper & Row.

Oliver, A. I. (1965). *Curriculum improvement: A guide to problems, principles, and procedures.* New York: Dodd, Mead.

ROBERT T. NASH
*University of Wisconsin,
Oshkosh*

## ECOLOGICAL EDUCATION FOR THE HANDICAPPED HOLISTIC APPROACH AND LEARNING DISABILITIES TEST-TEACH-TEST PARADIGM

## CORNELIA DE LANGE SYNDROME

Cornelia De Lange syndrome is a developmental disability first reported by Brachman in 1916 and further investigated by De Lange in 1933 (Goodman & Gorlin, 1977). It may also be referred to as *Amsterdam dwarfism* (Clarke & Clarke, 1975). Currently, no definitive test or genetic analysis to confirm the diagnosis exists. Such diagnosis rests on the presence or absence of a number of physical, cognitive, and behavioral characteristics.

Cornelia De Lange infants show a lower than normal birth weight and length, and can be described as failing to thrive. The majority are found to be functioning in the lower reaches of the moderately retarded range. A few reported cases have shown functioning levels approaching the low average range.

These children appear remarkably similar in appearance, substantiating the probability of a genetic etiology as well as a syndrome. Nearly all of the children show thick curly eyebrows, long eyelashes, and increased facial hair. They have thin lips forming a downward slanting mouth, with smaller than normal-sized limbs, hands, feet, and head. Many exhibit a characteristic low-pitched gravelly voice early in infancy (Smith & Jones, 1982).

Behaviorally, these children may demonstrate autisticlike behaviors as well as the potential for self-abusive behaviors. They may be stubborn and difficult to manage and may bruise easily, an observation that may be of particular interest to the special educator. The syndrome tends to be relatively uncommon, with reported incidence rates varying from 1:30,000 to 1:50,000 live births (Goodman, 1977).

### REFERENCES

Clarke, A., & Clarke, D. B. (1975). *Mental deficiency, the changing perspectives* (3rd ed.). New York: Free Press.

Goodman, R., & Gorlin, R. (1977). *Atlas of the face of genetic disorders.* St. Louis: Mosby.

Smith, D., & Jones, R. (1982). *Recognizable patterns of human malformation* (3rd ed.). Philadelphia: Saunders.

JOHN E. PORCELLA
*Rhinebeck Country School,
Rhinebeck, New York*

## AUTISM

## CORRECTIONAL EDUCATION

The Correctional Education Association (1983) defined correctional education as a coordinated system of individualized learning services and activities conducted within the walls of a correctional facility. Services are provided by certified educational staff and are designed to meet the identified needs of the inmate population in the areas of basic education leading to a high-school credential; vocational training geared toward obtaining entry-level skills and maintaining competitive employment; and development of attitudes, skills, and abilities in the context of sociopersonal development.

It is difficult to summarize the types of correctional education programs available in institutions because services vary among and within states. Few states provide comprehensive educational services to meet the identified educational needs. Usually, a state will focus on just a few program areas such as higher education or adult education.

Estimates indicate that 85 to 95% of the incarcerated adults do not have high-school diplomas. Many of them can neither read nor write after completing their sentences (Loeffler & Martin, 1982). From a survey conducted by Bell (1979), it was found that 50% of the adults in federal and state institutions were illiterate. Researchers such as Roberts (1973) state that the average inmate is unable to complete a job application, read and understand newspapers, or apply for an automobile operator's license (Day & McCane, 1982). In addition, 70% of the inmates have had no vocational training prior to sentencing. The National Advisory Council on Vocational Education found that the typical inmate is male, poor, and with less than 10 years of schooling. Gehring (1980) described correctional students as frequently afflicted by special learning and/or drug-related problems, accustomed to violence, and lacking in academic skills.

According to the U.S. Department of Justice (1983), the incarceration rate for individuals not completing elementary school is 259 per 1000 for males between the ages of 20 to 29 years; for elementary school graduates, it is 83 per 1000; for those completing 9 to 11 years in school, it is 70 per 1000; for high-school graduates, it decreased to 11 per 1000; and for persons with 16 years of schooling, the rate drops to 1 per 1000.

Numerous research studies on correctional education

programs have documented the effectiveness of both juvenile and adult correctional programs (Correctional Education Association, 1983). Correctional education programs have resulted in increased employment and improved quality of life for released inmates.

A major difficulty facing correctional educational administrators stems from the fact that the quantity of existing correctional education programs is insufficient to meet the needs of the hundreds of thousands of men, women, and children who are incarcerated in correctional institutions throughout the United States. The lack of public support and financial resources for correctional education programs severely limit the extent of correctional program effectiveness.

## REFERENCES

Bell, R. (1979, June). *Correctional education program for inmates* (National Evaluation Programs, Phase I). Washington, DC: U.S. Department of Justice.

Correctional Education Association. (1983). Lobbying for correctional education: A guide to action. (Available from Correctional Education Association, 1400 20th Street, NW, Washington, DC 20009.)

Day, S. R., & McCane, M. R. (1982). *Vocational education in corrections* (Information Series 237, 11–12). Columbus, OH: State University, National Center for Research in Vocational Education.

Gehring, T. (1980, Sept.). Correctional education and the U.S. Department of Education. *Journal of Correctional Education, 35*(4), 137–141.

Karcz, S., & Sabatino, D. A. (in press). Correctional education: Selected problems and practices. In K. D. Gadow & I. Bialer (Eds.), *Advances in learning and behavioral disabilities*. Greenwich, CT: JAI Press.

Loeffler, C. A., & Martin, T. C. (1982, April). *The functional illiterate: Is correctional education doing its job?* Huntsville, TX: Marloe Research.

Roberts, A. R. (1973). *Readings in prison education*. Springfield, IL: Thomas.

U.S. Department of Justice (1983, Oct.). *Report to the nation on crime and justice: The data* (NCJ-87060, p. 37). Rockville, MD: Bureau of Justice Statistics.

STAN A. KARCZ
*University of Wisconsin, Stout*

CORRECTIONAL SPECIAL EDUCATION
JUVENILE DELINQUENCY
RIGHT TO EDUCATION

## CORRECTIONAL SPECIAL EDUCATION

Over 500,000 criminal offenders are currently housed in the nation's 559 state and federal prisons and 3493 local jails. Of this population, approximately 72,000 are incarcerated in state juvenile correctional facilities, jails, and group homes. In addition, almost 2 million persons are under community supervision instead of in confinement (Bureau of Justice Statistics, 1983). This rate of incarceration is among the highest in the world.

A large portion of the incarcerated population is handicapped for educational purposes. For example, Morgan's (1979) survey indicated that 42% of incarcerated juveniles meet PL 94-142 definitional criteria as handicapped. Surveys of adult correctional facilities in Oregon (Hurtz & Heintz, 1979) and Louisiana (Klinger, Marshall, Price, & Ward, 1983) suggest similar proportions of handicapped persons in adult prisons, for example, between 30 and 50%.

Correctional education, which consists of formal educational programs ranging from basic literacy training to postsecondary vocational and university education, is offered in the vast majority of correctional facilities in the United States. Such programs typically are voluntary in adult facilities, but mandatory for juveniles. The administrative regulations for PL 94-142 specifically include correctional education programs in the mandate for a free and appropriate public education for handicapped persons 21 years of age and under; however, less than 10% of the state departments of juvenile and adult corrections are in compliance (Coffey, 1983). States not in compliance are experiencing heightened pressure through litigation (Wood, 1984) and administrative sanction to provide special education programs. Increased interest in correctional special education is reflected in federally funded demonstration and training projects, receipt of PL 94-142 state flow-through monies by correctional education programs, and the development of training programs for correctional special educators.

In 1984 the Correctional/ Special Education Training (C/SET) Project staff (Rutherford, Nelson, & Wolford, 1985) surveyed the 85 state departments of juvenile and/ or adult corrections and the 50 state departments of education to determine the number of handicapped offenders in juvenile and adult correctional facilities.

There are 33,190 individuals incarcerated in state juvenile correctional facilities. Of this number, 30,681 or 92%, are in correctional education programs. The estimated number of handicapped juvenile offenders is 9443, or 28% of the total incarcerated population. The number of juveniles receiving special education services is 7750, or 23% of the number of juveniles in corrections. Thus, according to state administrators' estimates, approximately 80% of handicapped juvenile offenders are being served.

In addition to the data collected concerning handicapped offenders in juvenile corrections, data were also collected relative to services for handicapped inmates in state adult correctional facilities. An estimated 117,000 of those in adult corrections are under the age of 22 (Gerry, 1985) and thus potentially eligible for special education services under PL 94-142.

Of the 399,636 adults in state corrections programs, approximately 118,158 or 30% are receiving correctional education services. Based on data reported by 31 states, the estimated number of handicapped offenders in adult corrections is 41,590 or 10%, 4313 of whom, or less than 1%, are receiving special education services.

Currently a need exists for correctional special education services in juvenile and adult correctional institutions, raising the question of what constitutes an effective correctional special education program. Some researchers (e.g., Gerry, 1985; Smith & Hockenberry, 1980; Smith, Ramirez, & Rutherford, 1983) have delineated essential compliance issues with regard to implementation of PL 94-142 in correctional education programs. There are six factors that are important to the implementation of meaningful correctional special education programs. These are (1) procedures for conducting functional assessments of the skills and learning needs of handicapped offenders; (2) the existence of a curriculum that teaches functional academic and daily living skills; (3) the inclusion of vocational special education in the curriculum; (4) the existence of transitional programs and procedures between correctional programs and the public schools or the world of work; (5) the presence of a comprehensive system for providing institutional and community services to handicapped offenders; and (6) the provision of in-service and preservice training for correctional educators in special education.

## REFERENCES

Bureau of Justice Statistics (1983). *Report to the nation on crime and justice: The data.* Washington, DC: U.S. Department of Justice.

Coffey, O. D. (1983). Meeting the needs of youth from a corrections viewpoint. In S. Braaten, R. B. Rutherford, & C. A. Kardash (Eds.), *Programming for adolescents with behavioral disorders* (pp. 79–84). Reston, VA: Council for Children with Behavioral Disorders.

Gerry, M. H. (1985). *Monitoring the special education programs of correctional institutions.* Washington, DC: U.S. Department of Education.

Hurzt, R., & Heintz, E. I. (1979). Incidence of specific learning disabilities at Oregon State Correctional Institution. Paper presented at the National Institute of Corrections Conference, Portland, OR.

Klinger, J. H., Marshall, G. M., Price, A. W., & Ward, K. D. (1983). A pupil appraisal for adults in the Louisiana Department of Corrections. *Journal of Correctional Education, 34* (2) 46–48.

Morgan, D. J. (1979). Prevalence and types of handicapping conditions found in juvenile correctional institutions: A national survey. *Journal of Special Education, 13,* 283–295.

Rutherford, R. B., Nelson, C. M., & Wolford, B. I. (1985). Special education in the most restrictive environment: Correctional/ special education. *Journal of Special Education, 19,* 60–71.

Smith, B. J., & Hockenberry, C. M. (1980). Implementing the Education for All Handicapped Children Act, P.L. 94-142, in youth corrections facilities: Selected issues. In F. J. Weintraub, A. Abeson, J. Ballard, & M. L. LaVor (Eds.), *Public policy and the education of exceptional children* (pp. 1–36). Reston, VA: Council for Exceptional Children.

Smith, B. J., Ramirez, B., & Rutherford, R. B. (1983). Special education in youth correctional facilities. *Journal of Correctional Education, 34,* 108–112.

Wood, F. J. (1984). *The law and correctional education.* Tempe, AZ: Correctional Special Education Training Project.

ROBERT B. RUTHERFORD, JR.
*Arizona State University*

**CORRECTIONAL EDUCATION**
**JUVENILE DELINQUENCY**

# COUNCIL FOR CHILDREN WITH BEHAVIORAL DISORDERS

Founded in 1961, the Council for Children with Behavioral Disorders (CCBD), a subdivision of the Council for Exceptional Children, is the professional organization of teachers, teacher trainers, administrators, psychologists, and parents concerned with the education and treatment of behaviorally disordered and emotionally disturbed children and youth. Members of the organization assist in developing appropriate educational programs for behaviorally disordered students.

CCBD has three major functions coordinated by three standing committees of its executive committee; regional services and membership, legislation, and publications. The regional services and membership committee coordinates regional, state, and local chapters of CCBD to further the professional development of members and provide advocacy activities for behaviorally disordered children and youth. The legislation committee furthers these advocacy efforts at a national level through lobbying and legislative support efforts on behalf of these youngsters. The publications committee coordinates the publication efforts of the council through the professional journal *Behavioral Disorders,* the CCBD *Monograph Series on Severe Behavior Disorders of Children and Youth*, the *Programming for Adolescents with Behavioral Disorders* series, and the *Teaching: Behaviorally Disorders Disordered Youth* practitioner's monograph series.

Currently, with a membership of 6000, CCBD is the third largest of the Council for Exceptional Children's 13 divisions. CCBD has evolved into the primary advocacy organization for students whose behavioral and emotional problems bring them in conflict with the schools and the community. It is also the primary professional organization for those who educate and treat these students.

ROBERT B. RUTHERFORD, JR.
*Arizona State University*

# COUNCIL FOR EXCEPTIONAL CHILDREN

The Council for Exceptional Children (CEC) is the world's largest professional organization dedicated to the welfare of exceptional children. The CEC was founded in 1922 at

Teachers' College, Columbia University. Today, its United States and Canadian membership includes approximately 50,000 persons, with 962 local chapters, 46 student associations, and 57 state or province federations. The organization is further divided into 13 special interest groups, including divisions on the physically handicapped, behavior disorders, mental retardation, communication disorders, learning disabilities, visually handicapped, talented and gifted, early childhood education, special education administration, career development, technology and media, educational diagnostic services, and teacher education.

Recently, CEC has been highly visible as an advocate for federal legislation and funding for the gifted and the handicapped. The organization issues two respected periodicals, *Exceptional Children* and *Teaching Exceptional Children*. The former is more research and policy oriented, while the latter is geared more toward practitioners' needs. In addition, several hundred books, multimedia packages, bibliographies, and fact sheets are available from CEC. Access to nearly one half a million references on handicapped and gifted children can be obtained from ERIC (Educational Resources Information Center) and CEC Information Services. Each year, a national convention sponsored by CEC attracts thousands of professionals, paraprofessionals, and parents. In the past few years, CEC has sponsored successful topical workshops devoted to areas such as microcomputer use in special education, black exceptional children, and early childhood special education. Periodic international conferences are also sponsored by CEC.

The CEC's founding in 1922 was predated by other organizations concerned with the handicapped; Convention of American Instructors of the Deaf, 1850; American Association of Instructors of the Blind, 1853; Conference of Executives of American Schools for the Deaf, 1863; American Association on Mental Deficiency, 1876; American Association to Promote the Teaching of Speech to the Deaf; 1890; and National Education Association's Department of Special Education, 1897. The CEC was founded the same year that a related organization, the National Association for the Study and Education of Exceptional Children, was disbanded. Four years earlier, the National Education Association (NEA) discontinued its Department of Special Education.

Elizabeth E. Farrell, who had been active in NEA's special education activities earlier, other Teachers' College faculty, and advanced students in the 1922 summer session at Columbia, formed CEC at a meeting on August 10 in a downtown New York restaurant. The early years found an organization without a true central office, limited funds, and a heavy reliance on volunteers for its existence. Various internal and external problems nearly ended CEC in its first two decades.

Wooden (1980) claims that one of the organization's strength was its system of local chapters. Grass-roots leadership was developed through planning and carrying out of professional activities at the local level. A sense of the *whole child* developed among members: since CEC's interests were broader than early groups with single-category interests. After the 1930s depression, CEC began to stabilize with the nation. Reorganization of the council's internal structure and a better financial situation allowed for expansion of CEC's role and activities. Today, despite some decline in membership from its peak in the 1970s, CEC is respected as a leader and advocate in its field. It works cooperatively with other organizations to promote the education and welfare of all exceptional children and youth. The Council for Exceptional Children's headquarters are now located in Reston, Virginia.

### REFERENCE

Wooden, H. Z. (1980a). Growth of a social concept. *Exceptional Children, 47*(1), 40–46.

JOHN D. WILSON
*Elwyn Institutes, Elwyn,
Pennsylvania*

## COUNCIL FOR LEARNING DISABILITIES

In 1968 educators formed the Division for Children with Learning Disabilities (DCLD) within the Council for Exceptional Children (CEC) (Hallahan, Kauffman, & Lloyd, 1985). Both groups believed that without a name to identify a group of children who did not fit into any other handicapping condition, there would be difficulty in obtaining needed funds for special services.

During the early 1980s emerged the realization that not only did children have learning disabilities but so did adults. Consequently, the Division for Children with Learning Disabilities became the Council for Learning Disabilities (CLD). Besides this change of name, CLD changed its affiliation: as it seceded from the Council for Exceptional Children (Lerner, 1985). The majority of CLD's membership voted to become a separate and independent organization.

Conferences and newsletters sponsored by CLD provide a valuable means of sharing information and serve as a stimulus for research, program development, and advocacy. In addition, CLD formed a strong national lobbying group to promote legislative recognition of learning disabilities.

### REFERENCES

Hallahan, D. P., Kauffman, J. M., & Lloyd, J. W. (1985). *Introduction to learning disabilities*. Englewood Cliffs, NJ: Prentice-Hall.

Learner, J. W. (1985). *Learning disabilities*. Dallas: Houghton Mifflin.

JOSEPH M. RUSSO
*Hunter College, City University
of New York*

## COUNCIL OF ADMINISTRATORS OF SPECIAL EDUCATION (CASE)

The Council of Administrators of Special Education (CASE) was founded in 1952 as a division of the Council for Exceptional Children. The CASE membership (currently 34,000) includes current members of the Council for Exceptional Children. They are administrators, directors, supervisors, or coordinators of state and local, public and private special education programs, schools, or classes, or faculty of programs preparing special education administrators. The purpose of the CASE is to promote professional leadership, provide opportunity for the study of problems common to its members, and provide information for developing improved services to exceptional children. The CASE has 27 state federations in the United States and Canada.

Through its publications program, the CASE disseminates a quarterly newsletter and provides copies of selected research publications. It also has initiated the CASE Dissemination Packet Services and a series of issue papers. The office of the executive director is at Indiana University, ES 3108, 902 West New York Street, Indianapolis, IN 46223.

SHIRLEY A. JONES
*Virginia Polytechnic Institute
and State University*

## COUNSELING THE HANDICAPPED

With so much emphasis placed on handicapped individuals' educational, adaptive behavior, and social skill needs, their emotional needs are often forgotten. Indeed, handicapped individuals often have issues that affect their lives that could be addressed and resolved through the counseling process. For example, some mentally retarded individuals experience feelings of frustration because of their handicap and its limitations and could benefit from counseling support. Learning-disabled students, given the peer rejection sometimes associated with their academic difficulties, also might benefit from therapeutic attention. And clearly, counseling should be a central intervention for behaviorally and emotionally disturbed persons.

While the need for counseling with the handicapped is apparent, the specific counseling techniques or approaches that are most effective under defined circumstances are not empirically evident. From a comprehensive diagnostic and treatment perspective, the multimodal approach of Lazarus (1976) has been used with handicapped children. Using Lazarus's *BASIC ID* modalities (behavior, affect, sensation, images, cognition, interpersonal relationships, and drugs/biological functioning), handicapped children's comprehensive social-emotional needs are analyzed and a counseling and psychotherapy program is developed to address the modalities most critical to the identified issues. Keat (1979) has also proposed a multimodal therapy ap-

proach, which he has used with learning-disabled children, summarized by the acronym HELPING (health, emotions-feelings, learning-school, personal relationships, imagination-interests, need to know-think, guidance of antecedents-behaviors-consequences). Again, primary concerns in the modality areas are identified and then targeted for counseling support.

From a purely counseling perspective, a number of therapeutic approaches are available. Prout and Brown (1983) identified six major theoretical approaches to counseling and psychotherapy that can be adopted when handicapped individuals are the primary clients: behavior therapy, reality therapy, person-centered therapy, rational-emotive therapy, Adlerian therapy, and psychoanalytic/psychodynamic therapy. Behavior therapy has been especially useful with behaviorally disturbed individuals. Using operant or classical conditioning, cognitive, or social learning behavioral approaches, positive behaviors are taught and/or reinforced while disruptive or disturbing behaviors are altered or extinguished. The other psychotherapeutic approaches have been used, in addition to the behavioral, for emotionally disturbed individuals who manifest an assortment of affectively based difficulties and issues. Additionally, all of these approaches can be applied to the emotional issues that often coexist or result from other handicapping conditions.

Besides the psychotherapeutic approaches, a number of more specialized approaches are available when counseling handicapped individuals. Briefly reviewed in Reynolds and Gutkin (1982), these include family therapy approaches, sociodrama, developmental therapy, art therapy, music therapy, and holistic or milieu therapy. Again, these approaches often become part of a comprehensive program that addresses handicapped children's educational, social-emotional, affective, family, and adaptive needs. In many cases, the use of counseling occurs only as an afterthought to what is otherwise a comprehensive program. Clearly, the possibility that handicapped children have related or separate counseling needs must be emphasized in research programs and in applied settings.

### REFERENCES

Keat, D. B. (1979). *Multimodal therapy with children.* New York: Pergamon.

Lazarus, A. A. (1976). *Multimodal behavior therapy.* New York: McGraw-Hill.

Prout, H. T., & Brown, D. T. (1983). *Counseling and psychotherapy with children and adolescents.* Tampa, FL: Mariner

Reynolds, C. R., & Gutkin, T. B. (1982). *The handbook of school psychology.* New York: Wiley.

HOWARD M. KNOFF
*University of South Florida*

**BEHAVIOR MODIFICATION
FAMILY THERAPY
PSYCHOTHERAPY**

## CRATTY, BRYANT J. (1929–      )

As an assistant, associate, and full professor of kinesiology at the University of Southern California since 1961, Bryant Cratty has done research on perceptual and motor development and its relationship to the human personality. He developed programs for the neurologically impaired in the early 1960s that expanded to research of learning games to aid slow learners to acquire academic skills.

**Bryant J. Cratty**

In 1970, Cratty published *Perceptual and Motor Development in Infants and Children*, which traced motor development from infancy to adolescence and gave specific teaching suggestions. In *Motor Activity and the Education of Retardates*, Cratty offered detailed curriculum guides, including relaxation and motor activities that would assist a child in gaining self-confidence.

Cratty has published over 55 books and monographs (many translated into 15 languages and braille) that range from graduate texts in motor development and learning to applied sports psychology. He has also published over 100 articles in domestic and foreign journals and lectured in 20 countries.

### REFERENCES

Cratty, B. J. (1975). *Motor activity and the education of retardates* (2nd ed.). Philadelphia, PA: Lea and Febiger.

Cratty, B. J. (1980). *Adapted physical education for handicapped children and youth*. Denver, CO: Love.

Cratty, B. J. (1985). *Active learning*, (2nd ed.). Englewood Cliffs, NJ: Prentice-Hall.

Cratty, B. J. (1986). *Perceptual and motor development in infants and children* (3rd ed.). Englewood Cliffs, NJ: Prentice-Hall.

ELAINE FLETCHER-JANZEN
*Texas A&M University*

## CREATIVE PROBLEM SOLVING (CPS)

Creative problem solving (CPS) is a structured model for using knowledge and imagination to arrive at a creative, innovative, or effective solution to a problem. Developed by Alex F. Osborn (1953), the original process consisted of three steps: fact finding, including problem definition and preparation; idea finding, including idea production and idea development; and solution finding, including evaluation and adoption. Parnes (1967) developed and refined this sequential problem-solving process into a five-step comprehensive model that incorporates findings from applied and theoretical research on creative thinking and behavior. The five steps are fact finding, problem finding, idea finding, solution finding, and acceptance finding.

Also known as the Osborn-Parnes Model, CPS is the most widely used method to encourage the application of creative thinking skills in the solving of problems. Fundamental to the CPS process is the principle of deferred judgment. This principle is based on Osborn's original notion that when judgment is withheld during ideation, at least 70% more good ideas are produced (Osborn, 1953). Throughout the process both divergent thinking and convergent thinking constantly occur as the problem solver moves from one step to the next. The CPS process proceeds in the following manner. Prior to the first step, there is the "mess" or preparation stage during which the identification or recognition of a situation of personal importance is determined. In fact finding, the emphasis is on gathering all possible background information that may help to define the real problem. Data are collected, facts about the situation are explored, and what is known about the situation is sought out and analyzed. Judgment is deferred until all alternatives have been exhausted. The next step focuses on the problem.

In problem finding, the emphasis is on restating the problem for solution. The problem is examined from a wide variety of perspectives, redefined, narrowed, and analyzed. As the problem is being defined, it is recommended that the phrase "In what ways might I . . ." (IWWMI) be used to encourage more ideas and further elaborations. Again, it is important that judgment be deferred so that thoughts about the problem may flow freely. Sometimes new facts or data will cause a return to step one for more fact finding.

Once the problem has been satisfactorily defined, step three, or idea finding, occurs. Here the intent is to generate many ideas and possible solutions. It is especially important during this phase to defer judgment. Many techniques may be used to generate a quantity of ideas. The most popular is brainstorming, or storming the mind, to generate new and frequently innovative ideas. Application of the four cardinal rules of brainstorming are a must to ensure that ideas flow freely before they are judged for their merits. The rules of brainstorming are (1) rule out criticism; (2) welcome freewheeling or wild ideas; (3) seek quantity; and (4) seek combination and improvement. Other techniques that may be used here and throughout the five steps to encourage the production of ideas are idea-spurring questions, morphological analyses, synectics, attribute listing, scampering, and free association.

In step four, solution finding, the goal is to choose those alternatives that seem to provide the greatest potential for solving the problem. Criteria for evaluating solutions are developed and applied to each possible solution. The best idea, or combination of ideas, to solve the problem is chosen. Ideas not chosen should not be discarded for they may be used later.

The final step, acceptance finding, involves preparations to put the idea into use. The challenge is to make it acceptable. This involves developing a plan for carrying out an idea and for selling and promoting it. Considerations must be given to all factors that may aid or hinder the implementation of the plan.

Parnes (1967) has emphasized the importance of knowledge and imagination in creative productivity. Through the Creative Problem Solving Institute, in university classes, and in many other settings, he has successfully demonstrated that the process is easy to learn and applicable to many situations. College students, government officials, business persons, artists, educators, parents, and children exemplify the types of people who have learned to apply the set of skills in CPS to the solution of practical problems.

The literature on CPS is extensive. Reviews of the CPS process have been completed by Parnes (1981) and Noller (1977), among others. Edwards (1986) has provided an extensive review of information on approaches to enhance creative thinking and ideation during the CPS process.

## REFERENCES

Edwards, M. O. (1986). *Idea power: Time tested methods to stimulate your imagination*. Buffalo, NY: Bearly.

Noller, R. B. (1977). *Scratching the surface of creative problem solving*. Buffalo, NY: D.O.K.

Osborn, A. F. (1953). *Applied imagination*. New York: Scribner.

Parnes, S. J. (1967). *Creative behavior guidebook*. New York: Scribner.

Parnes, S. J. (1981). *The magic of your mind*. Buffao, NY: Bearly.

MARY M. FRASIER
*University of Georgia*

**CREATIVE PROBLEM SOLVING INSTITUTE**
**CREATIVITY**
**SOCIODRAMA**
**TORRANCE, E. PAUL**

# CREATIVE PROBLEM SOLVING INSTITUTE (CPSI)

The Creative Problem Solving Institute (CPSI) is a multidisciplinary, multilevel program designed to familiarize participants with the principles and techniques of creative problem solving (CPS). Founded in 1955 by Alex Osborn, the institute is sponsored by the Creative Education Foundation in cooperation with the State University College, Buffalo. In its first years the institute's program was based on brainstorming, a procedure introduced by Osborn to facilitate creative thinking in a group. Osborn's (1953) notion was that "most of us can work better creatively when teamed up with the right partner because collaboration tends to induce effort, and also to spur our automatic power of association" (p. 72). His conceptualization of the creative problem-solving process included three steps: (1) fact finding, (2) idea finding, and (3) solution finding (Osborn, 1953).

Sidney J. Parnes, who succeeded Osborn as the director of the institute, retained the basic principles of the original model while extending the process to encompass a more eclectic approach. Kitano and Kirby (1986) summarized Parnes's approach as follows: "The Model consists of six steps and incorporates a variety of research-supported techniques for stimulating creativity, including brainstorming, synectics, incubation, imaging, deferred judgment, forced relationships and practice" (p. 205). The six steps as outlined by Parnes (1977) are objective finding, fact finding, problem finding, idea finding, solution finding, and acceptance finding.

The annual summer institute has four major areas: (1) the Springboard Program, (2) the CPSI Youth Program, (3) the Extending Program, and (4) the Leadership Development Program Facilitating Creative Problem Solving. The Springboard Program and the CPSI Youth Program (ages 7 to 16) are designed for participants who have little or no previous experience in the study of creative problem solving. The Extending Program is designed to help participants expand their options through a variety of approaches to creativity. This program consists of different interest groups in which participants practice skills in the creative problem-solving process. The Leadership Development Program emphasizes self-growth and the development of skills for teaching creative problem solving to others.

In addition to annual summer institutes, regional Creative Problem Solving institutes, symposiums, and workshops are held throughout the year. The CPSI attracts people from business, education, and government to its summer institutes and other programs. Participants receive training from specialists with varied experiences in fields associated with creativity.

## REFERENCES

Kitano, M. K., & Kirby, D. F. (1986). *Gifted education: A comprehensive review*. Boston: Little, Brown.

Osborn, A. F. (1953). *Applied imagination: Principles and procedures of creative problem-solving* (rev. ed.). New York: Scribner.

Parnes, S. J. (1977). Guiding creative action. *Gifted Child Quarterly, 21*(4), 460–476.

MARY M. FRASIER
*University of Georgia*

**CONCEPT FORMATION**
**CREATIVE PROBLEM SOLVING**
**OSBORN, ALEXANDER F.**

## CREATIVE STUDIES PROGRAM

The Creative Studies Program was inaugurated in September 1969 by Stanley J. Parnes at Buffalo (N.Y.) State University College to enhance various aspects of college students' present and future behaviors both in college and the general community (Parnes & Noller, 1972a). Parnes et al. developed the Creative Studies Program curriculum based on an earlier project, Creative Problem Solving.

The Creative Problem Solving curriculum is a five-step process (fact finding, problem finding, idea finding, solution finding, and acceptance finding) that emphasizes the generation of a variety of alternatives prior to selecting or implementing a solution (Maher, 1982). The general purposes of the Creative Problem Solving Model are (1) to provide a sequential process that will enable an individual to work from an accumulation of information to arrive at a creative, innovative, or effective solution, and (2) to improve students' overall creative behavior (Maher, 1982).

In implementing the Creative Studies Project curriculum at Buffalo State, Noller and Parnes (1972) developed a 2-year, 4-semester curriculum. The first year of the curriculum provided the students with hands-on experience in creativity. Such experiences were provided through a variety of instructional procedures, including the use of discussions, creative media (e.g., sculpture, art, dance), films, and guest leaders (Noller & Parnes, 1972). The second year of the project provided the students an opportunity to lead others through the project's curriculum.

The Creative Studies Program appears to be a successful method to increase the creative performance of college students (Maher, 1982; Parnes & Noller, 1972b). These students do better in school, perform better on three out of five mental operations (cognition, divergent production, and convergent production) in Guilford's Structure of Intellect Model (Guilford, 1967), and are more productive in nonacademic settings calling for creative performance. Torrance (1972) notes that the Creative Problem Solving curriculum or its modifications (e.g., the Creative Studies Program) is successful in teaching children to think creatively 91 to 92% of the time.

## REFERENCES

Guilford, J. P. (1967). *The nature of human intelligence.* New York: McGraw-Hill.

Maher, C. J. (1982). *Teaching models in the education of the gifted.* Rockville, MD: Aspen.

Noller, R. B., & Parnes, S. J. (1972). Applied creativity: The Creative Studies Project: Part III—The curriculum. *Journal of Creative Behavior, 6,* 275–294.

Parnes, S. J., & Noller, R. B. (1972a). Applied creativity: The Creative Studies Project: Part I—The development. *Journal of Creative Behavior, 6,* 11–22.

Parnes, S. J., & Noller, R. B. (1972b). Applied creativity: The Creative Studies Project: Part II—Results of the two-year program. *Journal of Creative Behavior, 6,* 164–186.

Torrance, E. P. (1972). Can we teach children to think creatively? *Journal of Creative Behavior, 6,* 114–143.

JOHN R. BEATTIE
*University of North Carolina,
Charlotte*

**CREATIVITY**
**CREATIVITY TESTS**

## CREATIVITY

Creativity is a complex and multifaceted phenomenon of human behavior. Theories explaining creativity have ranged from those that define it as the innovative combination of knowledge and imagination applied to the solution of problems to those that view creativity as an "unconscious process through which libidinal or aggressive energies are converted into culturally sanctioned behaviors" (Freud, 1924).

MacKinnon (1978) has properly observed that one should not seek to choose from among the several meanings for the best single definition of creativity; it is a concept that carries all of the meanings that have been offered and will likely carry many more as investigations continue. Current positions on the meaning of creativity suggest a holistic view for, as Clark (1983) has observed, none of the theories thus far provide a complete picture. Her rationale for organizing the various theories into four areas of human functioning—thinking, feeling, sensing, and intuiting—is based on her perception that none of the theories provide a complete picture. The position she takes is that each perception may be only a fragment of the total. It is only through their integration that creativity is possible.

The creative process, person, product, and environment are the vantage points from which creativity is most often discussed. What happens in the creative process? Wallas (1926) described the process as consisting of four stages: preparation, incubation, illumination, and verification. Torrance defined the process as "one of becoming sensitive to or aware of problems . . . bringing together available information . . . searching for solutions . . . and communicating the results" (Torrance & Myers, 1970, p. 22).

While Taylor (1960) supported the notion of stages, he added that creativity exists at five levels with each level involving different psychological processes that may change the steps in the process. The five levels are (1) expressive creativity, a form of spontaneous expression without reference to originality and quality of the product; (2) technical or productive creativity, where the emphasis is on skill rather than spontaneity and novelty; (3) inventive creativity, with an emphasis on the new use of old things; (4) innovative creativity, where new ideas or principles are developed; and (5) emergentive creativity, which describes creative formulation using the most abstract ideational principles or assumptions underlying a body of art or science. Guilford (1959), emphasizing divergent thinking as the essence of creativity, identified generalized sensitivity to problems, fluency, flexibility, originality, redefinition, and elaboration as important components.

Research into hemispheric functioning has provided the most recent perspectives on creativity and the creative process. The notion that creative individuals are right-hemisphere dominant while logical, rational thinkers are left-hemisphere dominant has led to current theories that define the creative act as the result of interactions between hemispheres. For detailed reviews of current studies on hemisphericity, the reader is referred to Clark (1983) or Kitano and Kirby (1986).

Creative products may be ideas, works of art, scientific theories, or even building designs, provided certain criteria are met. According to MacKinnon (1978), these criteria include originality or novelty and relevance to a problem, situation, or goal. In addition, the answer that the product yields must be aesthetically pleasing and must create new conditions of human existence that transcend and transform traditional views and experiences.

Consistent among the many descriptions of creative persons are traits and behaviors such as unusual sensitivity to their environment, independence in thinking, nonconforming in their behaviors, and persistence at tasks. Creative people tend to be open to new ideas and experiences and less accepting of traditional points of view. Exploring ideas for their own sake, a marked sense of humor, a high tolerance for ambiguity, and strong self-confidence in their own work are other common traits of highly creative people.

An environment or situation that is open and accepting is critical for the release and development of creative potential. Kneller (1966) suggested that the main obstacles to creativity appear to be cultural and biological. Arieti (1976) presented the concept of the creativogenic society to describe his holistic view of cultural traits that support the development of creativity. Such a society is distinguished by its lack of emphasis on immediate gratification, its tolerance for and interest in divergent points of view, and its use of incentives and rewards for creativity. Torrance (1962) has suggested that other important variables are those that encourage unusual questions and ideas and those that allow performance to occur without constant threat of evaluation.

The debate regarding the nature of the relationship between creativity and intelligence has not been conclusively resolved. Kitano and Kirby (1986) contend that there is at least a conceptual agreement among researchers that creativity is distinguishable from general intelligence. That is, "an individual can be extremely bright but uncreative, or highly creative but not necessarily intellectually gifted" (Kitano & Kirby, 1986, p. 192). It has been estimated that an IQ of at least 120 is generally necessary for high creativity. IQ levels may vary according to the nature of the creative act.

Much of the discussion regarding the relationship between creativity and intelligence relates to assessment. There have been several measures developed to assess creativity, but questions still arise regarding whether creativity should be measured by recognized achievement or by tests of divergent or creative thinking. The most frequently used measure of creativity is the Torrance Tests of Creative Thinking (1974), which provides a single score index of creative potential on both the figural and verbal versions. Other measures of creativity are batteries developed by Guilford (1959) and by Wallach and Kogan (1965).

Leading proponents of the search for methods to teach creative thinking have been Parnes (1967) and Torrance (1979). Parnes developed the Creative Problem Solving Process, a five-step method combining knowledge and imagination in problem solving. Torrance (1979) created a three-stage instructional model—the Incubation Model—which integrates creativity objectives with content objectives. Clark (1983) and Kitano and Kirby (1986) provide further information on methods to teach creativity.

## REFERENCES

Arieti, S. (1976). *Creativity: The magic synthesis.* New York: Basic Books.

Clark, B. (1983). *Growing up gifted* (2nd ed.). Columbus, OH: Merrill.

Freud, S. (1924). The relations of the poet to day-dreaming. In *Collected papers* (Vol. 2). London: Hogarth. (Original work published 1908)

Guilford, J. P. (1959). Three faces of intellect. *American Psychology, 14,* 469–479.

Kitano, M. K., & Kirby, D. F. (1986). *Gifted education: A comprehensive view.* Boston: Little, Brown.

Kneller, G. F. (1966). *The art and science of creativity.* New York: Holt, Rinehart, & Winston.

MacKinnon, D. W. (1978). *In search of human effectiveness.* Buffalo, NY: Creative Education Foundation.

Parnes, S. J. (1967). *Creative behavior guidebook.* New York: Scribner.

Stein, M. I. (1974). *Stimulating creativity: Vol I. Individual procedures.* New York: Academic.

Taylor, I. A. (1960). The nature of the creative process. In P. Smith (Ed.), *Creativity: An examination of the creative process.* New York: Hastings House.

Torrance, E. P. (1962). *Guiding creative talent.* Englewood Cliffs, NJ: Prentice-Hall.

Torrance, E. P. (1974). *Torrance Tests of Creative Thinking: Norms-technical manual.* Bensenville, IL: Scholastic Testing Service.

Torrance, E. P. (1979). An instructional model for enhancing incubation. *Journal of Creative Behavior, 13*(1), 23–35.

Torrance, E. P., & Myers, R. E. (1970). *Creative learning and teaching.* New York: Dodd, Mead.

Wallach, M. A., & Kogan, N. (1965). *Modes of thinking in young children.* New York: Holt, Rinehart, & Winston.

Wallas, G. (1926). *The art of thought.* New York: Harcourt Brace Jovanovich.

MARY M. FRASIER
*University of Georgia*

**CREATIVE STUDY PROGRAM**
**GIFTED CHILDREN**
**TORRANCE, PAUL**

# CREATIVITY TESTS

Creativity tests have been in widespread application for more than 50 years in research on cognitive skills and in the identification of gifted and talented children for participation in special education programs. However, it was the tremendous increase of interest in giftedness and creativity and concomitant funding of such research from about 1953 to 1963 that fueled research in the area. Major conceptual advances occurred during this period as Torrance began studying creativity in earnest and such classic and influential works as Guilford's (1959) *Three Faces of Intellect* and Getzels and Jackson's (1962) *Intelligence and Creativity* were published. Guilford was most influential in proposing the concept of convergent and divergent thinking, the latter being closely associated with creative thinking. Getzels and Jackson changed the dominant views of the relationship between IQ and creativity by postulating, based on their extensive study, that creativity was far more independent of IQ than previously believed, especially at the upper IQ levels. This work paved the way for the development of modern creativity tests. Creativity tests have changed very little since their growth spurt during the 1960s.

Most of the tests of creativity currently available were developed in the course of large-scale research projects on the nature of creativity. The two major batteries to be developed were the University of Southern California tests, devised by Guilford et al. as part of the Aptitute Research

Project, and the Torrance Tests of Creative Thinking, devised by E. Paul Torrance in his efforts to design curriculum and teaching methods for the improvement of creative functioning in children. Torrance's research program has been designated the Georgia Studies of Creative Behavior since the late 1960s.

These tests and many others are commercially available and often used in the assessment of creativity; however, many psychometricians consider all such tests to be experimental (Anastasi, 1982). The items in creativity tests, with very few exceptions (such as the Welsh Figure Preference Test), are open-ended and thus on the subjective side of the scoring continuum. It is particularly important for this reason to assess the interscorer reliability of creativity tests before placing them into practice. Normative data for creativity tests generally fall significantly short of what has become the accepted psychometric standard for good tests of intelligence and achievement. Reliability and validity data are extensive for some tests such as the Torrance Tests of Creative Thinking, but for others they are extremely limited. The Torrance tests have been used in more than 1000 published studies and doctoral dissertations. Even with the large body of research on this scale, the relationship between measurement of creativity with existing tests and major variables of personality, intelligence, and creativity on the job or in other settings remains unclear.

The major creativity scales attempt to measure multiple dimensions of creativity, including such variables as fluency, originality, unusual responses, flexibility, resistance to premature closure, etc. It remains unclear whether these dimensions are sufficiently independent to warrant differentiation in the measurement process. The measurement of creativity also has been found to be relatively task specific; i.e., performance on creativity measures does not generalize well to tasks outside of the test and the test setting.

Despite these problems, the use of creativity tests continue to be a popular activity in programs for the gifted and talented. Creativity has proven a difficult concept to master and the state of the psychometric data regarding creativity tests generally reflects the nature of the concept. Creativity tests are probably better than most psychometricians believe (Bennett, 1972; Wallach, 1968). The relatively weak results of research on this genre of tests, compared with the outcome of research on tests of intelligence and academic achievement, are more reflective of the difficult nature of the concept than of any inherent weakness in the major scales in use today such as the Torrance Tests of Creative Thinking.

## REFERENCES

Anastasi, A. (1982). *Psychological testing* (5th ed.). New York: Macmillan.

Bennett, G. K. (1972). Review of the Remote Associates Test. In O. K. Buros (Ed.), *Seventh mental measurements yearbook.* Highland Park, NJ: Gryphon.

Guilford, J. P. (1959). Three faces of intellect. *American Psychologist, 14,* 469–479.

Getzels, J. W., & Jackson, P. W. (1962). *Creativity and intelligence.* New York: Wiley.

Wallach, M. A. (1968). Review of the Torrance Test of Creative Thinking. *American Educational Research Journal, 5,* 272–281.

CECIL R. REYNOLDS
*Texas A&M University*

**CREATIVE PROBLEM SOLVING**
**TORRANCE, E. PAUL**
**TORRANCE TESTS OF CREATIVE THINKING**
**WELSH FIGURE PREFERENCE TEST**
**(SEE ALSO SPECIFIC TEST TITLES)**

# CRETINISM

Cretinism is a metabolic endocrine abnormality that is caused by a thyroid gland disorder. It exists in many forms. Athyrotic hypothyroidism is the congenital absence or partial absence of the thyroid gland. Endemic cretinism is a dietary deficiency of iodine. Familial hypothyroidism is an inborn error of thyroid metabolism and iodine transport. Intrauterine hypothyroidism occurs in infants whose mothers were on antithyroid therapy during pregnancy. Prior to the advent of diets containing iodine and the addition of iodine to table salt within the last hundred years, the endemic form was most common in areas where iodine-rich seafoods were difficult to obtain, for example, the mountainous regions of western Europe and the midwestern United States.

Individuals with untreated congenital hypothyroidism have characteristic features: wide-set eyes, broad nose bridge, and protruding tongue. The head appears to be oversized. The abdomen is large and protrudes with frequent umbilical hernia. Extremities look as though they are shortened and there is general low muscle tone. Mental retardation is a frequent result of the untreated condition.

Felix Platter (1536–1614), a Swiss physician, was one of the first to note the existence of endemic cretinism. In the early part of the sixteenth century, a Swiss physician, Aureolus Theophrastus Bombastus Von Hohenheim, better known as Paracelsus (1493–1541), observed that cretinism was associated with mental retardation. Wolfgang Hoefer (1614–1681), a court physician in Vienna, offered the first extensive description of cretinism. He contended that cretinism could be attributed primarily to food and a poor education.

Throughout the nineteenth century, governments in central Europe expended resources and attention on the investigation and treatment of cretinism. Johann Jacob Guggenbuhl (1816–1863), a Swiss physician, devoted his life to the "cure and prophylaxis" of cretinism. During this time cretinism was viewed as typifying all forms of mental deficiency. The first journal on mental deficiency, which was published in 1850, was entitled *Beobachtungen tuber den Cretinismus (Observations of Cretinism).*

Owing to the work of Thomas Curling in 1860 and Charles Fogge in 1870, cretinism was identified as related to hypothyroidism. The English physician George Murray developed the first thyroid treatment in 1891. However, etiological and pathological subtleties remained unknown and unappreciated until the twentieth century. In 1975, Dr. Jean H. Dussault from Quebec developed the screening test for neonatal hypothyroidism that is used in the United States today.

Treatment consists of replacement of the thyroid hormone, thyroxin, with synthetic preparations. The results of treatment depend not only on the length of time before treatment is begun but on the severity and type of hypothyroidism. Occurring in one in every 6000 children, hypothyroidism is one of the most common inborn errors of metabolism. The direct result of early identification is the opportunity for early treatment. This, in turn, allows children born with hypothyroidism to develop normally, obviating the need for special education.

## REFERENCES

Dussault, J. H., Coulombe, P., Laberge, C., Letarte, J., Guyda, H., & Khoury, K., (1975). Preliminary report on a mass screening program for neonatal hypothyroidism. *Journal of Pediatrics, 86,* 670–674.

Gearheart, B. R., & Litton, F. W. (1975). *The trainable retarded: A foundations approach.* St. Louis: Mosby.

Kanner, L. (1967). Historical review of mental retardation (1800–1965). *American Journal of Mental Deficiency, 72,* 165–189.

Klein, A. H., Meltzer, S., & Kenny, F. M. (1972). Improved prognosis in congenital hypothyroidism treated before age 3 months. *Journal of Pediatrics, 81,* 912–915.

Prehem, H. J., & Cegelka, P. T. (1982). *Mental retardation: From categories to people.* Columbus, OH: Merrill.

Scheerenberger, R. C. (1983). *A history of mental retardation.* Baltimore, MD: Brookes.

CAROLE REITER GOTHELF
*Hunter College, City University*
*of New York*

**HYPOTHYROIDISM**
**INBORN ERRORS OF METABOLISM**

# CRI DU CHAT SYNDROME (CAT CRY SYNDROME)

Discovered by Jerome Lejeune, director of the department of genetics at the University of Paris, and his coworkers, Gautier and Turpin, in 1963, cri du chat syndrome is associated with a partial deletion of one of the chromosomes in the B group; specifically, there is a deletion of the short arm of chromosome 5 (5p-). Cri du chat syndrome is the most frequently reported of the autosomal deletion syndromes. The name was derived from the characteristic high-pitched, mewing cry, closely resembling the cry of a kitten, that is heard in the immediate newborn period, lasts several weeks, and then disappears with the exception of some cases, in which the catlike cry persists into adulthood.

Affected infants show low birth weight, failure to thrive, hypotonia, microcephaly, a round or moon-faced appearance with hypertelorism (wide-set eyes), antimongoloid or downward sloping palpebral fissures with or without epicanthal folds, strabismus, and a broad-based nose. Ears are low-set and abnormally shaped with malformations, including narrow external canals and preauricular tags. Micrognathia, a short neck, and varying degrees of syndactyly are present. Various types of congenital heart defects and abnormal dermatoglyphics are frequently noted. Major diagnostic features include severe mental retardation and markedly delayed motor development.

A significant number of cri du chat infants survive to adulthood and continue to demonstrate microcephaly. They also have short stature, facial asymmetry, dental malocclusions, skeletal problems such as scoliosis, eye defects, and a waddling gait. These individuals are at or below the trainable level. As school-aged children, they are found in classes for the moderately and severely retarded. According to Gearheart and Litton (1975), the incidence of cri du chat is not known. Berg et al. (1970) found that 7 of the 744 patients with IQs below 35 had this defect. Goodman and Gorlin (1970) reported that a preponderance of patients were female.

No treatment is presently available for this syndrome. As with other chromosome defects, prevention is associated with amniocentesis and genetic counseling. The possibility of a recurrence of the syndrome in another member of the family is rare unless the condition is due to a translocation chromosome. Most cases of cri du chat syndrome are sporadic, with about 13% originating from a balanced carrier parent who is phenotypically normal.

## REFERENCES

Berg, J. M., McCreary, B. D., Ridler, M. A., & Smith, G. F., (1970). *The deLange syndrome.* Oxford, England: Pergamon.

Berkow, R. (Ed.). (1982). *The Merck manual of diagnosis and therapy* (14th ed.). Rahway, NJ: Merck Sharp & Dohme Research Laboratories.

Cegelka, P. T., & Prehn, H. J. (1982). *Mental retardation: From categories to people.* Columbus, OH: Merrill.

Gearheart, B. R., & Litton, F. W. (1975). *The trainable retarded: A foundations approach.* St. Louis, MO: Mosby.

Goodman, R. M., & Gorlin, R. J. (1970). *The face in genetic disorders.* St. Louis, MO: Mosby.

Holmes, L. B., Moses H. W., Halldorsson, S., Mack, C., Pavt, S. S., & Matzilevich, B. (1972). *Mental retardation: An atlas of diseases with associated physical abnormalities.* New York: Macmillan.

Lejuene, J., Gautier, M., & Turpin, R. (1959). *Les chromosomes humains en culture des tissues: Competes rendus hebdomadaires des seances de l'Academie des Sciences* (pp. 248–602). Paris: l'Academie des Sciences.

Zellweger, H., & Ionasescu, V. (1978). Genetics of mental retardation. In C. H. Carter (Ed.), *Medical aspects of mental retardation* (2nd ed.). Springfield, IL: Thomas.

CATHERINE HALL RIKHYE
*Hunter College, City University
of New York*

## CHROMOSOMAL ABNORMALITIES
## MENTAL RETARDATION

# CRIME AND THE HANDICAPPED

Public Law 94-142 mandated that educational services be provided to all handicapped youths no matter where they reside. Johnson (1979) indicates that about one third of incarcerated youths are thought to have serious learning disabilities, in contrast to only 16% of the unincarcerated population.

Morgan (1979) conducted a study to produce a national profile of handicapping conditions. He sent questionnaires to administrators of juvenile correctional facilities in 50 states and 5 U.S. territories. Among the respondents, only 6 did not provide most of the requested information; 204 institutions responded. Among the findings, Morgan reports that:

1. Compared to the national incidence of handicapped children (12.3%), 42.4% of delinquent children committed to correctional institutions were found to have some type of handicapping condition.
2. The handicapping conditions with the highest incidence rates in correctional facilities were emotional disturbance (16.23%), learning disabilities (10.59%), and educable mental retardation (7.69%).

Morgan (1979) indicates that the figure 42% is inflated. Keilitz and Miller (1980) combined results of several studies, including Morgan's (1979), and concluded that those studies suggest that (1) prevalence estimates of the major categories of emotional disorders, learning disabilities, and mental retardation are of greater magnitude than expected on the basis of estimates of prevalence among the general student population; and (2) the great difference in prevalence of handicapping conditions between those youths outside and inside the justice system remains even when study design problems and bias are minimized.

Much speculation exists as to the relationship between criminal behavior and handicapping conditions. Siegal and Senna (1981) assign theories that attempt to determine the cause of delinquency into four categories: individualized, social structure, social process, and social reaction. Unfortunately, the variables and factors that impact on these theories are the same that are used to describe the educable mentally retarded and the emotionally handicapped.

Keilitz and Miller (1980) present three rationales as the most prominent explanations of the disproportionate prevalence of handicapping conditions among youths in the justice system. The three are school failure, suspectibility, and differential treatment.

Despite these attempts to account for unexpectedly high prevalence, there is no definitive explanation for the disproportionate number of handicapped youths in the justice system. There is clear evidence that services (Johnson, 1979) mandated under PL 94-142 must be provided and that these services have not been fully implemented. The problem of handicapping conditions as they relate to crime is serious and needs much more attention, especially in the areas of research, programs, and prevention (Brown & Robbins, 1979).

## REFERENCES

Brown, S., & Robbins, M. (1979). Serving the special education needs of students in correctional facilities. *Exceptional Children, 45*, 574–579.

Johnson, J. (1979). An essay on incarcerated youth: An oppressed group. *Exceptional Children, 45*(7), 566–571.

Keilitz, I., & Miller, S. L. (1980). Handicapped adolescents and young adults in the justice system. *Exceptional Education Quarterly, 1*(2), 117–126.

Morgan, D. I. (1979). Prevalence and type of handicapping conditions found in juvenile correctional institutions: A national survey. *Journal of Special Education, 13*, 283–295.

Siegal, L. J., & Senna, J. J. (1981). *Juvenile delinquency: Theory, practice, and law*. St. Paul, MN: West.

PHILIP E. LYON
*College of St. Rose*

EDUCATIONALLY DISADVANTAGED
JUVENILE DELINQUENCY

# CRISIS INTERVENTION

Crisis intervention is a service spontaneously available to individuals and students who are in need of immediate assistance (Kelly & Vergason, 1978). Caplan defines a crisis as a sudden onset of behavioral imbalance in a child where previous function was stable (Caplan, 1963). The intent of intervention in a crisis is to provide knowledge of coping behaviors of enduring value. According to Swanson and Reinert (1976), a child in conflict is one "whose manifested behavior has a deleterious effect on his/her personal or educational development and/or the personal or educational development of his peers" (p. 5).

Intervention at the point of disruption or crisis is not new. Traditionally, the crisis was handled by an administrator or teacher. According to Long, Morse, and Newman (1976):

> the problem is these are usually of a reflexive and haphazard type. From our analysis of acts and reactions in the school setting it appears that a good many leave much to be desired. Since they usually lack an awareness of the underlying conditions, they are reactions to symptoms, often with a curbing intention. (p. 232) also these crisis situations may be only "a crisis to the teacher who is the consumer of the behavior." (p. 325)

The crisis concept has changed in four ways. The first is in consultation, which has gone from supervisory to strategic planning. In other words, clinicians and teachers work together toward resolution. The second is in the use of the helping teacher, who becomes responsible for the disturbed child. The third change is in the style of interviewing proposed by Redl called life space interviewing (LSI). The fourth change occurs in a system to manage the confrontation situations that are found in secondary education.

The holding of crisis meetings is one way to develop a positive, success-oriented classroom. When disruptions such as fights, serious arguments, misunderstandings, and expressions of angry feelings (verbal or physical) occur, impromptu crisis meetings help students understand and resolve serious conflicts (Redl, 1959). These meetings, which involve only those students who were actually involved in the problem situation, can take place in the classroom, lunchroom, or playground. To conduct a crisis meeting, the following steps are usually taken:

1. *Cooling Off.* Students should be given a few minutes to cool off if they are very upset and not ready to engage in thoughtful discussion. If necessary, students can be sent to their desks, a quiet area, or the principal's office.

2. *Setting Rules.* The meeting is initiated by speaking in a calm manner. Ground rules for the discussion are set. These may include avoiding arguing and listening to what each person has to say.

3. *Listening Actively.* The student is asked to describe the incident, what led up to the incident, and how he or she feels. After listening carefully, the listener rephrases what the student has said to show understanding. Other students may be asked to summarize or repeat what the first student said. Then the second student is asked to give his or her recollection of the incident. During the active listening phase, the main goal is to obtain a clarification of what happened and how the participants are feeling.

Helping students clarify their feelings may also serve to drain off some anger or frustration.

4. *Exploring Problem.* At this step, the problem is considered at length. Questions such as how the problem could have been avoided, what can be done the next time the problem begins, and what consequences should be expected (Glass et al., 1982) can be addressed.

Another resource is the crisis or helping teacher. Gearheart and Weishahn find that this teacher

> provides temporary support and control to troubled students when they are unable or unwilling to cope with the demands of the regular classroom. The type of service the Crisis Teacher provides requires that he/she be available at the time of the crisis. Working closely with the regular classroom teachers, he/she provides support, reassurance, and behavioral management strategies. Troubled students come and go on either a regular or an episodic basis, depending on the needs of the students. When the teacher is not dealing with a crisis, he/she can be helping less troubled students academically and behaviorally. He/she can make referrals to supportive services, provide the needed intensive assistance for the more severely troubled students, and follow up on specific recommendations. The crisis teacher becomes an active partner with the teacher, mental health personnel, and parents in helping this student. (p. 223)

Another form of crisis intervention is the life space interviewing (LSI) method which was developed to help teachers become effective in talking to children and to help teachers use these skills as a specific management tool (L'Abate & Curtis, 1975). There are two main goals: clinical exploitation of life events and immediate emotional first aid. There are both long-range and immediate goals. This kind of therapy may help the student to express hostility, frustration, or aggression; provide support while helping the student to avoid panic or guilt; help the student to maintain relationships; allow teachers to supervise behavior and ensure conformity to rules; and help teachers in settling complex situations (L'Abate & Curtis, 1975). Bernstein (1963) in L'Abate and Curtis (1975) provides some guidelines for LSI:

1. Be polite
2. Do not tower above a child; bend down to him
3. Be sure of yourself
4. Use "why" sparingly
5. Encourage talk about the actual situation
6. Help the child to avoid being overwhelmed by shame or guilt by minimizing the problem
7. Help the child to express his or her feelings about the situation
8. Be aware of the kind of thinking demanded by a particular situation
9. Work with the child to make the situation better
10. Allow the child time to ask questions

L'Abate and Curtis (1975) list some limitations of LSI:

1. It requires the teacher to have an ability to understand human behavior in more of an art than a science form.
2. It often requires more time than a regular classroom teacher with 30 students has to spare; this is where the helping teacher could assist.
3. It requires education and cooperation among all members of the school staff.

The resource classroom is yet another way to help exceptional children. Here the child is provided with instruction and emotional support by the resource teacher for part of the day. The child may move between the classrooms and receive instruction from both teachers. It is even possible that the child can be placed on a limited day schedule in cases where he or she cannot handle either the resource or regular classroom. In summary, crisis intervention can be the most appropriate kind of action if all psychological, sociological, and educational knowledge is applied at the correct moment in time.

### REFERENCES

Caplan, G. (1963). Opportunities for school psychologists in the primary prevention. *Mental Hygiene, 47*(4), 525–539.

Gearheart, B. R., & Weishahn, M. W. (1980). *The handicapped student in the regular classroom.* St. Louis: Mosby.

Glass, R., Christiansen, J., & Christiansen, J. L. (1982). *Teaching exceptional students in the regular classroom.* Boston: Little, Brown.

Kelly, L. J., & Vergason, G. A. (1978). *Dictionary for special education and rehabilitation.* Denver: Love.

L'Abate, L., & Curtis, L. T. (1975). *Teaching the exceptional child.* Philadelphia: Saunders.

Long, H. J., Morse, W. C., & Newman, R. G. (1976). *Conflict in the classroom: The education of emotionally disturbed children.* Belmont, CA: Wadsworth.

Redl, F. (1959). Concept of the life space interview. *American Journal of Orthopsychiatry, 29* (1) 1–18.

Swanson, L. H., & Reinert, H. R. (1979). *Teaching strategies for children in conflict curriculum methods, and materials.* St. Louis: Mosby.

RICHARD E. HALMSTAD
*University of Wisconsin, Stout*

## LIFE SPACE INTERVIEWING
REDL, FRITZ

## CRISIS TEACHER

The concept of the crisis teacher/helping teacher was initiated, according to Long, Morse, and Newman (1976), as the result of the efforts of a staff of elementary teachers in a high problematic school. The crisis teacher is first an educator trained in psychoeducational theory and practice who provides direct assistance to regular classroom teachers and students that might exhibit disruptive (crisis) behaviors. Ultimately, this educator will enhance the learning environment by providing a liaison between the crisis teacher and the regular classroom teacher. This brings to the classroom teacher immediate peer help as opposed to the consultants, such as the school psychologist, school counselor, or principal, ordinarily sought out.

Historically, crises had been met by sending the students involved to the principal's office. Frequently, this procedure would yield less than adequate results for various reasons. First, the principal is often uninformed of the events leading up to the classroom crisis. Second, the principal's administrative responsibilities may make him or her unavailable when needed most. Third, the repressive nature of being sent to the principal's office may, in some instances, exacerbate the problem. In addition, resorting to this method of crisis resolution in some instances results in an inadvertent reinforcer being applied to the situation.

Regular classroom teachers are cognizant of the needs expressed by all students in their classrooms and as such understand that not all children manifest disruptive behaviors at all times. However, teachers are aware that every child in the classroom has the right to an equal share of his or her time. Since disruptive children cannot always be physically removed from the classroom and other students have educational needs to be met, the crisis teacher concept seems to meet the purpose of addressing the one who needs help, while keeping the classroom teacher in continuing interaction with other students.

Immediate help from a crisis teacher is also seen as an effort to interject a process that would promote a more expedient method of handling psychoeducational problems manifested by the disruptive student. Prior to such a process being developed, regular classroom teachers resorted to punishment and then waited until a staffing could be arranged to receive advice from a psychologist, nurse, counselor, special education teacher, or other team member. Again, the regular classroom teacher was faced with receiving well-meaning but delayed corrective suggestions that proved inappropriate to their needs. As cited by Reynolds and Birch (1977), such advice was often impractical. Teachers knew what to do but did not have the resources to implement the course of action advocated by a team to which the teacher was not always a contributing member.

If direct assistance is essential to the regular classroom teacher, then the training of the crisis teacher is crucial to the effectiveness of the position. It is suggested that the crisis teacher becomes a part of the school staff and, as such, an educator trained in psychoeducational programs that specifically qualify the individual to interact positively with regular classroom teachers and students dur-

ing crises. This interaction requires the crisis teacher to possess a wealth of expertise concerning the theory and application of psychological concepts. Of equal importance, however, is the individual's ability to apply sound special education practices within the classroom setting. Here then, we have a new resource person to provide the regular classroom teacher with direct help (psychoeducational) in crisis situations.

While the crisis teacher's training encompasses a psychoeducational emphasis, it should be noted that the main thrust within this role remains one of service to the whole individual in his or her development. As such, the crisis teacher must be cognizant of a variety of specific interventions such as remedial instruction, tutoring, group activities, art, music, psychodrama, role-playing, "big brother" and "big sister" activities, and problem-solving activities (Shea, 1978). The crisis teacher must have competencies along with knowledge of behavioral, psychodynamic, and environmental interventions in order to adequately confront and correct most disruptive classroom dilemmas.

Of equal importance to offering direct assistance to students is the crisis teacher's responsibility to staff members, parents, and community-based agencies. Consultations with each group is essential. Acting as a liaison between child, teacher, parent, and community not only lends support through direct aid and remediation but will, through time, lead to provisions for the establishment of programs for future education and the therapeutic needs of troubled students. Modifications of the unhealthy aspects of the learning environment also becomes a responsibility of the crisis teacher, as well as generating plans to develop new programs to enhance a positive psychoeducational atmosphere that will foster sound mental health (Shea, 1978).

Long, Morse, and Newman (1976) has suggested the crisis/helping teacher model include the following features: (1) emphasizes direct assistance to pupils; (2) has an eclectic approach to intervention strategies; (3) is concerned with the prevention of problems as well as their remediation; (4) tends to be broadly concerned with the total life space of the child rather than targeted on specific discrepancies or deficits. It appears that the concept of the crisis teacher has had a positive effect in that it tends to promote healthy self-concepts and lends itself to future self-management and authentic human relationships.

An important footnote includes the crisis teacher's ability to know when an incident is not a crisis and does not warrant his or her attention., Of importance then is to avoid conceiving of all events of a disruptive nature as being catastrophic and in need of special attention. The following is a summary of the steps recognized by Morse in the development of the helping/crisis teacher model as presented by Reynolds and Birch (1977):

1. The majority of the faculty recognizes that the dis-

ruptive behavior of a number of pupils provides a barrier between the pupils and the teachers.

2. The teachers examine carefully the establishment of special classes for these children.

3. An in-depth analysis of needs results in the realization that what the faculty needs and what special education can provide are not compatible for the following reasons: the number of disruptive students that make teachers feel incompetent and discouraged usually is one or two per class; even the most difficult students are not that way all of the time; teachers have already learned to assess and thus anticipate problems; trials at repressing disruptive behavior through harsh verbal means, removal of privileges, and other forms of punishment have failed; advice from personnel such as psychologists, counselors, and administrators provide verbal encouragement but little in the way of actual help.

4. After an analysis of the classroom situation, the children, and teacher effectiveness, it is concluded that direct in-class help is needed in a form that provides a person capable of working with children who are in, or close to, a crisis. The training of this person should be that of a teacher and a specialist, with emphasis on learning disabilities and behavior disorders. Help should be present right in the school—not from an itinerant or central office base. The helping teacher should neither be under rigidly scheduled external control nor tied to a classroom of children. Flexibility for direct and timely cooperative work with a regular class teacher should have high priority. Sometimes the most helpful immediate action might be removal of a child from the regular class for conference or a quiet time under the visual supervision of the helping teacher. At other times, the helper might conduct the regular class while the teacher is attending to a problem in the class. The actual daily duties of the helping teacher must develop out of the needs of the particular school, its pupils, and community resources.

## REFERENCES

Long, N. J., Morse, W. C., & Newman, R. G. (1976). *Conflict in the classroom: The education of emotionally, disturbed children* (3rd ed.). Belmont, CA: Wadsworth.

Reynolds, M. C., & Birch, J. W. (1977). *Teaching exceptional children in all America's schools*. Reston, VA: Council for Exceptional Children.

Shea, T. M. (1978). *Teaching children and youth with behavior disorders*. St. Louis: Mosby.

RICHARD E. HALMSTAD
*University of Wisconsin, Stout*

**CRISIS INTERVENTION**
**RESOURCE ROOM**
**SPECIAL CLASS**

## CRISSEY, MARIE SKODAK (1910–      )

Born in Lorain, Ohio, Marie Skodak Crissey obtained her BS and MA degrees from Ohio State University in 1931. She was an Institute of International Education fellow at the University of Budapest in 1931–1932. Crissey became interested in factors influencing development of intelligence and school achievement partly through the influence of Henry H. Goddard and Sidney Pressey. Her PhD was in developmental psychology from the University of Iowa in 1938.

She is well known for her still frequently cited classic research (Skodak, 1939; Skodak & Skeels, 1949) on the heredity-environment issue, which countered the then widely held concept of genetically determined and fixed IQ. She found that the IQs of adopted children correlated more highly with the estimated intelligence of their biological rather than their adoptive parents, but that their actual level of intelligence was closer to that of their adoptive parents. Thus her research showed both hereditary and environmental influences on intelligence, and demonstrated that favorable home environment could raise levels of intelligence. From an applied standpoint, she emphasized the potential effectiveness of environmental intervention programs to stimulate the development of children from deprived backgrounds.

During her professional career, Crissey developed special education programs, intervention programs for handicapped and deprived children, vocational guidance programs for high school students, and vocational rehabilitation services for the handicapped. She was at the Child Guidance Center at Flint, Michigan, from 1938 to 1946 and was director of school psychology and special education at Dearborn, Michigan, from 1949 to 1969. She has had a private practice in psychology since 1942 (Anonymous, 1984). She is a fellow of the American Association of Mental Deficiency and of five divisions of the American Psychological Association. Among her numerous awards are the Joseph P. Kennedy International Award for research in mental retardation in 1968 and a citation for distinguished service from the American Psychological Association in 1972.

## REFERENCES

Anonymous. (1984). Crissey, Marie Skodak. In R. Corsini (Ed.), *Encyclopedia of psychology* (Vol. 2). New York: Wiley.

Skodak, M. (1939). Children in foster homes: A study of mental development. *University of Iowa Studies in Child Welfare, 16*(1).

Skodak, M., & Skeels, H. M. (1949). A final follow-up study of one hundred adopted children. *Journal of Genetic Psychology, 75,* 85–125.

ROBERT T. BROWN
*University of North Carolina,
Wilmington*

# CRITERION-REFERENCED TESTING

Criterion-referenced testing is a method for examining a person's performance with respect to a standard or criterion. It is commonly contrasted with norm-referenced testing, in which a person's performance is compared with that of other persons who make up a norm group. While this concept has been used in pedagogy for millennia, it has been most recently formalized by Glaser and Klaus (1962). In their conception, a criterion is a level of performance achieved only when the person being examined is able to perform certain tasks. These tasks have been determined to be necessary for learning. During the course of study there may be many criteria, which may be viewed as stages or intermediate steps. The assessment of the performance on the tasks necessary to achieve criteria is commonly called criterion referenced testing (CRT).

In the late 1960s criterion-referencing became commonly associated with mastery (Popham & Husek, 1969; Glass, 1978), especially with minimum-competency testing. In this variant, CRT is intended to classify persons into those who can and those who cannot perform at some minimally acceptable level. At the current time, at least 39 states in the United States require some form of minimum-competency testing. Purposes for the testing include issuing of high-school diplomas, passage to high school from junior high, and comparison of classes and schools for various political purposes. While the latter reason is almost never formally stated, it is common practice in many states to publish building- or district-level average test performance. These are then compared with state "competitors." There have been numerous proposals to link teacher salaries to their classrooms' performance on such tests. In only a few isolated school districts have such procedures been established.

The major issues in CRT are definition of the content, development of the tests, evaluation of test characteristics, and standard setting. A useful text on these issues has been compiled by Berk (1984a); it contains current thinking by researchers in the CRT field.

Definition of the content for criterion-referenced tests is closely tied to instruction. If one uses the Glaser and Husek concept of CRT, a careful analysis of the tasks being required of the students forms the basis for the test. Those tasks are separated either hierarchically or organizationally into stages or steps. Tests are constructed that sample the behaviors the student must exhibit to demonstrate

knowledge or mastery for each step. In hierarchical content, the student must know certain content or be able to perform certain tasks before the next content or task can be attempted. Many courses in mathematics exhibit such structure. Other content may have an organizational sequence that is not inherent to it such as English literature. It may be studied historically, thematically, or by type such as poetry, novel, and essay. Criterion-referenced testing may be used to indicate level of achievement for each part. Nitko (1984) refers to ordering and definition for domains. A domain may be ordered or unordered and well-defined or ill-defined. He asserts that CRT should be used only with well-defined content domains.

There has been relatively little research on developing items or questions for CRTs, and most test developers have used item-writing technology developed for norm-referenced achievement tests. Roid and Haladyna (1980) have attempted to develop an item-writing technology using algorithms for sentence writing. Other proposed approaches are based on mapping and on factor analysis (Roid, 1984). Future efforts are certain to use computers in the generation of items for CRTs.

Analysis of item and test characteristics has received some attention from psychometricians. Both classical reliability theory and item characteristic curve theory have been applied to the analysis of items and of the entire test. Reliability of CRT tests has been derived for test scores (Berk, 1984b) and for the classification decision (Subkoviak, 1984).

A major debate erupted in the latter 1970s over the issue of standards setting: Can standards be set and who sets them? Glass (1978) argued that the arbitrariness of standard setting results in poor educational practice and that test scores should be interpreted in other, unspecified ways. Numerous authors argued for standard setting, and several techniques, notably owed to Nedelsky, Angoff, and Ebel, have been developed. Shepard (1984) gives an overview of the issues and the techniques.

## REFERENCES

Berk, R. A. (Ed.). (1984a). *A guide to criterion-referenced test construction.* Baltimore, MD: Johns Hopkins University Press.

Berk, R. A. (1984b). Conducting the item analysis. In R. A. Berk (Ed.), *A guide to criterion-referenced test construction* (pp. 97–143). Baltimore, MD: Johns Hopkins University Press.

Glaser, R. (1963). Instructional technology and the measurement of learning outcomes. Some questions. *American Psychologist, 18,* 519–521.

Glaser, R., & Klaus, D. J. (1962). Proficiency measurement: Assessing human performance. In R. M. Gagne (Ed.). *Psychological Principles in Systems Development* (pp. 419–474) New York: Holt, Reinhart & Winston.

Glass, G. V. (1978). Standards and criteria. *Journal of Educational Measurmeent, 59,* 602–605.

Nitko, A. J. (1984). Defining "Criterion-Referenced Test." In R.

A. Berk (Ed.), *A guide to criterion-referenced test construction* (pp. 8–28). Baltimore, MD: Johns Hopkins University Press.

Popham, W. J., & Husek, T. R. (1969). Implications of criterion-referenced measurement. *Journal of Educational Measurement. 6*, 1–9.

Roid, G. H. (1984). Generating the test items. In R. A. Berk (Ed.), *A guide to criterion-referenced test construction* (pp. 49–77). Baltimore, MD: Johns Hopkins University Press.

Roid, G. H., & Haladyna, T. M. (1980). The emergence of an item-writing technology. *Review of Educational Research, 50*, 293–314.

Shepard, L. A. (1984). Setting performance standards. In R. A. Berk (Ed.), *A guide to criterion-referenced test construction* (pp. 169–198). Baltimore, MD: Johns Hopkins University Press.

Subkoviak, M. J. (1984). Estimating the reliability of mastery nonmastery classifications. In R. A. Berk (Ed.), *A guide to criterion referenced test construction* (pp. 267–291). Baltimore, MD: Johns Hopkins University Press.

VICTOR L. WILLSON
*Texas A&M University*

## MINIMUM COMPETENCY TESTING
## NORM REFERENCED TESTING

## CRONBACH, LEE J. (1916–    )

Lee J. Cronbach attended Fresno College, gaining his BA degree in 1934. After completing his MA degree at the University of California, Berkeley, in 1937, he attended the educational psychology program at the University of Chicago, gaining his PhD in 1940.

In 1940 Cronbach went to the State College of Washington as instructor in the department of psychology. He stayed there until 1946, advancing to the rank of assistant professor. During World War II, he was involved with the University of California division of War Research at San Diego, serving as research psychologist. After the war, Cronbach spent three years (1946–1948) as assistant professor of education at the University of Chicago. In 1948 Cronbach went to the University of Illinois, where he remained until 1964.

Cronbach is well known for his work on tests and measurement in psychology. He served the American Psychological Association as chairman of its Committee on Test Standards (1950–1953) and served on the Committee on Psychological Tests. His book, *Essentials of Psychological Testing*, is considered a classic in the field.

Cronbach is also well known for his work as coinvestigator on the Terman Study of Children of High Ability, a project he joined in 1963. That study was a long-term longitudinal study of intellectually gifted students. The study has demonstrated much of what we know of the lives and productivity of the intellectually gifted. It has dispelled many of the common stereotypes surrounding the intellectually gifted.

### REFERENCES

Cronbach, L. J. (1960). *Essentials of psychological testing*. (2nd ed.) New York: Harper & Brothers.

Cronbach, L. J., & Gleser, G. C. (1965). *Psychological test and personnel decisions*. (2nd ed.). Champaign: University of Illinois Press.

RAND B. EVANS
*Texas A&M University*

## CROSS CATEGORICAL PROGRAMMING

Public Law 94-142 identifies 11 categories of special-needs students. The categories include deaf, deaf-blind, hard of hearing, mentally retarded, multihandicapped, orthopedically impaired, other health impaired, seriously emotionally disturbed, specific learning disability, speech impaired, and visually impaired (Federal Register, 1977). The most common practice is for educational agencies to group children and youth based on these categories of exceptionality. For example, a school district may have a resource program that serves learning-disabled adolescents. It may also have two self-contained classrooms, one for moderately mentally retarded youngsters and one for severely emotionally disturbed youths.

Alternately, it is becoming increasingly common for school districts and special education cooperatives to group students with diverse handicaps in a single classroom or program. One classroom, for example, may serve both moderately mentally retarded and severely emotionally disturbed youths. A resource program may serve both mildly mentally retarded and learning-disabled individuals. The practice of grouping children and youth with diverse handicaps is referred to as cross categorical programming.

The rationale for developing cross categorical programs is based on theoretical and practical issues. With reference to the theoretical basis, a number of experts have written that students with different exceptional labels are more alike than they are different (Gardner, 1977; Schloss, 1984). Consequently, many of the teaching methods used today with one group of exceptional students have been, and continue to be, used with other groups (Hallahan & Kauffman, 1976). Emphasizing this point, the vast majority of categorical special education methods and materials texts contain similar teaching strategies (Hallahan & Kauffman, 1976). There has been a recent proliferation of generic methods texts that purport to contain instructional techniques suitable for a majority of handicapped individuals (Hammill & Bartell, 1986; Mercer & Mercer, 1985; Schloss & Sedlak, 1986).

Another compelling theoretical rationale for cross categorical instruction is provided by professionals with a behavioral orientation. These professionals emphasize that a common set of learning principles may be used to predict and influence the growth and development of individuals with a range of learning and behavioral features. As a result, the precise instructional needs of an individual should dictate instructional objectives and methodology, not general special education labels (Smith, Neisworth, & Hunt, 1984).

With reference to pragmatic issues, many school districts are not sufficiently large to staff separate classes for each category of exceptionality. For example, a rural school district may contain only 200 junior-high-school-aged students. Given current estimates, one would expect to find only nine learning-disabled youngsters, four mentally retarded youngsters, and one severely emotionally disturbed youth. It would not be feasible to staff three separate classrooms for each category. Consequently, the school district may choose to combine the 14 learners into one cross categorical classroom.

Cross categorical programs, or programs that serve students with diverse exceptional labels in the same setting, are becoming increasingly prevalent. Theoretically, categorical labels may be less useful for instructional grouping than for specific behavioral descriptions. Also, a common set of learning strategies may be useful for all handicapped persons. Many school districts find it to be administratively expedient to group children and youth with different exceptional labels.

## REFERENCES

Federal Register. (1977, Aug.). Washington, DC: U.S. Government Printing Office.

Gardner, W. I. (1977). *Learning and behavioral characteristics of exceptional children and youth: A humanistic behavioral approach.* Boston: Allyn & Bacon.

Hallahan, D. P., & Kauffman, J. M. (1976). *Introduction to learning disabilities: A psycho-behavioral approach.* Englewood Cliffs, NJ: Prentice-Hall.

Hammill, D. D., & Bartel, N. R. (1986). *Teaching children with learning and behavior problems.* (6th ed.). Boston: Allyn & Bacon.

Mercer, C. D., & Mercer, A. R. (1985). *Teaching students with learning problems.* Columbus, OH: Merrill.

Schloss, P. J. (1984). *Social development of exceptional children and youth.* Rockville, MD: Aspen Systems.

Schloss, P. J., & Sedlak, R. (1986). *Instructional methods for mildly handicapped children and youth.* Boston: Allyn & Bacon.

Smith, B. M., Neisworth, J. T., & Hunt, F. M. (1984). *The exceptional child: A functional approach.* New York: McGraw-Hill.

PATRICK J. SCHLOSS
*Pennsylvania State University*

## INDIVIDUALIZATION OF INSTRUCTION
## LEAST RESTRICTIVE ENVIRONMENT

## CROSS CULTURAL SPECIAL EDUCATION

Public Law 94-142 was implemented to provide equal educational opportunities for all handicapped children. Legislation and litigation continues to focus on educational opportunities for exceptional children, however, equal educational opportunity is not a reality for all. Many exceptional students continue to be discriminated against or receive inadequate services based soley on their race, social class, or creed (Heward & Orlansky, 1984).

In attempts to overcome these discriminating factors, it is necessary only to look at the basic premise on which special education relies; each individual student must be considered for his or her unique and special needs. Application of this premise across cultural boundaries will assist special educators in their attempt to provide equal educational opportunities for all exceptional children.

It seems unlikely that any teacher would possess the skills or background to deal adequately with the unique aspects of the many and varied cultures that may be encountered. As such, it may be useful to use as many community resources as possible in any attempt to meet these culturally diverse needs. King-Stoops (1980) devised a strategy for working with children of migrant farmers. She suggests that high school or college students with similar migrant backgrounds be used as aides or volunteers in the classroom setting. While King-Stoops speaks only to migrant children, it seems clear that such an approach could be easily and successfully used with a wide variety of cultures. While this may serve well in certain circumstances, this strategy may be impossible to implement in all settings. Heward and Orlansky (1984) suggest that the implementation of effective instructional techniques would likely benefit all students regardless of cultural background. It is important to note that effective instruction is based on and stems from effective assessment. The potential for culturally biased assessment must also be considered in developing an instructional plan and throughout the implementation of that plan.

## REFERENCES

Heward, W. L., & Orlansky, M. D. (1984). *Exceptional children.* Columbus, OH: Merrill.

King-Stoops, J. (1980). *Migrant education: Teaching the wandering ones.* Bloomington, IN: Phi Delta Kappa.

JOHN R. BEATTIE
*University of North Carolina,
Charlotte*

## CULTURAL BIAS IN TESTING
## SYSTEM OF MULTICULTURAL PLURALISTIC ASSESSMENT

## CROSS MODALITY TRAINING

Cross modality training refers to teaching the neurological process of converting information received through one input modality to another system within the brain. The process is also referred to as intersensory integration, intermodal transfer, and transducing. Cross modality integration problems have been linked historically to learning disabilities. It has been hypothesized that certain learners may process visual and auditory information accurately when each type of information is presented distinctly, but that those students may be deficient in tasks requiring them to shift or cross information between sensory systems (Chalfant & Scheffelin, 1969).

Reading, where the learner must relate visual symbols to auditory equivalents, is one academic domain for which cross modal integration is required. Johnson and Myklebust (1978) proposed that some reading disorders are due to an inability to make such conversions within the neurosensory system. It also has been proposed that disabilities such as apraxia, or the inability to plan and execute appropriate motor action, are related to inadequate cross modality integration because the child must convert an auditory memory of a word into motor output (Lerner, 1985).

Cross modality training programs have been devised to address intersensory integration problems. For example, Frostig (1965, 1968) advocated cross modality exercises, including activities such as describing a picture (visual to auditory), following spoken directions (auditory to motor), and feeling objects through a curtain and drawing their shapes on paper (tactile to visual-motor). Currently, scant research is available to support the use of cross modality training as a strategy to improve students' academic skills. Additionally, few, if any, tests are designed to assess cross-modal perception.

## REFERENCES

Chalfant, J., & Scheffelin, M. (1969). *Central processing dysfunction in children* (NINDS Monograph NO. 9). Bethesda, MD: U.S. Department of Health, Education, and Welfare.

Frostig, M. (1965). Corrective reading in the classroom. *Reading Teacher, 18*, 573–580.

Frostig, M. (1968). Education for children with learning disabilities. In H. Myklebust (Ed.), *Progress in learning disabilities*. New York: Grune & Stratton.

Johnson, D., & Myklebust, H. (1967). *Learning disabilities: Educational principles and practices*. New York: Grune & Stratton.

Lerner, J. W. (1985). *Learning disabilities: Theories, diagnosis, and teaching strategies*. Boston: Houghton Mifflin.

DOUGLAS FUCHS
LYNN S. FUCHS
*Peabody College, Vanderbilt University*

**FROSTIG REMEDIAL PROGRAM**
**MULTISENSORY INSTRUCTION**

# CROUZON'S SYNDROME (CRANIOFACIAL DYSOSTOSIS) (CS)

Crouzon's syndrome (CS) is believed to be a congenital disability that follows a pattern of autosomal dominance. The major physical characteristics are a result of premature closing of the skull, which causes cranial deformity, widely spaced eyes (which may protrude), and a misshapened face. The nasal bridge may be flat and the nose beaked with underdeveloped nasal sinuses. Malformation of the ear canals and eyes as a result of hypertension and orbital deformity is said to occur in 70 to 80% of the cases (along with optic atrophy); this may cause visual and hearing problems. The upper jaw and bones of the midface may be underdeveloped and the lower jaw may be prominent. Crowding, misalignment of upper teeth, and an enlarged tongue may cause some problems with eating and speech development. Higher incidence of infections also may occur, and in some cases congenital heart disease has been reported. Mental retardation may be noted in some children, but most have average mental abilities. In rare instances, spina bifida may be present (Carter, 1978).

Some related services may be necessary if visual, aural, and motor problems exist. Speech therapy will probably be required. In addition, psychological and guidance counseling may be required because of the physical appearance of the child. Mainstreamed placement with support services is often the proper educational approach for CS children.

## REFERENCES

Carter, C. (Ed.). (1978). *Medical aspects of mental retardation* (2nd ed.). Springfield, IL: Thomas.

Goodman, R., & Gorlin, R. (1977). *Atlas of the face in genetic disorders* (2nd ed.). St. Louis: Mosby.

SALLY L. FLAGLER
*University of Oklahoma*

# CRUICKSHANK, WILLIAM M. (1915–     )

William M. Cruickshank received his BA in 1937 from Eastern Michigan University, his MA in 1938 from the University of Chicago, and his PHD in 1945 from the University of Michigan.

Cruickshank was the founder and director of the Division of Special Education and Rehabilitation and distinguished professor at Syracuse University from 1946 to 1967. He subsequently became director of the Institute for the Study of Mental Health and Related Disabilities and professor of child and family health, psychology, and education at the University of Michigan from 1967 to the present.

William M. Cruickshank

The language develops as they attempt to imitate the speech sounds of adults. Since twins spend an inordinate amount of time together, they begin to understand approximations of mature language and reinforce each other for use of this lesser form of communication. Cryptophasia retards normal language development.

CECIL R. REYNOLDS
*Texas A&M University*

**LANGUAGE DELAYS**
**LANGUAGE DISORDERS**
**TWINS**

Since 1937 Cruickshank's main interests have been in the area of brain-injured children, neurologically handicapped children, and the neurophysiological characteristics of accurately defined learning-disabled children. Author of over 200 books, articles, and edited books (some of which are translated in several languages), Cruickshank's major publications include *Teaching Methods for Brain-Injured and Hyperactive Children* (1961), *Learning Disabilities in Home, School, and Community* (1977), and *Psychoeducational Foundations of Learning Disabilities* (1973).

Holder of six honorary doctoral degrees, he has taught in many countries and continues as a visiting professor and lecturer. As the founder, first president (1975–1985), and executive director of the International Academy for Research in Learning Disabilities, Cruickshank remains an international authority on the problems of learning-disabled children and youths worldwide.

## REFERENCES

Cruickshank, W. M. (1977). *Learning disabilities in home, school, and community* (rev. ed.). Syracuse, NY: Syracuse University.

Cruickshank, W. M., et al. (1961). *Teaching methods for brain-injured and hyperactive children.* Syracuse, NY: Syracuse University

STAFF

## CRYPTOPHASIA

Cryptophasia is a language disorder characteristic of twins. Twins often have delayed language development accompanied by what appears to be a jargon that only the twins understand. This jargon is a form of imitation of adult language with its own syntax, a type of "pidgin." The language may become elaborate and complex but remains, for the most part, understandable only to the twins.

## CRYSTALLIZED *v.* FLUID INTELLIGENCE

The theory of fluid and crystallized intelligence was proposed over 40 years ago by Raymond Cattell. It is based on the work of Charles Spearman (1932), who concluded that intelligence has a unitary, comprehensive ability common to all tests. He called his universal factor "g" for general ability factor.

This factor was the basis for the two-factor theory proposed by Cattell. This theory states that every mental test measures two factors: a general factor g, which is common to all tests, and a specific factor s, which is peculiar to each test (Cattell, 1963). Cattell defined intelligence by dividing the general ability factor into two categories. These are now designated crystallized intelligence ($Gc$) and fluid intelligence ($Gf$).

Cattell and Horn (1978) suggested that $Gf$ is the major measurable outcome of the influence of biological factors and that $Gc$ is the primary manifestation of educational and cultural influence. They indicated that fluid intelligence pertains to the individual ability to perceive and extract rules and relationships, while crystallized intelligence arises from the individual application of fluid intelligence in learning symbols, language, and mathematics. Cattell and Horn suggested that $Gf$ may be determined by heredity, and may be defined by tasks in which analytical ability is emphasized, while $Gc$ is determined by education, and is similar to achievement in that it is the accumulated knowledge of an individual.

Fluid and crystallized intelligence may be measured by determining a person's ability for learning and problem solving. $Gf$ can be measured with figure analogies, block designs, and memory span. $Gc$ would be the product of $Gf$ in content areas such as vocabulary, general information, authentic skill, and scholastic achievement (Cattell & Horn, 1978).

Research by Lansdell (1962) has indicated that $Gc$ and $Gf$ have been applicable in program planning for individuals with neurological impairment Lansdell found that the effects of general brain damage will be similar in both fluid and crystallized abilities, but more pronounced in fluid abilities. This may result in deficits in abstract reasoning as opposed to specific knowledge.

Other studies have attempted to link evidence and theory from cognitive psychology to individual differences. Kneif and James (1978) found that if students showed lower general ability, instruction focused on fluid ability would be more helpful for learning math concepts. If students showed higher general ability, instruction focused on crystallized ability would be more helpful. This indicates that we can, on occasion, capitalize on crystallized abilities.

Current research on *Gf* and *Gc* is focused on ability factors and cognitive processes (Lansman, 1982), primacy/recency components of short-term memory (Crawford & Stankov, 1983), and speed of information processing in sixth graders. This last study (Jenkinson, 1983) measured memory scanning and picture identification. It eliminated the effects of *Gf* and *Gc* and failed to support any causal relationship between fluid and crystallized abilities.

## REFERENCES

Cattell, R. B. (1963). Theory of fluid and crystallized intelligence: A critical experiment. *Journal of Educational Psychology, 54,* 1–22.

Cattell, R. B., & Horn, J. L. (1978). A check on the theory of fluid and crystallized intelligence. *Journal of Educational Measurement, 15,* 139.

Crawford, J., & Stankov, L. (1983). Fluid and crystallized intelligence and primacy/recency components of short-term memory. *Intelligence, 7,* 227–252.

Jenkinson, J. L. (1983). Is speed of information processing related to fluid or to crystallized intelligence? *Intelligence, 7,* 91–106.

Kneif, L. M., & James, M. A. (1978). Interaction of general, fluid, and crystallized ability and instruction in 6th grade mathematics. *Journal of Educational Psychology, 70,* 319–323.

Lansdell, H. (1962). Laterality of verbal intelligence in the brain. *Science, 135,* 922–923.

Lansman, M., Donaldson, G., Hunt, E., & Yantis, S. (1982). Ability factors and cognitive processes. *Intelligence, 6,* 347–386.

Spearman, C. (1932). *The abilities of man.* London: Macmillan.

STEVEN GUMERMAN
*Temple University*

## INTELLIGENCE
## INTELLIGENCE QUOTIENT

## CUED SPEECH

Cued speech was developed in 1967 by R. Orin Cornett at Gallaudet College in Washington, DC. It was designed to clarify ambiguity experienced by severely and profoundly hearing-impaired individuals relying on lipreading as a means of comprehending speech (Evans, 1982). During

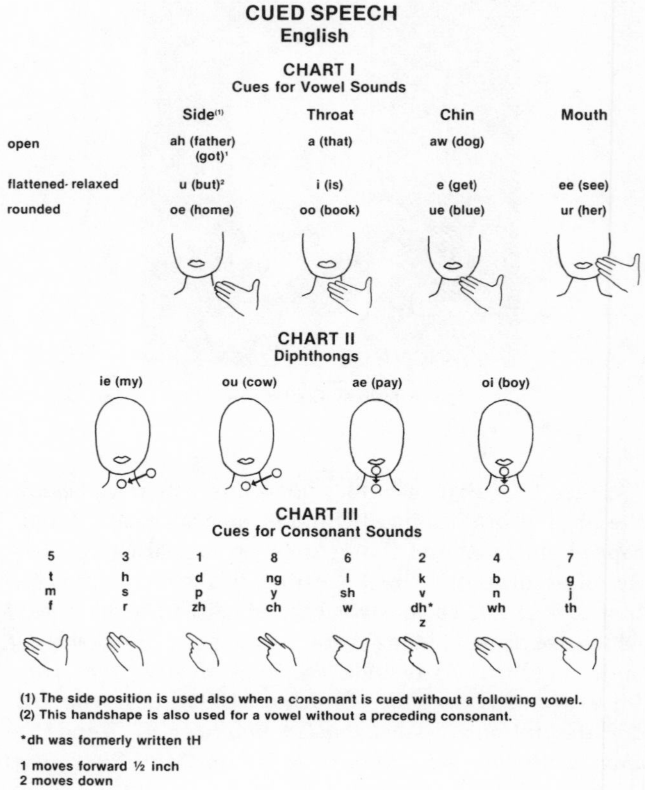

**CUED SPEECH**
English

**CHART I**
Cues for Vowel Sounds

| | Side(1) | Throat | Chin | Mouth |
|---|---|---|---|---|
| open | ah (father) (got)¹ | a (that) | aw (dog) | |
| flattened- relaxed | u (but)² | i (is) | e (get) | ee (see) |
| rounded | oe (home) | oo (book) | ue (blue) | ur (her) |

**CHART II**
Diphthongs

ie (my)   ou (cow)   ae (pay)   oi (boy)

**CHART III**
Cues for Consonant Sounds

| 5 | 3 | 1 | 8 | 6 | 2 | 4 | 7 |
|---|---|---|---|---|---|---|---|
| t | h | d | ng | l | k | b | g |
| m | s | p | y | sh | v | n | j |
| f | r | zh | ch | w | dh* z | wh | th |

(1) The side position is used also when a consonant is cued without a following vowel.
(2) This handshape is also used for a vowel without a preceding consonant.

*dh was formerly written tH

1 moves forward ½ inch
2 moves down

Cued speech—English.

speechreading, hearing-impaired individuals may confuse many sounds such as /p/, /m/, and /b/, because they are visually similar. Users of cued speech attempt to overcome this confusion by providing a visual supplement to information presented through speechreading.

This system includes 12 hand signals or cues (presented in the Figure). Four cues are hand positions that differentiate between groups of vowel sounds. A hand can be placed at the side of the face, the throat, the chin, or the corner of the mouth. Eight cues, based on American Sign Language (ASL) hand shapes, are hand configurations used to visually differentiate between groups of consonants (Wilbur, 1979). For example, a full hand represents the /m/, /f/, and /t/ sounds, whereas the extension of only the index finger represents the /d/, /p/, and /zh/ sounds. An auditory signal is visually supplemented by superimposing a consonant hand configuration on a vowel hand position. For example, the words *mitt* and *bit* may appear similar to the hearing-impaired speech reader; however, these words are cued differently. *Mitt* is cued with a full hand positioned at the throat, whereas *bit* is cued by placing a "b" hand shape at the throat.

Use of cued speech requires training for both the sender and the hearing-impaired individual. Cornett (1967) reports that an average of approximately 12 to 20 hours is required to develop proficient use of cued speech. Actually, time will vary with the individual learner and fluency comes with practice.

There are advantages and disadvantages associated with the use of cued speech. Its advantages include an adherence to the philosophy of oralism. Cued speech supplements information presented through speechreading; however, it cannot be used and understood in the absence of speech. In addition, use of cued speech has been associated with increases in speechreading accuracy (Clarke & Ling, 1976; Ling & Clarke, 1975), vocabulary, and intelligibility (Rupert, 1969). Disadvantages include the questionable phonetic competence of users, lack of transfer potential to reading (Wilbur, 1979), and an overdependence on cues (Clarke & Ling, 1976).

## REFERENCES

Clarke, B. R., & Ling, D. (1976). The effects of using cued speech: A follow-up study. *Volta Review, 78,* 23–34.

Cornett, R. O. (1967). Cued speech. *American Annals of the Deaf, 112,* 3–13.

Evans, L. (1982). *Total communication: Structure and strategy.* Washington, DC: Gallaudet College Press.

Ling, D., & Clarke, B. R. (1975). Cued speech: An evaluative study. *American Annals of the Deaf, 120,* 480–488.

Rupert, J. (1969). Kindergarten program using cued speech at the Idaho School for the Deaf. *Proceedings of the 44th Meeting of American Instructors of the Deaf,* Berkeley, CA.

Wilbur, R. B. (1979). *American Sign Language and sign systems.* Baltimore, MD: University Park Press.

MAUREEN A. SMITH
*Pennsylvania State University*

SIGN LANGUAGE
TOTAL COMMUNICATION

# CUISENAIRE RODS

Cuisenaire rods, named for the Belgian mathematician who designed them, consist of a set of small colored wooden rods of varying lengths. Gattegno, a British psychologist, popularized their use for both mathematics and language instruction through combinations of size and color. Karambelas (1971) described how the rods are used in language instruction.

There have been many studies of the use of Cuisenaire rods in mathematics instruction. Hawkins (1984) introduced the relationship in the Pythagorean theorem to low-ability seventh graders using Cuisenaire rods. Sweetland (1984) used the rods in teaching multiplication of fractions. LeBlanc (1976) designed a teacher preparation program in elementary school mathematics using Cuisenaire rods as the vehicle for actively engaging prospective teachers in mathematics with the goal of applying that math-

ematics in the elementary school. McDonald (1981) incorporated the rods in teaching binomial expressions and Ginther (1970) designed applications of the rods in advanced mathematics. Urion (1979) developed a Cuisenaire rod activity for generating approximations of pi. Knowles (1979) described the use of the rods and the calculator in examining decimals that result from division of whole numbers. Ewbank (1978) and Hater (1970) drew attention to the use of color in mathematics instruction including Cuisenaire rods, number lines, magic squares, and combinatorial problems. Davidson (1977) suggested uses for the rods in teaching mathematics from basic arithmetic through algebra.

Brooks (1977) described a game for two teams that uses dice, meter sticks, and Cuisenaire rods. The games provide practice in number facts, regrouping, and use of the rods in relation to the metric system. Shively and Holz (1975) used the rods to illustrate finite mathematical systems. Steiner (1975) designed activities with Cuisenaire rods, Dienes Blocks, and Papy's minicomputer. Sheffelin and Seltzer (1974) described a workshop for 300 participants on the use of Cuisenaire rods with learning-disabled children. Kamps (1970) tested portions of Piaget's model for the development of operational conservation and measurement of length with 102 second-grade students from three different cities. One group had participated in the American Association for the Advancement of Science—A Process Approach science program in grades Kindergarten through 2, one group had received limited experience in linear measurement, and one group had used Cuisenaire rods in grades 1 and 2. A Kruskal-Wallis one-way analysis of variance revealed no significant difference at the .05 level among the three groups of students.

## REFERENCES

Brooks, M. J. (1977). The one-meter dash. *Arithmetic Teacher, 24*(4), 327–328.

Davidson, P. S. (1977). Rods can help children learn at all grade levels. *Learning, 6*(3), 86–88.

Ewbank, W. A. (1978). The use of color for teaching mathematics. *Arithmetic Teacher, 26*(1), 53–57.

Ginther, J. L. (1970). An application of Cuisenaire rods in advanced mathematics. *School Science & Mathematics, 70*(3), 250–253.

Hater, M. A. (1970). Investigation of color in the Cuisenaire rods. *Perceptual & Motor Skills, 31*(2), 441–442.

Hawkins, V. J. (1984). The Pythagorean theorem revisited: Weighing the results. *Arithmetic Teacher, 32*(4), 36–37.

Kamps, K. G. (1970). An investigation of portions of a model for acquisition of conservation and measurement of length based on performance of selected second grade children on six Piaget-type tasks. *Research in Education* (Ann Arbor, MI: University Microfilms, SEO15002).

Karambelas, J. (1971). Teaching foreign languages "the silent way." *Association of Departments of Foreign Languages Bulletin, 3*(1), 41.

Knowles, F. (1979). Coloured rods, a calculator, and decimals. *Mathematics Teaching, 86,* 28–29.

LeBlanc, J. F. (1976). *Addition and subtraction Mathematics-methods program unit.* Bloomington, IN: Mathematics Education Development Center, Indiana University.

McDonald, J. R. (1981). Sharing teaching ideas: Factor cards: A device for GFC; A model of 3-space; Discovery in advanced algebra with concrete models. *Mathematics Teacher, 74*(5), 349–358.

Sheffelin, M. A., & Seltzer, C. (1974). Math manipulatives for learning disabilities. *Academic Therapy, 9*(5), 357–362.

Shively, J. E., & Holz, A. W. (1975). Finite operational systems for elementary students. *School Science & Mathematics, 75*(2), 191–196.

Steiner, H. G. (1975). Mathematical analysis of Piaget's grouping concept. Papy's minicomputer as a grouping. *International Journal of Mathematical Education in Science & Technology, 5*(2), 241–250.

Sweetland, R. D. (1984). Understanding multiplication of fractions. *Arithmetic Teacher, 32*(1), 48–52.

Urion, D. K. (1979). Using the Cuisenaire rods to discover approximations of pi. *Arithmetic Teacher, 27*(4), 17.

FREDRICKA K. REISMAN
*Drexel University*

# CULTURAL BIAS IN TESTING

The cultural test bias hypothesis is the contention that racial and ethnic group differences in mental test scores are the result of inherent flaws in the tests themselves. These flaws bias, or cause systematic error, in a manner that causes ethnic minorities to earn low scores. Mean differences in scores among groups are then interpreted as artifacts of the test and not as reflecting any real differences in mental abilities or skills.

Mean differences in mental test scores across race are some of the most well-established phenomena in psychological research on individual differences. One of the primary explanations of these differences is that they are produced by people who are reared in very different environments, with lower scoring groups having been relatively deprived of the quantity and quality of stimulation received in the formative years by higher scoring groups. Another explanation is that lower scoring groups reflect a difference in the genetic potential for intellectual performance. Most contemporary views take an environment X genetic interaction approach.

Cultural bias in testing has existed as a potential explanation at least since it was raised by Sir Cyril Burt (1921), with occasional papers on the issue appearing over the years. It was not widely accepted as a serious hypothesis until the late 1960s, when the Association of Black Psychologists (ABP) called for a moratorium on the use of psychological tests with minorities and disadvantaged students, particularly with regard to placement in special education programs. In 1969 the ABP issued an official policy statement encouraging parents of black children to refuse to allow their children or themselves to be evaluated on any achievement, intelligence, aptitude, or performance test.

The primary objections to the testing of minorities on the basis of race or cultural bias in the tests have been classified by Reynolds (1982a) into six categories as follows:

1. *Inappropriate Content.* Black or other minority children have not been exposed to the material on the test questions or other stimulus materials. The tests are geared toward white middle-class homes and values.

2. *Inappropriate Standardization Samples.* Ethnic minorities are underrepresented in the collection of normative reference group data. In the early years, it was not unusual for standardization samples of major tests to be all white.

3. *Examiner and Language Bias.* Since most psychologists are white and primarily speak only standard English, they intimidate blacks and other minorities. They are also unable to communicate accurately with minority children. Lower test scores for minorities, then, are said to reflect this intimidation and difficulty in the communication process, not lower ability levels.

4. *Inequitable Social Consequences.* As a result of bias in educational and psychological tests, minority group members, who are already at a disadvantage in the educational and vocational markets because of past discrimination, are disproportionately relegated to dead-end educational tracks and thought unable to learn. *Labeling effects* also fall into this category.

5. *Measurement of Different Constructs.* Related to item (1), this position asserts that the tests are measuring significantly different attributes when used with children from other than the white middle-class culture.

6. *Differential Predictive Validity.* While tests may accurately predict a variety of outcomes for white middle-class children, they fail to predict at an acceptable level any relevant criteria for minority group members. Corollary to this objection is a variety of competing positions regarding the selection of an appropriate, common criterion against which to validate tests across cultural groupings. Scholastic or academic attainment levels are considered by a variety of black psychologists to be biased as to criteria.

These actions by the ABP had several positive effects. Prior to the call for a moratorium on testing of minorities, little actual research existed in the area. Much research was prompted by the ABP position as it brought the race bias hypothesis to the forefront of explanations of race differences in intelligence. Also in response to this call for a moratorium, the American Psychological Association Board of Scientific Affairs had a committee appointed to study the use of tests with disadvantaged students. The committee, headed by T. Anne Cleary, gave its official report in the form of an article in American Psychologist (Cleary, Humphreys, Kendrick, & Wesman, 1975).

Research on race bias in testing was, and continues to be, of major importance to psychology as well as to society. The cultural test bias hypothesis is probably one of the most crucial scientific questions facing psychology today (Reynolds, 1981). If this hypothesis ultimately is accepted as correct, then the past 100 years or so of research into the psychology of individual differences (or differential psychology, the basic psychological science underlying all fields of applied psychology) must be dismissed as artifactual, or at least as confounded, since such research is based on standard psychometric methodology. Race bias in testing is being tested in the judicial courts as well as in the scholarly court of open inquiry. Two major court decisions, known as *Larry P.* (1979) and *PASE* (1980), have given conflicting opinions regarding the issues. Of two federal district courts, one decided that intelligence tests are racially biased and the other decided they are not biased.

Contrary to the position of the late 1960s, considerable research is now available regarding race bias in testing. For the most part, this research has failed to support the test bias hypothesis, revealing that (1) well-constructed, well-standardized educational and psychological tests predict future performance in an essentially equivalent manner across race for U.S.-born ethnic minorities; (2) the internal psychometric structure of the tests is essentially invariant with regard to race; and (3) the content of these tests is about equally appropriate across these groups.

Race bias in testing is one of the most controversial and violently emotional issues in psychology. It will not be resolved entirely on the basis of research and data, as tests have unquestionably been abused in their past use with minority groups. Much of the controversy centers around the placement of minority children in special education programs. Thus, special consideration must be given to ensure that the misuses and abuses of the past are thwarted by "intelligent testing" (Kaufman, 1979). A general review of race bias in testing can be found in Jensen (1980). Specialty reviews of race bias in employment testing have been done by Hunter et al. (1979), and of bias in the testing of children by Reynolds (1982a). A book-length debate of the issues can be found in Reynolds and Brown (1984). Methodology for investigating most aspects of cultural bias in testing relevant to special education is reviewed in Reynolds (1982b).

## REFERENCES

Burt, C. (1921). *Mental and scholastic tests*. London: P.S.Kiy.

Cleary, T. A., Humphreys, L. G., Kendrick, S. A., & Wesman, A.
(1975). Educational uses of tests with disadvantaged students. *American Psychologist, 30,* 15–41.

Hunter, J. E., Schmidt, F. L., & Hunter, R. (1979). Differential validity of employment tests by race: A comprehensive review and analysis. *Psychological Bulletin, 86,* 721–735.

Jensen, A. R. (1980). *Bias in mental testing*. New York: Free Press.

Kaufman, A. S. (1979). Intelligence testing with the WISC-R. *Interscience*. New York: Wiley.

Reynolds, C. R. (1981). In support of bias in mental testing and scientific inquiry. *Behavioral & Brain Sciences, 3,* 352.

Reynolds, C. R. (1982a). The problem of bias in psychological assessment. In C. R. Reynolds & T. B. Gutkin (Eds.), *The handbook of school psychology*. New York: Wiley.

Reynolds, C. R. (1982b). Methods for detecting construct and predictive bias. In R. A. Berk, (Ed.), *Handbook of methods for detecting test bias*. Baltimore, MD: Johns Hopkins University Press.

Reynolds, C. R., & Brown, R. T. (1984). *Perspectives on bias in mental testing*. New York: Wiley.

CECIL R. REYNOLDS
*Texas A&M University*

**LARRY P.**
**MARSHALL *v.* GEORGIA**
**PASE *v.* HANNON**


# CULTURAL DEPRIVATION

See EARLY EXPERIENCE AND CRITICAL PERIODS; See SOCIOECONOMIC STATUS.


# CULTURE-FAIR TEST

The items on many widely used tests of intellectual ability appear to require knowledge and experience that is widespread in western civilization but lacking in other cultures. If one wishes to use a test with diverse cultural groups or to compare the performance of people in different cultures, a test containing culture-specific items clearly lacks content validity. In response to this difficulty, Cattell (1933) developed a test consisting of novel problem-solving items that do not occur in any culture. He called it a culture-free test of intelligence. In later editions the name was changed to culture-fair intelligence test in recognition of the fact that any test must depend on certain basic cultural experiences. Later, Cattell (1963) developed the theory of fluid and crystallized intelligence to distinguish between the basic abilities measured by a culture-reduced test and the accumulated cultural learning measured by a culture-loaded test.

The basic idea of a culture-fair test is to measure general intelligence with items that do not appear to depend on experiences that differ among the cultural groups to be tested. By use of items involving figural analogies, matrices, mazes, gestalt completion, and the like, it is possible to construct psychometrically adequate scales that correlate very highly with more culture-loaded tests of intellectual ability within an appropriate cultural group. The presumption is that these tests continue to measure the same ability when used with other cultural groups for which the culture-loaded test is not appropriate.

In the recent controversy over differences in intelligence among racial and ethnic groups within the United States, the issue of test bias has become a major point of contention. It has frequently been asserted that the observed differences in average test scores of racial groups are the result of different cultural experiences, and that this causes differences in performance on the culture-loaded tests. In other words, the tests are biased or not culture-fair. The evidence relating to this issue has been reviewed in detail by Jensen (1980) and in Reynolds and Brown (1984). A critical part of the evidence is that apparently culture-fair tests show the same pattern of group differences as do more culture-loaded tests.

## REFERENCES

Cattell, R. B. (1933). *The Cattell intelligence tests, scales 1, 2 and 3*. London: Harrap.

Cattell, R. B. (1963). Theory of fluid and crystallized intelligence: A crucial experiment. *Journal of Educational Psychology, 54,* 7–22.

Jensen, A. R. (1980). *Bias in mental testing*. New York: Free Press.

Reynolds, C. R., & Brown, R. T. (Eds.) (1984). *Perspectives on bias in mental testing*. New York: Plenum.

ROBERT C. NICHOLS
DIANE JARVIS
*State University of New York,*
*Buffalo*

CULTURAL BIAS IN TESTING

# CULTURAL-FAMILIAL RETARDATION

The term cultural-familial retardation has long been used to indicate mild retardation of unknown etiology that is associated with a family history of mild retardation, and a home environment that provides adverse experiences that are believed to inhibit mental development. The word cultural suggests an environmental basis; familial implies a genetic origin. Synonyms include sociocultural or psychosocial, intrinsic, subcultural, endogenous, and familial retardation. Individuals in this population usually have IQs in the range of mild retardation (about 55 to 70), have no demonstrable biological pathology to account for the retardation, usually have a parent or sibling who is re-tarded, and come from low socioeconomic status homes (Westling, 1986).

The specific cause of cultural-familial retardation is uncertain, but it probably involves interactive factors; each factor alone is not sufficient to explain the intellectual and behavioral deficits. The present consensus is that the interactions among psychosocial, environmental, and genetic factors are so great and begin so early in life that one cannot place responsibility on any single cause in individual cases (Grossman, 1983). A few decades ago it was believed that this type of retardation was inherited, and environmental factors were discounted. Polygenic inheritance is suggested because this type of retardation is not randomly distributed among the poverty stricken, but most often found in families where the mother is retarded.

Mild retardation is less common in children born to healthy, mature women than in children born to adolescent mothers, women who are malnourished, or women who get poor prenatal care and are thus especially vulnerable to infections, trauma, and prenatal intoxications. Children born to such mothers have a relatively high incidence of prematurity and/or low birth weight, factors that are related to problems in physical and intellectual development. However, most children born to such women, or born prematurely, are not retarded.

Specific environmental factors include extreme malnourishment during early infancy, severe early social isolation, very large families with closely spaced births, very harsh or abusive discipline, severe neglect, marked parental ignorance about health care, chaotic or highly disorganized family life, and extremely inadequate educational opportunities. However, the severe malnutrition during late pregnancy and early infancy that causes retardation in underdeveloped countries is virtually unknown in America and the other factors listed are found in families where there is no retardation.

Educable or mildly retarded (EMR) children without known biological cause for the retardation follow the normal sequence of physical and intellectual development. Retarded children go through the usual Piaget sequences of cognitive development, but more slowly. Very few reach the formal operations stage that normal children reach around age 12 (Inhelder, 1968; Zigler & Balla, 1982). Usually EMR students master basic academic skills. On intelligence and academic achievement tests they tend to have low scores on most subtests of the scales, in contrast to learning-disabled children, who may score low on one or two subtests (and who are more likely to come from middle-class families). The EMR students require more trials to learn new skills than normal children, perhaps because of attentional and short-term memory difficulties or failure to develop effective strategies for learning and problem solving (Warren & Taylor, 1984).

In the past, many dropped out of school early, but now most complete high school, usually in special education programs that focus on occupational skills during adolescence. It has been estimated that although poor children make up about 80% of the educable mentally retarded students in schools, only about 10% of American children living in poverty will be classified as mildly retarded (Haywood, Burns, Arbitman-Smith, & Delclos, 1984). Children from such families may also contribute to normal, slow-learning, and gifted populations (Richardson, 1968).

Some psychologists and educators have proposed that much of the responsibility for retardation in culturally disadvantaged families is with the environment outside the home, particularly the educational system. Mildly retarded students have been called "six-hour retarded children," implying that they are retarded only during school hours; however, there is little evidence for assuming that those children cope as well as others outside of school. Criticism of schools is partially based on the fact that prevalence studies have shown a higher percentage of identified cases during school years than before or after those years (Richardson, 1968). School demands may tax the abilities of mildly retarded individuals more than some activities of later life; for example, good reading comprehension and high mathematics are important, but they are not essential for some occupations. If we classify as retarded any adults who are competitive and consistently employed full-time, many former EMR students would not be considered retarded as adults, whatever an earlier classification, and whatever their IQs as adults. Levine (1985) reported a high correlation between stress and anxiety, especially for unemployed mildly retarded adults; therefore, personality factors as well as job skills and IQ may be relevant in the classification of adults.

Some sociologists and educators have argued that children in this group are not really retarded, but that intelligence tests are biased against poor children, especially minority ones. This argument seems to ignore the fact that some children from the same families and communities are successful with the same test items that others fail. Careful empirical evaluations of tests and test items offer little support for claims of test bias in well-constructed, properly standardized tests (Reynolds, 1983). Modifying (raising) scores because of economic disadvantages would merely make it more difficult for low-scoring and disadvantaged students to meet eligibility criteria for services they need.

Many misconceptions about cultural-familial retardation stem from interpretations and misinterpretations of the work of Henry Herbert Goddard. Publicity after the publication of *The Kallikaks* (Goddard, 1912) led to fear and prejudice toward retarded persons, especially those from poor families. The Kallikak study was part of a large study of over 300 families in which feeblemindedness was reported in two or more members of the same primary family for several generations. Goddard described an attractive young Caucasian woman to whom he gave the pseudonym of Deborah Kallikak (adapted from Greek words meaning good and bad) and her relatives in two lines of descent traced from Martin Kallikak, a Revolutionary War soldier. One line, from Martin's marriage to

a prominent woman, was filled with outstanding citizens. Deborah's line, said to be from Martin's mating with a barmaid, had feeblemindedness, poverty, shiftlessness, illegitimacy, and alcoholism in each generation. Descriptions of Deborah's mental development and her skills as an adult make it clear that she functioned at a retarded level; she could do embroidery and simple carpentry, and manage second-grade academic work. Broad media coverage of Goddard's conclusion that retardation was hereditary was overgeneralized and assumed to apply to all persons from low-income families. Interpretations of Goddard's work influenced state sterilization laws and the placement of state schools for the retarded in remote areas as protection for the schools and for society. By 1950 practices and law had changed. Goddard's work was reevaluated by modern research criteria, and was sharply criticized (Smith, 1985). During the 1960s and 1970s, some psychologists took a strong environmentalist position.

Children in the cultural-familial group look much like other children and are usually not recognized as retarded by their families during preschool years. They are more likely than others to need eyeglasses and to have frequent illnesses or other health problems (perhaps related to inadequate health care and habits).

Follow-up studies of former students in EMR classes indicate that as adults, many meet the demands of society more easily than they did school demands. From 40 to 80% are employed as adults, but employment is likely to be in unskilled or semiskilled work and incomes may be at or below the poverty level. Whether similar adults who received no special education fare as well is uncertain, but the evidence suggests that they may not.

Edgerton et al. studied the community life of retarded adults. They used repeated interviews and direct observations in 1960–1961, 1972–1973, and 1983 (Edgerton, Bollinger, & Herr, 1984). Case histories and descriptions of the original 48 persons described in *The Cloak of Competence* (Edgerton, 1967) indicate that those studied belong to the cultural-familial group. Edgerton found them to be on the lower end of the continuum on almost every index of economic and social functioning. They lived in slum areas, under deplorable conditions, had very little job security and few marketable skills. Almost all had found a "benefactor" (spouse, relative, or friend) to help them cope with the stresses of everyday life such as losing jobs or friends, having illnesses and financial problems. Life was not easy for them, but many of the 15 adults (mean age 56) remaining in 1983 reported at least moderate satisfaction with life.

Since mid-century, extensive efforts have been made to interrupt the vicious cycle of poverty, social incompetence, and prejudice associated with cultural-familial retardation. The establishment of the federal Office of Economic Opportunity (OEO) in the 1960s illustrates a massive effort to provide health, educational, and social intervention. The OEO's most visible and enduring program is Project Head Start: a preschool program for young children. Federal and state programs have had impact, but have not even approached the goal of reducing mental retardation by half, as was predicted in 1962 by the President's Panel on Mental Retardation. Project Head Start is now one of the largest health service providers for young children in America. It has been very successful in health areas, but its effects on intellectual functioning and academic achievement are less certain. However, there have been positive results in federally funded research in rigorously controlled experimental preschool programs. In addition, a collaborative study of the pooled data from 11 major studies on the long-term effects of early educational intervention projects designed to prevent the progressive decline in cognitive skills of children from low-income families (primarily minorities) suggests that carefully planned early intervention may have a positive effect on school competence. The competence was measured by assignment to special education programs or repeated grades, the development of abilities as measured by standardized tests, and the effect of attitudes and values of children and on families, both measured by questionnaires (Lazar & Darlington, 1982).

Experimental educational interventions designed to reverse retardation and other severe learning problems in school-age students are exemplified by studies using the Instrumental Enrichment "mediated learning experience" approach developed in Israel (Feuerstein, Rand, Hoffman, & Miller, 1980) and used at several North American sites by Haywood of Vanderbilt University (Haywood & Arbitman-Smith, 1981). Both the American and the Israeli investigators reported positive effects from the use of Instrumental Enrichment, particularly for adolescents with severe educational disadvantages.

Studies of socially competent children who are at high risk for retardation may provide especially useful information. Werner and Smith (1982) described the "resilient" children in a 20-year study of 698 multiracial children in Hawaii. The resilient children grew to successful, competent adulthood despite poverty, parents with little formal education, and a good deal of stress. Factors associated with resilience were fewer serious childhood illnesses, development of more internal locus of control, well-spaced families of less than five children, and high-achievement motivation.

Das (1973), who has lived in several cultures, has suggested that the technology and cultural demands of society may be important factors in determining whether individuals are classified as mildly retarded. He noted that "biases" in the West emphasize verbal abilities and reasoning, and that the educational systems selectively refer children showing deficiencies in these areas for special education. School experiences are an integral part of a child's growth and development; they transmit the values of the majority culture. Cultural-familial children generally are less adept in language and reasoning than those from higher socioeconomic status families; thus, they start school at a disadvantage. In a technological society in which high-level verbal and reasoning skills are needed and valued, these children begin at a disadvantage that might not be such a problem in a simpler society. It is unlikely that we will soon prevent cultural-familial retardation in America, but progress is being made in reducing associated medical problems and perhaps ameliorating some of the severe learning and educational problems of children from families in which the risk of cultural-familial retardation is high.

## REFERENCES

Das, J. P. (1973). Cultural deprivation and cognitive competence. In N. R. Ellis (Ed.), *International review of research in mental retardation*. Vol. 6. New York: Academic.

Edgerton, R. B. (1967). *The cloak of competence: Stigma in the lives of the mentally retarded.* Berkeley: University of California Press.

Edgerton, R. B., Bollinger, M., & Herr, B. (1984). The cloak of competence: After two decades. *American Journal of Mental Deficiency, 88,* 345–351.

Feurerstein, R., Rand, Y., Hoffman, M. B., & Miller, R. (1980). *Instrumental enrichment.* Baltimore, MD: University Park Press.

Goddard, H. H. (1912). *The Kallikak family: A Study in the heredity of feeble-mindedness.* New York: Macmillan.

Grossman, H. J. (Ed.). (1983). *Classification in mental retardation.* Washington, DC: American Association on Mental Deficiency.

Haywood, H. C., & Arbitman-Smith, R. (1981). Modification of cognitive functions in slow learning adolescents. In P. Mittler (Ed.), *Frontiers of knowledge in mental retardation: Social, educational, and behavioral aspects.* Baltimore, MD: University Park Press.

Haywood, H. C., Burns, S., Arbitman-Smith, R., & Delclos, V. R. (1984). Forward to fundamentals; Learning and the 4th R. *Peabody Journal of Education, 61*(3), 6–35.

Inhelder, B. (1968). *The diagnosis of reasoning in the mentally retarded* (translated by W. B. Stephens). New York: Day.

Lazar, I., & Darlington, R. (1982). Lasting effects of early education: A report from the consortium for longitudinal studies. *Monographs of the Society for Research in Child Development, 47*(serial nos. 2–3).

Levine, H. G. (1985). Situational anxiety and everyday life experiences of mildly mentally retarded adults. *American Journal of Mental Deficiency, 90,* 27–83.

Reynolds, C. R. (1983). Test bias: In God we trust; all others must have data. *Journal of Special Education, 17,* 241–260.

Richardson, S. A. (1968). The influence of social-environmental and nutritional factors on mental ability. In N. S. Scrimshaw & J. E. Gordon (Eds.), (1968). *Malnutrition, Learning, and Behavior.* Cambridge, MA: MIT Press.

Smith, J. D. (1985). *Minds made feeble: The myth and legacy of the Kallikaks.* Rockville, MD: Aspen.

Warren, S. A., & Taylor, R. L. (1984). Education of children with learning problems. *Symposium on learning disorders, pediatric clinics of North America.* Philadelphia: Saunders.

Werner, E. E., & Smith, R. S. (1982). *Vulnerable but invincible: A longitudinal study of resilient children and youth.* New York: McGraw-Hill.

Westling, D. L. (1986). *Introduction to Mental Retardation*. Englewood Cliffs, NJ: Prentice-Hall.

Zigler, E., & Balla, D. (1982). Introduction: The developmental approach to mental retardation. In E. Zigler & D. Balla. *Mental retardation: The development-difference controversy*. Hillside, NJ: Erlbaum.

SUE ALLEN WARREN
*Boston University*

**EDGERTON, R.**
**EDUCABLE MENTALLY RETARDED**
**GODDARD, H. H.**
**MENTAL RETARDATION**
**TRAINABLE MENTALLY RETARDED**

## CUMULATIVE DEFICIT HYPOTHESIS

The cumulative deficit hypothesis was originally advanced to account for the progressive decline in IQ with age observed in English canal boat children (Gordon, 1923) and in children in the mountains of Virginia (Sherman and Key, 1932). The hypothesis is that cultural disadvantage has a constant inhibiting effect on intellectual development so that its effects accumulate over time, resulting in a progressively increasing gap between advantaged and disadvantaged children. The basic hypothesis has been elaborated on by Deutsch (1967) and others to suggest that later learning depends on skills developed earlier in life. The lack of prerequisite skills makes it increasingly difficult for disadvantaged children to keep up with their age group; it also makes the cumulative deficit increasingly difficult to change. This line of reasoning has led to an emphasis on beginning compensatory education programs at an early age.

Beginning with Klineberg (1963), the cumulative deficit hypothesis has been offered by a number of writers as an explanation for the average ability-test-score differences observed between black and white populations in the United States. The controversy surrounding the racial issue has focused increased attention on the hypothesis and on the evidence concerning whether or not the test-score differences between blacks and whites increases with age. The literature has been reviewed by Jensen (1974), who concluded that, when all of the methodological complexities are taken into account, there is no evidence of an increasing gap in ability between blacks and whites.

Most studies of cumulative deficit have used cross-sectional data in which children of different ages are tested at the same time. For example, the influential *Equality of Educational Opportunity* study (Coleman, et al., 1966) was specifically designed to test the cumulative deficit hypothesis. Large representative samples of white, black, Asian, and American Indian school children in rural and urban areas of all regions of the United States were tested in first, third, sixth, ninth, and twelfth grades. Some early interpretations of this study concluded that a cumulative deficit had been found, since the report emphasized the increasing lag of minorities in grade-level-equivalent scores. For example, the report stated, "at grade 6 the average Negro is approximately 1½ years behind the average white . . . at grade 12, he is approximately 3¼ years behind the average white" (p. 273). However, the report correctly pointed out that grade-equivalent scores are not an equal-interval scale, and they are more variable for all students at higher grade levels. When appropriately expressed in standard-deviation units, the average score for blacks was about one standard deviation below that for whites at all grade levels. The only increasing deficit in standard-deviation units in this study was for blacks in the rural southeastern United States. The critical issue in evaluating a cross-sectional study is whether the samples of children of different ages are truly comparable. Differences between advantaged and disadvantaged children in rates of school dropout, migration, age-in-grade, and other factors can affect the results.

More dependable conclusions can usually be drawn from longitudinal studies in which the same children are tested repeatedly at different times over a period of years. For example, Rosenfeld and Hilton (1971) compared groups of black and white pupils tested on a battery of scholastic achievement tests at grades 5, 7, 9, and 11. The results were not consistent for all tests, but an increasing gap between blacks and whites was found for both verbal and quantitative abilities. The authors suggested that the increasing deficit for blacks could be due to the fact that most of the whites were in an academic curriculum, while most of the blacks were in a nonacademic curriculum.

Another methodology for investigating the cumulative deficit hypothesis is to compare scores of older and younger siblings. By using siblings within the same family, many of the sources of error in cross-sectional and longitudinal studies are effectively controlled. For example, Jensen (1974) studied IQ differences among all sibling pairs in elementary grades in Berkley, California, controlling for birth order and family size. About 40% of the sibling pairs were black. The black siblings showed a small increasing gap in verbal IQ compared with the white siblings, but there was no increasing gap for nonverbal IQ.

The increasing gap between advantaged and disadvantaged groups is characteristic of a specific population at a specific time, like the birthrate or the average family income. Its presence or absence at one time and place is no guarantee that it will or will not be observed at another. When Jensen (1977) repeated his sibling analysis using data from a rural community in the southeastern United States, where the cultural difference between blacks and whites is much greater than it is in Berkley, a substantial increasing gap between the races was found.

From all of these studies one might conclude that extreme environmental disadvantage, as may exist for canal boat children and black children in the rural Southeast, seems to result in a cumulative deficit. The cumulative deficit hypothesis, however, does not seem sufficient to explain most of the group differences that are observed.

## REFERENCES

Coleman, J. S., Campbell, E. Q., Mood, A., Hobson, C. J., McPartland, J., Wenfeld, F. D., & York, R. L. (1966). *Equality of educational opportunity*. Washington, DC: U.S. Office of Education.

Deutsch, M. (1967). *The disadvantaged child*. New York: Basic Books.

Gordon, H. (1923). *Mental and scholastic tests among retarded children* (Education Pamphlet 44, Board of Education, London). London: Her Majesty's Stationary Office.

Jensen, A. R. (1974). Cumulative deficit: A testable hypothesis? *Developmental Psychology, 10,* 996–1019.

Jensen, A. R. (1977). Cumulative deficit in IQ of blacks in the rural south. *Developmental Psychology, 13,* 184–191.

Klineberg, O. (1963). Negro-white differences in intelligence test performance: A new look at an old problem. *American Psychologist, 18,* 198–203.

Rosenfeld, M., & Hilton, T. L. (1971). Negro-white differences in adolescent educational growth. *American Educational Research Journal, 8,* 267–283.

Sherman, M., & Key, C. B. (1932). The intelligence of isolated mountain children. *Child Development, 3,* 279–290.

ROBERT C. NICHOLS
DIANE JARVIS
*State University of New York,
Buffalo*

## POVERTY, RELATIONSHIP TO SPECIAL EDUCATION
## SOCIOECONOMIC IMPACT OF DISABILITIES
## SOCIOECONOMIC STATUS

# CURRICULUM

Educational curriculum is what students learn, or the content of instruction (Howell, in press). Historically, the curriculum of U.S. public education was specified in broad, global terms, addressing abstract notions such as Americanization and instilling of democratic values in youths (Mulhern, 1959). In the twentieth century, however, developments in learning theory such as Thorndike's demonstration of the specificity of transfer promoted a reconceptualization of learning from concurrent strengthening of global faculties to sequential mastery of numerous, definite, and particularized skills and knowledge (Fuchs & Deno, 1982). This reconceptualization has led to alternative ways of specifying school curricula for distinct behavioral outcomes (Bloom, Hastings, & Madaus, 1971). Current curriculum statements typically represent carefully sequenced, calibrated, and organized sets of tasks, regularly called objectives (Johnson, 1967).

In special education, as in regular education, curriculum is derived from an analysis of the needs of society. This analysis, however, renders considerably different instructional focuses for mildly and severely handicapped students. For the mildly handicapped, analysis of the needs of society results in a curriculum similar, if not identical, to that of normally developing pupils; it includes curricular tasks such as reading, writing, and mathematics. For the more severely handicapped, this analysis results in a curriculum that addresses basic survival skill requirements. These alternative educational focuses often are referred to as developmental curriculum (which identifies tasks for normally performing children) (Snell, 1983) and functional curriculum (which addresses skills necessary for ultimate attainment of self-sufficiency) (Holvoet, Guess, Mulligan, & Brown, 1980).

For the mildly handicapped student, the curriculum may be resequenced, broken down into smaller tasks, reorganized, or taught via dramatically different instructional strategies. Two alternative ways of addressing curriculum for the mildly handicapped have been referred to as the task analytic approach and the ability training model (Ysseldyke & Salvia, 1974). With the task analytic approach, the curriculum is approached by breaking down terminal tasks into sets of subskills, which are addressed separately and sequentially and ultimately synthesized into final tasks of the curriculum (Howell, in press). With the ability training model, hierarchies of abilities that are prerequisite to mastery of basic reading, writing, and mathematics skills such as perceptual-motor or psycholinguistic abilities are hypotheseized. These abilities are addressed before the standard school curriculum is taught. In both cases, however, the ultimate curriculum, or the final educational objective, remains constant and is consonant with the curricular goals of the mainstream educational environment.

In contradistinction, the functional curriculum of the more severely handicapped population is determined more individually. It addresses objectives that (1) represent the practical or functional skills most likely to be needed currently or in the near future; (2) span the four instructional domains of domestic, leisure/recreational, community, and vocational skills; (3) are suitable for the student's chronological age; and (4) address the pupil's current performance levels and are reasonably thought to be attainable (Snell, 1983). The basic assumptions of a functional curriculum for the severely handicapped are that the school's responsibility is to teach skills that optimize a person's independent and responsible functioning in society (Hawkins & Hawkins, 1981). For the severely handicapped, these skills must be chosen from a group of tasks and activities that have a high probability of being required and that increase self-sufficiency (Brown et al., 1979).

## REFERENCES

Bloom, B. S., Hastings, J. T., & Madaus, G. F. (1981). *Handbook on formative and summative evaluation of student learning.* New York: McGraw-Hill.

Brown, L., Branston, M. B., Hamre-Nietupski, S., Pumpian, I., Certo, N., & Gruenewald, L. (1979). A strategy for developing chronological age appropriate and functional curricular content for severely handicapped adolescents and young adults. *Journal of Special Education, 13*, 81–90.

Fuchs, L. S., & Deno, S. L. (1982). *Developing goals and objectives for educational programs.* Washington, DC: American Association of Colleges for Teacher Education.

Hawkins, R. P., & hawkins, K. K. (1981). Parental observation on the education of severely retarded children: Can it be done in the classroom? *Analysis & Intervention in Developmental Disabilities, 1*, 13–22.

Holvoet, J., Guess, D., Mulligan, M., & Brown, F. (1980). The Individualized Curriculum Sequencing model (II): A teaching strategy for severely handicapped students. *Journal of the Association for the Severely Handicapped, 5*, 337–351.

Howell, K. W. (in press). Direct assessment of academic performance. In L. S. Fuchs & D. Fuchs (Eds.), Linking assessment to instruction. *School Psychology Review.*

Johnson, M. (1967). Definitions and models in curriculum theory. *Educational Theory, 7*, 127–140.

Mulhern, J. (1959). *A history of education* (2nd ed.). New York: Ronald.

Snell, M. E. (1983). *Systematic instruction of the moderately and severely handicapped* (2nd ed.). Columbus, OH: Merrill.

Ysseldyke, J. E., & Salvia, J. (1974). Diagnostic prescriptive teaching: Two models. *Exceptional Children, 41*, 181–185.

LYNN S. FUCHS
*Peabody College, Vanderbilt University*

## ANNUAL GOALS
## CURRICULUM FOR THE MILDLY HANDICAPPED
## CURRICULUM FOR THE SEVERELY HANDICAPPED

## CURRICULUM, AGE APPROPRIATE

See AGE APPROPRIATE CURRICULUM.

## CURRICULUM-BASED ASSESSMENT (CBA)

With curriculum-based assessment (CBA), instructional materials and course content are employed as the basis for testing. During the past decade, CBA has been used with increasing frequency to assess students' learning progress and to evaluate the effectiveness of educational programs (Fuchs & Fuchs, 1986).

Although commercial norm-referenced tests continue as a mainstay in special education placement and program evaluation activity (Goh, Teslow, & Fuller, 1981), these traditional tests suffer from some important weaknesses, including (1) poor psychometric properties and inadequate conceptualization (Ysseldyke, 1979); (2) poor relationship to instructional content and educational objectives (Jenkins & Pany, 1978; Zigmond & Silverman, 1984); and (3) insufficient alternative forms to permit ongoing progress monitoring.

As an alternative to commercial norm-referenced tests, CBA addresses at least the last two problems (Fuchs, 1986). With CBA, measurement procedures are designed to match students' programmatic objectives. Alternative test forms are drawn directly from curricula specified in objectives and are administered repeatedly. Student progress data are evaluated with reference to the performance criteria specified in objectives and with respect to classroom peers' progress within the same curriculum. Individualized programs are tested formatively and modified over time as required to ensure effective instructional programs and attainment of objectives.

Therefore, CBA is based on the following set of assumptions: (1) the instructional and curricular validity of CBA is stronger than with traditional assessment methods; (2) each student's needs are defined best in terms of the context of local educational programs; (3) the essential measure of educational success is the student's progress in the school's curriculum; and (4) the appropriate reference group with which to judge the adequacy of students' rates of curricular progress is their local school district peers' progress through the same material (Deno, 1985).

Research indicates that at least some forms of ongoing CBA can be used effectively to address several different assessment functions. It can be used reliably to identify pupils in need of special education (Marston, Tindal, & Deno, 1984; Tindal & Marston, 1986), to specify target skills for students and write useful individual educational program goals and objectives (Fuchs, Deno, & Mirkin, 1984), to monitor pupil progress toward goals and formatively develop effective instructional programs (Fuchs & Fuchs, in press a), and to evaluate the effectiveness of special education programs on an individual and district-wide basis (Tindal & Marston, 1986).

## REFERENCES

Deno, S. L. (1985). Curriculum-based measurement: The emerging alternative. *Exceptional Children, 52*, 219–232.

Fuchs, L. S. (1986). Monitoring progress among mildly handicapped pupils: Review of current practice and research. *Remedial & Special Education, 7*(5), 5–12.

Fuchs, L. S., Deno, S. L., & Mirkin, P. K. (1984). The effects of frequent curriculum-based measurement and evaluation on pedagogy, student achievement and student awareness of learning. *American Educational Research Journal, 21*, 449–460.

Fuchs, L. S., & Fuchs, D. (1986). Curriculum-based assessment of progress toward long- and short-term goals. *Journal of Special Education, 20*, 69–82.

Fuchs, L. S., & Fuchs, D. (in press c). Effects of systematic formative evaluation: A meta-analysis. *Exceptional Children*.

Goh, D. S., Teslow, C. J., & Fuller, G. B. (1981). The practices of psychological assessment among school psychologists. *Professional Psychology, 12*, 699–706.

Jenkins, J. R., & Pany, D. (1978). Standardized achievement tests: How useful for special education? *Exceptional Children, 44*, 448–453.

Marston, D., Tindal, G., & Deno, S. L. (1984). Eligibility for learning disability services: A direct and repeated measurement approach. *Exceptional Children, 50*, 554–555.

Tindal, G., & Marston, D. (1986). Approaches to assessment. In J. Torgeson & B. Wong (Eds.), *Psychological and educational perspectives on learning disabilities*. Orlando, FL: Academic.

Ysseldyke, J. E. (1979). Psychoeducational assessment of decision making. In J. E. Ysseldyke & P. K. Mirkin (Eds.), *Proceedings of the Minnesota Roundtable Conference on Assessment of Learning Disabled Children* (Monograph No. 8) (pp. 15–36). Minneapolis: University of Minnesota Institute for Research on Learning Disabilities.

Zigmond, N., & Silverman, R. (1984). Informal assessment for program planning and evaluation in special education. *Educational Psychologist, 19*, 163–171.

LYNN S. FUCHS
DOUGLAS FUCHS
*Peabody College, Vanderbilt
University*

AGE-APPROPRIATE CURRICULUM
ASSESSMENT
NORM-REFERENCED TESTING

# CURRICULUM FOR THE MILDLY HANDICAPPED IN SPECIAL EDUCATION

The definition of curriculum varies in the literature but in the broadest sense, it is used in the field in two ways: (1) to indicate a plan for the education of learners, and (2) to identify a field of study. The word curriculum comes from a Latin root meaning race course; it can be regarded as the standardized ground covered by students in their race for a diploma (Zais, 1976).

Special education curriculum for the mildly handicapped learner consists of learning tasks, activities, or assignments that are directed toward increasing a student's knowledge or skills in a specific content or subject area. It is the special educator's task to identify the differences between the regular and special education curriculum and to make educational decisions based on available assessment data.

The decision to provide variation in content may be less significant in educating mildly handicapped learners than the decision to provide variation in the conditions under which learning can be best facilitated. A critical issue involves the determination of the need for compensatory versus remedial curricula (Case, 1975). Many of the strategies and techniques used with mildly handicapped learners in special education overlap with Chapter I, other remedial programs, and regular education.

Mainstreaming has encouraged efforts to help the over 70% of special education students who spend at least part of the day in regular classrooms to master the regular curriculum or "face curricular isolationism" (O'Connell-Mason & Raison, 1982).

This special education curriculum must be coordinated with regular education curriculum, which in turn must be modified or changed at times to accommodate students with different learning styles. The curricula must be designed to meet the particular needs and characteristics of the individuals who are to learn various contents.

Howell, Kaplan, and O'Connell (1979) indicate that to date, the research has not demonstrated the superiority of one type of curriculum modification over another. However, there are a number of general types of modifications that have been found useful: (1) eliminate or reduce the subjects in the student's curriculum; (2) develop or identify an alternative curriculum; (3) alter expectations for the quantity or quality of work; (4) teach subject matter more slowly; (5) teach only the most essential subject matter; (6) develop a parallel curriculum; (7) provide a supplemented curriculum; or (8) adjust materials and/or response modes.

Growth in the field of special education curriculum for the mildly handicapped learner has become an integral part of regular education. It is clear that the similarities are greater than the differences. The same principles and procedures, with some modifications, can be used to instruct all children. All children can reach their potential given the opportunity, effective teaching, and proper resources (Berdine & Blackhurst, 1985).

## REFERENCES

Berdine, W. H., & Blackhurst, A. E. (1985). *An introduction to special education*. Boston: Little, Brown.

Case, R. (1975). Gearing the demands of instruction to the developmental capacities of the learner. *Review of Educational Research, 45*, 3–9.

Howell, K. W., Kaplan, J. S., & O'Connell, C. Y., (1979). *Evaluating exceptional children: A task analysis approach*. Columbus, OH: Merrill.

O'Connell-Mason, C., & Raison, S. B. (1982). *Curriculum assessment and modification*. Washington, DC: American Association of Colleges for Teacher Education.

Zais, R. S. (1976). *Curriculum: Principles and foundations*. New York: Harper & Row.

DEBORAH A. SHANLEY
*Medgar Evers College, City
University of New York*

AGE-APPROPRIATE CURRICULUM
MAINSTREAMING
TASK ANALYSIS

# CURRICULUM FOR THE SEVERELY HANDICAPPED

Educational curriculum is what students learn, or the content of instruction (Howell, in press). Historically, the curriculum of U.S. public education was specified in broad, global terms, addressing abstract notions such as Americanization and instilling of democratic values in youths (Mulhern, 1959). In the twentieth century, however, developments in learning theory such as Thorndike's demonstration of the specificity of transfer promoted a reconceptualization of learning from concurrent strengthening of global faculties to sequential mastery of numerous, definite, and particularized skills and knowledge (Fuchs & Deno, 1982). This reconceptualization has led to alternative ways of specifying school curricula for distinct behavioral outcomes (Bloom, Hastings, & Madaus, 1971). Current curriculum statements typically represent carefully sequenced, calibrated, and organized sets of tasks, regularly called objectives (Johnson, 1967).

In special education, as in regular education, curriculum is derived from an analysis of the needs of society. For the severely handicapped individual, this analysis results in curriculum that addresses basic survival skill requirements. This educational focus, which represents an alternative to the normal or developmental educational curriculum (Snell, 1983), is referred to as a functional curriculum. The basic assumptions of a functional curriculum for the severely handicapped are that the school's responsibility is to teach skills that optimize a person's independent and responsible functioning in society (Hawkins & Hawkins, 1981) and that, for the severely handicapped, these skills must be chosen from a group of tasks and activities that have a high probability of being required and that increase self-sufficiency (Brown et al., 1979).

This functional curriculum is determined individually and addresses objectives that (1) represent practical or functional skills most likely to be needed currently or in the near future; (2) are suitable for the student's chronological age; (3) address the pupil's current performance levels and are reasonably thought to be attainable; and (4) span four instructional domains (Snell, 1983).

The four domains of instructional content are domestic, leisure/recreational, community, and vocational. The domestic domain includes skills performed in and around the home, including self-care, clothing care, housekeeping, cooking, and yard work. In the leisure-recreational domain are skills needed to engage in spectator or participant activities performed for self-pleasure. Skills required in the community domain include street crossing, using public transportation, shopping, eating in restaurants, and using other public facilities such as parks. The vocational domain addresses skills necessary for employment such as appropriate work dress and demeanor, assembly line behavior, interviewing for jobs, completing work applications, and punctuality.

The process of determining appropriate functional curricula on an individual basis has been conceptualized as comprising five steps (Brown et al., 1979): (1) selecting curriculum domains; (2) identifying and surveying current and future natural environments; (3) dividing the relevant environments into subenvironments; (4) inventorying these subenvironments for the relevant activities performed there; and (5) examining the activities to isolate the skills required for their performance.

To address the functional curriculum for the severely handicapped, instructional strategies typically have been based on behavioral methodology. The intructional process begins with a descriptive analysis of the environmental events subsequent to, antecedent to, or during recurring behavioral events, with the purpose of identifying possible discriminative and reinforcing stimuli. Then, a task analysis of terminal objectives is conducted; in it subskills necessary for successful mastery of the final objectives are identified. Next, subskill instructional objectives are established and initial teaching strategies are specified. Then ongoing assessments of pupils' progress toward goals are collected as the instructional hypothesis is implemented. Finally, ongoing assessment data are evaluated and employed formatively to redesign instructional procedures in order to increase the probability of goal attainment.

## REFERENCES

Bloom, B. S., Hastings, J. T., & Madaus, G. F. (1981). *Handbook on formative and summative evaluation of student learning.* New York: McGraw-Hill.

Brown, L., Branston, M. B., Hamre-Nietupski, S., Pumpian, I., Certo, N., & Gruenewald, L. (1979). A strategy for developing chronological age appropriate and functional curricular content for severely handicapped adolescents and young adults. *Journal of Special Education, 13,* 81–90.

Fuchs, L. S., & Deno, S. L. (1982). *Developing goals and objectives for educational programs.* Washington, DC: American Association of Colleges for Teacher Education.

Hawkins, R. P., & Hawkins, K. K. (1981). Parental observation on the education of severely retarded children: Can it be done in the classroom? *Analysis & Intervention in Developmental Disabilities, 1,* 13–22.

Holvoet, J., Guess, D., Mulligan, M., & Brown, F. (1980). The Individualized Curriculum Sequencing model (II): A teaching strategy for severely handicapped students. *Journal of the Association for the Severely Handicapped, 5,* 337–351.

Howell, K. W. (in press). Direct assessment of academic performance. In L. S. Fuchs and D. Fuchs (Eds.), Linking assessment to instruction. *School Psychology Review.*

Johnson, M. (1967). Definitions and models in curriculum theory. *Educational Theory, 7,* 127–140.

Mulhern, J. (1959). *A history of education* (2nd ed.). New York: Ronald.

Snell, M. E. (1983). *Systematic instruction of the moderately and severely handicapped* (2nd ed.). Columbus, OH: Merrill.

LYNN S. FUCHS
*Peabody College, Vanderbilt University*

CURRICULUM
CURRICULUM FOR THE MILDLY HANDICAPPED
FUNCTIONAL INSTRUCTION
FUNCTIONAL SKILLS

## CURRICULUM IN EARLY CHILDHOOD INTERVENTION

The curricula used in early intervention vary depending on the needs of the children served. Generally, however, they address developmental areas critical to the child's psychological/behavioral maturation and later school success (Bailey & Wolery, 1984). Early intervention curricula are likely to emphasize motor, cognitive, language, social, and self-help skill development. Early intervention instructors will likely address the development of gross and fine motor skills, eating and self-help skills, toileting, dressing, and undressing. A distinction has been made between developmental and functional approaches in early childhood curricula. The first emphasizes developmental progress; the second is more concerned with training for independent functioning (Bailey & Wolery, 1984).

The purposes of early intervention curricula are to develop, habilitate, or accelerate young children's development. In the case of handicapped children, the intent is to minimize the effects of children's disabilities on later development and learning and academic performance. With mildly to moderately handicapped children, early curriculum is more likely to emphasize developmental training. With more severely handicapped children, the emphasis is likely to be on functional training, for example, facilitating independent functioning.

There is considerable interaction between the various curriculum areas in any particular instructional approach. For example, eating training involves fine motor, social, and communication skill development as well as self-help training. A variety of curricula for early intervention are currently available. Few of them are distinguished by validation efforts. Bailey, Jens, and Johnson, (1983) have published a recent review of infant curricula.

### REFERENCES

Bailey, D. B., Jens, K. G., & Johnson, N. (1983). Curricula for handicapped infants. In F. Fewell & S. G. Garwood (Eds.), *Educating handicapped infants*. Rockville, MD: Aspen.

Bailey, D. B., Jr., & Wolery, M. (1984). *Teaching infants and preschoolers with handicaps*. Columbus, OH: Merrill.

MARY MURRAY
*Journal of Special Education,
Ben Salem, Pennsylvania*

EARLY IDENTIFICATION OF HANDICAPPED CHILDREN
PRESCHOOL ASSESSMENT
PRESCHOOL SPECIAL EDUCATION

## CUSTODIAL CARE OF THE HANDICAPPED

Organized care for the handicapped goes back no more than 150 years. If we consider the handicapped to include the insane, mentally infirm, orphans, the poor, and those found to be criminal in nature, then we can easily locate the second American Revolution as during the Jackson presidency (Rothman, 1971). Prior to this period, care of handicapped individuals was managed primarily by families, neighbors, and friends of the handicapped. In the case of criminals, the offenders were put to death.

During the Jacksonian period large institutions were constructed in Boston, New York, and Philadelphia. Almshouses for the poor were constructed in smaller communities. Governmental agencies and the wealthy provided funds for the erection of insane asylums. Soon the medical profession was actively using the asylums as an integral part of care for the insane. It was also during this time that penitentiaries proliferated throughout the East Coast states. In addition, homes built with public funds and other types of asylums were constructed for orphans and delinquent children. in Rothman's (1971) *Discovery of the Asylum*, we find ample documentation of reform during the Jacksonian period. As Rothman has stated, this period could appropriately be referred to as "the age of the asylum."

Interested investigators have claimed that the growth of institutions in America for the insane, orphans, poor, criminals, and, one could hypothesize, the mentally retarded, paralleled the growth of psychiatry. It was 300 years prior to the advent of the first U.S. institutions that we find King Henry VIII taking the old monastery of St. Mary of Bethlehem in London, England, and reserving it solely for the care of the mentally ill. One can assume that at that time little was known about any differentiation of diagnosis between the mentally disturbed and the mentally retarded. Thus, the idiot and the insane were probably treated much the same. St. Mary's provided deplorable conditions and inadequate care for the infirm. Other asylums soon appeared in Mexico (1566), France (1641), Moscow (1764), and Vienna (the famous Lunatics' Tower, 1784). All of these institutions were the forerunners of similar edifices in America. Many of the first institutions were nothing more than a modification of a penal institution. An example of such early primitive care can be seen in the description of Lunatics' Tower:

> It was an ornately decorated tower within which were square rooms. The doctors and keepers lived in the square rooms, while the patients were confined in the spaces between the walls of the square rooms and the outside of the tower. The patients were put on exhibit to the public for a small fee. (Coleman, 1984)

An account (Coleman, 1984) of the LaBicetre Hospital in Paris is said to be representative of most institutions for the insane throughout the eighteenth century.

The patients were ordinarily shackled to the walls of their dark, unlighted cells by iron collars which held them flat against the wall and permitting little movement. Oftimes, there were also iron hoops around the waists of the patients and both their hands and feet were chained. Although these chains usually permitted enough movement that the patients could feed themselves out of bowls, they often kept them from being able to lie down at night. Since little was known about dietetics, and the patients were presumed to be animals anyway, little attention was paid to whether they were adequately fed or to whether the food was good or bad. The cells were furnished only with straw and were never swept or cleaned; the patient remained in the midst of all the accumulated ordure. No one visited the cells except at feeding time, no provision was made for warmth, and even the most elementary gestures of humanity were lacking. (modified from Selling, 1943)

What is striking to the reader is the never ending stream of trends in the care of the handicapped, often instituted in the name of progress. In fact, care was generally for profit, coercion, incarceration, or medical validation. Historical accounts indicate that while benevolence was the primary motivation for the creation of institutional care, society also needed to seek stability from social disruption.

Humanitarian reform of institutions both in Europe and America occurred on a small scale during the eighteenth century. Pinel's experiments at LaBicetre included removing the chains, adding sunlit rooms, extending kindness, and including freedom to exercise. Reactions by patients were recorded as overwhelmingly positive by even the most seriously disturbed (Zilboorg & Henry, 1941, p. 3232). William Tuke, an English Quaker, also provided a humane environment, at the York Retreat in England, while in America Benjamin Rush, the founder of American psychiatry, provided care in a more benevolent manner. Such examples of humane treatment, however, are isolated, as most institutions continued to treat their residents much like animals and such labels as "snake pits" and "schools for unimprovable or unteachable idiots" were not uncommon.

Notable among Americans who created a moral cognizance of existing deplorable conditions was Dorothea Dix (1802–1887). In her famous *Memorial*, submitted to the U.S. Congress in 1848, she remarked that she had observed

more than 9000 idiots, epileptics, and insane in the United States, destitute of appropriate care and protection . . . bound with galling chains; bowed beneath fetters and heavy iron balls attached to drag chains, lacerated with ropes, scourged with rods, and terrified beneath storms of execration and cruel blows; now subject to jibes and scorn and torturing tricks; now abandoned to the most outrageous violations. (Zilboorg & Henry, 1941, pp. 583–584)

This message was repeated often as Dix and her followers

became instrumental in improving conditions throughout the United States, Canada, and Scotland. She is credited with establishing 32 hospitals. Unfortunately, most asylums continued to be unfit for humans.

It was not until the late 1800s that the mentally retarded were beginning to be seen as a group separate, at least in name, from other of society's deviant groups. There is reason to suspect that the mentally retarded had often been punished severely and in some instances hanged for criminal activities beyond their comprehension. The first institutions constructed solely for the mentally retarded seem to have been built for educational purposes. These temporary boarding school-type facilities were established primarily for the "improvables." The schools rejected admittance to those who could not be cured and returned to their families. Even the famed Fernald State School sought to create an institution that would not serve uncurables. When the effort to educate the mentally retarded and return them to society failed, retarded individuals' care deteriorated. The retarded were viewed as subhuman and unable to be taught productive skills. The failure was probably due to the unrealistically high expectations of complete recovery.

The perception of failure and disappointment prevailed after these early attempts at cure failed. Along with this perception came a dramatic change in the care of retarded individuals. People that had the potential to be developmentally changed were treated accordingly, while those thought of as having subhuman qualities were treated as animals.

State schools and institutions soon gave way to asylums. In 1893 the Custodial Asylum for Unteachable Idiots was founded in Rome, New York. Governor Butler of Massachusetts said:

A well-fed, well-cared for idiot is a happy creature. An idiot awakened to his condition is a miserable one. . . . It is earnestly urged that the best disposal to be made of this large class of the permanently disabled is to place it in custodial departments of institutions for the feebleminded persons . . . under the same merciful system that inspires hope and help for the lowest of humanity. (Kerlin, 1888 quoted in Kugel & Shearer, 1976)

It was also during this time (1885) that Illinois built a facility to provide for custodial care; the states of Iowa and Connecticut followed. Intentions were noble. There was an implied protectiveness associated with each state's appropriation for an asylum (Kugel & Shearer, 1976, p. 52). History, however, has recorded the opposite to have been the case.

In the early 1900s perceptions of the mentally retarded again changed and custodial care was said to have deteriorated. The moron and imbecile were soon made the source of all social ills. Leaders in the field such as M. W. Barr, a past president of the American Association for Mental Deficiency (AAMD), issued indictments of imbeciles as a threat to home and community. Calling for action, Johnson (1901) spoke bluntly when he stated that in order to prevent the propagation of idiocy and imbecility it might be "necessary to kill them or to resort to the knife" (Kugel & Shearer, 1976, p. 57). With attitudes such as these, it is little wonder that retarded individuals received deplorable care for the next 50 years.

The severely retarded were gradually dehumanized and moved to the back wards. These wards as well as other asylum cells were filthy and overcrowded. Such facilities were often referred to as the land of the living dead. In the fall of 1965 Senator Robert Kennedy visited several of his state's institutions; he was appalled at the conditions he encountered. Additional investigations by Blatt (1970) further delineated the horrors: "in toilets, I frequently saw urinals ripped out, sinks broken and toilet bowls backed up . . . I found incredible overcrowding" (p. 13). The national average cost of caring for the mentally retarded in 1962 was less than $5 per day per patient. Some states managed to lower that to less than $2.50 per day.

Blatt (1970) further described conditions in several institutions. He saw 7 foot by 7 foot isolation cells that seldom included beds, washstands, or toilets. Restraints were common. There were alarming shortages of staff and one supervisor for each 100 severely retarded individuals was not uncommon. It is small wonder that patients were locked up, restrained, or sedated. The odors of the wards and dayrooms were overpowering even though rooms were hosed down daily to move the human excretions to sewers located in the center of the rooms.

Blatt's (1966) photographic essay, "Christmas in Purgatory" did much to alert professionals and the general public to the deplorable conditions existing for the institutionalized retarded. Those pictures of the stark gray, high walls, barred windows, beds pushed head to head, patients lying unclothed in feces, and rooms full of young children, left their mark. The ensuing years have seen a movement away from those custodial conditions. Even in the 1960s, many institutions such as the Seaside, also chronicled by Blatt, were providing residential treatment that encouraged more and better trained staff, family participation, fewer closed wards, sunlit areas, medical and dental attention, and daily hygienic care. Within the last 20 years, the mentally retarded have been part of a deinstitutionalization movement unlike that of any era in U.S. history. Residential homes for the handicapped are commonplace and the U.S. educational system now provides especially designed curricula to teach basic independent living skills. In addition, government-supported projects have proliferated throughout the United States and now include not only programs for assessment and training but opportunities in employment that were nonexistent only a few years ago.

## REFERENCES

Blatt, B., & Kaplan, F. (1966). *Christmas in purgatory*. Boston: Allyn & Bacon.

Blatt, B. (1970). *Exodus from pandemonium*. Boston: Allyn & Bacon.

Coleman, J. C., Butcher, J. N., & Carson, R. C. (1984). *Abnormal psychology and modern life* (7th ed.). Glenview, IL: Scott, Foresman.

Kugel, R. B., & Shearer, A. (Eds.). (1976). *Changing patterns in residential services for the mentally retarded*. Washington, DC: President's Committee on Mental Retardation.

Rothman, D. J. (1971). *The discovery of the asylum*. Boston: Little, Brown.

Selling, L. S. (1943). *Men against madness*. New York: Garden City Books.

Zilboorg, G., & Henry, G. W. (1941). *A history of medical psychology*. New York: Norton.

RICHARD E. HALMSTAD
*University of Wisconsin, Stout*

**DEINSTITUTIONALIZATION
INSTITUTIONALIZATION**

# CYLERT

Cylert (Pemoline) is a mild central nervous system stimulant medication that is used in the management of hyperactive children. While the onset of effectiveness of Cylert has been found to be slower than that of some other central nervous system stimulants, it also has been found to have a longer half-life, 12 hours compared with 4 hours for other stimulants (Ross & Ross, 1982). Because of this longer half-life, Cylert need be administered only on a once-daily basis. For hyperactive children, this eliminates the social stigma associated with taking medication at school. In addition, parents are better able to supervise drug administration, thereby reducing the possibility of drug abuse and increasing the probability of compliance. Another advantage of Cylert therapy over other psychostimulants in pediatric populations is its long duration of therapeutic action without sympathomimetic cardiovascular effects. In fact, therapeutic effects of Cylert have been found to be similar to those of amphetamines and methylphenidate (Ross & Ross, 1982). Clinical trials have yielded data to indicate that Cylert enhances short-term memory, attentiveness to cognitive and academic tasks, and social functioning (Ross & Ross, 1982).

As with other psychostimulants, one concern with Cylert administration has been the occurrence of side effects. While mild side effects, including insomnia, headaches, anorexia, abdominal pains, dizziness, and nausea have been reported, of greater concern is the elevation of liver enzymes, which sometimes necessitates the withdrawal of medication. Severe dysphoric effects following the cessation of Cylert also have been reported in some isolated cases (Brown, Borden, Spunt, & Medenis, 1985).

## REFERENCES

Brown, R. T., Borden, K. A., Spunt, A. L., & Medenis, R. (1985). Depression following Pemoline withdrawal in a hyyperactive child. *Clinical Pediatrics, 24,* 174.

Ross, D. M. & Ross, S. A. (1982). *Hyperactivity: Current issues, research and theory* (2nd ed.). New York: Wiley-Interscience.

RONALD T. BROWN
*Emory University School
of Medicine*

## HYPERACTIVITY
## MEDICAL MANAGEMENT

## CYSTIC FIBROSIS

Cystic fibrosis is a fatal genetic disorder that involves almost all organ systems. Pulmonary infection and obstruction generally cause most of the complications and are ultimately the cause of death (Doershuk & Stern, 1982). Repeated hospitalizations and crises, financial burdens, as well as the fatal nature of the disease itself, have an extreme emotional impact on the child and his or her family. Parents must deal with the anxiety, depression, and self-blame associated with having a terminally ill child with an illness that is genetically determined. These parents may become overprotective and have difficulty allowing the child to engage in age-appropriate activities.

Frequent hospitalizations along with physical difficulties such as chronic cough, clubbed fingertips, shortness of breath, and short stature clearly set the cystic fibrosis child apart from his or her peers. Although the disease apparently has little effect on intellectual functioning, the child may fall behind his or her peers academically if home instruction is not instituted during absences from school. Adolescence may be a particularly difficult period for both child and parents. The increasingly debilitating nature of the disease may thwart the child's natural striving for independence and make planning for the future difficult (Wright, Schaefer, & Solomons, 1979).

## REFERENCES

Doershuk, C. F., & Stern, R. C. (1982). Cystic fibrosis. In S. S. Gellis & B. M. Kagan (Eds.), *Current pediatric therapy* (Vol. 10 pp. 207–218). Philadelphia: Saunders.

Wright, L., Schaefer, A. B., & Solomons, G. (1979). *Encyclopedia of pediatric psychology.* Baltimore, MD: University Park Press.

ALICE G. FRIEDMAN
*University of Oklahoma Health
Sciences Center*

LOGAN WRIGHT
*University of Oklahoma*

ADAPTED PHYSICAL EDUCATION
CYSTIC FIBROSIS FOUNDATION
HEALTH MAINTENANCE PROCEDURES

## CYSTIC FIBROSIS FOUNDATION

The Cystic Fibrosis Foundation is a voluntary, nonprofit health organization that supports research about and treatment for cystic fibrosis. The foundation was founded in 1955 by a small group of parents of children with cystic fibrosis. The foundation currently supports more than 125 centers throughout the United States that provide specialized diagnosis and long-term, high-quality care for victims of cystic fibrosis.

The foundation actively supports research activities and professional education in the area of cystic fibrosis. Recent research efforts have focused both on developing more effective treatments for cystic fibrosis and on identifying the basic genetic defect that is responsible for the disease. The foundation also supports a fellowship program to train clinical and basic scientists in an effort to encourage scholars to focus on the complications of cystic fibrosis (Cystic Fibrosis Foundation Annual Report, 1985). The Cystic Fibrosis Foundation has both state and local chapters. To locate a local chapter, contact the headquarters of the foundation at the following address: Cystic Fibrosis Foundation, 6000 Executive Boulevard, Suite 510, Rockville, MD 20852, (301) 881-9130.

## REFERENCE

Cystic Fibrosis Foundation. (1985). *Annual report for the fiscal year 1985.* Rockville, MD.

ALICE G. FRIEDMAN
*University of Oklahoma Health
Sciences Center*

## CYTOMEGALOVIRUS

The cytomegalovirus is a filterable DNA virus in the family of herpes viruses. It is responsible for the infectious disease known as cytomegalic inclusion disease. The virus is not easily eliminated and persists in host tissues for months, years, or even a lifetime. It produces a chronic infection with a variable incubation period, outcome, and course. The infection may be a significant form of congenital disease in newborns whose immune system is incompletely developed or in adults who are immunosuppressed.

There are two patterns of infection: localized and generalized. In the localized form, inclusion bodies are found only in the salivary glands; this clinical entity sometimes is referred to as generalized salivary gland disease. The second, generalized, form is represented in two principal types: that accompanied by necrotizing and calcifying encephalitis and that associated with enlargement of the spleen and the liver, lymphadenopathy, and blood dyscrasias. There is increasing recognition of the association of this infection with acquired immune deficiency syndrome (AIDS). Where there is significant cerebral damage, there is often ocular involvement.

It is generally agreed that the virus is widespread; the localized form of the disease is both frequent in occurrence and asymptomatic. Ten to thirty-two percent of autopsied infants show evidence of localized disease. Although the generalized form of the disease may occur in adults, it is characteristically seen in infants and children, occurring in up to 1% of children. Cytomegalovirus has been detected in up to 90% of immunosuppressed kidney transplant patients; active infection may predispose these patients to bacterial superinfection and transplant rejection. The virus also alters the immune system, although apparently only during the acute phase of infection; the mechanism for immunosuppression is not fully understood.

Because many organs may be affected in generalized disease, the clinical features are variable. Usually there is an acute or subacute febrile illness, and infants are likely to have been premature. There may be severe jaundice and bleeding tendencies, and enlargement of the spleen and liver is frequent. Pneumonia and renal involvement often are present. In the encephalitic form, hydrocephalus and chorioretinitis occur. Most infected infants succumb to encephalitic disease. Among those who survive, mental or motor retardation, microcephaly, seizures, and ocular involvement are common. Ocular lesions include microcornea, chorioretinitis, pseudocolobomas of the retina, retinal hemorrhage, pale optic discs, uveitis, keratoconjunctivitis, and dacryoadenitis.

The diagnosis is best established by recovery of the virus from the urine, saliva, or aqueous humor of the eye. Congenital toxoplasmosis is difficult to differentiate, but radiologic evidence of periventricular calcification suggests cytomegalic inclusion disease. Other diseases to be differentiated include generalized bacterial infection, herpes simplex encephalitis, congenital liver deformities, and diseases of the reticuloendothelial system. No treatment has been effective in controlling this disease. Several antiviral medications used to control the herpes virus have been tried with minimal success.

## REFERENCES

Friedlaender, M. H. (1963). Immunology of infections systemic diseases that affect the eye. In T. D. Duane & E. A. Jaeger (Eds.), *Biomedical foundations of Ophthalmology*. Hagerstown, MD: Harper & Row.

Walsh, F. B., & Hoyt, W. F. (1969). *Clinical neuro-ophthalmology*. Baltimore, MD: Williams & Wilkins.

GEORGE R. BEAUCHAMP
*Cleveland Clinic Foundation*

## HERPES

# D

## DAILY LIVING SKILLS

The term daily living skills refers to those skills that individuals use in their personal self-care and occasionally in their interactions with others. A wide range of specific behaviors may be included under each of these headings. The skills might appear to be very straightforward (e.g., grasping a brush handle) or extremely complex (e.g., developing healthy eating habits). The range of skills and behaviors that are often included under the rubric of daily living skills is best conceptualized as points along a continuum. At one end of the continuum essential daily living skills might include toileting, feeding, and dressing. Moving along the continuum toward increasing independence, a second level of skills could include hand washing, toothbrushing, etc. Daily living skills that might be taught at a higher level of independence include menstrual hygiene, shaving, and other more complex tasks.

As the student masters behaviors that are taught at fundamental levels, these newly acquired behaviors become the building material for future skill development. The end result of effective instruction in the skills that students use day to day is seen in the student's mastery of more complex conceptually oriented skills (e.g., sexual awareness, diet planning) that frequently subsume previously mastered skills. The goal in teaching these skills is to assist the exceptional needs learner in the development of more normative abilities. As these skills are taught and mastered, the student is more likely to gain access to more normative age-appropriate environments and interactions with others.

Nonexceptional children typically learn these skills (as a matter of course) through the instruction and modeling of parents, siblings, and peers, and through their own natural exploration of their environment. The exceptional child, however, often has handicaps that impair his or her ability to observe, explore, internalize, and use the skills that might otherwise be acquired. Physical handicaps may prevent the exceptional child from making use of information that he or she is able to absorb. The emotionally disordered child may exhibit problem behaviors that actively interfere with the learning of daily living skills. In addition, some exceptional children, notably those in institutions and segregated classrooms, may lack role models and/or access to the type of environments that allow the sort of exploration and experimentation necessary for the acquisition of daily living skills. Indeed, some environments actually discourage the development of such skills by prohibiting, in the interest of efficiency, neatness, etc., the exceptional individual from becoming involved in any aspect of his or her own care. Thus, the exceptional child often requires systematic instruction and/or various forms of environmental adaptation to enable him or her to reach the full development of potential in the area of daily living skills. As Bigge and O'Donnell (1976) have pointed out, not only is it necessary to teach exceptional children daily living skills in order to enable them to cope effectively with their present day-to-day experiences, but it is also necessary to provide them with the chance to survive in society and contribute to it. Failure to assist exceptional children in learning these skills can only result in their becoming unnecessarily dependent adults.

Owing to the complexity, the uniqueness of mental and physical conditions and limitations, and the variety of skills to be taught, a wide range of goals exists in the area of daily living skills. Some children may become self-reliant; others may be able to accomplish only the most basic of daily living tasks (Bigge & O'Donnell, 1976). In addition, the techniques used in teaching these skills will vary widely in accordance with the child's abilities, attention, motor imitation, and verbal comprehension (Snell, 1978).

Prior to beginning training in daily living skills, there must be an initial period of assessment. At times it will be more efficient to first strengthen verbal skills, attending, and imitation. Likewise, behaviors such as those that are disruptive, aggressive, or nonresponsive may not only interfere with the teaching process but may lead to inaccurate test results and confused training methods. Thus, these behaviors are best decreased or eliminated before assessment begins. The assessment itself should produce not only a detailed analysis of existing daily living skills and needs, but also an estimate of additional factors that might affect training—current level of development and functioning in relevant areas, physical limitations, problem behaviors, and practical considerations such as accessibility of needed facilities and specialized equipment.

Once the assessment is complete, the child's individual needs can be clearly defined and appropriate goals set. A task analysis of the skill(s) to be taught can then be completed and any necessary adaptive equipment (e.g., a special spoon handle or clothing with velcro fastenings) can be obtained. Following this, the child is guided through the successive steps, with assistance being gradually cut back until the child is able to perform the task independently. The issues of generalization and maintenance are of utmost importance in the teaching of daily living skills. Many of the skills that are taught in this area have not been encouraged in other environments or have not been taught in a fashion that promotes their maintenance over time. Thus, although a well-intentioned teacher might instruct a student to a level of independence in bathing himself or herself, the lack of a bathtub in the home setting does not allow for generalization or maintenance of this skill.

Teachers of exceptional needs learners must at all times consider the learning characteristics of the student in conjunction with the potential for the new behavior. Accurate goal development, ongoing assessment, and planned strategies for teaching and maintaining behaviors increases the potential for effective teaching of daily living skills to exceptional needs learner (Sulzer-Azaroff & Mayer, 1977).

REFERENCES

Bigge, J. L., & O'Donnell, J. G. (1976). *Teaching individuals with physical and multiple disabilities.* Columbus, OH: Merrill.

Snell, M. E. (1978). *Systematic instruction of the moderately and severely handicapped.* Columbus, OH: Merrill.

Sulzer-Azaroff, B., & Mayer, G. R. (1977). *Applying behavior-analysis procedures with children and youth.* New York: Holt, Rinehart & Winston.

Laura Kinzie Brutting
J. Todd Stephens
*University of Wisconsin,
Madison*

**ECOLOGICAL ASSESSMENT
FUNCTIONAL DOMAINS
FUNCTIONAL SKILLS TRAINING**

# DANCE THERAPY

Dance therapy is a method by which movement is incorporated into a therapeutic or educational program. As a therapy approach, dance has been used to enhance traditional methods of medical and verbal group therapies with numerous populations, including the aged, the mentally ill, and the mentally retarded. Dance especially useful with the retarded because it does not require verbal abilities (Rogers, 1977). Benefits noted through informal observations of dance therapy programs have included improvements in general motility, speech patterns, locomotion, and social ability (Barteneiff & Lewis, 1980). Dance therapy has also resulted in reduction of muscle tension and trait anxiety (Kline et al., 1978).

Dance has also been used in a broader context to promote physical and social development. Crain, Eisenhart, and McLaughlin (1984) implemented a dance program with mildly retarded adolescent students that included movement orientation, movement exploration, dance foundations, rhythms, and traditional dances. They noted improvements for 11 of 13 participants in areas of physical and social development.

Dance therapy is useful with special populations both as an adjunct to normal group verbal therapies and as a method to enhance physical, social, and educational development.

REFERENCES

Barteneiff, I., & Lewis, D. (1980). *Body movement: Coping with the environment.* New York: Gordon & Breach.

Crain, C., Eisenhart, M., & McLaughlin, J. (1984). The application of a multiple measurement approach to investigate the effects of a dance program on educable mentally retarded adolescents. *Research Quarterly for Exercise & Sport, 55,* 231–236.

Kline, F., Burgoyne, R. W., Staples, F., Moredock, P., Snyder, V., & Ioerger, M. (1978). A report on the use of movement therapy for chronic, severely disabled outpatients. *Art Psychotherapy, 5,* 181–183.

Rogers, S. B. (1977). Contributions of dance therapy in a treatment program for retarded adolescents and adults. *Art Psychotherapy, 4,* 195–197.

Christine A. Espin
*University of Minnesota*

**RECREATION FOR THE HANDICAPPED
RECREATIONAL THERAPY**

# DATA-BASED INSTRUCTION

Data-based instruction is a way of describing, measuring, and assessing behavior for instructional purposes. The system is based on the behavioral theories of B. F. Skinner (1938). Data-based instruction emerged from the concept of precision teaching. Precision teaching involves operationally defining behavior and measuring, recording, and assessing behavior to determine the success of an instructional program (Idol-Maestas 1983).

Lilly (1979) listed the eight basic steps of data-based instruction. The first step is to define the instructional problem in behavioral terms. The use of behavioral terms allows the teacher to pinpoint specific descriptions of behaviors that need addressing. The behavior should be defined in such a manner that anyone observing the child would be able to determine what the behavior is and when it occurs.

The second step involves assessing the problem so the teacher will have some idea of the student's present level of performance before intervention. There must be a pattern of behavior established during baseline. Therefore, one to five instances of baseline data of each behavior is required. Baseline data collected before intervention will serve as a measure of the student's progress after intervention has been implemented.

Once the behavior has been defined and baseline data collected, the next step is to state the objectives of the instructional program. What are the teacher's expectations as a result of the educational intervention? These objectives should be clear and specific. In breaking down instructional objectives into teachable components, instructional objectives may become simple and clear or complex and detailed. Therefore, some objectives may need to be broken down into small teachable steps. This process is called task analysis. In the determination of teaching-learning procedures, the teacher should determine the instructional strategies that will be used. In data-based instruction there are no specific instructional strategies that must be used. Any strategy that produces good results is acceptable. The emphasis is placed on determining the instructional objectives first; then instructional strategies and materials are selected based on the objectives.

Once the instructional program is implemented, it is very important to collect data on a continuous basis. This information is used to assess the effectiveness of the instructional program. The more often the data are collected, the more reliable and consistent the information. These data should be collected in the same manner as the baseline data to ensure appropriateness and the accuracy of the conclusions. Lilly (1977) states that it is important for the teacher to record the data so that it can be used for instructional decisions. Recording the data is done by charting the information on a graph. There are many formats used to chart data, however, the most important consideration is that the data display a visual presentation of the student's behavior for a specific amount of time.

The data that has been collected over time is used to make decisions concerning the effectiveness of the instructional program. The following guidelines are suggested by Lilly (1979).

1. Allow enough time for an instructional procedure to have an effect (at least 1 week).
2. Do not allow a student to continue more than 2 or 3 weeks without making progress.
3. When progress does not occur, blame the instruction program, not the child.
4. When progress does occur, celebrate with everyone involved.
5. Use progress charts in discussing school programs with parents. (p. 112)

In addition, Lilly (1977) states that it is essential to ask the following questions during instructional decision time.

1. Is progress sufficient to justify continuation of the present instructional procedures?
2. Do progress data indicate that the instructional objectives and/or methodology is appropriate or inappropriate for the student?
3. Is the criterion level appropriate for the instructional objective?
4. If the objective is reached, what is the appropriate next step? (p. 112)

## REFERENCES

Idol-Maestas, L. (1983). *Special educator's consultation handbook.* Rockville, MD: Aspen.

Lilly, M. S. (1977). Evaluating individual education programs. In S. Torres (Ed.), *A primer on individualized education programs for handicapped children* (pp. 26–30). Reston VA: Council for Exceptional Children.

Lilly, M. S. (1979). Learning and behavior problems, current trends. In M. S. Lilly (Ed.), *Children with exceptional needs: A survey of special education.* New York: Holt, Rinehart & Winston.

Skinner, B. F. (1938). *The behavior of organisms.* New York: Appleton Century.

JANICE HARPER
*North Carolina Central University*

## DIAGNOSTIC PRESCRIPTIVE TEACHING
## PRECISION TEACHING

## DAY-CARE CENTERS

Formal day-care programs originated during the Industrial Revolution with custodial care in factory rooms for young children of working mothers. Early in this century, the Salvation Army in Baltimore and Hull House in Chicago began day-care programs for infants and children of working mothers. Beginning in 1933, the Federal Work Relief Project supported Emergency Nursery Schools (ENS) as a way of providing jobs for unemployed teachers. The ENS programs were similar to the later Head Start programs in that they were for preschool children, offered medical services, emphasized nutrition, and provided inservice staff training; however, ENS emphasized nurturing care while Head Start emphasizes more formal education. When the ENS program ended, day care for mothers working in war industries was funded under the Lanham Act until 1946. Other day-care programs were supported by industry during World War II. None of those early programs were intended for handicapped children, but probably some with mild problems were admitted.

Programs exclusively for disabled children excluded from school began in the 1950s. Sponsored and conducted by parent groups, most were for moderately retarded children. In the 1960s the Massachusetts Department of Mental Health added a day-care program to its preschool program because many severely retarded children were excluded from schools. Very few private preschools, kindergartens, or public schools accepted children with severe handicaps until the late 1970s. Most blind, deaf, severely retarded, and severely physically impaired children could stay at home without day-care services or go to a state-supported residential facility. After implementation of PL 94-142 in 1977, school systems supported educational programs that replaced (and were often similar to) the private day-care facilities for school-age children. Then day-care services were developed for preschool- and postschool-age handicapped groups. This is noted in the American Association on Mental Deficiency's definition of day care: "extended care services provided on an ongoing basis for individuals residing in the community and not eligible for school programs or workshops; involves social, physical, recreational, and personal-care training and activity" (Grossman, 1983, p. 167). Since the term day care is associated with young children, some facilities for older clients are labeled by such terms as activity centers. The basic aim for day care is to provide supervised activities designed for personal growth and recreation, not to prepare clients for vocations; thus, goals differentiate day-care centers from workshops and schools.

Efforts at integrating handicapped and nonhandicapped preschool day-care programs have increased in recent years (Guralnick, 1978). A national survey of day-care facilities for young children and infants showed that some handicapped children were eligible for integrated services. About 21% of the centers reported accepting physically and emotionally handicapped children; about 14% would accept retarded children (Coelen, Galantz, & Calore, 1979). The tendency for separation of handicapped from nonhandicapped children is still reflected in professional literature, with almost no mention of handicaps in day-care journals and books. A few booklets (e.g., Granato, 1972) offer common-sense suggestions for day-care providers working with integrated handicapped children.

Empirical studies evaluating the effects of day-care programs for handicapped children and adults are rare, but comments on scientific and social policy issues in a book by Zigler and Gordon (1982) suggest that the research trend is toward identifying factors associated with different outcomes rather than simply attempting to determine whether day care is good for children.

## REFERENCES

Coelen, C., Galantz, F., & Calore, D. (1979). *Day care centers in the United States: A national profile*. Cambridge, MA: Abt Associates.

Granato, S. (1972). *Day care: Serving children with special needs*. Washington, DC: U.S. Government Printing Office.

Grossman, H. J. (1983). *Classification in mental retardation*. Washington, DC: American Association on Mental Deficiency.

Guralnick, M. J. (1978). *Early intervention and the integration of handicapped and nonhandicapped children*. Baltimore, MD: University Park Press.

Zigler, E. F., & Gordon, E. W. (Eds.) (1982). *Day care: Scientific and social issues*. Boston: Auburn House.

SUE ALLEN WARREN
*Boston University*

**HEAD START**
**LEAST RESTRICTIVE ENVIRONMENT**
**MAINSTREAMING**
**RESPITE CARE**

## DAYDREAMING

The literature on daydreaming from the special educator's perspective tends to fall into three catagories. In the first, daydreaming is seen as a symptom of disability. In the second, it is associated with creativity and giftedness. In the third, it is reported to be an effective therapeutic device. As a symptom of disability, daydreaming is associated with both physical and cognitive disorders. It has been suggested that a central nervous system dysfunction may cause a lag in brain structure development leading to behavior such as daydreaming that inhibits learning. Petite mal epileptic seizures are also often mistaken for daydreaming. As a result, medical screening might be appropriate for chronic daydreamers. Cognitively, Blanton (1983) and others classify daydreaming as an immature behavior—along with hyperactivity, distractibility, impulsivity, procrastination, messiness, and sloppiness—that becomes a problem in educational situations. Besides possible physiological causes, inordinate daydreaming may be due to deep emotional problems or to a student's inability to focus attention on a task for any length of time.

Suggested treatments for problem daydreaming vary as widely as suggested causes. Mock et al. (1982) found that among hyperactive students with distractible cognitive styles (characterized by daydreaming, slow response time, and high error rates), the use of ritalin improved performance on some school-related tasks, decreasing both decision time and error rates. Practical suggestions for teachers include calling the student's attention to the task at hand in some inconspicuous way such as placing a hand on the student's paper or using physical proximity to convey expectations. Operant conditioning can be effective as well, using reward points or some other positive reinforcement when students finish tasks. Allowing students to choose activities that are inherently interesting to them also fosters prolonged attention.

If daydreaming needs to be overcome in some students,

it seems that it should be fostered in others. The connection between fantasy and creativity is widely recognized. Daydreaming seems to accompany the period of incubation that precedes creative production. Fred Kekule's discovery of the molecular structure of benzene is a common example of the power of relaxed, unguided fantasy. Guides for parents of gifted children consistently recommend allowing their children time to daydream, even though, like the learning disabled, gifted children must often be encouraged to stay on task. These two views of daydreaming—as a creative tool for gifted children and as an obstacle for the learning disabled—may be understood in light of recent findings by Kanter (1982). After controlling for IQ, Kanter found that frequent daydreamers are slow in response production and weak in verbal creativity, but gifted in visual creative abilities. Treatments vary as educators try to overcome the former with the learning disabled and foster the latter in the gifted.

Daydreaming itself has been used in a variety of ways as a clinical device. Programmed imaging, as McQueen (1983) describes it, is often used to develop skills in the psychomotor domain. Subjects practice basketball free throws in their mind's eye, for example, before going onto the court. Controlled experiments have shown this to be highly effective. Guided daydreaming, which until recently was a more common technique in Europe than in the United States, is controlled by someone who stays outside the activities of the participants. The leader, usually a teacher or therapist, talks the subjects through an experience. This is often useful for relaxation and as an aid to memory, self-awareness, and clarifying goals or realizing internal conflicts. Once a subject becomes adept at disciplined daydreaming, it can be used as a powerful tool. Therapists have reported decreased incidence of depression, phobias, and psychosomatic disorders in patients trained to use their imaginations. It has also aided those who have trouble making decisions. Subjects are encouraged to imagine possible scenarios that might occur in consequence of a variety of decisions and then choose the most desirable. Neurotic or otherwise undesirable behaviors have also been modified with clinical use of imagery. One technique is to have the subjects practice substitute behaviors mentally before incorporating them into their daily activities. A more extreme method is the use of aversive imagery techniques, in which highly negative mental pictures are evoked to discourage maladaptive behaviors such as compulsive stealing (Singer, 1974).

## REFERENCES

Blanton, G. H. (1983, Feb.). *Social and emotional development of learning disabled children.* Paper presented at the annual convention of the Association for Children and Adults with Learning Disabilities, (ERIC Document Reproduction Service No. ED 232 336), Washington, DC.

Kanter, S. (1982). Divergent thinking abilities as a function of daydreaming frequency. *Journal for the Education of the Gifted, 5*(1), 12–23.

McQueen, D. (1983, March). *Imaging as a heuristic.* Paper presented at the annual meeting of the Conference on College Composition and Communication, Detroit, MI (ERIC Document Reproduction Service No. ED 234 429).

Mock, K. R., Swanson, J. M., & Kinsbourne, M. (1978, March). *Stimulant effect on matching familiar figures: Changes in impulsive and distractible cognitive styles.* Paper presented at the annual meeting of the American Educational Research Association, Toronto, Canada (ERIC Document Reproduction Service No. ED 160 189).

Singer, J. L. (1974). *Imagery and daydream methods in psychotherapy and behavior modification.* New York: Academic.

JANET S. BRAND
Hunter College, City University
of New York

**HYPNOSIS**
**IMAGERY**

# DEAF

The word deaf is applied to persons who cannot hear or suffer from a major hearing impairment. In classical writings as well as in common talk, until only a few years ago, the word deaf frequently had a strongly pejorative connotation, either in its figurative sense of deaf to the word of God or in locutions such as deaf and dumb. The latter clearly indicated a belief that those who are deaf from birth also have an intellectual defect. The term deaf-mute (used either as an adjective or as a noun), carried the notion of a double infirmity, until it was realized that the absence of speech, in those born deaf, was not related to a deficiency of the vocal organs and was only the consequence of the lack of hearing. Deaf now is used alone mostly since a majority of deaf persons have no other infirmity aside from possibly a general language deficiency.

There is as yet no universally accepted definition of the different categories of hearing impairment. All the existing classifications are based on the mean speech range frequency thresholds obtained for the best ear by pure tone. The classification of the Bureau International d'Audiophonologie (BIAP; International Office for Audiophonology) is based on the mean hearing loss for 500, 1000, and 2000 Hz (ISO standards). It uses the terms recommended by the World Health Organization for the grading of all types of impairments: mild (20–40 dB), moderate (40–70 dB), severe (70–90 dB), and profound (more than 90 dB). The last category is itself divided in three subgroups, since there are large differences in the possibilities of residual hearing use among those whose average loss is only slightly superior to 90 dB and those who have a more than 100 dB hearing loss. Other classifications use different gradings and terms for the less than 70 dB categories, but there is fair agreement concerning the definition of the severe and profound groups.

Pure-tone audiometry, however, provides only a partial picture of the residual hearing capacity. It does not reflect the variable potential gain that can be brought by adequate hearing aid fitting. Several authors such as Pollack (1964), advocate the aided audiogram as a more meaningful measure of functional hearing capacity. Even this, however, does not reflect the qualitative aspects of residual hearing, which may vary extensively among individuals with the same pure-tone audiometric thresholds. Some insight about the quality of hearing may be gained by investigation of psychoacoustic tuning curves (Harrison, 1984), but these measures cannot presently be applied to small children because they require the subjects' active and informed cooperation.

These difficulties in establishing a well-founded functional classification have led several authors to adopt simpler general definitions for educational purposes. According to the Conference of Executives of American Schools for the Deaf (Frisina, 1974), a deaf person is one whose hearing is disabled to an extent (usually 70 dB International Standards Organization or greater) that precludes the understanding of speech through the ear alone, without or with the use of a hearing aid; a hard-of-hearing person is one whose hearing is disabled to an extent (usually 35 to 69 dB International Standards Organization) that makes difficult, but does not preclude, the understanding of speech through the ear alone, without or with a hearing aid.

It is necessary to stress the importance in both of these definitions of the word usually, since there is a large overlap in the degree of pure-tone hearing loss of people who functionally correspond to one or the other category. Recently, Quigley and Kretschmer (1982) stated that for educational purposes, "a deaf child or adult is one who sustained a profound (91 dB or greater) primarily sensorineural hearing impairment prelingually" (p. 2). This trend toward considering as deaf only those with a larger than 90 dB hearing impairment is probably related to development of early intervention programs and improvement of hearing aids, resulting in earlier and better spoken language acquisition for an increasing number of the less profoundly hearing impaired.

In addition to the former definitions, the definition that was adopted by a UNESCO experts' committee (1985) introduces the notion of relativity of deafness to prevalent socioeconomic conditions:

> To be considered as *deaf* those children whose spontaneous speech and language development have been very much retarded or is completely absent due to their severe hearing impairment or a hearing impairment combined with a lack of training and/or technical amplification. In countries with ad-

equate resources for diagnosis, training, and provision of hearing aids, some children with hearing impairment would not be included in the above-mentioned group, whereas they would be regarded as functionally deaf in countries lacking these resources. (p. 5)

Other terms such as auditorially impaired or deficient, acoustically impaired, hypoacoustic, or, in French, demisourd (half deaf), are used either as synonyms for deaf and hearing impaired or to designate a category of the latter. The word cophotic, limited to the medical profession, is applied to those ears that have completely lost their auditory function.

The World Health Organization recommends that a distinction be made in all physical or mental defects, among impairment, disability, and handicap. Deaf children and adults are impaired in having a pathological auditory system. They are consequently disabled by difficulty in perceiving speech and environmental sounds. This disability can make them more or less severely handicapped by limiting their overall personal and social functioning. Some types of impairment, those owed to conductive hearing loss, can be alleviated or cured by medical and/or surgical therapy. For most deaf persons, as defined by the Conference of Executives of American Schools for the deaf, the physical impairment is due to inner ear or nervous system damage and is irreversible. The disability can, however, be reduced by appropriate hearing aid fitting, training, and, in the case of children, education. The handicap can be lessened or even eliminated in two ways: through the reduction of the disability or through the functioning in a sociocultural group where hearing is not necessary.

Among deaf and hard-of-hearing children and adults, it is important to distinguish between those who were affected from birth or shortly thereafter (before language was established) and those who became hearing impaired later on. These groups are commonly called prelingually and postlingually deaf, respectively. The prelingually deaf child cannot acquire language by the same natural process as the normally hearing. Their auditory pathways in the brain, as well as those parts of the cerebral cortex concerned with the processing of spoken language, are not adequately stimulated in the early years most favorable for language development. This lack of adequate stimulation during the sensitive period not only results in great difficulties in the acquisition of spoken language skills, but may also produce permanent structural changes in the central nervous system. These changes could diminish the capacity of the brain to efficiently process speech-linked information later on, even if normal hearing could be restored, or artificial hearing produced (Périer et al., 1984).

Because of the interference of deafness with language acquisition prelingually deaf children and adults markedly differ from the postlingually deafened. The latter have a sensory impairment that interferes with their ability to perceive speech and other sounds, but they have a normally and completely developed language function. Although the quality of their speech may become distorted after some time because of the lack of auditory feedback, they usually remain intelligible. Their reading and writing capacities remain intact. By contrast, prelingually deaf children have such difficulties in acquiring spoken language that most of them, when they leave school as adolescents or young adults, have a linguistic insufficiency in addition to their sensory impairment (Conrad, 1979). Not only are they deficient in oral language skills, but also in reading and writing capacities. This linguistic insufficiency constitutes a serious handicap for their integration within the society of the normally hearing. It can, however, be attenuated and largely prevented by early and adequate education. When this includes sign language, a normal linguistic function may be developed in that modality, allowing full participation in the sociocultural life of the deaf community.

Deafness is related to a physical impairment, like other disabilities requiring rehabilitative and educational measures. It differs, however, from all these by a unique feature: the fact that this disability has given birth to a specific language, sign language (Bellugi (1972). Just as a wide variety of spoken languages have evolved among the normally hearing world population, different sign languages have originated among the scattered communities of deaf people (Stokoe, 1972). However, many western world sign languages have a partly common trunk because of the important influence of the Abbé de l'Epée, the first educator of the deaf to recognize, in the late eighteenth century in France, the sign language of the deaf. There are, therefore, more common or similar signs among western sign languages than there are common or similar words in spoken languages. This facilitates communication among deaf people of different nationalities.

The use of sign language eliminates all handicaps for those who are proficient in it. Indeed, it is the normally hearing individual who becomes handicapped when he or she tries to participate in a group where sign language is the principal or only mode of communication. The common language is a powerful bond that largely contributes to the creation of a group identity. This tendency is strengthened when the group is a minority subjected to strong social pressure. This is particularly true for the deaf, since sign language was not recognized as a proper language until several linguists such as William Stokoe (1972), Ursula Bellugi (1972), and others brought forward the convincing results of their research. They demonstrated that sign languages of the deaf are as worthy of esteem and respect as vocal languages, possessing all the attributes of the latter except oral realization. Among these attributes are not only grammatical correctness, arbitrariness, and double articulation, but also more affective qualities such as the capacity to express humor and poetry.

In the past, many deaf individuals did not themselves realize the value of their manual language (Meadow, 1980). They were influenced by the hearing society's contempt for what was regarded as a primitive and crude mode of communication, incapable of expressing abstraction and therefore unsuitable for high-level intellectual processes. The new status of sign language has done much not only to promote its diffusion and enrichment, but also to upgrade its users' self-confidence and self-esteem. This has given new impetus to deaf organizations and prompted the birth of such movements as Deaf Pride. This movement promulgates the notion that the deaf are equal but different and want this difference to be recognized and taken into account in the organization of society as a whole. Sign language supports deaf culture, mainly characterized by social and artistic events. It is, however, more appropriate to speak of cultural values rather than of a complete culture since the deaf share many ingredients of the hearing majorities' cultures such as their literature and their religions.

While some of the deaf reject spoken language and refuse to make any efforts at participation in sociocultural activities with the hearing, most of them aspire to bilingualism (i.e., the use of both sign and spoken languages) and biculturalism. Better information for society at large and sensitization to the rightful demands of the deaf has contributed in recent years to strengthening biculturalism. An important event in bringing the deaf to the attention of the hearing world was the success of Mark Medoff's play Children of a Lesser God, in which a deaf actress held the principal part. The play was awarded the Tony Award for best play of the year in 1980.

According to many psychologists and sociolinguists, it is important for the personality structure of severely and profoundly hearing-impaired individuals that they identify themselves as deaf. The realization that they are different, but not inferior, allows them to direct all their energies in a positive direction, rather than striving toward the unattainable goal of trying to be like the hearing. According to this view, deaf children of hearing parents (who represent more than 90% of deaf children) should be given the opportunity at an early age for social intercourse with deaf adults who can serve as realistic models. For many deaf adults, sign language is essential for the full expression of their personality. As a consequence, they deeply feel their belonging to the deaf community and cherish the values of deaf culture.

Other deaf adults, while not denying their hearing impairments, prefer to stress all that they have in common with the normally hearing. Making the most of their spoken language receptive and expressive skills, however imperfect, they choose to forget their deafness and make others forget it as often as possible. To hold their place in normally hearing society, they accept that they must make special efforts and that they must sometimes suffer setbacks. This does not change their self-image of "more similar than different" and does not prevent them from enjoying a rewarding social life. For these, being deaf remains a nuisance and nothing else. They do not feel especially attracted to the deaf community and sign language.

The degree of hearing impairment and its date of onset relative to language acquisition are both important factors in determining whether a given individual will identify as deaf or not. Most of the hard of hearing who can acquire efficient language skills without too much difficulty, and most of the postlingually deaf who possess language do not join the deaf community. Conversely, many of the prelingually deaf have great difficulty in acquiring spoken language and never feel completely at home in the company of the normally hearing. They make up the largest part of the deaf community. However, several hard-of-hearing or postlingually deaf individuals are also attracted by sign language and deaf culture, while several of the profoundly deaf who have developed strong attachments to the normally hearing do not especially seek the company of other deaf people.

## REFERENCES

Bellugi, U. (1972). Studies in sign language. In: T. J. O'Rourke (Ed.), *Psycholinguistics and total communication: The state of the art. American Annals of the Deaf*, pp. 68–74.

Conrad, R. (1979). *The deaf school child*. London: Harper & Row.

Frisina, R. (1974). *Report of the committee to redefine deaf and hard of hearing for educational purposes*. (Mimeo).

Harrison, R. V. (1984). Objective measures of cochlear frequency selectivity in animals and in man. A review. *Acta Neurological Belgica, 84*, 213–232.

Meadow, K. P. (1980). *Deafness and child development*. London: Arnold.

Périer, O., Alegria, J., Buyse, M., D'Alimonte, G., Gilson, D., & Serniclaes, W. (1984). Consequences of auditory deprivation in animals and humans. *Acta Oto-Laryngologica* (Suppl. 411), 60–70.

Pollack, D. (1964). Acoupedics: A uni-sensory approach to auditory training. *Volta Review, 66*, 400–409.

Quigley, S. P., & Kretschmer, R. E. (1982). *The education of deaf children: Issues, theory and practice*. London: Arnold.

Stokoe, W. C. (1972). *Semiotics and human sign language*. Paris: Mouton.

UNESCO. (1985). *Consultation on alternative approaches for the education of the deaf*. Paris: UNESCO Headquarters.

OLIVIER PÉRIER
*Université Libre de Bruxelles,
Centre Comprendre et
Parler, Belgium*

## CONDUCTIVE HEARING LOSS
## DEAF EDUCATION

## DEAF, INTERPRETERS FOR

See INTERPRETERS FOR THE DEAF.

## DEAF-BLIND

There exists a broad range of visual and auditory impairments among deaf-blind persons, indicating an enormous diversity in the severity of disabilities within this population. The term deaf-blind covers persons with severe visual and hearing disabilities who are unable to profit from special programs designed solely for deaf or blind children and youths (*Federal Register*, 1975). It is estimated that there are approximately 6000 deaf-blind persons in the United States (Sims-Tucker & Jensema, 1984). Approximately 36% of these individuals were born deaf-blind during the great rubella epidemic of 1963–1965. Maternal rubella, heredity, and meningitis are among the top three causes of deaf-blindness in the United States. Additionally, deaf-blind persons often are afflicted with congenital heart disease and mental retardation (Vernon, Grieve, & Shaver, 1980).

Deaf-blindness has often been associated with Helen Keller and her teacher Anne Sullivan (Lash, 1980). Although some deaf-blind people function within or above normal intelligence, many require extraordinary educational training. The separate handicaps are not additive but multiplicative in nature (Warren, 1984), and often cause severe learning problems. Deaf-blind children have often been referred to as the most difficult group of children to educate (Sims-Tucker & Jensema, 1984). They frequently engage in stereotypic behaviors that interfere with learning and communication. In an attempt to meet the special needs of this population, Regional Centers for Services for Deaf-Blind Children was established in 1967 (Sims-Tucker & Jensema, 1984).

Educational programming for deaf-blind children, including assessment and evaluation, continues to be a difficult task. The trend in educating children with severe handicaps has emphasized a more functional curriculum (Brown et al., 1979). Similarly, educators of deaf-blind children are turning to these curricular approaches for developing intervention programs in such areas as self-help, prevocational and vocational skills, communication, and sensory development (Vadasy & Fewell, 1984). Programming developed by Van Dijk (1971) has provided teachers, parents, and therapists with an invaluable communication curriculum that incorporates movement theory, which is often associated with the coactive movement. In addition, the emphasis on visual as well as auditory training can be seen in educational programs developed by Goetz and Utley (undated) and Efron and DuBoff (1979).

The combined efforts of professionals have made a tremendous impact on the current provisions of educational programs for deaf-blind children. Nonetheless, there exists a clear need for continued research in the areas of developing and refining effective intervention techniques for deaf-blind children and youths.

## REFERENCES

Brown, L., Branston, M., Hamre-Nietupski, S., Pumpian, I., Certo, N., & Gruenewald, L. (1979). A strategy for developing chronological age appropriate and functional curricular content for severely handicapped adolescents and young adults. *Journal of Special Education, 13*, 81–90.

Efron, M., & DuBoff, B. (1979). *A vision guide for teachers of deaf-blind children.* Raleigh, NC: South Atlantic Regional Center for Services to Deaf-Blind Children.

Goetz, L., & Utley, B. (undated). *Auditory assessment and program manual for severely handicapped deaf-blind students.* Parsons, KS: Words & Pictures.

Lash, J. P. (1980). *Helen and teacher: The story of Helen Keller and Anne Sullivan Macy.* New York: Delacorte.

Lockett, T., & Rudolph, J. (1980). Deaf-blind children with maternal rubella: Implications for adult services. *American Annals of the Deaf, 125*, 1000–1006.

Sims-Tucker, B., & Jensema, C. (1984). Severely and profoundly auditorially/visually impaired students: The deaf-blind population. In P. Valletutti & B. Sims-Tucker (Eds.), *Severely and profoundly handicapped students: Their nature and needs* (pp. 269–317). Baltimore, MD: Brookes.

Vadasy, P., & Fewell, R. (1984). Predicting the futures of deaf-blind adolescents: Their living and vocational options. *Education of the Visually Handicapped, 16*, 12–19.

Van Dijk, J. (1971). Learning difficulties and deaf-blind children. *Proceedings of the Fourth International Conference on Deaf-Blind Children.* Watertown, MA: Perkins School for the Blind.

Vernon, M., Grieve, B., & Shaver, K. (1980). Handicapping conditions associated with the congenital rubella syndrome. *American Annals of the Deaf, 125*(8), 993–997.

Warren, D. (1984). *Blindness and early childhood development.* New York: American Foundation for the Blind.

VIVIAN I. CORREA
*University of Florida*

**DEAF**
**KELLER, HELEN**
**MOVEMENT THERAPY**
**VISUALLY HANDICAPPED**

# DEAF EDUCATION

The history of deaf education is relatively short because no records exist of organized teaching in prehistoric times or in the ancient civilizations of Egypt, Greece, and Rome.

Although a few records exist of previous isolated examples of deaf individuals reaching some degree of education, Pedro Ponce de Leon (1520–1584) is generally considered to be the first teacher of the deaf. A Benedictine monk, he was entrusted with the education of several deaf children of Spanish nobility, and received wide publicity as a result of his successes. The records concerning the first teachers of the deaf are full of information showing that many of the techniques used today find their roots in the work of those pioneers. The reader is referred to the excellent survey by Moores (1978) for a review. However, it is necessary to mention the Abbott de l'Epée and Samuel Heinicke, because confrontation between their methods was at the heart of the oral versus manual controversy that has profoundly divided deaf educators for two centuries.

De l'Epée established the first public school for the deaf in the world, in 1755, in his Paris home. He started it when he was asked to give religious instruction to deaf twin sisters who used signs to communicate between them. De l'Epée understood that gestures could express human thought as much as spoken language and believed sign language to be the natural language of the deaf. He, therefore, set out to learn it from his pupils, but felt compelled to supplement their natural signs by newly formed "methodical" signs in order to obtain a complete sign counterpart of French syntax and morphology. The teaching of articulation was regarded by him as of lesser importance than that of signs and written language.

Samuel Heinicke taught several deaf children as a private tutor in different parts of Germany and established a school in Leipzig in 1778. He prided himself on being able to teach his pupils to speak clearly, and was strongly opposed to the teaching of written before spoken language, which he considered the only appropriate vehicle of thought. Heinicke and his followers Graser and Hill bitterly criticized de l'Epée's method, considering speech to be the first priority of teaching and sign language detrimental to that cause.

Controversy between the advocates of oralism and manualism, which started with de l'Epée and Heinicke, was lively during most of the nineteenth century, not only in Europe, but also in the United States. The first school for the deaf in the United States was founded by Thomas Hopkins Gallaudet, in 1847, with Laurent Clerc, a deaf teacher trained in Paris by de l'Epée's successor, Sicard. Other manual schools were created along the same lines, most of them paying little or no attention to the teaching of speech and articulation. Other U.S. educators responded with the creation of strictly oral schools. The controversy between manual and oral methods was later embodied by two exceptional personalities: Edward Miner Gallaudet (Thomas's son) and Alexander Graham Bell. The former was convinced of the importance of spoken as well as sign language and was instrumental in establishing an oral-manual combined method in most American schools. Bell observed that education of the deaf in residential schools isolated them from the hearing society, and claimed that sign language was detrimental to the acquisition of English. He advocated the elimination of both sign language and the deaf teachers who used it.

In 1880 an international congress of educators of the deaf convened in Milan, Italy. It adopted two resolutions:

1. Considering the unquestionable superiority of speech over signs for the most perfect knowledge of language, the oral method must be preferred to the gestual method.

2. Considering that the simultaneous use of signs and speech has the disadvantage of being noxious to speech, to lip reading, and to the precision of ideas, the purely oral method must be preferred.

These resolutions were enforced in all European countries, but in the United States Edward Gallaudet opposed Bell and managed to restrict their application. Not only did he maintain a school system using the combined oral-manual method, but he was also able to educate teachers of the deaf in this method at the National Deaf Mute College, Washington, DC; that school was to become the present Gallaudet College. From that time on, the opposition between Bell and Gallaudet increased. It led to the formation of two rival groups of schools and teachers: the exclusively oral and the combined oral-manual.

In Europe, oral education continued to prevail, unchallenged, during more than half of the twentieth century. After World War II, progress in electroacoustic technology gave new impetus to oralism. Hopes arose that auditory training with sophisticated apparatus and efficient individual hearing aids combined with lip reading would enable hearing-impaired children to develop their speech skills, both receptively and expressively, to a much larger extent then previously. Whetnall and Fry in London (1964) and the John Tracy Clinic in Los Angeles (Thielman, 1970), among many others, considered that early intervention would allow most deaf children to attend ordinary schools for the normally hearing or special units attached to those schools. The integration—or mainstreaming—movement that they initiated progressively gathered more and more strength in Great Britain, then in the United States and continental Europe.

It is generally accepted today that many hearing-impaired children, with early education, proper hearing aid fitting, and continued support, can successfully be educated with the normally hearing (Nix, 1976; Webster & Ellwood, 1985). While the degree of hearing loss is an important factor in determining which hearing-impaired children can be mainstreamed, it is generally recognized that this factor is by no means decisive in itself. Some profoundly deaf children can succeed in ordinary schools, while others with more residual hearing may not be able to do so (Périer et al., 1980). There is, therefore, no con-

sensus concerning the proportion of deaf and hard-of-hearing children that should be integrated. The present situation varies greatly among nations. In some such as Italy, the official policy is that all handicapped children should be mainstreamed. Other countries, like West Germany, maintain separate special school systems for the profoundly deaf and the hard of hearing, so that even the majority of the latter are not educated with the normally hearing. Several developing countries where special education has yet to be organized view mainstreaming as a tempting alternative to the building and maintaining of special schools. Caution against the excesses of such a trend is voiced by numerous educators of the deaf, who argue that most of the profoundly deaf will continue to need special education. The pros and cons of mainstreaming have been aptly described by Meadow (1980), who argues that the options should carefully be weighed for each child.

Sign language interpretation services for the deaf have been developed primarily in the United States to assist the deaf in all circumstances in which they may benefit from them. Legal provisions ensuring that a deaf child has the right to the best possible education has made it possible in some cases to provide support services in schools or universities, allowing more deaf children and students to be mainstreamed than was formerly possible. In addition to sign language interpretation, other forms of interpretation are beginning to be developed in some countries: oral interpretation and oral interpretation with cued speech.

While the trend toward mainstream education has steadily increased over the years, the hope that early speech and hearing training would solve the language and education difficulties of most hearing-impaired children has proved overly optimistic. Several studies, among them Conrad's (1979), demonstrated that whatever method was used, whether oral or manual, the majority of deaf school graduates reached a mean reading age equivalent only to that of 9- to 10-year-old hearing children. Thus, the existing methods had not prevented relative failure to develop good command of the societal language (English in this case), even in its written form. Other studies reviewed by Quigley & Kretschmer (1982) showed that deaf children of deaf parents who had had signs as their first language were not disadvantaged in the oral skills and had slightly but significantly better gradings in overall language evaluation when compared with deaf children of hearing parents.

These results, together with the rehabilitation of sign language, were largely instrumental in the birth and development of the total communication (TC) philosophy. This, as defined by Denton (1970), is the right of a deaf child to learn to use all forms of communication available to develop language competence. This includes the full spectrum: child-devised gestures, speech, formal sign language, finger spelling, speech reading, reading, writing, as well as any other methods that may be developed in the future. Every deaf child should also be provided with the opportunity to learn to use any remnant of residual hearing he or she may have by employing the best possible electronic equipment for amplifying sound. Many schools in the United States, and a growing number throughout the world, have adhered to the principle of TC, although there are various interpretations of its meaning. More and more infant programs throughout the world are using it from the earliest age; many are urging parents to learn to communicate with their children through signs in addition to speech. Such combination of signs and speech has been termed bimodal communication by Schlesinger (1978).

Several types of manual aids other than signs are used to facilitate the reception or the production of spoken language. While many educators are using these or some form of bimodal communication for the profoundly deaf, others continue to use exclusively oral methods.

The Table is an attempt at classification of the methods currently used. It must be borne in mind, however, that various combinations are possible; some techniques developed within the framework of a given method are applicable in other contexts. For instance, in some Belgian centers, cued speech (3.1) is used in combination with bimodal communication (4.1) and with the verbo-tonal method (1). Five groups can be distinguished: auditory, oral, oral plus manual aids, combined, and manual.

1. Auditory unisensory or acoupedic methods rely on auditory training to develop spoken language. Speech reading is either not encouraged or suppressed during training periods (Pollack, 1964). In the verbo-tonal method (Guberina et al., 1972), perception of acoustic features through the tactile sense is used in addition to hearing. The auditory global approach of Calvert and Silverman (1975) stands at the margin between the acoupedic and the oral-aural, since "the primary, although not always the exclusive, channel for speech development is auditory."

2. Oral also called oral-aural (Simmons-Martin, 1972). Auditory perception and speech reading are used as well as other modalities, but signs are excluded. Ling (1976) describes systematic speech development procedure primarily based on audition though not neglecting tactile and visual support, as in Calvert and Silverman's multisensory approach, used when the auditory global is not sufficient. Van Uden's maternal reflective method (1970) insists on the necessity of active oral-aural dialogue and natural prosody.

3.1 Oral-aural plus lip-reading complements. In cued speech (Cornett, 1967) and related systems, the oral-aural approach is combined with a system of hand shapes executed near the mouth, synchronously with speech. The hand brings only that part of the information that is not supplied by lip reading. The combination of this information allows the deaf child to unequivocally identify by sight the speech sounds and syllables that the hearing identify through the ear (Nicholls & Ling, 1982; Périer et al., 1986).

3.2 Oral-aural plus manual representation of phonemes. In the French Borel-Maisonny method (1979), and in the German Phonembestimmte Manual System (PMS) of Schulte (1974), the oral-aural methodology is aided by contrived gestures that correspond to some of the characteristics of speech sounds and thus help in their identification and production. The gestures bring independent information that is not linked to lip reading.

3.3 Oral-aural plus finger spelling. These are the U.S. Rochester (Scouten, 1942) and U.S.S.R. neo-oralism (Morkovin, 1960) methods. Finger spelling is executed by the teacher simultaneously with speech; the child is asked to accompany his or her own speech by finger spelling. Since the latter is a representation of written language, reading and writing are strongly emphasized.

4.1 Unilingual bimodal communication or simultaneous method. One language, that of the hearing society and of most deaf children's parents, is simultaneously expressed in speech and signs. There are numerous varieties of signed representations of spoken language. Some are close to the regional sign language of the deaf, differing mostly in word order; others use additional signs to convey syntactical and morphological information; still others are wholly contrived (Crystal & Craig, 1978).

4.2 Bilingual bimodal communication. Spoken language in an oral-aural approach is used in certain situations by hearing persons, while sign language is used in other situations by deaf and hearing persons. In early education, it is often considered acceptable for hearing parents who have not yet mastered sign language to use those signs they have learned in combination with their spoken language (Bouvet, 1981; Erting, 1978).

5. Visual unisensory communication by sign language alone. While no educators advocate that deaf children should not learn the major societal language, a few favor the exclusive use of sign language for early education. Only when sign language is firmly established as a first language is the majority's societal language taught as a

Classifications of Methods Used in Deaf Education

| 1. Auditory | Auditory unisensory or acoupedic |
| 2. Oral | Oral-aural, multisensory |
| 3. Oral + Manual Aids | 3.1 Oral-aural + lip-reading complements |
| | 3.2 Oral-aural + manual representation of phonemes |
| | 3.3 Oral-aural + finger spelling |
| 4. Combined | 4.1 Unilingual bimodal communication or simultaneous method |
| | 4.2 Bilingual bimodal communication |
| 5. Manual | Visual unisensory communication by sign language alone |

second language (Ahlgren, 1980). In some programs, teaching is first done in the written form, spoken language being delayed (Mali & Rickli, 1983).

The status of deaf education in 1985 is characterized by a great vitality and a large diversity, although the antagonism between methods has somewhat abated. The oral-manual controversy is not as bitter as before, with most people on each side now recognizing the merits of the other (Tervoort, 1982a, 1982b). The question today is not so much of a choice between exclusively oral and combined oral-manual methods as of deciding for whom, when, how, and how much each modality should be used. General agreement exists on the paramount importance of early detection, assessment, and intervention, including proper hearing aid fitting and maintenance. The role of parents as the first educators of their deaf children, already stressed by Whetnall and Fry and the John Tracy Clinic, is now widely recognized (UNESCO, 1985). Their full participation is essential for the success of any method. Parents should, therefore, be thoroughly informed about the different programs available so that they can make their own choices. The fact that more than 90% of deaf children's parents are normally hearing must be taken into account in any decision about education policy. Whichever method is adopted, and whether priority is given to speech or sign, educators of today all have common goals: to enable deaf children to acquire the mastery of language needed to assert their personalities and attain full accomplishment; to bring deaf children to complete literacy, through which they will be able to reach the degree of academic achievement corresponding to their intellectual capacities and personal motivation.

## REFERENCES

Ahlgren, E. (1980). The sign language group in Stockholm. In E. Ahlgren & Bengman (Eds.), Papers from the first international symposium on the sign language research (pp. 3–7). Leksand.

Borel-Maisonny, S. (1979). *Absence d'expression verbale*. Paris: A.R.P.L.O.E.

Bouvet, D. (1981). *La Parole de l'enfant sourd*. Paris: Presses Universitaires de France, Collection Le Fil Rouge.

Calvert, D. R., & Silverman, S. R. (1975). *Speech and deafness: A text for learning and teaching*. Washington, DC: A. G. Bell Association.

Conrad, R. (1979). *The deaf school child*. London: Harper & Row.

Cornett, R. O. (1967). Cued speech. *American Annals of the Deaf, 112*, pp. 3–13.

Crystal, D., & Craig, E. (1978). Contrived sign language. In I. M. Schlesinger & L. Namir (Eds.), *Sign language of the deaf* (pp. 141–168). New York: Academic.

Denton, D. (1970). Remarks in support of a system of total communication for deaf children. Communication Symposium. Frederick, MD: Maryland School for the Deaf.

Erting, C. (1978). Language policy and deaf ethnicity in the United States. *Sign Language Studies, 19*, 139–152.

Guberina, P., Skaric, I., & Zaga, B. (1972). *Case studies in the use of restricted bands of frequencies in auditory rehabilitation of the deaf*. Zagreb, Yugoslavia: Institute of Phonetics Faculty of Arts.

Ling, D. (1976). *Speech and the hearing-impaired child: Theory and practice*. Washington, DC: A. G. Bell Association.

Malé, A., & Rickli, F. (1983). *Introduction au bilinguisme: Langue des signes française—français oral, à l'école de Montbrillant*. Geneva, Switzerland: Département de l'Instruction Publique.

Moores, D. F. (1978). *Educating the deaf: Psychology, principles, and practices*. Boston: Houghton Mifflin.

Morkovin, B. (1960). Experiment in teaching deaf preschool children in the Soviet Union. *Volta Review, 62*, 260–268.

Nicholls, G. H., & Ling, D. (1982). Cued speech and the reception of spoken language. *Journal of Speech and Hearing Research, 25*, 262–269.

Nix, G. (1976). *Mainstream education for hearing impaired children and youth*. New York: Grune & Stratton.

Périer, O., Capouillez, J. M., & Paulissen, D. (1980). The relationship between the degree of auditory deficiency and the possibility of successful mainstreaming in schools for hearing children. In H. Hartmann, (Ed.), *1st International Congress of the Hard of Hearing* (pp. 348–353). Hamburg: Deutscher Schwerhorigenbund.

Périer, O., Charlier, B., Hage, C., & Alegria, J. (1986). Evaluation of the effects of prolonged cued speech practice upon the reception and internal processing of spoken language. *Proceedings of the 1985 International Congress of Educators of the Deaf*, Manchester, England.

Pollack, D. (1964). Acoupedics: An unisensory approach to auditory training. *Volta Review, 66*, 400–409.

Quigley, S. P., & Kretschmer, R. F. (1982). *The education of deaf children: Issues, theory and practice*. London: Arnold.

Schlesinger, H. S. (1978). The acquisition of bimodal language. In I. M. Schlesinger & L. Namir (Eds.), *Sign language of the deaf*. New York: Academic.

Schulte, K. (1974). *The phonemetransmitting manual system* (PMS). Heidelberg: Julius Verlag.

Scouten, E. (1942). *A revaluation of the Rochester method*. Rochester, NY: Rochester School for the Deaf.

Simmons-Martin, A. (1972). The oral/aural procedure: Theoretical basis and rationale. *Volta Review, 74*, 541–551.

Tervoort, B. T. (1982a). Communication and the deaf. *Proceedings of the International Congress on Education of the Deaf*, (pp. 219–229), Hamburg. Heidelberg: Julius Verlag.

Tervoort, B. T. (1982b). The future: Oralism versus manualism? *Proceedings of the International Congress on Education of the Deaf* (pp. 544–547), Hamburg. Heidelberg: Julius Verlag.

Thielman, V. (1970). John Tracy Clinic correspondence course for parents of preschool deaf children. *Proceedings of the International Congress on Education of the Deaf* (pp. 156–158), Stockholm.

UNESCO (1985). Consultation on alternative approaches for the education of the deaf. Paris: UNESCO.

Van Uden, A. (1970). New realizations in the light of the pure oral method. *Volta Review, 72*, 524–536.

Webster, A., & Ellwood, J. (1985). *The hearing-impaired child in the ordinary school*. London: Croom Helm.

Whetnall, E., & Fry, D. (1964). *The deaf child*. Springfield, IL: Thomas.

OLIVIER PÉRIER
*Université Libre de Bruxelles,
and Centre Comprendre et
Parler Belgium*

AMERICAN SIGN LANGUAGE
DEAF
FINGERSPELLING
TOTAL COMMUNICATION

## DEBORAH P. *v.* TURLINGTON

*Deborah P.* (1979) is the federal district court case that struck down the competency testing program requirements for high-school graduation in the state of Florida. Deborah P. represented the class of all students in the state who were in danger of failing the test, including students of all ethnic backgrounds. The federal district court found that the competency testing program was unconstitutional for two reasons. The program had failed to provide students with adequate notice of the changes in requirements for a diploma, and the program was held to be racially discriminatory under the Fourteenth Amendment. According to the court, the competency testing program tended to perpetutate preexisting patterns of racial discrimination within the Florida school system. Children in special education programs were not specifically addressed in *Deborah P.*, however, similar issues may be raised if special education students are required to pass competency tests or denied diplomas on the basis of testing programs that discriminate on the basis of race or handicapping condition.

### REFERENCE

*Deborah P. v. Turlington* (1979). #78-892-CIV-T-C, U.S. District Court, Middle District, Tampa Division, July 12 (slip opinion).

CECIL R. REYNOLDS
*Texas A&M University*

## DECERTIFICATION

The passing of PL 94-142 brought about not only an increased awareness of special education students, but also an increased number of students being served in the special education classroom. Recently, however, federal and state education budgets have been drastically reduced. Consequently, it has become necessary to cut certain educational spending procedures. One such cut has been directed at limiting the number of students receiving special education services, especially those referred to as mildly handicapped (Boyan, 1985).

This reduction of spending and ultimately of services has been attempted in several ways. First, states have changed their eligibility criteria for placement in certain programs (Boyan, 1985); i.e., states have made it more difficult to place a child in a special education setting. A second cost-cutting attempt has been the increase in cross-categorical programs. The emphasis of these programs is on serving mildly handicapped students rather than categorically placed students. This approach has gained considerable support as it seems to provide appropriate services while reducing the budget.

In any attempt to decertify students, certain events are likely to take place. First, parents of children who no longer receive services may remove their children from the public school setting and place their children instead in a school specifically designed for certain types of handicapped students. Another possibility is increased litigation. Parents may well claim that their child is being inappropriately served in the regular classroom setting. Finally, it appears that there may be additional litigation brought by parents of children who are not and never have been certified. These parents may claim that their normal child is unable to receive his or her maximum educational opportunities in the regular classroom when the teacher must spend an inordinate amount of time with the decertified student. The decertification issue is far from being resolved.

### REFERENCE

Boyan, C. (1985). California's new eligibility criteria: Legal and program implications. *Exceptional Children, 52*, 131–141.

JOHN R. BEATTIE
*University of North Carolina,
Charlotte*

## DECROLY, OVIDE (1871–1932)

Ovide Decroly, a Belgian physician whose hospital work brought him into contact with many handicapped children, reasoned that the best treatment for such children would be a sound educational program. He established a special school for "the retarded and abnormal" in 1901. A few years later, he founded a school for normal children, where he demonstrated that the methods he was using successfully with handicapped children were equally effective with the nonhandicapped.

Decroly's educational methods were unique. The cornerstone of his method was what he called the "center of interest." Centers of interest were developed around four basic needs: food, protection from the elements, defense against common dangers, and work. Emphasis was placed on learning through activities that grow out of the interests and needs of the students. As much as a year's study could grow out of one topic or theme.

Decroly's work profoundly influenced the European concept of education for both normal and handicapped children. Many of his ideas were similar to those of John Dewey, but Decroly was more a practitioner than a philosopher and his foremost contribution was the establishment of schools that served as models of education based on the needs of children.

## REFERENCES

Hamaide, A. (1924). *The Decroly class*. New York: Dutton.
Kajava, K. (1951). *The traditional European school and some recent experiments in the new education*. Doctoral dissertation. New York: Columbia University.

PAUL IRVINE
*Katonah, New York*

# DEFECTIVE SPEECH

See SPEECH.

# DEFINITION OF HANDICAPPING CONDITIONS

See SPECIFIC HANDICAP.

# DEINSTITUTIONALIZATION

Deinstitutionalization is a movement based on the principles of normalization. Handicapped individuals, mostly the retarded and emotionally handicapped, are moved out of institutions into alternative community living arrangements. Wolfensberger (1972), one of the most outspoken advocates of both deinstitutionalization and normalization, maintains that normalization refers not to treatment but to services, situations, and attitudes that will bring about humane care for the handicapped. This practice calls for small, community-based group homes that would permit residents to participate in local activities and be closer to their families as opposed to long-term, total life care in institutions. Community residential facilities are small in size, house an equally small number of persons, and are meant to be either a permanent residence or a transitional training residence for retarded adults. These facilities range in design from loosely supervised apartments to group homes with live-in house parents (Baker, Seltzer, & Seltzer, 1977).

The trend toward deinstitutionalization of retarded persons began approximately 25 years ago when President Kennedy remarked that the practice of institutionalized segregation from the rest of society was immoral. In 1974 President Nixon announced the goal of returning half of all institutionalized retarded individuals to community settings (Braddock, 1977). The basic construct for the deinstitutionalization movement includes: (1) the creation and maintenance of environments that do not impose excessive restrictions on disabled persons; (2) the creation of arrangements that bring persons as close as possible to the social and cultural mainstream; and (3) guarantees that the human and legal rights of disabled citizens are protected (Neufeld, 1979, p. 115).

Discouraging facts regarding trends toward deinstitutionalization have been identified. Braddock (1977) notes that there are too few community-based residences to receive individuals ready to leave institutions. Directors of institutions believe that over half of their present residents could live successfully in community-based facilities. Neufeld (1979) maintains that deinstitutionalization activities have failed because they have been organized within geographical and population units that are too large.

Neufeld (1979) suggests several deinstitutionalization procedures for promoting this concept. These include (1) placing strong initiatives in the hands of local communities; (2) identifying small geographical service areas containing a relatively small population base; (3) establishing community human service boards with legislative authority to receive funds and operate programs; (4) allowing only highly specialized medical treatment facilities to exist at a regional, multicounty level; (5) giving local human service boards and local providers backup support in the form of training and technical assistance from regional facilities and state agencies; and (6) recognizing that community programs should be developed in order to stabilize the population in institutions (p. 124).

For deinstitutionalization to produce effective results, several issues should be considered. Adequate alternatives that are properly designed, properly maintained, and properly supervised should be developed. In addition, comprehensive evaluations of the individual's ability to succeed in a community-based facility should be made.

## REFERENCES

Baker, B. L., Seltzer, G. B., & Seltzer, M. M. (1977). *As close as possible. Community residences for retarded adults*. Boston: Little, Brown.
Braddock, D. (1977). *Opening closed doors: The deinstitutionalization of disabled individuals*. Reston, VA: Council of Exceptional Children.

Neufeld, G. R. (1979). Deinstitutionalization procedures. In R. Wiegerink & J. W. Pelosi (Eds.), *Developmental disabilities: The DD movement* (pp. 115–126). Baltimore, MD: Brookes.

Wolfensberger, W. (1972). *The principle of normalization in human services.* Toronto, Ontario: National Institute on Mental Retardation.

CECELIA STEPPE-JONES
*North Carolina Central
University*

**COMMUNITY-BASED SERVICES**
**COMMUNITY RESIDENTIAL PROGRAMS**
**NORMALIZATION**
**REHABILITATION**

# DELACATO, CARL H. (1923–          )

Carl H. Delacato received his BS in education at West Chester State College in 1945. He continued his education, receiving an MS in education at the University of Pennsylvania in 1948. In 1952 he received his EdD at the University of Pennsylvania. He founded and directed Chestnut Hill Reading Clinic in 1948.

Delacato's major areas of study are neurological organization and patterning. Patterning is also known as the Doman Delacato-Treatment Method for children with neurological disabilities (Delacato, 1968). The central theory of the Doman-Delacato Treatment Method is based on the neurological organization of the individual. Delacato (1968) defined neurological organization as a physiologically optimum condition that exists uniquely and most completely in man and is the result of total and uninterrupted ontogenetic development. Delacato (1968) feels that language problems could be diagnosed, treated, and prevented through the assessment and modification of neurological organization. Some of Delacato's major works and writings include *The Diagnosis and Treatment of Speech and Reading Problems* and *Neurological Organization and Reading.*

**REFERENCES**

Delacato, C. H. (1966). *Neurological organization and reading.* Springfield, IL: Thomas.

Delacato, C. H. (1968). *The diagnosis and treatment of speech and reading problems.* Springfield, IL: Thomas.

ELIZABETH JONES
*Texas A&M University*

# DELAYED LANGUAGE

See LANGUAGE DELAYS.

# DE LEON, PEDRO

See PONCE DE LEON, PEDRO DE.

# DE L'EPÉE, ABBÉ CHARLES MICHEL (1712–1789)

Abbé Charles Michel de l'Epée founded in Paris in 1755 the first public school for the deaf, the *Institution Nation-*

**Carl H. Delacato**

**Abbé Charles Michel de l'Epée**

*ale des Sourds Muets*. The Abeé developed a systematic language of signs based on the earlier work of Jacob Rodrigues Pereire. His system of signs was the basis of the instructional system in the United States' first school for the deaf, the American School for the Deaf. It is still in use today in modified form.

**REFERENCE**

Lane, H. (1984). *When the mind hears*. New York: Random House.

PAUL IRVINE
*Katonah, NY*

# DELINQUENCY AND SPECIAL EDUCATION

According to Abeson (1977) and Messinger (1976), juvenile delinquents with handicapping conditions have not been given sufficient consideration in the application of the provisions of PL 94-142, the Education for All Handicapped Children Act of 1975. This lack of attention and lack of appropriate special education services is complicated by the confusion surrounding the term juvenile delinquent. This term is variously applied—to predelinquents (e.g., youths misbehaving in school or those who have truant behavior and are suspended); to youths in trouble with the law (e.g., in custody or arrested); to youths detained by the courts; to youths on probation (a form of supervision that bypasses the need for incarceration); to incarcerated youths; and to youths on parole (a form of supervision after incarceration). Despite the confusion of the term, under each circumstance previously described, the juvenile delinquent with a handicapping condition is entitled to a special education program. However, to date there have been only a few documented predelinquent special education programs, no police/school special education programs, only a few court detention/special education programs, only a few probation/special education programs, and only a few parole/special education programs. On a more positive note, there is evidence of a growing number of correctional institution special education programs (Karcz, 1984).

Underutilization of the provisions of PL 94-142 by decision makers in law enforcement agencies, court detention programs, probation programs, parole programs, and, to a lesser extent, correctional institutions is probably owed to the fact that these officials are not fully aware of the law. Furthermore, Hockenberry (1980) suggests that education agencies at the various levels of government may wish to seek interagency policy agreements among those public agencies charged with the responsibility of providing services to youths with handicapping conditions

who commit a delinquent or status offense. Coffey (1983) reports a major reason that PL 94-142 is more problematic for corrections officials and other justice personnel is that the law was written for public schools. As a result, it is almost impossible to apply many of its provisions to schools in correctional institutions.

Despite these shortcomings, youths with handicapping conditions are generally receiving some provision of special education services within the correctional institutions. In 1984 Nelson, Rutherford, and Wolford reported on a Correctional/Special Education Training (C/SET) Project that surveyed available educational programs in juvenile and adult correctional institutions. The survey involved 85 state departments of corrections, juvenile and/or adult divisions, and 50 state special education offices. The C/SET determined that 92% of the 33,190 incarcerated juveniles received educational programs. The number of juvenile offenders with handicapping conditions served was 7750; that number constituted 80% of the total estimated handicapped juvenile population. Of the 399,636 adults incarcerated in 1984, the estimated number of adult offenders with handicapping conditions was 41,590. The number of adult offenders with handicapping conditions served was 4313, or approximately 10% of the adult special education population (or 1% of the total adult population). Comprehensive data about model special programs in correctional institutions are still unavailable. The federally funded C/SET Project is expected to remedy this situation. The C/SET has as one of its goals "to identify model correctional education programs which represent the most promising special education practices" (Karcz & Sabatino, 1986).

Several studies are available that address the effectiveness of special education programs in corrections. Bachara and Zaba (1978) found that the juvenile offenders who were offered remediation in the form of special education, tutoring, or perceptual-motor training exhibited a significantly lower recidivism rate than those who were not offered these programs. Other researchers of the juvenile delinquent population have found that there exists an overall impoverishment of adaptive skill behaviors for this population (Berman & Siegal, 1976).

According to Brown & Robbins (1979), correctional education programs for special education students can be improved if the following issues are addressed: (1) recognition of handicapped youths by committing courts; (2) appropriate testing; (3) possible revision of PL 94-142 criteria to account for the uniqueness of the correctional setting, e.g., rapid turnover of juvenile inmates (an average of 7 months in the institution); (4) specific certification and preservice needs of teachers in correctional education programs; (5) the need for research to create a program data base on which to develop additional programs for handicapped youths in the correctional system; (6) the need for developing institutional/school reentry procedures for students; and (7) the need to develop agreements among two or more agencies serving handicapped inmates.

## REFERENCES

Abeson, A., & Zettel, J. (1977, Oct.). The end of the quiet revolution: The Education for All Handicapped Children Act of 1975. *Exceptional Children, 44*(12), 114–128.

Bachara, G. H., & Zaba, J. N. (1978). Learning disabilities and juvenile delinquency. *Journal of Learning Disability, 11,* 58–62.

Berman, A. & Siegal, A. (1976). Adaptive and learning skills in juvenile delinquents. A neuropsychological analysis. *Journal of Learning Disabilities, 9,* 51–53.

Brown, S. M., & Robbins, M. J. (1979). Serving the special education needs of students in correctional facilities. *Exceptional Children, 49,* 574–579.

Coffey, O. D. (1983). Meeting the needs of handicapped youth in correctional facilities. *Journal of Vocational Special Needs Education, 34,* 13–14.

Hockenberry, C. M. (1980). *Education of adjudicated handicapped youth: Policy issues and implications* (ERIC IAP No. 79-8). Reston, VA: Eric Clearinghouse on Handicapped and Gifted Children.

Karcz, S. A. (1984). *The impact of a special education related service on selected behavior of detained handicapped youth.* Unpublished doctoral dissertation. Syracuse, NY: University of Syracuse.

Karcz, S., & Sabatino, D. A. (1986). Correctional education: Selected problems and practices. In K. D. Gadow and I. Bialer (Eds.), *Advances in learning and behavioral disabilities.* Greenwich, CT: JAI Press, 5, 203–245.

Messinger, J. F. (1976, Aug.). Juvenile delinquents: A relatively untapped population for special education professionals. *Behavioral Disorders, 2*(7), 124–126.

Nelson, C. M., Rutherford, R. B., & Wolford, B. T. (1985). *Juvenile and adult correctional special education data* (Correctional/Special Education Training [C/SET] Project). Washington, DC: U.S. Department of Education.

STAN A. KARCZ
*University of Wisconsin, Stout*

## JUVENILE COURT SYSTEM & THE HANDICAPPED
## JUVENILE DELINQUENCY

## DELINQUENTS, HANDICAPPING CONDITIONS AMONG

By the 1960s and early 1970s, increasing attention and research had focused on the psychological characteristics of juvenile delinquents (Murphy, 1986). The implementation of the Education for All Handicapped Children Act of 1975 (PL 94-142) intensified this interest and brought the plight of handicapped delinquents into the special education arena. Although this law required that handicapped students be appropriately educated, it lacked specific guidelines governing services to handicapped delinquents. As a result, agencies have been able to avoid dealing with the complex task of providing services to this population (Murphy, 1986).

Estimates of prevalence of handicapping conditions among juvenile delinquents vary dramatically (Crawford, 1982; Murphy, 1986). These disparities largely can be attributed to methodological inconsistencies in identification of the major handicapping conditions (i.e., learning disabilities, emotional disturbance, and mental retardation). Further methodological inconsistencies exist in defining juvenile delinquency. The criteria for identifying juvenile delinquents are not uniform across state departments of correction (Murphy, 1986). Indeed, differential diagnosis of handicapping conditions as well as juvenile delinquency appear, in part, to be a state phenomenon.

Though tenuous, the accumulated body of research indicates that the prevalence of handicapping conditions among juvenile delinquents is disproportionate to that reported in nondelinquent populations (Crawford, 1982; Keiltz & Dunivant, 1986; Murphy, 1986). However, the actual prevalence of the major handicaps among juvenile delinquents is difficult to establish. This difficulty can be attributed to the lack of uniform procedures in identifying handicapping conditions and juvenile delinquency. These findings have important implications concerning the identification and servicing of handicapped delinquents under the provisions of the Education for All Handicapped Children Act (Murphy, 1986). Educational handicaps and delinquency among adolescents are almost certainly related, although causality has not been established.

## REFERENCES

Crawford, D. (1982). *Prevalence of handicapped juveniles in the justice system: A study of the literature.* Phoenix, AZ: Research & Development Training Institutes.

Keiltz, I., & Dunivant, N. (1986). The relationship between learning disability and juvenile delinquency: Current state of knowledge. *Remedial & Special Education, 7*(3), 18–26.

Murphy, D. A. (1986). The prevalence of handicapping conditions among juvenile delinquents. *Remedial & Special Education, 7,* 7–17.

HARRISON C. STANTON
*Texas A&M University*

## JUVENILE DELINQUENCY
## LEARNING DISABILITIES

## DE LORENZO, MARIA E. G. E. (1927–  )

Maria E. De Lorenzo is a noted Uruguayan special educator. She obtained her BA in education at Teacher's College, Montevideo, Uruguay (1941), and her MA in clinical psychology at the University of Michigan, Ann Arbor (1948). She served as director of School N.1 for mentally retarded children (1949–1967) and as a member of the National Board of Elementary Education in Uruguay from 1967 to 1972. From 1966 to the present, De Lorenzo has been chief of the Mental Retardation Unit of the Inter-American Children's Institute, a specialized agency of the Organization of American States.

She frequently acts as a consultant for numerous international organizations such as the United Nations, the Organization of American States, Partners of the Americas, the President's Committee on Mental Retardation (U.S.), and the International League of Societies for Persons with Mental Handicaps. Since 1967, De Lorenzo has been a member of various U.N. organizations, among them the World Health Organization, U.N. Educational, Scientific, and Cultural Organization, and U.N. International Children's Emergency Fund. She is a member of numerous professional associations and of the editorial boards of the *International Journal of Rehabilitation Research*, the *Journal of Learning, Disabilities,* and the *Infant Mental Health Journal*.

De Lorenzo received numerous honors and special appointments, e.g., the Joseph P. Kennedy Award (1966), the Leadership Award for Achievements in Mental Deficiency (1976), and the Award of Merit granted by the President's Committee on Mental Retardation (1977). She also received the associate researcher *honoris causa* at the Research Department of the Bureau of Child Research, University of Kansas (1972). In 1978, De Lorenzo was invited to be the main speaker at the opening session of the World Congress on Future Special Education, organized by Council for Exceptional Children in Sterling, Scotland.

Ivan Z. Holowinsky
*Rutgers University*

## DELTA SCHOOL/BUTTONWOOD FARMS, INC.

Buttonwood Farms was established in 1958 to serve students with social and emotional disorders. The corporation publishes the quarterly *Journal of Special Education*, which reviews trends in the field, provides an update on the state of the arts, and discusses research and educational techniques for the handicapped. Buttonwood Farms conducts seminars throughout the school year that feature psychological reviews, testing approaches, and educational workshops.

The Buttonwood Farms corporation operates the Delta School, located in Philadelphia, Pennsylvania. The Delta School serves students at the elementary and secondary levels who have emotional disorders and learning problems. The curriculum provides an intensive educational experience that coordinates the student's individual educational plan with concepts related to learning and understanding the world of work. These objectives are achieved through tutorial instruction, academic programs, and remedial approaches. The Delta School program emphasizes career awareness and community work programs. The ancillary services include counseling, adaptive physical education, speech and language therapies, industrial arts, and vocational guidance. For information, write the Delta School, Buttonwood Farms, Inc., 3515 Woodhaven Road, Philadelphia, PA 19154.

### REFERENCE

Sargent, J. K. (1982). *The directory of exceptional children* (9th ed.). Boston: Porter Sargent.

Paul C. Richardson
*Elwyn Institutes,
Elwyn, Pennsylvania*

## DEMOGRAPHY OF SPECIAL EDUCATION

Demographic characteristics relating to handicapped children and youths include (1) the number and types of handicapped children and youths served; (2) the services received by these children and youths; (3) the personnel who provide services; and (4) the settings in which special education and related services are provided.

During the school year 1984–1985, 4,363,031 handicapped children and youths were receiving special education services. Of this number, 1,839,292 were learning disabled, 1,129,417 were speech impaired, 717,785 were mentally retarded, 373,207 were emotionally disturbed, 71,230 were hard of hearing/deaf, 71,780 were multihandicapped, 58,835 were orthopedically impaired, 69,118 were other health impaired, 30,375 were visually handicapped, and 1,992 were deaf-blind. The total number of handicapped children and youths served represents an increase of 21,632 students from the previous school year (1983–1984). This increase primarily was the result of an increase in the learning-disabled population and reduction in the number of students in several other categories (e.g., mentally retarded, speech impaired). In terms of age, the largest proportion of increase was evidenced by children ages 3 to 5 (243,087 in 1983–1984 to 259,483 in 1984–1985) and youths ages 18 to 21 (186,393 in 1983–1984 to 192,438 in 1984–1985).

The number of personnel employed to work with handicapped children and youths generally has paralleled the

| Handicapping Condition | Total Served | Regular Classes (%) | Separate Classes (%) | Separate Schools (%) | Other Environments (%) |
|---|---|---|---|---|---|
| Learning disabled | 1,790,923 | 77.27 | 21.21 | 1.33 | 0.18 |
| Speech impaired | 1,120,012 | 93.32 | 4.76 | 1.34 | 0.58 |
| Mentally retarded | 713,785 | 29.63 | 56.09 | 13.62 | 0.66 |
| Emotionally disturbed | 358,736 | 44.04 | 36.51 | 19.96 | 2.48 |
| Hard of hearing/deaf | 70,472 | 38.68 | 35.96 | 24.33 | 1.02 |
| Multihandicapped | 59,188 | 13.96 | 46.28 | 36.54 | 3.22 |
| Orthopedically impaired | 58,348 | 36.76 | 38.42 | 17.33 | 7.48 |
| Other health impaired | 53,914 | 42.25 | 27.20 | 9.88 | 20.68 |
| Visually handicapped | 28,710 | 57.10 | 18.02 | 23.91 | 0.98 |
| Deaf-blind | 2,019 | 12.83 | 30.36 | 54.33 | 2.48 |
| Noncategorical | 27,669 | 55.47 | 35.12 | 4.77 | 4.63 |

growth or decline of specific categories:

**SPECIAL EDUCATION TEACHERS EMPLOYED**

| | 1976–1977 | 1982–1983 | 1983–1984 |
|---|---|---|---|
| Learning disabled | 44,003 | 82,625 | 89,756 |
| Speech impaired | 18,392 | 19,632 | 20,600 |
| Mentally retarded | 71,681 | 61,452 | 58,727 |
| Emotionally disturbed | 21,709 | 26,967 | 28,225 |
| Hard of hearing/deaf | 8,789 | 8,224 | 8,144 |
| Multihandicapped | — | 5,240 | 5,769 |
| Orthopedically impaired | 5,344 | 4,383 | 4,643 |
| Other health impaired | 4,975 | 3,079 | 3,174 |
| Visually handicapped | 3,470 | 3,275 | 3,047 |
| Deaf-blind | — | 898 | 786 |
| Noncategorical | — | 25,305 | 24,919 |
| All conditions | 179,804 | 241,079 | 247,791 |

Other categories of personnel engaged in providing special education or related services also have shown marked change:

**SCHOOL STAFF**

| | 1976–1977 | 1982–1983 | 1983–1984 |
|---|---|---|---|
| Social workers | 5,881 | 7,659 | 7,586 |
| Occupational therapists | 1,401 | 2,380 | 2,490 |
| Recreational therapists | 504 | 751 | 595 |
| Physical therapists | — | 1,962 | 2,109 |
| Teacher aides | 66,876 | 102,722 | 105,394 |
| Physical education coordinators | 5,014 | 3,815 | 3,694 |
| Supervisors | 10,161 | 11,607 | 11,846 |
| Other noninstructional | 17,479 | 45,124 | 41,353 |
| Psychologists | 9,950 | 14,513 | 14,811 |
| Diagnostic staff | 7,781 | 6,145 | 6,562 |
| Speech pathologists | 11,032 | 20,152 | 20,838 |
| Audiologists | 470 | 794 | 773 |
| Work-study coordinators | 5,473 | 5,478 | 5,781 |
| Vocational education teachers | 1,384 | 1,585 | 2,678 |
| All staff | 151,649 | 224,684 | 226,505 |

In addition, the demographic characteristics of handicapped children and youths can be portrayed through the different educational environments in which these students receive special education and related services. Special education and related services are offered in regular classes, separate classes, separate schools, and other environments:

**ALL HANDICAPPING CONDITIONS** (School Year 1983–1984)

| Regular Classes | Separate Classes | Separate Schools | Other Environments |
|---|---|---|---|
| 2,910,515 | 1,070,427 | 260,601 | 43,156 |
| (67.93%) | (24.98%) | (6.08%) | (1.01%) |

The proportion of handicapped children and youths served in each environment is dependent on the specific handicapping condition. (See table at top of page).

When examined by age groups, young handicapped children (ages 3 to 5) are served in more restrictive settings than older children and youths (ages 6 to 17). This may be the result of fewer regular education programs for young children, which, in turn, requires the establishment of separate programs for young handicapped children.

## REFERENCES

U.S. Department of Education. (1985). *Seventh annual report to Congress on the implementation of the Education of the Handicapped Act.* Washington, DC: Author.

U.S. Department of Education. (1986). *Eighth annual report to Congress on the implementation of the Education of the Handicapped Act.* Washington, DC: Author.

MARTY ABRAMSON
*University of Wisconsin, Stout*

## SPECIAL EDUCATION, FEDERAL IMPACT ON
*See* POLITICS AND SPECIAL EDUCATION

## DENDRITES

A typical neuron is depicted in the Figure below. The nucleus of the cell, called the soma or perikaryon, has various protruding elements. The main protruding element is the axon.

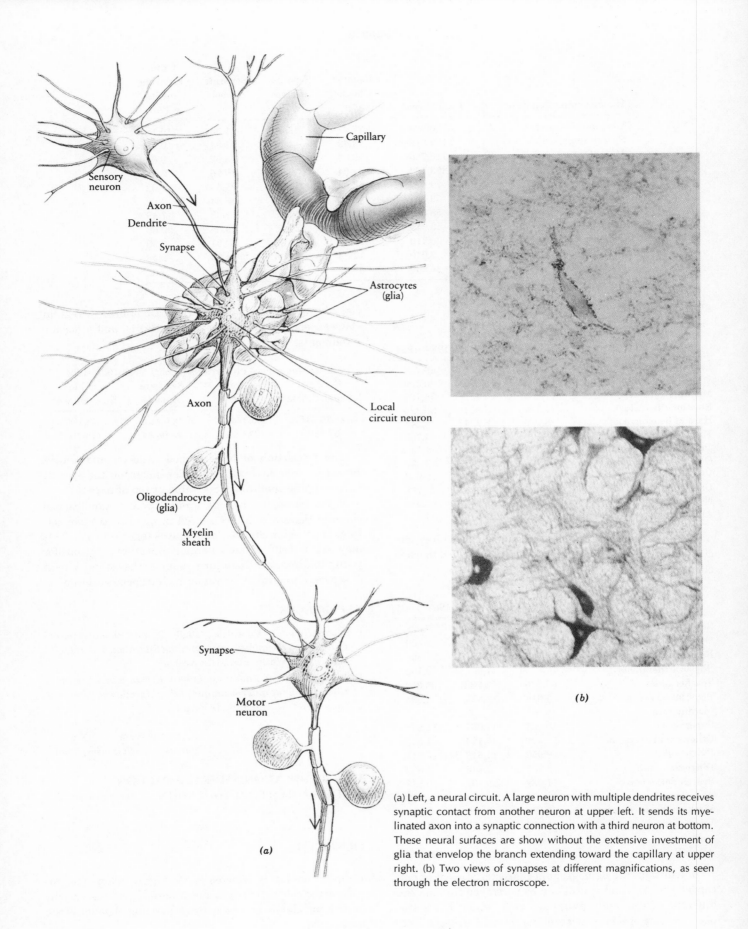

Labels on figure (a):

Sensory neuron

Axon

Dendrite

Synapse

Capillary

Astrocytes (glia)

Local circuit neuron

Axon

Oligodendrocyte (glia)

Myelin sheath

Synapse

Motor neuron

*(a)*

*(b)*

(a) Left, a neural circuit. A large neuron with multiple dendrites receives synaptic contact from another neuron at upper left. It sends its myelinated axon into a synaptic connection with a third neuron at bottom. These neural surfaces are show without the extensive investment of glia that envelop the branch extending toward the capillary at upper right. (b) Two views of synapses at different magnifications, as seen through the electron microscope.

Typically surrounding the soma, except where the axon exits, are a variety of smaller protruding elements that form the dendritic network of the neuron. The dendrites have an appearance somewhat akin to branches of a leafless tree and *dendron* is the Greek stem meaning tree. The dendrites serve as the neurotransmitter receptacle sites, as does the soma itself, from neurotransmitter release from the axon of a different neuron. The synaptic termination actually occurs on little spines that arise from the dendrite. These spines are numerous. For example, a single motor neuron may have as many as 4000 spines on its dendrites. Although it was originally assumed that the dendrite served a rather passive role in neuronal transmission, it is now speculated that the dendritic processes play a much more dynamic and active role in neurotransmission (Cooper, Bloom, & Roth, 1978; Cotman & McGaugh, 1980) and neurobehavioral (i.e., learning) functions.

## REFERENCES

Cooper, J. R., Bloom, F. E., & Roth, R. H. (1978). *The biochemical basis of neuropharmacology* (3rd ed.). New York: Oxford University Press.

Cotman, C. W., & McGaugh, J. L. (1980). *Behavioral neuroscience.* New York: Academic.

ERIN D. BIGLER
*Austin Neurological Clinic*
*University of Texas, Austin*

## CENTRAL NERVOUS SYSTEM GLIAL CELLS

## DENO, EVELYN N. (1911–     )

As a developmental psychologist, Evelyn Deno has specialized in the design and delivery of helping services for handicapped children and their parents. As a preschool, elementary, and college teacher of 17 years, Deno earned her MA in 1950, and PhD in 1958, in child development and clinical psychology from the University of Minnesota, where she taught graduate-level classes in child development. She then went on to become director of special education and rehabilitation for the Minneapolis public schools. She returned to the University of Minnesota in 1967 as professor of educational psychology and director of the Psycho-Educational Center. She was also co-director of the Leadership Training Institute for the USOE Bureau of Professional Development.

Best known for her "cascade of special education services" concept and diagram, Deno has always seen the need for "helping service systems and political agents to promote a more compatible match between individual aspirations and the constraining social and physical environmental realities" (personal communication, August 27, 1985). She has applied developmental theory to see

how people with special adjustment problems can be helped to survive in a culture and society inclined to regard deviance from the "norm" (or what is expected) as a problem of the deviant one, not a challenge to society's ability and obligation to respect individual differences." (personal communication, August 27, 1985)

Deno's current interests lie with the adjustment problems of older persons and the design and implementation of programs for them to serve as counselors to their peers, tutors, and as "special friends" to learning-disabled and emotionally disturbed children. She has received a number of awards for outstanding contributions in her field. Service delivery models designed and tested under her direction have been designated as national service prototypes.

ELAINE FLETCHER-JANZEN
*Texas A&M University*

## DENTISTRY AND THE HANDICAPPED CHILD

Dental disease represents a serious health problem for many handicapped children. A comprehensive survey by the National Center for Health Statistics (1979) estimated that oral disease is 40% higher among mentally retarded individuals, across all ages, than in the population at large. In a more recent report (Callahan, 1983a), the incidence of dental disease was almost 20% higher in the mentally retarded population than in comparably aged nonhandicapped individuals.

The physical consequences and personal discomfort of dental disorders and untreated oral diseases for handicapped individuals are obvious; they include pain, oral abscesses, and loss of teeth. The educational and social implications are, perhaps, just as important. Bad teeth, gum disorders, etc. can cause bad breath and cosmetic disabilities and thus make the social acceptance of handicapped children and adults more difficult. The cosmetic implications of good dental health for the handicapped have been recognized by many states that provide dental care to vocational rehabilitation clients, though the need for services usually outstrips the resources available to meet them.

A number of diverse physiological social and economic factors have been identified as being responsible for the greater degree of dental and oral disorders in handicapped populations. Malformations and abnormal development of certain teeth are thus coincidental with certain types of handicapping conditions. Particular dental difficulties have been found to be associated with various types of handicapping conditions. Individuals with Down's syndrome have been found to experience a relatively low incidence of tooth decay but a high incidence of periodontal or gum disease (Pugliese, 1978); while the gums of many epileptic individuals have been found to overgrow as a consequence of dilantin use (Nowaka, 1976). Neurological seizures or motor disabilities may result in head injuries that cause serious damage to oral structures. Motor impairments, limited cognitive understanding of the importance of good dental habits, and poor motivation often limit the carrying out of oral hygiene practices by handicapped children and frustrate parents' training and monitoring efforts.

The strained economic conditions of many handicapped children is another reason for the high incidence of oral disease in special education populations. Many handicapped children come from socioeconomically disadvantaged families that are not likely to emphasize the precepts of oral hygiene in their daily living or to afford dental care. Furthermore, there has been a reduction of dental support for such families in Medicaid programs. Indeed, the federal government, under Title XIX, does not require that states provide any dental services to adult Medicaid recipients.

Additionally, until recently, barrier restrictions, difficulties in patient management, and negative attitudes have limited receptivity in dental professionals with regard to the provision of services to difficult patients. Difficulties in patient management and negative attitudes on the part of dental health professionals negatively affect the provision of dental care to difficult to treat handicapped patients. As recently as 1977, only 200 out of 1000 dentists in a metropolitan area were identified as either accepting or interested in accepting handicapped patients (Callahan, 1983b). Beyond such problems, even when willing and proficient service providers are available, parents of handicapped children and agencies serving them are often unaware of their availability.

Specific difficulties with respect to preventing or ameliorating dental problems and oral disease in handicapped students are attributable to the attitudes of school personnel generally and special education personnel in particular. There is very little attention paid to the dental/oral needs and problems of handicapped children in our schools currently. This is in part a consequence of changing conditions of service provision to handicapped children. Increasingly, as that provision has moved from segregated circumstances such as institutions in which health care considerations are predominant over educational ones, to the less restrictive environments of day and public school programs, there has been a decided shift from concern with the physical (care) needs of handicapped schoolchildren to their specific instructional needs. While the health professionals and special education teachers serving special education populations undoubtedly recognize the needs of handicapped children for good oral training

and dental health care, they are not likely to emphasize these in their day to day individualized education plan practices. Present-day special education requires the provision of so many mandated educational services that the laborious training of children in instructionally peripheral areas of brushing, flossing, etc. is likely to be neglected.

The 1970s were a particularly active period with respect to comprehensive investments of time and effort in improving dental care for handicapped individuals. One of the most important efforts in this respect was the funding by the Robert Wood Johnson Foundation during 1974–1978 of 11 dental schools across the country. This funding was to support the development of comprehensive dental school training programs relative to the provision of services to handicapped individuals; i.e., to develop specialized skills and technology, to create positive attitude change in dental professionals, to develop referral and service delivery capabilities at dental schools, and to institutionalize aspects of these programs at dental schools following funding.

Evaluation of these projects revealed decreased anxiety in faculty, staff, and students in working with handicapped students, increased ability to communicate with the handicapped regarding their dental problems, and improved dental care practices. Positive attitude changes were reported in persons affected by the program, e.g., decreased fear and anxiety, as well as a better understanding of handicapped dental patients. A comprehensive report on the Robert Wood Johnson Foundation's program, the most ambitious privately funded one to date, is available from the Educational Testing Service (Campbell et al., 1982).

Apropos of the Robert Wood Johnson Foundation's work, Stiefel and Truelove (1985) recently reported on the 5-year postgraduate program at the University of Washington that resulted in significant cognitive changes and gains in confidence respecting the treatment of handicapped individuals by dentists, dental hygienists, and assistants who participated in a postgraduate program.

While there has been a steady if meager stream of publications concerning the dental management of handicapped children, a resurgence of interest is to be observed in the work of such investigators as Price (1978) and Pugliese (1978). Much of this interest, as might be expected, has been in the direction of preventive dentistry, and in the participation of home, school, and community in the dental management of handicapped individuals. Callahan (1983a, 1983b), among others, has emphasized that effective dental care for handicapped individuals must go beyond the improvement of dental services per se and improved technology to improving the willingness of dental practitioners to engage school and other service providers in the dental care of handicapped students. Callahan emphasizes the value of preventive services that will improve the dental status of the handicapped and reduce the costs of their dental care. For those handicapped individuals who will remain school and community based (this means most handicapped children and adults), programs of comprehensive preventive dental care should be emphasized over those of costly treatment.

What can be accomplished through preventive programs has been demonstrated through model outreach programs implemented by the National Foundation of Dentistry for the Handicapped (Callahan, 1983b). These programs have incorporated daily oral hygiene programs into the practices at a variety of special education schools, sheltered workshops, and group homes at relatively modest costs. They rely on periodic screening to detect dental disorders while they are still easily manageable. They use referral networks to coordinate the delivery of dental treatment to those handicapped individuals who require it. Most important, they use teachers, counselors, vocational rehabilitation personnel, houseparents, and other service personnel, in addition to those from the dental professions, on their service delivery teams. Similar concerted efforts might be valuable in bringing special education and special educators fully into the teaching and training of oral hygiene methods and precepts.

Recent interest in applying dental and oral hygiene principles in work with more severely handicapped populations is evidenced by the work of Feldman and Elliot (1981). Finally, because the vast majority of special education students these days reside at home, it is encouraging to observe recent efforts directed toward parents as oral hygiene trainers and monitors. Thus an article by Stark et al. (1985) provides guidelines to parents respecting their children's dental needs with regard to nutrition, medication, visits to the dentist, and the inculcation of proper dental care habits.

## REFERENCES

Callahan, W. P. (1983a). Dental disease: A continuing education problem for the disabled individual. *Journal of Special Education, 17,* 355–359.

Callahan, W. P. (1983b). The effectiveness of instructional programming on the reduction of dental diseases in mentally retarded individuals. *Mental Retardation, 21,* 260–262.

Campbell, J. Y., Esser, B. F., & Flaugher, R. L. (1982). *Evaluation of a program for training dentists in the care of handicapped patients* (Report No. QAT24225). Princeton, NJ: Educational Testing Service.

*Dentistry and the handicapped.* (1981). (Videotape). Denver: LADOCA.

Feldman, D., & Elliot, T. A. (1981). A multidimensional oral hygiene curriculum for the severelyi and profoundly handicapped. *Journal of Special Education Technology, 4,* 33–45.

Nowak, A. J. (1976). *Dentistry for the handicapped patient.* St. Louis: Mosby.

Price, J. H. (1978). Dental health education for the mentally and physically handicapped. *Journal of School Health, 48,* 171–173.

Pugliese, R. (1978). Oral health status in a group of mentally retarded patients. *Rhode Island Dental Journal, 11,* 6–9.

Stark, J., Markel, G., Black, C. M., & Greenbaum, J. (1985). Day to day dental care: A parents' guide. *Exceptional Parent, 15,* 15–17.

Stiefel, D. J. (1980). Dental care for the handicapped at the University of Washington. *Journal of Dental Medicine, 44,* 141–145.

Stiefel, D. J., & Truelove, E. L. (1985). A postgraduate dental training program for treatment of persons with disabilities. *Journal of Dental Education, 49,* 85–90.

U.S. Public Health Service. (1980). *Special report on dental care for handicapped people.* Arlington, VA: Rehabilitation Services Administration, U.S. Department of Health, Education, and Welfare.

U.S. Department of Health, Education, and Welfare, Public Health Service. (1979). *Basic data on dental examination findings of persons.* Hyattesville, MD: National Center for Health Statistics.

DAVID C. MANN
*St. Francis Hospital,*
*Pittsburgh, Pennsylvania*

**BRUXISM**
**INDIVIDUAL EDUCATION PLAN (IEP)**
**SELF-HELP TRAINING**

## DENVER DEVELOPMENTAL SCREENING TEST (DDST)

The Denver Developmental Screening Test (DDST) is an individually administered, norm-referenced device intended for early detection of developmental delays in children aged 2 weeks to 6 years. The test is composed of 105 items organized into four broad developmental areas: the personal-social area, including tasks such as responding to others, playing cooperatively, and caring for oneself; the fine motor-adaptive area, including tasks such as drawing, copying designs, and manipulating blocks; the language area, including tasks involving the ability to hear, imitate, understand, and use language; and the gross motor area, including tasks such as walking forward and backward, balancing, and throwing and catching a ball.

On the test record form, the tasks of each general area are ordered along a developmental continuum reflecting increasing age and difficulty. Each item is clearly marked on the continuum to show the ages at which 25, 50, 75, and 90% of the norm group successfully performed the task. Items are scored in pass-fail format and a judgment about the child's general developmental status is made by evaluating the number of delays (failure of an item that is passed by 90% of children who are younger) evidenced during testing.

Test reviewers have consistently credited the DDST with being an appropriate screening instrument for the early identification of possible delayed development. Reliability and validity are thought to be adequate for a screening instrument, although the standardization sample composition (Denver residents only) has raised some questions about the adequacy of the test's norms (Moriarty, 1978; Salvia & Ysseldyke, 1985; Walker, Bonner, & Milling, 1985; Werner, 1978).

## REFERENCES

Moriarty, A. E. (1978). Review of the Denver Developmental Screening Test. In O. K. Buros (Ed.), *The seventh mental measurements yearbook* (pp. 733–734). Highland, Park, NJ: Gryphon Press.

Salvia, J. & Ysseldyke, J. E. (1985). *Assessment in special and remedial education* (3rd ed.). Boston: Houghton Mifflin.

Walker, C. E., Bonner, B., & Milling, L. (1985). Review of the Denver Developmental Screening Test. In D. J. Keyser & R. C. Sweetland (Eds.), *Test critiques*: Vol. I (pp. 239–251). Kansas City, MO: Test Corporation of America.

Werner, E. E. (1978). Review of the Denver Developmental Screening Test. In O. K. Buros (Ed.), *The seventh mental measurement yearbook* (pp. 734–736). Highland Park, NJ: Gryphon Press.

GEORGE MCCLOSKEY
*American Guidance Service,
Circle Pines, Minnesota*

## DEPAKENE

Depakene is an antiepileptic agent known generically as valproic acid. Depakene is the most recently introduced anticonvulsant medication. It differs both chemically and in clinical action from most other anticonvulsants (Goldensohn, Glaser, & Goldberg, 1984). Generally this medication is used either as the sole or adjunctive treatment for simple (petit mal) and complex absence seizures as well as generalized seizure disorders. The precise mechanism by which Depakene works is unknown; however, some research has suggested that its activity is related to increased brain levels of gamma-aminobutyric acid.

While there is little research on the behavioral effects of Depakene, uncontrolled trials suggest that it may improve visual-motor coordination (Schlack, 1974), alertness, and school performance (Barnes & Bower, 1975). Nausea and gastrointestinal irritation are common side effects of Depakene, but these can be controlled through dosage or by giving the drug with food. If Depakene is given with other medications, particularly phenobarbital, there can be extreme, temporary sedation as well as awkward motor movements. Some of the more extreme side effects include a disruption of platelet functioning, liver damage, and pancreas failure, all of which have the po-

tential to be fatal. For these reasons, Depakene typically is held in reserve as a medication of final resort for those individuals with seizures that cannot be controlled by other medication.

## REFERENCES

Barnes, S. E., & Bower, B. D. (1975). Sodium valproate in the treatment of intractible childhood epilepsy. *Developmental Medicine and Child Neurology, 17,* 175–181.

Goldensohn, E. S., Glaser, G. H., & Goldberg, M. A. (1984). Epilepsy. In L. P. Rowland (Ed.), *Merritt's textbook of neurology* (7th ed.) (pp. 629–650). Philadelphia: Lea & Febiger.

Schlack, H. G. (1974). Ergenye in the treatment of epilepsy. *Therapiewoche, 24,* 39–42.

RICHARD A. BERG
*West Virginia University
Medical Center, Charleston
Division*

ANTICONVULSANTS
EPILEPSY

## DEPRESSION

The word depression has many different meanings. In psychiatry, depression may range from a transient, momentary feeling of emotional dejection to a severe disorder that can stop a person from functioning, cause a slowdown of body processes, and even, in some cases, lead to death. When does depression cease to be a normal condition and become an abnormal clinical state? Researchers and clinicians view a combination of intensity, severity, and duration of depressive symptoms in the identification of clinical depression.

The onset of clinical depression is usually signaled by a depressed mood and/or loss of interest in usual activities. Symptoms may include anxiety, crying, slowed thinking, suicidal tendencies, and feelings of guilt, worthlessness, and hopelessness. When these symptoms persist more than two weeks, a clinical depression may be occurring. Depression can be associated with another psychiatric disorder such as schizophrenia or alcoholism, or with a physical illness, for instance, a viral disease or an endocrine disorder. However, clinical depressions often exist without any other intermediary disturbance. It is these conditions, the clinical depressive syndromes, which include unipolar and bipolar disorders (the latter is also known as manic-depressive illness) and cyclothymic and dysthymic disorders (the latter is also known as depressive neurosis), that are the major focus of current research and clinical attention.

For some time it had been thought that depression was more common to late-middle and old age, but more recent surveys indicate that a higher proportion of younger persons are depressed than previously believed, that depression occurs as much or more in the 20 to 40 age range as in older persons, and that depression in infants, children, and adolescents has been underidentified. In general, clinical depression is twice as common in women as in men. Possible reasons for this are genetic, sociocultural, and hormonal. Diagnostic practices and the willingness for women to seek help more frequently than men may also contribute. All of these possibilities are receiving a great deal of research attention.

Four to ten percent of the American public now suffers from an identifiable depressive disorder. Over the course of a lifetime, perhaps 25% of the population will experience a major depressive episode. In fact, clinical depression is so prevalent in the United States that most people have a friend or relative who has suffered or is suffering from some variant of the disorder.

There are a number of effective treatments available for clinical depressions; these include several specific forms of psychotherapy, a variety of antidepressant drugs and lithium, combinations of drugs and psychotherapy, and electroconvulsive treatment (ECT). The preferred treatment depends on the type and severity of the depression and on factors such as the physical condition and age of the depressed person. Many people are helped by treatment, although all treatments do not work equally well for all people. Some people with recurrent unipolar or bipolar disorders have been helped substantially by long-term maintenance treatment.

Approximately 50% of people who have had a major clinical depressive episode never experience another one. For the remaining 50%, the course is variable: there may be a few episodes with intervals of many years of normal functioning, episodes may be more frequent, or they may cluster. For some, the frequency of episodes will increase with advancing age. Most individuals who have one or more manic episodes will eventually also have a depressive episode. For these individuals, the course is similarly variable. Adequate treatment can minimize or reduce the severity of the episode in many cases. Treatment may take a medical form; for example, medication may be given to address the chemical imbalance that has been stimulated by the depression. As mentioned earlier, ECT may be employed with major depressions that have not been responsive to other treatments. Treatment forms will typically be combined with psychotherapeutic attention to environmental and cognitive issues presented by the person, or this modality may be sufficient in and of itself.

Long-term follow-up studies of persons with serious clinical depressions not associated with other psychiatric disorders have found a suicide rate of 15%. A greater percentage of women attempt suicide, but a greater percentage of men successfully complete the act. The depressed individual considered an especially high suicide risk is a white male over the age of 45 who is separated, widowed, or divorced, lives alone, and is unemployed or retired. A number of researchers have found that the likelihood of completed suicide in depressed people is related to hopelessness and negative expectations about the future rather than to other symptoms. With treatment, these feelings can often be overcome.

There seems to be no single outstanding cause of clinical depressions. Rather, there are a variety of factors, some of which may have more weight in certain types of depressions than others. Among these factors are genetic predisposition, biological imbalances or abnormalities, personality characteristics, learned behavior and thought patterns, stressful life events, social and economic class, culture, age, and sex.

CHARLES P. BARNARD
*University of Wisconsin, Stout*

# DEPRIVATION, BIONEURAL RESULTS OF

The term deprivation is usually used to mean the absence or reduction of normal sensory input to the nervous system. Its meaning is sometimes extended to include restriction or suppression of opportunities for normal motoric activities associated with exploration, play, and social intercourse. The bioneural results of deprivation have mostly been investigated through animal experiments.

The visual system has been studied extensively. Various changes reviewed by Vrensen and De Groot (1974) have been observed in the visual cortex of animals reared in the dark. Monocular deprivation has been shown to produce more salient changes than binocular; competition between the two sides seems to be a more important factor than deprivation per se. The changes are particularly marked, and largely irreversible, when deprivation occurs during a critical period of early life. The best known examples are the protracted loss of vision through one eye in kittens (Wiesel & Hubel, 1965) and monkeys (Hubel et al., 1976), resulting from a brief period of interference with that eye's function shortly after birth. Stimulation of the deprived eye no longer elicits normal activity in the visual area of the brain because this has become reorganized in favor of the other eye.

In the auditory system, complete suppression of input is impossible without destruction of both inner ears, since otherwise there is always some perception of the sounds produced in the animal's own body. Temporary restriction of auditory stimuli can be achieved by rearing in a sound-attenuated environment or by interfering with the external or middle ear structures that transmit sound to the inner ear. Both methods produce perturbations of the auditory function and neuronal alterations of brain stem auditory nuclei (Webster & Webster, 1979). Significant changes in the microscopic structure of the auditory cortex have been observed in mutant mice with hereditary deafness owed to inner ear degeneration (Périer et al., 1984). As in the visual system, there are critical or sensitive periods of development during which plasticity is greatest and the results of deprivation most evident (Eggermont, 1986).

Nonspecific reduction of sensory stimulation is achieved by rearing animals in standard or isolated laboratory conditions as opposed to environmental complexity. In these experiments, there is a reduction of the normal span of sensory experiences, motor activities, and social exchanges. Behavioral differences as well as differences in cerebral structures are observed. Both have been extensively reviewed by Walsch (1980, 1981a, 1981b).

In man, the counterpart of animal experiments on the visual system is functional amblyopia, a condition observed in some children who have suffered from unattended squinting or other conditions interfering with the vision of one eye. Even after correction of the pathological condition, the deprived eye may remain largely nonfunctional. Partial auditory deprivation is a frequent occurrence in small children as a result of serous otitis media. It seems to cause long-lasting learning difficulties, even after normal hearing has been restored. All degrees of hearing loss, from mild to profound, might affect the human auditory pathways and cortex, as shown in animals. These possible effects in man have been discussed by Ruben & Rapin (1980). Studies in language development indicate that infants possess a capacity for making phonetic distinctions which must, to persist, be confirmed by the corresponding sounds of language spoken in their environment. Some studies indicate that children with congenital or early acquired hearing loss might lose this early competence (Serniclaes, et al., 1984).

Examples of extreme multisensory and social deprivation in man are afforded by "wolf" children and exceptional cases such as that of Genie, a girl maintained in isolation for years by psychotic parents (Curtiss, 1977). The complexity of such cases as well as the lack of sufficient information about their early life make their interpretation difficult. Less severe but more frequent deprivation situations occur in hospitalism (Spitz, 1945) and in poorly stimulating familial background. It is probable, though yet unproven, that these have bioneural consequences in addition to the well-known psychological ones.

## REFERENCES

Curtiss, S. (1977). *Genie, a psycholinguistic study of a modern day "wild child."* New York: Academic.

Eggermont, J. (1986). Critical periods in auditory development. Proceedings of the Nijmegen Workshop. *Acta Otolaryngologica* (Stockholm) (Suppl., in press).

Hubel, D. H., Wiesel, T. N., & LeVay S. (1976). Functional architecture of area 17 in normal and monocularly deprived Macaque monkeys. *Cold Spring Harbor Symposium on Quantitative Biology. 40,* 581–589.

Périer, O., Alegria, J., Buyse, M., D'Alimonte, G., Gilson, D., & Serniclaes, W. (1984). Consequences of auditory deprivation in animals and humans. *Acta Otolaryngologica* (Stockholm), *411,* 60–70.

Ruben, R. J., & Rapin, I. (1980). Plasticity of the developing auditory system. *Annals of Otology Rhinology and Laryngology, 89,* 303–311.

Serniclaes, W., D'Alimonte, G., & Alegria, J. (1984). Production and perception of French stops by moderately deaf subjects. *Speech Communication, 3,* 185–198.

Spitz, R. A. (1945). Hospitalism—An enquiry into the genesis of psychiatric conditions in early childhood. *Psychoanalytic Study of the Child, 1,* 53–74.

Vrensen, G., & De Groot, D. (1974). The effect of dark rearing and its recovery on synaptic terminals in the visual cortex of rabbits. A quantitative electron microscopic study. *Brain Research, 78,* 263–278.

Walsch, R. (1980). Effects of environmental complexity and deprivation on brain chemistry and physiology: A review. *International Journal of Neuroscience, 11,* 77–89.

Walsch, R. (1981a). Effects of environmental complexity and deprivation on brain anatomy and histology: A review. *International Journal of Neuroscience, 12,* 33–51.

Walsch, R. (1981b). Sensory environments, brain damage, and drugs: A review of interactions and mediating mechanisms. *International Journal of Neuroscience, 14,* 129–137.

Webster, D. B., & Webster, M. (1979). Effects of neonatal conductive hearing loss on brain stem auditory nuclei. *Annals of Otology Rhinology, & Laryngoly, 88,* 684–688.

OLIVIER PÉRIER
*Université Libre de Bruxelles*
*Comprendre et Parler, Brussels*
*Belgium*

**EARLY EXPERIENCE & CRITICAL PERIODS**
**GENIE**
**LANGUAGE, ABSENCE OF**
**LANGUAGE DELAYS**

## DESENSITIZATION

Desensitization is a procedure that combines guided participation, modeling, and the graduated approach to a desired response (e.g., shaping). The technique has been used primarily with fear responses in children and adults, and its primary targets have been phobic reactions to various stimuli. While undergoing this therapy, the individual is first introduced to the process by beginning under the least demanding conditions. The therapist models the desired behavior and the individual is guided through his or her responses. These responses are gradually modified to approximate the real circumstances under which the feared stimuli might be encountered. The gradual modification takes place with the therapist modeling each successive response and guiding the student through the appropriate response. The therapist also makes encouraging statements and uses other reinforcing methods (Kratochwill, 1975). These supportive techniques are gradually withdrawn. The two procedures used are generally referred to as shaping a correct response and fading the prompts that have been used to support the acquisition of the behavior (Alberto & Troutman, 1982).

Desensitization, as a behavioral procedure, has a substantive body of research to support its feasibility in fear reduction treatment. As desensitization makes use of treatment technology (e.g., shaping, fading, prompting, modeling, and reinforcement), which is known to be effective with the acquisition of other adaptive behaviors, we would expect it to be effective in training individuals to respond in acceptable ways to stimuli that have in the past provoked maladaptive responses. Desensitization, however, is not a typical in-school program. Although the treatment technology may be commonly used in school settings, the application to fear or phobic responses is generally provided in settings other than the classroom. Therefore, desensitization is a procedure that combines several common behavioral techniques to assist in the development of appropriate responses to currently feared situations (e.g., riding in a bus, entering a swimming pool, going to a movie).

### REFERENCES

Alberto, P. A., & Troutman, A. C. (1982). *Applied behavior analysis for teachers*. Columbus, OH: Merrill.

Kratochwill, T. R. (1975). Contact desensitization. In A. S. Bellack & M. Hersen (Eds.), *Dictionary of behavior therapy techniques*, New York: Pergamon.

LYLE E. BARTON
*Kent State University*

**BEHAVIOR MODIFICATION
FEARS AND PHOBIAS**

## DES LAURIERS, AUSTIN M. (1917–    )

Austin M. Des Lauriers received his PhD in 1942 from the University of Montreal. His areas of research have been in school psychology, autism, and schizophrenia.

From 1967 to 1970 he served as professor and director of research and training at the University of Missouri Medical Center, Kansas City. Since 1979 he has served as professor and director of the Child Study Center at Ottawa, where he also maintains a private practice.

Des Lauriers' research interests have dealt in particular with topics of childhood schizophrenia (Des Lauriers, 1962) and autism. His book, *Your Child Is Asleep* (1969), is considered a classic in the field. Des Lauriers holds that the autistic child's condition and behavior (in an arrested form) involve the same conflicts that a normal child experiences. He holds the education of an autistic child is an "awakening."

### REFERENCES

Des Lauriers, A. M. (1962). *The experience of reality in childhood schizophrenia*. New York: I.V.P.

Des Lauriers, A. M., & Carlson, C. F. (1969). *Your child is asleep: Early infantile autism*. Homewood, IL: Dorsey.

RICK GONZALES
*Texas A&M University*

## DES LAURIERS–CARLSON HYPOTHESIS

In 1969 Austin Des Lauriers and Carole Carlson found that the reticular activating system was involved in the cause of early infantile autism. They proposed an imbalance in the relationship between the reticular activating system and the limbic system. The limbic system, which is involved in emotion, motivation, and reinforcement, is inhibited by the reticular activating system, rendering the autistic child unable to make associations between behavior and positive or negative consequences. The work of Des Lauriers and Carlson came after Kanner (1943) identified the behavioral characteristics of children who were qualitatively different from other childhood clinical populations. These symptoms included the inability to develop relationships, a delay in speech acquisition, echolalia, and repetitive play activities. These have become identifying characteristics of early infantile autism.

The etiology of early infantile autism was once thought to be based on abnormal family relationships and early parenting experiences (Kanner, 1943). There have since been many theories that attempt to understand the complicated disorder. Findings are mixed and tentative. The focus has included abnormal parenting and family relationships, the social environment, and biochemical and organic deficits as contributing factors.

Although much of the early research focused on family and environmental causes, more recent research identifies possible involvement with neurochemistry, developmental biology, neurophysiology, and neuroanatomy (Hanson & Gottesman, 1976). In 1983 Gillberg and Gillberg reported an increase in pre and perinatal hazards that are suggestive of brain dysfunction in infantile autism. Recent advances in cytogenetics have resulted in the identification of a specific biological marker or fragile site on the X chromosome. These are indicators that there is a coexistence of autism with the fragile X chromosome, suggesting an etiological link (August & Lockhart, 1984).

Sherman, Nass, and Shapiro (1984) researched cerebral blood flow in autistic children. Their research suggested depressed gray matter cerebral blood flow in autistic subjects; this may reflect their mental retardation. These findings lend support to the hypothesis of Damasio and Maurer (1978), who suggested that autism is the result of abnormalities of the mesolimbic dopaminergic system.

Currently, it is generally accepted that early infantile autism is a behavioral syndrome reflecting abnormal brain functioning (Sherman, Nass, & Shapiro, 1984). These findings present a challange for special educators who are involved in the education and treatment of autistic persons. McDonald and Sheperd (1976) reported that teachers play a major role in educating autistic children using criterion-referenced assessment and behavior teaching practices in a comprehensive program. This work has led to the current involvement of special education in the treatment of autism.

Treatment for early infantile autism has included family therapy, behavior modification, and special education. These methods are all helpful in providing the child with a chance to continue to develop and provide support to the family. Des Lauriers and Carlson used body stimulation as a way to make contact with the autistic child. They suggested that stimulation would be pleasurable and gratifying to the child. Psychotropic drugs also have been indicated in behavior management. The long-term prognosis for early infantile autism is poor. Most cases require lifetime management. While no special specific cause can be found, current theories have advanced our knowledge of early infantile autism. The current challenge is for psychologists, special educators, and parents to work together in a multidisciplinary fashion to provide opportunities for growth for the autistic child through education and to guide the families toward a better understanding of long-term care.

## REFERENCES

August, J. A., & Lockhart, H. L. (1984). Familial autism and the fragile X chromosome. *Journal of Autism & Developmental Disorders, 14,* 197–203.

Damasio, A. R., & Maurer, R. G. (1978). A neurological model for children with autism. *Archives of Neurology, 35,* 771–776.

Des Lauriers, A. M., & Carlson, C. F. (1969). *Your child is asleep: Early infantile autism.* Homewood, IL: Dorsey.

Gillberg, C., & Gillberg, C. I. (1983). Infantile autism: A total population study of reduce optimality in the pre-peri and neonatal period. *Journal of Autism & Developmental Disorders, 13,* 153–166.

Hanson, D. R., & Gottesman, I. I. (1976). The genetics, if any, of infantile autism and childhood schizophrenia. *Journal of Autism & Developmental Disorders, 6,* 209, 231.

Kanner, L. (1943). Autistic disturbances of affective contact. *Nervous Child, 2,* 217–250.

McDonald, J. E., & Sheperd, G. (1976). The autistic child, a challenge for educators. *Psychology in the Schools, 13,* 248–256.

Sherman, M., & Nass, R., & Shapiro, T. (1984). Brief report: Regional cerebral blood flow in autism. *Journal of Autistic & Developmental Disorders, 14,* 439–446.

STEVEN GUMERMAN
*Temple University*

AUTISM
RETICULAR SYSTEM

## DESPERT, JULIETTE L. (1892–1982)

Juliette L. Despert, MD, child psychiatrist, and researcher, received her education in her native France and in the United States. During her many years as a practicing psychiatrist, she contributed numerous articles to professional journals and published over half a dozen books, including *The Emotionally Disturbed Child: An Inquiry into Family Patterns, Schizophrenia in Childhood,* and *Children of Divorce,* and developed the Despert Fables.

## REFERENCES

Despert, J. L. (1953). *Children of divorce.* New York: Doubleday.

Despert, J. L. (1968). *Schizophrenia in childhood.* New York: Brunner.

Despert, J. L. (1970). *The emotionally disturbed child: An inquiry into family patterns.* New York: Doubleday.

PAUL IRVINE
*Katonah, New York*

## DESTRUCTIVE BEHAVIORS

To specify all acts in which persons engage that could be considered destructive is impossible; the topography of various destructive behaviors is at least as diverse as the people who exhibit them. A number of factors mitigate against a universally acceptable definition of destructive behaviors and are generally accounted for in operational definitions of such acts. There are at least three elements that should be implicitly or explicitly incorporated into operational definitions of destructive behaviors. One element is that of intentionality. For example, a child who accidently breaks a dish is not generally considered destructive, but one who deliberately breaks a dish is considered destructive. Second, characteristics of the behavior itself (e.g., intensity, frequency) play a definitional role. For instance, children who occasionally bite their fingernails are not considered to be self-destructive, while those who often bite their hands until they bleed generally are considered self-destructive. Third, situational factors influence definitions. Persons who intentionally break a glass in a restaurant are considered destructive; in contrast, in some wedding ceremonies the intentional breaking of a glass is a socially sanctioned event.

In addition to such definitional considerations, a discussion of destructive behaviors is further complicated by the diverse types of behaviors subsumed under this general heading. One scheme to organize the literature on destructive behaviors is to consider two primary dimensions: whether the acts are committed by groups or by individuals and whether the acts are directed toward objects, other persons, or self. This organizational scheme, far from perfect, results in the following six major classes of destructive behaviors: (1) destructive acts committed by groups against objects in the environment (e.g., school-wide problems of vandalism); (2) destructive acts committed by groups against other people (e.g., gang warfare); (3) destructive acts committed by groups against the members of the group (e.g., mass suicides); (4) destructive acts committed by an individual against objects in the environment (e.g., a child destroys materials); (5) destructive acts committed by an individual against other persons (e.g., a child assaults others); and (6) destructive acts committed by individuals against themselves (e.g., a child engages in self-injurious behavior).

A multitude of treatment programs that have successfully reduced various types of destructive behaviors have been reported. These programs have ranged in scope from large district-wide programs to reduce vandalism to interventions that have reduced the destructive behavior of a single individual. Likewise, the programs have varied a great deal according to the procedures used. As in the case with selecting any procedure to reduce behavior, a host of ethical, moral, legal, empirical, and practical issues must be attended to (see Foxx, 1982; Polsgrove, 1983; Repp, 1983). In the following paragraphs, effective programs for reducing various destructive behaviors are briefly discussed in approximate order of increasing intrusiveness. It should be stressed, however, that ineffective programs, regardless of their level of intrusiveness, should never be perpetuated.

There have been many examples of positively-based programs to reduce destructive behaviors. An interesting large-scale program to reduce acts of vandalism was reported by Mayer, Butterworth, Nefpaktitis, and Sulzer-Azaroff (1983). Selected teachers in 18 schools participated in workshops and consultation sessions. Over the three-year study, the teachers significantly increased their rates of praise. Acts of vandalism were significantly reduced and decreases in other disruptive and destructive student behaviors were also observed. Russo, Cataldo, and Cushing (1981) reported that positively reinforcing compliance resulted in decreased acts of self-destruction among three children, although no contingencies were in effect for the self-destructive behaviors. Using a DRO procedure (reinforcement delivered for nonoccurrence of behavior), Frankel, Moss, Schofield, and Simmons (1976) eliminated aggressive and self-destructive acts.

Extinction combined with positive reinforcement was used by Martin and Treffry (1970) to eliminate poor posture and self-destructive behaviors in a 16-year-old partially paralyzed mentally retarded girl with cerebral palsy. She was positioned in such a manner that if she slouched she was not visible to the persons administering the reinforcers. If she was engaging in self-destructive behaviors, she was also not reinforced.

A variety of destructive behaviors exhibited by five mentally retarded boys were reduced by a nonexclusionary timeout procedure (Foxx & Shapiro, 1978). A number of advantages are associated with this technique compared with other forms of timeout procedures.

An overcorrection procedure (a punishment technique involving the correction of the undesirable behavior followed by practicing the desirable behavior) was used by Foxx and Azrin (1972) to eliminate the destructive behavior of a profoundly retarded adult female. Other punishment procedures (e.g., contingent electric shock, aromatic ammonia, citric acid, etc.) have also been used to decrease destructive behaviors.

Irrespective of the particular type of destructive behavior, these responses merit our best professional interventions. A variety of treatments (in addition to the ones mentioned here) have proven successful, but careful attention to aspects of individual cases is essential.

## REFERENCES

Foxx, R. M. (1982). *Decreasing behaviors of severely retarded and autistic persons.* Champaign, IL: Research Press.

Foxx, R. M., & Azrin, N. H. (1972). Restitution: A method of eliminating aggressive-disruptive behavior of retarded and brain damaged patients. *Behavior Research and Therapy, 10,* 15–27.

Foxx, R. M., & Shapiro, S. T. (1978). The timeout ribbon: A nonexclusionary timeout procedure. *Journal of Applied Behavior Analysis, 11,* 125–136.

Frankel, F., Moss, D., Schofield, S., & Simmons, J. Q. (1976). Use of differential reinforcement to suppress self-injurious and aggressive behavior. *Psychological Reports, 39,* 843–849.

Martin, G. L., & Treffry, D. (1970). Treating self-destruction and developing self-care skills with a severely retarded girl: A case study. *Psychological Aspects of Disability, 17,* 125–131.

Mayer, G. R., Butterworth, T., Nafpaktitis, M., & Sulzer-Azaroff, B. (1983). Preventing school vandalism and improving discipline: A three-year study. *Journal of Applied Behavior Analysis, 16,* 355–369.

Polsgrove, L. (Ed.). (1983). Aversive control in the classroom. *Exceptional Education Quarterly, 3*(4).

Repp, A. C. (1983). *Teaching the mentally retarded.* Englewood Cliffs, NJ: Prentice-Hall.

Russo, D. C., Cataldo, M. F., & Cushing, P. J. (1981). Compliance training and behavioral covariation in the treatment of multiple behavior problems. *Journal of Applied Behavior Analysis, 14,* 209–222.

JAMES P. KROUSE
*Clarion University of
Pennsylvania*

**ACTING OUT**
**APPLIED BEHAVIOR ANALYSIS**
**EMOTIONAL DISORDERS**
**REALITY THERAPY**

## DETROIT TESTS OF LEARNING APTITUDE (DTLA)

The Detroit Tests of Learning Aptitude (DTLA) were originally developed by Harry Baker and Bernice Leland in an attempt to determine psychological strengths and weaknesses (McLoughlin & Lewis, 1981). The DTLA contains 19 subtests and the authors suggest that at least 9 but no more than 13 subtests be administered to an individual student. Students' raw scores are converted to mental age scores. The manual suggests that the median of these mental ages be used to calculate a ratio IQ (Silverstein, 1978). However, since the subtests administered from the DTLA are often chosen to locate areas in which the student is having difficulty, McLoughlin and Lewis (1981) recommend that an IQ score not be calculated.

The original DTLA is of questionable value in assessing students' aptitude. For example, standardization of the test was conducted on only 50 students per grade level and only in Detroit (Compton, 1980; Silverstein, 1978). While test-retest reliability is reported to be 0.96 after 5 months and 0.68 after 2 to 5 years, no interrater reliability is included (McLoughlin & Lewis, 1981). Additionally, no information regarding validity is included. Finally, the original DTLA is difficult to administer. The directions are sometimes vague and subjective judgments are often required in the scoring procedures (McLoughlin & Lewis, 1981).

In response to these criticisms, Hammill redeveloped the DTLA, creating the DTLA-2 (Hammill, 1985). The DTLA-2 contains 11 subtests (word opposites, sensitive imitation, oral directions, word sequences, story construction, design reproduction, object sequences, symbolic relations, conceptual matching, word fragments, and letter sequences), all of which are administered. Test administration time varies from 50 minutes to 2 hours.

Test results are reported in terms of raw scores, percentiles, standard scores, and composite score quotients. Composite quotients are determined by combining different sets of subtest scores. These composite scores include verbal aptitude, nonverbal aptitude, conceptual aptitude, structural aptitude, attention-enhanced aptitude, attention-reduced aptitude, motor-enhanced aptitude, motor-reduced aptitude, and overall aptitude.

In response to the limited standardization of the original DTLA, Hammill administered the DTLA-2 to a sample of 1532 students, ages 6 to 17, living in 30 states (Hammill, 1985). Internal consistency reliability for the DTLA-2 subtests ranged from 0.81 to 0.95 with 88% of the subtests above 0.80 and 38% at or above 0.90. The reliability coefficients for the composite scores ranged from 0.95 to 0.97. Test-retest reliability of the subtests ranged from 0.63 to 0.91 but test-retest reliability of the composite scores ranged from 0.80 to 0.94. The manual reports that adequate content validity, criterion-related validity, and construct validity are present in the DTLA-2. Since the DTLA-2 is relatively new, no statements as to its effectiveness as yet appear in the literature. Its overall benefits to the field are still to be determined.

### REFERENCES

Compton, C. (1980). *A guide to 65 tests for special education.* Belmont, CA: Fearon Education.

Hammill, D. D. (1985). *The Detroit Tests of Learning Aptitude-2* Austin, TX: Pro-Ed.

McLoughlin, J. A., & Lewis, R. B. (1981). *Assessing special students.* Columbus, OH: Merrill.

Silverstein, A. B. (1978). Review of the Detroit Tests of Learning Aptitudes. In O. K. Buros (Ed.), *The eighth mental measurements yearbook.* Highland Park, NJ: Gryphon.

JOHN R. BEATTIE
*University of North Carolina,
Charlotte*

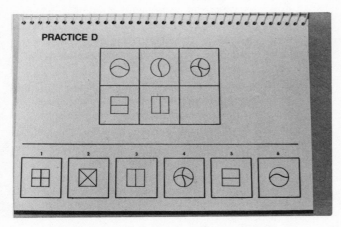

A practice item from the Detroit Test of Learning Aptitude Revision, the DTLA-2.

# DEVELOPING COUNTRIES AND SPECIAL EDUCATION

See MIDDLE EAST, SPECIAL EDUCATION IN THE.

# DEVELOPING UNDERSTANDING OF SELF AND OTHERS—REVISED (DUSO-R)

Developing Understanding of Self and Others-Revised (DUSO-R) is an improved version of the 1970 DUSO. Dinkmeyer and Dinkmeyer (1982) developed the DUSO program to increase understanding of social and emotional behavior in preschool and early primary age children. It is a program of activities and materials that uses puppets, songs, stories, discussion, and role playing to help children grow in their understanding of self and others as well as to recognize their needs and goals. Two different kits are provided, DUSO–1 for grades Kindergarten to 2 and DUSO–2 for grades 3 to 4; they differ only in the degree of complexity presented. There are 41 goals assessed in three major units. The units are (1) developing understanding of self; (2) developing understanding of others; and (3) developing understanding of choices. Each of the 41 goals uses songs, guided fantasies, dramatic play activities, problem situations, and feeling world activities (Goldman, 1984).

The DUSO-R has several improvements over the original DUSO. Stories and songs have been updated to be more reflective of current issues. Pictures featuring minority groups, handicapped persons, and the elderly are used to depict problem situations and show these people as responsible problem solvers. Also, males and females are portrayed as equal in capabilities. A new feature, Guided Fantasy, involves a combination of muscle relaxation and visual imagery to guide a child through presented situations. Another new feature is a set of activity sheets. These sheets can be sent home with the child to show to or do with the parents. Retained was the simplicity that allows easy administration with no special training. A guidebook is provided for the examiner; it is recommended that it be read thoroughly prior to administering the program. Teachers, counselors, and other guidance faculty are capable of administering the DUSO-R. Average administration time is 30 to 40 minutes.

The DUSO-R is a colorful, easily administered program that assesses three main subject areas (Krismann, 1983): affective education, guidance and counseling, and health. It is based on an inquiry, experiential, and discussion approach to learning. The program can be used to teach appropriate social skills and problem-solving techniques, as well as to give insight into self-concept and interpersonal relationships. It can be used with emotionally disturbed and disabled children as well as normal children. As it is more of a teaching instrument than a testing instrument, objective interpretations are based on individual responses rather than norms. The DUSO-R can be a useful, valuable tool that can be added to a teacher's daily, weekly, or periodic schedule.

## REFERENCES

Dinkmeyer, D., & Dinkmeyer, D., Jr. (1984). *Developing Understanding of Self and Others-D-1* and *D-2* (rev. eds.). Circle Pines, MN: American Guidance Services.

Goldman, S. J. (1984). Developing Understanding of Self and Others-Revised. *School Counselor, 31,* 486–488.

Krismann, C. (1983). Developing Understanding of Self and Others-Revised. *Social Science Education Consortium* (Suppl.), 39–40.

LISA J. SAMPSON
*Eastern Kentucky University*

COUNSELING THE HANDICAPPED
SOCIAL SKILLS

# DEVELOPMENTAL APHASIA

Developmental aphasia (developmental dysphasia) is but one of several terms used to refer to language disorders in children attributed to presumed central nervous system pathology. The terms childhood aphasia, congenital aphasia, and central auditory dysfunction (Bloom & Lahey, 1978; Lubert, 1981) are among others used by psychologists, speech-language pathologists, neurologists, and other professionals who have investigated childhood language disorders. These terms have been used to differentiate an acquired loss of established language from a developmental failure of normal language acquisition.

Etiology is usually unknown. Some researchers have speculated that concomitants of accidents, disease, or developmental deviations may be responsible for disruptions in the processing of auditory stimuli (Myklebust, 1971a).

Children who have been labeled dysphasic have been noted to display attentional deficits and have difficulty in focusing. They may process auditory information at a slower rate than normal children. Difficulty in discriminating speech sounds in minimal contrast pairs is reported frequently. Figure-ground problems may result in difficulties in sorting out important from irrelevant auditory signals. Inaccurate reporting of the sequence of auditory stimuli is another characteristic commonly reported by investigators.

Understanding auditory-verbal language is basic to the development of verbal expression, reading, and writing.

Difficulty in processing auditory stimuli noted in dysphasic children is reflected in histories of delayed onset of speech, in slower than normal acquisition of grammatical structures (Bloom & Lahey, 1978), and sometimes in word-finding problems (Myklebust, 1971b). Bloom and Lahey note that although language acquisition is delayed in aphasic children, they seem to acquire grammatical rules in a pattern similar to that of normally developing children.

A discrepancy between measured verbal and nonverbal abilities on intelligence tests is a common finding among children labeled dysphasic. Myklebust (1971b) cautions diagnosticians not to rely on results of a single test. Instruments that measure vocabulary comprehension, grammatical comprehension, auditory memory span, and various aspects of expressive language skills are needed to obtain a comprehensive picture of a child's linguistic strengths and weaknesses.

## REFERENCES

Bloom, L., & Lahey, M. (1978). *Language development and language disorders*. New York: Wiley.

Lubert, N. (1981). Auditory perceptual impairments in children with specific language disorders: A review of the literature. *Journal of Speech and Hearing Disorders, 46*, 3–9.

Myklebust, H. (1971a). Childhood aphasia: An evolving concept. In L. E. Travis (Ed.), *The handbook of speech pathology and audiology* (pp. 1181–1201). New York: Appleton-Century-Crofts.

Mykelbust, H. (1971b). Childhood aphasia: Identification, diagnosis, remediation. In L. E. Travis (Ed.), *The handbook of speech pathology and audiology* (pp. 1203–1217). New York: Appleton-Century-Crofts.

K. Sandra Vanta
*Cleveland Public Schools,
Cleveland, Ohio*

APHASIA
DYSPHASIA

# DEVELOPMENTAL DELAY

Historically, our understanding of human development as a dynamic, continuous process owes much to the pioneering research of Arnold Gesell (1925). Following years of clinical research observing and recording infant and child behavior, Gesell established a series of developmental norms. These age-related profiles described the sequence of normal motor development and adaptive, language, and personal-social behaviors of the average child. In addition, viewing school life from a developmental perspective, he emphasized maturational readiness as well as overall adjustment to school as a critical determinant of children's academic performance in reading, writing, and arithmetic

(Gesell, 1946). Although urging conservation application of the developmental norms owing to the variable rate at which children normally develop, Gesell emphasized the value of developmental diagnosis as a means of identifying abnormal development (Gesell, 1925).

The concept of developmental delay refers to a maturational lag, an abnormal, slower rate of development in which a child demonstrates a functioning level below that observed in normal children of the same age (Thompson & O'Quinn, 1979). Suggesting no cerebral dysfunction or structural damage, proponents of the concept maintain that discrepant abilities manifested by the delayed child occur because of neurological immaturity associated with slower development (Golden & Wilkening, 1986; Lerner, 1985; Thompson & O'Quinn, 1979).

In the field of childhood exceptionalities, developmental delay is associated with theories of mental retardation, learning disabilities, and attention deficit disorder. Evidence supporting the existence of developmental delay and its relationship to exceptionality are found repeatedly in the literature. Although controversial and refuted by many, some researchers in each subfield support the concept.

Zigler & Balla (1982) associates developmental delay with the intellectual functioning of the retarded child. Zigler identifies cultural-familial retarded children as those who function intellectually at the low end of the normal distribution, who make up 75% of the retarded population, and who are unaffected by organic impairments. Zigler maintains that cultural-familial retarded children, unlike the organically impaired, develop cognitively and intellectually like normal children. He posits that similar sequential development and within-stage cognitive functioning exist in normal and cultural-familial retarded children. He claims that differences occur only in the rate of development and upper level of cognitive growth finally reached. According to Zigler, a normal and a retarded child matched for developmental level demonstrate similar cognitive processing regardless of age and IQ differences.

Developmental delay also has been associated with the learning-disabled child's academic failure. According to certain theorists (Lerner, 1985; Ross, 1976), the learning-disabled child's failure to achieve academically at levels predicted by intelligence tests may be due to a maturational lag in the neurological processes necessary for successful academic achievement. Some children may require extra time to mature before entering academic work. Lerner (1985) reported studies identifying the learning-disabled child as immature. In one longitudinal study of perceptual functioning, results indicated the existence and later disappearance of processing deficits among learning-disabled children (Silver & Hagin, 1966). Individuals who had early difficulty in spatial orientation and other perceptual functions apparently caught up and were functioning normally as adults.

Ross (1976) suggests that "learning disabilities may thus be viewed as the result of delayed development in the capacity to employ and sustain selective attention" (pp. 60–61). As a result of an inability to filter background distractions and attend to academic skills, the child fails to learn the necessary skills and becomes handicapped in school. Although Ross (1976) maintains that individual differences in the rate at which children develop the ability to use selective attention may cause learning disabilities, he also reports that a number of theorists attribute learning disabilities to a lag in perceptual development. Although tests of various programs designed to improve perceptual functioning have not resulted in improved academic skills (Hammill, Goodman, & Wiederholt, 1974), some theorists still maintain that lags in perceptual-motor functioning underlie many problems children have in learning academic material.

Finally, attention deficit disorder (ADD) has been associated with a delay in neurological and physical maturation (Reid & Hresko, 1981; Ross & Ross, 1976), resulting in characteristics similar to those of younger children. Since most children with attention deficits also have learning disabilities, Routh's (1986) reports that both groups have problems in selectively attending to relevant stimuli are not surprising (Ross, 1976; Ross & Ross, 1982; Routh, 1986). Routh (1986) describes children with ADD as developmentally immature in several areas, including span of apprehension, vigilance, and resistance to distraction. Particularly with the hyperactive child, viewing the delay as temporary with the idea that the child will catch up may be a misconception. Although Routh, Schroeder, and O'Tuama (1974) report findings of decreased hyperactivity with age, other studies indicate that hyperactivity frequently persists into adolescence with an attendant lack of academic achievement (Reid & Hresko, 1981).

Developmental delay as an explanation for impaired specific or general intellectual deficits is questioned by many. Although controversial, much research supports the theoretical assumptions underlying Zigler's developmental position of cultural-familial retardation (Weisz & Yeates, 1981). Assuming the validity of research findings, Weiss and Weisz (1986) support the assumption that non-organically retarded individuals "should not be regarded as 'abnormal' but as manifesting a developmental delay." They additionally argue that they "are quantitatively different from nonretarded individuals, not qualitatively different" (pp. 372–373).

The view that developmental delay is generally responsible for learning disabilities and attention deficit disorders is controversial. Although some studies report an apparent age-related disappearance of spatial-perceptual dysfunctioning (Silver & Hagin, 1966), many view the notion that delayed individuals may catch up as faulty (Hynd & Obrzut, 1986). Indeed, Ross (1976) views the child who is delayed in developing selective attention as one who will

undoubtedly have suffered many years of academic failure and incurred tremendous damage in self-confidence and self-esteem. The likelihood of catching up seems remote at best.

## REFERENCES

Gesell, A. (1925). *The mental growth of the pre-school child.* New York: Macmillan.

Gesell, A., & Ilg, F. L. (1946). *The child from five to ten.* New York: Harper & Brothers.

Golden, C. J., & Wilkening, G. N. (1986). Neuropsychological bases of exceptionality. In R. T. Brown & C. R. Reynolds (Eds.), *Psychological perspectives on childhood exceptionalities: A handbook* (pp. 61–90). New York: Wiley.

Hammill, D., Goodman, L., & Wiederholt, J. L. (1974). Visual-motor processes. Can we train them? *Reading Teacher, 27,* 469–478.

Hynd, G. W., & Obrzut, J. E. (1986). Exceptionality: Historical antecedents and present positions. In R. T. Brown & C. R. Reynolds (Eds.), *Psychological perspectives on childhood exceptionality: A handbook* (pp. 3–27), New York: Wiley.

Lerner, J. (1985). *Learning disabilities: Theory, diagnosis & teaching strategies* (4th ed.). Boston: Houghton Mifflin.

Reid, D. K., & Hresko, W. P. (1981). *A cognitive approach to learning disabilities.* New York: McGraw-Hill.

Ross, A. O. (1976). *Psychological aspects of learning disabilities and reading disorders.* New York: McGraw-Hill.

Ross, D. M., & Ross, S. A. (1982). *Hyperactivity: Research, theory, and action* (2nd ed.). New York: Wiley.

Routh, D. K. (1986). Attention deficit disorder. In R. T. Brown & C. R. Reynolds (Eds.), *Psychological perspectives on childhood exceptionality: A handbook* (pp. 467–507). New York: Wiley.

Routh, D. K., Schroeder, C. S., & O'Tuama, L. A. (1974). Development of activity level in children. *Developmental Psychology, 10,* 163–168.

Silver, A. A., & Hagin, R. A. (1966). Maturation of perceptual functions in children with specific reading disability. *Reading Teacher, 19,* 253–259.

Thompson, R. J., & O'Quinn, A. N. (1979). *Developmental disabilities.* New York: Oxford University Press.

Weiss, B., & Weisz, J. R. (1986). General cognitive deficits: Mental retardation. In R. T. Brown & C. R. Reynolds (Eds.), *Psychological perspectives on childhood exceptionality: A handbook* (pp. 344–390). New York: Wiley.

Weisz, J. R., & Yeates, K. O. (1981). Cognitive development in retarded and nonretarded persons: Piagetian tests of the similar structure hypothesis. *Psychological Bulletin, 90,* 153–178.

Zigler, E., & Balla, D. (1982). *Mental retardation: The developmental-difference controversy.* Hillsdale, NJ: Erlbaum.

SHIRLEY PARKER WELLS
*University of North Carolina,*
*Wilmington*

## GESELL, ARNOLD

## LEARNING DISABILITIES

MENTAL RETARDATION
PERCEPTUAL DEVELOPMENT (LAG IN)


# DEVELOPMENTAL DISABILITIES

Developmental disabilities is a generic term that refers to "all of the lifelong disabling conditions that require similar treatment or helping services and that occurred prior to age 22" (Ehlers, Prothero, & Langone, 1982). According to Boggs (1972), the concept of developmental disabilities has no etiological basis and includes all children and adults with a substantial continuing disability originating in childhood. The term is not to include disabilities that effectively could be overcome with rehabilitation or that are not both apparent and disabling prior to age 18. This concept of developmental disabilities has evolved since its inception in 1969 from a coalition of representatives of the National Association for Retarded Children, American Association on Mental Deficiency (AAMD), National Association of Coordinators of State Programs for the Mentally Retarded, National Association of State Mental Health Program Directors, Council for Exceptional Children, and United Cerebral Palsy Association. The concept of developmental disabilities was introduced by this coalition because of three major concerns: (1) the emphasis on categories of exceptionality, (2) the narrow focus in federal legislation for the handicapped on mental retardation, and (3) the absence of any proposals by the Nixon administration for legislative action on behalf of the handicapped.

In regard to categorization, Boggs (1972) cites the following reasons for professional concern: (1) the high degree of coincidence in the same individuals of the most common disabling conditions (mental retardation, cerebral palsy, epilepsy, childhood schizophrenia, and other neurological and sensory disorders), (2) the exactitude of diagnostic semantics and the degree to which diagnosis could be manipulated when it was a factor in eligibility for service, and (3) the growing professional opinion against fragmenting services that call for similarly trained personnel. These concerns also are reflected in a report of the President's Committee on Mental Retardation (1968), which calls for people and organizations interested in specific handicapping conditions to work together to promote more effective services.

A second concern was that earlier legislation related to the handicapped focused primarily on persons with mental retardation while many persons with needs similar to the mentally retarded were being neglected (Ehlers et al., 1982). Also, training of professionals funded by previous legislation was primarily clinical and did not foster an interdisciplinary approach to providing services to the handicapped.

A third concern that influenced the coalition was the "vacillation and declining support from the Johnson administration" for programs for the mentally retarded and the lack of "any special thought . . . given to the needs in mental retardation" by the Nixon administration. (Boggs, 1972, pp. 184–185). While the coalition formed was, according to Boggs, "an ongoing legislative alliance" (p. 186), it represented professionals concerned not only with legislative issues but also with current thinking regarding provision of services for the handicapped. Consequently, members of the coalition sought to develop a legislative program with goals reflective of professional and consumer program objectives.

In 1969 the concept of developmental disabilities as previously described by Boggs was introduced by this coalition; its members developed an amendment to the Mental Retardation Facilities Act (PL 88-164). The reasons for amending PL 88-164, according to Boggs, were as follow: (1) to give states greater incentive to continue planning and greater authority to use federal funds in accordance with state plans, (2) to expand the list of eligible services and not have the services tied to a specialized facility, (3) to have available monies allocated in response to the same plan, and (4) to use a functional approach associating the handicapped by common service needs to define eligibility for service rather than categorization by diagnosis.

In the proposed legislation the term mental retardation was replaced by the term developmental disabilities. Developmental disability was seen as a functional definition of a person needing specific services. According to a report issued by the President's Committee on Mental Retardation (1976), the rationale for use of the term developmental disability was to avoid categorical fractioning of service organizations and funding among similar and overlapping disabilities and to clearly distinguish developmental disabilities from the field of mental health. This concept as incorporated into the Developmental Disabilities Services and Facilities Construction Amendments of 1970 (PL 91-517) is broader than the one (mental retardation) used in previous legislation, but it does not reflect a truly functional definition of developmental disabilities. The definition is as follows:

> A disability attributable to mental retardation, cerebral palsy, epilepsy, or other neurological condition . . . closely related to mental retardation or to require treatment similar to that required for mentally retarded individuals, which disability originates before such individual attains age eighteen, which has continued or can be expected to continue indefinitely, and which constitutes a substantial handicap to such individuals.

The concept of developmental disabilities as reflected in this legislation has been criticized because while expanding the population eligible for services, it is still essentially categorical. Neisworth and Smith (1974) point out that the definition as used in PL 91-517 lacks precision and includes requirements based on assumptions that "invite inconsistent and tenuous interpretations and applications" (p. 345). They further point out the lack of functionality in the definition and suggest a redefinition of developmental disabilities that would, in their opinion, lead to more specificity and reliability of interpretation and implementation:

Developmental disability refers to significantly deficient locomotor, communicative, adjustive, or academic functioning that is manifested during the developmental period, and that has continued or can be expected to continue indefinitely. (p. 346)

Since the introduction of the term developmental disability in federal legislation, it has been altered so that the definition used in recent legislation more clearly reflects the concept held by the coalition. The first alteration occurred when autism, any other condition closely related to mental retardation or requiring similar services and treatment, and dyslexia resulting from other disabilities included in the definition were added to the earlier definition and used in the Developmentally Disabled Assistance and Bill of Rights Act (PL 94-103). However, this altered definition still did not reflect the thinking of the coalition or address issues described by Neisworth and Smith.

A major alteration occurred when the National Task Force on the Definition of Developmental Disabilities was established in response to one of the requirements of PL 94-103. According to Thompson and O'Quinn (1979), members of this task force opposed the use of the term developmental disabilities as a "catch-all for an arbitrary collection of existing labels or conditons" (p. 14) and advocated a generic or functional definition be formulated to cut across specific categories or conditions. Members of this task force defined the developmentally disabled as "a group of people experiencing a chronic disability which substantially limits their functioning in a variety of broad areas of major life activity central to independent living" (p. 14). Subsequently, the thinking of the task force was reflected in the Rehabilitation Comprehensive Services and Developmental Disabilities Amendments of 1978 (PL 95-602) and retained in the Developmental Disabilities Act of 1984 (PL 98-527). The definition reads as follows:

The term developmental disability means a severe, chronic disability of a person which:
—is attributable to a mental or physical impairment or combination of mental and physical impairments;
—is manifested before the person attains age twenty-two;
—is likely to continue indefinitely;
—results in substantial functional limitations in three or more of the following areas of major life activities:
(i) self-care, (ii) receptive and expressive language, (iii) learn-

ing, (iv) mobility, (v) self-direction, (vi) capacity for independent living, and (vii) economic sufficiency; and
—reflects the person's need for a combination and sequence of special, interdisciplinary, or generic care, treatment, or other services which are of lifelong or extended duration and are individually planned and coordinated.

Seltzer (1983) describes this definition as functionally oriented with emphasis on chronicity, age-specific onset, multiple areas of functional limitations, and need for an extended array of long-term services from a multiplicity of service providers. Seltzer points to this functional orientation as an advantage of this latest definition but cites its lack of operational clarity as a disadvantage. However, Seltzer goes on to point out that with use and the development of operational guidelines, the disadvantages are hoped to diminish.

The term developmental disability has been incorporated into various classification systems. The American Association on Mental Deficiency (AAMD) includes developmental disability in the *Manual of Terminology and Classification in Mental Retardation* (Grossman, 1977) and *Classification in Mental Retardation* (Grossman, 1983). The definitions correspond to the one first introduced in 1970 (PL 91-602), which is categorical and restrictive. A major difference between these definitions is the concept of etiology of developmental disabilities. In the earlier edition, developmental disabilities are described as attributable to various disorders, while in the later definition developmental disabilities are described as associated with specific disorders. Developmental disability was added to the *Thesaurus of ERIC Descriptors* (Houston, 1984) in June 1977, and is defined as a

category in federal legislation referring to disabilities resulting from mental retardation, cerebral palsy, epilepsy, autism or other neurological conditions closely related to mental retardation that originate before age 18 and are considered a substantial handicap to normal functioning. (p. 69)

Neither the AAMD nor the ERIC definitions are functional or reflective of the original concept proposed by the coalition or the definition incorporated into federal legislation in 1978.

The overlap in various definitions of developmental disabilities and other handicapping conditions has caused considerable confusion. Grossman (1983) points out that basic characteristics of mental retardation overlap with the legislative definition of developmental disabilities. Grossman goes on to say that the areas of limitations described in the legislative definition of developmental disabilities apply to more severe forms of mental retardation and to some mildly retarded individuals during certain periods of their lives. Grossman describes the parallel aspects of mental retardation and developmental disabilities as that of being developmental in origin and stressing impairment in adaptive behavior. He also indicates that the subgroup of persons with more severe forms of mental retardation will have a permanent and substantial handicap, as do many children with autism and cerebral palsy. Thus persons in this subgroup may be considered developmentally disabled. However, those with milder mental retardation and less severe conditions of cerebral palsy, epilepsy, and autism would fall outside the definition of developmental disability.

In summary, the concept of developmental disability is a generic one that evolved from the area of mental retardation and focuses on the needs of persons with serious and ongoing disabilities that originated before age 22. Thompson and O'Quinn (1979) point out that as the concept of developmental disabilities continues to evolve, efforts at defining developmental disabilities are likely to continue as well.

## REFERENCES

Boggs, E. M. (1972). Federal legislation 1966–1971. In J. Wortis (Ed.), *Mental retardation: An annual review* (Vol. 4). New York: Grune & Stratton.

Ehlers, W. H., Prothero, J. C., & Langone, J. (1982). *Mental retardation and other developmental disabilities* (3rd ed.), Columbus, OH: Merrill.

Grossman, H. J. (Ed.). (1977). *Manual of terminology and classification in mental retardation*. Washington, DC: American Association on Mental Deficiency.

Grossman, H. J. (Ed.), (1983). *Classification in mental retardation*. Washington, DC: American Association on Mental Deficiency.

Houston, J. E. (1984). *Thesaurus of ERIC descriptors*. Phoenix, AZ: Oryx.

Neisworth, J. T., & Smith, R. M. (1974). An analysis and redefinition of "developmental disabilities." *Exceptional Children, 40*, 345–347.

President's Committee on Mental Retardation. (1968). *MR68—The edge of change*. Washington, DC: U.S. Government Printing Office.

President's Committee on Mental Retardation. (1976). *MR76—Mental retardation past and present*. Washington, DC: U.S. Government Printing Office.

Seltzer, G. B. (1983). Systems of classification. In J. L. Matson, & J. A. Mulick. (Eds.) *Handbook of mental retardation*. New York: Pergamon.

Thompson, R. J., & O'Quinn, A. N. (1979). *Developmental disabilities*. New York: Oxford University Press.

ELEANOR BOYD WRIGHT
*University of North Carolina,
Wilmington*

**AAMD**
**CEREBRAL PALSY**
**MENTAL RETARDATION**
**PHYSICAL HANDICAP**

# DEVELOPMENTAL DISABILITIES ACT

The Developmental Disabilities Act of 1984 is federal legislation that amended Title I of the Mental Retardation Facilities and Community Health Centers Construction Act of 1963. The statute (administered as PL 98-527) was enacted to revise and extend the provisions of the 1963 legislation to ensure (1) that persons with developmental disabilities receive the care, treatment, and other services necessary to enable them to achieve their maximum potential through increased independence, productivity, and integration into the community, and (2) the establishment and operation of a system that coordinates, monitors, plans, and evaluates services that provide the protection of the legal and human rights of persons with developmental disabilities (U.S. Congress, 1984).

Specifically, the Developmental Disabilities Act of 1984 is intended to:

Assist in the provision of comprehensive services to persons with developmental disabilities, with priority to those persons whose needs are not otherwise met by programming available through the Rehabilitation Act of 1973 or other health, education, or welfare programs.

Aid states in conducting planning activities.

Make grants to public and private nonprofit agencies for the purpose of establishing model programs, demonstrating innovative habilitation techniques, and training professional and paraprofessional personnel to serve the developmentally disabled population.

Distribute grant funds for the administration and operation of interdisciplinary training and service centers, identified as university affiliated facilities.

Award grants in support of the protection and advocacy system administered by each state to promote and sustain the legal and human rights of all persons with developmental disabilities.

Two important provisions of the 1984 statute require that states receiving Federal Development Disabilities Act funds (1) establish a central advocacy and oversight body, a state planning council, and (2) have in effect an individualized habilitation plan for each developmentally delayed citizen receiving services from the programs. Congress has authorized an annual federal expenditure of $87 million through fiscal year 1987 to support the various programs established under the Development Disabilities Act of 1984.

GEORGE JAMES HAGERTY
*Stonehill College*

# LEGAL REGULATIONS OF SPECIAL EDUCATION

## DEVELOPMENTAL DISABILITIES LEGAL RESOURCE CENTER

See PROTECTION AND ADVOCACY SYSTEM—DEVELOPMENTALLY DISABLED (P&A).

## DEVELOPMENTAL DYSLEXIA

Developmental dyslexia is typically perceived as a complex heterogeneous reading disorder. It appears to stem from a selective disturbance of the maturation of neurological functions thought to be responsible for the acquisition of reading and writing skills. It is genetically determined and thus distinct from acquired alexia from traumatic brain injury (Gaddes, 1976). Critical components of the disorder that are relative to the individual's unique patterns of intrinsic abilities and extrinsic assets dictate that the dyslexic must have at least average intelligence; sufficient cultural and linguistic opportunity; emotional stability; access to appropriate instruction; and approximately normal sensory acuity (Rourke & Gates, 1981). Prognosis of relative success in compensating for the disorder's consequences is based on early identification, delineation of the individual's unique pattern of strengths and weaknesses, capitalization on unique educational strategies, and concomitant appropriate sociocultural/familial support systems.

More than 80 years' worth of published material (Benton, 1980) has been generated by the disorder; its history has been rich with conflicting information. To state that developmental dyslexia has been a confusing disorder would be diplomatic at best; however, continued research in the differentiation of subtypes, longitudinal studies on developmental changes, technological advances related to etiology, and empirical results from promising intervention programs continue to refine conceptualizations of dyslexia.

The origin of the term dyslexia has been attributed to Kausmaul, who in 1877 defined the word *alexia* as word blindness. In 1891 Dejerine provided autopsy data on individuals who had suffered cerebrovascular injury and were left with reading disabilities. In 1896 Morgan described a famous dyslexic case study concerning an intelligent 14-year-old male who could not read or write but could perform algebra. These studies indicated specific deficits or abnormal development of the angular gyrus region in the dominant hemisphere (Dalby, 1979).

In 1900 Hinshelwood reported that the disorder caused partial or complete loss of visual memory for letters and words. In 1901 Nettleship observed that a disproportion-

ate number of males had dyslexia, the disorder tended to run in families, and there was the presence of a linguistic factor. Four years later, Fisher recommended implementation of a "look and say" method of instruction for individuals who had a phonemic analysis deficit. This remediation used global word recognition. Interestingly, he also advocated teaching children to write with their left hands, based on the assumption that the right hemisphere subserved the learning process in children with faulty left hemispheres. Marie, in 1906, disagreed with the localizationist theories of brain functioning, then the prevalent school of thought, which assumed specific behaviors were attributed to specific brain areas. He argued that there could not be specific centers for reading because reading was a new development in humans (Pirozzolo, 1981).

Educational and clinical psychologists' interest in dyslexia gained momentum during the first two decades of the twentieth century. Research focused on the basic underlying factors that presumably caused failure in learning to read, and two schools of thought emerged. The first emphasized the relation of perceptual and cognitive disabilities and the second concentrated on environmental factors (Benton, 1980). A new perspective on dyslexia was formulated by Orton toward the end of the second decade.

Orton related reading disability to a defective interhemispheric organization of cerebral function. It was assumed to be the result of a faulty maturational process of establishing specialization of function in a single hemisphere. The consequences of incomplete hemispheric dominance were said to lead to confusion and failure to read effectively (Johnson & Myklebust, 1967).

Behavioral and personality disorders in dyslexics were investigated in the 1930s. It was assumed that psychotherapy should be the primary mode of intervention before and during educational remediation. In the early 1940s, Werner and Strauss (Dalby, 1979) stated that brain damage was present, whether or not detectable by neurological means, as long as similar behavior patterns were exhibited. They initiated the term minimal brain damage (MBD), which, unfortunately, was embraced by zealous individuals who then attributed MBD to the entire population of persons with learning disorders. Without substantial evidence to support the conclusion that brain damage existed minimally, dissimilar disorders were erroneously lumped together (e.g., attention deficit disorders, developmental dyslexia). The devastating impact of these erroneous labels was unfortunately incurred by the child (Hobbs, 1975).

To complicate this picture further, incidence rates for dyslexics in the general population ranged from 10 to 30%, as reported in the voluminous post-World War II research on dyslexia. It became clear, however, that many researchers had failed to differentiate specific reading disability from failure to read owing to other factors (e.g., lack of normal intelligence, primary sensory impairments, lack of adequate educational and cultural opportunities, and emotional instability). The field of developmental dyslexia became clouded, and, as Benton and Pearl (1978) note, this large volume of research did little to differentiate distinct subtypes of dyslexia. The concept of dyslexia appeared to mean different things to different people. Adams (1967) found 23 definitions of dyslexia in the literature and he argued for abandonment of the term. It has been observed that the particular way in which research in developmental dyslexia is conducted stems directly from its definition, and if that definition is not one that is commonly accepted, researchers' results will differ accordingly (Rourke, 1976).

From the 1960s to the present, research proceeded by varied means. Renewed interest in Orton's work followed advances in asymmetrical hemispheric specialization research (e.g., dichotic listening, dichaptic discrimination, and tachistoscopic methods). Medical technology has furthered investigations in the neurological basis of dyslexia by means of electroencephalography, computerized tomography scanning, cerebral blood flow studies, positron emission tomography, and autopsies on dyslexic and normal brains. Current research in the educational/neuropsychological literature (Hynd & Obrzut, 1981; Knights & Bakker, 1976) has supported the involvement of higher cortical impairment in developmental dyslexia. There are a select few that contend that dyslexia stems from subcortical impairment involving the cerebellar-vestibular system (Frank & Levinson, 1973); however, independent validation of this research has not yet been published.

Evidence from research on pre- and perinatal events in relation to dyslexia has demonstrated the importance of this period on the child's development. However, there is no strong evidence to substantiate that abnormalities in this period lead directly to specific reading disability. Extensive data from twin research (Herschel, 1978) showed a genetic basis to developmental dyslexia, although there is little evidence to support particular biochemical, physiological, or behavioral attributes linked specifically to dyslexia.

Sex differences are apparent in that males are disproportionately represented in reading-disabled populations. Data exist that indicate even normal girls are more adept at the learning-to-read process than normal boys. Anatomical data further substantiate those claims, since myelination occurred more rapidly in the left hemisphere for girls and the right hemisphere for boys (Dalby, 1979). Other sex differences have been hypothesized to be maturational lags in hemispheric specialization shifts in the learning-to-read process (Rourke, 1982), where girls pass through the stages faster than boys (Gaddes, 1976). These hypotheses suggest that the right hemisphere-mediated functions may have a critical role in the initial stages of the acquisition of the reading process, whereas the left hemisphere-mediated functions may be more efficient in using a routinized mode that stems from that acquisition. This right-to-left shift in hemispheric specialization may be a function of increased competence with the learning-to-read process.

The current perspective on developmental dyslexia has focused on more stringent methods of research in the identification of distinct subtypes (Rourke & Gates, 1981). Converging data from this body of research suggested a need for a multidimensional definition; it was clear that appropriate identification of dyslexics could not be made solely on the basis of poor reading achievement with approximately average intelligence (Yule & Rutter, 1976). The presence of differences in the types of dyslexia necessitates different strategies of educational interventions. Recognition of these differences became more pronounced following multivariate analyses of clinical neuropsychological methods (Petrauskas & Rourke, 1979) and important developmental changes described in longitudinal research (Satz, Taylor, Friel, & Fletcher, 1978).

The neuropsychological evidence has suggested the presence of several subtypes of dyslexic readers, two of which are fairly distinct in older children and adults: auditory-linguistic deficient (dysphonetic) readers and visual-spatial deficient (dyseidetic) readers, as described by Pirozzolo (1981). Others have described a mixed dyslexic group (both dysphonetic and dyseidetic), an unspecified group (of which subcortical impairment cannot be completely ruled out), and a normal group.

Hartlage and Telzrow (1983) have elucidated various means of using neuropsychological data for successful educational intervention. They hypothesized that a child's neuropsychological strengths should be emphasized in matching complementary curricula to that pattern, without total rejection of tasks using weaker neuropsychological abilities. As an example, auditory-linguistic deficient dyslexics typically have stronger right hemisphere-mediated functions; thus, a "whole word" or "look and say" method of reading would be recommended. This would occur without rejecting the teaching of sounds of letters and blends when decoding new words. Other techniques (Aaron & Poostay, 1982) advocate a careful review of the individual child's functional behaviors. Task analysis of these behaviors indicates where the functional breakdown has occurred in the learning process and represents the focus of intervention.

## REFERENCES

Aaron, I. E., & Poostay, E. J. (1982). Strategies for reading disorders. In C. R. Reynolds & T. B. Gutkin (Eds.), *The handbook of school psychology* (pp. 410–435). New York: Wiley.

Adams, R. B. (1967). *Dyslexia: A discussion of its definition.* Paper prepared for the second meeting of the Federal Government's

Attack on Dyslexia. Washington, DC: Bureau of Research, U.S. Office of Education.

Benton, A. L. (1980). Dyslexia: Evolution of a concept. *Bulletin of the Orton Society, 30,* 10–26.

Benton, A. L., & Pearl, D. (1978). *Dyslexia: An appraisal of current knowledge.* New York: Oxford University Press.

Dalby, J. T. (1979). Deficit or delay: Neuropsychological models of developmental dyslexia. *Journal of Special Education, 3,* 239–264.

Frank, J., & Levinson, H. (1973). Dysmetric dyslexia and dyspraxia: Hypothesis and study. *Journal of the American Academy of Child Psychiatry, 12,* 690–701.

Gaddes, W. H. (1976). Prevalence estimates and the need for definition of learning disabilities. In R. Knights & D. Bakker (Eds.), *The neuropsychology of learning disorders: Theoretical approaches* (pp. 3–24). Baltimore, MD: University Park Press.

Hartlage, L. C., & Telzrow, C. F. (1983). The neuropsychological basis of educational intervention. *Journal of Learning Disabilities, 16,* 521–523.

Herschel, M. (1978). Dyslexia revisted: A review. *Human Genetics, 40,* 115–134.

Hobbs, N. (1975). *The futures of children: Categories, labels, and their consequences.* San Francisco: Jossey-Bass.

Hynd, G. W., & Obrzut, J. E. (1981). *Neuropsychological assessment and the school-age child: Issues and procedures.* New York: Grune & Stratton.

Johnson, D. J., & Myklebust, H. R. (1967). *Learning disabilities: Educational principles and practices.* New York: Grune & Stratton.

Knights, R., & Bakker, D. (1976). *The neuropsychology of learning disorders: Theoretical approaches.* Baltimore, MD: University Park Press.

Petrauskas, R. J., & Rourke, B. P. (1979). Identification of subtypes of retarded readers: A neuropsychological multivariate approach. *Journal of Clinical Neuropsychology, 1,* 17–37.

Pirozzolo, F. J. (1981). Language and brain: Neuropsychological aspects of developmental reading disability. *School Psychology Review, 3,* 350–355.

Rourke, B. P. (1976). Reading retardation in children: Developmental lag or deficit? In R. Knights & D. Bakker (Eds.), *The neuropsychology of learning disorders: Theoretical approaches* (pp. 125–137). Baltimore, MD: University Park Press.

Rourke, B. P. (1982). Central processing deficiencies in children: Toward a developmental neuropsychological model. *Journal of Clinical Neuropsychology, 4,* 1–18.

Rourke, B. P., & Gates, R. D. (1981). Neuropsychological research and school psychology. In G. W. Hynd & J. E. Obrzut (Eds.), *Neuropsychological assessment and the school-age child: Issue and procedures* (pp. 3–25). New York: Grune & Stratton.

Satz, P., Taylor, H. G., Friel, J., & Fletcher, J. M. (1978). Some developmental and predictive precursors of reading disabilities: A six year follow-up. In A. L. Benton & D. Pearl (Eds.), *Dyslexia: An appraisal of current knowledge* (pp. 313–347). New York: Oxford University Press.

Yule, W., & Rutter, M. (1976). Epidemiological and social implications of specific reading retardation. In R. Knights & D. Bak-

ker (Eds.), *The neuropsychology of learning disorders: Theoretical approaches* (pp. 25–39). Baltimore, MD: University Park Press.

SCOTT W. SAUTTER
*Peabody College,*
*Vanderbilt University*

BRAIN DAMAGE
NEUROLOGICAL ORGANIZATION
READING DISORDERS
READING REMEDIATION

## DEVELOPMENTALLY DISABLED ASSISTANCE AND BILL OF RIGHTS ACT OF 1975

See PUBLIC LAW 94-103.

## DEVELOPMENTAL MILESTONES

Adults who have kept infant diaries have watched with pride as their children reached particular developmental milestones. The first responsive smile, the initial unsure steps, and the dawning of language are three of the most obvious milestones. Psychologists take an interest in these early milestones, but their perspective extends beyond the infant years to the whole life span. Their research includes a host of physical, biological, mental, emotional, and social milestones which, taken together, form a normative picture of the child's development.

Milestones that involve a physical or biological change are the most salient because the newly acquired behavior is so clear. One day infants are holding onto the coffee table investigating magazines or curios, and the next day they are launching themselves into a void where no support exists. This adventure constitutes the first step. The first step, typically achieved at 11.7 months is, however, a culmination of the series of physical milestones outlined in the Table below (Bayley, 1969). This table gives the average age when infants master the physical skills that precede walking as well as an age range when different children master the skills. Notice that these normal ranges are often several months apart. For example, occasionally children will pull themselves to a standing position at the age of 5 months. At the other end of the scale, some perfectly normal children do not accomplish this same feat until they are a year old. This range of normality attests to the individual differences that exist in attaining all developmental milestones.

Another physical sequence that psychologists have described in detail is the development of grasping (see Table). Newborns have a reflexive grasp and will close

Physical Milestones

| Walking | Mean Age for Mastery (Months) | Range of Ages for Mastery (Months) | Fine Motor Grasping | Mean Age for Mastery (Months) | Range of Ages for Mastery (Months) |
|---|---|---|---|---|---|
| Crawling movements | .4 | .1–3 | Holds onto red ring | .8 | .3–3 |
| Sits with support | 2.3 | 1–5 | Arm thrusts in play | .8 | .3–2 |
| Pulls self to sitting | 5.3 | 4.–8 | Opens hands | 2.7 | .7–6 |
| Prewalking progression | 7.1 | 5.–11 | Grasps with palm | 3.7 | 2–7 |
| Pulls to standing position | 8.1 | 5.–12 | Partially opposes thumb | 4.9 | 4–8 |
| Walks with help | 9.6 | 7–12 | Reaches with one hand | 5.4 | 4–8 |
| Stands alone | 11.0 | 9–16 | Reaches for pellet | 5.6 | 4–8 |
| Walks alone | 11.7 | 9–17 | Thumb opposed to finger | 6.9 | 5–9 |
| | | | Finger prehension | 7.4 | 6–10 |
| | | | Pincer prehension | 8.9 | 7–12 |

their palms around any object. In the first few months of life, infants bat at objects in their environment. By 4 months of age, infants have stopped batting at objects and have developed fluid eye-hand coordination (White, 1971). Now they can direct their hands efficiently to an object they see, open their fist en route and, once contact is made, grasp the object with their palms. The palmar grasp works well for handling wooden blocks and rattles, but it is not efficient for picking up small objects. The pincer grasp, where the thumb and forefinger are delicately opposed, will supplant the palmar grasp at approximately 9 months of age (Bayley, 1969).

Infants engage in a lot of rhythmical behaviors—repetitious kicking, rocking, waving, and bouncing. These rhythmical behaviors form a transition between reflexive, uncoordinated behavior and behaviors that are precise and controlled. Rocking on the hands, for example, can be observed shortly before the child begins to crawl. Bouncing on the legs precedes the first steps (Thelen, 1981). These progressions make sense if we view them as a consequence of the developments taking place in the brain.

At birth, the brain weighs about 12 ounces (350 grams). Most of this brain tissue is generated in the last 3 months of pregnancy. In fact, forming the 10 billion cells that comprise the human brain means that during the last months of pregnancy and the first months of life, about 250,000 neurons must be generated each minute (Cowan, 1979). In the first 2 years of life, the weight of the brain will triple, reflecting a surge in the number of dendrites (Conel, 1967). As the infant matures, the dendrites intertwine into more extensive networks, until each neuron is connected by its dendrites with thousands of other cells. When one cell is activated, the effect can be spread through the entire dendritic network.

This brief sketch of how the brain develops fits into Thelen's discussion of rhythmical behavior. She argues that the development of the brain presages the physical developments we regard as milestones. In newborns, the brain's neurons are relatively isolated, hence the child's

behaviors are reflexive and uncoordinated. As the dendritic networks begin to form, the child's behavior takes on more rhythmical patterns. At this point, the child will practice activating a particular part of the body in a rhythmical way. When neuronal networks for a particular area mature, physical skills will be controlled by the infant and will be integrated with the actions of other parts of the body (Hofer, 1981). Many of the milestones in physical development reflect, then, the developmental milestones of the brain.

Changes in the brain trigger other biological milestones. The hypothalamus, a small area of the brain that monitors and controls the release of hormones, can be characterized as the master controller for puberty (Grumbach, 1975). In males, the growth spurt, the deepening of the voice, and the appearance of secondary sex characteristics are obvious signals that the hormonal changes of puberty have begun. In females, menstruation is the most salient indication of the change from girlhood to womanhood, although girls also go through a growth spurt at the beginning of puberty. The female growth spurt peaks at approximately 12 years of age. In males, the period of fastest growth is approximately 14 years of age (Tanner & Eveleth, 1975). The timing of the growth spurt depends heavily on genetic factors, but is certainly influenced by a host of environmental variables such as diet and economic status (Tanner & Eveleth, 1975).

The impact of environmental factors on a biological milestone is most obvious in the case of menstruation. In many European countries, the age of menarch (first menstruation) during the late 1800s was approximately 16 years. In contemporary western cultures, menstruation typically begins 3 years earlier (Tanner & Eveleth, 1975). In the United States, for example, the mean age for menarche is 12.8 years (Warren, 1983). These marked changes in the age of menarch are attributed to better nutrition, more favorable socioeconomic conditions, and improvements in general health.

The physical and biological milestones that have been

described are relatively easy to identify because they are characterized by unique or discrete changes. Many mental milestones appear gradually and are more difficult to identify because they are so subtle. To psychologists interested in cognitive development, however, these milestones have become as obvious as the pincer grasp of infancy or the growth spurt of puberty.

The sensory motor period of development refers to the first 2 years of life. During this period, the child changes dramatically, from a wordless newborn, whose behaviors are primarily reflexive, to a talking 2 year old who has developed an amazing mastery of the immediate environment. In these 2 growth-filled years, the biggest mental milestones are the development of the object concept and the beginnings of language.

The object concept, described by Piaget (1954), reflects the infant's growing mental awareness. In the first few months of life, the infant is unconcerned about the comings and goings of people and objects. "Out of sight, out of mind" is an appropriate description for the infant's understanding of objects. Shortly after the first 6 months, infants' behaviors begin to change. Now, when their mothers disappear, infants stare at the doorway. They may cry, hoping that the combination of looking and crying will make their mother reappear. This change in behavior signals the realization, on the infant's part, that their mother is a separate entity.

Piaget (1954) followed the development of the object concept in his own three children. Using an infant version of hide-and-seek, he hid his children's favorite toy under a cloth or pillow. The hiding involved no deception; the infant could follow the toy visually as Piaget slowly slid it under the cover. Prior to 8 months, Piaget's children often reached for the cloth, but abandoned the search in a moment or two. By 10 months, however, they quickly pulled the cloth away and grabbed the toy. Piaget interpreted this change as indicating that his children could hold an image of the toy in their memories long enough to search for the object. They had developed a concept of an object that endured even when the object disappeared.

The object concept is a landmark in the development of memory. Once infants can represent objects in their minds, they are no longer limited to a reacting role; they can plan a course of action. Combine this initiative with the fact that 8 to 10 month olds have some mobility and you have the foundation for the avid exploration and curiosity of the 2 year old. The exploration and action of the 2 year old may seem like play to adults, and it is; but it is play with a serious purpose. It serves as the foundation for the abstract logic that is still many years in the future (Langer, 1980).

It is not coincidental that the second milestones of infancy, the child's first word, appears shortly after the object concept. In order to name an object, you must have a clear concept of that object. In most children, the appearance of the first word occurs between 10 and 15 months

(de Villiers & de Villiers, 1979). But these early words are tied to a specific context and really do not function as symbols. For example, Nicky at 13 months would wave and say "bye-bye" when his father left for work in the morning. But Nicky couldn't say "bye-bye" without waving. "Bye-bye" was associated with the morning, the waving, and the father leaving (Anisfeld, 1984). It took several more months for Nicky to use "bye-bye" in a symbolic way, to mean goodbye.

With the acquisition of language, the child moves into a period called the intuitive or preoperational stage of mental development. This stage of development, which lasts from approximately 2 to 5 years, stands in stark contrast to the sensory motor period because language begins to direct the child's behavior. The preoperational period begins with a child whose language skills are just emerging and ends with a child who relies on language instead of action to understand the world (Anisfeld, 1984). Two and 3 year olds buttress their beginning language skills by combining words and actions. These toddlers comprehend an airplane by saying "airplane," sticking out their arms, running around the room, and making sounds like a roaring engine. The action of imitating the airplane helps them form an image of an airplane and helps them attach the label "airplane" to the scene. Similarly, 3 and 4 year olds playing with blocks or dolls keep a running monologue going to describe the action they are orchestrating. By tying language to the action-based concepts that were developed during the sensory motor period, the child can gain confidence in the use of language. When language emerges as the primary means of understanding the world, the child's behavior changes dramatically. Four year olds who ask their parents endless questions about the car, the refrigerator, the dog, and the weather, are demonstrating that they can now learn about the world using language. When language skills are mature, the child is ready to transcend the constraints of time and space, to think about situations that cannot be experienced, and to let logic become the guide to mental operations.

Between 5 and 7 years of age, a third mental milestone is reached—concrete operational thought. Having mastered language and action, children begin to operate symbolically. They classify and order their environments and, in the process, enhance their awareness of the world. Understanding the days of the week and the months of the year allows adults to bring order to the daily chaos of life. Knowing that it is Monday supplies a great deal of information. It is the beginning of the week, tomorrow is Tuesday, and the weekend is 5 days away. The knowledge that today is Monday allows us to draw many other conclusions, because Monday is part of a larger organization of knowledge encompassing months, seasons, and years. Preoperational children lack these higher level organizations. But with the onset of concrete operational thought, children begin to sort out the world, order it for their use, and develop multilayered concepts (Kuhn, 1972). The baseball cards and coin collections that abound during the early elementary years are a testimony to the child's developing classification skills. Being able to order information is just as important as being able to classify. People can be tall, average, or short. Outdoor temperatures can range from over 100 degrees to well below zero. Students' examinations are ordered from "As" to "Fs." Establishing an order to information and assigning numbers to that order is a second way of organizing the world. This skill, called seriation, also emerges during the period of concrete operational thought.

The real hallmark of concrete operational thought, however, is not the skill of classification or seriation, but the ability to transform information. One woman can simultaneously be mother, Mrs. Lindsay, and Aunt Carol, and each of these classifications is appropriate. A pet can be Spot, an Irish Setter, a dog, and a mammal. Each label is understood as part of a larger organization. The concrete operational child not only uses language to guide actions, but coordinates different bits of information. We see this skill in a child's developing sense of humor (McGhee, 1979). Once children understand that words can be used in several contexts, they can appreciate the following joke:

Waiter, What's this fly doing in my soup?
It looks like the breaststroke, sir.

Mastering concrete operations moves the child toward more logical thought processes, but the advances of concrete operational thought are really a stepping stone to the culmination of mental development—formal operational thought. Formal thought processes are the final mental milestone; they begin between 12 and 16 years of age (Inhelder & Piaget, 1958). During this period of development, mental operations are completely integrated and thought attains a flexibility unrealized at the earlier stages. Students can abstract from the reality of a problem and consider alternatives to a problem. Furthermore, they can systematically test their ideas and discover which of several hypotheses is correct. As formal thought proceeds, adolescents can evaluate and transform hypothetical statements such as, "If this is Los Angeles, then the freeways are jammed." Most adolescents can logically extend this statement to include, "If the freeways are empty, this cannot be Los Angeles" (Moshman, 1979). As is obvious from this example, individuals who have reached the milestone of formal operations frequently move beyond the actual information given. As a result, they can speculate about worlds that do not exist, they can evaluate political systems they have not experienced, and they can predict technological advances that will not materialize for years. The thought processes foreshadowed by the toddler's exploration come to fruition in the balanced, flexible, cohesive thought of formal operations.

Human infants are helpless and need parental care and protection to survive. This evolutionary necessity may have prompted the development of the specific signs and signals that infants use to keep their mothers nearby (Bowlby, 1980). The first social smile, noticed by all parents, is part of a larger system known as the attachment behavioral system. The purpose of this system is to make sure the infant is safe. By using different attachment behaviors, infants signal their need for attention, express preferences for particular people, object angrily if they are separated from an attachment figure, and seek comfort from their attachment object when the environment is threatening (Main, 1981).

The newborn can signal the mother (or primary caretaker) by crying. Mothers are so tuned to this signal that their heart rate speeds up when their infant begins crying (Donovan, Leavitt, & Balling, 1978). Mothers all over the world respond to their infants' cries by going to their babies, picking them up, and cuddling them. Smiling is another attachment behavior. When the mother is near, the infant's smile strengthens and continues the social interaction between mother and infant. From the second month of life, infants begin to smile broadly at their mothers and indicate their pleasure by bicycling movements of their arms and legs. Most parents find this combination irresistible and immediately interact with their child. Infants also signal their parents by reaching, clinging, crawling, and walking. Once toddlers are mobile, they can take a more active role in maintaining proximity to their mothers. The popular image of the child peeping from behind mother's skirts is an example of the child seeking the mother when the environment seems threatening.

The formation of strong caretaker-infant attachments during the first year of life bodes well for social development in the toddler and preschool years. When a secure attachment exists, toddlers seem competent and self-assured as they explore their environments. Infants who are securely attached become preschoolers who are regarded as leaders and sought by other children as playmates (Bronson, 1981). The continuing effects of a secure attachment are easily explained. A secure attachment indicates a caring, trusting relationship between the mother and infant. In all likelihood, this positive relationship will continue into the toddler, preschool, and school years (Bretherton & Waters, 1985).

The attachment behavioral system carries over into peer relationships. A positive relationship with the mother seems to set the stage for the development of friendships. Friendships that involve cooperation and communication typically begin to develop during the preschool years. In fact, preschoolers can engage in the full spectrum of social interaction—cooperation, competition, aggression, affiliation, and altruism. Preschoolers can communicate, but more important, they can listen. If they need more information, they can ask questions. This ability to interact and carry on a dialogue is often the beginning of social relationships.

Despite the existence of basic social skills, the preschooler's social repertoire looks rather meager when compared with the school-age child's. Whereas friendships in preschool are a matter of convenience, stable, long-term friendships exist among elementary school children. Whether children are skillful at making friends at this age period depends on their ability to establish a common ground and exchange information as well as their ability to resolve conflicts and communicate (Gottman, 1983).

By adolescence, friends become confidants. Typically, teenage friends are the same age, the same sex, the same race, and have some common interest (Berndt, 1982). Being a friend now carries a measure of responsibility. Friends demand loyalty and require support. This kind of interpersonal commitment was not part of friendships during earlier periods of development.

Developmental milestones take many forms. The rapid physical changes that occur during infancy and the biological milestones that herald a new period of life are readily identified because they represent an abrupt break with the past. Mental development is characterized by just as many milestones, but they tend to emerge gradually. The object concept, the first word, and concrete operational thought processes are each noticeable points on the continuous tableau of development. As with most milestones, cognitive advances represent both the culmination of earlier processes and the foundation for further development. Social and emotional milestones include attachment behaviors and friendships. The first cries for attention and the devoted camaraderie of adolescence are both milestones that attest to the child's interactions with others. Examined together, the succession of physical, mental, and social milestones chart an individual's progress on the road of life.

## REFERENCES

Anisfeld, M. (1984). *Language development from birth to three.* Hillsdale, NJ: Erlbaum.

Bayley, N. (1969). *Manual for the Bayley scales of infant development.* New York: Psychological Corporation.

Berndt, T. J. (1982). The features and effects of friendship in early adolescence. *Child Development, 53,* 1447–1460.

Bowlby, J. (1980). *Attachment and loss: (Loss, sadness, and depression).* (Vol. 3). New York: Basic Books.

Bretherton, I., & Waters, E. (1985). Growing points of attachment theory and research. *Monographs for the Society for Research in Child Development, 50,* (209).

Bronson, W. C. (1981). *Toddlers' behavior with agemates: Issues of interaction, cognition, and affect.* Norwood, NJ: Ablex.

Conel, J. L. (1967). *The postnatal development of the human cortex.* (Vol. 8). Cambridge, MA: Harvard University Press.

Cowan, W. M. (1979). The development of the brain. *Scientific American, 241,* 112–133.

de Villiers, P. A., & de Villiers, J. G. (1979). *Early language.* Cambridge, MA: Harvard University Press.

Donovan, W. A., Leavitt, L. A., & Balling, J. D. (1978). Maternal physiological responses to infant signals. *Psychophysiology, 15,* 68–74.

Gottman, J. M. (1983). How children become friends. *Monographs of the Society for Research in Child Development, 48,* (201).

Grumbach, M. M. (1975). Onset of puberty. In S. R. Berenberg (Ed.), *Puberty: Biologic and psychosocial components.* Leiden, Netherlands: Stenfert Kroese.

Hofer, M. A. (1981). *The roots of human behavior.* San Francisco: Freeman.

Inhelder, B., & Piaget, J. (1958). *The growth of logical thinking from childhood to adolescence.* New York: Basic Books.

Kuhn, D. (1972). Mechanisms of change in the development of cognitive structures. *Child Development, 43,* 833–844.

Langer, J. (1980). *The origins of logic: Six to twelve months.* New York: Academic.

Main, M. (1981). Avoidance in the service of attachment. In K. Immelmann, G. W. Barlow, L. Petrinovich, & M. Main (Eds.), *Behavioral development: The Bielefeld Interdisciplinary Project.* London: Cambridge University Press.

McGhee, P. E. (1979). *Humor: Its origin and development.* San Francisco: Witt, Freeman.

Moshman, D. (1979). Development of formal hypothesis-testing ability. *Developmental Psychology, 15,* 104–112.

Piaget, J. (1954). *The construction of reality in the child.* New York: Ballantine.

Tanner, J. M., & Eveleth, P. B. (1975). Variability between populations in growth and development at puberty. In S. R. Berenberg (Ed.), *Puberty: Biologic and psychosocial components.* Leiden, Netherlands: Stenfert Kroese.

Thelen, E. (1981). Rhythmical behavior in infancy: An ethological perspective. *Developmental Psychology, 17,* 237–257.

Warren, M. P. (1983). Physical and biological aspects of puberty. In J. Brooks-Gunn and A. C. Petersen (Eds.), *Girls at puberty.* New York: Plenum.

White, B. L. (1971). *Human infants: Experience and psychological development.* Englewood Cliffs, NJ: Prentice-Hall.

CAROL TOMLINSON-KEASEY
*University of California,
Riverside*

## DEVELOPMENTAL NORMS

Developmental norms describe the position of an individual along a continuum of development. Two fundamental types of developmental norms are age equivalents and grade equivalents. They are obtained by administering a test to several successive age or grade groups; the average, or typical, performance of each age or grade group is subsequently determined and becomes the norm for a particular age or grade group (Anastasi, 1982).

A number of human traits demonstrate growth with increasing age, including abstract intelligence, vocabulary or language acquisition, and motor skill development.

Age equivalents have frequently been used to interpret performance for age-related traits. The average test score obtained by successive age or grade groups is determined based on the performance of a carefully selected sample of individuals. The age (in years and months) for which a particular test score was the average becomes the age equivalent for that particular test score; e.g., a child who answered 35 questions correctly on a receptive language test received an age equivalent of 4-6, meaning that 35 was the average, or typical, score for children aged 4 years, 6 months tested in the norming program. The term mental age refers to an age equivalent obtained from an intelligence test. A child with a mental age of 6 years, 3 months, for example, performed as well as the average child aged 6 years, 3 months.

Skills that develop as a direct result of school instruction such as reading or mathematics have frequently been assessed with tests that yield grade equivalents. The typical, or average, performance of successive grade groups is determined for a carefully selected sample of pupils. The grade for which a certain test score was the average becomes the grade equivalent for that particular test score (Thorndike & Hagen, 1977); e.g., a pupil who answered 40 questions correctly on a mathematics concepts test received a grade equivalent of 6.2, meaning that 40 was the average score for pupils in the second month of grade 6.

Age and grade equivalents have come into disfavor for a number of reasons:

1. They represent scales having unequal units because human traits typically develop faster in the earlier years and slow down in adolescence and adulthood. Thus, the difference in performance between ages 3 and 4, e.g., may be much greater than the difference in performance between ages 14 and 15 for a particular trait. Similarly, the difference in performance between grade equivalents 1.0 and 2.0 may be much greater than that between 8.0 and 9.0. This characteristic makes interpretation difficult.

2. They are not as rich in meaning as within-group norms (standard scores and percentile ranks) because they "match" the individual's performance to the age or grade group for which that performance was just average.

3. They can imply a level of functioning or skill development that is misleading. A fifth-grade pupil who receives a reading comprehension grade equivalent of 10.8 is not necessarily reading at the same level as a student in the eighth month of the tenth grade. The grade equivalent of 10.8 is to some extent a contrivance of the grade equivalent score scale and simply means the pupil is reading very well for a fifth grader (Cronbach, 1984). Grade equivalents are especially difficult to interpret when obtained from group achievement tests. Mental ages for adoles-cence and adulthood likewise do not describe actual performance at those ages and often represent an arbitrary and artificial extension of the mental age scale.

In summary, age and grade equivalents are developmental norms that, when interpreted cautiously, can sometimes provide useful information; however, within-group norms such as standard scores and percentile ranks are the preferred method of test interpretation.

## REFERENCES

Anastasi, A. (1982). *Psychological testing* (5th ed.). New York: Macmillan.

Cronbach, L. J. (1984). *Essentials of psychological testing* (4th ed.). New York: Harper & Row.

Thorndike, R. L., & Hagen, E. P. (1977). *Measurement and evaluation in psychology and education*. New York: Wiley.

GARY J. ROBERTSON
*American Guidance Service,*
*Circle Pines, Minnesota*

**GRADE EQUIVALENTS**
**NORM REFERENCED TESTING**

# DEVELOPMENTAL OPTOMETRY

The relationship between vision, sight, and learning took on a new meaning in 1922 when A. M. Skeffington, an optometrist who help found the Postgraduate Optometric Extension Program, lectured on the concept that Snellen visual acuity (sight) and visual effectiveness (vision) were not one in the same. In the 1930s George Crow and Margaret Eberl expanded this concept by instituting the use of preventive lenses and visual training to enhance visual abilities, promote visual efficiency, and reduce or eliminate visual anomalies such as amblyopia, strabismus, and binocular dysfunction. At the same time, the American Optometric Association published a pamphlet, "It is a Cruel Test," stating that "Optometry is not interested in merely whether the child sees well—it is interested in whether he sees efficiently."

Clinical studies in the visual development of the school-age child took a dramatic step forward in the 1940s at the Clinic of Child Development at Yale University. Gesell, Ilg et al. established that the eye and the other sensory modalities take turns in the development of the mind. Gesell et al. stated that vision is so fundamental in the growth of the mind that the body takes hold of the physical world with his eyes long before he takes hold with his hands. The eyes lead in the patterning of behavior.

The team at the Clinic of Child Development Center observed visual behavior from the earliest stages. It was noted, for example, that the newborn eyes wander without a stimulus. However, after a few hours, the child can often fixate briefly. By 16 weeks the eyes are leading the other senses, but they also begin to team with the hands. Through these observations, it was established that visual development began at birth despite the fact that vision appeared to be a "fleeting, discontinuous performance."

At the Child Development Center, Getman also developed, applied, and modified optometric techniques to test the visual development of the child from 21 to 48 months. These new tests and modifications were necessitated by the fact that adult testing procedures were of little value in the testing of children.

Getman found that monocular and binocular fixation, near and far point shifting of attention, and depth perception and spatial awareness develop and increase throughout childhood at varying rates. The studies revealed the importance of how the visual mechanism is involved in the total performance of the child. The concept of developmental vision that Getman and Kephart elaborated on also established a causal relationship between early motor patterns and the development of binocularity. Therefore, any delay or omission in development could result not only in binocular defects but in amblyopias and anisometropias. According to Solan (1979) any deviation from the normal ontogeny of motor and sensory maturation is considered to be significant.

Renshaw, Getman, and Skeffington studied the retinoscopic reflex during reading in conjunction with the lie detector test. They noted that when reading, stress could be revealed by the blood pressure, respiration, galvanic skin response, and retinoscopic reflex. These studies, along with the work of Huebal, Wiesel, and others, established that vision is not just genetically endowed; it develops. The concept of function altering structure rather than structure altering function became embodied in developmental vision theory. Solan (1979) states that by integrating the concepts of Myklebust, Strauss, Werner, Birch, Kephart, Piaget, Jensen, and others, the developmental optometrist is able to construct a diagnostic and therapeutic regimen. Developmental and perceptual therapy provides a child experiencing a learning disability with those characteristics normally associated with good students who are efficient learners.

The optometrist specializing in the field of developmental vision includes in the basic vision examination a careful case history that covers any significant information on the prenatal, perinatal, and postnatal disorders and any delays in the developmental milestones. The visual examination includes the standard testing procedures such as visual acuity, ocular health status of the eyes, binocular status, refractive status, and accommodative facility. Additional tests may probe the child's concept of laterality, directionality, dominance, eye-hand coordination, and visual perception.

Training of the child with developmental vision prob-

lems encompasses the standard visual training procedures. These include enhancement of ocular motility, stereopsis, eye-hand coordination, and accommodation. Additional techniques may emphasize bilateral and binocular integration.

The optometrist, as Solan (1979) states, blends professional and intellectual skills to develop in the learning-disabled child a suitable level of visual functional readiness for learning, the sensory-motor skills necessary for a child to respond to classroom instruction, and cognitive skills and conceptual tempo required for assimilation and generalization in learning reasoning and problem solving.

### REFERENCES

Barsch, R. H. (1964, January). The role of cognition in movement. *Optometric Child Vision Care & Guidance, 8*(4), 17–23.

Gesell, A., Halverson, A. Z., & Amstruda, C. (1940). *The first five years of life.* New York: Harper & Brothers.

Gesell, A., Ilg, F. L., & Bullis, G. E. (1949). *Vision: Its development in infant and child.* New York: Harper & Brothers.

Getman, G. (1960). *Techniques and diagnostic criteria for the optometric care of children's vision,* Duncan, OK: Occupational Education Programs.

Getman, G. (1962). *How to develop your child's intelligence.* Luverne, MI: Privately printed.

Getman, G., & Bullis, G. (1950). *Developmental vision* (Vol. 1). Duncan, OK: OEP.

Getman, G., & Kephart, N. (1957). *Developmental vision* (Vol. 2). Duncan, OK: OEP.

Kephart, N. C. (1960). *The slow learner in the classroom.* Columbus, OH: Charles E. Merril.

Lavatelli, C. (1973). *Piaget's theory applied to an early childhood curriculum.* Boston: Center for Media Development.

Piaget, J., & Inhelder, B. (1956). *The child's conception of space.* London: Routledge & Kegan Paul.

Skeffington, A. (1957). *Developmental vision* (Vol. 1). Duncan, OK: OEP.

Solan, H. (1979) *Learning disabilities: The role of the developmental optometrist. 50*(11), 1265. St. Louis: American Optometric Association.

BRUCE P. ROSENTHAL
*State University of New York,*
*College of Optometry*

## DEVELOPMENTAL PSYCHOLOGY

*Developmental Psychology* is a publication of the American Psychological Association. Founded in 1968, its first editor was Boyd R. McCandless of Emory University.

The journal's primary purpose is to publish reports of empirical research on topics pertaining to developmental psychology. Developmental psychology is defined as including variables pertaining to growth and development broadly cast. Not only chronological age and physical growth variables are included, but also other factors, such as sex and socioeconomic status.

*Developmental Psychology* is published bimonthly. Manuscripts may be sent to *Developmental Psychology,* American Psychological Association, 1200 Seventeenth Street, NW, Washington, DC 20036.

ELIZABETH JONES
*Texas A&M University*

## DEVELOPMENTAL TEST OF VISUAL-MOTOR INTEGRATION

The Developmental Test of Visual-Motor Integration (VMI) (Beery, 1982) is widely used in schools and research. The test consists of 24 geometric forms beginning with simple lines and figures and ending with complex patterns. A booklet contains the forms with a place beneath each figure for the child's drawing. The VMI may be used for group or individual screening of children, primarily between the ages of 4 and 13. The standardization sample consisted of 3090 children between ages 2 and 19.

Scoring of the VMI is straightforward. Criteria for a successful performance are presented along with examples of both passing and failing drawings. In addition, norms from other developmental schedules and age trends are provided. Tables enable the determination of scaled scores (mean of 10 and a standard deviation of 3) and percentiles.

Interrater reliability is reported to be generally high. The median test-retest reliability coefficient is .81. Studies of internal consistency reliability have a median of .79. A large number of research studies are available that report on various aspects of validity, including the use of the VMI as a readiness measure (Simner, 1983), the developmental progression of drawings, the effects of ethnicity on performance, and the relationship of the VMI to cognitive measures and various handicapping conditions.

### REFERENCES

Beery, K. E. (1982). *Revised administration, scoring, and teaching manual for the Developmental Test of Visual-Motor Integration.* Cleveland, OH: Modern Curriculum.

Simner, M. L. (1983). The warning signs of school failure: An updated profile of the at-risk kindergarten child. *Topics in Early Childhood Special Education, 3,* 17–27.

DAVID W. BARNETT
*University of Cincinnati*

## DEVELOPMENTAL TEST OF VISUAL PERCEPTION (DTVP)

The Developmental Test of Visual Perception (DTVP) by Marianne Frostig was designed to measure five operationally defined perceptual skills: eye-motor coordination, figure ground, constancy of shape, position in space, and spatial relationships. It was created to determine the presence of learning disabilities in children ages 3 through 8. Individual and group administration forms are available. Administration time averages from 30 to 45 minutes; the objective scoring takes an additional 5 to 10 minutes. Only a skilled psychologist should give the test, otherwise unacceptable reductions in reliability can occur (Darnell, 1985).

The test is criticized on several levels. The norms presented are outdated and nonrepresentative of the general population. A total of 2100 southern California children were used. They were predominantly middle-class white children between ages 3 and 9. There were no blacks and few Mexican-American or Asian children included in the sample. Limited reliability and validity data are available. Reliability data reveal a reasonable test-retest correlation when the whole test is examined (.80), however, correlations of the independent subtests are weak (.48). This could indicate that the individual subtests are relatively unstable; this detracts from the author's statement of independent trait measurements (Sabatino, 1985). Predictive validity is limited to the position in space subtest and its ability to predict language arts or math concepts relationships (Colarusso et al., 1975). The DTVP is severely limited by its norms and standardization. Overall, the DTVP should be considered a useful addition to a more intensive test battery, but never a sole determinant for perceptual assessment or intervention.

### REFERENCES

Colarruso, R. P., Martin, H., & Hartung, J. (1975). Specific visual perception skills as long term predictors of academic success. *Journal of Learning Disabilities, 4,* 279–283.

Darnell, R. (1985). Review of the Marianne Frostig Developmental Test of Visual Perception. In J. V. Mitchell, Jr. (Ed.), *The ninth mental measurements yearbook* (Vol. 2). Lincoln: University of Nebraska Press.

Frostig, M. et al. (1963). *The Marianne Frostig Developmental Test of Visual Perception.* Palo Alto, CA: Consulting Psychologist.

Sabatino, D. (1985). Review for Marianne Frostig Developmental Test of Visual Perception. In J. V. Mitchell, Jr. (Ed.), *The ninth mental measurements yearbook.* Lincoln: University of Nebraska Press.

LISA J. SAMPSON
*Eastern Kentucky University*

# DEVELOPMENTAL THERAPY

Developmental therapy is a method of educating severely socially, emotionally, and behaviorally handicapped children. It has normal social-emotional development as its goal. Developmental sequences in behavior, social communication, socialization, and cognition provide the framework for the curriculum. Devised by Mary M. Wood and associates (1979, 1986), developmental therapy links theory and research about normal social-emotional development to classroom practices. It was first demonstrated in 1970 at the Rutland Psychoeducational Center in Athens, Georgia, in a collaborative effort between the public school system, the mental health system, the University of Georgia, and the U.S. Department of Education.

Developmental therapy has been used successfully with severely emotionally disturbed and autistic children from age 2 to 16 years in preschool, elementary, middle school, and high-school classes. It also has been used effectively in day-treatment settings and residential facilities. Educators have adapted aspects of developmental therapy to resource rooms, self-contained classrooms, and regular education classes. It has extensive applications in the therapeutic arts, including art, music, and recreation therapies. It has also been adapted for use in camp settings and leisure programs, and for parents in home programs with autistic children. It was approved by the U.S. Office of Education, National Institute of Education Joint Dissemination Review Panel in 1975 as an exemplary educational program with documented effectiveness. It received validation again in 1981 from the same panel as an exemplary training model for teachers.

The foundation for developmental therapy is based on theory and research about social, emotional, cognitive, communication, and behavioral development. There is agreement that social knowledge, language, and judgment play important roles in governing behavior and that these are acquired through social experience. There also is agreement that the quality of interactions with others influences the form behavior will take. In addition, developmental theorists provide the concept of ordered, sequential processes in thinking, feeling, behaving, and relating from infancy through adolescence. Their work provides a reference for understanding the extent to which social and affective skills can be taught and the limitations that can be expected at any particular stage (Erikson, 1977; Flavell, 1977; Kohlberg, 1983; Piaget, 1977). Social learning and behavioral theorists provide knowledge about the impact of others on the development of self-control and self-regulated behavior. Studies of modeling, imitation, punishment, discipline, aggression by adults toward children, and the role of reasoning in behavioral management provide understanding about how social behavior emerges (Bandura, 1977; Turiel, 1983; Selman, 1980). Psychoanalytic theorists focus on feelings, anxieties, defense mechanisms, ego functions, and relationships with adults (Freud, 1965; Loevinger, 1976; Maccoby, 1980). These major constructs from different theoretical orientations have been integrated into the practices of developmental therapy.

Students are grouped for developmental therapy according to their stage of social-emotional development. Groups range in size from 4 to 12 students, with the smaller groups used for students at lower developmental stages and those with severe psychopathology. Each group is conducted by a lead teacher-therapist and a support teacher aide. The goals and specific program (treatment) objectives and procedures for each stage are based on individual assessment of each student's social-emotional development. Characteristic roles for adults and the activities, materials, schedules, and behavior management strategies are specified by the stage.

The instrument used to assess each student's social-emotional development is the Developmental Therapy Objectives Rating Form (DTORF). This instrument provides specific individual education plan (IEP) short-term objectives and long-range program goals. Since the first field testing, the DTORF has been used with several thousand students ages 2 to 16 with a range of handicapping conditions, including children who are autistic, mentally retarded, severely multihandicapped, deaf, schizophrenic, nonhandicapped, and gifted.

Several studies provide evidence about the effectiveness of developmental therapy. One series involving 73 severely emotionally disturbed students used parents' ratings (Kaufman, Paget, & Wood, 1981); effectiveness was defined as a statistically significant reduction in severe problem behavior from time of enrollment to termination and 2 years later. Results showed a large and statistically significant reduction in severe problem behavior at the time of termination and 2 years later. Significant reductions were found to occur regardless of age, race, sex, parents' income, and length of time in the program. Another series of studies followed the progress of 106 preschool children receiving developmental therapy in different settings (Wood & Swan, 1978). Effectiveness in these studies was defined as gains in percentages of DTORF objectives mastered. Gains occurred in all four settings: a day-treatment program, a psychoeducational program for autistic students, a resource room in a public day-care facility, and a mainstreamed setting in a Head Start program. In another study of 127 moderately to severely disturbed students receiving developmental therapy. A preestablished criterion of a gain of one half of one standard deviation for DTORF was set as acceptable progress in a 10-week period. This expectation was achieved by 68% of the students.

## REFERENCES

Bandura, A. (1977). *Social learning theory*. Englewood Cliffs, NJ: Prentice-Hall.

Erikson, E. H. (1977). *Toys and reasons.* New York: Norton.

Flavell, J. H. (1977). *Cognitive development.* Englewood Cliffs, NJ: Prentice-Hall.

Freud, A. (1965). *Normality and pathology in childhood: Assessment of development.* New York: International Universities Press.

Kaufman, A., Paget, C., & Wood, M. M. (1981). Effectiveness of developmental therapy for severely emotionally disturbed children. In F. H. Wood (Ed.), *Perspectives for a new decade: Education's responsibility for seriously emotionally disturbed and behaviorally disordered children and youth.* Reston, VA: Council for Exceptional Children.

Kohlberg, L. (1983). *Essays on moral development.* (Vol. 2). San Francisco: Harper & Row.

Loevinger, J. (1976). *Ego development.* San Francisco: Jossey-Bass.

Maccoby, E. E. (1980). *Social development.* New York: Harcourt, Brace & Jovanovich.

Piaget, J. (1977). *The development of thought.* New York: Viking.

Selman, R. (1980). *The growth of interpersonal understanding.* New York: Holt, Rinehart & Winston.

Turiel, E. (1983). *The development of social knowledge.* Cambridge, MA: Cambridge University Press.

Wood, M. M. (1979). *The developmental therapy objectives: A self-instructional workbook.* Austin, TX: Pro Ed.

Wood, M. M. (1986). *Developmental therapy in the classroom.* Austin, TX: Pro Ed.

Wood, M. M. & Swan, W. W. (1978). A developmental approach to educating the disturbed young child. *Behavioral Disorders, 3,* 197–209.

MARY M. WOOD
*University of Georgia*

EMOTIONAL DISORDERS
SOCIAL DEVELOPMENT
SOCIAL LEARNING THEORY

# DEVEREUX FOUNDATION, THE

The Devereux School was founded in 1912 by Helena T. Devereux (1885–1975), who had been a public school teacher and resigned her position to begin a school for emotionally disturbed and mentally retarded children. The school was chartered as a Pennsylvania nonprofit foundation in 1938; it maintains its corporate headquarters in Devon, Pennsylvania (suburban Philadelphia). Currently, the foundation operates in Arizona, Arkansas, California, Connecticut, Delaware, Georgia, Massachusetts, New Jersey, Texas, and at several sites in southeastern Pennsylvania. Approximately 2000 children and adolescents are served by Devereux at all of its locations. Devereux schools and treatment centers are licensed, approved, and/or accredited by numerous state and national agencies. According to the Foundation's publications, in addition to the emotionally disturbed and mentally retarded, special programs are available for children, adolescents, and young adults with diagnoses including psychosis, aphasia, specific reading disabilities, brain injury, autism, schizophrenia, and underachievement (Sargent, 1984).

In addition to its educational and treatment services, Devereux has been involved in various research and publishing efforts. Recent publications include the Devereux Behavior Rating Scales (child, adolescent and elementary school versions) and the Individual Motor Achievement Guided Education (IMAGE) program (Sargent, 1984).

**REFERENCE**

Sargent, J. K. (1984). *The directory for exceptional children* (10th ed.). Boston: Porter Sargent.

JOHN D. WILSON
*Elwyn Institutes,
Elwyn, Pennsylvania*

# DEVIATION IQ

A standard score, known as a deviation IQ, was introduced to overcome the technical problems inherent in the ratio IQ. A standard score is obtained by converting raw test scores from a standardization sample to a normalized score distribution with a fixed mean and standard deviation. Deviation IQs typically have a mean of 100 and a standard deviation of the authors' choosing such as 15 for Wechsler tests and 16 for the Stanford-Binet. There is no difference between Wechsler and Binet IQs in the 90 to 110 range, but the further the score from average, the greater the difference, as illustrated in the Table below. Standard scores are used to convert ordinal to interval data. Standard (normalized) scores provide equal variability at each age level and standard scores from one test can be directly compared with standard scores from another. In individual assessment, David Wechsler introduced the deviation IQ with his Wechsler-Bellevue scale in 1939. (The deviation IQ had been used with some group tests earlier.) Wechsler chose to use a standard score with a standard deviation of 15 (instead of 16, the median standard deviation of the contemporary Binet) because most people are more familiar with units of 5 (i.e., 5, 10, 15) than of 4 (i.e., 4, 8, 12, 16). Today most test authors use a deviation IQ with a standard deviation of either 15 or 16, but some use 20 and even 24.

Because of the popularity among professionals of the concept of the standard score with a mean of 100 and a standard deviation of 15 or 16, and because of the lack of popularity of the letters I and Q, some contemporary test authors have changed the name of the score from IQ to Learning Quotient (LQ), General Cognitive Index (GCI), Mental Processing Composite, etc. Whatever standard scores may be called, when they are derived from a test

Percentile Rank Equivalents for Deviation IQs with Standard Deviations of 15, 16, and 20[a]

| Percentile Rank | Wechsler 15z + 100 | Stanford-Binet 16z + 100 | ASVAB 20z + 100 |
|---|---|---|---|
| 0.1 | 55 | 52 | 40 |
| 0.9 | 65 | 62 | 53 |
| 2.0 | 69 | 67 | 59 |
| 2.9 | 72 | 70 | 62 |
| 5.0 | 75 | 74 | 67 |
| 9.7 | 81 | 79 | 74 |
| 14.7 | 84 | 83 | 79 |
| 25.8 | 90 | 90 | 87 |
| 40.1 | 96 | 96 | 95 |
| 50.0 | 100 | 100 | 100 |
| 59.9 | 104 | 104 | 105 |
| 74.2 | 110 | 110 | 113 |
| 84.1 | 115 | 116 | 120 |
| 90.3 | 120 | 121 | 126 |
| 95.0 | 125 | 126 | 133 |
| 97.1 | 129 | 130 | 138 |
| 98.0 | 131 | 133 | 141 |
| 98.9 | 135 | 137 | 146 |
| 99.9 | 145 | 148 | 160 |

[a] Wechsler refers to Wechsler Preschool and Primary Scale of Intelligence, Wechsler Intelligence Scale for Children—Revised, and the Wechsler Adult Intelligence Scale—Revised. Stanford-Binet refers to the 1972 and 1985 editions only. ASVAB is the common abbreviation for the Armed Services Vocational Assessment Battery.

of mental ability, they are interpreted in the same way as deviation IQs, i.e., as indicating where the individual stands in relation to others of his or her age on the content of the test.

It should be noted that the Wechsler-Bellevue (predecessor of the Wechsler Adult Intelligence Scale) was developed for adults rather than children/adolescents and that mental test raw scores for average adults are very little higher than those of adolescents. Since the average raw score at age 50 is actually a little lower than of age 20, it makes no sense to refer to someone as having reached a mental age of 50 or to divide such a score by chronological age. With adults, as with children, a deviation IQ is a convenient index for indicating the current level of intellectual development and functioning (as later qualified). By mid-adolescence and for many predictions, tests with norms based on educational status may be better than those based on age.

Since an IQ is a score from a test and since the content of tests of mental ability differ not only from each other but also within a test from childhood to adolescence, the term IQ should be preceded by the name of the test from which it was derived and accompanied by the age at which it was obtained. As a score, an IQ indicates both an individual's ability level at a given point in time and the relationship of the individual's score to those obtained by others of his or her age. As such, an IQ should be considered as a descriptive rather than an explanatory term. An

IQ can be used to help understand a person's current level of cognitive functioning associated with learning in the mainstream culture. Scores from mental ability scales are to some extent reflections of previous learning within the culture in which the test was standardized, and they are predictors of subsequent educational performance in that culture over the next few years.

IQs are often thought of as indicators of scholastic or educational aptitude. However, they do not reflect important variables such as mechanical, motor, musical, and artistic aptitudes. IQs do not reflect skills in building or maintaining inter- or intrapersonal relationships. Only to a limited extent do IQs reflect such catalytic variables as persistence, enthusiasm for a particular kind of effort, or divergent thinking. Decisions about an individual need to be based on more than scores from one test of cognitive ability.

JOSEPH L. FRENCH
*Pennsylvania State University*

## INTELLIGENCE QUOTIENT

## RATIO IQ

## DEXEDRINE

(Dexedrine sulfate), an amphetamine, is used in the treatment of attention deficit disorder with hyperactivity, narcolepsy, and as short-term therapy for exogenous obesity. Although amphetamines are known to work as central nervous stimulants, the mechanism whereby they produce mental and behavioral effects in children is not known. Adverse reactions can include palpitations and rapid heartbeat; euphoria, restlessness, and insomnia; and exacerbation of motor and vocal tics and Tourette's syndrome. Overdose may result in assaultiveness, confusion, hallucinations, and panic states usually followed by fatigue and depression.

A brand name of Smith Kline and French, Dexedrine is available in 5 mg tablets; 5, 10, and 15 mg sustained released capsules, and elixir. Recommended dosage for attention deficit disorder with hyperactivity in children 6 years of age and older is to start with 5 mg once or twice daily, with daily dosage to be raised, if needed, in increments of 5 mg at weekly intervals, typically not to exceed a total of 40 mg per day.

### REFERENCE

*Physicians' desk reference.* (1984). (pp. 1878–1880). Oradell, NJ: Medical Economics.

LAWRENCE C. HARTLAGE
*Evans, Georgia*

## ATTENTION DEFICIT DISORDER

## DEXTROAMPHETAMINE

Dextramphetamine sulfate is an amphetamine that may be used in the treatment of attention deficit disorder with hyperactivity. Other uses, adverse reactions, and overdose symptoms are listed under the entry *Dexedrine*, a brand name. Generic dextroamphetamine is distributed by Rexar Pharmaceutical Corporation in 5 and 10 mg scored tablets.

### REFERENCE

*Physicians' desk reference* (1984) (pp. 1587–1588). Oradell, NJ: Medical Economics.

LAWRENCE C. HARTLAGE
*Evans, Georgia*

## DIABETES

Diabetes is a chronic metabolic disease affecting approximately 12 million Americans. Common symptoms of diabetes include extreme hunger and thirst, frequent urination, irritability, weakness, fatigue, nausea, and high blood and urine sugar levels. Two major types of diabetes have been identified. Type I, or insulin dependent diabetes, was formerly called juvenile-onset because it usually occurred in children and adolescents. Type II, or noninsulin dependent, was formerly called maturity-onset. In Type I diabetes, the pancreas does not function properly, resulting in little to no insulin production and a build-up of sugar in the bloodstream. Treatment involves insulin injections, diet, and regular exercise. Approximately 1 million Americans are Type I diabetics. It is thought that there is a genetic predisposition for diabetes. At present there is no known cure. Obesity and stress can contribute to the onset of diabetes.

Hypoglycemia (low blood sugar) and hyperglycemia (high blood sugar) are the two most common emergencies encountered by diabetics. Hypoglycemia occurs when the blood sugar drops too low because of too much insulin, not enough food, or too much exercise. Symptoms include anger or bad temper, sudden staggering and poor coordination, pale color, disorientation, confusion, and sweating, eventually leading to stupor or unconsciousness, also called insulin shock. This condition is treated by administering some form of sugar such as fruit juice or candy. If unconsciousness occurs, a child should receive emergency medical care.

Hyperglycemia occurs when there is too little insulin, when infection or illness is present, or when too much food or drink is consumed. Symptoms of hyperglycemia include drowsiness, extreme thirst and frequent urination, fruity or wine-smelling breath, heavy breathing, flushed skin, vomiting, and eventually stupor or unconsciousness, called a diabetic coma. Treatment of this condition is usually the administration of insulin with the supervision of a health-care professional.

Some diabetics develop complications such as retinopathy, that sometimes result in blindness, diabetic neuropathy or nerve disease, diabetic nephropathy or kidney disease, cardiovascular disease, or respiratory failure. Diabetes and its complications is the number three cause of nonaccidental death among children in the United States (Wright, Schafer, & Solomons, 1979).

It has been suggested by researchers that by the time a child reaches the developmental age of 12, and sometimes as early as 8 or 10, he or she should be able to take over the responsibilities of doing his or her own urine or blood sugar tests and administration of insulin. Keep in mind that children in special education classes may reach these developmental ages at slower rates and thus may be more reliant on teachers and parents for assistance in complying with their diabetic regimen. In such cases teachers must be aware of the regimen. Parents should inform teachers about their child's needs, which may include a special diet, especially at lunch and snack time, time to run tests and take insulin injections, exercise, and signs of emergency, especially hyperglycemia and hypoglycemia. However, teachers should make every effort not to separate the child from the peer group. The diabetic child has the same needs for support, encouragement, and understanding as other children and should be encouraged to participate in all activities. When treats are offered, the teacher might offer a "diabetic" treat such as raisins, peanuts, or sugarless candy or gum.

Compliance with the diabetic treatment regimen is usually difficult for a child and it may be more difficult for a child in special education who does not understand all of the rules of diabetes. It is important in this case that the teacher and school staff work with the child's parents to understand the special needs and restrictions diabetes places on the child. Teachers need to be aware of the diabetic child's developmental age and work with the child to develop responsibility, independence, and self-reliance compatible with his or her age of development. Should parents prove either unsophisticated or unresponsive, direct teacher-physician contact becomes essential.

### REFERENCES

American Diabetes Association. (1984). *A word to . . . teachers and school staff*. Alexandria, VA: Author.

American Diabetes Association. (1984). *Your child has diabetes: What you should know*. Alexandria, VA: Author.

American Diabetes Association (1984). An introduction: *What you need to know about diabetes*. Alexandria, VA: Author.

Carpenter, J. (1976). *Diabetes: A handicap*. Unpublished manuscript.

Wright, L., Schafer, A., & Solomons, G. (1979). *Encyclopedia of pediatric psychology*. Baltimore, MD: University Park Press.

JANET CARPENTER
LOGAN WRIGHT
*University of Oklahoma*

**FAMILY RESPONSE TO HANDICAP**
**HEALTH PROBLEMS OF THE HANDICAPPED**

# DIAGNOSIS IN SPECIAL EDUCATION

Diagnosis is an essential step in the process of identifying those children in need of special education services. A recent source (Matarazzo, & Pankratz, 1984) defines psychological diagnosis as "(1) the process of classifying information relevant to an individual's emotional and behavioral state, and (2) the name assigned the state, taken generally from a commonly accepted classification system (p. 369)." Based on this definition, diagnosis in special education involves taking the information obtained through the assessment of a student's emotional, behavioral, academic, and intellectual functioning and classifying that information based on some accepted diagnostic system. The specific diagnostic system used determines the specific classification or name given to that student's level of functioning or condition.

The diagnostic procedure traditionally employed in special education has been one based on a medical model (Reynolds, 1984; Ysseldyke & Algozzine, 1982). This model is one borrowed from psychological diagnostic systems. It consists of preparing catalogs of systems of various special and remedial conditions and determining the extent to which an individual has characteristics similar to those of the known condition (Ysseldyke & Algozzine, 1982). According to Reynolds (1984), the focus has been on "intrapsychic causes of psychological dysfunction to the exclusion of extrapersonal factors, and on the deficiencies and weaknesses of individuals rather than on their strengths (p. 453)."

There have been many problems associated with the use of this type of a diagnostic model in special education. One problem centers around the fact that a wide variety of diagnostic systems have been developed. This has resulted in a situation in which the assessment of one student can produce very different diagnoses depending on the diagnostic system being referred to. There also tends to be considerable variations among the diagnoses of individuals classified under the same diagnostic system

(Edgar & Hayden, 1985; Reynolds, 1984). These inconsistencies have made the process of special education diagnosis complicated and controversial.

The passage of PL 94-142, the Education for All Handicapped Children Act of 1975, has had a major impact on the process of diagnosis in special education. Public Law 94-142 provides a system of definitions by which individuals eligible for special education can be identified and classified. In general, it defines those children for whom special education is warranted in the following way:

> Handicapped children means those children evaluated as being mentally retarded, hard of hearing, deaf, speech impaired, visually handicapped, seriously emotionally disturbed, orthopedically impaired, other health impaired, deaf-blind, multihandicapped, or as having specific learning disabilities, who because of those impairments need special education and related services.

The specific handicaps used in this definition are then further defined as follows:

> "Deaf" means a hearing impairment which is so severe that the child is impaired in processing linguistic information through hearing, with or without amplification, which adversely affects educational performance.

> "Deaf-blind" means concomitant hearing and visual impairments, the combination of which causes such severe communication and other developmental and educational problems that they cannot be accommodated in special education programs soley for deaf or blind children.

> "Hard of hearing" means a hearing impairment, whether permanent or fluctuating, which adversely affects a child's educational performance but which is not included under the definition of "deaf" in this section.

> "Mentally retarded" means significantly subaverage general intellectual functioning existing concurrently with deficits in adaptive behavior and manifested during the development period, which adversely affects a child's educational performance.

> "Multihandicapped" means concomitant impairments (such as mentally retarded-blind, mentally retarded-orthopedically impaired, etc.), the combination of which causes such severe educational problems that they cannot be accommodated in special education programs soley for one of the impairments. The term does not include deaf-blind children.

> "Orthopedically impaired" means a severe orthopedic impairment which adversely affects a child's educational performance. The term includes impairments caused by congenital anomaly (e.g., clubfoot, absence of some member, etc.), impairments caused by disease (e.g., poliomyelitis, bone tuberculosis, etc.), and impairments from other causes (e.g., cerebral palsy, amputations, and fractures or burns which cause contractures).

> "Other health impaired" means limited strength, vitality, or alertness, due to chronic or acute health problems such as a heart condition, tuberculosis, rheumatic fever, nephritis, asthma, sickle cell anemia, hemophilia, epilepsy, lead poi-

soning, leukemia, or diabetes, which adversely affects a child's educational performance.

"Seriously emotionally disturbed" is defined as follows:

(1) The term means a condition exhibiting one or more of the following characteristics over a long period of time and to a marked degree, which adversely affects educational performance:

(a) An inability to learn which cannot be explained by intellectual, sensory, or health factors

(b) An inability to build or maintain satisfactory interpersonal relationships with peers and teachers

(c) Inappropriate types of behavior or feelings under normal circumstances

(d) A general pervasive mood of unhappiness or depression or

(e) A tendency to develop physical symptoms or fears associated with personal or school problems

(2) The term includes children who are schizophrenic or autistic. The term does not include children who are socially maladjusted, unless it is determined that they are seriously emotionally disturbed.

"Specific learning disability" means a disorder in one or more of the basic psychological processes involved in understanding or in using language, spoken or written, which may manifest itself in an imperfect ability to listen, think, speak, read, write, spell, or to do mathematical calculations. The term includes such conditions as perceptual handicaps, brain injury, minimal brain dysfuunction, dyslexia, and developmental aphasia. The term does not include children who have learning problems which are primarily the result of visual, hearing, or motor handicaps, of mental retardation, or of environmental, cultural, or economic disadvantage.

"Speech impaired" means a communication disorder, such as stuttering, impaired articulation, a language impairment, or a voice impairment, which adversely affects a child's educational performance.

"Visually handicapped" means a visual impairment which, even with correction, adversely affects a child's educational performance. The term includes both partially seeing and blind children.

Shortly after PL 94-142 was passed, debates ensued over some of the definitions used in that law. The greatest controversy has been over the definition given for learning disabilities. Those required to implement this law felt that the category of learning disabled needed to be defined more precisely. Therefore, the 1977 *Federal Register* attempted to specify the regulations for defining and identifying the learning disabled students under PL 94-142. According to the 1977 *Federal Register*, a determination of learning disability

is made based on (1) whether a child does not achieve commensurate with his or her age and ability when provided with appropriate educational experiences and (2) whether the child has a severe discrepancy between achievement and intellectual ability in one or more of seven areas relating to communication skills and mathematical abilities. These concepts are to be interpreted on a case by case basis by the qualified

evaluation team members. The team must decide that the discrepancy is not primarily the result of (1) visual, hearing, or motor handicaps; (2) mental retardation; (3) emotional disturbance; or (4) environmental, cultural, or economic disadvantage.

While this definition has provided more guidance, it has still left it up to the individual state education departments to decide what criteria would be used to determine a severe discrepancy. As a result, there is a great diversity of criteria being used by the different state departments for the diagnosis of learning disabilities (Reynolds, 1984; Mercer, Hughes, & Mercer, 1985).

A recent study (Mercer, et al., 1985) of the 50 state departments of education focused on the different criteria used to diagnose learning disabilities. It was found that 44% of the states use the 1977 definition of learning disability without modification, whereas another 28% use it with a slight variation. A different definition is used by 24% of the states, and 4% of the states do not use a learning disability definition. Several states use more than one definition. It was found that there are six components commonly used in the process of defining and/or identifying learning disabilities. Three of these components (academic problem, exclusion, and discrepancy) were found to be increasing in usage while the other three components (process, neurological, and intelligence) were decreasing in usage. These components are identified as follows. The intelligence component focuses on the ability level or range of the person being identified. The process-language component focuses on that aspect of the 1977 definition that deals with identifying a process deficit that is manifested in a language disorder. The academic component is usually reported within four areas: reading, writing, spelling, and arithmetic. The exclusion component focuses on those characteristics that exclude children from being identified as learning disabled. This includes handicaps such as visual and auditory impairment, motor impairment, mental retardation, emotional disturbance, and environmental disadvantages that are the primary cause of the learning disability. The neurological component focuses onthe consideration of central nervous system impairment in relation to learning-disabled students. The discrepancy component focuses on the discrepancy between a child's estimated ability and his or her academic performance.

There is a great amount of diversity from state to state as to the degree to which each of these components is incorporated into the measurement model used in defining and identifying learning-disabled children. Reynolds (1984) has also noted that there have been varying levels of expertise with which these models have been implemented. Both of these factors have contributed to differences in the proportions of children served as learning disabled in the various states. Figures can easily vary from less than 2% to more than 35% of a random sample of the population, depending on which state's criteria are being applied (Reynolds, 1984).

According to Hammill, Larsen, Leigh, and McNutt (1981), the National Joint Committee for Learning Disabilities was also dissatisfied with the learning disabilities definition as presented in PL 94-142. They felt that while this definition served the educational community well by providing a basis for federal and state funding for instructional services for school-aged children, it had inherent weaknesses. Those weaknesses made it unacceptable as a definition that could be used to delimit a field as broad and complex as that of learning disabilities. They proposed a new definition of learning disabilities as follows:

Learning disabilities is a generic term that refers to a heterogeneous group of disorders manifested by significant difficulties in the acquisition and use of listening, speaking, reading, writing, reasoning, or mathematical abilities. These disorders are intrinsic to the individual and presumed to be due to central nervous system dysfunction. Even though a learning disability may occur concomitantly with other handicapping conditions (e.g., sensory impairment, mental retardation, social and emotional disturbance) or environmental influences (e.g., cultural differences, insufficient/inappropriate instruction, psychogenic factors), it is not the direct result of those conditions or influences.

This definition varies from the one given in five major ways. It does not include the use of the term children, therefore allowing for the recognition of learning-disabled adults. It does not include the phrase "basic psychological process," thus placing more emphasis on the cause of the learning problem as being intrinsic to the affected person. Spelling is not listed as a manifestation of a specific disorder but is instead subsumed under written expression. This definition also does not include a list of conditions (i.e., perceptual handicaps, brain injury, etc.) since these conditions are themselves ill-defined and invite more controversy, confusion, and misinterpretation. Finally, there is no exclusion clause so as to clarify that learning disabilities can occur in conjunction with other handicapping conditions, as long as these conditions are not the direct or primary cause of the disability.

Another diagnostic system has been developed by the American Psychiatric Association and published most recently in the Diagnostic and Statistical Manual of Mental Disorders (DSM III; 1983). This system classifies childhood or adolescent disorders into the following five major groups and subgroups:

I. Intellectual
    Mental retardation
II. Behavioral Covert
    Attention deficit disorder
    Conduct disorder
III. Emotional
    Anxiety disorders of childhood or adolescence
    Other disorders of infancy, childhood, or adolescence
IV. Physical
    Eating disorders
    Stereotyped movement disorders
    Other disorders with physical manifestations
V. Developmental
    Pervasive developmental disorders
    Specific developmental disorders

Each of these major groups and subgroups is defined and the diagnostic criteria for each subgroup are given. The following is a brief summary of the definition of each of these subgroups.

The essential features of mental retardation are (1) significantly subaverage general intellectual functioning, (2) resulting in, or associated with, deficits or impairments in adaptive behavior, with (3) onset before the age of 18. This diagnosis is made regardless of whether or not there is a coexisting mental or physical disorder. Mental retardation is further differentiated into the following subtypes:

| Subtype | IQ level | Corresponding educational category |
| --- | --- | --- |
| Mild | 50–70 | Educable |
| Moderate | 35–49 | Trainable |
| Severe | 20–34 | |
| Profound | Below 20 | |

The essential features of attention deficit disorder are signs of developmentally inappropriate inattention and impulsivity. There are two subtypes of the disorder: attention deficit disorder with hyperactivity and attention deficit disorder without hyperactivity. There is also a residual subtype for individuals once diagnosed as having attention deficit disorder with hyperactivity in which hyperactivity is no longer present, but other signs of the disorder persist. Onset is typically by the age of 3, although it may not come to a professional's attention until the child enters school. Academic difficulties are common and social functioning may also be impaired.

The essential feature of a conduct disorder is a repetitive and persistent pattern of conduct in which either the basic rights of others or major age-appropriate societal norms or rules are violated. There are four subtypes based on the presence or absence of adequate social bonds and the presence or absence of a pattern of aggressive antisocial behavior. These subtypes are undersocialized, aggressive; undersocialized, nonaggressive; socialized, aggressive; and socialized, nonaggressive. Frequent features of all four subtypes include difficulties at home and in the community; precocious sexual activity; low self-esteem; blaming others for difficulties; unusually early smoking, drinking, etc.; poor frustration tolerance, irritability, and temper outbursts; below age and intelligence in academic achievement; and attentional difficulties.

The anxiety disorders of childhood or adolescence include three different disorders in which anxiety is the predominant clinical feature. In the first two categories, separation anxiety disorder and avoidant disorder of childhood or adolescence, the anxiety is focused on specific situations. In the third category, overanxious disorder, the anxiety is generalized to a variety of situations.

There are five categories of other disorders of infancy, childhood, or adolescence defined in DSM III. The essential features of the reactive attachment disorder of infancy are poor emotional and physical development, with onset before 8 months of age, because of a lack of adequate caretaking. The disturbance is not due to a physical disorder, mental retardation, or infantile autism. The essential feature of the schizoid disorder of childhood or adolescence is a defect in the capacity to form social relationships that is not due to any other mental disorder. The essential feature of elective mutism is continuous refusal to speak in almost all social situations, including at school, despite ability to comprehend spoken language and to speak. The essential feature of an oppositional disorder is a pattern of disobedient, negativistic, and provocative opposition to authority figures. The oppositional attitude is toward family members, particularly the parents, and toward teachers. This oppositional attitude is persistent even when it is destructive to the interests and well-being of the child or adolescent. The essential feature of an identity disorder is severe subjective distress regarding inability to reconcile aspects of the self into a relatively coherent and acceptable sense of self. The symptoms last at least 3 months and result in impairment in social or academic functioning.

The rating disorders subclass is characterized by gross disturbances in eating behavior. It includes anorexia nervosa, bulimia, pica, pumination, disorder of infancy, and atypical eating disorder.

The essential feature of stereotyped movement disorders is an abnormality of gross motor movement. The disorders all involve tics and include transient tic disorder, chronic motor tic disorder, and tourette's disorder. A tic is defined as an involuntary rapid movement of a functionally related group of skeletal muscles or the involuntary production of noises or words.

Other disorders with physical manifestations include stuttering (speech), functional enuresis and functional encopresis, sleepwalking disorder, and sleep terror disorder. These categories were included because formerly, psychological conflict was thought to play a central role in all of these disorders and it was thought that these conditions were almost always associated with other signs of psychopathology. This remains an issue of controversy.

Pervasive developmental disorders are characterized by distortions in the development of multiple basic psychological functions that are involved in the development of social skills and language, such as attention, perception, reality testing, and motor movement. Included in this subgroup is infantile autism (full syndrome present and residual state) and childhood onset pervasive develop-

mental disorder (full syndrome present and residual state).

The subclass of specific developmental disorders is for disorders of specific areas of development not owed to another disorder. It includes developmental reading disorder, developmental arithmetic disorder, developmental language disorder (expressive and receptive type), developmental articulation disorder, and mixed specific developmental disorder.

As these definitions indicate, DSM III places much more emphasis on emotional aspects of conditions than does PL 94-142. The DSM III is not primarily concerned with any educational implications that these conditions might have, which, as seen earlier, is the main emphasis of PL 94-142. Therefore, these two diagnostic systems are based on two different theoretical bases; this explains some of the basic differences in their diagnostic criteria. For example, PL 94-142's definition of emotional disturbance is very general and includes only those conditions directly related to the school situations as compared with the more detailed and comprehensive set of definitions given by DSM III.

The DSM III definition of mental retardation is also more detailed than that given by PL 94-142. It follows closely the definition presented by the American Association on Mental Deficiency (AAMD) in its *Manual on Terminology and Classification* (Grossman, 1983). That definition states:

> Mental retardation refers to significantly subaverage general intellectual functioning existing concurrently with deficits in adaptive behavior and manifested during the developmental period.

Significantly subaverage general intellectual functioning is defined as a score on a standardized intelligence test that is 70 or below.

The AAMD diagnostic and classification system of mental retardation was first developed in 1961. With each revision there has been added an increasing amount of emphasis on the role of adaptive behavior in the diagnosis of mental retardation. This emphasis has influenced almost all other diagnostic systems, including those in DSM III and PL 94-142. For example, all three definitions include aspects of intellectual functioning and adaptive behavior. However, PL 94-142 again emphasizes the effects of this condition on educational achievement, while DSM III and AAMD emphasize more of the psychological impact of this condition on adaptive behavior.

It is obvious that there is much diversity in the diagnosis of the mildly mentally retarded, learning disabled, and emotionally disturbed. According to Edgar and Hayden (1985), these handicapping conditions belong to a large percent of the total handicapped population and are the ones that are most difficult to quantify. These categories are basically indistinguishable from one another, and the population of children within these categories is indistinguishable from the larger group of children with general learning problems (e.g., disadvantaged, slow learner, etc.).

Each of these nonquantifiable categories has a history of problems in terms of the criteria used in their identification. For example, mild retardation is defined based on an IQ; there has been continual criticism of the use of IQ tests with minority population (Edgar & Hayden, 1985). The high percentage of minority students diagnosed as mentally retarded has brought charges from some that the traditional IQ tests cannot be reliably used to diagnose mental retardation. It has also been virtually impossible to define the distinction between seriously emotionally disturbed and socially maladjusted. There are no quantitative measures available for determining who is seriously emotionally disturbed. Emotional disturbance tends to be a socially defined condition, as does mild mental retardation and learning disabilities. Many of the problems associated with the diagnosis of learning disabilities have already been discussed. Edgar and Hayden (1985) feel that the only quantifiable aspect of the learning disabled definition is low achievement, which could classify 20 to 30% of all school-age children. Reynolds (1984) concludes that a large segment of children being served as learning disabled may not, in fact, be learning disabled. These are usually the intellectually borderline and low average children. According to Reynolds (1984), this is due, in part, to the diversity of models of severe discrepancy as well as to biases in the referral process favoring low IQ, low-achieving children. Reynolds (1984) suggests that a regression model of severe discrepancy be adopted to answer the question of whether there is a severe discrepancy between the achievement level of the student in question and the achievement level of all other children with the same IQ.

Diagnosis in special education has attempted to follow the traditional model of psychological diagnosis. However, this model has not proven to be an effective one for special education. One of the main criticisms of this diagnostic system has been its inability to provide reliable and valid classifications of the conditions involved in special education diagnosis. Conditions such as mental retardation, emotional disturbance, and learning disabilities have not been quantifiably defined and are therefore difficult to classify. Despite these serious flaws, the concept of formal diagnosis is still considered to be of vital importance. Therefore, alternatives to the medical model are being proposed. For example, Reynolds et al. (1984) advocates a reciprocal deterministic model that goes beyond the diagnosis of the internal characteristics of an individual to include the diagnosis of that individual's behavior and environment and the interaction of those three factors. This may or may not be the direction of the future of diagnosis in special education. It does seem clear that the unsatisfactory status of the current diagnostic systems would indicate that some change in direction is needed so that diagnosis in special education can become more valid and reliable.

## REFERENCES

American Psychiatric Association. (1980). *Diagnostic and statistical manual of mental disorders* (3rd ed.). Washington, DC: Author.

Edgar, E., & Hayden, A. H. (1985). Who are the children special education should serve? And how many children are there? *Journal of Special Education, 18,* 523–539.

Grossman, H. J. (Ed.). (1983). *Classification in mental retardation.* Washington, DC: American Association on Mental Deficiencies.

Hammill, D. D., Larsen, S. C., Leigh, J., & McNult, G. (1981). A new definition of learning disabilities. *Learning Disabilities Quarterly, 4,* 336–342.

Matarazzo, J. D., & Pankratz, L. D. (1984). Diagnosis. In R. J. Corsini (Ed.), *Encyclopedia of psychology* (pp. 369–372). New York: Wiley.

Mercer, C. D., Hughes, C., & Mercer, A. R. (1985). Learning disabilities definitions used by state education departments. *Learning Disabilities Quarterly, 8,* 45–55.

Reynolds, C. R. (1984). Critical measurement issues in learning disabilities. *Journal of Special Education, 18,* 451–475.

Reynolds, C. R., Gutkin, T. B., Elliot, S. N., & Witt, J. C. (1984). *School psychology: Essentials of theory and practice.* New York: Wiley.

Ysseldyke, J. E., & Algozzine, B. (1982). *Critical issues in special and remedial education.* Boston: Houghton Mifflin.

Lori E. Unruh
*Eastern Kentucky University*

AAMD
DIAGNOSTIC & STATISTICAL MANUAL
MENTAL STATUS
SEVERE DISCREPANCY ANALYSIS

# DIAGNOSTIC AND STATISTICAL MANUAL OF MENTAL DISORDERS (DSM III)

The most widely used system for psychiatric diagnosis and classification in the United States is the third edition of the *Diagnostic and Statistical Manual of Mental Disorders* (DSM-III; American Psychiatric Association, 1980). *The Diagnostic and Statistical Manual of Mental Disorders* was initially published in 1952 (DSM-I), with the first revision appearing in 1968 (DSM-II). All revisions of DSM were developed for use with children, adolescents, and adults.

There are a number of features of DSM-III that represent improvements over its predecessors. In DSM-III, an attempt was made to provide clear criteria for reaching a diagnosis. Specific descriptions of each disorder are listed, including core symptoms, a subset of additional symptoms, duration of the problems, age of onset, course, predisposing factors, and requirements for a differential diagnosis. Earlier versions had resulted in considerable unreliability in making a diagnosis by relying too heavily on clinical judgments in matching patients to a general description of the disorder.

A second feature of DSM-III is that it was designed to be primarily atheoretical so that it would appeal to a broad group of clinicians. There is a greater emphasis on presenting symptoms rather than etiology. This is in contrast to the first and second editions, which emphasized a psychoanalytic orientation to the etiology of many of the disorders that were listed.

A major change in DSM-III is its use of a multiaxial classification system. In contrast to DSM-II, which used only a single diagnostic dimension involving the primary psychiatric disorder displayed by the individual, DSM-III provides five independent axes or dimensions designed to give a more comprehensive evaluation of the individual. Axis I classifies the person in terms of the major psychiatric syndrome displayed. In Axis II it is determined whether there is any accompanying personality disorder in the case of adults or a developmental disorder in the case of children. The presence of a physical condition that might be of importance in the diagnosis and/or management of the psychiatric disorder is noted in Axis III. In Axis IV, the individual is classified with respect to the degree of psychosocial stress experienced during the previous year. Finally, Axis V rates the highest level of adaptive functioning displayed by the individual. In summary, the first three axes represent the primary diagnostic evaluation. Axes IV and V are included to provide additional information for use in treatment planning and predicting outcome.

While DSM-III is considered to be a marked improvement over the previous editions, a number of criticisms and limitations have been noted about this document (e.g., Garmezy, 1978; Schacht & Nathan, 1977). One concern has been the reliability of establishing a diagnosis with DSM-III. Data from initial field tests would suggest that the multiaxial diagnostic system has enhanced the reliability of clinical judgments with adults (Spitzer, Endicott, & Robins, 1978). However, research on the diagnosis of childhood disorders has been less encouraging (Cantwell, Russell, Mattison, & Will, 1979).

The validity of the DSM-III categories has also been questioned. There are approximately 85 new disorders listed in DSM-III compared with DSM-II. These new disorders are clinically derived and are not based on empirically defined patterns of dysfunctional behavior. While some of these categories have "face validity," it remains to be shown that these syndromes are actually displayed in clinical populations.

There is another criticism about DSM-III that is particularly relevant to children: it includes areas not typically regarded as mental disorders such as developmental disorders and learning disabilities. Concerns have been expressed that children diagnosed with specific developmental or learning problems will be diagnosed and stigmatized as having a mental disorder (Rutter & Shaffer, 1980).

## REFERENCES

American Psychiatric Association. (1980). *Diagnostic and statistical manual of mental disorders* (3rd ed.). Washington, DC: Author.

Cantwell, D. P., Russell, T., Mattison, R., & Will, L. (1979). A comparison of DSM-II and DSM-III in the diagnosis of childhood psychiatric disorders. I. Agreement with expected diagnosis. *Archives of General Psychiatry, 36,* 1208–1213.

Garmezy, N. (1978). DSM-III. Never mind the psychologists: Is it good for the children? *Clinical Psychologist, 31,* 3–6.

Rutter, M. & Shaffer, D. (1980). DSM-III. A step forward or back in terms of the classification of child psychiatric disorders? *Journal of the American Academy of Child Psychiatry, 19,* 371–394.

Schacht, T., & Nathan, P. E. (1977). But is it good for the psychologist? Appraisal and status of DSM-III. *American Psychologist, 32,* 1017–1025.

Spitzer, R. L., Endicott, J., & Robins, E. (1978). Research diagnostic criteria: Rationale and reliability. *Archives of General Psychiatry, 35,* 773–782.

LAWRENCE J. SIEGEL
*University of Texas Medical
Branch, Galveston*

**CLINICAL PSYCHOLOGY**
**MENTAL ILLNESS**
**MENTAL STATUS EXAMS**

# DIAGNOSTIC PRESCRIPTIVE TEACHING

Diagnostic prescriptive teaching "refers to the practice of formulating instructional prescriptions on the basis of differential diagnostic results" (Arter & Jenkins, 1979, p. 518). Although any educational plan for an individual learner should spring from assessment, diagnostic prescriptive teaching has had a more specific meaning. The key idea underlying diagnostic prescriptive teaching is that a given diagnostic pattern is linked differentially to a specific instructional strategy (methods, materials, techniques, etc.). That a given set of assessment findings implies an accompanying set of instructional strategies is assumed.

In the early 1970s, when ability training began to receive criticism from within the field of learning diabilities (Hammill, 1972; Hammill, Goodman, & Wiederholt, 1974), Ysseldyke and Salvia (1974) suggested that diagnostic prescriptive teaching should be based on one of two theoretical models. The first model is the ability training model. From this perspective, the diagnosed strengths and weaknesses are conceptualized primarily as perceptual or psycholinguistic in nature and understood to be the basis for academic skills. Training programs are then differentially prescribed to improve the underlying abilities demonstrating weaknesses. For example, if a student is diagnosed as expressing figure-ground errors, the prescribed educational plan would include remedial figure-ground activities, without any "advice" from the diagnostic pattern to suggest how teaching the ability will or should relate to the level of academic skill. The second model is the task analysis model. From this perspective, the diagnosis or assessment targets are the specific academic skills for the purpose of identifying the skills within the learner's repertoire. The goal of instruction is then the attainment of those new or missing skills. For example, if assessment identifies a student knows only 75% of the addition facts through 10, the prescription is that the student should be taught the remaining 25% without any "advice" from the assessment results of how those skills should be taught.

Since the early 1970s, diagnostic prescriptive teaching has taken on a meaning broader than the two theoretical models. Smead and Schwartz (1982) have developed a model that is integrative in nature. Moving beyond the ability training model with its focus nearly completely on perceptual or psycholinguistic processes. They have identified three learner-focused areas from which diagnostic information has relevance for instruction: motivational-emotional, cognitive-perceptual, and neurological-physical. In a similar manner, they have focused on a greater variety of dimensions than did those previously concerned solely with the application of task analysis to special education. In addition, they have suggested that a third set of factors must be considered: the environmental characteristics of the learning situation, which include sociological, emotional, pedagological, contingency, standing patterns of behavior, and physical factors. Finally, they have suggested that the interactions among these three sets of factors—learner focused, task focused, and environmental focused—must also be diagnosed and related to the instructional prescription.

Thus, diagnostic prescriptive teaching has become better understood with the realization that a series of diagnostic patterns with related prescribed activities is simplistic given the complexity and variety of learners, tasks, and environments—and how they interact. Prescribed instructional goals must flow from assessment, addressing the learner and his/her style of learning, the skills or abilities that must be learned, and the situation and contingencies under which learning will be best facilitated.

## REFERENCES

Arter, J. A., & Jenkins, J. R. (1979). Differential diagnosis-prescriptive teaching: A critical appraisal. *Review of Educational Research, 49,* 517–555.

Hammill, D. (1972). Training visual perceptual processes. *Journal of Learning Disabilities, 5,* 39–44.

Hammill, D., Goodman, L., & Wiederholt, J. L. (1974). Visual-motor processes: Can we train them? *Exceptional Children, 41,* 5–14

Smead, V. S., & Schwartz, N. H. (1982, Aug.). *An integrative model for instructional planning.* Paper presented at the 19th Annual Meeting of the American Psychological Association, Washington, DC.

Ysseldyke, J. E., & Salvia, J. (1974). Diagnostic-prescriptive teaching: Two models. *Exceptional Children, 41,* 17–32.

STEVEN R. TIMMERMANS
*Mary Free Bed Hospital
and Rehabilitation Center,
Grand Rapids, Michigan*

**DIAGNOSTIC REMEDIAL APPROACH**
**DIAGNOSTIC TEACHING**
**DIRECT INSTRUCTION**

# DIAGNOSTIC READING

See DIAGNOSTIC READING SCALE.

# DIAGNOSTIC READING SCALES: REVISED EDITION

The Diagnostic Reading Scales are an integrated series of tests designed to provide a standardized evaluation of students' silent and oral reading levels and auditory comprehension. Additionally, it can be used to determine instructional and independent reading level and an estimate of reading potential. The scales have a range of use from the elementary levels for normal and up through senior high school for poor readers.

The test is designed to be administered individually. The test package consists of an examiner's manual, which describes administration, scoring, and interpretation procedures; the test book, which is composed of three word recognition lists, reading passages, and supplementary phonics tests; and an examiner's record booklet, which duplicates the test book and contains the information the examiner uses to score student responses.

The battery measures the nature and extent of word attack skills and sight vocabulary, and provides an estimate of the student's instructional level (which is different from an Informal Reading Inventory (IRI) estimate). Scoring the test is simple, but the interpretation should be done by someone with a strong background in the treatment and diagnosis of reading difficulties. The test can be given in one or two sittings. Total administration and scoring time is about 45 minutes.

## REFERENCES

Diagnostic reading scales (1978) (revised ed.). In O. K. Buros (Ed.), *The eighth mental measurements yearbook* (Vol. II, pp. 1240–1244). Highland Park, NJ: Gryphon Press.

*Examiner's manual: Diagnostic reading scales* (1981). Montery, CA: CTB/McGraw-Hill.

RONALD V. SCHMELZER
*Eastern Kentucky University*

## DIAGNOSTIC REMEDIAL APPROACH

The diagnostic remedial approach is the foundation of special education. Children are included or excluded from special education on a basis of the relationship between their present levels of functioning and the eligibility criteria established by state and local standards. Children who meet eligibility criteria are entitled to a free and appropriate public education. The formulation of an appropriate education plan based on data and information developed during the diagnosis should provide a direct and identifiable linkage between learner characteristics and program implementation (McDaniels, 1979).

Historically, there has been considerable debate among special educators as to the validity of the diagnostic remedial approach. This can be attributed to two factors. First, there are numerous views as to what constitutes a satisfactory diagnosis and just as many divergent views as to what constitutes a valid remedial approach. One seldom knows whether the diagnostic approach was developed before, after, or concurrent with the development of the remedial approach.

Second, there have been few combinations that have truly validated the diagnostic remedial relationship. What tends to be more common is that one selects a set of tests, administers them, and then makes decisions as to what would be a valid remedial approach. The selection of both the test battery and the remedial approach are more likely to be a function of user knowledge and training than the validity of the tests or the treatments.

There have been approaches where individuals or teams developed both the instruments to conduct the diagnosis and the methods and materials to implement the treatment. These have often included techniques designed to train selected abilities. Special educators have commonly referred to this perspective as the process approach. Considerable controversy has surrounded this particular perspective, even to the point that critics and supporters disagree on the use and interpretations of the available data (Kavale, 1981; Larsen, Parker, & Hammill, 1982).

Another approach is characterized by direct curriculum-based assessments of the child, the establishment of a performance baseline, and direct intervention for the problem. This approach tends to focus directly on the problem identified by the teacher. The remedial alternatives are designed to move the youngster from a lower level of performance to a higher level.

It is ironic that the process approach, which was designed to relate diagnosis to remediation, is the approach that has been subjected to the greatest amount of investigation and the greatest amount of criticism and skepticism. Is this because there is only limited potential in the diagnostic remedial approach or is it because the developers failed to establish the proper combinations of diagnostic and remedial approaches? Is it possible that both the diagnostic and remedial approaches are too global and fail to provide information about the children such that remedial approaches can be properly selected (McKinney & Feagans, 1984)?

To date, for some unexplained reason, special education continues to receive large numbers of referrals and seems to have about the same number of children for whom diagnostic remedial approaches are recommended. The diagnostic remedial models do not seem to have increased the ability of the field to prevent difficulties; nor have they provided evidence of any generalizable approach to the amelioration of the difficulties children manifest.

Diagnosis is a process that begins with the general and proceeds to the specific. Each step in the process should lead to a more careful delineation of learner characteristics. Unfortunately, this is not the dominant model of special education. Special education directs much more of its resources to the determination of eligibility criteria than it does to the detailed acquisition of individual learner characteristics. Should this emphasis continue, it is doubtful that meaningful diagnostic remedial approaches can ever be developed.

The diagnostic process is predicated on the availability of valid and reliable instruments. Test developers accentuate statistical qualities and place great emphasis on reliability. What is seemingly lacking is a stress on test interpretation that is as reliable as the test itself. If five different people are provided with valid and reliable information and all five interpret this information differently, there can be no consistency in the diagnostic remedial approach. To assist users, test developers often make generalized remedial recommendations. Many of these lack validity and some tend to misguide the user.

Diagnosis needs to include at least three components. One component ought to include the determination of cognitive characteristics, including intelligent behavior, information processing, and cognitive maturity. A second component ought to include the assessment of skill and meanings specific to the referral (e.g., language) in areas related to the primary referral factor. A third component should seek out information relative to personal-social status and the interrelationships of these to ecological considerations.

The diagnostician needs to be aware of the hierarchy of instruments and techniques that will allow for different levels of analyses of each child. Such a case would exist if a group or individualized standardized reading test was administered, the results interpreted, and a more specific decoding or comprehension inquiry conducted. Should the individual evidence more complex problems, measures of learning and responses to instruction could be integrated into the diagnostic process. The more elaborate and comprehensive the diagnosis, the more difficulty there will be in reaching agreement as to its treatment implications.

The term remediation is generally defined to mean modification of an inappropriate behavior to an appropriate one or assistance to a child to close a gap or "catch up." An example of the former might exist when a child inappropriately subtracts from left to right and an instructor shows him or her a correct left-to-right procedure. Another example might exist when a child inappropriately subtracts from left to right and an instructor informs him or her that the only correct procedure is to subtract from right to left. Note that two different approaches were undertaken to correct the same behavior. An example of the latter would be supplemental assistance such as found in Chapter 1 programs or in long-term assignments to a resource center. Here the child is often assisted to meet the requirements of the regular class. Efforts are directed toward the regular curriculum and instructional practices are extremely similar to those in the regular class (e.g., the extended use of worksheets).

A major difficulty with the selection and implementation of the various remedial approaches is an inability to specify which youngsters are best suited to which programs and to predict the amount of progress each child should be expected to make. Further, specialists are often at a loss to explain why one child makes progress while other does not.

Remedial approaches in special education fall into three classes. One is a process-oriented approach, often referred to as an indirect approach, in which certain traits (e.g., psycholinguistic abilities) are remediated in the hope that performance on related traits (e.g., reading) will be improved. A second approach, traditionally referred to as the direct approach, focuses directly on a target behavior (e.g., vocabulary building) and every effort is made to improve performance on that specific behavior. A third approach stresses the development of self-monitoring and self-enhancing capabilities, some of which are called metacognitive training (Cherkes-Julkowski, 1985), strategy training (Hallahan & Sapona, 1983), and learning to learn. All approaches need further study. The ultimate validation of the diagnostic remedial relationship will represent a contribution to special education that is second to none.

## REFERENCES

Cherkes-Julkowski, M. (1985). Metacognitive considerations in mathematics instruction for the learning disabled. In J. Cawley (Ed.), *Cognitive strategies and mathematics for the learning disabled* (pp. 117–138). Rockville, MD: Aspen Systems.

Hallahan, D., & Sapona, R. (1983). Self-monitoring of attention with learning disabled children: Past research and current issues. *Journal of Learning Disabilities, 16*, 616–620.

Kavale, K. (1981). Functions of the Illinois Test of Psycholinguistic Abilities (ITPA): Are they trainable? *Exceptional Children, 47*, 496–510.

Larsen, S. C., Parker, R. M., & Hammill, D. D. (1982). Effectiveness of psycholinguistic training: A response to Kavale. *Exceptional Children, 49*, 60–67.

McDaniels, G. (1979). DAS information bulletin #50. Washington, DC: Bureau of Education for the Handicapped.

McKinney, J. D., & Feagans, L. (1984). *Classification and intervention with learning disability subtypes*. Unpublished document. Chapel Hill, NC: Frank Porter Graham Child Development Center.

JOHN F. CAWLEY
JAMES H. MILLER
*University of New Orleans*

DIAGNOSIS
DIAGNOSTIC PRESCRIPTIVE TEACHING
DIRECT INSTRUCTION
REMEDIAL EDUCATION

# DIAGNOSTIC TEACHING

Diagnostic teaching is the name given an instructional process used to discover the instructional and environmental conditions under which student learning is most productive. Diagnostic teaching is also referred to as clinical teaching and data-based instructional decision making.

Diagnostic teaching differs from a diagnostic-prescriptive model of instruction. In a diagnostic-prescriptive approach, a student's achievement and learning characteristics are assessed. Subsequently, recommendations for instructional delivery are drawn from this information. This model relies on inference from a static data base (e.g., test information) for prediction of optimal instructional arrangements. In common use, such a model often fails to make use of information gained during the instructional process.

Diagnostic teaching, although sometimes included as a step in a diagnostic-prescriptive model of instruction (Reynolds & Birch, 1977), is more commonly viewed as an alternative assessment system. Like a diagnostic-prescriptive approach, diagnostic teaching makes use of test information about a student's achievement and learning characteristics, but it differs from a diagnostic-prescriptive model in a number of significant ways.

Diagnostic teaching is a process of systematic discovery rather than prediction. Reisman (1982), in discussing application of diagnostic teaching to mathematics, describes a process with five steps: (1) identify strengths and weaknesses in mathematics; (2) hypothesize reasons for achievement and nonachievement; (3) formulate instructional objectives; (4) teach to the objectives; and (5) evaluate student learning.

Zigmond, Vallecorsa, and Silverman (1983) propose a model of diagnostic teaching that is similar to that of Reisman but that is more detailed; it contains 12 discrete steps. Other and different models of diagnostic teaching are available. Differences tend to be in the thoroughness of description. Most have a set of common characteristics.

Diagnostic teaching is a cyclical process that is continued throughout the duration of student instruction. It is used to find the most effective match of learner characteristics and instructionally relevant variables. However, there is a recognition that because the difficulty of material and the demands of schooling change over time, the most appropriate combinations of instructional variables will change over time as well.

Since diagnostic teaching is an ongoing process, the diagnostician is most properly a skilled teacher rather than a diagnostic specialist who does not have continual contact with the student. The child's teacher is also in the best position to judge whether student performance or a particular instructional interchange is typical and of significance or merely an exception to the norm. The teacher's ability to note student habits and learning strategies, likes and dislikes, reactions to grouping arrangements, etc., provides the basis on which trial modifications in instruction can be made.

Diagnostic teaching requires the diagnostician to be familiar with a variety of different curricular approaches. For any given approach, the diagnostician must be able to determine where the student might encounter difficulty. This allows the teacher to provide instruction at an appropriate level of difficulty using curricula that require different student behaviors, capacities, and experiences. Howell & Kaplan (1980) demonstrate how basic skills can be analyzed for use in diagnostic teaching.

Diagnostic teaching also requires the diagnostician to be familiar with instructional variables that can be used differently in conjunction with various curricular approaches. Among these are engaged time, the immediacy and nature of performance feedback, grouping practices, and presentation and questioning techniques. For example, one exploratory combination within the diagnostic teaching process might be an increase in the engaged time a student spends being directly taught (instructional variables) phonics (curricular approach). If student learning did not meet expectations, one or more of the critical variables would be systematically altered.

Historically, the effects of different instructional combinations have been judged subjectively by the diagnostic teacher. The decision whether to continue instruction or to test another combination of variables was equally subjective. During the past decade, there has been a growing sophistication in the use of student performance data to judge instructional effect more effectively. There also has also been an increase in the sophistication of decision rules that can be used to guide the course of diagnostic teaching.

Procedures for the collection of student performance data are integral to most models of diagnostic teaching. These range from the use of special recording paper and elaborate techniques for performance analysis (White & Haring, 1980) to the use of checklists and behavioral tallies (Zigmond, Vallecorsa, & Silverman, 1983). Decision rules are usually presented within the context of a particular model but generally indicate what to do if student performance is deficient and how long instruction should continue before some systematic modification in instruction is made.

### REFERENCES

Howell, K. W., & Kaplan, J. S. (1980). *Diagnosing basic skills*. Columbus, OH: Merrill.

Reisman, F. K. (1982). *A guide to the diagnostic teaching of arithmetic*. Columbus, OH: Merrill.

Reynolds, M. C., & Birch, J. W. (1977). *Teaching exceptional children in all America's schools*. Reston, VA: Council for Exceptional Children.

White, O. R., & Haring, N. G. (1980). *Exceptional teaching*. Columbus, OH: Merrill.

Zigmond, N., Vallecorsa, A., & Silverman, R. (1983). *Assessment for instructional planning in special education*. Englewood Cliffs, NJ: Prentice-Hall.

STEVEN A. CARLSON
*Beaverton Schools, Beaverton, Oregon*

**DIAGNOSTIC PRESCRIPTIVE TEACHING
DIRECT INSTRUCTION
TEACHER EFFECTIVENESS**

# DIALYSIS AND SPECIAL EDUCATION

Dialysis, the process of flushing kidney wastes by artificial means in cases of acute or chronic renal failure, has been increasingly used with children during the last 25 years. Dialysis methodology is viewed as a drastic mode of treatment for children, necessitated in advanced cases of kidney disease prior to, or as the result of, failed transplantation (Czaczkes & De-Nour, 1979).

While individual differences make generalization difficult, Whitt (1984) indicates that the complex and time-

consuming dialysis schedule places most children at educational and emotional risk, as the time spent in hemodialysis treatment interrupts the normal pace and
progress of the child's schooling. Hobbs and Perrin (1985)
found the result of this loss of school time and educational
opportunity to be academic underachievement and missed
and splintered basic skills. In addition, the disruption of
normal school progress and success weakens children's
emotional stability and their feelings of competence and
control (Stapleton, 1983).

During periods of school attendance, the primary role
of special education is to maintain the independence of the
child in dialysis. This is best accomplished by providing
resource assistance to allow that child to function effectively within the regular classroom whenever possible
while remediating educational weaknesses and gaps
(Kleinberg, 1982). As the school experience for the dialysis
child represents one of the few opportunities for that child
to be in control of the environment, to gain competence
and skill, and to prepare for the future in a normalized
setting, special education must be used to modify programs, instruction, and the learning environment to ensure optimal educational progress (Van Osdol, 1982).

Special education services are also required for those
periods of time (each week) during which a child is
undergoing hemodialysis. Children in such treatment report concerns with the boredom imposed by the length of
the sessions and the anxiety associated with the process
and its discomforts (Amonette, 1984). Special education
must provide instructional materials and programs for
children to be used during treatment to relieve anxiety
and boredom and effective home and hospital instructors
to apply them. Recent technological advances in microcomputer and telecommunication strategies hold promise
for upgrading the educational experience for the dialysis
student during nonattendance periods.

## REFERENCES

Amonette, L. (1984). *Kidney dialysis patients discover new hope through ABE Program.* Paper presented at the National Adult Education Conference, Louisville, KY.

Czaczkes, J. W., & De-Nour, A. K. (1979). *Chronic hemodialysis as a way of life.* New York: Brunner/Mazel.

Hobbs, N., & Perrin, J. M. (Eds.). (1985). *Issues in the care of children with chronic illness.* San Francisco: Jossey-Bass.

Kleinberg, S. (1982). *Educating the chronically ill child.* Balti-more, MD: Aspen Systems.

Stapleton, S. (1983). Recognizing powerlessness: Causes and in-dicators in patients with chronic renal failure. In J. F. Miller (Ed.), *Coping with chronic illness: Overcoming powerlessness.* Philadelphia: Davis.

Van Osdol, W. R. (1982). *Introduction to exceptional children* (3rd ed.). Dubuque, IA: Brown.

Whitt, J. K. (1984). End stage renal disease. In M. G. Eisenberg, L. C. Sutkin, & M. A. Jansen (Eds.), *Chronic illness and dis-

*ability through the life span: Effects on self and family.* New York: Springer.

RONALD S. LENKOWSKY
*Hunter College, City University of New York*

**ADAPTIVE PHYSICAL EDUCATION
PHYSICAL DISABILITIES**

# DIANA v. STATE BOARD OF EDUCATION

*Diana* (1970) and *Guadalupe* v. *Tempe Elementary School District* (1972) were highly similar cases that were never actually brought to trial but that have nevertheless had a significant impact on special education assessment and placement procedures. In each case, civil rights organi-zations filed suit in federal courts on behalf of all bilingual students attending classes for the mildly mentally re-tarded (or the respective state's cognate designation). Both cases noted disproportionate representation of bilingual, Spanish-surnamed children in programs for the mentally retarded. Additionally, the plaintiffs in each case argued that intelligence tests administered in English to Spanish-speaking children were the principal reason for the ov-errepresentation. Other charges were made raising con-cerns about the quality of programs for the mentally re-tarded in both cases and violations of the equal protection clause of the Fourteenth Amendent to the U.S. Consti-tution, including lack of due process considerations. As Reschly (1979) has noted, in both cases the school districts involved were engaged in unsound, unprofessional as-sessment procedures and had developed much of their spe-cial education processes around what most in the field would consider bad professional practice.

Each case was resolved on the basis of similar consent decrees, agreements entered into by each party and then certified by the court to avoid further litigation. Issues regarding the quality of direct service were virtually ig-nored in the decrees, which centered on assessment and placement procedures. In *Diana,* for example, the consent decree certified by the court required assessment of each child's primary language competence; if the primary lan-guage was found to be other than English, tests used in the assessment had to be nonverbal, translated, or ad-ministered using an interpreter. The decree also required that unfair portions of English language tests were to be deleted and more influence accorded to the results of non-verbal intelligence tests when placement decisions were being made.

*Guadalupe,* in the consent decree, mandated the same changes in testing practices as *Diana. Guadalupe* went on to add four additional statements:

1. IQ tests were not to be the exclusive or the primary basis for the diagnosis of mild mental retardation.
2. Adaptive behavior in other than school settings would be assessed.
3. Due process procedures were to be developed and instituted before individual assessment or any movement toward diagnosis and placement could occur.
4. Special education would be provided to each child in the most normal setting or environment possible.

Since *Diana* and *Guadalupe* were settled by consent decrees, no judicial opinion is available and there are no findings to be reviewed and discussed. Neither case set legal precedent. Both were strongly influential, however, in subsequent legislation passed at the state and federal levels. Wording from the two decrees is now commonplace in many state and federal regulations governing the education of the handicapped.

## REFERENCE

Reschly, D. J. (1979). Nonbiased assessment. In G. Phye & D. Reschly (Eds.), *School psychology: Perspectives and issues.* New York: Academic.

CECIL R. REYNOLDS
*Texas A&M University*

CONSENT DECREE
EDUCATION FOR ALL HANDICAPPED CHILDREN ACT OF 1975
EQUAL PROTECTION
LARRY P.
MARSHALL *v.* GEORGIA

## DIAZEPAM

Diazepam (Valium) is a minor tranquilizer with relatively few side effects compared with other psychotropic medications. It is prescribed primarily with adult populations for symptoms of anxiety. Although the use of diazepam continues to be widespread (i.e., 77 million prescriptions were filled in retail pharmacies in one year) (Yaffe & Danish, 1977), few studies regarding its therapeutic efficacy can be found in pediatric literature. Clinically, diazepam seems to be prescribed infrequently as a psychotropic, particularly as an antianxiety drug in children.

While diazepam is used only infrequently as a psychotropic agent in pediatric populations, it is often used as an adjunct in the treatment of seizure disorders. When administered intravenously in repeated dosages as deemed necessary, diazepam has been found to be effective in the initial management of uncontrolled, continuous seizures, or status epilepticus (Behrman, Vaughn, Victor, & Nelson, 1983). In general, diazepam is not used in the long-term management of seizure disorders because of the likelihood of the development of tolerance to the drug. Tolerance often develops very rapidly, sometimes as quickly as 3 to 14 days after initiation of therapy (Behrman et al., 1983). Increasing the dosage when the tolerance develops may help control the seizures, but, frequently, side effects such as drowsiness, ataxia, and slurred speech make the increased dosage intolerable. Occasionally, diazepam may be indicated therapeutically in the treatment of petit mal seizures, refractory to Zarontin and other agents, and in combination with phenobarbital and phenytoin in the treatment of seizures associated with central nervous system disease (Behrman et al., 1983).

Diazepam has been used to some extent in the treatment of sleep disturbances in children. It should be noted that insomnia and night waking, although common in childhood, are typically transitory. The practitioner must carefully rule out other dysfunctions such as phobic and separation disorders, as well as psychosocial stressors that may result in sleep disturbances. Further, psychostimulant medications used during the day for the treatment of hyperactivity may also cause sleep disturbances (Brown & Borden, in press). However, if the etiology of the sleep disturbance is an identifiable stressor that cannot be alleviated, the short-term use of diazepam at low dosages, administered in a single dose at bedtime, may be a temporary treatment for both the child and the parent (Shaffer & Ambrosini, 1985). Diazepam may also be particularly effective for those sleep disturbances termed parasomnias, they include nightmares, sleep terrors, and sleepwalking. Since these disorders typically dissipate with age, the need for continued medication must be reassessed frequently.

The side effects attributed to diazepam are often further elaborations of the desired therapeutic effects. Those of primary concern include disinhibition, incoordination, drowsiness, and depression (Jaffe & Magnuson, 1985; Rapoport, Mikkelsen, & Werry, 1978). Both physiological and psychological dependence may also develop as a function of prolonged usage (Rapoport et al., 1978). Following prolonged usage, diazepam should be discontinued slowly with decreasing dosages because seizures may occur in response to abrupt withdrawal.

## REFERENCES

Behrman, R. E., Vaughn, V. C., Victor, B., & Nelson, W. E. (1983). Convulsive disorders. In R. Behrman & V. Vaughn (Eds.), *Nelson textbook of pediatrics* (pp. 1531–1545). Philadelphia: Saunders.

Brown, R. T., & Borden, K. A. (in press). Neuropsychological effects of stimulant medication on children's learning and behavior. In C. R. Reynolds (Ed.), *Child neuropsychology: Techniques of diagnosis and treatment.* New York: Plenum.

Jaffe, S., & Magnuson, J. V. (1985). Anxiety disorders. In J. Wiener (Ed.), *Diagnosis and psychopharmacology of childhood and adolescent disorders* (pp. 199–214). New York: Wiley.

Rapoport, J. L., Mikkelsen, E. J., & Werry, J. S. (1978). Antimanic, antianxiety, hallucinogenic, and miscellaneous drugs. In J. Werry (Ed.), *Pediatric psychopharmacology* (pp. 316–355). New York: Brunner/Mazel.

Shaffer, D., & Ambrosini, P. J. (1985). Enuresis and sleep disorders. In J. Wiener (Ed.), *Diagnosis and psychopharmacology of childhood and adolescent disorders* (pp. 305–331). New York: Wiley.

Yaffe, S. J., & Danish, M. (1977). The classification and pharmacology of psychoactive drugs in childhood and adolescence. In J. Wiener (Ed.), *Psychopharmacology in childhood and adolescence* (pp. 41–57). New York: Basic Books.

RONALD T. BROWN
SANDRA B. SEXON
*Emory University School
of Medicine*

ANTICONVULSANTS
PHENOBARBITAL
TRANQUILIZERS
ZARONTIN

## DICHOTIC LISTENING

Dichotic listening involves the simultaneous presentation of similar stimuli to both ears. An advantage of one ear over another is assumed by faster or more correct recall for a given ear. This technique has been used to draw conclusions concerning an individual subject's auditory asymmetry and cerebral lateralization for a given stimuli. Originally devised by Broadbent (1954) to examine auditory attention and memory deficits, the dichotic listening paradigm was later adapted by Kimura (1961) to examine hemispheric lateralization of language.

The method involves the presentation of stimulus pairs (e.g., sentences, digits, words, consonant-vowel-consonant [CVC] syllables) with equal intensity to both ears. At the end of the sequence, the subject is instructed to select from a known set of alternatives or to recall what was heard. The subject is not typically required to report the ear to which the signal was presented.

Research using a dichotic listening task has typically focused on "ear advantages" or the number of correct responses for each ear. Most normal (nonbrain injured) individuals demonstrate a right ear advantage (REA) (left-hemisphere) for verbal material and a left ear advantage (LEA) for nonverbal material (Kimura, 1961). This effect is thought to reflect the functional specialization of the cerebral hemisphere opposite the favored ear. Neurologically, this favored access is due to greater numbers of

contralateral ear to hemisphere connections and a blocking of ipsilateral signals.

The dichotic listening paradigm has been demonstrated to have both clinical and research application. Clinical use of dichotic listening tasks attempt to differentiate disorders that involve the central auditory system (at the cerebral level) from those that are primarily peripheral (sensory organs). It is expected that achieved scores will be lower for input presented to the ear that is contralateral to a temporal lobe lesion than scores for input presented to the ear ipsilateral to the lesion. This difference in scores is referred to as the lesion or contralateral effect (Speaks, Niccum, & Van Tasell, 1985).

The majority of the research has examined functional lateralization in normal subjects. Dichotic listening is useful in such study because it is noninvasive and hence it allows the investigation of functioning in normal subjects. Attempts have also been made to associate reading disorders with reversed or incomplete cerebral lateralization based on performance on dichotic listening tasks. Findings, however, have been inconsistent, with some researchers suggesting incomplete cerebral dominance for poor readers (Zurif & Carson, 1970) and others indicating a REA for both normal and reading-disabled students (Sparrow & Satz, 1970; Hynd, Obrzut, Weed, & Hynd, 1979). These differences may be attributed to the methodological and conceptual difficulties that have plagued research in this area (Satz, 1976). Clearly, caution must be observed when inferring cerebral lateralization from dichotic listening tasks for children with reading disorders.

## REFERENCES

Broadbent, D. E. (1954). The role of auditory localization in attention and memory span. *Journal of Experimental Psychology, 47*, 191–196.

Hynd, G. W., Obrzut, J. W., Weed, W., & Hynd, C. R. (1979). Development of cerebral dominance: Dichotic listening asymmetry in normal and learning disabled children. *Journal of Experimental Child Psychology, 28*, 445–454.

Kimura, D. (1961). Cerebral dominance and the perception of verbal stimuli. *Canadian Journal of Psychology, 15*, 166–171.

Satz, P. (1976). Cerebral dominance and reading disability: An old problem revisited. In R. M. Knights & D. J. Bakker (Eds.), *The neuropsychology of learning disorders: theoretical approaches* (pp. 273–297). Baltimore, MD: University Park Press.

Sparrow, S., & Satz, P. (1970). Dyslexia, laterality and neuropsychological development. In D. J. Bakker and P. Satz (Eds.), *Specific reading disability: Advances in theory and method* (pp. 41–60). Rotterdam: Rotterdam University Press.

Speaks, C., Niccum, N., & Van Tasell, D. (1985). Effects of stimulus material on the dichotic listening performance of patients with sensorineural hearing loss. *Journal of Speech & Hearing Research, 28*, 16–25.

Zurif, E. F., & Carson, G. (1970). Dyslexia in relation to cerebral dominance and temporal analysis. *Neuropsychologia, 8*, 351–361.

ARLENE I. RATTAN
*Ball State University*

RAYMOND S. DEAN
*Ball State University*
*Indiana University School*
*of Medicine*

## CEREBRAL FUNCTION, LATERALIZATION OF DEVELOPMENTAL DYSLEXIA

## DICTIONARY OF OCCUPATIONAL TITLES

The *Dictionary of Occupational Titles* is prepared and published by the U.S. Department of Labor, Employment and Training Administration. It provides comprehensive occupational information to serve the labor market in job placement, employment counseling, and guidance. Concise standardized definitions (17,500) are alphabetized by title with coding arrangements for occupational classifications. Blocks of jobs are assigned to one of 550 occupational groups using a 5- or 6-digit code. Skilled, semi-skilled, or unskilled categories are specified. The format for each definition is occupational code number; occupational title; industry designation; alternate title (if any); body of the definitional lead statement; task element statement; undefined related title (if any).

Consumers may reproduce any part of this public document without special permission from the federal government. Source credit is requested but not required. The *Dictionary of Occupational Titles* has 1371 pages.

### REFERENCE

U.S. Department of Labor, Employment, and Training Administration. (1977). *Dictionary of occupational titles* (4th ed.). Washington, DC: Author.

C. MILDRED TASHMAN
*College of St. Rose*

## DIFFERENTIAL APTITUDE TESTS (DAT), FORMS V AND W

The differential aptitude tests (Forms V and W) are an integrated battery of eight aptitude tests that provide a basis for educational and vocational guidance in junior and senior high schools. They may also be used with adults. They are based on the premise that sound guidance requires a variety of information concerning an individual's strengths and interests. The battery provides nine scores: verbal reasoning (30 minutes, 50 items); numerical ability (30 minutes, 40 items); abstract reasoning (20 minutes, 45 items); clerical speed and accuracy (2,3-minute tests, 200 total items); mechanical reasoning (30 minutes, 70 items); space relations (25 minutes, 60 items); spelling (10 minutes, 90 items); and language usage (20 minutes, 50 items).

The spelling and language usage tests are achievement rather than aptitude tests. The battery may be administered in two long sessions or six shorter sessions. The tests are easy to administer and can be given by anyone familiar with standardized testing procedures. Scoring may be done either by hand or by machine. Percentiles and stanines are included for both males and females in grades 8 through 12. The DAT battery has proven useful over the years. This relatively new revision should be even more useful to school counselors, psychologists, and other specialized personnel. The test requires interpretation by personnel trained in vocational guidance.

### REFERENCE

Differential aptitude tests (1978). In O. K. Buros (Ed.), *The eighth mental measurements yearbook.* (Vol. II, pp. 654–665). Highland Park, NJ: Gryphon Press.

RONALD V. SCHMELZER
*Eastern Kentucky University*

## DILANTIN

Dilantin is an antiepileptic drug that can be useful in the treatment of seizure disorders. Generically, it is known as phenytoin. It was introduced in 1938 by Merritt and Putnam, who discovered its anticonvulsant activity in animals. It has proven remarkably effective in treating both partial seizures and generalized tonic-clonic seizure activity. Dilantin appears to work primarily in the motor cortex of the brain; it acts to inhibit the spread of seizure activity by preventing the extension of seizure activity from abnormally discharging neurons to surrounding cells. It is thought that Dilantin tends to stabilize the threshold of neurons against the hyperexcitability caused by excessive stimulation or environmental changes that can lead to seizures. Additionally, Dilantin appears to reduce brain stem center activity responsible for the tonic phase of tonic clonic (grand mal) seizures.

Some minor toxic symptoms such as gastric discomfort and nausea are frequent at the onset of Dilantin therapy. These tend to disappear rapidly. In children, a common effect of chronic use is gingival hyperplasia, which may cause bleeding gums. This condition generally can be prevented by good oral hygiene. Hirsutism occurs frequently, and may be aesthetically distressing, especially in girls. Toxic reactions to Dilantin include blurring of vision or ataxia. The onset of pruritus (severe itching), rash, or fever is an indication for immediate drug withdrawal, as liver damage or bone marrow suppression may occur, as may a syndrome resembling systemic lupus.

## REFERENCE

Goldensohn, E. S., Glaser, G. H., & Goldberg, M. A. (1984). Epilepsy. In L. P. Rowland (Ed.), *Merritt's textbook of neurology* (7th ed., pp. 629–650). Philadelphia: Lea & Febiger.

RICHARD A. BERG
*West Virginia University
Medical Center, Charleston
Division*

ANTICONVULSANTS
EPILEPSY

## DIPLEGIA

Diplegia is a topographic term used to describe a movement disorder predominantly affecting the lower extremities, with only mild involvement of the upper extremities. The term diplegia frequently is used as a description of a kind of cerebral palsy in which the arms are less involved than in a quadriplegia and more involved than in a paraplegia. The term quadriplegia indicates both arms and both legs are involved to a similar degree, and the term paraplegia denotes involvement of both legs only.

Clinical practice suggests the term diplegia is somewhat misleading, as the primary emphasis truly is on the movement disorder of the lower extremities; however, the upper extremities show so little involvement that a casual observer may not detect deficits that could impair function seriously. Often these deficits are sensory-motor-vestibular in nature and interfere with acquisition of fine motor skills such as dressing and handwriting.

The etiology of diplegia may be developmental delay, anoxia, trauma, jaundice, neonatal seizures, reflex suppression, or other factors that suggest the possibility of certain progressive biochemical disorders or spinocerebellar degenerative diseases. Differential diagnosis by a skilled pediatric neurologist, with ongoing follow-up by appropriate therapists, is essential to provide appropriate medical and educational intervention for children with diplegia.

## REFERENCE

Berkow, R. (Ed.). (1982). *The Merck manual of diagnosis and therapy.* (14th ed.). Rahway, NJ: Merck, Sharp & Dohme.

RACHAEL J. STEVENSON
*Bedford, Ohio*

CHOREA
DYSKINESIA
NEUROPSYCHOLOGY

## DIPLOPIA

The basis for understanding diplopia (double vision) requires an appreciation of the physiologic mechanisms of binocularity within the visual cortex (Records, 1979). Evidence suggests there are four classes of cortical neuronal receptive fields for common visual direction—monocular left eye, monocular right eye, binocular corresponding, and binocular disparate. Presumably, each neuron derives stimulation from a specific visual direction; the visual direction is unambiguous for all classes except binocular disparate, where it falls between the visual directions of the two monocular receptive fields for that neuron. Consider stimuli to two eyes, presented on corresponding retinal points and moved gradually away in disparity; in time, fusion breaks and diplopia is perceived. When stimuli are presented to corresponding points only, as with a point of light, binocular corresponding neurons and monocular right and left neurons are stimulated. All three types have the same visual direction label and there is no conflict, resulting in single vision. When a small disparity is introduced, some binocular disparate neurons are stimulated and binocular corresponding neurons should cease responding. However, the monocular right and left neurons each are stimulated for a visual direction slightly to either side of the mean visual direction for binocular disparate neurons. These are integrated with a third set of responses from the binocular disparate neuron; therefore there should be a range of small disparities for which binocular response gives a unitary perception of a fused stimulus. In essence, it is this disparity that permits stereopsis, a specialized form of depth perception.

Diplopia may be physiologic or pathologic (Von Noorden, 1985). Physiologic diplopia is normal and results from stimulation and appreciation of objects simultaneously with the area of disparities that may be fused within the cortex and those outside. Object points in visual space stimulating corresponding retinal elements may be constructed to form a plane known as horopter. Both in front of and behind this plane is Panum's fusional space, an area in space that can be integrated cortically without perceiving objects as double. Physiologic diplopia occurs outside this space, and may be appreciated by observing an object in the distance and holding a pencil near. While attending to the distant object, the pencil will be seen as double. Most of the time, physiologic diplopia is cortically suppressed and not appreciated. Its clinical significance is twofold. Occasionally, schoolchildren become aware of and concerned about physiologic diplopia; reassurance is warranted. Second, diplopia may be useful from a diagnostic and therapeutic perspective in the presence of strabismus.

Pathological diplopia may be characterized as either monocular or binocular. Monocular diplopia results from defects in the refractive media or retinal pathology. Examples are high astigmatic refractive error, cataract, ectopic lens position, or macular edema. If diplopia is binocular, image positions may be separated horizontally, vertically, or obliquely; may vary with different directions of gaze and head position; and may be constant or variable.

Extraocular muscle paresis in adults almost always yields diplopia. However, patients with strabismus from early life rarely perceive diplopia. A series of adaptive mechanisms in infancy and childhood avoid this symptom: abnormal head position, binocular rivalry, suppression, and abnormal retinal correspondence. In the presence of a weak extraocular muscle, moving the head to a position that avoids the field of action of the paretic muscle often will prevent diplopia; therefore, an abnormal head position may be an indicator of extraocular muscle paresis. Binocular rivalry is a function that can be present normally or abnormally. When viewing with one eye through a monocular telescope or microscope, it often is unnecessary to close the other eye to avoid confusion of images. This cortical phenomenon, known as retinal rivalry, is a normal adaptation to avoid diplopia. In the presence of strabismus, particularly in a strabismic circumstance where there is alternation of fixation from one eye to the other, retinal rivalry is apparently the operant mechanism. In a constant strabismic circumstance, one eye assumes fixation to the exclusion of the other, and the image from the deviating eye is suppressed. Suppression is a mechanism, largely limited to infancy and youth, one consequence of which is decreased vision (amblyopia). Thus, amblyopia develops and is treatable in infancy and early childhood; however, once maturation of the system is complete (about age 9 years), amblyopia is neither a threat nor effectively treated.

Where strabismus is of early onset and longstanding duration, the cortical adaptation of abnormal retinal correspondence may ensue. In this instance, noncorresponding retinal points are cortically integrated, presumably to avoid diplopia. Thus diplopia may be monocular or binocular, physiologic or pathologic. The presence of diplopia may be detrimental to school performance. It is generally avoidable by closing one eye, and this behavior may be observed. Generally, however, adaptations are readily achieved to conditions producing diplopia in children, and the symptom does not represent a significant barrier to learning.

## REFERENCES

Records, R. E. (1979). *Physiology of the human eye and visual system*. Hagerstown, MD: Harper & Row.

Von Noorden, G. K. (1985). *Binocular vision and ocular motility*. St. Louis: Mosby.

GEORGE R. BEAUCHAMP
*Cleveland Clinic Foundation,
Cleveland, Ohio*

# DIRECT INSTRUCTION

The term direct instruction arose from two complementary lines of research and development. Rosenshine (1976) introduced the term into the mainstream of educational research. His synthesis of many classroom observation studies indicated that students consistently demonstrate higher reading achievement scores when their teachers do the following:

1. Devote substantial time to active instruction
2. Break complex skills and concepts into small, easy-to-understand steps and systematically teach in a step-by-step fashion
3. Ensure that all students operate at a high rate of success
4. Provide immediate feedback to students about the accuracy of their work
5. Conduct much of the instruction in small groups to allow for frequent student-teacher interactions

The other source of direct instruction derives from the work of curriculum developers rather than researchers. In the early 1960s in Israel, Smilarsky taught preschoolers from peasant immigrant families from surrounding Arab nations. The method, called direct promotion, taught in a direct manner toward specific goals. In the mid-1960s Bereiter and Engelmann (1966) formed an academically oriented preschool based on direct-instruction principles. In the late 1960s, Engelmann articulated the concept of direct instruction in the form of specific curricular materials and in a comprehensive model for teaching low-performing students. Direct instruction was incorporated as part of the acronym for DISTAR (Direct Instruction System for Teaching and Remediation) and as part of the title of the direct instruction model that took part in the U.S. Office of Education Follow Through Project. The key to direct instruction, as envisioned by Engelmann and his colleagues, is a comprehensive intervention, addressing teacher expectations for student learning, the curriculum, teaching skills, time spent engaged in academic activities, administrative support, and parental involvement.

At the heart of the direct instruction intervention was the conviction that student faialure could be prevented or at least remedied, regardless of the label placed on the child. The empirical basis for this conviction is found in a number of sources, ranging from an annotated bibliography of 188 articles and books on direct instruction in special education (Fabre, 1983) to an article reviewing 20 direct instruction studies in special education in Australia (Maggs & Maggs, 1979). Other sources include a review of special education studies in the United States (Gersten, 1985) and an overview of articles on direct instruction (Carnine, 1983). These various reports frequently emphasize the academic gains of students in direct instruction (ABT Associates, 1977).

The national evaluation of the Follow Through (FT) Project yielded another finding that surprised many educators:

> The performance of FT children in direct instruction sites on the affective measures is an unexpected result. The direct instruction model does not explicitly emphasize affective outcomes of instruction, but the sponsor has asserted that they will be the consequence of effective teaching. Critics of the model have predicted that the emphasis on tightly controlled instruction might discourage children from freely expressing themselves, and thus inhibit the development of self-esteem and other affective skills. In fact, this is not the case. (ABT Associates, 1977, p. 73)

These outcomes reflect the basic philosophy of direct instruction: student failures are school failures. School failures are not remedied by showing teachers research findings in an attempt to increase teacher expectations; however, teachers need well-designed curricular materials, substantial instructional time to teach students, and teaching techniques for motivating and helping students who are making numerous mistakes.

Curricular materials guide teachers in explaining, reviewing, and giving practice on academic content. Direct instruction materials are designed in part to minimize student confusions. In a simple example, subtracting 3942 from 6000 often confuses students as they try to rename in one column at a time. In direct instruction, students rewrite 600 tens as 599 tens and 1 ten in a single step:

$$
\begin{array}{r}
599+1 \\
\cancel{6}\cancel{0}\cancel{0}0 \\
-\underline{3942} \\
\end{array}.
$$

Recognizing that 600 = 599 + 1 is much less confusing than crossing out successive zeroes and rewriting the value represented by each renamed zero.

Direct instruction materials also teach students strategies that allow them to handle a wide range of tasks. In intermediate spelling, students learn a few rules and 655 word roots; they then can spell over 10,000 words. The instructional design principles are articulated in several books: *Theory of Instruction* (Engelmann & Carnine, 1982), *Direct Instruction Reading* (Carnine & Silbert, 1979), *Direct Instruction Mathematics* (Silbert, Carnine, & Stein, 1981), and *Applied Psychology for Teachers: A Behavioral Cognitive Approach* (Becker, in press).

Direct instruction teaching techniques are designed to maximize the quality and amount of academic engaged time. The amount of time is increased by showing teachers how to schedule instructional time more effectively and how to keep students attending by using reinforcement, rapid pacing, challenges, etc. The quality of learning is particularly influenced by how teachers react to student errors. For memorization errors, teachers give the answers and periodically review the missed questions. For errors reflecting inappropriate strategy selection or application, the teacher asks questions based on prior instruction to guide the student in using the strategy to arrive at an appropriate answer.

Familarity with direct instruction curriculas and teaching techniques requires intensive staff development. Staff development occurs primarily in individual teachers' classrooms. A supervisor observes and sets priorities for training on teaching techniques. A supervisor might model a correction procedure with a teacher's students one day, observe the teacher applying the procedure immediately, and then return a few days later to see whether the teacher is comfortable with the procedure. If the teacher has mastered the correction procedure, the supervisor will commence training in the next teaching technique on the priority list.

Supervision of direct instruction can be difficult. Supervisors must have tact as well as skill in diagnosing teaching deficiencies, identifying and prioritizing remedies, modeling and prompting remedies, and managing their time efficiently in order to spend sufficient time making classroom observations.

Administrative support is needed to select and train supervisors and establish their roles with teachers. Because direct instruction supervision is so intensive, administrative support is often needed until teachers realize that the supervisor's role is primarily to assist teachers, not to evaluate them. The problems administrators can face in implementing innovative programs like direct instruction (Carnine, in press) are diverse, with the solutions taking different forms at each stage of the change process. Student growth in the cognitive and affective domains can more than compensate for the difficulties teachers and administrators encounter in implementing direct instruction.

## REFERENCES

ABT Associates. (1977). *Education as experimentation: A planned variation model.* (Vol. 4). Cambridge, MA: Authors.

Bereiter, C., & Engelmann, S. (1966). *Teaching disadvantaged children in the preschool.* Engelwood Cliffs, NJ: Prentice-Hall.

Carnine, D. W., & Silbert, J. (1979). *Direct instruction reading.* Columbus, OH: Merrill.

Carnine, D. (1983). Direct instruction: In search of instructional solutions for educational problems. In D. Carnine, D. Elkind, D. Melchenbaum, R. Lisieben, & F. Smith (Eds.), *Interdisciplinary voices in learning disabilities and remedial education* (pp. 1–66). Austin, TX: Pro-Ed.

Carnine, D. W. (in press). Barriers to improving reading instruction. In S. J. Samuels & P. D. Pearson (Eds.), *Building exemplary reading programs.* Newark, DE: International Reading Association.

Engelmann, S., & Carnine, D. W. (1982). *Theory of instruction.* New York: Irvington.

Fabre, T. (1983). *The application of direct instruction in special education: An annotated bibliography.* University of Oregon.

Gersten, R. (1985). Direct instruction with special education students: A review of evaluation research. *Journal of Special Education, 19,* 42–58.

Maggs, A., & Maggs, R. K. (1979). Direct instruction research in Australia. *Journal of Special Education Technology, 81 (3),* 26–34.

Rosenshine, B. (1976). Classroom instruction. In N. L. Gage (Ed.), Psychology of teaching: The 77th yearbook of the National Society for the Study of Education. Chicago, IL: National Society for the Study of Education.

Silbert, J., Carnine, D. W., & Stein, M. (1981). *Direct instruction mathematics.* Columbus, OH: Merrill.

DOUGLAS CARNINE
*University of Oregon*

**DISTAR**
**READING REMEDIATION**

# DIRECTORY OF FACILITIES FOR THE LEARNING DISABLED, ANNUAL

See ANNUAL DIRECTORY OF FACILITIES FOR THE LEARNING DISABLED.

# DISABILITY

The term disability is derived from the Latin prefix *dis-*, meaning negation, separation, lack of, or opposite of; and the Latin *habilitas*, meaning fitness, and *habere*, indicating to have or to be easily handled. Disability today indicates the lack of power or ability to do something. It is usually regarded as a negative attribute. The prefix contributes to our English word some of the connotations of its association with Dis, the god of the underworld in Roman mythology with whom the Greeks identified Pluto, and with Hades and the realm of the dead.

Some writers distinguish disability from impairment and handicap. Wright (1960) views a disability as mainly a medical condition; however, she sees a handicap reflecting the demands placed on an individual in a particular situation. An individual may indeed have a disability but may not have a handicap except in certain situations. Wright's elaboration on the significance of physical disability is essential reading for persons interested in a psychological perspective of body physique.

Stevens (1962) has formulated a taxonomy for special education in which he distinguishes among disability, impairment, and handicap. Stevens regards disability as a loss of function, impairment as tissue damage or disease, and handicap as "the burden which is imposed on the learner when confronted with educational situations which cannot be resolved by reason of body dysfunction or impairment" (p. 65). While the progression may be from tissue damage to loss of function to certain situational difficulties, Stevens argues that the extent or severity of any disability cannot be directly predicted from evaluation of the impairment only. Nor can the behavior one exhibits, or the burden that one elects to carry or that is assigned by society to a person with a certain disability or impairment, be accurately determined from knowledge about the disability only. Disabilities in motion, sensation, intelligence, emotion, and physiological processes do not necessarily translate into specific handicaps in situations requiring mobility, communication, healthy self-concept, or social interaction skills. Figure 1 lists the components Stevens has identified as the subdivisions of the three terms he considers the educationally significant somatopsychological variants.

1. Somatopsychological variants
    1.1. Handicap
        1.1.1 Motility
        1.1.2 Communication
        1.1.3 Self-concept
        1.1.4 Social interaction
    1.2 Disability
        1.2.1 Motion
        1.2.2 Sensation
        1.2.3 Intelligence
        1.2.4 Emotion
        1.2.5 Physiological processes
    1.3 Impairment
2. Educationally significant attributes of somatopsychological disorders
    2.1 Nature of condition
    2.2 Nature of therapeutic process
    2.3 Psychological aspects
    2.4 Social considerations
    2.5 Cultural considerations
3. Special education procedures
    3.1 Modifications of laws
    3.2 Finance
    3.3 Instructional modifications
    3.4 Noninstructional services
    3.5 Administrative modifications
    3.6 Ancillary services
    3.7 Other

Figure 1. Summary of a taxonomy of special education (from G. D. Stevens, 1962. *Taxonomy of special education for children with body disorders.* Pittsburgh: Department of Special Education and Rehabilitation, University of Pittsburgh).

The World Health Organization (WHO) has recently made efforts to clarify terms and extend the medical model of disease per se to account for the consequences of disease (1980). Researchers for WHO began working in the early 1970s on a classification system that would extend the medical model and facilitate the recognition of the contributions of medical services, rehabilitation agencies, and social welfare personnel to the care of people with conditions that interfere with everyday life, especially those people who have chronic, progressive, and irreversible conditions. The medical model of disease may be illustrated as:

$$etiology \rightarrow pathology \rightarrow manifestation$$

(WHO, 1980, p. 10).

The extended model may be presented as:

$$disease \rightarrow impairment \rightarrow disability \rightarrow handicap$$

(WHO, 1980, p. 11).

Disability in the WHO classification system denotes the "consequences of impairment in terms of functional performance and activity by the individual" (p. 14). An impairment is defined as "any loss or abnormality of psychological, physiological, or anatomical structure or function" (p. 47). Handicap is defined as "a disadvantage for a given individual, resulting from an impairment or a disability, that limits or prevents the fulfillment of a role that is normal (depending on age, sex, and social and cultural factors) for that individual" (p. 183). Thus impairment represents "exteriorization of a pathological state" (p. 47) and occurs at the tissue level; disability refers to "excesses or deficiencies of customarily expected activity, performance, and behavior" (p. 142) and is located at the level of the person; and handicap "reflects the consequences for the individual—cultural, social, economic, and environmental—that stem from the presence of impairment and disability" (p. 183). Figure 2 outlines of the components of the WHO proposed classification system.

In the present context of special education and rehabilitation, the term disability is frequently changed to the adjectival form and used to describe individuals. Thus we hear talk about disabled persons. Note, however, the affect of this change; instead of considering a disability or the lack of power to act, attention is directed to people who are characterized as not having power to act, with no distinction as to what actions might be limited. Wright (1960), in her discussion of physical disabilities, has pointed out the distinction between calling someone a physically disabled person as opposed to a person with a physical disability: "it is precisely the perception of a person with a physical disability as a *physically disabled person* that has reduced all his life to the disability aspects

| Impairment | Disability | Handicap |
|---|---|---|
| Intellectual | Behavior | Orientation |
| Psychological | Communication | Physical independ- |
| Language | Personal care | ence |
| Aural | Locomotor | Mobility |
| Ocular | Body disposition | Occupation |
| Visceral | Dexterity | Social integration |
| Skeletal | Situational | Economic self-suffi- |
| Disfiguring | Particular skills | ciency |
| Generalized, sen- | Other | Other |
| sory, and other | | |
| impairments | | |

Figure 2. Consequences of disease (from World Health Organization, 1980. *International classification of impairments, disabilities, and handicaps: A manual of classification relating to the consequences of disease.* Geneva, Switzerland: World Health Organization).

of his physique. The short cut distorts and undermines" (p. 8). Consider the impact of further streamlining our language when we talk about the disabled and characterize as disabled an entire group of people who may share nothing other than their membership in the amorphous group labeled disabled. A common example is the group called the learning disabled (LD); the extreme heterogeneity among the individual group members is obscured by the blanket term or its abbreviation to LD.

Attempts to define the term disability and differentiate it from related terms is more than an exercise in semantics. Precise definitions are needed for determining who is eligible for services; what the incidence and prevalence of conditions are; what projected health care, educational, rehabilitation, and welfare assistance may be required from a local, state, national, or international perspective; and what efforts might facilitate the development of appropriate housing and employment opportunities. It seems likely that as long as the term disability carries a strong pejorative connotation, attempts will be made to limit its denotation and increase the objectivity of its meaning.

## REFERENCES

Stevens, G. D. (1962). *Taxonomy in special education for children with body disorders*. Pittsburgh: Department of Special Education and Rehabilitation, University of Pittsburgh.

World Health Organization. (1980). *International classification of impairments, disabilities, and handicaps: A manual of classification relating to the consequences of disease.* Geneva, Switzerland: Author.

Wright, B. (1960). *Physical disability—A psychological approach.* New York: Harper & Row.

MARJORIE E. WARD
*Ohio State University*

## HANDICAPPED, DEFINITION
## LABELING

# DISADVANTAGED CHILD

Who are the disadvantaged? How narrow or broad does our *definition* need to be to adequately encompass this concept? How do we educate this population? What new skills will the teacher preparation colleges and universities need to require? How much of a role, if any, should the state or federal government play in financing new programs? With each new journal, textbook, or conversation, educators asked these general questions as well as hundreds of more detailed questions concerning the specific cultural criteria making up the disadvantaged, the role of language development, and related curricula changes needed expressly for this group.

According to Ornstein (1976) most educators when speaking or writing about the disadvantaged take it on themselves to "categorize them somewhat arbitrarily into one or more of the following areas of deprivation: economic, racial, geographic, social, cultural, cognitive, and/or emotional" (p. 5). Most writings about the disadvantaged first gained attention during the 1940s and 1950s; lower-class youths and racial minorities were identified as the populace of this educationally disenfranchised group of learners. Historically we can identify the roots of this population in terms of their educational needs, but it was not until the mid 1960s that writers such as Riessman and Havighurst had their turns at defining the characteristics that constitute this deprived population. As indicated by Riessman (1962), the terms culturally deprived, educationally deprived, deprived, underprivileged, disadvantaged, lower class, and lower socioeconomic group, could all be used interchangeably.

Ornstein (1976) has presented an interesting and basic critique of the attempts made by Havighurst and Riessman to provide us with the characteristics of the disadvantaged. Havighurst began by attempting to provide the traditional conceptualization of the disadvantaged that grew out of the earliest of writings. The disadvantaged youth is seen as coming primarily from a low-income family and most likely from a racial minority. Havighurst emphasizes the social, economic, and personal handicaps of the disadvantaged and sees this youth at the lowest end of several strata. Ornstein interprets this as providing the unwary reader with a convenient label that is essentially laden with negativism.

On the other hand, we have Ornstein's interpretation of what he refers to as a positive trend exemplified in Riessman's (1962) classic book. *The Culturally Deprived Child*, in which he views the disadvantaged youth as having many positive characteristics. With the emphasis now on a more positive outlook, readers are encouraged to note and develop qualities within this population such as physical orientation, hidden verbal ability, creative potential, group cohesiveness informality, and sense of humor.

Although Riessman has made great efforts to identify some characteristics that might be construed as potentially positive qualities, he also is cognizant of the negative criteria used by Havighurst and others. An examination of *The Culturally Deprived Child* (1962), results in the reader's awareness that Reissman understood the enormity of the problems encountered by the deprived children of our nation.

Karnes, Reid, & Jones (1971), in the Guidance Monograph Series, provide us with an approach to the identification process in that they refer to a difference between middle class and lower class in only the six areas of (1) self-concept, (2) motivation, (3) social behavior, (4) language, (5) intellectual functioning, and (6) physical fitness. With such broad categories, each educator can conceivably provide us with information applicable to either the Havighurst or Riessman model. In addition, the term disadvantaged youth is also seen as being too nebulous and having a degree of relativism that in turn reduces the selection process for innovative educational programs to confront this issue. Loss of objectivity in the identification and ultimate selection of students for educational enrichment often results in failure to meet the program's goals.

Without many of the precise criteria needed to identify the disadvantaged population, the educational community moved ahead with special programs with a financial base from congressional legislation. In 1965 Congress passed the Elementary and Secondary Education Act and for the first time in U.S. history, federal financial support was provided to both public and nonpublic schools. From this legislation came Title I—Education of Children of Low-Income Families. Title I was designed to support and provide financial incentives for special programs to meet the special needs of socially and educationally deprived children of low-income families. Other means of financial support to improve the teaching of disadvantaged students came from ESEA, Title III, and the National Defense Education Act, Title XI.

Programs that were funded for the disadvantaged first included in-service programs to retrain teachers in meeting the challenges presented by the disadvantaged in all areas of the curriculum. Once the children from low-income families were identified and assessed, they were generally found to have come from home environments that did not promote preschool educational activities. They also manifested inadequate language development and reading skills, possessed insufficient motivation to pursue vocational goals, had histories of poor daily nutrition and hygienic habits, and generally had a distrust of educational systems.

Specific learning characteristics of the deprived or disadvantaged student might include many of the following: (1) oriented to the physical and visual rather than to the oral; (2) content-centered rather than form-centered; (3) externally oriented rather than introspective; (4) problem-centered rather than abstract-centered; (5) inductive rather than deductive; (6) spatial rather than temporal; (7) slow, careful, patient, and persevering (in areas of importance) rather than quick, clever, facile, and flexible; (8) inclined to communicate through actions rather than words; (9) deficient in auditory attention and interpretation skills; (10) oriented toward concrete application of what is learned; (11) short attention span; (12) characteristic gaps in knowledge and learning; (13) lacking experiences of receiving approval for success in tasks (Conte & Grimes, 1969).

Meeting the needs of the disadvantaged child is a relatively new educational approach when viewed within the context of America's education history. Efforts to define this population were not without conflict, and massive expenditures of monies by the federal government has also stirred controversy.

Assessment instruments were designed and administered to select specific populations to meet government guidelines. Programs proliferated throughout the United States and children from lower socioeconomic levels were finally being provided with equal educational opportunities.

**REFERENCES**

Conte, J. M., & Grimes, G. H. (1969). *Media and the culturally different.* Washington, DC: National Education Association.

Karnes, M. B., Reid, J., & Jones, G. R. (1971). *The culturally disadvantaged student and guidance.* Boston: Houghton Mifflin.

Ornstein, A. C. (1976). Who are the disadvantaged? In J. H. Cull & R. E. Hardy (Eds.), *Problems of disadvantaged and deprived youth,* (pp. 5–15). Springfield, IL: Thomas.

Riessman, F. (1962). *The culturally deprived child.* New York: Harper & Row.

RICHARD E. HALMSTAD
*University of Wisconsin, Stout*

# DISCIPLINE

The noun discipline comes from the Latin word *disciplina*, meaning teaching, learning. However, a more common use of the word connotes either training that corrects or molds or punishment for transgressions against societal or parental rules.

Discipline begins with the efforts of parents to teach the mores of their culture. Almost all of this early discipline begins when the infant becomes mobile and can therefore behave in ways that parents believe need to be changed. Early parental discipline usually focuses on behavioral control, e.g., not touching the untouchable or not running in the street. Difficulties can arise if parents think that the child can control a behavior that the child in fact cannot—at least not at that age. A good example of this is toilet training of toddlers. Parents continue to carry the responsibility for disciplining children until they enter school. From the time children enter school until

they leave, teachers endeavor to discipline children as well.

Parents seem to discipline their children either through power-assertion techniques or through love-oriented techniques (Hoffman, 1970). In the former style of parental discipline, power assertion, the parent uses physical punishment, deprives the child of material objects or privileges, directly applies force, or threatens. Control is exercised by taking advantage of greater physical strength and/or control of home environment.

Love withdrawal, a form of love-oriented discipline, uses direct but nonphysical expressions of anger or disappointment when the child misbehaves. For example, the parent may discipline by explicitly stating negative feelings, ignoring, isolating, or turning away from the child.

The use of power-assertive discipline such as spanking or love-oriented techniques such as withdrawal of affection may produce resentment or anxiety and cause the child to focus attention on his or her own negative consequences. These procedures are punitive rather than altruistic, i.e., they decrease the child's appreciation of another person's distress.

Through induction, another form of love-oriented parental discipline, the parent appeals to the child's affection or respect for another. In essence, the child may be reminded that someone else will be hurt, disappointed, or suffer from his or her actions.

In comparison, inductive discipline is a nonpunitive technique that communicates the harm caused by a child's actions and encourages the child to place himself or herself in the victim's place. Hoffman (1975) believes that children are likely to develop a strong altruistic orientation if their parents often use inductive disciplinary techniques.

Another perspective on discipline is espoused by William Glasser (1969). Glasser suggests that children be allowed to determine their own discipline and to set consequences for their behavior. Adults (parents, teachers, etc.) who use Glasser's style of discipline often play a low-key role that reduces immediate application of reward and punishment and supplants both with discussion in which the adult serves as mediator for decision making.

While Glasser's approach may be effective with bright, middle-class, high-school students, it may not be effective with young children or with older adolescents who have grown up in a lower-class setting. If children have not developed the requisite skills for deciding on a socially competent course of action when disciplinary decisions are required, this approach is not suggested. The effectiveness of each technique varies, perhaps influenced most by such factors as the age and cultural background of the child.

On entering the school setting, previously learned behavior patterns emerge when children are faced with adapting to participating in a room where waiting, sharing, instruction, and learning must take place. The term control is often viewed as a convenient catch all for what should be termed classroom management. One is never sure whether the meaning is intended in the broad sense (to cover all of classroom management), or the literal sense, that of keeping pupil behavior so curbed that the classroom is totally teacher-dominated.

Discipline, like control, is often incorrectly used to mean various aspects of classroom management. Good discipline may be considered maintaining an orderly, strict classroom. Strong discipline may be considered teacher behavior that is rigid, firm, and unbending.

A more acceptable use of the term in the educational setting would describe discipline as an imposition of self-control in order to promote efficient habits of learning, proper conduct, consideration for others, and a positive learning environment.

Classroom management (control) is a major factor contributing to the success of a teacher. A distinction between discipline and classroom management is, therefore, necessary. Relative to classroom management, instruction (teaching) is regarded as conducting reading, spelling, and mathematics lessons, doing science experiments, etc. Conversely, when students do not conduct themselves appropriately or treat each other courteously and respectfully, disciplinary action is required. Hence, classroom management may be perceived primarily in the negative sense of correcting pupil misbehavior, keeping a watchful eye for evidence of wrong doing, and disciplining pupils rather than a process involving the interaction of classroom resources, instruction, and learning.

To maintain discipline in the classroom, the student must be given as much independence as the teacher and child can tolerate. Classroom management should yield neither highly structured teacher-dominated environments nor completely permissive ones. To facilitate the development of self-control and discipline, a teacher's managerial style should attempt to promote active participation and a positive learning environment.

## REFERENCES

Glasser, W. (1969). *Schools without failure.* New York: Harper & Row.

Hoffman, M. L. (1970). Moral development. In P. H. Mussen (Ed.), *Carmicheal's manual of child psychology* (3rd ed., Vol. 2). New York: Wiley.

Hoffman, M. L. (1975). Altruistic behavior and the parent-child relationships. *Journal of Personality & Social Psychology, 40,* 121–137.

MICHAEL J. ASH
JOSE LUIS TORRES
*Texas A&M University*

**CLASSROOM MANAGEMENT**
**SELF-CONTROL CURRICULUM**
**SELF-MONITORING**

## DISCREPANCY ANALYSIS

See LEARNING DISABILITIES, SEVERE DISCREPANCY ANALYSIS IN.

## DISCREPANCY FROM GRADE

Discrepancy model analysis is used in the assessment of learning disabilities to determine if a difference exists between the level of achievement and ability. Levels of achievement and intelligence are measured reliably by using standardized tests. Results, however, may not always be accurate owing to error in measurement. Attempts to measure discrepancy may also be complicated by age or grade level. A discrepancy of one year at the third grade for a 9 year old is more severe than a similar discrepancy for a 16 year old.

Several techniques using expectancy analysis are used in quantifying learning disabilities (Mercer, 1983). They are the mental grade method, the learning quotient method, and the Harris method. Harris (1961) provided a method to determine an individual's reading expectancy grade (RE). The examiner subtracts five years from the individual's mental age:

$$RE = MA - 5$$

To determine if a discrepancy exists, a comparison is made between the individual's reading expectancy and the present reading level. The learning quotient method was developed by Myklebust (1968); it includes mental age, chronological age, and grade age (GA). The learning quotient is the ratio between the present achievement age and expectancy age with a score of 89 or below resulting in classification as learning disabled.

A third technique once commonly used to determine discrepancy in learning disabilities was proposed by Harris (1970). This method includes both mental age and chronological age but gives priority to mental age:

$$EA = \frac{2MA + CA}{3}$$

These methods for determining discrepancy have been criticized in that difference scores between two tests were less reliable than each score separately (Salvia & Clark, 1973). It has also been noted that a large number of children might exhibit discrepancy by pure chance. These techniques were also criticized because of their failure with nonreaders.

## REFERENCES

Harris, I. (1961). *Emotional blocks to learning.* New York: Free Press.

Harris, A. J. (1970). *How to increase reading ability* (5th ed.). New York: McKay.

Mercer, C. D. (1983). *Students with learning disabilities* (2nd ed.). Columbus, OH: Merrill.

Myklebust, H. (1968). Learning disabilities: Definition and overview. In H. Myklebust (Ed.), *Progress in learning disabilities*. New York: Grune & Stratton.

Salvia, J., & Clark, J. (1973). Use of deficits to identify the learning disabled. *Exceptional Children, 39*, 305–308.

CRAIG D. SMITH
*Georgia College*

CLASSIFICATION, SYSTEMS OF
GRADE EQUIVALENTS
LEARNING DISABILITIES
LEARNING DISABILITIES, PROBLEMS IN DEFINITION OF
LEARNING DISABILITIES, SEVERE DISCREPANCY
  ANALYSIS IN DIAGNOSIS OF

## DISCRIMINANT ANALYSIS

Discriminant analysis is a statistical technique used to predict group membership from two or more interval dependent variables. It is similar to multiple regression in conception. For example, a researcher might be interested in determining if dyslexic students are distinguishable from other learning-disabled students using the subtests of the WISC-R. Discriminant analysis can be used to determine the optimal set of weights for the WISC-R subtests that maximally separate the two groups on a new variable composed of the weighted sum of the WISC-R subtests.

Discriminant analysis may also be viewed as a data reduction technique. Instead of needing a large number of variables to categorize subjects, the researcher applies discriminant analysis so that a new variable or set of variables is created that uses the information of the original variables. The new variables are linear combinations, or weighted sums, of the original variables. It is anticipated that fewer new variables are needed than in the original set, hence the idea of data reduction. Mathematically, more than one unique solution to the problem is possible. The number of solutions will be equal to the smaller of two numbers: the number of predictors or the degrees of freedom for groups (number of groups minus one). Each solution corresponds to a new variable independent statistically of all the other new solution variables. For two groups there is only one solution since the smaller of the two numbers is equal to one (two groups minus one). This solution is also equal to the multiple regression of the group variable (mathematically defined as, for example, one or two on the predictor variables. The regression weights and the discriminant analysis weights in this case are identical.

For three or more groups, there will be two or more solutions to the problem of maximally distinguishing between the groups. Each solution corresponds to constructing a straight line on which the groups differ most in the sense of squared distance from the mean of the groups on the line. Each solution line is perpendicular in a Euclidean geometric sense from each other solution line. Computer programs are used to solve these problems, and the programs are designed to find the best solution first. The best solution is one in which the variance between the groups is greatest in relation to average variance within the groups for all possible lines. Once this solution is found, the next one is found from the residuals of fit to the first solution. A statistical test, Wilks lambda, is a multivariate analog to the ratio of the sum of squares within groups to the sum of the squares' total. An F-test may be used to test significance. For each new solution, test the additional error reduced in a manner similar to that employed in multiple regression to test a new predictor's additional contribution to prediction. Also, stepwise procedures can be employed in discriminant analysis to select the subset of predictors that maximally separate the groups. Predictors that do not contribute to separation in a given solution are dropped.

Discriminant analysis is widely used in both social and physical sciences. Its mathematical solutions are straightforward for a computer; discriminant analysis programs for microcomputers are now also available.

### REFERENCES

Cohen, J., & Cohen, P. (1983). *Applied multiple regression/correlation analysis for the social sciences* (3rd ed.). Hillsdale, NJ: Erlbaum.

Pedhazur, E. (1982). *Multiple regression in behavioral research* (2nd ed.). New York: Holt, Rinehart & Winston.

VICTOR L. WILLSON
*Texas A&M University*

FACTOR ANALYSIS
MULTIPLE REGRESSION
WISC-WISC-R

## DISCRIMINATION LEARNING

Discrimination learning refers to the process of learning to respond differentially to relevant dimensions of a stimulus event. As a fundamental construct of behaviorally oriented learning explanations, this type of learning emphasizes events that occur before a behavior(s); the relationship of these events to the strength and contextual appropriateness of the behavior(s); and the resulting consequences that serve to maintain, strengthen, or punish the behavior(s).

During the teaching of discriminations, a stimulus event is presented to the student. Following this presentation, the student independently or, if necessary, with prompts, exhibits a behavioral response. If the behavior that the individual engages in is appropriate relative to the stimulus event, the learner is rewarded with a potentially reinforcing outcome. If the behavior is not appropriate with regard to the stimulus event, the consequent alternatives might include not attending to the response (ignoring), or systematic presentation of consequences aimed at reducing the future probability of the behavior occurring (punishment).

As a function of the consequences that occur in this S > R > C relationship, the stimulus events that have historically led to reinforcement become cues for the learner to engage in particular behaviors that will result in rewarding consequences. These stimulus events are referred to as discriminative stimuli ($S^D$). Conversely, those stimulus events that have not resulted in reinforcement ($S^\Delta$) do not cue the individual to respond. Discrimination learning, then, teaches an individual when to engage in a particular behavior to obtain desirable outcomes, and by contrast clarifies when behavior will not lead to desirable consequences.

The teaching of discriminations constitutes one of the major tasks for individuals who are involved in educating the exceptional needs learner. While this type of learning is often assumed to take place in an almost incidental fashion, with most exceptional learners this outcome is not as likely. A host of variables, including diverse cognitive skills, inconsistent learning opportunities, and nefarious reinforcement contingencies, may interact to limit such individuals' development of accurate discriminations. Effective educational service delivery for the exceptional child or youth often necessitates the use of more systematic methods of teaching discriminations.

Planned teaching of discriminations has involved simple to complex presentations of the attributes of the stimulus events (e.g., size, shape, volume, color, or combinations of these) and varied reinforcement schedules (e.g., movement from fixed to variable schedules of reinforcement) aimed at strengthening the discriminative potential of the stimulus event. Following accurate individualized assessment, discriminations are taught beginning at a level that increases the opportunity for success. Based on continuing assessment, teaching complexity is systematically moved in the direction of more normative skill development.

Teaching of discriminated responses has been used in vocationally oriented curricula, social skills programs, and many other curriculum areas targeted for the exceptional needs learner. By teaching individuals to exhibit specified behaviors under certain stimulus conditions, many of the inconsistent and inappropriate behaviors exhibited by this diverse group have been strengthened or replaced with more environmentally appropriate responses. For a comprehensive explanation of discrimination learning, the reader is referred to texts by Alberto and Troutman (1977) and Sulzer-Azaroff and Mayer (1977). Both texts provide clear examples of the application of this learning principle to educational programming.

## REFERENCES

Alberto, P. A., & Troutman, A. C. (1977). *Applied behavior analysis for teachers: Influencing student performance*. Columbus, OH: Merrill.

Sulzer-Azaroff, B., & Mayer, G. R. (1977). *Applying behavior-analysis procedures with children and youth*. New York: Holt, Rinehart & Winston.

J. Todd Stephens
*University of Wisconsin,
Madison*

APPLIED BEHAVIOR ANALYSIS
BEHAVIOR MODIFICATION
DATA BASE INSTRUCTION
PRECISION TEACHING

# DISPROPORTIONALITY

Disproportionality in special education denotes unequal percentages of students with various demographic characteristics in special education classifications and programs. Disproportionality most often occurs in the mildly handicapping classifications of mild mental retardation (MMR), emotionally disturbed (ED), and specific learning disability (SLD), or in programs for the talented and gifted (TAG). The demographic variables in which disproportionality is most often observed, and sometimes seen as a problem, are ethnic/racial status, sex, and socioeconomic status. Disproportionality related to these student characteristics is well known, but highly controversial (Reschly, 1986).

The most widely studied disproportionality phenomenon is the overrepresentation of minorities, males, and economically disadvantaged students in the exceptional child classification of MMR. The same groups are also overrepresented, according to some studies, in programs for the SLD and ED. However, the overrepresentation in SLD and ED is rarely of the same magnitude as in MMR.

In the Table, data compiled from a Federal Office of Civil

National Projections from 1978 OCR Survey

|                              | Minority (%) | White (%) | Hispanic (%) | Black (%) |
| ---------------------------- | ------------ | --------- | ------------ | --------- |
| *Classification*             |              |           |              |           |
| Mildly mentally retarded     | 2.54         | 1.07      | 0.98         | 3.46      |
| Seriously emotionally disturbed | 0.42      | 0.29      | 0.29         | 0.50      |
| Learning disabled            | 2.29         | 2.32      | 2.58         | 2.23      |
| Speech impaired              | 1.82         | 2.04      | 1.78         | 1.87      |
| Total (mildly handicapped)   | 7.07         | 5.72      | 5.63         | 8.06      |

*Source:* Based on Finn (1982), Table 1, p. 324 and Table 3, p. 330.

Rights (OCR) survey of school districts in the United States, reported in a National Academy of Sciences monograph (Heller, Holtzman, & Messick, 1982), are presented. The OCR survey results are the only data source for a national summary of disproportionality in special education programs for the mildly handicapped. These national results indicate that the only significant area of disproportionality is MMR, where the percentage of black students classified as MMR is three times the percentage of white students so classified. Relatively equal percentages of black, white, and Hispanic students are found in all other classifications except for ED, where black students are again overrepresented, but the numbers of students are small. The national results also indicate that Hispanic students are not overrepresented in special education programs for the mildly handicapped, an apparent reversal of a phenomenon that led earlier to placement bias litigation in Arizona and California.

Other studies have indicated minority disproportionality in SLD and ED. For example, data for the state of Florida presented in the *S1 v. Turlington* trial (1986) indicated that black students were overrepresented in SLD, ED, and MMR.

Males and economically disadvantaged students generally are overrepresented in special education programs for the MMR. This overrepresentation sometimes approaches a ratio of two males for every female in SLD, ED, and MMR programs. Although studied far less frequently, overrepresentation of economically disadvantaged students is at least as ubiquitous as minority overrepresentation. Indeed, minority overrepresentation is probably best understood as reflecting the effects of poverty circumstances (Reschly, 1986).

The disproportionate representation of students in TAG programs is a virtual mirror image of representation in programs for the mildly handicapped. Economically disadvantaged minority students are underrepresented in programs for the gifted. The degree of underrepresentation is highly variable, but for black students, it is approximately the same as the degree of overrepresentation in programs for the mildly handicapped. The representation of males and females is approximately equal in TAG programs except in very specialized programs that attempt to select the markedly gifted (IQ greater than 150) or in programs for markedly advanced students in the areas of science and mathematics. In the latter kinds of programs, there is considerable underrepresentation of females, a phenomenon that also evokes considerable controversy.

Disproportionality statistics are easily confused and often distorted. In the *Larry P.* case, undisputed facts established that black students constituted 10% of the total enrollment in California, but 25% of the MMR enrollment. However, only 1% of all California black students were in MMR programs. These seeming disparities arise from the low base rate of MMR (and other exceptional conditions) and the failure to clearly distinguish between percent of group in the general population (10%), percent of group in the program (1%), and percent of the program by group (25%) (Reschly, 1986). Interpretation of disproportionality statistics must carefully distinguish among these different percentages.

The two general causes of disproportionality suggested in the literature are bias or discrimination and genuine individual differences. In short, the disproportionality is seen by some as a reflection of genuine differences among students and by others as a reflection of pernicious bias and discrimination from a variety of sources.

Allegations of bias or discrimination generally implicate the processes and procedures in which students are selected to be considered for placement in various kinds of programs. Thus bias or discrimination has been alleged in referral procedures, in the assessment process and assessment instruments (especially in intelligence tests), and in decision making by persons responsible for classification and placement decisions. Results of research on referral, assessment process and procedures, and decision making are far from definitive or unequivocal. Thus far, there is little evidence that bias or discrimination is a primary cause of disproportionality (Bickel, 1982; Reschly, 1986).

There is ample evidence establishing an association between extreme poverty and the incidence of mild mental retardation. This evidence has been gathered over the past 80 years with different racial or ethnic groups throughout western Europe and the United States. The MMR is to a large degree a phenonemon of poverty, but the vast majority of poor persons are not mildly mentally retarded (Reschly, 1986). The mechanisms whereby poverty increases risk for mild mental retardation are not clearly understood, but a variety of conditions are implicated (Robinson & Robinson, 1976).

Explanations for the sex disproportionality within the mildly handicapped and in certain types of programs for the gifted are far less clear, but no less controversial. These explanations range from constitutional factors (e.g., suggesting that the greater susceptibility of males to various constitutional disorders explains the overrepresentation of males in the mildly handicapped classifications) to the hypothesis that lower amounts of testosterone in females might account for the underrepresentation of women in programs for extremely advanced students in science and mathematics. Experiential or environmental influences are also suggested for sex disproportionality, e.g., suggestions that sex-typed behavior accounts for greater male referral for learning problems as well as fewer females excelling in math and science. Again, definitive, unequivocal results have not been established, and probably cannot be established in the foreseeable future.

Disproportionality, whether it involves overrepresentation of black students in programs for the mildly retarded or underrepresentation of women in programs for mathematically precocious youths, should be seen as a symptom, but only a symptom. Factors that might lead to disproportionality should be investigated, including possible bias or discrimination in procedures and processes whereby students are selected or placed in various programs. Disproportionality as such, however, does not indicate whether the differences arise from genuine variations in performance of persons or from bias or discrimination.

Disproportionality, particularly overrepresentation of minority students in programs for the mildly mentally retarded, has provoked extensive and enormously expensive litigation beginning in about 1968 and continuing through the late 1980s (Bersoff, 1982; Prasse & Reschly, 1986; Reschly, 1986). The common features of the placement bias cases are (1) overrepresentation of minority students, usually blacks, in self-contained MMR special classes; (2) class-action suits filed in federal district courts; and (3) allegations of bias in various aspects of the referral, preplacement evaluation, and classification/placement decision making. The outcomes of these cases have been extremely diverse, ranging from judicial decrees banning overrepresentation and forbidding the use of individually administered intelligence tests in certain circumstances to judicial decrees indicating that overrepresentation as such is not discriminatory and upholding the use of IQ tests along with other measures as an important protection for all children in the referral and classification/placement process. Federal circuit courts have upheld trial decisions in two cases, *Larry P.* v. *Riles* (1984) and *Marshall* v. *Georgia* (1985). However, the *Larry P.* and *Marshall* opinions reached opposite conclusions on a similar set of issues. Further litigation is likely.

Research methods designed to develop valid ways to screen, refer, and classify/place students that also eliminate disproportionality have been unsuccessful to date. Methods that eliminate disproportionality have, to date, been less reliable and valid. Processes and procedures that maintain the integrity of programs in meeting the needs of students, apply reliable and valid screening, referral, and classification/placement procedures, and lead to the elimination of disproportionality have been and probably will continue to be unattainable.

## REFERENCES

Bersoff, D. N. (1982). The legal regulation of school psychology. In C. R. Reynolds & T. B. Gutkin (Eds.), *The handbook of school psychology* (pp. 1043–1074). New York: Wiley.

Bickel, W. E. (1982). Classifying mentally retarded students: A review of placement practice in special education. In K. A. Heller, W. H. Holtzman, & S. Messick (Eds.), *Placing children in special education: A strategy for equity* (pp. 182–229). Washington, DC: National Academy.

Finn, J. D. (1982). Patterns in special education placement as revealed by OCR surveys. In R. A. Heller, W. H. Holtzman, & S. Messick, (Eds.), *Placing children in special education: A strategy for equity* (pp. 322–381). Washington, DC: National Academy.

Heller, K., Holtzman, W., & Messick, S. (Eds.), (1982). *Placing children in special education: A strategy for equity*. Washington, DC: National Academy.

Prasse, D. P., & Reschly, D. J. (1986). *Larry P*: A case of segregation, testing, or program efficacy? *Exceptional Children, 52*, 333–346.

Reschly, D. J. (1986). Economic and cultural factors in childhood exceptionality. In R. T. Brown & C. R. Reynolds (Eds.), *Psychological perspectives on childhood exceptionality: A handbook* (pp. 423–466). New York: Wiley-Interscience.

Robinson, N., & Robinson, H. (1976). *The mentally retarded child* (2nd ed.). New York: McGraw-Hill.

DANIEL J. RESCHLY
*Iowa State University*

**CULTURAL BIAS IN TESTS**
**LARRY P.**
**MARSHALL *v.* GEORGIA**
**NONDISCRIMINATORY ASSESSMENT**

# DISTAR

DISTAR (Direct Instructional System for Teaching and Remediation) is a product name for an instructional system published by Science Research Associates Inc. (SRA). From 1964 to 1966, Siegfried Engelmann and Carl Bereiter developed the teaching methods used in the DISTAR program, which is based on a task analysis of basic skills and presentation of materials in a direct teaching model. In 1967 SRA contracted with Engelmann to develop, write, and test DISTAR reading, language, and arithmetic materials. His coauthors were Elaine Bruner, reading; Douglas Carnine, arithmetic; and Jean Osborn and Therese Engelmann, language. In 1968 Wesley Becker joined Engelmann's Follow-Through Project and in 1969 they formed the Engelmann-Becker Corporation, a private non-profit organization providing teacher training in the Engelmann-Becker instructional model and the production of materials for Follow-Through sites. Although developmental work took place at the Engelmann-Becker Corporation, product development for DISTAR per se was and is performed under contract between SRA and the individual authors involved. Siegfried Engelmann became and remains professor of special education at the University of Oregon and codirector of the Direct Instruction Follow-Through Program (Brinckerhoff, 1983; Guinet, 1971; Kim, Berger, & Kratochvil, 1972; Moodie & Hoen, 1972).

The DISTAR system was originally designed to teach basic skills and concepts in reading, arithmetic, and language to disadvantaged preschoolers (Guinet, 1971). However, the scope has broadened to include average, above average, learning-disabled, and educable and trainable mentally retarded children (Kim et al., 1972). Current reviews of research (Cotton & Savard, 1982; Gersten, 1981) have revealed that the direct instruction method has proven successful with socioeconomically disadvantaged primary age children and special education students through age 13.

The system is grounded in the ideas that children learn what they are taught, that the necessary basic skills and concepts are the same for all children, that IQ is a function of teaching, and that it is possible to teach all of the necessary skills and concepts by means of a suitable instructional program. The required small group instruction ensures maximum student participation. Immediate reinforcement or correction ensures the prevention of error patterns (*Direct Instruction Management Handbook*, 1981; Guinet, 1971; Kim et al., 1972; Moodie & Hoen, 1972). The 30-minute lessons consisting of verbal interaction between teacher and students provide immediate teacher feedback. Lessons are carefully sequenced in a step-by-step fashion requiring mastery of basic skills before presentation of more complex ones. The well-defined small learning stages ensure daily successes that reinforce student self-concept. Limited visuals control distractions and are provided only at the end of lessons as rewards. The rewards are similar to the worksheets completed in class and taken home in recognition of doing well (Williamson, 1970). The presentation of tasks and the use of praise is highly structured. The teacher's manual instructs the teacher how to present the tasks, what to say, what signals and cues to use, what to expect from the children, and how to correct errors. The DISTAR premise that all children will learn if taught properly requires that all teachers use the DISTAR materials and follow the DISTAR methods of instruction to ensure student success (*Direct Instruction Management Handbook*, 1981; Guinet, 1971).

## REFERENCES

Brinckerhoff, L. (1983, Spring). Siegfried Engleman-Prophet or Profiteer. *ADI NEWS*, p. 1.

Cotton, K., & Savard, W. G. (1982). *Direct instruction: Research on school effectiveness project*. Portland, OR: Northwest Regional Educational Lab. (ERIC Document Reproduction Service No. ED 214 909).

*Direct instruction management handbook*. (1981). Chicago: Science Research Associates.

Gersten, R. M. (1981, April). *Direct instruction programs in special education settings: A review of evaluation research findings*. Paper presented at the annual international convention of the Council for Exceptional Children, New York. (ERIC Document Reproduction Service No. ED 204 957).

Guinet, L. (1971). *Evaluation of DISTAR materials in three junior learning assistance classes* (Report No. 71–16). Vancouver, BC: Board of School Trustees, Department of Planning and Evaluation. (ERIC Document Reproduction Service No. ED 057 105)

Kim, Y., Berger, B. J., & Kratochvil, D. W. (1972). *DISTAR instructional system* (Report No. OEC-0-70-4892). Washington, DC: Office of Education, Office of Program Planning and Evaluation. (ERIC Document Reproduction Service No. ED 061 632)

Moodie, A., & Hoen, R. (1972). *Evaluation of DISTAR programs in learning assistance classes of Vancouver 1971–72* (Report No. 72–18). Vancouver, BC: Board of School Trustees, Department of Planning and Evaluation. (ERIC Document Reproduction Service No. ED 088 911).

Williamson, F. (1970). *DISTAR Reading—Research and Experiment*. Urbana: University of Illinois. (ERIC Document Reproduction Service No. ED 045 318).

MARY D'IPPOLITO
*Montgomery County
Intermediate Unit,
Norristown, Pennsylvania*

**DIRECT INSTRUCTION
FOLLOW THROUGH**

# DISTRACTIBILITY

Attention is considered the most basic prerequisite for learning (Hewett, Taylor, & Artuso, 1969). As a disorder of attention, distractibility has been extensively studied by special educators and psychologists. Distractibility represents a construct that cannot be directly measured but rather must be based on inferences from gross behavioral observations of a child's behavior or performance on a particular task. Operational definitions of distractibility therefore differ and measurement is often imprecise. For example, some researchers and practitioners define distractibility as poor performance on an attentionally demanding task such as matching similar figures, while others define it as diminished performance when a distraction is introduced. Whether a child who is observed to be looking away from a task is inferred to be distractible or rather contemplating the task by considering a relevant idea illustrates the difficulty with precise measurement. Despite these definitional and methodological problems, research has advanced our understanding of the diagnosis, etiology, and treatment of distractibility.

Definitions of distractibility include difficulty in tuning out or forced responsiveness to unessential or extraneous stimulation such as environmental noises or stimuli such as hunger pangs, that may produce a motor activity within the individual (Cruickshank, Bentzen, Ratzeburg, & Tannhauser, 1961). In a classroom setting, distractibility typically refers to behavior that reflects the child's interest in things other than those on which the child should be concentrating (Bryan, 1974).

In the research literature, distractibility has been assessed by a variety of methods in a number of different settings (Whalen, 1983). Methods have included assessing performance as a child works in a room containing colorful and interesting distractors or, after introducing extraneous auditory or visual stimuli, while performing the task. The administration of a variety of laboratory games and procedures, the use of standardized behavior rating scales such as the Connors Teacher and Parent Rating Scale (Goyette, Connors, & Ulrich, 1978), and the analysis of results from individually administered intelligence tests (Kaufman, 1979) represent other methods reported in the research literature. Assessments have been conducted in the home, classroom, playground, playroom, and during the administration of individual intelligence and achievement tests (Bryan, 1974; Milich, Loney, & Landau, 1982).

Behaviors that reflect distractibility vary greatly depending on the task, type of distraction, setting, and the individual child. Evidence suggests that children are differentially distracted by some environmental stimuli or tasks but not others, and that they are distracted in some settings but not others (Tarver & Hallahan, 1974). Relating to the task variable, tasks that require a high degree of voluntary attention or those characterized as being less interesting to the child such as attending to a math or reading lesson are more likely to elicit distractible behavior than those tasks that require a low degree of voluntary attention such as playing with toys or drawing a picture of the child's choice. A difference also exists between auditory and visual tasks in the amount of distractibility that may be induced. In addition, a distraction that is more central to a task is more likely to interfere with a child's performance than a distraction that is more peripheral (Ricks & Mirsky, 1974). For example, children working independently at their desks completing reading worksheets are more likely to be distracted by the oral reading of a small reading group across the room than by a classmate sitting next to them jostling papers. The setting is also an important interacting variable in the eliciting of distractible behavior. A child may be distracted by a certain stimulus in one setting but not in another. For example, the noise from an overhead fluorescent light may distract a child in art class but not during math. The degree of structure provided in a particular setting is also related to the eliciting of distractible behavior, with distractibility more likely to occur in more unstructured settings.

Various characteristics of the child are also associated with whether distractible behavior occurs. The very same task and distracting stimuli in the identical setting may elicit distractible behaviors in one child but not another. Based on teacher and parent ratings in the home and classroom and observations during individual testing sessions, children with a wide variety of learning handicaps are found to exhibit greater distractibility than their nonhandicapped peers (Krupski, 1981). These groups include all functioning levels of the mentally retarded (Zigler, 1973), low achievers (Soli & Devine, 1976), and children with centrencephalic epilepsy (Campanelli, 1970). Distractibility is often associated with hyperactivity. However, investigators (Douglas, 1972, 1974) have failed to support the assumption that all hyperactive children are distractible.

The presumed causes of distractibility are many and varied. There exists some evidence for a developmental trend in distractibility, with children becoming less distractible as they grow older (Well, Lorch, & Anderson, 1980). Distractibility in boys has also been associated with congenital characteristics such as minor physical anomalies as well as gross motor incoordination (O'Donnell, O'Neill, & Staley, 1979). Other suspected etiologies include metabolic disturbances interacting with diet (Wunderlich, 1981), gross brain damage or an underlying neurological condition such as minimal brain dysfunction, and environmental variables such as child-rearing practices. Ross (1976) postulates that distractibility is due to a delayed development in selective attention.

Selective attention refers to a child's age-appropriate ability to focus on relevant information in the environment while excluding irrelevant or distracting information. As a child is listening to a teacher-directed lesson in the classroom, numerous stimuli impinge on the child's senses such as the noise from the overhead lights, the child's classmate across the row shifting in his or her chair, or a feeling of hunger. In order for the child to learn and attend to the teacher, the child must screen out all the irrelevant stimuli and focus on the relevant stimuli. The ability to screen out the irrelevant while focusing on the relevant stimuli requires selective attention.

Although there exists wide agreement that attention/distractibility and learning are strongly related, the precise nature of this relationship remains unclear. Distractibility has been demonstrated to negatively affect memory (Torgesen, 1981), and achievement in arithmetic and reading (Stedman, Lawlis, & Cortner, 1978). The exhibiting of distractible behaviors also affects adult behavior, with distractible children eliciting greater amounts of attention and instruction from adults in a one-to-one setting but less attention and interaction in a group setting (Ianna, Hallahan, & Bell, 1982). Distractibility typically occurs following head trauma in children and in adults.

The most common types of interventions for distractibility are pharmacotherapy, consisting of the administration of stimulant medication such as Ritalin and Mellaril (Gadow, 1981), and behavior-management techniques. Behavior-management techniques include making rewards contingent on attentive behaviors and cognitive behavioral interventions such as self-instruction, self-correction, and self-monitoring (Kneedler & Hallahan, 1981). Other types of interventions have included reducing distracting input by environmental modifications such as changing the seating arrangement (Sandoval, 1982), having youngsters work in plain, nonstimulating cubicles, changing the student's diet (Wunderlich, 1981), and introducing sensory integrative therapy, which involves gross, fine and visual-motor activities (Ainsa, 1983). Although all of these interventions have enjoyed some success, the most successful are pharmacotherapy and behavior management. Further, although these two types of interventions have often reduced distractibility in particular children, they frequently do not produce increases in learning unless they are combined with increased direct academic instruction.

## REFERENCES

Ainsa, T. (1983). Sensory integration: A home intervention program. *Academic Therapy, 18,* 495–498.

Bryan, T. S. (1974). An observational analysis of classroom behaviors of children with learning disabilities. *Journal of Learning Disabilities, 7,* 35–43.

Capanelli, P. (1970). Sustained attention in brain damaged children. *Exceptional Children, 36,* 317–323.

Cruickshank, W. M., Bentzen, F. A., Ratzeburg, F. H., & Tannhauser, R. (1961). *A teaching method for brain-injured and hyperactive children.* Syracuse, NY: Syracuse University Press.

Douglas, V. I. (1972). Stop, look and listen: The problem of sustained attention and impulse control in hyperactive and normal children. *Canadian Journal of Behavioral Science, 4,* 259–282.

Douglas, V. I. (1974). Sustained attention and impulse control: Implications for the handicapped child. In J. A. Swets & L. L. Elliott (Eds.), *Psychology and the handicapped child* (DHEW, Pub. No. (OE) 73-05000). Washington, DC: U.S. Department of Education and Welfare.

Gadow, K. (1981). Effects of stimulant drugs on attention and cognitive deficits. *Exceptional Child Quarterly, 2*(3), 83–93.

Goyette, C. H., Connors, C. K., & Ulrich, R. F. (1978). Normative data on revised Connors parent and teacher rating scales. *Journal of Abnormal and Child Psychology, 6,* 221–236.

Hewett, F. M., Taylor, F. D., & Artuso, D. A. (1969). The Santa Monica Project. Evaluation of an engineered classroom design with emotionally disturbed children. *Exceptional Children, 33,* 523–529.

Ianna, S. O., Hallahan, D. P., & Bell, R. Q. (1982). The effects of distractible child behavior on adults in a problem-solving setting. *Learning Disabilities Quarterly, 5,* 126–132.

Kaufman, A. S. (1979). *Intelligent testing with the WISC-R.* New York: Wiley.

Kneedler, R. D., & Hallahan, D. P. (1981). Self-monitoring of on-task behavior with learning-disabled children: Current studies and directions. *Exceptional Child Quarterly, 2*(3), 73–82.

Krupski, A. (1981, Aug.). *Variations in attention as a function of classroom task demands.* Paper presented at the meeting of the American Psychological Association, Los Angeles, CA.

Milich, R., Loney, J., & Landau, S. (1982). Independent dimensions of hypractivity and aggression: A validation with playroom observation data. *Journal of Abnormal Psychology, 91,* 183–198.

O'Donnell, J. P., O'Neill, S. O., & Staley, A. (1979). Congenital correlates of distractibility. *Journal of Abnormal Child Psychology, 7,* 465–470.

Ricks, N. L., & Mirsky, A. F. (1974). Sustained attention and the effects of distraction in underachieving second grade children. *Journal of Education, 156,* 4–17.

Ross, A. O. (1976). *Psychological aspects of learning disabilities and reading disorders.* New York: McGraw-Hill.

Sandoval, J. (1982). Hypreactive children. 12 Ways to help them in the classroom. *Academic Therapy, 18,* 107–113.

Soli, S. D., & Devine, V. T. (1976). Behavioral correlates of achievements: A look at high and low achievers. *Journal of Educational Psychology, 68,* 335–341.

Stedman, J. M., Lawlis, G. F., & Cortner, R. H. (1978). Relationships between WISC-R factors, Wide Range Achievement Test scores, and visual-motor maturation in children referred for psychological evaluation. *Journal of Consulting & Clinical Psychology, 46,* 869–872.

Tarver, S. G., & Hallahan, D. P. (1974). Attention deficits in children with learning disabilities: A review. *Journal of Learning Disabilities, 1,* 560–569.

Torgesen, J. K. (1981). Relationship between memory and attention in learning disabilities. *Exceptional Child Quarterly, 2*(3), 51–59.

Well, A. D., Lorch, E. P., & Anderson, D. R. (1980). Developmental trends in distractibility: Is absolute or proportional decrement the appropriate measure of interference? *Journal of Experimental Child Psychology, 30,* 109–124.

Whalen, C. K. (1983). Hyperactivity, learning problems, and the attention deficit disorders. In T. H. Ollendick & M. Hersen (Eds.), *Handbook of child psychopathology* (pp. 151–199). New York: Plenum.

Wunderlich, R. C. (1981). Nutrition and learning. *Academic Therapy, 16,* 303–307.

Zigler, C. (1973). Why retarded children do not perform up to the level of their ability. In R. M. Allen, A. D. Cortazzo, & R. P. Toister (Eds.), *Theories of cognitive development: Implications for the mentally retarded* (pp. 13–35). Coral Cables, FL: University of Miami Press.

MARK E. SWERDLIK
*Illinois State University*

## ATTENTION DEFICIT DISORDER

CONNORS RATING SCALE
HYPERKINESIS
IMPULSE CONTROL
WECHSLER INTELLIGENCE SCALE FOR CHILDREN—
  REVISED

## DIVORCE AND SPECIAL EDUCATION

Since the mid 1970s, the impact of parental divorce on children has been an area of primary concern for professionals in psychology and education. This interdisciplinary consensus has been generated in part by alarming Census descriptions of rapidly changing adult lifestyles. For example, Census reports indicate that the divorce rate more than doubled from 1970 to 1981 and more than tripled from 1960 to 1981. Since these figures do not account for those who were divorced and remarried at the time of the survey, they actually underestimate the total incidence of divorce in our society. Similarly, the incidence of single-parent child rearing has also increased markedly, from 11.9% in 1970 to 22.5% in 1983. These figures do not include those who have previously experienced a single-parent situation but are now living in reconstituted two-parent families. Single-parent families resulting specifically from divorce and separation have increased by 111% from 1970 to 1983; in 1983, 90% of one-parent families were headed by mothers (U.S. Bureau of the Census, 1979, 1982a, 1982b, 1984). Projecting future trends, Glick and Norton (1977) estimate that if these levels of divorce continue, 40% of current marriages will end in divorce. Hetherington (1979) projects that 40 to 50% of children born in the past decade will spend some time living in a single-parent family.

Practitioners have also been sensitized by firsthand experience in clinics and schools where maladaptive child behaviors and poor school performance appear with disproportionate frequency among children from divorced households. However, professionals in these applied settings have received limited help from researchers, who have only recently begun to study the relationship between divorce and subsequent child adjustment.

A central issue is whether adjustment to divorce represents a transitory stressor or is associated with long-term disorders. Longitudinal studies provide a consensus that divorce should be conceptualized as a multistage process (Hetherington, Cox, & Cox, 1978, 1985; Wallerstein, 1985; Wallerstein & Kelly, 1974). These studies, conducted over periods of 6 and 10 years, respectively, reveal complex interactions and altered family relationships that result in long-term maladjustment for children. They also illustrate substantial age and sex differences in adjustment.

Wallerstein and Kelly (Kelly & Wallerstein, 1976; Wallerstein, 1984, 1985; Wallerstein & Kelly, 1974, 1975, 1976, 1980a, 1980b) conducted a 10-year longitudinal study of 131 children residing in Marin County, California, whose parents were divorced. This was a nonclinical sample of children, ages 2½ to 18 years, from white, middle-class families. Clinical interviews were conducted just after separation, and at 1-, 5-, and 10-year intervals following divorce. Initial results revealed that children responded differently by age. At the 1-year follow-up, adjustment problems persisted, although most adolescents had made adequate adjustments (attributed to distancing from parents and successful mastery experiences during the past year). At the 5-year follow-up, variables that mediate children's adjustment to divorce were identified—resolution of parental conflict, child's relationship with noncustodial parent, quality of parenting by custodial parent, personality and coping skills of the child, child's support system, diminished anger and depression in the child, and age and sex of the child. A positive relationship with the father was more important for boys than girls. Results of the 10-year follow-up (of 113 original subjects) confirmed the long-term impact of divorce. Difficulties at 10 years were characterized by poor parenting (diminished capacity to parent) and an overburdened child (taking on of adult responsibility).

Hetherington, Cox, and Cox (Hetherington, 1979; Hetherington, Cox, & Cox, 1978, 1979a, 1979b, 1982, 1985) used a sample of 96 divorced- and intact-family preschool-age children from white, middle-class families in Virginia. Children were assessed at 2 months, and 1, 2, and 6 years after divorce. A comprehensive, multifactored, multisource approach to assessment was used to assess sex-role typing and cognitive and social development of the child.

Results indicated severe disorganization and stress during the first year. Difficulties were evident in parenting behavior and child adjustment. Divorced parents were less able than nondivorced parents to cope with parenting. They made fewer maturity demands, were less consistent in discipline, used less reasoning, communicated less with the child, and displayed less interaction with and affection toward the child. Children were more dependent, disobedient, aggressive, demanding, unaffectionate, and whining. Mother-son relationships were particularly affected, characterized by a cycle of poor parenting, child aggression, coercive parenting, increased negative child behavior, and parental feelings of helplessness and incompetence. By 2 years, most of the negative effects had abated. Factors that facilitated adjustment included low parental conflict and parental agreement on child rearing. Results at 6 years (which included a remarried sample) indicated that divorce had a more negative impact on boys and remarriage had a more negative impact on girls. Externalizing problems were more stable across time for boys and internalizing problems more stable for girls. Divorced-family children experienced more negative life changes, which were, in turn, related to more behavior problems at follow-up.

Kurdek et al. (Kurdek, 1981, 1983, 1985, in press; Kurdek & Berg, 1983; Kurdek, Blisk, & Siesky, 1981; Kurdek & Siesky, 1980a, 1980b; Kurdek & Sinclair, 1985) examined the role of cognitive mediators in children's adjustment to divorce. Their initial study included a sample of 70 divorced-family children, mean age of 9.92 years, from white middle-class families in Dayton, Ohio, whose parents were members of Parents Without Partners. Results revealed that children's adjustment to divorce was facilitated by an internal locus of control, accurate perceptions of social situations (i.e., understanding of interpersonal relations), low interpersonal stress, and good father-child relationships. They found that children's reasoning about divorce was linked to the development of logical and social reasoning. Further, level of cognitive understanding determined whether the child's thinking about divorce was nonegocentric; focused on parents' thoughts, feelings, and intentions; and was grounded in an appreciation of the complex dynamics of interpersonal relations.

Using a national sample of 18,000 elementary and secondary students from 14 states, Brown (1980) compared one-parent (divorced, separated, widowed, unmarried) and two-parent families. Global measures of adjustment such as grade point average, attendance, suspensions, truancy, and referral for discipline problems were obtained from school records. Findings indicated that the impact for elementary-aged children was evident on behavioral (e.g., suspensions and truancy) and academic indexes. For high-school children, differences were evident on behavioral indexes (e.g., expulsions, tardiness, suspensions); however, there appeared to be little impact on academic achievement.

The research of Stolberg et al. (Stolberg, in press; Stolberg & Anker, 1983; Stolberg & Bush, 1985; Stolberg & Cullen, 1983; Stolberg, Kiluk, & Garrison, in press) has focused on environmental factors that mediate children's adjustment to divorce, including such factors as parenting skills, visitation, and family changes associated with divorce. Local samples obtained through Parents Without Partners, newspaper ads, and schools were used. They found parenting skills, frequency of life changes, and marital hostility to be successful predictors of prosocial skills and psychopathology of divorced-family children. Parenting skills (of the mother/custodial parent) were found to be the single most significant influence on child adjustment, particularly affecting prosocial skills. There was no direct relationship between parent and child adjustment when effects of parenting skills were removed.

Furstenberg et al. (Furstenberg et al., 1983; Furstenberg & Spanier, 1984) used data from a national sociological study of children's well being. The representative sample included 1300 U.S. children (ages 11 to 16) and their families, and subsequent subsamples of divorced and remarried families. Findings from this study revealed a racial difference in divorce and remarriage rates, with blacks one and a half times as likely to divorce but less

likely to remarry than whites (remarriage rate: one out of eight for blacks, four out of seven for whites). Frequent contact (at least once per week) of the child with the noncustodial parent was evident in only 17% of the divorced sample. Those variables that best predicted amount of contact with the noncustodial parent, irrespective of the child's sex, included provision of child support and residential propinquity, which were positively related to amount of contact, and length of time since separation, which was negatively related.

Findings from other studies relevant to determinants of children's postdivorce adjustment indicate that adjustment is facilitated by availability of the noncustodial parent and a positive relationship with the custodial parent (Hess & Camara, 1979); parent-child discussion of divorce-related topics (Jacobson, 1978a, 1978b); low interpersonal hostility prior to separation (Berg & Kelly, 1979; Jacobson, 1978a, 1978b, 1978c); and more time spent with the father (Jacobson, 1978a, 1978c).

In reviewing the literature on remarriage, Kurdek and Sinclair (1985) conclude that similarities exist between children's adjustment to divorce and to remarriage in that children from both situations (compared with those in intact families) exhibit higher deviance rates, more difficulty in management, and lower self-esteem, as do their parents. Although findings are conflicting, past research generally indicates that (1) remarriage does not necessarily stabilize the family; (2) children reexperience the disruption associated with divorce when parents remarry; and (3) the parent's situation in reference to role strain does not necessarily improve with remarriage.

Critical reviews of past research have consistently indicated severe methodological limitations (Atkeson, Forehand, & Rickard, 1982; Clingempeel & Reppucci, 1982; Kurdek, 1981, 1983). Major limitations include (1) small and biased samples that limit generalizability of the findings; (2) inadequate or nonexistent control groups, which precludes the study of divorce-specific effects; (3) failure to control for socioeconomic status in comparisons between divorced and intact families; and (4) failure to include multimethod, multifactored criteria to control for measurement bias.

The NASP-KSU (National Association of School Psychologists—Kent State University) Impact of Divorce Project was directed at minimizing the limitations of the cited research in order to provide more definitive conclusions about the long-term impact of divorce on children (Guidubaldi, 1983, in press; Guidubaldi & Cleminshaw, 1985; Guidubaldi, Cleminshaw, & Perry, 1985; Guidubaldi, Cleminshaw, Perry, & Mcloughlin, 1983; Guidubaldi, Cleminshaw, Perry, & Nastasi, 1984; Guidubaldi, Cleminshaw, Perry, Nastasi, & Lightel, 1986; Guidubaldi & Nastasi, 1984; Guidubaldi & Perry, 1985, in press; Guidubaldi, Perry, & Cleminshaw, 1984; Guidubaldi, Perry, & Nastasi, in press). Results on 699 children from 38 states at the initial data-gathering period (Time-1) demonstrated more conclusively than previous studies that, during middle childhood (ages 6 to 11), youths are adversely affected by divorce. Because the average length of time in a single-parent home at Time-1 was 3.98 years (sd = 2.54), these effects were interpreted as long term. Specific criteria on which children from divorced homes performed more poorly than those from intact homes are as follows: (1) social-behavioral measures from parent and teacher ratings of peer popularity status, anxiety, dependency, aggression, withdrawal, inattention, and locus of control; (2) Wechsler IQ scores; (3) Wide Range Achievement Test scores in reading, spelling, and math; (4) school performance indexes, including grades in reading and math and repeating of a school grade; (5) adaptive behaviors (measured by the Vineland Teacher Rating Scale) in the areas of daily living, social skills, and communication; and (6) physical health ratings of the children in the study as well as of parents and siblings. Intact-family children showed superior performance on 21 of 27 social competence criteria and 8 of 9 academic competence criteria. Additionally, analyses revealed that divorced-family children were far more likely to have been previously referred to a school psychologist, to have been retained in grade, and to be in special class placements, including programs for reading difficulties.

Definition of the sequelae of divorce is a complex process, and assessment must therefore include not only multidimensional aspects of child and parent adjustment but also a longitudinal-ecological approach. The NASP-KSU study thus included follow-up samples of 229 children at 2- and 3-year intervals, and examined environmental factors as mediators of children's postdivorce adjustment. Major findings from this nationwide study are as follows:

1. The negative, differential effects of divorce on children and young adolescents are long term where the average length of time since divorce was 6.41 years (sd = 2.35) at Time-2 of this study.

2. Children's reactions to divorce are especially influenced by sex and age, with boys during late childhood and early adolescence being more adversely affected on multiple criteria than 6- and 7-year-old boys. Late childhood and young adolescent girls were much better adjusted than those at the 6- and 7-year age levels.

3. Single-parent, divorced-family households have significantly less income than intact families. This difference accounts for significant academic achievement variance between divorced- and intact-family children.

4. The socioeconomic measures of parents' educational and occupational levels moderate some of children's divorce adjustment. This is especially apparent in regard to the educational level of the same sex parent.

5. A positive relationship with both the custodial and noncustodial parent predicted positive adjustment for both girls and boys of divorce concurrently and across time. The noncustodial parent-child relationship was noticeably more important for boys.

6. More frequent and reliable visitation with the noncustodial parent (typically, the father) was associated with better adjustment for both girls and boys.

7. Diminished degree of conflict between parents predicted improved children's adjustment, especially for boys across time to early adolescence.

8. Authoritarian (i.e., punitive) child-rearing styles in comparison with authoritative (i.e., more democratic) and permissive styles predicted more adverse child adjustment, especially for boys.

9. The home routines of less television viewing, regular bedtimes, maternal employment, and helpfulness of maternal grandfather predict positive adjustment for both boys and girls.

10. Family support factors that promote positive postdivorce adjustment are availability of helpful relatives, including in-laws, availability of friends, paid child care assistance such as nursery schools and babysitters, and participation in occupational and educational endeavors by the custodial parent.

11. When the total sample of male and female divorced-family children are considered, school environment variables of smaller school population, safe and orderly atmosphere, fewer miles bused to school, and traditional rather than open classroom structure are associated with better adjustment. However, several school and classroom climate factors relate to better adjustment for girls only. These include safe and orderly environment, frequent monitoring of student progress, high expectations for academic achievement, and time on task.

The impact of divorce on children has appropriately become a central concern of mainstreamed education. Special educators perhaps need to focus even more on this rapidly increasing disruption of children's lives. As evidenced in the NASP-KSU nationwide study, children in special education programs disproportionately come from divorced, single-parent homes. Income levels, home routines, and parental supports are adversely affected by this condition and children from these homes, particularly boys, show overwhelming evidence of maladjustment in both academic and social-emotional areas of performance. Understanding conditions that can ameliorate the negative impact of divorce on children may be one of the most critical bases for development of preventive mental health interventions as well as remedial techniques for children already identified as special.

## REFERENCES

Atkeson, B. M., Forehand, R. L., & Rickard, K. M. (1982). The effects of divorce on children. In B. B. Lahey & A. E. Kazdin

(Eds.), *Advances in clinical child psychology* (Vol. 5). New York: Plenum.

Baumrind, D. (1972). Socialization and instrumental competence in young children. In I. B. Weiner & D. Elkind (Eds.), *Readings in child development* (pp. 178–195). New York: Wiley.

Berg, B., & Kelly, R. (1979). The measured self-esteem of children from broken, rejected, and accepted families. *Journal of Divorce, 2*, 263–369.

Brown, B. F. (1980). A study of the school needs of children from one-parent families. *Phi Delta Kappan, 62*, 537–540.

Clingempeel, W. G., & Reppucci, N. D. (1982). Joint custody after divorce: Major issues and goals for research. *Psychological Bulletin, 91*, 102–127.

Furstenberg, F. F., Nord, C. W., Peterson, J. L., & Zill, N. (1983). The life course of children of divorce: Marital disruption and parental contact. *American Sociological Review, 48*, 656–668.

Furstenberg, F. F., & Spanier, G. B. (1984). *Recycling the family*. Beverly Hills, CA: Sage.

Glick, P. C., & Norton, A. J. (1977). Marrying, divorcing and living together in the U.S. today. *Population Bulletin, 5*, 32.

Guidubaldi, J. (1983, July). Divorce research clarifies issues: A report on NASP's nationwide study. *Communique, 10*, 1–3.

Guidubaldi, J. (in press). Differences in children's divorce adjustment across grade level and gender: A report from the NASP-Kent State University Nationwide Project. In S. Wolchik & P. Karoly (Eds.), *Children of divorce: Perspectives on adjustment*. Lexington, MA: Lexington.

Guidubaldi, J., & Cleminshaw, H. (1985). Divorce, family health and child adjustment. *Family Relations, 34*, 35–41.

Guidubaldi, J., Cleminshaw, H., & Perry, J. (1985). The relationship of parental divorce to health status of parents and children. *Special Services in the Schools, 1*, 73–81.

Guidubaldi, J., Cleminshaw, H. K., Perry, J. D., & Mcloughlin, C. S. (1983). The impact of parental divorce on children: Report of the nationwide NASP study. *School Psychology Review, 12*, 300–323.

Guidubaldi, J., Cleminshaw, H. K., Perry, J., & Nastasi, B. (1984). Impact of family support systems on children's academic and social functioning after divorce. In G. Rowe, J. DeFrain, H. Lingrin, R. MacDonald, N. Stinnet, S. Van Zandt, & R. Williams (Eds.), *Family strengths 5: Continuity and diversity* (pp. 191–207). Newton, MA: Education Development Center.

Guidubaldi, J., Cleminshaw, H. K., Perry, J. D., Nastasi, B. K., & Lightel, J. (1986). The role of selected family environment factors in children's post-divorce adjustment. *Family Relations, 35*, 141–151.

Guidubaldi, J., & Nastasi, B. (1984, April). Classroom climate and post-divorce child adjustment. In J. Guidubaldi (Chair), *Factors related to academic and social adjustment of elementary grade divorced-family children*. Symposium conducted at the annual convention of the American Educational Research Association, New Orleans.

Guidubaldi, J., & Perry, J. D. (1985). Divorce and mental health sequelae for children: A two-year follow-up of a nationwide sample. *Journal of the American Academy of Child Psychiatry, 24*, 531–537.

Guidubaldi, J., & Perry, J. D. (in press). Assessment of adolescents' divorce adjustment and custody arrangements. In R. G.

Harrington (Ed.), *Testing adolescents*. Kansas City: Test Corporation of America.

Guidubaldi, J., Perry, J. D., & Cleminshaw, H. K. (1984). The legacy of parental divorce: A nationwide study of family status and selected mediating variables on children's academic and social competencies. In B. B. Lahey & A. E. Kazdin (Eds.), *Advances in clinical child psychology* (Vol. 7, pp. 109–151). New York: Plenum.

Guidubaldi, J., Perry, J. D., & Nastasi, B. K. (in press). Growing up in a divorced family: Initial and long-term perspectives on children's adjustment. In S. Oskamp (Ed.), *Annual review of social psychology*, Beverly Hills, CA: Sage.

Hess, R. D., & Camara, K. A. (1979). Post-divorce family relationships as mediating factors in the consequences of divorce for children. *Journal of Social Issues, 35*(4), 79–96.

Hetherington, E. M. (1979). Divorce: A child's perspective. *American Psychologist, 34*, 851–858.

Hetherington, E. M., Cox, M., & Cox, R. (1978). The aftermath of divorce. In J. H. Stevens, Jr., & M. Mathews (Eds.), *Mother-child, father-child relationships* (pp. 149–176). Washington, DC: National Association for Education of Young Children.

Hetherington, E. M., Cox, M., & Cox, R. (1979a). Family interaction and the social-emotional and cognitive development of children following divorce. In V. Vaughn & T. Brazelton (Eds.), *The family setting priorities*. New York: Science and Medicine.

Hetherington, E. M., Cox, M., & Cox, R. (1979b). Play and social interaction in children following divorce. *Journal of Social Issues, 35*, 26–49.

Hetherington, E. M., Cox, M., & Cox, R. (1982). Effects of divorce on parents and children. In M. E. Lamb (Ed.), *Nontraditional families: Parenting and child development* (pp. 233–288). Hillsdale, NJ: Erlbaum.

Hetherington, E. M., Cox, M., & Cox, R. (1985). Long-term effects of divorce and remarriage on the adjustment of children. *Journal of the American Academy of Child Psychiatry, 24*, 518–530.

Jacobson, D. S. (1978a). The impact of marital separation/divorce on children. I. Parent-child separation and child adjustment. *Journal of Divorce, 1*(4), 341–360.

Jacobson, D. S. (1978b). The impact of marital separation/divorce on children: II. Interparent hostility and child adjustment. *Journal of Divorce, 2*, 3–19.

Jacobson, D. S. (1978c). The impact of marital separation/divorce on children: III. Parent-child communication and child adjustment, and regression analysis of findings from overall study. *Journal of Divorce, 2*, 175–194.

Kelly, J. B., & Wallerstein, J. S. (1976). The effects of parental divorce: Experiences of the child in early latency. *American Journal of Orthopsychiatry, 46*, 20–23.

Kurdek, L. A. (1981). An integrative perspective on children's divorce adjustment. *American Psychologist, 36*, 856–866.

Kurdek, L. A. (Ed.). (1983). *Children and divorce*. San Francisco: Jossey-Bass.

Kurdek, L. A. (1985). Children's reasoning about parental divorce. In R. D. Ashmore & D. M. Brodzinsky (Eds.), *Perspectives on the family* (pp. 1–48). Hillsdale, NJ: Erlbaum.

Kurdek, L. A. (in press). Cognitive mediators of children's adjustment to divorce. In S. Wolchick & D. Karoly (Eds.), *Chil-*

*dren of divorce: Perspectives on adjustment.* New York: Gardner.

Kurdek, L. A., & Berg, B. (1983). Correlates of children's adjustment to their parents' divorces. In L. A. Kurdek (Ed.), *Children and divorce* (pp. 47–60). San Francisco: Jossey-Bass.

Kurdek, L. A., Blisk, D., & Siesky, A. E. (1981). Correlates of children's long-term adjustment to their parents' divorce. *Developmental Psychology, 17,* 565–579.

Kurdek, L. A., & Siesky, A. E. (1980a). Sex role self-concepts of single divorced parents and their children. *Journal of Divorce, 3,* 249–261.

Kurdek, L. A., & Siesky, A. E. (1980b). Children's perceptions of their parents' divorce. *Journal of Divorce, 3,* 339–378.

Kurdek, L. A., & Sinclair, R. (1985). *The relation between adolescent adjustment and family structure, grade, and gender.* Unpublished manuscript, Wright State University, Department of Psychology, Dayton, OH.

Stolberg, A. L. (in press). Prevention programs for divorcing families. In L. Bond (Ed.), *Vermont Conference on the Primary Prevention of Psychopathology.*

Stolberg, A., & Anker, J. (1983). Cognitive and behavioral changes in children resulting from parental divorce and consequent environmental changes. *Journal of Divorce, 7,* 23–41.

Stolberg, A. L., & Bush, J. P. (1985). A path analysis of factors predicting children's divorce adjustment. *Journal of Clinical Child Psychology, 14,* 49–54.

Stolberg, A. L., & Cullen, P. M. (1983). Preventive interventions for families of divorce: Divorce Adjustment Project. In L. A. Kurdek (Ed.), *Children and divorce* (pp. 71–82). San Francisco: Jossey-Bass.

Stolberg, A. L., Kiluk, D., & Garrison, K. M. (in press). A temporal model of divorce adjustment with implications for primary prevention. In S. M. Auerbach & A. L. Stolberg (Eds.), *Issues in clinical and community psychology: Crisis intervention with children and families.* Washington, DC: Hemisphere.

U.S. Bureau of the Census. (1979). *Divorce, child custody, and child support* (Current Population Reports, Series P-23, No. 84). Washington, DC: U.S. Government Printing Office.

U.S. Bureau of the Census. (1982a). *Household and family characteristics: March 1981* (Current Population Reports, Series P-20, No. 371). Washington, DC: U.S. Government Printing Office.

U.S. Bureau of the Census. (1982b). *Marital status and living arrangements: March 1981* (Current Population Reports, Series P-20, No. 372). Washington, DC: U.S. Government Printing Office.

U.S. Bureau of the Census. (1984). *Marital status and living arrangements: March 1983* (Current Population Reports, Series P-20). Washington, DC: U.S. Government Printing Office.

Wallerstein, J. S. (1984). Children of divorce: Preliminary report of a ten-year follow-up of young children. *American Journal of Orthopsychiatry, 54,* 444–453.

Wallerstein, J. S. (1985). Children of divorce: Preliminary report of a ten-year follow-up of older children and adolescents. *Journal of the American Academy of Child Psychiatry, 24,* 545–553.

Wallerstein, J. S., & Kelly, J. B. (1974). The effects of parental divorce: The adolescent experience. In E. Anthony & C. Kou-panik (Eds.), *The child and his family* (Vol. 3, pp. 479–505). New York: Wiley.

Wallerstein, J. S., & Kelly, J. B. (1975). The effects of parental divorce: Experiences of the preschool child. *Journal of the American Academy of Child Psychiatry, 14,* 600–616.

Wallerstein, J. S., & Kelly, J. B. (1976). The effects of parental divorce experiences of the child in later latency. *American Journal of Orthopsychiatry, 46,* 256–267.

Wallerstein, J. S., & Kelly, J. B. (1980a). California's children of divorce. *Psychology Today, 13,* 66–67.

Wallerstein, J. S., & Kelly, J. B. (1980b). *Surviving the break-up: How children and parents cope with divorce.* New York: Basic Books.

JOHN GUIDUBALDI
BONNIE K. NASTASI
*Kent State University*

## DIX, DOROTHEA L. (1802–1887)

Dorothea Dix, a humanitarian and social reformer, was responsible for major reforms in the care of the mentally ill in the United States and abroad. Shocked by the common practice of incarcerating mentally ill people in jails with criminals, she spent a year and a half investigating conditions in her home state of Massachusetts and, in 1843, reported her findings to the state legislature. Her description of the abhorrent conditions that existed (including the use of chains for restraint) and her argument that mentally ill persons could be properly treated and cared for only in hospitals, resulted in substantial enlargement of the state hospital at Worcester, which was one of only eight mental hospitals in the United States at that time. Capitalizing on her success in Massachusetts,

**Dorthea L. Dix**

Dix turned her attention to other states and countries. She was responsible for the construction of 32 hospitals in the United States and others in Canada, Europe, and Japan.

During the Civil War, Dix served as superintendent of women nurses, the highest office held by a woman during the war. After the war she returned, at age 65, to her work with hospitals. In 1881 she retired to the New Jersey State Hospital at Trenton, the first hospital established through her efforts, where she remained until her death.

## REFERENCE

Marshall, H. E. (1937). *Dorothea Dix, forgotten samaritan.* Chapel Hill, NC: University of North Carolina Press.

PAUL IRVINE
*Katonah, New York*

## DOCTORAL TRAINING IN SPECIAL EDUCATION

Over 80 special education programs in colleges and universities in the United States award the doctoral degree (Sindelar & Schloss, 1986). The common purpose of these programs is to prepare leaders for the field, but the programs themselves are as diverse as the roles their graduates assume. Many local, state, and federal administrators, college and university teacher trainers, scholars, and researchers hold the doctorate in special education. Both the doctor of philosophy (PhD) and the doctor of education (DEd or EdD) are awarded. Although the PhD is considered an academic degree and the DEd a professional degree, this distinction does not hold up in practice because many prominent scholars hold the DEd and many practitioners the PhD.

Students are typically selected for doctoral training on the basis of their potential for success in advanced graduate training and the potential they exhibit as special education leaders. Programs frequently use the previous academic achievement of their applicants and Graduate Record Examination scores (or both) to predict success in advanced graduate work. Leadership potential is evaluated through previous professional experience, professional references, and, occasionally, statements of professional goals (by which the seriousness of an applicant's intent may be judged). Typically, admission is competitive.

A program of study is planned under the direction of an advisor (or major professor) and a supervisory committee. The program typically derives from the aspirations of the student and the strengths of the program offerings. In addition to special education course work, doctoral programs may include concentrations in a related field of study or cognate area and work in research methodology and statistics. The successful completion of coursework, however, represents only a fraction of the formal requirements that a doctoral candidate must meet. Many programs require a qualifying examination before formal admission to candidacy and, later in the program, a comprehensive examination to determine mastery of the program of studies. Doctoral programs culminate with the completion of an independent research project and the preparation and defense of the dissertation. The supervisory committee evaluates the student's performance at each of these checkpoints.

These formal requirements represent only part of what students learn during their doctoral studies. Many have the opportunity (often as graduate assistants) to develop skills in teaching, supervision, administration, and research. Initially, their participation in these activities is guided by the faculty. With experience, candidates may take on more responsibility and operate with greater independence. Many programs provide financial support for graduate assistants with funds from leadership preparation grants awarded by the U.S. Department of Education's Office of Special Education and Rehabilitative Services.

The importance of these informal experiences in the full preparation of doctoral students was established in an analysis of the credentials of recent graduates. Rose, Cullinan, and Heller (1984) reported that recent graduates who were considered competitive applicants for college and university positions had published at least three articles, presented more than four papers at national conferences, written or assisted in the writing of two grant applications, taught at least one course independently, and conducted numerous workshops and consultancies. Clearly, there is much to be accomplished beyond the formal requirements of a doctoral program for its graduates to compete successfully in the academic job market.

Finally, it must be emphasized that leadership preparation programs have undertaken a critical self-evaluation in response to the common and difficult problems they face: the quantity and quality of students, the poor focus of their offerings, faculty dissatisfaction, and low faculty productivity (Prehm, 1984). With regard to this final concern, recent research (Schloss & Sindelar, in press) has shown that productive researchers are the exception and not the rule, even for faculties of doctoral-granting programs. The recent efforts of the Higher Education Consortium for Special Education, an organization representing institutions with comprehensive programs in special education, in developing indicators of quality in leadership training represent a positive first step in addressing these issues.

## REFERENCES

Prehm, H. J. (1984). Preparation for leadership in personnel preparation. *Teacher Education & Special Education*, 7, 59–65.

Rose, T. L., Cullinan, D., & Heller, H. W. (1984). A consumer's report of special education doctoral programs. *Teacher Education & Special Education, 7*, 88–91.

Schloss, P. J., & Sindelar, P. T. (in press). Publication frequencies of departments conferring the PhD in special education. *Teacher Education and Special Education.*

Sindelar, P. T., & Schloss, P. J. (1986). The reputations of doctoral training program in special education. *Journal of Special Education, 20*, 49–59.

PAUL T. SINDELAR
*Florida State University*

## SUPERVISION IN SPECIAL EDUCATION
## SPECIAL NET
## TEACHER CENTERS

## DOG GUIDES FOR THE BLIND

The use of dogs to guide blind persons has a long history. However, it was not until after World War I that the dog was systematically trained to guide blinded German veterans. The veterans were taught to follow the trained dog's movements through the use of a specially designed harness.

An American, Dorothy Harrison Eustis, living in Switzerland, described the use of German shepherds as dog guides for the blind in a 1927 article published in the *Saturday Evening Post*. One of the Americans who got in touch with Eustis after the publication of the article was Morris Frank, a young man from Tennessee who had been recently blinded. He persuaded Eustis to have a dog trained for him and traveled to Switzerland to be trained with the dog.

After Frank's success with the first American dog guide, the legendary Buddy, Eustis returned to the United States in 1929 and established The Seeing Eye Inc., the first school to train dog guides for the blind in America. The twenty-second edition of the American Foundation for the Blind *Directory of Agencies Serving the Blind in the United States* lists eight programs in the United States that prepare dog guides. There are similar training programs throughout the world.

The dog guide, because of a variety of limitations, provides mobility assistance to only about 1% of the blind population (Whitstock, 1980). Personal preferences, remaining vision, vocation, and life circumstances often dictate the advisability of the use of a dog guide. Very few school-aged visually impaired persons use dog guides, although the practice is not prohibited.

### REFERENCES

American Foundation for the Blind. (1984). *Directory of agencies serving the visually handicapped in the U.S.* (22nd ed.). New York: Author.

Whitstock, R. H. (1980). Dog guides. In R. L. Welsh & B. B. Blasch (Eds.), *Foundations of orientation and mobility*. New York: American Foundation for the Blind.

GIDEON JONES
*Florida State University*

## AMERICAN FOUNDATION FOR THE BLIND
## MOBILITY TRAINING

## DOLCH WORD LIST

The Dolch Word List of 220 common words constitutes over 65% of the words found in elementary reading materials and 50% of all reading materials (Dolch, 1960). These high-frequency words form the framework for all reading materials. The list, developed by Edward W. Dolch, includes prepositions, conjunctions, pronouns, adjectives, adverbs, and the most common verbs. There are no nouns included in this list since each noun, according to Dolch, is tied to subject matter (Johns, 1971). The list is comprised of structure words, words that hold language together, as opposed to content words.

The average third-grade reader should be able to identify these 220 service words at sight. Many of the words have irregular spellings and cannot be learned by picture cues. Dolch (1939) reports that if the reader is able to recognize more than half the words at the sight reading rate of 120 words per minute, he or she will have confidence and will be able focus on the meaning of the material.

The Dolch Word List is frequently used as a diagnostic tool to identify poor readers. Many retarded readers are deficient in recognizing and understanding the proper use of these words. The list also services as the basis of remedial instruction. Garrard Publishers produces several materials, Popper Words, Basic Sight Vocabulary Cards, and Basic Sight Word Test, based on the list.

### REFERENCES

Dolch, E. W. (1939). *A manual of remedial reading*. Champaign, IL: Garrard.

Dolch, E. W. (1960). *Teaching primary reading*. Champaign, IL: Garrard.

Johns, J. L. (1971). The Dolch Basic Word List—Then and now. *Journal of Reading Behavior, 3*, 35–40.

JOYCE E. NESS
*Montgomery County
Intermediate Unit,
Norristown, Pennsylvania*

## READING DISORDERS
## READING REMEDIATION

## DOLL, EDGAR A. (1889–1968)

Edgar A. Doll joined the staff of the Training School at Vineland, New Jersey, as research and clinical psychologist in 1913. There he worked with E. R. Johnstone and H. H. Goddard in the Vineland Laboratory: the first laboratory devoted solely to the study of mental retardation.

Following service in World War I, three years with New Jersey's State Department of Classification and Education, completion of the doctorate in psychology at Princeton University, and two years of teaching at Ohio State University, Doll returned to Vineland as director of research. His studies of social competence led to the publication, in 1935, of the *Vineland Social Maturity Scale*, a revolutionary instrument that provided an objective basis for measuring social functioning which was more useful than mental age for classifying people for purposes of training and care.

**Edgar A. Doll**

Doll left Vineland in 1949 to serve as coordinator of research for the Devereux Schools. He was later consulting psychologist for the Bellingham, Washington, public schools. He served as president of the American Association of Applied Psychology, the American Association on Mental Deficiency, and the American Orthopsychiatric Association.

### REFERENCES

Doll, E. A. (1953). *The measurement of social competence: A manual for the Vineland Social Maturity Scale.* Minneapolis: Educational Test Bureau.

Doll, E. E. (1969). Edgar Arnold Doll, 1889–1968. *American Journal of Mental Deficiency, 73,* 680–682.

PAUL IRVINE
*Katonah, New York*

## DOMAN, GLENN (1919–    )

Glenn Doman is internationally known for his interests in child brain development and function. He attended Drexel Institute in 1938 and went on to graduate from the University of Pennsylvania School of Physical Therapy in 1965. He was certified at the perceptor level in human brain development in 1969.

**Glenn Doman**

During the past 30 years Doman has studied children. He founded and was director of the Institutes for Achievement of Human Potential, 1955–1981; he is currently chairman of the board. He is known for the formulation of the Doman-Delacato treatment method for children with neurological disabilities. The treatment was popular during the 1960s. The theory stresses that an individual's development in mobility, vision, audition, and language follows specific neurological stages that are correlated with anatomical progress.

Doman's publications include *How to Teach Your Baby to Read*, available in 15 languages; a children's book, *Nose Is Not Toes; What to Do About Your Brain Injured Child;* and *How to Multiply Your Baby's Intelligence.*

### REFERENCES

Doman, G. (1964a). *How to teach your baby to read.* New York: Random House.

Doman, G. (1964b). *Nose is not toes.* London: Jonathan Cape.

Doman, G. (1974). *What to do about your brain injured child.* New York: Doubleday.

Doman, G. (1984). *How to multiply your baby's intelligence.* New York: Doubleday.

ROBERTA C. STOKES
*Texas A&M University*

## DOPAMINE

Dopamine (DA) is a catecholamine class neurotransmitter. Dopamine has been one of the most studied neurotransmitters because of observed roles for DA in schizophrenia, tardive dyskinesia, and Parkinson's disease. Dopaminergic pathways are located throughout the limbic system (area of the brain often associated with emotional reactivity and memory), the basal ganglia (area of the brain associated with motor timing and complex integration), and frontal brain areas. Animal studies of DA depletion and studies of neurological disorders with motor manifestations (i.e., Parkinson's disease) produce results supportive of DA's contributory role in brain systems involved in normal locomotion (Seiden & Dykstra, 1977). Similarly, researchers working with drugs that stimulate DA in animal brains have noted increases in spontaneous aggression during chemical stimulation of DA receptor sites (Senault, 1970). Introduction of haloperidol (Haldol), a DA-blocking agent, reduces the frequency of such fighting (Leavitt, 1982). The role of DA in sexual activity appears similar; that is, increased availability of DA increases sexual behavior in rats. In humans, however, the latter effect appears more indirect. When L-Dopa, a precursor of DA, was administered to male Parkinson's patients, its observed effect on sexual potency appeared more the result of removing other disabling motor symptoms than a result of direct stimulation of libido (Leavitt, 1982). In addition, DA appears to play a role in the regulation of food intake. Investigators (Seiden & Dykstra, 1977) also have noted a role for DA in the maintenance of avoidance behavior and in the facilitation of behavior on positive reinforcement schedules.

**REFERENCES**

Leavitt, F. (1982). *Drugs and behavior*. New York: Wiley.

Seiden, L. S., & Dykstra, L. A. (1977). *Psychopharmocology: A biochemical and behavioral approach*. New York: Van Nostrand Reinhold.

Senault, B. (1970). Comportement d'aggressivité intraspécifique induit par l'apomorphine chez le rat. *Psychopharmocologia, 18,* 271–287.

ROBERT F. SAWICKI
*Lake Erie Institute of
Rehabilitation, Lake Erie,
Pennsylvania*

**HALDOL**
**TRANQUILIZERS**

# DOUBLE-BLIND DESIGN

One frequently encountered problem in research involving the administration of medication, particularly psychotropic drugs, is that some children or adults may be improved solely as a function of their knowledge that a drug has been administered. The degree to which this effect, frequently referred to as a placebo effect, is present and affecting the outcome of research is unknown and uncon-

trolled in any specific situation. Experimenters may also be influenced by administration of medication, particularly if the researcher developed the pharmaceutical agent or has other subjective reasons to be biased toward a particular outcome. In such cases, investigators may observe differential rates of behavioral or physiological change in those subjects receiving medication in comparison with those individuals receiving no drug therapy (Babbie, 1979). In either of these cases, the subject's or experimenter's expectation of a certain outcome represents a threat to the validity of the research design. Validity is compromised when the effect of the drug administered is confounded with the expectation of what, if any, the effects of the drug might be.

To control for the effect of patients merely taking medication, as would be the case if those taking medication were compared with a nonmedicated control group, subjects who are not receiving an active drug substance are administered a placebo that appears identical to the active medication in every regard, with the exception that its active ingredients are inert. Thus, the drug under study is not present in the placebo dose and the patients are unaware of whether their medication is in fact active or a placebo. In research terminology, then, the patients are blind to their own drug condition. In order to control for the effect of experimenter bias, it is also necessary for the investigators who administer medication and those who evaluate the outcome (the presence or absence of the drug effect) to be blind to the drug condition of the patients. When these precautions are followed, the research design is said to employ a double-blind procedure, since neither the patients nor the researchers are cognizant of the drug condition to which patients may be assigned (Sprague, 1979).

Obviously, there must be records of which patients have received active medication and which have received placebos in order for the results of the study to be interpretable. However, it is critical that this information not be available to researchers who may have contact with the patients or to the patients themselves until after the study has been completed. Thus, by following a strict double-blind research design, drug effects may be distinguished from actual patient and experimenter expectations regarding the drug under investigation (Sprague, 1979). Unless these two types of effects can be separated, the validity of such a study would be compromised seriously (Sprague, 1979; Sprague & Werry, 1971).

In summary, the double-blind condition exists when neither the subject involved nor the investigator evaluating the drug trial is cognizant of the control condition (placebo) or the active pharmacological intervention. Such a procedure precludes the investigator's expectations and hopes from influencing any physiological or behavioral changes that may occur as a function of active pharmacotherapy (Sprague, 1979).

In reviews of the massive literature pertaining to the psychopharmacology of hyperactive and mentally retarded populations, Sprague (Sprague, 1979; Sprague & Werry, 1971) has underscored that the use of double-blind procedures is a minimum requisite in evaluating psychotropic drugs for these groups. Nonetheless, ethical considerations may preclude withholding an effective medication for a child despite the requirements of rigorous empirical research. Thus, investigators must carefully weigh the mandates of controlled clinical trials research with the special needs of some children. Moreover, some research (Whalen & Henker, 1980) in the field of pediatric psychopharmacology has provided rather convincing evidence to suggest that the notion of being administered any pill, whether placebo or active medication, exerts a specific effect on children's views of personal causality. This is particularly true for hyperactive or conduct-disordered children (Ross & Ross, 1982). Should these findings be upheld in future research, the use of active medication as well as both a placebo and a no-pill condition will in fact be necessary in clinical trials, particularly those that involve stimulant medications or other psychotropic drugs prescribed for behavior disorders in children.

## REFERENCES

Babbie, E. R. (1979). *The practice of social research*. Belmont, CA: Wadsworth.

Ross, D. M., & Ross S. A. (1982). *Hyperactivity*. New York: Wiley.

Sprague, R. L. (1979). Assessment of intervention. In R. L. Trites (Ed.), *Hyperactivity in children: Etiology, measurement and treatment implications* (pp. 217–229). Baltimore, MD: University Park Press.

Sprague, R. L., & Werry, J. S. (1971). Methodology of psychopharmacological studies with the retarded. In N. R. Ellis (Ed.), *International review of research in mental retardation* (Vol. 5). New York: Academic.

Whalen, C. K., & Henker, B. (1980). *Hyperactive children: The social ecology of identification and treatment*. New York: Academic.

MARTHA ELLEN WYNNE
*Loyola University of Chicago*

RONALD T. BROWN
*Emory University School
of Medicine*

ABAB DESIGN
HAWTHORNE EFFECT
RESEARCH

# DOWN, J. (JOHN) LANGDON, (1828–1896)

J. (John) Langdon Down, an English physician, in 1866 described the condition that he called mongolism and that is now known as Down syndrome or Down's syndrome. Although there had been earlier descriptions in the med-

ical literature of individuals who appeared to belong to the same category, Down is credited with the discovery and description of this clinical entity.

Down was concerned with the prevention of mental retardation. He recommended attention to good parental health and sound prenatal care and child-rearing practices. He advocated education for mentally retarded individuals and recognized the efficacy of early training.

## REFERENCES

Down, J. L. (1866). Observations on an ethnic classification of idiots. *London Hospital Clinical Lecture Reports, 3*, 259–262.

Down, J. L. (1887). *Mental affectations of childhood and youth*. London: Churchill.

Penrose, L. S., & Smith, G. F. (1966). *Down's anomaly*. Boston: Little, Brown.

PAUL IRVINE
*Katonah, New York*

# DOWN'S SYNDROME

Down's syndrome, a chromosomal anomaly, accounts for one-third of all cases of genetic-origin mental retardation (Hayden & Beck, 1981). Zarfas and Wolf (1979) reported a frequency of 2/1000 live births. The Centers for Disease Control in Atlanta currently report statistics of 1/1000. In 1866 J. Langdon Down, the first person to describe the characteristics of the syndrome, believed that the condition was a regression to a more primitive racial type. He coined the term mongolism. The term is derogatory to both the individual with Down's syndrome and the Mongolian race. However, Down's recognition of the pattern of characteristics clearly delineated the condition as a distinct and separate entity (Pueschel, Canning, Murphy, & Zausmer, 1978).

Of the more than 50 known characteristics (Koch & Koch, 1974), the most common are a small skull with a flat back of head; slanting, almond-shaped eyes; white speckled irises; flat-bridged nose and ears slightly smaller than average; small mouth with protruding, fissured tongue; drooping corners of the mouth; shortness of stature; stubby hands; little finger curved inward; a single crease along the palm of the hand rather than the average double palm crease; fingerprints and footprints differing from the norm; hypotonia (too little muscle tone); and an unsteady, jerky gait (See Figure 1). Not all characteristics are present in each Down's syndrome individual and some of the symptoms may be less pronounced. Some level of mental retardation is inevitable but the degree of mental retardation may vary greatly. Studies have shown that cognitive development advances steadily until it levels off at mental ages of about $3\frac{1}{2}$ to 5 years (Cornwell & Birch, 1969; Zeaman & House, 1962). Connally (1978) suggests that despite the generally found IQ deficit, the abilities of

Figure 1.  Children with Down's syndrome often, but not always, have appealing features as do these children.

Down's syndrome children are not as limited as once suggested. Some IQs may be as high as borderline normal. Skill development may continue well into the third and fourth decade but abstract abilities may remain severely limited (Cornwell, 1974).

Lejeune, Gautur, and Turpin (1963) discovered that individuals with Down's syndrome had 47 rather than 46 chromosomes in each cell. All of the types of chromosomal abnormalities that cause Down's syndrome result in an extra 21 chromosomes, or trisomy 21. Hereditary types account for less than 4%. In such cases, genetic counseling can be given. Amniocentesis may be helpful, as Down's syndrome is detectable in utero.

Nondisjunction, the most common form of Down's syndrome, found in 95% of afflicted persons, is not inherited. Trisomy 21 occurs when in place of the chromosome 21 pair, there is a trisomy (three individual 21 chromosomes). Nondisjunction can occur during formation of the egg or the sperm, or during the first few cell divisions after conception. The older the female, the more likely Down's syndrome will occur (See Figure 2). During aging, the ova are exposed to stressors that may damage the chromosomes. Recent studies that examined chromosomes from both parents indicate that there may be a link between the age of the male and Down's syndrome as well (Pueschel, 1982).

Translocation, the inherited form of Down's syndrome, occurs during normal cell reproduction when two chromosomes overlap and break at the point of contact. Instead of reuniting properly, the broken ends unite with the wrong chromosome. The translocation usually occurs between the 14th and 21st chromosomes. A 14th may break and unite with a 21st or may become attached to a 21st without breaking, resulting in an abnormal chromosome (a 14–21 combination). The abnormal chromosome will reproduce itself. Therefore, an individual who inherits it will

be a carrier of translocation Down's syndrome. Either a male or female can be a carrier, but it is more common in the female (Koch & Koch, 1974).

Mosaicism is the least common type of Down's syndrome. The mosaic has some normal 46 chromosome cells and some abnormal 47 chromosome cells, as detailed by Koch and Koch (1974). At some point during prenatal cell division (mitosis), and after a number of normal cells are produced, a mutation occurs. Generally, the result is a milder form of Down's syndrome. In some cases, a mosaic may have normal intelligence and exhibit few or no Down's syndrome characteristics. This type of Down's syndrome is not initially hereditary and there is little chance that it will occur in a second birth to the same parents. However, mosaics can pass on Down's syndrome to their offspring.

Although the exact cause of Down's syndrome is unknown, possible causes include radiation, gene mutation, viruses, drugs and other chemicals, autoimmune mechanisms, existing aberrations, aged gametes, and factors such as economic, thermal, temporal, and geographic conditions (American Association of Mental Deficiency, 1983). Advances in technology have made it possible to photomicrograph and more accurately study chromosomes.

Careful medical attention using a preventive medical approach is important as there are a number of medical problems associated with Down's syndrome. Common are the following: respiratory infections, thyroid disorders, congenital heart disease, intestinal obstruction of the duodenum, underdeveloped sex organs, and skeletal abnormalities (Pueschel et al., 1978; Smith & Berg, 1976). Life expectancy for Down's syndrome individuals is much higher today than in the past. These individuals may survive into their 60s and 70s (Kasparyan, 1977).

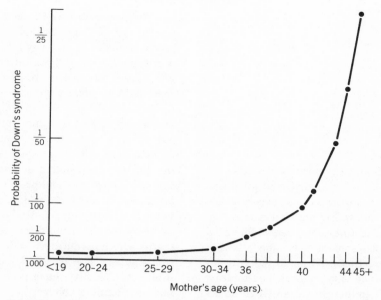

Figure 2. Incidence of Down's syndrome as a function of mother's age at birth.

Parent support is a vital need (Turnbull & Turnbull, 1978) to ensure that infant stimulation programs emphasizing self-help skills, language acquisition, feeding, toilet training, and positive socialization, are provided. Down's syndrome individuals are educable and should have exposure to their nonhandicapped peers from their early years. Generally, there is no reason that most Down's syndrome individuals cannot attend regular preschools and later local neighborhood schools. In the past, professionals advised parents to place their Down's syndrome child in 24-hour institutional care based on the false assumption that the Down's syndrome individual would be severely or profoundly retarded. Custodial care is seldom warranted unless severe medical, psychological, or social problems occur. Carefully supervised, comprehensive special education, K–12, should include prevocational and vocational skill development. Adult living may include working in a sheltered workshop or in a well-organized and supervised private work place in business or industry. The greatest general development is found in Down's syndrome individuals who are reared at home and well stimulated (Connally, 1978). Optimum progress occurs when facilities are positive and training begins early and is comprehensive.

## REFERENCES

American Association of Mental Deficiency. (1983). Classification in mental retardation (rev.). *American Journal of Mental Deficiency, 89,* 242–256.

Centers for Disease Control. (1985, September). *Birth defect monitoring progress data* (Congenital Malformation Survey Report). Washington, DC: Department of Health and Human Services.

Connally, J. (1978). Intelligence levels of Down's syndrome children. *American Journal of Mental Deficiency, 83,* 193–196.

Cornwell, A. C. (1974). Development of language abstraction and numerical concept formation in Down's syndrome children. *American Journal of Mental Deficiency, 79,* 179–190.

Cornwell, A. C., & Birch, H. G. (1969). Psychological and social development in home reared children with Down syndrome (mongolism). *American Journal of Mental Deficiency, 74,* 314–350.

Hayden, A. H., & Beck, G. R. (1981). Finding and educating high risk infants. In R. Meyer, C. Ramsey, & P. Throames (Eds.), *Finding and educating high risk infants* (pp. 19–51). Baltimore, MD: University Park.

Kasparyan, A. (1977). Prolonged survival in Down syndrome. *Journal of American Medical Association, 237*(17), 1827.

Koch, R., & Koch, K. (1974). *Understanding the mentally retarded child: A new approach.* New York: Random House.

Lejeune, J., Gautur, M., & Turpin, R. (1963). Study of the somatic chromosomes of nine mongoloid idiot children. In S. H. Bayer (Ed.), *Papers on human genetics* (pp. 238–240). Englewood Cliffs, NJ: Prentice-Hall.

Pines, M. (1982). Infant stimulation. *Psychology Today, 7,* 48–53.

Pueschel, S. (1982). *A study of the young child with Down syndrome.* New York: Human Science.

Pueschel, S., Canning, C., Murphy, A., & Zausmer, E. (1978). *Down syndrome growing and learning.* Fairway: Andrews, McMeel, & Parker.

Smith, G. F., & Berg, J. M. (1976). *Down's anomaly.* New York: Churchill Livingstone.

Turnbull, A., & Turnbull, H. (1978). *Parents speak out: Growing with a handicapped child.* Columbus, OH: Merrill.

Zarfas, D. E., & Wolf, L. C. (1979). Maternal age patterns and the incidence of Down's syndrome. *American Journal of Mental Deficiency, 83,* 353–359.

Zeaman, D., & House, B. (1962). Mongoloid mental age is proportional to log cognitive age. *Child Development, 33,* 481–488.

SALLY E. PISARCHICK
*Cuyahoga Special Education
Service Center, Maple
Heights, Ohio*

GENETIC COUNSELING
MENTAL RETARDATION
MOSAICISM
TRISOMY 21

## DRAW-A-PERSON

The draw-a-person (DAP) is an assessment technique used with both children and adults for a variety of purposes. Harris (1963) provided a set of instructions, a scoring system, and norms for using the technique as a measure of children's intelligence. The test has also been widely used as a projective personality assessment technique following a suggestion by Machover (1949). Although specific instructions vary, the examinee is typically asked to draw a picture of a person. The examiner provides as little structure as possible; however, if necessary, the subject is encouraged to draw an entire person and not to use stick figures. The subject is then asked to draw a person of the opposite sex. These basic instructions are often embellished to include a drawing of oneself and an inquiry phase during which the subject may be asked to make up a story about the person in the drawing or to explain various details included in the picture. Several scoring systems have been developed (Shaffer, Duszynski, & Thomas, 1984), however, a global rating of the overall level of adjustment appears to be the most reliable method of interpreting the DAP (Swenson, 1968).

### REFERENCES

Harris, D. B. (1963). *Children's drawings as measures of intellectual maturity*. New York: Harcourt, Brace, & World.

Machover, K. (1949). *Personality projection in the drawing of the human figure*. Splringfield, IL: Thomas.

Shaffer, J., Duszynski, K., & Thomas, C. (1984). A comparison of three methods for scoring figure drawings. *Journal of Personality Assessment, 48*, 245–254.

Swenson, C. H. (1968). Empirical evaluation of human figure drawings. 1957–1966. *Psychological Bulletin, 70*, 20–44.

ROBERT G. BRUBAKER
*Eastern Kentucky University*

BENDER GESTALT
HOUSE TREE PERSON
KINETIC FAMILY DRAWING

## DROPOUT

A dropout is generally considered to be an individual who leaves school before graduation. Yet, Block, Covill-Servo, and Rosen (1978) found a serious problem with this definition and the reporting of dropouts. They found many inconsistancies in the way school districts define and report dropouts. New York defines a dropout as "any pupil who leaves school prior to graduation for any reason except death and does not enter another school" (Block, Covill-Servo, & Rosen, 1978, p. 15). Under this definition, an average of 25% of the students entering high school drop out.

Reasons for leaving school include a dislike of school, involuntary exclusion, academic problems, problems with teachers, marriage, and pregnancy. These reasons are determined ex post facto and do not have a high predictive value in identifying potential dropouts. Most dropouts are 16 years old and from families with lower socioeconomic status where parental attitudes toward education and parental supervision are low. Dropouts generally are of lower intellectual ability, have poor personal-social skills, and have academic problems.

The consequences of dropping out of school are seen when compared with the results of graduating. Dropouts generally earn significantly less money and are more likely to be unemployed. Contributing to these effects is the finding that dropouts have no postsecondary training because, as an entrance requirement, most postsecondary training programs require a high-school diploma or equivalent.

### REFERENCE

Block, E. E., Covill-Servo, J., & Rosen, M. F. (1978). *Failing students—Failing schools: A study of dropouts and discipline in New York State*. Rochester, NY: Statewide Youth Advocacy Project.

DANIEL R. PAULSON
*University of Wisconsin, Stout*

## DRUG ABUSE

Historically, the term drug abuse has been used to describe the use or abuse of and dependence on or addiction to psychoactive drugs other than alcoholic beverages. This included both the legally prescribed (licit) chemical-compound pharmaceuticals and the organic and chemical illegal (illicit) compounds. Although use, abuse, and dependence have distinct definitions, drug abuse has been used as the traditional generic term. Within the past decade the term substance abuse has become more accepted, as it includes the traditional licit and illicit drug compounds, alcoholic beverages, and nontraditional compounds such as glue and volatile solvents, abused by sniffing and inhalation.

Notwithstanding the wide inclusion of substances beyond the early definition and intent of the descriptor drug abuse, the *Diagnostic and Statistical Manual of Mental Disorders* Third Edition (DSM III; American Psychiatric Association, 1980) clearly defines the term substance use disorders. It delineates the substances, licit and illicit, the conditions and periods of use, and the symptoms needed for a patient to be diagnosed as having a substance use disorder.

The original term of drug abuse resulted from the clear separation of alcohol from those chemical and organic compounds with psychoactive (mechanism of action in the brain) properties. In part, this separation was a direct result of the legislative need to tax, regulate, and control the alcoholic beverage industry immediately following the repeal of prohibition in the United States. It was also a result, in part, of the need to regulate and control drugs other than alcohol that were used for medicinal purposes and produced by the growing pharmaceutical industry. The second aspect of this separation came from the common idea on the part of the general population that alcohol use was a socially acceptable and legal endeavor, whereas drug use was either prescribed and controlled by the medical community for therapeutic reasons or an illegal and criminal activity when used socially or recreationally (Ray, 1978).

The proliferation of numerous over-the-counter, non-prescription drugs in the past 20 years and the rediscovery of the euphoric, mood-altering properties of certain organic substances have added to the increasing numbers of pharmaceutical drugs available in the United States. A plethora of legal and illegal combinations and patterns of use, abuse, and dependency have resulted. This trend and the growing awareness of the dangers of habitual drug taking have created a new direction in the concept of drug abuse. The broader concept of substance abuse, and more recently chemical dependency, embraces a category that includes all psychoactive compounds, licit and illicit, chemical and organic, and discriminates among the user, abuser, and chemically dependent person.

Until the general population becomes aware of the number and variety of psychoactive substances having potential to be abused and produce life difficulties, the term drug abuse will no doubt continue to be used. However, although not a misnomer in the general sense, it fails to communicate all aspects of the multifaceted nature of use, abuse, and dependency.

## REFERENCES

American Psychiatric Association. (1980). *Diagnostic and statistical manual of mental disorders* (3rd ed.). Washington, DC: Author.

Ray, O. S. (1978). *Drugs, society and human behavior* (2nd ed.). St. Louis: Mosby.

L. WORTH BOLTON
*Cape Fear Substance Abuse Center, Wilmington, North Carolina*

AL-ANON
ALCOHOL AND DRUG ABUSE PATTERNS
CHEMICALLY DEPENDENT YOUTH
SUBSTANCE ABUSE

## DRUGS

See SPECIFIC DRUG.

## DRUG THERAPY

Drug therapy may be broadly described as the administration of medications designed to alter behaviors, thoughts, or moods that interfere with adaptive functioning. A voluminous amount has been written on the topic of drug therapy with children; no attempt is made to review this literature in depth here. Excellent sources may be found in the reviews by Barkley (1983), Campbell and Small (1978), Conners and Werry (1979), Gadow (1979), Sprague and Ullmann (1981), and Sroufe (1975) and in meta-analyses by Kavale (1982) and Kavale and Nye (1984). Drug therapy is the most common medical intervention for altering the behavior of children. Despite its relatively short history (usually traced to the mid-1930s), drug treatment is widely practiced today. Exact prevalence data do not exist, yet most estimates indicate that in any given year about 2% of all schoolchildren receive medication for hyperactivity alone.

It is important to recognize limitations inherent in general discussions of drug effects. A variety of factors, such as the nature of the dependent measures used in particular studies, control of placebo and expectancy effects, the effects of situational factors, dosage level, and numerous individual subject variables (e.g., metabolism, severity of problem, etc.), preclude the possibility of listing universal effects of various drugs. Neither the intended effects nor the undesirable side effects discussed here are seen in all persons receiving drug therapy. The major categories of drugs most often used with handicapped children are anticonvulsants, stimulants, antipsychotics, and antidepressants. Of these classes of drugs, stimulants are the most frequently prescribed.

Anticonvulsants are used in the treatment of disorders such as epilepsy. Beyond their use as antiepileptics, there is little evidence indicating desirable effects of these drugs. In fact, research indicates that adverse short-term side effects such as anxiety, nausea, and increased disorganization may result from these medications.

Ritalin (methylphenidate), Dexedrine (dextroamphetamine), and Cylert (magnesium pemoline) are the stimulants most often prescribed for hyperactivity. Used for this purpose, these drugs have sparked the most controversy and also have been the most thoroughly researched of all psychoactive medications. Many earlier researchers referred to the calming effects of stimulants with hyperactive children as paradoxical, and suggested this response had diagnostic merit. However, because increased sustained attention is seen in both hyperactive and non-hyperactive children who are given stimulants, the paradoxical effect and its diagnostic implications have been seriously questioned.

Other frequently reported effects of stimulants include improvement in impulse control, increased compliance, and decreased disruptive behavior. The learning of new skills or improvements in memory or intelligence test performance are generally not influenced beyond that which can be ascribed to improvements in attention. Adverse side effects associated with stimulants include increases in heart rate and blood pressure, insomnia, decreases in appetite, heightened emotionality, nervous habits, and assorted somatic complaints (e.g., headaches, stomach aches). One potential side effect, although rare, is the risk of producing an irreversible form of Tourette's syndrome.

Antipsychotics are most often used to treat extreme excitability, stereotypic behavior, delusions, hallucinations, and other schizophrenic characteristics. Among a number of possible negative side effects of antipsychotics are impairments in learning, enuresis, drowsiness, retarded speech and movement, rashes, sensitivity to sunlight, drooling, and tardive dyskinesia.

Antidepressants are generally prescribed to children to treat hyperactivity (when the use of stimulants is not appropriate), enuresis, and anxiety. In reports of the efficacy of antidepressants, it is generally concluded that both enuresis and anxiety (e.g., school phobia) respond to drug therapy but only while the drug is administered. Reported side effects include dry mouth, decreased appetite, nausea, seizures, and even death in rare instances.

Drug therapy has perhaps engendered more controversy and polemics than any other single type of treatment for children. Although beneficial in some instances as an adjunct to other treatments, there are a number of valid considerations regarding drug therapy: (1) Although they may be moderated by changes in dose or type of drug given, side effects do occur. (2) Many children do not respond to drug therapy. (3) Drugs are not as specific in their effects as are other available treatments. (4) Important questions concerning generalization and maintenance of improvements made during drug therapy as well as long-term effects of receiving medication need to be answered. (5) Reliance on external controls may not be desirable. (6) A host of ethical concerns are inherent in the administration of drugs. (7) Court decisions and state regulations have influenced the use of drugs.

In sum, the following conclusions appear justified. Alternative treatments must be attempted before drug therapy is initiated; drug therapy alone is insufficient; careful monitoring by both physicians and persons in the child's daily environment of both intended and unintended effects is essential; the prolonged use of psychoactive medications should be minimized; medications should not be used as punishment, as an alternative for active programming, or in dosages larger than necessary.

## REFERENCES

Barkley, R. A. (1983). Hyperactivity. In R. J. Morris & T. R. Kratochwill (Eds.), *The practice of child therapy* (pp. 87–112). New York: Pergamon.

Campbell, M., & Small, A. M. (1978). Chemotherapy. In B. B. Wolman, J. Egan, & A. O. Ross (Eds.), *Handbook of treatment of mental disorders in childhood and adolescence* (pp. 9–27). Englewood Cliffs, NJ: Prentice-Hall.

Conners, C. K., & Werry, J. S. (1979). Pharmacotherapy. In H. C. Quay & J. S. Werry (Eds.), *Psychopathological disorders of childhood* (2nd ed., pp. 336–386). New York: Wiley.

Gadow, K. D. (1979). *Children on medication: A primer for school personnel.* Reston, VA: Council for Exceptional Children.

Kavale, K. A. (1982). The efficacy of stimulant drug treatment for hyperactivity: A meta-analysis. *Journal of Learning Disabilities, 15,* 280–289.

Kavale, K. A., & Nye, C. (1984). The effectiveness of drug treatment for severe behavior disorders: A meta-analysis. *Behavioral Disorders, 9,* 117–130.

Sprague, R. L., & Ullmann, R. (1981). Psychoactive drugs and child management. In J. M. Kauffman & D. P. Hallahan (Eds.), *Handbook of special education* (pp. 749–766). Englewood Cliffs, NJ: Prentice-Hall.

Sroufe, L. A. (1975). Drug treatment of children with behavior problems. In F. Horowitz (Ed.), *Review of child development research* (Vol. 4, pp. 347–407). Chicago: University of Chicago Press.

JAMES P. KROUSE
*Clarion University of
Pennsylvania*

## ANTICONVULSANTS, SEE SPECIFIC DRUG

# DUE PROCESS

Due process is the shorthand term applied to the procedural safeguard and due process procedures stated in Sections 121a.500–121a.514 of the PL 94-142 regulations. These procedures offer parents the right to share with schools in decision making that could result in their children's being found eligible for and placed in special education classes. Because these placements may segregate children from the typical school environment, courts and PL 94-142 have mandated that schools follow particular procedures to ensure that parents have the opportunity to review and give their consent to changes in their child's educational program. Bersoff (1978) and Kotin (1978) provide a discussion of the legal theory underlying the due process requirements.

The due process requirements can be classified under six headings: prior notice, opportunity to examine records, independent educational evaluation, informed consent, impartial due process hearing and appeal, and surrogate parents. First, the educational agency must provide written notice a reasonable time before any action is initiated to propose or reject (e.g., when parents request special education for their child) a change in the identification, evaluation, or educational placement of a child (Section 121a.504). The notice must be written in the parents' native language or other mode of communication such as braille and in a way that results in parents understanding the notice. The notice must contain a description of the action proposed or refused by the agency, an explanation of why such action was considered, a description of any options to be considered in making a decision, and a full explanation of all procedural safeguards available to the parents. These procedural safeguards allow the parents, at no cost, the opportunity to inspect and review all education records of their child and to obtain an independent educational evaluation conducted by a qualified examiner who is not employed by the agency. The intent of these provisions is to fully inform parents.

With this information, the parents are presumed able to give voluntary informed consent to the actions proposed. Section 121a.504 requires that consent be obtained before the agency conducts a preplacement evaluation and before initial special education placement.

When parents and schools disagree about any issue concerning the evaluation, placement, or educational program for a special education student, either party may request an impartial due process hearing. A hearing officer is presented evidence under conditions that are similar to those in a court. Either party can call witnesses and cross-examine. A verbatim record is taken of the proceedings. The hearing officer writes a decision that may be appealed to the state education agency and, if desired, to a civil court. Given the emotional and financial costs of this procedure, several states have initiated a mediation process as an alternative for settling disputes before a due process hearing is conducted; however, mediation is not a substitute for a due process hearing. Recent U.S. Department of Education Reports to Congress (1984, 1985, 1986) have reported on the extent to which mediations are used and have described issues concerning implementation.

Finally, public agencies are required to identify surrogate parents to represent a handicapped child when no parent or guardian can be located. Several issues have been raised about this requirement, such as qualifications to be a surrogate parent, training for this role, and liability protection, among others (U.S. Department of Education, 1977).

## REFERENCES

Bersoff, D. N. (1978). Procedural safeguards. In L. G. Morra (Ed.), *Developing criteria for the evaluation of due process procedural safeguards provision of Public Law 94-142 (pp. 63–142).* Washington, DC: U.S. Office of Education.

Kotin, L. (1978). Recommended criteria and assessment techniques for the evaluation by LEAs of their compliance with the notice and consent requirements of P.L. 94-142. In L. G. Morra (Ed.), *Developing criteria for the evaluation of due process procedural safeguards provision of Public Law 94-142* (pp. 143–178). Washington, DC: U.S. Office of Education.

U.S. Department of Education. (1984). *Fifth annual report to Congress on the implementation of Public Law 94-142: The Education for All Handicapped Children Act.* Washington DC: Author.

U.S. Department of Education. (1985). *Sixth annual report to Congress on the implementation of Public Law 94-142: The Education for All Handicapped Children Act.* Washington, DC: Author.

U.S. Department of Education. (1986). *Seventh annual report to Congress on the implementation of Public Law 94-142: The Education for All Handicapped Children Act.* Washington, DC: Author.

U.S. Department of Health, Education, and Welfare. (1977). Education of handicapped children: Implementation of Part B of the Education of the Handicapped Act. *Federal Register, 42*(163), 42474–42518.

ROLAND K. YOSHIDA
*Fordham University*

INFORMED CONSENT
LEGAL REGULATIONS OF SPECIAL EDUCATION
PUBLIC LAW 94-142
SURROGATE PARENTS

## DUNN, LLOYD M. (1917–    )

Lloyd Dunn was born in Saskatchewan, Canada, and received his U.S. citizenship in 1963. He obtained his BEd in 1949 and his MEd in 1950 at the University of Saskatchewan. In 1953, he received his PhD in special education at the University of Illinois. From 1953 to 1969, he was on the faculty of Peabody College, now part of Vanderbilt University. Dunn is currently affiliate professor of education at the University of Hawaii, and semiretired. He is a past president of and has received the Wallin award of the Council for Exceptional Children.

His major works are in the areas of psychometrics, language development, and education of the mentally retarded. Dunn (1968) has taken the position that much of the past and present practices of special education for minority children who are labeled mildly retarded are morally and educationally wrong. He believes that regular class placement without special education services is needed for most such children (Dunn, 1968). He was an early advocate of small, special-purpose residential facilities for the more severely retarded, rather than large, impersonal state residential institutions (Dunn, 1963).

Dunn is best known for the textbook *Exceptional Children in the Schools*, the article "Special Education for the Mildly Retarded—Is Much of It Justifiable!" such tests as the Peabody Picture Vocabulary Test and the Peabody Individual Achievement Test, and such instructional programs as the Peabody Language Development Kits and the Peabody Early Experiences Kit.

### REFERENCES

Dunn, L. M. (1963). *Exceptional children in the schools*. New York: Holt, Rinehart, & Winston.

Dunn, L. M. (1968). Special education for the mildly retarded— Is much of it justifiable! *Exceptional Children, 35*, 5–22.

Dunn, L. M., & Dunn, L. M. (1981). *Peabody Picture Vocabulary Test—Revised*. Circle Pines, MN: American Guidance Service.

ELIZABETH JONES
*Texas A&M University*

## DURRELL ANALYSIS OF READING DIFFICULTY

The *Durrell Analysis of Reading Difficulty*, now in its third edition (1980), was developed by D. D. Durrell and J. H. Catterson to provide an estimate of general reading achievement. Among the components in the *Durrell Analysis* are oral reading, silent reading, and listening comprehension subtests, composed of primary- and intermediate-grade paragraphs and literal questions. Also contained in the oral reading subtest is a checklist for monitoring such oral reading behaviors as fluency, enunciation, expression, and word identification. A test of imagery is an optional component in the silent reading subtest.

Vocabulary and word identification skills can be diagnosed by several components of the *Durrell Analysis*. There is the word recognition/word analysis subtest, which can be used to measure sight vocabulary, and the listening vocabulary subtest, consisting of words drawn from categories in Roget's (1941) *Thesaurus*. In addition, there are tests of pronunciation of word segments (i.e., letters, blends, prefixes, and suffixes), spelling, and auditory analysis of words or word segments. At the primary level, the visual memory of words subtest diagnoses children's ability to identify a word or word segment shown for a few seconds; at the intermediate level, children are required to reproduce a word after it has been displayed.

For nonreaders or problem readers, *Durrell* provides the prereading phonics abilities inventories, which can be used to assess such reading skills as naming lowercase letters, identifying phonemes in spoken words, or writing letters from dictation.

### REFERENCES

Durrell, D. D., & Catterson, J. H. (1980). *Durrell analysis of reading difficulty* (3rd ed.). Cleveland, OH: Psychological Corporation.

Roget, P. M. (1941). *Thesaurus of words and phrases*. New York: Grosset & Dunlap.

PATRICIA A. ALEXANDER
*Texas A&M University*

## DUSO

See DEVELOPING UNDERSTANDING OF SELF AND OTHERS.

## DWARFISM

Dwarfism is a condition of extreme smallness of stature in an individual. There are several kinds of dwarfism, and systems of categorization vary. In general, however, two distant types exist: dwarfism, usually seen in specific groups such as pygmies, in which individuals have normal psychic development, physiological functioning, and regular physical proportions; and dwarfism owed to a disorder of the pituitary gland, also called hypopituitarism (Guyton, 1977).

Guyton (1977) describes several kinds of pituitary disorders in which the rate of secretion of one or more of the eight hormones produced by this gland is affected. Disorders in the production of human growth hormone during childhood can lead to childhood dwarfism. Hypopituitarism can be caused by genetic factors in which normal parents may produce an individual with dwarfism. In this type of dwarfism, the individual usually is of normal intelligence with disproportionate growth of body parts, usually the legs. Some of these cases are marked by sexual immaturity as well.

A variety of metabolic disturbances owed to organic disease may also result in hypopituitarism, and may result in mental deficiency as well as suppressed growth. In recent years, experimentation with human growth hormone obtained from cadavers has resulted in near normal growth in children with hypopituitarism. Various organizations have been formed recently to promote acceptance and understanding of "little people" (as they prefer to be called) and to dissipate stereotypical ideas that have arisen from the centuries of sideshow ostracism that little people have received (Ablon, 1984).

## REFERENCES

Ablon, J. (1984). *Little people in America: The social dimension of dwarfism.* New York: Praeger.

Guyton, A. C. (1977). *Basic human physiology.* Philadelphia: Saunders.

BERNICE ARRICALE
*Hunter College, City University
of New York*

## PHYSICAL ANOMALIES

## DYSCALCULIA

Dyscalculia is a term that applies to disturbances of quantitative thinking stemming from dysfunction of the central nervous system. The term precludes limited intellectual capacity, primary language disorders, anxiety, or poor teaching as causes of arithmetic failure. Kosc (1974) describes developmental dyscalculia as a disorder owed to heredity or congenital impairment of the brain centers that are the organic substrates of mathematical abilities. In cases of developmental dyscalculia, these abilities fail to develop within the normal limits of time and sequence. The term acalculia generally is used to describe an acquired disorder of calculating ability resulting from traumatic brain damage (Gaddes, 1980).

Studies of traumatically brain-damaged adults indicate that specific areas of damage are associated with specific arithmetical disabilities. Lesions of the parieto-occipital areas of the left hemisphere are likely to be related to disabilities in counting, ordering, or reading numbers. Posterior right hemisphere lesions may result in spatial difficulties associated with poor computation skills (Lezak, 1983). While these studies give insight into the organic origins of developmental dyscalculia, precise localization is difficult to ascertain. However, limited postmortem study suggests that developmental dyscalculia is related to abnormality or underdevelopment of parietal, temporal, and occipital cortices of both hemispheres and the intracerebral mechanisms associated with hearing and language (Gaddes, 1980).

Kosc identifies specific disturbances that may be indicative of dyscalculia. These may occur in clusters or individually and include verbal disturbances in which students cannot designate numerals or mathematical terms by name; disturbances of visuo-spatial organization in which students are unable to manipulate objects abstractly to determine relative sizes, shapes, and amounts; disturbances related to reading and writing numerals and operational symbols; disturbances of concept formation in which students are unable to understand mathematical concepts and relationships among numbers; and operational disturbances in which students are unable to compute.

The symptoms of dyscalculia frequently appear with other impaired symbolic functions of the brain, including dyslexia and dysgraphia. Gaddes classifies these disturbances as deficits in language (auditory-gnostic), reading (reading-gnostic), or spatial imagery. He suggests that developmental problems in auditory language probably are more devastating to arithmetic competence than deficiencies in any of the other psychological processes because inner language, conceptual growth, and incidental learning are impaired.

Johnson and Myklebust (1967) describe additional nonverbal behavioral correlates that occur frequently in the dyscalculic population. Many dyscalculic children are deficient in visual-spatial organization and nonverbal integration. They may have excellent auditory abilities and excel in word reading; however, it is not unusual for these children to encounter difficulty in higher levels of reading comprehension (Rourke & Strang, 1983). Johnson and Myklebust suggest this is due to an inability to integrate certain types of nonverbal experience. some dyscalculics have a disturbance in body image and lack a strong sense of direction (Badian, 1983). They may have disturbances in visual-motor integration, either for writing or for nonverbal motor skills (Cohn, 1971). Frequently, dyscalculics are poor in social perception and in making judgments; they may be unable to pick up or give nonverbal cues, often a part of social communication (Bryan, 1977). Badian reports a high correlation of sociability with arithmetic achievement.

Rourke and Strang (1983) suggest the existence of subtypes of arithmetical disabilities on the basis of neuropsychological characteristics. Research has demonstrated that children who have similarly low levels of performance in arithmetic may differ widely in neuropsychological abilities and deficiencies (Rourke & Finlayson, 1978; Rourke & Strang, 1978). Children who performed poorly on most measures of verbal and auditory-perceptual abilities made arithmetical errors involving memory for number facts, sequencing steps necessary to do complex written computation, and word problems. Their deficient language skills were reflected in these errors. Conversely, those children who performed poorly on visual-spatial, visual-perceptual, complex psychomotor, and bilateral tactile-perceptual tasks showed an impoverished understanding of mathematical concepts; difficulty with column alignment, number formation, and directionality; and general visual-spatial disorganization. It is possible that different and additional subtypes may emerge as a result of further research in this area.

The existence of different sets of central processing

skills in dyscalculic children points to the importance of differential diagnosis and the selection of appropriate methods of intervention and instruction. Johnson and Myklebust stress the use of auditory verbalization as a mediating process to help children with visual-spatial problems learn numerical relationships they are unable to generalize through observation and manipulation. This theory is consistent with recent data suggesting that teaching approaches emphasizing neuropsychological strengths in the instruction of specific academic subjects may result in the greatest gains for individual students (Hartlage & Telzrow, 1983).

## REFERENCES

Badian, N. A. (1983). Dyscalculia and nonverbal disorders of learning. In H. R. Myklebust (Ed.), *Progress in learning disabilities* (Vol. 5, pp. 235–264). New York: Grune & Stratton.

Bryan, T. (1977). Learning disabled children's comprehension of nonverbal communication. *Journal of Learning Disabilities*, *10*, 501–506.

Cohn, R. (1971). Arithmetic and learning disabilities. In H. R. Myklebust (Ed.), *Progress in learning disabilities* (Vol. 2, pp. 322–389). New York: Grune & Stratton.

Gaddes, W. H. (1980). *Learning disabilities and brain function: A neuropsychological approach* (2nd ed.). New York: Springer-Verlag.

Hartlage, L. C., & Telzrow, C. F. (1983). The neuropsychological bases of educational intervention. *Journal of Learning Disabilities*, *16*(9), 521–528.

Johnson, D. J., & Myklebust, H. R. (1967). *Learning disabilities: Educational principles and practices*. New York: Grune & Stratton.

Kosc, L. (1974). Developmental dyscalculia. *Journal of Learning Disabilities*, *7*(3), 164–177.

Lezak, M. D. (1983). *Neuropsychological assessment* (2nd ed.). New York: Oxford University Press.

Rourke, B. P., & Finlayson, M. A. J. (1978). Neuropsychological significance of variations in patterns of academic performance: Verbal and visual-spatial abilities. *Journal of Abnormal Child Psychology*, *6*, 121–133.

Rourke, B. P., & Strang, J. D. (1978). Neuropsychological significance of variations in patterns of academic performance: Motor, psychomotor, and tactile-perceptual abilities. *Journal of Pediatric Psychology*, *3*, 62–66.

Rourke, B. P., & Strang, J. D. (1983). Subtypes of reading and arithmetical disabilities: A neuropsychological analysis. In M. Rutter (Ed.), *Developmental neuropsychiatry* (pp. 473–488). New York: Guilford Press.

Barbara S. Speer
*Shaker Heights City School
District, Ohio*

## ARITHMETIC REMEDIATION
## MATHEMATICS, LEARNING DISABILITIES AND

# DYSCOPIA

See APRAXIA.

# DYSFLUENCY

See STUTTERING.

# DYSGRAPHIA

Dysgraphia is the impaired ability to express ideas in writing (Gaddes, 1980). The ability to communicate thoughts to others through the written word is a highly complex process involving the integration of auditory, visual, and motor skills (Myklebust, 1965). The nature of the underlying deficits in dysgraphia is related to one or more of these factors. Writing disturbances are commonly observed when children are required to copy written or printed material, write words and sentences to dictation, or write spontaneously (Luria, 1966).

To learn to write, children must have developed many prerequisite skills in language, perception, sequencing, memory, and motor coordination. Slowed or delayed development interferes with the acquisition of readiness skills needed for writing (Myklebust, 1965). Writing requires a variety of verbal functions, including verbal comprehension and expression, auditory phonetic discrimination, oral sequencing, and verbal memory. A deficit in any one of these functions may result in impaired ability to convey ideas in spontaneous writing while the ability to copy accurately remains unimpaired (Johnson & Myklebust, 1967).

Children who have acquired a limited vocabulary, have poor reading skills, and have difficulty using grammar and syntax usually are unable to organize and translate their thoughts into writing. Written selections tend to be short and concrete. Words frequently are omitted or poorly organized into sentences; verbs and pronouns are misused; and errors in grammar, capitalization, and punctuation are displayed (Johnson & Myklebust, 1967).

Children with auditory discrimination deficits have difficulty distinguishing the sounds in words and confuse similarly sounding letters. Spontaneous writing and writing to dictation frequently reveal misspellings characterized by the omission and insertion of letters and syllables (Luria, 1973). Children who cannot hear the sequence of sounds in words are unable to write letters in the correct order. Auditory memory problems often are associated with this difficulty (Gaddes, 1980).

Writing also requires many nonverbal functions, including visual discrimination, visual-spatial orientation, visual memory, motor control, and visual-motor integration. Impairments in these skills not only are evidenced in writing to dictation and writing spontaneously, but are manifested in difficulty reproducing and copying written or printed materials (Johnson & Myklebust, 1967). Writing requires children to visually recognize and distinguish the differences between letters and words. Children with visual-spatial disturbances frequently confuse letters of the same shape but different orientation, make directional errors, and have difficulty maintaining horizontal and vertical positions.

Impaired visual memory is reflected in an inability to recall and reproduce the visual image or sequence of letters and words. Children with memory problems often can copy but lack the ability to write spontaneously or from dictation because they cannot visually remember letter and word forms (Johnson & Myklebust, 1967). Visual skills must be integrated and coordinated with motor skills. Children with disorders of motor control may be able to read and may possess the auditory and visual skills needed for writing but are unable to make the appropriate motor movements needed to produce letters and words (Luria, 1973; Myklebust, 1965). Motor dysfunction is revealed in two different ways. Some children write so rapidly and carelessly that the quality of their writing is poor, perhaps even illegible. In contrast, other children write very slowly and with considerable effort but are able to produce well-formed letters and acceptable writing. These children typically have difficulty with written assignments since they require an unusual amount of time to complete their work (Orton, 1937).

## REFERENCES

Gaddes, W. H. (1980). *Learning disabilities and brain function: A neuropsychological approach.* New York: Springer-Verlag.

Johnson, D. J., & Myklebust, H. R. (1967). *Learning disabilities: Educational principles and practices.* New York: Grune & Stratton.

Luria, A. R. (1966). *Higher cortical functions in man.* New York: Basic Books.

Luria, A. R. (1973). *The working brain.* New York: Basic Books.

Myklebust, H. R. (1965). *Development and disorders of written language* (Vol. I). New York: Grune & Stratton.

Orton, S. T. (1937). *Reading, writing, and speech problems in children.* New York: Norton.

MARILYN P. DORNBUSH
*Atlanta, Georgia*

**VISUAL-MOTOR AND VISUAL-PERCEPTUAL PROBLEMS**
**WRITING DISORDERS**
**WRITING REMEDIATION**

# DYSKINESIA

Dyskinesia refers to a difficulty in performing voluntary movements. Dyskinetic syndromes refer to a large group of different problems that interfere with the performance of voluntary motion. When used in descriptions of cerebral palsy, the dyskinetic syndrome may include the slow writhing movements of athetosis, which affects extremities; the proximal and trunk movements (dystonia); or the abrupt, sudden, unpatterned choreiform movements. In this context, the dyskinesia is most apparent with emotional tension and disappears during sleep. Such movements are felt to be due to pathological states of the basal ganglion and associated neurological systems (Berkow, 1982).

Tardive dyskinesia sometimes is used to describe a kind of involuntary movement of the jaw or other tremors, including rigidity that contributes to difficulty in performance of voluntary movements. Tardive dyskinesia may result from adverse side effects of certain antipsychotic drugs (Berkow, 1982). Dyskinesis intermittens sometimes is used to describe a movement difficulty owed to poor circulation (Hensyl, 1982). Since all of the aforementioned terms are medical and imply special cause/effect relationships, the use of these terms is most appropriate within a medical context. Observations of such movement disorders by teachers or therapists should be communicated to appropriate medical personnel in a clear, descriptive manner.

## REFERENCES

Berkow, R. (Ed.). (1982). *The Merck manual of diagnosis and therapy.* (14th ed.). Rahway, NJ: Merck, Sharp & Dohme.

Hensyl, W. R. (Ed.). (1982). *Stedman's medical dictionary* (24th ed.). Baltimore, MD: Williams & Wilkins

RACHAEL J. STEVENSON
*Bedford, Ohio*

**CEREBRAL PALSY**
**CHOREA**

# DYSLEXIA

Dyslexia, in the broadest sense, describes an inability to extract meaning from the written word. However, it is used most often to describe an impairment or loss of the ability to read owing to central nervous system dysfunction. This dysfunction may be acquired from traumatic brain injury, or it may be developmental in nature, stemming from congenital deficits (Gaddes, 1980). Rabinovitch (1962) differentiates between primary reading retardation, which reflects a basic disturbed pattern of neurological organization, and secondary reading retardation, in which the capacity to read is intact but is used insufficiently because of exogenous factors. The primary reading retardation described by Rabinovitch corresponds to specific or developmental dyslexia, defined by the World Federation of Neurology in 1968 as "a disorder manifested by difficulty in learning to read despite conventional instructions, adequate intelligence, and socio-cultural opportunity. It is dependent upon fundamental cognitive disabilities which are frequently of constitutional origin" (Critchley, 1970). Critchley differentiates developmental dyslexia from other reading problems, ascribing to it the following characteristics: persistence into adulthood; specific reading and spelling errors; familial incidence; greater incidence in males; the absence of signs of serious brain damage or perceptual defects; the absence of significant psychogenesis; failure to read despite conventional techniques of instruction; the presence of average or above average intelligence.

Scientific opinion regarding the etiology of dyslexia has changed over the years. In the 1920s the prevalent theory stated that dyslexia was not caused by a defect in the structure of the central nervous system, but rather by a delay of functional development, or maturational lag. In 1925 Samuel Orton again placed the emphasis on the structure of the brain. In working with retarded patients, Orton made a connection between reading disorders and physical traits such as left-handedness and ambidexterity. He concluded that a basic state of ambiguous cerebral dominance, physiological in nature, was the cause of many defects in language development (Orton, 1937).

In recent years research from the fields of neurology and neuropsychology has led to the hypothesis that specific reading disorders are related to differences in cerebral structure. Determination of the specific location of brain lesions and analysis of concomitant clinical symptoms have provided information suggesting the existence of several subtypes of neuropsychological reading disorders (Gaddes, 1980; Luria, 1973). Lesions in the parieto-occipital zones of the dominant left hemisphere are associated with an inability to perceive written symbols. Left temporal lobe damage may affect auditory analysis and synthesis. Bakker (1983) describes a theory formulated by Masland suggesting that dyslexics have difficulty with interhemispheric transfer of function. Overdevelopment of one hemisphere may impede the functional development of the other, and Masland believes that both left- and right-hemisphere strategies are involved in the reading process.

Evidence of heterogeneity in the dyslexic population points to the importance of differential diagnosis, followed by appropriate remedial strategy. Johnson and Myklebust (1967) identify two subtypes of reading problems based on deficits in the central auditory and visual processes prerequisite to reading. The visual dyslexic may exhibit visual discrimination difficulties, reversal tendencies, and visual memory disorders, while the auditory dyslexic is unable to relate visual symbols to their auditory equivalents and has difficulty synthesizing sounds into words. Myklebust (1978) adds to the list of subtypes inner language dyslexia, in which the child can read the words but fails to understand their meaning, and intermodal dyslexia, in which auditory and visual cognitive processes fail to work together. Boder (1971) suggests the existence of three subtypes of dyslexia based on analyses of reading and spelling errors: dyseidetic or visuo-spatial dyslexia; dysphonetic or auditory dyslexia; and mixed dyslexia.

Although there is some disagreement about appropriate remedial strategies for these subtypes, most experts generally agree that visuo-spatial dyslexics profit from a phonovisual or tactile-kinesthetic approach, while auditory dyslexics make better progress using a whole-word approach in initial stages of instruction. Children showing characteristics of mixed dyslexia are severely handicapped and need to be taught initially through tactile-kinesthetic means, and subsequently through multi-sensory procedures.

Recent cytoarchitechtonic investigation into anatomical differences between dyslexic and nondyslexic brains indicates that anomalous lateralization and asymmetry may be characteristic of dyslexia (Galaburda, 1983). Geschwind (1983) theorized that overproduction of the male hormone, testosterone, may influence neuronal migration in the developing brain, causing asymmetrical development favoring the right side. This may result in right hemisphere dominance for language, a condition frequently seen in dyslexic populations. Further research is needed to test these theories.

## REFERENCES

Bakker, D. J. (1983). Hemispheric specialization and specific reading retardation. In M. Rutter (Ed.), *Developmental neuropsychiatry* (pp. 498–506). New York: Guilford Press.

Boder, E. (1971). Developmental dyslexia: Prevailing diagnostic concepts and a new diagnostic approach. In H. R. Myklebust (Ed.), *Progress in learning disabilities* (Vol. 2, pp. 293–321). New York: Grune & Stratton.

Critchley, M. (1970). *The dyslexic child.* London: Heinemann.

Gaddes, W. H. (1980). *Learning disabilities and brain function: A neuropsychological approach* (2nd ed.). New York: Springer-Verlag.

Galaburda, A. (1983). Developmental dyslexia: Current anatomical research. *Annals of Dyslexia, 33,* 41–53.

Geschwind, N. (1983). Biological associations of left-handedness. *Annals of Dyslexia, 33,* 29–40.

Johnson, D. J., & Myklebust, H. R. (1967). *Learning disabilities: Educational principles and practices.* New York: Grune & Stratton.

Luria, A. R. (1973). *The working brain.* Harmondsworth, England: Penguin.

Myklebust, H. R. (1978). Toward a science of dyslexiology. In H. R. Myklebust (Ed.), *Progress in learning disabilities* (Vol. 4, pp. 1–39). New York: Grune & Stratton.

Orton, S. T. (1937). *Reading, writing and speech problems in children.* New York: Norton.

Rabinovitch, R. D. (1962). Dyslexia: Psychiatric considerations. In J. Money (Ed.), *Reading disability: Progress and research needs in dyslexia* (pp. 73–79). Baltimore, MD: Johns Hopkins Press.

BARBARA S. SPEER
*Shaker Heights City School
District, Ohio*

CEREBRAL SPECIALIZATION
BODER TEST OF READING SPELLING PATTERNS
DEVELOPMENTAL DYSLEXIA
NEUROLOGICAL ORGANIZATION
READING DISORDERS
READING REMEDIATION

# DYSLEXIA, DEVELOPMENTAL

See DEVELOPMENTAL DYSLEXIA.

# DYSLOGIC SYNDROME

Dyslogia refers to an impairment in the ability to express ideas in speech (*Blakiston's*, 1979; Hinsie & Campbell, 1960). Most authors, however, use the term to denote an impairment in the ability to use language that is of a central nervous system etiology and cannot be explained by specific sensory deficits (e.g., deafness) or mental deficiency (Nicolosi, Harryman, & Kresheck, 1978). Hence dyslogia is a seldom used synonym for aphasia. Eisenson (1972) used the term dyslogia to describe youngsters with congenital or developmental aphasia. He argued that by definition aphasia denotes a loss of language function, and thus use of this term to describe children who had never developed language would not be accurate. Hence, in the strictest use, dyslogic syndrome refers to children with congenital or developmental aphasia (Eisenson, 1972).

Eisenson (1972) indicates such children are not mentally retarded, deaf, or hard of hearing, and not severely autistic, although at times children with dyslogic syndrome may exhibit behaviors indicative of all these conditions. Perceptual deficits, particularly in the auditory modality, are evident, and these may be uniquely related to the processing of speech. Impairments in the ability to sequence, particularly of a temporal nature, are present. Performance on nonverbal tests of intelligence is reported to be within normal limits (Eisenson, 1972).

Rapin and Allen (1983) described seven developmental language syndromes identified from their clinical samples: phonologic-syntactic syndrome; severe expressive syndrome with good comprehension; verbal auditory agnosia; mute autistic syndrome; autistic syndrome with echolalia; semantic-pragmatic syndrome without autism; and syntatic pragmatic syndrome. The authors state that all syndromes are characterized by delayed onset of expressive speech and impaired communicative intent (pragmatics). Three of Rapin and Allen's syndrome may be similar to Eisenson's description of the dyslogic syndrome: phonologic-syntactic syndrome; severe expressive syndrome with good comprehension; and syntactic-pragmatic syndrome. Each of these is characterized by severe expressive language deficits in absence of autisticlike behavior.

## REFERENCES

*Blakiston's Gould medical dictionary* (4th ed.) (1979). New York: McGraw-Hill.

Eisenson, J. (1972). *Aphasia in children.* New York: Harper & Row.

Hinsie, L. E., & Campbell, R. J. (1960)). *Psychiatric dictionary* (3rd ed.). New York: Oxford University Press.

Nicolosi, L., Harryman, E., & Kresheck, J. (1978). *Terminology of communication disorders.* Baltimore, MD: Williams & Wilkens.

Rapin, I., & Allen, D. A. (1983). Developmental language disorders: Nosologic considerations. In U. Kirk (Ed.), *Neuropsychology of language, reading, and spelling* (pp. 155–184). New York: Academic.

CATHY F. TELZROW
*Cuyahoga Special Education
Service Center, Maple
Heights, Ohio*

APHASIA
DEVELOPMENTAL APHASIA
DYSPHASIA
LANGUAGE DISORDERS

# DYSMETRIA

Dysmetria is a term derived from the Greek *dys-* (difficult) and *metron* (measure). It refers to a condition in which an individual has difficulty in gauging distance for bodily movements. Dysmetria is a form of dysergia, in which an individual is unable to stop muscular movement at a desired point. Signs of dysmetria are elicited by asking the afflicted individual to raise both arms rapidly, stopping at the shoulders so the arms are extended horizontally. Difficulty in controlling the range of movement in such a task may be indicative of dysmetria. In some expressions of dysmetria, the individual may overshoot the intended goal (hypermetria). Undershooting the intended goal is referred to as hypometria. Individuals with dysmetria may perform rapid, brusque movements with more force than is typically seen in voluntary movement. Dysmetria may be associated with cerebellar dysfunction.

## REFERENCES

*Blakiston's Gould medical dictionary* (4th ed.). (1979). New York: McGraw-Hill.

*Dorland's illustrated medical dictionary* (26th ed.). (1981). Philadelphia: Saunders.

*Mosby's medical and nursing dictionary* (1983). St. Louis: Mosby.

CATHY F. TELZROW
*Cuyahoga Special Education
Service Center, Maple
Heights, Ohio*

**ATAXIA
GAIT DISTURBANCES**

## DYSMORPHIC FEATURES

Dysmorphic features are those physical anomalies that identify the presence of congenital syndromes or acquired disabilities. Dysmorphic features may be present in a variety of body parts, including the head, face, hands, and feet. Most congenital syndromes are associated with dysmorphic features that are specific to and, in fact, represent signs of the condition. Dysmorphic features associated with Down's syndrome, for example, include a single palmar crease (Simian crease) on one or both hands, epicanthus, and microcephaly (Kelly, 1975). Apert's syndrome, another condition frequently associated with mental retardation, is characterized by syndactyly (webbing) of the hands and feet and a flat, narrow head owing to closure of the bony sutures (Batshaw & Perret, 1981). Some dysmorphic features (e.g., anencephaly or absence of the cortical brain tissues) are severe and typically result in death (Batshaw & Perret, 1981).

While dysmorphic features may occur in the absence of any known syndrome and without apparent mental or physical impairment, in most cases such anomalies are suggestive of moderate to severe impairment. Dysmorphic features may represent malformations that occur during the first trimester (Batshaw & Perret, 1981). Malformations may result from genetic abnormalities (e.g., Down's syndrome, phenylketonuria); cell migration defects (e.g., cleft palate, spina bifida); maternal infection (e.g., rubella, cytomegalovirus); drugs (e.g., fetal alcohol syndrome, fetal dilantin syndrome); and other teratogens (Batshaw & Perret, 1981; Casey & Collie, 1984). The presence of dysmorphic features often is used to infer level and type of associated impairment. A study of the relationship between physical appearance and mental retardation syndromes reported that atypical appearance increases with the severity of mental retardation; greater atypical appearance is associated with more severe organic impairment in populations of severely and profoundly retarded persons; and mildly retarded persons with positive neurologic findings demonstrated greater degrees of atypical appearance (Richardson, Koller, & Katz, 1985).

Dysmorphic features of a less severe nature also have been identified in populations of mildly handicapped children. Waldrop and Halverson (1971) described findings from five separate studies in which congenital anomalies such as epicanthus, curved fifth digits, and a wide gap between the first and second toes were associated with hyperactive behavior in children. The authors suggest that "the same factors operating in the first weeks of pregnancy influenced the occurrence of *both* the morphological aberrations and the predisposition for impulsive, fast-moving behavior" (Waldrop & Halverson, 1971, p. 343). Subsequent studies demonstrated such minor physical anomalies could be identified in infants, were stable over time, and were associated with infant irritability (Quinn, Renfield, Burg, & Rapaport, 1977). While these and other authors (e.g., Rosenberg & Weller, 1973) suggest minor congenital anomalies may be useful in predicting at-risk status for mild learning problems, other findings suggest the quality of the child's environment may represent an important intervening variable (LaVeck, Hammond, Telzrow, LaVeck, 1983).

## REFERENCES

Batshaw, M. L., & Perret, Y. M. (1981). *Children with handicaps: A medical primer*. Baltimore, MD: Brooks.

Casey, P. H., & Collie, W. R. (1984). Severe mental retardation and multiple congenital anomalies of uncertain cause after extreme parental exposure to 2, 4-D. *The Journal of Pediatrics, 104*, 313–315.

Kelly, T. E. (1975). The role of genetic mechanisms in childhood handicaps. In R. H. A. Haslam & P. J. Valletutti (Eds.), *Medical problems in the classroom* (pp. 193–215). Baltimore: University Park Press.

LaVeck, F., Hammond, M. A., Telzrow, R., & LaVeck, G. D. (1983). Further observations on minor anomalies and behavior in different home environments. *Journal of Pediatric Psychology, 8*, 171–179.

Quinn, P. O., Renfield, M., Burg, C., & Rapaport, J. L. (1977). Minor physical anomalies: A newborn screening and 1-year follow-up. *Journal of Child Psychiatry, 16*, 662–669.

Richardson, S. A., Koller, H., & Katz, M. (1985). Appearance and mental retardation: Some first steps in the development and application of a measure. *American Journal of Mental Deficiency, 89*, 475–484.

Rosenberg, J. B., & Weller, G. M. (1973). Minor physical anomalies and academic performance in young school-children. *Developmental Medicine & Child Neurology, 15*, 131–135.

Waldrop, M. F., & Halverson, C. F. (1971). Minor physical anomalies and hyperactive behavior in young children. In J.

Hellmuth (Ed.), *The exceptional infant* (Vol. 2, pp. 343–380). New York: Brunner/Mazel.

CATHY F. TELZROW
*Cuyahoga Special Education
Service Center, Maple
Heights, Ohio*

**CONGENITAL DISORDERS
MINOR PHYSICAL ANOMALIES
PHYSICAL ANOMALIES**

# DYSNOMIA

Dysnomia and anomia are used interchangeably to denote problems in finding and using an intended word. Eisenson (1973) defines dysnomia as "difficulty in invoking an appropriate term regardless of its part of speech" (p. 19). It is frequently evidenced in dysphasic patients as a residual of central nervous system dysfunction. The dysphasic individual may substitute a word related by class or function to the intended word (e.g., knife for fork, (Eisenson, 1973). Fewer problems were noted on common words than those used less frequently in the language (Jenkins, Jiménez-Pabón, Shaw, & Sefer, 1975).

A dysphasic individual tends to talk around the elusive word and sometimes may remark that he or she knows it but cannot say it. He or she may attempt a gesture to illustrate the word's meaning or may give several functional cues, sometimes achieving successful recall through associations. Some dysphasics recognize the word when it is said to them. Word-finding difficulties also have been found among learning-disabled children with language disorders (Wiig & Semel, 1984) and among children diagnosed as being developmentally dysphasic (Myklebust, 1971). In such cases, the child cannot name an object or picture, but is aware of the error and can recognize the intended word when it is supplied because auditory monitoring processes are intact (Myklebust, 1971).

Dysnomic difficulties are evident in picture-naming tasks, characterized by use of an associated word (e.g., door for key). Use of an opposite such as "brother" for "sister" also is a common error in both children and adults. Verbal association tasks that require a child to name items within categories (e.g., animals) may produce rapid naming of several items and then either silence or incorrect responses. Errors may occur on words that a child has evidenced knowing on previous occasions (Wiig & Semel, 1984). German (1982) studied 8-to-11-year-old learning-disabled children to identify types of substitutions unique to this group when the children were unable to retrieve words. The strongest pattern noted was the substitution of a word of lesser complexity and with wider application (e.g., "string" for "rein"); the weakest pattern was the rep-

etition of initial sound(s) of a related word before the target word was uttered (e.g., "br, br, comb").

Word-finding problems in spontaneous speech may be signaled by inappropriate pauses, use of filler ("um" and "er") and nonmeaningful phrases ("whatchama call it"), substitution of a functional description (circumlocution), or overuse of nonspecific words ("stuff," "place," "something," "thing") (Wiig & Semel, 1984). Classroom tasks involving rhyming words, silent picture naming, matching initial-, medial-, and final-consonant sounds, and look-say methods of reading may prove troublesome for dysnomic children (Wiig, Semel, & Nystrom, 1982). German (1982) suggests that a thorough evaluation of a child's pattern of word substitutions may prove helpful in intervention techniques.

## REFERENCES

Eisenson, J. (1973). *Adult aphasia: Assessment and treatment.* New York: Appleton-Century-Crofts.

German, D. (1982). Word-finding substitutions in children with learning disabilities. *Language, Speech & Hearing Services in Schools, 13,* 223–230.

Jenkins, J. J., Jiménez-Pabón, E., Shaw, R. E., & Sefer, J. W. (1975). *Schuell's aphasia in adults: Diagnosis, prognosis, and treatment.* Hagerstown, MD: Harper & Row.

Myklebust, H. (1971). Childhood aphasia: An evolving concept. In L. E. Travis (Ed.), *The handbook of speech pathology and audiology,* (pp. 1181–1201). New York: Appleton-Century-Crofts.

Wiig, E., & Semel, E. (1984). *Language assessment and intervention for the learning disabled* (2nd ed.). Columbus, OH: Merrill.

Wiig, E., Semel, E., & Nystrom, L. A. (1982). Comparison of rapid naming abilities in language learning disabled and academically achieving eight-year olds. *Language, Speech & Hearing Services in Schools, 13,* 11–25.

K. SANDRA VANTA
*Cleveland Public Schools,
Cleveland, Ohio*

**APHASIA
SPEECH AND LANGUAGE HANDICAPS**

# DYSSOCIAL REACTION

The dyssocial reaction was classified in the *Diagnostic and Statistical Manual of Mental Disorders,* 2nd edition (DSM II), of the American Psychiatric Association's nomenclature of behavior disorders within the major category of personality disorders as a primary personality disturbance. It should be noted that the third revision of DSM no longer contains the classification of dyssocial reaction.

Wolman (1965) described dyssocial personalities as those who manifest a "disregard for and conflict with the social code as a result of having lived their lives in an abnormal moral environment" (p. 1058). These individuals' behaviors are dominated by criminal values but they display good ego strength. Coleman, Butcher, and Carson (1980) described the dyssocial offender synonymously with the professional criminal. These individuals are frequently reared in a subcultural setting that promotes deviant codes of behavior.

Not surprisingly, the dyssocial individual will generally show little or no personality decompensation other than that to which the criminal or delinquent might adhere to because of their subcultural code of conduct. Although not immune to other mental disorders, dyssocial offenders generally protect themselves through emotional insulation and a strong deviant social support system. Other diagnoses previously used to describe this personality have included pseudosocial personality and psychopathic personality with asocial and amoral trends.

Criteria cited by Wicks (1974) to identify the dyssocial personality include: (1) an individual reared in an urban area where the only observable successful people were criminals; (2) an individual brought up in a structural (small and independent) society where people made their own laws, often in disregard of the social norms of the rest of society; and (3) an individual whose past background lends itself to the production of a person oblivious to the laws of society. Wick's summary comment is that dyssocial individuals are truly products of their environments.

The hypothesis that crime and delinquency are intimately and perhaps causally related to a deviant society directs us to the differential association theory suggested by E. H. Sutherlund. He notes that the basic processes of socialization are the same for all individuals. We come to construe and accept the values, attitudes, and standards admired and promoted by meaningful others. It follows that the individual who becomes a professional criminal usually learns through training in ways similar to those in which legitimate professionals learn. The developing adolescent is reinforced not only through contact with peers but, more important by observing successful criminal adults living and flourishing financially in the same subculture. As witnesses to these role models, the developing youth accepts the behaviors as worthy of emulation and duplication. The youth comes into adulthood fully cognizant of the behavior patterns that produce admiration and adulation from the subculture's population.

Historically, we cite Sutherland and Cressey (1966) as contributing significantly to the concept of the subculture's degree of influence on the development and training of the professional criminal. The antecedent of this contribution is housed in Sutherland's classic textbook *Introduction to Criminology*, first published in 1924. Several editions later Sutherland proposed his theory of differential association, which, in effect, supports the cultural-deviant explanation of criminal and delinquent behavior. Sutherland's earliest writings seem to have been influenced by the French criminologist Gabrial Tarde, who had suggested that "laws of imitation" are instrumental in the development of criminal behavior. Sutherland's textbooks included chapters devoted to the principle of differential association and, according to Cressey (1970), each revision of the text until the 1947 edition included revisions concerning the etiological factors of crime.

Differential association parallels not only the American Psychiatric Association's description of the etiologic foundations of the dyssocial reactions, but it also parallels discussions of Durkheim's anomie theory. This explanation of criminal causality includes the normalization of crime in the sense that criminal behavior stops being seen as a sign or result of individual or cultural pathology. Instead, the behavior becomes explicable as a form of normal learned behavior in the right social milieu. Therefore, blame for criminal activity was placed on the socioeconomic structure of society. According to both Bottomley (1979) and Cressey (1970), Sutherland's works received a great amount of attention and controversy for much of the 1950s and 1960s. Articles criticizing the ideas of Sutherland continued during that period, and the responsibility of defending those principles fell to Cressey (*Introduction to Criminology*, 8th edition, 1970).

In essence, the nine propositions cited by Sutherland in 1947 support a major statement on causality that says one will adopt criminal or delinquent patterns of behavior as a result of an inordinate number of definitions favorable to law violation (Carey & McAnany, 1984). The following nine propositions supporting differential association are briefly stated. The reader is encouraged to pursue an in-depth discussion of them in Sutherland and Cressey (1970).

1. Criminal behavior is learned.
2. Criminal behavior is learned in interaction with other persons in a process of communication.
3. The principal part of the learning of criminal behavior occurs within intimate personal groups.
4. When criminal behavior is learned, the learning includes techniques of committing the crime—which are sometimes very complicated, sometimes very simple; and the specific direction of motives, drives, rationalization, and attitudes.
5. The specific direction of motives and drives is learned from the definitions of legal codes as favorable and/or unfavorable.
6. A person becomes delinquent because of an excess of definitions favorable to violation of law over definitions unfavorable to violation of law.
7. Differential associations may vary in frequency, duration, priority, and intensity.
8. The process of learning criminal behavior by association with criminal and anticriminal patterns in-

volves all of the mechanisms that are involved in any other learning process.

9. Though criminal behavior is an expression of general needs and values, it is not explained by those general needs and values, since noncriminal behavior is an expression of those same needs and values.

The nine propositions are heavily laden with behaviorally oriented vocabulary. The process of learned behaviors is relied on to such a significant degree that opposition from dissenting schools of thought was inevitable. Response to much of this opposition is provided by Cressey (1970). It should be added, however, that a general perusal of the literature leads to praise for Sutherland's contributions into the etiologic understanding of criminally motivated behavior.

## REFERENCES

Bottomley, A. K. (1979). *Criminology in focus.* New York: Harper & Row.

Carey, J. T., & McAnany, P. D. (1984). *Introduction to juvenile delinquency.* Englewood Cliffs, NJ: Prentice-Hall.

Coleman, J. C. (1972). *Abnormal psychology and modern life* (4th ed.). Glenview, IL: Scott, Foresman.

Coleman, J. C., Butcher, J. N., & Carson, R. C. (1980). *Abnormal psychology and modern life* (6th ed.). Glenview, IL: Scott, Foresman.

Hinsie, L., & Campbell, R. J. (1970). *Psychiatric dictionary* (4th ed.). London: Oxford Press.

Sutherland, E. H., & Cressey, D. R. (1966). *Principles of criminology* (7th ed.). New York: Lippincott.

Sutherland, E. H., & Cressey, D. R. (1970). *Criminology* (8th ed.). New York: Lippincott.

Wicks, R. J. (1974). *Applied psychology for law enforcement and correction officers.* New York: McGraw-Hill.

Wolman, B. B. (Ed.) (1965). *Handbook of clinical psychology.* New York: McGraw-Hill.

RICHARD E. HALMSTAD
*University of Wisconsin, Stout*

## DIAGNOSTIC AND STATISTICAL MANUAL OF MENTAL DISORDERS III (DSM III)
## MENTAL ILLNESS
## PERSONALITY ASSESSMENT

# DYSPEDAGOGIA

Dyspedagogia refers to poor teaching. It has been cited as a major cause of reading retardation and other learning disorders. Though the term is used as one of the etiologic agents for a wide array of problems, dyspedagogia is most commonly associated with the field of learning disabilities (Epstein et al., 1980).

Early research in reading disorders and learning disabilities looked for psychophysiological dysfunctions or psychological information-processing deficits as the cause of a child's inefficient learning. Once various forms of testing established a supposed etiology, specific treatment regimens were to flow directly from the diagnosis. Although this approach to special and remedial education, often referred to as ability training, has been questioned (Ysseldyke, 1973), it remains a dominant force in practice. Learning problems were seen as based in the individual child, whether because of psychoneurological dysfunction or sociocultural disadvantage. Improper choice of teaching materials or methodology, or an inappropriate match between learning style and pedagogy, were rarely viewed as contributing factors in a student's academic retardation.

Cohen (1971) cites Harris's research (1968) on teaching beginning reading as an early example of dyspedagogia as an etiological agent in poor reading achievement. When comparisons were made between different beginning reading programs, matching classrooms across and within each program, the achievement discrepancies were greater between classrooms using the same program than across the different types of beginning reading programs. This was generally interpreted to indicate that the teacher variable is a more powerful determinant of student achievement than the actual programs or materials employed.

Cohen (1971) believes that dyspedagogia is the norm for most children, both in regular and special education. Many children, however, learn well enough despite poor or inappropriate teaching. The problem lies in the fact that those children who come to the educational setting with negatively predisposing social, psychological, neurological, or linguistic differences need effective, intensive teaching, and will suffer inordinately from dyspedagogia. The presenting background problems are not ignored, but the burden falls on educators to minimize their deleterious effects on learning by providing sound, skill-oriented instruction.

Currently, as a result of recent research in regular education on effective teaching (e.g., Brophy, 1979; Rosenshine, 1978), a good deal of attention is being given to issues such as direct instruction, time on task, academically engaged time, instructional management, performance monitoring, success-oriented learning, feedback, reflective teaching, and related practices. This research may offer promise for special education (Englert, 1984; Goodman, 1985; Rieth et al., 1979).

## REFERENCES

Brophy, J. E. (1979). Teacher behavior and its effects. *Journal of Educational Psychology, 71,* 733–750.

Cohen, S. A. (1971). Dyspedagogia as a cause of reading retardation: Definition and treatment. In B. Bateman (Ed.), *Learning disorders* (Vol. 4). Seattle, WA: Special Child Publications.

Englert, C. S. (1984). Effective direct instruction practices in special education settings. *Remedial & Special Education, 5*(2) 38–47.

Epstein, M. H., Cullinan, D., Hessen, E. I., & Lloyd, J. (1980). Understanding children with learning disabilities. *Child Welfare, 59*(1), 3–14.

Goodman, L. (1985). The effective schools movement and special education. *Teaching Exceptional Children, 17*, 102–105.

Harris, A., Morrison, C., Serwa, B., & Gold, L. (1968). *A continuation of the craft project: Comparing approaches with disadvantaged urban Negro children in primary grades* (U.S.O.E. #6-10-063). New York: City University of New York.

Rieth, H. J., Polsgrove, L., & Semmel, M. I. (1979). Relationship between instructional time and academic achievement: Implications for research and practice. *Education Unlimited, 1*(6), 53–56.

Rosenshine, B. (1978). *Academic engaged time, content covered and direct instruction* (ERIC Document #152 776). Champaign, IL: University of Illinois.

Ysseldyke, J. E. (1973). Diagnostic-prescriptive teaching: The search for aptitude-treatment interactions. In L. Mann & D. Sabatino (Eds.), *First review of special education*. New York: Grune & Stratton.

JOHN D. WILSON
*Elwyn Institutes,*
*Elwyn, Pennsylvania*

# DYSPHASIA

Dysphasia is commonly defined as language impairment secondary to central nervous system pathology that affects all levels of linguistic functioning. The terms dysphasia and aphasia have been used interchangeably in the literature, with asphasia occurring more often.

Brookshire (1978) states the most common causes are cerebrovascular accident (stroke), head trauma (penetration wound such as that of a gunshot, or nonpenetration wound such as that resulting from a blow to the head), bacterial or viral infection, and brain abscess or tumor that affects the dominant cerebral hemisphere (the left in most cases).

Dysphasics display impairments of language comprehension, language formulation, and verbal expression. Symptoms are complex and all linguistic modalities are affected. The dysphasic will demonstrate auditory problems to some degree. Reduced auditory attention span, difficulty in discriminating words with similar sounds, and problems in abstraction resulting in impaired understanding of word meanings may be present. A patient's verbal attempts may be hindered by word-finding difficulties. Many researchers note that fewer errors occur in common words than in those occurring less frequently in the language.

Some dysphasics display problems with retrieving the grammatical structures necessary to construct a message. Function words such as prepositions, conjunctions, and articles are particularly troublesome. In some cases, the limitations may cause telegraphic speech. So-called automatic speech such as prayers, overlearned social greetings, clichés, and expletives are usually intact. Some dysphasics have difficulties with repeating; others echo when a message is not understood. Perseverations also may be noted. Word association problems may be responsible for a dysphasic producing a word opposite of the expected response (e.g., yes for no).

A dysphasic may transpose syllables in words (e.g., tevalison for television), or substitute inappropriate sounds that may be related to a word associated to that which was intended (e.g., telescoping floor and rug into "flug"). Eisenson (1973) refers to such substitution errors as paraphasias, and notes that in some cases, a patient may create a new word (neologism).

Alexia refers to reading difficulties and errors generally parallel to those noted in a patient's understanding of spoken language. Agraphia refers to writing difficulties, and, once again, errors similar to those noted in a patient's speech are noted in writing (Eisenson, 1973; Jenkins et al., 1975). Because no system operates in isolation, other concomitants of central nervous system dysfunction may be seen in dysphasics. Hemiparesis or hemiplegia are frequently a result of the cerebral assault. If the oral musculature is affected, slurring of speech may occur. Dysarthria is a disturbance in sound production caused by disturbances in the central or peripheral nervous systems (Eisenson, 1973). Apraxias of speech also affect articulation, but motor programming difficulties are responsible in this condition. Disturbances in visual and proprioceptive processes also may be present and cause changes in informational intake.

Many classification systems of dysphasia have been proposed. Some are based on presumed site of lesion, some on behavioral aspects of the condition, while others address diagnostic-predictive aspects. Interested readers will find discussions of classification systems in Eisenson (1973) and Brookshire (1978).

## REFERENCES

Brookshire, R. H. (1978). *An introduction to aphasia* (2nd ed.). Minneapolis, MN: BRK.

Eisenson, J. (1973). *Adult aphasia: Assessment and treatment.* New York: Appleton-Century-Crofts.

Jenkins, J. J., Jimenez-Pabon, E., Shaw, R. E., & Sefer, J. W. (1975). *Schuell's aphasia in adults: Diagnosis, prognosis, and treatment.* Hagerstown, MD: Harper & Row.

K. SANDRA VANTA
*Cleveland Public Schools,*
*Cleveland, Ohio*

**ALEXIA**
**DSYNOMIA**
**EXPRESSIVE DSYPHASIA**

# DYSPHASIA, EXPRESSIVE

See EXPRESSIVE DYSPHASIA.


# DYSPRAXIA

(See APRAXIA).


# DYSTONIA MUSCULORUM DEFORMANS (DMD)

Dystonia musculorum deformans (DMD) is a progressive neurological disease primarily reflected in movement disorders. In addition to impaired motor function, twisting of the limbs is often seen. In its early stages, DMD may be mistaken for hysteria or psychosomatic movement disturbances. Well learned, previously smooth, coordinated movements become difficult and awkward in appearance. Individuals in the early stages of DMD may lose the previously acquired ability to write legibly; one hand may be affected prior to the other, even more confusing in the early stages of the disorder. Other apparently confusing symptoms appear; some children may be able to walk backward and even run without visible difficulty, but ordinary forward walking may be severely impaired (Hartlage & Hartlage, 1986). Children with DMD are often misdiagnosed as having emotional disorders. Proper diagnosis requires not only a psychological assessment but a thorough evaluation by a pediatric neurologist. Children with DMD have a serious orthopedic neuromuscular disorder that requires adaptive physical education and other accommodations at school in order for the child to function successfully in formal educational environments. Placement in a special education classroom is not typically required.

## REFERENCE

Hartlage, P. L., & Hartlage, L. C. (1986). Epilepsy and other neurological and neuromuscular handicaps. In R. T. Brown & C. R. Reynolds (Eds.), *Psychological perspectives on childhood exceptionality*. New York: Wiley-Interscience.

CECIL R. REYNOLDS
*Texas A&M University*


# ADAPTIVE PHYSICAL EDUCATION

# E

## EAR AND HEARING

The ear is the sensory organ of hearing, and hearing is the sense by which sound waves are recognized and interpreted. The ear can be divided into four parts: the outer, middle, and inner ear, and central pathways. Sound waves enter the outer ear via the auricle (or pinna) on the side of the head and then go through the ear canal (external auditory meatus) to the middle ear. The middle ear consists of the eardrum (tympanic membrane) and three articulated bones (malleus, incus, and stapes), collectively called the ossicles, which extend from the eardrum to the inner ear. The middle ear transforms the acoustic energy of the sound waves impinging on the eardrum to mechanical energy.

The inner ear is divided into a vestibular (balance) and cochlear (hearing) section. The cochlea consists of three fluid-filled ducts. The middle duct contains the Organ of Corti, which houses the sensory nerve endings for hearing. The cochlea transforms the mechanical sound wave energy from the middle ear to electrical energy to initiate a neural response. The neural response of the cochlea is carried by the central auditory pathways to the brain. The central pathways consist of the auditory nerve (eighth cranial nerve), which starts in the inner ear, interacts with neural complexes in the brain stem, and terminates in Heschel's gyri, which is the primary auditory reception center in the temporal cortex on each side of the brain.

### REFERENCES

Moore, B. C. J. (1982). *An introduction to the psychology of hearing* (2nd ed.). New York: Academic.

Pickles, J. O. (1982). *An introduction to the physiology of hearing.* New York: Academic.

THOMAS A. FRANK
*Pennsylvania State University*

DEAF
DEAF EDUCATION

## EARLY CHILDHOOD, SPECIAL EDUCATION TOPICS IN

*Topics in Early Childhood Special Education* (TECSE) began in 1981. Originally published by Aspen Systems Corporation, the journal was sold in 1983 to PRO-ED, Inc. Published four times a year, each issue is devoted to discussions of a different topic pertaining to some aspect of educating young children and infants who evidence problems in learning. Articles are peer-reviewed. Editorial offices are located at: TECSE, C/O PRO-ED, 5341 Industrial Oaks Blvd., Austin, TX 78735.

DONALD D. HAMMILL
*PRO-ED, Inc.,*
*Austin, Texas*

## EARLY EXPERIENCE AND CRITICAL PERIODS

Early experience and critical periods have traditionally been given important roles in intellective, personality, social, and emotional development. Briefly, early experience is viewed as having greater and more lasting impact on development than merely prior experience. Events that occur during certain discrete early critical periods, during which development is rapidly occurring, may have irreversible effects on later behavior. A partial list of proposed critical periods is in the Table. Summaries of supporting research are in Denenberg (1972) and Scott (1978).

Persisting influence of early experience is implicit in the continuity position on development, which dominated both psychology and education for much of the twentieth century. It holds that later development is continuous with, and thus grows out of, earlier behavior, which in turn is molded by early experience. As an example, Pasamanick and Knoblock (1961) proposed a continuum of reproductive casualty: the degree of perinatal insult suffered by a newborn directly relates to the degree of later impairment it will show. Thus, early plasticity and response to stimulation is replaced by later rigidity and resistance to change. The proposed generality of the continuity view was well expressed by Kelly (1955): "Whether one is an extreme hereditarian, an environmentalist, a constitutionalist, or an orthodox psychoanalyst, he is not likely to anticipate major changes in personality after the first years of life" (p. 659).

Beginning in the 1950s and 1960s, however, and burgeoning in the 1970s and 1980s, a number of researchers and theorists began to produce data and reviews of pre-

561

Some Suggested Behavioral Critical Periods

| Species | Early Manipulation | Later Effect |
|---|---|---|
| Precocial birds | Exposure to parent surrogate | Filial imprinting |
| Birds | Exposure to potential mate | Sexual imprinting |
| Mammals | Hormone presentation or removal | Sexual and agonistic behavior |
| Songbirds | Exposure to adult song; surgery | Acquisition of adult song |
| Mice | Exposure to noise | Susceptibility to audiogenic seizures |
| Cats and monkeys | Visual environment | Pattern vision; brain structure and function |
| Rats and mice | Mild stress | Resistance to stress |
| Rats | Rearing environment | Learning; brain structure and function |
| Dogs and monkeys | Social environment | Sexual and social behavior |
| Sheep and goats | Social environment | Mother-infant bond |
| Human infants and children | Exposure to toxins | Intellective and sensory functioning |
| Human children | Exposure to language; brain damage | Language acquisition |
| Humans | Social environment | Caretaker-infant bond |
| Human children | Rearing environment | Social, emotional, intellective functioning |

vious research that supported the noncontinuity view that early experience and behavior did not necessarily predispose humans—or nonhumans for that matter—to particular later behavior (Brim & Kagan, 1980; Emde & Harmon, 1984; Erikson, 1950; Kagan, 1984; Kagan, Kearsley, & Zelazo, 1978; Kagan & Moss, 1962). As one example, Sameroff and Chandler (1975) found little evidence to suggest that degree of perinatal insult directly caused degree of later impairment. Most children who had suffered low or even moderate degrees of perinatal insult could not be differentiated from those who had suffered none. Problems were shown by children whose perinatal insult was combined with inadequate caretaking behavior. Sameroff and Chandler proposed a dynamic and interactive "continuum of caretaking casualty" to replace Pasamanick and Knoblock's linear "continuum of reproductive casualty." Lerner (1986) has provided a thoughtful discussion of the continuity-noncontinuity dispute.

Emphasis on early experience and critical periods initially came independently from two distinct disciplines, psychoanalysis and biology. In virtually all of his writings on psychoanalysis and the psychodynamic theory of personality development, Sigmund Freud proposed that trau-

matic emotional experiences in infancy and early childhood had lasting, usually permanent, effects on personality. Such experiences, often of a sexual nature and involving the parents, were repressed into the unconscious where they later manifested themselves as neurotic behaviors. Freud viewed personality development as essentially complete and set by 6 years of age (Freud, 1938). Freud's views persist in many contemporary psychodynamically oriented theorists and practitioners. Some in the Freudian tradition extended psychodynamic theory to account for psychoses. Bettelheim (1967), for example, proposed that autistic children withdraw into themselves and shut out others as a defense against their cold, hostile parents. Generations of parents were blamed for their children's schizophrenia and autism as well as other less disturbed behaviors. Others (Bowlby, 1951) proposed that early maternal deprivation would lead to later maladjusted behavior.

The biological concept of critical periods refers to times, generally in prenatal development, when organ systems are undergoing rapid differentiation. Early in embryonic development, tissue transplanted from a donor site to a host site develops as appropriate to the host site. If transplanted later, however, the tissue continues to develop as appropriate to the original donor site, demonstrating an irreversible loss of plasticity. Teratogens introduced during these critical periods activate irreversible changes in development, frequently producing gross abnormalities. Organ systems have individual, but largely overlapping, critical periods. Most end shortly after the embryonic period (8 weeks of gestation), but those for the central nervous system, eyes, and external genitalia extend well after birth. The classic, if tragic, example of a brief critical period for teratogenic action is that of thalidomide, a mild tranquilizer. Depending on when it was taken by the pregnant woman, between days 34 and 50 past her last menstrual period, thalidomide produced various finger, limb, external ear, and other anomalies in the fetus. Ingestion before day 34 or after day 50 had essentially no effect.

The ethologist Konrad Lorenz (1937) observed that newly hatched precocial birds such as ducklings and goslings appeared to form filial attachments that could not be reversed by later experiences only during short periods of time early in life. He thus provided evidence for a behavioral critical period. Later research (Hess, 1959) corroborated Lorenz's work. Further, particular experience seems to affect a variety of behaviors only if presented at particular times, and deprivation of experience beyond a certain point appears permanently to alter certain behaviors (see Table). Researchers proposed, for example, that (1) early, but not later, rearing in complex environments improves rats' problem-solving performance and increases their brain weight; (2) rearing monkeys in social isolation for 1 year hinders permanently their acquisition of appropriate social behavior; (3) exposure to particular auditory stimuli during certain early periods only primes mice to have audiogenic seizures in later life; (4) human infants become imprinted or attached to their mothers only in the first 6 months of life; and (5) mothers can become adequately attached to their infants only in the first few days of life.

In an important theoretical paper, Scott (1962) proposed a "general principle of organization" that integrated biological and psychological critical periods:

> Once a system becomes organized, whether it is the cells of the embryo that are multiplying and differentiating or the behavior patterns of a young animal that are becoming organized through learning, it becomes progressively more difficult to reorganize the system. That is, organization inhibits reorganization. Further, organization can be strongly modified only when active processes are still going on, and this accounts for critical periods of development. (p. 11)

Regardless of the seeming wealth of evidence for the importance of early experience and critical periods, a variety of research suggests that many purported permanent effects are neither enduring nor irreversible and that others are not as time limited as originally thought. Some of that evidence can be enumerated as follows:

1. Early feeding, toilet-training, and other experiences are not correlated with later behavior. In addition, although a few behaviors are stable over age, little consistency in personality is seen from infancy or even early childhood to adulthood (Kagan & Moss, 1962).

2. No overall continuum of reproductive casualty exists. In addition to Sameroff and Chandler's emphasis on interaction between infant characteristics and caretakers' behavior, perinatal insult appears to affect development according to threshold, rather than continuous model. Most children appear to recover from mild perinatal insult; recovery from severe insult is much less likely.

3. Some types of early experiences thought to be permanent are reversible under certain conditions and do not operate in the restricted time frame once proposed. For example, ducklings will show strong imprinting long after the normal end of the critical period if allowed sufficient time to follow the object (Brown, 1975). Of particular interest, monkeys raised in isolation for a year will develop a considerable amount of normal social behavior if put in the unusual therapeutic context of living with a young monkey (Suomi & Harlow, 1972).

4. A number of severely deprived children have shown surprising degrees of intellective and social development after initiation of intensive therapy (Clarke & Clarke, 1976; Skuse, 1984). Genie, a severely deprived child, is of particular interest because of her acquisition of language long after the purported critical period had ended.

5. Proposed critical periods for attachment of infants to their caretakers, and vice versa, have not been found by a variety of researchers.

6. Little evidence suggests that severe behavior disorders, particularly autism, result from aberrant parental behavior; organic factors are thought to be largely responsible.

7. As early deprivation does not necessarily produce irreversible deficits, so early enrichment does not necessarily produce lasting gains. Brief early intervention does not inoculate children against adverse environmental factors. On the other hand, programs such as Head Start do produce meaningful changes in children's behavior, and highly intrusive compensatory programs, such as the Abcedarian Project have produced dramatic results.

8. Maternal deprivation, in and of itself, does not provide lasting deleterious effects on children (Rutter, 1981).

Although early experience still is viewed as playing an important role in human development, its role is not as pervasive as once thought. Evidence for critical periods in some areas of development is strong (Colombo, 1982). Further, evidence that change in normal development occurs throughout life and that effects of extreme deprivation can be partially countered with intensive therapy should not be misread as implying that plasticity is equivalent across life. Humans are more responsive to many types of experience at a relatively early age. Indeed, MacDonald (1985) suggests that plasticity declines with age and that more intense therapy may be necessary with older individuals. Similarly, Brown (1986) proposes a continuum of therapeutic environments, suggesting that the greater the degree of early impairment, the greater—and more unusual—may be the needed intervention. Recovery from some early experiences will occur only in response to therapies that are not part of the normal environment. Recovery from others that involve manifest brain damage may not be possible under any condition. A question of considerable current interest is whether recovery from early brain damage is more complete than recovery after later damage. Further, we need to distinguish between different types of early experiences and critical periods (Brown, 1981). Areas where adverse early experiences have disrupted a developing organic system will be more resistant to therapy than areas where the experiences have resulted in the learning of particular behaviors. Early interference with organization of an organ system is likely to be permanent, whereas interference with the organization of behavior through learning can be overcome through relearning.

Parents should not be blamed for their children's autistic or schizophrenic behavior, nor should complete recovery of most such children, particularly autistic ones, be expected. Much recovery from early psychological deprivation or adverse conditions can be effected with sensitive and intensive therapy. Psychodynamic explanations of childhood and adult behavior in terms of infant experiences have little scientific support. Early intervention programs can be effective in increasing the intellective, emotional, and social development of high-risk infants and children, but they need to be intensive and long term (Bricker, Bailey, & Bruder, 1984). Finally, therapy or rehabilitation of children with manifest brain damage should be undertaken as soon as realistically possible in order to effect maximum recovery.

## REFERENCES

Bettelheim, B. (1967). *The empty fortress: Infantile autism and the birth of the self*. New York: Free Press.

Bowlby, J. (1951). Maternal care and child health. *Bulletin of the World Health Organization, 3*, 355–534.

Bricker, D., Bailey, E., & Bruder, M. B. (1984). The efficacy of early intervention and the handicapped infant: A wise or wasted resource. In M. Wolraich & D. K. Routh (Eds.). *Advances in developmental and behavioral pediatrics* (Vol. 5). (pp. 331–371). Greenwich, CT: JAI.

Brim, O. G., Jr., & Kagan, J. (Eds.). (1980). *Constancy and change in human development*. Cambridge, MA: Harvard University Press.

Brown, R. T. (1975). Following and visual imprinting in ducklings across a wide age range. *Developmental Psychobiology, 8*, 187–191.

Brown, R. T. (1986). Etiology and development of exceptionality. In R. T. Brown & C. R. Reynolds (Eds.), *Psychological perspectives on childhood exceptionality: A handbook*. New York: Wiley.

Brown, R. T. (1981). *Should we be sensitive about critical periods?* Annual meeting of the Psychonomic Society.

Clarke, A. M., & Clarke, A. D. B. (Eds.). (1976). *Early experience: Myth and evidence*. New York: Free Press.

Colombo, J. (1982). The critical period concept: Research, methodology, and theoretical issues. *Psychological Bulletin, 91*, 260–275.

Denenberg, V. H. (Ed.). (1972). *The development of behavior*. Sunderland, MA: Sinauer.

Emde, R. N., & Harmon, R. J. (Eds.). (1984). *Continuities and discontinuities in development*. New York: Plenum.

Erikson, E. (1950). *Childhood and society*. New York: Norton.

Freud, S. (1938). *A general introduction to psychoanalysis*. New York: Garden City.

Hess, E. H. (1959). Imprinting. *Science, 130*, 133–141.

Kagan, J. (1984). *The nature of the child*. New York: Basic Books.

Kagan, J., Kearsley, R. B., & Zelazo, P. Z. (1978). *Infancy: Its place in human development*. Cambridge, MA: Harvard University Press.

Kagan, J., & Moss, H. A. (1962). *Birth to maturity*. New York: Wiley.

Kelly, E. L. (1955). Consistency of the adult personality. *American Psychologist, 10*, 659–681.

Lerner, R. M. (1986). *Concepts and theories of human development* (2nd ed.). New York: Random House.

Lorenz, K. (1937). The companion in the bird's world. *Auk, 54*, 245–273.

MacDonald, K. (1985). Early experience, relative plasticity, and social development. *Developmental Review, 5*, 99–121.

Pasamanick, B., & Knoblock, H. (1966). Retrospective studies on the epidemiology of reproductive casualty: Old and new. *Merrill-Palmer Quarterly, 12*, 7–26.

Rutter, M. (1981). *Maternal deprivation reassessed* (2nd ed.). New York: Penguin.

Sameroff, A. J., & Chandler, M. J. (1975). Reproductive risk and the continuum of caretaking casualty. In F. D. Horowitz, M. Hetherington, S. Scarr-Salapotek, & G. Siegel (Eds.), *Review of child development research* (Vol. 4). Chicago: University of Chicago Press.

Scott, J. P. (1952). Critical periods in behavioral development. *Science, 138*, 949–958.

Scott, J. P. (Ed.). (1978). *Critical periods*. Straudsburg, PA: Dowden, Hutchinson, & Ross.

Skuse, D. (1984). Extreme deprivation in early childhood-II. Theoretical issues and a comparative review. *Journal of Child Psychology & Psychiatry, 25*, 543–572.

Suomi, S., & Harlow, H. (1972). Social rehabilitation of isolate-reared monkeys. *Developmental Psychology, 6*, 487–496.

ROBERT T. BROWN
*University of North Carolina,
Wilmington*

ABCEDARIAN PROJECT
BRAIN DAMAGE
ETIOLOGY
GENIE
HEAD START
THALIDOMIDE

# EARLY IDENTIFICATION OF HANDICAPPED CHILDREN

Early identification became a topic of increasing interest with the community mental health movement of the 1960s and again with the passage of PL 94-142 in 1975. This law contained components requiring that schools take aggressive action to identify handicapped children needing services; it recommended that such children be provided services from ages 4 through 19, and severely handicapped children from birth through age 21. In addition, several early childhood intervention programs that targeted at-risk children began yielding impressive evidence by the late 1970s of the cost-effectiveness of early intervention (Edmiaston & Mowder, 1985).

Effective early intervention programs require identification methods with high predictive validity. Given possible undesirable outcomes (such as labeling effects) and the extensive costs of intervention programs, the number of false positives (students predicted to become handicapped but who do not) should be kept low (Mercer, Algozzine, & Trifiletii, 1979b). The identification procedure must also be cost-efficient; screening procedures should use readily available information or tests that are quick and inexpensive to administer.

An example of a possible cost-efficient method is to use data contained on children's birth certificates. Finkelstein and Ramey (1985) used such data, including the mother's age, education, and previous live births now dead; the child's birth order, race, and birth weight; and the month in which prenatal care was begun. The data were used to predict which of 1000 children would be handicapped at first grade. Handicapped was defined as having scores more than one standard deviation below the mean on the Peabody Picture Vocabulary Test and on the Myklebust Pupil Rating Scale. Although using birth certificate data correctly identified almost all (81%) of the actual handicapped students, only 15% of the group predicted to be handicapped actually were. This procedure cannot be used as the sole method of early identification, but it may represent a first screen in a series of ever more extensive screening tests. There appear to be many inexpensive techniques that can be used to identify the students most at-risk, but most of these methods yield too many false positives (Mercer, Algozzine, & Trifiletti, 1979a).

There have been a large number of attempts to construct easily administered tests and test batteries that accurately identify children needing special services. Mercer et al. (1979a) reviewed 70 studies, only 15 of which allowed computation of false positives and false negatives. In these studies, screening instruments included the Evanston Early Identification Scale, the Wide Range Achievement Test (WRAT), the Metropolitan Reading Readiness Test, and the Bender-Gestalt, as well as batteries composed of visual-motor, language, gross motor, and cognitive measures. Intervals between administration of the screening and criterion measures ranged from 8 months to 7 years. Median accuracy rates (percentage of all subjects correctly identified) were 75% for single instruments, 79% for batteries, and 80% for teacher perceptions. Mercer et al. indicate that developmental history, socioeconomic status, and teacher perception of skill deficits are strong predictors of later learning difficulty. They suggest that screening should take place in mid-kindergarten, as this allows intervention to begin at the earliest time that teacher ratings become reliable as predictors. Share, Jorm, Maclean, and Matthews (1984) provide data indicating that more than half the variance in first grade reading scores can be predicted by direct assessment of phonemic naming and letter copying in kindergarten; Mercer et al. suggest that

useful ratings of these skills can be made by classroom teachers, freeing professional examiners' time.

## REFERENCES

Edmiaston, R. K., & Mowder, B. A. (1985). Early identification for handicapped children: Efficacy issues and data for school psychologists. *Psychology in the Schools, 22,* 171–178.

Finkelstein, N. W., & Ramey, C. T. (1985). Information from birth certificates as a risk index for educational handicap. *American Journal of Mental Deficiency, 84,* 546–552.

Meisels, S. J., Wiske, M. S., & Tivaran, T. (1984). Predicting school performance with the Early Screening Inventory. *Psychology in the Schools, 21,* 25–33.

Mercer, C. D., Algozzine, B., & Trifiletti, J. J. (1979a). Early identification—An analysis of the research. *Learning Disabilities Quarterly, 2*(2), 12–24.

Mercer, C. D., Algozzine, B., & Trifiletti, J. J. (1979b). Early identification: Issues and considerations. *Exceptional Children, 46,* 52–54.

Share, D. L., Jorm, A. F., Maclean, R., & Matthews, R. (1984). Sources of individual differences in reading acquisition. *Journal of Educational Psychology, 76,* 1309–1324.

JOHN MACDONALD
*Eastern Kentucky University*

**PREREFERRAL INTERVENTIONS**
**PRESCHOOL ASSESSMENT**
**PRESCHOOL SCREENING**

# EARLY INFANTILE AUTISM

See AUTISM.

# EASTERN EUROPE, SPECIAL EDUCATION IN

As a rule, educational administration and administration of special education services in East European countries are centralized within respective ministries of education. In Bulgaria (People's Republic of Bulgaria), exceptional children are included within the system of general preschool education. There are facilities for deaf, hard of hearing, blind, visually handicapped, and speech-disordered children. Lipkowski (1968) estimated that exceptional children in Bulgaria comprise 1.1% of the general population. Special schools exist for children ages 4 to 7 with children 7 to 15 attending eight grades of auxiliary schools (Dziedzic, 1968). Deaf and hard-of-hearing preschoolers are referred for consultation and pedagogical help to the centers of rehabilitation (Noskova & Kuznyetsova, 1980).

Children who need speech therapy are trained in special kindergartens as well as in special therapy clinics. In addition to speech therapy, those children also receive clinical counseling. There are also special kindergartens for mentally retarded children. The main goal of the preschool education of the handicapped is the preparation of exceptional children for entrance into various types of special schools. Visually handicapped children beginning at age 5 are placed in special classes within public schools. Children with mild handicapping conditions are educated with nonhandicapped children.

Diagnosis of exceptionalities in school-age children in Bulgaria is made by medico-pedagogical committees consisting of physicians, psychologists, defectologists, and educators. If the commission is unable to agree on a diagnosis, the child in question is referred to a diagnostic camp for up to three weeks of evaluation. Special committees are set up for a comprehensive evaluation of preschoolers. To upgrade qualifications of the members of medico-pedagogical committees, in-service training is systematically organized for them.

In Czechoslovakia (Czechoslovak Socialist Republic), the Ministries of Education of the Czech and Slovak Socialist Republics have administrative responsibility for schools. Ideological, political, and pedagogical management of education is centralized in national ministries of education. They issue curricula, sanction syllabuses for all subjects, and approve textbooks and texts (Holmes, 1980).

Compulsory education extends from ages 6 to 16 (Banach, 1979). It has been estimated in Czechoslovakia that the total number of exceptional children comprises 2.3% of the general population (Lipkowski, 1968). There exist various schools for exceptional children, including for the mentally retarded (special kindergartens, auxiliary schools, apprentice schools); for children with speech, hearing, and visual defects; and for physically handicapped children (Kabele, 1978). The government makes attendance compulsory in kindergarten for children who are 3 years of age and who have perceptual mental and physical defects. They remain there until they are able to be placed in the basic 9-year schools. Within a basic 9-year school, specialized classes are established for children who have developmental dyslexia as well as for children with perceptual and motor defects. Special schools are also established for educable mentally retarded children. When it is not clear whether children are educable, they are placed in special auxiliary schools and classes where long-term observation can take place.

In Czechoslovakia health officials monitor infants with high-risk potential from birth through 3 years. The monitoring is the responsibility of district pediatricians. Children with various defects are referred for additional examinations by physicians and psychologists. Programming for children 3 or older is conducted by a district psychoeducational committee. Comprehensive evaluation includes medical diagnosis, psychological evaluation of cognitive abilities, and educational evaluation of educability and learning potential. As a rule, a diagnostic study team includes physicians, psychologists, defectologists and educators.

Special classes are taught by experienced teachers qualified to teach first through fifth grade of the basic 9-year school; they have specialized preparation for the area of deficiency in question. When needed, home instruction is provided up to 2 teaching hours per week. Teacher education takes place in one of 12 colleges of education. Teachers have to pass examinations in ideological-political knowledge, psychology of education, music, physical education, art, language, and mathematics (Holmes, 1980). Research relative to exceptional children is published in *Psychologia & Patopsychologia Dietata* (*Psychology and Psychopathology of Children*), a quarterly publication devoted to research on exceptional children.

Efforts on behalf of exceptional children in Hungary (Magyaroszag People's Republic) began toward the end of the nineteenth century. A pamphlet describing mental retardation and institutions for the mentally retarded was published in 1884 by Frim, the founder of the first Hungarian institute for the mentally retarded. The first kindergarten for blind children opened in 1908. The current system of special education includes auxiliary schools, schools for severely retarded, deaf, hard-of-hearing, blind, visually handicapped, and physically disabled children. Educational programs for exceptional children are designed according to the chronological age of the child and category of disability. Exceptional children 3 to 6 years of age attend preschool special education classes. Children between 6 and 14 years of age attend special classes for the retarded in supplementary schools. Moderately retarded children between ages 6 and 8 attend preparatory schools, and mildly retarded children between ages 8 and 16 attend the "practical" schools (Dziedzic, 1968). Children between 3 months and 3 years are eligible for training in preschool facilities. Special kindergartens exist for blind and deaf children, children with motor difficulties, and children who are mentally retarded (Noskova & Kuznyetsova, 1980). Children with severe speech disorders can be assigned into a program at 3 years of age, and in cases of mild speech disorders at ages 4 or 5. It is estimated that in 1978, there were 8000 mentally retarded children in Hungary, comprising 2.3% of all school-age children (Zamsky & Shakhovskaya, 1980). Mildly mentally retarded children and children in auxiliary schools receive general vocational preparation. Assessment for placement into special education programs is conducted by interdisciplinary teams consisting of physicians, psychologists, and defectologists.

The Institute of Therapeutic Pedagogy in Budapest was organized in 1900 and continues to train teacher-defectologists. All students are trained in the pedology of the mentally retarded. They can also add areas of specialization such as pedagogy of the deaf, blind, emotionally disturbed, physically handicapped, and speech disabled. The course work for teacher-defectologists lasts 4 years. Since 1972 the institute has added a specialized defectological research and consultation service (Noskova & Kuznyetsova, 1980). The institute provides comprehensive evaluations of infants and preschool children who manifest high-risk potential for disability, preparation of instructor-defectologists familiar with early identification and intervention, and research work with young children. The institute works closely with children's hospitals and educational facilities. Currently, 59% of special education teachers in Hungary have defectological preparation. The Budapest institute maintains exchange programs with the Moscow Pedagogical Institute.

In Rumania (Rumanian People's Republic), the education and training of the mildly handicapped is the responsibility of the ministries of education and labor. Severely handicapped children and those in need of custodial care are the responsibility of the ministry of health. Children are selected for special school placement by evaluation committees consisting of a pediatrician, neurologist, psychologist, psychiatrist, special class teacher, and general education teachers. Since 1959 industrial establishments have been requested to reserve from 3 to 5% of their available positions for the handicapped and graduates of special schools (Lipkowski, 1968). Mentally retarded children ages 4 to 7 attend preschool classes. Mentally retarded children from ages 7 to 14 attend elementary special education schools. Older children attend residential special vocational schools (Dziedzic, 1968). Every school maintains students' records, which are transferred to the employer on graduation. The educational system in Rumania was reorganized in 1979. The emphasis shifted toward a close integrated relationship between education and vocational preparation (Boyanjiu, 1985).

In Yugoslavia (Socialist Federal Republic of Yugoslavia), special schools are part of general public education from 3 to 18 years of age. The number of children in special schools varies from 50 to 400. Depending on the category of handicapping condition, the number of children in a single class varies from 8 (hard of hearing) to 15 (mentally retarded, mild). The staff of each special school consists of a principal, assistant principal, speech therapist, psychologist, social worker, and pediatrician. Also depending on the category of handicapping condition, other professionals are assigned such as a neuropsychologist for a school of mentally retarded children and an ophthalmologist for a school for the visually handicapped (Rozanova, 1974). In general, the mildly handicapped attend auxiliary or special schools for 8 years. For youngsters who reach 12 years of age, education emphasizes vocational preparation.

There are special schools for the mentally retarded, visually and auditorially handicapped, orthopedically handicapped, and behaviorally disordered. Additionally, there are preschool facilities for handicapped children. An interesting innovation is the placement of children from undesirable homes into foster homes. This system of "alternate families" is viewed as an important part of the rehabilitation of exceptional children (Rozanova, 1974). An effort has been noted since 1969 in Yugoslavia to mainstream mildly handicapped children. Children are evaluated for placement into special programs by the child study teams that consist of pediatricians, educational psychologists, clinical psychologists, social workers, and special educators.

Special educators are prepared in two-year schools (after graduation from high school) or 4-year schools. Two-year schools for special educators exist in Belgrade and Lublany. Four-year schools exists in Zagreb. The curriculum for special educators includes general and child psychology, anatomy, physiology, "special" psychology, introduction to psychodiagnosis, psychopathology, and special education (Rozanova, 1974). Special educators publish their studies in *Special School*, a journal that appears six times a year.

## REFERENCES

Banach, C. (1979). Reorganization of the system of education in Czechoslovakia. *Badania O'swiatowe (Educational Research)*, *4*(16), 132–136.

Boyanjiu, K. (1985). Rumanian communist party policy in the sphere of peoples education and characteristics of labor education, occupational training and social involvement of exceptional children and youth. *Defectologia, 2*, 58–62.

Dziedzic, S. (1986). Educational care of the severely retarded. *Szkota Specjalna (Special School)*, *3*, 206–222.

Holmes, B. (Ed.). (1980). *International yearbook of education* (Vol. 32). Paris: UNESCO.

Kabele, F. (1978). *Czechoslovakia in economic aspects of special education.* Paris: UNESCO.

Lipkowski, O. (1968). Current status and developmental tendencies of special education in Europe. *Szkola Specjalna (Special School)*, *3*, 223–238.

Noskova, L. P., & Kuznyetsova, G. V. (1980). Diagnosis of developmental disorders and the state of preschool upbringing of abnormal children in the socialist countries. *Defectologia, 3*, 83–88.

Rozanova, T. V. (1974). Problems of special education in Yugoslavia. *Defectologia, 3*, 49–57.

Zamsky, C., & Shakhovskaya, S. (1980). With Hungarian defectologists. *Defectologia, 3*, 88–93.

IVAN Z. HOLOWINSKY
*Rutgers University*

## CANADA, SPECIAL EDUCATION IN
## CENTRAL AMERICA, SPECIAL EDUCATION IN
## CHINA, SPECIAL EDUCATION IN

# EATING DISORDERS

Two eating disorders are of major concern, anorexia nervosa and bulimia. Anorexia nervosa (starvation due to nerves) is a condition in which an individual eats little or no food for prolonged periods. Bulimia (ox hunger) is a condition in which an individual alternately binges (grossly overeats) and purges (rids the body of food or fluids through such things as induced vomiting or abuse of laxatives) or engages in excessive exercising although weak and fatigued (Halmi, 1983). Bulimics commonly chew and spit out food (Mitchell, et al., 1985). In both disorders, no physical basis for the abnormal eating can be found. Further, both can be life threatening, are increasing in incidence, and are serious problems for medical and psychological professionals. Other eating disorders, involving the eating of specific nonfood substances such as clay (pica), will not be discussed here.

Although famous and tragic cases such as that of Karen Carpenter have made anorexia familiar, little can confidently be said about specific etiology or overall effective treatment. Bulimia is still more difficult because even seriously affected individuals may appear normal to outside observers. However, some general etiological factors and occasionally effective treatments can be described. Further, anorexics and bulimics commonly share certain personality characteristics and frequently have families with a particular complex of unhealthy attitudes and behaviors. The most obvious difference between the two groups is in physical appearance: anorexics are emaciated, whereas bulimics may be of average or even above average weight.

Anorexia and bulimia are largely disorders of middle- and upper-class adolescent females. Anorexia occurs approximately nine times more often in women than in men, and may affect 1/100 white women between the ages of 12 and 18 years (Neuman & Halvorson, 1983). Bulimia is more common than anorexia and may affect 5% of college women and 1% of young employed women (Hart & Ollendick, 1985). Twenty to 30% of college women may engage in bulimic behavior. The most common age of onset for anorexia is early adolescence, whereas bulimia generally appears somewhat later, peaking at about age 18 (Neuman & Halvorson, 1983).

Diagnostic criteria for anorexia nervosa may be summarized as involving intense fear of becoming obese, which does not diminish as weight loss progresses; disturbed body image (e.g., feeling fat even when emaciated); loss of at least 25% of original or projected weight; and refusal to maintain normal body weight. Those for bulimia include recurrent episodes of secretive binge eating (rapid consumption of a large amount of food in a short period of time); termination of binging by abdominal pain, sleep, social interruption, or self-induced vomiting; repeated attempts to lose weight by severe diets, self-induced vomiting, or use of cathartics or diuretics; frequent weight fluctuations owing to alternating binges and fasts; awareness that the eating pattern is abnormal and fear of not being able to stop eating voluntarily; and depressed mood and self-deprecating thoughts following eating binges (for detailed criteria, see American Psychiatric Association, 1980).

Anorexics are subject to numerous complications, including malnutrition, edema, amenorrhea, loss of hair, hyperactivity, hypoglycemia, vitamin deficiencies, constipation, weakness, and fatigue. In extreme, death may result from starvation, electrolyte depletion, or cardiac arrhythmia (Neuman & Halvorson, 1983).

Bulimia leads to a variety of physiological complications, including cardiac irregularities, kidney dysfunction, neurological abnormalities, gastrointestinal pain, salivary gland enlargement (appearance of a chipmunk), edema and bloating, electrolyte imbalance, amenorrhea, dermatological complaints, and finger clubbing or swelling. Finger abnormalities result from pressure against the mouth during self-induced vomiting. Abuse of laxatives can lead to permanent nerve damage in the colon, chronic vomiting, serious dental and oropharyngeal problems, and stomach overloading and resulting overexpansion to stomach rupture. Several of these complications can result in death.

Anorexic and bulimic sufferers share many behaviors and concerns. They are terrified of becoming obese and measure their worth and self-esteem by how much they weigh and how much their stomachs protrude. Both tend to be perfectionists, overdemanding of themselves, and very success-oriented. Low self-esteem and fear of rejection, especially by the opposite sex, are common.

Both have difficulty allowing anyone to become emotionally close to them. Bulimics are typically helpless, ineffective, have low self-esteem, are nonassertive, have maturity fears, tension management problems, and difficulty in identifying or describing internal states (Johnson & Flach, 1985). Bulimics' relationships tend to be superficial and lack genuineness; they are very good at distancing themselves from people while seeming to be friendly and sociable. A common underlying fearful belief is, "If this person really gets to know me, he or she won't like me." Bulimics frequently fear sexual rejection or "not being good enough to please a man." Bulimics may additionally overidentify with femininity. Drug abuse among bulimics and their families occurs at a high rate (Herzog, 1982). Motivation for change is extremely difficult to maintain.

Many anorexics were model children who were "people pleasers." They tend to be introverted, well behaved, compulsive, self-critical, and very conscientious. As the disorder progresses, anorexics frequently become suspicious, indecisive, stubborn, unsociable, and disliking of any change. Phobic, depressive, or hysterical features are also common. Perceptions of events often become very distorted.

The specific etiologies of anorexia nervosa and bulimia are not known, but both are thought to be biopsychosocial diseases. Unknown biological predispositions may interact with both individual psychological states and needs and our culture's emphasis, especially for females, on thinness as a worthy or desirable characteristic (Wooley & Wooley, 1985). Several potential etiological factors can be described.

According to Bruch (1978), in the past 20 years the average female under 30 years of age has become heavier; at the same time, the ideal shape for women has been in the direction of being thinner. To be thin is to increase women's desirability both in their eyes and the eyes of others. The result is demonstrated in the mushrooming of the weight reduction industry and the numerous books and magazine articles that have appeared on losing weight and dieting.

Wooley and Wooley (1985) quote from Ambrose Bierce's *Devil's Dictionary*: "To men a man is but a mind, who cares what face he carries? Or what form he wears? But woman's body *is* the woman." For many centuries females' cultural conditioning has tied self-esteem to physical attractiveness. Many therapists think that recent cultural emphasis on "thinness is beautiful and good" has contributed to the increased incidence of eating disorders (Wooley & Wooley, 1985). The message to women in particular is that in order to be popular, attractive, accepted, sexy, healthy, and desired in the world of work, they must be thin. The ideal of feminine beauty increasingly conforms each year to the adolescent male physique, implying emulation of men both behaviorally and physically (Wooley & Wooley, 1985). This change may be due to broader social changes involving competition between women and men for prestige and power. Also involved for many young women is the resolution of intense identification conflicts with their parents. Young women today are the first generation raised by extremely weight-conscious mothers who additionally view themselves as failures by current social standards of beauty.

Bruch (1985) says that cultural emphasis for slimness as a determining factor does not explain the more severe disturbance of "frantic preoccupation with excessive slenderness of the anorexic." She believes that the changing status of expectations for women is important in understanding the etiology. Females, says Bruch, who have been raised as "clinging vines" and future wives, and who find themselves during their teens with the expectation to demonstrate that they are women of achievement, may find that they are filled with self-doubt and uncertainty. By bowing to the dictum to be thin, they are validating that they deserve respect.

Anorexia can begin with a stressful life situation for which the young woman does not possess appropriate coping skills. Real or perceived rejection, sexual engagements, or a loss of some kind frequently precedes development of the disorder. Any change can be catastrophic for an anorexic. Worrying about performing perfectly and being socially accepted often results in situations in which anorexics find themselves out of control. Magical thinking is common.

According to Bemis and colleagues, who have studied hypothalamic functions in anorexics, starvation may actually damage the hypothalamus, and emotional stress may interfere with hypothalamic functioning. Further, psychological aberrations associated with anorexia may be relatively independent expressions of a primary hypothalamic deficiency that is of unknown origin (Bemis, 1978).

Women may be biologically more susceptible to eating disorders than men since women tend to demonstrate greater appetite fluctuations when confronted by stress. Also, through socialization, women are more likely than men to inhibit expression of negative feelings, leading to internal stress. This internal stress may exacerbate a biological predisposition.

Certain family factors facilitate the development of anorexia. If a parent has had the disorder or is either extremely thin or obese, the chances of a young woman becoming anorexic increase (Neuman & Halvorson, 1983). In families of anorexics, food is usually a primary issue. The family may use food for other than nutritional purposes. For example, eating may be a way of dealing with personal problems or negative or positive feelings, or it may be a method of presenting the appearance of one great big happy family. Power struggles over eating are extremely common.

Families of anorexics show certain personality patterns, although no one appears consistently. Mothers are frequently intrusive and dominating and have experienced clinical depressions, whereas fathers appear passive and aloof from the family. Less frequently, these patterns may be reversed (Neuman & Halvorson, 1983).

Family interpersonal dynamics are a significant contributing factor. Features that appear to be correlated with the development of the disorder are rigidity, lack of conflict resolution, overprotectiveness, and enmeshment (appearing to be a very close family). Keeping the peace at any cost is a high priority in these families; conflicts are not dealt with openly. In many families of anorexics, the anorexic generally feels powerless and ineffective, and behaves primarily on the basis of what other people want or need. Often the family has not encouraged or allowed the young woman to develop her autonomy or individuality. Only compliance is tolerated. Anorexia may develop as a result of a young woman's attempt to take control of her own life and achieve her own sense of identity. She learns that one thing she can control is her weight.

In some cases the family unconsciously does not want the child to grow up. This message is received by the child, who in turn exhibits anorexic behavior, which then leads to failure to develop secondary sexual characteristics. Some anorexics enjoy being viewed as special by their families. Thus being anorexic can bring a great deal of attention, leading to self-perpetuation of the disorder.

Adolescent peer memberships are viewed as being critical in making the transition from childhood to adulthood. Some investigators have noted that anorexics have few if any close peer friendships (Neuman & Halvorson, 1983). Adolescent anorexics' overdependence and involvement with their families may prevent the formation of normal adolescent peer relationships. Thus, these youngsters may be at great disadvantage in making the essential developmental transition to adulthood.

The etiology of bulimia is not understood. Much of what has been said about anorexia nervosa is generally thought to be applicable to bulimia. Families of bulimics are characterized by enmeshment but are at the same time disengaged. There is high family conflict with low emphasis on self-expression, especially expression of conflict. Achievement is emphasized at the expense of intellectual and social activities (Johnson & Flach, 1985).

Fifty percent of women diagnosed and treated for anorexia nervosa can be expected to recover completely within 2 to 5 years. Nutritional improvement or recovery can be expected in approximately two thirds of treated cases. Usually, after adequate body weight has been attained, menstruation will resume within a year.

As many as half of all anorexics experience a relapse. Approximately 38% may be rehospitalized at some point during the next 2 years. Three to 25% of anorexia nervosa cases end in death from medical complications or suicide. This disorder has the highest death rate in psychiatry.

Usually the longer the bulimic has been ill, the more difficult it will be for her to overcome the disorder. Also, as mentioned previously, lack of motivation for change makes working with bulimics on an outpatient basis difficult. Numerous difficulties in addition to the motivation problem interfere with recovery. Bulimia seems to have an addictive quality that is usually not seen in anorexia. Many therapists believe that treatment is likely to fail if this addictive quality is not dealt with. The bulimic behavior itself is a strong and immediate reinforcer. Finally, continual dieting often results in compensatory overeating, which appears to have a physiological component.

No consensus exists regarding the most effective form of treatment for eating disorders (Vandereycken & Meermann, 1984). Therapists have used behavioral therapy, diet counseling, cognitive therapy, cognitive-behavioral treatment, trance therapy, group and individual psychotherapy, drug treatment, and family therapy with varying degrees of success (Garner & Garfinkel, 1985). Whatever the treatment approach, the usual goals are aimed at increasing confidence and self-esteem, challenging irrational or "anorexic" thinking, developing autonomy, and teaching coping skills. Further, Vandereycken and Meermann (1984, p. 219) suggest that the "best guarantees of success in therapy are a constructive patient/therapist working relationship and an explicit but consistent treatment plan/contract."

Hospitalization becomes necessary when outpatient therapy fails to reverse an impasse or a deteriorating physical or psychological course. The therapist assumes considerable physical and psychological control and responsibility for the care of the hospitalized anorexic. A weight restoration program is usually initiated in which the anorexic is expected to gain at least 1 pound a week until she achieves a target weight consisting of 95% of her ideal weight (Anderson, Morse, & Santmyer, 1985).

Psychotherapy combined with the restoration of weight through direct management of the anorexic's eating is effective in varying degrees. The anorexic has, through her disorder, avoided dealing with several important issues that need to be addressed in psychotherapy. These include individuation, assuming responsibility, separation, becoming an adult, making career and other decisions, dealing with the loss of one's own life.

As is true with anorexia nervosa, cognitive, cognitive-behavior, family, drug, group, and individual psychological treatment approaches have all been used with bulimics, also with varying degrees of success (Garner & Garfinkel, 1985). However, at this time it is not known whether any intervention actually influences the long-term outcome. Without proper motivation, bulimia is difficult to treat successfully.

Certain beliefs and values seem to be very important in the maintenance of these conditions. One of these is the belief that weight and shape are extremely important and need to be closely controlled at all cost. A change in these psychopathological beliefs and values concerning body weight and shape may be necessary for complete recovery. Self-help and support groups such as Overeaters Anonymous may be valuable.

Because eating-disordered individuals are usually perfectionists, teachers can help by advising and encouraging them to take fewer courses and to balance academic loads by combining difficult classes with classes that are less demanding. If hospitalization becomes necessary and the anorexic student expresses fear that she will be unable to maintain her academic standing, the teacher can point out that usually hospital personnel are more than willing to assist the patient by administering academic tests and by making arrangements to see that other academic requirements are met. Major treatment centers as well as many hospitals have educational components and academic teachers on their staff.

## REFERENCES

American Psychiatric Association. (1980). *Diagnostic and statistical manual of mental disorders* (3rd ed.). Washington, DC: Author.

Anderson, A. E., Morse, C., & Santmyer, K. (1985). Inpatient treatment for anorexia nervosa. In D. M. Garner & P. E. Garfinkel (Eds.), *Handbook of psychotherapy for anorexia nervosa and bulimia* (pp. 311–343). New York: Guilford.

Bemis, K. M. (1978). Current approaches to the etiology and treatment of anorexia nervosa. *Psychological Bulletin, 35,* 593–617.

Bruch, H. (1978). *The golden cage. The enigma of anorexia nervosa.* Cambridge, MA: Harvard University Press.

Bruch, H. (1985). Four decades of eating disorders. In D. M. Garner & P. E. Garfinkel (Eds.), *Handbook of psychotherapy for anorexia nervosa and bulimia* (pp. 7–18). New York: Guilford.

Garner, D. M., & Garfinkel, P. E. (Eds.). (1985). *Handbook of psychotherapy for anorexia nervosa and bulimia.* New York: Guilford.

Halmi, K. A. (1983). Advances in anorexia nervosa. In M. Wolraich & D. K. Routh (Eds.), *Advances in development and behavioral pediatrics* (Vol. 4, pp. 1–23). Greenwich, CT: Jai Press.

Hart, K. J., & Ollendick, T. H. (1985). Prevalence of bulimia in working and university women. *American Journal of Psychiatry, 142,* 851–854.

Herzog, D. B. (1982). Bulimia: The secretive syndrome. *Psychosomatics, 23,* 481–487.

Johnson, C., & Flach, A. (1985). Family characteristics of 105 patients with bulimia. *American Journal of Psychiatry, 142,* 1321–1324.

Mitchell, J. E., Halsukami, D., Eckert, E. D., & Pyle, R. L. (1985). Characteristics of 275 patients with bulimia. *American Journal of Psychiatry, 142*(4), 251–255.

Neuman, P. A., & Halvorson, P. S. (1983). *Anorexia nervosa and bulimia: A handbook for counselors and therapists.* New York: Van Nostrand Reinhold.

Vandereycken, W., & Meermann, R. (1984). *Anorexia nervosa: A clinician's guide to treatment.* Berlin: de Gruyter.

Wooley, S. C., & Wooley, O. W. (1985). Intensive outpatient and residential treatment for bulimia. In D. M. Garner & P. E. Garfinkel (Eds.), *Handbook of psychotherapy for anorexia nervosa and bulimia* (pp. 391–430). New York: Guilford.

C. SUE LAMB
*University of North Carolina, Wilmington*

FAMILY COUNSELING
MALNUTRITION
PICA

# ECHOLALIA

Echolalia is "the repetition of a word or group of words just spoken by another person" (Fay, 1980a, p. 25). Echolalia has been noted in those with degenerative brain disease, psychosis (both children and adults), Gilles de la Tourette syndrome, childhood dysphasia, severe mental retardation, and some forms of aphasia, as well as in some congenitally blind children (Fay, 1980a). It is a prominent characteristic of all of these children's speech, with the vast majority who eventually acquire speech having a history of echoing. Many children who acquire normal speech and language practice some echolalia during the developmental speech and language period of infancy and early childhood. Echolalic behaviors generally disappear by 2½ to 3 years (Fay, 1980a; Van Riper, 1963).

Studies of echolalic behaviors suggest that they reflect language comprehension deficits. Studies cited by Paccia and Curcio (1982) and by Fay (1980a) report that young children and autistic children frequently echo nonsense syllables or highly abstract words. David and Graber (1977) report more appropriate responses and less echolalia for easier linguistic tasks in their mentally retarded subjects. A message may be repeated in its entirety or partially, with repetition usually following immediately after the initial presentation.

Delayed echolalia is the repetition of utterances made by oneself or others; the utterances are stored and repeated at a later time, ranging from minutes to weeks. Repetition of television commercials by autistic children is an example. Unlike immediate repetitions, delayed echolalia may serve a communicative purpose. Children have been reported to use stored utterances to express an intention or to verbalize a behavioral self-reminder (Fay, 1980b).

Echolalics sometimes grammatically or semantically restructure a repeated utterance. Such mitigated echolalia may evidence improvement in understanding. Mitigated repetitions are heard in autistic children, but they comprise only a small percentage of their echolalia (Fay, 1980b). An echoed utterance preceded or followed by an appropriate self-formulated comment evidences comprehension. The repetition seems to facilitate understanding in much the same manner as in normal adults and children when confronted with difficult messages.

## REFERENCES

David, L. D., & Graber, N. B. (1977). An analysis of linguistically induced echolalia in two mentally retarded children. *Ohio Journal of Speech & Hearing, 12,* 103–113.

Fay, W. H. (1980a). Aspects of speech. In R. L. Schiefelbush (Ed.), *Language intervention series* (Vol. 5, pp. 21–50). Baltimore, MD: University Park Press.

Fay, W. H. (1980b). Aspects of language. In R. L. Schiefelbush (Ed.), *Language intervention series* (Vol. 5, pp. 53–85). Baltimore, MD: University Park Press.

Paccia, J. M., & Curcio, F. (1982). Language processing and forms of immediate echolalia in autistic children. *Journal of Speech & Hearing Research, 25,* 42–47.

Van Riper, C. (1963). *Speech correction: Principles and methods.* Englewood Cliffs, NJ: Prentice-Hall.

K. SANDRA VANTA
*Cleveland Public Schools, Cleveland, Ohio*

AUTISM
AUTISTIC BEHAVIOR
SPEECH AND LANGUAGE HANDICAPS

# ECHOPRAXIA

Echopraxia can be defined as the involuntary imitation of movements made by another person. The echolalia of the autistic child, in which the child echo-speaks phrases and words, might be viewed as a specific kind of echopraxia. Another echo of movement that is specific to some hearing-impaired persons has been observed clinically. In this form, the individual imitates the facial and mouth movements of the speaker. These movements may be a means of reinforcing meaning and subsequent content for the hearing-impaired individual. Echopraxia is also "a common symptom in the catatonic form of schizophrenia" (Campbell, 1981).

Clinical experience suggests that the neural mechanisms involved in these examples of echopraxia are different from true voluntary imitation. The latter represents a developmental landmark and has a voluntary quality that probably reflects the involvement of higher cortical centers. The phenomenon of echopraxia is also associated with different neural mechanisms than mirrored movements, which are observed when voluntary movements of one hand of an individual are accompanied by simultaneous identical movements of the opposite hand. This kind of movement may reflect a delay in inhibition related to specialization of one hand as a holder and the other hand as a doer. Young children with mirrored hand movements may find skilled motor tasks such as writing particularly difficult. The neurological significance of echopraxia and related movement disorders is best determined by a skilled neurologist on an individual basis (Chusid, 1978).

## REFERENCES

Campbell, R. J. (1981). *Psychiatric dictionary*. (5th ed.). New York: Oxford University Press.

Chusid, J. G. (1978). *Correlative neuroanatomy and functional neurology* (16th ed.). Los Angeles: Lang Medical.

RACHAEL J. STEVENSON
*Bedford, Ohio*

**CHILDHOOD SCHIZOPHRENIA**
**ECHOLALIA**

# ECOLOGICAL ASSESSMENT

The purpose of ecological assessment is to understand the complex interactions that occur between an individual who is the focus of assessment and his or her environment. Representing what is essentially an expansion of traditional behavior assessment techniques, ecological behavior assessment is similar to behavioral assessment with two important distinctions. First, in ecological behavior assessment, emphasis is placed on the quantification of behavior and its controlling environmental factors from a systems level perspective. That is, rather than focusing exclusively on molecular units of targeted behaviors and consequences directly responsible for their maintenance, the goal of ecological behavior assessment is to generate an understanding of the total behavior-environment system. This "system mapping" is typically accomplished through the measurement of behaviors and persons other than those to which an intervention is to be applied. For example, research conducted by Wahler and his associates (Wahler, 1975) in which observational data were taken on a variety of child behaviors has suggested that behavioral interventions targeted at a single response are likely to result in complex patterns of collateral and inverse changes in behavior within a child's repertoire. Second, in ecological behavior assessment, emphasis is placed on the measurement of existing patterns of teacher and student behavior with the goal of using this information in the development of intervention alternatives.

Given the complexity of the classroom ecology, how then is it possible to adequately assess the myriad interactions among behaviors of students, behaviors of students and teachers, and behaviors of students and teachers and the physical environment? With the finite nature of the assessment process and the functionally infinite possibilities for behavior-setting interactions, such a task would indeed be formidable. Fortunately, by drawing on concepts employed in the area of statistical analysis, the task need not be that of documenting all interactions but merely of observing those that contribute to a significant proportion of variance in possible classroom behavior.

The following steps then are presented as suggestions in the ecological assessment of behavior in any classroom setting. First, it is important to assess teacher expectations for what constitues "good" and "bad" regularities in classroom behavior. Because teachers are typically the rule makers for such behavior, and because they are the individuals most responsible for making decisions regarding behavior appropriateness, assessment of their expectations is likely to provide an important criterion by which to evaluate intervention success.

Second, once teacher expectations for student behavior have been identified, the next step is to assess regularities in student behavior that actually exist in the classroom setting. Here it is necessary to identify and observe multiple categories of student behavior at both the individual and group level. Because of the emphasis of ecological behavior assessment on molar units of student behavior (i.e., patterns of behavior that occur across students), techniques such as momentary time sampling, sequential interval time sampling of several students chosen at random, self-monitoring, and review of permanent products may be useful in obtaining frequency measures at the group level. Whatever the technique employed, one goal of ecological behavioral assessment is to identify relative frequencies of both appropriate and inappropriate classroom behaviors that are descriptive for the class as a whole.

The third and perhaps most important task in the ecological assessment of classroom behavior is the identification of regularities in teacher behaviors. Whether they are aware of it or not, teachers play critical roles in the establishment of classroom ecology. They generate rules for behavior that are specific to the classroom setting and deliver consequences to children in accordance with these rules.

The fourth and final step in the ecological assessment of classroom behavior involves the assessment of behavioral processes. Specifically, once regularities in both teacher and student behavior have been identified, the issue becomes one of determining just how the behaviors in which the teacher engages are used to consequence the behaviors in which students engage. Through an ecological mapping of contigencies common to classroom settings, it becomes possible to draw comparisons between behaviors that teachers would like to encourage in students and behaviors that they actually do encourage through their interactions.

Ecological assessment can be time-consuming and complex, but it is often a rewarding process for truly understanding the behavior of children. The present summary draws heavily on the work of Kounin (1970), Gump (1975), Martens and Witt (in press), and Reynolds, Gutkin, Elliott, and Witt (1984). The interested reader is referred to these sources for additional detail on the application of the ecological perspective to assessment.

## REFERENCES

Gump, P. V. (1975). Ecological psychology and children. In M. Hetherington (Ed.), *Review of child development research.* (Vol. 5). Chicago: University of Chicago Press.

Kounin, J. S. (1970). *Discipline and group management in classrooms.* New York: Holt, Rinehart & Winston.

Martens, B. K., & Witt, J. C. (in press). On the ecological validity of behavior modification. In J. C. Witt, S. N. Elliott, & F. M. Gresham (Eds.), *The handbook of behavior therapy in education.* New York: Plenum.

Reynolds, C. R., Gutkin, T. B., Elliott, S. N., & Witt, J. C. (1984). *School psychology: Essentials of theory and practice.* New York: Wiley.

Wahler, R. G. (1975). Some structural aspects of deviant child behavior. *Journal of Applied Behavior Analysis, 8,* 27–42.

JOSEPH C. WITT
*Louisiana State University*

## APPLIED BEHAVIOR ANALYSIS
## CLINICAL INTERVIEW

# ECOLOGICAL EDUCATION FOR THE HANDICAPPED

Ecology refers, generally, to the study of the relationship between an organism and its environment. Although the roots of ecology as a field of study are found in early anthropology, the application of ecological theories, models, and principles in special education is relatively new. The first attempt to examine the interaction of environmental effects and certain handicapped persons, and to specify related treatment approaches, is found in the works of Heinz Werner, Alfred A. Strauss, Lora Lehtinen, and William M. Cruickshank. These researchers of the 1940s, 1950s, and 1960s, studied brain-injured children and adults and the effects that various environmental stimuli had on their learning and overall behavior. An important concept derived from their research was the idea of the "stimulus-reduced" environment, first prescribed for classically brain-injured adults and children, then extended to certain "exogenous" mentally retarded children, and finally to children with "minimal brain damage" or learning disabilities. Although this work began in the 1940s, these researchers, and those who built on their pioneering efforts, did not refer formally to their efforts as ecological in nature. The term ecology itself, derived primarily from the biological sciences, surfaced as an educational variable with studies of emotionally disturbed children in the late 1960s and early 1970s.

The most notable contributions to the field include the work of Hobbs (1966) with Project Re-Ed and the University of Michigan studies in child variance (Feagans, 1972). Project Re-Ed recognized that many of the socialization problems experienced by so-called emotionally disturbed children did not have a locus within the child. Rather, problems existed in the interaction between the labeled child and the important social institutions in which he or she acted. Since there was a bad fit between child and environment (i.e., home, family, school, community), it was necessary to remove the child temporarily from this failure situation, not just to work with the child, but also to change contributing factors in the environment. While specially trained teachers aided the student, social services personnel and mental health consultants worked with the significant others in the child's world before re-merging the two again. Segregation was to be as brief as possible; normalization was always the goal.

The Michigan work, accomplished within the university's Institute for Mental Retardation and Related Disorders, reviewed, integrated, and synthesized the research, theories, and conceptual models bearing on childhood emotional disturbance. The group then developed and implemented various dissemination and training activities based on their synthesis of differing approaches to emotional disturbance. Though ecological theory was only one of six major approaches studied, the Michigan efforts helped in large part to enhance the role of ecological theory in special education.

Broadly, the ecological approach to the study and treatment of emotionally disturbed and other handicapped children attempts to break down traditional views of handicaps as something found exclusively in the involved child. The disturbance is not intrinsic per se, but a description of the interaction of a particular child with a particular environment. The search is for the source of the mismatch in the ecosystem. The study of the child occurs not in the sterility of the psychological laboratory, but in the naturalistic, real-world, holistic settings in which the child's problems occur. This is not to deny that emotional disturbance, or mental retardation, or learning disabilities are not real, or that problems in learning or adjustment that certain children experience may not have contributing neurological or biochemical substrata. The ecological focus in special education tries to show that looking only at internal factors cannot give the whole picture, and that treatment approaches based on simplified, historical, etiological views can limit the success parents and professionals might have with handicapped learners.

Since a purely medical or psychological explanation alone is not sought when handicapped students are viewed through ecological theory, a multidisciplinary team approach to diagnosis, classification, education, and treatment emerges. Special education ecologists look not only at how the child acts on his or her environment, but how the environment in its broadest sense acts on the child. Rather than overemphasize causal factors, proponents of the ecological approach seek to find or establish a state of equilibrium between child and surroundings. Specific coping skills may be taught to bring about a greater match between the child's behavior and the expectations placed on him or her by the physical and social environment. Rather than just attempting to change, or cure, what is purportedly going on within the child, the ecological special educator seeks to study the cultural relativity of the child's behavior, and to promote cultural conformity and adaptation (or synomorphy) between child and environment. The focus is on the reciprocity of behavior and reaction. Algozzine, Schmid and Mercer (1981) ask: is the disturbance merely in the eye of the beholder? Is the child really disturbed, or just disturbing?

The ecological approach to special education goes by many names. It has been termed environmental psychology, architectural psychology, ecological psychology, sociophysical technology, person-environment relations, man-environment studies, and environmental design cybernetics (Preiser & Taylor, 1983). Ecological principles have been used to examine not only brain-injured and socially/emotionally maladjusted students, but also children and youths with other handicapping conditions. Some of these studies found, for example, that the mere proximity of toys led to greater interaction and gradual expansion of the recreation setting for severely/profoundly handicapped individuals (Wehman, 1978). Other writers (Marsh & Price, 1980) looked into the interaction of environmental variables such as flexibility of school settings and information reception or reading disabilities and academic achievement, in secondary-age learning-disabled youth. Sarason and Doris (1979) coined the phrase "iatrogenic educable mental retardation" in describing the school-related disabilities found in learners from lower socioeconomic status backgrounds. Autistic, brain-injured, and normal children have been shown to demonstrate differential social responses to the density of the class or group setting in which they are placed (Hutt & Viazey, 1966). Even classroom lighting amounts and types have been examined to determine any possible effects they may have on student learning and behavior (Fletcher, 1983). As Zentall (1983) notes, professionals place regular and special education students in learning environments for about 1100 hours per year, without any empirical basis for the design of that environment—a design that, to a large extent, can be modified or controlled.

Though special and regular educators have shown cognizance of the environmental needs of certain physically and sensorily handicapped children (e.g., preferential seating for the hard of hearing, plant modifications for the physically handicapped, magnifiers and enlarged materials for partially sighted students), they still have not totally embraced the prosthetic environments described by behavioral engineers such as Ogden Lindsley (1964). Ecologists in the field would claim that special educators should continue to move away from the former child-focus approach, and more toward a pedagogy in which they test, observe, and teach in the real-world settings where skills must ultimately be generalized and successfully demonstrated if they are to say that learning truly has occurred (Hutchins & Renzaglia, 1983).

## REFERENCES

Algozzine, B., Schmid, R., & Mercer, C. D. (1981). *Childhood behaviors disorders: Applied research and educational practice.* Rockville, MD: Aspen.

Feagans, L. (1972). Ecological theory as a model for constructing a theory of emotional disturbance. In W. C. Rhodes and M. L. Tracy (Eds.), *A study in child variance* (Vol. 1). Ann Arbor: University of Michigan.

Fletcher, D. (1983). Effects of classroom lighting on the behavior of exceptional children. *Exceptional Education Quarterly, 4*(2), 75–89.

Hobbs, N. L. (1966). Helping disturbed children: Psychological and ecological strategies. *American Psychologist, 21,* 1105–1115.

Hutchins, M. P., & Renzaglia, A. (1983). Environmental considerations for severely handicapped individuals: The needs and the questions. *Exceptional Education Quarterly, 4*(2), 67–71.

Hutt, C., & Viazey, J. M. (1966). Differential effects of group density on social behavior. *Nature, 209,* 1371–1372.

Lindsley, O. R. (1964). Direct measurement and prosthesis of retarded behavior. *Journal of Education, 147,* 62–81.

Marsh, G. E., & Price, B. J. (1980). *Methods for teaching the mildly handicapped.* St. Louis: Mosby.

Preiser, W. F. E., & Taylor, A. (1983). The habitability framework: Linking human behavior and physical environment in special education. *Exceptional Education Quarterly, 4*(2), 1–15.

Sarason, S. B., & Doris, J. (1979). *Educational handicaps, public policy and social history.* New York: Free Press.

Wehman, P. (1978). Effects of different environmental conditions on leisure time activity of the severely and profoundly handicapped. *Journal of Special Education, 12*(2), 183–193.

Zentall, S. S. (1983). Learning environments: A review of physical and temporal factors. *Exceptional Education Quarterly, 4*(2), 90–115.

JOHN D. WILSON
*Elwyn Institutes,
Elwyn, Pennsylvania*

ECOLOGICAL ASSESSMENT

# ECONOMICS ISSUES: EDUCATION FOR THE HANDICAPPED

The language assuring a free education to all handicapped children to age 21 constitutes the major economic issue confronting special education today. The dollars necessary are public revenue monies in a changing mix of local, state, and federal responsibility. Special education has become a major expenditure of tax resources. Five years ago the *federal expenditure* on special education was $5 billion annually. Today, the best estimates are that the figure has more than doubled. With legislatively mandated special education services, the question of how to meet the rising costs of special education confronts local, state, and federal governments and all taxpayers.

Financially speaking, special education equals excess cost. Excess cost is the dollar amount needed to educate a handicapped student in contrast to a nonhandicapped student. In an East to West Coast gradual sweep of the United States following World War I, various states passed legislation enabling school districts to offer services for the blind and the deaf. The impetus was, as always, not provided by special educators but parental pressure on state legislatures. Many states, as early as 1803 in Massachusetts, had funded residential facilities. Extending state monies on an excess cost basis for deaf and blind students to remain in local communities seemed reasonable, if for no other reason than the fact that nearly 90% of the funding was from local monies. The state contribution in support of the excess cost factor did not concern even the most conservative state legislatures.

States expanded their legislation and excess cost support to the educable mentally retarded and the physically handicapped before World War II. These handicapped, particularly in the polio period, were considered to have lifelong chronic disabilities with a medical basis. That fact

was important in the minds of the various state legislators who were more interested in the public welfare than the educational value of the programs they were supporting. The percentages of handicapped children supported in various states remained controlled, if by no other factor than the dollar amount allocated each year for services.

Following World War II, states added a support basis for speech and hearing and school psychological services. Twenty years later, services would be further expanded to include a variety of therapies and support services, including resource room teachers. The basis for these expansions were still related to the average daily membership of special education or regular education students, or the number of classroom units within a district. These two bases enabled states to provide for a conservative growth estimate each year. In the late 1960s programs and services for the neurologically handicapped began to come under the category learning disabilities.

A dramatic example can be seen in the contrast between a continual decline in children counted as mentally retarded (from 969,547 for school year 1976–1977 to 650,534 in school year 1983–1984) and the substantial and continuing increase in the children counted as learning disabled (from 797,213 in school year 1976–1977 to 1,811,489 in school year 1983–1984). In addition, the increase in the learning disability category has accounted for the greatest proportion of the increase in the total national handicapped child count.

The amount of excess cost has now exceeded $1800 per handicapped child served. Of that total, the federal, state, and local shares were 14, 55, and 31% respectively. Given that special education has a tradition of being funded as an excess cost factor over normal state and local costs, who should fund that excess cost? The shift through the years has been from the state to the federal government. There is the opinion, if not direction, by conservative political thinking that costs should shift back to states and local areas. That would mean increased property taxes, usually very unpopular.

One of the major reasons that special education has become an economic issue is that the regularly expanding services, particularly for secondary and postsecondary students, require additional costs each year. Although national data on the number of handicapped secondary students served are not currently available, child counts from all 50 states show that the number of postsecondary-aged handicapped students (18 to 21 years old) served by the public schools has increased by over two-thirds in the last five years, with 186,393 served in school year 1983–1984.

That does not mean that the percentage of handicapped students constituting the 17 to 23% dropout rate in the secondary schools each year has lessened, only that the cost has increased. The critics of special education are asking with a stronger voice if such expenditures are worthwhile. Special educators do not have an answer.

Indeed, most special educators reject the idea of cost/benefit ratio studies, where expenditures would be examined in the light of earned income. While the cost of educating the handicapped child is twice that of educating a nonhandicapped child, little else is known. The one exception is the cost of public school special education versus institutionalization. The average cost of keeping a retarded child in an institution is slightly in excess of $10,000 per year. The cost of keeping a delinquent in an institution for a month is $15,000. The cost in 1973 for deinstitutionalization of an already institutionalized child was $5000 per year. A longitudinal follow-up study showed substantial net savings to the community through deinstitutionalization of up to $20,800 per person over a 10-year period.

The real rationale for deinstitutionalization is the earning power of the handicapped person. Between 75 and 90% of all mildly retarded persons become self-supporting. Nearly 40% of the severely disabled report some degree of self-support. That raises a major issue. The dollar cost in terms of the gain in self-sufficiency for the severely retarded is extremely high in contrast to other disability groups.

The future earnings of the mildly retarded educated in special education since 1970 is $6 of earnings for each dollar spent. If, however, the cost of continued program support in contrast to earning is calculated, then the cost benefit ratio is near $12 for every dollar spent. That figure is regarded as accurate because the national average of cost benefit ratio for adults receiving rehabilitation is $13.50 to $1 since 1971. The cost benefit ratio for the moderately retarded drops to 1.1.

Another type of cost benefit analysis is the period in years it would require a handicapped person to pay back society in tax dollars. The pay back period differs radically for different types of handicaps. For instance, it requires a person receiving speech therapy 2 to 3 years of employment to pay back the dollars spent on the excess cost of his or her education. A severely retarded child would require 2 to 7 years. The mean pay back estimates fix the cost of 11 years of special education at $52,722, with the direct tax payment at $89,680, or a net long-term savings of $36,958 in taxes generated over expenditures per person.

The adult rehabilitation literature sees a cost benefit ratio of $10.20 earned for each dollar spent as a low, and something in excess of $14 as a high. Factors influencing these figures are inflation, number of persons served, employability, job market, severity of disability, and economic issues related to the gross national product. It is not good enough to say that handicapped students, given a productive life through special education, generate some $30,000 plus on taxes over the excess cost of that education. The bottom line is what it would have cost society to have maintained them as adults.

DAVID A. SABATINO
*West Virginia College
of Graduate Studies*

SPECIAL EDUCATION, FEDERAL IMPACT ON
SPECIAL EDUCATION, LEGAL REGULATION OF

## EDGERTON, ROBERT B. (1931–    )

Robert Edgerton was introduced to the study of mental retardation at the Pacific State Hospital, California, after completing his PhD in anthropology (1960) from the University of California, Los Angeles (UCLA). He has taught at UCLA since that time in the departments of psychiatry and anthropology, becoming professor in 1972 and an administrator of socio-behavioral studies in the Mental Retardation Research Center in 1970.

Edgerton provided major contributions to the study of mental retardation primarily through his intensive and atypical methods of research. As a strong advocate of participant/observation and the qualitative approach to gathering scientific data, he conducted research using anthropological perspectives and methodologies.

At a time when deinstitutionalization is in practice, the qualitative results of Edgerton's research have been useful for social policy evaluation. He has provided insights into the everyday lives of mentally retarded persons that directly affect the design of community residential policies and criteria for reinstitutionalization. Author of over 75 books, articles, and monographs, Edgerton's principal publications include *The Cloak of Competence, Mental Retardation,* and *Environments and Behavior: The Adaptation of Mentally Retarded Persons.*

### REFERENCES

Edgerton, R. B. (1967). *The cloak of competence.* Berkeley and Los Angeles: University of California Press.

Edgerton, R. B. (1979). *Mental retardation.* Cambridge, MA: Harvard University Press.

Kernan, K., Begab, M., & Edgerton, R. B. (Eds.). (1983). *Environments and behavior: The adaptation of mentally retarded persons.* Baltimore, MD: University Park Press.

ELAINE FLETCHER-JANZEN
*Texas A&M University*

## EDUCABILITY

In its broadest sense, educability refers to the likelihood of a handicapped child benefiting from and progressing in a course of education. As such, it is appropriate to refer to the educability of a blind child or a hearing child. However, the concept is most closely related to mental retardation and has become part of the classificatory nomenclature in that area. In fact, the concept of educability can be viewed as the driving force behind the development and growth of psychometrics.

In 1904 Alfred Binet was charged with developing a process by which children unlikely to pass a standard curriculum could be identified and placed in alternative settings or excluded altogether. Working from a viewpoint that normal children achieved certain developmental stages at predictable rates, Binet and his associate Theodore Simon developed an instrument for evaluating a child's mental age. This allowed for projections of the child's functioning in school and for more heterogeneous groupings.

While the concept of mental retardation had long been accepted as a separate entity, Binet's scale had the unexpected side effect of demonstrating that the differences were on a quantitative continuum rather than being qualitatively distinct. A new group of individuals who fell between the normal and the retarded emerged. MacMillan (1977) points out that such individuals were unable to be identified prior to intelligence testing, since they were generally able-bodied, socially competent, and normal looking. Only when placed in academic situations were their learning difficulties brought to the attention of school authorities.

Just as this group of individuals is identified only in relation to school performance, it is this same sphere that causes the greatest obstacles to them, creating what the President's Committee on Mental Retardation has termed the "six-hour retarded child." This is the child who is considered retarded only during that period of the day that he or she is in school, and who is indistinguishable from others for the remaining time. By extension, many of these individuals are "cured" simply by leaving school and entering the work force.

Further underscoring the relationship between educational setting and classification is the fact that the American Association on Mental Deficiency's *Manual on Terminology and Classification of Mental Retardation* (Grossman, 1973) does not include any term for educable mentally retarded despite the fact that this is the most common designation for public school children in special classes for the mentally retarded. The definition of educable mentally retarded varies from state to state. Sedlak and Sedlak (1985) present a listing of criteria that serves to demonstrate the diversity to be found in such a classification. They list some common traits that set this group apart from so-called normal learners. These include reduced learning potential, attentional and memory deficits, decreased ability to profit from incidental learning, and atypical motivational characteristics. In addition, these individuals often have marked language difficulties and decreased personal/social skills. Lambert, Wilcox, and Gleason (1974) and Sedlak and Sedlak (1985) provide more in-depth analyses of the issues related to assessment, programming, and expectations for these children.

## REFERENCES

Grossman, H. J. (1973). *Manual on terminology and classification in mental retardation.* Washington, DC: American Association on Mental Deficiency.

Lambert, N. M., Wilcox, M. R., & Gleason, W. P. (1974). *The educationally retarded child: Comprehensive assessment and planning for slow learners and the educable mentally retarded.* New York: Grune & Stratton.

MacMillan, D. C. (1977). *Mental retardation in school and society.* Boston: Little, Brown.

Sedlak, R. A., & Sedlak, D. M. (1985). *Teaching the educable mentally retarded.* Albany: State University of New York Press.

DENNIS M. FLANAGAN
*Montgomery County
Intermediate Unit,
Norristown, Pennsylvania*

**AAMD
MENTAL RETARDATION
SIX-HOUR RETARDED CHILD**

## EDUCABLE MENTALLY RETARDED

Educable mentally retarded (EMR) individuals are often identified early in their elementary school careers as being unable to fully profit from a regular educational curriculum and school experience. Supported by special education programming, which often includes academic instruction and socialization experiences in regular classroom settings (mainstreaming), EMR students can achieve academically through an advanced elementary grade level; can learn and adaptively practice independent social living skills in the community; and can use specific job training to attain partial or total financial self-support as adults (Kirk & Gallagher, 1983).

All retarded individuals are characterized by a general intellectual functioning that is significantly below average, concurrent deficits in adaptive behavior, and the presence of these conditions during childhood or early adolescence, for instance, prior to age 18 (Grossman, 1977). These characteristics pertain to EMR individuals but, more specifically, their IQ scores range between 68 to 75 (depending on the IQ test used), and their adaptive behavior skills can facilitate the independent living and financial self-support potentials described previously.

Physically, EMR children most resemble their typical peers, with an expected range of height and weight from below to above average. Nonetheless, they do tend to have slightly more vision, hearing, and neurological difficulties, as well as slight delays in their developmental milestones. With respect to language development, EMR children are often delayed. They tend to develop language at a slower pace, and some research suggests that this development is more delayed than their intellectual and/or cognitive abilities would predict (Cromer, 1974). Socially, EMR individuals tend to have more failures than their typical peers, avoid some (new) situations to prevent additional failures, expect more failure, and function below their mental age expectations in new situations (Kauffman & Payne, 1975). Vocationally, many studies show that approximately 80% of EMR adults function capably in unskilled or semiskilled occupations.

Estimates of the total 1985 U.S. population suggest that approximately 3% are mentally retarded. Of that group, about 89% are thought to be educable. These data estimate that there are 6,408,000 EMR individuals of all ages, with 2,492,000 below age 21 and 3,916,000 above 21.

Because of their cognitive and language difficulties, educational programs for EMR children and adolescents are often adapted to maximize success. These adaptations generally include structured, unambigious directions and learning situations; carefully sequenced activities that result from task analyses of broad goals into manageable (for the individual) intermediate goals; sufficient time for the child to practice and overlearn presented material; and positive reinforcement when even small successes are attained. EMR individuals can learn basic reading and math skills; can follow directions and complete job or other applications; and can express their feelings, beliefs, and attitudes. While education is often focused on functional and community survival skills and basic communication (oral and written), EMR individuals can be challenged to achieve beyond these levels if positive motivation and self-concept levels dictate. Clearly, EMR individuals have a wide range of skills and developmental abilities. Their educational, social, and vocational training should reflect individualization, and expectations for them should be based on their skills and potentials—not stereotypes or generalizations.

### REFERENCES

Cromer, R. F. (1974). Receptive language in the mentally retarded: Processes and diagnostic distinctions. In R. L. Schiefelbusch & L. L. Lloyds (Eds.), *Language perspectives-retardation, acquisition, and intervention*. Baltimore, MD: University Park Press.

Grossman, H. (Ed.). (1977). *Manual on terminology and classification in mental retardation*. Washington, DC: American Association on Mental Deficiency.

Kauffman, J., & Payne, J. (Eds.) (1975). *Mental retardation: Introduction and personal perspectives*. Columbus, OH: Charles E. Merrill.

Kirk, S. A., & Gallagher, J. J. (1983). *Educating exceptional children* (4th ed.). Boston: Houghton Mifflin.

HOWARD M. KNOFF
*University of South Florida*

**MENTAL RETARDATION**
**TRAINABLE MENTALLY RETARDED**

# EDUCATEUR

The educateur, sometimes referred to as the psychoeducateur, is a trained generalist whose primary concern goes beyond that of the traditional teacher's interest in student learning to include a focus on the personality and emotional development of the child (Morse & Smith, 1980). The role of the educateur dates to the years immediately following World War II, when the presence of large numbers of displaced emotionally disturbed children (victims of the psychological traumas of war) were identified in France and Scotland (Daly, 1985). Inadequate numbers of qualified mental health workers to meet the many needs of these children led to the development of a new profession, that of the educateur, a professional trained in the skills of teaching, social work, psychology, and recreation.

In the mid 1950s in Canada, Guindon (1973) adapted the European educateur model for use with delinquent and emotionally handicapped children and youths. Guindon's psychoeducateur intervention had an ecological orientation, emphasizing the significance of change in the child's environment and using interventions associated with other perspectives.

Drawing from a combination of psychodynamic and developmental approaches, educateur treatment seeks to restructure completely all activities and relationships in the child's environment. To accomplish this, the child is placed in a residential setting for an average period of 18 months. Here, the educateur initially works to provide a highly structured environment with maximum external control. Then external controls are gradually reduced with concomitant increase in flexibility and individual expression for the child.

Linton (1971) described the educateur working in these specialized facilities as being trained to effect positive changes by focusing specifically on the interaction between child and environment and on the natural support systems such as family and community. Thus the educateur functions as a child advocate and environmental change agent to reduce discord and restore harmony in a manner that ultimately permits complete withdrawal of external intervention. The educateur's goal is to help the child acquire problem-solving skills and behavioral repertoires for successfully meeting both known and unfamiliar situations (Goocher, 1975).

Project Re-ED (Hobbs, 1982) is considered by some individuals to represent an Americanized version of the educateur model with the term teacher-counselor replacing educateur. For those individuals interested in acquiring educateur skills, Daly (1985) reports that at least four American colleges or universities (Ohio State University, Southern Connecticut State College, Western Michigan University, and the University of Virginia) provide training programs using the term educateur. The training in these programs includes recreation, special education, and behavioral sciences as well as an internship in a child service agency.

## REFERENCES

Daly, P. M. (1985). The educateur: An atypical childcare worker. *Behavioral Disorders, 11*, 35–41.

Goocher, B. E. (1975). Behavioral applications of an educateur model in child care. *Child Care Quarterly, 4*, 84–92.

Guindon, J. (1973). The reeducation process. *International Journal of Mental Health, 2*(1), 15–26, 27–32.

Hobbs, N. (1982). *The troubled and troubling child.* San Francisco: Jossey-Bass.

Linton, T. E. (1971). The education model: A theoretical model: A theoretical monograph. *Journal of Special Education, 5,* 155–190.

Morse, W., & Smith, J. (1980). *Understanding child variance.* Reston, VA: Council for Exceptional Children.

KATHY L. RUHL
*Pennsylvania State University*

## PROJECT RE-ED

## EDUCATIONAL AND PSYCHOLOGICAL MEASUREMENT

*Educational and Psychological Measurement* is a quarterly journal devoted to the development and application of measures of individual differences. Articles published in the journal are divided into three sections.

The first section consists of articles reporting the results of research investigations into problems in the measurement of individual differences in education and psychology. Articles include investigations on known or new statistical and psychometric procedures, the psychometric characteristics of tests, descriptions of testing programs, and the use of tests and measurements in education, industry, and government.

The second section is devoted to validity studies on new or existing tests for measuring individual differences. This section is published at least twice a year, in the summer and winter issues. It is an excellent source for consumers or researchers wishing to obtain current validity information on new or newly revised tests.

A third section is devoted to computer studies, with reports on the use(s) of already existing or new computer programs available on a mainframe, mini-, or microcomputer. These programs may be used for carrying out computations in statistical analyses when assessing the measurement of individual differences.

The address of the journal's office is Educational and Psychological Measurement, Box 6856, College Station, Durham, NC 27708.

GWYNETH M. BOODOO
*Texas A&M University*

## EDUCATIONAL DIAGNOSTICIAN

An educational diagnostician is an individual who often functions as a member of the multidisciplinary team that determines whether a child is eligible for special education programs. The educational diagnostician differs from the school psychologist both in preparation and function. Generally, the educational diagnostician is a certified or licensed regular or special education teacher with three or more years of experience in the classroom. Graduate training, typically a two-semester master of education program, is focused on content and techniques concerned with diagnosis and remediation of learning problems. The school psychologist is generally not a certified or licensed teacher but has graduate or advanced graduate training of two or more years, the focus of which is on the content and techniques related to assessment of intellectual and behavioral functioning of children and training in psychological interventions including both direct and indirect service delivery. While most states offer certification for school psychologists, fewer states actually offer formal certification, licensure, or endorsement for educational diagnosticians.

The role of the educational diagnostician has been influenced by the Education for All Handicapped Children Act of 1975 (PL 94-142) and state legislation and/or regulations. The school psychologist performed some of the functions of educational diagnosis prior to the recent development of the position of educational diagnostician. The terms educational diagnostician and educational specialist are often used interchangeably.

Federal and state requirements for assessment of current levels of educational performance, the prohibition of a single test score in determining eligibility, and the requirement that eligibility for special education be made by a multidisciplinary team have increased the demand for educational diagnosticians in most states. Eligibility for special education generally requires team consideration of educational, social, psychological, and medical information.

McLeod (1983) suggests the purpose of educational diagnosis is to answer a generic question about how the child may be helped to learn basic school skills effectively. Specific questions, while differing from child to child, generally include further questioning about how the child learns, why he or she is failing, and what can be done about it. Determination of learning style—visual or aural—is seen as a basic need in the diagnostic process.

Rote learning versus learning through insight should also be specified.

Hargrove and Poteet (1984) specify assessment, diagnostic, and prescriptive activities as the components of educational evaluations. In conducting the evaluation, the diagnostician uses the three basic skills of looking, listening, and questioning. Tools and techniques used by the diagnostician include rating scales, interviews, observations, tests, and clinical judgment.

In most school districts using educational diagnosticians, their primary role relates to the evaluation of students referred for special education programs or services, though in most states they are prohibited from working with emotionally disturbed children, a task more suited to the school psychologist. The educational diagnostician can perform a valuable function in working with other students who may be experiencing learning problems but who would not be considered in need of special education.

### REFERENCES

Hargrove, L. J., & Poteet, J. A. (1984). *Assessment in special education*. Englewood Cliffs, NJ: Prentice-Hall.

McLeod, J. (1983). The art and science of educational diagnosis. *Exceptional Child, 30*, 57–66.

PHILIP R. JONES
*Virginia Polytechnic Institute and State University*

MULTIDISCIPLINARY TEAMS
SCHOOL PSYCHOLOGY

# EDUCATIONALLY DISADVANTAGED

According to the Office of Elementary and Secondary Education, educationally deprived children are children whose educational attainment is below the level that is appropriate for children their age. These children are often referred to as educationally disadvantaged. A cause for this scholastic retardation in depressed areas is attributed to the attitudes and behavior of school personnel (Passow, 1967). These children often come from culturally deprived homes that fail to equip the children to fit into and adapt well into the school environment (Passow, 1967). Daniels (1967) adds that the disadvantaged have become handicapped because of social or environmental conditions in their ability to learn and to acquire skills and abilities for coping with the problems of earning a living and enjoying a satisfying life. He accepts the estimate that the disadvantaged constitute 25% of the school population and in larger cities 30 to 40%.

Title I of the Elementary and Secondary Education Act was designed to overcome the debilitating burdens placed on educationally disadvantaged students by certain school personnel and culturally deprived families. Title I was one in a series of legislative efforts aimed at addressing the needs of the culturally disadvantaged. Some of the others were the Civil Rights Act of 1964, the Economic Opportunity Act of 1964, the Vocational Act of 1963, and the National Defense Act (revised in 1965). Additional related legislation aimed at reducing discrimination policies toward the educationally disadvantaged and other specific targeted populations were Title IX of the Education Amendments of 1972 (PL 92-318), the Education for All Handicapped Children Act (PL 94-142), and the Rehabilitation Act of 1973 (PL 93-112).

Chapter 1 of PL 97-35 addresses the issue of financial assistance to meet the educational needs of disadvantaged children. This legislation replaced Title I of the Elementary and Secondary Act of 1965. Chapter I continues to be the main legislation addressing the educational needs of deprived children. The act will fund local education agency school programs to meet the needs of educationally deprived children. According to PL 97-35:

> Such programs and projects may include the acquisition of equipment and instructional materials, employment of special instructional and counseling and guidance personnel, employment and training of teacher aides, payments to teachers in amounts in excess of regular salary schedules (as a bonus for service in schools serving project areas), the training of teachers, the construction, where necessary, of school facilities, other expenditures authorized under Title I . . . .

Passow's (1967) assessment of the underlying causes for educational deprivation and cultural deprivation still appear to be valid, even though much federal legislation has been written to address this American educational need. Passow has stated that "their problems stem from poverty and unemployment; segregation, discrimination, and lack of equal opportunity in housing and employment, as well as education; discontinuities with the 'dominant' culture, rising out of difference in life style, child rearing practices and skills for urban living; and inadequate educational attainment of those skills essential in a technical society." Promising practices, he states, fall into nine categories: in-service education and recruitment, reading, summer programs, community-school aspects, guidance activities, early admissions programs, team teaching programs, special placement classes, and job-retraining programs. The challenge for schools in developing promising practices is to keep in mind the question, How can the school educate inner city children out of their subcultures into society's mainstream while preserving and developing their individuality and diversity, as well as the positive elements of their cultures?

The current literature suggests that schools can increase their effectiveness by changing their focus from considering the culturally disadvantaged as disadvantaged to considering them as culturally different. This shift in focus permits one to accept the fact that the culturally different may continue having disadvantages but they also have benefits for society. Programs that include emphasis on the benefits to society by the culturally different are basically encompassed in the concept of multicultural education.

Rodriguez (1983) defines multicultural education as education that values cultural pluralism. Multicultural education recognizes that cultural diversity is a valuable resource and should be extended into American society. Schools should not melt away cultural differences or merely tolerate cultural pluralism. Each cultural unit lives as part of an interrelated whole. According to Bennett (1986), the goal of multicultural education is to change the total educational environment so that it will develop competencies in multiple cultures and provide members of all cultural groups with equal educational opportunity. Equity is at the heart of multicultural education.

It appears, therefore, that effective programming for the educationally disadvantaged can be enhanced if the needs of the disadvantaged are perceived in an educational milieu that also recognizes the benefits to society of the students' culture.

## REFERENCES

Bennett, C. I. (1986). *Comprehensive multicultural education: Theory and practice*, Boston: Allyn & Bacon. p. 53.

Daniels, W. G. (1967). Some essential ingredients in educational programs for the socially disadvantaged. In J. Hellmuth (Ed.), *Disadvantaged child. Vol. 1: Special child* (pp. 202–221). Seattle, WA: Seattle Seguin School.

Passow, H. A. (1967). Education of the culturally deprived child. In J. Hellmuth (Ed.), *Disadvantaged child, Special child*. Seattle, WA: Seguin School.

Rodriguez, F. (1983). *Education in a multicultural society*. Lanham, MD: University Press of America.

STAN A. KARCZ
*University of Wisconsin, Stout*

CULTURAL BIAS IN TESTING
PLURALISM, CULTURAL

## EDUCATIONAL PRODUCTS INFORMATION EXCHANGE (EPIE)

Established in 1967 and chartered by the New York Board of Regents, the Educational Products Information Exchange (EPIE) is devoted to helping educators effectively select and use instructional materials. Its members are primarily educational practitioners in local school districts.

The EPIE is a source of information, advocacy, and training concerning instructional materials. The organization has emphasized the need for consumers and producers to examine products with respect to the congruence of instructional design, intrinsic quality dimensions, practicality, and user effects. A central feature of this advocacy is the systematic application of "learner verification and revision," which involves testing to ensure that a product does what its producer claims and what teachers expect it to do. The EPIE's product evaluation procedures are based on a sophisticated analyses, a user review system, and a comprehensive list of criteria.

The EPIE Institute publishes a newsletter, "Epiegram," which reviews research findings derived from product development and evaluation studies and from practitioners' uses of products. The EPIE Institute may be contacted at 475 Riverside Drive, New York, New York 10027.

JUDY SMITH-DAVIS
*Counterpoint Communications Company, Reno, Nevada*

## EDUCATIONAL RESOURCES INFORMATION CENTER

The Educational Resources Information Center (ERIC) is a national information system that provides access to the literature of education. Operating since 1965 and funded by the National Institute of Education, the ERIC system consists of a coordinating staff in Washington, DC, and 16 clearinghouses located at universities or professional organizations, each specializing in a major area of the field of education. The clearinghouse responsible for selecting, acquiring, cataloguing, abstracting, and indexing documents related to handicapped and gifted children is located at the Council for Exceptional Children (CEC) in Reston, Virginia.

The 16 clearinghouses prepare abstracts of relevant documents for two monthly ERIC publications. *Current Index to Journals in Education* (CIJE), a guide to current periodical literature in education, covers approximately 780 major educational and education-related journals; *Resources in Education* (RIE), a guide to other current literature in education, covers research findings, project and technical reports, speeches, unpublished manuscripts, and books. The clearinghouses also prepare interpretive summaries and annotated bibliographies on high-interest topics. The ERIC Clearinghouse on Handicapped and Gifted Children prepares a quarterly publication, *Exceptional Child Education Resources* (ECER), that includes indexes and abstracts of material included in both RIE and CIJE. The RIE and CIJE can be searched manually using author, subject, and institution indexes; they are also available for on-line computer searching through major commercial database brokerage systems. The ERIC system also produces a thesaurus of descriptors used to index documents. Documents indexed and abstracted in RIE are available from the ERIC Document Reproduction Service, except when noted, in both microfiche and paper copy, or in microfiche only. The ERIC microfiche collections are maintained at numerous university libraries across the country.

LINDA J. STEVENS
*University of Minnesota*

## COUNCIL FOR EXCEPTIONAL CHILDREN

## EDUCATIONAL TESTING SERVICE (ETS)

Educational Testing Service (ETS) is a nonprofit corporation established in 1947; it originally intended to carry out the College Entrance Examination Board (CEEB) testing program. The ETS also was involved in assisting the testing functions of the Carnegie Corporation and the American Council on Education. In addition to providing contract services to these, and now many other agencies (ETS develops and is responsible for carrying out the Law School Admissions Test, Graduate Record Examination, and numerous other programs), ETS has a world-renowned research and development staff. In recent years, ETS has undergone a streamlining that has reduced its basic research programs and led to a cutback in all research and development activities not aimed at marketable products, a change that represents a great loss to testing and to measurement theory.

The largest percentage of ETS's activity is devoted to developing, administering, scoring, and reporting services for the Scholastic Aptitude Test (SAT). The SAT is administered regularly at more than 5000 testing centers to more than 1 million college applicants each year. The use of ETS-administered admissions testing programs periodically stirs great controversy, mostly centering around charges of unfairness to certain classes of individuals.

In all of its testing programs, ETS regularly makes accommodations for handicapped individuals. Not only are readers or recorded tests provided for the blind and for the dyslexic, but protheses and special administrative procedures for orthopedically handicapped individuals are provided as well; such special arrangements must be requested far in advance of the intended testing date.

Recently ETS has become heavily involved in competency testing and examinations for licensure and certification of professions. The ETS prepares exams for teachers and has proposed competency exams for school psychologists as well.

CECIL R. REYNOLDS
*Texas A&M University*

## EDUCATION AND TRAINING OF THE MENTALLY RETARDED (ETMR)

*Education and Training of the Mentally Retarded* (ETMR) is the quarterly journal published by the Division on Mental Retardation, The Council for Exceptional Children. The journal began its twentieth volume in 1985. Content focuses on the education and welfare of retarded persons through data-based and expository articles as well as critical reviews of the literature. The editorial policy statement places major emphasis on identification and assessment, educational programming, characteristics, training of instructional personnel, habilitation, prevention, community understanding, and legislation. Editorial offices are located at 1920 Association Drive, Reston, VA 22091.

PHILIP R. JONES
*Virginia Polytechnic Institute
and State University*

## EDUCATION AND TREATMENT OF CHILDREN (ETC)

*Education and Treatment of Children* (ETC) is a referred, scholarly journal published quarterly by Clinical Psychology Publishing Company for the Pressley Ridge School in Pittsburgh, Pennsylvania. The journal's goal is to disseminate reliable information related to educational and treatment services for children and youths. Manuscripts accepted for publication are judged on their relevance to a variety of child care professionals for improving the effectiveness of teaching and training techniques.

The responsibilities of the editorship of *ETC* are shared by R. F. Dickie and Daniel Hursh in cooperation with several specific area editors. The scholarly review process is further facilitated by 10 editors and numerous individuals serving on the editorial review board. These individuals include academicians, educators, practitioners, and others representing most geographic areas of the United States and portions of Canada.

Since its initial publication in 1976, ETC has published manuscripts describing a wide variety of experimental studies as well as nonexperimental procedures and/or services and programs for exceptional and normal children and youths. A considerable portion of each issue is devoted to reviews of books and other published materials in the areas of education and treatment of children and youths. The content of the journal is informative and practical for practitioner and researcher alike and should prove useful in improving treatment practices.

JULIA A. HICKMAN
*University of Texas, Austin*

## EDUCATION APPERCEPTION TEST

The Education Apperception Test (EAT) was developed by two school psychologists (Thompson & Sones, 1973) as an analogue to projective storytelling tasks such as the Children's Apperception Test. It focused on children's perception of school and the educative process. The test consists of 18 black and white pictures depicting children in ambiguous school and school-related circumstances. According to the authors (Thompson & Sones, 1973), the selection of pictures was based on their relevance to significant areas of school and school-related activities. The children shown in the EAT are of middle elementary school ages. Despite a 1973 publication date and the authors personally taking the pictures, they appear archaic.

The EAT was developed on the basis of the traditional projective hypothesis, which contends that when presented with ambiguous stimuli, various needs, drive states, and underlying, subconscious personality characteristics will dictate the nature of the individual's response. Fundamental to this hypothesis is the premise that the individual is free to choose any of an infinite number of responses but the various internal states noted dictate the individual's final choices. The EAT pictures were chosen and designed on the basis of the work experiences of the authors. Administration and interpretation of the EAT follow essentially the format of other projective storytelling procedures and are reviewed in most basic measurement texts (Anastasi, 1982).

The use of the term test in the title of the EAT seems inappropriate. It is a technique for exploring personality variables without norms or standard scores of any kind. No validity data are presented in the manual and the use of the EAT as anything other than a structured interview procedure, possibly in a research setting, is inappropriate. As a structured interview technique, the EAT may be useful in helping to understand children's behavior and learning problems associated with school and academic-related concerns.

### REFERENCES

Anastasi, A. (1982). *Psychological testing*. New York: Macmillan.
Thompson, J. M., & Sones, R. A. (1973). *Education Apperception Test*. Los Angeles: Western Psychological Services.

CECIL R. REYNOLDS
*Texas A&M University*

PERSONALITY ASSESSMENT
SERIOUSLY EMOTIONALLY DISTURBED
VALIDITY

## EDUCATION FOR ALL HANDICAPPED CHILDREN ACT OF 1975 (PL 94-142)

The federal government's role in the education of handicapped children began in the 1960s with legislation au-

thorizing support for the training of teachers of the deaf and for the provision of speech pathologists and audiologists for individuals with speech and hearing impairments (PL 87-276). A genuine commitment to education occurred in 1965 with passage of the Elementary and Secondary Education Act (ESEA; PL 89-10) and subsequent passage of PL 89-313 (Federal Assistance to State Operated and Supported Schools for the Handicapped). The ESEA authorized funds to local education agencies to establish programs for educationally deficient children. Public Law 89-313 offered grants to state agencies for the provision of education to children who receive their education in state-operated or state-supported facilities.

In 1966 ESEA again was amended (PL 89-750) to provide for the establishment of the National Technical Institute for the Deaf and the Model Secondary School for the Deaf. Moreover, the amended ESEA established the Bureau of Education for the Handicapped within the Office of Education. This office was to administer all programs operated for the benefit of the handicapped. The 1967 amendments to ESEA (PL 90-247) created regional resource centers to provide assessment for handicapped learners as well as additional funds for training special education personnel.

With the amendments to the Vocational Education Act of 1968 (PL 90-576), 10% of the funds authorized under the Act were to be used for vocational education programs for handicapped students. The Handicapped Children's Early Education Assistance Act (PL 90-538) also was enacted in 1968 to establish model programs for young handicapped children.

During the 1970s legislation for the handicapped expanded. The Education Amendments of 1974 (PL 93-380) authorized an increase in the basic state grant program from $100 to $660 million. These amendments required that each state establish a goal of providing full educational opportunities for handicapped children. In addition, the amendments affirmed the educational rights of handicapped children. One year later, on November 29, 1975, the Education for All Handicapped Children Act (PL 94-142) was signed into law. This legislation reaffirmed and strengthened the educational rights of handicapped children and increased the financial commitment of the federal government.

The Act provides for a contribution on the part of the federal government to the education of handicapped children. Specifically, states are entitled to a percentage of the national average per pupil expenditure (NAPPE) in public elementary and secondary schools multiplied by the number of handicapped children, ages 3 to 21, in the state who are receiving special education and related services. The initial amount available was 5% of the NAPPE for fiscal year 1982 and was to have risen to 40% of the NAPPE. Congress did not fully fund this part of the Act. It is estimated that federal funds account for approximately 12% of the total per pupil expenditure for handicapped students. States may count up to 12% of their handicapped school-age population for entitlement purposes.

To qualify for funds under the Act, each state must have a state plan that:

Assures that all handicapped children have a right to a free and appropriate public education

Establishes policies and procedures that ensure the provision of a full educational opportunity to all handicapped children

Provides for the identification and location of all handicapped children

Provides for the maintenance of records pertaining to the individualized education program for each handicapped child

Establishes procedural safeguards to ensure that handicapped and nonhandicapped are educated together to the maximum extent appropriate, and that testing and evaluation are not discriminatory

Ensures that all education programs in a state are under the general supervision of the state education agency

Provides for consultation with individuals concerned with the education of handicapped children

Specific assurances and procedures that must be provided in the state plan may be found in Section 613 of the Act.

The primary purpose of the Act was to ensure that all handicapped children had "available to them a free and appropriate public education which emphasize(d) special education and related services designed to meet their unique needs." The concept of free and appropriate public education included education at public expense that met appropriate state standards and that was provided in conjunction with an individualized education program.

Section 615 of the Act requires that procedural safeguards be put in place. These safeguards are intended to ensure that:

Parents/guardians may examine relevant records relating to the identification, evaluation, and placement of the child

Parents/guardians may obtain an independent evaluation

Each child has a surrogate parent appointed whenever the parents/guardians are unknown

Parents/guardians receive prior written notice when a change in the identification, evaluation, or placement of the child is anticipated

Parents/guardians have an opportunity to present complaints related to the identification, evaluation, placement, or provision of a free appropriate public education

The remainder of this section describes the hearings and appeals procedures available to parents/guardians. These procedures range from due process hearings held by a local or state educational agency to civil actions initiated against local or state education agencies.

To enforce compliance with either provisions of the Act or the state implementation plan, federal funds can be withheld by the U.S. Department of Education. This remedy is not available to individuals but is available as an administrative remedy where substantial noncompliance is noted.

Evaluation of the Act is provided for in Section 618. In conjunction with Section 617, which authorizes the hiring of up to 20 individuals to engage in data collection and evaluation activities, Section 618 requires the commissioner (now the secretary) to evaluate the impact of the program and the effectiveness of state efforts. Specific information requirements include (1) the number of handicapped children, by state and handicapping category, who are receiving a free appropriate public education; (2) the number of handicapped children, by state and handicapping category, who are receiving special education and related services in regular education settings, in separate classes, separate school settings, or other environments; (3) the number of handicapped children enrolled in public or private institutions; (4) the amount of federal, state, and local expenditures available for special education and related services; and (5) the number of personnel by disability category employed and needed to adequately carry out the act. This information, as well as information pertaining to the progress being made in the implementing the Act, is to be transmitted to Congress by February 1 of each year.

Section 619 of the Act provides an incentive to states to serve young handicapped children. By providing special education and related services to children ages 3 through 5, each state may receive an amount up to $300 per child. The actual amount per child under this program, like that provided for under the basic entitlement, is dependent on the actual amount of dollars appropriated for the program.

The key provisions of PL 94-142 include the concepts of a free appropriate public education, least restrictive environment, and the individualized education program (IEP). Free appropriate public education (FAPE) is "special education and related services which are provided at public expense . . . in conformity with an individualized education program." The responsibility for FAPE rests with the local education agency (LEA), although state education agencies, under the general supervision requirements of the act, are responsible for ensuring that local agencies provide FAPE to all handicapped students.

LEAs must have an IEP in place at the beginning of each school year for those handicapped children receiving special education. Newly identified handicapped children, that is those needing special education and related services, must have an IEP developed and in place within 30 days of the determination that special education is needed.

The IEP is the mechanism by which goals and objectives are established, programs planned, and student progress followed. In developing, reviewing, and revising the IEP on an annual basis, the Act requires that a public agency official other than the child's teacher (e.g., an LEA official), the child's teacher, and the child's parent(s) be present. Where appropriate, the child may participate. Information in the IEP must include:

Current levels of educational performance

A statement of annual goals

Specific services to be provided to the child

The date that services will be initiated and the likely length of such services

Criteria and schedules for determining whether objectives have been achieved

Special education and related services must be provided in the least restrictive environment, to the extent appropriate. The Act does not require that handicapped children be educated entirely in regular classes or that all handicapped children have a part of their education provided in regular classes. Decisions about what constitutes the least restrictive environment are made for each handicapped child based on the child's needs and requirements for an educational program.

In addition to the procedural safeguards noted (notice to parents of a handicapped child of their legal rights and the school district's intent to initiate a change in the evaluation, program, or placement of a child), other procedural safeguards are provided by law. For example, testing and evaluation of children suspected of having a handicapping condition must be conducted by trained personnel and administered in the child's native language so as not to be racially or culturally discriminatory. Testing and evaluation cannot consist of the administration of a single instrument that becomes the sole criterion for determining the program for a child. Should parents disagree with the evaluation procedures or outcomes, they have the right to an independent evaluation, at public expense, unless the LEA establishes that its hearing was appropriate. Apart from civil proceedings, parents may request an impartial due process hearing involving the identification, evaluation, placement, or provision of a free appropriate public education. This hearing is conducted by a third party, not a direct employee of the local or state education agency. Either the parents or the local education agency may appeal the hearing officer's decision to the state education agency.

Under the general supervision authority contained in the Act, state education agencies are required to monitor local education agencies, private school placements of handicapped children, and all other state agencies (e.g.,

prisons, state institutions) to ensure compliance with the provisions of the Act. The state education agency must conduct on-site visits, examine local education records, and collect data. The procedures used to engage in compliance and monitoring activities are a part of the state plan (Section 613) and are subject to periodic review by the U.S. Department of Education, Special Education Programs. Public Law 94-142 was reauthorized in 1983 and was revised and incorporated under PL 98-199. The full text of the law is given in the Appendix.

MARTY ABRAMSON
*University of Wisconsin, Stout*

**FREE APPROPRIATE PUBLIC EDUCATION**
**INDIVIDUAL EDUCATION PLAN**
**LEAST RESTRICTIVE ENVIRONMENT**
**PARENTS OF THE HANDICAPPED**

## EDUCATION FOR "OTHER HEALTH IMPAIRED" CHILDREN

"Other Health Impaired" children include those pupils whose health problems severely affect their learning. Federal law designates this group as children with severe orthopedic impairments, illnesses of a chronic or acute natue that requires a prolonged convalescence or which limits that child's vitality and strength, congenital anomalies (e.g., spina bifida and clubfoot), other physical causes (e.g., amputation and cerebral palsy), and other health problems including, but not limited to hemophilia, asthma, severe anemia, and diabetes. This category constitutes about 4% of children classified as handicapped (Ysseldyke & Algozzine, 1984). Unfortunately, the terminology used for children suffering other health impairments does not indicate any commonality in student need, as the categorization is based on recognizable differences in condition and not on necessary educational interventions (Reynolds & Birch, 1982).

Other health impairments may be the result of congenital defects or adventitious (acquired) disabilities. The tremendous heterogeneity associated with the term requires attention to the one obvious common factor of such children, a physical condition that interferes with normal functioning. This limits the child's opportunity to participate fully in learning activities by affecting the body's supply of strength and energy or the removal of wastes, reducing mobility, and creating severe problems in growth and development (Kneedler, 1984).

Although the continuum of degree may range from mild to severe, educational principles for other health impaired children include:

1. Placement and education within the mainstream of

the public school to the maximum capability of the child. In addition, for those children requiring a special class, school, or home/hospital instruction, directing efforts to return them as soon as possible to regular education (Heron & Harris, 1982).

2. Architectural modifications including the removal of all architectural barriers for full school integration and the modification of classroom structure and environment to allow optimal mobility and exploration.

3. Parent and family education is assumed by the school to provide for coordination of effort, resources, and services.

4. Trained teachers and paraprofessionals who will assist other health impaired children within the school setting.

5. Coordination and utilization of all necessary support and resource personnel by school districts serving such children include transportation modifications, physical and occupational therapy, adaptive physical education, and vocational education and counseling (Gearheart & Weishahn, 1980).

## REFERENCES

Gearheart, B. R., & Weishahn, M. W. (1980). *The handicapped child in the regular classroom* (2nd ed.). St. Louis: Mosby.

Heron, T. E., & Harris, K. C. (1982). *The Educational consultant: Helping professionals, parents, and mainstreamed students.* Boston, Mass: Allyn & Bacon.

Kneedler, R. D., Hallahan, D. P., & Kauffman, J. M. (1984). *Special education for today.* Englewood Cliffs, NJ: Prentice-Hall.

Reynolds, M. C., & Birch, J. W. (1982). *Teaching exceptional children in all America's schools.* Reston, Va: Council for Exceptional Children.

Ysseldyke, J. E., & Algozzine, B. (1984). *Introduction to special education.* Boston, Mass: Houghton Mifflin.

RONALD S. LENKOWSKY
*Hunter College, City University of New York*

CATEGORICAL EDUCATION
CEREBRAL PALSY
EDUCATION FOR THE TERMINALLY ILL
OTHER HEALTH IMPAIRED
SPINA BIFIDA

## EDUCATION FOR THE HANDICAPPED LAW REPORT (EHLR)

*Education for the Handicapped Law Report* (EHLR) is a compilation of current documents concerning special education law. The *EHLR* loose-leaf volumes contain federal statutes and regulations relevant to the education of handicapped children and youths; policy letters, state monitoring reports, rulings, and other documents issued by the Office for Civil Rights and Special Education Programs in the U.S. Department of Education; major court decisions; and current decisions of administrative hearings and appeals from selected state educational agencies.

Other features of the *EHLR* are lists of relevant cases pending before or acted on by the U.S. Supreme Court during each term, a newsletter that reports events and items of special interest, and directories of groups and agencies involved or interested in education of the handicapped. The binder contents are continually updated by 24 supplements annually. The extensive *EHLR* indexes serve as a convenient search system for users.

SHIRLEY A. JONES
*Virginia Polytechnic Institute and State University*

## EDUCATION FOR THE TERMINALLY ILL

The teacher confronted by the crisis of a terminally ill child is faced with a complex and difficult situation. The role of the educator requires interaction with the life-threatened child and that child's family, peers, and classmates. Medical and technological advances have increased the life expectancy of terminally ill children and allowed many to return to school during periods of remission or control of their illness (Desy-Spinetta & Spinetta, 1983). To be helped and comforted by a return to the familiar atmosphere of school, the dying child requires the active support and assistance of school personnel (Eklof, 1984).

There are several stages of instruction to be observed in the education of terminally ill children. The initial phase should begin with the instruction and counseling of those who will teach them. It is necessary for educators to face, express, and deal with their own feelings toward death and dying before they can effectively identify and meet the emotional needs and presenting problems of such children. Denial, avoidance, fear, and helplessness are attitudes commonly encountered in unprepared teachers that directly affect the quality of the terminally ill child's experiences in school (Cairns, 1980). Instructional modules devoted to teacher self-awareness and the reality of facing and coping with death and dying are recommended for inclusion in teacher preparation programs (Sirvis, 1981).

As terminally ill children often choose a caring adult other than a parent with whom to communicate and express their feelings, the second stage in teacher preparation must be familiarization and understanding of the psychological stages encountered by the terminally ill and the "language of feelings" employed by such children. Professionals must be aware of the different ways children may select to communicate those feelings in order to be helpful and supportive (Kubler-Ross, 1983).

The second phase in a comprehensive education program for the terminally ill must address the needs and fears of the peers and classmates of the dying child. Wass and Corr (1982) stress the need for curriculum units on death and terminal illness to prepare teachers to instruct on such topics, while Jeffrey and Lansdown (1982) also recommend the inclusion of curriculum units on death and dying for both regular and special education class pupils.

The final phase in educating the terminally ill child offers directed strategies for the teacher. These include: (1) the maintenance of regular classroom routines for such children and the continued application of rules, limits, and reasonable goal-setting (Noore, 1981); (2) the use by teachers of such methods as life space interviews, adjunctive therapy, expressive writing, bibliotherapy (literature), role playing, magic circle discussions, art therapy, and play therapy to cope with the child's presenting problems (Ainsa, 1981); (3) the preparation by teachers to deal effectively with behaviors that may range from withdrawal to defiance while helping friends and classmates grieve and recover on the death of the child; (4) the maintenance by teachers of a primary role and the fulfillment of teaching responsibilities while emphasizing views in the classroom that stress maintaining meaning in the life of the terminally ill child (Stuecher, 1980).

## REFERENCES

Ainsa, T. (1981). Teaching the terminally ill child. *Education, 101,* 397–401.

Cairns, N. (1980). The dying child in the classroom. *Essence: Issues in the study of aging, dying, and death, 4,* 25–32.

Desy-Spinetta, P., & Spinetta, J. J. (1983). The child with cancer returns to school: Preparing the teacher. In J. E. Schowalter, P. R. Patterson, M. Tallmer, A. H. Kutscher, S. V. Gullo, & D. Peretz (Eds.), *The child and death,* New York: Columbia University Press.

Eklof, M. (1984). The terminally ill child: How peers, parents and teachers can help. *PTA Today, 10,* 8–9.

Jeffrey, P., & Lansdown, R. (1982). The role of the special school in the care of the dying child. *Developmental Medicine & Child Neurology, 24,* 693–696.

Kubler-Ross, E. (1983). *On children and death.* New York: Macmillan.

Noore, N. (1981). The damaged child. *Journal for Special Educators, 17,* 376–380.

Sirvis, B. (1981). Death and dying: An instructional module for special educators. *Dissertation Abstracts International,* Order no. 76-21039, *39,* 164 pp.

Wass, H., & Corr, C. A. (1982). *Helping children cope with death: guidelines and resources.* New York: Hemisphere.

RONALD S. LENKOWSKY
*Hunter College, City University
of New York*

FAMILY COUNSELING
FAMILY RESPONSE TO A HANDICAPPED CHILD
PHYSICAL HANDICAPS

# EDUCATION OF THE BLIND/VISUALLY HANDICAPPED

Educationally significant, noncorrectable vision impairments are prevalent in approximately 1 student in 1000. The U.S. Department of Education (1985) reports that approximately 32,000 students between the ages of 3 and 21 are identified as visually handicapped. Educators use one of two basic classifications in identifying students who are visually handicapped: blind and visually impaired/low vision. Those who are blind may have no light perception or may have some light perception without projection. The low-vision learner is considered severely impaired (even with corrective assistance such as glasses), but is able to read print (often in modified form).

According to Kirk and Gallagher (1986), research on the impact of visual handicaps indicates that, for the vast majority of students, (1) intellectual abilities are not markedly affected; (2) the perception of other senses is not substantially different from that of seeing persons; (3) language development is affected only in those areas where the meanings of words are dependent on visual concepts; and (4) self-esteem and self-confidence are not distorted except when a peer group has negatively influenced the individual's attitude.

The influence of recent social and educational movements to serve disabled citizens in less restrictive settings has realized a particular impact on the education of visually handicapped students. Prior to 1960, approximately 80% of visually handicapped learners were prepared in residential schools; currently over 70% of visually handicapped learners are served in local educational programs. The integration of visually handicapped students into regular school environments such as the innovative local programming promoted by Barraga (1983) focuses on adaptations in the presentation of learning experiences, modifications in instructional materials, and refinements in the learning environment.

Depending on the nature and severity of the visual handicap, Reynolds and Birch (1982) have identified the continuum of services that should be available to appropriately serve the blind or low-vision student placed in local school programs. The range of services and other resources includes specialized instruction directed to the unique learning needs and style of the visually impaired. This instruction may be offered by consultants, itinerant teachers, resource teachers, or specially assisted regular classroom teachers or teacher aides. Particularly important in the development of effective programming for this population is the substitution of auditory or tactual learning programs to compensate for the loss of visual capabilities.

The range of services also includes instruction in orientation and mobility and the availability of readily accessible programs and facilities. To ensure the maximum possible classroom integration, modifications in facility structure, classroom arrangement, and lighting may be necessary. In addition, specialized materials and technologies such as braille, advanced reading machines (e.g., Kurzweil Reader, Optacon), recorded information, and large print documents and magnifiers are offered, along with comprehensive early intervention programming for infants and young children and a strong, ongoing program of career preparation and placement.

### REFERENCES

Barraga, N. (1903). *Visual handicaps and learning* (rev. ed.). Austin, TX: Exceptional Resources.

Kirk, S. A., & Gallagher, J. J. (1986). *Educating exceptional children* (5th ed.). Boston: Houghton Mifflin.

Reynolds, M. C., & Birch, J. W. (1982). *Teaching exceptional children in all America's schools* (rev. ed.). Reston, VA: Council for Exceptional Children.

U.S. Department of Education. (1985). *Seventh annual report to Congress on the implementation of the Education of the Handicapped Act.* Washington, DC: U.S. Government Printing Office.

GEORGE JAMES HAGERTY
*Stonehill College*

### VISUAL IMPAIRMENT

## EDUCATION WEEK

*Education Week* is a weekly newspaper published 42 times during the typical academic year. It is published by Editorial Projects in Education Inc., a Washington, DC based corporation, and edited by Ronald Wolk. Subscriptions are $48 per year. *Education Week* carries news, comment, and editorials of interest and concern to professional educators and researchers in the field. The paper monitors budgetary concerns and federal policy. Special education news is regularly included, as are position papers on topics of special interest such as learning disabilities diagnosis and mainstreaming. Letters to the editor and commentary on current events in education and previously published news items, features, or commentaries are accepted. Classified ads and listings of job openings are also included.

CECIL R. REYNOLDS
*Texas A&M University*

## EEG ABNORMALITIES

Electrical changes in the brain that manifest in EEG abnormalities represent the heart of the epileptic attack

(Dodrill, 1981). During the evaluation of a patient, it is not uncommon to find an abnormal EEG when there is no overt evidence of a seizure disorder. The criteria for determining the presence of a seizure disorder in an individual with an abnormal EEG are rarely stated explicitly. Hill (1957) has reported that a high percentage of schizophrenic patients show paroxysmal abnormalities in their EEGs (e.g., synchronous spikes, spike and wave complexes, and slow wave bursts). The relationship between an abnormal EEG and behavioral disturbances in nonepileptic individuals is more difficult to define. It also has been demonstrated that commonly used drugs can often cause EEG changes that can mimic seizure activity (Fink, 1963; Ulett, Heusler, & Word, 1965). Some of these changes are described in the Table below.

Defining the limits of normality in an EEG presents a major problem with which clinicians and investigators have struggled for years. There is no doubt that spikes, spike-wave discharges, focal slowing with phase reversal, and paroxysmal activity during wakefulness are always abnormal; however, there are many instances and EEG patterns that do not contain any of the above but still may be considered abnormal. In patients who drink alcohol heavily or who have received tranquilizers or other medications, EEG abnormalities may be seen and represent the effect of these drugs or withdrawal from them. EEG abnormalities seen in some psychopathic individuals with a history of aggressive behavior may be due to brain damage. Positive electroencephalographic abnormalities and brain damage thus may be a result and not the cause of emotional disturbance. Even with these possibilities there

Effect of Commonly Used Drugs on the EEG[a]

| Drug Type | Effect on Basic Frequencies | EEG Changes Synchronization | New Waves | Persistence After Drug Discontinued |
|---|---|---|---|---|
| Phenothiazine | Beta slowing (occasional) | Increased | High voltage sharp | 6–10 weeks |
| Tricyclics | Increased beta | Increased | Sharp | Unknown |
| Barbiturates | Increased beta; slowing | Increased in low doses; decreased in high doses | Spindles | 3–6 weeks |
| Meprobamate | Increased beta | Increased | Spindles | 3–6 weeks |
| Benzodiazepines | Increased beta | Increased | Fast, sharp | 3–6 weeks |

[a] All of the these drugs except barbiturates tend to increase preexisting dysrhythmias. Withdrawal from high levels of barbiturates and meprobamate can induce increased slowing, synchronization, and paroxysmal activity, and may result in seizures.

remains impressive literature correlating EEG abnormalities with certain psychiatric symptomatology.

In a large study of unselected, nonepileptic individuals, it was possible to differentiate those with abnormal EEGs from those with normal EEGs on the basis of their symptoms (Tucker, Detre, Harrow, & Glaser, 1965). Symptoms classically associated with schizophrenia were significantly more common in psychiatric patients with abnormal EEGs; they included impaired associations, flattened affect, religiosity, persecutory and somatic delusions, auditory hallucinations, impaired personal habits, and destructive-assaultive behavior. The group with abnormal EEGs also exhibited symptoms normally associated with neurological diseases such as time disorientation, perseveration, recent memory difficulties, and headaches. Neurotic and depressed individuals had approximately the same incidence of abnormal EEGs as the general population (18%).

Research by Wilkus and Dodrill (1976) demonstrated that increasing involvement of the brain with epileptiform discharges (epilepticlike EEG abnormalities) is related to decreased cognitive performance. Furthermore, the decreased performances associated with this condition are conspicuously widespread and involve many different kinds of functions. The EEGs of epileptics have been studied with respect to abnormalities in rhythm frequency. Generally, decreased abilities were associated with slower rhythm frequencies. Dodrill and Wilkus (1976) studied the performance of a large group of epileptic individuals on a broad range of tests and found that performance was not substantially decreased until the dominant posterior rhythm frequency dropped below 8 Hz, when performance decreased precipitously. Although decreased abilities were seen across a wide range of skills, those requiring simultaneous attention and complex mental manipulations showed the greatest losses. Finally, it is worth mentioning that although generalized nonepileptiform EEG abnormalities tend to demonstrate the most potent relationships with performance, they have been the least investigated (Dodrill, 1981).

## REFERENCES

Dodrill, C. B. (1981). Neuropsychology of epilepsy. In S. B. Filskov & T. J. Boll (Eds.), *Handbook of clinical neuropsychology* (pp. 366–395). New York: Wiley.

Dodrill, C. B., & Wilkus, R. J. (1976). Neuropsychological correlates of the electroencephalogram in epileptics: II. The waking posterior rhythm and its interaction with epileptiform activity. *Epilepsia, 17,* 101–109.

Fink, M. (1963). Quantitative EEG in human psychopharmacology: Drug patterns. In G. H. Glaser (Ed.), *EEG and behavior* (pp. 143–169). New York: Basic Books.

Hill, D. (1957). Electroencephalogram in schizophrenia. In R. Richter (Ed.), *Schizophrenia: Somatic aspects* (pp. 30–72). London: Pergamon.

Tucker, G. J., Detre, T., Harrow, M., & Glaser, G. H. (1965). Behavior and symptoms of psychiatric patients and the electroencephalogram. *Archives of General Psychiatry, 12,* 278–292.

Ulett, G. A., Heusler, A. F., & Word, T. J. (1965). The effect of psychotropic drugs on the EEG of the chronic psychotic patient. In W. P. Wilson (Ed.), *Applications of electroencephalography in psychiatry: A symposium* (pp. 23–36). Durham, NC: Duke University Press.

Wilkus, R. J., & Dodrill, C. B. (1976). Neuropsychological correlates of the electroencephalogram in epileptics. I. Topographic distribution and average rate of epileptiform activity. *Epilepsia, 17,* 89–100.

RICHARD A. BERG
*West Virginia University*
*Medical Center, Charleston*
*Division*

**EPILEPSY**
**NEUROPSYCHOLOGY**

## EEOC

See EQUAL EMPLOYMENT OPPORTUNITY COMMISSION.

## EFFECTIVENESS OF SPECIAL EDUCATION

The question of the effectiveness of special education brings to mind Dickens' opening lines in *A Tale of Two Cities:* "It was the best of times, it was the worst of times." Much the same can be said about the effectiveness of special education: it is effective, it is not effective. The reasons for this equivocation are varied. One primary source is the vaguely defined parameters of the group labeled mildly handicapped. For some 90% of pupils labeled mildly handicapped who fall under the rubric of educable mentally retarded (EMR), learning disabled (LD), or behaviorally disordered (BD), there is considerable controversy surrounding specific identification criteria; the result is a lack of homogeneous classification. The heterogeneity present in these populations makes it difficult to assess treatment effectiveness even though these groups are presumed to possess similar problems. Those children with sensory deficits, physical disabilities, or severe and profound handicaps do not suffer from as many classification problems. Their conditions are better defined and more specific than the arbitrary and nonspecific symptoms that surround the mildly handicapped. This does not mean that it is impossible to treat conditions difficult to diagnose. It does mean, however, that the differences across mildly handicapped populations may mask specific treatment effectiveness, and, consequently, not provide an accurate picture of intervention efficacy in general. Therefore, it is possible for special education to be both effective and ineffective.

The problem is not the lack of research investigating the effectiveness of special education practices but rather the lack of definitive conclusions that may be drawn from such research. The *Illinois Test of Psycholinguistic Abilities* (ITPA) has served as the clinical model for a variety of intervention programs. It provides a good example of the difficulties inherent in deciding on the effectiveness of special education. The ITPA programs were based on the assumption that language is comprised of discrete components that can be trained. This last assumption has been the subject of debate in a series of reviews (Hammill & Larsen, 1974, 1978; Lund, Foster, & McCall-Perez, 1978; Minskoff, 1975; Newcomer, Larsen, & Hammill, 1975). The tenor of this debate may be gleaned from summary statements from two reviews, one pro and the other con. On the positive side:

> Our analysis indicates that some studies show significant positive results as measured by the ITPA, some studies show positive results in the areas remediated, and some do not show results from which any conclusions can be drawn. It is, therefore, not logical to conclude either that all studies in psycholinguistic training are effective or that all studies in psycholinguistic training are not effective. (Lund et al., 1978, p. 317)

On the negative side:

> The cumulative results of the pertinent research have failed to demonstrate that psycholingusitc training has value, at least, with the ITPA as the criterion for successful training. It is important to note that, regardless of the reevaluation by propsycholinguistic educators, the current state of the research strongly questions the efficacy of psycholinguistic training and suggests that programs designed to improve psycholinguistic functioning need to be viewed cautiously and monitored with great care. (Hammill & Larsen, 1978, p. 413)

The rhetoric in the debate became increasingly enmeshed in trivial controversy and polemics abounded, but the primary question about the effectiveness of psycholinguistic training was not answered convincingly. Many other issues related to the effectiveness of special education could be used to illustrate the fragility of research findings. If all such issues were reviewed, the conclusion to be drawn would be the same: special education is both effective and ineffective.

In an effort to delineate more fully the magnitude of the effectiveness (or the ineffectiveness) of special education, methods of quantitative research synthesis have been developed; they add clarity, explicitness, and definition to the review process. Because such methods, which have come to be known as meta-analysis (Glass, McGaw, & Smith, 1981), increase the objectivity, verifiability, and replicability of the review process, the conclusions drawn are more systematic and unequivocal. Meta-analysis is based on a metric "effect size" (*ES*), which transforms individual study data into standard deviation units (z-scores). The individual *ES* calculations may then be combined and recombined into different aggregations that reveal important information about the problem under study. For example, suppose a hypothetical evaluation of a special education intervention (temporal centripetal therapy) revealed an average ES ($\overline{ES}$) of +1.00. This would indicate a one standard deviation superiority of the treatment group. This can be illustrated by two separate but overlapping distributions, as shown in the Figure below. This relationship suggests that the average treated child was better off than 84% of the control (comparison) group, while only 16% of the control group was better off than the average treated child.

By summarizing the findings of several meta-analyses investigating the effectiveness of special education, it is possible to delineate the magnitude of treatment efficacy for common practices in special education, and place the question of the effectiveness of special education into a different context. For example, in the long-standing debate over the efficacy of psycholinguistic training, previous reviews could not settle the issue and it remained unclear whether psycholinguistic training was a viable treatment alternative.

Kavale (1981) performed a meta-analysis on 34 studies investigating psycholinguistic training effectiveness. The 34 studies yielded 240 *ES*'s, which produced an overall $\overline{ES}$ of .39. This finding was based on data representing approximately 1850 subjects who averaged 7.5 years of age with a mean IQ of 82 and who received an average of 50 hours of psycholinguistic training. Thus, the average subject receiving psycholinguistic training stands at approximately the 65th percentile of subjects receiving no special psycholinguistic training; the latter remain at the 50th percentile.

Table 1 presents $\overline{ES}$'s classified by ITPA subtest. If subtests where the data are thin (i.e., 5 or fewer *ES*'s) are eliminated, than five of the nine subtests show modest, albeit positive, effects. It is questionable whether these

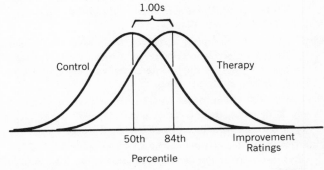

Illustration of the findings from a hypothetical study assessing the efficacy of temporal centripetal therapy.

Table 1. Average Effect Sizes for ITPA Subtests

| ITPA Subtest | Mean Effect Size | Number of Effect Sizes |
|---|---|---|
| Auditory reception | .21 | 20 |
| Visual reception | .21 | 20 |
| Auditory association | .44 | 24 |
| Visual association | .39 | 21 |
| Verbal expression | .63 | 24 |
| Manual expression | .54 | 23 |
| Grammatic closure | .30 | 21 |
| Visual closure | .48 | 5 |
| Auditory sequential memory | .32 | 21 |
| Visual sequential memory | .27 | 21 |
| Auditory closure | −.05 | 3 |
| Sound blending | .38 | 3 |

psycholinguistic abilities respond to training at a level that would warrant continuation of such training. The case is different for four abilities: auditory and visual association, verbal and manual expression. For these psycholinguistic abilities, training improves functioning from 15 to 23 percentile ranks at the center of the distribution. Thus, the average trained subject would be better off than approximately 65 to 73% of untrained subjects on associative or expressive abilities.

The findings of this meta-analysis appear to cast serious doubt on previous conclusions such as "the overwhelming consensus of research evidence concerning the effectiveness of psycholinguistic training is that it remains essentially nonvalidated. . . ." (Hammill & Larsen, 1978, p. 412). Findings for ITPA total score and subtest scores provided validation for the benefits of psycholinguistic training. Clearly, the findings regarding the receptiveness to intervention of the expressive constructs, particularly verbal expression, and the representational level subtests are encouraging since they embody the "language" aspects of the ITPA and, ultimately, productive language bahavior.

For a basic area like language, the average elementary school pupil gains about one standard deviation ($\overline{ES}$ = +1.00) over the school year and exceeds about 84% of the pupils' scores made on a language achievement measure at the beginning of the school year. The approximately 60% success rate for training verbal expression is thus substantial, and is particularly important for EMR and LD children, who are likely to manifest difficulties in this area. In fact, roughly 50 hours of psycholinguistic training produce benefits on the verbal expression subtest ($\overline{ES}$ = .63) exceeding that which would be expected from half a year of schooling in language achievement ($\overline{ES}$ = .50).

In concrete terms, improvement of this magnitude translates into perhaps an additional half-dozen correct responses on a test like the ITPA. If these six items are considered proxies for hundreds of skills, abilities, and bits of information, then an improvement in these seemingly

few items is significant. Consider an analogous situation: a child with IQ 130 answers perhaps nine more information questions or nine more vocabulary items on the WISC-R than a child with IQ 100. Does this suggest that the difference between IQ 100 and IQ 130 is nine bits of knowledge? Certainly, the abilities involved transcend nine pieces of information. Likewise, improvement on a test of verbal expression represents more than the expected increase of six items since it comprises a complex amalgam of language abilities.

The example provided by psycholinguistic training reveals that questions about the effectiveness of special education are not easily answered. When considering the effectiveness of psycholinguistic training, the answer was not a simple positive or negative response but rather a differential response resulting in the conclusion that psycholinguistic training is effecive, psycholinguistic training is not effective. The methods of meta-analysis were used to investigate the effectiveness of other special education practices with the findings summarized in Table 2 (see Kavale & Forness, 1985, for a complete description except for the modality model.) Two other process training strategies were investigated; the findings were not optimistic. Perceptual motor training activities have a long history in special education (since the days of Itard and Sequin) and widely disseminated clinical evidence has acknowledged their efficacy. The overall ES was .082, which

Table 2. Effectiveness of Special Education Practices

| Practice | Studies | Effect Size | Rank (%) |
|---|---|---|---|
| Psycholinguistic training | 34 | | |
| Reception | | .21 | 58 |
| Association | | .44 | 67 |
| Expression | | .63 | 74 |
| Perceptual-motor training | 180 | | |
| Perceptual | | .17 | 57 |
| Achievement | | .01 | 50 |
| Cognitive | | .03 | 51 |
| Modality model | 39 | | |
| Assessment | | .51 | 70 |
| Teaching | | .14 | 56 |
| Special vs. regular class | 50 | | |
| EMR | | −.14 | 44 |
| LD/BD | | .29 | 61 |
| Stimulant | 135 | | |
| Behavioral | | .80 | 79 |
| Intelligence | | .39 | 65 |
| Achievement | | .38 | 65 |
| Psychotropic medication | 70 | | |
| Behavioral | | .28 | 59 |
| Cognitive | | .74 | 71 |
| Feingold diet | 23 | | |
| Behavioral | | .29 | 61 |
| Attention | | .02 | 51 |
| Achievement | | −.05 | 48 |

Table 3. Average Effect Sizes for Perceptual-Motor Training Programs

| Training Program | Mean Effect Size | Number of Effect Sizes |
|---|---|---|
| Barsch | .157 | 18 |
| Cratty | .113 | 27 |
| Delacato | .161 | 79 |
| Frostig | .096 | 173 |
| Getman | .124 | 48 |
| Kephart | .064 | 132 |
| Combination | .057 | 78 |
| Other | −.021 | 82 |

means that the average trained subject, at the end of treatment, was better off than 53% of control subjects, a gain only slightly better than no treatment at all. Additionally, of 637 ES measurements, 48% were negative, suggesting that the probability of obtaining a positive response to training is only slightly better than chance.

Examination of Table 2 reveals perceptual motor training to have essentially no effect on achievement and cognitive outcomes and only a modest effect on the areas to which the training is directed (i.e., perceptual-motor processes). The data were combined and recombined but, regardless of how global or discrete the aggregation, perceptual motor training presented essentially zero effects and nothing indicative of any selected benefits.

Perceptual-motor training programs, have taken a variety of forms and the names associated with these programs read like a roster from a special education hall of fame. The $\overline{ES}$'s for the various training methods are shown in Table 3. Again the findings offer a bleak picture; there is nothing even hinting at positive effects. Thus, contrary to the suggestion that the available evidence does not allow either a positive or negative evaluation of perceptual-motor training (Hallahan & Cruickshank, 1973), this meta-analysis indicated that the necessary empirical evidence is presently available. It is not premature to draw definitive conclusions regarding the efficacy of perceptual-motor interventions since the available research offers the negative evidence necessary for questioning the value of perceptual-motor training. Yet, the deep historical roots and strong clinical tradition will make difficult the removal of perceptual-motor training from its prominent position as a treatment technique.

Modality instruction is another popular process strategy in special education (Kavale & Forness, in press). Based on the search for aptitude × treatment interactions, the modality model evaluates modal preferences (visual or auditory) to determine particular learning styles, which are then used in differential programming ephasizing the use of visual or auditory materials. The findings summarized in Table 2 do not offer support for the modality model. In terms of modality assessments, the original $\overline{ES}$

was .93, which approached the one standard difference typically used for establishing groups. When corrected for measurement effort in the tests used for assessing modality preferences (average $r = .56$), however, the level of group differentiation is reduced. Instead of differentiating better than 8 out of 10 cases, group differentiation was no better than 7 out of 10 cases. Thus, only 70% of the subjects could be clearly differentiated; this suggests considerable overlap between subjects exhibiting a modality preference and those not exhibiting such a preference.

With respect to modality teaching, the $\overline{ES}$ of .14 translates into only a 6 percentile rank improvement. This indicates a 56% level of improvement, which is only slightly above chance (50%) and suggests conversely that 44% of the subjects did not reveal any gain with modality teaching. Furthermore, 35% of the ES measurements were negative, indicating that in better than one-third of the cases, subjects receiving instruction matched to their preferred learning modality actually did less well than control subjects receiving no specially modified instruction. These findings were similar across modalities (i.e., auditory, visual, kinesthetic), across standardized achievement measures, and across reading skills.

Although intuitively appealing, little empirical support for the modality model was found. With respect to modality assessment, groups seemingly differentiated on the basis of modality preferences actually revealed considerable overlap, and it was problematic whether any of the presumed differences could really be deemed preferences. On the instructional side, little (or no) gain in reading achievement was found when instructional methods were matched to preferred learning modality. Only modest improvement was demonstrated for either auditory, visual, or kinesthetic teaching methods.

A possible explanation for the ineffectiveness of modality teaching is the difficulty in isolating instructional practices and materials as either primarily auditory or visual. All modalities appear to influence strongly the learning process and only in extreme cases (e.g., sensory deficits) can instruction be really differentiated on the basis of modality. Possibly, as there is less group differentiation in terms of modality preferences, modality factors per se make only a minor contribution to the constellation of factors producing individual differences in learning.

The remainder of the $\overline{ES}$'s in Table 2 reveal that a majority are below .50, suggesting that the aggregate findings across a variety of special education practices represent less than one-half standard deviation advantage for the treated groups when compared with untreated groups.

Exceptions include special class placement, where the overall $\overline{ES}$ of −.12 implies a disadvantage for the special class. Approximately 58% of the ES's were negative: in more than half the cases, special classes were less effective. Since the average comparison regular class subjects would be at the 50th percentile, the effects of approximately two years, on average, of special class placement were ($\overline{\text{ES}}$ = −.12), to reduce the relative standing of the average special class pupil by 5 percentile ranks. Although both achievement ($\overline{\text{ES}}$ = .15) and social/personality (ES = −.11) outcomes were negative, differential effects were found for student classification. Special class placement was most disadvantageous for handicapped children whose primary problem was lowered IQ levels (i.e., EMR with an $\overline{\text{ES}}$ of −.14 and the slow learner [IQ 75–90] with an $\overline{\text{ES}}$ of −.34). The average LD or BD pupil in a special class was better off than 61% of those placed in a regular class ($\overline{\text{ES}}$ = +.29). Thus, unconditional judgments about mainstreaming must be tempered lest the special education field find itself in a morass similar to that created by the nature-nurture debate over intelligence.

Although this appears to be a significant finding, it raises the disturbing question of why some pupils placed in special classes are slightly worse off (in terms of achievement and social/personality adjustment) than they would have been had they been left in regular classrooms. The significant variable appears to be intelligence. If the child is placed in a special class because of a low IQ, it may lower teacher expectations for performance, which results in less effort on the teachers' part and less learning on the child's part (Braun, 1976; Rosenthal & Jacobson, 1968; Rosenthal & Rubin, 1978). The lowered expectancy, be it conscious or unconscious, diverts instructional efforts away from academic pursuits toward a maintenance function.

On the other hand, the normal intelligence of LD and BD/ED pupils (at least, by definition) apparently does not dampen teacher expectation. Teachers apparently take a more optimistic view and make a greater effort to improve academic functioning. Perhaps this effort represents the "real" special education—not a system seeking the status quo but a system focusing on individual learning needs and abilities in order to design the most effective program of academic remediation necessary to overcome academic deficits. Consequently, special education must seek not new technology but a frame of reference emphasizing the potential for growth in all its clientele. Such a posture will allow the "special" in special education to operate more effectively.

The difficulties imposed by sample variability in special education is revealed in the findings related to drug effectiveness. Severe BD treated with psychotropic medication ($\overline{\text{ES}}$ = .30) do not appear as amenable to treatment as those with hyperactivity who are treated with stimulant medication ($\overline{\text{ES}}$ = .59). These findings suggest that approximately 72% of hyperactive children would be better off than placebo-treated controls, compared with 62% of drug-treated children with severe behavior disorders. The most obvious explanation for the average 10 percentile rank advantage found for drug-treated hyperactive children is severity level. It appears that the more severe BD (e.g., psychosis, schizophrenia), although revealing

modest positive gains, cannot be expected to improve as much as milder BD (e.g., those with hyperactivity), who have almost twice the level of improvement. Conversely, this same explanation may account for the differences found in the cognitive area.

By summarizing a large number of studies with a single index, it is possible to compare different interventions for the same problem. For example, the $\overline{\text{ES}}$ for the Feingold diet (.12) translates into a 5 percentile rank improvement for diet treatment of hyperactivity, which is less than one-fourth as large as the 22 percentile rank gain shown for stimulant medication. Although, across studies, the average ages and IQs were similar for drug-treated and diet-treated subjects, the average duration of treatment differed: 39 versus 10 weeks. In relation to $\overline{\text{ES}}$ (.12 vs. .59), these comparisons suggest that stimulant drug treatment is approximately five times as effective in about one-fourth the time when compared with the Feingold diet. Such comparisons provide perspective and bring greater insight into the problem of special education's effectiveness.

Besides the aggregate $\overline{\text{ES}}$, another important statistic is the standard deviation (SD) associated with each $\overline{\text{ES}}$. While the $\overline{\text{ES}}$ is an average of the individual ES measurements in a set, the SD is a sort of average of how distant the individual ES measurements in a distribution are removed from the mean itself. When considering $\overline{\text{ES}}$ and SD, meta-analysis findings may be taken as yielding a form of expectation ($\overline{\text{ES}}$ ± SD) for the phenomenon under study. This expectation means that under similar circumstances the special education practice should reveal an effect approximating the $\overline{\text{ES}}$, but as the circumstances change, the resulting effect is likely to demonstrate variability within the boundaries defined by the SD.

The overall $\overline{\text{ES}}$ and associated SD are displayed in an efficacy summary in Table 4. Examination of Table 4 reveals a disconcerting fact: the associated SDs are typically as great as or even greater than the $\overline{\text{ES}}$'s. This suggests that the variability of treatment effectiveness is typically greater than the average effectiveness of that treatment. In most cases, the intervention exhibited greater variability than it did average effectiveness, which suggests that from one setting to the next the effect of any intervention can vary from negative to zero to positive over a wide range. Although all education models (i.e., programs

Table 4. Special Education Efficacy Summary

| Practice | Mean Effect Size | Standard Deviation |
|---|---|---|
| Psycholinguistic training | .39 | .54 |
| Perceptual-motor training | .08 | .27 |
| Modality model | .28 | .34 |
| Special class placement | −.12 | .65 |
| Stimulant drugs | −.59 | .61 |
| Psychotropic drugs | .30 | .75 |
| Feingold diet | .12 | .42 |

of what to teach, when, how and the like) reveal learning and achievement to be variable (Dunkin & Biddle, 1974; Gage, 1976; Peterson & Walberg, 1979), special education appears to be marked by even greater variability. Special education practices are more variable than beneficial in the effects they produce; this means that a special education intervention that works in one place may or may not work in another. The variability inherent in special education practices is compounded by the fact that it is essentially indeterminate. Special education interventions may or may not produce benefits, but the final outcome is largely unpredictable. An integral part of meta-analysis is to correlate *ES* with important study features (e.g., age, sex, IQ level, socioeconomic status, diagnosis, setting, treatment duration, and the like) to determine the magnitude of the relationship among these factors. If some features correlated substantially with *ES*, then it would be possible to predict where a particular intervention might be effective (or not effective). For example, if the correlation between the *ES* for the Feingold diet and age were significant, then it would be possible to delimit specific age levels where diet treatment would possess a greater probability of success. Unfortunately, in no area of special education were the correlations of a magnitude that permit useful predictions. Thus, special education is highly variable and that variability is not easily predicted.

Special education then is not characterized by precise relationships wherein the efficacy of any intervention is easily calculated (e.g., do A in circumstance X and Y, and do B in circumstance Z). Although this may appear to be a serious shortcoming, practical applications in special education do not require prescriptive pronouncement; i.e., a single course of action under a wide range of circumstances. Because special education is unpredictable, it must be approached with a degree of uncertainty. The uncertainty introduces risk into the system (i.e., not knowing whether the intervention will work or not), and means that it is necessary for the practice of special education be based on rational action. Such rational action demands that the special education practitioner possess a variety of options in order to remain flexible and versatile in the face of uncertainty. When it is realized that the success or failure of special education is contingent on relatively uncontrolled (and unknown) factors, the task of the practitioner becomes one of minimizing the risk by providing the most satisfactory solution for the child's problem under the present circumstances. The best means of achieving a satisfactory solution is to replace dogmatic beliefs with an array of rational choices that interpose between the intricate concatenation of events involved in the special education teaching-learning process and the practitioner's wisdom and experience. Given the nature of special education, it is likely that intervention practices will remain variable and unpredictable. Consequently, when considering the question of the effectiveness of special education, it is also likely that the answer will remain, it is effective, it is not effective. The equivocation necessary when evaluating special education practice means that for the practitioner, it is the best of times, it is the worst of times.

## REFERENCES

Braun, C. (1976). Teacher expectations—Socio-psychological dynamics. *Review of Educational Research, 46,* 185–213.

Dunkin, M. J., & Biddle, B. J. (1974). *The study of teaching.* New York: Holt, Rinehart & Winston.

Gage, N. L. (Ed.). (1976). *The psychology of teaching methods: The 75th yearbook of the National Society for the Study of Education, Part I.* Chicago: University of Chicago Press.

Glass, G. V., McGaw, B., & Smith, M. L. (1981). *Meta-analysis in social research.* Beverly Hills, CA: Sage.

Hallahan, D. P., & Cruickshank, W. M. (1973). *Psychoeducational foundations of learning disabilities.* Englewood Cliffs, NJ: Prentice-Hall.

Hammill, D. D., & Larsen, S. C. (1974). The effectiveness of psycholinguistic training. *Exceptional Children, 41,* 5–14.

Hammill, D. D., & Larsen, S. C. (1978). The effectiveness of psycholinguistic training: A reaffirmation of position. *Exceptional Children, 44,* 402–414.

Kavale, K. A. (1981). Functions of the Illinois Test of Psycholinguistic Abilities (ITPA): Are they trainable? *Exceptional Children, 47,* 496–510.

Kavale, K. A., & Forness, S. R. (1985). *The science of learning disabilities.* San Diego, CA: College-Hill.

Kavale, K. A., & Forness, S. R. (in press). A matter of substance over style: A quantitative synthesis assessing the efficacy of modality testing and teaching. *Exceptional Children.*

Lund, K. A., Foster, G. E., & McCall-Perez, F. C. (1978). The effectiveness of psycholinguistic training: A reevaluation. *Exceptional Children, 44,* 310–319.

Minskoff, E. (1975). Research on psycholinguistic training: Critique and guidelines. *Exceptional Children, 42,* 136–144.

Newcomer, P., Larsen, S. C., & Hammill, D. D. (1975). A response. *Exceptional Children, 42,* 144–148.

Peterson, P. L., & Walberg, H. J. (Eds.). (1979). *Research on teaching: Concepts, findings, and implications.* Berkeley, CA: McCutchan.

Rosenthal, R., & Jacobson, L. (1968). *Pygmalion in the classroom.* New York: Holt, Rinehart & Winston.

Rosenthal, R., & Rubin, D. B. (1978). Interpersonal expectance effects: The first 345 studies. *Behavioral and Brain Sciences, 3,* 377–415.

Kenneth A. Kavale
*University of Iowa*

**PERCEPTUAL TRAINING**
**PSYCHOLINGUISTICS**
**STANDARD DEVIATION**
**RESEARCH IN SPECIAL EDUCATION**

## EGBERT, ROBERT L. (1923–          )

Robert L. Egbert received his BS and MS degrees from Utah State University. He then attended Cornell University, Ithaca, New York, where he obtained his doctorate in 1949.

Egbert is currently a professor of education at the University of Nebraska, Lincoln and is a recipient of the 1986 Edward C. Pomery award for outstanding contribution to teacher education. He has served as president on the board of directors of AACTE. He is presently a member of the board of directors of High/Scope Educational Research Foundation.

Egbert was director of the National Commission for Excellence in Teacher Education. He has published many articles and reports dealing with improvement and change in teacher education for use both regionally and nationally (Egbert, 1971, 1974, 1985*a*). He was staff director in the preparation of the report "A Call for Change in Teacher Education" in 1985).

## REFERENCES

Egbert, R. L. (1971). Follow through. *National Elementary Principal, 51*, 104–109.

Egbert, R. L. (1974). Improving teacher education through the use of research information. *Journal of Teacher Education, 35*(4), 9–11.

Egbert, R. L. (1985*a*). The practice of preservice teacher education. *Journal of Teacher Education, 36*, 16–22.

Egbert, R.L. (1985). *A call for change in teacher education.* National Commission for Excellence in Teacher Education.

ROBERTA C. STOKES
*Texas A&M University*

# EISENSON, JON J. (1907–        )

Jon J. Eisenson received his BSS from the College of the City of New York in 1928, his MA from Columbia University in 1930, and his PhD in clinical psychology also from Columbia University in 1935. In his early years as a psychologist he felt one must understand the nature of language, its relationship to thinking and learning, and how it is used and abused by human beings if one is to understand the human behavior of normal or handicapped persons.

His major fields of interest include language and the brain, aphasia, stuttering, dyslexia, and communication of both the normal and abnormal. Eisenson served as the assistant chief clinical psychologist in the War Department in 1944–1945 during World War II. Since then, his primary interests have been with the effects of brain damage on language behavior and developing techniques for recovery, reading problems (dyslexia), congenital and acquired.

Eisenson's principle publications include *Aphasia in Children*, which discusses the problems of severely lin-

Jon J. Eisenson

guistically impaired children with the diagnosis of aphasia, and *Communicative Disorders in Children*, which is a book intended for professionals who wish to improve the communicative abilities of children whose impairments are of such a degree that normal communication is interfered with, *Adult Aphasia*, acquired as a result of disease or accident, and *Reading for Meaning*, a psycholinguistic approach to the teaching of reading.

Eisenson has published many articles and books and is an experienced teacher and guest lecturer. He is strongly interested in reading and plans to continue researching the problems of reading in the future. By avocation, he writes poetry for children and for adults (Eisenson, 1985).

## REFERENCES

Eisenson, J. J. (1983). *Voice and diction.* (5th ed.). New York: Macmillan.

Eisenson, J. J. (1984). *Adult aphasia.* (2nd ed.). Englewood Cliffs, NJ: Prentice-Hall.

Eisenson, J. J. (1984). *Language and speech disorders in children.* Elmsford, NY: Pergamon.

Eisenson, J. J. (1985). *My special zoo.* Tulsa, Oklahoma: Modern Education.

Eisenson, J. J. (1985). *Reading for meaning.* Tulsa, Oklahoma: Modern Education.

Eisenson, J. J., & Ogilvie, M. (1983). *Communication disorders.* (5th ed.). New York: Macmillan.

STAFF

# ELABORATED *v.* RESTRICTED VERBAL CODES

The expressions "elaborated" and "restricted" code were introduced by the British sociologist Basil Bernstein in 1974 and were defined:

on a linguistic level, in terms of the probability of predicting for any one speaker which syntactic elements will be used to organize meaning. In the case of an elaborated code, the speaker will select from a relatively extensive range of alternatives and therefore the probability of predicting the pattern of organizing elements is considerably reduced. In the case of a restricted code, the number of these alternatives is often severely limited and the probability of predicting the pattern is greatly increased. (pp. 76–77).

Bernstein hypothesized that these different codes were functions of different social structures. Comparisons of groups of middle-class and working-class children showed significant differences for grammatical and lexical features. Middle-class children used a significantly higher proportion of subordinations, complex verbal stems, the passive voice, uncommon adjectives, adverbs and conjunctions, and the pronoun I.

In later publications, Bernstein refined and extended his theory. A code was then said to be "a regulative principle controlling speech realizations in diverse social contexts" (Bernstein, 1974, p. 12). "Elaborated codes give access to universalitic orders of meaning, which are less context bound, whereas restricted codes give access to particularistic orders of meaning, which are far more context bound, that is, tied to a particular context" (p. 197).

The four contexts Bernstein cites are the regulative, instructional, imaginative, and interpersonal. In each of these contexts, speech variants can be observed that are characteristically elaborated or restricted, (codes cannot be observed because they belong to the deep structure of communication). The variants are elaborated if they appear to be selected from a wide range of syntactic alternatives that can be used in various contexts (universality); they are restricted if they are chosen from a much more limited, therefore more predictable, number of possibilities. The distinction between speech variants and codes is important because elaborated speech variants can appear in elaborated and restricted codes, as can restricted variants. What distinguishes the codes is the relative frequency of the two types of variants in both codes.

As social roles are first learned in the family, the way socialization occurs is of crucial importance for the development of one or the other coding activity. Bernstein distinguished two kinds of families. Person-oriented families, in which the child learns to play his or her part among the other members of the family, are more likely to endow a child with an elaborated code. The child growing up in a positional family, in which roles are preestablished, is less likely to learn to adapt his or her language to that of interlocutors and, as a consequence, is more likely to build up a restricted code.

Berstein insists that a restricted code is not in itself inferior to an elaborated code. The main problem for working-class children belonging to families that seem to be predominantly of the positional type is that their restricted code will consitute a severe handicap when they go to school. "For the schools are predicated on elaborated code and its system of social relationships. Although an elaborated code does not entail any specific value system, the value system of the middle class penetrates the texture of the very learning context itself" (Bernstein, 1974, p. 186).

Bernstein was critized, on the one hand, for the vagueness of his definitions and the crudeness of the linguistic distinctions he operated with, and on the other hand, for having given scientific support to the theory of linguistic deprivation (Labov, 1970) and eventually to compensatory education programs (Bereiter & Engelmann, 1966). The latter criticism does not seem to be justified, as it ignores the evolution in Bernstein's ideas after 1962.

### REFERENCES

Bereiter, G., & Engelmann, S. (1966). *Teaching disadvantaged children in the pre-school.* Englewood Cliffs, NJ: Prentice-Hall.

Bernstein, B. (1974). *Class, codes and control* (Vol. 1). London: Routledge & Kegan Paul.

Dittmar, N. (1973). *Sociolinguistics. A critical survey of theory and application.* London: Arnold.

Labov, W. (1970). The logic of non-standard English. In J. Alatis (Ed.), *Report of the 20th Annual Round Table Meeting on Linguistics and Language Studies.* Washington, DC: Georgetown University Press.

S. De Vriendt
*Vrije Universiteit Brussels,
Brussels, Belgium*

## EXPRESSIVE LANGUAGE DISORDERS
## LANGUAGE DEFICIENCIES AND DEFICITS
## LANGUAGE DELAYS

# ELAVIL

Elavil is the trade name for the generic tricyclic antidepressant amitriptyline. Elavil and other tricyclic antidepressants (TCA) usually are prescribed for endogenous depressions. These are affective disorders that present with vegetative disturbance (i.e., psychomotor slowing, poor appetite/weight loss, loss of sexual interest) and usually cannot be ascribed to a situational cause. Persons with endogenous depression often have positive familial histories for an affective disorder.

Therapeutically, TCAs are intended to reduce symptom intensity, increase mood elevation and physical activity, reestablish appetite and sleep patterns, and, in general, facilitate activity levels that will promote social adjustment (Blum, 1984). Such effects are assumed to be a result of TCA's blocking brain amine re-uptake, thus making more of the various catecholamines available at their specific receptor sites (Seiden & Dykstra, 1977).

Elavil differs from other TCAs in that it tends to produce greater sedation and a greater degree of anticholinergic side effects: visual blurring, urinary retention, constipation, concentration difficulties (Katzung, 1982). The TCAs are not often used in the treatment of children, because children appear to be more at risk for cardiovascular side effects and seizure-facilitating side effects of high doses (Blum, 1984). However, in titrated doses, TCAs have been used to treat enuresis and severe obsessive-compulsive disorders in children (Detre & Jarecki, 1971).

## REFERENCES

Blum, K. (1984). *Handbook of abusable drugs*. New York: Gardner Press.

Detre, T. P., & Jarecki, G. H. (1971). *Modern psychiatric treatment*. Philadelphia: Lippincott.

Katzung B. G. (1982). *Basic and clinical pharmacology*. Los Altos, CA: Lange Medical.

Seiden, L. S., & Dykstra, L. A. (1977). *Psychopharmocology: A biochemical and behavioral approach*. New York: Van Nostrand Reinhold.

ROBERT F. SAWICKI
*Lake Erie Institute of
Rehabilitation, Lake Erie,
Pennsylvania*

DOPAMINE
HALDOL
TRANQUILIZERS

## ELECTIVE MUTISM

Elective mutism is a psychological disorder most often encountered in early childhood. It is marked by the refusal of the individual to speak. The child has both the physical capacity to produce speech and comprehends the spoken language. To maintain a diagnosis of elective mutism, according to the *Diagnostic and Statistical Manual of Mental Disorders* of the American Psychiatric Association (DSM-III, 1980), more pervasive developmental disorders, including language disorders and mental retardation, must first be eliminated as primary diagnoses.

While elective mutism is generally regarded as a disorder primarily found in the preschool and younger elementary school child, an adolescent variation of mutism has been identified by Kaplan and Escoll (1973). However, as its discussion precedes the more contemporary psychiatric definition, it is not elaborated on.

Symptomatology indicative of elective mutism was first identified in German literature in the late nineteenth century by Kussmaul, who referred to it as *aphasia voluntaria*, although the present term of elective mutism was not used until 1934 by Tramer (Silver, 1985). Careful review of the literature indicates the presence of elective mutism in many countries such as Israel (Hesse, 1981;

Meijer, 1979), Great Britain (Wilkins, 1985), Switzerland (Hesselman, 1983), Canada (Zondlo & Scanlan, 1983), France (Myquel, et al., 1982), and Japan (Ohi, et al., 1982). The variety of languages and represented in this childhood disorder suggests that culture does not have an overwhelming influence on its development. Rather, elective mutism is psychogenic, with its etiology linked to socioemotional and other developmental factors.

The withholding of speech demonstrated by the electively mute may be situational, with the child often speaking at home but refusing to verbalize with strangers and particularly others at school. The reticence encountered on initial contact with the child may be misinterpreted by the teacher as shyness in a normal child and thus ignored. For this reason, the child's problems may be ignored in school, with the more disruptive and aggressive child commanding greater attentiveness on the part of the teacher, school-based guidance teams, and the administration. As the symptomatology often serves a purpose to the parents, they may not initiate contact with the school to relate any other circumstances with regard to their child's withholding of speech. While this symptom may be used to gain attention by some children, the lack of conspicuousness serves a protective function by reducing fear of others (Reed, 1963); it is maintained by the reinforcing value that it serves when the child is ignored. Wergeland (1979) noted that while shyness is indicative of the electively mute even in adolescence, it is likely the result of early family experiences. In a study involving 11 children admitted to a psychiatric clinic, it was noted that prior admission for elective mutism had occurred some 8 to 18 years before. The families of the admitted children were typified by shyness, reservation, social isolation, and overprotection. The last two factors may be of particular importance to the special educator, as many handicapped children are overprotected and more likely to be engaged in a parent-child symbolic relationship, thus stifling their development of independence. The social isolation sometimes maintained by the family with a handicapped member is also a recognizable factor.

Hayden (1980) identifies this symbiosis in some children who are elective mutes. In a study involving 68 children, Hayden noted 31 who displayed a strong symbiotic relationship with a primary caregiver, usually the mother. He termed this form of the disorder symbiotic mutism. Additionally, he identified speech phobic mutism, involving the child's fear of hearing his or her own voice; reactive mutism, characterized as a reaction to a single trauma; and passive-aggressive mutism, where silence is used for the purpose of manipulation. Where reactive mutism is identified, it may have resulted from the child's reaction to trauma during early stages of speech acquisition. Subsequent development may be accompanied by impoverished expressive language, even many years after the mutism has ceased. Symbiotic and passive-aggressive mutism are often associated with child-family relations in which withholding speech is a means of gaining control over the domination of a parent figure. Speech-phobic mutism is often accompanied by conditioned anxiety responses by the child on hearing his or her own voice. In general, in addition to the situational reticence, elective mutes have often been shown to be highly anxious, with rigid body posture and physical tension.

The treatment of elective mutism depends on the provision of a nonthreatening milieu at home and in the situations under which the behaviors become manifest. Attempts to be intrusive into the child's silence only serve to strengthen the resistance and will generally result in greater withdrawal and the absence of speech.

Most effective approaches to the reduction of learned anxiety responses and, in particular, elective mutism, fall under the rubric of behavior modification. Desensitization, a treatment technique by which the individual is gradually introduced to the anxiety-eliciting stimulus (Bandura, 1969), has been shown to be the method of choice. Such an approach should be undertaken only with the involvement of the parent, the teacher, and a psychologist familiar with the child and the techniques to be employed. Kupietz et al. (1982) recommends a stimulus-fading approach involving four phases. The initial phase is conducted with the parent engaging the child in conversation within the school setting. The assumption being made is that the parent is the figure with whom the child has had most experience in verbalizing. The second phase includes the teacher as a passive participant, "observing the session unobtrusively, and gradually increasing her proximity to the child in ensuing sessions" (p. 1073). The third phase involves the parent serving as an intermediary through which the teacher asks the child questions. In phase four, the teacher and child verbally interact in the presence of a limited number of children. The rate at which progress is made from one phase to a subsequent phase is dependent on the acceptance by the child of the transition from the sole participation of the parent to the presence of strangers in the anxiety-eliciting situation. In applying such an approach, psychodynamic factors must be considered. As parental symbiotic needs may have contributed to the mutism, the parents must be allowed to see the safety and advantage to the child's separation from them via this verbal engagement with others. A concerted, joint effort combining an understanding of the home and family dynamics with systematic behavioral intervention is needed to alter elective mutism in children and adolescents.

## REFERENCES

American Psychiatric Association (1980). *Diagnostic and statistical manual of mental disorders* DSM III. Washington, DC: Author.

Bandura, A. (1969). *Principles of behavior modification.* New York: Holt, Rinehart & Winston.

Hayden, T. L. (1980). Classification of elective mutism. *Journal of the American Academy of Child Psychiatry, 19,* 18–33.

Hesse, P. P. (1981). Colour, form and silence: A formal analysis of drawings of a child who did not speak. *Arts in Psychotherapy, 8,* 175–184.

Hesselman, S. (1983). Elective mutism in children 1877–1981. A literary summary. *Acta Paedopsychiatra, 49,* 297–310.

Kaplan, S. I., & Escoll, P. (1973). Treatment of two silent adolescent girls. *Journal of the American Academy of Child Psychiatry, 12,* 59–71.

Kupietz, S. S., & Schwartz, I. L. (1982). Elective mutism: Evaluation and treatment of three cases. *New York State Journal of Medicine, 82,* 1073–1076.

Meijer, A. (1979). Elective mutism in children. *Israeli Annals of Psychiatry, 17,* 93–100.

Myquel, M., & Granon, M. (1982). Le mutisme electif extrafamilial chez l'enfant. *Neuropsychiatre Enfant Adolesce, 30,* 329–339.

Ohi, M., Fujita, T., Tanaka, T., & Kobayashi, I. (1982). A clinical and psychopathological consideration on elective mutism in adolescence: Five cases who have poor volition to seek socialization. *Seishin Shinkeigaku Zasshi, 84,* 114–133.

Reed, C. F. (1963). Elective mutism in children: A reappraisal. *Journal of Child Psychology & Psychiatry, 4,* 99–107.

Silver, L. B. (1985). Speech disorders. In H. J. Kaplan & B., Sadock (Eds.), *Comprehensive textbook of psychiatry/IV* (pp. 1716–1721). Baltimore, MD: Williams & Wilkins.

Wergeland, H. (1979). Elective mutism. *Acta Psychiatrica Scandivavica, 59,* 218–228.

Wilkins, R. (1985). A comparison of elective mutism and emotional disorders in children. *British Journal of Psychiatry, 146,* 198–203.

Zondlo, F. C., & Scanlan, J. M. (1983). Elective mutism in a 26 year old deaf female. *Canadian Journal of Psychiatry, 28,* 49–51.

ELLIS I. BAROWSKY
*Hunter College, City University of New York*

**LANGUAGE DISORDERS**
**MUTISM**

# ELECTROCONVULSIVE THERAPY (ECT)

Though developed as a treatment for schizophrenia, electroconvulsive therapy (ECT) has not been consistently demonstrated to be a successful intervention for that disorder. Major affective disorders, however, have been amenable to a course of ECT; thus, it is considered an adjunctive somatic therapy in the treatment of depression. As described by the American Psychiatric Association Task Force on Electroconvulsive Therapy (1978), a course of ECT consists of a series of treatments, usually 6 to 10, occurring two to three times per week. During each treatment, a major motor seizure is induced. Electrode placement has evolved from bitemporal placement (Cerletti &

Bini, 1938) to unilateral placement over the nondominant hemisphere (Goldman, 1949; Lancaster, Steinert, & Frost, 1958). The latter placement was an attempt to avoid the gross confusional symptoms created by bilateral placement or unilateral placement over the dominant hemisphere.

In reviewing studies that compare ECT with various drug treatment groups, ECT was found to be significantly superior in the treatment of endogenous depression. The ECT groups demonstrated 86.7% positive response compared with 58.1 to 79.3% positive response in the drug treatment groups (Kiloh, 1982). Studies suggest the improvement noted among endogenously depressed persons is not merely from the ambience of the ECT treatment context, but appears to be related to the aftereffects of the electrical stimulation.

Though beneficial effects have been reported subsequent to a course of ECT, the cost-benefit question involved in the treatment has not been resolved. The majority of reviews suggest that no permanent structural changes may be attributed directly to the electrical stimulation. Memory disturbance (both retrograde and anterograde) appears severe immediately after treatment; however, memory processes appear to reintegrate between 1 and 3 months following cessation of treatment (Halliday, et al., 1968; Squire, 1977). Electrode placement is related to both the degree and the modality of memory interference. Bitemporal placement produces the greatest interference, which disrupts both verbal and nonverbal recall. Unilateral electrode placement appears to produce effects consistent with assumed brain-behavior interactions (i.e., dominant placement produces greater interference in verbal recall, while nondominant placement produces greater interference in nonverbal recall).

Interactive effects also have been reported between pretreatment cognitive style and residual brain effects (O'Connor, Colter, & Shaw, 1984). For example, right unilateral ECT affected frame dependence on the Rod and Frame Test (Mansueto & Adevai, 1967) for subjects who were initially judged field independent, but it did not affect the performance of subjects who were initially judged field dependent.

## REFERENCES

American Psychiatric Association Task Force on Electroconvulsive Therapy (1978, Sept.) *Electroconvulsive therapy*. Task Force Report 14. Washington, DC: Author.

Cerletti, U., & Bini, L. (1938). L'electroshock. *Archivo Generale di Neurologia Psichiatria e Psychoanalisi, 19*, 266–268.

Goldman, D. (1949). Brief stimulus electroshock therapy. *Journal of Nervous & Mental Disease, 110*, 36–45.

Halliday, A. M., Davison, K., Browne, M. W., & Keeger, L. C. (1968). A comparison of the effects on depression and memory of bilateral ECT and unilateral ECT to the dominant and nondominant hemispheres. *British Journal of Psychiatry, 114*, 997–1012.

Kiloh, L. G. (1982). Electroconvulsive therapy. In E. S. Paykel (Ed.), *Handbook of affective disorders* (pp. 262–275). New York: Guilford Press.

Lancaster, N. P., Steinert, R. R., & Frost, I. (1958). Unilateral electronconvulsive therapy. *Journal of Mental Science, 104*, 221–227.

Mansueto, C. S., & Adevai, G. (1967). Development and evaluation of a portable rod and frame test. *Journal of Psychosomatic Research, 11*, 207–211.

O'Connor, K. P., Colter, N., & Shaw, J. C. (1984). Cognitive style, cortical function, and electroconvulsive therapy. *Journal of Nervous & Mental Disease, 172*, 711–717.

Squire, L. R. (1977). ECT and memory loss. *American Journal of Psychiatry, 134*, 997–1001.

ROBERT F. SAWICKI
*Lake Erie Institute of
Rehabilitation, Lake Erie,
Pennsylvania*

**BRAIN ORGANIZATION
DEPRESSION
EEG ABNORMALITIES**

## ELECTROENCEPHALOGRAPH

An electroencephalograph is a machine that is used to measure the electrical activity of the brain. Fluctuations in brain electrical activity are recorded by electrodes attached to the scalp. The placement of the electrodes has been standardized for clinical use and is accepted internationally (Jasper, 1958). The potentials of the brain are shown on paper in a record called an electroencephalogram (EEG). The amplitude of the brain's electrical activity is small; it is measured in microvolts (millionths of a volt) and must be amplified by the electroencephalograph. The fluctuations in voltage that appear on the EEG have a fairly rhythmic character. The wavelike patterns that are produced will vary with the brain region being recorded as well as with the age and state of alertness of the patient.

The primary information in the EEG is its frequency, which varies from 0.5 to 60 Hz (cycles per second). Attempts have been made to provide rough categories for the classification of frequency. The characteristic pattern for adults in the waking state is dominated by the so-called alpha frequencies, a roughly sinusoidal shape pattern ranging from 8 to 12.5 Hz. Current usage usually identifies five frequency bands that are used in both clinical practice and research, particularly sleep research: delta, 0.5–4 Hz; theta, 4–8 Hz; alpha, 8–13 Hz; beta 1, 13–20 Hz; and beta 2, 20–40 Hz (Greenfield & Sternbach, 1972).

As a general rule, it is possible to predict what sort of brain wave pattern an individual will produce in the absence of brain damage. Variations from expected patterns can constitute a basis for postulating impaired brain functioning. Lewinsohn (1973) notes that the major pathologic changes include waves that are too fast, too slow, or too flat, with all of these conditions being either focal or diffuse.

A major limitation of the EEG is that normal-appearing records may be obtained in the presence of clear-cut evidence of severe organic brain disease (Chusid, 1976). Additionally, about 15 to 20% of the normal population produce abnormal EEG recordings (Mayo Clinic, 1976). Diagnostically, EEGs have been found to be about 60% accurate (Filskov & Goldstein, 1974). EEGs have proven most useful in the diagnosis of seizure disorders.

## REFERENCES

Chusid, J. G. (1976). *Correlative neuroanatomy and functional neurology*, Los Altos, CA: Lange Medical Publications.

Filskov, S. B., & Goldstein, S. G. (1974). Diagnostic validity of the Halstead-Reitan Neuropsychological Battery. *Journal of Consulting & Clinical Psychology, 42*, 382–388.

Greenfield, N. S., & Sternbach, R. A. (1972). *Handbook of psychophysiology*, New York: Holt, Rinehart & Winston.

Jasper, H. H. (1958). The ten twenty electrode system of the International Federation. *Electroencephalaography & Clinical Neurophysiology, 10*, 371–375.

Lewinsohn, P. M. (1973). *Psychological assessment of patients with brain injury*, Washington, DC: Division of Research, Department of Health, Education and Welfare.

Mayo Clinic. (1976). *Clinical examinations in neurology*. Philadelphia: Saunders.

RICHARD A. BERG
*West Virginia University
Medical Center, Charleston
Division*

**ABSENCE SEIZURES
EPILEPSY
GRAND MAL SEIZURES**

# ELECTROMECHANICAL SWITCHES

Simple technologies like electromechanical switches and battery interrupters are an easy and relatively inexpensive means of providing physically disabled students with access to battery-operated toys, small appliances, assistive communication devices, and computers. Electromechanical switches, which are often referred to simply as controls, can be purchased or made in a variety of styles, sizes, and shapes. The majority of physically disabled students use some type of push switch. The selection of a particular switch is based on the student's movement capabilities and the device the switch will operate.

Battery-operated toys with electromechanical switches are interesting and fun for physically disabled and sensory-impaired students. They are effective in teaching cause-effect relationships and independent environmental control and motor skills such as reaching and grasping. Switches attached to toys can also provide one way for a student to practice using an adaptation for computer access.

LINDA MCCORMICK
*University of Hawaii*

**COMPUTER USE WITH THE HANDICAPPED
ELECTRONIC COMMUNICATION AIDS**

# ELECTRONIC COMMUNICATION AIDS

Electronic communication aids consist of several related electronic components used by nonspeaking persons to communicate. These components are the communication aid, an interface, and an output device. An interface is a device used by a nonspeaking person to control the communication aid. The interface could consist of a simple on/off electronic switch, a headstick pointer, or a computer keyboard. An electronic signal is sent to a communication aid, which processes and may display the selected message signal. The symbol can be indicated by a small light emitting diode (LED) light, an electronic pointer, or liquid crystal display (LCD) display. The message can then be sent to one or more output devices such as a computer printer or speech synthesizer.

Electronic communication aids can be categorized by implementation level and by symbol selection technique (Harris & Vanderheiden, 1980). There are two implementation levels: simple and independent. Simple electronic aids consist of an interface and the communication aid. No output devices are used. An example of a simple electronic device is a joystick interface, which controls a light indicator on a vocabulary display. The disadvantage of a simple electronic system is that the listener must be present to observe the communication aid, and must sequence the selected symbols together to understand the message. Independent electronic aids are similar to simple electronic aids except that a spoken or written output device is added. This allows the nonspeaking person to communicate without listener assistance. These devices may or may not be portable.

Symbol selection methods for electronic communication aids can be categorized as direct selection or scanning selection systems. Direct selection allows the nonspeaking user to directly choose symbols for communication. Fingerpointing, pointing with a headstick, or typing on a keyboard are direct selection methods. Scanning selection systems are designed for persons with very limited motor control. The interface for a scanning system is typically a simple electronic switch. When the switch is activated, the communication aid will scan the available symbols one at a time. The nonspeaking person then uses the switch to stop the scanning once the symbol to be communicated is reached.

Most advanced electronic communication aids use a process called encoding for symbol selection. Through encoding, large numbers of vocabulary words or messages can be accessed by combining a few symbols into simple codes. The symbols might be picture cues, letter cues, written words, or numbers. For example, the symbol combination *eat + A* could be an encoded combination that produces "I would like an apple" on the output device; *eat + B* would produce "I would like a banana"; and *play + B* would produce "Let's play ball." Through advances in electronic technology and computer software, many electronic communication aids can now easily be customized to meet the handicapped user's needs. The user can develop messages, decide on what codes will be used to access the messages, and store the messages for later use. Messages and codes can be added, deleted, or revised at any time by the user. These advanced systems are expensive but are cost effective since a single system is capable of growing and changing as the user's needs and skills change over time.

## REFERENCES

Harris, D., & Vanderheiden, G. (1980). Augmentative communication techniques. In R. L. Schiefelbush (Ed.), *Nonspeech language and communication: Analysis and intervention.* Baltimore, MD: University Park Press.

Vanderheiden, G. (1985). *Nonvocal communication resource book* (revised ed.), Madison, WI: Trace Research and Development Center, University of Wisconsin.

SHARON L. GLENNEN
*Pennsylvania State University*

## AUGMENTATIVE COMMUNICATION SYSTEMS
## COMMUNICATION BOARDS

# ELECTRONIC TRAVEL AIDS

Blind persons who travel independently rely on essentially three kinds of travel aids: long canes, dog guides, and electronic travel aids. Electronic travel aids serve as guidance devices that extend the range of perception of the environment beyond the fingertip, tip of the long cane, or handle of the dog guide's harness. These sensory aids enable the blind person to determine the approximate elevation, dimensions, azimuth, and possibly surface texture of objects detected within the range that the ultrasonic or electromagnetic waves penetrate. Information put out as auditory sounds or tactile vibrations permits the user to decide whether to avoid direct contact with the source of the signal, make contact with it, or simply use it as a reference point for orientation and navigation purposes.

Of the four most commonly used electronic travel aids, three are considered secondary aids that complement and enrich information received from the long cane or dog guide. The Russell Pathsounder is a small battery-operated unit that can be mounted on the user's chest. The unit emits ultrasonic waves that penetrate the area in front of the unit to a distance of 6 ft. If the invisible waves hit an object and produce an echo picked up by the receiver in the unit, then an auditory and/or vibrating signal is triggered. The chest unit vibrates until the object appears in the inner protection zone less than inches from the traveler's chest. Once within that zone, the vibrator in the back of the neck strap is activated to signal the closer proximity. The auditory warning signal is a buzzing sound that switches to a high-pitched beep when objects enter the inner protection zone. The Pathsounder can supplement the long cane by protecting the upper body. Wheelchair users also find the device helpful (Farmer, 1980).

The Sonicguide developed in New Zealand is another secondary aid that provides protection for the vulnerable area between the knees and the head. The unit emits pulses of ultrasonic waves from a source mounted in eyeglass frames. The pitch of the sound represents distance from an object within a 20-ft range; the stereophonic effect reveals location to the left or right of the head direction; and the sound quality or timbre suggests characteristics of the surface texture (Mellor, 1981).

The Mowat Sensor is a small hand-held sonar device that can be used to detect landmarks, openings, and specific objects like bus stop signs or water fountains. The Mowat Sensor has two ranges of operation extending to 13 ft. When an object appears within range, the entire unit vibrates at a rate related to the distance of the object (Farmer, 1980).

The LASER (light amplification by stimulated emission of radiation) cane is considered both a primary and secondary aid. It is an adaptation of the long cane with three built-in laser sources that send out beams of infa red light in three directions. The beams are only 1 in. wide at 10 ft from the source to permit rather precise location of objects. The upward beam detects objects in line with the head, the forward beam locates objects in the direct line of travel, and the downward beam picks up drop-offs such as curbs or stairs (Farmer, 1980). For a more detailed discussion of mobility aids in general and electronic travel aids in particular, see Farmer's chapter on mobility devices in Welsh and Blasch (1980).

## REFERENCES

Farmer, L. (1980). Mobility devices. In R. Welsh & B. Blasch (Eds.), *Foundations of orientation and mobility.* New York: American Foundation for the Blind.

Mellor, C. M. (1981). *Aids for the 80's: What they are and what they do*. New York: American Foundation for the Blind.

MARJORIE E. WARD
*The Ohio State University*

MOBILITY TRAINING
VISION TRAINING

# ELEMENTARY AND SECONDARY EDUCATION ACT (ESEA)

The Elementary and Secondary Education Act (ESEA; PL 89-10) of 1965 included the first major program of federal assistance to local school districts (Eidenberg & Morey, 1969). Title I of ESEA, amended and renamed Chapter 1 of the Education Consolidation and Improvement Act (ECIA) in 1981, provides federal grants through states to school districts based on the number of children from families in poverty. The grants are to provide compensatory education services to educationally deprived children. Children are determined to be eligible for services based not on family income but on local determination, within federal guidelines, that they are educationally disadvantaged.

Also included in this statute is the authorization for the Chapter 1 state agency program for handicapped children in state-operated or state-supported schools. Grants are made to the states to provide supplementary educational services based on the number of handicapped children in such programs. This authority predates the Education for All Handicapped Children Act (PL 94-142) and was aimed primarily at children in institutional settings. Children served in Chapter 1 state agency programs are subject to all the requirements of PL 94-142. For purposes of federal reimbursement, however, a handicapped child may be counted in either the Chapter 1 state agency grant (250,000 children in December 1984) or in the PL 94-142 state grant (4.1 million children in December 1984), but not both.

## REFERENCES

Eidenberg, E., & Morey, R. (1969). *An act of congress*. New York: Norton.

Rehab Group. (1979). *Assessment of educational programs in state-supported and state-operated agencies*. Falls Church, VA: Author.

Riddle, W. (1985). *Elementary and Secondary Education Act: A condensed history of the original law and major amendments*. Washington, DC: Congressional Research Service.

JAMES R. RICCIUTI
*United States Office of
Management and Budget*

EDUCATION FOR ALL HANDICAPPED CHILDREN ACT OF 1975
LEGAL REGULATIONS OF SPECIAL EDUCATION

# ELLIS, NORMAN R. (1924– )

Norman R. Ellis, born in Springville, Alabama, September 14, 1924, is known for his theoretical work on mental retardation, for research on memory and learning by persons with mental retardation, and for editing major works on mental retardation. He is a major proponent of the difference or deficit theory, which proposes that people with mental retardation have mental processes that are in some ways qualitatively different from those of persons with normal intelligence. From this model, it follows that the goal of research should be to discover and study those processes that predict differences in intellectual ability. In the area of research, Ellis is credited with formulating the stimulus trace deficit theory, which states that short-term memory deficits of subjects who are mentally retarded are due to rapid deterioration of stimulus traces in the brain. He also proposed a three-stage model of memory: primary memory, secondary memory, and tertiary memory (Borkowski, Peck, & Damberg, 1983; Detterman, 1983). Ellis is editor of major works on mental retardation, including two editions of the *Handbook in Mental Deficiency* (1963, 1979) and 13 volumes of *International Review of Research in Mental Retardation* (1966–1986). He is the author of nearly 100 scholarly articles.

Ellis received his BA degree in 1951 from Howard College, an MA in general experimental psychology from the University of Alabama in 1952, and a PhD from Louisiana State University in 1956 in general experimental psychology. He is professor of psychology and director of the doctoral training program in mental retardation and developmental disabilities, University of Alabama. He previously held positions at George Peabody College, Louisiana State University, and State Colony and Training School, Pineville, Louisiana.

Ellis is a fellow of the American Association on Mental Deficiency and American Psychological Association. He received the American Association on Mental Deficiency Award for Outstanding Research in 1972 and the Edgar A. Doll Award for Outstanding Research from the American Psychological Association in 1986. He has received numerous awards from the University of Alabama. He is listed in the twelfth edition of *American Men and Women in Science*.

## REFERENCES

Borkowski, J. G., Peck, V. A., & Damberg, P. R. (1983). Attention, memory, and cognition. In J. L. Matson & J. A. Mulick (Eds.), *Handbook of mental retardation* (pp. 479–497). New York: Pergamon.

Detterman, K. D. (1983). Some trends in research design. In J. L. Matson & J. A. Mulick (Eds.), *Handbook of research in mental retardation* (pp. 527–539). New York: Pergamon.

Ellis, N. R. (Ed.). (1963). *Handbook in mental deficiency*. New York: McGraw-Hill.

Ellis, N. R. (Ed.). (1979). *Handbook of mental deficiency* (2nd ed.). Hillsdale, NJ: Erlbaum.

Ellis, N. R. (Ed.). (1966–1986). *International review of research in mental retardation* (Vols. 1–13). New York: Academic.

ELEANOR BOYD WRIGHT
*University of North Carolina,
Wilmington*

## ELWYN INSTITUTES

Elwyn Institutes was founded in 1852. It is located on a 400-acre campus near Media, Pennsylvania. It is a comprehensive service facility, and it provides day and residential programs for children and adults who are learning handicapped, developmentally delayed, retarded, deaf/blind, neurologically disabled, brain damaged, visually impaired, physically handicapped, deaf, hard of hearing, or multihandicapped and deaf.

Elwyn Institutes' continuum of services features rehabilitation programs that coordinate residential and community living arrangements with special education, vocational training, and sequential programs that lead to independence in the community. Students in residence live in modern living accommodations on campus and in apartments within the local communities.

Elwyn Institutes maintains programs in Philadelphia, Wilmington, Delaware, Fountain Valley, California, and Israel. Management and administrative supervision is provided at the American Institute for Mental Studies, also known as the Vineland Training School in Vineland, New Jersey.

Elwyn Institutes' educational programs are offered to students with day and residential accommodations from preschool years through to 21 years. These programs provide a wide range of educational services, including comprehensive evaluations, preschool programs, daycare facilities, and elementary and secondary levels of education and training. Ancillary services include audiological evaluations, speech and language therapy, mobility training, occupational therapy, psychiatric and psychological services, and medical and dental care.

Elwyn Institutes is located at 111 Elwyn Road, Elwyn, PA 19063.

### REFERENCE

Sargent, J. K. (1982). *The directory for exceptional children* (9th ed.). Boston: Porter Sargent.

PAUL C. RICHARDSON
*Elwyn Institutes, Elwyn,
Pennsylvania*

## EMBEDDED FIGURES TEST (EFT)

The Embedded Figures Test (EFT) was designed to measure individual differences in cognitive style, specifically, field dependence-independence. Developed by Herman Witkin in 1950, the EFT requires subjects to locate a simple geometric figure embedded within a larger, more complex figure. Field-independent subjects are able to perform this task more quickly than field-dependent subjects. A recent review by LaVoie (1985) suggested that the EFT may be related to learning and instructional preferences and serve as an indicator of analytic ability. Witkin, Moore, Goodenough, and Cox (1977) also discussed the educational implications of cognitive style.

Test materials include 24 complex figure cards (two sets of 12, Form A and Form B), a set of eight simple figure cards, and a stylus used by the subject to trace the embedded figure. An average time of disembedding is calculated (total search time divided by 12) and converted into a standard score. Reliability studies indicate good internal consistency and test-retest stability. The test correlates significantly with more cumbersome measures of field dependence. The EFT can be used with individuals ages 12 and up, however, adaptations of the test are available for younger children (the Children's Embedded Figures Test for ages 5 through 11 and the Preschool Embedded Figures Test for ages 3 through 5). There is also a group test. All four versions are available from Consulting Psychologists Press, Inc.

### REFERENCES

LaVoie, A. L. (1985). Embedded Figures Test. In D. J. Keyser & R. C. Sweetland (Eds.), *Test critiques* (Vol. II). Kansas City, MO: Test Corrporation of America.

Witkin, H. A. (1950). Individual differences in ease of perception of embedded figures. *Journal of Personality, 19,* 1–15.

Witkin, H. A., Moore, C. A., Goodenough, D. R., & Cox, P. W. (1977). Field-dependent and field-independent cognitive styles and their educational implications. *Review of Educational Research, 47,* 1–64.

ROBERT G. BRUBAKER
*Eastern Kentucky University*

**ASSESSMENT**
**VISUAL PERCEPTION AND DISCRIMINATION**

## EMOTIONAL DISORDERS

The greatest amount of progress on behalf of the emotionally disturbed (ED) has occurred in the twentieth century. Assessment instruments, residential schools for the emotionally disturbed, special classes in public schools, child guidance clinics, juvenile courts and legal statutes specifically written for delinquent and abused children, and hundreds of texts dealing with the etiology, diagnosis, and treatment of children are all products of the twentieth century.

By the 1960s and 1970s, dramatic progress had been made on behalf of children and youth. Behavior modification techniques became a popular treatment method and ecological approaches to treatment of the disturbed child were developed. Public Law 94-142 mandated an appropriate education for all children. Efforts were made to deinstitutionalize children and to mainstream them in the public schools. By the late 1970s and early 1980s, a family systems approach to treatment of the disturbed child came into vogue. Today efforts are being made to educate the emotionally disturbed child in the classroom and to supplement education with a therapeutic treatment program.

The problems in defining normal functioning in children make it difficult to classify abnormalities. This is particularly the case in emotional disturbance, where behavioral rather than academic criteria are primarily employed. Stemming from the realities of providing educational remediation, however, Bower (1969) spearheaded efforts to conceptualize emotional disturbances in children. He provided a practical definition consisting of the following five characteristics: (1) learning problems are not explained by intellectual, sensory, or health factors; (2) there are difficulties in initiating and maintaining interpersonal relationships; (3) behavioral or emotional reactions are not appropriate to circumstances; (4) there is pervasive unhappiness or depression; and (5) there is the development of physical symptoms or fears related to school or personal problems. Any one or more of these five characteristics occurring to a marked extent over a long period of time are sufficient for diagnosis. Bower's criteria were adopted verbatim in PL 94-142 Public Law 94-142 additionally labeled schizophrenic and autistic children as seriously emotionally disturbed and differentiated socially maladjusted from emotionally disturbed children. Autistic children were dropped from the emotionally disturbed category and placed in the health-impaired category in 1981.

Despite its official sanction as a category of childhood exceptionality, the label emotional disturbance has evoked considerable debate in the literature. It has been reported that the differentiation of emotional and behavioral disorders in children is difficult to make (Boyle & Jones, 1985), and that the distinction between primary and secondary emotional disturbance in learning disabilities is similarly confused (Chandler & Jones, 1983). Inadequacies in definition may have resulted in the underdetection and underserving of emotionally disturbed children (Long & McQueen, 1984). Although Bower (1981) has openly discussed the nebulous nature of basing a classification category on disturbances in emotion, he has continued to advocate the application of the revised term emotionally handicapped and his original diagnostic criteria.

Incidence rates of emotional disturbances, or the number of newly diagnosed cases at any point in time, are practically nonexistent because of the difficulties in accurately defining the onset and duration of childhood psychiatric disorders. Estimates of prevalence, or the number of existing cases at any point in time, however, are available and are based on data collected from educational and psychiatric perspectives.

A recent comprehensive report summarized the prevalence rates of exceptional children (Zill, 1985) as reported by the National Center for Education Statistics from 1976 to 1985. The number of emotionally disturbed children receiving special education services during the 1982–1983 school year was 352,000, or just under 1% of the total school enrollment. This represents a nearly 25% increase from the 1976–1977 school year. These data, however, are likely a gross underestimate of the prevalence rate. Teacher estimates of children in need of services for emotional disturbance vary between 2.7 and 4% of total school enrollment. Support for an even higher prevalence rate is available in a review of psychiatric research that reported that the prevalence of globally defined "clinical maladjustment" in children was no lower than 11.9% (Gould, Wunsch-Hitzig, & Dohrenwend, 1981). The prevalence rate probably lies somewhere between estimates obtained from teachers and estimates obtained from psychiatric research indicating that emotional disturbance is a significant problem in childhood populations.

A number of individual difference variables have been identified as significant correlates of childhood emotional disturbance. Sex is a particularly important factor. Males are more likely than females to be identified throughout the school years, with more males receiving the psychiatric diagnosis of conduct disorder and more females receiving the psychiatric diagnoses of specific emotional disorders, especially during adolescence (Offord, 1983). Racial and family characteristics have also been implicated. Blacks are more likely than whites to be identified, and identification varies inversely with parent education level as well as family socioeconomic status (Zill, 1985). The importance of family variables is supported by the strong association between childhood psychiatric diagnoses in general and broken homes, marital discord, and parental deviance (Offord, 1983).

The etiology of mild to moderate emotional disturbances may not always be precise, but two major causative factors seem to predominate. These include socioenvironmental factors and biological factors. Genetic factors are important, but from the information to date, only the more severe forms of psychopathology seem to result from a genetic predisposition. This will be discussed in the section on seriously emotionally disturbed children.

*Etiology.* In the last quarter of the twentieth century, marked changes are occurring in the family as we know it today. Single-parent families, blended families ("his and her children" in second marriages), parents working outside the home, "latchkey" children, apartment living, and family mobility all contribute to socioenvironmental factors as one of the major etiologies of emotional disturbances in children. Parental deprivation or distortions in parent-child relationships as a result of parental psychopathology are all too common. Many children are seriously neglected, and/or emotionally, physically, and even sexually abused by a parent or surrogate parent. Chronic neglect of a pervasive nature can and does affect the child's emotional and personal development. Physically and sexually abused children often exhibit depression or emotional agitation, poor self-image, cognitive deficits, and difficulties interrelating with peers (Willis, 1985).

Children and youth reared in extreme poverty are at higher risk for developing personality disorders and delinquent behavior. These disadvantaged children often exhibit cognitive delays. Thus, early school performance may be deficient, which may further accentuate a negative self-image.

In the biological realm, children with chronic health or other physical disorders may create added stress within the family. The exceptional child may be overprotected or rejected. In addition, the parent(s) may feel ambivalent toward the child. Any or all of these reactions can lead to maladaptive parental behaviors that can then create problems for the child and family.

A child's temperament may also determine, to an extent, a predilection toward emotional problems, especially if the child's temperament does not match parental and other environmental expectations. Nine temperament characteristics are described by Thomas, Chess, and Birch (1968): activity level, approach-withdrawal, rhythmicity, adaptibility, mood, threshold, intensity, distractibility, persistence, and attention span. A difficult child is characterized by being slow to adapt to change, withdrawing from new stimuli, exhibiting a negative mood, manifesting biological irregularity, and demonstrating a high level of expressiveness. The difficult child is more likely to develop behavior disorders because his or her ability to interact with the environment and others is not always easy and nonstressful. This child may be at greater risk for abuse merely because he or she is, by nature, difficult. Children who present with neurological dysfunction or brain damage as the result of prematurity, pre- or postnatal infections, complications during pregnancy, and head trauma owed to accidents or injuries, may present with a diagnosis of emotional disturbance.

*Classification of ED.* Bowers' (1969) definition of emotional disturbance provides a set of criteria for labeling and differentiating a group of children who may respond to educational remediation. From a psychiatric perspective, however, the label emotional disturbance encompasses a wide range of childhood psychopathology. A number of different psychiatric disorders are included; they are the product of disparate etiologies and respond differentially

to the treatment strategies that are available. Once a child receives the categorical label of emotionally disturbed, it is important to provide a more specific psychiatric diagnosis to facilitate effective treatment.

A brief discussion of some of the major childhood psychiatric syndromes included under the emotional disturbance label follows. The reader is referred to texts on childhood psychopathology or exceptionality by Achenbach (1982), Brown and Reynolds (1986), and Steinhauer and Rae-Grant (1983), and to the third edition of the *Diagnostic and Statistical Manual of Mental Disorders* of the American Psychiatric Association (DSM-III) (1980) for more specific and comprehensive information.

Childhood depression has been recognized as a viable diagnosis in recent years. Estimates of prevalence vary according to diagnostic criteria, but one recent study placed the prevalence rate of depression at just over 5% for elementary school-aged children (Leftowitz & Tesiny, 1985). The rising incidence of suicide in children and adolescents is undoubtedly linked to increasing rates of childhood depression. With pervasive unhappiness or depression included as one of the diagnostic criteria for emotional disturbance, it is clear that childhood depression or depressive affect related to other psychological problems will appear frequently in groups of emotionally disturbed children.

Childhood depression differs from adult depression along a number of lines. The major presenting complaints in children are extreme sadness and accompanying withdrawal. Masked versions, in which the presenting complaints involve acting out behaviors, are not uncommon. Vegetative symptoms do not occur as frequently in children as they do in adults. However, both acute and chronic depression in children have been reported. The withdrawn, uncommunicative child is definitely a candidate for this diagnosis. Rapid, unexplained increases in acting out behaviors also necessitate consideration of an underlying depressive reaction.

A number of childhood psychiatric problems are linked directly to anxiety disorders. Anxiety may be the primary symptom or reactions to anxiety may produce somatic complaints and/or behavioral changes.

Phobias occur when anxiety and its somatic or behavioral concomitants are displayed in the presence of a feared object or situation. School phobia is a specific phobic reaction resulting from fears about school experiences, about separation from parents, or a combination of both. Panic disorder and generalized anxiety reactions refer to more global anxiety responses that are not linked to specific aspects of the environment yet may reflect underlying emotional conflict. In post traumatic stress disorder, symptoms based on both anxiety and depression occur following a traumatic event that a child reexperiences repeatedly on a psychological level. With the incidence of child abuse increasing, the latter diagnosis is appearing more frequently in populations of emotionally disturbed children.

Other childhood disorders such as psychosomatic disorders may be seen in the special education child. Psychosomatic disorders are any physical conditions that can be initiated, exacerbated, or prolonged by psychosocial factors (Schaefer, Millman, & Levine, 1979).

The notion that health-related problems are caused by the interaction of biological, social, and psychological factors constitutes the cornerstone of psychosomatic disorders. Indeed, psychosomatic dysfunction is one of the major causes of school absence. For example, the child who presents with asthma, gastrointestinal disorders such as ulcers, diarrhea, vomiting, or abdominal pain, migraine headaches or hypertension, skin disorders such as dermatitis, and even hysterical symptoms may manifest an exaggeration of symptoms secondary to emotional stress. The stress may result from environmental demands, learning problems, or parent-child problems. Basically, physical symptoms that are rooted in or exacerbated by emotional conflict are the primary presenting complaints in psychosomatic disorders. Preexisting physiological vulnerability, such as ulcers or asthma, can be worsened by emotional stresses within the individual or family.

Children who have a history of multiple or prolonged hospitalization, or a history of chronic illness, may also present with emotional disturbance secondary to the trauma of medical surgeries or procedures. The effects of hospitalization and physical illness on the developing child can be understood best by reading Willis, Elliot, and Jay (1982).

Personality disorders are characterized by maladaptive and inflexible patterns of behaviors, thoughts, and emotions that affect an individual's functioning across situations and time. The symptoms of personality disorders are ego syntonic, meaning that they are not viewed by the individual as problematic. They are diagnosed more frequently in adults than in children because rapid developmental changes in children complicate predictions regarding stability of functioning. Childhood precursors of personality disorders have been applied as specific diagnoses in childhood populations.

Based on symptom clusters, personality disorders and their childhood precursors have been grouped into three categories (Steinhauer & Berman, 1983). The first group is defined by emotional constriction, rigidity, aloofness, and the inability to maintain interpersonal relationships. Schizoid disorders of childhood and adolescence are included in this category, as well as schizoid, paranoid, and schizotypal personality disorders. The second group is defined by dramatic, emotional, self-centered, and unstable behaviors. Identity disorders of childhood and adolescence and conduct disorders are the childhood precursors within this category. Histrionic, narcissitic, and antisocial personality disorders are also included. Intrapsychic struggles between anxiety and defenses against anxiety characterize the third group. Avoidant disorder and oppositional disorder are diagnoses applied to children manifesting these characteristics. Avoidant, dependent,

compulsive, and passive-aggressive are labels used to describe fully developed personality disorders based on these intrapsychic struggles.

Children who present with a behavior disorder are often seen in the school setting. This population differs from children who present with social maladjustment when the following criteria are present: the presence of guilt or anxiety; a specific etiology; and responsiveness to treatment. Often these children experience enormous frustration, intrapsychic conflicts, poor self-esteem, feelings of failure, and high anxiety levels. They may act out their frustrations in an aggressive way (Group for the Advancement of Psychiatry, 1966); as opposed to socially maladjusted children, they frequently feel remorse for their aggressive acts.

Immature behaviors displayed in the school setting (thumb sucking, crying, whining, negativism, baby talk) are often seen in children under stress and are indicative of some underlying, perhaps transient, problem occurring at home or elsewhere in the child's environment. Some children who have been overprotected by their parents may be bright, but immature in their social and environmental behavior. The withdrawn child does not interact with peers, is often viewed as a loner, is overly shy, and may be deficient in social skills. The immature or withdrawn child requires intervention but does not necessarily require individual treatment.

*Treatment.* Since there is no cookbook method of treating all disorders with which a child might present, the mental health professional treating an emotionally disturbed child must consider a number of factors when planning treatment strategies. It is not within the scope of this section to advocate one therapeutic orientation over another. Rather, an overview of psychodynamic therapy, behavior therapy, family and group therapy, and parent consultation will be presented.

Psychodynamic therapy deals with the underlying psychological causes creating a child's disturbance rather than overt symptoms. Feelings, fantasies, and fears are played out by the child in play therapy. The therapist may make dynamic interpretations of the child's verbal or nonverbal communication. It is hoped that the interpretations will make the child aware of unconscious thoughts and feelings that perpetuate his or her overt symptoms and that change in behavior may result from this therapeutic and educational style of interaction. In behavior therapy, the notion is that all behavior is learned and that some children learn maladaptive ways of interacting or relating or do not learn appropriate behaviors and social skills. The behavior therapist focuses on symptoms rather than causes, and seeks to actively manipulate the unacceptable behavior. This is an excellent technique to use when children present with discrete symptoms or present with a paucity of verbal insight skills. Relaxation training, a specific behavioral technique, might be used to aid children who are experiencing stress and other tension-related disorders.

Group psychotherapy is especially helpful for children

experiencing peer or social interaction problems, since in group therapy usually two or more children are seen by a therapist. The orientation of the group can be behavioral, psychodynamic, or supportive, but the goal of the therapist is usually to increase the child's awareness and control of his or her emotions.

The decision to treat a child in the context of family therapy is made when the therapist perceives the family as maintaining and perpetuating the child's problem. The therapist attempts to identify and modify maladaptive family patterns that perpetuate the child's problems (Jay, Waters, & Willis, 1986). Parent consultation is also used to teach parents means of modifying behavior at home, to offer advice on child rearing, to explain a child's behavior, and to give support. A more detailed account of treatment methods used with children can be found in Jay, Waters, and Willis (1986).

## REFERENCES

Achenbach, T. M. (1982). *Developmental psychopathology*. New York: Wiley.

American Psychiatric Association (1980). *Diagnostic and statistical manual of mental disorders* (3rd ed.) (DSM III). Washington, DC: Author.

Bower, E. M. (1969). *Early identification of emotionally handicapped children in school* (2nd ed.). Springfield, IL: Thomas.

Bower, E. M. (1981). *Early identification of emotionally handicapped children in school* (3rd ed.). Springfield, IL: Thomas.

Boyle, M. H., & Jones, S. C. (1985). Selecting measures of emotional and behavioral disorders of childhood for use in general populations. *Journal of Child Psychology & Psychiatry, 26*, 137–159.

Brown, R. T., & Reynolds, C. R. (1986). *Psychological perspectives on childhood exceptionality*. New York: Wiley.

Chandler, H. N., & Jones, K. (1983). Learning disabled or emotionally disturbed: Does it make any difference? *Journal of Learning Disabilities, 16*, 432–434.

Gould, M. S., Wunsch-Hitzig, R., & Dohrenwend, B. (1981). Estimating the prevalence of childhood psychopathology. *Journal of the American Academy of Child Psychiatry, 20*, 462–476.

Group for the Advancement of Psychiatry. (1966). *Psychopathological disorders in childhood: Theoretical considerations and a proposed classification* (Vol. 6, Report No. 2). New York: Author.

Jay, S., Waters, D. B., & Willis, D. J. (1986). The emotionally exceptional. In R. T. Brown & C. R. Reynolds (Eds.), *Psychological perspectives on childhood exceptionality*. New York: Wiley.

Leftowitz, M. M., & Tesiny, E. P. (1985). Depression in children: Prevalence and correlates. *Journal of Consulting & Clinical Psychology, 53*, 647–656.

Long, K. A., & McQueen, D. V. (1984). Detection and treatment of emotionally disturbed children in schools: Problems and theoretical perspectives. *Journal of Clinical Psychology, 40*, 378–390.

Offord, D. R. (1983). Classification and epidemiology in child psychiatry: Status and unresolved problems. In P. D. Steinhauer & Q. Rae-Grant (Eds.), *Psychological problems of the child in the family* (2nd ed.). New York: Basic Books.

Schaefer, C. E., Millman, H. L., Levine, G. (1979). *Therapies for psychosomatic disorders in children*. San Francisco. Jossey-Bass.

Steinhauer, P. D., & Berman, G. (1983). Anxiety, neurotic, and personality disorders in children. In P. D. Steinhauer & Q. Rae-Grant (Eds.), *Psychological problems of the child in the family* (2nd ed.), pp. 230–257). New York: Basic Books.

Steinhauer, P. D., & Rae-Grant, Q. (Eds.). (1983). *Psychological problems of the child in the family* (2nd ed.). New York: Basic Books.

Thomas, A., Chess, S., & Birch, H. G. (1968). *Temperament and behavior disorders in children*. New York: New York University Press.

Willis, D. J. (1985). *Psychological investigation of physical and sexual abuse of children*. Presidential address. Los Angeles: American Psychological Association.

Willis, D. J., Elliot, C., & Jay, S. (1982). Psychological effects of physical illness and its concomitants. In P. Magrab (Ed.), *Handbook for the practice of pediatric psychology*. New York: Wiley.

Wright, L., Schaefer, A. B., & Solomons, G. (1979). *Encyclopedia of pediatric psychology*. Baltimore, MD: University Park Press.

Zill, N. (1985). *The school-age handicapped*. Prepared by Child Trends, incorporated under Department of Education contract number 300-83-0198. Washington, DC: U.S. Department of Education.

DIANE J. WILLIS
E. WAYNE HOLDEN
*University of Oklahoma Health
Sciences Center*

CONDUCT DISORDER
CHILDHOOD PSYCHOSIS
CHILDHOOD SCHIZOPHRENIA
PSYCHONEUROTIC DISORDERS
SERIOUSLY EMOTIONALLY DISTURBED

## EMOTIONAL LABILITY

Emotional lability refers to rapidly shifting or unstable emotions (American Psychiatric Association, 1980). It is a psychiatric term that developed from attempts to classify the qualitative aspects of inappropriate emotional functioning in clinical cases. Lability has been most frequently applied in descriptions of serious emotional disturbance where rapid changes in emotional status are readily apparent. Unstable emotions are also characteristic of less severe psychopathologies and can be used to describe normal children's functioning during periods of stress or crisis. Sustained emotional lability, however, is considered to be pathological and results from a number of different causative factors. The primary etiological agents in children are fragile central nervous system functioning and frustration in meeting environmental demands (Swanson & Willis, 1979).

Some familiarity with the psychiatric terminology used to describe emotion (Kaplan, Freedman, Saddock, 1980) is needed to clearly understand the role of lability in the description of a child's functioning. Mood refers to sustained internal sensations that are stable and influence all aspects of an individual's functioning. Affect, on the other hand, is the immediate expression of emotion that is attached to specific environmental events. Affect can vary from situation to situation, while mood is pervasive emotional tone occurring across situations. The outward manifestations of affect are the basis for describing emotional responding. Lability refers to changes in affect that are repetitious and abrupt; both negative and positive affect may be displayed. Emotional responding is intense and typically does not fit environmental demands. Lability can be contrasted with other terms used to describe affective expression. Restricted affect is characterized by a reduction in the range and intensity of responding; blunted affect refers to a severe reduction in the intensity of responding; and flat affect is the complete absence of emotional responding.

Children receiving special education services who are classified emotionally disturbed are at greatest risk for displaying emotional lability. Unstable emotions are a primary diagnostic feature in a number of childhood psychiatric conditions included under the emotional disturbance label. Other categories of childhood exceptionality, however, are not exempt from rapidly shifting or unstable emotions. Labile affect is frequently displayed secondary to cognitive disturbance in learning-disabled and mentally retarded children. Emotional lability may also be present in children with sensory handicaps or physical handicaps owed to frustrations with meeting environmental demands. Even gifted children can display emotional lability when they are not appropriately challenged in the classroom setting. It is clear that emotional lability can be applied to all categories of childhood exceptionality and not restricted to children who have been diagnosed with a psychiatric condition.

## REFERENCES

American Psychiatric Association. (1980). *A psychiatric glossary* (5th ed.). Boston: Little, Brown.

Kaplan, H. I., & Freedman, A. M., & Saddock, B. J. (1980). *Comprehensive textbook of psychiatry/III*. Baltimore, MD: Williams & Wilkins.

Sawnson, M., & Willis, D. J. (1979). *Understanding exceptional children and youth*. Chicago: Rand McNally.

E. WAYNE HOLDEN
DIANE J. WILLIS
*University of Oklahoma Health
Sciences Center*

ACTING OUT
EMOTIONAL DISORDERS
SERIOUSLY EMOTIONALLY DISTURBED

## ENCEPHALITIS

Encephalitis is an inflammation or infection of the brain, as contrasted with meningitis, which is an infection of the meninges or tissue covering the brain and spinal cord. Numerous types of encephalitides have been identified, and these tend to be classified by the etiologic agent. The two most common types are viral encephalitis, which is the result of a virus infection, and postinfectious encephalitis, which occurs as a complication of another infectious disease (e.g., chicken pox, measles). Encephalitis lethargica (also known as Von Economo's disease or sleeping sickness) is a rarely occurring type of encephalitis that appears in epidemics, generally in the spring of the year (Brown, 1971; Thomson, 1979). The last known outbreak of encephalitis lethargica occurred in Great Britain in the 1920s; it is presumed to be associated with a viral infection that attacks cortical and subcortical brain structures (Thomson, 1979).

A large number of viruses have been identified as etiologic agents in encephalitis. These viruses are categorized according to their mode of transmission. Enteroviruses are spread from person to person via respiratory infection or hand to mouth contact (e.g., coxsackievirus). Other viruses are acquired from infected animals such as mosquitoes or ticks. A third type of virus is spread by arthropods and requires a cycle in the arthropod host (R. T. Johnson, 1979). The herpes simplex virus has been reported to be the most common source of nonepidemic encephalitis (Kaufman, 1981). In newborns, infection may occur as a result of an active genital herpes infection in the mother (Baringer, 1979).

Common symptoms of encephalitis include headache, neck pain, nausea, vomiting, fever, and lethargy (*Mosby's*, 1983). Convulsions may occur, and paralysis in the head, neck, or body may be evident (Brown, 1971). Severe neurologic disturbances of affect may be associated with encephalitis. These include aggressiveness and violence (Lechtenberg, 1982), irritability (*Mosby's*, 1983), delusions and sexual indiscretions (Lechtenberg, 1982), and olfactory and gustatory hallucinations (Baringer, 1979).

The course of encephalitis is highly variable, and is associated with the etiologic agent and age of onset, among other factors. Mortality rates for victims of herpes simplex encephalitis are reported to be as high as 30 to 70% (Baringer, 1979). Survivors tend to demonstrate significant neurologic impairment of memory, cognition, and behavior, although total recovery in selected individuals has been reported (Baringer, 1979). Mortality rates for St. Louis and western encephalitides are much lower, approximately 10% of those afflicted (R. T. Johnson, 1979), although higher rates may occur in infants below 1 year. More than half the children surviving western equine encephalitis are reported to have significant neurologic sequelae, including mental retardation, spastic paralyses, and behavioral problems (K. M. Johnson, 1979). Many survivors of encephalitis may require special education or related services. Because of the variable sequelae associated with this condition, a multifactored evaluation is essential to planning an appropriate educational program.

## REFERENCES

Baringer, J. R. (1979). Herpes simplex encephalitis. In P. B. Beeson, W. McDermott, J. B. Wyngaarden (Eds.), *Cecil textbook of medicine* (pp. 821–824). Philadelphia: Saunders.

Brown, J. A. C. (1971). *The Stein and Day international medical encyclopedia.* New York: Stein & Day.

Johnson, K. M. (1979). Arthropod-borne viral encephalitides. In P. B. Beeson, W. McDermott, & J. B. Wyngaarden (Eds.), *Cecil textbook of medicine* (pp. 283–292). Philadelphia: Saunders.

Johnson, R. T. (1979). Viral meningitis and encephalitis. In P. B. Beeson, W. McDermott, & J. B. Wyngaarden (Eds.), *Cecil textbook of medicine* (pp. 817–821). Philadelphia: Saunders.

Kaufman, D. M. (1981). *Clinical neurology for psychiatrists.* New York: Grune & Stratton.

Lechtenberg, R. (1982). *The psychiatrist's guide to diseases of the nervous system.* New York: Wiley.

*Mosby's medical and nursing dictionary.* (1983). St. Louis: Mosby.

Thomson, W. A. R. (1979). *Black's medical dictionary* (32nd ed.). New York: Barnes & Noble.

CATHY F. TELZROW
*Cuyahoga Special Education
Service Center, Maple
Heights, Ohio*

## HERPES
## MENINGITIS

## ENCOPRESIS

Encopresis refers to the repeated (voluntary or involuntary) passage of feces into places not socially appropriate among persons for whom there is no organic pathology. According to the diagnostic criteria of DSM-III (American Psychiatric Association, 1982), a minimum of one monthly event must occur after age 4; others (e.g., Bawkin & Bawkin, 1972) consider 2 to be the youngest age at which encopresis can be diagnosed. Reported prevalence estimates range from 1 to 5%, depending on the particular sample studied (i.e., children in the general population or in institutional settings). Encopresis is more prevalent among males than females.

Four major types of encopresis are discussed in the literature. As with enuresis, a distinction between primary and secondary encopresis is often made. This refers to whether the child has previously displayed bowel control. A second major distinction is made between nonretentive and retentive encopresis. Nonretentive encopresis refers to children who produce normal stools but pass them into their clothes or some other inappropriate place. In contrast, retentive encopresis refers to children who retain feces in the bowel. Such stool retention can result in relaxed sphincter muscles and a distended colon, resulting in periodic soilings because the child has adapted to the sensations of a full rectum.

Encopresis has been examined primarily from three different perspectives. From the medical perspective, encopresis is viewed as a result of inadequacies in the structure or function of the physiological mechanisms necessary for bowel control (Wicks-Nelson & Israel, 1984). According to the psychodynamic view, encopresis is a symptom of more fundamental conflicts such as fear of castration, coercive toilet training, or aggression toward parents (Ayllon, Simon, & Wildman, 1975). From the behavioral perspective, primary encopresis is seen as a result of the failure to consistently apply training procedures, while secondary encopresis is viewed as a result of either reinforcement that maintains soiling, or a lack of reinforcement for appropriate toileting (Doleys, 1979).

Although the treatment of encopresis has not received the attention given the treatment of enuresis, research from these three perspectives has been reported. Medical treatments include the use of medications, laxatives, and enemas, often in combination with dietary changes. Doleys (1979) has pointed out a number of weaknesses in reports of medical treatments. Medical treatments are generally considered less effective than other available interventions (Doleys, 1979; Siegel, 1983). Likewise, little empirical evidence supports the efficacy of psychotherapy for treating encopresis (Wicks-Nelson & Israel, 1984; Siegel, 1983).

A variety of behavioral treatments are supported by empirical evidence. Effective behavioral programs for encopresis have used positive reinforcement for appropriate toileting (Bach & Moylan, 1975), punishment (Ferinden & Van Handel, 1970), biofeedback (Kohlenberg, 1973), and a combination of procedures (Lyon, 1984). In brief, the behavioral literature indicates several successful procedures that also result in generalization of appropriate toileting behavior across situations and maintenance of desirable behavior. In designing behavioral treatments, Siegel (1983) urges maintaining regular contact with parents, using positive reinforcement for appropriate toileting in conjunction with any punishment procedure used, carefully considering restricted use of laxatives, and planning for possible relapses.

## REFERENCES

American Psychiatric Association. (1982). *Desk reference to the diagnostic criteria from the diagnostic and statistical manual of mental disorders* (3rd ed.). Washington, DC: Author.

Ayllon, T., Simon, S. J., & Wildman, R. W. (1975). Instructions and reinforcement in the elimination of encopresis: A case study. *Journal of Behavior Therapy & Experimental Psychiatry, 6,* 235–238.

Bach, R., & Moylan, J. J. (1975). Parents administer behavior therapy for inappropriate urination and encopresis. *Journal of Behavior Therapy & Experimental Psychiatry, 6,* 239–241.

Bawkin, H., & Bawkin, R. M. (1972). *Behavior disorders in children* (4th ed.). Philadelphia: Saunders.

Doleys, D. M. (1979). Assessment and treatment of childhood encopresis. In A. J. Finch & P. C. Kendall (Eds.), *Clinical treatment and research in child psychopathology.* New York: Spectrum.

Ferinden, W., & Van Handel, D. (1970). Eliminating the soiling behavior in an elementary school child through the application of aversive techniques. *Journal of School Psychology, 8,* 267–269.

Kohlenberg, R. J. (1973). Operant conditioning of human anal sphincter pressure. *Journal of Applied Behavior Analysis, 6,* 201–208.

Lyon, M. A. (1984). Positive reinforcement and logical consequences in the treatment of classroom encopresis. *School Psychology Review, 13,* 238–243.

Siegel, L. J. (1983). Psychosomatic and psychophysiological disorders. In R. J. Morris & T. R. Kratochwill (Eds.), *The practice of child therapy* (pp. 253–286). New York: Pergamon.

Wicks-Nelson, R., & Israel, A. C. (1984). *Behavior disorders of childhood.* Englewood Cliffs, NJ: Prentice-Hall.

JAMES P. KROUSE
*Clarion University of
Pennsylvania*

**APPLIED BEHAVIOR ANALYSIS
ENURESIS**

# ENDORPHINS

Endorphin is a term proposed by Goldstein (1976) to apply to all endogenous peptides that exhibit pharmacological properties like morphine. Since the first report by Hughes in 1975 of the isolation of a morphinelike substance in brain tissue, there has been much research and speculation as to the biological function of these peptides. Many of the first studies concentrated on locating and identifying the compounds. In addition to brain tissue, endorphins have also been found in the pituitary gland and gastrointestinal tract (Cooper, Bloom, & Roth, 1982). Within the brain, endorphins have been located in a number of areas. In particular, high concentrations have been found in areas involved in pain perception, memory, and arousal of emotions (Synder, 1977).

Considerable effort has also been made to understand the physiological and behavioral effects of the endorphins. Injection of endorphins produces many of the same physiological effects of morphine such as analgesia, hypother-

mia, nausea, vomiting, muscular rigidity, and severe akinesia (Cooper et al., 1982).

It has been theorized (and it is a widely held view) that the endogenous opiate system is relatively inactive during normal conditions and exerts an effect only under specific environmental or physiological circumstances (Amir, Brown, & Amit, 1980). However, determining the behavioral effects of the endorphins and the conditions under which they do exert an effect has been a controversial endeavor. The number of whole animal effects that have been attributed to the endorphinergic system has grown considerably in the last decade, but still remains open to much more comprehensive analysis. In addition to pain perception, proposed physiological properties that may be regulated by endorphins include blood pressure, body temperature, respiration, eating and drinking, sexual activity, and memory (Cooper et al., 1982). There have also been reports suggesting that disruption of this system may be involved in some mental disorders, but the evidence for this is even more equivocal than for other roles (McGeer, Eccles, & McGeer, 1978).

Akil (1977) has hypothesized that the endorphins evolved from primitive systems involved with pain and stress modulation and later become important in drives, emotions, and mood states, and in interfacing sensory and hormonal mechanisms. Preliminary studies do suggest that the role of the endorphins is multiple and involves much more than dulling the sensation of pain. It is likely that the endorphins are involved in analgesia, metabolism, affective states, and the processing of sensory information, though at present it is too early to draw any conclusions.

## REFERENCES

Akil, H. (1977). Opiates: Biological mechanisms. In J. D. Barchas, P. A. Berger, R. D. Ciaranello, & G. R. Elliot (Eds.), *Psychopharmacology: From theory to practice.* New York: Oxford University Press.

Amir, S., Brown, Z. W., & Amit, Z. (1980). The role of endorphins in stress: Evidence and speculations. *Neuroscience & Biobehavioral Reviews, 4,* 77–86.

Cooper, J. R., Bloom, F. E., & Roth, R. H. (1982). *The biochemical basis of neuropharmacology.* New York: Oxford University Press.

Goldstein, A. (1976). Opioid peptides (endorphins) in pituitary and brain. *Science, 193,* 1081–1086.

Hughes, J. (1975). Isolation of an endogenous compound from the brain with pharmacological properties similar to morphine. *Brain Research, 88,* 295–308.

McGeer, P. L., Eccles, J. C., & McGeer, E. G. (1978). *Molecular neurobiology of the mammalian brain.* New York: Plenum.

Synder, S. H. (1977, March). Opiate receptors and internal opiates. *Scientific American,* pp. 44–56.

POLLY E. SANDERSON
*Research Triangle Institute,
Research Triangle Park,
North Carolina*

METABOLIC DISORDERS
STRESS AND THE HANDICAPPED STUDENT

## ENDOCRINE DISTURBANCES

Diabetes mellitus (a disease of the pancreas) and delayed growth are two common endocrine disturbances. In healthy individuals, the pancreas secretes insulin in response to the amount of glucose in the blood. Insulin is essential in helping the glucose enter the cell for use in cell growth. In children with diabetes, this insulin/glucose regulatory mechanism is lost and insulin is produced/released in insufficient amounts. Thus, the child must rely on an external source of insulin that is injected daily into an arm or thigh. The child must eat the right amount of certain foods in order to regulate his or her blood glucose and thus insulin requirements.

Such regimentation of daily insulin injections and diet can pose problems for children and their families. Arguments can occur between the child and parents over diet, regular testing of blood or urine glucose, and insulin injections. Child/parent conflict may be accompanied by poor academic performance or other behavioral problems. Poor diabetic control also may negatively affect the child's energy level, concentration, and neuropsychological functioning (Rosenbloom, 1984).

Management of the child's diabetes may be a significant source of stress and friction in some families, especially those in which adolescent diabetics use their disease management as an outlet for demonstrating independence and individuation from parents. Some children are embarrassed by their illness and are teased by peers. If the diabetes is not well controlled, the child may miss school frequently; in that case, he or she should have the opportunity for homebound education. Even though most children with diabetes lead a relatively normal life, some continue to feel different, and all such children, in reality, have some diabetes-required regimentation that their peers do not share (Stein & Jessop, 1984). For example, they need to eat three meals per day, to avoid a sugar overload, and to awaken early for an insulin injection. The child and his or her parents should be consulted to determine the diabetic student's individual academic and personal requirements at school.

Delayed growth or short stature is another common endocrine disturbance. Most children with this disturbance eventually will have normal stature, but the onset of their pubertal development is delayed. A smaller group of children have specific hormonal deficits such as Turner's syndrome (a chromosomal abnormality in girls) and hypopituitarism (insufficient quantities of growth hormone).

Girls with Turner's syndrome have some difficulties with spatial relationships; these difficulties can affect school performance in areas such as geometry or geography (Holmes, Karlsson, & Thompson, 1985). It should be emphasized that a girl with Turner's syndrome who is bright and functioning well in other areas may compensate for this difficulty, although these areas still may be much harder for her than for her peers.

Relatively few data exist regarding types of behavioral problems or cognitive deficits in children with hypopituitarism. A variety of areas of the brain may be involved for children with this problem. Ideally, a child with hypopituitarism should receive a comprehensive neuropsychological assessment of academic achievement, cognitive ability, memory, motor and sensory functioning, and social abilities. Beacuse of the markedly small size of these children, they may be teased by their peers and their parents may expect less of them. These children may compensate by becoming the "class clown" or "school mascot." The educator should make note of his or her own reactions to the student with short stature to ensure that the student is treated according to age rather than size.

Interpersonal difficulties may occur in children with short stature as they enter adolescence. Inability to participate in age-appropriate activities and low self-esteem may result in behavior problems, withdrawal from social contacts, or poor school performance (Holmes, Karlsson, & Thompson, 1985). Some of these children are able to cope well with their dwarfism by finding areas in which they excel.

### REFERENCES

Holmes, C. S., Karlsson, J. A., & Thompson, R. G. (1985). Social and school competencies in children with short stature: Longitudinal patterns. *Journal of Developmental and Behavioral Pediatrics, 6*(5), 263–267.

Rosenbloom, A. L. (1984). Primary and subspeciality care of diabetes mellitus in children and youth. *Pediatric Clinics of North America, 31,* 107–117.

Stein, R. E., & Jessop, D. J. (1984). General issues in the care of children with chronic physical conditions. *Pediatric Clinics of North America, 31,* 189–198.

SAMUEL LEBARON
LONNIE K. ZELTZER
*University of Texas Health
Science Center, San Antonio*

DIABETES
DWARFISM
FAMILY RESPONSE TO A HANDICAPPED CHILD

## ENGLEMANN, SIEGFRIED E. (1931–    )

Siegfried E. Englemann obtained his BA in education at the University of Illinois in 1955. He was a research associate at the University of Illinois from 1964 to 1966; from

1966 to 1977 he was a senior educational specialist at the University of Illinois. From 1970 to 1974 he was associate professor at the University of Oregon. Since 1974 he has been a professor of special education at the University of Oregon.

Englemann's major area of study is working with disadvantaged children in the classroom setting. Englemann and Bereiter (1966) believe that the "how" of educating disadvantaged children is as important as the "what," and that to fail in developing more effective teaching methods is perhaps to fail completely in equalizing the educational attainment of children from differing cultural backgrounds. Englemann and Bereiter (1966) also feel that direct instruction is a thoroughly feasible and highly effective way of teaching needed academic skills to the young. The most important side effect of the direct teaching is the development of self-conscious pride and confidence in one's own ability to learn and think.

Some of Englemann's major works include *Teaching: A Basic Course in Applied Psychology, Teaching I: Classroom Management,* and *Teaching II: Cognitive Learning and Instruction.* He also contributed chapters to many books and has written over 80 articles, including "Observations on the Use of Direct Instruction with Young, Disadvantaged Children," "Teaching Formal Operations to Preschool Children," and many others.

## REFERENCES

Becker, W. C., Englemann, S. E., & Thomas, D. R. (1969). *Teaching: A basic course in applied psychology.* Chicago: Science Research Associates.

Englemann, S. E. (1969). *Preventing failure in the primary grades*: Chicago: Science Research Associates.

Englemann, S. E., & Bereiter, C. (1966). Observations on the use of direct instructions with young, disadvantaged children. *Journal of School Psychology, 4*(3), 55–62.

ELIZABETH JONES
*Texas A&M University*

## ENGINEERED CLASSROOM

The engineered classroom designed by Frank M. Hewett is a developmental strategy for educating children with maladaptive behavior. Hewett (1968) identifies other strategies, sensory-neurological, psychodynamic-interpersonal, and behavior modification, as having contributed successfully to the amelioration of some emotionally handicapped students' problem behaviors, but found that all had limitations relating to their goals or methodologies. The engineered classroom is designed to provide a more complete strategy in terms of establishing goals and procedures for the treatment of handicapped students in educational settings. Although the original concept was

applied to work with emotionally handicapped students, Hewett (1968) expresses a belief that many of the components of the engineered classroom could also be applied to students classified as mentally handicapped and learning disabled.

The engineered classroom is designed as a "learning triangle" consisting of curriculum, conditions, and consequences (Hewett & Forness, 1984). Three fundamental precepts underlie the engineered classroom curriculum:

1. Teachers need to think and provide instruction in small steps.
2. The steps are basic to instruction.
3. The steps and procedures are to be sequential.

The curriculum areas are designed as a sequence of instruction for developing students' learning competence. The five levels in the sequence include goals and activities designed to develop students' skills in attending to tasks, responding to tasks, following ordered steps in tasks, exploring the environment, interacting socially with others, and attaining mastery of basic academic skills. The conditions under which the curriculum is to be implemented entail a set of variables to be controlled by the teacher or "engineer." These include *when* students are to complete tasks, *where* they are to complete tasks, *how* students are to complete tasks, *how long* they are to work on tasks, *how much* teachers expect students to do, and *how well* students are to complete a task. The third component of the learning triangle, consequences for behavior, is provided in the form of positive reinforcement or punishment based on the completion or incompletion of tasks.

Within each of the curricular levels of learning competence, Hewett and Taylor (1980) describe specific goals and methods. The first four levels focus on getting the individual child ready to learn; the fifth level focuses on the child gaining social approval; and the sixth level focuses on the attainment of basic adaptive skills for the school environment. At the attention level, skills are developed in auditory and visual discrimination, auditory and visual memory, and task attention. To develop these skills, Hewett recommends that teachers carefully design the environment by removing distracting stimuli and accenting focal stimuli. Therefore, students are cued to attend only to stimuli relevant to the task at hand. In addition, concrete instructional materials are recommended, particularly with students at higher academic levels. (At higher levels, traditional academics is treated in a more abstract fashion that may confuse or frustrate handicapped learners.) Educational tasks are to be presented in small, discrete units to prevent overwhelming students with the amount or magnitude of tasks.

At the response level, motor coordination, verbal and nonverbal language, and task response skills are developed. Development of response skills helps students to interact more appropriately by improving basic response systems used in educational settings. This is accomplished by teachers providing extensive cues to guide responding (errorless learning) and by controlling requirements for success (successive approximations). In addition, response barriers are reduced by building motor and language response skills.

The order level consists of following directions and school adjustment tasks. Students are required to demonstrate skills in locating, copying from a model, and following multistep directions. The process of skill development entails students determining starting points for specific tasks and following tasks through to completion. Teachers must present task procedures clearly to students to minimize confusion or conflict. Perceptual motor training tasks are used frequently to develop order-level competence.

The next level within the curriculum, the exploratory level, is designed to develop active participation in classroom and community activities and students' knowledge of their environment. Objectives at this level focus on students demonstrating curiosity about objects, events, and experiences available to them. Teachers expose students to a wide range of multisensory experiences and encourage them to use their sensory channels to explore and learn about their environment. As with other levels, the teacher structures the choices available to students to reduce confusion and conflict. Activities with predictable outcomes are used to develop an understanding of cause/effect relationships. Discovering predictable cause and effect relationships helps students' awareness of reality and reduces fantasy experiences. This focus on reality helps students to overcome irrational fears and misperceptions about their world. Science and art activities are used as vehicles to guide students to explore the world around them (Hewett, 1968; Hewett & Taylor, 1980).

At the social level of learning competence, students develop skills in establishing and maintaining relationships with peers, teachers, and significant others (Hewett & Taylor, 1980). Students' positive self-concepts are also developed in terms of self-confidence, reactions to frustration, and emotional mood. Teachers structure activities to encourage communication among students and with others in the environment. Students use novel communication devices (e.g., walkie-talkies, invisible ink, telephones) to participate in activities requiring cooperation and communication between two or more individuals. Cooperative activities also are used to develop turn-taking skills and tolerance for delays in receiving rewards. Development and maintenance of appropriate social behaviors are facilitated through modeling, coaching, and role-playing techniques. Also, between-student competition is replaced by within-student competition.

The mastery level entails development of the basic academic skills needed to function successfully in school. Skill areas include reading, written language, mathematics,

and vocational skills. There is an emphasis on structuring learning through the use of extensive response cues and consequences. Extensive use of errorless learning strategies is typical at this level. The specific structure of individual tasks is determined by the operations associated with the task and deals primarily with the *how* and *how well* conditions. Mastery level assignments are broken down into tiny steps to encourage and simplify learning.

One of the most salient characteristics of the engineered classroom is the physical arrangement of its learning centers (part of the conditions side of the learning triangle). The room is structured to encourage the development of skills within different levels of the curriculum. The order center includes tables and storage cabinets in one corner of the room. The activities for this center emphasize active participation, direction following, and task completion. Attention and response level activities are also included at the order center. The communication center consists of tables, chairs, and record player. Activities for this center are based on luck rather than skill and focus on minimizing competition and encouraging waiting turns. Social competence activities are also conducted at this center. The exploratory center features art and science activities. Consequently, this area of the classroom contains tables, chairs, sink, and storage cabinets for art materials and science equipment. The activities are geared toward multisensory discovery of environmental stimuli and the learning of cause/effect relationships. The fourth area, the mastery center, is located in the center of the classroom and includes individual student desks and adjacent study booths. Instructional activities for basic academics are presented in this area.

Consequences for behavior are an additional component of the engineered classroom. Behavior in the engineered classroom is followed by either positive consequences or punishment. Students are rewarded for appropriate behaviors through task-embedded reinforcement (e.g., acquisition of knowledge, knowledge of results, multisensory stimulation, task completion) or external reinforcers provided by the teacher (e.g., tangible reinforcers, points, social approval). The primary punishment techniques include response cost, time-out, and overcorrection. Teachers monitor behavior through the use of a check-mark system that features a work record card. Teachers give or withhold check marks contingently for a 15-minute fixed interval. Each instructional hour, therefore, is divided into three 15-minute work periods, each followed by a 5-minute monitoring period (Hewett & Taylor, 1980).

## REFERENCES

Hewett, F. M. (1968). *The emotionally disturbed child in the classroom.* Boston: Allyn & Bacon.

Hewett, F. M., & Forness, S. R. (1984). *Education of exceptional learners* (3rd ed.). Boston: Allyn & Bacon.

Hewett, F. M., & Taylor, F. D. (1980). *The emotionally disturbed child in the classroom: The orchestration of success* (2nd ed.). Boston: Allyn & Bacon.

LAWRENCE J. O'SHEA
*University of Florida*

BEHAVIOR MODIFICATION
CLASSROOM MANAGEMENT
MULTISENSORY INSTRUCTION
VAKT

## ENGLISH AS A SECOND LANGUAGE (ESL) WITH HANDICAPPED STUDENTS

The special needs of handicapped limited English-speaking (LEP) and non-English-speaking (NEL) children began to receive some attention in the 1970s as a result of the special education and bilingual education legislation. The suspicion that minority children were overrepresented in special education classes was confirmed and the validity of many instruments used to evaluate minority children was called into question (Mercer, 1973). It became increasingly clear that school districts could not continue to operate on the premise that cultural-linguistic minority children's limited proficiency in English is the sole cause of their academic difficulties and that placement can be based solely on a child's English language skills. Despite pleas for education reform to accommodate linguistic and ethnic minorities, it was not until the 1980s that there was some evidence (in some geographic areas) that bilingual and special education could form a viable partnership.

A new field of bilingual special education has begun to emerge (Baca & Cervantes, 1984), but provision of appropriate assessment and educational services for handicapped limited English-speaking and non-English-speaking students continues to be fraught with problems. For more than a decade, researchers and practitioners have acknowledged the importance of distinguishing a language difference from a language disorder, and have stressed the importance of understanding and accepting cultural and linguistic differences; but there are still many theoretical and practical issues in regard to how and by whom these students should be served.

Assessment is a major issue. The language assessment of minority children is complicated by the problems of language assessment in general and the particular challenge of distinquishing among differences, disordes, and delays (Erickson, 1985). Another major issue is whether handicapped students who also happen to be speakers of a language other than English should be served by special education personnel or English as a second language (ESL) teachers. Still another issue is appropriate instructional strategies. Past strategies emphasized direct teaching, including patterning drills and listen-say approaches, with little concern for meaning. There is presently a trend toward learning through context, initially stressing development of comprehension rather than imitation and contrived production (Erickson, 1985).

### REFERENCES

Baca, L. M., & Cervantes, H. T. (Eds.). (1984). *The bilingual special education interface*. St. Louis: Times Mirror/Mosby.

Erickson, J. G. (1985). How many languages do you speak? An overview of bilingual education. *Topics in Language Disorders, 5*(4), 1–14.

Mercer, J. R. (1973). *Labeling the mentally retarded*. Berkeley, CA: University of California Press.

LINDA MCCORMICK
*University of Hawaii*

BILINGUAL EDUCATION
CULTURAL BIAS IN TESTS

## ENGRAMS

Psychologists have long questioned how information is stored and subsequently retrieved from the brain. As early as 1900, Müller and Pelzeker argued that memory involves an unobservable physical change in the central nervous system that becomes relatively permanent as a result of repeated presentation of information. In keeping with this notion, most neurobiological theories of memory have hypothesized the existence of a memory trace or engram. Generally, this term is used to denote the relatively permanent structural or biochemical change in the brain consistent with the long-term storage of information (Hillgard & Bower, 1975). Information in short-term memory, on the other hand, appears to be less stable and is inaccessible unless converted into the enduring long-term store.

Retrieval of the memory trace is seen to be based on a reactivation of the same physical structure or biochemical conditions that were responsible for the initial storage or encoding process (Bloch & Laroche, 1984). This reactivation process seems to be triggered by stimuli that are the same or similar to the original stimulus event. From this point of view, both storage and retrieval are based on similar "neuronal circuits."

At the psychological level, investigations have suggested that people encode both the orthographic (visual) characteristics and verbal attributes of a given stimulus input (Dean, Garabedian, & Yekovich, 1983). While many have hypothesized that verbal information in long-term memory is stored predominantly on the basis of abstract conceptual properties, a recent investigation by Dean, Gray, and Yekovich (under review) showed that more superficial attributes of the presentation (i.e., visual or auditory components) also play a prominent role in the encoding process. Moreover, the results of this investigation lend support to the notion that stimuli under some conditions may be stored as "literal copy." This conclusion appears to be consistent with the engram notion in that both refer to the relative permanence of a memory trace.

In the same study, it was observed that when words were presented without verbal context, learners tended to retrieve verbal stimuli on the basis of nonsemantic visual features rather than semantic elements. This research suggests that individuals may identify previously presented verbal information on the basis of the presence or absence of a visual memory trace. These results also lend support to the hypothesis that information may be dual encoded, such that verbal information is stored on the basis of its verbal-abstract meaning as well as the visual features of stimuli (Paivio, 1971).

Clearly, neurobiological theories of memory storage and retrieval seem to be compatible with psychological models of long-term memory. Hilgard and Bower (1975) provide a more detailed presentation of the interaction between these two theoretical approaches.

## REFERENCES

Bloch, V., & Laroche, S. (1984). Facts and hypotheses related to the search for the engram. In G. Lynch, J. L. McGaugh, & N. M. Weinberger (Eds.), *Neurobiology of learning and memory* (249–260). New York: Guilford Press.

Dean, R. S., Garabedian, A. A., & Yekovich, F. R. (1983). The effects of modality shifts on proactive interference in long-term memory. *Contemporary Educational Psychology, 8,* 28–45.

Dean, R. S., Gray, J. W., & Yekovich, F. R. (under review). Modality effects in long-term memory. *Journal of Experimental Psychology: Human Learning & Memory.*

Hillgard, E. R., & Bower, G. H. (1975). *Theories of Learning.* Englewood Cliffs, NJ: Prentice-Hall.

Müller, G. E., & Pilzecker, A. (1900). Experimentelle beitrage zur lehre von gedachtniss. *Zeitschrift fur Psychologie, 1,* 1–300.

Paivio, A. (1971). *Imagery and verbal processes.* New York: Holt, Rinehart & Winston.

JEFFREY W. GRAY
*Ball State University*

RAYMOND S. DEAN
*Ball State University*
*Indiana University School*
*of Medicine*

## MEMORY DISORDERS

## ENRICHMENT

Enrichment is a term that is frequently used to denote one form or approach to differentiating instruction for gifted youth. It is also often used to denote supplementary curriculum for youth at any level of ability. When the term refers to a form of instruction for gifted youth, it may be defined, by contrast, with terms such as acceleration, individualization, or grouping. These terms may, however, relate chiefly to administrative arrangements just as enrichment may relate to an approach that administratively refers to provision for the gifted by the regular teacher in a typical heterogeneous classroom. Administrative acceleration may simply refer to a gifted child's early admission to school, grade skipping in the elementary school, or early admission to college. Individualization may refer to the administrative arrangement of continuous progress in an ungraded school. Finally, grouping may refer to the gathering of all mathematically talented youth into a single "honors" mathematics class in seventh grade. While these administrative approaches may stem in part from concern with the nature or needs of gifted youth, they tend to acquire a functional autonomy that makes them independent alternatives or options, regardless of gifted youths' specific needs.

Massé and Gagné (1983) assert that proper definitions of the term enrichment and the associated terms, acceleration, individualization, and grouping, must grow out of consideration of the special and unique characteristics of the gifted and their correlated special needs. They noted, however, that lists of characteristics of gifted (and talented) youths can be extensive and even contradictory. From their own review of research on characteristics of the gifted they concluded that there are four basic and pervasive characteristics: (1) rapid learning; (2) ease in learning complex material; (3) diversity of interests; and (4) depth of specific interests. Renzulli's (1979) three-ring conception of giftedness would probably be similar in stressing the components of ability (rapid learning, complex learning and task commitment) and depth of interest, but Renzulli's third component, creative ability, is probably not reflected in Massé and Gagné's concept. However, in his enrichment triad instructional model, Renzulli (1977) proposed a Type 1 enrichment that provides gifted youths with an opportunity for exploratory learning in areas of varied interests. Such activity might meet the need generated by the characteristic of "varied interests" noted by Massé and Gagné. Type II enrichment in the triad model refers to group instructional activities to teach thinking and feeling processes, while Type III refers to enrichment through opportunities to investigate real problems. Type III probably relates well to Massé and Gagné's characteristic of the gifted, depth of specific interest.

Stanley (1979) proposed four types of enrichment. The first is busywork, or simply more of the same type of work done by all students. A second type is irrelevant academic enrichment, which is supplementary instruction that pays no attention to the special talents or characteristics of gifted youth. The third type is cultural enrichment, which ignores the student's talents or abilities but offers curriculum in the arts and foreign languages. The fourth type, relevant enrichment, provides special instruction directly related to gifted youths' special talents or characteristics (e.g., an enriched mathematics course for mathematically talented youths). In contrast to these four types of enrichment, Stanley proposes that acceleration is always vertical, moving a gifted youth to higher levels. In contrast to his use of the term of vertical to refer to acceleration, the term horizontal is often used to refer to enrichment. Stanley characterizes it as a process of teaching more content but at the same level of difficulty or complexity.

Tannenbaum (1983) argued that enrichment for the gifted always requires a curriculum that is differentiated from the regular curriculum in that it is designed to meet the special needs of gifted youths. Tannenbaum (1983) went on to propose an enrichment matrix that can be used to design curriculum for the gifted. The matrix calls for five type of content adjustment: (1) expansion of basic skills; (2) teaching core content in less time; (3) broadening the knowledge base; (4) teaching content related to the teacher's special expertise; (5) out-of-school mentoring experiences. The matrix also attends to higher level thinking skills and social-affective modification. These modifications can be applied to all curricular areas.

The term enrichment is best used to refer to curriculum experiences that are supplements to or replacements for the regular curriculum. Enrichment for the gifted should be designed to meet their specific needs and their capacity to learn more and more complex material. The term acceleration refers to learning or delivery processes: instruction or learning earlier than normal and at a faster pace. Administrative acceleration should be used to meet the needs of gifted youths for instruction at a level that matches their readiness or achievement levels and their need to learn rapidly or at a faster pace. However, it should also be recognized that gifted youths do not wait for the school to initiate acceleration. Alone or with the help of parents or siblings, they learn new skills or information ahead of the normal schedule. At home and at school, they usually comprehend and learn new skills and information much more rapidly than other youths.

The ideal educational program for gifted youths offers a combination of enriched curriculum and accelerated instruction. That is, these students are allowed to move into higher and appropriate levels of the regular school curriculum, to be taught at a pace that matches their capacity to learn, and to experience an enriched or augmented curriculum that meets their need for extended and more complex learning.

## REFERENCES

Massé, P., & Gagné, F. (1983). Observations on enrichment and acceleration. In B. M. Shore, F. Gagne, S. Larivee, R. H. Tali, & R. E. Tremblay (Eds.), *Face to face with giftedness* (pp. 395–413). New York: Trillium.

Renzulli, J. S. (1977). *The enrichment triad model: A guide for developing defensible programs for the gifted and talented.* Mansfield Center, CT: Creative Learning Press.

Renzulli, J. S. (1979). *What makes giftedness.* Los Angeles, CA: National State Leadership Training Institute for the Gifted/Talented.

Stanley, J. C. (1979). Identifying and nurturing the intellectually gifted. In W. C. George, S. J. Cohn, & J. C. Stanley (Eds.), *Educating the gifted, acceleration and enrichment* (pp. 172–180). Baltimore, MD: Johns Hopkins University Press.

Tannenbaum, A. J. (1983). *Gifted children, psychological and educational perspectives.* New York: Macmillan.

JOHN F. FELDHUSEN
*Purdue University*

## ACCELERATED PLACEMENT OF GIFTED CHILDREN
## GIFTED AND TALENTED CHILDREN

## ENRICHMENT TRIAD MODEL

The Enrichment Triad Model is a teaching-learning model developed by J. S. Renzulli (1977) specifically for teaching gifted children. Renzulli's model is designed to be used with students who have three interacting clusters of traits—creativity, high ability, and task commitment. Identified students with these traits take part in a program based on three interrelated categories of enrichment that are depicted in the Figure below. These categories include (1) Type I, general exploratory activities: (2) Type II, group training activities; and (3) Type III, individual and small group investigations of real problems. The first two categories (Types I and II) are considered appropriate for all learners, whereas the third category (Type III) con-

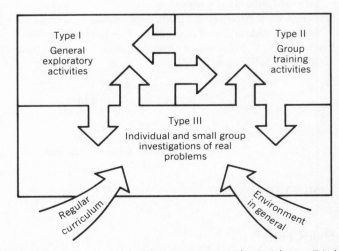

The Enrichment Triad Model. (*Source*: From *The Enrichment Triad Model* by J. S. Renzulli. Copyright 1977 by Creative Learning Press. Reprinted by permission.)

sists of advanced-level experiences that gifted students pursue on a self-selected basis.

Type I enrichment consists of general exploratory experiences that are designed to expose students to a variety of topics or areas of study that are not ordinarily covered in the regular curriculum. This type of enrichment is provided through a variety of activities such as interest or learning centers, audio-visual materials, field trips, guest speakers, or teacher demonstrations.

In Type II enrichment, the teacher uses special methods, materials, and instructional techniques that are specifically designed to develop higher level thinking processes, research skills, and processes related to personal and social development. These are exercises that will help students to deal more effectively with content and to solve problems in a variety of areas and new situations.

Advanced-level Type III enrichment, individual and small group investigations, is the major focus of this model, since it is the type of activity considered especially appropriate for gifted students. During this activity, students are encouraged to gather new data, use the authentic methods of researchers in particular fields of knowledge, and share the results of their work with appropriate audiences. According to Renzulli (1977), when students have superior potential for performance in particular areas of sincere interest, they "must be allowed the opportunity to pursue topics therein to unlimited levels of inquiry" (p. 17). To develop his model, Renzulli investigated the characteristics of eminent adults (Roe, 1952), studied Ward's (1961) ideas for inquiry, and adopted Bruner's (1960) and Torrance's (1965) conclusions that young children are able to engage in critical and creative investigations.

In her comprehensive review of teaching-learning models, Maker (1982) provides judgments on the advantages and disadvantages of the model. She explains that an important advantage of the triad is its overall program framework designed specifically for use in gifted programs. "The most obvious disadvantage of the *Triad* model," she claims, "is its newness and the lack of research on its effectiveness as a total approach" (p. 232).

To obtain additional information related to the model, Renzulli requests that interested persons write to him at the University of Connecticut, Storrs, CT 06268.

## REFERENCES

Bruner, J. S. (1960). *The process of education.* Cambridge, MA: Harvard University Press.

Maker, C. J. (1982). *Teaching models in education of the gifted.* Rockville, MD: Aspen.

Renzulli, J. S. (1977). *The Enrichment Triad Model.* Wethersfield, CT: Creative Learning Press.

Roe, A. (1952). *The making of a scientist.* New York: Dodd & Mead.

Torrance, E. P. (1965). *Gifted children in the classroom.* New York: Macmillan.

Ward, V. S. (1961). *Educating the gifted: An axiomatic approach.* Columbus, OH: Merrill.

JUNE SCOBEE
*University of Houston, Clear Lake*

**GIFTED AND TALENTED CHILDREN**
**GIFTED CHILDREN**
**RENZULLI, J. S.**

# ENURESIS

Enuresis may be broadly defined as the repeated involuntary voiding of urine that occurs beyond the age at which bladder control is expected and for which there is no organic or urologic explanation. According to the American Psychiatric Association (1982), diagnostic criteria include at least two events per month for children between the ages of 5 and 6, or at least one monthly episode for older children. However, many (e.g., Campbell, 1970; Doleys, 1977; Eufemia, Wesolowski, Trice, & Tseng, 1984) note that children as young as 3 years old may be considered enuretic.

Childhood enuresis is classified as either nocturnal (occurring during sleep) or diurnal (occurring during waking hours). Distinctions have also been made between primary enuresis (child has always been enuretic) and secondary enuresis (child loses previously acquired control). According to Sorotzkin (1984), the view that secondary enuresis is related to higher levels of psychological stress or organic etiology is not based on empirical evidence. Furthermore, the lack of prognostic value of distinguishing primary and secondary enuresis also attests to not making such a distinction.

Reported prevalence estimates vary greatly. In a review of literature, Siegel (1983) reports that there are more than 3 million enuretic children in America. He also states that approximately 20% of all children are nocturnal enuretics at age 5, with half of these children remaining enuretic at age 10. Most researchers report that enuresis is about twice as prevalent among males than females.

Enuresis has been studied from a variety of theoretical perspectives. Although there are many variants of the psychoanalytic orientation, all share the assumption that enuresis is merely the symptomatic expression of intrapsychic problems. For example, enuresis has been variously viewed as an expression of repressed sexual drives, an act of displaced aggression against parents, a masochistic expulsion of destructive energy, a functional equivalent of a fetish, and a desire for regression that frequently occurs with the birth of a sibling or separation (Mountjoy, Ruben, & Bradford, 1984; Sorotzkin, 1984). Siegel (1983) concludes that empirical evidence does not support the view of enuresis as a symptom of underlying psychological disturbance.

A number of biological factors have been studied in relation to enuresis. The maturational lag hypothesis, for example, posits that neurological immaturity is responsible for primary enuresis; this perspective has been seriously questioned, however, since nearly all 5-year-old nocturnal enuretics have occasional dry nights, indicating maturation has occurred (Sorotzkin, 1984). Other biological variables that have been implicated include genetic factors, infections, atypical sleep patterns, and small functional bladder capacities (Sorotzkin, 1984). Of these factors, diminished functional bladder capacity is most supported by research although even that support is equivocal.

From a behavioral perspective, enuresis is essentially viewed as the failure to appropriately respond to both physiological and environmental cues for urination. Current behavioral theories consider both classical and operant factors.

Although a diverse array of treatments for enuresis have been reported (e.g., drug therapy, psychotherapy, hypnotherapy, fluid restrictive diets, elimination diets, and surgery), behavioral approaches have unquestionably received the most empirical attention. Among the many behavioral treatments, the most frequently employed are urine alarm procedures, retention control training, and treatment packages that incorporate multiple components.

The urine alarm procedure involves the use of an apparatus by which an alarm is activated at the onset of urination. While the device was originally developed for (and most often used for) treating nocturnal enuresis, it has been adapted and used to treat diurnal enuresis as well. There is some disagreement regarding whether the procedure represents classical conditioning (i.e., after repeated pairings of the bell, which causes the child to awaken and inhibit urination and heed full bladder cues, distention of the bladder eventually acquires discriminative stimulus properties) or operant conditioning (i.e., the bell is an aversive stimulus that is avoided by inhibiting urination and awakening). Empirical evidence attests to the efficacy of the procedure. Doleys (1985) reports that typical data indicate a 75% success rate, with relapse rates of 40%; reapplication of the procedure is typically successful with 60 to 70% of those who initially relapse. Procedural variations such as gradually requiring the child to drink large quantities prior to bedtime and using an intermittent schedule of alarm presentation have yielded higher success rates and/or lower relapse rates (Doleys, 1977).

Retention-control training is a procedure in which the child is required to refrain from urinating for progressively longer periods of time. It is based on the premise that such training increases functional bladder capacity

(i.e., the volume at which evacuating contractions occur). Although some evidence exists to support the procedure, it has not proven universally successful (Doleys, 1977; Siegel, 1983).

A multicomponent treatment for nocturnal enuresis is the dry-bed training procedure of Azrin, Sneed, and Foxx (1974). Among the features of this intensive program are the use of a urine alarm, increased intake of liquids, retention control training, practice in toileting, positive reinforcement for appropriate urination, hourly awakenings, and verbal reprimands and positive practice overcorrection for accidents. The dry-pants training program (Azrin & Foxx, 1974) is directed at diurnal enuresis and is procedurally similar to the dry-bed program. The total program is regarded as highly successful; however, program modifications such as eliminating the alarm should be made with caution (Eufemia et al., 1984; Siegel, 1983; Sorotzkin, 1984).

## REFERENCES

American Psychiatric Association. (1982). *Desk reference to the diagnostic criteria from diagnostic and statistical manual of mental disorders* (3rd ed.). Washington, DC: Author.

Azrin, N. H., & Foxx, R. M. (1974). *Toilet training in less than a day*. New York: Simon & Schuster.

Azrin, N. H., Sneed, T. J., & Foxx, R. M. (1974). Dry-bed training: Rapid elimination of childhood enuresis. *Behaviour Research and Therapy, 12*, 147–156.

Campbell, M. F. (1970). Neuromuscular neuropathy. In M. F. Campbell & T. H. Harrison (Eds.), *Urology* (Vol. 2, pp. 1935–1948). Philadelphia: Saunders.

Doleys, D. M. (1977). Behavioral treatment of nocturnal enuresis in children: A review of the recent literature. *Psychological Bulletin, 84*, 30–54.

Doleys, D. M. (1985). Bell and pad conditioning. In A. S. Bellack & M. Hersen (Eds.), *Dictionary of behavior therapy techniques* (pp. 46–48). New York: Pergamon.

Eufemia, R. L., Wesolowski, M. D., Trice, A. D., & Tseng, M. S. (1984). The long and short term effects of dry bed training. *Education and Treatment of Children, 7*, 61–66.

Mountjoy, P. T., Ruben, D. H., & Bradford, T. S. (1984). Recent technological advances in the treatment of enuresis: Theory and research. *Behavior Modification, 8*, 291–315.

Siegel, L. J. (1983). Psychosomatic and psychophysiological disorders. In R. J. Morris & T. R. Kratochwill (Eds.), *The practice of child therapy* (pp. 253–286). New York: Pergamon.

Sorotzkin, B. (1984). Nocturnal enuresis: Current perspectives. *Clinical Psychology Review, 4*, 293–315.

JAMES P. KROUSE
*Clarion University of Pennsylvania*

**APPLIED BEHAVIOUR ANALYSIS**
**ENCOPRESIS**